POCKET
SPANISH
DICTIONARY

SPANISH ▶ ENGLISH   ENGLISH ▶ SPANISH

Collins
An Imprint of HarperCollinsPublishers

third edition/tercera edición 1999

© HarperCollins Publishers 1995, 1999
© William Collins Sons & Co. Ltd. 1990

latest reprint 2000

HarperCollins Publishers
P.O. Box, Glasgow G4 0NB, Great Britain

The HarperCollins website address is
www.**fire**and**water**.com

Collins® and Bank of English® are registered trademarks
of HarperCollins Publishers Limited

ISBN 0 00 470773-7

HarperCollins Publishers, Inc.
10 East 53rd Street, New York, NY 10022

ISBN 0-06-095660-7

CIP information is available on request

The HarperCollins USA website address is
www.harpercollins.com

Typeset by Morton Word Processing Ltd, Scarborough

*Printed and bound in Great Britain by Caledonian International
Book Manufacturing Ltd, Glasgow, G64*

editors/redactores
Mike Gonzalez • Alicia de Benito de Harland
Soledad Pérez-López • José Ramón Parrondo

contributors/colaboradores
Bob Grossmith • Teresa Álvarez García
Sharon Hunter • Claire Evans

editorial staff/redacción
Joyce Littlejohn • Val McNulty

series editor/colección dirigida por
Lorna Sinclair Knight

INTRODUCTION

We are delighted that you have decided to buy the Collins Pocket Spanish Dictionary, and hope you will enjoy and benefit from using it at home, at school, on holiday or at work.

The innovative use of colour guides you quickly and efficiently to the word you want, and the comprehensive wordlist provides a wealth of modern and idiomatic phrases not normally found in a dictionary this size.

In addition, the supplement provides you with guidance on using the dictionary, along with entertaining ways of improving your dictionary skills.

We hope that you will enjoy using it and that it will significantly enhance your language studies.

Note on trademarks

ABREVIATURAS

ABBREVIATIONS

adjetivo, locución adjetiva	**adj**	adjective, adjectival phrase
abreviatura	**ab(b)r**	abbreviation
adverbio, locución adverbial	**adv**	adverb, adverbial phrase
administración, lengua administrativa	**ADMIN**	administration
agricultura	**AGR**	agriculture
América Latina	**AM**	Latin America
anatomía	**ANAT**	anatomy
arquitectura	**ARQ, ARCH**	architecture
artículo	**art**	article
el automóvil	**AUT(O)**	the motor car and motoring
aviación, viajes aéreos	**AVIAT**	flying, air travel
biología	**BIO(L)**	biology
botánica, flores	**BOT**	botany
inglés británico	**BRIT**	British English
química	**CHEM**	chemistry
comercio, finanzas, banca	**COM(M)**	commerce, finance, banking
comparativo	**compar**	comparative
informática	**COMPUT**	computers
conjunción	**conj**	conjunction
construcción	**CONSTR**	building
compuesto	**cpd**	compound element
cocina	**CULIN**	cookery
definido	**def**	definite
demostrativo	**demos**	demonstrative
economía	**ECON**	economics
electricidad, electrónica	**ELEC**	electricity, electronics
enseñanza, sistema escolar y universitario	**ESCOL**	schooling, schools and universities
España	**ESP**	Spain
especialmente	**esp**	especially
exclamación, interjección	**excl**	exclamation, interjection
femenino	**f**	feminine
lengua familiar (! vulgar)	**fam(!)**	informal usage (! particularly offensive)
ferrocarril	**FERRO**	railways
uso figurado	**fig**	figurative use
fotografía	**FOTO**	photography
(verbo inglés) del cual la partícula es inseparable	**fus**	(phrasal verb) where the particle is inseparable
generalmente	**gen**	generally
geografía, geología	**GEO**	geography, geology
geometría	**GEOM**	geometry
indefinido	**indef**	indefinite
lengua familiar (! vulgar)	**inf(!)**	informal usage
infinitivo	**infin**	infinitive
informática	**INFORM**	computers
interrogativo	**interr**	interrogative
invariable	**inv**	invariable
irregular	**irreg**	irregular
lo jurídico	**JUR**	law

ABREVIATURAS

ABBREVIATIONS

América Latina	LAM	Latin America
gramática, lingüística	LING	grammar, linguistics
masculino	m	masculine
matemáticas	MAT(H)	mathematics
medicina	MED	medical term, medicine
masculino/femenino	m/f	masculine/feminine
lo militar, ejército	MIL	military matters
música	MUS	music
sustantivo, nombre	n	noun
navegación, náutica	NAUT	sailing, navigation
sustantivo numérico	num	numeral noun
complemento	obj	(grammatical) object
	o.s.	oneself
peyorativo	pey, pej	derogatory, pejorative
fotografía	PHOT	photography
fisiología	PHYSIOL	physiology
plural	pl	plural
política	POL	politics
participio de pasado	pp	past participle
preposición	prep	preposition
pronombre	pron	pronoun
psicología, psiquiatría	PSICO, PSYCH	psychology, psychiatry
tiempo pasado	pt	past tense
química	QUIM	chemistry
ferrocarril	RAIL	railways
religión, lo eclesiástico	REL	religion, church service
	sb	somebody
enseñanza, sistema escolar y universitario	SCH	schooling, schools and universities
singular	sg	singular
España	SP	Spain
	sth	something
sujeto	su(b)j	(grammatical) subject
subjuntivo	subjun	subjunctive
superlativo	superl	superlative
tauromaquia	TAUR	bullfighting
también	tb	also
técnica, tecnología	TEC(H)	technical term, technology
telecomunicaciones	TELEC, TEL	telecommunications
televisión	TV	television
imprenta, tipografía	TIP, TYP	typography, printing
inglés norteamericano	US	American English
verbo	vb	verb
verbo intransitivo	vi	intransitive verb
verbo pronominal	vr	reflexive verb
verbo transitivo	vt	transitive verb
zoología, animales	ZOOL	zoology
marca registrada	®	registered trademark
indica un equivalente cultural	≈	introduces a cultural equivalent

SPANISH PRONUNCIATION

Consonants

b	[b, ß]	**b**oda **b**om**b**a la**b**or	see notes on **v** below
c	[k]	**c**aja	**c** before **a**, **o** or **u** is pronounced as in **c**at
ce, ci	[θe, θi]	**c**ero **c**ielo	**c** before **e** or **i** is pronounced as in **th**in
ch	[tʃ]	**ch**iste	**ch** is pronounced as **ch** in **ch**air
d	[d, ð]	**d**anés ciu**d**a**d**	at the beginning of a phrase or after **l** or **n**, **d** is pronounced as in English. In any other position it is pronounced like **th** in **th**e
g	[g, ɣ]	**g**afas pa**g**a	**g** before **a**, **o** or **u** is pronounced as in **g**ap, if at the beginning of a phrase or after **n**. In other positions the sound is softened
ge, gi	[xe, xi]	**g**ente **g**irar	**g** before **e** or **i** is pronounced similar to **ch** in Scottish lo**ch**
h		**h**aber	**h** is always silent in Spanish
j	[x]	**j**ugar	**j** is pronounced similar to **ch** in Scottish lo**ch**
ll	[ʎ]	ta**ll**e	**ll** is pronounced like the **lli** in mi**lli**on
ñ	[ɲ]	ni**ñ**o	**ñ** is pronounced like the **ni** in o**ni**on
q	[k]	**q**ue	**q** is pronounced as **k** in **k**ing
r, rr	[r, rr]	quita**r** ga**rr**a	**r** is always pronounced in Spanish, unlike the silent **r** in dance**r**. **rr** is trilled, like a Scottish **r**
s	[s]	quizá**s** i**s**la	**s** is usually pronounced as in pa**ss**, but before **b**, **d**, **g**, **l**, **m** or **n** it is pronounced as in ro**s**e
v	[b, ß]	**v**ía di**v**idir	**v** is pronounced something like **b**. At the beginning of a phrase or after **m** or **n** it is pronounced as **b** in **b**oy. In any other position the sound is softened
z	[θ]	tena**z**	**z** is pronounced as **th** in **th**in

f, k, l, m, n, p, t and **x** are pronounced as in English.

Vowels

a	[a]	p**a**ta	not as long as **a** in f**a**r. When followed by a consonant in the same syllable (i.e. in a closed syllable), as in am**a**nte, the **a** is short, as in b**a**t
e	[e]	m**e**	like **e** in th**ey**. In a closed syllable, as in g**e**nte, the **e** is short as in p**e**t
i	[i]	p**i**no	as in m**ea**n or mach**i**ne
o	[o]	l**o**	as in l**o**cal. In a closed syllable, as in c**o**ntrol, the **o** is short as in c**o**t
u	[u]	l**u**nes	as in r**u**le. It is silent after **q**, and in **gue, gui**, unless marked **güe, güi** e.g. anti**güe**dad, when it is pronounced like **w** in **w**olf

Semivowels

i, y	[j]	b**i**en h**i**elo **y**unta	pronounced like **y** in **y**es
u	[w]	h**u**evo f**u**ento antig**ü**edad	unstressed **u** between consonant and vowel is pronounced like **w** in **w**ell. See also notes on **u** above

Diphthongs

ai, ay	[ai]	b**ai**le	as **i** in r**i**de
au	[au]	**au**to	as **ou** in sh**ou**t
ei, ey	[ei]	bu**ey**	as **ey** in gr**ey**
eu	[eu]	d**eu**da	both elements pronounced independently [e] + [u]
oi, oy	[oi]	h**oy**	as **oy** in t**oy**

Stress

The rules of stress in Spanish are as follows:

(a) when a word ends in a vowel or in **n** or **s**, the second last syllable is stressed: pa**ta**ta, pa**ta**tas, **co**me, **co**men

(b) when a word ends in a consonant other than **n** or **s**, the stress falls on the last syllable: pa**red**, ha**blar**

(c) when the rules set out in (a) and (b) are not applied, an acute accent appears over the stressed vowel: co**mún**, geogra**fía**, in**glés**

In the phonetic transcription, the symbol ['] precedes the syllable on which the stress falls.

PRONUNCIACIÓN INGLESA

Vocales y diptongos

	Ejemplo inglés	*Ejemplo español/explicación*
ɑː	f**a**ther	Entre **a** de p**a**dre y **o** de n**o**che
ʌ	b**u**t, c**o**me	**a** muy breve
æ	m**a**n, c**a**t	Con los labios en la posición de **e** en p**e**na se pronuncia el sonido **a** parecido a la **a** de c**a**rro
ə	fath**er**, **a**go	Vocal neutra parecida a una **e** u **o** casi mudas
əː	b**ir**d, h**ear**d	Entre **e** abierta, y **o** cerrada, sonido alargado
ɛ	g**e**t, b**e**d	Como en p**e**rro
ɪ	**i**t, b**i**g	Más breve que en s**i**
iː	t**ea**, s**ee**	Como en f**i**no
ɔ	h**o**t, w**a**sh	Como en t**o**rre
ɔː	s**aw**, **a**ll	Como en p**o**r
u	p**u**t, b**oo**k	Sonido breve, más cerrado que b**u**rro
uː	t**oo**, y**ou**	Sonido largo, como en **u**no
aɪ	fl**y**, h**igh**	Como en fr**ai**le
au	h**ow**, h**ou**se	Como en p**au**sa
ɛə	th**ere**, b**ear**	Casi como en v**ea**, pero el segundo elemento es la vocal neutra [ə]
eɪ	d**ay**, ob**ey**	**e** cerrada seguida por una **i** débil
ɪə	h**ere**, h**ear**	Como en man**ía**, mezclándose el sonido **a** con la vocal neutra [ə]
əu	g**o**, n**o**te	[ə] seguido por una breve **u**
ɔɪ	b**oy**, **oi**l	Como en v**oy**
uə	p**oor**, s**ure**	**u** bastante larga más la vocal neutra [ə]

Consonantes

	Ejemplo inglés	*Ejemplo español/explicación*
b	**b**ig, lo**bb**y	Como en tum**b**a
d	men**d**e**d**	Como en con**d**e, an**d**ar
g	**g**o, **g**et, bi**g**	Como en **g**rande, **g**ol
dʒ	**g**in, ju**dg**e	Como en la **ll** andaluza y en **G**eneralitat (catalán)
ŋ	si**ng**	Como en ví**n**culo
h	**h**ouse, **h**e	Como la jota hispanoamericana
j	**y**oung, **y**es	Como en **y**a
k	**c**ome, mo**ck**	Como en **c**aña, Es**c**ocia
r	**r**ed, t**r**ead	Se pronuncia con la punta de la lengua hacia atrás y sin hacerla vibrar
s	**s**and, ye**s**	Como en ca**s**a, **s**esión
z	ro**s**e, **z**ebra	Como en de**s**de, mi**s**mo
ʃ	**sh**e, ma**ch**ine	Como en **ch**ambre (francés), ro**x**o (portugués)
tʃ	**ch**in, ri**ch**	Como en **ch**ocolate
v	**v**alley	Como en f, pero se retiran los dientes superiores vibrándolos contra el labio inferior
w	**w**ater, **wh**ich	Como en la **u** de h**u**evo, p**u**ede
ʒ	vi**s**ion	Como en **j**ournal (francés)
θ	**th**ink, my**th**	Como en re**c**eta, **z**apato
ð	**th**is, **th**e	Como en la **d** de habla**d**o, verda**d**

p, f, m, n, l, t iguales que en español
El signo * indica que la r final escrita apenas se pronuncia en inglés británico cuando la palabra siguiente empieza con vocal. El signo ['] indica la sílaba acentuada.

SPANISH VERB TABLES

1 Gerund *2* Imperative *3* Present *4* Preterite *5* Future *6* Present subjunctive *7* Imperfect subjunctive *8* Past participle *9* Imperfect. *Etc* indicates that the irregular root is used for all persons of the tense, e.g. **oír**: *6* oiga *etc* = oigas, oigamos, oigáis, oigan. Forms which consist of the unmodified verb root + verb ending are not shown, e.g. *ac*ertamos, *ac*ertáis.

acertar *2* acierta *3* acierto, aciertas, acierta, aciertan *6* acierte, aciertes, acierte, acierten

acordar *2* acuerda *3* acuerdo, acuerdas, acuerda, acuerdan *6* acuerde, acuerdes, acuerde, acuerden

advertir *1* advirtiendo *2* advierte *3* advierto, adviertes, advierte, advierten *4* advirtió, advirtieron *6* advierta, adviertas, advierta, advirtamos, advirtáis, adviertan *7* advirtiera *etc*

agradecer *3* agradezco *6* agradezca *etc*

aparecer *3* aparezco *6* aparezca *etc*

aprobar *2* aprueba *3* apruebo, apruebas, aprueba, aprueban *6* apruebe, apruebes, apruebe, aprueben

atravesar *2* atraviesa *3* atravieso, atraviesas, atraviesa, atraviesan *6* atraviese, atravieses, atraviese, atraviesen

caber *3* quepo *4* cupe, cupiste, cupo, cupimos, cupisteis, cupieron *5* cabré *etc* *6* quepa *etc* *7* cupiera *etc*

caer *1* cayendo *3* caigo *4* cayó, cayeron *6* caiga *etc* *7* cayera *etc*

calentar *2* calienta *3* caliento, calientas, calienta, calientan *6* caliente, calientes, caliente, calienten

cerrar *2* cierra *3* cierro, cierras, cierra, cierran *6* cierre, cierres, cierre, cierren

COMER *1* comiendo *2* come, comed *3* como, comes, come, comemos, coméis, comen *4* comí, comiste, comió, comimos, comisteis, comieron *5* comeré, comerás, comerá, comeremos, comeréis, comerán *6* coma, comas, coma, comamos, comáis, coman *7* comiera, comieras, comiera, comiéramos, comierais, comieran *8* comido *9* comía, comías, comía, comíamos, comíais, comían

conocer *3* conozco *6* conozca *etc*

contar *2* cuenta *3* cuento, cuentas, cuenta, cuentan *6* cuente, cuentes, cuente, cuenten

costar *2* cuesta *3* cuesto, cuestas, cuesta, cuestan *6* cueste, cuestes, cueste, cuesten

dar *3* doy *4* di, diste, dio, dimos, disteis, dieron *7* diera *etc*

decir *2* di *3* digo *4* dije, dijiste, dijo, dijimos, dijisteis, dijeron *5* diré *etc* *6* diga *etc* *7* dijera

etc *8* dicho

despertar *2* despierta *3* despierto, despiertas, despierta, despiertan *6* despierte, despiertes, despierte, despierten

divertir *1* divirtiendo *2* divierte *3* divierto, diviertes, divierte, divierten *4* divirtió, divirtieron *6* divierta, diviertas, divierta, divirtamos, divirtáis, diviertan *7* divirtiera *etc*

dormir *1* durmiendo *2* duerme *3* duermo, duermes, duerme, duermen *4* durmió, durmieron *6* duerma, duermas, duerma, durmamos, durmáis, duerman *7* durmiera *etc*

empezar *2* empieza *3* empiezo, empiezas, empieza, empiezan *4* empecé *6* empiece, empieces, empiece, empecemos, empecéis, empiecen

entender *2* entiende *3* entiendo, entiendes, entiende, entienden *6* entienda, entiendas, entienda, entiendan

ESTAR *2* está *3* estoy, estás, está, están *4* estuve, estuviste, estuvo, estuvimos, estuvisteis, estuvieron *6* esté, estés, esté, estén *7* estuviera *etc*

HABER *3* he, has, ha, hemos, han *4* hube, hubiste, hubo, hubimos, hubisteis, hubieron *5* habré *etc* *6* haya *etc* *7* hubiera *etc*

HABLAR *1* hablando *2* habla, hablad *3* hablo, hablas, habla, hablamos, habláis, hablan *4* hablé, hablaste, habló, hablamos, hablasteis, hablaron *5* hablaré, hablarás, hablará, hablaremos, hablaréis, hablarán *6* hable, hables, hable, hablemos, habléis, hablen *7* hablara, hablaras, hablara, habláramos, hablarais, hablaran *8* hablado *9* hablaba, hablabas, hablaba, hablábamos, hablabais, hablaban

hacer *2* haz *3* hago *4* hice, hiciste, hizo, hicimos, hicisteis, hicieron *5* haré *etc* *6* haga *etc* *7* hiciera *etc* *8* hecho

instruir *1* instruyendo *2* instruye *3* instruyo, instruyes, instruye, instruyen *4* instruyó, instruyeron *6* instruya *etc* *7* instruyera *etc*

ir *1* yendo *2* ve *3* voy, vas, va, vamos, vais, van *4* fui, fuiste, fue, fuimos, fuisteis, fueron *6* vaya, vayas, vaya, vayamos, vayáis, vayan

7 fuera *etc* **9** iba, ibas, iba, íbamos, ibais, iban

jugar *2* juega *3* juego, juegas, juega, juegan *4* jugué *6* juegue *etc*

leer *1* leyendo *4* leyó, leyeron *7* leyera *etc*

morir *1* muriendo *2* muere *3* muero, mueres, muere, mueren *4* murió, murieron *6* muera, mueras, muera, muramos, muráis, mueran *7* muriera *8* muerto

mostrar *2* muestra *3* muestro, muestras, muestra, muestran *6* muestre, muestres, muestre, muestren

mover *2* mueve *3* muevo, mueves, mueve, mueven *6* mueva, muevas, mueva, muevan

negar *2* niega *3* niego, niegas, niega, niegan *4* negué *6* niegue, niegues, niegue, neguemos, neguéis, nieguen

ofrecer *3* ofrezco *6* ofrezca *etc*

oír *1* oyendo *2* oye *3* oigo, oyes, oye, oyen *4* oyó, oyeron *6* oiga *etc* *7* oyera *etc*

oler *2* huele *3* huelo, hueles, huele, huelen *6* huela, huelas, huela, huelan

parecer *3* parezco *6* parezca *etc*

pedir *1* pidiendo *2* pide *3* pido, pides, pide, piden *4* pidió, pidieron *6* pida *etc* *7* pidiera *etc*

pensar *2* piensa *3* pienso, piensas, piensa, piensan *6* piense, pienses, piense, piensen

perder *2* pierde *3* pierdo, pierdes, pierde, pierden *6* pierda, pierdas, pierda, pierdan

poder *1* pudiendo *2* puede *3* puedo, puedes, puede, pueden *4* pude, pudiste, pudo, pudimos, pudisteis, pudieron *5* podré *etc* *6* pueda, puedas, pueda, puedan *7* pudiera *etc*

poner *2* pon *3* pongo *4* puse, pusiste, puso, pusimos, pusisteis, pusieron *5* pondré *etc* *6* ponga *etc* *7* pusiera *etc* *8* puesto

preferir *1* prefiriendo *2* prefiere *3* prefiero, prefieres, prefiere, prefieren *4* prefirió, prefirieron *6* prefiera, prefieras, prefiera, prefiramos, prefiráis, prefieran *7* prefiriera *etc*

querer *2* quiere *3* quiero, quieres, quiere, quieren *4* quise, quisiste, quiso, quisimos, quisisteis, quisieron *5* querré *etc* *6* quiera, quieras, quiera, quieran *7* quisiera *etc*

reír *2* ríe *3* río, ríes, ríe, ríen *4* rio, rieron *6* ría, rías, ría, riamos, riáis, rían *7* riera *etc*

repetir *1* repitiendo *2* repite *3* repito, repites, repite, repiten *4* repitió, repitieron *6* repita *etc* *7* repitiera *etc*

rogar *2* ruega *3* ruego, ruegas, ruega, ruegan *4* rogué *6* ruegue, ruegues, ruegue, roguemos, roguéis, rueguen

saber *3* sé *4* supe, supiste, supo, supimos, supisteis, supieron *5* sabré *etc* *6* sepa *etc* *7* supiera *etc*

salir *2* sal *3* salgo *5* saldré *etc* *6* salga *etc*

seguir *1* siguiendo *2* sigue *3* sigo, sigues, sigue, siguen *4* siguió, siguieron *6* siga *etc* *7* siguiera *etc*

sentar *2* sienta *3* siento, sientas, sienta, sientan *6* siente, sientes, siente, sienten

sentir *1* sintiendo *2* siente *3* siento, sientes, siente, sienten *4* sintió, sintieron *6* sienta, sientas, sienta, sintamos, sintáis, sientan *7* sintiera *etc*

SER *2* sé *3* soy, eres, es, somos, sois, son *4* fui, fuiste, fue, fuimos, fuisteis, fueron *6* sea *etc* *7* fuera *etc* *9* era, eras, era, éramos, erais, eran

servir *1* sirviendo *2* sirve *3* sirvo, sirves, sirve, sirven *4* sirvió, sirvieron *6* sirva *etc* *7* sirviera *etc*

soñar *2* sueña *3* sueño, sueñas, sueña, sueñan *6* sueñe, sueñes, sueñe, sueñen

tener *2* ten *3* tengo, tienes, tiene, tienen *4* tuve, tuviste, tuvo, tuvimos, tuvisteis, tuvieron *5* tendré *etc* *6* tenga *etc* *7* tuviera *etc*

traer *1* trayendo *2* traigo *4* traje, trajiste, trajo, trajimos, trajisteis, trajeron *6* traiga *etc* *7* trajera *etc*

valer *2* val *3* valgo *5* valdré *etc* *6* valga *etc*

venir *2* ven *3* vengo, vienes, viene, vienen *4* vine, viniste, vino, vinimos, vinisteis, vinieron *5* vendré *etc* *6* venga *etc* *7* viniera *etc*

ver *3* veo *6* vea *etc* *8* visto *9* veía *etc*

vestir *1* vistiendo *2* viste *3* visto, vistes, viste, visten *4* vistió, vistieron *6* vista *etc* *7* vistiera *etc*

VIVIR *1* viviendo *2* vive *3* vivo, vives, vive, vivimos, vivís, viven *4* viví, viviste, vivió, vivimos, vivisteis, vivieron *5* viviré, vivirás, vivirá, viviremos, viviréis, vivirán *6* viva, vivas, viva, vivamos, viváis, vivan *7* viviera, vivieras, viviera, viviéramos, vivierais, vivieran *8* vivido *9* vivía, vivías, vivía, vivíamos, vivías, vivían

volver *2* vuelve *3* vuelvo, vuelves, vuelve, vuelven *6* vuelva, vuelvas, vuelva, vuelvan *8* vuelto

VERBOS IRREGULARES EN INGLÉS

present	pt	pp	present	pt	pp
arise	arose	arisen	feed	fed	fed
awake	awoke	awoken	feel	felt	felt
be (am, is, are; being)	was, were	been	fight	fought	fought
			find	found	found
bear	bore	born(e)	flee	fled	fled
beat	beat	beaten	fling	flung	flung
become	became	become	fly (flies)	flew	flown
begin	began	begun	forbid	forbade	forbidden
behold	beheld	beheld	forecast	forecast	forecast
bend	bent	bent	forego	forewent	foregone
beseech	besought	besought	foresee	foresaw	foreseen
beset	beset	beset	foretell	foretold	foretold
bet	bet, betted	bet, betted	forget	forgot	forgotten
bid	bid, bade	bid, bidden	forgive	forgave	forgiven
bind	bound	bound	forsake	forsook	forsaken
bite	bit	bitten	freeze	froze	frozen
bleed	bled	bled	get	got	got, (US) gotten
blow	blew	blown			
break	broke	broken	give	gave	given
breed	bred	bred	go (goes)	went	gone
bring	brought	brought	grind	ground	ground
build	built	built	grow	grew	grown
burn	burnt, burned	burnt, burned	hang	hung, hanged	hung, hanged
burst	burst	burst	have (has; having)	had	had
buy	bought	bought			
can	could	(been able)	hear	heard	heard
cast	cast	cast	hide	hid	hidden
catch	caught	caught	hit	hit	hit
choose	chose	chosen	hold	held	held
cling	clung	clung	hurt	hurt	hurt
come	came	come	keep	kept	kept
cost	cost	cost	kneel	knelt, kneeled	knelt, kneeled
creep	crept	crept			
cut	cut	cut	know	knew	known
deal	dealt	dealt	lay	laid	laid
dig	dug	dug	lead	led	led
do (3rd person: he/she/it does)	did	done	lean	leant, leaned	leant, leaned
			leap	leapt, leaped	leapt, leaped
draw	drew	drawn			
dream	dreamed, dreamt	dreamed, dreamt	learn	learnt, learned	learnt, learned
drink	drank	drunk	leave	left	left
drive	drove	driven	lend	lent	lent
dwell	dwelt	dwelt	let	let	let
eat	ate	eaten	lie (lying)	lay	lain
fall	fell	fallen	light	lit, lighted	lit, lighted

present	pt	pp	present	pt	pp
lose	lost	lost	spell	spelt, spelled	spelt, spelled
make	made	made			
may	might	—	spend	spent	spent
mean	meant	meant	spill	spilt, spilled	spilt, spilled
meet	met	met			
mistake	mistook	mistaken	spin	spun	spun
mow	mowed	mown, mowed	spit	spat	spat
must	(had to)	(had to)	split	split	split
pay	paid	paid	spoil	spoiled, spoilt	spoiled, spoilt
put	put	put			
quit	quit, quitted	quit, quitted	spread	spread	spread
			spring	sprang	sprung
read	read	read	stand	stood	stood
rid	rid	rid	steal	stole	stolen
ride	rode	ridden	stick	stuck	stuck
ring	rang	rung	sting	stung	stung
rise	rose	risen	stink	stank	stunk
run	ran	run	stride	strode	stridden
saw	sawed	sawn	strike	struck	struck, stricken
say	said	said			
see	saw	seen	strive	strove	striven
seek	sought	sought	swear	swore	sworn
sell	sold	sold	sweep	swept	swept
send	sent	sent	swell	swelled	swollen, swelled
set	set	set			
shake	shook	shaken	swim	swam	swum
shall	should	—	swing	swung	swung
shear	sheared	shorn, sheared	take	took	taken
shed	shed	shed	teach	taught	taught
shine	shone	shone	tear	tore	torn
shoot	shot	shot	tell	told	told
show	showed	shown	think	thought	thought
shrink	shrank	shrunk	throw	threw	thrown
shut	shut	shut	thrust	thrust	thrust
sing	sang	sung	tread	trod	trodden
sink	sank	sunk	wake	woke	woken
sit	sat	sat	waylay	waylaid	waylaid
slay	slew	slain	wear	wore	worn
sleep	slept	slept	weave	wove, weaved	woven, weaved
slide	slid	slid			
sling	slung	slung	wed	wedded, wed	wedded, wed
slit	slit	slit			
smell	smelt, smelled	smelt, smelled	weep	wept	wept
			win	won	won
sow	sowed	sown, sowed	wind	wound	wound
speak	spoke	spoken	wring	wrung	wrung
speed	sped, speeded	sped, speeded	write	wrote	written

LOS NÚMEROS

NUMBERS

un, uno(a)	1	one
dos	2	two
tres	3	three
cuatro	4	four
cinco	5	five
seis	6	six
siete	7	seven
ocho	8	eight
nueve	9	nine
diez	10	ten
once	11	eleven
doce	12	twelve
trece	13	thirteen
catorce	14	fourteen
quince	15	fifteen
dieciséis	16	sixteen
diecisiete	17	seventeen
dieciocho	18	eighteen
diecinueve	19	nineteen
veinte	20	twenty
veintiuno	21	twenty-one
veintidós	22	twenty-two
treinta	30	thirty
treinta y uno(a)	31	thirty-one
treinta y dos	32	thirty-two
cuarenta	40	forty
cuarenta y uno(a)	41	forty-one
cincuenta	50	fifty
sesenta	60	sixty
setenta	70	seventy
ochenta	80	eighty
noventa	90	ninety
cien, ciento	100	a hundred, one hundred
ciento uno(a)	101	a hundred and one
doscientos(as)	200	two hundred
doscientos(as) uno(a)	201	two hundred and one
trescientos(as)	300	three hundred
trescientos(as) uno(a)	301	three hundred and one
cuatrocientos(as)	400	four hundred
quiniento(as)	500	five hundred
seiscientos(as)	600	six hundred
setecientos(as)	700	seven hundred
ochocientos(as)	800	eight hundred
novecientos(as)	900	nine hundred
mil	1000	a thousand
mil dos	1002	a thousand and two
cinco mil	5000	five thousand
un millón	1000000	a million

LOS NÚMEROS

NUMBERS

primer, primero(a), 1º, 1er (1ª, 1era)   first, 1st
segundo(a), 2º (2ª)   second, 2nd
tercer, tercero(a), 3º (3ª)   third, 3rd
cuarto(a), 4º (4ª)   fourth, 4th
quinto(a), 5º (5ª)   fifth, 5th
sexto(a), 6º (6ª)   sixth, 6th
séptimo(a)   seventh
octavo(a)   eighth
noveno(a)   ninth
décimo(a)   tenth
undécimo(a)   eleventh
duodécimo(a)   twelfth
decimotercio(a)   thirteenth
decimocuarto(a)   fourteenth
decimoquinto(a)   fifteenth
decimosexto(a)   sixteenth
decimoséptimo(a)   seventeenth
decimoctavo(a)   eighteenth
decimonoveno(a)   nineteenth
vigésimo(a)   twentieth
vigésimo(a) primero(a)   twenty-first
vigésimo(a) segundo(a)   twenty-second
trigésimo(a)   thirtieth
centésimo(a)   hundredth
centésimo(a) primero(a)   hundred-and-first
milésimo(a)   thousandth

Números Quebrados etc

Fractions etc

un medio   a half
un tercio   a third
dos tercios   two thirds
un cuarto   a quarter
un quinto   a fifth
cero coma cinco, 0,5   (nought) point five, 0.5
tres coma cuatro, 3,4   three point four, 3.4
diez por cien(to)   ten per cent
cien por cien   a hundred per cent

Ejemplos

Examples

va a llegar el 7 (de mayo)   he's arriving on the 7th (of May)
vive en el número 7   he lives at number 7
el capítulo/la página 7   chapter/page 7
llegó séptimo   he came in 7th

N.B. In Spanish the ordinal numbers from 1 to 10 are commonly used; from 11 to 20 rather less; above 21 they are rarely written and almost never heard in speech. The custom is to replace the forms for 21 and above by the cardinal number.

LA HORA

¿qué hora es?

es/son

medianoche, las doce (de la noche)	
la una (de la madrugada)	
la una y cinco	
la una y diez	
la una y cuarto *or* quince	
la una y veinticinco	
la una y media *or* treinta	
las dos menos veinticinco, la una treinta y cinco	
las dos menos veinte, la una cuarenta	
las dos menos cuarto, la una cuarenta y cinco	
las dos menos diez, la una cincuenta	
mediodía, las doce (de la tarde)	
la una (de la tarde)	
las siete (de la tarde)	

medianoche, las doce (de la noche)
la una (de la madrugada)
la una y cinco
la una y diez
la una y cuarto *or* quince
la una y veinticinco
la una y media *or* treinta
las dos menos veinticinco, la una treinta y cinco
las dos menos veinte, la una cuarenta
las dos menos cuarto, la una cuarenta y cinco
las dos menos diez, la una cincuenta
mediodía, las doce (de la tarde)
la una (de la tarde)

las siete (de la tarde)

¿a qué hora?

a medianoche
a las siete

en veinte minutos
hace quince minutos

THE TIME

what time is it?

it's o *it is*

midnight, twelve p.m.
one o'clock (in the morning), one (a.m.)
five past one
ten past one
a quarter past one, one fifteen
twenty-five past one, one twenty-five
half-past one, one thirty
twenty-five to two, one thirty-five

twenty to two, one forty
a quarter to two, one forty-five

ten to two, one fifty
twelve o'clock, midday, noon
one o'clock (in the afternoon), one (p.m.)
seven o'clock (in the evening), seven (p.m.)

(at) what time?

at midnight
at seven o'clock

in twenty minutes
fifteen minutes ago

ESPAÑOL - INGLÉS
SPANISH - ENGLISH

A, a

a [a] (*a+el = al*) *prep* **1** (*dirección*) to; **fueron ~ Madrid/Grecia** they went to Madrid/Greece; **me voy ~ casa** I'm going home

2 (*distancia*): **está ~ 15 km de aquí** it's 15 kms from here

3 (*posición*): **estar ~ la mesa** to be at table; **al lado de** next to, beside; *ver tb* **puerta**

4 (*tiempo*): **~ las 10/~ medianoche** at 10/midnight; **~ la mañana siguiente** the following morning; **~ los pocos días** after a few days; **estamos ~ 9 de julio** it's the ninth of July; **~ los 24 años** at the age of 24; **al año/~ la semana** (*AM*) a year/week later

5 (*manera*): **~ la francesa** the French way; **~ caballo** on horseback; **~ oscuras** in the dark

6 (*medio, instrumento*): **~ lápiz** in pencil; **~ mano** by hand; **cocina ~ gas** gas stove

7 (*razón*): **~ 30 ptas el kilo** at 30 pesetas a kilo; **~ más de 50 km/h** at more than 50 kms per hour

8 (*dativo*): **se lo di ~ él** I gave it to him; **vi al policía** I saw the policeman; **se lo compré ~ él** I bought it from him

9 (*tras ciertos verbos*): **voy ~ verle** I'm going to see him; **empezó ~ trabajar** he started working *o* to work

10 (*+infin*): **al verle, le reconocí inmediatamente** when I saw him I recognized him at once; **el camino ~ recorrer** the distance we (*etc*) have to travel; **¡~ callar!** keep quiet!; **¡~ comer!** let's eat!

abad, esa [a'ßað, 'ðesa] *nm/f* abbot/abbess; **~ía** *nf* abbey

abajo [a'ßaxo] *adv* (*situación*) (down) below, underneath; (*en edificio*) downstairs; (*dirección*) down, downwards; **el piso de ~** the downstairs flat; **la parte de ~** the lower part; **¡~ el gobierno!** down with the government!; **cuesta/río ~** downhill/downstream; **de arriba ~** from top to bottom; **el ~ firmante** the undersigned; **más ~** lower *o* further down

abalanzarse [aßalan'θarse] *vr*: **~ sobre** *o* **contra** to throw o.s. at

abandonado, a [aßando'naðo, a] *adj* derelict; (*desatendido*) abandoned; (*desierto*) deserted; (*descuidado*) neglected

abandonar [aßando'nar] *vt* to leave; (*persona*) to abandon, desert; (*cosa*) to abandon, leave behind; (*descuidar*) to neglect; (*renunciar a*) to give up; (*INFORM*) to quit; **~se** *vr*: **~se a** to abandon o.s. to; **abandono** *nm* (*acto*) desertion, abandonment; (*estado*) abandon, neglect; (*renuncia*) withdrawal, retirement; **ganar por abandono** to win by default

abanicar [aßani'kar] *vt* to fan; **abanico** *nm* fan; (*NAUT*) derrick

abaratar [aßara'tar] *vt* to lower the price of; **~se** *vr* to go *o* come down in price

abarcar [aßar'kar] *vt* to include, embrace; (*AM*) to monopolize

abarrotado, a [aßarro'taðo, a] *adj* packed

abarrotar [aßarro'tar] *vt* (*local, estadio, teatro*) to fill, pack

abarrotero, a [aßarro'tero, a] (*AM*) *nm/f* grocer; **abarrotes** *nmpl* (*AM*) groceries, provisions

abastecer [aßaste'θer] *vt*: **~ (de)** to supply (with); **abastecimiento** *nm* supply

abasto [a'ßasto] *nm* supply; **no dar ~ a** to be unable to cope with

abatido, a [aβa'tiðo, a] *adj* dejected, downcast

abatimiento [aβati'mjento] *nm* (*depresión*) dejection, depression

abatir [aβa'tir] *vt* (*muro*) to demolish; (*pájaro*) to shoot *o* bring down; (*fig*) to depress; **~se** *vr* to get depressed; **~se sobre** to swoop *o* pounce on

abdicación [aβðika'θjon] *nf* abdication

abdicar [aβði'kar] *vi* to abdicate

abdomen [aβ'ðomen] *nm* abdomen; **abdominales** *nmpl* (*tb: ejercicios abdominales*) sit-ups

abecedario [aβeθe'ðarjo] *nm* alphabet

abedul [aβe'ðul] *nm* birch

abeja [a'βexa] *nf* bee

abejorro [aβe'xorro] *nm* bumblebee

abertura [aβer'tura] *nf* = **apertura**

abeto [a'βeto] *nm* fir

abierto, a [a'βjerto, a] *pp de* **abrir** ♦ *adj* open; (*AM*) generous

abigarrado, a [aβiɣa'rraðo, a] *adj* multi-coloured

abismal [aβis'mal] *adj* (*fig*) vast, enormous

abismar [aβis'mar] *vt* to humble, cast down; **~se** *vr* to sink; **~se en** (*fig*) to be plunged into

abismo [a'βismo] *nm* abyss

abjurar [aβxu'rar] *vi*: **~ de** to abjure, forswear

ablandar [aβlan'dar] *vt* to soften; **~se** *vr* to get softer

abnegación [aβneɣa'θjon] *nf* self-denial

abnegado, a [aβne'ɣaðo, a] *adj* self-sacrificing

abocado, a [aβo'kaðo, a] *adj*: **verse ~ al desastre** to be heading for disaster

abochornar [aβotʃor'nar] *vt* to embarrass

abofetear [aβofete'ar] *vt* to slap (in the face)

abogado, a [aβo'ɣaðo, a] *nm/f* lawyer; (*notario*) solicitor; (*en tribunal*) barrister (*BRIT*), attorney (*US*); **~ defensor** defence lawyer *o* attorney (*US*)

abogar [aβo'ɣar] *vi*: **~ por** to plead for; (*fig*) to advocate

abolengo [aβo'lengo] *nm* ancestry, lineage

abolición [aβoli'θjon] *nf* abolition

abolir [aβo'lir] *vt* to abolish; (*cancelar*) to cancel

abolladura [aβoʎa'ðura] *nf* dent

abollar [aβo'ʎar] *vt* to dent

abominable [aβomi'naβle] *adj* abominable

abonado, a [aβo'naðo, a] *adj* (*deuda*) paid(-up) ♦ *nm/f* subscriber

abonar [aβo'nar] *vt* (*deuda*) to settle; (*terreno*) to fertilize; (*idea*) to endorse; **~se** *vr* to subscribe; **abono** *nm* payment; fertilizer; subscription

abordar [aβor'ðar] *vt* (*barco*) to board; (*asunto*) to broach

aborigen [aβo'rixen] *nm/f* aborigine

aborrecer [aβorre'θer] *vt* to hate, loathe

abortar [aβor'tar] *vi* (*malparir*) to have a miscarriage; (*deliberadamente*) to have an abortion; **aborto** *nm* miscarriage; abortion

abotonar [aβoto'nar] *vt* to button (up), do up

abovedado, a [aβoβe'ðaðo, a] *adj* vaulted, domed

abrasar [aβra'sar] *vt* to burn (up); (*AGR*) to dry up, parch

abrazar [aβra'θar] *vt* to embrace, hug

abrazo [a'βraθo] *nm* embrace, hug; **un ~** (*en carta*) with best wishes

abrebotellas [aβreβo'teʎas] *nm inv* bottle opener

abrecartas [aβre'kartas] *nm inv* letter opener

abrelatas [aβre'latas] *nm inv* tin (*BRIT*) *o* can opener

abreviar [aβre'βjar] *vt* to abbreviate; (*texto*) to abridge; (*plazo*) to reduce; **abreviatura** *nf* abbreviation

abridor [aβri'ðor] *nm* bottle opener; (*de latas*) tin (*BRIT*) *o* can opener

abrigar [aβri'ɣar] *vt* (*proteger*) to shelter; (*suj: ropa*) to keep warm; (*fig*) to cherish

abrigo [a'βriɣo] *nm* (*prenda*) coat, overcoat; (*lugar protegido*) shelter

abril [a'βril] *nm* April

abrillantar [aβriʎan'tar] *vt* to polish

abrir [a'βrir] *vt* to open (up) ♦ *vi* to open; **~se** *vr* to open (up); (*extenderse*) to open out; (*cielo*) to clear; **~se paso** to find *o* force a way through

abrochar [aβro'tʃar] *vt* (*con botones*) to button (up); (*zapato, con broche*) to do up

abrumar [aβru'mar] *vt* to overwhelm; (*sobrecargar*) to weigh down

abrupto, a [a'βrupto, a] *adj* abrupt; (*empinado*) steep

absceso [aβs'θeso] *nm* abscess

absentismo [aβsen'tismo] *nm* absenteeism

absolución [aβsolu'θjon] *nf* (*REL*) absolution; (*JUR*) acquittal

absoluto, a [aβso'luto, a] *adj* absolute; **en ~** not at all

absolver [aβsol'βer] *vt* to absolve; (*JUR*) to pardon; (: *acusado*) to acquit

absorbente [aβsor'βente] *adj* absorbent; (*interesante*) absorbing

absorber [aβsor'βer] *vt* to absorb; (*embeber*) to soak up

absorción [aβsor'θjon] *nf* absorption; (*COM*) takeover

absorto, a [aβ'sorto, a] *pp de* **absorber** ♦ *adj* absorbed, engrossed

abstemio, a [aβs'temjo, a] *adj* teetotal

abstención [aβsten'θjon] *nf* abstention

abstenerse [aβste'nerse] *vr*: **~ (de)** to abstain *o* refrain (from)

abstinencia [aβsti'nenθja] *nf* abstinence; (*ayuno*) fasting

abstracción [aβstrak'θjon] *nf* abstraction

abstracto, a [aβs'trakto, a] *adj* abstract

abstraer [aβstra'er] *vt* to abstract; **~se** *vr* to be *o* become absorbed

abstraído, a [aβstra'iðo, a] *adj* absent-minded

absuelto [aβ'swelto] *pp de* **absolver**

absurdo, a [aβ'surðo, a] *adj* absurd

abuchear [aβutʃe'ar] *vt* to boo

abuelo, a [a'βwelo, a] *nm/f* grandfather/mother; **~s** *nmpl* grandparents

abulia [a'βulja] *nf* apathy

abultado, a [aβul'taðo, a] *adj* bulky

abultar [aβul'tar] *vi* to be bulky

abundancia [aβun'danθja] *nf*: **una ~ de** plenty of; **abundante** *adj* abundant, plentiful

abundar [aβun'dar] *vi* to abound, be plentiful

aburguesarse [aβurɣe'sarse] *vr* to become middle-class

aburrido, a [aβu'rriðo, a] *adj* (*hastiado*) bored; (*que aburre*) boring; **aburrimiento** *nm* boredom, tedium

aburrir [aβu'rrir] *vt* to bore; **~se** *vr* to be bored, get bored

abusar [aβu'sar] *vi* to go too far; **~ de** to abuse

abusivo, a [aβu'siβo, a] *adj* (*precio*) exorbitant

abuso [a'βuso] *nm* abuse

abyecto, a [aβ'jekto, a] *adj* wretched, abject

acá [a'ka] *adv* (*lugar*) here; **¿de cuándo ~?** since when?

acabado, a [aka'βaðo, a] *adj* finished, complete; (*perfecto*) perfect; (*agotado*) worn out; (*fig*) masterly ♦ *nm* finish

acabar [aka'βar] *vt* (*llevar a su fin*) to finish, complete; (*consumir*) to use up; (*rematar*) to finish off ♦ *vi* to finish, end; **~se** *vr* to finish, stop; (*terminarse*) to be over; (*agotarse*) to run out; **~ con** to put an end to; **~ de llegar** to have just arrived; **~ por hacer** to end (up) by doing; **¡se acabó!** it's all over!; (*¡basta!*) that's enough!

acabóse [aka'βose] *nm*: **esto es el ~** this is the last straw

academia [aka'ðemja] *nf* academy; **académico, a** *adj* academic

acaecer [akae'θer] *vi* to happen, occur

acallar [aka'ʎar] *vt* (*persona*) to silence; (*protestas, rumores*) to suppress

acalorado, a [akalo'raðo, a] *adj* (*discusión*) heated

acalorarse [akalo'rarse] *vr* (*fig*) to get heated

acampar [akam'par] *vi* to camp

acantilado [akanti'laðo] *nm* cliff

acaparar [akapa'rar] *vt* to monopolize; (*acumular*) to hoard

acariciar [akari'θjar] *vt* to caress; (*esperanza*) to cherish

acarrear [akarre'ar] *vt* to transport; (*fig*) to cause, result in

acaso [a'kaso] *adv* perhaps, maybe; **(por) si ~** (just) in case

acatamiento [akata'mjento] *nm* respect; (*ley*) observance

acatar [aka'tar] *vt* to respect; (*ley*) obey

acatarrarse [akata'rrarse] *vr* to catch a cold

acaudalado, a [akauða'laðo, a] *adj* well-off

acaudillar [akauði'ʎar] *vt* to lead, command

acceder [akθe'ðer] *vi*: **~ a** (*petición etc*) to agree to; (*tener acceso a*) to have access to; (*INFORM*) to access

accesible [akθe'siβle] *adj* accessible

acceso [ak'θeso] *nm* access, entry; (*camino*) access, approach; (*MED*) attack, fit

accesorio, a [akθe'sorjo, a] *adj, nm* accessory

accidentado, a [akθiðen'taðo, a] *adj* uneven; (*montañoso*) hilly; (*azaroso*) eventful ♦ *nm/f* accident victim

accidental [akθiðen'tal] *adj* accidental; **accidentarse** *vr* to have an accident

accidente [akθi'ðente] *nm* accident; **~s** *nmpl* (*de terreno*) unevenness *sg*

acción [ak'θjon] *nf* action; (*acto*) action, act; (*COM*) share; (*JUR*) action, lawsuit; **accionar** *vt* to work, operate; (*INFORM*) to drive

accionista [akθjo'nista] *nm/f* shareholder, stockholder

acebo [a'θeβo] *nm* holly; (*árbol*) holly tree

acechar [aθe'tʃar] *vt* to spy on; (*aguardar*) to lie in wait for; **acecho** *nm*: **estar al acecho (de)** to lie in wait (for)

aceitar [aθei'tar] *vt* to oil, lubricate

aceite [a'θeite] *nm* oil; (*de oliva*) olive oil; **~ra** *nf* oilcan; **aceitoso, a** *adj* oily

aceituna [aθei'tuna] *nf* olive

acelerador [aθelera'ðor] *nm* accelerator

acelerar [aθele'rar] *vt* to accelerate

acelga [a'θelɣa] *nf* chard, beet

acento [a'θento] *nm* accent; (*acentuación*) stress

acentuar [aθen'twar] *vt* to accent; to stress; (*fig*) to accentuate

acepción [aθep'θjon] *nf* meaning

aceptable [aθep'taβle] *adj* acceptable

aceptación [aθepta'θjon] *nf* acceptance; (*aprobación*) approval

aceptar [aθep'tar] *vt* to accept; (*aprobar*) to approve

acequia [a'θekja] *nf* irrigation ditch

acera [a'θera] *nf* pavement (*BRIT*), sidewalk (*US*)

acerca [a'θerka]: **~ de** *prep* about, concerning

acercar [aθer'kar] *vt* to bring *o* move nearer; **~se** *vr* to approach, come near

acerico [aθe'riko] *nm* pincushion

acero [a'θero] *nm* steel

acérrimo, a [a'θerrimo, a] *adj* (*partidario*) staunch; (*enemigo*) bitter

acertado, a [aθer'taðo, a] *adj* correct; (*apropiado*) apt; (*sensato*) sensible

acertar [aθer'tar] *vt* (*blanco*) to hit; (*solución*) to get right; (*adivinar*) to guess ♦ *vi* to get it right, be right; **~ a** to manage to; **~ con** to happen *o* hit on

acertijo [aθer'tixo] *nm* riddle, puzzle

achacar [atʃa'kar] *vt* to attribute

achacoso, a [atʃa'koso, a] *adj* sickly

achantar [atʃan'tar] (*fam*) *vt* to scare, frighten; **~se** *vr* to back down

achaque *etc* [a'tʃake] *vb ver* **achacar** ♦ *nm* ailment

achicar [atʃi'kar] *vt* to reduce; (*NAUT*) to bale out

achicharrar [atʃitʃa'rrar] *vt* to scorch, burn

achicoria [atʃi'korja] *nf* chicory

aciago, a [a'θjaɣo, a] *adj* ill-fated, fateful

acicalar [aθika'lar] *vt* to polish; (*persona*) to dress up; **~se** *vr* to get dressed up

acicate [aθi'kate] *nm* spur

acidez [aθi'ðeθ] *nf* acidity

ácido, a ['aθiðo, a] *adj* sour, acid ♦ *nm* acid

acierto *etc* [a'θjerto] *vb ver* **acertar** ♦ *nm* success; (*buen paso*) wise move; (*solución*) solution; (*habilidad*) skill, ability

aclamación [aklama'θjon] *nf* acclamation; (*aplausos*) applause

aclamar [akla'mar] *vt* to acclaim; (*aplaudir*) to applaud

aclaración [aklara'θjon] *nf* clarification, explanation

aclarar [akla'rar] *vt* to clarify, explain; (*ropa*) to rinse ♦ *vi* to clear up; **~se** *vr* (*explicarse*) to understand; **~se la garganta** to clear one's throat

aclaratorio, a [aklara'torjo, a] *adj* explanatory

aclimatación [aklimata'θjon] *nf* acclimatization

aclimatar [aklima'tar] *vt* to acclimatize; **~se** *vr* to become acclimatized

acné [ak'ne] *nm* acne

acobardar [akoβar'ðar] *vt* to intimidate

acodarse [ako'ðarse] *vr*: **~ en** to lean on

acogedor, a [akoxe'ðor, a] *adj* welcoming; (*hospitalario*) hospitable

acoger [ako'xer] *vt* to welcome; (*abrigar*) to shelter; **~se** *vr* to take refuge

acogida [ako'xiða] *nf* reception; refuge

acometer [akome'ter] *vt* to attack; (*emprender*) to undertake; **acometida** *nf* attack, assault

acomodado, a [akomo'ðaðo, a] *adj* (*persona*) well-to-do

acomodador, a [akomoða'ðor, a] *nm/f* usher(ette)

acomodar [akomo'ðar] *vt* to adjust; (*alojar*) to accommodate; **~se** *vr* to conform; (*instalarse*) to install o.s.; (*adaptarse*): **~se (a)** to adapt (to)

acompañar [akompa'ɲar] *vt* to accompany; (*documentos*) to enclose

acondicionar [akondiθjo'nar] *vt* to arrange, prepare; (*pelo*) to condition

acongojar [akongo'xar] *vt* to distress, grieve

aconsejar [akonse'xar] *vt* to advise, counsel; **~se** *vr*: **~se con** to consult

acontecer [akonte'θer] *vi* to happen, occur; **acontecimiento** *nm* event

acopio [a'kopjo] *nm* store, stock

acoplamiento [akopla'mjento] *nm* coupling, joint; **acoplar** *vt* to fit; (*ELEC*) to connect; (*vagones*) to couple

acorazado, a [akora'θaðo, a] *adj* armour-plated, armoured ♦ *nm* battleship

acordar [akor'ðar] *vt* (*resolver*) to agree, resolve; (*recordar*) to remind; **~se** *vr* to agree; **~se (de algo)** to remember (sth); **acorde** *adj* (*MUS*) harmonious ♦ *nm* chord; **acorde con** (*medidas etc*) in keeping with

acordeón [akorðe'on] *nm* accordion

acordonado, a [akorðo'naðo, a] *adj* (*calle*) cordoned-off

acorralar [akorra'lar] *vt* to round up, corral

acortar [akor'tar] *vt* to shorten; (*duración*) to cut short; (*cantidad*) to reduce; **~se** *vr* to become shorter

acosar [ako'sar] *vt* to pursue relentlessly; (*fig*) to hound, pester; **acoso** *nm* harassment; **acoso sexual** sexual harassment

acostar [akos'tar] *vt* (*en cama*) to put to bed; (*en suelo*) to lay down; **~se** *vr* to go to bed; to lie down; **~se con uno** to sleep with sb

acostumbrado, a [akostum'braðo, a] *adj* usual; **~ a** used to

acostumbrar [akostum'brar] *vt*: **~ a uno a algo** to get sb used to sth ♦ *vi*: **~ (a) hacer** to be in the habit of doing; **~se** *vr*: **~se a** to get used to

acotación [akota'θjon] *nf* marginal note; (*GEO*) elevation mark; (*de límite*) boundary mark; (*TEATRO*) stage direction

ácrata ['akrata] *adj, nm/f* anarchist

acre ['akre] *adj* (*olor*) acrid; (*fig*) biting ♦ *nm* acre

acrecentar [akreθen'tar] *vt* to increase, augment

acreditar [akreði'tar] *vt* (*garantizar*) to

vouch for, guarantee; (*autorizar*) to authorize; (*dar prueba de*) to prove; (COM: *abonar*) to credit; (*embajador*) to accredit; **~se** *vr* to become famous

acreedor, a [akree'ðor, a] *adj*: **~ de** worthy of ♦ *nm/f* creditor

acribillar [akriβiˈʎar] *vt*: **~ a balazos** to riddle with bullets

acróbata [aˈkroβata] *nm/f* acrobat

acta [ˈakta] *nf* certificate; (*de comisión*) minutes *pl*, record; **~ de nacimiento/de matrimonio** birth/marriage certificate; **~ notarial** affidavit

actitud [aktiˈtuð] *nf* attitude; (*postura*) posture

activar [aktiˈβar] *vt* to activate; (*acelerar*) to speed up

actividad [aktiβiˈðað] *nf* activity

activo, a [akˈtiβo, a] *adj* active; (*vivo*) lively ♦ *nm* (COM) assets *pl*

acto [ˈakto] *nm* act, action; (*ceremonia*) ceremony; (TEATRO) act; **en el ~** immediately

actor [akˈtor] *nm* actor; (JUR) plaintiff ♦ *adj*: **parte ~a** prosecution

actriz [akˈtriθ] *nf* actress

actuación [aktwaˈθjon] *nf* action; (*comportamiento*) conduct, behaviour; (JUR) proceedings *pl*; (*desempeño*) performance

actual [akˈtwal] *adj* present(-day), current; **~idad** *nf* present; **~idades** *nfpl* (*noticias*) news *sg*; **en la ~idad** at present; (*hoy día*) nowadays

actualizar [aktwaliˈθar] *vt* to update, modernize

actualmente [aktwalˈmente] *adv* at present; (*hoy día*) nowadays

actuar [akˈtwar] *vi* (*obrar*) to work, operate; (*actor*) to act, perform ♦ *vt* to work, operate; **~ de** to act as

acuarela [akwaˈrela] *nf* watercolour

acuario [aˈkwarjo] *nm* aquarium; (ASTROLOGÍA): **A~** Aquarius

acuartelar [akwarteˈlar] *vt* (MIL) to confine to barracks

acuático, a [aˈkwatiko, a] *adj* aquatic

acuchillar [akutʃiˈʎar] *vt* (TEC) to plane (down), smooth

acuciante [akuˈθjante] *adj* urgent

acuciar [akuˈθjar] *vt* to urge on

acudir [akuˈðir] *vi* (*asistir*) to attend; (*ir*) to go; **~ a** (*fig*) to turn to; **~ en ayuda de** to go to the aid of

acuerdo *etc* [aˈkwerðo] *vb ver* **acordar** ♦ *nm* agreement; **¡de ~!** agreed!; **de ~ con** (*persona*) in agreement with; (*acción, documento*) in accordance with; **estar de ~** to be agreed, agree

acumular [akumuˈlar] *vt* to accumulate, collect

acuñar [akuˈɲar] *vt* (*moneda*) to mint; (*frase*) to coin

acupuntura [akupunˈtura] *nf* acupuncture

acurrucarse [akurruˈkarse] *vr* to crouch; (*ovillarse*) to curl up

acusación [akusaˈθjon] *nf* accusation

acusar [akuˈsar] *vt* to accuse; (*revelar*) to reveal; (*denunciar*) to denounce

acuse [aˈkuse] *nm*: **~ de recibo** acknowledgement of receipt

acústica [aˈkustika] *nf* acoustics *pl*

acústico, a [aˈkustiko, a] *adj* acoustic

adaptación [aðaptaˈθjon] *nf* adaptation

adaptador [aðaptaˈðor] *nm* (ELEC) adapter

adaptar [aðapˈtar] *vt* to adapt; (*acomodar*) to fit

adecuado, a [aðeˈkwaðo, a] *adj* (*apto*) suitable; (*oportuno*) appropriate

adecuar [aðeˈkwar] *vt* to adapt; to make suitable

a. de J.C. *abr* (= *antes de Jesucristo*) B.C.

adelantado, a [aðelanˈtaðo, a] *adj* advanced; (*reloj*) fast; **pagar por ~** to pay in advance

adelantamiento [aðelantaˈmjento] *nm* (AUTO) overtaking

adelantar [aðelanˈtar] *vt* to move forward; (*avanzar*) to advance; (*acelerar*) to speed up; (AUTO) to overtake ♦ *vi* to go forward, advance; **~se** *vr* to go forward, advance

adelante [aðeˈlante] *adv* forward(s), ahead ♦ *excl* come in!; **de hoy en ~** from now

on; **más ~** later on; (*más allá*) further on
adelanto [aðeˈlanto] *nm* advance; (*mejora*) improvement; (*progreso*) progress
adelgazar [aðelɣaˈθar] *vt* to thin (down) ♦ *vi* to get thin; (*con régimen*) to slim down, lose weight
ademán [aðeˈman] *nm* gesture; **ademanes** *nmpl* manners; **en ~ de** as if to
además [aðeˈmas] *adv* besides; (*por otra parte*) moreover; (*también*) also; **~ de** besides, in addition to
adentrarse [aðenˈtrarse] *vr*: **~ en** to go into, get inside; (*penetrar*) to penetrate (into)
adentro [aˈðentro] *adv* inside, in; **mar ~** out at sea; **tierra ~** inland
adepto, a [aˈðepto, a] *nm/f* supporter
aderezar [aðereˈθar] *vt* (*ensalada*) to dress; (*comida*) to season; **aderezo** *nm* dressing; seasoning
adeudar [aðeuˈðar] *vt* to owe; **~se** *vr* to run into debt
adherirse [aðeˈrirse] *vr*: **~ a** to adhere to; (*partido*) to join
adhesión [aðeˈsjon] *nf* adhesion; (*fig*) adherence
adicción [aðikˈθjon] *nf* addiction
adición [aðiˈθjon] *nf* addition
adicto, a [aˈðikto, a] *adj*: **~ a** addicted to; (*dedicado*) devoted to ♦ *nm/f* supporter, follower; (*toxicómano etc*) addict
adiestrar [aðjesˈtrar] *vt* to train, teach; (*conducir*) to guide, lead; **~se** *vr* to practise; (*enseñarse*) to train o.s.
adinerado, a [aðineˈraðo, a] *adj* wealthy
adiós [aˈðjos] *excl* (*para despedirse*) goodbye!, cheerio!; (*al pasar*) hello!
aditivo [aðiˈtiβo] *nm* additive
adivinanza [aðiβiˈnanθa] *nf* riddle
adivinar [aðiβiˈnar] *vt* to prophesy; (*conjeturar*) to guess; **adivino, a** *nm/f* fortune-teller
adj *abr* (= *adjunto*) encl.
adjetivo [aðxeˈtiβo] *nm* adjective
adjudicación [aðxuðikaˈθjon] *nf* award; adjudication

adjudicar [aðxuðiˈkar] *vt* to award; **~se** *vr*: **~se algo** to appropriate sth
adjuntar [aðxunˈtar] *vt* to attach, enclose; **adjunto, a** *adj* attached, enclosed ♦ *nm/f* assistant
administración [aðministraˈθjon] *nf* administration; (*dirección*) management; **administrador, a** *nm/f* administrator; manager(ess)
administrar [aðminisˈtrar] *vt* to administer; **administrativo, a** *adj* administrative
admirable [aðmiˈraβle] *adj* admirable
admiración [aðmiraˈθjon] *nf* admiration; (*asombro*) wonder; (*LING*) exclamation mark
admirar [aðmiˈrar] *vt* to admire; (*extrañar*) to surprise; **~se** *vr* to be surprised
admisible [aðmiˈsiβle] *adj* admissible
admisión [aðmiˈsjon] *nf* admission; (*reconocimiento*) acceptance
admitir [aðmiˈtir] *vt* to admit; (*aceptar*) to accept
admonición [aðmoniˈθjon] *nf* warning
adobar [aðoˈβar] *vt* (*CULIN*) to season
adobe [aˈðoβe] *nm* adobe, sun-dried brick
adoctrinar [aðoktriˈnar] *vt*: **~ en** to indoctrinate with
adolecer [aðoleˈθer] *vi*: **~ de** to suffer from
adolescente [aðolesˈθente] *nm/f* adolescent, teenager
adonde [aˈðonde] *conj* (to) where
adónde [aˈðonde] *adv* = **dónde**
adopción [aðopˈθjon] *nf* adoption
adoptar [aðopˈtar] *vt* to adopt
adoptivo, a [aðopˈtiβo, a] *adj* (*padres*) adoptive; (*hijo*) adopted
adoquín [aðoˈkin] *nm* paving stone
adorar [aðoˈrar] *vt* to adore
adormecer [aðormeˈθer] *vt* to put to sleep; **~se** *vr* to become sleepy; (*dormirse*) to fall asleep
adornar [aðorˈnar] *vt* to adorn
adorno [aˈðorno] *nm* ornament; (*decoración*) decoration
adosado, a [aðoˈsaðo, a] *adj*: **casa**

adosada semi-detached house
adquiero etc vb ver **adquirir**
adquirir [aðki'rir] vt to acquire, obtain
adquisición [aðkisi'θjon] nf acquisition
adrede [a'ðreðe] adv on purpose
adscribir [aðskri'ßir] vt to appoint
adscrito pp de **adscribir**
aduana [a'ðwana] nf customs pl
aduanero, a [aðwa'nero, a] adj customs
cpd ♦ nm/f customs officer
aducir [aðu'θir] vt to adduce; (dar como
prueba) to offer as proof
adueñarse [aðwe'narse] vr: ~ **de** to take
possession of
adulación [aðula'θjon] nf flattery
adular [aðu'lar] vt to flatter
adulterar [aðulte'rar] vt to adulterate
adulterio [aðul'terjo] nm adultery
adúltero, a [a'ðultero, a] adj adulterous
♦ nm/f adulterer/adulteress
adulto, a [a'ðulto, a] adj, nm/f adult
adusto, a [a'ðusto, a] adj stern; (austero)
austere
advenedizo, a [aðßene'ðiθo, a] nm/f
upstart
advenimiento [aðßeni'mjento] nm arrival;
(al trono) accession
adverbio [að'ßerßjo] nm adverb
adversario, a [aðßer'sarjo, a] nm/f
adversary
adversidad [aðßersi'ðað] nf adversity;
(contratiempo) setback
adverso, a [að'ßerso, a] adj adverse
advertencia [aðßer'tenθja] nf warning;
(prefacio) preface, foreword
advertir [aðßer'tir] vt to notice; (avisar): ~
a uno de to warn sb about o of
Adviento [að'ßjento] nm Advent
advierto etc vb ver **advertir**
adyacente [aðja'θente] adj adjacent
aéreo, a [a'ereo, a] adj aerial
aerobic [ae'roßik] nm aerobics sg
aerodeslizador [aeroðesliθa'ðor] nm
hovercraft
aeromozo, a [aero'moθo, a] (AM) nm/f air
steward(ess)
aeronáutica [aero'nautika] nf aeronautics
sg
aeronave [aero'naße] nm spaceship
aeroplano [aero'plano] nm aeroplane
aeropuerto [aero'pwerto] nm airport
aerosol [aero'sol] nm aerosol
afabilidad [afaßili'ðað] nf friendliness;
afable adj affable
afamado, a [afa'maðo, a] adj famous
afán [a'fan] nm hard work; (deseo) desire
afanar [afa'nar] vt to harass; (fam) to
pinch; ~**se** vr: ~**se por hacer** to strive to
do
afear [afe'ar] vt to disfigure
afección [afek'θjon] nf (MED) disease
afectación [afekta'θjon] nf affectation;
afectado, a adj affected
afectar [afek'tar] vt to affect
afectísimo, a [afek'tisimo, a] adj
affectionate; **suyo** ~ yours truly
afectivo, a [afek'tißo, a] adj (problema
etc) emotional
afecto [a'fekto] nm affection; **tenerle** ~ **a**
uno to be fond of sb
afectuoso, a [afek'twoso, a] adj
affectionate
afeitar [afei'tar] vt to shave; ~**se** vr to
shave
afeminado, a [afemi'naðo, a] adj
effeminate
Afganistán [afvanis'tan] nm Afghanistan
afianzamiento [afjanθa'mjento] nm
strengthening; security
afianzar [afjan'θar] vt to strengthen; to
secure; ~**se** vr to become established
afiche [a'fitʃe] (AM) nm poster
afición [afi'θjon] nf fondness, liking; **la** ~
the fans pl; **pinto por** ~ I paint as a
hobby; **aficionado, a** adj keen,
enthusiastic; (no profesional) amateur
♦ nm/f enthusiast, fan; amateur; **ser**
aficionado a algo to be very keen on o
fond of sth
aficionar [afiθjo'nar] vt: ~ **a uno a algo** to
make sb like sth; ~**se** vr: ~**se a algo** to
grow fond of sth
afilado, a [afi'laðo, a] adj sharp
afilar [afi'lar] vt to sharpen

afiliarse [afi'ljarse] vr to affiliate
afín [a'fin] adj (parecido) similar; (conexo) related
afinar [afi'nar] vt (TEC) to refine; (MUS) to tune ♦ vi (tocar) to play in tune; (cantar) to sing in tune
afincarse [afin'karse] vr to settle
afinidad [afini'ðað] nf affinity; (parentesco) relationship; **por ~** by marriage
afirmación [afirma'θjon] nf affirmation
afirmar [afir'mar] vt to affirm, state; **afirmativo, a** adj affirmative
aflicción [aflik'θjon] nf affliction; (dolor) grief
afligir [afli'xir] vt to afflict; (apenar) to distress; **~se** vr to grieve
aflojar [aflo'xar] vt to slacken; (desatar) to loosen, undo; (relajar) to relax ♦ vi to drop; (bajar) to go down; **~se** vr to relax
aflorar [aflo'rar] vi to come to the surface, emerge
afluente [aflu'ente] adj flowing ♦ nm tributary
afluir [aflu'ir] vi to flow
afmo, a abr (= afectísimo(a) suyo(a)) Yours
afónico, a [a'foniko, a] adj: **estar ~** to have a sore throat; to have lost one's voice
aforo [a'foro] nm (de teatro etc) capacity
afortunado, a [afortu'naðo, a] adj fortunate, lucky
afrancesado, a [afranθe'saðo, a] adj francophile; (pey) Frenchified
afrenta [a'frenta] nf affront, insult; (deshonra) dishonour, shame
África ['afrika] nf Africa; **africano, a** adj, nm/f African
afrontar [afron'tar] vt to confront; (poner cara a cara) to bring face to face
afuera [a'fwera] adv out, outside; **~s** nfpl outskirts
agachar [aɣa'tʃar] vt to bend, bow; **~se** vr to stoop, bend
agalla [a'ɣaʎa] nf (ZOOL) gill; **tener ~s** (fam) to have guts
agarradera [aɣarra'ðera] (esp AM) nf handle

agarrado, a [aɣa'rraðo, a] adj mean, stingy
agarrar [aɣa'rrar] vt to grasp, grab; (AM) to take, catch; (recoger) to pick up ♦ vi (planta) to take root; **~se** vr to hold on (tightly)
agarrotar [aɣarro'tar] vt (persona) to squeeze tightly; (reo) to garrotte; **~se** vr (motor) to seize up; (MED) to stiffen
agasajar [aɣasa'xar] vt to treat well, fête
agazaparse [aɣaθa'parse] vr to crouch down
agencia [a'xenθja] nf agency; **~ inmobiliaria** estate (BRIT) o real estate (US) agent's (office); **~ de viajes** travel agency
agenciarse [axen'θjarse] vr to obtain, procure
agenda [a'xenda] nf diary
agente [a'xente] nm/f agent; (de policía) policeman/policewoman; **~ inmobiliario** estate agent (BRIT), realtor (US); **~ de seguros** insurance agent
ágil ['axil] adj agile, nimble; **agilidad** nf agility, nimbleness
agilizar [axili'θar] vt (trámites) to speed up
agitación [axita'θjon] nf (de mano etc) shaking, waving; (de líquido etc) stirring; (fig) agitation
agitado, a [axi'taðo, a] adj hectic; (viaje) bumpy
agitar [axi'tar] vt to wave, shake; (líquido) to stir; (fig) to stir up, excite; **~se** vr to get excited; (inquietarse) to get worried o upset
aglomeración [aɣlomera'θjon] nf: **~ de tráfico/gente** traffic jam/mass of people
aglomerar [aɣlome'rar] vt to crowd together; **~se** vr to crowd together
agnóstico, a [aɣ'nostiko, a] adj, nm/f agnostic
agobiar [aɣo'βjar] vt to weigh down; (oprimir) to oppress; (cargar) to burden
agolparse [aɣol'parse] vr to crowd together
agonía [aɣo'nia] nf death throes pl; (fig)

agony, anguish

agonizante [aɣoni'θante] *adj* dying

agonizar [aɣoni'θar] *vi* to be dying

agosto [a'ɣosto] *nm* August

agotado, a [aɣo'taðo, a] *adj* (*persona*) exhausted; (*libros*) out of print; (*acabado*) finished; (*COM*) sold out

agotador, a [aɣota'ðor, a] *adj* exhausting

agotamiento [aɣota'mjento] *nm* exhaustion

agotar [aɣo'tar] *vt* to exhaust; (*consumir*) to drain; (*recursos*) to use up, deplete; **~se** *vr* to be exhausted; (*acabarse*) to run out; (*libro*) to go out of print

agraciado, a [aɣra'θjaðo, a] *adj* (*atractivo*) attractive; (*en sorteo etc*) lucky

agradable [aɣra'ðaβle] *adj* pleasant, nice

agradar [aɣra'ðar] *vt*: **él me agrada** I like him

agradecer [aɣraðe'θer] *vt* to thank; (*favor etc*) to be grateful for; **agradecido, a** *adj* grateful; **¡muy agradecido!** thanks a lot!; **agradecimiento** *nm* thanks *pl*; gratitude

agradezco *etc vb ver* **agradecer**

agrado [a'ɣraðo] *nm*: **ser de tu** *etc* **~** to be to your *etc* liking

agrandar [aɣran'dar] *vt* to enlarge; (*fig*) to exaggerate; **~se** *vr* to get bigger

agrario, a [a'ɣrarjo, a] *adj* agrarian, land *cpd*; (*política*) agricultural, farming

agravante [aɣra'βante] *adj* aggravating
♦ *nm*: **con el ~ de que ...** with the further difficulty that ....

agravar [aɣra'βar] *vt* (*pesar sobre*) to make heavier; (*irritar*) to aggravate; **~se** *vr* to worsen, get worse

agraviar [aɣra'βjar] *vt* to offend; (*ser injusto con*) to wrong; **~se** *vr* to take offence; **agravio** *nm* offence; wrong; (*JUR*) grievance

agredir [aɣre'ðir] *vt* to attack

agregado, a [aɣre'ɣaðo, a] *nm/f*: **A~** ≈ teacher (*who is not head of department*)
♦ *nm* aggregate; (*persona*) attaché

agregar [aɣre'ɣar] *vt* to gather; (*añadir*) to add; (*persona*) to appoint

agresión [aɣre'sjon] *nf* aggression

agresivo, a [aɣre'siβo, a] *adj* aggressive

agriar [a'ɣrjar] *vt* to (turn) sour; **~se** *vr* to turn sour

agrícola [a'ɣrikola] *adj* farming *cpd*, agricultural

agricultor, a [aɣrikul'tor, a] *nm/f* farmer

agricultura [aɣrikul'tura] *nf* agriculture, farming

agridulce [aɣri'ðulθe] *adj* bittersweet; (*CULIN*) sweet and sour

agrietarse [aɣrje'tarse] *vr* to crack; (*piel*) to chap

agrimensor, a [aɣrimen'sor, a] *nm/f* surveyor

agrio, a ['aɣrjo, a] *adj* bitter

agrupación [aɣrupa'θjon] *nf* group; (*acto*) grouping

agrupar [aɣru'par] *vt* to group

agua ['aɣwa] *nf* water; (*NAUT*) wake; (*ARQ*) slope of a roof; **~s** *nfpl* (*de piedra*) water *sg*, sparkle *sg*; (*MED*) water *sg*, urine *sg*; (*NAUT*) waters; **~s abajo/arriba** downstream/upstream; **~ bendita/ destilada/potable** holy/distilled/drinking water; **~ caliente** hot water; **~ corriente** running water; **~ de colonia** eau de cologne; **~ mineral (con/sin gas)** (carbonated/uncarbonated) mineral water; **~ oxigenada** hydrogen peroxide; **~s jurisdiccionales** territorial waters

aguacate [aɣwa'kate] *nm* avocado (pear)

aguacero [aɣwa'θero] *nm* (heavy) shower, downpour

aguado, a [a'ɣwaðo, a] *adj* watery, watered down

aguafiestas [aɣwa'fjestas] *nm/f inv* spoilsport, killjoy

aguanieve [aɣwa'njeβe] *nf* sleet

aguantar [aɣwan'tar] *vt* to bear, put up with; (*sostener*) to hold up ♦ *vi* to last; **~se** *vr* to restrain o.s.; **aguante** *nm* (*paciencia*) patience; (*resistencia*) endurance

aguar [a'ɣwar] *vt* to water down

aguardar [aɣwar'ðar] *vt* to wait for

aguardiente [aɣwar'ðjente] *nm* brandy,

liquor

aguarrás [aɣwa'rras] *nm* turpentine

agudeza [aɣu'ðeθa] *nf* sharpness; (*ingenio*) wit

agudizar [aɣuði'θar] *vt* (*crisis*) to make worse; **~se** *vr* to get worse

agudo, a [a'ɣuðo, a] *adj* sharp; (*voz*) high-pitched, piercing; (*dolor, enfermedad*) acute

agüero [a'ɣwero] *nm*: **buen/mal ~** good/ bad omen

aguijón [aɣi'xon] *nm* sting; (*fig*) spur

águila ['aɣila] *nf* eagle; (*fig*) genius

aguileño, a [aɣi'leɲo, a] *adj* (*nariz*) aquiline; (*rostro*) sharp-featured

aguinaldo [aɣi'naldo] *nm* Christmas box

aguja [a'ɣuxa] *nf* needle; (*de reloj*) hand; (*ARQ*) spire; (*TEC*) firing-pin; **~s** *nfpl* (*ZOOL*) ribs; (*FERRO*) points

agujerear [aɣuxere'ar] *vt* to make holes in

agujero [aɣu'xero] *nm* hole

agujetas [aɣu'xetas] *nfpl* stitch *sg*; (*rigidez*) stiffness *sg*

aguzar [aɣu'θar] *vt* to sharpen; (*fig*) to incite

ahí [a'i] *adv* there; **de ~ que** so that, with the result that; **~ llega** here he comes; **por ~** that way; (*allá*) over there; **200 o por ~** 200 or so

ahijado, a [ai'xaðo, a] *nm/f* godson/ daughter

ahínco [a'inko] *nm* earnestness

ahogar [ao'ɣar] *vt* to drown; (*asfixiar*) to suffocate, smother; (*fuego*) to put out; **~se** *vr* (*en el agua*) to drown; (*por asfixia*) to suffocate

ahogo [a'oɣo] *nm* breathlessness; (*fig*) financial difficulty

ahondar [aon'dar] *vt* to deepen, make deeper; (*fig*) to study thoroughly ♦ *vi*: **~ en** to study thoroughly

ahora [a'ora] *adv* now; (*hace poco*) a moment ago, just now; (*dentro de poco*) in a moment; **~ voy** I'm coming; **~ mismo** right now; **~ bien** now then; **por ~** for the present

ahorcar [aor'kar] *vt* to hang

ahorita [ao'rita] (*fam: esp AM*) *adv* right now

ahorrar [ao'rrar] *vt* (*dinero*) to save; (*esfuerzos*) to save, avoid; **ahorro** *nm* (*acto*) saving; **ahorros** *nmpl* (*dinero*) savings

ahuecar [awe'kar] *vt* to hollow (out); (*voz*) to deepen; **~se** *vr* to give o.s. airs

ahumar [au'mar] *vt* to smoke, cure; (*llenar de humo*) to fill with smoke ♦ *vi* to smoke; **~se** *vr* to fill with smoke

ahuyentar [aujen'tar] *vt* to drive off, frighten off; (*fig*) to dispel

airado, a [ai'raðo, a] *adj* angry

airar [ai'rar] *vt* to anger; **~se** *vr* to get angry

aire ['aire] *nm* air; (*viento*) wind; (*corriente*) draught; (*MUS*) tune; **~s** *nmpl*: **darse ~s** to give o.s. airs; **al ~ libre** in the open air; **~ acondicionado** air conditioning; **airearse** *vr* (*persona*) to go out for a breath of fresh air; **airoso, a** *adj* windy; draughty; (*fig*) graceful

aislado, a [ais'laðo, a] *adj* isolated; (*incomunicado*) cut-off; (*ELEC*) insulated

aislar [ais'lar] *vt* to isolate; (*ELEC*) to insulate

ajardinado, a [axarði'naðo, a] *adj* landscaped

ajedrez [axe'ðreθ] *nm* chess

ajeno, a [a'xeno, a] *adj* (*que pertenece a otro*) somebody else's; **~ a** foreign to

ajetreado, a [axetre'aðo, a] *adj* busy

ajetreo [axe'treo] *nm* bustle

ají [a'xi] (*AM*) *nm* chil(l)i, red pepper; (*salsa*) chil(l)i sauce

ajillo [a'xiʎo] *nm*: **gambas al ~** garlic prawns

ajo ['axo] *nm* garlic

ajuar [a'xwar] *nm* household furnishings *pl*; (*de novia*) trousseau; (*de niño*) layette

ajustado, a [axus'taðo, a] *adj* (*tornillo*) tight; (*cálculo*) right; (*ropa*) tight(-fitting); (*resultado*) close

ajustar [axus'tar] *vt* (*adaptar*) to adjust; (*encajar*) to fit; (*TEC*) to engage; (*IMPRENTA*) to make up; (*apretar*) to tighten; (*concertar*) to agree (on); (*reconciliar*) to reconcile; (*cuentas, deudas*) to settle ♦ *vi* to fit; ~**se** *vr*: ~**se a** (*precio etc*) to be in keeping with, fit in with; ~ **las cuentas a uno** to get even with sb

ajuste [a'xuste] *nm* adjustment; (*COSTURA*) fitting; (*acuerdo*) compromise; (*de cuenta*) settlement

al [al] (= **a** +**el**) *ver* **a**

ala ['ala] *nf* wing; (*de sombrero*) brim; (*futbolista*) winger; ~ **delta** *nf* hang-glider

alabanza [ala'ßanθa] *nf* praise

alabar [ala'ßar] *vt* to praise

alacena [ala'θena] *nf* kitchen cupboard (*BRIT*), kitchen closet (*US*)

alacrán [ala'kran] *nm* scorpion

alambique [alam'bike] *nm* still

alambrada [alam'braða] *nf* wire fence; (*red*) wire netting

alambrado [alam'braðo] *nm* = **alambrada**

alambre [a'lambre] *nm* wire; ~ **de púas** barbed wire

alameda [ala'meða] *nf* (*plantío*) poplar grove; (*lugar de paseo*) avenue, boulevard

álamo ['alamo] *nm* poplar; ~ **temblón** aspen

alarde [a'larðe] *nm* show, display; **hacer ~ de** to boast of

alargador [alarxa'ðor] *nm* (*ELEC*) extension lead

alargar [alar'var] *vt* to lengthen, extend; (*paso*) to hasten; (*brazo*) to stretch out; (*cuerda*) to pay out; (*conversación*) to spin out; ~**se** *vr* to get longer

alarido [ala'riðo] *nm* shriek

alarma [a'larma] *nf* alarm

alarmar *vt* to alarm; ~**se** to get alarmed; **alarmante** [alar'mante] *adj* alarming

alba ['alßa] *nf* dawn

albacea [alßa'θea] *nm/f* executor/executrix

albahaca [al'ßaka] *nf* basil

Albania [al'ßanja] *nf* Albania

albañil [alßa'ɲil] *nm* bricklayer; (*cantero*) mason

albarán [alßa'ran] *nm* (*COM*) delivery note, invoice

albaricoque [alßari'koke] *nm* apricot

albedrío [alße'ðrio] *nm*: **libre ~** free will

alberca [al'ßerka] *nf* reservoir; (*AM*) swimming pool

albergar [alßer'var] *vt* to shelter

albergue *etc* [al'ßerve] *vb ver* **albergar** ♦ *nm* shelter, refuge; ~ **juvenil** youth hostel

albóndiga [al'ßondiva] *nf* meatball

albornoz [alßor'noθ] *nm* (*de los árabes*) burnous; (*para el baño*) bathrobe

alborotar [alßoro'tar] *vi* to make a row ♦ *vt* to agitate, stir up; ~**se** *vr* to get excited; (*mar*) to get rough; **alboroto** *nm* row, uproar

alborozar [alßoro'θar] *vt* to gladden; ~**se** *vr* to rejoice

alborozo [alßo'roθo] *nm* joy

álbum ['alßum] (*pl* ~**s**, ~**es**) *nm* album; ~ **de recortes** scrapbook

alcachofa [alka'tʃofa] *nf* artichoke

alcalde, esa [al'kalde, esa] *nm/f* mayor(ess)

alcaldía [alkal'dia] *nf* mayoralty; (*lugar*) mayor's office

alcance *etc* [al'kanθe] *vb ver* **alcanzar** ♦ *nm* reach; (*COM*) adverse balance

alcantarilla [alkanta'riʎa] *nf* (*de aguas cloacales*) sewer; (*en la calle*) gutter

alcanzar [alkan'θar] *vt* (*algo: con la mano, el pie*) to reach; (*alguien: en el camino etc*) to catch up (with); (*autobús*) to catch; (*suj: bala*) to hit, strike ♦ *vi* (*ser suficiente*) to be enough; ~ **a hacer** to manage to do

alcaparra [alka'parra] *nf* caper

alcayata [alka'jata] *nf* hook

alcázar [al'kaθar] *nm* fortress; (*NAUT*) quarter-deck

alcoba [al'koßa] *nf* bedroom

alcohol [al'kol] *nm* alcohol; ~ **metílico** methylated spirits *pl* (*BRIT*), wood alcohol (*US*); **alcohólico, a** *adj, nm/f* alcoholic

alcoholímetro [alko'limetro] *nm* Breathalyser ® (*BRIT*), drunkometer (*US*)

alcoholismo [alko'lismo] *nm* alcoholism

alcornoque [alkor'noke] nm cork tree; (fam) idiot

alcurnia [al'kurnja] nf lineage

aldaba [al'daβa] nf (door) knocker

aldea [al'dea] nf village; **~no, a** adj village cpd ♦ nm/f villager

aleación [alea'θjon] nf alloy

aleatorio, a [alea'torjo, a] adj random

aleccionar [alekθjo'nar] vt to instruct; (adiestrar) to train

alegación [alexa'θjon] nf allegation

alegar [ale'xar] vt to claim; (JUR) to plead ♦ vi (AM) to argue

alegato [ale'xato] nm (JUR) allegation; (AM) argument

alegoría [alexo'ria] nf allegory

alegrar [ale'xrar] vt (causar alegría) to cheer (up); (fuego) to poke; (fiesta) to liven up; **~se** vr (fam) to get merry o tight; **~se de** to be glad about

alegre [a'levre] adj happy, cheerful; (fam) merry, tight; (chiste) risqué, blue; **alegría** nf happiness; merriment

alejamiento [alexa'mjento] nm removal; (distancia) remoteness

alejar [ale'xar] vt to remove; (fig) to estrange; **~se** vr to move away

alemán, ana [ale'man, ana] adj, nm/f German ♦ nm (LING) German

Alemania [ale'manja] nf: **~ Occidental/ Oriental** West/East Germany

alentador, a [alenta'ðor, a] adj encouraging

alentar [alen'tar] vt to encourage

alergia [a'lerxja] nf allergy

alero [a'lero] nm (de tejado) eaves pl; (de carruaje) mudguard

alerta [a'lerta] adj, nm alert

aleta [a'leta] nf (de pez) fin; (de ave) wing; (de foca, DEPORTE) flipper; (AUTO) mudguard

aletargar [aletar'xar] vt to make drowsy; (entumecer) to make numb; **~se** vr to grow drowsy; to become numb

aletear [alete'ar] vi to flutter

alevín [ale'βin] nm fry, young fish

alevosía [aleβo'sia] nf treachery

alfabeto [alfa'βeto] nm alphabet

alfalfa [al'falfa] nf alfalfa, lucerne

alfarería [alfare'ria] nf pottery; (tienda) pottery shop; **alfarero, a** nm/f potter

alféizar [al'feiθar] nm window-sill

alférez [al'fereθ] nm (MIL) second lieutenant; (NAUT) ensign

alfil [al'fil] nm (AJEDREZ) bishop

alfiler [alfi'ler] nm pin; (broche) clip

alfiletero [alfile'tero] nm needlecase

alfombra [al'fombra] nf carpet; (más pequeña) rug; **alfombrar** vt to carpet; **alfombrilla** nf rug, mat

alforja [al'forxa] nf saddlebag

algarabía [alɣara'βia] (fam) nf gibberish; (griterío) hullabaloo

algas ['alɣas] nfpl seaweed

álgebra ['alxeβra] nf algebra

álgido, a ['alxiðo, a] adj (momento etc) crucial, decisive

algo ['alɣo] pron something; anything ♦ adv somewhat, rather; **¿~ más?** anything else?; (en tienda) is that all?; **por ~ será** there must be some reason for it

algodón [alɣo'ðon] nm cotton; (planta) cotton plant; **~ de azúcar** candy floss (BRIT), cotton candy (US); **~ hidrófilo** cotton wool (BRIT), absorbent cotton (US)

algodonero, a [alɣoðo'nero, a] adj cotton cpd ♦ nm/f cotton grower ♦ nm cotton plant

alguacil [alɣwa'θil] nm bailiff; (TAUR) mounted official

alguien ['alɣjen] pron someone, somebody; (en frases interrogativas) anyone, anybody

alguno, a [al'ɣuno, a] adj (delante de nm: **algún**) some; (después de n): **no tiene talento ~** he has no talent, he doesn't have any talent ♦ pron (alguien) someone, somebody; **algún que otro libro** some book or other; **algún día iré** I'll go one o some day; **sin interés ~** without the slightest interest; **~ que otro** an occasional one; **~s piensan** some (people) think

alhaja [a'laxa] nf jewel; (tesoro) precious

object, treasure

alhelí [ale'li] *nm* wallflower, stock

aliado, a [a'ljaðo, a] *adj* allied

alianza [a'ljanθa] *nf* alliance; (*anillo*) wedding ring

aliar [a'ljar] *vt* to ally; **~se** *vr* to form an alliance

alias ['aljas] *adv* alias

alicates [ali'kates] *nmpl* pliers; **~ de uñas** nail clippers

aliciente [ali'θjente] *nm* incentive; (*atracción*) attraction

alienación [aljena'θjon] *nf* alienation

aliento [a'ljento] *nm* breath; (*respiración*) breathing; **sin ~** breathless

aligerar [alixe'rar] *vt* to lighten; (*reducir*) to shorten; (*aliviar*) to alleviate; (*mitigar*) to ease; (*paso*) to quicken

alijo [a'lixo] *nm* consignment

alimaña [ali'maɲa] *nf* pest

alimentación [alimenta'θjon] *nf* (*comida*) food; (*acción*) feeding; (*tienda*) grocer's (shop); **alimentador** *nm*: **alimentador de papel** sheet-feeder

alimentar [alimen'tar] *vt* to feed; (*nutrir*) to nourish; **~se** *vr* to feed

alimenticio, a [alimen'tiθjo, a] *adj* food *cpd*; (*nutritivo*) nourishing, nutritious

alimento [ali'mento] *nm* food; (*nutrición*) nourishment

alineación [alinea'θjon] *nf* alignment; (*DEPORTE*) line-up

alinear [aline'ar] *vt* to align; **~se** *vr* (*DEPORTE*) to line up; **~se en** to fall in with

aliñar [ali'ɲar] *vt* (*CULIN*) to season; **aliño** *nm* (*CULIN*) dressing

alioli [ali'oli] *nm* garlic mayonnaise

alisar [ali'sar] *vt* to smooth

aliso [a'liso] *nm* alder

alistarse [alis'tarse] *vr* to enlist; (*inscribirse*) to enrol

aliviar [ali'βjar] *vt* (*carga*) to lighten; (*persona*) to relieve; (*dolor*) to relieve, alleviate

alivio [a'liβjo] *nm* alleviation, relief

aljibe [al'xiβe] *nm* cistern

allá [a'ʎa] *adv* (*lugar*) there; (*por ahí*) over there; (*tiempo*) then; **~ abajo** down there; **más ~** further on; **más ~ de** beyond; **¡~ tú!** that's your problem!

allanamiento [aʎana'mjento] *nm*: **~ de morada** burglary

allanar [aʎa'nar] *vt* to flatten, level (out); (*igualar*) to smooth (out); (*fig*) to subdue; (*JUR*) to burgle, break into

allegado, a [aʎe'ɣaðo, a] *adj* near, close
♦ *nm/f* relation

allí [a'ʎi] *adv* there; **~ mismo** right there; **por ~** over there; (*por ese camino*) that way

alma ['alma] *nf* soul; (*persona*) person

almacén [alma'θen] *nm* (*depósito*) warehouse, store; (*MIL*) magazine; (*AM*) shop; **(grandes) almacenes** *nmpl* department store *sg*; **almacenaje** *nm* storage

almacenar [almaθe'nar] *vt* to store, put in storage; (*proveerse*) to stock up with; **almacenero** *nm* (*AM*) shopkeeper

almanaque [alma'nake] *nm* almanac

almeja [al'mexa] *nf* clam

almendra [al'mendra] *nf* almond; **almendro** *nm* almond tree

almíbar [al'miβar] *nm* syrup

almidón [almi'ðon] *nm* starch; **almidonar** *vt* to starch

almirante [almi'rante] *nm* admiral

almirez [almi're θ] *nm* mortar

almizcle [al'miθkle] *nm* musk

almohada [almo'aða] *nf* pillow; (*funda*) pillowcase; **almohadilla** *nf* cushion; (*TEC*) pad; (*AM*) pincushion

almohadón [almoa'ðon] *nm* large pillow; bolster

almorranas [almo'rranas] *nfpl* piles, haemorrhoids

almorzar [almor'θar] *vt*: **~ una tortilla** to have an omelette for lunch ♦ *vi* to (have) lunch

almuerzo *etc* [al'mwerθo] *vb ver* **almorzar**
♦ *nm* lunch

alocado, a [alo'kaðo, a] *adj* crazy

alojamiento [aloxa'mjento] *nm* lodging(s)

(pl); (viviendas) housing
alojar [alo'xar] vt to lodge; **~se** vr to lodge, stay
alondra [a'londra] nf lark, skylark
alpargata [alpar'ɣata] nf rope-soled sandal, espadrille
Alpes ['alpes] nmpl: **los ~** the Alps
alpinismo [alpi'nismo] nm mountaineering, climbing; **alpinista** nm/f mountaineer, climber
alpiste [al'piste] nm birdseed
alquilar [alki'lar] vt (suj: propietario: inmuebles) to let, rent (out); (: coche) to hire out; (: TV) to rent (out); (suj: alquilador: inmuebles, TV) to rent; (: coche) to hire; **"se alquila casa"** "house to let (BRIT) o for rent (US)"
alquiler [alki'ler] nm renting; letting; hiring; (arriendo) rent; hire charge; **~ de automóviles** car hire; **de ~** for hire
alquimia [al'kimja] nf alchemy
alquitrán [alki'tran] nm tar
alrededor [alreðe'ðor] adv around, about; **~ de** around, about; **mirar a su ~** to look (round) about one; **~es** nmpl surroundings
alta ['alta] nf (certificate of) discharge; **dar de ~** to discharge
altanería [altane'ria] nf haughtiness, arrogance; **altanero, a** adj arrogant, haughty
altar [al'tar] nm altar
altavoz [alta'ßoθ] nm loudspeaker; (amplificador) amplifier
alteración [altera'θjon] nf alteration; (alboroto) disturbance
alterar [alte'rar] vt to alter; to disturb; **~se** vr (persona) to get upset
altercado [alter'kaðo] nm argument
alternar [alter'nar] vt to alternate ♦ vi to alternate; (turnar) to take turns; **~se** vr to alternate; to take turns; **~ con** to mix with; **alternativa** nf alternative; (elección) choice; **alternativo, a** adj alternative; (alterno) alternating; **alterno, a** adj alternate; (ELEC) alternating
Alteza [al'teθa] nf (tratamiento) Highness

altibajos [alti'ßaxos] nmpl ups and downs
altiplanicie [altipla'niθje] nf high plateau
altiplano [alti'plano] nm = **altiplanicie**
altisonante [altiso'nante] adj high-flown, high-sounding
altitud [alti'tuð] nf height; (AVIAT, GEO) altitude
altivez [alti'ßeθ] nf haughtiness, arrogance; **altivo, a** adj haughty, arrogant
alto, a ['alto, a] adj high; (persona) tall; (sonido) high, sharp; (noble) high, lofty ♦ nm halt; (MUS) alto; (GEO) hill; (AM) pile ♦ adv (de sitio) high; (de sonido) loud, loudly ♦ excl halt!; **la pared tiene 2 metros de ~** the wall is 2 metres high; **en alta mar** on the high seas; **en voz alta** in a loud voice; **las altas horas de la noche** the small o wee hours; **en lo ~ de** at the top of; **pasar por ~** to overlook
altoparlante [altopar'lante] (AM) nm loudspeaker
altruismo [altru'ismo] nm altruism
altura [al'tura] nf height; (NAUT) depth; (GEO) latitude; **la pared tiene 1.80 de ~** the wall is 1 metre 80cm high; **a estas ~s** at this stage; **a estas ~s del año** at this time of the year
alubia [a'lußja] nf bean
alucinación [aluθina'θjon] nf hallucination
alucinar [aluθi'nar] vi to hallucinate ♦ vt to deceive; (fascinar) to fascinate
alud [a'luð] nm avalanche; (fig) flood
aludir [alu'ðir] vi: **~ a** to allude to; **darse por aludido** to take the hint
alumbrado [alum'braðo] nm lighting; **alumbramiento** nm lighting; (MED) childbirth, delivery
alumbrar [alum'brar] vt to light (up) ♦ vi (MED) to give birth
aluminio [alu'minjo] nm aluminium (BRIT), aluminum (US)
alumno, a [a'lumno, a] nm/f pupil, student
alunizar [aluni'θar] vi to land on the moon

alusión [alu'sjon] *nf* allusion

alusivo, a [alu'siβo, a] *adj* allusive

aluvión [alu'βjon] *nm* alluvium; (*fig*) flood

alverja [al'βerxa] (*AM*) *nf* pea

alza [ˈalθa] *nf* rise; (*MIL*) sight

alzada [al'θaða] *nf* (*de caballos*) height; (*JUR*) appeal

alzamiento [alθa'mjento] *nm* (*rebelión*) rising

alzar [al'θar] *vt* to lift (up); (*precio, muro*) to raise; (*cuello de abrigo*) to turn up; (*AGR*) to gather in; (*IMPRENTA*) to gather; ~**se** *vr* to get up, rise; (*rebelarse*) to revolt; (*COM*) to go fraudulently bankrupt; (*JUR*) to appeal

ama [ˈama] *nf* lady of the house; (*dueña*) owner; (*institutriz*) governess; (*madre adoptiva*) foster mother; ~ **de casa** housewife; ~ **de llaves** housekeeper

amabilidad [amaβili'ðað] *nf* kindness; (*simpatía*) niceness; **amable** *adj* kind; nice; **es usted muy amable** that's very kind of you

amaestrado, a [amaes'traðo, a] *adj* (*animal: en circo etc*) performing

amaestrar [amaes'trar] *vt* to train

amago [a'maɣo] *nm* threat; (*gesto*) threatening gesture; (*MED*) symptom

amainar [amai'nar] *vi* (*viento*) to die down

amalgama [amal'ɣama] *nf* amalgam; **amalgamar** *vt* to amalgamate; (*combinar*) to combine, mix

amamantar [amaman'tar] *vt* to suckle, nurse

amanecer [amane'θer] *vi* to dawn ♦ *nm* dawn; ~ **afiebrado** to wake up with a fever

amanerado, a [amane'raðo, a] *adj* affected

amansar [aman'sar] *vt* to tame; (*persona*) to subdue; ~**se** *vr* (*persona*) to calm down

amante [a'mante] *adj*: ~ **de** fond of ♦ *nm/f* lover

amapola [ama'pola] *nf* poppy

amar [a'mar] *vt* to love

amargado, a [amar'ɣaðo, a] *adj* bitter

amargar [amar'ɣar] *vt* to make bitter; (*fig*) to embitter; ~**se** *vr* to become embittered

amargo, a [a'marɣo, a] *adj* bitter; **amargura** *nf* bitterness

amarillento, a [amari'ʎento, a] *adj* yellowish; (*tez*) sallow; **amarillo, a** *adj, nm* yellow

amarrar [ama'rrar] *vt* to moor; (*sujetar*) to tie up

amarras [a'marras] *nfpl*: **soltar** ~ to set sail

amasar [ama'sar] *vt* (*masa*) to knead; (*mezclar*) to mix, prepare; (*confeccionar*) to concoct; **amasijo** *nm* kneading; mixing; (*fig*) hotchpotch

amateur [ˈamatur] *nm/f* amateur

amazona [ama'θona] *nf* horsewoman; **A~s** *nm*: **el A~s** the Amazon

ambages [am'baxes] *nmpl*: **sin** ~ in plain language

ámbar [ˈambar] *nm* amber

ambición [ambi'θjon] *nf* ambition; **ambicionar** *vt* to aspire to; **ambicioso, a** *adj* ambitious

ambidextro, a [ambi'ðekstro, a] *adj* ambidextrous

ambientación [ambjenta'θjon] *nf* (*CINE, TEATRO etc*) setting; (*RADIO*) sound effects

ambiente [am'bjente] *nm* (*tb fig*) atmosphere; (*medio*) environment

ambigüedad [ambiɣwe'ðað] *nf* ambiguity; **ambiguo, a** *adj* ambiguous

ámbito [ˈambito] *nm* (*campo*) field; (*fig*) scope

ambos, as [ˈambos, as] *adj pl, pron pl* both

ambulancia [ambu'lanθja] *nf* ambulance

ambulante [ambu'lante] *adj* travelling *cpd*, itinerant

ambulatorio [ambula'torio] *nm* state health-service clinic

amedrentar [ameðren'tar] *vt* to scare

amén [a'men] *excl* amen; ~ **de** besides

amenaza [ame'naθa] *nf* threat

amenazar [amena'θar] *vt* to threaten ♦ *vi*: ~ **con hacer** to threaten to do

amenidad [ameni'ðað] *nf* pleasantness

ameno, a [a'meno, a] *adj* pleasant
América [a'merika] *nf* America; **~ del
Norte/del Sur** North/South America; **~
Central/Latina** Central/Latin America;
americana *nf* coat, jacket; *ver tb*
americano; **americano, a** *adj, nm/f*
American
amerizar [ameri'θar] *vi* (*avión*) to land (on
the sea)
ametralladora [ametraʎa'ðora] *nf*
machine gun
amianto [a'mjanto] *nm* asbestos
amigable [ami'vaßle] *adj* friendly
amígdala [a'mixðala] *nf* tonsil;
amigdalitis *nf* tonsillitis
amigo, a [a'mixo, a] *adj* friendly ♦ *nm/f*
friend; (*amante*) lover; **ser ~ de algo** to
be fond of sth; **ser muy ~s** to be close
friends
amilanar [amila'nar] *vt* to scare; **~se** *vr* to
get scared
aminorar [amino'rar] *vt* to diminish;
(*reducir*) to reduce; **~ la marcha** to slow
down
amistad [amis'taö] *nf* friendship; **~es** *nfpl*
(*amigos*) friends; **amistoso, a** *adj*
friendly
amnesia [am'nesja] *nf* amnesia
amnistía [amnis'tia] *nf* amnesty
amo ['amo] *nm* owner; (*jefe*) boss
amodorrarse [amoðo'rrarse] *vr* to get
sleepy
amoldar [amol'dar] *vt* to mould; (*adaptar*)
to adapt
amonestación [amonesta'θjon] *nf*
warning; **amonestaciones** *nfpl* (*REL*)
marriage banns
amonestar [amones'tar] *vt* to warn; (*REL*)
to publish the banns of
amontonar [amonto'nar] *vt* to collect, pile
up; **~se** *vr* to crowd together;
(*acumularse*) to pile up
amor [a'mor] *nm* love; (*amante*) lover;
hacer el ~ to make love; **~ propio** self-
respect
amoratado, a [amora'taðo, a] *adj* purple
amordazar [amorða'θar] *vt* to muzzle;

(*fig*) to gag
amorfo, a [a'morfo, a] *adj* amorphous,
shapeless
amoroso, a [amo'roso, a] *adj* affectionate,
loving
amortajar [amorta'xar] *vt* to shroud
amortiguador [amortigwa'ðor] *nm* shock
absorber; (*parachoques*) bumper; **~es**
nmpl (*AUTO*) suspension *sg*
amortiguar [amorti'ɣwar] *vt* to deaden;
(*ruido*) to muffle; (*color*) to soften
amortización [amortiθa'θjon] *nf* (*de
deuda*) repayment; (*de bono*) redemption
amotinar [amoti'nar] *vt* to stir up, incite
(to riot); **~se** *vr* to mutiny
amparar [ampa'rar] *vt* to protect; **~se** *vr*
to seek protection; (*de la lluvia etc*) to
shelter; **amparo** *nm* help, protection; **al
amparo de** under the protection of
amperio [am'perjo] *nm* ampère, amp
ampliación [amplja'θjon] *nf* enlargement;
(*extensión*) extension
ampliar [am'pljar] *vt* to enlarge; to extend
amplificación [amplifika'θjon] *nf*
enlargement; **amplificador** *nm*
amplifier
amplificar [amplifi'kar] *vt* to amplify
amplio, a ['ampljo, a] *adj* spacious; (*de
falda etc*) full; (*extenso*) extensive; (*ancho*)
wide; **amplitud** *nf* spaciousness; extent;
(*fig*) amplitude
ampolla [am'poʎa] *nf* blister; (*MED*)
ampoule
ampuloso, a [ampu'loso, a] *adj*
bombastic, pompous
amputar [ampu'tar] *vt* to cut off,
amputate
amueblar [amwe'ßlar] *vt* to furnish
amurallar [amura'ʎar] *vt* to wall up *o* in
anacronismo [anakro'nismo] *nm*
anachronism
anales [a'nales] *nmpl* annals
analfabetismo [analfaße'tismo] *nm*
illiteracy; **analfabeto, a** *adj, nm/f*
illiterate
analgésico [anal'xesiko] *nm* painkiller,
analgesic

análisis [a'nalisis] *nm inv* analysis
analista [ana'lista] *nm/f* (*gen*) analyst
analizar [anali'θar] *vt* to analyse
analogía [analo'xia] *nf* analogy
analógico, a [ana'loxiko, a] *adj* (*INFORM*) analog; (*reloj*) analogue (*BRIT*), analog (*US*)
análogo, a [a'naloxo, a] *adj* analogous, similar
ananá(s) [ana'na(s)] (*AM*) *nm* pineapple
anaquel [ana'kel] *nm* shelf
anarquía [anar'kia] *nf* anarchy; **anarquismo** *nm* anarchism; **anarquista** *nm/f* anarchist
anatomía [anato'mia] *nf* anatomy
anca ['anka] *nf* rump, haunch; **~s** *nfpl* (*fam*) behind *sg*
ancho, a ['antʃo, a] *adj* wide; (*falda*) full; (*fig*) liberal ♦ *nm* width; (*FERRO*) gauge; **ponerse ~** to get conceited; **estar a sus anchas** to be at one's ease
anchoa [an'tʃoa] *nf* anchovy
anchura [an'tʃura] *nf* width; (*extensión*) wideness
anciano, a [an'θjano, a] *adj* old, aged ♦ *nm/f* old man/woman; elder
ancla ['ankla] *nf* anchor; **~dero** *nm* anchorage; **anclar** *vi* to (drop) anchor
andadura [anda'ðura] *nf* gait; (*de caballo*) pace
Andalucía [andalu'θia] *nf* Andalusia; **andaluz, a** *adj*, *nm/f* Andalusian
andamiaje [anda'mjaxe] *nm* = **andamio**
andamio [an'damjo] *nm* scaffold(ing)
andar [an'dar] *vt* to go, cover, travel ♦ *vi* to go, walk, travel; (*funcionar*) to go, work; (*estar*) to be ♦ *nm* walk, gait, pace; **~se** *vr* to go away; **~ a pie/a caballo/en bicicleta** to go on foot/on horseback/by bicycle; **~ haciendo algo** to be doing sth; **¡anda!** (*sorpresa*) go on!; **anda por** *o* **en los 40** he's about 40
andén [an'den] *nm* (*FERRO*) platform; (*NAUT*) quayside; (*AM*: *de la calle*) pavement (*BRIT*), sidewalk (*US*)
Andes ['andes] *nmpl*: **los ~** the Andes
Andorra [an'dorra] *nf* Andorra
andrajo [an'draxo] *nm* rag; **~so, a** *adj* ragged

anduve *etc* [an'duße] *vb ver* **andar**
anécdota [a'nekðota] *nf* anecdote, story
anegar [ane'ɣar] *vt* to flood; (*ahogar*) to drown; **~se** *vr* to drown; (*hundirse*) to sink
anejo, a [a'nexo, a] *adj*, *nm* = **anexo**
anemia [a'nemja] *nf* anaemia
anestesia [anes'tesja] *nf* (*sustancia*) anaesthetic; (*proceso*) anaesthesia
anexar [anek'sar] *vt* to annex; (*documento*) to attach; **anexión** *nf* annexation; **anexionamiento** *nm* annexation; **anexo, a** *adj* attached ♦ *nm* annexe
anfibio, a [an'fißjo, a] *adj* amphibious ♦ *nm* amphibian
anfiteatro [anfite'atro] *nm* amphitheatre; (*TEATRO*) dress circle
anfitrión, ona [anfi'trjon, ona] *nm/f* host(ess)
ángel ['anxel] *nm* angel; **~ de la guarda** guardian angel; **tener ~** to be charming; **angelical** *adj*, **angélico, a** *adj* angelic(al)
angina [an'xina] *nf* (*MED*) inflammation of the throat; **~ de pecho** angina; **tener ~s** to have tonsillitis
anglicano, a [angli'kano, a] *adj*, *nm/f* Anglican
anglosajón, ona [anglosa'xon, ona] *adj* Anglo-Saxon
angosto, a [an'gosto, a] *adj* narrow
anguila [an'gila] *nf* eel
angula [an'gula] *nf* elver, baby eel
ángulo ['angulo] *nm* angle; (*esquina*) corner; (*curva*) bend
angustia [an'gustja] *nf* anguish; **angustiar** *vt* to distress, grieve
anhelar [ane'lar] *vt* to be eager for; (*desear*) to long for, desire ♦ *vi* to pant, gasp; **anhelo** *nm* eagerness; desire
anidar [ani'ðar] *vi* to nest
anillo [a'niʎo] *nm* ring; **~ de boda** wedding ring
animación [anima'θjon] *nf* liveliness; (*vitalidad*) life; (*actividad*) activity; bustle
animado, a [ani'maðo, a] *adj* lively;

(*vivaz*) animated; **animador, a** *nm/f*
(*TV*) host(ess), compère; (*DEPORTE*)
cheerleader

animadversión [animaðßer'sjon] *nf* ill-
will, antagonism

animal [ani'mal] *adj* animal; (*fig*) stupid
♦ *nm* animal; (*fig*) fool; (*bestia*) brute

animar [ani'mar] *vt* (*BIO*) to animate, give
life to; (*fig*) to liven up, brighten up,
cheer up; (*estimular*) to stimulate; **~se** *vr*
to cheer up; to feel encouraged;
(*decidirse*) to make up one's mind

ánimo ['animo] *nm* (*alma*) soul; (*mente*)
mind; (*valentía*) courage ♦ *excl* cheer up!

animoso, a [ani'moso, a] *adj* brave; (*vivo*)
lively

aniquilar [aniki'lar] *vt* to annihilate,
destroy

anís [a'nis] *nm* aniseed; (*licor*) anisette

aniversario [anißer'sarjo] *nm* anniversary

anoche [a'notʃe] *adv* last night; **antes de**
~ the night before last

anochecer [anotʃe'θer] *vi* to get dark
♦ *nm* nightfall, dark; **al ~** at nightfall

anodino, a [ano'ðino, a] *adj* dull,
anodyne

anomalía [anoma'lia] *nf* anomaly

anonadado, a [anona'ðaðo, a] *adj*:
estar/quedar/sentirse ~ to be
overwhelmed *o* amazed

anonimato [anoni'mato] *nm* anonymity

anónimo, a [a'nonimo, a] *adj*
anonymous; (*COM*) limited ♦ *nm* (*carta*)
anonymous letter; (: *maliciosa*) poison-
pen letter

anormal [anor'mal] *adj* abnormal

anotación [anota'θjon] *nf* note;
annotation

anotar [ano'tar] *vt* to note down;
(*comentar*) to annotate

anquilosamiento [ankilosa'mjento] *nm*
(*fig*) paralysis; stagnation

anquilosarse [ankilo'sarse] *vr* (*fig:*
persona) to get out of touch; (*método,*
costumbres) to go out of date

ansia ['ansja] *nf* anxiety; (*añoranza*)
yearning; **ansiar** *vt* to long for

ansiedad [ansje'ðað] *nf* anxiety

ansioso, a [an'sjoso, a] *adj* anxious;
(*anhelante*) eager; **~ de** *o* **por algo**
greedy for sth

antagónico, a [anta'ʏoniko, a] *adj*
antagonistic; (*opuesto*) contrasting;
antagonista *nm/f* antagonist

antaño [an'taɲo] *adv* long ago, formerly

Antártico [an'tartiko] *nm*: **el ~** the
Antarctic

ante ['ante] *prep* before, in the presence
of; (*problema etc*) faced with ♦ *nm* (*piel*)
suede; **~ todo** above all

anteanoche [antea'notʃe] *adv* the night
before last

anteayer [antea'jer] *adv* the day before
yesterday

antebrazo [ante'ßraθo] *nm* forearm

antecedente [anteθe'ðente] *adj* previous
♦ *nm* antecedent; **~s** *nmpl* (*JUR*): **~s**
penales criminal record; (*procedencia*)
background

anteceder [anteθe'ðer] *vt* to precede, go
before

antecesor, a [anteθe'sor, a] *nm/f*
predecessor

antedicho, a [ante'ðitʃo, a] *adj*
aforementioned

antelación [antela'θjon] *nf*: **con ~** in
advance

antemano [ante'mano]: **de ~** *adv*
beforehand, in advance

antena [an'tena] *nf* antenna; (*de televisión*
etc) aerial; **~ parabólica** satellite dish

anteojo [ante'oxo] *nm* eyeglass; **~s** *nmpl*
(*AM*) glasses, spectacles

antepasados [antepa'saðos] *nmpl*
ancestors

anteponer [antepo'ner] *vt* to place in
front; (*fig*) to prefer

anteproyecto [antepro'jekto] *nm*
preliminary sketch; (*fig*) blueprint

anterior [ante'rjor] *adj* preceding,
previous; **~idad** *nf*: **con ~idad a** prior to,
before

antes ['antes] *adv* (*con prioridad*) before
♦ *prep*: **~ de** before ♦ *conj*: **~ de ir/de**

que te vayas before going/before you go; **~ bien** (but) rather; **dos días ~** two days before o previously; **no quiso venir ~** she didn't want to come any earlier; **tomo el avión ~ que el barco** I take the plane rather than the boat; **~ que yo** before me; **lo ~ posible** as soon as possible; **cuanto ~ mejor** the sooner the better

antiaéreo, a [antia'ereo, a] *adj* anti-aircraft

antibalas [anti'βalas] *adj inv*: **chaleco ~** bullet-proof jacket

antibiótico [anti'βjotiko] *nm* antibiotic

anticiclón [antiθi'klon] *nm* anticyclone

anticipación [antiθipa'θjon] *nf* anticipation; **con 10 minutos de ~** 10 minutes early

anticipado, a [antiθi'paðo, a] *adj* (*pago*) advance; **por ~** in advance

anticipar [antiθi'par] *vt* to anticipate; (*adelantar*) to bring forward; (*COM*) to advance; **~se** *vr*: **~se a su época** to be ahead of one's time

anticipo [anti'θipo] *nm* (*COM*) advance

anticonceptivo, a [antikonθep'tiβo, a] *adj, nm* contraceptive

anticongelante [antikonxe'lante] *nm* antifreeze

anticuado, a [anti'kwaðo, a] *adj* out-of-date, old-fashioned; (*desusado*) obsolete

anticuario [anti'kwarjo] *nm* antique dealer

anticuerpo [anti'kwerpo] *nm* (*MED*) antibody

antídoto [an'tiðoto] *nm* antidote

antiestético, a [anties'tetiko, a] *adj* unsightly

antifaz [anti'faθ] *nm* mask; (*velo*) veil

antigualla [anti'ɣwaʎa] *nf* antique; (*reliquia*) relic

antiguamente [antiɣwa'mente] *adv* formerly; (*hace mucho tiempo*) long ago

antigüedad [antiɣwe'ðað] *nf* antiquity; (*artículo*) antique; (*rango*) seniority

antiguo, a [an'tiɣwo, a] *adj* old, ancient; (*que fue*) former

Antillas [an'tiʎas] *nfpl*: **las ~** the West Indies

antílope [an'tilope] *nm* antelope

antinatural [antinatu'ral] *adj* unnatural

antipatía [antipa'tia] *nf* antipathy, dislike; **antipático, a** *adj* disagreeable, unpleasant

antirrobo [anti'rroβo] *adj inv* (*alarma etc*) anti-theft

antisemita [antise'mita] *adj* anti-Semitic ♦ *nm/f* anti-Semite

antiséptico, a [anti'septiko, a] *adj* antiseptic ♦ *nm* antiseptic

antítesis [an'titesis] *nf inv* antithesis

antojadizo, a [antoxa'ðiθo, a] *adj* capricious

antojarse [anto'xarse] *vr* (*desear*): **se me antoja comprarlo** I have a mind to buy it; (*pensar*): **se me antoja que** I have a feeling that

antojo [an'toxo] *nm* caprice, whim; (*rosa*) birthmark; (*lunar*) mole

antología [antolo'xia] *nf* anthology

antorcha [an'tortʃa] *nf* torch

antro ['antro] *nm* cavern

antropófago, a [antro'pofaɣo, a] *adj, nm/f* cannibal

antropología [antropolo'xia] *nf* anthropology

anual [a'nwal] *adj* annual

anuario [a'nwarjo] *nm* yearbook

anudar [anu'ðar] *vt* to knot, tie; (*unir*) to join; **~se** *vr* to get tied up

anulación [anula'θjon] *nf* annulment; (*cancelación*) cancellation

anular [anu'lar] *vt* (*contrato*) to annul, cancel; (*ley*) to revoke, repeal; (*suscripción*) to cancel ♦ *nm* ring finger

Anunciación [anunθja'θjon] *nf* (*REL*) Annunciation

anunciante [anun'θjante] *nm/f* (*COM*) advertiser

anunciar [anun'θjar] *vt* to announce; (*proclamar*) to proclaim; (*COM*) to advertise

anuncio [a'nunθjo] *nm* announcement; (*señal*) sign; (*COM*) advertisement; (*cartel*) poster

anzuelo [an'θwelo] *nm* hook; (*para pescar*) fish hook

añadidura [aɲaði'ðura] *nf* addition, extra; **por ~** besides, in addition

añadir [aɲa'ðir] *vt* to add

añejo, a [a'ɲexo, a] *adj* old; (*vino*) mellow

añicos [a'ɲikos] *nmpl:* **hacer ~** to smash, shatter

añil [a'ɲil] *nm* (*BOT, color*) indigo

año ['aɲo] *nm* year; **¡Feliz A~ Nuevo!** Happy New Year!; **tener 15 ~s** to be 15 (years old); **los ~s 90** the nineties; **~ bisiesto/escolar** leap/school year; **el ~ que viene** next year

añoranza [aɲo'ranθa] *nf* nostalgia; (*anhelo*) longing

apabullar [apaβu'ʎar] *vt* (*tb fig*) to crush, squash

apacentar [apaθen'tar] *vt* to pasture, graze

apacible [apa'θiβle] *adj* gentle, mild

apaciguar [apaθi'ɣwar] *vt* to pacify, calm (down)

apadrinar [apaðri'nar] *vt* to sponsor, support; (*REL*) to be godfather to

apagado, a [apa'ɣaðo, a] *adj* (*volcán*) extinct; (*color*) dull; (*voz*) quiet; (*sonido*) muted, muffled; (*persona: apático*) listless; **estar ~** (*fuego, luz*) to be out; (*RADIO, TV etc*) to be off

apagar [apa'ɣar] *vt* to put out; (*ELEC, RADIO, TV*) to turn off; (*sonido*) to silence, muffle; (*sed*) to quench

apagón [apa'ɣon] *nm* blackout; power cut

apalabrar [apala'βrar] *vt* to agree to; (*contratar*) to engage

apalear [apale'ar] *vt* to beat, thrash

apañar [apa'ɲar] *vt* to pick up; (*asir*) to take hold of, grasp; (*reparar*) to mend, patch up; **~se** *vr* to manage, get along

aparador [apara'ðor] *nm* sideboard; (*AM: escaparate*) shop window

aparato [apa'rato] *nm* apparatus; (*máquina*) machine; (*doméstico*) appliance; (*boato*) ostentation; **~ de facsímil** facsimile (machine), fax; **~ digestivo** (*ANAT*) digestive system; **~so,**

a *adj* showy, ostentatious

aparcamiento [aparka'mjento] *nm* car park (*BRIT*), parking lot (*US*)

aparcar [apar'kar] *vt, vi* to park

aparear [apare'ar] *vt* (*objetos*) to pair, match; (*animales*) to mate; **~se** *vr* to make a pair; to mate

aparecer [apare'θer] *vi* to appear; **~se** *vr* to appear

aparejado, a [apare'xaðo, a] *adj* fit, suitable; **llevar** *o* **traer ~** to involve; **aparejador, a** *nm/f* (*ARQ*) master builder

aparejo [apa'rexo] *nm* harness; rigging; (*de poleas*) block and tackle

aparentar [aparen'tar] *vt* (*edad*) to look; (*fingir*): **~ tristeza** to pretend to be sad

aparente [apa'rente] *adj* apparent; (*adecuado*) suitable

aparezco *etc vb ver* **aparecer**

aparición [apari'θjon] *nf* appearance; (*de libro*) publication; (*espectro*) apparition

apariencia [apa'rjenθja] *nf* (*outward*) appearance; **en ~** outwardly, seemingly

apartado, a [apar'taðo, a] *adj* separate; (*lejano*) remote ♦ *nm* (*tipográfico*) paragraph; **~ (de correos)** post office box

apartamento [aparta'mento] *nm* apartment, flat (*BRIT*)

apartamiento [aparta'mjento] *nm* separation; (*aislamiento*) remoteness, isolation; (*AM*) apartment, flat (*BRIT*)

apartar [apar'tar] *vt* to separate; (*quitar*) to remove; **~se** *vr* to separate, part; (*irse*) to move away; to keep away

aparte [a'parte] *adv* (*separadamente*) separately; (*además*) besides ♦ *nm* aside; (*tipográfico*) new paragraph

aparthotel [aparto'tel] *nm* serviced apartments

apasionado, a [apasjo'naðo, a] *adj* passionate

apasionar [apasjo'nar] *vt* to excite; **le apasiona el fútbol** she's crazy about football; **~se** *vr* to get excited

apatía [apa'tia] *nf* apathy

apático, a [a'patiko, a] *adj* apathetic

Apdo *abr* (= *Apartado (de Correos)*) PO Box

apeadero [apea'ðero] *nm* halt, stop, stopping place

apearse [ape'arse] *vr* (*jinete*) to dismount; (*bajarse*) to get down *o* out; (AUTO, FERRO) to get off *o* out

apechugar [apetʃu'ɣar] *vr*: ~ **con algo** to face up to sth

apedrear [apeðre'ar] *vt* to stone

apegarse [ape'ɣarse] *vr*: ~ **a** to become attached to; **apego** *nm* attachment, devotion

apelación [apela'θjon] *nf* appeal

apelar [ape'lar] *vi* to appeal; ~ **a** (*fig*) to resort to

apellidar [apeʎi'ðar] *vt* to call, name; **~se** *vr*: **se apellida Pérez** her (sur)name's Pérez

apellido [ape'ʎiðo] *nm* surname

apelmazarse [apelma'θarse] *vr* (*masa, arroz*) to go hard; (*prenda de tana*) to shrink

apenar [ape'nar] *vt* to grieve, trouble; (AM: *avergonzar*) to embarrass; **~se** *vr* to grieve; (AM) to be embarrassed

apenas [a'penas] *adv* scarcely, hardly ♦ *conj* as soon as, no sooner

apéndice [a'pendiθe] *nm* appendix; **apendicitis** *nf* appendicitis

aperitivo [aperi'tiβo] *nm* (*bebida*) aperitif; (*comida*) appetizer

apero [a'pero] *nm* (AGR) implement; **~s** *nmpl* farm equipment *sg*

apertura [aper'tura] *nf* opening; (POL) liberalization

apesadumbrar [apesaðum'brar] *vt* to grieve, sadden; **~se** *vr* to distress o.s.

apestar [apes'tar] *vt* to infect ♦ *vi*: ~ (**a**) to stink (of)

apetecer [apete'θer] *vt*: ¿**te apetece un café?** do you fancy a (cup of) coffee?; **apetecible** *adj* desirable; (*comida*) appetizing

apetito [ape'tito] *nm* appetite; **~so, a** *adj* appetizing; (*fig*) tempting

apiadarse [apja'ðarse] *vr*: ~ **de** to take pity on

ápice ['apiθe] *nm* whit, iota

apilar [api'lar] *vt* to pile *o* heap up; **~se** *vr* to pile up

apiñarse [api'ɲarse] *vr* to crowd *o* press together

apio ['apjo] *nm* celery

apisonadora [apisona'ðora] *nf* steamroller

aplacar [apla'kar] *vt* to placate; **~se** *vr* to calm down

aplanar [apla'nar] *vt* to smooth, level; (*allanar*) to roll flat, flatten

aplastante [aplas'tante] *adj* overwhelming; (*lógica*) compelling

aplastar [aplas'tar] *vt* to squash (flat); (*fig*) to crush

aplatanarse [aplata'narse] *vr* to get lethargic

aplaudir [aplau'ðir] *vt* to applaud

aplauso [a'plauso] *nm* applause; (*fig*) approval, acclaim

aplazamiento [aplaθa'mjento] *nm* postponement

aplazar [apla'θar] *vt* to postpone, defer

aplicación [aplika'θjon] *nf* application; (*esfuerzo*) effort

aplicado, a [apli'kaðo, a] *adj* diligent, hard-working

aplicar [apli'kar] *vt* (*ejecutar*) to apply; **~se** *vr* to apply o.s.

aplique *etc* [a'plike] *vb ver* **aplicar** ♦ *nm* wall light

aplomo [a'plomo] *nm* aplomb, self-assurance

apocado, a [apo'kaðo, a] *adj* timid

apodar [apo'ðar] *vt* to nickname

apoderado [apoðe'raðo] *nm* agent, representative

apoderarse [apoðe'rarse] *vr*: ~ **de** to take possession of

apodo [a'poðo] *nm* nickname

apogeo [apo'xeo] *nm* peak, summit

apolillarse [apoli'ʎarse] *vr* to get moth-eaten

apología [apolo'xia] *nf* eulogy; (*defensa*) defence

apoltronarse [apoltro'narse] *vr* to get

lazy

apoplejía [apople'xia] *nf* apoplexy, stroke

apoquinar [apoki'nar] (*fam*) *vt* to fork out, cough up

aporrear [aporre'ar] *vt* to beat (up)

aportar [apor'tar] *vt* to contribute ♦ *vi* to reach port; **~se** *vr* (*AM: llegar*) to arrive, come

aposento [apo'sento] *nm* lodging; (*habitación*) room

aposta [a'posta] *adv* deliberately, on purpose

apostar [apos'tar] *vt* to bet, stake; (*tropas etc*) to station, post ♦ *vi* to bet

apóstol [a'postol] *nm* apostle

apóstrofo [a'postrofo] *nm* apostrophe

apoyar [apo'jar] *vt* to lean, rest; (*fig*) to support, back; **~se** *vr*: **~se en** to lean on; **apoyo** *nm* (*gen*) support; backing, help

apreciable [apre'θjaßle] *adj* considerable; (*fig*) esteemed

apreciar [apre'θjar] *vt* to evaluate, assess; (*COM*) to appreciate, value; (*persona*) to respect; (*tamaño*) to gauge, assess; (*detalles*) to notice

aprecio [a'preθjo] *nm* valuation, estimate; (*fig*) appreciation

aprehender [apreen'der] *vt* to apprehend, detain

apremiante [apre'mjante] *adj* urgent, pressing

apremiar [apre'mjar] *vt* to compel, force ♦ *vi* to be urgent, press; **apremio** *nm* urgency

aprender [apren'der] *vt, vi* to learn

aprendiz, a [apren'diθ, a] *nm/f* apprentice; (*principiante*) learner; **~ de conductor** learner driver; **~aje** *nm* apprenticeship

aprensión [apren'sjon] *nm* apprehension, fear; **aprensivo, a** *adj* apprehensive

apresar [apre'sar] *vt* to seize; (*capturar*) to capture

aprestar [apres'tar] *vt* to prepare, get ready; (*TEC*) to prime, size; **~se** *vr* to get ready

apresurado, a [apresu'raðo, a] *adj* hurried, hasty; **apresuramiento** *nm* hurry, haste

apresurar [apresu'rar] *vt* to hurry, accelerate; **~se** *vr* to hurry, make haste

apretado, a [apre'taðo, a] *adj* tight; (*escritura*) cramped

apretar [apre'tar] *vt* to squeeze; (*TEC*) to tighten; (*presionar*) to press together, pack ♦ *vi* to be too tight

apretón [apre'ton] *nm* squeeze; **~ de manos** handshake

aprieto [a'prjeto] *nm* squeeze; (*dificultad*) difficulty; **estar en un ~** to be in a fix

aprisa [a'prisa] *adv* quickly, hurriedly

aprisionar [aprisjo'nar] *vt* to imprison

aprobación [aproßa'θjon] *nf* approval

aprobar [apro'ßar] *vt* to approve (of); (*examen, materia*) to pass ♦ *vi* to pass

apropiación [apropja'θjon] *nf* appropriation

apropiado, a [apro'pjaðo, a] *adj* appropriate

apropiarse [apro'pjarse] *vr*: **~ de** to appropriate

aprovechado, a [aproße'tʃaðo, a] *adj* industrious, hard-working; (*económico*) thrifty; (*pey*) unscrupulous; **aprovechamiento** *nm* use; exploitation

aprovechar [aproße'tʃar] *vt* to use; (*explotar*) to exploit; (*experiencia*) to profit from; (*oferta, oportunidad*) to take advantage of ♦ *vi* to progress, improve; **~se** *vr*: **~se de** to make use of; to take advantage of; **¡que aproveche!** enjoy your meal!

aproximación [aproksima'θjon] *nf* approximation; (*de lotería*) consolation prize; **aproximado, a** *adj* approximate

aproximar [aproksi'mar] *vt* to bring nearer; **~se** *vr* to come near, approach

apruebo *etc vb ver* **aprobar**

aptitud [apti'tuð] *nf* aptitude

apto, a ['apto, a] *adj* suitable

apuesta [a'pwesta] *nf* bet, wager

apuesto, a [a'pwesto, a] *adj* neat, elegant

apuntador [apunta'ðor] *nm* prompter

apuntalar [apunta'lar] *vt* to prop up

apuntar [apun'tar] vt (con arma) to aim at; (con dedo) to point at o to; (anotar) to note (down); (TEATRO) to prompt; **~se** vr (DEPORTE: tanto, victoria) to score; (ESCOL) to enrol

apunte [a'punte] nm note

apuñalar [apuɲa'lar] vt to stab

apurado, a [apu'raðo, a] adj needy; (difícil) difficult; (peligroso) dangerous; (AM) hurried, rushed

apurar [apu'rar] vt (agotar) to drain; (recursos) to use up; (molestar) to annoy; **~se** vr (preocuparse) to worry; (darse prisa) to hurry

apuro [a'puro] nm (aprieto) fix, jam; (escasez) want, hardship; (vergüenza) embarrassment; (AM) haste, urgency

aquejado, a [ake'xaðo, a] adj: **~ de** (MED) afflicted by

aquél, aquélla [a'kel, a'keʎa] (pl **aquéllos, as**) pron that (one); (pl) those (ones)

aquel, aquella [a'kel, a'keʎa] (pl **aquellos, as**) adj that; (pl) those

aquello [a'keʎo] pron that, that business

aquí [a'ki] adv (lugar) here; (tiempo) now; **~ arriba** up here; **~ mismo** right here; **~ yace** here lies; **de ~ a siete días** a week from now

aquietar [akje'tar] vt to quieten (down), calm (down)

ara ['ara] nf: **en ~s de** for the sake of

árabe ['araβe] adj, nm/f Arab ♦ nm (LING) Arabic

Arabia [a'raβja] nf: **~ Saudí** o **Saudita** Saudi Arabia

arado [a'raðo] nm plough

Aragón [ara'ɣon] nm Aragon; **aragonés, esa** adj, nm/f Aragonese

arancel [aran'θel] nm tariff, duty; **~ de aduanas** customs (duty)

arandela [aran'dela] nf (TEC) washer

araña [a'raɲa] nf (ZOOL) spider; (lámpara) chandelier

arañar [ara'ɲar] vt to scratch

arañazo [ara'ɲaθo] nm scratch

arar [a'rar] vt to plough, till

arbitraje [arβi'traxe] nm arbitration

arbitrar [arβi'trar] vt to arbitrate in; (DEPORTE) to referee ♦ vi to arbitrate

arbitrariedad [arβitrarje'ðað] nf arbitrariness; (acto) arbitrary act; **arbitrario, a** adj arbitrary

arbitrio [ar'βitrjo] nm free will; (JUR) adjudication, decision

árbitro ['arβitro] nm arbitrator; (DEPORTE) referee; (TENIS) umpire

árbol ['arβol] nm (BOT) tree; (NAUT) mast; (TEC) axle, shaft; **arbolado, a** adj wooded; (camino etc) tree-lined ♦ nm woodland

arboleda [arβo'leða] nf grove, plantation

arbusto [ar'βusto] nm bush, shrub

arca ['arka] nf chest, box

arcada [ar'kaða] nf arcade; (de puente) arch, span; **~s** nfpl (náuseas) retching sg

arcaico, a [ar'kaiko, a] adj archaic

arce ['arθe] nm maple tree

arcén [ar'θen] nm (de autopista) hard shoulder; (de carretera) verge

archipiélago [artʃi'pjelaɣo] nm archipelago

archivador [artʃiβa'ðor] nm filing cabinet

archivar [artʃi'βar] vt to file (away); **archivo** nm file, archive(s) (pl)

arcilla [ar'θiʎa] nf clay

arco ['arko] nm arch; (MAT) arc; (MIL, MUS) bow; **~ iris** rainbow

arder [ar'ðer] vi to burn; **estar que arde** (persona) to fume

ardid [ar'ðið] nm ploy, trick

ardiente [ar'ðjente] adj burning, ardent

ardilla [ar'ðiʎa] nf squirrel

ardor [ar'ðor] nm (calor) heat; (fig) ardour; **~ de estómago** heartburn

arduo, a ['arðwo, a] adj arduous

área ['area] nf area; (DEPORTE) penalty area

arena [a'rena] nf sand; (de una lucha) arena; **~s movedizas** quicksand sg

arenal [are'nal] nm (arena movediza) quicksand

arengar [aren'ɡar] vt to harangue

arenisca [are'niska] nf sandstone; (cascajo) grit

arenoso, a [are'noso, a] *adj* sandy

arenque [a'renke] *nm* herring

argamasa [arɣa'masa] *nf* mortar, plaster

Argel [ar'xel] *n* Algiers; **Argelia** *nf* Algeria; **argelino, a** *adj, nm/f* Algerian

Argentina [arxen'tina] *nf:* **(la) ~** Argentina

argentino, a [arxen'tino, a] *adj* Argentinian; (*de plata*) silvery ♦ *nm/f* Argentinian

argolla [ar'xoʎa] *nf* (large) ring

argot [ar'ɣo] (*pl* **~s**) *nm* slang

argucia [ar'xuθja] *nf* subtlety, sophistry

argüir [ar'xwir] *vt* to deduce; (*discutir*) to argue; (*indicar*) to indicate, imply; (*censurar*) to reproach ♦ *vi* to argue

argumentación [arxumenta'θjon] *nf* (line of) argument

argumentar [arxumen'tar] *vt, vi* to argue

argumento [arxu'mento] *nm* argument; (*razonamiento*) reasoning; (*de novela etc*) plot; (*CINE, TV*) storyline

aria ['arja] *nf* aria

aridez [ari'δeθ] *nf* aridity, dryness

árido, a ['ariðo, a] *adj* arid, dry; **~s** *nmpl* (*COM*) dry goods

Aries ['arjes] *nm* Aries

ario, a ['arjo, a] *adj* Aryan

arisco, a [a'risko, a] *adj* surly; (*insociable*) unsociable

aristócrata [aris'tokrata] *nm/f* aristocrat

aritmética [arit'metika] *nf* arithmetic

arma ['arma] *nf* arm; **~s** *nfpl* arms; **~ blanca** blade, knife; (*espada*) sword; **~ de fuego** firearm; **~s cortas** small arms

armada [ar'maða] *nf* armada; (*flota*) fleet

armadillo [arma'ðiʎo] *nm* armadillo

armado, a [ar'maðo, a] *adj* armed; (*TEC*) reinforced

armador [arma'ðor] *nm* (*NAUT*) shipowner

armadura [arma'ðura] *nf* (*MIL*) armour; (*TEC*) framework; (*ZOOL*) skeleton; (*FÍSICA*) armature

armamento [arma'mento] *nm* armament; (*NAUT*) fitting-out

armar [ar'mar] *vt* (*soldado*) to arm; (*máquina*) to assemble; (*navío*) to fit out; **~la, ~ un lío** to start a row, kick up a fuss

armario [ar'marjo] *nm* wardrobe; (*de cocina, baño*) cupboard

armatoste [arma'toste] *nm* (*mueble*) monstrosity; (*máquina*) contraption

armazón [arma'θon] *nf o m* body, chassis; (*de mueble etc*) frame; (*ARQ*) skeleton

armería [arme'ria] *nf* gunsmith's

armiño [ar'miɲo] *nm* stoat; (*piel*) ermine

armisticio [armis'tiθjo] *nm* armistice

armonía [armo'nia] *nf* harmony

armónica [ar'monika] *nf* harmonica

armonioso, a [armo'njoso, a] *adj* harmonious

armonizar [armoni'θar] *vt* to harmonize; (*diferencias*) to reconcile ♦ *vi:* **~ con** (*fig*) to be in keeping with; (*colores*) to tone in with, blend

arnés [ar'nes] *nm* armour; **arneses** *nmpl* (*de caballo etc*) harness *sg*

aro ['aro] *nm* ring; (*tejo*) quoit; (*AM: pendiente*) earring

aroma [a'roma] *nm* aroma, scent

aromático, a [aro'matiko, a] *adj* aromatic

arpa ['arpa] *nf* harp

arpía [ar'pia] *nf* shrew

arpillera [arpi'ʎera] *nf* sacking, sackcloth

arpón [ar'pon] *nm* harpoon

arquear [arke'ar] *vt* to arch, bend; **~se** *vr* to arch, bend

arqueología [arkeolo'xia] *nf* archaeology; **arqueólogo, a** *nm/f* archaeologist

arquero [ar'kero] *nm* archer, bowman

arquetipo [arke'tipo] *nm* archetype

arquitecto [arki'tekto] *nm* architect; **arquitectura** *nf* architecture

arrabal [arra'ßal] *nm* suburb; (*AM*) slum; **~es** *nmpl* (*afueras*) outskirts

arraigado, a [arrai'yaðo, a] *adj* deep-rooted; (*fig*) established

arraigar [arrai'var] *vt* to establish ♦ *vi* to take root; **~se** *vr* to take root; (*persona*) to settle

arrancar [arran'kar] *vt* (*sacar*) to extract, pull out; (*arrebatar*) to snatch (away); (*INFORM*) to boot; (*fig*) to extract ♦ *vi* (*AUTO, máquina*) to start; (*ponerse en marcha*) to get going; **~ de** to stem from

arranque etc [a'rranke] vb ver **arrancar**
♦ nm sudden start; (AUTO) start; (fig) fit,
outburst

arrasar [arra'sar] vt (aplanar) to level,
flatten; (destruir) to demolish

arrastrado, a [arras'traðo, a] adj poor,
wretched; (AM) servile

arrastrar [arras'trar] vt to drag (along);
(fig) to drag down, degrade; (suj: agua,
viento) to carry away ♦ vi to drag, trail on
the ground; **~se** vr to crawl; (fig) to
grovel; **llevar algo arrastrado** to drag sth
along

arrastre [a'rrastre] nm drag, dragging

arre ['arre] excl gee up!

arrear [arre'ar] vt to drive on, urge on ♦ vi
to hurry along

arrebatado, a [arreßa'taðo, a] adj rash,
impetuous; (repentino) sudden, hasty

arrebatar [arreßa'tar] vt to snatch (away),
seize; (fig) to captivate; **~se** vr to get
carried away, get excited

arrebato [arre'ßato] nm fit of rage, fury;
(éxtasis) rapture

arrecife [arre'θife] nm (tb: ~ de coral) reef

arredrarse [arre'ðrarse] vr: **~ (ante algo)**
to be intimidated (by sth)

arreglado, a [arre'ɣlaðo, a] adj (ordenado)
neat, orderly; (moderado) moderate,
reasonable

arreglar [arre'ɣlar] vt (poner orden) to tidy
up; (algo roto) to fix, repair; (problema) to
solve; **~se** vr to reach an understanding;
arreglárselas (fam) to get by, manage

arreglo [a'rreɣlo] nm settlement; (orden)
order; (acuerdo) agreement; (MUS)
arrangement, setting

arrellanarse [arreʎa'narse] vr: **~ en** to sit
back in/on

arremangar [arreman'gar] vt to roll up,
turn up; **~se** vr to roll up one's sleeves

arremeter [arreme'ter] vi: **~ contra** to
attack, rush at

arrendamiento [arrenda'mjento] nm
letting; (alquilar) hiring; (contrato) lease;
(alquiler) rent; **arrendar** vt to let, lease;
to rent; **arrendatario, a** nm/f tenant

arreos [a'rreos] nmpl (de caballo) harness
sg, trappings

arrepentimiento [arrepenti'mjento] nm
regret, repentance

arrepentirse [arrepen'tirse] vr to repent;
~ de to regret

arrestar [arres'tar] vt to arrest; (encarcelar)
to imprison; **arresto** nm arrest; (MIL)
detention; (audacia) boldness, daring;
arresto domiciliario house arrest

arriar [a'rrjar] vt (velas) to haul down;
(bandera) to lower, strike; (cable) to pay
out

PALABRA CLAVE
---

arriba [a'rrißa] adv 1 (posición) above;
desde ~ from above; **~ de todo** at the
very top, right on top; **Juan está ~** Juan
is upstairs; **lo ~ mencionado** the
aforementioned
2 (dirección): **calle ~** up the street
3: **de ~ abajo** from top to bottom; **mirar
a uno de ~ abajo** to look sb up and
down
4: **para ~: de 5000 pesetas para ~** from
5000 pesetas up(wards)
♦ adj: **de ~: el piso de ~** the upstairs flat
(BRIT) o apartment; **la parte de ~** the top
o upper part
♦ prep: **~ de** (AM) above; **~ de 200
dólares** more than 200 dollars
♦ excl: **¡~!** up!; **¡manos ~!** hands up!; **¡~
España!** long live Spain!

---

arribar [arri'ßar] vi to put into port;
(llegar) to arrive

arribista [arri'ßista] nm/f parvenu(e),
upstart

arriendo etc [a'rrjendo] vb ver **arrendar**
♦ nm = **arrendamiento**

arriero [a'rrjero] nm muleteer

arriesgado, a [arrjes'xaðo, a] adj
(peligroso) risky; (audaz) bold, daring

arriesgar [arrjes'xar] vt to risk; (poner en
peligro) to endanger; **~se** vr to take a risk

arrimar [arri'mar] vt (acercar) to bring
close; (poner de lado) to set aside; **~se** vr

to come close o closer; **~se a** to lean on

arrinconar [arrinko'nar] vt (colocar) to put in a corner; (enemigo) to corner; (fig) to put on one side; (abandonar) to push aside

arrodillarse [arroði'ʎarse] vr to kneel (down)

arrogancia [arro'ɣanθja] nf arrogance; **arrogante** adj arrogant

arrojar [arro'xar] vt to throw, hurl; (humo) to emit, give out; (COM) to yield, produce; **~se** vr to throw o hurl o.s.

arrojo [a'rroxo] nm daring

arrollador, a [arroʎa'ðor, a] adj overwhelming

arrollar [arro'ʎar] vt (AUTO etc) to run over, knock down; (DEPORTE) to crush

arropar [arro'par] vt to cover, wrap up; **~se** vr to wrap o.s. up

arroyo [a'rrojo] nm stream; (de la calle) gutter

arroz [a'rroθ] nm rice; **~ con leche** rice pudding

arruga [a'rruɣa] nf (de cara) wrinkle; (de vestido) crease

arrugar [arru'ɣar] vt to wrinkle; to crease; **~se** vr to get creased

arruinar [arrwi'nar] vt to ruin, wreck; **~se** vr to be ruined, go bankrupt

arrullar [arru'ʎar] vi to coo ♦ vt to lull to sleep

arsenal [arse'nal] nm naval dockyard; (MIL) arsenal

arsénico [ar'seniko] nm arsenic

arte ['arte] (gen m en sg y siempre f en pl) nm art; (maña) skill, guile; **~s** nfpl (bellas **~s**) arts

artefacto [arte'fakto] nm appliance

arteria [ar'terja] nf artery

artesanía [artesa'nia] nf craftsmanship; (artículos) handicrafts pl; **artesano, a** nm/f artisan, craftsman/woman

ártico, a ['artiko, a] adj Arctic ♦ nm: **el Á~** the Arctic

articulación [artikula'θjon] nf articulation; (MED, TEC) joint; **articulado, a** adj articulated; jointed

articular [artiku'lar] vt to articulate; to join together

artículo [ar'tikulo] nm article; (cosa) thing, article; **~s** nmpl (COM) goods

artífice [ar'tifiθe] nm/f (fig) architect

artificial [artifi'θjal] adj artificial

artificio [arti'fiθjo] nm art, skill; (astucia) cunning

artillería [artiʎe'ria] nf artillery

artillero [arti'ʎero] nm artilleryman, gunner

artilugio [arti'luxjo] nm gadget

artimaña [arti'maɲa] nf trap, snare; (astucia) cunning

artista [ar'tista] nm/f (pintor) artist, painter; (TEATRO) artist, artiste; **~ de cine** film actor/actress; **artístico, a** adj artistic

artritis [ar'tritis] nf arthritis

arveja [ar'ßexa] (AM) nf pea

arzobispo [arθo'ßispo] nm archbishop

as [as] nm ace

asa ['asa] nf handle; (fig) lever

asado [a'saðo] nm roast (meat); (AM: barbacoa) barbecue

asador [asa'ðor] nm spit

asadura [asa'ðura] nf entrails pl, offal

asalariado, a [asala'rjaðo, a] adj paid, salaried ♦ nm/f wage earner

asaltante [asal'tante] nm/f attacker

asaltar [asal'tar] vt to attack, assault; (fig) to assail; **asalto** nm attack, assault; (DEPORTE) round

asamblea [asam'blea] nf assembly; (reunión) meeting

asar [a'sar] vt to roast

asbesto [as'ßesto] nm asbestos

ascendencia [asθen'denθja] nf ancestry; (AM) ascendancy; **de ~ francesa** of French origin

ascender [asθen'der] vi (subir) to ascend, rise; (ser promovido) to gain promotion ♦ vt to promote; **~ a** to amount to; **ascendiente** nm influence ♦ nm/f ancestor

ascensión [asθen'sjon] nf ascent; (REL): **la A~** the Ascension

ascenso [as'θenso] *nm* ascent; (*promoción*) promotion

ascensor [asθen'sor] *nm* lift (*BRIT*), elevator (*US*)

ascético, a [as'θetiko, a] *adj* ascetic

asco ['asko] *nm*: **¡qué ~!** how revolting *o* disgusting; **el ajo me da ~** I hate *o* loathe garlic; **estar hecho un ~** to be filthy

ascua ['askwa] *nf* ember; **estar en ~s** to be on tenterhooks

aseado, a [ase'aðo, a] *adj* clean; (*arreglado*) tidy; (*pulcro*) smart

asear [ase'ar] *vt* to clean, wash; to tidy (up)

asediar [ase'ðjar] *vt* (*MIL*) to besiege, lay siege to; (*fig*) to chase, pester; **asedio** *nm* siege; (*COM*) run

asegurado, a [asexu'raðo, a] *adj* insured

asegurador, a *nm/f* insurer

asegurar [asexu'rar] *vt* (*consolidar*) to secure, fasten; (*dar garantía de*) to guarantee; (*preservar*) to safeguard; (*afirmar, dar por cierto*) to assure, affirm; (*tranquilizar*) to reassure; (*tomar un seguro*) to insure; **~se** *vr* to assure o.s., make sure

asemejarse [aseme'xarse] *vr* to be alike; **~ a** to be like, resemble

asentado, a [asen'taðo, a] *adj* established, settled

asentar [asen'tar] *vt* (*sentar*) to seat, sit down; (*poner*) to place, establish; (*alisar*) to level, smooth down *o* out; (*anotar*) to note down ♦ *vi* to be suitable, suit

asentir [asen'tir] *vi* to assent, agree; **~ con la cabeza** to nod (one's head)

aseo [a'seo] *nm* cleanliness; **~s** *nmpl* (*servicios*) toilet *sg* (*BRIT*), cloakroom *sg* (*BRIT*), restroom *sg* (*US*)

aséptico, a [a'septiko, a] *adj* germ-free, free from infection

asequible [ase'kiβle] *adj* (*precio*) reasonable; (*meta*) attainable; (*persona*) approachable

aserradero [aserra'ðero] *nm* sawmill; **aserrar** *vt* to saw

asesinar [asesi'nar] *vt* to murder; (*POL*) to

assassinate; **asesinato** *nm* murder; assassination

asesino, a [ase'sino, a] *nm/f* murderer, killer; (*POL*) assassin

asesor, a [ase'sor, a] *nm/f* adviser, consultant

asesorar [aseso'rar] *vt* (*JUR*) to advise, give legal advice to; (*COM*) to act as consultant to; **~se** *vr*: **~se con** *o* **de** to take advice from, consult; **asesoría** *nf* (*cargo*) consultancy; (*oficina*) consultant's office

asestar [ases'tar] *vt* (*golpe*) to deal, strike

asfalto [as'falto] *nm* asphalt

asfixia [as'fiksja] *nf* asphyxia, suffocation

asfixiar [asfik'sjar] *vt* to asphyxiate, suffocate; (*COM*) to act as consultant to be asphyxiated, suffocate; **~se** *vr* to be asphyxiated, suffocate

asgo *etc vb ver* **asir**

así [a'si] *adv* (*de esta manera*) in this way, like this, thus; (*aunque*) although; (*tan pronto como*) as soon as; **~ que** so; **~ como** as well as; **~ y todo** even so; **¿no es ~?** isn't it?, didn't you? *etc*; **~ de grande** this big

Asia ['asja] *nf* Asia; **asiático, a** *adj, nm/f* Asian, Asiatic

asidero [asi'ðero] *nm* handle

asiduidad [asiðwi'ðað] *nf* assiduousness; **asiduo, a** *adj* assiduous; (*frecuente*) frequent ♦ *nm/f* regular (customer)

asiento [a'sjento] *nm* (*mueble*) seat, chair; (*de coche, en tribunal etc*) seat; (*localidad*) seat, place; (*fundamento*) site; **~ delantero/trasero** front/back seat

asignación [asixna'θjon] *nf* (*atribución*) assignment; (*reparto*) allocation; (*sueldo*) salary; **~ (semanal)** pocket money

asignar [asix'nar] *vt* to assign, allocate

asignatura [asixna'tura] *nf* subject; course

asilado, a [asi'laðo, a] *nm/f* inmate; (*POL*) refugee

asilo [a'silo] *nm* (*refugio*) asylum, refuge; (*establecimiento*) home, institution; **~ político** political asylum

asimilación [asimila'θjon] *nf* assimilation

asimilar [asimi'lar] *vt* to assimilate

asimismo [asi'mismo] *adv* in the same

way, likewise

asir [a'sir] *vt* to seize, grasp

asistencia [asis'tenθja] *nf* audience; (*MED*) attendance; (*ayuda*) assistance; **asistente** *nm/f* assistant; **los asistentes** those present; **asistente social** social worker

asistido, a [asis'tiðo, a] *adj*: ~ **por ordenador** computer-assisted

asistir [asis'tir] *vt* to assist, help ♦ *vi*: ~ **a** to attend, be present at

asma ['asma] *nf* asthma

asno ['asno] *nm* donkey; (*fig*) ass

asociación [asoθja'θjon] *nf* association; (*COM*) partnership; **asociado, a** *adj* associate ♦ *nm/f* associate; (*COM*) partner

asociar [aso'θjar] *vt* to associate

asolar [aso'lar] *vt* to destroy

asomar [aso'mar] *vt* to show, stick out ♦ *vi* to appear; **~se** *vr* to appear, show up; ~ **la cabeza por la ventana** to put one's head out of the window

asombrar [asom'brar] *vt* to amaze, astonish; **~se** *vr* (*sorprenderse*) to be amazed; (*asustarse*) to get a fright; **asombro** *nm* amazement, astonishment; (*susto*) fright; **asombroso, a** *adj* astonishing, amazing

asomo [a'somo] *nm* hint, sign

aspa ['aspa] *nf* (*cruz*) cross; (*de molino*) sail; **en ~** X-shaped

aspaviento [aspa'ßjento] *nm* exaggerated display of feeling; (*fam*) fuss

aspecto [as'pekto] *nm* (*apariencia*) look, appearance; (*fig*) aspect

aspereza [aspe'reθa] *nf* roughness; (*agrura*) sourness; (*de carácter*) surliness; **áspero, a** *adj* rough; bitter, sour; harsh

aspersión [asper'sjon] *nf* sprinkling

aspiración [aspira'θjon] *nf* breath, inhalation; (*MUS*) short pause; **aspiraciones** *nfpl* (*ambiciones*) aspirations

aspirador [aspira'ðor] *nm* = **aspiradora**

aspiradora [aspira'ðora] *nf* vacuum cleaner, Hoover ®

aspirante [aspi'rante] *nm/f* (*candidato*) candidate; (*DEPORTE*) contender

aspirar [aspi'rar] *vt* to breathe in ♦ *vi*: ~ **a** to aspire to

aspirina [aspi'rina] *nf* aspirin

asquear [aske'ar] *vt* to sicken ♦ *vi* to be sickening; **~se** *vr* to feel disgusted; **asqueroso, a** *adj* disgusting, sickening

asta ['asta] *nf* lance; (*arpón*) spear; (*mango*) shaft, handle; (*ZOOL*) horn; **a media ~** at half mast

asterisco [aste'risko] *nm* asterisk

astilla [as'tiλa] *nf* splinter; (*pedacito*) chip; **~s** *nfpl* (*leña*) firewood *sg*

astillero [asti'λero] *nm* shipyard

astringente [astrin'xente] *adj, nm* astringent

astro ['astro] *nm* star

astrología [astrolo'xia] *nf* astrology; **astrólogo, a** *nm/f* astrologer

astronauta [astro'nauta] *nm/f* astronaut

astronave [astro'naße] *nm* spaceship

astronomía [astrono'mia] *nf* astronomy; **astrónomo, a** *nm/f* astronomer

astucia [as'tuθja] *nf* astuteness; (*ardid*) clever trick

asturiano, a [astu'rjano, a] *adj, nm/f* Asturian

astuto, a [as'tuto, a] *adj* astute; (*taimado*) cunning

asumir [asu'mir] *vt* to assume

asunción [asun'θjon] *nf* assumption; (*REL*): **A~** Assumption

asunto [a'sunto] *nm* (*tema*) matter, subject; (*negocio*) business

asustar [asus'tar] *vt* to frighten; **~se** *vr* to be (*o become*) frightened

atacar [ata'kar] *vt* to attack

atadura [ata'ðura] *nf* bond, tie

atajar [ata'xar] *vt* (*enfermedad, mal*) to stop ♦ *vi* (*persona*) to take a short cut

atajo [a'taxo] *nm* short cut

atañer [ata'ɲer] *vi*: ~ **a** to concern

ataque *etc* [a'take] *vb ver* **atacar** ♦ *nm* attack; ~ **cardíaco** heart attack

atar [a'tar] *vt* to tie, tie up

atardecer [atarðe'θer] *vi* to get dark ♦ *nm* evening; (*crepúsculo*) dusk

atareado, a [atare'aðo, a] *adj* busy

atascar [atas'kar] *vt* to clog up; (*obstruir*) to jam; (*fig*) to hinder; **~se** *vr* to stall; (*cañería*) to get blocked up; **atasco** *nm* obstruction; (*AUTO*) traffic jam

ataúd [ata'uð] *nm* coffin

ataviar [ata'ßjar] *vt* to deck, array; **~se** *vr* to dress up

atavío [ata'ßio] *nm* attire, dress; **~s** *nmpl* finery *sg*

atemorizar [atemori'θar] *vt* to frighten, scare; **~se** *vr* to get scared

Atenas [a'tenas] *n* Athens

atención [aten'θjon] *nf* attention; (*bondad*) kindness ♦ *excl* (be) careful!, look out!

atender [aten'der] *vt* to attend to, look after ♦ *vi* to pay attention

atenerse [ate'nerse] *vr*: **~ a** to abide by, adhere to

atentado [aten'taðo] *nm* crime, illegal act; (*asalto*) assault; **~ contra la vida de uno** attempt on sb's life

atentamente [atenta'mente] *adv*: **Le saluda ~** Yours faithfully

atentar [aten'tar] *vi*: **~ a** *o* **contra** to commit an outrage against

atento, a [a'tento, a] *adj* attentive, observant; (*cortés*) polite, thoughtful

atenuante [ate'nwante] *adj* extenuating

atenuar [ate'nwar] *vt* (*disminuir*) to lessen, minimize

ateo, a [a'teo, a] *adj* atheistic ♦ *nm/f* atheist

aterciopelado, a [aterθjope'laðo, a] *adj* velvety

aterido, a [ate'riðo, a] *adj*: **~ de frío** frozen stiff

aterrador, a [aterra'ðor, a] *adj* frightening

aterrar [ate'rrar] *vt* to frighten; to terrify

aterrizaje [aterri'θaxe] *nm* landing

aterrizar [aterri'θar] *vi* to land

aterrorizar [aterrori'θar] *vt* to terrify

atesorar [ateso'rar] *vt* to hoard

atestado, a [ates'taðo, a] *adj* packed ♦ *nm* (*JUR*) affidavit

atestar [ates'tar] *vt* to pack, stuff; (*JUR*) to attest, testify to

atestiguar [atesti'ɣwar] *vt* to testify to, bear witness to

atiborrar [atiβo'rrar] *vt* to fill, stuff; **~se** *vr* to stuff o.s.

ático ['atiko] *nm* attic; **~ de lujo** penthouse (flat (*BRIT*) *o* apartment)

atinado, a [ati'naðo, a] *adj* (*sensato*) wise; (*correcto*) right, correct

atinar [ati'nar] *vi* (*al disparar*): **~ al blanco** to hit the target; (*fig*) to be right

atisbar [atis'ßar] *vt* to spy on; (*echar una ojeada*) to peep at

atizar [ati'θar] *vt* to poke; (*horno etc*) to stoke; (*fig*) to stir up, rouse

atlántico, a [at'lantiko, a] *adj* Atlantic ♦ *nm*: **el (océano) A~** the Atlantic (Ocean)

atlas ['atlas] *nm* atlas

atleta [at'leta] *nm* athlete; **atlético, a** *adj* athletic; **atletismo** *nm* athletics *sg*

atmósfera [at'mosfera] *nf* atmosphere

atolladero [atoʎa'ðero] *nm* (*fig*) jam, fix

atolondramiento [atolondra'mjento] *nm* bewilderment; (*insensatez*) silliness

atómico, a [a'tomiko, a] *adj* atomic

atomizador [atomiθa'ðor] *nm* atomizer; (*de perfume*) spray

átomo ['atomo] *nm* atom

atónito, a [a'tonito, a] *adj* astonished, amazed

atontado, a [aton'taðo, a] *adj* stunned; (*bobo*) silly, daft

atontar [aton'tar] *vt* to stun; **~se** *vr* to become confused

atormentar [atormen'tar] *vt* to torture; (*molestar*) to torment; (*acosar*) to plague, harass

atornillar [atorni'ʎar] *vt* to screw on *o* down

atosigar [atosi'ɣar] *vt* to harass, pester

atracador, a [ataka'ðor, a] *nm/f* robber

atracar [atra'kar] *vt* (*NAUT*) to moor; (*robar*) to hold up, rob ♦ *vi* to moor; **~se** *vr*: **~se (de)** to stuff o.s. (with)

atracción [atrak'θjon] *nf* attraction

atraco [a'trako] *nm* holdup, robbery

atracón [atra'kon] *nm*: **darse** *o* **pegarse**

un ~ **(de)** (fam) to stuff o.s. (with)

atractivo, a [atrak'tiβo, a] adj attractive
♦ nm appeal

atraer [atra'er] vt to attract

atragantarse [atraɣan'tarse] vr: ~ **(con)** to
choke (on); **se me ha atragantado el
chico** I can't stand the boy

atrancar [atran'kar] vt (puerta) to bar, bolt

atrapar [atra'par] vt (trap); (resfriado etc)
to catch

atrás [a'tras] adv (movimiento) back
(-wards); (lugar) behind; (tiempo)
previously; **ir hacia** ~ to go back(wards);
to go to the rear; **estar** ~ to be behind o
at the back

atrasado, a [atra'saðo, a] adj slow; (pago)
overdue, late; (país) backward

atrasar [atra'sar] vi to be slow; ~**se** vr to
remain behind; (tren) to be o run late;
atraso nm slowness; lateness, delay; (de
país) backwardness; **atrasos** nmpl (COM)
arrears

atravesar [atraβe'sar] vt (cruzar) to cross
(over); (traspasar) to pierce; to go
through; (poner al través) to lay o put
across; ~**se** vr to come in between;
(intervenir) to interfere

atravieso etc vb ver **atravesar**

atrayente [atra'jente] adj attractive

atreverse [atre'βerse] vr to dare;
(insolentarse) to be insolent; **atrevido, a**
adj daring; insolent; **atrevimiento** nm
daring; insolence

atribución [atriβu'θjon] nf: **atribuciones**
(POL) powers; (ADMIN) responsibilities

atribuir [atriβu'ir] vt to attribute;
(funciones) to confer

atribular [atriβu'lar] vt to afflict, distress

atributo [atri'βuto] nm attribute

atril [a'tril] nm (para libro) lectern; (MUS)
music stand

atrocidad [atroθi'ðað] nf atrocity, outrage

atropellar [atrope'ʎar] vt (derribar) to
knock over o down; (empujar) to push
(aside); (AUTO) to run over, run down;
(agraviar) to insult; ~**se** vr to act hastily;
atropello nm (AUTO) accident; (empujón)

push; (agravio) wrong; (atrocidad) outrage

atroz [a'troθ] adj atrocious, awful

ATS nm/f abr (= Ayudante Técnico
Sanitario) nurse

atto, a abr = **atento**

atuendo [a'twendo] nm attire

atún [a'tun] nm tuna

aturdir [atur'ðir] vt to stun; (de ruido) to
deafen; (fig) to dumbfound, bewilder

atusar [atu'sar] vt to smooth (down)

audacia [au'ðaθja] nf boldness, audacity;
audaz adj bold, audacious

audible [au'ðiβle] adj audible

audición [auði'θjon] nf hearing; (TEATRO)
audition

audiencia [au'ðjenθja] nf audience; **A~**
(JUR) High Court

audífono [au'ðifono] nm (para sordos)
hearing aid

auditor [auði'tor] nm (JUR) judge advocate;
(COM) auditor

auditorio [auði'torjo] nm audience; (sala)
auditorium

auge ['auxe] nm boom; (clímax) climax

augurar [auɣu'rar] vt to predict;
(presagiar) to portend

augurio [au'xurjo] nm omen

aula ['aula] nf classroom; (en universidad
etc) lecture room

aullar [au'ʎar] vi to howl, yell

aullido [au'ʎiðo] nm howl, yell

aumentar [aumen'tar] vt to increase;
(precios) to put up; (producción) to step
up; (con microscopio, anteojos) to magnify
♦ vi to increase, be on the increase; ~**se**
vr to increase, be on the increase;
aumento nm increase; rise

aun [a'un] adv even; ~ **así** even so; ~ **más**
even o yet more

aún [a'un] adv: ~ **está aquí** he's still here;
~ **no lo sabemos** we don't know yet;
¿**no ha venido** ~? hasn't she come yet?

aunque [a'unke] conj though, although,
even though

aúpa [a'upa] excl come on!

aureola [aure'ola] nf halo

auricular [auriku'lar] nm (TEL) earpiece,

receiver; **~es** *nmpl* (*para escuchar música etc*) headphones

aurora [au'rora] *nf* dawn

auscultar [auskul'tar] *vt* (*MED: pecho*) to listen to, sound

ausencia [au'senθja] *nf* absence

ausentarse [ausen'tarse] *vr* to go away; (*por poco tiempo*) to go out

ausente [au'sente] *adj* absent

auspicios [aus'piθjos] *nmpl* auspices

austeridad [austeri'ðað] *nf* austerity; **austero, a** *adj* austere

austral [aus'tral] *adj* southern ♦ *nm* monetary unit of Argentina

Australia [aus'tralja] *nf* Australia; **australiano, a** *adj*, *nm/f* Australian

Austria ['austrja] *nf* Austria; **austríaco, a** *adj*, *nm/f* Austrian

auténtico, a [au'tentiko, a] *adj* authentic

auto ['auto] *nm* (*JUR*) edict, decree; (: *orden*) writ; (*AUTO*) car; **~s** *nmpl* (*JUR*) proceedings; (: *acta*) court record *sg*

autoadhesivo [autoaðe'siβo] *adj* self-adhesive; (*sobre*) self-sealing

autobiografía [autoβjoɣra'fia] *nf* autobiography

autobús [auto'βus] *nm* bus

autocar [auto'kar] *nm* coach (*BRIT*), (passenger) bus (*US*)

autóctono, a [au'toktono, a] *adj* native, indigenous

autodefensa [autoðe'fensa] *nf* self-defence

autodeterminación [autoðetermina'θjon] *nf* self-determination

autodidacta [autoði'ðakta] *adj* self-taught

autoescuela [autoes'kwela] *nf* driving school

autógrafo [au'toɣrafo] *nm* autograph

autómata [au'tomata] *nm* automaton

automático, a [auto'matiko, a] *adj* automatic ♦ *nm* press stud

automotor, triz [automo'tor, 'triθ] *adj* self-propelled ♦ *nm* diesel train

automóvil [auto'moβil] *nm* (motor) car (*BRIT*), automobile (*US*); **automovilismo** *nm* (*actividad*) motoring; (*DEPORTE*) motor

racing; **automovilista** *nm/f* motorist, driver; **automovilístico, a** *adj* (*industria*) motor *cpd*

autonomía [autono'mia] *nf* autonomy; **autónomo, a** (*ESP*), **autonómico, a** (*ESP*) *adj* (*POL*) autonomous

autopista [auto'pista] *nf* motorway (*BRIT*), freeway (*US*), **~ de peaje** toll road (*BRIT*), turnpike road (*US*)

autopsia [au'topsja] *nf* autopsy, postmortem

autor, a [au'tor, a] *nm/f* author

autoridad [autori'ðað] *nf* authority; **autoritario, a** *adj* authoritarian

autorización [autoriθa'θjon] *nf* authorization; **autorizado, a** *adj* authorized; (*aprobado*) approved

autorizar [autori'θar] *vt* to authorize; (*aprobar*) to approve

autorretrato [autorre'trato] *nm* self-portrait

autoservicio [autoser'βiθjo] *nm* (*tienda*) self-service shop (*BRIT*) o store (*US*); (*restaurante*) self-service restaurant

autostop [auto'stop] *nm* hitch-hiking; **hacer ~** to hitch-hike; **~ista** *nm/f* hitch-hiker

autosuficiencia [autosufi'θjenθja] *nf* self-sufficiency

autovía [auto'βia] *nf* ≈ A-road (*BRIT*), dual carriageway (*BRIT*), ≈ state highway (*US*)

auxiliar [auksi'ljar] *vt* to help ♦ *nm/f* assistant; **auxilio** *nm* assistance, help; **primeros auxilios** first aid *sg*

Av *abr* (= *Avenida*) Av(e).

aval [a'βal] *nm* guarantee; (*persona*) guarantor

avalancha [aβa'lantʃa] *nf* avalanche

avance [a'βanθe] *nm* advance; (*pago*) advance payment; (*CINE*) trailer

avanzar [aβan'θar] *vt*, *vi* to advance

avaricia [aβa'riθja] *nf* avarice, greed; **avaricioso, a** *adj* avaricious, greedy

avaro, a [a'βaro, a] *adj* miserly, mean ♦ *nm/f* miser

avasallar [aβasa'ʎar] *vt* to subdue, subjugate

Avda *abr* (= *Avenida*) Av(e).
AVE ['aße] *nm abr* (= *Alta Velocidad Española*) ≈ bullet train
ave ['aße] *nf* bird; **~ de rapiña** bird of prey
avecinarse [aße0i'narse] *vr* (*tormenta, fig*) to be on the way
avellana [aße'ʎana] *nf* hazelnut; **avellano** *nm* hazel tree
avemaría [aßema'ria] *nm* Hail Mary, Ave Maria
avena [a'ßena] *nf* oats *pl*
avenida [aße'niða] *nf* (*calle*) avenue
avenir [aße'nir] *vt* to reconcile; **~se** *vr* to come to an agreement, reach a compromise
aventajado, a [aßenta'xaðo, a] *adj* outstanding
aventajar [aßenta'xar] *vt* (*sobrepasar*) to surpass, outstrip
aventura [aßen'tura] *nf* adventure; **aventurado, a** *adj* risky; **aventurero, a** *adj* adventurous
avergonzar [aßerɣon'θar] *vt* to shame; (*desconcertar*) to embarrass; **~se** *vr* to be ashamed; to be embarrassed
avería [aße'ria] *nf* (*TEC*) breakdown, fault
averiado, a [aße'rjaðo, a] *adj* broken down; **"~"** "out of order"
averiguación [aßeriɣwa'θjon] *nf* investigation; (*descubrimiento*) ascertainment
averiguar [aßeri'ɣwar] *vt* to investigate; (*descubrir*) to find out, ascertain
aversión [aßer'sjon] *nf* aversion, dislike
avestruz [aßes'truθ] *nm* ostrich
aviación [aßja'θjon] *nf* aviation; (*fuerzas aéreas*) air force
aviador, a [aßja'ðor, a] *nm/f* aviator, airman/woman
avicultura [aßikul'tura] *nf* poultry farming
avidez [aßi'ðeθ] *nf* avidity, eagerness; **ávido, a** *adj* avid, eager
avinagrado, a [aßina'xraðo, a] *adj* sour, acid
avión [a'ßjon] *nm* aeroplane; (*ave*) martin; **~ de reacción** jet (plane)
avioneta [aßjo'neta] *nf* light aircraft

avisar [aßi'sar] *vt* (*advertir*) to warn, notify; (*informar*) to tell; (*aconsejar*) to advise, counsel; **aviso** *nm* warning; (*noticia*) notice
avispa [a'ßispa] *nf* wasp
avispado, a [aßis'paðo, a] *adj* sharp, clever
avispero [aßis'pero] *nm* wasp's nest
avispón [aßis'pon] *nm* hornet
avistar [aßis'tar] *vt* to sight, spot
avituallar [aßitwa'ʎar] *vt* to supply with food
avivar [aßi'ßar] *vt* to strengthen, intensify; **~se** *vr* to revive, acquire new life
axila [ak'sila] *nf* armpit
axioma [ak'sjoma] *nm* axiom
ay [ai] *excl* (*dolor*) ow!, ouch!; (*aflicción*) oh!, oh dear!; **¡~ de mí!** poor me!
aya ['aja] *nf* governess; (*niñera*) nanny
ayer [a'jer] *adv, nm* yesterday; **antes de ~** the day before yesterday
ayote [a'jote] (*AM*) *nm* pumpkin
ayuda [a'juða] *nf* help, assistance ♦ *nm* page; **ayudante, a** *nm/f* assistant, helper; (*ESCOL*) assistant; (*MIL*) adjutant
ayudar [aju'ðar] *vt* to help, assist
ayunar [aju'nar] *vi* to fast; **ayunas** *nfpl*: **estar en ayunas** to be fasting; **ayuno** *nm* fast; fasting
ayuntamiento [ajunta'mjento] *nm* (*consejo*) town (*o* city) council; (*edificio*) town (*o* city) hall
azabache [aθa'ßatʃe] *nm* jet
azada [a'θaða] *nf* hoe
azafata [aθa'fata] *nf* air stewardess
azafrán [aθa'fran] *nm* saffron
azahar [aθa'ar] *nm* orange/lemon blossom
azar [a'θar] *nm* (*casualidad*) chance, fate; (*desgracia*) misfortune, accident; **por ~** by chance; **al ~** at random
azoramiento [aθora'mjento] *nm* alarm; (*confusión*) confusion
azorar [aθo'rar] *vt* to alarm; **~se** *vr* to get alarmed
Azores [a'θores] *nfpl*: **las ~** the Azores
azotar [aθo'tar] *vt* to whip, beat; (*pegar*) to spank; **azote** *nm* (*látigo*) whip;

(*latigazo*) lash, stroke; (*en las nalgas*) spank; (*calamidad*) calamity

azotea [aθo'tea] *nf* (flat) roof

azteca [aθ'teka] *adj, nm/f* Aztec

azúcar [a'θukar] *nm* sugar; **azucarado, a** *adj* sugary, sweet

azucarero, a [aθuka'rero, a] *adj* sugar *cpd*
♦ *nm* sugar bowl

azucena [aθu'θena] *nf* white lily

azufre [a'θufre] *nm* sulphur

azul [a'θul] *adj, nm* blue; ~ **marino** navy blue

azulejo [aθu'lexo] *nm* tile

azuzar [aθu'θar] *vt* to incite, egg on

B, b

B.A. *abr* (= *Buenos Aires*) B.A.

baba ['baβa] *nf* spittle, saliva; **babear** *vi* to drool, slaver

babero [ba'βero] *nm* bib

babor [ba'βor] *nm* port (side)

baboso, a [ba'βoso, a] (*AM: fam*) *adj* silly

baca ['baka] *nf* (*AUTO*) luggage *o* roof rack

bacalao [baka'lao] *nm* cod(fish)

bache ['batʃe] *nm* pothole, rut; (*fig*) bad patch

bachillerato [batʃiʎe'rato] *nm* higher *secondary school course*

bacteria [bak'terja] *nf* bacterium, germ

báculo ['bakulo] *nm* stick, staff

bagaje [ba'vaxe] *nm* baggage, luggage

Bahama [ba'ama]: **las (Islas) ~** *nfpl* the Bahamas

bahía [ba'ia] *nf* bay

bailar [bai'lar] *vt, vi* to dance; ~**ín, ina** *nm/f* (ballet) dancer; **baile** *nm* dance; (*formal*) ball

baja ['baxa] *nf* drop, fall; (*MIL*) casualty; **dar de ~** (*soldado*) to discharge; (*empleado*) to dismiss

bajada [ba'xaða] *nf* descent; (*camino*) slope; (*de aguas*) ebb

bajar [ba'xar] *vi* to go down, come down; (*temperatura, precios*) to drop, fall ♦ *vt* (*cabeza*) to bow; (*escalera*) to go down,

come down; (*precio, voz*) to lower; (*llevar abajo*) to take down; ~**se** *vr* (*de coche*) to get out; (*de autobús, tren*) to get off; ~ **de** (*coche*) to get out of; (*autobús, tren*) to get off

bajeza [ba'xeθa] *nf* baseness *no pl*; (*una ~*) vile deed

bajío [ba'xio] *nm* (*AM*) lowlands *pl*

bajo, a ['baxo, a] *adj* (*mueble, número, precio*) low; (*piso*) ground; (*de estatura*) small, short; (*color*) pale; (*sonido*) faint, soft, low; (*voz: en tono*) deep; (*metal*) base; (*humilde*) low, humble ♦ *adv* (*hablar*) softly, quietly; (*volar*) low ♦ *prep* under, below, underneath ♦ *nm* (*MUS*) bass; ~ **la lluvia** in the rain

bajón [ba'xon] *nm* fall, drop

bakalao [baka'lao] (*fam*) *nm* rave (music)

bala ['bala] *nf* bullet

balance [ba'lanθe] *nm* (*COM*) balance; (*: libro*) balance sheet; (*: cuenta general*) stocktaking

balancear [balanθe'ar] *vt* to balance ♦ *vi* to swing (to and fro); (*vacilar*) to hesitate; ~**se** *vr* to swing (to and fro); to hesitate; **balanceo** *nm* swinging

balanza [ba'lanθa] *nf* scales *pl*, balance; (*ASTROLOGÍA*): **B~** Libra; ~ **comercial** balance of trade; ~ **de pagos** balance of payments

balar [ba'lar] *vi* to bleat

balaustrada [balaus'traða] *nf* balustrade; (*pasamanos*) banisters *pl*

balazo [ba'laθo] *nm* (*golpe*) shot; (*herida*) bullet wound

balbucear [balβuθe'ar] *vi, vt* to stammer, stutter; **balbuceo** *nm* stammering, stuttering

balbucir [balβu'θir] *vi, vt* to stammer, stutter

balcón [bal'kon] *nm* balcony

balde ['balde] *nm* bucket, pail; **de ~** (for) free, for nothing; **en ~** in vain

baldío, a [bal'dio, a] *adj* uncultivated; (*terreno*) waste ♦ *nm* waste land

baldosa [bal'dosa] *nf* (*azulejo*) floor tile; (*grande*) flagstone; **baldosín** *nm* (small) tile

Baleares [baleˈares] *nfpl*: **las (Islas)** ~ the Balearic Islands

balido [baˈliðo] *nm* bleat, bleating

baliza [baˈliθa] *nf* (AVIAT) beacon; (NAUT) buoy

ballena [baˈʎena] *nf* whale

ballesta [baˈʎesta] *nf* crossbow; (AUTO) spring

ballet [baˈle] (*pl* ~s) *nm* ballet

balneario, a [balneˈarjo, a] *adj*: **estación balnearia** (AM) (bathing) resort ♦ *nm* spa, health resort

balón [baˈlon] *nm* ball

baloncesto [balonˈθesto] *nm* basketball

balonmano [balonˈmano] *nm* handball

balonvolea [balomboˈlea] *nm* volleyball

balsa [ˈbalsa] *nf* raft; (BOT) balsa wood

bálsamo [ˈbalsamo] *nm* balsam, balm

baluarte [baˈlwarte] *nm* bastion, bulwark

bambolear [bamboleˈar] *vi* to swing, sway; (silla) to wobble; ~**se** *vr* to swing, sway; to wobble; **bamboleo** *nm* swinging, swaying; wobbling

bambú [bamˈbu] *nm* bamboo

banana [baˈnana] (AM) *nf* banana; **banano** (AM) *nm* banana tree

banca [ˈbanka] *nf* (COM) banking

bancario, a [banˈkarjo, a] *adj* banking *cpd*, bank *cpd*

bancarrota [bankaˈrrota] *nf* bankruptcy; **hacer** ~ to go bankrupt

banco [ˈbanko] *nm* bench; (ESCOL) desk; (COM) bank; (GEO) stratum; ~ **de crédito/de ahorros** credit/savings bank; ~ **de arena** sandbank; ~ **de datos** databank

banda [ˈbanda] *nf* band; (pandilla) gang; (NAUT) side, edge; **la B~ Oriental** Uruguay; ~ **sonora** soundtrack

bandada [banˈdaða] *nf* (de pájaros) flock; (de peces) shoal

bandazo [banˈdaθo] *nm*: **dar** ~**s** to sway from side to side

bandeja [banˈdexa] *nf* tray

bandera [banˈdera] *nf* flag

banderilla [bandeˈriʎa] *nf* banderilla

banderín [bandeˈrin] *nm* pennant, small flag

bandido [banˈdiðo] *nm* bandit

bando [ˈbando] *nm* (edicto) edict, proclamation; (facción) faction; **los ~s** (REL) the banns

bandolera [bandoˈlera] *nf*: **llevar en** ~ to wear across one's chest

bandolero [bandoˈlero] *nm* bandit, brigand

banquero [banˈkero] *nm* banker

banqueta [banˈketa] *nf* stool; (AM: en la calle) pavement (BRIT), sidewalk (US)

banquete [banˈkete] *nm* banquet; (para convidados) formal dinner

banquillo [banˈkiʎo] *nm* (JUR) dock, prisoner's bench; (banco) bench; (para los pies) footstool

bañador [baɲaˈðor] *nm* swimming costume (BRIT), bathing suit (US)

bañar [baˈɲar] *vt* to bath, bathe; (objeto) to dip; (de barniz) to coat; ~**se** *vr* (en el mar) to bathe, swim; (en la bañera) to have a bath

bañera [baˈɲera] *nf* bath(tub)

bañero, a [baˈɲero, a] (AM) *nm/f* lifeguard

bañista [baˈɲista] *nm/f* bather

baño [ˈbaɲo] *nm* (en bañera) bath; (en río) dip, swim; (cuarto) bathroom; (bañera) bath(tub); (capa) coating

baqueta [baˈketa] *nf* (MUS) drumstick

bar [bar] *nm* bar

barahúnda [baraˈunda] *nf* uproar, hubbub

baraja [baˈraxa] *nf* pack (of cards); **barajar** *vt* (naipes) to shuffle; (fig) to jumble up

baranda [baˈranda] *nf* = **barandilla**

barandilla [baranˈdiʎa] *nf* rail, railing

baratija [baraˈtixa] *nf* trinket

baratillo [baraˈtiʎo] *nm* (tienda) junkshop; (subasta) bargain sale; (conjunto de cosas) secondhand goods *pl*

barato, a [baˈrato, a] *adj* cheap ♦ *adv* cheap, cheaply

baraúnda [baraˈunda] *nf* = **barahúnda**

barba [ˈbarβa] *nf* (mentón) chin; (pelo) beard

barbacoa [barßa'koa] *nf* (*parrilla*)
barbecue; (*carne*) barbecued meat
barbaridad [barßari'ðað] *nf* barbarity;
(*acto*) barbarism; (*atrocidad*) outrage; **una
~** (*fam*) loads; **¡qué ~!** (*fam*) how awful!
barbarie [bar'ßarje] *nf* barbarism,
savagery; (*crueldad*) barbarity
barbarismo [barßa'rismo] *nm* = **barbarie**
bárbaro, a [bar'ßaro, a] *adj* barbarous,
cruel; (*grosero*) rough, uncouth ♦ *nm/f*
barbarian ♦ *adv*: **lo pasamos ~** (*fam*) we
had a great time; **¡qué ~!** (*fam*) how
marvellous!; **un éxito ~** (*fam*) a terrific
success; **es un tipo ~** (*fam*) he's a great
bloke
barbecho [bar'ßetʃo] *nm* fallow land
barbero [bar'ßero] *nm* barber, hairdresser
barbilla [bar'ßiʎa] *nf* chin, tip of the chin
barbo ['barßo] *nm* barbel; **~ de mar** red
mullet
barbotear [barßote'ar] *vt, vi* to mutter,
mumble
barbudo, a [bar'ßuðo, a] *adj* bearded
barca ['barka] *nf* (*small*) boat; **~ pesquera**
fishing boat; **~ de pasaje** ferry; **~za** *nf*
barge; **~za de desembarco** landing craft
Barcelona [barθe'lona] *n* Barcelona
barcelonés, esa [barθelo'nes, esa] *adj* of
o from Barcelona
barco ['barko] *nm* boat; (*grande*) ship; **~
de carga** cargo boat; **~ de vela** sailing
ship
baremo [ba'remo] *nm* (*MAT, fig*) scale
barítono [ba'ritono] *nm* baritone
barman ['barman] *nm* barman
Barna *n* = **Barcelona**
barniz [bar'niθ] *nm* varnish; (*en la loza*)
glaze; (*fig*) veneer; **~ar** *vt* to varnish;
(*loza*) to glaze
barómetro [ba'rometro] *nm* barometer
barquero [bar'kero] *nm* boatman
barquillo [bar'kiʎo] *nm* cone, cornet
barra ['barra] *nf* bar, rod; (*de un bar, café*)
bar; (*de pan*) French stick; (*palanca*) lever;
~ de carmín *o* **de labios** lipstick; **~ libre**
free bar
barraca [ba'rraka] *nf* hut, cabin

barranco [ba'rranko] *nm* ravine; (*fig*)
difficulty
barrena [ba'rrena] *nf* drill; **barrenar** *vt* to
drill (through), bore; **barreno** *nm* large
drill
barrer [ba'rrer] *vt* to sweep; (*quitar*) to
sweep away
barrera [ba'rrera] *nf* barrier
barriada [ba'rrjaða] *nf* quarter, district
barricada [barri'kaða] *nf* barricade
barrida [ba'rriða] *nf* sweep, sweeping
barrido [ba'rriðo] *nm* = **barrida**
barriga [ba'rriɣa] *nf* belly; (*panza*) paunch;
barrigón, ona *adj* potbellied;
barrigudo, a *adj* potbellied
barril [ba'rril] *nm* barrel, cask
barrio ['barrjo] *nm* (*vecindad*) area,
neighborhood (*US*); (*en las afueras*)
suburb; **~ chino** red-light district
barro ['barro] *nm* (*lodo*) mud; (*objetos*)
earthenware; (*MED*) pimple
barroco, a [ba'rroko, a] *adj, nm* baroque
barrote [ba'rrote] *nm* (*de ventana*) bar
barruntar [barrun'tar] *vt* (*conjeturar*) to
guess; (*presentir*) to suspect; **barrunto**
nm guess; suspicion
bartola [bar'tola]: **a la ~** *adv*: **tirarse a la
~** to take it easy, be lazy
bártulos ['bartulos] *nmpl* things,
belongings
barullo [ba'ruʎo] *nm* row, uproar
basar [ba'sar] *vt* to base; **~se** *vr*: **~se en**
to be based on
báscula ['baskula] *nf* (*platform*) scales
base ['base] *nf* base; **a ~ de** on the basis
of; (*mediante*) by means of; **~ de datos**
(*INFORM*) database
básico, a ['basiko, a] *adj* basic
basílica [ba'silika] *nf* basilica

┌─────────────────┐
│ *PALABRA CLAVE* │
└─────────────────┘

bastante [bas'tante] *adj* **1** (*suficiente*)
enough; **~ dinero** enough *o* sufficient
money; **~s libros** enough books
2 (*valor intensivo*): **~ gente** quite a lot of
people; **tener ~ calor** to be rather hot
♦ *adv*: **~ bueno / malo** quite good/rather

bad; ~ **rico** pretty rich; **(lo) ~ inteligente (como) para hacer algo** clever enough o sufficiently clever to do sth

bastar [bas'tar] *vi* to be enough o sufficient; **~se** *vr* to be self-sufficient; **~ para** to be enough to; **¡basta!** (that's) enough!

bastardilla [bastar'ðiʎa] *nf* italics

bastardo, a [bas'tarðo, a] *adj, nm/f* bastard

bastidor [basti'ðor] *nm* frame; *(de coche)* chassis; *(TEATRO)* wing; **entre ~es** *(fig)* behind the scenes

basto, a ['basto, a] *adj* coarse, rough; **~s** *nmpl (NAIPES)* ≈ clubs

bastón [bas'ton] *nm* stick, staff; *(para pasear)* walking stick

bastoncillo [baston'θiʎo] *nm* cotton bud

basura [ba'sura] *nf* rubbish *(BRIT)*, garbage *(US)*

basurero [basu'rero] *nm (hombre)* dustman *(BRIT)*, garbage man *(US)*; *(lugar)* dump; *(cubo)* (rubbish) bin *(BRIT)*, trash can *(US)*

bata ['bata] *nf (gen)* dressing gown; *(cubretodo)* smock, overall; *(MED, TEC etc)* lab(oratory) coat

batalla [ba'taʎa] *nf* battle; **de ~** *(fig)* for everyday use

batallar [bata'ʎar] *vi* to fight

batallón [bata'ʎon] *nm* battalion

batata [ba'tata] *nf* sweet potato

batería [bate'ria] *nf* battery; *(MUS)* drums; **~ de cocina** kitchen utensils

batido, a [ba'tiðo, a] *adj (camino)* beaten, well-trodden ♦ *nm (CULIN)*: **~ (de leche)** milk shake

batidora [bati'ðora] *nf* beater, mixer; **~ eléctrica** food mixer, blender

batir [ba'tir] *vt* to beat, strike; *(vencer)* to beat, defeat; *(revolver)* to beat, mix; **~se** *vr* to fight; **~ palmas** to clap, applaud

batuta [ba'tuta] *nf* baton; **llevar la ~** *(fig)* to be the boss, be in charge

baúl [ba'ul] *nm* trunk; *(AUTO)* boot *(BRIT)*, trunk *(US)*

bautismo [bau'tismo] *nm* baptism, christening

bautizar [bauti'θar] *vt* to baptize, christen; *(fam: diluir)* to water down; **bautizo** *nm* baptism, christening

baya ['baja] *nf* berry

bayeta [ba'jeta] *nf* floorcloth

bayoneta [bajo'neta] *nf* bayonet

baza ['baθa] *nf* trick; **meter ~** to butt in

bazar [ba'θar] *nm* bazaar

bazofia [ba'θofja] *nf* trash

beato, a [be'ato, a] *adj* blessed; *(piadoso)* pious

bebé [be'ße] *(pl* **~s)** *nm* baby

bebedor, a [beße'ðor, a] *adj* hard-drinking

beber [be'ßer] *vt, vi* to drink

bebida [be'ßiða] *nf* drink; **bebido, a** *adj* drunk

beca ['beka] *nf* grant, scholarship

becario, a [be'karjo, a] *nm/f* scholarship holder, grant holder

bedel [be'ðel] *nm (ESCOL)* janitor; *(UNIV)* porter

béisbol ['beisßol] *nm (DEPORTE)* baseball

belén [be'len] *nm (de navidad)* nativity scene, crib; **B~** Bethlehem

belga ['belɣa] *adj, nm/f* Belgian

Bélgica ['belxika] *nf* Belgium

bélico, a ['beliko, a] *adj (actitud)* warlike; **belicoso, a** *adj (guerrero)* warlike; *(agresivo)* aggressive, bellicose

beligerante [belixe'rante] *adj* belligerent

belleza [be'ʎeθa] *nf* beauty

bello, a ['beʎo, a] *adj* beautiful, lovely; **Bellas Artes** Fine Art

bellota [be'ʎota] *nf* acorn

bemol [be'mol] *nm (MUS)* flat; **esto tiene ~es** *(fam)* this is a tough one

bencina [ben'θina] *(AM) nf (gasolina)* petrol *(BRIT)*, gasoline *(US)*

bendecir [bende'θir] *vt* to bless

bendición [bendi'θjon] *nf* blessing

bendito, a [ben'dito, a] *pp de* **bendecir** ♦ *adj* holy; *(afortunado)* lucky; *(feliz)* happy; *(sencillo)* simple ♦ *nm/f* simple soul

beneficencia [benefi'θenθja] *nf* charity
beneficiar [benefi'θjar] *vt* to benefit, be of benefit to; **~se** *vr* to benefit, profit; **~io, a** *nm/f* beneficiary
beneficio [bene'fiθjo] *nm* (*bien*) benefit, advantage; (*ganancia*) profit, gain; **~so, a** *adj* beneficial
benéfico, a [be'nefiko, a] *adj* charitable
beneplácito [bene'plaθito] *nm* approval, consent
benevolencia [beneβo'lenθja] *nf* benevolence, kindness; **benévolo, a** *adj* benevolent, kind
benigno, a [be'nixno, a] *adj* kind; (*suave*) mild; (*MED: tumor*) benign, non-malignant
berberecho [berβe'retʃo] *nm* (*ZOOL, CULIN*) cockle
berenjena [beren'xena] *nf* aubergine (*BRIT*), eggplant (*US*)
Berlín [ber'lin] *n* Berlin; **berlinés, esa** *adj* of o from Berlin ♦ *nm/f* Berliner
bermudas [ber'muðas] *nfpl* Bermuda shorts
berrear [berre'ar] *vi* to bellow, low
berrido [be'rriðo] *nm* bellow(ing)
berrinche [be'rrintʃe] (*fam*) *nm* temper, tantrum
berro ['berro] *nm* watercress
berza ['berθa] *nf* cabbage
besamel [besa'mel] *nf* (*CULIN*) white sauce, bechamel sauce
besar [be'sar] *vt* to kiss; (*fig: tocar*) to graze; **~se** *vr* to kiss (one another); **beso** *nm* kiss
bestia ['bestja] *nf* beast, animal; (*fig*) idiot; **~ de carga** beast of burden
bestial [bes'tjal] *adj* bestial; (*fam*) terrific; **~idad** *nf* bestiality; (*fam*) stupidity
besugo [be'suxo] *nm* sea bream; (*fam*) idiot
besuquear [besuke'ar] *vt* to cover with kisses; **~se** *vr* to kiss and cuddle
betún [be'tun] *nm* shoe polish; (*QUÍM*) bitumen
biberón [biβe'ron] *nm* feeding bottle
Biblia ['biβlja] *nf* Bible

bibliografía [biβljoɣra'fia] *nf* bibliography
biblioteca [biβljo'teka] *nf* library; (*mueble*) bookshelves; **~ de consulta** reference library; **~rio, a** *nm/f* librarian
bicarbonato [bikarβo'nato] *nm* bicarbonate
bicho ['bitʃo] *nm* (*animal*) small animal; (*sabandija*) bug, insect; (*TAUR*) bull
bici ['biθi] (*fam*) *nf* bike
bicicleta [biθi'kleta] *nf* bicycle, cycle; **ir en ~** to cycle
bidé [bi'ðe] (*pl* **~s**) *nm* bidet
bidón [bi'ðon] *nm* (*de aceite*) drum; (*de gasolina*) can

PALABRA CLAVE
---

bien [bjen] *nm* 1 (*bienestar*) good; **te lo digo por tu ~** I'm telling you for your own good; **el ~ y el mal** good and evil
2 (*posesión*): **~es** goods; **~es de consumo** consumer goods; **~es inmuebles** o **raíces/~es muebles** real estate *sg*/personal property *sg*
♦ *adv* 1 (*de manera satisfactoria, correcta etc*) well; **trabaja/come ~** she works/eats well; **contestó ~** he answered correctly; **me siento ~** I feel fine; **no me siento ~** I don't feel very well; **se está ~ aquí** it's nice here
2 (*frases*): **hiciste ~ en llamarme** you were right to call me
3 (*valor intensivo*) very; **un cuarto ~ caliente** a nice warm room; **~ se ve que ...** it's quite clear that ...
4: **estar ~: estoy muy ~ aquí** I feel very happy here; **está ~ que vengan** it's all right for them to come; **¡está ~!** lo **haré** oh all right, I'll do it
5 (*de buena gana*): **yo ~ que iría pero ...** I'd gladly go but ...
♦ *excl*: **¡~!** (*aprobación*) O.K.!; **¡muy ~!** well done!
♦ *adj inv* (*matiz despectivo*): **niño ~** rich kid; **gente ~** posh people
♦ *conj* 1: **~ ... ~: ~ en coche ~ en tren** either by car or by train
2: **no ~** (*esp AM*): **no ~ llegue te llamaré**

as soon as I arrive I'll call you
3: si ~ even though; *ver tb* **más**

---

bienal [bje'nal] *adj* biennial

bienaventurado, a [bjenaßentu'raðo, a] *adj (feliz)* happy, fortunate

bienestar [bjenes'tar] *nm* well-being, welfare

bienhechor, a [bjene'tʃor, a] *adj* beneficent ♦ *nm/f* benefactor/ benefactress

bienvenida [bjembe'niða] *nf* welcome; **dar la ~ a uno** to welcome sb

bienvenido [bjembe'niðo] *excl* welcome!

bife ['bife] *(AM) nm* steak

bifurcación [bifurka'θjon] *nf* fork

bifurcarse [bifur'karse] *vr (camino, carretera, río)* to fork

bigamia [bi'xamja] *nf* bigamy; **bígamo, a** *adj* bigamous ♦ *nm/f* bigamist

bigote [bi'xote] *nm* moustache; **bigotudo, a** *adj* with a big moustache

bikini [bi'kini] *nm* bikini; *(CULIN)* toasted ham and cheese sandwich

bilbaíno, a [bilßa'ino, a] *adj* from *o* of Bilbao

bilingüe [bi'lingwe] *adj* bilingual

billar [bi'ʎar] *nm* billiards *sg*; *(lugar)* billiard hall; *(mini-casino)* amusement arcade; **~ americano** pool

billete [bi'ʎete] *nm* ticket; *(de banco)* (bank)note *(BRIT)*, bill *(US)*; *(carta)* note; **~ sencillo, ~ de ida solamente** single *(BRIT) o* one-way *(US)* ticket; **~ de ida y vuelta** return *(BRIT) o* round-trip *(US)* ticket; **~ de 20 libras** £20 note

billetera [biʎe'tera] *nf* wallet

billetero [biʎe'tero] *nm* = **billetera**

billón [bi'ʎon] *nm* billion

bimensual [bimen'swal] *adj* twice monthly

bimotor [bimo'tor] *adj* twin-engined ♦ *nm* twin-engined plane

biodegradable [bioðexra'ðaßle] *adj* biodegradable

biografía [bjoxra'fia] *nf* biography; **biógrafo, a** *nm/f* biographer

biología [bjolo'xia] *nf* biology; **biológico, a** *adj* biological; **biólogo, a** *nm/f* biologist

biombo ['bjombo] *nm* (folding) screen

biopsia [bi'opsja] *nf* biopsy

biquini [bi'kini] *nm* bikini

birlar [bir'lar] *(fam) vt* to pinch

Birmania [bir'manja] *nf* Burma

birria ['birrja] *nf:* **ser una ~** *(película, libro)* to be rubbish

bis [bis] *excl* encore! ♦ *adv:* **viven en el 27 ~** they live at 27a

bisabuelo, a [bisa'ßwelo, a] *nm/f* great-grandfather/mother

bisagra [bi'saɣra] *nf* hinge

bisiesto [bi'sjesto] *adj:* **año ~** leap year

bisnieto, a [bis'njeto, a] *nm/f* great-grandson/daughter

bisonte [bi'sonte] *nm* bison

bisté [bis'te] *nm* = **bistec**

bistec [bis'tek] *nm* steak

bisturí [bistu'ri] *nm* scalpel

bisutería [bisute'ria] *nf* imitation *o* costume jewellery

bit [bit] *nm (INFORM)* bit

bizco, a ['biθko, a] *adj* cross-eyed

bizcocho [biθ'kotʃo] *nm (CULIN)* sponge cake

bizquear [biθke'ar] *vi* to squint

blanca ['blanka] *nf (MUS)* minim; **estar sin ~** to be broke; *ver tb* **blanco**

blanco, a ['blanko, a] *adj* white ♦ *nm/f* white man/woman, white ♦ *nm (color)* white; *(en texto)* blank; *(MIL, fig)* target; **en ~** blank; **noche en ~** sleepless night

blancura [blan'kura] *nf* whiteness

blandir [blan'dir] *vt* to brandish

blando, a ['blando, a] *adj* soft; *(tierno)* tender, gentle; *(carácter)* mild; *(fam)* cowardly; **blandura** *nf* softness; tenderness; mildness

blanquear [blanke'ar] *vt* to whiten; *(fachada)* to whitewash; *(paño)* to bleach ♦ *vi* to turn white; **blanquecino, a** *adj* whitish

blasfemar [blasfe'mar] *vi* to blaspheme, curse; **blasfemia** *nf* blasphemy

blasón [bla'son] *nm* coat of arms

bledo ['bleðo] *nm*: **me importa un ~** I couldn't care less

blindado, a [blin'daðo, a] *adj* (*MIL*) armour-plated; (*antibala*) bullet-proof; **coche** (*ESP*) *o* **carro** (*AM*) **~** armoured car

blindaje [blin'daxe] *nm* armour, armour-plating

bloc [blok] (*pl* **~s**) *nm* writing pad

bloque ['bloke] *nm* block; (*POL*) bloc; **~ de cilindros** cylinder block

bloquear [bloke'ar] *vt* to blockade; **bloqueo** *nm* blockade; (*COM*) freezing, blocking

blusa ['blusa] *nf* blouse

boato [bo'ato] *nm* show, ostentation

bobada [bo'ßaða] *nf* foolish action; foolish statement; **decir ~s** to talk nonsense

bobería [boße'ria] *nf* = **bobada**

bobina [bo'ßina] *nf* (*TEC*) bobbin; (*FOTO*) spool; (*ELEC*) coil

bobo, a ['boßo, a] *adj* (*tonto*) daft, silly; (*cándido*) naïve ♦ *nm/f* fool, idiot ♦ *nm* (*TEATRO*) clown, funny man

boca ['boka] *nf* mouth; (*de crustáceo*) pincer; (*de cañón*) muzzle; (*entrada*) mouth, entrance; **~s** *nfpl* (*de río*) mouth *sg*; **~ abajo/arriba** face down/up; **se me hace agua la ~** my mouth is watering

bocacalle [boka'kaʎe] *nf* (entrance to a) street; **la primera ~** the first turning *o* street

bocadillo [boka'ðiʎo] *nm* sandwich

bocado [bo'kaðo] *nm* mouthful, bite; (*de caballo*) bridle; **~ de Adán** Adam's apple

bocajarro [boka'xarro]: **a ~** *adv* (*disparar, preguntar*) point-blank

bocanada [boka'naða] *nf* (*de vino*) mouthful, swallow; (*de aire*) gust, puff

bocata [bo'kata] (*fam*) *nm* sandwich

bocazas [bo'kaθas] (*fam*) *nm inv* bigmouth

boceto [bo'θeto] *nm* sketch, outline

bochorno [bo'tʃorno] *nm* (*vergüenza*) embarrassment; (*calor*): **hace ~** it's very muggy; **~so, a** *adj* muggy; embarrassing

bocina [bo'θina] *nf* (*MUS*) trumpet; (*AUTO*) horn; (*para hablar*) megaphone

boda ['boða] *nf* (*tb*: **~s**) wedding, marriage; (*fiesta*) wedding reception; **~s de plata/de oro** silver/golden wedding

bodega [bo'ðeɣa] *nf* (*de vino*) cellar; (*depósito*) storeroom; (*de barco*) hold

bodegón [boðe'ɣon] *nm* (*ARTE*) still life

bofe ['bofe] *nm* (*tb*: **~s**: *de res*) lights

bofetada [bofe'taða] *nf* slap (in the face)

bofetón [bofe'ton] *nm* = **bofetada**

boga ['boɣa] *nf*: **en ~** (*fig*) in vogue

bogar [bo'ɣar] *vi* (*remar*) to row; (*navegar*) to sail

bogavante [boɣa'ßante] *nm* lobster

Bogotá [boɣo'ta] *n* Bogotá

bohemio, a [bo'emjo, a] *adj, nm/f* Bohemian

boicot [boi'kot] (*pl* **~s**) *nm* boycott; **~ear** *vt* to boycott; **~eo** *nm* boycott

boina ['boina] *nf* beret

bola ['bola] *nf* ball; (*canica*) marble; (*NAIPES*) (grand) slam; (*betún*) shoe polish; (*mentira*) tale, story; **~s** (*AM*) *nfpl* bolas *sg*; **~ de billar** billiard ball; **~ de nieve** snowball

bolchevique [boltʃe'ßike] *adj, nm/f* Bolshevik

boleadoras [bolea'ðoras] (*AM*) *nfpl* bolas *sg*

bolera [bo'lera] *nf* skittle *o* bowling alley

boleta [bo'leta] (*AM*) *nf* (*billete*) ticket; (*permiso*) pass, permit

boletería [bolete'ria] (*AM*) *nf* ticket office

boletín [bole'tin] *nm* bulletin; (*periódico*) journal, review; **~ de noticias** news bulletin

boleto [bo'leto] *nm* ticket

boli ['boli] (*fam*) *nm* Biro ®, pen

bolígrafo [bo'liɣrafo] *nm* ball-point pen, Biro ®

bolívar [bo'lißar] *nm* monetary unit of Venezuela

Bolivia [bo'lißja] *nf* Bolivia; **boliviano, a** *adj, nm/f* Bolivian

bollería [boʎe'ria] *nf* cakes *pl* and pastries *pl*

bollo ['boʎo] nm (pan) roll; (bulto) bump, lump; (abolladura) dent

bolo ['bolo] nm skittle; (píldora) (large) pill; **(juego de) ~s** nmpl skittles sg

bolsa ['bolsa] nf bag; (AM) pocket; (ANAT) cavity, sac; (COM) stock exchange; (MINERÍA) pocket; **de ~** pocket cpd; **~ de agua caliente** hot water bottle; **~ de aire** air pocket; **~ de papel** paper bag; **~ de plástico** plastic bag

bolsillo [bol'siʎo] nm pocket; (cartera) purse; **de ~** pocket(-size)

bolsista [bol'sista] nm/f stockbroker

bolso ['bolso] nm (bolsa) bag; (de mujer) handbag

bomba ['bomba] nf (MIL) bomb; (TEC) pump ♦ (fam) adj: **noticia ~** bombshell ♦ (fam) adv: **pasarlo ~** to have a great time; **~ atómica/de humo/de efecto retardado** atomic/smoke/time bomb

bombardear [bombarðe'ar] vt to bombard; (MIL) to bomb; **bombardeo** nm bombardment; bombing

bombardero [bombar'ðero] nm bomber

bombear [bombe'ar] vt (agua) to pump (out o up); **~se** vr to warp

bombero [bom'bero] nm fireman

bombilla [bom'biʎa] (ESP) nf (light) bulb

bombín [bom'bin] nm bowler hat

bombo ['bombo] nm (MUS) bass drum; (TEC) drum

bombón [bom'bon] nm chocolate

bombona [bom'bona] nf (de butano, oxígeno) cylinder

bonachón, ona [bona'tʃon, ona] adj good-natured, easy-going

bonanza [bo'nanθa] nf (NAUT) fair weather; (fig) bonanza; (MINERÍA) rich pocket o vein

bondad [bon'daθ] nf goodness, kindness; **tenga la ~ de** (please) be good enough to; **~oso, a** adj good, kind

bonificación [bonifika'θjon] nf bonus

bonito, a [bo'nito, a] adj pretty; (agradable) nice ♦ nm (atún) tuna (fish)

bono ['bono] nm voucher; (FIN) bond

bonobús [bono'βus] (ESP) nm bus pass

bonoloto [bono'loto] nf state-run weekly lottery

boquerón [boke'ron] nm (pez) (kind of) anchovy; (agujero) large hole

boquete [bo'kete] nm gap, hole

boquiabierto, a [bokia'βjerto, a] adj: **quedar ~** to be amazed o flabbergasted

boquilla [bo'kiʎa] nf (para riego) nozzle; (para cigarro) cigarette holder; (MUS) mouthpiece

borbotón [borβo'ton] nm: **salir a borbotones** to gush out

borda ['borða] nf (NAUT) (ship's) rail; **tirar algo/caerse por la ~** to throw sth/fall overboard

bordado [bor'ðaðo] nm embroidery

bordar [bor'ðar] vt to embroider

borde ['borðe] nm edge, border; (de camino etc) side; (en la costura) hem; **al ~ de** (fig) on the verge o brink of; **ser ~** (ESP: fam) to be rude; **~ar** vt to border

bordillo [bor'ðiʎo] nm kerb (BRIT), curb (US)

bordo ['borðo] nm (NAUT) side; **a ~** on board

borinqueño, a [borin'kenjo, a] adj, nm/f Puerto Rican

borla ['borla] nf (adorno) tassel

borrachera [borra'tʃera] nf (ebriedad) drunkenness; (orgía) spree, binge

borracho, a [bo'rratʃo, a] adj drunk ♦ nm/f (habitual) drunkard, drunk; (temporal) drunk, drunk man/woman

borrador [borra'ðor] nm (escritura) first draft, rough sketch; (goma) rubber (BRIT), eraser

borrar [bo'rrar] vt to erase, rub out

borrasca [bo'rraska] nf storm

borrico, a [bo'rriko, a] nm/f donkey/she-donkey; (fig) stupid man/woman

borrón [bo'rron] nm (mancha) stain

borroso, a [bo'rroso, a] adj vague, unclear; (escritura) illegible

bosque ['boske] nm wood; (grande) forest

bosquejar [boske'xar] vt to sketch; **bosquejo** nm sketch

bostezar [boste'θar] vi to yawn; **bostezo**

nm yawn

bota ['bota] *nf* (*calzado*) boot; (*para vino*) leather wine bottle; **~s de agua**, **~s de goma** Wellingtons

botánica [bo'tanika] *nf* (*ciencia*) botany; *ver tb* **botánico**

botánico, a [bo'taniko, a] *adj* botanical ♦ *nm/f* botanist

botar [bo'tar] *vt* to throw, hurl; (*NAUT*) to launch; (*AM*) to throw out ♦ *vi* to bounce

bote ['bote] *nm* (*salto*) bounce; (*golpe*) thrust; (*vasija*) tin, can; (*embarcación*) boat; **de ~ en ~** packed, jammed full; **~ de la basura** (*AM*) dustbin (*BRIT*), trashcan (*US*); **~ salvavidas** lifeboat

botella [bo'teʎa] *nf* bottle; **botellín** *nm* small bottle

botica [bo'tika] *nf* chemist's (shop) (*BRIT*), pharmacy; **~rio, a** *nm/f* chemist (*BRIT*), pharmacist

botijo [bo'tixo] *nm* (earthenware) jug

botín [bo'tin] *nm* (*calzado*) half boot; (*polaina*) spat; (*MIL*) booty

botiquín [boti'kin] *nm* (*armario*) medicine cabinet; (*portátil*) first-aid kit

botón [bo'ton] *nm* button; (*BOT*) bud; **~ de oro** buttercup

botones [bo'tones] *nm inv* bellboy (*BRIT*), bellhop (*US*)

bóveda ['boβeða] *nf* (*ARQ*) vault

boxeador [boksea'ðor] *nm* boxer

boxear [bokse'ar] *vi* to box

boxeo [bok'seo] *nm* boxing

boya ['boja] *nf* (*NAUT*) buoy; (*de caña*) float

boyante [bo'jante] *adj* prosperous

bozal [bo'θal] *nm* (*de caballo*) halter; (*de perro*) muzzle

bracear [braθe'ar] *vi* (*agitar los brazos*) to wave one's arms

bracero [bra'θero] *nm* labourer; (*en el campo*) farmhand

bragas ['braɣas] *nfpl* (*de mujer*) panties, knickers (*BRIT*)

bragueta [bra'ɣeta] *nf* fly, flies *pl*

braille [breil] *nm* braille

bramar [bra'mar] *vi* to bellow, roar;

bramido *nm* bellow, roar

brasa ['brasa] *nf* live *o* hot coal

brasero [bra'sero] *nm* brazier

Brasil [bra'sil] *nm*: **(el) ~** Brazil; **brasileño, a** *adj*, *nm/f* Brazilian

bravata [bra'ßata] *nf* boast

braveza [bra'ßeθa] *nf* (*valor*) bravery; (*ferocidad*) ferocity

bravío, a [bra'ßio, a] *adj* wild; (*feroz*) fierce

bravo, a ['braßo, a] *adj* (*valiente*) brave; (*feroz*) ferocious; (*salvaje*) wild; (*mar etc*) rough, stormy ♦ *excl* bravo!; **bravura** *nf* bravery; ferocity

braza ['braθa] *nf* fathom; **nadar a la ~** to swim (the) breast-stroke

brazada [bra'θaða] *nf* stroke

brazado [bra'θaðo] *nm* armful

brazalete [braθa'lete] *nm* (*pulsera*) bracelet; (*banda*) armband

brazo ['braθo] *nm* arm; (*ZOOL*) foreleg; (*BOT*) limb, branch; **luchar a ~ partido** to fight hand-to-hand; **ir cogidos del ~** to walk arm in arm

brea ['brea] *nf* pitch, tar

brebaje [bre'ßaxe] *nm* potion

brecha ['bretʃa] *nf* (*hoyo, vacío*) gap, opening; (*MIL, fig*) breach

brega ['breɣa] *nf* (*lucha*) struggle; (*trabajo*) hard work

breva ['breßa] *nf* early fig

breve ['breße] *adj* short, brief ♦ *nf* (*MUS*) breve; **~dad** *nf* brevity, shortness

brezo ['breθo] *nm* heather

bribón, ona [bri'ßon, ona] *adj* idle, lazy ♦ *nm/f* (*pícaro*) rascal, rogue

bricolaje [briko'laxe] *nm* do-it-yourself, DIY

brida ['briða] *nf* bridle, rein; (*TEC*) clamp; **a toda ~** at top speed

bridge [britʃ] *nm* bridge

brigada [bri'ɣaða] *nf* (*unidad*) brigade; (*trabajadores*) squad, gang ♦ *nm* ≈ staff-sergeant, sergeant-major

brillante [bri'ʎante] *adj* brilliant ♦ *nm* diamond

brillar [bri'ʎar] *vi* (*tb fig*) to shine; (*joyas*)

to sparkle

brillo ['briʎo] *nm* shine; *(brillantez)* brilliance; *(fig)* splendour; **sacar ~ a** to polish

brincar [brin'kar] *vi* to skip about, hop about, jump about; **está que brinca** he's hopping mad

brinco ['brinko] *nm* jump, leap

brindar [brin'dar] *vi*: **~ a o por** to drink (a toast) to ♦ *vt* to offer, present

brindis ['brindis] *nm inv* toast

brío ['brio] *nm* spirit, dash; **brioso, a** *adj* spirited, dashing

brisa ['brisa] *nf* breeze

británico, a [bri'taniko, a] *adj* British ♦ *nm/f* Briton, British person

brizna ['briθna] *nf (de hierba, paja)* blade; *(de tabaco)* leaf

broca ['broka] *nf (TEC)* drill, bit

brocal [bro'kal] *nm* rim

brocha ['brotʃa] *nf (large)* paintbrush; **~ de afeitar** shaving brush

broche ['brotʃe] *nm* brooch

broma ['broma] *nf* joke; **en ~** in fun, as a joke; **~ pesada** practical joke; **bromear** *vi* to joke

bromista [bro'mista] *adj* fond of joking ♦ *nm/f* joker, wag

bronca ['bronka] *nf* row; **echar una ~ a uno** to tick sb off

bronce ['bronθe] *nm* bronze; **~ado, a** *adj* bronze; *(por el sol)* tanned ♦ *nm* (sun)tan; *(TEC)* bronzing

bronceador [bronθea'ðor] *nm* suntan lotion

broncearse [bronθe'arse] *vr* to get a suntan

bronco, a ['bronko, a] *adj (manera)* rude, surly; *(voz)* harsh

bronquio ['bronkjo] *nm (ANAT)* bronchial tube

bronquitis [bron'kitis] *nf inv* bronchitis

brotar [bro'tar] *vi (BOT)* to sprout; *(aguas)* to gush (forth); *(MED)* to break out

brote ['brote] *nm (BOT)* shoot; *(MED, fig)* outbreak

bruces ['bruθes]: **de ~** *adv*: **caer o dar de ~** to fall headlong, fall flat

bruja ['bruxa] *nf* witch; **brujería** *nf* witchcraft

brujo ['bruxo] *nm* wizard, magician

brújula ['bruxula] *nf* compass

bruma ['bruma] *nf* mist; **brumoso, a** *adj* misty

bruñir [bru'ɲir] *vt* to polish

brusco, a ['brusko, a] *adj (súbito)* sudden; *(áspero)* brusque

Bruselas [bru'selas] *n* Brussels

brutal [bru'tal] *adj* brutal

brutalidad [brutali'ðað] *nf* brutality

bruto, a ['bruto, a] *adj (idiota)* stupid; *(bestial)* brutish; *(peso)* gross; **en ~** raw, unworked

Bs.As. *abr* (= *Buenos Aires*) B.A.

bucal [bu'kal] *adj* oral; **por vía ~** orally

bucear [buθe'ar] *vi* to dive ♦ *vt* to explore; **buceo** *nm* diving

bucle ['bukle] *nm* curl

budismo [bu'ðismo] *nm* Buddhism

buen [bwen] *adj m ver* **bueno**

buenamente [bwena'mente] *adv (fácilmente)* easily; *(voluntariamente)* willingly

buenaventura [bwenaßen'tura] *nf (suerte)* good luck; *(adivinación)* fortune

PALABRA CLAVE

bueno, a ['bweno, a] *adj (antes de nmsg:* **buen**) **1** *(excelente etc)* good; **es un libro ~, es un buen libro** it's a good book; **hace ~, hace buen tiempo** the weather is fine, it is fine; **el ~ de Paco** good old Paco; **fue muy ~ conmigo** he was very nice *o* kind to me

2 *(apropiado)*: **ser ~ para** to be good for; **creo que vamos por buen camino** I think we're on the right track

3 *(irónico)*: **le di un buen rapapolvo** I gave him a good *o* real ticking off; **¡buen conductor estás hecho!** some *o* a fine driver you are!; **¡estaría ~ que ...!** a fine thing it would be if ...!

4 *(atractivo, sabroso)*: **está ~ este bizcocho** this sponge is delicious;

Carmen está muy buena Carmen is gorgeous
5 (*saludos*): **¡buen día!, ¡~s días!** (good) morning!; **¡buenas (tardes)!** (good) afternoon!; (*más tarde*) (good) evening!; **¡buenas noches!** good night!
6 (*otras locuciones*): **estar de buenas** to be in a good mood; **por las buenas o por las malas** by hook or by crook; **de buenas a primeras** all of a sudden
♦ *excl*: **¡~!** all right!; **~, ¿y qué?** well, so what?

Buenos Aires *nm* Buenos Aires
buey [bwei] *nm* ox
búfalo ['bufalo] *nm* buffalo
bufanda [bu'fanda] *nf* scarf
bufar [bu'far] *vi* to snort
bufete [bu'fete] *nm* (*despacho de abogado*) lawyer's office
buffer ['bufer] *nm* (*INFORM*) buffer
bufón [bu'fon] *nm* clown
buhardilla [buar'ðiʎa] *nf* attic
búho ['buo] *nm* owl; (*fig*) hermit, recluse
buhonero [buo'nero] *nm* pedlar
buitre ['bwitre] *nm* vulture
bujía [bu'xia] *nf* (*vela*) candle; (*ELEC*) candle (power); (*AUTO*) spark plug
bula ['bula] *nf* (*papal*) bull
bulbo ['bulßo] *nm* bulb
bulevar [bule'ßar] *nm* boulevard
Bulgaria [bul'varja] *nf* Bulgaria; **búlgaro, a** *adj, nm/f* Bulgarian
bulla ['buʎa] *nf* (*ruido*) uproar; (*de gente*) crowd
bullicio [bu'ʎiθjo] *nm* (*ruido*) uproar; (*movimiento*) bustle
bullir [bu'ʎir] *vi* (*hervir*) to boil; (*burbujear*) to bubble
bulto ['bulto] *nm* (*paquete*) package; (*fardo*) bundle; (*tamaño*) size, bulkiness; (*MED*) swelling, lump; (*silueta*) vague shape
buñuelo [bu'ɲwelo] *nm* ≈ doughnut (*BRIT*), ≈ donut (*US*); (*fruta de sartén*) fritter
BUP [bup] *nm abr* (*ESP*: = *Bachillerato Unificado Polivalente*) *secondary education and leaving certificate for 14–17 age group*

buque ['buke] *nm* ship, vessel
burbuja [bur'ßuxa] *nf* bubble; **burbujear** *vi* to bubble
burdel [bur'ðel] *nm* brothel
burdo, a ['burðo, a] *adj* coarse, rough
burgués, esa [bur'xes, esa] *adj* middle-class, bourgeois; **burguesía** *nf* middle class, bourgeoisie
burla ['burla] *nf* (*mofa*) gibe; (*broma*) joke; (*engaño*) trick
burladero [burla'ðero] *nm* (bullfighter's) refuge
burlar [bur'lar] *vt* (*engañar*) to deceive ♦ *vi* to joke; **~se** *vr* to joke; **~se de** to make fun of
burlesco, a [bur'lesko, a] *adj* burlesque
burlón, ona [bur'lon, ona] *adj* mocking
burocracia [buro'kraθja] *nf* civil service
burócrata [bu'rokrata] *nm/f* civil servant
burrada [bu'rraða] *nf*: **decir/soltar ~s** to talk nonsense; **hacer ~s** to act stupid; **una ~** (*mucho*) a (hell of a) lot
burro, a ['burro, a] *nm/f* donkey/she-donkey; (*fig*) ass, idiot
bursátil [bur'satil] *adj* stock-exchange *cpd*
bus [bus] *nm* bus
busca ['buska] *nf* search, hunt ♦ *nm* (*TEL*) bleeper; **en ~ de** in search of
buscar [bus'kar] *vt* to look for, search for, seek ♦ *vi* to look, search, seek; **se busca secretaria** secretary wanted
busque *etc vb ver* **buscar**
búsqueda ['buskeða] *nf* = **busca** *nf*
busto ['busto] *nm* (*ANAT*, *ARTE*) bust
butaca [bu'taka] *nf* armchair; (*de cine, teatro*) stall, seat
butano [bu'tano] *nm* butane (gas)
buzo ['buθo] *nm* diver
buzón [bu'θon] *nm* (*en puerta*) letter box; (*en la calle*) pillar box

C, c

C. *abr* (= *centígrado*) C; (= *compañía*) Co.

c. *abr* (= *capítulo*) ch.

C/ *abr* (= *calle*) St

c.a. *abr* (= *corriente alterna*) AC

cabal [ka'ßal] *adj* (*exacto*) exact; (*correcto*) right, proper; (*acabado*) finished, complete; **~es** *nmpl*: **estar en sus ~es** to be in one's right mind

cábalas ['kaßalas] *nfpl*: **hacer ~** to guess

cabalgar [kaßal'ɣar] *vt, vi* to ride

cabalgata [kaßal'ɣata] *nf* procession

caballa [ka'ßaʎa] *nf* mackerel

caballeresco, a [kaßaʎe'resko, a] *adj* noble, chivalrous

caballería [kaßaʎe'ria] *nf* mount; (*MIL*) cavalry

caballeriza [kaßaʎe'riθa] *nf* stable; **caballerizo** *nm* groom, stableman

caballero [kaßa'ʎero] *nm* gentleman; (*de la orden de caballería*) knight; (*trato directo*) sir

caballerosidad [kaßaʎerosi'ðað] *nf* chivalry

caballete [kaßa'ʎete] *nm* (*ARTE*) easel; (*TEC*) trestle

caballito [kaßa'ʎito] *nm* (*caballo pequeño*) small horse, pony; **~s** *nmpl* (*en verbena*) roundabout, merry-go-round

caballo [ka'ßaʎo] *nm* horse; (*AJEDREZ*) knight; (*NAIPES*) queen; **ir en ~** to ride; **~ de vapor** o **de fuerza** horsepower; **~ de carreras** racehorse

cabaña [ka'ßaɲa] *nf* (*casita*) hut, cabin

cabaré [kaßa're] (*pl* **~s**) *nm* cabaret

cabaret [kaßa're] (*pl* **~s**) *nm* cabaret

cabecear [kaßeθe'ar] *vt, vi* to nod

cabecera [kaße'θera] *nf* head; (*IMPRENTA*) headline

cabecilla [kaße'θiʎa] *nm* ringleader

cabellera [kaße'ʎera] *nf* (head of) hair; (*de cometa*) tail

cabello [ka'ßeʎo] *nm* (*tb*: **~s**) hair

caber [ka'ßer] *vi* (*entrar*) to fit, go; **caben**

3 más there's room for 3 more

cabestrillo [kaßes'triʎo] *nm* sling

cabestro [ka'ßestro] *nm* halter

cabeza [ka'ßeθa] *nf* head; (*POL*) chief, leader; **~ rapada** skinhead; **~da** *nf* (*golpe*) butt; **dar ~das** to nod off; **cabezón, ona** *adj* (*vino*) heady; (*fam*: *persona*) pig-headed

cabida [ka'ßiða] *nf* space

cabildo [ka'ßildo] *nm* (*de iglesia*) chapter; (*POL*) town council

cabina [ka'ßina] *nf* cabin; (*de camión*) cab; **~ telefónica** telephone box (*BRIT*) o booth

cabizbajo, a [kaßiθ'ßaxo, a] *adj* crestfallen, dejected

cable ['kaßle] *nm* cable

cabo ['kaßo] *nm* (*de objeto*) end, extremity; (*MIL*) corporal; (*NAUT*) rope, cable; (*GEO*) cape; **al ~ de 3 días** after 3 days

cabra ['kaßra] *nf* goat

cabré *etc vb ver* **caber**

cabrear [kaßre'ar] (*fam*) *vt* to bug; **~se** *vr* (*enfadarse*) to fly off the handle

cabrío, a [ka'ßrio, a] *adj* goatish; **macho ~** (he-)goat, billy goat

cabriola [ka'ßrjola] *nf* caper

cabritilla [kaßri'tiʎa] *nf* kid, kidskin

cabrito [ka'ßrito] *nm* kid

cabrón [ka'ßron] *nm* cuckold; (*fam!*) bastard (*!*)

caca ['kaka] (*fam*) *nf* pooh

cacahuete [kaka'wete] (*ESP*) *nm* peanut

cacao [ka'kao] *nm* cocoa; (*BOT*) cacao

cacarear [kakare'ar] *vi* (*persona*) to boast; (*gallina*) to crow

cacería [kaθe'ria] *nf* hunt

cacerola [kaθe'rola] *nf* pan, saucepan

cachalote [katʃa'lote] *nm* (*ZOOL*) sperm whale

cacharro [ka'tʃarro] *nm* earthenware pot; **~s** *nmpl* pots and pans

cachear [katʃe'ar] *vt* to search, frisk

cachemir [katʃe'mir] *nm* cashmere

cacheo [ka'tʃeo] *nm* searching, frisking

cachete [ka'tʃete] *nm* (*ANAT*) cheek; (*bofetada*) slap (in the face)

cachiporra [katʃiˈporra] *nf* truncheon

cachivache [katʃiˈβatʃe] *nm* (*trasto*) piece of junk; **~s** *nmpl* junk *sg*

cacho [ˈkatʃo] *nm* (small) bit; (*AM: cuerno*) horn

cachondeo [katʃonˈdeo] (*fam*) *nm* farce, joke

cachondo, a [kaˈtʃondo, a] *adj* (*ZOOL*) on heat; (*fam: sexualmente*) randy; (: *gracioso*) funny

cachorro, a [kaˈtʃorro, a] *nm/f* (*perro*) pup, puppy; (*león*) cub

cacique [kaˈθike] *nm* chief, local ruler; (*POL*) local party boss; **caciquismo** *nm* system of control by the local boss

caco [ˈkako] *nm* pickpocket

cacto [ˈkakto] *nm* cactus

cactus [ˈkaktus] *nm inv* cactus

cada [ˈkaða] *adj inv* each; (*antes de número*) every; **~ día** each day, every day; **~ dos días** every other day; **~ uno/a** each one, every one; **~ vez más/menos** more and more/less and less; **uno de ~ diez** one out of every ten

cadalso [kaˈðalso] *nm* scaffold

cadáver [kaˈðaβer] *nm* (dead) body, corpse

cadena [kaˈðena] *nf* chain; (*TV*) channel; **trabajo en ~** assembly line work; **~ perpetua** (*JUR*) life imprisonment

cadencia [kaˈðenθja] *nf* rhythm

cadera [kaˈðera] *nf* hip

cadete [kaˈðete] *nm* cadet

caducar [kaðuˈkar] *vi* to expire; **caduco, a** *adj* expired; (*persona*) very old

caer [kaˈer] *vi* to fall (down); **~se** *vr* to fall (down); **me cae bien/mal** I get on well with him/I can't stand him; **~ en la cuenta** to realize; **su cumpleaños cae en viernes** her birthday falls on a Friday

café [kaˈfe] (*pl* **~s**) *nm* (*bebida, planta*) coffee; (*lugar*) café ♦ *adj* (*color*) brown; **~ con leche** white coffee; **~ solo** black coffee

cafetera [kafeˈtera] *nf* coffee pot

cafetería [kafeteˈria] *nf* (*gen*) café

cafetero, a [kafeˈtero, a] *adj* coffee *cpd*;

ser muy ~ to be a coffee addict

cagar [kaˈɣar] (*fam!*) *vt* to bungle, mess up ♦ *vi* to have a shit (!)

caída [kaˈiða] *nf* fall; (*declive*) slope; (*disminución*) fall, drop

caído, a [kaˈiðo, a] *adj* drooping

caiga *etc vb ver* **caer**

caimán [kaiˈman] *nm* alligator

caja [ˈkaxa] *nf* box; (*para reloj*) case; (*de ascensor*) shaft; (*COM*) cashbox; (*donde se hacen los pagos*) cashdesk; (: *en supermercado*) checkout, till; **~ de ahorros** savings bank; **~ de cambios** gearbox; **~ fuerte, ~ de caudales** safe, strongbox

cajero, a [kaˈxero, a] *nm/f* cashier; **~ automático** cash dispenser

cajetilla [kaxeˈtiʎa] *nf* (*de cigarrillos*) packet

cajón [kaˈxon] *nm* big box; (*de mueble*) drawer

cal [kal] *nf* lime

cala [ˈkala] *nf* (*GEO*) cove, inlet; (*de barco*) hold

calabacín [kalaβaˈθin] *nm* (*BOT*) baby marrow; (: *más pequeño*) courgette (*BRIT*), zucchini (*US*)

calabaza [kalaˈβaθa] *nf* (*BOT*) pumpkin

calabozo [kalaˈβoθo] *nm* (*cárcel*) prison; (*celda*) cell

calada [kaˈlaða] *nf* (*de cigarrillo*) puff

calado, a [kaˈlaðo, a] *adj* (*prenda*) lace *cpd* ♦ *nm* (*NAUT*) draught

calamar [kalaˈmar] *nm* squid *no pl*

calambre [kaˈlambre] *nm* (*tb:* **~s**) cramp

calamidad [kalamiˈðað] *nf* calamity, disaster

calar [kaˈlar] *vt* to soak, drench; (*penetrar*) to pierce, penetrate; (*comprender*) to see through; (*vela*) to lower; **~se** *vr* (*AUTO*) to stall; **~se las gafas** to stick one's glasses on

calavera [kalaˈβera] *nf* skull

calcar [kalˈkar] *vt* (*reproducir*) to trace; (*imitar*) to copy

calcetín [kalθeˈtin] *nm* sock

calcinar [kalθiˈnar] *vt* to burn, blacken

calcio ['kalθjo] nm calcium
calcomanía [kalkoma'nia] nf transfer
calculador, a [kalkula'ðor, a] adj
(persona) calculating
calculadora [kalkula'ðora] nf calculator
calcular [kalku'lar] vt (MAT) to calculate,
compute; ~ que ... to reckon that ...;
cálculo nm calculation
caldear [kalde'ar] vt to warm (up), heat
(up)
caldera [kal'dera] nf boiler
calderilla [kalde'riʎa] nf (moneda) small
change
caldero [kal'dero] nm small boiler
caldo ['kaldo] nm stock; (consomé)
consommé
calefacción [kalefak'θjon] nf heating; ~
central central heating
calendario [kalen'darjo] nm calendar
calentador [kalenta'ðor] nm heater
calentamiento [kalenta'mjento] nm
(DEPORTE) warm-up
calentar [kalen'tar] vt to heat (up); ~se vr
to heat up, warm up; (fig: discusión etc)
to get heated
calentura [kalen'tura] nf (MED) fever,
(high) temperature
calibrar [kali'ßrar] vt to gauge, measure;
calibre nm (de cañón) calibre, bore;
(diámetro) diameter; (fig) calibre
calidad [kali'ðað] nf quality; de ~ quality
cpd; en ~ de in the capacity of, as
cálido, a ['kaliðo, a] adj hot; (fig) warm
caliente etc [ka'ljente] vb ver calentar
♦ adj hot; (fig) fiery; (disputa) heated;
(fam: cachondo) randy
calificación [kalifika'θjon] nf qualification;
(de alumno) grade, mark
calificar [kalifi'kar] vt to qualify; (alumno)
to grade, mark; ~ de to describe as
calima [ka'lima] nf (cerca del mar) mist
cáliz ['kaliθ] nm chalice
caliza [ka'liθa] nf limestone
calizo, a [ka'liθo, a] adj lime cpd
callado, a [ka'ʎaðo, a] adj quiet
callar [ka'ʎar] vt (asunto delicado) to keep
quiet about, say nothing about; (persona,

opinión) to silence ♦ vi to keep quiet, be
silent; ~se vr to keep quiet, be silent;
¡cállate! be quiet!, shut up!
calle ['kaʎe] nf street; (DEPORTE) lane; ~
arriba/abajo up/down the street; ~ de
un solo sentido one-way street
calleja [ka'ʎexa] nf alley, narrow street;
callejear vi to wander (about) the
streets; callejero, a adj street cpd ♦ nm
street map; callejón nm alley, passage;
callejón sin salida cul-de-sac;
callejuela nf side-street, alley
callista [ka'ʎista] nm/f chiropodist
callo ['kaʎo] nm callus; (en el pie) corn; ~s
nmpl (CULIN) tripe sg
calma ['kalma] nf calm
calmante [kal'mante] nm sedative,
tranquillizer
calmar [kal'mar] vt to calm, calm down
♦ vi (tempestad) to abate; (mente etc) to
become calm
calmoso, a [kal'moso, a] adj calm, quiet
calor [ka'lor] nm heat; (agradable) warmth;
hace ~ it's hot; tener ~ to be hot
caloría [kalo'ria] nf calorie
calumnia [ka'lumnja] nf calumny, slander;
calumnioso, a adj slanderous
caluroso, a [kalu'roso, a] adj hot; (sin
exceso) warm; (fig) enthusiastic
calva ['kalßa] nf bald patch; (en bosque)
clearing
calvario [kal'ßarjo] nm stations pl of the
cross
calvicie [kal'ßiθje] nf baldness
calvo, a ['kalßo, a] adj bald; (terreno)
bare, barren; (tejido) threadbare
calza ['kalθa] nf wedge, chock
calzada [kal'θaða] nf roadway, highway
calzado, a [kal'θaðo, a] adj shod ♦ nm
footwear
calzador [kalθa'ðor] nm shoehorn
calzar [kal'θar] vt (zapatos etc) to wear;
(un mueble) to put a wedge under; ~se
vr: ~se los zapatos to put on one's
shoes; ¿qué (número) calza? what size
do you take?
calzón [kal'θon] nm (tb: calzones nmpl)

shorts; (AM: de hombre) (under)pants;
(: de mujer) panties
calzoncillos [kalθon'θiʎos] nmpl
underpants
cama ['kama] nf bed; ~ **individual/de
matrimonio** single/double bed
camafeo [kama'feo] nm cameo
camaleón [kamale'on] nm chameleon
cámara ['kamara] nf chamber; (habitación)
room; (sala) hall; (CINE) cine camera;
(fotográfica) camera; ~ **de aire** inner tube;
~ **de comercio** chamber of commerce; ~
frigorífica cold-storage room
camarada [kama'raða] nm comrade,
companion
camarera [kama'rera] nf (en restaurante)
waitress; (en casa, hotel) maid
camarero [kama'rero] nm waiter
camarilla [kama'riʎa] nf clique
camarón [kama'ron] nm shrimp
camarote [kama'rote] nm cabin
cambiable [kam'bjaßle] adj (variable)
changeable, variable; (intercambiable)
interchangeable
cambiante [kam'bjante] adj variable
cambiar [kam'bjar] vt to change; (dinero)
to exchange ♦ vi to change; ~**se** vr
(mudarse) to move; (de ropa) to change;
~ **de idea** to change one's mind; ~ **de
ropa** to change (one's clothes)
cambio ['kambjo] nm change; (trueque)
exchange; (COM) rate of exchange;
(oficina) bureau de change; (dinero
menudo) small change; **en** ~ on the other
hand; (en lugar de) instead; ~ **de divisas**
foreign exchange; ~ **de velocidades** gear
lever
camelar [kame'lar] vt to sweet-talk
camello [ka'meʎo] nm camel; (fam:
traficante) pusher
camerino [kame'rino] nm dressing room
camilla [ka'miʎa] nf (MED) stretcher
caminante [kami'nante] nm/f traveller
caminar [kami'nar] vi (marchar) to walk,
go ♦ vt (recorrer) to cover, travel
caminata [kami'nata] nf long walk; (por el
campo) hike

camino [ka'mino] nm way, road; (sendero)
track; **a medio** ~ halfway (there); **en el** ~
on the way, en route; ~ **de** on the way
to; ~ **particular** private road

Camino de Santiago

ℹ️ The **Camino de Santiago** is a
medieval pilgrim route stretching from
the Pyrenees to Santiago de Compostela in
north-west Spain, where tradition has it
the body of the Apostle James is buried.
Nowadays it is a popular tourist route as
well as a religious one.

camión [ka'mjon] nm lorry (BRIT), truck
(US); ~ **cisterna** tanker; **camionero, a**
nm/f lorry o truck driver
camioneta [kamjo'neta] nf van, light
truck
camisa [ka'misa] nf shirt; (BOT) skin; ~ **de
fuerza** straitjacket; **camisería** nf
outfitter's (shop)
camiseta [kami'seta] nf (prenda) tee-shirt;
(: ropa interior) vest; (de deportista) top
camisón [kami'son] nm nightdress,
nightgown
camorra [ka'morra] nf: **buscar** ~ to look
for trouble
campamento [kampa'mento] nm camp
campana [kam'pana] nf bell; ~ **de cristal**
bell jar; ~**da** nf peal; ~**rio** nm belfry
campanilla [kampa'niʎa] nf small bell
campaña [kam'paɲa] nf (MIL, POL)
campaign
campechano, a [kampe'tʃano, a] adj
(franco) open
campeón, ona [kampe'on, ona] nm/f
champion; **campeonato** nm
championship
campesino, a [kampe'sino, a] adj
country cpd, rural; (gente) peasant cpd
♦ nm/f countryman/woman; (agricultor)
farmer
campestre [kam'pestre] adj country cpd,
rural
camping ['kampin] (pl ~s) nm camping;
(lugar) campsite; **ir de** o **hacer** ~ to go

camping

campo ['kampo] *nm (fuera de la ciudad)* country, countryside; *(AGR, ELEC)* field; *(de fútbol)* pitch; *(de golf)* course; *(MIL)* camp; **~ de batalla** battlefield; **~ de deportes** sports ground, playing field

camposanto [kampo'santo] *nm* cemetery

camuflaje [kamu'flaxe] *nm* camouflage

cana ['kana] *nf* white o grey hair; **tener ~s** to be going grey

Canadá [kana'ða] *nm* Canada; **canadiense** *adj, nm/f* Canadian ♦ *nf* fur-lined jacket

canal [ka'nal] *nm* canal; *(GEO)* channel, strait; *(de televisión)* channel; *(de tejado)* gutter; **~ de Panamá** Panama Canal; **~izar** *vt* to channel

canalla [ka'naʎa] *nf* rabble, mob ♦ *nm* swine

canalón [kana'lon] *nm (conducto vertical)* drainpipe; *(del tejado)* gutter

canapé [kana'pe] *(pl* **~s)** *nm* sofa, settee; *(CULIN)* canapé

Canarias [ka'narjas] *nfpl:* **(las Islas) ~** the Canary Islands, the Canaries

canario, a [ka'narjo, a] *adj, nm/f (native)* of the Canary Isles ♦ *nm (ZOOL)* canary

canasta [ka'nasta] *nf (round)* basket; **canastilla** *nf* small basket; *(de niño)* layette

canasto [ka'nasto] *nm* large basket

cancela [kan'θela] *nf* gate

cancelación [kanθela'θjon] *nf* cancellation

cancelar [kanθe'lar] *vt* to cancel; *(una deuda)* to write off

cáncer ['kanθer] *nm (MED)* cancer; *(ASTROLOGÍA):* **C~** Cancer

cancha ['kantʃa] *nf (de baloncesto, tenis etc)* court; *(AM: de fútbol)* pitch

canciller [kanθi'ʎer] *nm* chancellor

canción [kan'θjon] *nf* song; **~ de cuna** lullaby; **cancionero** *nm* song book

candado [kan'daðo] *nm* padlock

candente [kan'dente] *adj* red-hot; *(fig: tema)* burning

candidato, a [kandi'ðato, a] *nm/f* candidate

candidez [kandi'ðeθ] *nf (sencillez)* simplicity; *(simpleza)* naiveté; **cándido, a** *adj* simple; naive

candil [kan'dil] *nm* oil lamp; **~ejas** *nfpl (TEATRO)* footlights

candor [kan'dor] *nm (sinceridad)* frankness; *(inocencia)* innocence

canela [ka'nela] *nf* cinnamon

canelones [kane'lones] *nmpl* cannelloni

cangrejo [kan'grexo] *nm* crab

canguro [kan'guro] *nm* kangaroo; **hacer de ~** to babysit

caníbal [ka'niβal] *adj, nm/f* cannibal

canica [ka'nika] *nf* marble

canijo, a [ka'nixo, a] *adj* frail, sickly

canino, a [ka'nino, a] *adj* canine ♦ *nm* canine (tooth)

canjear [kanxe'ar] *vt* to exchange

cano, a ['kano, a] *adj* grey-haired, white-haired

canoa [ka'noa] *nf* canoe

canon ['kanon] *nm* canon; *(pensión)* rent; *(COM)* tax

canónigo [ka'noniɣo] *nm* canon

canonizar [kanoni'θar] *vt* to canonize

canoso, a [ka'noso, a] *adj* grey-haired

cansado, a [kan'saðo, a] *adj* tired, weary; *(tedioso)* tedious, boring

cansancio [kan'sanθjo] *nm* tiredness, fatigue

cansar [kan'sar] *vt (fatigar)* to tire, tire out; *(aburrir)* to bore; *(fastidiar)* to bother; **~se** *vr* to tire, get tired; *(aburrirse)* to get bored

cantábrico, a [kan'taβriko, a] *adj* Cantabrian; **mar C~** Bay of Biscay

cantante [kan'tante] *adj* singing ♦ *nm/f* singer

cantar [kan'tar] *vt* to sing ♦ *vi* to sing; *(insecto)* to chirp ♦ *nm (acción)* singing; *(canción)* song; *(poema)* poem

cántara ['kantara] *nf* large pitcher

cántaro ['kantaro] *nm* pitcher, jug; **llover a ~s** to rain cats and dogs

cante ['kante] *nm:* **~ jondo** flamenco singing

cantera [kan'tera] nf quarry

cantidad [kanti'ðað] nf quantity, amount

cantimplora [kantim'plora] nf (frasco) water bottle, canteen

cantina [kan'tina] nf canteen; (de estación) buffet

canto ['kanto] nm singing; (canción) song; (borde) edge, rim; (de un cuchillo) back; ~ **rodado** boulder

cantor, a [kan'tor, a] nm/f singer

canturrear [kanturre'ar] vi to sing softly

canuto [ka'nuto] nm (tubo) small tube; (fam: droga) joint

caña ['kaɲa] nf (BOT: tallo) stem, stalk; (carrizo) reed; (vaso) tumbler; (de cerveza) glass of beer; (ANAT) shinbone; ~ **de azúcar** sugar cane; ~ **de pescar** fishing rod

cañada [ka'ɲaða] nf (entre dos montañas) gully, ravine; (camino) cattle track

cáñamo ['kaɲamo] nm hemp

cañería [kaɲe'ria] nf (tubo) pipe

caño ['kaɲo] nm (tubo) tube, pipe; (de albañal) sewer; (MUS) pipe; (de fuente) jet

cañón [ka'ɲon] nm (MIL) cannon; (de fusil) barrel; (GEO) canyon, gorge

caoba [ka'oβa] nf mahogany

caos ['kaos] nm chaos

cap. abr (= capítulo) ch.

capa ['kapa] nf cloak, cape; (GEO) layer, stratum; **so ~ de** under the pretext of; ~ **de ozono** ozone layer

capacidad [kapaθi'ðað] nf (medida) capacity; (aptitud) capacity, ability

capacitar [kapaθi'tar] vt: ~ **a algn para (hacer)** to enable sb to (do)

capar [ka'par] vt to castrate, geld

caparazón [kapara'θon] nm shell

capataz [kapa'taθ] nm foreman

capaz [ka'paθ] adj able, capable; (amplio) capacious, roomy

capcioso, a [kap'θjoso, a] adj wily, deceitful

capellán [kape'ʎan] nm chaplain; (sacerdote) priest

caperuza [kape'ruθa] nf hood

capicúa [kapi'kua] adj inv (número, fecha)

reversible

capilla [ka'piʎa] nf chapel

capital [kapi'tal] adj capital ♦ nm (COM) capital ♦ nf (ciudad) capital; ~ **social** share o authorized capital

capitalismo [kapita'lismo] nm capitalism; **capitalista** adj, nm/f capitalist

capitán [kapi'tan] nm captain

capitanear [kapitane'ar] vt to captain

capitulación [kapitula'θjon] nf (rendición) capitulation, surrender; (acuerdo) agreement, pact; **capitulaciones (matrimoniales)** nfpl marriage contract sg

capitular [kapitu'lar] vi to make an agreement

capítulo [ka'pitulo] nm chapter

capó [ka'po] nm (AUTO) bonnet

capón [ka'pon] nm (gallo) capon

capota [ka'pota] nf (de mujer) bonnet; (AUTO) hood (BRIT), top (US)

capote [ka'pote] nm (abrigo: de militar) greatcoat; (: de torero) cloak

capricho [ka'pritʃo] nm whim, caprice; ~**so, a** adj capricious

Capricornio [kapri'kornjo] nm Capricorn

cápsula ['kapsula] nf capsule

captar [kap'tar] vt (comprender) to understand; (RADIO) to pick up; (atención, apoyo) to attract

captura [kap'tura] nf capture; (JUR) arrest; **capturar** vt to capture; to arrest

capucha [ka'putʃa] nf hood, cowl

capullo [ka'puʎo] nm (BOT) bud; (ZOOL) cocoon; (fam) idiot

caqui ['kaki] nm khaki

cara ['kara] nf (ANAT, de moneda) face; (de disco) side; (descaro) boldness; ~ **a** facing; **de** ~ opposite, facing; **dar la** ~ to face the consequences; ¿~ **o cruz?** heads or tails?; ¡**qué** ~ **(más dura)!** what a nerve!

carabina [kara'βina] nf carbine, rifle; (persona) chaperone

Caracas [ka'rakas] n Caracas

caracol [kara'kol] nm (ZOOL) snail; (concha) (sea) shell

carácter [ka'rakter] (pl **caracteres**) nm

character; **tener buen/mal ~** to be good natured/bad tempered

característica [karakte'ristika] *nf* characteristic

característico, a [karakte'ristiko, a] *adj* characteristic

caracterizar [karakteri'θar] *vt* to characterize, typify

caradura [kara'ðura] *nm/f*: **es un ~** he's got a nerve

carajillo [kara'xiʎo] *nm* coffee with a dash of brandy

carajo [ka'raxo] (*fam!*) *nm*: **¡~!** shit! (*!*)

caramba [ka'ramba] *excl* good gracious!

carámbano [ka'rambano] *nm* icicle

caramelo [kara'melo] *nm* (*dulce*) sweet; (*azúcar fundida*) caramel

caravana [kara'ßana] *nf* caravan; (*fig*) group; (*AUTO*) tailback

carbón [kar'ßon] *nm* coal; **papel ~** carbon paper; **carboncillo** *nm* (*ARTE*) charcoal; **carbonero, a** *nm/f* coal merchant; **carbonilla** [-'niʎa] *nf* coal dust

carbonizar [karßoni'θar] *vt* to carbonize; (*quemar*) to char

carbono [kar'ßono] *nm* carbon

carburador [karßura'ðor] *nm* carburettor

carburante [karßu'rante] *nm* (*para motor*) fuel

carcajada [karka'xaða] *nf* (loud) laugh, guffaw

cárcel ['karθel] *nf* prison, jail; (*TEC*) clamp; **carcelero, a** *adj* prison *cpd* ♦ *nm/f* warder

carcoma [kar'koma] *nf* woodworm

carcomer [karko'mer] *vt* to bore into, eat into; (*fig*) to undermine; **~se** *vr* to become worm-eaten; (*fig*) to decay

cardar [kar'ðar] *vt* (*pelo*) to backcomb

cardenal [karðe'nal] *nm* (*REL*) cardinal; (*MED*) bruise

cardíaco, a [kar'ðiako, a] *adj* cardiac, heart *cpd*

cardinal [karði'nal] *adj* cardinal

cardo ['karðo] *nm* thistle

carearse [kare'arse] *vr* to come face to face

carecer [kare'θer] *vi*: **~ de** to lack, be in need of

carencia [ka'renθja] *nf* lack; (*escasez*) shortage; (*MED*) deficiency

carente [ka'rente] *adj*: **~ de** lacking in, devoid of

carestía [kares'tia] *nf* (*escasez*) scarcity, shortage; (*COM*) high cost

careta [ka'reta] *nf* mask

carga ['karßa] *nf* (*peso, ELEC*) load; (*de barco*) cargo, freight; (*MIL*) charge; (*responsabilidad*) duty, obligation

cargado, a [kar'ßaðo, a] *adj* loaded; (*ELEC*) live; (*café, té*) strong; (*cielo*) overcast

cargamento [karßa'mento] *nm* (*acción*) loading; (*mercancías*) load, cargo

cargar [kar'ßar] *vt* (*barco, arma*) to load; (*ELEC*) to charge; (*COM: algo en cuenta*) to charge; (*INFORM*) to load ♦ *vi* (*MIL*) to charge; (*AUTO*) to load (up); **~ con** to pick up, carry away; (*peso, fig*) to shoulder, bear; **~se** (*fam*) *vr* (*estropear*) to break; (*matar*) to bump off

cargo ['karßo] *nm* (*puesto*) post, office; (*responsabilidad*) duty, obligation; (*JUR*) charge; **hacerse ~ de** to take charge of *o* responsibility for

carguero [kar'ßero] *nm* freighter, cargo boat; (*avión*) freight plane

Caribe [ka'rißе] *nm*: **el ~** the Caribbean; **del ~** Caribbean

caribeño, a [kari'ßеɲo, a] *adj* Caribbean

caricatura [karika'tura] *nf* caricature

caricia [ka'riθja] *nf* caress

caridad [kari'ðað] *nf* charity

caries ['karjes] *nf inv* tooth decay

cariño [ka'riɲo] *nm* affection, love; (*caricia*) caress; (*en carta*) love ...; **tener ~ a** to be fond of; **~so, a** *adj* affectionate

carisma [ka'risma] *nm* charisma

caritativo, a [karita'tißo, a] *adj* charitable

cariz [ka'riθ] *nm*: **tener** *o* **tomar buen/mal ~** to look good/bad

carmesí [karme'si] *adj, nm* crimson

carmín [kar'min] *nm* lipstick

carnal [kar'nal] *adj* carnal; **primo ~** first cousin

carnaval [karnaˈβal] *nm* carnival

| carnaval |

ⓘ **Carnaval** *is the traditional period of fun, feasting and partying which takes place in the three days before the start of Lent ("Cuaresma"). Although in decline during the Franco years the carnival has grown in popularity recently in Spain. Cádiz and Tenerife are particularly well-known for their flamboyant celebrations with fancy-dress parties, parades and firework displays being the order of the day.*

carne [ˈkarne] *nf* flesh; (CULIN) meat; ~ **de cerdo/cordero/ternera/vaca** pork/lamb/veal/beef; ~ **de gallina** (fig): **se me pone la ~ de gallina sólo verlo** I get the creeps just seeing it

carné [karˈne] (pl ~s) *nm*: ~ **de conducir** driving licence (BRIT), driver's license (US); ~ **de identidad** identity card

carnero [karˈnero] *nm* sheep, ram; (carne) mutton

carnet [karˈne] (pl ~s) *nm* = **carné**

carnicería [karniθeˈria] *nf* butcher's (shop); (fig: matanza) carnage, slaughter

carnicero, a [karniˈθero, a] *adj* carnivorous ♦ *nm/f* (tb fig) butcher; (carnívoro) carnivore

carnívoro, a [karˈniβoro, a] *adj* carnivorous

carnoso, a [karˈnoso, a] *adj* beefy, fat

caro, a [ˈkaro, a] *adj* dear; (COM) dear, expensive ♦ *adv* dear, dearly

carpa [ˈkarpa] *nf* (pez) carp; (de circo) big top; (AM: de camping) tent

carpeta [karˈpeta] *nf* folder, file

carpintería [karpinteˈria] *nf* carpentry, joinery; **carpintero** *nm* carpenter

carraspear [karraspeˈar] *vi* to clear one's throat

carraspera [karrasˈpera] *nf* hoarseness

carrera [kaˈrrera] *nf* (acción) run(ning); (espacio recorrido) run; (competición) race; (trayecto) course; (profesión) career; (ESCOL) course

carreta [kaˈrreta] *nf* wagon, cart

carrete [kaˈrrete] *nm* reel, spool; (TEC) coil

carretera [karreˈtera] *nf* (main) road, highway; ~ **de circunvalación** ring road; ~ **nacional** ≈ A road (BRIT), ≈ state highway (US)

carretilla [karreˈtiʎa] *nf* trolley; (AGR) (wheel)barrow

carril [kaˈrril] *nm* furrow; (de autopista) lane; (FERRO) rail

carrillo [kaˈrriʎo] *nm* (ANAT) cheek; (TEC) pulley

carrito [kaˈrrito] *nm* trolley

carro [ˈkarro] *nm* cart, wagon; (MIL) tank; (AM: coche) car

carrocería [karroθeˈria] *nf* bodywork, coachwork

carroña [kaˈrroɲa] *nf* carrion *no pl*

carroza [kaˈrroθa] *nf* (carruaje) coach

carrusel [karruˈsel] *nm* merry-go-round, roundabout

carta [ˈkarta] *nf* letter; (CULIN) menu; (naipe) card; (mapa) map; (JUR) document; ~ **de ajuste** (TV) test card; ~ **de crédito** credit card; ~ **certificada** registered letter; ~ **marítima** chart; ~ **verde** (AUTO) green card

cartabón [kartaˈβon] *nm* set square

cartel [karˈtel] *nm* (anuncio) poster, placard; (ESCOL) wall chart; (COM) cartel; ~**era** *nf* hoarding, billboard; (en periódico etc) entertainments guide; **"en ~era"** "showing"

cartera [karˈtera] *nf* (de bolsillo) wallet; (de colegial, cobrador) satchel; (de señora) handbag; (para documentos) briefcase; (COM) portfolio; **ocupa la ~ de Agricultura** she is Minister of Agriculture

carterista [karteˈrista] *nm/f* pickpocket

cartero [karˈtero] *nm* postman

cartilla [karˈtiʎa] *nf* primer, first reading book; ~ **de ahorros** savings book

cartón [karˈton] *nm* cardboard; ~ **piedra** papier-mâché

cartucho [karˈtutʃo] *nm* (MIL) cartridge

cartulina [kartuˈlina] *nf* card

casa ['kasa] *nf* house; (*hogar*) home; (*COM*) firm, company; **en ~** at home; **~ consistorial** town hall; **~ de huéspedes** boarding house; **~ de socorro** first aid post

casado, a [ka'saðo, a] *adj* married ♦ *nm/f* married man/woman

casamiento [kasa'mjento] *nm* marriage, wedding

casar [ka'sar] *vt* to marry; (*JUR*) to quash, annul; **~se** *vr* to marry, get married

cascabel [kaska'ßel] *nm* (small) bell

cascada [kas'kaða] *nf* waterfall

cascanueces [kaska'nweθes] *nm inv* nutcrackers *pl*

cascar [kas'kar] *vt* to crack, split, break (open); **~se** *vr* to crack, split, break (open)

cáscara ['kaskara] *nf* (*de huevo, fruta seca*) shell; (*de fruta*) skin; (*de limón*) peel

casco ['kasko] *nm* (*de bombero, soldado*) helmet; (*NAUT: de barco*) hull; (*ZOOL: de caballo*) hoof; (*botella*) empty bottle; (*de ciudad*): **el ~ antiguo** the old part; **el ~ urbano** the town centre; **los ~s azules** the UN peace-keeping force, the blue berets

cascote [kas'kote] *nm* rubble

caserío [kase'rio] *nm* hamlet; (*casa*) country house

casero, a [ka'sero, a] *adj* (*pan etc*) home-made ♦ *nm/f* (*propietario*) landlord/lady; **ser muy ~** to be home-loving; **"comida casera"** "home cooking"

caseta [ka'seta] *nf* hut; (*para bañista*) cubicle; (*de feria*) stall

casete [ka'sete] *nm o f* cassette

casi ['kasi] *adv* almost, nearly; **~ nada** hardly anything; **~ nunca** hardly ever, almost never; **~ te caes** you almost fell

casilla [ka'siʎa] *nf* (*casita*) hut, cabin; (*AJEDREZ*) square; (*para cartas*) pigeonhole; **casillero** *nm* (*para cartas*) pigeonholes *pl*

casino [ka'sino] *nm* club; (*de juego*) casino

caso ['kaso] *nm* case; **en ~ de ...** in case of ...; **en ~ de que ...** in case ...; **el ~ es**

que the fact is that; **en ese ~** in that case; **hacer ~ a** to pay attention to; **hacer** *o* **venir al ~** to be relevant

caspa ['kaspa] *nf* dandruff

cassette [ka'sete] *nm o f* = **casete**

casta ['kasta] *nf* caste; (*raza*) breed; (*linaje*) lineage

castaña [kas'taɲa] *nf* chestnut

castañetear [kastaɲete'ar] *vi* (*dientes*) to chatter

castaño, a [kas'taɲo, a] *adj* chestnut (-coloured), brown ♦ *nm* chestnut tree

castañuelas [kasta'ɲwelas] *nfpl* castanets

castellano, a [kaste'ʎano, a] *adj, nm/f* Castilian ♦ *nm* (*LING*) Castilian, Spanish

castidad [kasti'ðað] *nf* chastity, purity

castigar [kasti'var] *vt* to punish; (*DEPORTE*) to penalize; **castigo** *nm* punishment; (*DEPORTE*) penalty

Castilla [kas'tiʎa] *nf* Castile

castillo [kas'tiʎo] *nm* castle

castizo, a [kas'tiθo, a] *adj* (*LING*) pure

casto, a ['kasto, a] *adj* chaste, pure

castor [kas'tor] *nm* beaver

castrar [kas'trar] *vt* to castrate

castrense [kas'trense] *adj* (*disciplina, vida*) military

casual [ka'swal] *adj* chance, accidental; **~idad** *nf* chance, accident; (*combinación de circunstancias*) coincidence; **¡qué ~idad!** what a coincidence!

cataclismo [kata'klismo] *nm* cataclysm

catador, a [kata'ðor, a] *nm/f* wine taster

catalán, ana [kata'lan, ana] *adj, nm/f* Catalan ♦ *nm* (*LING*) Catalan

catalizador [kataliθa'ðor] *nm* catalyst; (*AUT*) catalytic convertor

catalogar [katalo'var] *vt* to catalogue; **~ a algn (de)** (*fig*) to categorize sb (as)

catálogo [ka'taloxo] *nm* catalogue

Cataluña [kata'luɲa] *nf* Catalonia

catar [ka'tar] *vt* to taste, sample

catarata [kata'rata] *nf* (*GEO*) waterfall; (*MED*) cataract

catarro [ka'tarro] *nm* catarrh; (*constipado*) cold

catástrofe [ka'tastrofe] *nf* catastrophe

catear [kate'ar] *(fam) vt (examen, alumno)* to fail

cátedra ['kateðra] *nf (UNIV)* chair, professorship

catedral [kate'ðral] *nf* cathedral

catedrático, a [kate'ðratiko, a] *nm/f* professor

categoría [katexo'ria] *nf* category; *(rango)* rank, standing; *(calidad)* quality; **de ~** *(hotel)* top-class

categórico, a [kate'xoriko, a] *adj* categorical

cateto, a ['kateto, a] *(pey) nm/f* peasant

catolicismo [katoli'θismo] *nm* Catholicism

católico, a [ka'toliko, a] *adj, nm/f* Catholic

catorce [ka'torθe] *num* fourteen

cauce ['kauθe] *nm (de río)* riverbed; *(fig)* channel

caucho ['kautʃo] *nm* rubber; *(AM: llanta)* tyre

caución [kau'θjon] *nf* bail; **caucionar** *vt (JUR)* to bail, go bail for

caudal [kau'ðal] *nm (de río)* volume, flow; *(fortuna)* wealth; *(abundancia)* abundance; **~oso, a** *adj (río)* large

caudillo [kau'ðiʎo] *nm* leader, chief

causa ['kausa] *nf* cause; *(razón)* reason; *(JUR)* lawsuit, case; **a ~ de** because of

causar [kau'sar] *vt* to cause

cautela [kau'tela] *nf* caution, cautiousness; **cauteloso, a** *adj* cautious, wary

cautivar [kauti'ßar] *vt* to capture; *(atraer)* to captivate

cautiverio [kauti'ßerjo] *nm* captivity

cautividad [kautißi'ðað] *nf* = **cautiverio**

cautivo, a [kau'tißo, a] *adj, nm/f* captive

cauto, a ['kauto, a] *adj* cautious, careful

cava ['kaßa] *nm champagne-type wine*

cavar [ka'ßar] *vt* to dig

caverna [ka'ßerna] *nf* cave, cavern

cavidad [kaßi'ðað] *nf* cavity

cavilar [kaßi'lar] *vt* to ponder

cayado [ka'jaðo] *nm (de pastor)* crook; *(de obispo)* crozier

cayendo *etc vb ver* **caer**

caza ['kaθa] *nf (acción: gen)* hunting; *(: con fusil)* shooting; *(una ~)* hunt, chase; *(animales)* game ♦ *nm (AVIAT)* fighter

cazador, a [kaθa'ðor, a] *nm/f* hunter; **cazadora** *nf* jacket

cazar [ka'θar] *vt* to hunt; *(perseguir)* to chase; *(prender)* to catch

cazo ['kaθo] *nm* saucepan

cazuela [ka'θwela] *nf (vasija)* pan; *(guisado)* casserole

CD *abbr (= compact disc)* CD

CD-ROM *abbr m* CD-ROM

CE *nf abr (= Comunidad Europea)* EC

cebada [θe'ßaða] *nf* barley

cebar [θe'ßar] *vt (animal)* to fatten (up); *(anzuelo)* to bait; *(MIL, TEC)* to prime

cebo ['θeßo] *nm (para animales)* feed, food; *(para peces, fig)* bait; *(de arma)* charge

cebolla [θe'ßoʎa] *nf* onion; **cebolleta** *nf* spring onion; **cebollín** *nm* spring onion

cebra ['θeßra] *nf* zebra

cecear [θeθe'ar] *vi* to lisp; **ceceo** *nm* lisp

ceder [θe'ðer] *vt* to hand over, give up, part with ♦ *vi (renunciar)* to give in, yield; *(disminuir)* to diminish, decline; *(romperse)* to give way

cedro ['θeðro] *nm* cedar

cédula ['θeðula] *nf* certificate, document

cegar [θe'xar] *vt* to blind; *(tubería etc)* to block up, stop up ♦ *vi* to go blind; **~se** *vr*: **~se (de)** to be blinded (by)

ceguera [θe'xera] *nf* blindness

CEI *abbr (= Confederación de Estados Independientes)* CIS

ceja ['θexa] *nf* eyebrow

cejar [θe'xar] *vi (fig)* to back down

celador, a [θela'ðor, a] *nm/f (de edificio)* watchman; *(de museo etc)* attendant

celda ['θelda] *nf* cell

celebración [θeleßra'θjon] *nf* celebration

celebrar [θele'ßrar] *vt* to celebrate; *(alabar)* to praise ♦ *vi* to be glad; **~se** *vr* to occur, take place

célebre ['θelebre] *adj* famous

celebridad [θeleßri'ðað] *nf* fame; *(persona)* celebrity

celeste [θe'leste] *adj (azul)* sky-blue

celestial [θeles'tjal] *adj* celestial, heavenly

celibato [θeli'βato] *nm* celibacy

célibe ['θeliβe] *adj, nm/f* celibate

celo[1] ['θelo] *nm* zeal; *(REL)* fervour; *(ZOOL)*: **en ~** on heat; **~s** *nmpl* jealousy *sg*; **tener ~s** to be jealous

celo[2] ['θelo] *nm* Sellotape ®

celofán [θelo'fan] *nm* cellophane

celoso, a [θe'loso, a] *adj* jealous; *(trabajador)* zealous

celta ['θelta] *adj* Celtic ♦ *nm/f* Celt

célula ['θelula] *nf* cell; **~ solar** solar cell

celulitis [θelu'litis] *nf* cellulite

celuloide [θelu'loiðe] *nm* celluloid

cementerio [θemen'terjo] *nm* cemetery, graveyard

cemento [θe'mento] *nm* cement; *(hormigón)* concrete; *(AM: cola)* glue

cena ['θena] *nf* evening meal, dinner

cenagal [θena'xal] *nm* bog, quagmire

cenar [θe'nar] *vt* to have for dinner ♦ *vi* to have dinner

cenicero [θeni'θero] *nm* ashtray

cenit [θe'nit] *nm* zenith

ceniza [θe'niθa] *nf* ash, ashes *pl*

censo ['θenso] *nm* census; **~ electoral** electoral roll

censura [θen'sura] *nf* (POL) censorship

censurar [θensu'rar] *vt* (idea) to censure; *(cortar: película)* to censor

centella [θen'teʎa] *nf* spark

centellear [θenteʎe'ar] *vi* (metal) to gleam; *(estrella)* to twinkle; *(fig)* to sparkle

centenar [θente'nar] *nm* hundred

centenario, a [θente'narjo, a] *adj* centenary; hundred-year-old ♦ *nm* centenary

centeno [θen'teno] *nm* (BOT) rye

centésimo, a [θen'tesimo, a] *adj* hundredth

centígrado [θen'tixraðo] *adj* centigrade

centímetro [θen'timetro] *nm* centimetre (BRIT), centimeter (US)

céntimo ['θentimo] *nm* cent

centinela [θenti'nela] *nm* sentry, guard

centollo [θen'toʎo] *nm* spider crab

central [θen'tral] *adj* central ♦ *nf* head office; *(TEC)* plant; *(TEL)* exchange; **~ eléctrica** power station; **~ nuclear** nuclear power station; **~ telefónica** telephone exchange

centralita [θentra'lita] *nf* switchboard

centralizar [θentrali'θar] *vt* to centralize

centrar [θen'trar] *vt* to centre

céntrico, a ['θentriko, a] *adj* central

centrifugar [θentrifu'xar] *vt* to spin-dry

centrista [θen'trista] *adj* centre *cpd*

centro ['θentro] *nm* centre; **~ comercial** shopping centre; **~ juvenil** youth club

centroamericano, a [θentroameri'kano, a] *adj, nm/f* Central American

ceñido, a [θe'ɲiðo, a] *adj* (chaqueta, pantalón) tight(-fitting)

ceñir [θe'ɲir] *vt* (rodear) to encircle, surround; *(ajustar)* to fit (tightly)

ceño ['θeɲo] *nm* frown, scowl; **fruncir el ~** to frown, knit one's brow

CEOE *nf abr* (ESP: = Confederación Española de Organizaciones Empresariales) ≈ CBI (BRIT), employers' organization

cepillar [θepi'ʎar] *vt* to brush; *(madera)* to plane (down)

cepillo [θe'piʎo] *nm* brush; *(para madera)* plane; **~ de dientes** toothbrush

cera ['θera] *nf* wax

cerámica [θe'ramika] *nf* pottery; *(arte)* ceramics

cerca ['θerka] *nf* fence ♦ *adv* near, nearby, close; **~ de** near, close to

cercanías [θerka'nias] *nfpl* (afueras) outskirts, suburbs

cercano, a [θer'kano, a] *adj* close, near

cercar [θer'kar] *vt* to fence in; *(rodear)* to surround

cerciorar [θerθjo'rar] *vt* (asegurar) to assure; **~se** *vr* (asegurarse) to make sure

cerco ['θerko] *nm* (AGR) enclosure; *(AM)* fence; *(MIL)* siege

cerdo, a ['θerðo, a] *nm/f* pig/sow

cereal [θere'al] *nm* cereal; **~es** *nmpl* cereals, grain *sg*

cerebro [θe'reβro] *nm* brain; *(fig)* brains *pl*

ceremonia [θere'monja] *nf* ceremony; **ceremonial** *adj, nm* ceremonial;

ceremonioso, a [θere'monjoso, a] *adj* ceremonious
cereza [θe're θa] *nf* cherry
cerilla [θe'riʎa] *nf* (*fósforo*) match
cernerse [θer'nerse] *vr* to hover
cero ['θero] *nm* nothing, zero
cerrado, a [θe'rraðo, a] *adj* closed, shut; (*con llave*) locked; (*tiempo*) cloudy, overcast; (*curva*) sharp; (*acento*) thick, broad
cerradura [θerra'ðura] *nf* (*acción*) closing; (*mecanismo*) lock
cerrajero [θerra'xero] *nm* locksmith
cerrar [θe'rrar] *vt* to close, shut; (*paso, carretera*) to close; (*grifo*) to turn off; (*cuenta, negocio*) to close ♦ *vi* to close, shut; (*la noche*) to come down; **~se** *vr* to close, shut; **~ con llave** to lock; **~ un trato** to strike a bargain
cerro ['θerro] *nm* hill
cerrojo [θe'rroxo] *nm* (*herramienta*) bolt; (*de puerta*) latch
certamen [θer'tamen] *nm* competition, contest
certero, a [θer'tero, a] *adj* (*gen*) accurate
certeza [θer'teθa] *nf* certainty
certidumbre [θerti'ðumßre] *nf* = **certeza**
certificado [θertifi'kaðo] *nm* certificate
certificar [θertifi'kar] *vt* (*asegurar, atestar*) to certify
cervatillo [θerßa'tiʎo] *nm* fawn
cervecería [θerßeθe'ria] *nf* (*fábrica*) brewery; (*bar*) public house, pub
cerveza [θer'ßeθa] *nf* beer
cesante [θe'sante] *adj* redundant
cesar [θe'sar] *vi* to cease, stop ♦ *vt* (*funcionario*) to remove from office
cesárea [θe'sarea] *nf* (*MED*) Caesarean operation *o* section
cese ['θese] *nm* (*de trabajo*) dismissal; (*de pago*) suspension
césped ['θespeð] *nm* grass, lawn
cesta ['θesta] *nf* basket
cesto ['θesto] *nm* (*large*) basket, hamper
cetro ['θetro] *nm* sceptre
cfr *abr* (= *confróntese*) cf.
chabacano, a [tʃaßa'kano, a] *adj* vulgar, coarse

chabola [tʃa'ßola] *nf* shack; **barrio de ~s** shanty town *sg*
chacal [tʃa'kal] *nm* jackal
chacha ['tʃatʃa] (*fam*) *nf* maid
cháchara ['tʃatʃara] *nf* chatter; **estar de ~** to chatter away
chacra ['tʃakra] (*AM*) *nf* smallholding
chafar [tʃa'far] *vt* (*aplastar*) to crush; (*plan etc*) to ruin
chal [tʃal] *nm* shawl
chalado, a [tʃa'lado, a] (*fam*) *adj* crazy
chalé [tʃa'le] (*pl* **~s**) *nm* villa; ≈ detached house
chaleco [tʃa'leko] *nm* waistcoat, vest (*US*); **~ salvavidas** life jacket
chalet [tʃa'le] (*pl* **~s**) *nm* = **chalé**
champán [tʃam'pan] *nm* champagne
champaña [tʃam'paɲa] *nm* = **champán**
champiñón [tʃampi'ɲon] *nm* mushroom
champú [tʃam'pu] (*pl* **champúes, champús**) *nm* shampoo
chamuscar [tʃamus'kar] *vt* to scorch, sear, singe
chance ['tʃanθe] (*AM*) *nm* chance
chancho, a ['tʃantʃo, a] (*AM*) *nm/f* pig
chanchullo [tʃan'tʃuʎo] (*fam*) *nm* fiddle
chandal [tʃan'dal] *nm* tracksuit
chantaje [tʃan'taxe] *nm* blackmail
chapa ['tʃapa] *nf* (*de metal*) plate, sheet; (*de madera*) board, panel; (*AM: AUTO*) number (*BRIT*) *o* license (*US*) plate; **~do, a** *adj*: **~do en oro** gold-plated
chaparrón [tʃapa'rron] *nm* downpour, cloudburst
chapotear [tʃapote'ar] *vi* to splash about
chapurrear [tʃapurre'ar] *vt* (*idioma*) to speak badly
chapuza [tʃa'puθa] *nf* botched job
chapuzón [tʃapu'θon] *nm*: **darse un ~** to go for a dip
chaqueta [tʃa'keta] *nf* jacket
chaquetón [tʃake'ton] *nm* long jacket
charca ['tʃarka] *nf* pond, pool
charco ['tʃarko] *nm* pool, puddle
charcutería [tʃarkute'ria] *nf* (*tienda*) shop selling chiefly pork meat products; (*productos*) cooked pork meats *pl*

charla ['tʃarla] *nf* talk, chat; (*conferencia*) lecture

charlar [tʃar'lar] *vi* to talk, chat

charlatán, ana [tʃarla'tan, ana] *nm/f* (*hablador*) chatterbox; (*estafador*) trickster

charol [tʃa'rol] *nm* varnish; (*cuero*) patent leather

chascarrillo [tʃaska'rriʎo] (*fam*) *nm* funny story

chasco ['tʃasko] *nm* (*desengaño*) disappointment

chasis ['tʃasis] *nm inv* chassis

chasquear [tʃaske'ar] *vt* (*látigo*) to crack; (*lengua*) to click; **chasquido** *nm* crack; click

chatarra [tʃa'tarra] *nf* scrap (metal)

chato, a ['tʃato, a] *adj* flat; (*nariz*) snub

chaval, a [tʃa'βal, a] *nm/f* kid, lad/lass

checo, a ['tʃeko, a] *adj, nm/f* Czech ♦ *nm* (*LING*) Czech

checo(e)slovaco, a [tʃeko(e)slo'βako, a] *adj, nm/f* Czech, Czechoslovak

Checo(e)slovaquia [tʃeko(e)slo'βakja] *nf* Czechoslovakia

cheque ['tʃeke] *nm* cheque (*BRIT*), check (*US*); **~ de viajero** traveller's cheque (*BRIT*), traveler's check (*US*)

chequeo [tʃe'keo] *nm* (*MED*) check-up; (*AUTO*) service

chequera [tʃe'kera] (*AM*) *nf* chequebook (*BRIT*), checkbook (*US*)

chicano, a [tʃi'kano, a] *adj, nm/f* chicano

chícharo ['tʃitʃaro] (*AM*) *nm* pea

chichón [tʃi'tʃon] *nm* bump, lump

chicle ['tʃikle] *nm* chewing gum

chico, a ['tʃiko, a] *adj* small, little ♦ *nm/f* (*niño*) child; (*muchacho*) boy/girl

chiflado, a [tʃi'flaðo, a] *adj* crazy

chiflar [tʃi'flar] *vt* to hiss, boo

Chile ['tʃile] *nm* Chile; **chileno, a** *adj, nm/f* Chilean

chile ['tʃile] *nm* chilli pepper

chillar [tʃi'ʎar] *vi* (*persona*) to yell, scream; (*animal salvaje*) to howl; (*cerdo*) to squeal

chillido [tʃi'ʎiðo] *nm* (*de persona*) yell, scream; (*de animal*) howl

chillón, ona [tʃi'ʎon, ona] *adj* (*niño*) noisy; (*color*) loud, gaudy

chimenea [tʃime'nea] *nf* chimney; (*hogar*) fireplace

China ['tʃina] *nf:* **(la) ~** China

chinche ['tʃintʃe] *nf* (*insecto*) (bed)bug; (*TEC*) drawing pin (*BRIT*), thumbtack (*US*) ♦ *nm/f* nuisance, pest

chincheta [tʃin'tʃeta] *nf* drawing pin (*BRIT*), thumbtack (*US*)

chino, a ['tʃino, a] *adj, nm/f* Chinese ♦ *nm* (*LING*) Chinese

chipirón [tʃipi'ron] *nm* (*ZOOL, CULIN*) squid

Chipre ['tʃipre] *nf* Cyprus; **chipriota** *adj, nm/f* Cypriot

chiquillo, a [tʃi'kiʎo, a] *nm/f* (*fam*) kid

chirimoya [tʃiri'moja] *nf* custard apple

chiringuito [tʃirin'xito] *nm* small open-air bar

chiripa [tʃi'ripa] *nf* fluke

chirriar [tʃi'rrjar] *vi* to creak, squeak

chirrido [tʃi'rriðo] *nm* creak(ing), squeak(ing)

chis [tʃis] *excl* sh!

chisme ['tʃisme] *nm* (*habladurías*) piece of gossip; (*fam: objeto*) thingummyjig

chismoso, a [tʃis'moso, a] *adj* gossiping ♦ *nm/f* gossip

chispa ['tʃispa] *nf* spark; (*fig*) sparkle; (*ingenio*) wit; (*fam*) drunkenness

chispear [tʃispe'ar] *vi* (*lloviznar*) to drizzle

chisporrotear [tʃisporrote'ar] *vi* (*fuego*) to throw out sparks; (*leña*) to crackle; (*aceite*) to hiss, splutter

chiste ['tʃiste] *nm* joke, funny story

chistoso, a [tʃis'toso, a] *adj* funny, amusing

chivo, a ['tʃiβo, a] *nm/f* (billy-/nanny-)goat; **~ expiatorio** scapegoat

chocante [tʃo'kante] *adj* startling; (*extraño*) odd; (*ofensivo*) shocking

chocar [tʃo'kar] *vi* (*coches etc*) to collide, crash ♦ *vt* to shock; (*sorprender*) to startle; **~ con** to collide with; (*fig*) to run into, run up against; **¡chócala!** (*fam*) put it there!

chochear [tʃotʃe'ar] *vi* to dodder, be senile

chocho, a [ˈtʃotʃo, a] *adj* doddering, senile; (*fig*) soft, doting

chocolate [tʃokoˈlate] *adj, nm* chocolate; **chocolatina** *nf* chocolate

chofer [tʃoˈfer] *nm* = **chófer**

chófer [ˈtʃofer] *nm* driver

chollo [ˈtʃoʎo] (*fam*) *nm* bargain, snip

choque *etc* [ˈtʃoke] *vb ver* **chocar** ♦ *nm* (*impacto*) impact; (*golpe*) jolt; (*AUTO*) crash; (*fig*) conflict; **~ frontal** head-on collision

chorizo [tʃoˈriθo] *nm* hard pork sausage, (type of) salami

chorrada [tʃoˈrraða] (*fam*) *nf*: **¡es una ~!** that's crap! (*!*); **decir ~s** to talk crap (*!*)

chorrear [tʃorreˈar] *vi* to gush (out), spout (out); (*gotear*) to drip, trickle

chorro [ˈtʃorro] *nm* jet; (*fig*) stream

choza [ˈtʃoθa] *nf* hut, shack

chubasco [tʃuˈßasko] *nm* squall

chubasquero [tʃußasˈkero] *nm* lightweight raincoat

chuchería [tʃutʃeˈria] *nf* trinket

chuleta [tʃuˈleta] *nf* chop, cutlet

chulo [ˈtʃulo] *nm* (*de prostituta*) pimp

chupar [tʃuˈpar] *vt* to suck; (*absorber*) to absorb; **~se** *vr* to grow thin

chupete [tʃuˈpete] *nm* dummy (*BRIT*), pacifier (*US*)

chupito [tʃuˈpito] (*fam*) *nm* shot

churro [ˈtʃurro] *nm* (type of) fritter

chusma [ˈtʃusma] *nf* rabble, mob

chutar [tʃuˈtar] *vi* to shoot (at goal)

Cía *abr* (= *compañía*) Co.

cianuro [θjaˈnuro] *nm* cyanide

cicatriz [θikaˈtriθ] *nf* scar; **~arse** *vr* to heal (up), form a scar

ciclismo [θiˈklismo] *nm* cycling

ciclista [θiˈklista] *adj* cycle *cpd* ♦ *nm/f* cyclist

ciclo [ˈθiklo] *nm* cycle

ciclón [θiˈklon] *nm* cyclone

cicloturismo [θiklotuˈrismo] *nm*: **hacer ~** to go on a cycling holiday

ciego, a [ˈθjeɣo, a] *adj* blind ♦ *nm/f* blind man/woman

cielo [ˈθjelo] *nm* sky; (*REL*) heaven; **¡~s!**

good heavens!

ciempiés [θjemˈpjes] *nm inv* centipede

cien [θjen] *num ver* **ciento**

ciénaga [ˈθjenaχa] *nf* marsh, swamp

ciencia [ˈθjenθja] *nf* science; **~s** *nfpl* (*ESCOL*) science *sg*; **~-ficción** *nf* science fiction

cieno [ˈθjeno] *nm* mud, mire

científico, a [θjenˈtifiko, a] *adj* scientific ♦ *nm/f* scientist

ciento [ˈθjento] (*tb:* **cien**) *num* hundred; **pagar al 10 por ~** to pay at 10 per cent

cierre *etc* [ˈθjerre] *vb ver* **cerrar** ♦ *nm* closing, shutting; (*con llave*) locking; **~ de cremallera** zip (fastener)

cierro *etc vb ver* **cerrar**

cierto, a [ˈθjerto, a] *adj* sure, certain; (*un tal*) a certain; (*correcto*) right, correct; **~ hombre** a certain man; **ciertas personas** certain *o* some people; **sí, es ~** yes, that's correct

ciervo [ˈθjerßo] *nm* deer; (*macho*) stag

cierzo [ˈθjerθo] *nm* north wind

cifra [ˈθifra] *nf* number; (*secreta*) code

cifrar [θiˈfrar] *vt* to code, write in code

cigala [θiˈɣala] *nf* Norway lobster

cigarra [θiˈɣarra] *nf* cicada

cigarrillo [θiɣaˈrriʎo] *nm* cigarette

cigarro [θiˈɣarro] *nm* cigarette; (*puro*) cigar

cigüeña [θiˈɣweɲa] *nf* stork

cilíndrico, a [θiˈlindriko, a] *adj* cylindrical

cilindro [θiˈlindro] *nm* cylinder

cima [ˈθima] *nf* (*de montaña*) top, peak; (*de árbol*) top; (*fig*) height

cimbrearse [θimbreˈarse] *vr* to sway

cimentar [θimenˈtar] *vt* to lay the foundations of; (*fig: fundar*) to found

cimiento [θiˈmjento] *nm* foundation

cinc [θink] *nm* zinc

cincel [θinˈθel] *nm* chisel; **~ar** *vt* to chisel

cinco [ˈθinko] *num* five

cincuenta [θinˈkwenta] *num* fifty

cine [ˈθine] *nm* cinema

cineasta [θineˈasta] *nm/f* film director

cinematográfico, a [θinematoˈɣrafiko, a] *adj* cine-, film *cpd*

cínico, a ['θiniko, a] *adj* cynical ♦ *nm/f* cynic

cinismo [θi'nismo] *nm* cynicism

cinta ['θinta] *nf* band, strip; *(de tela)* ribbon; *(película)* reel; *(de máquina de escribir)* ribbon; ~ **adhesiva** sticky tape; ~ **de vídeo** videotape; ~ **magnetofónica** tape; ~ **métrica** tape measure

cintura [θin'tura] *nf* waist

cinturón [θintu'ron] *nm* belt; ~ **de seguridad** safety belt

ciprés [θi'pres] *nm* cypress (tree)

circo ['θirko] *nm* circus

circuito [θir'kwito] *nm* circuit

circulación [θirkula'θjon] *nf* circulation; *(AUTO)* traffic

circular [θirku'lar] *adj, nf* circular ♦ *vi, vt* to circulate ♦ *vi (AUTO)* to drive; **"circule por la derecha"** "keep (to the) right"

círculo ['θirkulo] *nm* circle; ~ **vicioso** vicious circle

circuncidar [θirkunθi'dar] *vt* to circumcise

circundar [θirkun'dar] *vt* to surround

circunferencia [θirkunfe'renθja] *nf* circumference

circunscribir [θirkunskri'βir] *vt* to circumscribe; ~**se** *vr* to be limited

circunscripción [θirkunskrip'θjon] *nf* *(POL)* constituency

circunspecto, a [θirkuns'pekto, a] *adj* circumspect, cautious

circunstancia [θirkuns'tanθja] *nf* circumstance

cirio ['θirjo] *nm* (wax) candle

ciruela [θi'rwela] *nf* plum; ~ **pasa** prune

cirugía [θiru'xia] *nf* surgery; ~ **estética** *o* **plástica** plastic surgery

cirujano [θiru'xano] *nm* surgeon

cisne ['θisne] *nm* swan

cisterna [θis'terna] *nf* cistern, tank

cita ['θita] *nf* appointment, meeting; *(de novios)* date; *(referencia)* quotation

citación [θita'θjon] *nf (JUR)* summons *sg*

citar [θi'tar] *vt* to make an appointment with; *(JUR)* to summons; *(un autor, texto)* to quote; ~**se** *vr*: **se citaron en el cine** they arranged to meet at the cinema

cítricos ['θitrikos] *nmpl* citrus fruit(s)

ciudad [θju'ðað] *nf* town; *(más grande)* city; ~**anía** *nf* citizenship; ~**ano, a** *nm/f* citizen

cívico, a ['θiβiko, a] *adj* civic

civil [θi'βil] *adj* civil ♦ *nm (guardia)* policeman

civilización [θiβiliθa'θjon] *nf* civilization

civilizar [θiβili'θar] *vt* to civilize

civismo [θi'βismo] *nm* public spirit

cizaña [θi'θaɲa] *nf (fig)* discord

cl. *abr* (= *centilitro*) cl.

clamar [kla'mar] *vt* to clamour for, cry out for ♦ *vi* to cry out, clamour

clamor [kla'mor] *nm* clamour, protest

clandestino, a [klandes'tino, a] *adj* clandestine; *(POL)* underground

clara ['klara] *nf (de huevo)* egg white

claraboya [klara'βoja] *nf* skylight

clarear [klare'ar] *vi (el día)* to dawn; *(el cielo)* to clear up, brighten up; ~**se** *vr* to be transparent

clarete [kla'rete] *nm* rosé (wine)

claridad [klari'ðað] *nf (del día)* brightness; *(de estilo)* clarity

clarificar [klarifi'kar] *vt* to clarify

clarinete [klari'nete] *nm* clarinet

clarividencia [klariβi'ðenθja] *nf* clairvoyance; *(fig)* far-sightedness

claro, a ['klaro, a] *adj* clear; *(luminoso)* bright; *(color)* light; *(evidente)* clear, evident; *(poco espeso)* thin ♦ *nm (en bosque)* clearing ♦ *adv* clearly ♦ *excl (tb:* ~ **que sí)** of course!

clase ['klase] *nf* class; ~ **alta/media/ obrera** upper/middle/working class; ~**s particulares** private lessons, private tuition *sg*

clásico, a ['klasiko, a] *adj* classical

clasificación [klasifika'θjon] *nf* classification; *(DEPORTE)* league (table)

clasificar [klasifi'kar] *vt* to classify

claudicar [klauði'kar] *vi* to give in

claustro ['klaustro] *nm* cloister

cláusula ['klausula] *nf* clause

clausura [klau'sura] *nf* closing, closure;

clausurar vt (congreso etc) to bring to a close

clavar [kla'ßar] vt (clavo) to hammer in; (cuchillo) to stick, thrust

clave ['klaße] nf key; (MUS) clef

clavel [kla'ßel] nm carnation

clavícula [kla'ßikula] nf collar bone

clavija [kla'ßixa] nf peg, dowel, pin; (ELEC) plug

clavo ['klaßo] nm (de metal) nail; (BOT) clove

claxon ['klakson] (pl ~s) nm horn

clemencia [kle'menθja] nf mercy, clemency

cleptómano, a [klep'tomano, a] nm/f kleptomaniac

clérigo ['kleriɣo] nm priest

clero ['klero] nm clergy

cliché [kli'tʃe] nm cliché; (FOTO) negative

cliente, a ['kljente, a] nm/f client, customer

clientela [kljen'tela] nf clientele, customers pl

clima ['klima] nm climate

climatizado, a [klimati'θaðo, a] adj air-conditioned

clímax ['klimaks] nm inv climax

clínica ['klinika] nf clinic; (particular) private hospital

clip [klip] (pl ~s) nm paper clip

clítoris ['klitoris] nm inv (ANAT) clitoris

cloaca [klo'aka] nf sewer

cloro ['kloro] nm chlorine

club [klub] (pl ~s o ~es) nm club; ~ de jóvenes youth club

cm abr (= centímetro, centímetros) cm

C.N.T. (ESP) abr = Confederación Nacional de Trabajo

coacción [koak'θjon] nf coercion, compulsion; **coaccionar** vt to coerce

coagular [koaɣu'lar] vt (leche, sangre) to clot; ~**se** vr to clot; **coágulo** nm clot

coalición [koali'θjon] nf coalition

coartada [koar'taða] nf alibi

coartar [koar'tar] vt to limit, restrict

coba ['koßa] nf: **dar ~ a uno** to soft-soap sb

cobarde [ko'ßarðe] adj cowardly ♦ nm coward; **cobardía** nf cowardice

cobaya [ko'ßaja] nf guinea pig

cobertizo [koßer'tiθo] nm shelter

cobertura [koßer'tura] nf cover

cobija [ko'ßixa] (AM) nf blanket

cobijar [koßi'xar] vt (cubrir) to cover; (proteger) to shelter; **cobijo** nm shelter

cobra ['koßra] nf cobra

cobrador, a [koßra'ðor, a] nm/f (de autobús) conductor/conductress; (de impuestos, gas) collector

cobrar [ko'ßrar] vt (cheque) to cash; (sueldo) to collect, draw; (objeto) to recover; (precio) to charge; (deuda) to collect ♦ vi to be paid; **cóbrese al entregar** cash on delivery

cobre ['koßre] nm copper; ~**s** nmpl (MUS) brass instruments

cobro ['koßro] nm (de cheque) cashing; **presentar al** ~ to cash

cocaína [koka'ina] nf cocaine

cocción [kok'θjon] nf (CULIN) cooking; (en agua) boiling

cocear [koθe'ar] vi to kick

cocer [ko'θer] vt, vi to cook; (en agua) to boil; (en horno) to bake

coche ['kotʃe] nm (AUTO) car (BRIT), automobile (US); (de tren, de caballos) coach, carriage; (para niños) pram (BRIT), baby carriage (US); **ir en** ~ to drive; ~ **celular** Black Maria, prison van; ~ **de bomberos** fire engine; ~ **fúnebre** hearse; **coche-cama** (pl **coches-cama**) nm (FERRO) sleeping car, sleeper

cochera [ko'tʃera] nf garage; (de autobuses, trenes) depot

coche restaurante (pl **coches restaurante**) nm (FERRO) dining car, diner

cochinillo [kotʃi'niʎo] nm (CULIN) suckling pig, sucking pig

cochino, a [ko'tʃino, a] adj filthy, dirty ♦ nm/f pig

cocido [ko'θiðo] nm stew

cocina [ko'θina] nf kitchen; (aparato) cooker, stove; (acto) cookery; ~ **eléctrica/de gas** electric/gas cooker; ~

francesa French cuisine; **cocinar** *vt, vi* to cook

cocinero, a [koθi'nero, a] *nm/f* cook

coco ['koko] *nm* coconut

cocodrilo [koko'ðrilo] *nm* crocodile

cocotero [koko'tero] *nm* coconut palm

cóctel ['koktel] *nm* cocktail

codazo [ko'ðaθo] *nm:* **dar un ~ a uno** to nudge sb

codicia [ko'ðiθja] *nf* greed; **codiciar** *vt* to covet; **codicioso, a** *adj* covetous

código ['koðiɣo] *nm* code; **~ de barras** bar code; **~ civil** common law; **~ de (la) circulación** highway code; **~ postal** postcode

codillo [ko'ðiʎo] *nm* (*ZOOL*) knee; (*TEC*) elbow (joint)

codo ['koðo] *nm* (*ANAT, de tubo*) elbow; (*ZOOL*) knee

codorniz [koðor'niθ] *nf* quail

coerción [koer'θjon] *nf* coercion

coetáneo, a [koe'taneo, a] *adj, nm/f* contemporary

coexistir [koe(k)sis'tir] *vi* to coexist

cofradía [kofra'ðia] *nf* brotherhood, fraternity

cofre ['kofre] *nm* (*de joyas*) case; (*de dinero*) chest

coger [ko'xer] (*ESP*) *vt* to take (hold of); (*objeto caído*) to pick up; (*frutas*) to pick, harvest; (*resfriado, ladrón, pelota*) to catch ♦ *vi*: **~ por el buen camino** to take the right road; **~se** *vr* (*el dedo*) to catch; **~se a algo** to get hold of sth

cogollo [ko'ɣoʎo] *nm* (*de lechuga*) heart

cogote [ko'ɣote] *nm* back *o* nape of the neck

cohabitar [koaβi'tar] *vi* to live together, cohabit

cohecho [ko'etʃo] *nm* (*acción*) bribery; (*soborno*) bribe

coherente [koe'rente] *adj* coherent

cohesión [koe'sjon] *nm* cohesion

cohete [ko'ete] *nm* rocket

cohibido, a [koi'βiðo, a] *adj* (*PSICO*) inhibited; (*tímido*) shy

cohibir [koi'βir] *vt* to restrain, restrict

coincidencia [koinθi'ðenθja] *nf* coincidence

coincidir [koinθi'ðir] *vi* (*en idea*) to coincide, agree; (*en lugar*) to coincide

coito ['koito] *nm* intercourse, coitus

coja *etc vb ver* **coger**

cojear [koxe'ar] *vi* (*persona*) to limp, hobble; (*mueble*) to wobble, rock

cojera [ko'xera] *nf* limp

cojín [ko'xin] *nm* cushion; **cojinete** *nm* (*TEC*) ball bearing

cojo, a *etc* [ˈkoxo, a] *vb ver* **coger** ♦ *adj* (*que no puede andar*) lame, crippled; (*mueble*) wobbly ♦ *nm/f* lame person, cripple

cojón [ko'xon] (*fam*) *nm:* **¡cojones!** shit! (*!*); **cojonudo, a** (*fam*) *adj* great, fantastic

col [kol] *nf* cabbage; **~es de Bruselas** Brussels sprouts

cola ['kola] *nf* tail; (*de gente*) queue; (*lugar*) end, last place; (*para pegar*) glue, gum; **hacer ~** to queue (up)

colaborador, a [kolaβora'ðor, a] *nm/f* collaborator

colaborar [kolaβo'rar] *vi* to collaborate

colada [ko'laða] *nf:* **hacer la ~** to do the washing

colador [kola'ðor] *nm* (*de líquidos*) strainer; (*para verduras etc*) colander

colapso [ko'lapso] *nm* collapse; **~ nervioso** nervous breakdown

colar [ko'lar] *vt* (*líquido*) to strain off; (*metal*) to cast ♦ *vi* to ooze, seep (through); **~se** *vr* to jump the queue; **~se en** to get into without paying; (*fiesta*) to gatecrash

colcha ['koltʃa] *nf* bedspread

colchón [kol'tʃon] *nm* mattress; **~ inflable** *o* **neumático** air bed, air mattress

colchoneta [koltʃo'neta] *nf* (*en gimnasio*) mat; (*de playa*) air bed

colección [kolek'θjon] *nf* collection; **coleccionar** *vt* to collect; **coleccionista** *nm/f* collector

colecta [ko'lekta] *nf* collection

colectivo, a [kolek'tiβo, a] *adj* collective,

joint ♦ *nm* (*AM*) (small) bus

colega [ko'leɤa] *nm/f* colleague

colegial, a [kole'xjal, a] *nm/f* schoolboy/girl

colegio [ko'lexjo] *nm* college; (*escuela*) school; (*de abogados etc*) association; ~ **electoral** polling station; ~ **mayor** hall of residence

---

colegio

A **colegio** *is normally a private primary or secondary school. In the state system it means a primary school although these are also called* **escuelas**. *State secondary schools are called* **institutos**.

---

colegir [kole'xir] *vt* to infer, conclude

cólera ['kolera] *nf* (*ira*) anger ♦ *nm* (*MED*) cholera; **colérico, a** [ko'leriko, a] *adj* irascible, bad-tempered

colesterol [koleste'rol] *nm* cholesterol

coleta [ko'leta] *nf* pigtail

colgante [kol'ɤante] *adj* hanging ♦ *nm* (*joya*) pendant

colgar [kol'ɤar] *vt* to hang (up); (*ropa*) to hang out ♦ *vi* to hang; (*TELEC*) to hang up

cólico ['koliko] *nm* colic

coliflor [koli'flor] *nf* cauliflower

colilla [ko'liʎa] *nf* cigarette end, butt

colina [ko'lina] *nf* hill

colisión [koli'sjon] *nf* collision; ~ **de frente** head-on crash

collar [ko'ʎar] *nm* necklace; (*de perro*) collar

colmar [kol'mar] *vt* to fill to the brim; (*fig*) to fulfil, realize

colmena [kol'mena] *nf* beehive

colmillo [kol'miʎo] *nm* (*diente*) eye tooth; (*de elefante*) tusk; (*de perro*) fang

colmo ['kolmo] *nm*: **¡es el ~!** it's the limit!

colocación [koloka'θjon] *nf* (*acto*) placing; (*empleo*) job, position

colocar [kolo'kar] *vt* to place, put, position; (*dinero*) to invest; (*poner en empleo*) to find a job for; ~**se** *vr* to get a

job

Colombia [ko'lombja] *nf* Colombia; **colombiano, a** *adj, nm/f* Colombian

colonia [ko'lonja] *nf* colony; (*de casas*) housing estate; (*agua de* ~) cologne

colonización [koloniθa'θjon] *nf* colonization; **colonizador, a** [koloniθa'ðor, a] *adj* colonizing ♦ *nm/f* colonist, settler

colonizar [koloni'θar] *vt* to colonize

coloquio [ko'lokjo] *nm* conversation; (*congreso*) conference

color [ko'lor] *nm* colour

colorado, a [kolo'raðo, a] *adj* (*rojo*) red; (*LAM: chiste*) rude

colorante [kolo'rante] *nm* colouring

colorear [kolore'ar] *vt* to colour

colorete [kolo'rete] *nm* blusher

colorido [kolo'riðo] *nm* colouring

columna [ko'lumna] *nf* column; (*pilar*) pillar; (*apoyo*) support

columpiar [kolum'pjar] *vt* to swing; ~**se** *vr* to swing; **columpio** *nm* swing

coma ['koma] *nf* comma ♦ *nm* (*MED*) coma

comadre [ko'maðre] *nf* (*madrina*) godmother; (*chismosa*) gossip; **comadrona** *nf* midwife

comandancia [koman'danθja] *nf* command

comandante [koman'dante] *nm* commandant

comarca [ko'marka] *nf* region

comba ['komba] *nf* (*curva*) curve; (*cuerda*) skipping rope; **saltar a la** ~ to skip

combar [kom'bar] *vt* to bend, curve

combate [kom'bate] *nm* fight; **combatiente** *nm* combatant

combatir [komba'tir] *vt* to fight, combat

combinación [kombina'θjon] *nf* combination; (*QUÍM*) compound; (*prenda*) slip

combinar [kombi'nar] *vt* to combine

combustible [kombus'tiβle] *nm* fuel

combustión [kombus'tjon] *nf* combustion

comedia [ko'meðja] *nf* comedy; (*TEATRO*) play, drama

comediante [kome'ðjante] nm/f (comic) actor/actress

comedido, a [kome'ðiðo, a] adj moderate

comedor, a [kome'ðor, a] nm (habitación) dining room; (cantina) canteen

comensal [komen'sal] nm/f fellow guest (o diner)

comentar [komen'tar] vt to comment on

comentario [komen'tarjo] nm comment, remark; (literario) commentary; ~s nmpl (chismes) gossip sg

comentarista [komenta'rista] nm/f commentator

comenzar [komen'θar] vt, vi to begin, start; ~ **a hacer algo** to begin o start doing sth

comer [ko'mer] vt to eat; (DAMAS, AJEDREZ) to take, capture ♦ vi to eat; (almorzar) to have lunch; **~se** vr to eat up

comercial [komer'θjal] adj commercial; (relativo al negocio) business cpd; **comercializar** vt (producto) to market; (pey) to commercialize

comerciante [komer'θjante] nm/f trader, merchant

comerciar [komer'θjar] vi to trade, do business

comercio [ko'merθjo] nm commerce, trade; (negocio) business; (fig) dealings pl

comestible [komes'tiβle] adj eatable, edible; **~s** nmpl food sg, foodstuffs

cometa [ko'meta] nm comet ♦ nf kite

cometer [kome'ter] vt to commit

cometido [kome'tiðo] nm task, assignment

comezón [kome'θon] nf itch, itching

cómic ['komik] nm comic

comicios [ko'miθjos] nmpl elections

cómico, a ['komiko, a] adj comic(al) ♦ nm/f comedian

comida [ko'miða] nf (alimento) food; (almuerzo, cena) meal; (de mediodía) lunch

comidilla [komi'ðiʎa] nf: **ser la ~ de la ciudad** to be the talk of the town

comienzo etc [ko'mjenθo] vb ver **comenzar** ♦ nm beginning, start

comillas [ko'miʎas] nfpl quotation marks

comilona [komi'lona] (fam) nf blow-out

comino [ko'mino] nm: **(no) me importa un ~** I don't give a damn

comisaría [komisa'ria] nf (de policía) police station; (MIL) commissariat

comisario [komi'sarjo] nm (MIL etc) commissary; (POL) commissar

comisión [komi'sjon] nf commission

comité [komi'te] (pl ~s) nm committee

comitiva [komi'tiβa] nf retinue

como ['komo] adv as; (tal ~) like; (aproximadamente) about, approximately ♦ conj (ya que, puesto que) as, since; **¡~ no!** of course!; **~ no lo haga hoy** unless he does it today; **~ si** as if; **es tan alto ~ ancho** it is as high as it is wide

cómo ['komo] adv how?, why? ♦ excl what?, I beg your pardon? ♦ nm: **el ~ y el porqué** the whys and wherefores

cómoda ['komoða] nf chest of drawers

comodidad [komoði'ðað] nf comfort; **venga a su ~** come at your convenience

comodín [komo'ðin] nm joker

cómodo, a ['komoðo, a] adj comfortable; (práctico, de fácil uso) convenient

compact disc nm compact disk player

compacto, a [kom'pakto, a] adj compact

compadecer [kompaðe'θer] vt to pity, be sorry for; **~se** vr: **~se de** to pity, be o feel sorry for

compadre [kom'paðre] nm (padrino) godfather; (amigo) friend, pal

compañero, a [kompa'ɲero, a] nm/f companion; (novio) boy/girlfriend; **~ de clase** classmate

compañía [kompa'ɲia] nf company

comparación [kompara'θjon] nf comparison; **en ~ con** in comparison with

comparar [kompa'rar] vt to compare

comparecer [kompare'θer] vi to appear (in court)

comparsa [kom'parsa] nm/f (TEATRO) extra

compartimiento [komparti'mjento] nm (FERRO) compartment

compartir [kompar'tir] vt to share; (dinero,

comida etc) to divide (up), share (out)

compás [kom'pas] *nm* (*MUS*) beat, rhythm; (*MAT*) compasses *pl*; (*NAUT etc*) compass

compasión [kompa'sjon] *nf* compassion, pity

compasivo, a [kompa'sißo, a] *adj* compassionate

compatibilidad [kompatißili'ðað] *nf* compatibility

compatible [kompa'tißle] *adj* compatible

compatriota [kompa'trjota] *nm/f* compatriot, fellow countryman/woman

compendiar [kompen'djar] *vt* to summarize; **compendio** *nm* summary

compenetrarse [kompene'trarse] *vr* to be in tune

compensación [kompensa'θjon] *nf* compensation

compensar [kompen'sar] *vt* to compensate

competencia [kompe'tenθja] *nf* (*incumbencia*) domain, field; (*JUR, habilidad*) competence; (*rivalidad*) competition

competente [kompe'tente] *adj* competent

competición [kompeti'θjon] *nf* competition

competir [kompe'tir] *vi* to compete

compilar [kompi'lar] *vt* to compile

complacencia [kompla'θenθja] *nf* (*placer*) pleasure; (*tolerancia excesiva*) complacency

complacer [kompla'θer] *vt* to please; **~se** *vr* to be pleased

complaciente [kompla'θjente] *adj* kind, obliging, helpful

complejo, a [kom'plexo, a] *adj, nm* complex

complementario, a [komplemen'tarjo, a] *adj* complementary

completar [komple'tar] *vt* to complete

completo, a [kom'pleto, a] *adj* complete; (*perfecto*) perfect; (*lleno*) full ♦ *nm* full complement

complicado, a [kompli'kaðo, a] *adj* complicated; **estar ~ en** to be mixed up

in

cómplice ['kompliθe] *nm/f* accomplice

complot [kom'plo(t)] (*pl* **~s**) *nm* plot

componer [kompo'ner] *vt* (*MUS, LITERATURA, IMPRENTA*) to compose; (*algo roto*) to mend, repair; (*arreglar*) to arrange; **~se** *vr*: **~se de** to consist of; **componérselas para hacer algo** to manage to do sth

comportamiento [komporta'mjento] *nm* behaviour, conduct

comportarse [kompor'tarse] *vr* to behave

composición [komposi'θjon] *nf* composition

compositor, a [komposi'tor, a] *nm/f* composer

compostura [kompos'tura] *nf* (*actitud*) composure

compra ['kompra] *nf* purchase; **ir de ~s** to go shopping; **comprador, a** *nm/f* buyer, purchaser

comprar [kom'prar] *vt* to buy, purchase

comprender [kompren'der] *vt* to understand; (*incluir*) to comprise, include

comprensión [kompren'sjon] *nf* understanding; **comprensivo, a** *adj* (*actitud*) understanding

compresa [kom'presa] *nf*: **~ higiénica** sanitary towel (*BRIT*) o napkin (*US*)

comprimido, a [kompri'miðo, a] *adj* compressed ♦ *nm* (*MED*) pill, tablet

comprimir [kompri'mir] *vt* to compress

comprobante [kompro'ßante] *nm* proof; (*COM*) voucher; **~ de recibo** receipt

comprobar [kompro'ßar] *vt* to check; (*probar*) to prove; (*TEC*) to check, test

comprometer [komprome'ter] *vt* to compromise; (*poner en peligro*) to endanger; **~se** *vr* (*involucrarse*) to get involved

compromiso [kompro'miso] *nm* (*obligación*) obligation; (*cometido*) commitment; (*convenio*) agreement; (*apuro*) awkward situation

compuesto, a [kom'pwesto, a] *adj*: **~ de** composed of, made up of ♦ *nm* compound

computador [komputa'ðor] *nm*
computer; **~ central** mainframe
computer; **~ personal** personal computer
computadora [komputa'ðora] *nf* =
computador
cómputo ['komputo] *nm* calculation
comulgar [komul'var] *vi* to receive
communion
común [ko'mun] *adj* common ♦ *nm*: **el ~**
the community
comunicación [komunika'θjon] *nf*
communication; (*informe*) report
comunicado [komuni'kaðo] *nm*
announcement; **~ de prensa** press release
comunicar [komuni'kar] *vt*, *vi* to
communicate; **~se** *vr* to communicate;
está comunicando (*TEL*) the line's
engaged (*BRIT*) o busy (*US*);
comunicativo, a *adj* communicative
comunidad [komuni'ðað] *nf* community;
~ autónoma (*POL*) autonomous region;
C~ Económica Europea European
Economic Community
comunión [komu'njon] *nf* communion
comunismo [komu'nismo] *nm*
communism; **comunista** *adj*, *nm/f*
communist

PALABRA CLAVE

con [kon] *prep* **1** (*medio, compañía*) with;
comer ~ cuchara to eat with a spoon;
pasear ~ uno to go for a walk with sb
2 (*a pesar de*): **~ todo, merece nuestros
respetos** all the same, he deserves our
respect
3 (*para ~*): **es muy bueno ~ los
niños** he's very good with (the) children
4 (*+infin*): **~ llegar tan tarde se quedó
sin comer** by arriving so late he missed
out on eating
♦ *conj*: **~ que: será suficiente ~ que le
escribas** it will be sufficient if you write
to her

---

conato [ko'nato] *nm* attempt; **~ de robo**
attempted robbery
concebir [konθe'βir] *vt*, *vi* to conceive

conceder [konθe'ðer] *vt* to concede
concejal, a [konθe'xal, a] *nm/f* town
councillor
concentración [konθentra'θjon] *nf*
concentration
concentrar [konθen'trar] *vt* to
concentrate; **~se** *vr* to concentrate
concepción [konθep'θjon] *nf* conception
concepto [kon'θepto] *nm* concept
concernir [konθer'nir] *vi* to concern; **en
lo que concierne a ...** as far as ... is
concerned; **en lo que a mí concierne** as
far as I'm concerned
concertar [konθer'tar] *vt* (*MUS*) to
harmonize; (*acordar: precio*) to agree;
(*: tratado*) to conclude; (*trato*) to arrange,
fix up; (*combinar: esfuerzos*) to coordinate
♦ *vi* to harmonize, be in tune
concesión [konθe'sjon] *nf* concession
concesionario [konθesjo'narjo] *nm*
(licensed) dealer, agent
concha ['kontʃa] *nf* shell
conciencia [kon'θjenθja] *nf* conscience;
tener/tomar ~ de to be/become aware
of; **tener la ~ limpia/tranquila** to have a
clear conscience
concienciar [konθjen'θjar] *vt* to make
aware; **~se** *vr* to become aware
concienzudo, a [konθjen'θuðo, a] *adj*
conscientious
concierto *etc* [kon'θjerto] *vb ver*
concertar ♦ *nm* concert; (*obra*) concerto
conciliar [konθi'ljar] *vt* to reconcile
concilio [kon'θiljo] *nm* council
conciso, a [kon'θiso, a] *adj* concise
concluir [konklu'ir] *vt*, *vi* to conclude;
~se *vr* to conclude
conclusión [konklu'sjon] *nf* conclusion
concluyente [konklu'jente] *adj* (*prueba,
información*) conclusive
concordar [konkor'ðar] *vt* to reconcile
♦ *vi* to agree, tally
concordia [kon'korðja] *nf* harmony
concretar [konkre'tar] *vt* to make
concrete, make more specific; **~se** *vr* to
become more definite
concreto, a [kon'kreto, a] *adj*, *nm* (*AM*)

concrete; **en ~** (*en resumen*) to sum up; (*especificamente*) specifically; **no hay nada en ~** there's nothing definite

concurrencia [konku'rrenθja] *nf* turnout

concurrido, a [konku'rriðo, a] *adj* (*calle*) busy; (*local, reunión*) crowded

concurrir [konku'rrir] *vi* (*juntarse*: *ríos*) to meet, come together; (: *personas*) to gather, meet

concursante [konkur'sante] *nm/f* competitor

concurso [kon'kurso] *nm* (*de público*) crowd; (*ESCOL, DEPORTE, competencia*) competition; (*ayuda*) help, cooperation

condal [kon'dal] *adj*: **la Ciudad C~** Barcelona

conde ['konde] *nm* count

condecoración [kondekora'θjon] *nf* (*MIL*) medal

condecorar [kondeko'rar] *vt* (*MIL*) to decorate

condena [kon'dena] *nf* sentence

condenación [kondena'θjon] *nf* condemnation; (*REL*) damnation

condenar [konde'nar] *vt* to condemn; (*JUR*) to convict; **~se** *vr* (*REL*) to be damned

condensar [konden'sar] *vt* to condense

condesa [kon'desa] *nf* countess

condición [kondi'θjon] *nf* condition; **condicional** *adj* conditional

condicionar [kondiθjo'nar] *vt* (*acondicionar*) to condition; **~ algo a** to make sth conditional on

condimento [kondi'mento] *nm* seasoning

condolerse [kondo'lerse] *vr* to sympathize

condón [kon'don] *nm* condom

conducir [kondu'θir] *vt* to take, convey; (*AUTO*) to drive ♦ *vi* to drive; (*fig*) to lead; **~se** *vr* to behave

conducta [kon'dukta] *nf* conduct, behaviour

conducto [kon'dukto] *nm* pipe, tube; (*fig*) channel

conductor, a [konduk'tor, a] *adj* leading, guiding ♦ *nm* (*FÍSICA*) conductor; (*de*

vehículo) driver

conduje *etc vb ver* **conducir**

conduzco *etc vb ver* **conducir**

conectado, a [konek'taðo, a] *adj* (*INFORM*) on-line

conectar [konek'tar] *vt* to connect (up); (*enchufar*) plug in

conejillo [kone'xiʎo] *nm*: **~ de Indias** (*ZOOL*) guinea pig

conejo [ko'nexo] *nm* rabbit

conexión [konek'sjon] *nf* connection

confección [confe(k)'θjon] *nf* preparation; (*industria*) clothing industry

confeccionar [konfekθjo'nar] *vt* to make (up)

confederación [konfeðera'θjon] *nf* confederation

conferencia [konfe'renθja] *nf* conference; (*lección*) lecture; (*TEL*) call

conferir [konfe'rir] *vt* to award

confesar [konfe'sar] *vt* to confess, admit

confesión [konfe'sjon] *nf* confession

confesionario [konfesjo'narjo] *nm* confessional

confeti [kon'feti] *nm* confetti

confiado, a [kon'fjaðo, a] *adj* (*crédulo*) trusting; (*seguro*) confident

confianza [kon'fjanθa] *nf* trust; (*seguridad*) confidence; (*familiaridad*) intimacy, familiarity

confiar [kon'fjar] *vt* to entrust ♦ *vi* to trust

confidencia [konfi'ðenθja] *nf* confidence

confidencial [konfiðen'θjal] *adj* confidential

confidente [konfi'ðente] *nm/f* confidant/e; (*policial*) informer

configurar [konfixu'rar] *vt* to shape, form

confín [kon'fin] *nm* limit; **confines** *nmpl* confines, limits

confinar [konfi'nar] *vi* to confine; (*desterrar*) to banish

confirmar [konfir'mar] *vt* to confirm

confiscar [konfis'kar] *vt* to confiscate

confite [kon'fite] *nm* sweet (*BRIT*), candy (*US*)

confitería [konfite'ria] *nf* (*tienda*) confectioner's (shop)

confitura [konfi'tura] *nf* jam
conflictivo, a [konflik'tiβo, a] *adj (asunto, propuesta)* controversial; *(país, situación)* troubled
conflicto [kon'flikto] *nm* conflict; *(fig)* clash
confluir [kon'flwir] *vi (ríos)* to meet; *(gente)* to gather
conformar [konfor'mar] *vt* to shape, fashion ♦ *vi* to agree; **~se** *vr* to conform; *(resignarse)* to resign o.s.
conforme [kon'forme] *adj (correspondiente)* ~ **con** in line with; *(de acuerdo)*: **estar ~s (con algo)** to be in agreement (with sth) ♦ *adv* as ♦ *excl* agreed! ♦ *prep*: ~ **a** in accordance with; **quedarse ~ (con algo)** to be satisfied (with sth)
conformidad [konformi'ðað] *nf (semejanza)* similarity; *(acuerdo)* agreement; **conformista** *adj, nm/f* conformist
confortable [konfor'taβle] *adj* comfortable
confortar [konfor'tar] *vt* to comfort
confrontar [konfron'tar] *vt* to confront; *(dos personas)* to bring face to face; *(cotejar)* to compare
confundir [konfun'dir] *vt (equivocar)* to mistake, confuse; *(turbar)* to confuse; **~se** *vr (turbarse)* to get confused; *(equivocarse)* to make a mistake; *(mezclarse)* to mix
confusión [konfu'sjon] *nf* confusion
confuso, a [kon'fuso, a] *adj* confused
congelado, a [konxe'laðo, a] *adj* frozen; **~s** *nmpl* frozen food(s); **congelador** *nm (aparato)* freezer, deep freeze
congelar [konxe'lar] *vt* to freeze; **~se** *vr (sangre, grasa)* to congeal
congeniar [konxe'njar] *vi* to get on *(BRIT)* o along *(US)* well
congestión [konxes'tjon] *nf* congestion
congestionar [konxestjo'nar] *vt* to congest
congoja [kon'goxa] *nf* distress, grief
congraciarse [kongra'θjarse] *vr* to ingratiate o.s.
congratular [kongratu'lar] *vt* to congratulate
congregación [kongreβa'θjon] *nf* congregation
congregar [kongre'ɣar] *vt* to gather together; **~se** *vr* to gather together
congresista [kongre'sista] *nm/f* delegate, congressman/woman
congreso [kon'greso] *nm* congress
congrio ['kongrjo] *nm* conger eel
conjetura [konxe'tura] *nf* guess; **conjeturar** *vt* to guess
conjugar [konxu'ɣar] *vt* to combine, fit together; *(LING)* to conjugate
conjunción [konxun'θjon] *nf* conjunction
conjunto, a [kon'xunto, a] *adj* joint, united ♦ *nm* whole; *(MUS)* band; **en ~** as a whole
conjurar [konxu'rar] *vt (REL)* to exorcise; *(fig)* to ward off ♦ *vi* to plot
conmemoración [konmemora'θjon] *nf* commemoration
conmemorar [konmemo'rar] *vt* to commemorate
conmigo [kon'miɣo] *pron* with me
conmoción [konmo'θjon] *nf* shock; *(fig)* upheaval; ~ **cerebral** *(MED)* concussion
conmovedor, a [konmoße'ðor, a] *adj* touching, moving; *(emocionante)* exciting
conmover [konmo'ßer] *vt* to shake, disturb; *(fig)* to move
conmutador [konmuta'ðor] *nm* switch; *(AM: TEL: centralita)* switchboard; *(: central)* telephone exchange
cono ['kono] *nm* cone
conocedor, a [konoθe'ðor, a] *adj* expert, knowledgeable ♦ *nm/f* expert
conocer [kono'θer] *vt* to know; *(por primera vez)* to meet, get to know; *(entender)* to know about; *(reconocer)* to recognize; **~se** *vr (una persona)* to know o.s.; *(dos personas)* to (get to) know each other
conocido, a [kono'θiðo, a] *adj* (well-)known ♦ *nm/f* acquaintance
conocimiento [konoθi'mjento] *nm*

knowledge; (MED) consciousness; **~s** *nmpl* (*saber*) knowledge *sg*

conozco *etc vb ver* **conocer**

conque ['konke] *conj* and so, so then

conquista [kon'kista] *nf* conquest; **conquistador, a** *adj* conquering ♦ *nm* conqueror

conquistar [konkis'tar] *vt* to conquer

consagrar [konsa'ɣrar] *vt* (REL) to consecrate; (*fig*) to devote

consciente [kons'θjente] *adj* conscious

consecución [konseku'θjon] *nf* acquisition; (*de fin*) attainment

consecuencia [konse'kwenθja] *nf* consequence, outcome; (*coherencia*) consistency

consecuente [konse'kwente] *adj* consistent

consecutivo, a [konseku'tiβo, a] *adj* consecutive

conseguir [konse'ɣir] *vt* to get, obtain; (*objetivo*) to attain

consejero, a [konse'xero, a] *nm/f* adviser, consultant; (POL) councillor

consejo [kon'sexo] *nm* advice; (POL) council; **~ de administración** (COM) board of directors; **~ de guerra** court martial; **~ de ministros** cabinet meeting

consenso [kon'senso] *nm* consensus

consentimiento [konsenti'mjento] *nm* consent

consentir [konsen'tir] *vt* (*permitir, tolerar*) to consent to; (*mimar*) to pamper, spoil; (*aguantar*) to put up with ♦ *vi* to agree, consent; **~ que uno haga algo** to allow sb to do sth

conserje [kon'serxe] *nm* caretaker; (*portero*) porter

conservación [konserβa'θjon] *nf* conservation; (*de alimentos, vida*) preservation

conservador, a [konserβa'ðor, a] *adj* (POL) conservative ♦ *nm/f* conservative

conservante [konser'ßante] *nm* preservative

conservar [konser'ßar] *vt* to conserve, keep; (*alimentos, vida*) to preserve; **~se** *vr*

to survive

conservas [kon'serßas] *nfpl* canned food(s) (*pl*)

conservatorio [konserßa'torjo] *nm* (MUS) conservatoire, conservatory

considerable [konsiðe'raßle] *adj* considerable

consideración [konsiðera'θjon] *nf* consideration; (*estimación*) respect

considerado, a [konsiðe'raðo, a] *adj* (*atento*) considerate; (*respetado*) respected

considerar [konsiðe'rar] *vt* to consider

consigna [kon'siɣna] *nf* (*orden*) order, instruction; (*para equipajes*) left-luggage office

consigo *etc* [kon'siɣo] *vb ver* **conseguir** ♦ *pron* (*m*) with him; (*f*) with her; (Vd) with you; (*reflexivo*) with o.s.

consiguiendo *etc vb ver* **conseguir**

consiguiente [konsi'ɣjente] *adj* consequent; **por ~** and so, therefore, consequently

consistente [konsis'tente] *adj* consistent; (*sólido*) solid, firm; (*válido*) sound

consistir [konsis'tir] *vi*: **~ en** (*componerse de*) to consist of

consola [kon'sola] *nf* (*mueble*) console table; (*de videojuegos*) console

consolación [konsola'θjon] *nf* consolation

consolar [konso'lar] *vt* to console

consolidar [konsoli'ðar] *vt* to consolidate

consomé [konso'me] (*pl* **~s**) *nm* consommé, clear soup

consonante [konso'nante] *adj* consonant, harmonious ♦ *nf* consonant

consorcio [kon'sorθjo] *nm* consortium

conspiración [konspira'θjon] *nf* conspiracy

conspirador, a [konspira'ðor, a] *nm/f* conspirator

conspirar [konspi'rar] *vi* to conspire

constancia [kon'stanθja] *nf* constancy; **dejar ~ de** to put on record

constante [kons'tante] *adj, nf* constant

constar [kons'tar] *vi* (*evidenciarse*) to be clear o evident; **~ de** to consist of

constatar [konsta'tar] *vt* to verify

consternación [konsterna'θjon] *nf* consternation

constipado, a [konsti'paðo, a] *adj*: **estar ~** to have a cold ♦ *nm* cold

constitución [konstitu'θjon] *nf* constitution; **constitucional** *adj* constitutional

constituir [konstitu'ir] *vt* (*formar, componer*) to constitute, make up; (*fundar, erigir, ordenar*) to constitute, establish

constituyente [konstitu'jente] *adj* constituent

constreñir [konstre'ɲir] *vt* (*restringir*) to restrict

construcción [konstruk'θjon] *nf* construction, building

constructor, a [konstruk'tor, a] *nm/f* builder

construir [konstru'ir] *vt* to build, construct

construyendo *etc vb ver* **construir**

consuelo [kon'swelo] *nm* consolation, solace

cónsul ['konsul] *nm* consul; **consulado** *nm* consulate

consulta [kon'sulta] *nf* consultation; (*MED*): **horas de ~** surgery hours

consultar [konsul'tar] *vt* to consult

consultorio [konsul'torjo] *nm* (*MED*) surgery

consumar [konsu'mar] *vt* to complete, carry out; (*crimen*) to commit; (*sentencia*) to carry out

consumición [konsumi'θjon] *nf* consumption; (*bebida*) drink; (*comida*) food; **~ mínima** cover charge

consumidor, a [konsumi'ðor, a] *nm/f* consumer

consumir [konsu'mir] *vt* to consume; **~se** *vr* to be consumed; (*persona*) to waste away

consumismo [konsu'mismo] *nm* consumerism

consumo [kon'sumo] *nm* consumption

contabilidad [kontaβili'ðað] *nf* accounting, book-keeping; (*profesión*) accountancy; **contable** *nm/f* accountant

contacto [kon'takto] *nm* contact; (*AUTO*) ignition

contado, a [kon'taðo, a] *adj*: **~s** (*escasos*) numbered, scarce, few ♦ *nm*: **pagar al ~** to pay (in) cash

contador [konta'ðor] *nm* (*aparato*) meter; (*AM: contante*) accountant

contagiar [konta'xjar] *vt* (*enfermedad*) to pass on, transmit; (*persona*) to infect; **~se** *vr* to become infected

contagio [kon'taxjo] *nm* infection; **contagioso, a** *adj* infectious; (*fig*) catching

contaminación [kontamina'θjon] *nf* contamination; (*polución*) pollution

contaminar [kontami'nar] *vt* to contaminate; (*aire, agua*) to pollute

contante [kon'tante] *adj*: **dinero ~ (y sonante)** cash

contar [kon'tar] *vt* (*páginas, dinero*) to count; (*anécdota, chiste etc*) to tell ♦ *vi* to count; **~ con** to rely on, count on

contemplación [kontempla'θjon] *nf* contemplation

contemplar [kontem'plar] *vt* to contemplate; (*mirar*) to look at

contemporáneo, a [kontempo'raneo, a] *adj, nm/f* contemporary

contendiente [konten'djente] *nm/f* contestant

contenedor [kontene'ðor] *nm* container

contener [konte'ner] *vt* to contain, hold; (*retener*) to hold back, contain; **~se** *vr* to control *o* restrain o.s.

contenido, a [konte'niðo, a] *adj* (*moderado*) restrained; (*risa etc*) suppressed ♦ *nm* contents *pl*, content

contentar [konten'tar] *vt* (*satisfacer*) to satisfy; (*complacer*) to please; **~se** *vr* to be satisfied

contento, a [kon'tento, a] *adj* (*alegre*) pleased; (*feliz*) happy

contestación [kontesta'θjon] *nf* answer, reply

contestador [kontesta'ðor] *nm*: **~ automático** answering machine

contestar [kontes'tar] *vt* to answer, reply;

(*JUR*) to corroborate, confirm

contexto [kon'te(k)sto] *nm* context

contienda [kon'tjenda] *nf* contest

contigo [kon'tivo] *pron* with you

contiguo, a [kon'tivwo, a] *adj* adjacent, adjoining

continente [konti'nente] *adj, nm* continent

contingencia [kontin'xenθja] *nf* contingency; (*riesgo*) risk; **contingente** *adj, nm* contingent

continuación [kontinwa'θjon] *nf* continuation; **a ~** then, next

continuar [konti'nwar] *vt* to continue, go on with ♦ *vi* to continue, go on; **~ hablando** to continue talking *o* to talk

continuidad [kontinwi'ðað] *nf* continuity

continuo, a [kon'tinwo, a] *adj* (*sin interrupción*) continuous; (*acción perseverante*) continual

contorno [kon'torno] *nm* outline; (*GEO*) contour; **~s** *nmpl* neighbourhood *sg*, surrounding area *sg*

contorsión [kontor'sjon] *nf* contortion

contra ['kontra] *prep, adv* against ♦ *nm inv* con ♦ *nf*: **la C~** (*de Nicaragua*) the Contras *pl*

contraataque [kontraa'take] *nm* counter-attack

contrabajo [kontra'βaxo] *nm* double bass

contrabandista [kontraβan'dista] *nm/f* smuggler

contrabando [kontra'βando] *nm* (*acción*) smuggling; (*mercancías*) contraband

contracción [kontrak'θjon] *nf* contraction

contracorriente [kontrako'rrjente]: (**a**) **~** *adv* against the current

contradecir [kontraðe'θir] *vt* to contradict

contradicción [kontraðik'θjon] *nf* contradiction

contradictorio, a [kontraðik'torjo, a] *adj* contradictory

contraer [kontra'er] *vt* to contract; (*limitar*) to restrict; **~se** *vr* to contract; (*limitarse*) to limit o.s.

contraluz [kontra'luθ] *nf*: **a ~** against the light

contrapartida [kontrapar'tiða] *nf*: **como ~ (de)** in return (for)

contrapelo [kontra'pelo]: **a ~** *adv* the wrong way

contrapesar [kontrape'sar] *vt* to counterbalance; (*fig*) to offset; **contrapeso** *nm* counterweight

contraportada [kontrapor'taða] *nf* (*de revista*) back cover

contraproducente [kontraproðu'θente] *adj* counterproductive

contrariar [kontra'rjar] *vt* (*oponerse*) to oppose; (*poner obstáculo*) to impede; (*enfadar*) to vex

contrariedad [kontrarje'ðað] *nf* (*obstáculo*) obstacle, setback; (*disgusto*) vexation, annoyance

contrario, a [kon'trarjo, a] *adj* contrary; (*persona*) opposed; (*sentido, lado*) opposite ♦ *nm/f* enemy, adversary; (*DEPORTE*) opponent; **al/por el ~** on the contrary; **de lo ~** otherwise

contrarreloj [kontrarre'lo] *nf* (*tb*: **prueba ~**) time trial

contrarrestar [kontrarres'tar] *vt* to counteract

contrasentido [kontrasen'tiðo] *nm*: **es un ~ que él ...** it doesn't make sense for him to ...

contraseña [kontra'sena] *nf* (*INFORM*) password

contrastar [kontras'tar] *vt, vi* to contrast

contraste [kon'traste] *nm* contrast

contratar [kontra'tar] *vt* (*firmar un acuerdo para*) to contract for; (*empleados, obreros*) to hire, engage; **~se** *vr* to sign on

contratiempo [kontra'tjempo] *nm* setback

contratista [kontra'tista] *nm/f* contractor

contrato [kon'trato] *nm* contract

contravenir [kontraβe'nir] *vi*: **~ a** to contravene, violate

contraventana [kontraβen'tana] *nf* shutter

contribución [kontriβu'θjon] *nf* (*municipal etc*) tax; (*ayuda*) contribution

contribuir [kontriβu'ir] *vt, vi* to

contribute; (*COM*) to pay (in taxes)
contribuyente [kontriβu'jente] *nm/f*
(*COM*) taxpayer; (*que ayuda*) contributor
contrincante [kontrin'kante] *nm*
opponent
control [kon'trol] *nm* control; (*inspección*)
inspection, check; **~ador, a** *nm/f*
controller; **~ador aéreo** air-traffic
controller
controlar [kontro'lar] *vt* to control;
(*inspeccionar*) to inspect, check
controversia [kontro'βersja] *nf*
controversy
contundente [kontun'dente] *adj*
(*instrumento*) blunt; (*argumento, derrota*)
overwhelming
contusión [kontu'sjon] *nf* bruise
convalecencia [kombale'θenθja] *nf*
convalescence
convalecer [kombale'θer] *vi* to
convalesce, get better
convaleciente [kombale'θjente] *adj, nm/f*
convalescent
convalidar [kombali'ðar] *vt* (*título*) to
recognize
convencer [komben'θer] *vt* to convince
convencimiento [kombenθi'mjento] *nm*
(*certidumbre*) conviction
convención [komben'θjon] *nf* convention
conveniencia [kombe'njenθja] *nf*
suitability; (*conformidad*) agreement;
(*utilidad, provecho*) usefulness; **~s** *nfpl*
(*convenciones*) conventions; (*COM*)
property *sg*
conveniente [kombe'njente] *adj* suitable;
(*útil*) useful
convenio [kom'benjo] *nm* agreement,
treaty
convenir [kombe'nir] *vi* (*estar de acuerdo*)
to agree; (*venir bien*) to suit, be suitable
convento [kom'bento] *nm* convent
convenza *etc vb ver* **convencer**
converger [komber'xer] *vi* to converge
convergir [komber'xir] *vi* = **converger**
conversación [kombersa'θjon] *nf*
conversation
conversar [komber'sar] *vi* to talk,

converse
conversión [komber'sjon] *nf* conversion
convertir [komber'tir] *vt* to convert
convicción [kombik'θjon] *nf* conviction
convicto, a [kom'bikto, a] *adj* convicted
convidado, a [kombi'ðaðo, a] *nm/f* guest
convidar [kombi'ðar] *vt* to invite
convincente [kombin'θente] *adj*
convincing
convite [kom'bite] *nm* invitation;
(*banquete*) banquet
convivencia [kombi'βenθja] *nf*
coexistence, living together
convivir [kombi'βir] *vi* to live together
convocar [kombo'kar] *vt* to summon, call
(together)
convocatoria [komboka'torja] *nf* (*de
oposiciones, elecciones*) notice; (*de huelga*)
call
convulsión [kombul'sjon] *nf* convulsion
conyugal [konju'val] *adj* conjugal;
cónyuge ['konjuxe] *nm/f* spouse
coñac [ko'na(k)] (*pl* **~s**) *nm* cognac,
brandy
coño ['kono] (*fam!*) *excl* (*enfado*) shit! (*!*);
(*sorpresa*) bloody hell! (*!*)
cooperación [koopera'θjon] *nf*
cooperation
cooperar [koope'rar] *vi* to cooperate
cooperativa [koopera'tiβa] *nf* cooperative
coordinadora [koorðina'ðora] *nf* (*comité*)
coordinating committee
coordinar [koorði'nar] *vt* to coordinate
copa ['kopa] *nf* cup; (*vaso*) glass; (*bebida*):
(**tomar una**) **~** (to have a) drink; (*de
árbol*) top; (*de sombrero*) crown; **~s** *nfpl*
(*NAIPES*) ≈ hearts
copia ['kopja] *nf* copy; **~ de respaldo** *o*
seguridad (*INFORM*) back-up copy;
copiar *vt* to copy
copioso, a [ko'pjoso, a] *adj* copious,
plentiful
copla ['kopla] *nf* verse; (*canción*) (*popular*)
song
copo ['kopo] *nm*: **~ de nieve** snowflake;
~s de maíz cornflakes
coqueta [ko'keta] *adj* flirtatious,

coquettish; **coquetear** *vi* to flirt

coraje [ko'raxe] *nm* courage; (*ánimo*) spirit; (*ira*) anger

coral [ko'ral] *adj* choral ♦ *nf* (*MUS*) choir ♦ *nm* (*ZOOL*) coral

coraza [ko'raθa] *nf* (*armadura*) armour; (*blindaje*) armour-plating

corazón [kora'θon] *nm* heart

corazonada [koraθo'naða] *nf* impulse; (*presentimiento*) hunch

corbata [kor'ßata] *nf* tie

corchete [kor'tfete] *nm* catch, clasp

corcho ['kortfo] *nm* cork; (*PESCA*) float

cordel [kor'ðel] *nm* cord, line

cordero [kor'ðero] *nm* lamb

cordial [kor'ðjal] *adj* cordial; **~idad** *nf* warmth, cordiality

cordillera [korði'ʎera] *nf* range (of mountains)

Córdoba ['korðoßa] *n* Cordova

cordón [kor'ðon] *nm* (*cuerda*) cord, string; (*de zapatos*) lace; (*MIL etc*) cordon

cordura [kor'ðura] *nf*: **con ~** (*obrar, hablar*) sensibly

corneta [kor'neta] *nf* bugle

cornisa [kor'nisa] *nf* (*ARQ*) cornice

coro ['koro] *nm* chorus; (*conjunto de cantores*) choir

corona [ko'rona] *nf* crown; (*de flores*) garland; **coronación** *nf* coronation; **coronar** *vt* to crown

coronel [koro'nel] *nm* colonel

coronilla [koro'niʎa] *nf* (*ANAT*) crown (of the head)

corporación [korpora'θjon] *nf* corporation

corporal [korpo'ral] *adj* corporal, bodily

corpulento, a [korpu'lento a] *adj* (*persona*) heavily-built

corral [ko'rral] *nm* farmyard

correa [ko'rrea] *nf* strap; (*cinturón*) belt; (*de perro*) lead, leash

corrección [korrek'θjon] *nf* correction; (*reprensión*) rebuke; **correccional** *nm* reformatory

correcto, a [ko'rrekto, a] *adj* correct; (*persona*) well-mannered

corredizo, a [korre'ðiθo, a] *adj* (*puerta etc*) sliding

corredor, a [korre'ðor, a] *nm* (*pasillo*) corridor; (*balcón corrido*) gallery; (*COM*) agent, broker ♦ *nm/f* (*DEPORTE*) runner

corregir [korre'xir] *vt* (*error*) to correct; **~se** *vr* to reform

correo [ko'rreo] *nm* post, mail; (*persona*) courier; **C~s** *nmpl* Post Office *sg*; **~ aéreo** airmail; **~ electrónico** electronic mail, e-mail

correr [ko'rrer] *vt* to run; (*cortinas*) to draw; (*cerrojo*) to shoot ♦ *vi* to run; (*líquido*) to run, flow; **~se** *vr* to slide, move; (*colores*) to run

correspondencia [korrespon'denθja] *nf* correspondence; (*FERRO*) connection

corresponder [korrespon'der] *vi* to correspond; (*convenir*) to be suitable; (*pertenecer*) to belong; (*concernir*) to concern; **~se** *vr* (*por escrito*) to correspond; (*amarse*) to love one another

correspondiente [korrespon'djente] *adj* corresponding

corresponsal [korrespon'sal] *nm/f* correspondent

corrida [ko'rriða] *nf* (*de toros*) bullfight

corrido, a [ko'rriðo, a] *adj* (*avergonzado*) abashed; **3 noches corridas** 3 nights running; **un kilo ~** a good kilo

corriente [ko'rrjente] *adj* (*agua*) running; (*dinero etc*) current; (*común*) ordinary, normal ♦ *nf* current ♦ *nm* current month; **~ eléctrica** electric current

corrija *etc vb ver* **corregir**

corrillo [ko'rriʎo] *nm* ring, circle (of people); (*fig*) clique

corro ['korro] *nm* ring, circle (of people)

corroborar [korroßo'rar] *vt* to corroborate

corroer [korro'er] *vt* to corrode; (*GEO*) to erode

corromper [korrom'per] *vt* (*madera*) to rot; (*fig*) to corrupt

corrosivo, a [korro'sißo, a] *adj* corrosive

corrupción [korrup'θjon] *nf* rot, decay; (*fig*) corruption

corsé [kor'se] *nm* corset

cortacésped [korta'θespeð] *nm* lawn mower

cortado, a [kor'taðo, a] *adj* (*gen*) cut; (*leche*) sour; (*tímido*) shy; (*avergonzado*) embarrassed ♦ *nm* coffee (with a little milk)

cortar [kor'tar] *vt* to cut; (*suministro*) to cut off; (*un pasaje*) to cut out ♦ *vi* to cut; **~se** *vr* (*avergonzarse*) to become embarrassed; (*leche*) to turn, curdle; **~se el pelo** to have one's hair cut

cortauñas [korta'uɲas] *nm inv* nail clippers *pl*

corte ['korte] *nm* cut, cutting; (*de tela*) piece, length ♦ *nf*: **las C~s** the Spanish Parliament; **~ y confección** dressmaking; **~ de luz** power cut

cortejar [korte'xar] *vt* to court

cortejo [kor'texo] *nm* entourage; **~ fúnebre** funeral procession

cortés [kor'tes] *adj* courteous, polite

cortesía [korte'sia] *nf* courtesy

corteza [kor'teθa] *nf* (*de árbol*) bark; (*de pan*) crust

cortijo [kor'tixo] *nm* farm, farmhouse

cortina [kor'tina] *nf* curtain

corto, a ['korto, a] *adj* (*breve*) short; (*tímido*) bashful; **~ de luces** not very bright; **~ de vista** short-sighted; **estar ~ de fondos** to be short of funds; **~circuito** *nm* short circuit; **~metraje** *nm* (*CINE*) short

cosa ['kosa] *nf* thing; **~ de** about; **eso es ~ mía** that's my business

coscorrón [kosko'rron] *nm* bump on the head

cosecha [ko'setʃa] *nf* (*AGR*) harvest; (*de vino*) vintage

cosechar [kose'tʃar] *vt* to harvest, gather (in)

coser [ko'ser] *vt* to sew

cosmético, a [kos'metiko, a] *adj, nm* cosmetic

cosquillas [kos'kiʎas] *nfpl*: **hacer ~** to tickle; **tener ~** to be ticklish

costa ['kosta] *nf* (*GEO*) coast; **C~ Brava** Costa Brava; **C~ Cantábrica** Cantabrian Coast; **C~ del Sol** Costa del Sol; **a toda ~** at all costs

costado [kos'taðo] *nm* side

costar [kos'tar] *vt* (*valer*) to cost; **me cuesta hablarle** I find it hard to talk to him

Costa Rica *nf* Costa Rica; **costarricense** *adj, nm/f* Costa Rican; **costarriqueño, a** *adj, nm/f* Costa Rican

coste ['koste] *nm* = **costo**

costear [koste'ar] *vt* to pay for

costero, a [kos'tero, a] *adj* (*pueblecito, camino*) coastal

costilla [kos'tiʎa] *nf* rib; (*CULIN*) cutlet

costo ['kosto] *nm* cost, price; **~ de la vida** cost of living; **~so, a** *adj* costly, expensive

costra ['kostra] *nf* (*corteza*) crust; (*MED*) scab

costumbre [kos'tumbre] *nf* custom, habit

costura [kos'tura] *nf* sewing, needlework; (*zurcido*) seam

costurera [kostu'rera] *nf* dressmaker

costurero [kostu'rero] *nm* sewing box *o* case

cotejar [kote'xar] *vt* to compare

cotidiano, a [koti'ðjano, a] *adj* daily, day to day

cotilla [ko'tiʎa] *nm/f* (*fam*) gossip; **cotillear** *vi* to gossip; **cotilleo** *nm* gossip(ing)

cotización [kotiθa'θjon] *nf* (*COM*) quotation, price; (*de club*) dues *pl*

cotizar [koti'θar] *vt* (*COM*) to quote, price; **~se** *vr*: **~se a** to sell at, fetch; (*BOLSA*) to stand at, be quoted at

coto ['koto] *nm* (*terreno cercado*) enclosure; (*de caza*) reserve

cotorra [ko'torra] *nf* parrot

COU [kou] (*ESP*) *nm abr* (= *Curso de Orientación Universitaria*) *1 year course leading to final school-leaving certificate and university entrance examinations*

coyote [ko'jote] *nm* coyote, prairie wolf

coyuntura [kojun'tura] *nf* juncture, occasion

coz [koθ] nf kick

crack [krak] nm (droga) crack

cráneo ['kraneo] nm skull, cranium

cráter ['krater] nm crater

creación [krea'θjon] nf creation

creador, a [krea'ðor, a] adj creative ♦ nm/f creator

crear [kre'ar] vt to create, make

crecer [kre'θer] vi to grow; (precio) to rise

creces ['kreθes]: **con ~** adv amply, fully

crecido, a [kre'θiðo, a] adj (persona, planta) full-grown; (cantidad) large

creciente [kre'θjente] adj growing; (cantidad) increasing; (luna) crescent ♦ nm crescent

crecimiento [kreθi'mjento] nm growth; (aumento) increase

credenciales [kreðen'θjales] nfpl credentials

crédito ['kreðito] nm credit

credo ['kreðo] nm creed

crédulo, a ['kreðulo, a] adj credulous

creencia [kre'enθja] nf belief

creer [kre'er] vt, vi to think, believe; ~**se** vr to believe o.s. (to be); ~ **en** to believe in; **¡ya lo creo!** I should think so!

creíble [kre'iβle] adj credible, believable

creído, a [kre'iðo, a] adj (engreído) conceited

crema ['krema] nf cream; ~ **pastelera** (confectioner's) custard

cremallera [krema'ʎera] nf zip (fastener)

crematorio [krema'torjo] nm (tb: **horno ~**) crematorium

crepitar [krepi'tar] vi to crackle

crepúsculo [kre'puskulo] nm twilight, dusk

cresta ['kresta] nf (GEO, ZOOL) crest

creyendo vb ver **creer**

creyente [kre'jente] nm/f believer

creyó etc vb ver **creer**

crezco etc vb ver **crecer**

cría etc ['kria] vb ver **criar** ♦ nf (de animales) rearing, breeding; (animal) young; ver tb **crío**

criadero [kria'ðero] nm (ZOOL) breeding place

criado, a [kri'aðo, a] nm servant ♦ nf servant, maid

criador [kria'ðor] nm breeder

crianza [kri'anθa] nf rearing, breeding; (fig) breeding

criar [kri'ar] vt (educar) to bring up; (producir) to grow, produce; (animales) to breed

criatura [kria'tura] nf creature; (niño) baby, (small) child

criba ['kriβa] nf sieve; **cribar** vt to sieve

crimen ['krimen] nm crime

criminal [krimi'nal] adj, nm/f criminal

crin [krin] nf (tb: ~**es** nfpl) mane

crío, a ['krio, a] (fam) nm/f (niño) kid

crisis ['krisis] nf inv crisis; ~ **nerviosa** nervous breakdown

crispar [kris'par] vt (nervios) to set on edge

cristal [kris'tal] nm crystal; (de ventana) glass, pane; (lente) lens; ~**ino, a** adj crystalline; (fig) clear ♦ nm lens (of the eye); ~**izar** vt, vi to crystallize

cristiandad [kristjan'dað] nf Christendom

cristianismo [kristja'nismo] nm Christianity

cristiano, a [kris'tjano, a] adj, nm/f Christian

Cristo ['kristo] nm Christ; (crucifijo) crucifix

criterio [kri'terjo] nm criterion; (juicio) judgement

crítica ['kritika] nf criticism; ver tb **crítico**

criticar [kriti'kar] vt to criticize

crítico, a ['kritiko, a] adj critical ♦ nm/f critic

Croacia [kro'aθja] nf Croatia

croar [kro'ar] vi to croak

cromo ['kromo] nm chrome

crónica ['kronika] nf chronicle, account

crónico, a ['kroniko, a] adj chronic

cronómetro [kro'nometro] nm stopwatch

croqueta [kro'keta] nf croquette

cruce etc ['kruθe] vb ver **cruzar** ♦ nm crossing; (de carreteras) crossroads

crucificar [kruθifi'kar] vt to crucify

crucifijo [kruθi'fixo] nm crucifix

crucigrama [kruθi'ɣrama] nm crossword

(puzzle)

crudo, a ['kruðo, a] *adj* raw; (*no maduro*) unripe; (*petróleo*) crude; (*rudo, cruel*) cruel ♦ *nm* crude (oil)

cruel [krwel] *adj* cruel; **~dad** *nf* cruelty

crujido [kru'xiðo] *nm* (*de madera etc*) creak

crujiente [kru'xjente] *adj* (*galleta etc*) crunchy

crujir [kru'xir] *vi* (*madera etc*) to creak; (*dedos*) to crack; (*dientes*) to grind; (*nieve, arena*) to crunch

cruz [kruθ] *nf* cross; (*de moneda*) tails *sg*; **~ gamada** swastika

cruzada [kru'θaða] *nf* crusade

cruzado, a [kru'θaðo, a] *adj* crossed ♦ *nm* crusader

cruzar [kru'θar] *vt* to cross; **~se** *vr* (*líneas etc*) to cross; (*personas*) to pass each other

Cruz Roja *nf* Red Cross

cuaderno [kwa'ðerno] *nm* notebook; (*de escuela*) exercise book; (*NAUT*) logbook

cuadra ['kwaðra] *nf* (*caballeriza*) stable; (*AM*) block

cuadrado, a [kwa'ðraðo, a] *adj* square ♦ *nm* (*MAT*) square

cuadrar [kwa'ðrar] *vt* to square ♦ *vi*: **~ con** to square with, tally with; **~se** *vr* (*soldado*) to stand to attention

cuadrilátero [kwaðri'latero] *nm* (*DEPORTE*) boxing ring; (*GEOM*) quadrilateral

cuadrilla [kwa'ðriʎa] *nf* party, group

cuadro ['kwaðro] *nm* square; (*ARTE*) painting; (*TEATRO*) scene; (*diagrama*) chart; (*DEPORTE, MED*) team; **tela a ~s** checked (*BRIT*) *o* chequered (*US*) material

cuádruple ['kwaðruple] *adj* quadruple

cuajar [kwa'xar] *vt* (*leche*) to curdle; (*sangre*) to congeal; (*CULIN*) to set; **~se** *vr* to curdle; to congeal; to set; (*llenarse*) to fill up

cuajo ['kwaxo] *nm*: **de ~** (*arrancar*) by the roots; (*cortar*) completely

cual [kwal] *adv* like, as ♦ *pron*: **el ~** *etc* which; (*persona: sujeto*) who; (: *objeto*) whom ♦ *adj* such as; **cada ~** each one;

déjalo tal ~ leave it just as it is

cuál [kwal] *pron interr* which (one)

cualesquier(a) [kwales'kjer(a)] *pl de* **cualquier(a)**

cualidad [kwali'ðað] *nf* quality

cualquier [kwal'kjer] *adj ver* **cualquiera**

cualquiera [kwal'kjera] (*pl* **cualesquiera**) *adj* (*delante de nm y f:* **cualquier**) any ♦ *pron* anybody; **un coche ~ servirá** any car will do; **no es un hombre ~** he isn't just anybody; **cualquier día/libro** any day/book; **eso ~ lo sabe hacer** anybody can do that; **es un ~** he's a nobody

cuando ['kwando] *adv* when; (*aún si*) if, even if ♦ *conj* (*puesto que*) since ♦ *prep*: **yo, ~ niño ...** when I was a child ...; **~ no sea así** even if it is not so; **~ más** at (the) most; **~ menos** at least; **~ no** if not, otherwise; **de ~ en ~** from time to time

cuándo ['kwando] *adv* when; **¿desde ~?, ¿de ~ acá?** since when?

cuantía [kwan'tia] *nf* (*importe: de pérdidas, deuda, daños*) extent

cuantioso, a [kwan'tjoso, a] *adj* substantial

┌─────────────────┐
│ *PALABRA CLAVE* │
└─────────────────┘

cuanto, a ['kwanto, a] *adj* **1** (*todo*): **tiene todo ~ desea** he's got everything he wants; **le daremos ~s ejemplares necesite** we'll give him as many copies as *o* all the copies he needs; **~s hombres la ven** all the men who see her

2: **unos ~s**: **había unos ~s periodistas** there were a few journalists

3 (*+más*): **~ más vino bebes peor te sentirás** the more wine you drink the worse you'll feel

♦ *pron*: **tiene ~ desea** he has everything he wants; **tome ~/~s quiera** take as much/many as you want

♦ *adv*: **en ~**: **en ~ profesor** as a teacher; **en ~ a mí** as for me; *ver tb* **antes**

♦ *conj* **1**: **~ más gana menos gasta** the more he earns the less he spends; **~ más joven más confiado** the younger you are the more trusting you are

2: en ~: en ~ llegue/llegué as soon as I arrive/arrived

cuánto, a ['kwanto, a] *adj (exclamación)* what a lot of; *(interr: sg)* how much?; (: *pl*) how many? ♦ *pron, adv* how; *(interr: sg)* how much?; (: *pl*) how many?; **¡cuánta gente!** what a lot of people!; **¿~ cuesta?** how much does it cost?; **¿a ~s estamos?** what's the date?; **Señor no sé ~s** Mr. So-and-So

cuarenta [kwa'renta] *num* forty

cuarentena [kwaren'tena] *nf* quarantine

cuaresma [kwa'resma] *nf* Lent

cuarta ['kwarta] *nf (MAT)* quarter, fourth; *(palmo)* span

cuartel [kwar'tel] *nm (MIL)* barracks *pl*; **~ general** headquarters *pl*

cuarteto [kwar'teto] *nm* quartet

cuarto, a ['kwarto, a] *adj* fourth ♦ *nm (MAT)* quarter, fourth; *(habitación)* room; **~ de baño** bathroom; **~ de estar** living room; **~ de hora** quarter (of an) hour; **~ de kilo** quarter kilo

cuatro ['kwatro] *num* four

Cuba ['kuβa] *nf* Cuba; **cubano, a** *adj, nm/f* Cuban

cuba ['kuβa] *nf* cask, barrel

cubata [ku'βata] *nm (fam)* large drink *(of rum and coke etc)*

cúbico, a ['kuβiko, a] *adj* cubic

cubierta [ku'βjerta] *nf* cover, covering; *(neumático)* tyre; *(NAUT)* deck

cubierto, a [ku'βjerto, a] *pp de* **cubrir** ♦ *adj* covered ♦ *nm* cover; *(lugar en la mesa)* place; **~s** *nmpl* cutlery *sg*; **a ~** under cover

cubil [ku'βil] *nm* den; **~ete** *nm (en juegos)* cup

cubito [ku'βito] *nm*: **~ de hielo** ice-cube

cubo ['kuβo] *nm (MATH)* cube; *(balde)* bucket, tub; *(TEC)* drum

cubrecama [kuβre'kama] *nm* bedspread

cubrir [ku'βrir] *vt* to cover; **~se** *vr (cielo)* to become overcast

cucaracha [kuka'ratʃa] *nf* cockroach

cuchara [ku'tʃara] *nf* spoon; *(TEC)* scoop;

~da *nf* spoonful; **~dita** *nf* teaspoonful

cucharilla [kutʃa'riʎa] *nf* teaspoon

cucharón [kutʃa'ron] *nm* ladle

cuchichear [kutʃitʃe'ar] *vi* to whisper

cuchilla [ku'tʃiʎa] *nf (large) knife; (de arma blanca)* blade; **~ de afeitar** razor blade

cuchillo [ku'tʃiʎo] *nm* knife

cuchitril [kutʃi'tril] *nm* hovel

cuclillas [ku'kliʎas] *nfpl*: **en ~** squatting

cuco, a ['kuko, a] *adj* pretty; *(astuto)* sharp ♦ *nm* cuckoo

cucurucho [kuku'rutʃo] *nm* cornet

cuello ['kweʎo] *nm (ANAT)* neck; *(de vestido, camisa)* collar

cuenca ['kwenka] *nf (ANAT)* eye socket; *(GEO)* bowl, deep valley

cuenco ['kwenko] *nm* bowl

cuenta *etc* ['kwenta] *vb ver* **contar** ♦ *nf (cálculo)* count, counting; *(en café, restaurante)* bill *(BRIT)*, check *(US)*; *(COM)* account; *(de collar)* bead; **a fin de ~s** in the end; **caer en la ~** to catch on; **darse ~ de** to realize; **tener en ~** to bear in mind; **echar la ~** to take stock; **~ corriente/de ahorros** current/savings account; **~ atrás** countdown; **~kilómetros** *nm inv* ≈ milometer; *(de velocidad)* speedometer

cuento *etc* ['kwento] *vb ver* **contar** ♦ *nm* story

cuerda ['kwerða] *nf* rope; *(fina)* string; *(de reloj)* spring; **dar ~ a un reloj** to wind up a clock; **~ floja** tightrope

cuerdo, a ['kwerðo, a] *adj* sane; *(prudente)* wise, sensible

cuerno ['kwerno] *nm* horn

cuero ['kwero] *nm* leather; **en ~s** stark naked; **~ cabelludo** scalp

cuerpo ['kwerpo] *nm* body

cuervo ['kwerβo] *nm* crow

cuesta *etc* ['kwesta] *vb ver* **costar** ♦ *nf* slope; *(en camino etc)* hill; **~ arriba/abajo** uphill/downhill; **a ~s** on one's back

cueste *etc vb ver* **costar**

cuestión [kwes'tjon] *nf* matter, question, issue

cueva ['kweβa] *nf* cave

cuidado [kwi'ðaðo] *nm* care, carefulness; (*preocupación*) care, worry ♦ *excl* careful!, look out!

cuidadoso, a [kwiða'ðoso, a] *adj* careful; (*preocupado*) anxious

cuidar [kwi'ðar] *vt* (*MED*) to care for; (*ocuparse de*) to take care of, look after ♦ *vi*: ~ **de** to take care of, look after; ~**se** *vr* to look after o.s.; ~**se de hacer algo** to take care to do sth

culata [ku'lata] *nf* (*de fusil*) butt

culebra [ku'leβra] *nf* snake

culebrón [kule'βron] (*fam*) *nm* (*TV*) soap(-opera)

culinario, a [kuli'narjo, a] *adj* culinary, cooking *cpd*

culminación [kulmina'θjon] *nf* culmination

culo ['kulo] *nm* bottom, backside; (*de vaso, botella*) bottom

culpa ['kulpa] *nf* fault; (*JUR*) guilt; **por ~ de** because of; **tener la ~ (de)** to be to blame (for); ~**bilidad** *nf* guilt; ~**ble** *adj* guilty ♦ *nm/f* culprit

culpar [kul'par] *vt* to blame; (*acusar*) to accuse

cultivar [kulti'βar] *vt* to cultivate

cultivo [kul'tiβo] *nm* (*acto*) cultivation; (*plantas*) crop

culto, a ['kulto, a] *adj* (*que tiene cultura*) cultured, educated ♦ *nm* (*homenaje*) worship; (*religión*) cult

cultura [kul'tura] *nf* culture

culturismo [kultu'rismo] *nm* body-building

cumbre ['kumbre] *nf* summit, top

cumpleaños [kumple'aɲos] *nm inv* birthday

cumplido, a [kum'pliðo, a] *adj* (*abundante*) plentiful; (*cortés*) courteous ♦ *nm* compliment; **visita de ~** courtesy call

cumplidor, a [kumpli'ðor, a] *adj* reliable

cumplimentar [kumplimen'tar] *vt* to congratulate

cumplimiento [kumpli'mjento] *nm* (*de un deber*) fulfilment; (*acabamiento*) completion

cumplir [kum'plir] *vt* (*orden*) to carry out, obey; (*promesa*) to carry out, fulfil; (*condena*) to serve ♦ *vi*: ~ **con** (*deberes*) to carry out, fulfil; ~**se** *vr* (*plazo*) to expire; **hoy cumple dieciocho años** he is eighteen today

cúmulo ['kumulo] *nm* heap

cuna ['kuna] *nf* cradle, cot

cundir [kun'dir] *vi* (*noticia, rumor, pánico*) to spread; (*rendir*) to go a long way

cuneta [ku'neta] *nf* ditch

cuña ['kuɲa] *nf* wedge

cuñado, a [ku'ɲaðo, a] *nm/f* brother-/sister-in-law

cuota ['kwota] *nf* (*parte proporcional*) share; (*cotización*) fee, dues *pl*

cupe *etc vb ver* **caber**

cupiera *etc vb ver* **caber**

cupo ['kupo] *vb ver* **caber** ♦ *nm* quota

cupón [ku'pon] *nm* coupon

cúpula ['kupula] *nf* dome

cura ['kura] *nf* (*curación*) cure; (*método curativo*) treatment ♦ *nm* priest

curación [kura'θjon] *nf* cure; (*acción*) curing

curandero, a [kuran'dero, a] *nm/f* quack

curar [ku'rar] *vt* (*MED: herida*) to treat, dress; (*: enfermo*) to cure; (*CULIN*) to cure, salt; (*cuero*) to tan; ~**se** *vr* to get well, recover

curiosear [kurjose'ar] *vt* to glance at, look over ♦ *vi* to look round, wander round; (*explorar*) to poke about

curiosidad [kurjosi'ðað] *nf* curiosity

curioso, a [ku'rjoso, a] *adj* curious ♦ *nm/f* bystander, onlooker

currante [ku'rrante] (*fam*) *nm/f* worker

currar [ku'rrar] (*fam*) *vi* to work

currículo [ku'rrikulo] = **curriculum**

curriculum [ku'rrikulum] *nm* curriculum vitae

cursi ['kursi] (*fam*) *adj* affected

cursillo [kur'siʎo] *nm* short course

cursiva [kur'siβa] *nf* italics *pl*

curso ['kurso] *nm* course; **en ~** (*año*)

current; (*proceso*) going on, under
way

cursor [kur'sor] *nm* (*INFORM*) cursor

curtido, a [kur'tiðo, a] *adj* (*cara etc*)
weather-beaten; (*fig: persona*)
experienced

curtir [kur'tir] *vt* (*cuero etc*) to tan

curva ['kurßa] *nf* curve, bend

cúspide ['kuspiðe] *nf* (*GEO*) peak; (*fig*) top

custodia [kus'toðja] *nf* safekeeping;
custody; **custodiar** *vt* (*conservar*) to take
care of; (*vigilar*) to guard

cutis ['kutis] *nm inv* skin, complexion

cutre ['kutre] (*fam*) *adj* (*lugar*) grotty

cuyo, a ['kujo, a] *pron* (*de quien*) whose;
(*de que*) whose, of which; **en ~ caso** in
which case

C.V. *abr* (= *caballos de vapor*) H.P.

D, d

D. *abr* (= *Don*) Esq.

Da. *abr* = **Doña**

dádiva ['daðißa] *nf* (*donación*) donation;
(*regalo*) gift; **dadivoso, a** *adj*
generous

dado, a ['daðo, a] *pp de* **dar** ♦ *nm* die; **~s**
nmpl dice; **~ que** given that

daltónico, a [dal'toniko, a] *adj* colour-
blind

dama ['dama] *nf* (*gen*) lady; (*AJEDREZ*)
queen; **~s** *nfpl* (*juego*) draughts *sg*

damnificar [damnifi'kar] *vt* to harm;
(*persona*) to injure

danés, esa [da'nes, esa] *adj* Danish
♦ *nm/f* Dane

danzar [dan'θar] *vt, vi* to dance

dañar [da'ɲar] *vt* (*objeto*) to damage;
(*persona*) to hurt; **~se** *vr* (*objeto*) to get
damaged

dañino, a [da'ɲino, a] *adj* harmful

daño ['daɲo] *nm* (*a un objeto*) damage; (*a
una persona*) harm, injury; **~s y
perjuicios** (*JUR*) damages; **hacer ~ a** to
damage; (*persona*) to hurt, injure;
hacerse ~ to hurt o.s.

PALABRA CLAVE

dar [dar] *vt* **1** (*gen*) to give; (*obra de
teatro*) to put on; (*film*) to show; (*fiesta*)
to hold; **~ algo a uno** to give sb sth *o* sth
to sb; **~ de beber a uno** to give sb a
drink

2 (*producir: intereses*) to yield; (*fruta*) to
produce

3 (*locuciones +n*): **da gusto escucharle**
it's a pleasure to listen to him; *ver tb*
paseo *y otros sustantivos*

4 (+*n: = perifrasis de verbo*): **me da asco**
it sickens me

5 (*considerar*): **~ algo por descontado/
entendido** to take sth for granted/as
read; **~ algo por concluido** to consider
sth finished

6 (*hora*): **el reloj dio las 6** the clock
struck 6 (o'clock)

7: **me da lo mismo** it's all the same to
me; *ver tb* **igual, más**

♦ *vi* **1**: **~ con: dimos con él dos horas
más tarde** we came across him two
hours later; **al final di con la solución** I
eventually came up with the answer

2: **~ en** (*blanco, suelo*) to hit; **el sol me
da en la cara** the sun is shining (right)
on my face

3: **~ de sí** (*zapatos etc*) to stretch, give

♦ **~se** *vr* **1**: **~se por vencido** to give up

2 (*ocurrir*): **se han dado muchos casos**
there have been a lot of cases

3: **~se a**: **se ha dado a la bebida** he's
taken to drinking

4: **se me dan bien/mal las ciencias** I'm
good/bad at science

5: **dárselas de**: **se las da de experto** he
fancies himself *o* poses as an expert

dardo ['darðo] *nm* dart

datar [da'tar] *vi*: **~ de** to date from

dátil ['datil] *nm* date

dato ['dato] *nm* fact, piece of information;
~s personales personal details

DC *abbr m* (= *disco compacto*) CD

d. de J.C. *abr* (= *después de Jesucristo*)
A.D.

PALABRA CLAVE
---

de [de] *prep* (*de+el* = **del**) **1** (*posesión*) of;
la casa ~ Isabel/mis padres Isabel's/my
parents' house; es ~ ellos it's theirs
2 (*origen, distancia, con números*) from;
soy ~ Gijón I'm from Gijón; ~ 8 a 20
from 8 to 20; salir del cine to go out of
o leave the cinema; ~ 2 en 2 2 by 2, 2 at
a time
3 (*valor descriptivo*): una copa ~ vino a
glass of wine; la mesa ~ la cocina the
kitchen table; un billete ~ 1000 pesetas
a 1000 peseta note; un niño ~ tres años
a three-year-old (child); una máquina ~
coser a sewing machine; ir vestido ~
gris to be dressed in grey; la niña del
vestido azul the girl in the blue dress;
trabaja ~ profesora she works as a
teacher; ~ lado sideways; ~ atrás/
delante rear/front
4 (*hora, tiempo*): a las 8 ~ la mañana at
8 o'clock in the morning; ~ día/noche
by day/night; ~ hoy en ocho días a week
from now; ~ niño era gordo as a child
he was fat
5 (*comparaciones*): más/menos ~ cien
personas more/less than a hundred
people; el más caro ~ la tienda the
most expensive in the shop; menos/más
~ lo pensado less/more than expected
6 (*causa*): del calor from the heat; ~
puro tonto out of sheer stupidity
7 (*tema*) about; clases ~ inglés English
classes; ¿sabes algo ~ él? do you know
anything about him?; un libro ~ física a
physics book
8 (*adj +de +infin*): fácil ~ entender easy
to understand
9 (*oraciones pasivas*): fue respetado ~
todos he was loved by all
10 (*condicional +infin*) if; ~ ser posible if
possible; ~ no terminarlo hoy if I *etc*
don't finish it today

dé *vb ver* **dar**
deambular [deambu'lar] *vi* to wander
debajo [de'βaxo] *adv* underneath; ~ de
below, under; por ~ de beneath
debate [de'βate] *nm* debate; **debatir** *vt*
to debate
deber [de'βer] *nm* duty ♦ *vt* to owe ♦ *vi*:
debe (de) it must, it should; ~es *nmpl*
(ESCOL) homework; debo hacerlo I must
do it; debe de ir he should go; ~se *vr*:
~se a to be owing *o* due to
debido, a [de'βiðo, a] *adj* proper, just; ~ a
due to, because of
débil ['deβil] *adj* (*persona, carácter*) weak;
(*luz*) dim; **debilidad** *nf* weakness;
dimness
debilitar [deβili'tar] *vt* to weaken; ~se *vr*
to grow weak
debutar [deβu'tar] *vi* to make one's debut
década ['dekaða] *nf* decade
decadencia [deka'ðenθja] *nf* (*estado*)
decadence; (*proceso*) decline, decay
decaer [deka'er] *vi* (*declinar*) to decline;
(*debilitarse*) to weaken
decaído, a [deka'iðo, a] *adj*: estar ~
(*abatido*) to be down
decaimiento [dekai'mjento] *nm*
(*declinación*) decline; (*desaliento*)
discouragement; (*MED: estado débil*)
weakness
decano, a [de'kano, a] *nm/f* (*de
universidad etc*) dean
decapitar [dekapi'tar] *vt* to behead
decena [de'θena] *nf*: una ~ ten (or so)
decencia [de'θenθja] *nf* decency
decente [de'θente] *adj* decent
decepción [deθep'θjon] *nf*
disappointment
decepcionar [deθepθjo'nar] *vt* to
disappoint
decidir [deθi'ðir] *vt, vi* to decide; ~se *vr*:
~se a to make up one's mind to
décimo, a ['deθimo, a] *adj* tenth ♦ *nm*
tenth
decir [de'θir] *vt* to say; (*contar*) to tell;
(*hablar*) to speak ♦ *nm* saying; ~se *vr*: se
dice que it is said that; ~ para *o* entre sí

to say to o.s.; **querer** ~ to mean;
¡dígame! (*TEL*) hello!; (*en tienda*) can I
help you?

decisión [deθi'sjon] *nf* (*resolución*)
decision; (*firmeza*) decisiveness

decisivo, a [deθi'siβo, a] *adj* decisive

declaración [deklara'θjon] *nf*
(*manifestación*) statement; (*de amor*)
declaration; ~ **de ingresos** *o* **de la renta**
o **fiscal** income-tax return

declarar [dekla'rar] *vt* to declare ♦ *vi* to
declare; (*JUR*) to testify; **~se** *vr* to propose

declinar [dekli'nar] *vt* (*gen*) to decline;
(*JUR*) to reject ♦ *vi* (*el día*) to draw to a
close

declive [de'kliβe] *nm* (*cuesta*) slope; (*fig*)
decline

decodificador [dekoðifika'ðor] *nm*
decoder

decolorarse [dekolo'rarse] *vr* to become
discoloured

decoración [dekora'θjon] *nf* decoration

decorado [deko'raðo] *nm* (*CINE, TEATRO*)
scenery, set

decorar [deko'rar] *vt* to decorate;
decorativo, a *adj* ornamental,
decorative

decoro [de'koro] *nm* (*respeto*) respect;
(*dignidad*) decency; (*recato*) propriety;
~so, a *adj* (*decente*) decent; (*modesto*)
modest; (*digno*) proper

decrecer [dekre'θer] *vi* to decrease,
diminish

decrépito, a [de'krepito, a] *adj* decrepit

decretar [dekre'tar] *vt* to decree; **decreto**
nm decree

dedal [de'ðal] *nm* thimble

dedicación [deðika'θjon] *nf* dedication

dedicar [deði'kar] *vt* (*libro*) to dedicate;
(*tiempo, dinero*) to devote; (*palabras:
decir, consagrar*) to dedicate, devote;
dedicatoria *nf* (*de libro*) dedication

dedo ['deðo] *nm* finger; ~ **(del pie)** toe; ~
pulgar thumb; ~ **índice** index finger; ~
corazón middle finger; ~ **anular** ring
finger; ~ **meñique** little finger; **hacer** ~
(*fam*) to hitch (a lift)

deducción [deðuk'θjon] *nf* deduction

deducir [deðu'θir] *vt* (*concluir*) to deduce,
infer; (*COM*) to deduct

defecto [de'fekto] *nm* defect, flaw;
defectuoso, a *adj* defective, faulty

defender [defen'der] *vt* to defend

defensa [de'fensa] *nf* defence ♦ *nm*
(*DEPORTE*) defender, back; **defensivo, a**
adj defensive; **a la defensiva** on the
defensive

defensor, a [defen'sor, a] *adj* defending
♦ *nm/f* (*abogado* ~) defending counsel;
(*protector*) protector

deficiencia [defi'θjenθja] *nf* deficiency

deficiente [defi'θjente] *adj* (*defectuoso*)
defective; ~ **en** lacking *o* deficient in; **ser
un** ~ **mental** to be mentally handicapped

déficit ['defiθit] (*pl* ~**s**) *nm* deficit

definición [defini'θjon] *nf* definition

definir [defi'nir] *vt* (*determinar*) to
determine, establish; (*decidir*) to define;
(*aclarar*) to clarify; **definitivo, a** *adj*
definitive; **en definitiva** definitively; (*en
resumen*) in short

deformación [deforma'θjon] *nf*
(*alteración*) deformation; (*RADIO etc*)
distortion

deformar [defor'mar] *vt* (*gen*) to deform;
~se *vr* to become deformed; **deforme**
adj (*informe*) deformed; (*feo*) ugly;
(*malhecho*) misshapen

defraudar [defrau'ðar] *vt* (*decepcionar*) to
disappoint; (*estafar*) to defraud

defunción [defun'θjon] *nf* death, demise

degeneración [dexenera'θjon] *nf* (*de las
células*) degeneration; (*moral*) degeneracy

degenerar [dexene'rar] *vi* to degenerate

degollar [dexo'ʎar] *vt* to behead; (*fig*) to
slaughter

degradar [deɣra'ðar] *vt* to debase,
degrade; **~se** *vr* to demean o.s.

degustación [deɣusta'θjon] *nf* sampling,
tasting

deificar [deifi'kar] *vt* to deify

dejadez [dexa'ðeθ] *nf* (*negligencia*)
neglect; (*descuido*) untidiness, carelessness

dejar [de'xar] *vt* to leave; (*permitir*) to

allow, let; (*abandonar*) to abandon, forsake; (*beneficios*) to produce, yield ♦ *vi*: ~ **de** (*parar*) to stop; (*no hacer*) to fail to; **no dejes de comprar un billete** make sure you buy a ticket; ~ **a un lado** to leave *o* set aside

dejo ['dexo] *nm* (*LING*) accent

del [del] (= **de+el**) *ver* **de**

delantal [delan'tal] *nm* apron

delante [de'lante] *adv* in front, (*enfrente*) opposite; (*adelante*) ahead; ~ **de** in front of, before

delantera [delan'tera] *nf* (*de vestido, casa etc*) front part; (*DEPORTE*) forward line; **llevar la ~ (a uno)** to be ahead (of sb)

delantero, a [delan'tero, a] *adj* front ♦ *nm* (*DEPORTE*) forward, striker

delatar [dela'tar] *vt* to inform on *o* against, betray; **delator, a** *nm/f* informer

delegación [deleɣa'θjon] *nf* (*acción, delegados*) delegation; (*COM: oficina*) office, branch; ~ **de policía** police station

delegado, a [dele'ɣaðo, a] *nm/f* delegate; (*COM*) agent

delegar [dele'ɣar] *vt* to delegate

deletrear [deletre'ar] *vt* to spell (out)

deleznable [deleθ'naβle] *adj* brittle; (*excusa, idea*) feeble

delfín [del'fin] *nm* dolphin

delgadez [delɣa'ðeθ] *nf* thinness, slimness

delgado, a [del'ɣaðo, a] *adj* thin; (*persona*) slim, thin; (*tela etc*) light, delicate

deliberación [deliβera'θjon] *nf* deliberation

deliberar [deliβe'rar] *vt* to debate, discuss

delicadeza [delika'ðeθa] *nf* (*gen*) delicacy; (*refinamiento, sutileza*) refinement

delicado, a [deli'kaðo, a] *adj* (*gen*) delicate; (*sensible*) sensitive; (*quisquilloso*) touchy

delicia [de'liθja] *nf* delight

delicioso, a [deli'θjoso, a] *adj* (*gracioso*) delightful; (*exquisito*) delicious

delimitar [delimi'tar] *vt* (*funciones, responsabilidades*) to define

delincuencia [delin'kwenθja] *nf* delinquency; **delincuente** *nm/f* delinquent; (*criminal*) criminal

delineante [deline'ante] *nm/f* draughtsman/woman

delinear [deline'ar] *vt* (*dibujo*) to draw; (*fig, contornos*) to outline

delinquir [delin'kir] *vi* to commit an offence

delirante [deli'rante] *adj* delirious

delirar [deli'rar] *vi* to be delirious, rave

delirio [de'lirjo] *nm* (*MED*) delirium; (*palabras insensatas*) ravings *pl*

delito [de'lito] *nm* (*gen*) crime; (*infracción*) offence

delta ['delta] *nm* delta

demacrado, a [dema'kraðo, a] *adj*: **estar** ~ to look pale and drawn, be wasted away

demagogo, a [dema'ɣoɣo, a] *nm/f* demagogue

demanda [de'manda] *nf* (*pedido, COM*) demand; (*petición*) request; (*JUR*) action, lawsuit

demandante [deman'dante] *nm/f* claimant

demandar [deman'dar] *vt* (*gen*) to demand; (*JUR*) to sue, file a lawsuit against

demarcación [demarka'θjon] *nf* (*de terreno*) demarcation

demás [de'mas] *adj*: **los ~ niños** the other children, the remaining children ♦ *pron*: **los/las ~** the others, the rest (of them); **lo ~** the rest (of it)

demasía [dema'sia] *nf* (*exceso*) excess, surplus; **comer en ~** to eat to excess

demasiado, a [dema'sjaðo, a] *adj*: ~ **vino** too much wine ♦ *adv* (*antes de adj, adv*) too; ~**s libros** too many books; ¡**esto es** ~! that's the limit!; **hace** ~ **calor** it's too hot; ~ **despacio** too slowly; ~**s** too many

demencia [de'menθja] *nf* (*locura*) madness; **demente** *nm/f* lunatic ♦ *adj* mad, insane

democracia [demo'kraθja] *nf* democracy

demócrata [de'mokrata] *nm/f* democrat;

democrático, a *adj* democratic
demoler [demo'ler] *vt* to demolish;
demolición *nf* demolition
demonio [de'monjo] *nm* devil, demon;
¡~**s!** hell!, damn!; ¿**cómo ~s?** how the
hell?
demora [de'mora] *nf* delay; **demorar** *vt*
(*retardar*) to delay, hold back; (*detener*) to
hold up ♦ *vi* to linger, stay on; ~**se** *vr* to
be delayed
demos *vb ver* **dar**
demostración [demostra'θjon] *nf* (MAT)
proof; (*de afecto*) show, display
demostrar [demos'trar] *vt* (*probar*) to
prove; (*mostrar*) to show; (*manifestar*) to
demonstrate
demudado, a [demu'ðaðo, a] *adj* (*rostro*)
pale
den *vb ver* **dar**
denegar [dene'var] *vt* (*rechazar*) to refuse;
(JUR) to reject
denigrar [deni'xrar] *vt* (*desacreditar,
infamar*) to denigrate; (*injuriar*) to insult

Denominación de Origen

i The **Denominación de Origen**,
abbreviated to **D.O.**, *is a prestigious
classification awarded to food products
such as wines, cheeses, sausages and hams
which meet the stringent quality and
production standards of the designated
region. D.O. labels serve as a guarantee of
quality.*

---

denotar [deno'tar] *vt* to denote
densidad [densi'ðað] *nf* density; (*fig*)
thickness
denso, a ['denso, a] *adj* dense; (*espeso,
pastoso*) thick; (*fig*) heavy
dentadura [denta'ðura] *nf* (set of) teeth
pl; ~ **postiza** false teeth *pl*
dentera [den'tera] *nf* (*sensación
desagradable*) the shivers *pl*
dentífrico, a [den'tifriko, a] *adj* dental
♦ *nm* toothpaste
dentista [den'tista] *nm/f* dentist
dentro ['dentro] *adv* inside ♦ *prep:* ~ **de**

in, inside, within; **por ~** (on the) inside;
mirar por ~ to look inside; ~ **de tres
meses** within three months
denuncia [de'nunθja] *nf* (*delación*)
denunciation; (*acusación*) accusation; (*de
accidente*) report; **denunciar** *vt* to
report; (*delatar*) to inform on *o* against
departamento [departa'mento] *nm*
(*sección administrativa*) department,
section; (AM: *apartamento*) flat (BRIT),
apartment
dependencia [depen'denθja] *nf*
dependence; (POL) dependency; (COM)
office, section
depender [depen'der] *vi:* ~ **de** to depend
on
dependienta [depen'djenta] *nf*
saleswoman, shop assistant
dependiente [depen'djente] *adj*
dependent ♦ *nm* salesman, shop assistant
depilar [depi'lar] *vt* (*con cera*) to wax;
(*cejas*) to pluck; **depilatorio** *nm* hair
remover
deplorable [deplo'raßle] *adj* deplorable
deplorar [deplo'rar] *vt* to deplore
deponer [depo'ner] *vt* to lay down ♦ *vi*
(JUR) to give evidence; (*declarar*) to make
a statement
deportar [depor'tar] *vt* to deport
deporte [de'porte] *nm* sport; **hacer ~** to
play sports; **deportista** *adj* sports *cpd*
♦ *nm/f* sportsman/woman; **deportivo, a**
adj (*club, periódico*) sports *cpd* ♦ *nm*
sports car
depositar [deposi'tar] *vt* (*dinero*) to
deposit; (*mercancías*) to put away, store;
~**se** *vr* to settle; ~**io, a** *nm/f* trustee
depósito [de'posito] *nm* (*gen*) deposit;
(*almacén*) warehouse, store; (*de agua,
gasolina etc*) tank; ~ **de cadáveres**
mortuary
depreciar [depre'θjar] *vt* to depreciate,
reduce the value of; ~**se** *vr* to depreciate,
lose value
depredador, a [depreða'ðor, a] *adj*
predatory ♦ *nm* predator
depresión [depre'sjon] *nf* depression

deprimido, a [depri'miðo, a] *adj* depressed

deprimir [depri'mir] *vt* to depress; **~se** *vr* (*persona*) to become depressed

deprisa [de'prisa] *adv* quickly, hurriedly

depuración [depura'θjon] *nf* purification; (*POL*) purge

depurar [depu'rar] *vt* to purify; (*purgar*) to purge

derecha [de'retʃa] *nf* right(-hand) side; (*POL*) right; **a la ~** (*estar*) on the right; (*torcer etc*) (to the) right

derecho, a [de'retʃo, a] *adj* right, right-hand ♦ *nm* (*privilegio*) right; (*lado*) right(-hand) side; (*leyes*) law ♦ *adv* straight, directly; **~s** *nmpl* (*de aduana*) duty *sg*; (*de autor*) royalties; **tener ~ a** to have a right to

deriva [de'riβa] *nf*: **ir** *o* **estar a la ~** to drift, be adrift

derivado [deri'βaðo] *nm* (*COM*) by-product

derivar [deri'βar] *vt* to derive; (*desviar*) to direct ♦ *vi* to derive, be derived; (*NAUT*) to drift ♦ **~se** *vr* to derive, be derived; to drift

derramamiento [derrama'mjento] *nm* (*dispersión*) spilling; **~ de sangre** bloodshed

derramar [derra'mar] *vt* to spill; (*verter*) to pour out; (*esparcir*) to scatter; **~se** *vr* to pour out; **~ lágrimas** to weep

derrame [de'rrame] *nm* (*de líquido*) spilling; (*de sangre*) shedding; (*de tubo etc*) overflow; (*pérdida*) leakage; (*MED*) discharge

derredor [derre'ðor] *adv*: **al** *o* **en ~ de** around, about

derretido, a [derre'tiðo, a] *adj* melted; (*metal*) molten

derretir [derre'tir] *vt* (*gen*) to melt; (*nieve*) to thaw; **~se** *vr* to melt

derribar [derri'βar] *vt* to knock down; (*construcción*) to demolish; (*persona, gobierno, político*) to bring down

derrocar [derro'kar] *vt* (*gobierno*) to bring down, overthrow

derrochar [derro'tʃar] *vt* to squander; **derroche** *nm* (*despilfarro*) waste, squandering

derrota [de'rrota] *nf* (*NAUT*) course; (*MIL, DEPORTE etc*) defeat, rout; **derrotar** *vt* (*gen*) to defeat; **derrotero** *nm* (*rumbo*) course

derruir [derru'ir] *vt* (*edificio*) to demolish

derrumbar [derrum'bar] *vt* (*edificio*) to knock down; **~se** *vr* to collapse

derruyendo *etc vb ver* **derruir**

des *vb ver* **dar**

desabotonar [desaβoto'nar] *vt* to unbutton, undo; **~se** *vr* to come undone

desabrido, a [desa'βriðo, a] *adj* (*comida*) insipid, tasteless; (*persona*) rude, surly; (*respuesta*) sharp; (*tiempo*) unpleasant

desabrochar [desaβro'tʃar] *vt* (*botones, broches*) to undo, unfasten; **~se** *vr* (*ropa etc*) to come undone

desacato [desa'kato] *nm* (*falta de respeto*) disrespect; (*JUR*) contempt

desacertado, a [desaθer'taðo, a] *adj* (*equivocado*) mistaken; (*inoportuno*) unwise

desacierto [desa'θjerto] *nm* mistake, error

desaconsejado, a [desakonse'xaðo, a] *adj* ill-advised

desaconsejar [desakonse'xar] *vt* to advise against

desacreditar [desakreði'tar] *vt* (*desprestigiar*) to discredit, bring into disrepute; (*denigrar*) to run down

desacuerdo [desa'kwerðo] *nm* disagreement, discord

desafiar [desa'fjar] *vt* (*retar*) to challenge; (*enfrentarse a*) to defy

desafilado, a [desafi'laðo, a] *adj* blunt

desafinado, a [desafi'naðo, a] *adj*: **estar ~** to be out of tune

desafinar [desafi'nar] *vi* (*al cantar*) to be *o* go out of tune

desafío *etc* [desa'fio] *vb ver* **desafiar** ♦ *nm* (*reto*) challenge; (*combate*) duel; (*resistencia*) defiance

desaforado, a [desafo'raðo, a] *adj* (*grito*) ear-splitting; (*comportamiento*) outrageous

desafortunadamente
[desafortunaða'mente] *adv* unfortunately
desafortunado, a [desafortu'naðo, a] *adj*
(*desgraciado*) unfortunate, unlucky
desagradable [desaɣra'ðaßle] *adj*
(*fastidioso, enojoso*) unpleasant; (*irritante*)
disagreeable
desagradar [desaɣra'ðar] *vi* (*disgustar*) to
displease; (*molestar*) to bother
desagradecido, a [desaɣraðe'θiðo, a] *adj*
ungrateful
desagrado [desa'ɣraðo] *nm* (*disgusto*)
displeasure; (*contrariedad*) dissatisfaction
desagraviar [desaɣra'ßjar] *vt* to make
amends to
desagüe [des'aɣwe] *nm* (*de un líquido*)
drainage; (*cañería*) drainpipe; (*salida*)
outlet, drain
desaguisado [desaɣi'saðo] *nm* outrage
desahogado, a [desao'ɣaðo, a] *adj*
(*holgado*) comfortable; (*espacioso*) roomy,
large
desahogar [desao'ɣar] *vt* (*aliviar*) to ease,
relieve; (*ira*) to vent; **~se** *vr* (*relajarse*) to
relax; (*desfogarse*) to let off steam
desahogo [desa'oɣo] *nm* (*alivio*) relief;
(*comodidad*) comfort, ease
desahuciar [desau'θjar] *vt* (*enfermo*) to
give up hope for; (*inquilino*) to evict;
desahucio *nm* eviction
desairar [desai'rar] *vt* (*menospreciar*) to
slight, snub
desaire [des'aire] *nm* (*menosprecio*) slight;
(*falta de garbo*) unattractiveness
desajustar [desaxus'tar] *vt* (*desarreglar*) to
disarrange; (*desconcertar*) to throw off
balance; **~se** *vr* to get out of order;
(*aflojarse*) to loosen
desajuste [desa'xuste] *nm* (*de máquina*)
disorder; (*situación*) imbalance
desalentador, a [desalenta'ðor, a] *adj*
discouraging
desalentar [desalen'tar] *vt* (*desanimar*) to
discourage
desaliento *etc* [desa'ljento] *vb ver*
desalentar ♦ *nm* discouragement
desaliño [desa'liɲo] *nm* slovenliness

desalmado, a [desal'maðo, a] *adj* (*cruel*)
cruel, heartless
desalojar [desalo'xar] *vt* (*expulsar, echar*)
to eject; (*abandonar*) to move out of ♦ *vi*
to move out
desamor [desa'mor] *nm* (*frialdad*)
indifference; (*odio*) dislike
desamparado, a [desampa'raðo, a] *adj*
(*persona*) helpless; (*lugar: expuesto*)
exposed; (*desierto*) deserted
desamparar [desampa'rar] *vt* (*abandonar*)
to desert, abandon; (*JUR*) to leave
defenceless; (*barco*) to abandon
desandar [desan'dar] *vt*: **~ lo andado** *o* **el
camino** to retrace one's steps
desangrar [desan'grar] *vt* to bleed; (*fig:
persona*) to bleed dry; **~se** *vr* to lose a lot
of blood
desanimado, a [desani'maðo, a] *adj*
(*persona*) downhearted; (*espectáculo,
fiesta*) dull
desanimar [desani'mar] *vt* (*desalentar*) to
discourage; (*deprimir*) to depress; **~se** *vr*
to lose heart
desapacible [desapa'θißle] *adj* (*gen*)
unpleasant
desaparecer [desapare'θer] *vi* (*gen*) to
disappear; (*el sol, la luz*) to vanish;
desaparecido, a *adj* missing;
desaparición *nf* disappearance
desapasionado, a [desapasjo'naðo, a]
adj dispassionate, impartial
desapego [desa'peɣo] *nm* (*frialdad*)
coolness; (*distancia*) detachment
desapercibido, a [desaperθi'ßiðo, a] *adj*
(*desprevenido*) unprepared; **pasar ~** to go
unnoticed
desaprensivo, a [desapren'sißo, a] *adj*
unscrupulous
desaprobar [desapro'ßar] *vt* (*reprobar*) to
disapprove of; (*condenar*) to condemn;
(*no consentir*) to reject
desaprovechado, a [desaproße'tʃaðo, a]
adj (*oportunidad, tiempo*) wasted;
(*estudiante*) slack
desaprovechar [desaproße'tʃar] *vt* to
waste

desarmar [desar'mar] *vt* (MIL, *fig*) to disarm; (TEC) to take apart, dismantle; **desarme** *nm* disarmament

desarraigar [desarrai'xar] *vt* to uproot; **desarraigo** *nm* uprooting

desarreglar [desarre'xlar] *vt* (*desordenar*) to disarrange; (*trastocar*) to upset, disturb

desarreglo [desa'rreɣlo] *nm* (*de casa, persona*) untidiness; (*desorden*) disorder

desarrollar [desarro'ʎar] *vt* (*gen*) to develop; **~se** *vr* to develop; (*ocurrir*) to take place; (FOTO) to develop; **desarrollo** *nm* development

desarticular [desartiku'lar] *vt* (*hueso*) to dislocate; (*objeto*) to take apart; (*fig*) to break up

desasir [desa'sir] *vt* to loosen

desasosegar [desasose'xar] *vt* (*inquietar*) to disturb, make uneasy; **~se** *vr* to become uneasy

desasosiego *etc* [desaso'sjeɣo] *vb ver* **desasosegar** ♦ *nm* (*intranquilidad*) uneasiness, restlessness; (*ansiedad*) anxiety

desastrado, a [desas'traðo, a] *adj* (*desaliñado*) shabby; (*sucio*) dirty

desastre [de'sastre] *nm* disaster; **desastroso, a** *adj* disastrous

desatado, a [desa'taðo, a] *adj* (*desligado*) untied; (*violento*) violent, wild

desatar [desa'tar] *vt* (*nudo*) to untie; (*paquete*) to undo; (*separar*) to detach; **~se** *vr* (*zapatos*) to come untied; (*tormenta*) to break

desatascar [desatas'kar] *vt* (*cañería*) to unblock, clear

desatender [desaten'der] *vt* (*no prestar atención a*) to disregard; (*abandonar*) to neglect

desatento, a [desa'tento, a] *adj* (*distraído*) inattentive; (*descortés*) discourteous

desatinado, a [desati'naðo, a] *adj* foolish, silly; **desatino** *nm* (*idiotez*) foolishness, folly; (*error*) blunder

desatornillar [desatorni'ʎar] *vt* to unscrew

desatrancar [desatran'kar] *vt* (*puerta*) to unbolt; (*cañería*) to clear, unblock

desautorizado, a [desautori'θaðo, a] *adj* unauthorized

desautorizar [desautori'θar] *vt* (*oficial*) to deprive of authority; (*informe*) to deny

desavenencia [desaβe'nenθja] *nf* (*desacuerdo*) disagreement; (*discrepancia*) quarrel

desayunar [desaju'nar] *vi* to have breakfast ♦ *vt* to have for breakfast; **desayuno** *nm* breakfast

desazón [desa'θon] *nf* anxiety

desazonarse [desaθo'narse] *vr* to worry, be anxious

desbandarse [desβan'darse] *vr* (MIL) to disband; (*fig*) to flee in disorder

desbarajuste [desβara'xuste] *nm* confusion, disorder

desbaratar [desβara'tar] *vt* (*deshacer, destruir*) to ruin

desbloquear [desβloke'ar] *vt* (*negociaciones, tráfico*) to get going again; (COM: *cuenta*) to unfreeze

desbocado, a [desβo'kaðo, a] *adj* (*caballo*) runaway

desbordar [desβor'ðar] *vt* (*sobrepasar*) to go beyond; (*exceder*) to exceed; **~se** *vr* (*río*) to overflow; (*entusiasmo*) to erupt

descabalgar [deskaβal'xar] *vi* to dismount

descabellado, a [deskaβe'ʎaðo, a] *adj* (*disparatado*) wild, crazy

descafeinado, a [deskafei'naðo, a] *adj* decaffeinated ♦ *nm* decaffeinated coffee

descalabro [deska'laβro] *nm* blow; (*desgracia*) misfortune

descalificar [deskalifi'kar] *vt* to disqualify; (*desacreditar*) to discredit

descalzar [deskal'θar] *vt* (*zapato*) to take off; **descalzo, a** *adj* barefoot(ed)

descambiar [deskam'bjar] *vt* to exchange

descaminado, a [deskami'naðo, a] *adj* (*equivocado*) on the wrong road; (*fig*) misguided

descampado [deskam'paðo] *nm* open space

descansado, a [deskan'saðo, a] *adj* (*gen*) rested; (*que tranquiliza*) restful

descansar [deskan'sar] *vt* (*gen*) to rest
♦ *vi* to rest, have a rest; (*echarse*) to lie
down

descansillo [deskan'siʎo] *nm* (*de escalera*)
landing

descanso [des'kanso] *nm* (*reposo*) rest;
(*alivio*) relief; (*pausa*) break; (*DEPORTE*)
interval, half time

descapotable [deskapo'taβle] *nm* (*tb:*
coche ~) convertible

descarado, a [deska'raðo, a] *adj*
shameless; (*insolente*) cheeky

descarga [des'karγa] *nf* (*ARQ , ELEC, MIL*)
discharge; (*NAUT*) unloading

descargar [deskar'γar] *vt* to unload;
(*golpe*) to let fly; **~se** *vr* to unburden o.s.;
descargo *nm* (*COM*) receipt; (*JUR*)
evidence

descaro [des'karo] *nm* nerve

descarriar [deska'rrjar] *vt* (*descaminar*) to
misdirect; (*fig*) to lead astray; **~se** *vr*
(*perderse*) to lose one's way; (*separarse*) to
stray; (*pervertirse*) to err, go astray

descarrilamiento [deskarrila'mjento] *nm*
(*de tren*) derailment

descarrilar [deskarri'lar] *vi* to be derailed

descartar [deskar'tar] *vt* (*rechazar*) to
reject; (*eliminar*) to rule out; **~se** *vr*
(*NAIPES*) to discard; **~se de** to shirk

descascarillado, a [deskaskari'ʎaðo, a]
adj (*paredes*) peeling

descendencia [desθen'denθja] *nf* (*origen*)
origin, descent; (*hijos*) offspring

descender [desθen'der] *vt* (*bajar: escalera*)
to go down ♦ *vi* to descend;
(*temperatura, nivel*) to fall, drop; **~ de** to
be descended from

descendiente [desθen'djente] *nm/f*
descendant

descenso [des'θenso] *nm* descent; (*de
temperatura*) drop

descifrar [desθi'frar] *vt* to decipher;
(*mensaje*) to decode

descolgar [deskol'γar] *vt* (*bajar*) to take
down; (*teléfono*) to pick up; **~se** *vr* to let
o.s. down

descolorido, a [deskolo'riðo, a] *adj*
faded; (*pálido*) pale

descompasado, a [deskompa'saðo, a]
adj (*sin proporción*) out of all proportion;
(*excesivo*) excessive

descomponer [deskompo'ner] *vt*
(*desordenar*) to disarrange, disturb; (*TEC*)
to put out of order; (*dividir*) to break
down (into parts); (*fig*) to provoke; **~se** *vr*
(*corromperse*) to rot, decompose; (*TEC*) to
break down

descomposición [deskomposi'θjon] *nf*
(*de un objeto*) breakdown; (*de fruta etc*)
decomposition; **~ de vientre** stomach
upset, diarrhoea

descompuesto, a [deskom'pwesto, a]
adj (*corrompido*) decomposed; (*roto*)
broken

descomunal [deskomu'nal] *adj* (*enorme*)
huge

desconcertado, a [deskonθer'taðo, a]
adj disconcerted, bewildered

desconcertar [deskonθer'tar] *vt*
(*confundir*) to baffle; (*incomodar*) to upset,
put out; **~se** *vr* (*turbarse*) to be upset

desconchado, a [deskon'tʃaðo, a] *adj*
(*pintura*) peeling

desconcierto *etc* [deskon'θjerto] *vb ver*
desconcertar ♦ *nm* (*gen*) disorder;
(*desorientación*) uncertainty; (*inquietud*)
uneasiness

desconectar [deskonek'tar] *vt* to
disconnect

desconfianza [deskon'fjanθa] *nf* distrust

desconfiar [deskon'fjar] *vi* to be
distrustful; **~ de** to distrust, suspect

descongelar [deskonxe'lar] *vt* to defrost;
(*COM, POL*) to unfreeze

descongestionar [deskonxestjo'nar] *vt*
(*cabeza, tráfico*) to clear

desconocer [deskono'θer] *vt* (*ignorar*) not
to know, be ignorant of

desconocido, a [deskono'θiðo, a] *adj*
unknown ♦ *nm/f* stranger

desconocimiento [deskonoθi'mjento]
nm (*falta de conocimientos*) ignorance

desconsiderado, a [deskonsiðe'raðo, a]
adj inconsiderate; (*insensible*) thoughtless

desconsolar [deskonso'lar] *vt* to distress; **~se** *vr* to despair

desconsuelo *etc* [deskon'swelo] *vb ver* **desconsolar** ♦ *nm* (*tristeza*) distress; (*desesperación*) despair

descontado, a [deskon'taðo, a] *adj*: **dar por ~ (que)** to take (it) for granted (that)

descontar [deskon'tar] *vt* (*deducir*) to take away, deduct; (*rebajar*) to discount

descontento, a [deskon'tento, a] *adj* dissatisfied ♦ *nm* dissatisfaction, discontent

descorazonar [deskoraθo'nar] *vt* to discourage, dishearten

descorchar [deskor'tʃar] *vt* to uncork

descorrer [desko'rrer] *vt* (*cortinas, cerrojo*) to draw back

descortés [deskor'tes] *adj* (*mal educado*) discourteous; (*grosero*) rude

descoser [desko'ser] *vt* to unstitch; **~se** *vr* to come apart (at the seams)

descosido, a [desko'siðo, a] *adj* (*COSTURA*) unstitched

descrédito [des'kreðito] *nm* discredit

descreído, a [deskre'iðo, a] *adj* (*incrédulo*) incredulous; (*falto de fe*) unbelieving

descremado, a [deskre'maðo, a] *adj* skimmed

describir [deskri'ßir] *vt* to describe; **descripción** [deskrip'θjon] *nf* description

descrito [des'krito] *pp de* **describir**

descuartizar [deskwarti'θar] *vt* (*animal*) to cut up

descubierto, a [desku'ßjerto, a] *pp de* **descubrir** ♦ *adj* uncovered, bare; (*persona*) bareheaded ♦ *nm* (*bancario*) overdraft; **al ~** in the open

descubrimiento [deskußri'mjento] *nm* (*hallazgo*) discovery; (*revelación*) revelation

descubrir [desku'ßrir] *vt* to discover, find; (*inaugurar*) to unveil; (*vislumbrar*) to detect; (*revelar*) to reveal, show; (*destapar*) to uncover; **~se** *vr* to reveal o.s.; (*quitarse sombrero*) to take off one's hat; (*confesar*) to confess

descuento *etc* [des'kwento] *vb ver*

descontar ♦ *nm* discount

descuidado, a [deskwi'ðaðo, a] *adj* (*sin cuidado*) careless; (*desordenado*) untidy; (*olvidadizo*) forgetful; (*dejado*) neglected; (*desprevenido*) unprepared

descuidar [deskwi'ðar] *vt* (*dejar*) to neglect; (*olvidar*) to overlook; **~se** *vr* (*distraerse*) to be careless; (*abandonarse*) to let o.s. go; (*desprevenirse*) to drop one's guard; **¡descuida!** don't worry!; **descuido** *nm* (*dejadez*) carelessness; (*olvido*) negligence

---

PALABRA CLAVE

---

desde ['desðe] *prep* **1** (*lugar*) from; **~ Burgos hasta mi casa hay 30 km** it's 30 kms from Burgos to my house

2 (*posición*): **hablaba ~ el balcón** she was speaking from the balcony

3 (*tiempo*: +*adv, n*): **~ ahora** from now on; **~ la boda** since the wedding; **~ niño** since I *etc* was a child; **~ 3 años atrás** since 3 years ago

4 (*tiempo*: +*vb, fecha*) since; for; **nos conocemos ~ 1992/ ~ hace 20 años** we've known each other since 1992/for 20 years; **no le veo ~ 1997/~ hace 5 años** I haven't seen him since 1997/for 5 years

5 (*gama*): **~ los más lujosos hasta los más económicos** from the most luxurious to the most reasonably priced

6: **~ luego (que no)** of course (not)

♦ *conj*: **~ que**: **~ que recuerdo** for as long as I can remember; **~ que llegó no ha salido** he hasn't been out since he arrived

---

desdecirse [desðe'θirse] *vr* to retract; **~ de** to go back on

desdén [des'ðen] *nm* scorn

desdeñar [desðe'ɲar] *vt* (*despreciar*) to scorn

desdicha [des'ðitʃa] *nf* (*desgracia*) misfortune; (*infelicidad*) unhappiness; **desdichado, a** *adj* (*sin suerte*) unlucky; (*infeliz*) unhappy

desdoblar [desðo'ßlar] *vt* (*extender*) to spread out; (*desplegar*) to unfold

desear [dese'ar] *vt* to want, desire, wish for

desecar [dese'kar] *vt* to dry up; **~se** *vr* to dry up

desechar [dese'tʃar] *vt* (*basura*) to throw out *o* away; (*ideas*) to reject, discard; **desechos** *nmpl* rubbish *sg*, waste *sg*

desembalar [desemba'lar] *vt* to unpack

desembarazar [desembara'θar] *vt* (*desocupar*) to clear; (*desenredar*) to free; **~se** *vr*: **~se de** to free o.s. of, get rid of

desembarcar [desembar'kar] *vt* (*mercancías etc*) to unload ♦ *vi* to disembark; **~se** *vr* to disembark

desembocadura [desemboka'ðura] *nf* (*de río*) mouth; (*de calle*) opening

desembocar [desembo'kar] *vi* (*río*) to flow into; (*fig*) to result in

desembolso [desem'bolso] *nm* payment

desembragar [desembra'var] *vi* to declutch

desembrollar [desembro'ʎar] *vt* (*madeja*) to unravel; (*asunto, malentendido*) to sort out

desemejanza [deseme'xanθa] *nf* dissimilarity

desempaquetar [desempake'tar] *vt* (*regalo*) to unwrap; (*mercancía*) to unpack

desempatar [desempa'tar] *vi* to replay, hold a play-off; **desempate** *nm* (*FÚTBOL*) replay, play-off; (*TENIS*) tie-break(er)

desempeñar [desempe'ɲar] *vt* (*cargo*) to hold; (*papel*) to perform; (*lo empeñado*) to redeem; **~ un papel** (*fig*) to play (a role)

desempeño [desem'peɲo] *nm* redeeming; (*de cargo*) occupation

desempleado, a [desemple'aðo, a] *nm/f* unemployed person; **desempleo** *nm* unemployment

desempolvar [desempol'ßar] *vt* (*muebles etc*) to dust; (*lo olvidado*) to revive

desencadenar [desenkaðe'nar] *vt* to unchain; (*ira*) to unleash; **~se** *vr* to break loose; (*tormenta*) to burst; (*guerra*) to break out

desencajar [desenka'xar] *vt* (*hueso*) to dislocate; (*mecanismo, pieza*) to disconnect, disengage

desencanto [desen'kanto] *nm* disillusionment

desenchufar [desentʃu'far] *vt* to unplug

desenfadado, a [desenfa'ðaðo, a] *adj* (*desenvuelto*) uninhibited; (*descarado*) forward; **desenfado** *nm* (*libertad*) freedom; (*comportamiento*) free and easy manner; (*descaro*) forwardness

desenfocado, a [desenfo'kaðo, a] *adj* (*FOTO*) out of focus

desenfrenado, a [desenfre'naðo, a] *adj* (*descontrolado*) uncontrolled; (*inmoderado*) unbridled; **desenfreno** *nm* wildness; (*de las pasiones*) lack of self-control

desenganchar [desengan'tʃar] *vt* (*gen*) to unhook; (*FERRO*) to uncouple

desengañar [desenga'ɲar] *vt* to disillusion; **~se** *vr* to become disillusioned; **desengaño** *nm* disillusionment; (*decepción*) disappointment

desenlace [desen'laθe] *nm* outcome

desenmarañar [desenmara'ɲar] *vt* (*fig*) to unravel

desenmascarar [desenmaska'rar] *vt* to unmask

desenredar [desenre'ðar] *vt* (*pelo*) to untangle; (*problema*) to sort out

desenroscar [desenros'kar] *vt* to unscrew

desentenderse [desenten'derse] *vr*: **~ de** to pretend not to know about; (*apartarse*) to have nothing to do with

desenterrar [desente'rrar] *vt* to exhume; (*tesoro, fig*) to unearth, dig up

desentonar [desento'nar] *vi* (*MUS*) to sing (*o* play) out of tune; (*color*) to clash

desentrañar [desentra'ɲar] *vt* (*misterio*) to unravel

desentumecer [desentume'θer] *vt* (*pierna etc*) to stretch

desenvoltura [desenßol'tura] *nf* ease

desenvolver [desenßol'ßer] *vt* (*paquete*) to unwrap; (*fig*) to develop; **~se** *vr* (*desarrollarse*) to unfold, develop;

(*arreglárselas*) to cope

deseo [de'seo] *nm* desire, wish; **~so, a** *adj*: **estar ~so de** to be anxious to

desequilibrado, a [desekili'ßraðo, a] *adj* unbalanced

desertar [deser'tar] *vi* to desert

desértico, a [de'sertiko, a] *adj* desert *cpd*

desesperación [desespera'θjon] *nf* (*impaciencia*) desperation, despair; (*irritación*) fury

desesperar [desespe'rar] *vt* to drive to despair; (*exasperar*) to drive to distraction ♦ *vi*: **~ de** to despair of; **~se** *vr* to despair, lose hope

desestabilizar [desestaßili'θar] *vt* to destabilize

desestimar [desesti'mar] *vt* (*menospreciar*) to have a low opinion of; (*rechazar*) to reject

desfachatez [desfatʃa'teθ] *nf* (*insolencia*) impudence; (*descaro*) rudeness

desfalco [des'falko] *nm* embezzlement

desfallecer [desfaʎe'θer] *vi* (*perder las fuerzas*) to become weak; (*desvanecerse*) to faint

desfasado, a [desfa'saðo, a] *adj* (*anticuado*) old-fashioned; **desfase** *nm* (*diferencia*) gap

desfavorable [desfaßo'raßle] *adj* unfavourable

desfigurar [desfiɣu'rar] *vt* (*cara*) to disfigure; (*cuerpo*) to deform

desfiladero [desfila'ðero] *nm* gorge

desfilar [desfi'lar] *vi* to parade; **desfile** *nm* procession

desfogarse [desfo'ɣarse] *vr* (*fig*) to let off steam

desgajar [desɣa'xar] *vt* (*arrancar*) to tear off; (*romper*) to break off; **~se** *vr* to come off

desgana [des'ɣana] *nf* (*falta de apetito*) loss of appetite; (*apatía*) unwillingness; **~do, a** *adj*: **estar ~do** (*sin apetito*) to have no appetite; (*sin entusiasmo*) to have lost interest

desgarrador, a [desɣarra'ðor, a] *adj* (*fig*) heartrending

desgarrar [desɣa'rrar] *vt* to tear (up); (*fig*) to shatter; **desgarro** *nm* (*en tela*) tear; (*aflicción*) grief

desgastar [desɣas'tar] *vt* (*deteriorar*) to wear away *o* down; (*estropear*) to spoil; **~se** *vr* to get worn out; **desgaste** *nm* wear (and tear)

desglosar [desɣlo'sar] *vt* (*factura*) to break down

desgracia [des'ɣraθja] *nf* misfortune; (*accidente*) accident; (*vergüenza*) disgrace; (*contratiempo*) setback; **por ~** unfortunately

desgraciado, a [desɣra'θjaðo, a] *adj* (*sin suerte*) unlucky, unfortunate; (*miserable*) wretched; (*infeliz*) miserable

desgravación [desɣraßa'θjon] *nf* (COM): **~ fiscal** tax relief

desgravar [desɣra'ßar] *vt* (*impuestos*) to reduce the tax *o* duty on

deshabitado, a [desaßi'taðo, a] *adj* uninhabited

deshacer [desa'θer] *vt* (*casa*) to break up; (TEC) to take apart; (*enemigo*) to defeat; (*diluir*) to melt; (*contrato*) to break; (*intriga*) to solve; **~se** *vr* (*disolverse*) to melt; (*despedazarse*) to come apart *o* undone; **~se de** to get rid of; **~se en lágrimas** to burst into tears

desharrapado, a [desarra'paðo, a] *adj* (*persona*) shabby

deshecho, a [des'etʃo, a] *adj* undone; (*roto*) smashed; (*persona*): **estar ~** to be shattered

desheredar [desere'ðar] *vt* to disinherit

deshidratar [desiðra'tar] *vt* to dehydrate

deshielo [des'jelo] *nm* thaw

deshonesto, a [deso'nesto, a] *adj* indecent

deshonra [des'onra] *nf* (*deshonor*) dishonour; (*vergüenza*) shame

deshora [des'ora]: **a ~** *adv* at the wrong time

deshuesar [deswe'sar] *vt* (*carne*) to bone; (*fruta*) to stone

desierto, a [de'sjerto, a] *adj* (*casa, calle, negocio*) deserted ♦ *nm* desert

designar [desiɣ'nar] *vt* (*nombrar*) to designate; (*indicar*) to fix

designio [de'siɣnjo] *nm* plan

desigual [desi'ɣwal] *adj* (*terreno*) uneven; (*lucha etc*) unequal

desilusión [desilu'sjon] *nf* disillusionment; (*decepción*) disappointment; **desilusionar** *vt* to disillusion; to disappoint; **desilusionarse** *vr* to become disillusioned

desinfectar [desinfek'tar] *vt* to disinfect

desinflar [desin'flar] *vt* to deflate

desintegración [desinteɣra'θjon] *nf* disintegration

desinterés [desinte'res] *nm* (*desgana*) lack of interest; (*altruismo*) unselfishness

desintoxicarse [desintoksi'karse] *vr* (*drogadicto*) to undergo detoxification

desistir [desis'tir] *vi* (*renunciar*) to stop, desist

desleal [desle'al] *adj* (*infiel*) disloyal; (*COM: competencia*) unfair; ~**tad** *nf* disloyalty

desleír [desle'ir] *vt* (*líquido*) to dilute; (*sólido*) to dissolve

deslenguado, a [deslen'gwaðo, a] *adj* (*grosero*) foul-mouthed

desligar [desli'ɣar] *vt* (*desatar*) to untie, undo; (*separar*) to separate; ~**se** *vr* (*de un compromiso*) to extricate o.s.

desliz [des'liθ] *nm* (*fig*) lapse; ~**ar** *vt* to slip, slide

deslucido, a [deslu'θiðo, a] *adj* dull; (*torpe*) awkward, graceless; (*deslustrado*) tarnished

deslumbrar [deslum'brar] *vt* to dazzle

desmadrarse [desma'ðrarse] (*fam*) *vr* (*descontrolarse*) to run wild; (*divertirse*) to let one's hair down; **desmadre** (*fam*) *nm* (*desorganización*) chaos; (*jaleo*) commotion

desmán [des'man] *nm* (*exceso*) outrage; (*abuso de poder*) abuse

desmandarse [desman'darse] *vr* (*portarse mal*) to behave badly; (*excederse*) to get out of hand; (*caballo*) to bolt

desmantelar [desmante'lar] *vt* (*deshacer*) to dismantle; (*casa*) to strip

desmaquillador [desmaki'ʎa'ðor] *nm* make-up remover

desmayar [desma'jar] *vi* to lose heart; ~**se** *vr* (*MED*) to faint; **desmayo** *nm* (*MED: acto*) faint; (: *estado*) unconsciousness

desmedido, a [desme'ðiðo, a] *adj* excessive

desmejorar [desmexo'rar] *vt* (*dañar*) to impair, spoil; (*MED*) to weaken

desmembrar [desmem'brar] *vt* (*MED*) to dismember; (*fig*) to separate

desmemoriado, a [desmemo'rjaðo, a] *adj* forgetful

desmentir [desmen'tir] *vt* (*contradecir*) to contradict; (*refutar*) to deny

desmenuzar [desmenu'θar] *vt* (*deshacer*) to crumble; (*carne*) to chop; (*examinar*) to examine closely

desmerecer [desmere'θer] *vt* to be unworthy of ♦ *vi* (*deteriorarse*) to deteriorate

desmesurado, a [desmesu'raðo, a] *adj* disproportionate

desmontable [desmon'taβle] *adj* (*que se quita: pieza*) detachable; (*que se puede plegar etc*) collapsible; folding

desmontar [desmon'tar] *vt* (*deshacer*) to dismantle; (*tierra*) to level ♦ *vi* to dismount

desmoralizar [desmorali'θar] *vt* to demoralize

desmoronar [desmoro'nar] *vt* to wear away, erode; ~**se** *vr* (*edificio, dique*) to collapse; (*economía*) to decline

desnatado, a [desna'taðo, a] *adj* skimmed

desnivel [desni'βel] *nm* (*de terreno*) unevenness

desnudar [desnu'ðar] *vt* (*desvestir*) to undress; (*despojar*) to strip; ~**se** *vr* (*desvestirse*) to get undressed; **desnudo, a** *adj* naked ♦ *nm/f* nude; **desnudo de** devoid *o* bereft of

desnutrición [desnutri'θjon] *nf* malnutrition; **desnutrido, a** *adj* undernourished

desobedecer [desoβeðe'θer] *vt, vi* to disobey; **desobediencia** *nf* disobedience

desocupado, a [desoku'paðo, a] *adj* at leisure; (*desempleado*) unemployed; (*deshabitado*) empty, vacant

desocupar [desoku'par] *vt* to vacate

desodorante [desoðo'rante] *nm* deodorant

desolación [desola'θjon] *nf* (*de lugar*) desolation; (*fig*) grief

desolar [deso'lar] *vt* to ruin, lay waste

desorbitado, a [desorβi'taðo, a] *adj* (*excesivo: ambición*) boundless; (*deseos*) excessive; (*: precio*) exorbitant

desorden [des'orðen] *nm* confusion; (*político*) disorder, unrest

desorganizar [desorɣani'θar] *vt* (*desordenar*) to disorganize; **desorganización** *nf* (*de persona*) disorganization; (*en empresa, oficina*) disorder, chaos

desorientar [desorjen'tar] *vt* (*extraviar*) to mislead; (*confundir, desconcertar*) to confuse; **~se** *vr* (*perderse*) to lose one's way

despabilado, a [despaβi'laðo, a] *adj* (*despierto*) wide-awake; (*fig*) alert, sharp

despabilar [despaβi'lar] *vt* (*el ingenio*) to sharpen ♦ *vi* to wake up; (*fig*) to get a move on; **~se** *vr* to wake up; to get a move on

despachar [despa'tʃar] *vt* (*negocio*) to do, complete; (*enviar*) to send, dispatch; (*vender*) to sell, deal in; (*billete*) to issue; (*mandar ir*) to send away

despacho [des'patʃo] *nm* (*oficina*) office; (*de paquetes*) dispatch; (*venta*) sale; (*comunicación*) message

despacio [des'paθjo] *adv* slowly

desparpajo [despar'paxo] *nm* self-confidence; (*pey*) nerve

desparramar [desparra'mar] *vt* (*esparcir*) to scatter; (*líquido*) to spill

despavorido, a [despaβo'riðo, a] *adj* terrified

despecho [des'petʃo] *nm* spite; **a ~ de** in spite of

despectivo, a [despek'tiβo, a] *adj* (*despreciativo*) derogatory; (*LING*) pejorative

despedazar [despeða'θar] *vt* to tear to pieces

despedida [despe'ðiða] *nf* (*adiós*) farewell; (*de obrero*) sacking

despedir [despe'ðir] *vt* (*visita*) to see off, show out; (*empleado*) to dismiss; (*inquilino*) to evict; (*objeto*) to hurl; (*olor etc*) to give out *o* off; **~se** *vr*: **~se de** to say goodbye to

despegar [despe'ɣar] *vt* to unstick ♦ *vi* (*avión*) to take off; **~se** *vr* to come loose, come unstuck; **despego** *nm* detachment

despegue *etc* [des'peɣe] *vb ver* **despegar** ♦ *nm* takeoff

despeinado, a [despei'naðo, a] *adj* dishevelled, unkempt

despejado, a [despe'xaðo, a] *adj* (*lugar*) clear, free; (*cielo*) clear; (*persona*) wide-awake, bright

despejar [despe'xar] *vt* (*gen*) to clear; (*misterio*) to clear up ♦ *vi* (*el tiempo*) to clear; **~se** *vr* (*tiempo, cielo*) to clear (up); (*misterio*) to become clearer; (*cabeza*) to clear

despellejar [despeʎe'xar] *vt* (*animal*) to skin

despensa [des'pensa] *nf* larder

despeñadero [despeɲa'ðero] *nm* (*GEO*) cliff, precipice

despeñarse [despe'ɲarse] *vr* to hurl o.s. down; (*coche*) to tumble over

desperdicio [desper'ðiθjo] *nm* (*despilfarro*) squandering; **~s** *nmpl* (*basura*) rubbish *sg* (BRIT), garbage *sg* (US); (*residuos*) waste *sg*

desperdigarse [desperði'xarse] *vr* (*rebaño, familia*) to scatter, spread out; (*granos de arroz, semillas*) to scatter

desperezarse [despere'θarse] *vr* to stretch

desperfecto [desper'fekto] *nm* (*deterioro*) slight damage; (*defecto*) flaw, imperfection

despertador [desperta'ðor] *nm* alarm clock

despertar [desper'tar] *nm* awakening ♦ *vt* (*persona*) to wake up; (*recuerdos*) to revive; (*sentimiento*) to arouse ♦ *vi* to awaken, wake up; **~se** *vr* to awaken, wake up

despiadado, a [despja'ðaðo, a] *adj* (*ataque*) merciless; (*persona*) heartless

despido *etc* [des'piðo] *vb ver* **despedir** ♦ *nm* dismissal, sacking

despierto, a *etc* [des'pjerto, a] *vb ver* **despertar** ♦ *adj* awake; (*fig*) sharp, alert

despilfarro [despil'farro] *nm* (*derroche*) squandering; (*lujo desmedido*) extravagance

despistar [despis'tar] *vt* to throw off the track *o* scent; (*confundir*) to mislead, confuse; **~se** *vr* to take the wrong road; (*confundirse*) to become confused

despiste [des'piste] *nm* absent-mindedness; **un ~** a mistake, slip

desplazamiento [desplaθa'mjento] *nm* displacement

desplazar [despla'θar] *vt* to move; (*NAUT*) to displace; (*INFORM*) to scroll; (*fig*) to oust; **~se** *vr* (*persona*) to travel

desplegar [desple'ɣar] *vt* (*tela, papel*) to unfold, open out; (*bandera*) to unfurl; **despliegue** *etc* [des'pleɣe] *vb ver* **desplegar** ♦ *nm* display

desplomarse [desplo'marse] *vr* (*edificio, gobierno, persona*) to collapse

desplumar [desplu'mar] *vt* (*ave*) to pluck; (*fam: estafar*) to fleece

despoblado, a [despo'ßlaðo, a] *adj* (*sin habitantes*) uninhabited

despojar [despo'xar] *vt* (*alguien: de sus bienes*) to divest of, deprive of; (*casa*) to strip, leave bare; (*alguien: de su cargo*) to strip of

despojo [des'poxo] *nm* (*acto*) plundering; (*objetos*) plunder, loot; **~s** *nmpl* (*de ave, res*) offal *sg*

desposado, a [despo'saðo, a] *adj, nm/f* newly-wed

desposar [despo'sar] *vt* to marry; **~se** *vr* to get married

desposeer [despose'er] *vt*: **~ a uno de** (*puesto, autoridad*) to strip sb of

déspota ['despota] *nm/f* despot

despreciar [despre'θjar] *vt* (*desdeñar*) to despise, scorn; (*afrentar*) to slight; **desprecio** *nm* scorn, contempt; slight

desprender [despren'der] *vt* (*broche*) to unfasten; (*olor*) to give off; **~se** *vr* (*botón: caerse*) to fall off; (*broche*) to come unfastened; (*olor, perfume*) to be given off; **~se de algo que ...** to draw from sth that ...

desprendimiento [desprendi'mjento] *nm* (*gen*) loosening; (*generosidad*) disinterestedness; (*de tierra, rocas*) landslide

despreocupado, a [despreoku'paðo, a] *adj* (*sin preocupación*) unworried, nonchalant; (*negligente*) careless

despreocuparse [despreoku'parse] *vr* not to worry; **~ de** to have no interest in

desprestigiar [despresti'xjar] *vt* (*criticar*) to run down; (*desacreditar*) to discredit

desprevenido, a [despreße'niðo, a] *adj* (*no preparado*) unprepared, unready

desproporcionado, a [desproporθjo'naðo, a] *adj* disproportionate, out of proportion

desprovisto, a [despro'ßisto, a] *adj*: **~ de** devoid of

después [des'pwes] *adv* afterwards, later; (*próximo paso*) next; **~ de comer** after lunch; **un año ~** a year later; **~ se debatió el tema** next the matter was discussed; **~ de corregido el texto** after the text had been corrected; **~ de todo** after all

desquiciado, a [deski'θjaðo, a] *adj* deranged

desquite [des'kite] *nm* (*satisfacción*) satisfaction; (*venganza*) revenge

destacar [desta'kar] *vt* to emphasize, point up; (*MIL*) to detach, detail ♦ *vi* (*resaltarse*) to stand out; (*persona*) to be outstanding *o* exceptional; **~se** *vr* to stand out; to be outstanding *o* exceptional

destajo [des'taxo] *nm*: **trabajar a ~** to do piecework

destapar [desta'par] *vt* (*botella*) to open; (*cacerola*) to take the lid off; (*descubrir*) to uncover; **~se** *vr* (*revelarse*) to reveal one's true character

destartalado, a [destarta'laðo, a] *adj* (*desordenado*) untidy; (*ruinoso*) tumbledown

destello [des'teʎo] *nm* (*de estrella*) twinkle; (*de faro*) signal light

destemplado, a [destem'plaðo, a] *adj* (*MUS*) out of tune; (*voz*) harsh; (*MED*) out of sorts; (*tiempo*) unpleasant, nasty

desteñir [deste'ɲir] *vt* to fade ♦ *vi* to fade; **~se** *vr* to fade; **esta tela no destiñe** this fabric will not run

desternillarse [desterni'ʎarse] *vr*: **~ de risa** to split one's sides laughing

desterrar [deste'rrar] *vt* (*exilar*) to exile; (*fig*) to banish, dismiss

destiempo [des'tjempo]: **a ~** *adv* out of turn

destierro *etc* [des'tjerro] *vb ver* **desterrar** ♦ *nm* exile

destilar [desti'lar] *vt* to distil; **destilería** *nf* distillery

destinar [desti'nar] *vt* (*funcionario*) to appoint, assign; (*fondos*) **~ (a)** to set aside (for)

destinatario, a [destina'tarjo, a] *nm/f* addressee

destino [des'tino] *nm* (*suerte*) destiny; (*de avión, viajero*) destination

destituir [destitu'ir] *vt* to dismiss

destornillador [destorniʎa'ðor] *nm* screwdriver

destornillar [destorni'ʎar] *vt* (*tornillo*) to unscrew; **~se** *vr* to unscrew

destreza [des'treθa] *nf* (*habilidad*) skill; (*maña*) dexterity

destrozar [destro'θar] *vt* (*romper*) to smash, break (up); (*estropear*) to ruin; (*nervios*) to shatter

destrozo [des'troθo] *nm* (*acción*)

destruction; (*desastre*) smashing; **~s** *nmpl* (*pedazos*) pieces; (*daños*) havoc *sg*

destrucción [destruk'θjon] *nf* destruction

destruir [destru'ir] *vt* to destroy

desuso [des'uso] *nm* disuse; **caer en ~** to become obsolete

desvalido, a [desβa'liðo, a] *adj* (*desprotegido*) destitute; (*sin fuerzas*) helpless

desvalijar [desβali'xar] *vt* (*persona*) to rob; (*casa, tienda*) to burgle; (*coche*) to break into

desván [des'βan] *nm* attic

desvanecer [desβane'θer] *vt* (*disipar*) to dispel; (*borrar*) to blur; **~se** *vr* (*humo etc*) to vanish, disappear; (*color*) to fade; (*recuerdo, sonido*) to fade away; (*MED*) to pass out; (*duda*) to be dispelled

desvanecimiento [desβaneθi'mjento] *nm* (*desaparición*) disappearance; (*de colores*) fading; (*evaporación*) evaporation; (*MED*) fainting fit

desvariar [desβa'rjar] *vi* (*enfermo*) to be delirious; **desvarío** *nm* delirium

desvelar [desβe'lar] *vt* to keep awake; **~se** *vr* (*no poder dormir*) to stay awake; (*preocuparse*) to be vigilant *o* watchful

desvelos [des'βelos] *nmpl* worrying *sg*

desvencijado, a [desβenθi'xaðo, a] *adj* (*silla*) rickety; (*máquina*) broken-down

desventaja [desβen'taxa] *nf* disadvantage

desventura [desβen'tura] *nf* misfortune

desvergonzado, a [desβerɣon'θaðo, a] *adj* shameless

desvergüenza [desβer'ɣwenθa] *nf* (*descaro*) shamelessness; (*insolencia*) impudence; (*mala conducta*) effrontery

desvestir [desβes'tir] *vt* to undress; **~se** *vr* to undress

desviación [desβja'θjon] *nf* deviation; (*AUTO*) diversion, detour

desviar [des'βjar] *vt* to turn aside; (*río*) to alter the course of; (*navío*) to divert, re-route; (*conversación*) to sidetrack; **~se** *vr* (*apartarse del camino*) to turn aside; (: *barco*) to go off course

desvío *etc* [des'βio] *vb ver* **desviar** ♦ *nm*

(*desviación*) detour, diversion; (*fig*) indifference

desvirtuar [desßir'twar] *vt* to distort

desvivirse [desßi'ßirse] *vr*: **~ por** (*anhelar*) to long for, crave for; (*hacer lo posible por*) to do one's utmost for

detallar [deta'ʎar] *vt* to detail

detalle [de'taʎe] *nm* detail; (*gesto*) gesture, token; **al ~** in detail; (*COM*) retail

detallista [deta'ʎista] *nm/f* (*COM*) retailer

detective [detek'tiße] *nm/f* detective

detener [dete'ner] *vt* (*gen*) to stop; (*JUR*) to arrest; (*objeto*) to keep; **~se** *vr* to stop; (*demorarse*): **~se en** to delay over, linger over

detenidamente [deteniða'mente] *adv* (*minuciosamente*) carefully; (*extensamente*) at great length

detenido, a [dete'niðo, a] *adj* (*arrestado*) under arrest ♦ *nm/f* person under arrest, prisoner

detenimiento [deteni'mjento] *nm*: **con ~** thoroughly; (*observar, considerar*) carefully

detergente [deter'xente] *nm* detergent

deteriorar [deterjo'rar] *vt* to spoil, damage; **~se** *vr* to deteriorate; **deterioro** *nm* deterioration

determinación [determina'θjon] *nf* (*empeño*) determination; (*decisión*) decision; **determinado, a** *adj* specific

determinar [determi'nar] *vt* (*plazo*) to fix; (*precio*) to settle; **~se** *vr* to decide

detestar [detes'tar] *vt* to detest

detractor, a [detrak'tor, a] *nm/f* slanderer, libeller

detrás [de'tras] *adv* behind; (*atrás*) at the back; **~ de** behind

detrimento [detri'mento] *nm*: **en ~ de** to the detriment of

deuda ['deuða] *nf* debt

devaluación [deßalwa'θjon] *nf* devaluation

devastar [deßas'tar] *vt* (*destruir*) to devastate

devoción [deßo'θjon] *nf* devotion

devolución [deßolu'θjon] *nf* (*reenvío*) return, sending back; (*reembolso*) repayment; (*JUR*) devolution

devolver [deßol'ßer] *vt* to return; (*lo extraviado, lo prestado*) to give back; (*carta al correo*) to send back; (*COM*) to repay, refund ♦ *vi* (*vomitar*) to be sick

devorar [deßo'rar] *vt* to devour

devoto, a [de'ßoto, a] *adj* devout ♦ *nm/f* admirer

devuelto *pp de* **devolver**

devuelva *etc vb ver* **devolver**

di *vb ver* **dar; decir**

día ['dia] *nm* day; **¿qué ~ es?** what's the date?; **estar/poner al ~** to be/keep up to date; **el ~ de hoy/de mañana** today/ tomorrow; **al ~ siguiente** (on) the following day; **vivir al ~** to live from hand to mouth; **de ~** by day, in daylight; **en pleno ~** in full daylight; **D~ de Reyes** Epiphany; **~ festivo** (*ESP*) *o* **feriado** (*AM*) holiday; **~ libre** day off

diabetes [dja'ßetes] *nf* diabetes

diablo ['djaßlo] *nm* devil; **diablura** *nf* prank

diadema [dja'ðema] *nf* tiara

diafragma [dja'fraɣma] *nm* diaphragm

diagnosis [djaɣ'nosis] *nf inv* diagnosis

diagnóstico [djaɣ'nostiko] *nm* = **diagnosis**

diagonal [djaɣo'nal] *adj* diagonal

diagrama [dja'ɣrama] *nm* diagram; **~ de flujo** flowchart

dial [djal] *nm* dial

dialecto [dja'lekto] *nm* dialect

dialogar [djalo'ɣar] *vi*: **~ con** (*POL*) to hold talks with

diálogo ['djaloɣo] *nm* dialogue

diamante [dja'mante] *nm* diamond

diana ['djana] *nf* (*MIL*) reveille; (*de blanco*) centre, bull's-eye

diapositiva [djaposi'tißa] *nf* (*FOTO*) slide, transparency

diario, a ['djarjo, a] *adj* daily ♦ *nm* newspaper; **a ~** daily; **de ~** everyday

diarrea [dja'rrea] *nf* diarrhoea

dibujar [dißu'xar] *vt* to draw, sketch; **dibujo** *nm* drawing; **dibujos animados** cartoons

diccionario [dikθjo'narjo] *nm* dictionary
dice *etc vb ver* **decir**
dicho, a ['ditʃo, a] *pp de* **decir** ♦ *adj:* **en ~s países** in the aforementioned countries ♦ *nm* saying
dichoso, a [di'tʃoso, a] *adj* happy
diciembre [di'θjembre] *nm* December
dictado [dik'taðo] *nm* dictation
dictador [dikta'ðor] *nm* dictator; **dictadura** *nf* dictatorship
dictamen [dik'tamen] *nm* (*opinión*) opinion; (*juicio*) judgment; (*informe*) report
dictar [dik'tar] *vt* (*carta*) to dictate; (*JUR: sentencia*) to pronounce; (*decreto*) to issue; (*AM: clase*) to give
didáctico, a [di'ðaktiko, a] *adj* educational
diecinueve [djeθi'nweße] *num* nineteen
dieciocho [djeθi'otʃo] *num* eighteen
dieciséis [djeθi'seis] *num* sixteen
diecisiete [djeθi'sjete] *num* seventeen
diente ['djente] *nm* (*ANAT, TEC*) tooth; (*ZOOL*) fang; (: *de elefante*) tusk; (*de ajo*) clove; **hablar entre ~s** to mutter, mumble
diera *etc vb ver* **dar**
diesel ['disel] *adj:* **motor ~** diesel engine
diestro, a ['djestro, a] *adj* (*derecho*) right; (*hábil*) skilful
dieta ['djeta] *nf* diet; **dietética** *nf:* **tienda de dietética** health food shop; **dietético, a** *adj* diet (*atr*), dietary
diez [djeθ] *num* ten
diezmar [djeθ'mar] *vt* (*población*) to decimate
difamar [difa'mar] *vt* (*JUR: hablando*) to slander; (: *por escrito*) to libel
diferencia [dife'renθja] *nf* difference; **diferenciar** *vt* to differentiate between ♦ *vi* to differ; **diferenciarse** *vr* to differ, be different; (*distinguirse*) to distinguish o.s.
diferente [dife'rente] *adj* different
diferido [dife'riðo] *nm:* **en ~** (*TV etc*) recorded
difícil [di'fiθil] *adj* difficult

dificultad [difikul'taθ] *nf* difficulty; (*problema*) trouble
dificultar [difikul'tar] *vt* (*complicar*) to complicate, make difficult; (*estorbar*) to obstruct
difteria [dif'terja] *nf* diphtheria
difundir [difun'dir] *vt* (*calor, luz*) to diffuse; (*RADIO, TV*) to broadcast; **~ una noticia** to spread a piece of news; **~se** *vr* to spread (out)
difunto, a [di'funto, a] *adj* dead, deceased ♦ *nm/f* deceased (person)
difusión [difu'sjon] *nf* (*RADIO, TV*) broadcasting
diga *etc vb ver* **decir**
digerir [dixe'rir] *vt* to digest; (*fig*) to absorb; **digestión** *nf* digestion; **digestivo, a** *adj* digestive
digital [dixi'tal] *adj* digital
dignarse [div'narse] *vr* to deign to
dignatario, a [diɣna'tarjo, a] *nm/f* dignitary
dignidad [diɣni'ðað] *nf* dignity
digno, a ['diɣno, a] *adj* worthy
digo *etc vb ver* **decir**
dije *etc vb ver* **decir**
dilapidar [dilapi'ðar] *vt* (*dinero, herencia*) to squander, waste
dilatar [dila'tar] *vt* (*cuerpo*) to dilate; (*prolongar*) to prolong
dilema [di'lema] *nm* dilemma
diligencia [dili'xenθja] *nf* diligence; (*ocupación*) errand, job; **~s** *nfpl* (*JUR*) formalities; **diligente** *adj* diligent
diluir [dilu'ir] *vt* to dilute
diluvio [di'lußjo] *nm* deluge, flood
dimensión [dimen'sjon] *nf* dimension
diminuto, a [dimi'nuto, a] *adj* tiny, diminutive
dimitir [dimi'tir] *vi* to resign
dimos *vb ver* **dar**
Dinamarca [dina'marka] *nf* Denmark
dinámico, a [di'namiko, a] *adj* dynamic
dinamita [dina'mita] *nf* dynamite
dínamo ['dinamo] *nf* dynamo
dineral [dine'ral] *nm* large sum of money, fortune

dinero [di'nero] *nm* money; ~ **contante, ~ efectivo** (ready) cash; ~ **suelto** (loose) change

dio *vb ver* **dar**

dios [djos] *nm* god; **¡D~ mío!** (oh,) my God!

diosa ['djosa] *nf* goddess

diploma [di'ploma] *nm* diploma

diplomacia [diplo'maθja] *nf* diplomacy; (*fig*) tact

diplomado, a [diplo'maðo, a] *adj* qualified

diplomático, a [diplo'matiko, a] *adj* diplomatic ♦ *nm/f* diplomat

diputación [diputa'θjon] *nf* (*tb:* ~ **provincial**) ≈ county council

diputado, a [dipu'taðo, a] *nm/f* delegate; (*POL*) ≈ member of parliament (*BRIT*), ≈ representative (*US*)

dique ['dike] *nm* dyke

diré *etc vb ver* **decir**

dirección [direk'θjon] *nf* direction; (*señas*) address; (*AUTO*) steering; (*gerencia*) management; (*POL*) leadership; ~ **única/prohibida** one-way street/no entry

directa [di'rekta] *nf* (*AUT*) top gear

directiva [direk'tiβa] *nf* (*DEP, tb:* **junta** ~) board of directors

directo, a [di'rekto, a] *adj* direct; (*RADIO, TV*) live; **transmitir en** ~ to broadcast live

director, a [direk'tor, a] *adj* leading ♦ *nm/f* director; (*ESCOL*) head(teacher) (*BRIT*), principal (*US*); (*gerente*) manager(ess); (*PRENSA*) editor; ~ **de cine** film director; ~ **general** managing director

dirigente [diri'xente] *nm/f* (*POL*) leader

dirigir [diri'xir] *vt* to direct; (*carta*) to address; (*obra de teatro, film*) to direct; (*MUS*) to conduct; (*negocio*) to manage; ~**se** *vr:* ~**se a** to go towards, make one's way towards; (*hablar con*) to speak to

dirija *etc vb ver* **dirigir**

discernir [disθer'nir] *vt* to discern

disciplina [disθi'plina] *nf* discipline

discípulo, a [dis'θipulo, a] *nm/f* disciple

disco ['disko] *nm* disc; (*DEPORTE*) discus; (*TEL*) dial; (*AUTO: semáforo*) light; (*MUS*) record; (*INFORM*): ~ **flexible/rígido** floppy/hard disk; ~ **compacto/de larga duración** compact disc/long-playing record; ~ **de freno** brake disc

disconforme [diskon'forme] *adj* differing; **estar** ~ **(con)** to be in disagreement (with)

discordia [dis'korðja] *nf* discord

discoteca [disko'teka] *nf* disco(theque)

discreción [diskre'θjon] *nf* discretion; (*reserva*) prudence; **comer a** ~ to eat as much as one wishes; **discrecional** *adj* (*facultativo*) discretionary

discrepancia [diskre'panθja] *nf* (*diferencia*) discrepancy; (*desacuerdo*) disagreement

discreto, a [dis'kreto, a] *adj* discreet

discriminación [diskrimina'θjon] *nf* discrimination

disculpa [dis'kulpa] *nf* excuse; (*pedir perdón*) apology; **pedir ~s a/por** to apologize to/for; **disculpar** *vt* to excuse, pardon; **disculparse** *vr* to excuse o.s.; to apologize

discurrir [disku'rrir] *vi* (*pensar, reflexionar*) to think, meditate; (*el tiempo*) to pass, go by

discurso [dis'kurso] *nm* speech

discusión [disku'sjon] *nf* (*diálogo*) discussion; (*riña*) argument

discutir [disku'tir] *vt* (*debatir*) to discuss; (*pelear*) to argue about; (*contradecir*) to argue against ♦ *vi* (*debatir*) to discuss; (*pelearse*) to argue

disecar [dise'kar] *vt* (*conservar: animal*) to stuff; (*: planta*) to dry

diseminar [disemi'nar] *vt* to disseminate, spread

diseñar [dise'ɲar] *vt, vi* to design

diseño [di'seɲo] *nm* design

disfraz [dis'fraθ] *nm* (*máscara*) disguise; (*excusa*) pretext; ~**ar** *vt* to disguise; ~**arse** *vr:* ~**arse de** to disguise o.s. as

disfrutar [disfru'tar] *vt* to enjoy ♦ *vi* to enjoy o.s.; ~ **de** to enjoy, possess

disgregarse [disre'ɣarse] *vr*

(*muchedumbre*) to disperse

disgustar [disɣusˈtar] *vt* (*no gustar*) to displease; (*contrariar, enojar*) to annoy, upset; **~se** *vr* (*enfadarse*) to get upset; (*dos personas*) to fall out

disgusto [disˈɣusto] *nm* (*contrariedad*) annoyance; (*tristeza*) grief; (*riña*) quarrel

disidente [disiˈðente] *nm* dissident

disimular [disimuˈlar] *vt* (*ocultar*) to hide, conceal ♦ *vi* to dissemble

disipar [disiˈpar] *vt* to dispel; (*fortuna*) to squander; **~se** *vr* (*nubes*) to vanish; (*indisciplinarse*) to dissipate

dislocarse [disloˈkarse] *vr* (*articulación*) to sprain, dislocate

disminución [disminuˈθjon] *nf* decrease, reduction

disminuido, a [disminuˈiðo, a] *nm/f*: **~ mental/físico** mentally/physically handicapped person

disminuir [disminuˈir] *vt* to decrease, diminish

disociarse [disoˈθjarse] *vr*: **~ (de)** to dissociate o.s. (from)

disolver [disolˈβer] *vt* (*gen*) to dissolve; **~se** *vr* to dissolve; (*COM*) to go into liquidation

dispar [disˈpar] *adj* different

disparar [dispaˈrar] *vt, vi* to shoot, fire

disparate [dispaˈrate] *nm* (*tontería*) foolish remark; (*error*) blunder; **decir ~s** to talk nonsense

disparo [disˈparo] *nm* shot

dispensar [dispenˈsar] *vt* to dispense; (*disculpar*) to excuse

dispersar [disperˈsar] *vt* to disperse; **~se** *vr* to scatter

disponer [dispoˈner] *vt* (*arreglar*) to arrange; (*ordenar*) to put in order; (*preparar*) to prepare, get ready ♦ *vi*: **~ de** to have, own; **~se** *vr*: **~se a** *o* **para hacer** to prepare to do

disponible [dispoˈniβle] *adj* available

disposición [disposiˈθjon] *nf* arrangement, disposition; (*INFORM*) layout; **a la ~ de** at the disposal of; **~ de ánimo** state of mind

dispositivo [disposiˈtiβo] *nm* device, mechanism

dispuesto, a [disˈpwesto, a] *pp de* **disponer** ♦ *adj* (*arreglado*) arranged; (*preparado*) disposed

disputar [dispuˈtar] *vt* (*carrera*) to compete in

disquete [disˈkete] *nm* floppy disk, diskette

distancia [disˈtanθja] *nf* distance

distanciar [distanˈθjar] *vt* to space out; **~se** *vr* to become estranged

distante [disˈtante] *adj* distant

distar [disˈtar] *vi*: **dista 5km de aquí** it is 5km from here

diste *vb ver* **dar**

disteis [ˈdisteis] *vb ver* **dar**

distensión [distenˈsjon] *nf* (*en las relaciones*) relaxation; (*POL*) détente; (*muscular*) strain

distinción [distinˈθjon] *nf* distinction; (*elegancia*) elegance; (*honor*) honour

distinguido, a [distinˈɡiðo, a] *adj* distinguished

distinguir [distinˈɡir] *vt* to distinguish; (*escoger*) to single out; **~se** *vr* to be distinguished

distintivo [distinˈtiβo] *nm* badge; (*fig*) characteristic

distinto, a [disˈtinto, a] *adj* different; (*claro*) clear

distracción [distrakˈθjon] *nf* distraction; (*pasatiempo*) hobby, pastime; (*olvido*) absent-mindedness, distraction

distraer [distraˈer] *vt* (*atención*) to distract; (*divertir*) to amuse; (*fondos*) to embezzle; **~se** *vr* (*entretenerse*) to amuse o.s.; (*perder la concentración*) to allow one's attention to wander

distraído, a [distraˈiðo, a] *adj* (*gen*) absent-minded; (*entretenido*) amusing

distribuidor, a [distriβuiˈðor, a] *nm/f* distributor; **distribuidora** *nf* (*COM*) dealer, agent; (*CINE*) distributor

distribuir [distriβuˈir] *vt* to distribute

distrito [disˈtrito] *nm* (*sector, territorio*) region; (*barrio*) district

disturbio [dis'turβjo] *nm* disturbance; (*desorden*) riot

disuadir [diswa'ðir] *vt* to dissuade

disuelto [di'swelto] *pp de* **disolver**

disyuntiva [disjun'tiβa] *nf* dilemma

DIU *nm abr* (= *dispositivo intrauterino*) IUD

diurno, a ['djurno, a] *adj* day *cpd*

divagar [diβa'var] *vi* (*desviarse*) to digress

diván [di'βan] *nm* divan

divergencia [diβer'xenθja] *nf* divergence

diversidad [diβersi'ðað] *nf* diversity, variety

diversificar [diβersifi'kar] *vt* to diversify

diversión [diβer'sjon] *nf* (*gen*) entertainment; (*actividad*) hobby, pastime

diverso, a [di'βerso, a] *adj* diverse; **~s libros** several books; **~s** *nmpl* sundries

divertido, a [diβer'tiðo, a] *adj* (*chiste*) amusing; (*fiesta etc*) enjoyable

divertir [diβer'tir] *vt* (*entretener, recrear*) to amuse; **~se** *vr* (*pasarlo bien*) to have a good time; (*distraerse*) to amuse o.s.

dividendos [diβi'ðendos] *nmpl* (*COM*) dividends

dividir [diβi'ðir] *vt* (*gen*) to divide; (*distribuir*) to distribute, share out

divierta *etc vb ver* **divertir**

divino, a [di'βino, a] *adj* divine

divirtiendo *etc vb ver* **divertir**

divisa [di'βisa] *nf* (*emblema*) emblem, badge; **~s** *nfpl* foreign exchange *sg*

divisar [diβi'sar] *vt* to make out, distinguish

división [diβi'sjon] *nf* (*gen*) division; (*de partido*) split; (*de país*) partition

divorciar [diβor'θjar] *vt* to divorce; **~se** *vr* to get divorced; **divorcio** *nm* divorce

divulgar [diβul'var] *vt* (*ideas*) to spread; (*secreto*) to divulge

DNI (*ESP*) *nm abr* (= *Documento Nacional de Identidad*) national identity card

DNI

ℹ The **Documento Nacional de Identidad** *is a Spanish ID card which must be carried at all times and produced on request for the police. It contains the*

holder's photo, fingerprints and personal details. It is also known as the **DNI** *or "carnet de identidad".*

Dña. *abr* (= *doña*) Mrs

do [do] *nm* (*MUS*) do, C

dobladillo [doβla'ðiλo] *nm* (*de vestido*) hem; (*de pantalón: vuelta*) turn-up (*BRIT*), cuff (*US*)

doblar [do'βlar] *vt* to double; (*papel*) to fold; (*caño*) to bend; (*la esquina*) to turn, go round; (*film*) to dub ♦ *vi* to turn; (*campana*) to toll; **~se** *vr* (*plegarse*) to fold (up), crease; (*encorvarse*) to bend

doble ['doβle] *adj* double; (*de dos aspectos*) two-faced ♦ *nm* double ♦ *nm/f* (*TEATRO*) double, stand-in; **~s** *nmpl* (*DEPORTE*) doubles *sg*; **con sentido ~** with a double meaning

doblegar [doβle'var] *vt* to fold, crease; **~se** *vr* to yield

doblez [do'βleθ] *nm* fold, hem ♦ *nf* insincerity, duplicity

doce ['doθe] *num* twelve; **~na** *nf* dozen

docente [do'θente] *adj*: **centro / personal ~** teaching establishment/staff

dócil ['doθil] *adj* (*pasivo*) docile; (*obediente*) obedient

docto, a ['dokto, a] *adj*: **~ en** instructed in

doctor, a [dok'tor, a] *nm/f* doctor

doctorado [dokto'raðo] *nm* doctorate

doctrina [dok'trina] *nf* doctrine, teaching

documentación [dokumenta'θjon] *nf* documentation, papers *pl*

documental [dokumen'tal] *adj, nm* documentary

documento [doku'mento] *nm* (*certificado*) document; **~ national de identidad** identity card

dólar ['dolar] *nm* dollar

doler [do'ler] *vt, vi* to hurt; (*fig*) to grieve; **~se** *vr* (*de su situación*) to grieve, feel sorry; (*de las desgracias ajenas*) to sympathize; **me duele el brazo** my arm hurts

dolor [do'lor] *nm* pain; (*fig*) grief, sorrow; **~ de cabeza** headache; **~ de estómago**

stomachache

domar [do'mar] *vt* to tame

domesticar [domesti'kar] *vt* = **domar**

doméstico, a [do'mestiko, a] *adj* (*vida, servicio*) home; (*tareas*) household; (*animal*) tame, pet

domiciliación [domiθilia'θjon] *nf*: ~ **de pagos** (*COM*) standing order

domicilio [domi'θiljo] *nm* home; ~ **particular** private residence; ~ **social** (*COM*) head office; **sin** ~ **fijo** of no fixed abode

dominante [domi'nante] *adj* dominant; (*persona*) domineering

dominar [domi'nar] *vt* (*gen*) to dominate; (*idiomas*) to be fluent in ♦ *vi* to dominate, prevail; ~**se** *vr* to control o.s.

domingo [do'mingo] *nm* Sunday

dominio [do'minjo] *nm* (*tierras*) domain; (*autoridad*) power, authority; (*de las pasiones*) grip, hold; (*de idiomas*) command

don [don] *nm* (*talento*) gift; ~ **Juan Gómez** Mr Juan Gómez, Juan Gómez Esq (*BRIT*)

Don/Doña

ⓘ The term **don** often abbreviated to **D./Dña** is placed before the first name as a mark of respect to an older or more senior person - eg Don Diego, Doña Inés. Although becoming rarer in Spain it is still used with names and surnames on official documents and formal correspondence - eg "Sr. D. Pedro Rodríguez Hernández", "Sra. Dña. Inés Rodríguez Hernández".

---

donaire [do'naire] *nm* charm

donar [do'nar] *vt* to donate

donativo [dona'tiβo] *nm* donation

doncella [don'θeʎa] *nf* (*criada*) maid

donde ['donde] *adv* where ♦ *prep*: **el coche está allí** ~ **el farol** the car is over there by the lamppost *o* where the lamppost is; **en** ~ where, in which

dónde ['donde] *adv interrogativo* where?; **¿a** ~ **vas?** where are you going (to)?;

¿**de** ~ **vienes?** where have you been?; **¿por** ~**?** where?, whereabouts?

dondequiera [donde'kjera] *adv* anywhere; **por** ~ everywhere, all over the place ♦ *conj*: ~ **que** wherever

doña ['doɲa] *nf*: ~ **Alicia** Alicia; ~ **Victoria Benito** Mrs Victoria Benito

dorado, a [do'raðo, a] *adj* (*color*) golden; (*TEC*) gilt

dormir [dor'mir] *vt*: ~ **la siesta** to have an afternoon nap ♦ *vi* to sleep; ~**se** *vr* to fall asleep

dormitar [dormi'tar] *vi* to doze

dormitorio [dormi'torjo] *nm* bedroom; ~ **común** dormitory

dorsal [dor'sal] *nm* (*DEPORTE*) number

dorso ['dorso] *nm* (*de mano*) back; (*de hoja*) other side

dos [dos] *num* two

dosis ['dosis] *nf inv* dose, dosage

dotado, a [do'taðo, a] *adj* gifted; ~ **de** endowed with

dotar [do'tar] *vt* to endow; **dote** *nf* dowry; **dotes** *nfpl* (*talentos*) gifts

doy *vb ver* **dar**

dragar [dra'ɣar] *vt* (*río*) to dredge; (*minas*) to sweep

drama ['drama] *nm* drama

dramaturgo [drama'turɣo] *nm* dramatist, playwright

drástico, a ['drastiko, a] *adj* drastic

drenaje [dre'naxe] *nm* drainage

droga ['droɣa] *nf* drug

drogadicto, a [droɣa'ðikto, a] *nm/f* drug addict

droguería [droɣe'ria] *nf* hardware shop (*BRIT*) *o* store (*US*)

ducha ['dutʃa] *nf* (*baño*) shower; (*MED*) douche; **ducharse** *vr* to take a shower

duda ['duða] *nf* doubt; **dudar** *vt, vi* to doubt; **dudoso, a** [du'ðoso, a] *adj* (*incierto*) hesitant; (*sospechoso*) doubtful

duela *etc vb ver* **doler**

duelo ['dwelo] *vb ver* **doler** ♦ *nm* (*combate*) duel; (*luto*) mourning

duende ['dwende] *nm* imp, goblin

dueño, a ['dweɲo, a] *nm/f* (*propietario*)

owner; (*de pensión, taberna*) landlord/
lady; (*empresario*) employer
duermo *etc vb ver* **dormir**
dulce ['dulθe] *adj* sweet ♦ *adv* gently,
softly ♦ *nm* sweet
dulzura [dul'θura] *nf* sweetness; (*ternura*)
gentleness
duna ['duna] *nf* (*GEO*) dune
dúo ['duo] *nm* duet
duplicar [dupli'kar] *vt* (*hacer el doble de*)
to duplicate; **~se** *vr* to double
duque ['duke] *nm* duke; **~sa** *nf* duchess
duración [dura'θjon] *nf* (*de película, disco
etc*) length; (*de pila etc*) life; (*curso: de
acontecimientos etc*) duration
duradero, a [dura'ðero, a] *adj* (*tela etc*)
hard-wearing; (*fe, paz*) lasting
durante [du'rante] *prep* during
durar [du'rar] *vi* to last; (*recuerdo*) to
remain
durazno [du'raθno] (*AM*) *nm* (*fruta*) peach;
(*árbol*) peach tree
durex ['dureks] (*AM*) *nm* (*tira adhesiva*)
Sellotape ® (*BRIT*), Scotch tape ® (*US*)
dureza [du'reθa] *nf* (*calidad*) hardness
duro, a ['duro, a] *adj* hard; (*carácter*)
tough ♦ *adv* hard ♦ *nm* (*moneda*) five
peseta coin *o* piece

E, e

E *abr* (= *este*) E
e [e] *conj* and
ebanista [eßa'nista] *nm/f* cabinetmaker
ébano ['eßano] *nm* ebony
ebrio, a ['eßrjo, a] *adj* drunk
ebullición [eßuʎi'θjon] *nf* boiling
eccema [ek'θema] *nf* (*MED*) eczema
echar [e'tʃar] *vt* to throw; (*agua, vino*) to
pour (out); (*empleado: despedir*) to fire,
sack; (*hojas*) to sprout; (*cartas*) to post;
(*humo*) to emit, give out ♦ *vi*: **~ a
correr/llorar** to run off/burst into tears;
~se *vr* to lie down; **~ llave a** to lock (up);
~ abajo (*gobierno*) to overthrow; (*edificio*)
to demolish; **~ mano a** to lay hands on;

~ una mano a uno (*ayudar*) to give sb a
hand; **~ de menos** to miss
eclesiástico, a [ekle'sjastiko, a] *adj*
ecclesiastical
eclipse [e'klipse] *nm* eclipse
eco ['eko] *nm* echo; **tener ~** to catch on
ecología [ekolo'xia] *nf* ecology;
ecológico, a *adj* (*producto, método*)
environmentally-friendly; (*agricultura*)
organic; **ecologista** *adj* ecological,
environmental ♦ *nm/f* environmentalist
economato [ekono'mato] *nm* cooperative
store
economía [ekono'mia] *nf* (*sistema*)
economy; (*carrera*) economics
económico, a [eko'nomiko, a] *adj*
(*barato*) cheap, economical; (*ahorrativo*)
thrifty; (*COM: año etc*) financial;
(: *situación*) economic
economista [ekono'mista] *nm/f*
economist
ECU [eku] *nm* ECU
ecuador [ekwa'ðor] *nm* equator; **(el) E~**
Ecuador
ecuánime [e'kwanime] *adj* (*carácter*)
level-headed; (*estado*) calm
ecuatoriano, a [ekwato'rjano, a] *adj,
nm/f* Ecuadorian
ecuestre [e'kwestre] *adj* equestrian
eczema [ek'θema] *nm* = **eccema**
edad [e'ðað] *nf* age; **¿qué ~ tienes?** how
old are you?; **tiene ocho años de ~** he is
eight (years old); **de ~ mediana/
avanzada** middle-aged/advanced in
years; **la E~ Media** the Middle Ages
edición [eði'θjon] *nf* (*acto*) publication;
(*ejemplar*) edition
edificar [eðifi'kar] *vt, vi* to build
edificio [eði'fiθjo] *nm* building; (*fig*)
edifice, structure
Edimburgo [eðim'burɣo] *nm* Edinburgh
editar [eði'tar] *vt* (*publicar*) to publish;
(*preparar textos*) to edit
editor, a [eði'tor, a] *nm/f* (*que publica*)
publisher; (*redactor*) editor ♦ *adj*: **casa ~a**
publishing house, publisher; **~ial** *adj*
editorial ♦ *nm* leading article, editorial;

casa ~ial publishing house, publisher

edredon [eðreˈðon] *nm* duvet

educación [eðukaˈθjon] *nf* education; (*crianza*) upbringing; (*modales*) (good) manners *pl*

educado, a [eðuˈkaðo, a] *adj*: **bien/mal ~** well/badly behaved

educar [eðuˈkar] *vt* to educate; (*criar*) to bring up; (*voz*) to train

EE. UU. *nmpl abr* (= *Estados Unidos*) US(A)

efectista [efekˈtista] *adj* sensationalist

efectivamente [efektiβaˈmente] *adv* (*como respuesta*) exactly, precisely; (*verdaderamente*) really; (*de hecho*) in fact

efectivo, a [efekˈtiβo, a] *adj* effective; (*real*) actual, real ♦ *nm*: **pagar en ~** to pay (in) cash; **hacer ~ un cheque** to cash a cheque

efecto [eˈfekto] *nm* effect, result; **~s** *nmpl* (*~s personales*) effects; (*bienes*) goods; (*COM*) assets; **en ~** in fact; (*respuesta*) exactly, indeed; **~ invernadero** greenhouse effect

efectuar [efekˈtwar] *vt* to carry out; (*viaje*) to make

eficacia [efiˈkaθja] *nf* (*de persona*) efficiency; (*de medicamento etc*) effectiveness

eficaz [efiˈkaθ] *adj* (*persona*) efficient; (*acción*) effective

eficiente [efiˈθjente] *adj* efficient

efusivo, a [efuˈsiβo, a] *adj* effusive; **mis más efusivas gracias** my warmest thanks

EGB (*ESP*) *nf abr* (*ESCOL*) = *Educación General Básica*

egipcio, a [eˈxipθjo, a] *adj, nm/f* Egyptian

Egipto [eˈxipto] *nm* Egypt

egoísmo [eɣoˈismo] *nm* egoism

egoísta [eɣoˈista] *adj* egoistical, selfish ♦ *nm/f* egoist

egregio, a [eˈɣrexjo, a] *adj* eminent, distinguished

Eire [ˈeire] *nm* Eire

ej. *abr* (= *ejemplo*) eg

eje [ˈexe] *nm* (*GEO, MAT*) axis; (*de rueda*)

axle; (*de máquina*) shaft, spindle

ejecución [exekuˈθjon] *nf* execution; (*cumplimiento*) fulfilment; (*MUS*) performance; (*JUR: embargo de deudor*) attachment

ejecutar [exekuˈtar] *vt* to execute, carry out; (*matar*) to execute; (*cumplir*) to fulfil; (*MUS*) to perform; (*JUR: embargar*) to attach, distrain (on)

ejecutivo, a [exekuˈtiβo, a] *adj* executive; **el (poder) ~** the executive (power)

ejemplar [exemˈplar] *adj* exemplary ♦ *nm* example; (*ZOOL*) specimen; (*de libro*) copy; (*de periódico*) number, issue

ejemplo [eˈxemplo] *nm* example; **por ~** for example

ejercer [exerˈθer] *vt* to exercise; (*influencia*) to exert; (*un oficio*) to practise ♦ *vi* (*practicar*): **~ (de)** to practise (as)

ejercicio [exerˈθiθjo] *nm* exercise; (*período*) tenure; **~ comercial** financial year

ejército [eˈxerθito] *nm* army; **entrar en el ~** to join the army, join up

ejote [eˈxote] (*AM*) *nm* green bean

┌─────────────────┐
│ *PALABRA CLAVE* │
└─────────────────┘

el [el] (*f* **la**, *pl* **los**, **las**, *neutro* **lo**) *art def* **1** the; **el libro/la mesa/los estudiantes** the book/table/students

2 (*con n abstracto: no se traduce*): **el amor/la juventud** love/youth

3 (*posesión: se traduce a menudo por adj posesivo*): **romperse el brazo** to break one's arm; **levantó la mano** he put his hand up; **se puso el sombrero** she put her hat on

4 (*valor descriptivo*): **tener la boca grande/los ojos azules** to have a big mouth/blue eyes

5 (*con días*) on; **me iré el viernes** I'll leave on Friday; **los domingos suelo ir a nadar** on Sundays I generally go swimming

6 (*lo +adj*): **lo difícil/caro** what is difficult/expensive; (= *cuán*): **no se da cuenta de lo pesado que es** he doesn't

realise how boring he is
♦ *pron demos* 1: **mi libro y el de usted**
my book and yours; **las de Pepe son
mejores** Pepe's are better; **no la(s)
blanca(s) sino la(s) gris(es)** not the
white one(s) but the grey one(s)
2: **lo de: lo de ayer** what happened
yesterday; **lo de las facturas** that
business about the invoices
♦ *pron relativo:* **el que** *etc* 1 (*indef*): **el
(los) que quiera(n) que se vaya(n)**
anyone who wants to can leave; **llévese
el que más le guste** take the one you
like best
2 (*def*): **el que compré ayer** the one I
bought yesterday; **los que se van** those
who leave
3: **lo que: lo que pienso yo/más me
gusta** what I think/like most
♦ *conj:* **el que: el que lo diga** the fact
that he says so; **el que sea tan vago me
molesta** his being so lazy bothers me
♦ *excl:* **¡el susto que me diste!** what a
fright you gave me!
♦ *pron personal* 1 (*persona: m*) him; (: *f*)
her; (: *pl*) them; **lo/las veo** I can see
him/them
2 (*animal, cosa: sg*) it; (: *pl*) them; **lo** (*o*
la) **veo** I can see it; **los** (*o* **las**) **veo** I can
see them
3: **lo** (*como sustituto de frase*): **no lo
sabía** I didn't know; **ya lo entiendo** I
understand now

él [el] *pron* (*persona*) he; (*cosa*) it; (*después
de prep: cosa*) it; **de ~** his
elaborar [elaβo'rar] *vt* (*producto*) to make,
manufacture; (*preparar*) to prepare;
(*madera, metal etc*) to work; (*proyecto etc*)
to work on *o* out
elasticidad [elastiθi'ðað] *nf* elasticity
elástico, a [e'lastiko, a] *adj* elastic;
(*flexible*) flexible ♦ *nm* elastic; (*un ~*)
elastic band
elección [elek'θjon] *nf* election; (*selección*)
choice, selection
electorado [elekto'raðo] *nm* electorate,

voters *pl*
electricidad [elektriθi'ðað] *nf* electricity
electricista [elektri'θista] *nm/f* electrician
eléctrico, a [e'lektriko, a] *adj* electric
electro... [elektro] *prefijo* electro...;
~cardiograma *nm* electrocardiogram;
~cutar *vt* to electrocute; **~do** *nm*
electrode; **~domésticos** *nmpl*
(electrical) household appliances;
~magnético, a *adj* electromagnetic
electrónica [elek'tronika] *nf* electronics *sg*
electrónico, a [elek'troniko, a] *adj*
electronic
elefante [ele'fante] *nm* elephant
elegancia [ele'xanθja] *nf* elegance, grace;
(*estilo*) stylishness
elegante [ele'xante] *adj* elegant, graceful;
(*estiloso*) stylish, fashionable
elegir [ele'xir] *vt* (*escoger*) to choose,
select; (*optar*) to opt for; (*presidente*) to
elect
elemental [elemen'tal] *adj* (*claro, obvio*)
elementary; (*fundamental*) elemental,
fundamental
elemento [ele'mento] *nm* element; (*fig*)
ingredient; **~s** *nmpl* elements, rudiments
elepé [ele'pe] (*pl* **~s**) *nm* L.P.
elevación [eleβa'θjon] *nf* elevation; (*acto*)
raising, lifting; (*de precios*) rise; (*GEO etc*)
height, altitude
elevar [ele'βar] *vt* to raise, lift (up); (*precio*)
to put up; **~se** *vr* (*edificio*) to rise;
(*precios*) to go up
eligiendo *etc vb ver* **elegir**
elija *etc vb ver* **elegir**
eliminar [elimi'nar] *vt* to eliminate,
remove
eliminatoria [elimina'torja] *nf* heat,
preliminary (round)
elite [e'lite] *nf* elite
ella ['eʎa] *pron* (*persona*) she; (*cosa*) it;
(*después de prep: persona*) her; (: *cosa*) it;
de ~ hers
ellas ['eʎas] *pron* (*personas y cosas*) they;
(*después de prep*) them; **de ~** theirs
ello ['eʎo] *pron* it
ellos ['eʎos] *pron* they; (*después de prep*)

them; **de ~** theirs

elocuencia [elo'kwenθja] *nf* eloquence

elogiar [elo'xjar] *vt* to praise; **elogio** *nm* praise

elote [e'lote] (*AM*) *nm* corn on the cob

eludir [elu'ðir] *vt* to avoid

emanar [ema'nar] *vi*: **~ de** to emanate from, come from; (*derivar de*) to originate in

emancipar [emanθi'par] *vt* to emancipate; **~se** *vr* to become emancipated, free o.s.

embadurnar [embaður'nar] *vt* to smear

embajada [emba'xaða] *nf* embassy

embajador, a [embaxa'ðor, a] *nm/f* ambassador/ambassadress

embalaje [emba'laxe] *nm* packing

embalar [emba'lar] *vt* to parcel, wrap (up); **~se** *vr* to go fast

embalsamar [embalsa'mar] *vt* to embalm

embalse [em'balse] *nm* (*presa*) dam; (*lago*) reservoir

embarazada [embara'θaða] *adj* pregnant ♦ *nf* pregnant woman

embarazo [emba'raθo] *nm* (*de mujer*) pregnancy; (*impedimento*) obstacle, obstruction; (*timidez*) embarrassment; **embarazoso, a** *adj* awkward, embarrassing

embarcación [embarka'θjon] *nf* (*barco*) boat, craft; (*acto*) embarkation, boarding

embarcadero [embarka'ðero] *nm* pier, landing stage

embarcar [embar'kar] *vt* (*cargamento*) to ship, stow; (*persona*) to embark, put on board; **~se** *vr* to embark, go on board

embargar [embar'var] *vt* (*JUR*) to seize, impound

embargo [em'barvo] *nm* (*JUR*) seizure; (*COM, POL*) embargo

embargue [em'barve] *etc vb ver* **embargar**

embarque *etc* [em'barke] *vb ver* **embarcar** ♦ *nm* shipment, loading

embaucar [embau'kar] *vt* to trick, fool

embeber [embe'ßer] *vt* (*absorber*) to absorb, soak up; (*empapar*) to saturate

♦ *vi* to shrink; **~se** *vr*: **~se en un libro** to be engrossed *o* absorbed in a book

embellecer [embeʎe'θer] *vt* to embellish, beautify

embestida [embes'tiða] *nf* attack, onslaught; (*carga*) charge

embestir [embes'tir] *vt* to attack, assault; to charge, attack ♦ *vi* to attack

emblema [em'blema] *nm* emblem

embobado, a [embo'ßaðo, a] *adj* (*atontado*) stunned, bewildered

embolia [em'bolja] *nf* (*MED*) clot

émbolo ['embolo] *nm* (*AUTO*) piston

embolsar [embol'sar] *vt* to pocket, put in one's pocket

emborrachar [emborra'tʃar] *vt* to make drunk, intoxicate; **~se** *vr* to get drunk

emboscada [embos'kaða] *nf* ambush

embotar [embo'tar] *vt* to blunt, dull; **~se** *vr* (*adormecerse*) to go numb

embotellamiento [emboteʎa'mjento] *nm* (*AUTO*) traffic jam

embotellar [embote'ʎar] *vt* to bottle

embrague [embote'ʎar] *vt* to bottle

embrague [em'braxe] *nm* (*tb*: **pedal de ~**) clutch

embriagar [embrja'var] *vt* (*emborrachar*) to make drunk; **~se** *vr* (*emborracharse*) to get drunk

embrión [em'brjon] *nm* embryo

embrollar [embro'ʎar] *vt* (*el asunto*) to confuse, complicate; (*implicar*) to involve, embroil; **~se** *vr* (*confundirse*) to get into a muddle *o* mess

embrollo [em'broʎo] *nm* (*enredo*) muddle, confusion; (*aprieto*) fix, jam

embrujado, a [embru'xaðo, a] *adj* bewitched; **casa embrujada** haunted house

embrutecer [embrute'θer] *vt* (*atontar*) to stupefy; **~se** *vr* to be stupefied

embudo [em'buðo] *nm* funnel

embuste [em'buste] *nm* (*mentira*) lie; **~ro, a** *adj* lying, deceitful ♦ *nm/f* (*mentiroso*) liar

embutido [embu'tiðo] *nm* (*CULIN*) sausage; (*TEC*) inlay

emergencia [emer'xenθja] *nf* emergency;

(*surgimiento*) emergence

emerger [emer'ver] *vi* to emerge, appear

emigración [emixra'θjon] *nf* emigration; (*de pájaros*) migration

emigrar [emi'xrar] *vi* (*personas*) to emigrate; (*pájaros*) to migrate

eminencia [emi'nenθja] *nf* eminence; **eminente** *adj* eminent, distinguished; (*elevado*) high

emisario [emi'sarjo] *nm* emissary

emisión [emi'sjon] *nf* (*acto*) emission; (*COM etc*) issue; (*RADIO, TV: acto*) broadcasting; (: *programa*) broadcast, programme (*BRIT*), program (*US*)

emisora [emi'sora] *nf* radio *o* broadcasting station

emitir [emi'tir] *vt* (*olor etc*) to emit, give off; (*moneda etc*) to issue; (*opinión*) to express; (*RADIO*) to broadcast

emoción [emo'θjon] *nf* emotion; (: *excitación*) excitement; (*sentimiento*) feeling

emocionante [emoθjo'nante] *adj* (*excitante*) exciting, thrilling

emocionar [emoθjo'nar] *vt* (*excitar*) to excite, thrill; (*conmover*) to move, touch; (*impresionar*) to impress

emotivo, a [emo'tiβo, a] *adj* emotional

empacar [empa'kar] *vt* (*gen*) to pack; (*en caja*) to bale, crate

empacho [em'patʃo] *nm* (*MED*) indigestion; (*fig*) embarrassment

empadronarse [empaðro'narse] *vr* (*POL: como elector*) to register

empalagoso, a [empala'ɣoso, a] *adj* cloying; (*fig*) tiresome

empalmar [empal'mar] *vt* to join, connect ♦ *vi* (*dos caminos*) to meet, join; **empalme** *nm* joint, connection; junction; (*de trenes*) connection

empanada [empa'naða] *nf* pie, pasty

empantanarse [empanta'narse] *vr* to get swamped; (*fig*) to get bogged down

empañarse [empa'narse] *vr* (*cristales etc*) to steam up

empapar [empa'par] *vt* (*mojar*) to soak, saturate; (*absorber*) to soak up, absorb;

~se *vr*: **~se de** to soak up

empapelar [empape'lar] *vt* (*paredes*) to paper

empaquetar [empake'tar] *vt* to pack, parcel up

empastar [empas'tar] *vt* (*embadurnar*) to paste; (*diente*) to fill

empaste [em'paste] *nm* (*de diente*) filling

empatar [empa'tar] *vi* to draw, tie; **empate** *nm* draw, tie

empecé *etc vb ver* **empezar**

empedernido, a [empeðer'niðo, a] *adj* hard, heartless; (*fumador*) inveterate

empedrado, a [empe'ðraðo, a] *adj* paved ♦ *nm* paving

empeine [em'peine] *nm* (*de pie, zapato*) instep

empellón [empe'ʎon] *nm* push, shove

empeñado, a [empe'naðo, a] *adj* (*persona*) determined; (*objeto*) pawned

empeñar [empe'nar] *vt* (*objeto*) to pawn, pledge; (*persona*) to compel; **~se** *vr* (*endeudarse*) to get into debt; **~se en** to be set on, be determined to

empeño [em'peno] *nm* (*determinación, insistencia*) determination, insistence; **casa de ~s** pawnshop

empeorar [empeo'rar] *vt* to make worse, worsen ♦ *vi* to get worse, deteriorate

empequeñecer [empekene'θer] *vt* to dwarf; (*minusvalorar*) to belittle

emperador [empera'ðor] *nm* emperor; **emperatriz** *nf* empress

empezar [empe'θar] *vt, vi* to begin, start

empiece *etc vb ver* **empezar**

empiezo *etc vb ver* **empezar**

empinar [empi'nar] *vt* to raise; **~se** *vr* (*persona*) to stand on tiptoe; (*animal*) to rear up; (*camino*) to climb steeply

empírico, a [em'piriko, a] *adj* empirical

emplasto [em'plasto] *nm* (*MED*) plaster

emplazamiento [emplaθa'mjento] *nm* site, location; (*JUR*) summons *sg*

emplazar [empla'θar] *vt* (*ubicar*) to site, place, locate; (*JUR*) to summons; (*convocar*) to summon

empleado, a [emple'aðo, a] *nm/f* (*gen*)

employee; (*de banco etc*) clerk

emplear [emple'ar] *vt* (*usar*) to use, employ; (*dar trabajo a*) to employ; **~se** *vr* (*conseguir trabajo*) to be employed; (*ocuparse*) to occupy o.s.

empleo [em'pleo] *nm* (*puesto*) job; (*puestos: colectivamente*) employment; (*uso*) use, employment

empobrecer [empoβre'θer] *vt* to impoverish; **~se** *vr* to become poor *o* impoverished

empollar [empo'ʎar] (*fam*) *vt*, *vi* to swot (up); **empollón, ona** (*fam*) *nm/f* swot

emporio [em'porjo] *nm* (*AM: gran almacén*) department store

empotrado, a [empo'traðo, a] *adj* (*armario etc*) built-in

emprender [empren'der] *vt* (*empezar*) to begin, embark on; (*acometer*) to tackle, take on

empresa [em'presa] *nf* (*de espíritu etc*) enterprise; (*COM*) company, firm; **~rio, a** *nm/f* (*COM*) businessman/woman

empréstito [em'prestito] *nm* (*public*) loan

empujar [empu'xar] *vt* to push, shove

empujón [empu'xon] *nm* push, shove

empuñar [empu'nar] *vt* (*asir*) to grasp, take (firm) hold of

emular [emu'lar] *vt* to emulate; (*rivalizar*) to rival

PALABRA CLAVE

---

en [en] *prep* **1** (*posición*) in; (*: sobre*) on; **está ~ el cajón** it's in the drawer; **~ Argentina/La Paz** in Argentina/La Paz; **~ la oficina/el colegio** at the office/school; **está ~ el suelo/quinto piso** it's on the floor/the fifth floor

2 (*dirección*) into; **entró ~ el aula** she went into the classroom; **meter algo ~ el bolso** to put sth into one's bag

3 (*tiempo*) in; on; **~ 1605/3 semanas/invierno** in 1605/3 weeks/winter; **~ (el mes de) enero** in (the month of) January; **~ aquella ocasión/época** on that occasion/at that time

4 (*precio*) for; **lo vendió ~ 20 dólares** he

sold it for 20 dollars

5 (*diferencia*) by; **reducir/aumentar ~ una tercera parte/un 20 por ciento** to reduce/increase by a third/20 per cent

6 (*manera*): **~ avión/autobús** by plane/bus; **escrito ~ inglés** written in English

7 (*después de vb que indica gastar etc*) on; **han cobrado demasiado ~ dietas** they've charged too much to expenses; **se le va la mitad del sueldo ~ comida** he spends half his salary on food

8 (*tema, ocupación*): **experto ~ la materia** expert on the subject; **trabaja ~ la construcción** he works in the building industry

9 (*adj + ~ + infin*): **lento ~ reaccionar** slow to react

---

enaguas [e'naɣwas] *nfpl* petticoat *sg*, underskirt *sg*

enajenación [enaxena'θjon] *nf*: **~ mental** mental derangement

enajenar [enaxe'nar] *vt* (*volver loco*) to drive mad

enamorado, a [enamo'raðo, a] *adj* in love ♦ *nm/f* lover

enamorar [enamo'rar] *vt* to win the love of; **~se** *vr*: **~se de alguien** to fall in love with sb

enano, a [e'nano, a] *adj* tiny ♦ *nm/f* dwarf

enardecer [enarðe'θer] *vt* (*pasiones*) to fire, inflame; (*persona*) to fill with enthusiasm; **~se** *vr*: **~se por** to get excited about; (*entusiasmarse*) to get enthusiastic about

encabezamiento [enkaβeθa'mjento] *nm* (*de carta*) heading; (*de periódico*) headline

encabezar [enkaβe'θar] *vt* (*movimiento, revolución*) to lead, head; (*lista*) to head, be at the top of; (*carta*) to put a heading to

encadenar [enkaðe'nar] *vt* to chain (together); (*poner grilletes a*) to shackle

encajar [enka'xar] *vt* (*ajustar*): **~ (en)** to fit (into); (*fam: golpe*) to take ♦ *vi* to fit (well); (*fig: corresponder a*) to match; **~se**

vr: **~se en un sillón** to squeeze into a chair

encaje [en'kaxe] *nm* (*labor*) lace

encalar [enka'lar] *vt* (*pared*) to whitewash

encallar [enka'ʎar] *vi* (*NAUT*) to run aground

encaminar [enkami'nar] *vt* to direct, send; **~se** *vr*: **~se a** to set out for

encantado, a [enkan'taðo, a] *adj* (*hechizado*) bewitched; (*muy contento*) delighted; **¡~!** how do you do, pleased to meet you

encantador, a [enkanta'ðor, a] *adj* charming, lovely ♦ *nm/f* magician, enchanter/enchantress

encantar [enkan'tar] *vt* (*agradar*) to charm, delight; (*hechizar*) to bewitch, cast a spell on; **me encanta eso** I love that; **encanto** *nm* (*hechizo*) spell, charm; (*fig*) charm, delight

encarcelar [enkarθe'lar] *vt* to imprison, jail

encarecer [enkare'θer] *vt* to put up the price of; **~se** *vr* to get dearer

encarecimiento [enkareθi'mjento] *nm* price increase

encargado, a [enkar'ɣaðo, a] *adj* in charge ♦ *nm/f* agent, representative; (*responsable*) person in charge

encargar [enkar'ɣar] *vt* to entrust; (*recomendar*) to urge, recommend; **~se** *vr*: **~se de** to look after, take charge of

encargo [en'karɣo] *nm* (*tarea*) assignment, job; (*responsabilidad*) responsibility; (*COM*) order

encariñarse [enkari'ɲarse] *vr*: **~ con** to grow fond of, get attached to

encarnación [enkarna'θjon] *nf* incarnation, embodiment

encarnizado, a [enkarni'θaðo, a] *adj* (*lucha*) bloody, fierce

encarrilar [enkarri'lar] *vt* (*tren*) to put back on the rails; (*fig*) to correct, put on the right track

encasillar [enkasi'ʎar] *vt* (*tb fig*) to pigeonhole; (*actor*) to typecast

encauzar [enkau'θar] *vt* to channel

encendedor [enθende'ðor] *nm* lighter

encender [enθen'der] *vt* (*con fuego*) to light; (*luz, radio*) to put on, switch on; (*avivar: pasiones*) to inflame; **~se** *vr* to catch fire; (*excitarse*) to get excited; (*de cólera*) to flare up; (*el rostro*) to blush

encendido [enθen'diðo] *nm* (*AUTO*) ignition

encerado [enθe'raðo] *nm* (*ESCOL*) blackboard

encerar [enθe'rar] *vt* (*suelo*) to wax, polish

encerrar [enθe'rrar] *vt* (*confinar*) to shut in, shut up; (*comprender, incluir*) to include, contain

encharcado, a [entʃar'kaðo, a] *adj* (*terreno*) flooded

encharcarse [entʃar'karse] *vr* to get flooded

enchufado, a [entʃu'faðo, a] (*fam*) *nm/f* well-connected person

enchufar [entʃu'far] *vt* (*ELEC*) to plug in; (*TEC*) to connect, fit together; **enchufe** *nm* (*ELEC: clavija*) plug; (: *toma*) socket; (*de dos tubos*) joint, connection; (*fam: influencia*) contact, connection; (: *puesto*) cushy job

encía [en'θia] *nf* gum

encienda *etc vb ver* **encender**

encierro *etc* [en'θjerro] *vb ver* **encerrar** ♦ *nm* shutting in, shutting up; (*calabozo*) prison

encima [en'θima] *adv* (*sobre*) above, over; (*además*) besides; **~ de** (*en*) on, on top of; (*sobre*) above, over; (*además de*) besides, on top of; **por ~ de** over; **¿llevas dinero ~?** have you (got) any money on you?; **se me vino ~** it took me by surprise

encina [en'θina] *nf* holm oak

encinta [en'θinta] *adj* pregnant

enclenque [en'klenke] *adj* weak, sickly

encoger [enko'xer] *vt* to shrink, contract; **~se** *vr* to shrink, contract; (*fig*) to cringe; **~se de hombros** to shrug one's shoulders

encolar [enko'lar] *vt* (*engomar*) to glue, paste; (*pegar*) to stick down

encolerizar [enkoleri'θar] *vt* to anger, provoke; **~se** *vr* to get angry

encomendar [enkomen'dar] *vt* to entrust, commend; **~se** *vr*: **~se a** to put one's trust in

encomiar [enko'mjar] *vt* to praise, pay tribute to

encomienda *etc* [enko'mjenda] *vb ver* **encomendar** ♦ *nf* (*encargo*) charge, commission; (*elogio*) tribute; **~ postal** (*AM*) parcel post

encontrado, a [enkon'traðo, a] *adj* (*contrario*) contrary, conflicting

encontrar [enkon'trar] *vt* (*hallar*) to find; (*inesperadamente*) to meet, run into; **~se** *vr* to meet (each other); (*situarse*) to be (situated); **~se con** to meet; **~se bien (de salud)** to feel well

encrespar [enkres'par] *vt* (*cabellos*) to curl; (*fig*) to anger, irritate; **~se** *vr* (*el mar*) to get rough; (*fig*) to get cross, get irritated

encrucijada [enkruθi'xaða] *nf* crossroads *sg*

encuadernación [enkwaðerna'θjon] *nf* binding

encuadernador, a [enkwaðerna'ðor, a] *nm/f* bookbinder

encuadrar [enkwa'ðrar] *vt* (*retrato*) to frame; (*ajustar*) to fit, insert; (*contener*) to contain

encubrir [enku'ßrir] *vt* (*ocultar*) to hide, conceal; (*criminal*) to harbour, shelter

encuentro *etc* [en'kwentro] *vb ver* **encontrar** ♦ *nm* (*de personas*) meeting; (*AUTO etc*) collision, crash; (*DEPORTE*) match, game; (*MIL*) encounter

encuesta [en'kwesta] *nf* inquiry, investigation; (*sondeo*) (public) opinion poll; **~ judicial** post mortem

encumbrar [enkum'brar] *vt* (*persona*) to exalt

endeble [en'deßle] *adj* (*argumento, excusa, persona*) weak

endémico, a [en'demiko, a] *adj* (*MED*) endemic; (*fig*) rife, chronic

endemoniado, a [endemo'njaðo, a] *adj* possessed (of the devil); (*travieso*) devilish

enderezar [endere'θar] *vt* (*poner derecho*) to straighten (out); (: *verticalmente*) to set upright; (*situación*) to straighten *o* sort out; (*dirigir*) to direct; **~se** *vr* (*persona sentada*) to straighten up

endeudarse [endeu'ðarse] *vr* to get into debt

endiablado, a [endja'ßlaðo, a] *adj* devilish, diabolical; (*travieso*) mischievous

endilgar [endil'xar] (*fam*) *vt*: **~le algo a uno** to lumber sb with sth; **~le un sermón a uno** to lecture sb

endiñar [endi'ɲar] (*fam*) *vt* (*bofetón*) to land, belt

endosar [endo'sar] *vt* (*cheque etc*) to endorse

endulzar [endul'θar] *vt* to sweeten; (*suavizar*) to soften

endurecer [endure'θer] *vt* to harden; **~se** *vr* to harden, grow hard

enema [e'nema] *nm* (*MED*) enema

enemigo, a [ene'miɣo, a] *adj* enemy, hostile ♦ *nm/f* enemy

enemistad [enemis'tað] *nf* enmity

enemistar [enemis'tar] *vt* to make enemies of, cause a rift between; **~se** *vr* to become enemies; (*amigos*) to fall out

energía [ener'xia] *nf* (*vigor*) energy, drive; (*empuje*) push; (*TEC, ELEC*) energy, power; **~ eolica** wind power; **~ solar** solar energy/power

enérgico, a [e'nerxiko, a] *adj* (*gen*) energetic; (*voz, modales*) forceful

energúmeno, a [ener'xumeno, a] (*fam*) *nm/f* (*fig*) madman/woman

enero [e'nero] *nm* January

enfadado, a [enfa'ðaðo, a] *adj* angry, annoyed

enfadar [enfa'ðar] *vt* to anger, annoy; **~se** *vr* to get angry *o* annoyed

enfado [en'faðo] *nm* (*enojo*) anger, annoyance; (*disgusto*) trouble, bother

énfasis ['enfasis] *nm* emphasis, stress

enfático, a [en'fatiko, a] *adj* emphatic

enfermar [enfer'mar] *vt* to make ill ♦ *vi* to fall ill, be taken ill

enfermedad [enferme'ðað] *nf* illness; **~ venérea** venereal disease

enfermera [enfer'mera] *nf* nurse

enfermería [enferme'ria] *nf* infirmary; *(de colegio etc)* sick bay

enfermero [enfer'mero] *nm* (male) nurse

enfermizo, a [enfer'miθo, a] *adj (persona)* sickly, unhealthy; *(fig)* unhealthy

enfermo, a [en'fermo, a] *adj* ill, sick ♦ *nm/f* invalid, sick person; *(en hospital)* patient

enflaquecer [enflake'θer] *vt (adelgazar)* to make thin; *(debilitar)* to weaken

enfocar [enfo'kar] *vt (foto etc)* to focus; *(problema etc)* to consider

enfoque *etc* [en'foke] *vb ver* **enfocar** ♦ *nm* focus.

enfrascarse [enfras'karse] *vr*: **~ en algo** to bury o.s. in sth

enfrentar [enfren'tar] *vt (peligro)* to face (up to), confront; *(oponer)* to bring face to face; **~se** *vr (dos personas)* to face o confront each other; *(DEPORTE: dos equipos)* to meet; **~se a** o **con** to face up to, confront

enfrente [en'frente] *adv* opposite; **la casa de ~** the house opposite, the house across the street; **~ de** opposite, facing

enfriamiento [enfria'mjento] *nm* chilling, refrigeration; *(MED)* cold, chill

enfriar [enfri'ar] *vt (alimentos)* to cool, chill; *(algo caliente)* to cool down; **~se** *vr* to cool down; *(MED)* to catch a chill; *(amistad)* to cool

enfurecer [enfure'θer] *vt* to enrage, madden; **~se** *vr* to become furious, fly into a rage; *(mar)* to get rough

engalanar [engala'nar] *vt (adornar)* to adorn; *(ciudad)* to decorate; **~se** *vr* to get dressed up

enganchar [engan'tʃar] *vt* to hook; *(dos vagones)* to hitch up; *(TEC)* to couple, connect; *(MIL)* to recruit; **~se** *vr (MIL)* to enlist, join up

enganche [en'gantʃe] *nm* hook; *(TEC)* coupling, connection; *(acto)* hooking (up); *(MIL)* recruitment, enlistment; *(AM:*

depósito) deposit

engañar [enga'ɲar] *vt* to deceive; *(estafar)* to cheat, swindle; **~se** *vr (equivocarse)* to be wrong; *(disimular la verdad)* to deceive o.s.

engaño [en'gaɲo] *nm* deceit; *(estafa)* trick, swindle; *(error)* mistake, misunderstanding; *(ilusión)* delusion; **~so, a** *adj (tramposo)* crooked; *(mentiroso)* dishonest, deceitful; *(aspecto)* deceptive; *(consejo)* misleading

engarzar [engar'θar] *vt (joya)* to set, mount; *(fig)* to link, connect

engatusar [engatu'sar] *(fam) vt* to coax

engendrar [enxen'drar] *vt* to breed; *(procrear)* to beget; *(causar)* to cause, produce; **engendro** *nm (BIO)* foetus; *(fig)* monstrosity

englobar [englo'βar] *vt* to include, comprise

engordar [engor'ðar] *vt* to fatten ♦ *vi* to get fat, put on weight

engorroso, a [engo'rroso, a] *adj* bothersome, trying

engranaje [engra'naxe] *nm (AUTO)* gear

engrandecer [engrande'θer] *vt* to enlarge, magnify; *(alabar)* to praise, speak highly of; *(exagerar)* to exaggerate

engrasar [engra'sar] *vt (TEC: poner grasa)* to grease; *(: lubricar)* to lubricate, oil; *(manchar)* to make greasy

engreído, a [engre'iðo, a] *adj* vain, conceited

engrosar [engro'sar] *vt (ensanchar)* to enlarge; *(aumentar)* to increase; *(hinchar)* to swell

enhebrar [ene'βrar] *vt* to thread

enhorabuena [enora'βwena] *excl*: **¡~!** congratulations! ♦ *nf*: **dar la ~ a** to congratulate

enigma [e'niɣma] *nm* enigma; *(problema)* puzzle; *(misterio)* mystery

enjabonar [enxaβo'nar] *vt* to soap; *(fam: adular)* to soft-soap

enjambre [en'xambre] *nm* swarm

enjaular [enxau'lar] *vt* to (put in a) cage; *(fam)* to jail, lock up

enjuagar [enxwa'ɣar] *vt* (*ropa*) to rinse (out)

enjuague *etc* [en'xwaɣe] *vb ver* **enjuagar**
♦ *nm* (MED) mouthwash; (*de ropa*) rinse, rinsing

enjugar [enxu'ɣar] *vt* to wipe (off); (*lágrimas*) to dry; (*déficit*) to wipe out

enjuiciar [enxwi'θjar] *vt* (JUR: *procesar*) to prosecute, try; (*fig*) to judge

enjuto, a [en'xuto, a] *adj* (*flaco*) lean, skinny

enlace [en'laθe] *nm* link, connection; (*relación*) relationship; (*tb*: ~ **matrimonial**) marriage; (*de carretera, trenes*) connection; ~ **sindical** shop steward

enlatado, a [enla'taðo, a] *adj* (*comida, productos*) tinned, canned

enlazar [enla'θar] *vt* (*unir con lazos*) to bind together; (*atar*) to tie; (*conectar*) to link, connect; (AM) to lasso

enlodar [enlo'ðar] *vt* to cover in mud; (*fig: manchar*) to stain; (: *rebajar*) to debase

enloquecer [enloke'θer] *vt* to drive mad ♦ *vi* to go mad; ~**se** *vr* to go mad

enlutado, a [enlu'taðo, a] *adj* (*persona*) in mourning

enmarañar [enmara'ɲar] *vt* (*enredar*) to tangle (up), entangle; (*complicar*) to complicate; (*confundir*) to confuse; ~**se** *vr* (*enredarse*) to become entangled; (*confundirse*) to get confused

enmarcar [enmar'kar] *vt* (*cuadro*) to frame

enmascarar [enmaska'rar] *vt* to mask; ~**se** *vr* to put on a mask

enmendar [enmen'dar] *vt* to emend, correct; (*constitución etc*) to amend; (*comportamiento*) to reform; ~**se** *vr* to reform, mend one's ways; **enmienda** *nf* correction; amendment; reform

enmohecerse [enmoe'θerse] *vr* (*metal*) to rust, go rusty; (*muro, plantas*) to get mouldy

enmudecer [enmuðe'θer] *vi* (*perder el habla*) to fall silent; (*guardar silencio*) to remain silent

ennegrecer [enneɣre'θer] *vt* (*poner negro*) to blacken; (*oscurecer*) to darken; ~**se** *vr*

to turn black; (*oscurecerse*) to get dark, darken

ennoblecer [ennoβle'θer] *vt* to ennoble

enojar [eno'xar] *vt* (*encolerizar*) to anger; (*disgustar*) to annoy, upset; ~**se** *vr* to get angry; to get annoyed

enojo [e'noxo] *nm* (*cólera*) anger; (*irritación*) annoyance; ~**so, a** *adj* annoying

enorgullecerse [enorɣuʎe'θerse] *vr* to be proud; ~ **de** to pride o.s. on, be proud of

enorme [e'norme] *adj* enormous, huge; (*fig*) monstrous; **enormidad** *nf* hugeness, immensity

enrarecido, a [enrare'θiðo, a] *adj* (*atmósfera, aire*) rarefied

enredadera [enreða'ðera] *nf* (BOT) creeper, climbing plant

enredar [enre'ðar] *vt* (*cables, hilos etc*) to tangle (up), entangle; (*situación*) to complicate, confuse; (*meter cizaña*) to sow discord among *o* between; (*implicar*) to embroil, implicate; ~**se** *vr* to get entangled, get tangled (up); (*situación*) to get complicated; (*persona*) to get embroiled; (AM: *fam*) to meddle

enredo [en'reðo] *nm* (*maraña*) tangle; (*confusión*) mix-up, confusion; (*intriga*) intrigue

enrejado [enre'xaðo] *nm* fence, railings *pl*

enrevesado, a [enreβe'saðo, a] *adj* (*asunto*) complicated, involved

enriquecer [enrike'θer] *vt* to make rich, enrich; ~**se** *vr* to get rich

enrojecer [enroxe'θer] *vt* to redden ♦ *vi* (*persona*) to blush; ~**se** *vr* to blush

enrolar [enro'lar] *vt* (MIL) to enlist; (*reclutar*) to recruit; ~**se** *vr* (MIL) to join up; (*afiliarse*) to enrol

enrollar [enro'ʎar] *vt* to roll (up), wind (up)

enroscar [enros'kar] *vt* (*torcer, doblar*) to coil (round), wind; (*tornillo, rosca*) to screw in; ~**se** *vr* to coil, wind

ensalada [ensa'laða] *nf* salad; **ensaladilla (rusa)** *nf* Russian salad

ensalzar [ensal'θar] *vt* (*alabar*) to praise,

extol; (*exaltar*) to exalt

ensamblaje [ensam'blaxe] *nm* assembly; (*TEC*) joint

ensanchar [ensan'tʃar] *vt* (*hacer más ancho*) to widen; (*agrandar*) to enlarge, expand; (*COSTURA*) to let out; ~**se** *vr* to get wider, expand; **ensanche** *nm* (*de calle*) widening

ensangrentar [ensangren'tar] *vt* to stain with blood

ensañar [ensa'ɲar] *vt* to enrage; ~**se** *vr*: ~**se con** to treat brutally

ensartar [ensar'tar] *vt* (*cuentas, perlas etc*) to string (together)

ensayar [ensa'jar] *vt* to test, try (out); (*TEATRO*) to rehearse

ensayo [en'sajo] *nm* test, trial; (*QUÍM*) experiment; (*TEATRO*) rehearsal; (*DEPORTE*) try; (*ESCOL, LITERATURA*) essay

enseguida [ense'ɣiða] *adv* at once, right away

ensenada [ense'naða] *nf* inlet, cove

enseñanza [ense'ɲanθa] *nf* (*educación*) education; (*acción*) teaching; (*doctrina*) teaching, doctrine

enseñar [ense'ɲar] *vt* (*educar*) to teach; (*mostrar, señalar*) to show

enseres [en'seres] *nmpl* belongings

ensillar [ensi'ʎar] *vt* to saddle (up)

ensimismarse [ensimis'marse] *vr* (*abstraerse*) to become lost in thought; (*AM*) to become conceited

ensombrecer [ensombre'θer] *vt* to darken, cast a shadow over; (*fig*) to overshadow, put in the shade

ensordecer [ensorðe'θer] *vt* to deafen ♦ *vi* to go deaf

ensortijado, a [ensorti'xaðo, a] *adj* (*pelo*) curly

ensuciar [ensu'θjar] *vt* (*manchar*) to dirty, soil; (*fig*) to defile; ~**se** *vr* to get dirty; (*niño*) to wet o.s.

ensueño [en'sweɲo] *nm* (*sueño*) dream, fantasy; (*ilusión*) illusion; (*soñando despierto*) daydream

entablar [enta'βlar] *vt* (*recubrir*) to board (up); (*AJEDREZ, DAMAS*) to set up;

(*conversación*) to strike up; (*JUR*) to file ♦ *vi* to draw

entablillar [entaβli'ʎar] *vt* (*MED*) to (put in a) splint

entallar [enta'ʎar] *vt* (*traje*) to tailor ♦ *vi*: **el traje entalla bien** the suit fits well

ente ['ente] *nm* (*organización*) body, organization; (*fam: persona*) odd character

entender [enten'der] *vt* (*comprender*) to understand; (*darse cuenta*) to realize ♦ *vi* to understand; (*creer*) to think, believe; ~**se** *vr* (*comprenderse*) to be understood; (*2 personas*) to get on together; (*ponerse de acuerdo*) to agree, reach an agreement; ~ **de** to know all about; ~ **algo de** to know a little about; ~ **en** to deal with, have to do with; ~**se mal** (*2 personas*) to get on badly

entendido, a [enten'diðo, a] *adj* (*comprendido*) understood; (*hábil*) skilled; (*inteligente*) knowledgeable ♦ *nm/f* (*experto*) expert ♦ *excl* agreed!; **entendimiento** *nm* (*comprensión*) understanding; (*inteligencia*) mind, intellect; (*juicio*) judgement

enterado, a [ente'raðo, a] *adj* well-informed; **estar ~ de** to know about, be aware of

enteramente [entera'mente] *adv* entirely, completely

enterar [ente'rar] *vt* (*informar*) to inform, tell; ~**se** *vr* to find out, get to know

entereza [ente'reθa] *nf* (*totalidad*) entirety; (*fig: carácter*) strength of mind; (: *honradez*) integrity

enternecer [enterne'θer] *vt* (*ablandar*) to soften; (*apiadar*) to touch, move; ~**se** *vr* to be touched, be moved

entero, a [en'tero, a] *adj* (*total*) whole, entire; (*fig: honesto*) honest; (: *firme*) firm, resolute ♦ *nm* (*COM: punto*) point; (*AM: pago*) payment

enterrador [enterra'ðor] *nm* gravedigger

enterrar [ente'rrar] *vt* to bury

entibiar [enti'βjar] *vt* (*enfriar*) to cool; (*calentar*) to warm; ~**se** *vr* (*fig*) to cool

entidad [enti'ðað] *nf* (*empresa*) firm, company; (*organismo*) body; (*sociedad*) society; (*FILOSOFÍA*) entity

entiendo *etc vb ver* **entender**

entierro [en'tjerro] *nm* (*acción*) burial; (*funeral*) funeral

entonación [entona'θjon] *nf* (*LING*) intonation

entonar [ento'nar] *vt* (*canción*) to intone; (*colores*) to tone; (*MED*) to tone up ♦ *vi* to be in tune

entonces [en'tonθes] *adv* then, at that time; **desde ~** since then; **en aquel ~** at that time; **(pues) ~** and so

entornar [entor'nar] *vt* (*puerta, ventana*) to half close, leave ajar; (*los ojos*) to screw up

entorpecer [entorpe'θer] *vt* (*entendimiento*) to dull; (*impedir*) to obstruct, hinder; (: *tránsito*) to slow down, delay

entrada [en'traða] *nf* (*acción*) entry, access; (*sitio*) entrance, way in; (*INFORM*) input; (*COM*) receipts *pl*, takings *pl*; (*CULIN*) starter; (*DEPORTE*) innings *sg*; (*TEATRO*) house, audience; (*billete*) ticket; (*COM*): **~s y salidas** income and expenditure; (*TEC*): **~ de aire** air intake *o* inlet; **de ~** from the outset

entrado, a [en'traðo, a] *adj*: **~ en años** elderly; **una vez ~ el verano** in the summer(time), when summer comes

entramparse [entram'parse] *vr* to get into debt

entrante [en'trante] *adj* next, coming; **mes/año ~** next month/year; **~s** *nmpl* starters

entraña [en'traɲa] *nf* (*fig: centro*) heart, core; (*raíz*) root; **~s** *nfpl* (*ANAT*) entrails; (*fig*) heart *sg*; **sin ~s** (*fig*) heartless; **entrañable** *adj* close, intimate; **entrañar** *vt* to entail

entrar [en'trar] *vt* (*introducir*) to bring in; (*INFORM*) to input ♦ *vi* (*meterse*) to go in, come in, enter; (*comenzar*): **~ diciendo** to begin by saying; **hacer ~** to show in; **no me entra** I can't get the hang of it

entre ['entre] *prep* (*dos*) between; (*más de dos*) among(st)

entreabrir [entrea'βrir] *vt* to half-open, open halfway

entrecejo [entre'θexo] *nm*: **fruncir el ~** to frown

entrecortado, a [entrekor'taðo, a] *adj* (*respiración*) difficult; (*habla*) faltering

entredicho [entre'ðitʃo] *nm* (*JUR*) injunction; **poner en ~** to cast doubt on; **estar en ~** to be in doubt

entrega [en'treɣa] *nf* (*de mercancías*) delivery; (*de novela etc*) instalment

entregar [entre'ɣar] *vt* (*dar*) to hand (over), deliver; **~se** *vr* (*rendirse*) to surrender, give in, submit; (*dedicarse*) to devote o.s.

entrelazar [entrela'θar] *vt* to entwine

entremeses [entre'meses] *nmpl* hors d'œuvres

entremeter [entreme'ter] *vt* to insert, put in; **~se** *vr* to meddle, interfere; **entremetido, a** *adj* meddling, interfering

entremezclar [entremeθ'klar] *vt* to intermingle; **~se** *vr* to intermingle

entrenador, a [entrena'ðor, a] *nm/f* trainer, coach

entrenarse [entre'narse] *vr* to train

entrepierna [entre'pjerna] *nf* crotch

entresacar [entresa'kar] *vt* to pick out, select

entresuelo [entre'swelo] *nm* mezzanine

entretanto [entre'tanto] *adv* meanwhile, meantime

entretejer [entrete'xer] *vt* to interweave

entretener [entrete'ner] *vt* (*divertir*) to entertain, amuse; (*detener*) to hold up, delay; **~se** *vr* (*divertirse*) to amuse o.s.; (*retrasarse*) to delay, linger; **entretenido, a** *adj* entertaining, amusing; **entretenimiento** *nm* entertainment, amusement

entrever [entre'βer] *vt* to glimpse, catch a glimpse of

entrevista [entre'βista] *nf* interview; **entrevistar** *vt* to interview;

entrevistarse *vr* to have an interview

entristecer [entriste'θer] *vt* to sadden, grieve; **~se** *vr* to grow sad

entrometerse [entrome'terse] *vr*: **~ (en)** to interfere (in *o* with)

entroncar [entron'kar] *vi* to be connected *o* related

entumecer [entume'θer] *vt* to numb, benumb; **~se** *vr* (*por el frío*) to go *o* become numb; **entumecido, a** *adj* numb, stiff

enturbiar [entur'βjar] *vt* (*el agua*) to make cloudy; (*fig*) to confuse; **~se** *vr* (*oscurecerse*) to become cloudy; (*fig*) to get confused, become obscure

entusiasmar [entusjas'mar] *vt* to excite, fill with enthusiasm; (*gustar mucho*) to delight; **~se** *vr*: **~se con** *o* **por** to get enthusiastic *o* excited about

entusiasmo [entu'sjasmo] *nm* enthusiasm; (*excitación*) excitement

entusiasta [entu'sjasta] *adj* enthusiastic ♦ *nm/f* enthusiast

enumerar [enume'rar] *vt* to enumerate

enunciación [enunθja'θjon] *nf* enunciation

enunciado [enun'θjaðo] *nm* enunciation

envainar [embai'nar] *vt* to sheathe

envalentonar [embalento'nar] *vt* to give courage to; **~se** *vr* (*pey: jactarse*) to boast, brag

envanecer [embane'θer] *vt* to make conceited; **~se** *vr* to grow conceited

envasar [emba'sar] *vt* (*empaquetar*) to pack, wrap; (*enfrascar*) to bottle; (*enlatar*) to can; (*embolsar*) to pocket

envase [em'base] *nm* (*en paquete*) packing, wrapping; (*en botella*) bottling; (*en lata*) canning; (*recipiente*) container; (*paquete*) package; (*botella*) bottle; (*lata*) tin (*BRIT*), can

envejecer [embexe'θer] *vt* to make old, age ♦ *vi* (*volverse viejo*) to grow old; (*parecer viejo*) to age; **~se** *vr* to grow old; to age

envenenar [embene'nar] *vt* to poison; (*fig*) to embitter

envergadura [emberɣa'ðura] *nf* (*fig*) scope, compass

envés [em'bes] *nm* (*de tela*) back, wrong side

enviar [em'bjar] *vt* to send

enviciarse [embi'θjarse] *vr*: **~ (con)** to get addicted (to)

envidia [em'biðja] *nf* envy; **tener ~ a** to envy, be jealous of; **envidiar** *vt* to envy

envío [em'bio] *nm* (*acción*) sending; (*de mercancías*) consignment; (*de dinero*) remittance

enviudar [embju'ðar] *vi* to be widowed

envoltura [embol'tura] *nf* (*cobertura*) cover; (*embalaje*) wrapper, wrapping; **envoltorio** *nm* package

envolver [embol'βer] *vt* to wrap (up); (*cubrir*) to cover; (*enemigo*) to surround; (*implicar*) to involve, implicate

envuelto [em'bwelto] *pp de* **envolver**

enyesar [enje'sar] *vt* (*pared*) to plaster; (*MED*) to put in plaster

enzarzarse [enθar'θarse] *vr*: **~ en** (*pelea*) to get mixed up in; (*disputa*) to get involved in

épica ['epika] *nf* epic

épico, a ['epiko, a] *adj* epic

epidemia [epi'ðemja] *nf* epidemic

epilepsia [epi'lepsja] *nf* epilepsy

epílogo [e'piloxo] *nm* epilogue

episodio [epi'soðjo] *nm* episode

epístola [e'pistola] *nf* epistle

época ['epoka] *nf* period, time; (*HISTORIA*) age, epoch; **hacer ~** to be epoch-making

equilibrar [ekili'βrar] *vt* to balance; **equilibrio** *nm* balance, equilibrium; **equilibrista** *nm/f* (*funámbulo*) tightrope walker; (*acróbata*) acrobat

equipaje [eki'paxe] *nm* luggage; (*avíos*): **~ de mano** hand luggage

equipar [eki'par] *vt* (*proveer*) to equip

equipararse [ekipa'rarse] *vr*: **~ con** to be on a level with

equipo [e'kipo] *nm* (*conjunto de cosas*) equipment; (*DEPORTE*) team; (*de obreros*) shift

equis ['ekis] *nf inv* (the letter) X

equitación [ekita'θjon] *nf* horse riding

equitativo, a [ekita'tiβo, a] *adj* equitable, fair

equivalente [ekiβa'lente] *adj, nm* equivalent

equivaler [ekiβa'ler] *vi* to be equivalent *o* equal

equivocación [ekiβoka'θjon] *nf* mistake, error

equivocado, a [ekiβo'kaðo, a] *adj* wrong, mistaken

equivocarse [ekiβo'karse] *vr* to be wrong, make a mistake; **~ de camino** to take the wrong road

equívoco, a [e'kiβoko, a] *adj* (*dudoso*) suspect; (*ambiguo*) ambiguous ♦ *nm* ambiguity; (*malentendido*) misunderstanding

era ['era] *vb ver* **ser** ♦ *nf* era, age

erais *vb ver* **ser**

éramos *vb ver* **ser**

eran *vb ver* **ser**

erario [e'rarjo] *nm* exchequer (*BRIT*), treasury

eras *vb ver* **ser**

erección [erek'θjon] *nf* erection

eres *vb ver* **ser**

erguir [er'xir] *vt* to raise, lift; (*poner derecho*) to straighten; **~se** *vr* to straighten up

erigir [eri'xir] *vt* to erect, build; **~se** *vr*: **~se en** to set o.s. up as

erizarse [eri'θarse] *vr* (*pelo: de perro*) to bristle; (: *de persona*) to stand on end

erizo [e'riθo] *nm* (*ZOOL*) hedgehog; **~ de mar** sea-urchin

ermita [er'mita] *nf* hermitage

ermitaño, a [ermi'taɲo, a] *nm/f* hermit

erosión [ero'sjon] *nf* erosion

erosionar [erosjo'nar] *vt* to erode

erótico, a [e'rotiko, a] *adj* erotic; **erotismo** *nm* eroticism

erradicar [erraði'kar] *vt* to eradicate

errante [e'rrante] *adj* wandering, errant

errar [e'rrar] *vi* (*vagar*) to wander, roam; (*equivocarse*) to be mistaken ♦ *vt*: **~ el camino** to take the wrong road; **~ el tiro** to miss

erróneo, a [e'rroneo, a] *adj* (*equivocado*) wrong, mistaken

error [e'rror] *nm* error, mistake; (*INFORM*) bug; **~ de imprenta** misprint

eructar [eruk'tar] *vt* to belch, burp

erudito, a [eru'ðito, a] *adj* erudite, learned

erupción [erup'θjon] *nf* eruption; (*MED*) rash

es *vb ver* **ser**

esa ['esa] (*pl* **esas**) *adj demos ver* **ese**

ésa ['esa] (*pl* **ésas**) *pron ver* **ése**

esbelto, a [es'βelto, a] *adj* slim, slender

esbozo [es'βoθo] *nm* sketch, outline

escabeche [eska'βetʃe] *nm* brine; (*de aceitunas etc*) pickle; **en ~** pickled

escabroso, a [eska'βroso, a] *adj* (*accidentado*) rough, uneven; (*fig*) tough, difficult; (: *atrevido*) risqué

escabullirse [eskaβuˈʎirse] *vr* to slip away, to clear out

escafandra [eska'fandra] *nf* (*buzo*) diving suit; (*~ espacial*) space suit

escala [es'kala] *nf* (*proporción, MUS*) scale; (*de mano*) ladder; (*AVIAT*) stopover; **hacer ~ en** to stop *o* call in at

escalafón [eskala'fon] *nm* (*escala de salarios*) salary scale, wage scale

escalar [eska'lar] *vt* to climb, scale

escalera [eska'lera] *nf* stairs *pl*, staircase; (*escala*) ladder; (*NAIPES*) run; **~ mecánica** escalator; **~ de caracol** spiral staircase

escalfar [eskal'far] *vt* (*huevos*) to poach

escalinata [eskali'nata] *nf* staircase

escalofriante [eskalo'frjante] *adj* chilling

escalofrío [eskalo'frio] *nm* (*MED*) chill; **~s** *nmpl* (*fig*) shivers

escalón [eska'lon] *nm* step, stair; (*de escalera*) rung

escalope [eska'lope] *nm* (*CULIN*) escalope

escama [es'kama] *nf* (*de pez, serpiente*) scale; (*de jabón*) flake; (*fig*) resentment

escamar [eska'mar] *vt* (*fig*) to make wary *o* suspicious

escamotear [eskamote'ar] *vt* (*robar*) to lift, swipe; (*hacer desaparecer*) to make disappear

escampar [eskam'par] *vb impers* to stop
raining

escandalizar [eskandali'θar] *vt* to
scandalize, shock; **~se** *vr* to be shocked;
(*ofenderse*) to be offended

escándalo [es'kandalo] *nm* scandal;
(*alboroto, tumulto*) row, uproar;
escandaloso, a *adj* scandalous,
shocking

escandinavo, a [eskandi'naßo, a] *adj,
nm/f* Scandinavian

escaño [es'kaɲo] *nm* bench; (*POL*) seat

escapar [eska'par] *vi* (*gen*) to escape, run
away; (*DEPORTE*) to break away; **~se** *vr* to
escape, get away; (*agua, gas*) to leak
(out)

escaparate [eskapa'rate] *nm* shop
window

escape [es'kape] *nm* (*de agua, gas*) leak;
(*de motor*) exhaust

escarabajo [eskara'ßaxo] *nm* beetle

escaramuza [eskara'muθa] *nf* skirmish

escarbar [eskar'ßar] *vt* (*tierra*) to scratch

escarceos [eskar'θeos] *nmpl* (*fig*): **en mis
~ con la política ...** in my dealings with
politics ...; **~ amorosos** love affairs

escarcha [es'kartʃa] *nf* frost

escarchado, a [eskar'tʃaðo, a] *adj* (*CULIN:
fruta*) crystallized

escarlata [eskar'lata] *adj inv* scarlet;
escarlatina *nf* scarlet fever

escarmentar [eskarmen'tar] *vt* to punish
severely ♦ *vi* to learn one's lesson

escarmiento *etc* [eskar'mjento] *vb ver*
escarmentar ♦ *nm* (*ejemplo*) lesson;
(*castigo*) punishment

escarnio [es'karnjo] *nm* mockery; (*injuria*)
insult

escarola [eska'rola] *nf* endive

escarpado, a [eskar'paðo, a] *adj*
(*pendiente*) sheer, steep; (*rocas*) craggy

escasear [eskase'ar] *vi* to be scarce

escasez [eska'seθ] *nf* (*falta*) shortage,
scarcity; (*pobreza*) poverty

escaso, a [es'kaso, a] *adj* (*poco*) scarce;
(*raro*) rare; (*ralo*) thin, sparse; (*limitado*)
limited

escatimar [eskati'mar] *vt* to skimp (on),
be sparing with

escayola [eska'jola] *nf* plaster

escena [es'θena] *nf* scene

escenario [esθe'narjo] *nm* (*TEATRO*) stage;
(*CINE*) set; (*fig*) scene; **escenografía** *nf*
set design

escepticismo [esθepti'θismo] *nm*
scepticism; **escéptico, a** *adj* sceptical
♦ *nm/f* sceptic

escisión [esθi'sjon] *nf* (*de partido, secta*)
split

esclarecer [esklare'θer] *vt* (*misterio,
problema*) to shed light on

esclavitud [esklaßi'tuð] *nf* slavery

esclavizar [esklaßi'θar] *vt* to enslave

esclavo, a [es'klaßo, a] *nm/f* slave

esclusa [es'klusa] *nf* (*de canal*) lock;
(*compuerta*) floodgate

escoba [es'koßa] *nf* broom; **escobilla** *nf*
brush

escocer [esko'θer] *vi* to burn, sting; **~se**
vr to chafe, get chafed

escocés, esa [esko'θes, esa] *adj* Scottish
♦ *nm/f* Scotsman/woman, Scot

Escocia [es'koθja] *nf* Scotland

escoger [esko'xer] *vt* to choose, pick,
select; **escogido, a** *adj* chosen, selected

escolar [esko'lar] *adj* school *cpd* ♦ *nm/f*
schoolboy/girl, pupil

escollo [es'koʎo] *nm* (*obstáculo*) pitfall

escolta [es'kolta] *nf* escort; **escoltar** *vt*
to escort

escombros [es'kombros] *nmpl* (*basura*)
rubbish *sg*; (*restos*) debris *sg*

esconder [eskon'der] *vt* to hide, conceal;
~se *vr* to hide; **escondidas** (*AM*) *nfpl*: **a
escondidas** secretly; **escondite** *nm*
hiding place; (*juego*) hide-and-seek;
escondrijo *nm* hiding place, hideout

escopeta [esko'peta] *nf* shotgun

escoria [es'korja] *nf* (*de alto horno*) slag;
(*fig*) scum, dregs *pl*

Escorpio [es'korpjo] *nm* Scorpio

escorpión [eskor'pjon] *nm* scorpion

escotado, a [esko'taðo, a] *adj* low-cut

escote [es'kote] *nm* (*de vestido*) low neck;

pagar a ~ to share the expenses

escotilla [esko'tiʎa] *nf* (*NAUT*) hatch(way)

escozor [esko'θor] *nm* (*dolor*) sting(ing)

escribir [eskri'ßir] *vt*, *vi* to write; **~ a máquina** to type; **¿cómo se escribe?** how do you spell it?

escrito, a [es'krito, a] *pp de* **escribir** ♦ *nm* (*documento*) document; (*manuscrito*) text, manuscript; **por ~** in writing

escritor, a [eskri'tor, a] *nm/f* writer

escritorio [eskri'torjo] *nm* desk

escritura [eskri'tura] *nf* (*acción*) writing; (*caligrafía*) (hand)writing; (*JUR: documento*) deed

escrúpulo [es'krupulo] *nm* scruple; (*minuciosidad*) scrupulousness;
escrupuloso, a *adj* scrupulous

escrutar [eskru'tar] *vt* to scrutinize, examine; (*votos*) to count

escrutinio [eskru'tinjo] *nm* (*examen atento*) scrutiny; (*POL: recuento de votos*) count(ing)

escuadra [es'kwaðra] *nf* (*MIL etc*) squad; (*NAUT*) fleet; (*de coches etc*) fleet;
escuadrilla *nf* (*de aviones*) squadron; (*AM: de obreros*) gang

escuadrón [eskwa'ðron] *nm* squadron

escuálido, a [es'kwaliðo, a] *adj* skinny, scraggy; (*sucio*) squalid

escuchar [esku'tʃar] *vt* to listen to ♦ *vi* to listen

escudilla [esku'ðiʎa] *nf* bowl, basin

escudo [es'kuðo] *nm* shield

escudriñar [eskuðri'ɲar] *vt* (*examinar*) to investigate, scrutinize; (*mirar de lejos*) to scan

escuela [es'kwela] *nf* school; **~ de artes y oficios** (*ESP*) ≈ technical college; **~ normal** teacher training college

escueto, a [es'kweto, a] *adj* plain; (*estilo*) simple

escuincle [es'kwinkle] (*AM: fam*) *nm/f* kid

esculpir [eskul'pir] *vt* to sculpt; (*grabar*) to engrave; (*tallar*) to carve; **escultor, a** *nm/f* sculptor/tress; **escultura** *nf* sculpture

escupidera [eskupi'ðera] *nf* spittoon

escupir [esku'pir] *vt*, *vi* to spit (out)

escurreplatos [eskurre'platos] *nm inv* plate rack

escurridizo, a [eskurri'ðiθo, a] *adj* slippery

escurridor [eskurri'ðor] *nm* colander

escurrir [esku'rrir] *vt* (*ropa*) to wring out; (*verduras, platos*) to drain ♦ *vi* (*líquidos*) to drip; **~se** *vr* (*secarse*) to drain; (*resbalarse*) to slip, slide; (*escaparse*) to slip away

ese ['ese] (*f* **esa**, *pl* **esos, esas**) *adj demos* (*sg*) that; (*pl*) those

ése ['ese] (*f* **ésa**, *pl* **ésos, ésas**) *pron* (*sg*) that (one); (*pl*) those (ones); **~ ... éste ...** the former ... the latter ...; **no me vengas con ésas** don't give me any more of that nonsense

esencia [e'senθja] *nf* essence; **esencial** *adj* essential

esfera [es'fera] *nf* sphere; (*de reloj*) face; **esférico, a** *adj* spherical

esforzarse [esfor'θarse] *vr* to exert o.s., make an effort

esfuerzo *etc* [es'fwerθo] *vb ver* **esforzar** ♦ *nm* effort

esfumarse [esfu'marse] *vr* (*apoyo, esperanzas*) to fade away

esgrima [es'ɣrima] *nf* fencing

esgrimir [esɣri'mir] *vt* (*arma*) to brandish; (*argumento*) to use

esguince [es'ɣinθe] *nm* (*MED*) sprain

eslabón [esla'ßon] *nm* link

eslip [es'lip] *nm* pants *pl* (*BRIT*), briefs *pl*

eslovaco, a [eslo'ßako, a] *adj*, *nm/f* Slovak, Slovakian ♦ *nm* (*LING*) Slovak, Slovakian

Eslovaquia [eslo'ßakja] *nf* Slovakia

esmaltar [esmal'tar] *vt* to enamel; **esmalte** *nm* enamel; **esmalte de uñas** nail varnish *o* polish

esmerado, a [esme'raðo, a] *adj* careful, neat

esmeralda [esme'ralda] *nf* emerald

esmerarse [esme'rarse] *vr* (*aplicarse*) to take great pains, exercise great care; (*afanarse*) to work hard

esmero [es'mero] *nm* (great) care
esnob [es'nob] (*pl* ~**s**) *adj* (*persona*) snobbish ♦ *nm/f* snob; ~**ismo** *nm* snobbery
eso ['eso] *pron* that, that thing *o* matter; ~ **de su coche** that business about his car; ~ **de ir al cine** all that about going to the cinema; **a** ~ **de las cinco** at about five o'clock; **en** ~ thereupon, at that point; ~ **es** that's it; **¡~ sí que es vida!** now that is really living!; **por** ~ **te lo dije** that's why I told you; **y** ~ **que llovía** in spite of the fact it was raining
esos ['esos] *adj demos ver* **ese**
ésos ['esos] *pron ver* **ése**
espabilar *etc* [espaßi'lar] = **despabilar** *etc*
espacial [espa'θjal] *adj* (*del espacio*) space *cpd*
espaciar [espa'θjar] *vt* to space (out)
espacio [es'paθjo] *nm* space; (*MUS*) interval; (*RADIO*, *TV*) programme (*BRIT*), program (*US*); **el** ~ space; ~**so, a** *adj* spacious, roomy
espada [es'paða] *nf* sword; ~**s** *nfpl* (*NAIPES*) spades
espaguetis [espa'xetis] *nmpl* spaghetti *sg*
espalda [es'palda] *nf* (*gen*) back; ~**s** *nfpl* (*hombros*) shoulders; **a** ~**s de uno** behind sb's back; **tenderse de** ~**s** to lie (down) on one's back; **volver la** ~ **a alguien** to cold-shoulder sb
espantajo [espan'taxo] *nm* = **espantapájaros**
espantapájaros [espanta'paxaros] *nm inv* scarecrow
espantar [espan'tar] *vt* (*asustar*) to frighten, scare; (*ahuyentar*) to frighten off; (*asombrar*) to horrify, appal; ~**se** *vr* to get frightened *o* scared; to be appalled
espanto [es'panto] *nm* (*susto*) fright; (*terror*) terror; (*asombro*) astonishment; ~**so, a** *adj* frightening; terrifying; astonishing
España [es'paŋa] *nf* Spain; **español, a** *adj* Spanish ♦ *nm/f* Spaniard ♦ *nm* (*LING*) Spanish
esparadrapo [espara'ðrapo] *nm* (sticking) plaster (*BRIT*), adhesive tape (*US*)
esparcimiento [esparθi'mjento] *nm* (*dispersión*) spreading; (*diseminación*) scattering; (*fig*) cheerfulness
esparcir [espar'θir] *vt* to spread; (*diseminar*) to scatter; ~**se** *vr* to spread (out); to scatter; (*divertirse*) to enjoy o.s.
espárrago [es'parraxo] *nm* asparagus
esparto [es'parto] *nm* esparto (grass)
espasmo [es'pasmo] *nm* spasm
espátula [es'patula] *nf* spatula
especia [es'peθja] *nf* spice
especial [espe'θjal] *adj* special; ~**idad** *nf* speciality (*BRIT*), specialty (*US*)
especie [es'peθje] *nf* (*BIO*) species; (*clase*) kind, sort; **en** ~ in kind
especificar [espeθifi'kar] *vt* to specify; **específico, a** *adj* specific
espécimen [es'peθimen] (*pl* **especímenes**) *nm* specimen
espectáculo [espek'takulo] *nm* (*gen*) spectacle; (*TEATRO etc*) show
espectador, a [espekta'ðor, a] *nm/f* spectator
espectro [es'pektro] *nm* ghost; (*fig*) spectre
especular [espeku'lar] *vt, vi* to speculate
espejismo [espe'xismo] *nm* mirage
espejo [es'pexo] *nm* mirror; ~ **retrovisor** rear-view mirror
espeluznante [espeluθ'nante] *adj* horrifying, hair-raising
espera [es'pera] *nf* (*pausa, intervalo*) wait; (*JUR: plazo*) respite; **en** ~ **de** waiting for; (*con expectativa*) expecting
esperanza [espe'ranθa] *nf* (*confianza*) hope; (*expectativa*) expectation; **hay pocas** ~**s de que venga** there is little prospect of his coming
esperar [espe'rar] *vt* (*aguardar*) to wait for; (*tener expectativa de*) to expect; (*desear*) to hope for ♦ *vi* to wait; to expect; to hope
esperma [es'perma] *nf* sperm
espesar [espe'sar] *vt* to thicken; ~**se** *vr* to thicken, get thicker
espeso, a [es'peso, a] *adj* thick; **espesor**

nm thickness

espía [es'pia] *nm/f* spy; **espiar** *vt* (*observar*) to spy on

espiga [es'piɣa] *nf* (*BOT: de trigo etc*) ear

espigón [espi'ɣon] *nm* (*BOT*) ear; (*NAUT*) breakwater

espina [es'pina] *nf* thorn; (*de pez*) bone; ~ **dorsal** (*ANAT*) spine

espinaca [espi'naka] *nf* spinach

espinazo [espi'naθo] *nm* spine, backbone

espinilla [espi'niʎa] *nf* (*ANAT: tibia*) shin(bone); (*grano*) blackhead

espinoso, a [espi'noso, a] *adj* (*planta*) thorny, prickly; (*asunto*) difficult

espionaje [espjo'naxe] *nm* spying, espionage

espiral [espi'ral] *adj, nf* spiral

espirar [espi'rar] *vt* to breathe out, exhale

espiritista [espiri'tista] *adj, nm/f* spiritualist

espíritu [es'piritu] *nm* spirit; **espiritual** *adj* spiritual

espita [es'pita] *nf* tap

espléndido, a [es'plendiðo, a] *adj* (*magnífico*) magnificent, splendid; (*generoso*) generous

esplendor [esplen'dor] *nm* splendour

espolear [espole'ar] *vt* to spur on

espoleta [espo'leta] *nf* (*de bomba*) fuse

espolón [espo'lon] *nm* sea wall

espolvorear [espolßore'ar] *vt* to dust, sprinkle

esponja [es'ponxa] *nf* sponge; (*fig*) sponger; **esponjoso, a** *adj* spongy

espontaneidad [espontanei'ðað] *nf* spontaneity

espontáneo, a [espon'taneo, a] *adj* spontaneous

esposa [es'posa] *nf* wife; ~**s** *nfpl* handcuffs; **esposar** *vt* to handcuff

esposo [es'poso] *nm* husband

espray [es'prai] *nm* spray

espuela [es'pwela] *nf* spur

espuma [es'puma] *nf* foam; (*de cerveza*) froth, head; (*de jabón*) lather; **espumadera** *nf* (*utensilio*) skimmer; **espumoso, a** *adj* frothy, foamy; (*vino*) sparkling

esqueleto [eske'leto] *nm* skeleton

esquema [es'kema] *nm* (*diagrama*) diagram; (*dibujo*) plan; (*FILOSOFÍA*) schema

esquí [es'ki] (*pl* ~**s**) *nm* (*objeto*) ski; (*DEPORTE*) skiing; ~ **acuático** water-skiing; **esquiar** *vi* to ski

esquilar [eski'lar] *vt* to shear

esquimal [eski'mal] *adj, nm/f* Eskimo

esquina [es'kina] *nf* corner

esquinazo [eski'naθo] *nm*: **dar** ~ **a algn** to give sb the slip

esquirol [eski'rol] *nm* blackleg

esquivar [eski'ßar] *vt* to avoid

esquivo, a [es'kißo, a] *adj* evasive; (*tímido*) reserved; (*huraño*) unsociable

esta ['esta] *adj* demos ver **este²**

está *vb* ver **estar**

ésta ['esta] *pron* ver **éste**

estabilidad [estaßili'ðað] *nf* stability; **estable** [es'taßle] *adj* stable

establecer [estaßle'θer] *vt* to establish; ~**se** *vr* to establish o.s.; (*echar raíces*) to settle (down); **establecimiento** *nm* establishment

establo [es'taßlo] *nm* (*AGR*) stable

estaca [es'taka] *nf* stake, post; (*de tienda de campaña*) peg

estacada [esta'kaða] *nf* (*cerca*) fence, fencing; (*palenque*) stockade

estación [esta'θjon] *nf* station; (*del año*) season; ~ **de autobuses** bus station; ~ **balnearia** seaside resort; ~ **de servicio** service station

estacionamiento [estaθjona'mjento] *nm* (*AUTO*) parking; (*MIL*) stationing

estacionar [estaθjo'nar] *vt* (*AUTO*) to park; (*MIL*) to station; ~**io, a** *adj* stationary; (*COM: mercado*) slack

estadio [es'taðjo] *nm* (*fase*) stage, phase; (*DEPORTE*) stadium

estadista [esta'ðista] *nm* (*POL*) statesman; (*ESTADÍSTICA*) statistician

estadística [esta'ðistika] *nf* figure, statistic; (*ciencia*) statistics *sg*

estado [es'taðo] *nm* (*POL: condición*) state; ~ **de ánimo** state of mind; ~ **de cuenta** bank statement; ~ **de sitio** state of siege;

~ **civil** marital status; ~ **mayor** staff; **estar en** ~ to be pregnant; **(los) E~s Unidos** *nmpl* the United States (of America) *sg*
estadounidense [estaðouni'ðense] *adj* United States *cpd*, American ♦ *nm/f* American
estafa [es'tafa] *nf* swindle, trick; **estafar** *vt* to swindle, defraud
estafeta [esta'feta] *nf* (*oficina de correos*) post office; ~ **diplomática** diplomatic bag
estáis *vb ver* **estar**
estallar [esta'ʎar] *vi* to burst; (*bomba*) to explode, go off; (*epidemia, guerra, rebelión*) to break out; ~ **en llanto** to burst into tears; **estallido** *nm* explosion; (*fig*) outbreak
estampa [es'tampa] *nf* print, engraving
estampado, a [estam'paðo, a] *adj* printed ♦ *nm* (*impresión: acción*) printing; (: *efecto*) print; (*marca*) stamping
estampar [estam'par] *vt* (*imprimir*) to print; (*marcar*) to stamp; (*metal*) to engrave; (*poner sello en*) to stamp; (*fig*) to stamp, imprint
estampida [estam'piða] *nf* stampede
estampido [estam'piðo] *nm* bang, report
están *vb ver* **estar**
estancado, a [estan'kaðo, a] *adj* stagnant
estancar [estan'kar] *vt* (*aguas*) to hold up, hold back; (*COM*) to monopolize; (*fig*) to block, hold up; **~se** *vr* to stagnate
estancia [es'tanθja] *nf* (*permanencia*) stay; (*sala*) room; (*AM*) farm, ranch; **estanciero** (*AM*) *nm* farmer, rancher
estanco, a [es'tanko, a] *adj* watertight ♦ *nm* tobacconist's (shop), cigar store (*US*)

Estanco

ⓘ *Cigarettes, tobacco, postage stamps and official forms are all sold under state monopoly in shops called an* **estanco**. *Although tobacco products can also be bought in bars and* **quioscos** *they are generally more expensive.*

estándar [es'tandar] *adj, nm* standard;

estandarizar *vt* to standardize
estandarte [estan'darte] *nm* banner, standard
estanque [es'tanke] *nm* (*lago*) pool, pond; (*AGR*) reservoir
estanquero, a [estan'kero, a] *nm/f* tobacconist
estante [es'tante] *nm* (*armario*) rack, stand; (*biblioteca*) bookcase; (*anaquel*) shelf; (*AM*) prop; **estantería** *nf* shelving, shelves *pl*
estaño [es'taɲo] *nm* tin

PALABRA CLAVE

---

estar [es'tar] *vi* **1** (*posición*) to be; **está en la plaza** it's in the square; **¿está Juan?** is Juan in?; **estamos a 30 km de Junín** we're 30 kms from Junín
2 (*+adj: estado*) to be; ~ **enfermo** to be ill; **está muy elegante** he's looking very smart; **¿cómo estás?** how are you keeping?
3 (*+gerundio*) to be; **estoy leyendo** I'm reading
4 (*uso pasivo*): **está condenado a muerte** he's been condemned to death; **está envasado en ...** it's packed in ...
5 (*con fechas*): **¿a cuántos estamos?** what's the date today?; **estamos a 5 de mayo** it's the 5th of May
6 (*locuciones*): **¿estamos?** (*¿de acuerdo?*) okay?; (*¿listo?*) ready?; **¡ya está bien!** that's enough!
7: ~ **de**: ~ **de vacaciones/viaje** to be on holiday/away *o* on a trip; **está de camarero** he's working as a waiter
8: ~ **para**: **está para salir** he's about to leave; **no estoy para bromas** I'm not in the mood for jokes
9: ~ **por** (*propuesta etc*) to be in favour of; (*persona etc*) to support, side with; **está por limpiar** it still has to be cleaned
10: ~ **sin**: ~ **sin dinero** to have no money; **está sin terminar** it isn't finished yet
♦ **~se** *vr*: **se estuvo en la cama toda la tarde** he stayed in bed all afternoon

estas ['estas] *adj demos ver* **este²**
éstas ['estas] *pron ver* **éste**
estatal [esta'tal] *adj* state *cpd*
estático, a [es'tatiko, a] *adj* static
estatua [es'tatwa] *nf* statue
estatura [esta'tura] *nf* stature, height
estatuto [esta'tuto] *nm* (*JUR*) statute; (*de ciudad*) bye-law; (*de comité*) rule
este¹ ['este] *nm* east
este² ['este] (*f* **esta**, *pl* **estos, estas**) *adj demos* (*sg*) this; (*pl*) these
esté *etc vb ver* **estar**
éste ['este] (*f* **ésta**, *pl* **éstos, éstas**) *pron* (*sg*) this (one); (*pl*) these (ones); **ése ... ~ ...** the former ... the latter ....
estelar [este'lar] *adj* (*ASTRO*) stellar; (*actuación, reparto*) star (*atr*)
estén *etc vb ver* **estar**
estepa [es'tepa] *nf* (*GEO*) steppe
estera [es'tera] *nf* mat(ting)
estéreo [es'tereo] *adj inv, nm* stereo; **estereotipo** *nm* stereotype
estéril [es'teril] *adj* sterile, barren; (*fig*) vain, futile; **esterilizar** *vt* to sterilize
esterlina [ester'lina] *adj*: **libra ~** pound sterling
estés *etc vb ver* **estar**
estética [es'tetika] *nf* aesthetics *sg*
estético, a [es'tetiko, a] *adj* aesthetic
estibador [estiβa'ðor] *nm* stevedore, docker
estiércol [es'tjerkol] *nm* dung, manure
estigma [es'tiɣma] *nm* stigma
estilarse [esti'larse] *vr* to be in fashion
estilo [es'tilo] *nm* style; (*TEC*) stylus; (*NATACIÓN*) stroke; **algo por el ~** something along those lines
estima [es'tima] *nf* esteem, respect
estimación [estima'θjon] *nf* (*evaluación*) estimation; (*aprecio, afecto*) esteem, regard
estimar [esti'mar] *vt* (*evaluar*) to estimate; (*valorar*) to value; (*apreciar*) to esteem, respect; (*pensar, considerar*) to think, reckon
estimulante [estimu'lante] *adj* stimulating ♦ *nm* stimulant

estimular [estimu'lar] *vt* to stimulate; (*excitar*) to excite
estímulo [es'timulo] *nm* stimulus; (*ánimo*) encouragement
estipulación [estipula'θjon] *nf* stipulation, condition
estipular [estipu'lar] *vt* to stipulate
estirado, a [esti'raðo, a] *adj* (*tenso*) (stretched *o* drawn) tight; (*fig: persona*) stiff, pompous
estirar [esti'rar] *vt* to stretch; (*dinero, suma etc*) to stretch out; **~se** *vr* to stretch
estirón [esti'ron] *nm* pull, tug; (*crecimiento*) spurt, sudden growth; **dar un ~** (*niño*) to shoot up
estirpe [es'tirpe] *nf* stock, lineage
estival [esti'βal] *adj* summer *cpd*
esto ['esto] *pron* this, this thing *o* matter; **~ de la boda** this business about the wedding
Estocolmo [esto'kolmo] *nm* Stockholm
estofado [esto'faðo] *nm* stew
estofar [esto'far] *vt* to stew
estómago [es'tomaɣo] *nm* stomach; **tener ~** to be thick-skinned
estorbar [estor'βar] *vt* to hinder, obstruct; (*molestar*) to bother, disturb ♦ *vi* to be in the way; **estorbo** *nm* (*molestia*) bother, nuisance; (*obstáculo*) hindrance, obstacle
estornudar [estornu'ðar] *vi* to sneeze
estos ['estos] *adj demos ver* **este²**
éstos ['estos] *pron ver* **éste**
estoy *vb ver* **estar**
estrado [es'traðo] *nm* platform
estrafalario, a [estrafa'larjo, a] *adj* odd, eccentric
estrago [es'traɣo] *nm* ruin, destruction; **hacer ~s en** to wreak havoc among
estragón [estra'ɣon] *nm* tarragon
estrambótico, a [estram'botiko, a] *adj* (*persona*) eccentric; (*peinado, ropa*) outlandish
estrangulador, a [estrangula'ðor, a] *nm/f* strangler ♦ *nm* (*TEC*) throttle; (*AUTO*) choke
estrangular [estrangu'lar] *vt* (*persona*) to

strangle; (*MED*) to strangulate

estratagema [estrata'xema] *nf* (*MIL*) stratagem; (*astucia*) cunning

estrategia [estra'texja] *nf* strategy; **estratégico, a** *adj* strategic

estrato [es'trato] *nm* stratum, layer

estrechamente [es'tretʃamente] *adv* (*íntimamente*) closely, intimately; (*pobremente: vivir*) poorly

estrechar [estre'tʃar] *vt* (*reducir*) to narrow; (*COSTURA*) to take in; (*abrazar*) to hug, embrace; **~se** *vr* (*reducirse*) to narrow, grow narrow; (*abrazarse*) to embrace; **~ la mano** to shake hands

estrechez [estre'tʃeθ] *nf* narrowness; (*de ropa*) tightness; **estrecheces** *nfpl* (*dificultades económicas*) financial difficulties

estrecho, a [es'tretʃo, a] *adj* narrow; (*apretado*) tight; (*íntimo*) close, intimate; (*miserable*) mean ♦ *nm* strait; **~ de miras** narrow-minded

estrella [es'treʎa] *nf* star; **~ de mar** (*ZOOL*) starfish; **~ fugaz** shooting star; **estrellado, a** *adj* (*forma*) star-shaped; (*cielo*) starry

estrellar [estre'ʎar] *vt* (*hacer añicos*) to smash (to pieces); (*huevos*) to fry; **~se** *vr* to smash; (*chocarse*) to crash; (*fracasar*) to fail

estremecer [estreme'θer] *vt* to shake; **~se** *vr* to shake, tremble; **estremecimiento** *nm* (*temblor*) trembling, shaking

estrenar [estre'nar] *vt* (*vestido*) to wear for the first time; (*casa*) to move into; (*película, obra de teatro*) to première; **~se** *vr* (*persona*) to make one's début; **estreno** *nm* (*CINE etc*) première

estreñido, a [estre'niðo, a] *adj* constipated

estreñimiento [estreni'mjento] *nm* constipation

estrépito [es'trepito] *nm* noise, racket; (*fig*) fuss; **estrepitoso, a** *adj* noisy; (*fiesta*) rowdy

estría [es'tria] *nf* groove

estribación [estriβa'θjon] *nf* (*GEO*) spur, foothill

estribar [estri'βar] *vi*: **~ en** to lie on

estribillo [estri'βiʎo] *nm* (*LITERATURA*) refrain; (*MUS*) chorus

estribo [es'triβo] *nm* (*de jinete*) stirrup; (*de coche, tren*) step; (*de puente*) support; (*GEO*) spur; **perder los ~s** to fly off the handle

estribor [estri'βor] *nm* (*NAUT*) starboard

estricto, a [es'trikto, a] *adj* (*riguroso*) strict; (*severo*) severe

estridente [estri'ðente] *adj* (*color*) loud; (*voz*) raucous

estropajo [estro'paxo] *nm* scourer

estropear [estrope'ar] *vt* to spoil; (*dañar*) to damage; **~se** *vr* (*objeto*) to get damaged; (*persona: la piel etc*) to be ruined

estructura [estruk'tura] *nf* structure

estruendo [es'trwendo] *nm* (*ruido*) racket, din; (*fig: alboroto*) uproar, turmoil

estrujar [estru'xar] *vt* (*apretar*) to squeeze; (*aplastar*) to crush; (*fig*) to drain, bleed

estuario [es'twarjo] *nm* estuary

estuche [es'tutʃe] *nm* box, case

estudiante [estu'ðjante] *nm/f* student; **estudiantil** *adj* student *cpd*

estudiar [estu'ðjar] *vt* to study

estudio [es'tuðjo] *nm* study; (*CINE, ARTE, RADIO*) studio; **~s** *nmpl* studies; (*erudición*) learning *sg*; **~so, a** *adj* studious

estufa [es'tufa] *nf* heater, fire

estupefaciente [estupefa'θjente] *nm* drug, narcotic

estupefacto, a [estupe'fakto, a] *adj* speechless, thunderstruck

estupendo, a [estu'pendo, a] *adj* wonderful, terrific; (*fam*) great; **¡~!** that's great!, fantastic!

estupidez [estupi'ðeθ] *nf* (*torpeza*) stupidity; (*acto*) stupid thing (to do)

estúpido, a [es'tupiðo, a] *adj* stupid, silly

estupor [estu'por] *nm* stupor; (*fig*) astonishment, amazement

estuve *etc vb ver* **estar**

esvástica [es'βastika] *nf* swastika

ETA ['eta] (*ESP*) *nf abr* (= Euskadi ta

Askatasuna) ETA

etapa [e'tapa] *nf* (*de viaje*) stage; (*DEPORTE*) leg; (*parada*) stopping place; (*fase*) stage, phase

etarra [e'tarra] *nm/f* member of ETA

etc. *abr* (= *etcétera*) etc

etcétera [et'θetera] *adv* etcetera

eternidad [eterni'ðað] *nf* eternity; **eterno, a** *adj* eternal, everlasting

ética ['etika] *nf* ethics *pl*

ético, a ['etiko, a] *adj* ethical

etiqueta [eti'keta] *nf* (*modales*) etiquette; (*rótulo*) label, tag

Eucaristía [eukaris'tia] *nf* Eucharist

eufemismo [eufe'mismo] *nm* euphemism

euforia [eu'forja] *nf* euphoria

eurodiputado, a [eurodipu'taðo, a] *nm/f* Euro MP, MEP

Europa [eu'ropa] *nf* Europe; **europeo, a** *adj, nm/f* European

Euskadi [eus'kaði] *nm* the Basque Country *o* Provinces *pl*

euskera [eus'kera] *nm* (*LING*) Basque

evacuación [eßakwa'θjon] *nf* evacuation

evacuar [eßa'kwar] *vt* to evacuate

evadir [eßa'ðir] *vt* to evade, avoid; **~se** *vr* to escape

evaluar [eßa'lwar] *vt* to evaluate

evangelio [eßan'xeljo] *nm* gospel

evaporar [eßapo'rar] *vt* to evaporate; **~se** *vr* to vanish

evasión [eßa'sjon] *nf* escape, flight; (*fig*) evasion; **~ de capitales** flight of capital

evasiva [eßa'sißa] *nf* (*pretexto*) excuse

evasivo, a [eßa'sißo, a] *adj* evasive, non-committal

evento [e'ßento] *nm* event

eventual [eßen'twal] *adj* possible, conditional (upon circumstances); (*trabajador*) casual, temporary

evidencia [eßi'ðenθja] *nf* evidence, proof; **evidenciar** *vt* (*hacer patente*) to make evident; (*probar*) to prove, show; **evidenciarse** *vr* to be evident

evidente [eßi'ðente] *adj* obvious, clear, evident

evitar [eßi'tar] *vt* (*evadir*) to avoid;

(*impedir*) to prevent

evocar [eßo'kar] *vt* to evoke, call forth

evolución [eßolu'θjon] *nf* (*desarrollo*) evolution, development; (*cambio*) change; (*MIL*) manoeuvre; **evolucionar** *vi* to evolve; to manoeuvre

ex [eks] *adj* ex-; **el ~ ministro** the former minister, the ex-minister

exacerbar [eksaθer'ßar] *vt* to irritate, annoy

exactamente [eksakta'mente] *adv* exactly

exactitud [eksakti'tuð] *nf* exactness; (*precisión*) accuracy; (*puntualidad*) punctuality; **exacto, a** *adj* exact; accurate; punctual; **¡exacto!** exactly!

exageración [eksaxera'θjon] *nf* exaggeration

exagerar [eksaxe'rar] *vt, vi* to exaggerate

exaltado, a [eksal'taðo, a] *adj* (*apasionado*) over-excited, worked-up; (*POL*) extreme

exaltar [eksal'tar] *vt* to exalt, glorify; **~se** *vr* (*excitarse*) to get excited *o* worked-up

examen [ek'samen] *nm* examination

examinar [eksami'nar] *vt* to examine; **~se** *vr* to be examined, take an examination

exasperar [eksaspe'rar] *vt* to exasperate; **~se** *vr* to get exasperated, lose patience

Exca. *abr* = **Excelencia**

excavadora [ekskaßa'ðora] *nf* excavator

excavar [ekska'ßar] *vt* to excavate

excedencia [eksθe'ðenθja] *nf*: **estar en ~** to be on leave; **pedir** *o* **solicitar la ~** to ask for leave

excedente [eksθe'ðente] *adj, nm* excess, surplus

exceder [eksθe'ðer] *vt* to exceed, surpass; **~se** *vr* (*extralimitarse*) to go too far

excelencia [eksθe'lenθja] *nf* excellence; **E~** Excellency; **excelente** *adj* excellent

excentricidad [eksθentriθi'ðað] *nf* eccentricity; **excéntrico, a** *adj, nm/f* eccentric

excepción [eksθep'θjon] *nf* exception; **excepcional** *adj* exceptional

excepto [eks'θepto] *adv* excepting, except (for)

exceptuar [eksθep'twar] *vt* to except, exclude

excesivo, a [eksθe'siβo, a] *adj* excessive

exceso [eks'θeso] *nm* (*gen*) excess; (*COM*) surplus; **~ de equipaje/peso** excess luggage/weight

excitación [eksθita'θjon] *nf* (*sensación*) excitement; (*acción*) excitation

excitado, a [eksθi'taðo, a] *adj* excited; (*emociones*) aroused

excitar [eksθi'tar] *vt* to excite; (*incitar*) to urge; **~se** *vr* to get excited

exclamación [eksklama'θjon] *nf* exclamation

exclamar [ekskla'mar] *vi* to exclaim

excluir [eksklu'ir] *vt* to exclude; (*dejar fuera*) to shut out; (*descartar*) to reject; **exclusión** *nf* exclusion

exclusiva [eksklu'siβa] *nf* (*PRENSA*) exclusive, scoop; (*COM*) sole right

exclusivo, a [eksklu'siβo, a] *adj* exclusive; **derecho ~** sole o exclusive right

Excmo. *abr* = **excelentísmo**

excomulgar [ekskomul'var] *vt* (*REL*) to excommunicate

excomunión [ekskomu'njon] *nf* excommunication

excursión [ekskur'sjon] *nf* excursion, outing; **excursionista** *nm/f* (*turista*) sightseer

excusa [eks'kusa] *nf* excuse; (*disculpa*) apology

excusar [eksku'sar] *vt* to excuse; **~se** *vr* (*disculparse*) to apologize

exhalar [eksa'lar] *vt* to exhale, breathe out; (*olor etc*) to give off; (*suspiro*) to breathe, heave

exhaustivo, a [eksaus'tiβo, a] *adj* (*análisis*) thorough; (*estudio*) exhaustive

exhausto, a [ek'sausto, a] *adj* exhausted

exhibición [eksiβi'θjon] *nf* exhibition, display, show

exhibir [eksi'βir] *vt* to exhibit, display, show

exhortar [eksor'tar] *vt*: **~ a** to exhort to

exigencia [eksi'xenθja] *nf* demand, requirement; **exigente** *adj* demanding

exigir [eksi'xir] *vt* (*gen*) to demand, require; **~ el pago** to demand payment

exiliado, a [eksi'ljaðo, a] *adj* exiled ♦ *nm/f* exile

exilio [ek'siljo] *nm* exile

eximir [eksi'mir] *vt* to exempt

existencia [eksis'tenθja] *nf* existence; **~s** *nfpl* stock(s) (*pl*)

existir [eksis'tir] *vi* to exist, be

éxito ['eksito] *nm* (*triunfo*) success; (*MUS etc*) hit; **tener ~** to be successful

exonerar [eksone'rar] *vt* to exonerate; **~ de una obligación** to free from an obligation

exorbitante [eksorβi'tante] *adj* (*precio*) exorbitant; (*cantidad*) excessive

exorcizar [eksorθi'θar] *vt* to exorcize

exótico, a [ek'sotiko, a] *adj* exotic

expandir [ekspan'dir] *vt* to expand

expansión [ekspan'sjon] *nf* expansion

expansivo, a [ekspan'siβo, a] *adj*: **onda ~** a shock wave

expatriarse [ekspa'trjarse] *vr* to emigrate; (*POL*) to go into exile

expectativa [ekspekta'tiβa] *nf* (*espera*) expectation; (*perspectiva*) prospect

expedición [ekspeði'θjon] *nf* (*excursión*) expedition

expediente [ekspe'ðjente] *nm* expedient; (*JUR: procedimiento*) action, proceedings *pl*; (: *papeles*) dossier, file, record

expedir [ekspe'ðir] *vt* (*despachar*) to send, forward; (*pasaporte*) to issue

expendedor, a [ekspende'ðor, a] *nm/f* (*vendedor*) dealer

expensas [eks'pensas] *nfpl*: **a ~ de** at the expense of

experiencia [ekspe'rjenθja] *nf* experience

experimentado, a [eksperimen'taðo, a] *adj* experienced

experimentar [eksperimen'tar] *vt* (*en laboratorio*) to experiment with; (*probar*) to test, try out; (*notar, observar*) to experience; (*deterioro, pérdida*) to suffer; **experimento** *nm* experiment

experto, a [eks'perto, a] *adj* expert, skilled ♦ *nm/f* expert

expiar [ekspi'ar] *vt* to atone for

expirar [ekspi'rar] *vi* to expire

explanada [ekspla'naða] *nf* (*llano*) plain

explayarse [ekspla'jarse] *vr* (*en discurso*) to speak at length; **~ con uno** to confide in sb

explicación [eksplika'θjon] *nf* explanation

explicar [ekspli'kar] *vt* to explain; **~se** *vr* to explain (o.s.)

explícito, a [eks'pliθito, a] *adj* explicit

explique *etc vb ver* **explicar**

explorador, a [eksplora'ðor, a] *nm/f* (*pionero*) explorer; (*MIL*) scout ♦ *nm* (*MED*) probe; (*TEC*) (*radar*) scanner

explorar [eksplo'rar] *vt* to explore; (*MED*) to probe; (*radar*) to scan

explosión [eksplo'sjon] *nf* explosion; **explosivo, a** *adj* explosive

explotación [eksplota'θjon] *nf* exploitation; (*de planta etc*) running

explotar [eksplo'tar] *vt* to exploit; to run, operate ♦ *vi* to explode

exponer [ekspo'ner] *vt* to expose; (*cuadro*) to display; (*vida*) to risk; (*idea*) to explain; **~se** *vr*: **~se a (hacer) algo** to run the risk of (doing) sth

exportación [eksporta'θjon] *nf* (*acción*) export; (*mercancías*) exports *pl*

exportar [ekspor'tar] *vt* to export

exposición [eksposi'θjon] *nf* (*gen*) exposure; (*de arte*) show, exhibition; (*explicación*) explanation; (*declaración*) account, statement

expresamente [ekspresa'mente] *adv* (*decir*) clearly; (*a propósito*) expressly

expresar [ekspre'sar] *vt* to express; **expresión** *nf* expression

expresivo, a [ekspre'sißo, a] *adj* (*persona, gesto, palabras*) expressive; (*cariñoso*) affectionate

expreso, a [eks'preso, a] *pp de* **expresar** ♦ *adj* (*explícito*) express; (*claro*) specific, clear; (*tren*) fast ♦ *adv*: **mandar ~** to send by express (delivery)

express [eks'pres] (*AM*) *adv*: **enviar algo ~** to send sth special delivery

exprimidor [eksprimi'ðor] *nm* squeezer

exprimir [ekspri'mir] *vt* (*fruta*) to squeeze; (*zumo*) to squeeze out

expropiar [ekspro'pjar] *vt* to expropriate

expuesto, a [eks'pwesto, a] *pp de* **exponer** ♦ *adj* exposed; (*cuadro etc*) on show, on display

expulsar [ekspul'sar] *vt* (*echar*) to eject, throw out; (*alumno*) to expel; (*despedir*) to sack, fire; (*DEPORTE*) to send off; **expulsión** *nf* expulsion; sending-off

exquisito, a [ekski'sito, a] *adj* exquisite; (*comida*) delicious

éxtasis ['ekstasis] *nm* ecstasy

extender [eksten'der] *vt* to extend; (*los brazos*) to stretch, hold out; (*mapa, tela*) to spread (out), open (out); (*mantequilla*) to spread; (*certificado*) to issue; (*cheque, recibo*) to make out; (*documento*) to draw up; **~se** *vr* (*gen*) to extend; (*persona: en el suelo*) to stretch out; (*epidemia*) to spread; **extendido, a** *adj* (*abierto*) spread out, open; (*brazos*) outstretched; (*costumbre*) widespread

extensión [eksten'sjon] *nf* (*de terreno, mar*) expanse, stretch; (*de tiempo*) length, duration; (*TEL*) extension; **en toda la ~ de la palabra** in every sense of the word

extenso, a [eks'tenso, a] *adj* extensive

extenuar [ekste'nwar] *vt* (*debilitar*) to weaken

exterior [ekste'rjor] *adj* (*de fuera*) external; (*afuera*) outside, exterior; (*apariencia*) outward; (*deuda, relaciones*) foreign ♦ *nm* (*gen*) exterior, outside; (*aspecto*) outward appearance; (*DEPORTE*) wing(er); (*países extranjeros*) abroad; **en el ~** abroad; **al ~** outwardly, on the surface

exterminar [ekstermi'nar] *vt* to exterminate; **exterminio** *nm* extermination

externo, a [eks'terno, a] *adj* (*exterior*) external, outside; (*superficial*) outward ♦ *nm/f* day pupil

extinguir [ekstin'gir] *vt* (*fuego*) to extinguish, put out; (*raza, población*) to wipe out; **~se** *vr* (*fuego*) to go out; (*BIO*) to die out, become extinct

extinto, a [eks'tinto, a] *adj* extinct
extintor [ekstin'tor] *nm* (fire) extinguisher
extirpar [ekstir'par] *vt* (MED) to remove (surgically)
extorsión [ekstor'sjon] *nf* extorsion
extra ['ekstra] *adj inv* (*tiempo*) extra; (*chocolate, vino*) good-quality ♦ *nm/f* extra ♦ *nm* extra; (*bono*) bonus
extracción [ekstrak'θjon] *nf* extraction; (*en lotería*) draw
extracto [eks'trakto] *nm* extract
extradición [ekstraði'θjon] *nf* extradition
extraer [ekstra'er] *vt* to extract, take out
extraescolar [ekstraesko'lar] *adj*:
actividad ~ extracurricular activity
extralimitarse [ekstralimi'tarse] *vr* to go too far
extranjero, a [ekstran'xero, a] *adj* foreign ♦ *nm/f* foreigner ♦ *nm* foreign countries *pl*; **en el ~** abroad
extrañar [ekstra'ɲar] *vt* (*sorprender*) to find strange *o* odd; (*echar de menos*) to miss; **~se** *vr* (*sorprenderse*) to be amazed, be surprised
extrañeza [ekstra'ɲeθa] *nf* (*rareza*) strangeness, oddness; (*asombro*) amazement, surprise
extraño, a [eks'traɲo, a] *adj* (*extranjero*) foreign; (*raro, sorprendente*) strange, odd
extraordinario, a [ekstraorði'narjo, a] *adj* extraordinary; (*edición, número*) special ♦ *nm* (*de periódico*) special edition; **horas extraordinarias** overtime *sg*
extrarradio [ekstra'rraðjo] *nm* suburbs
extravagancia [ekstraβaɣa'vanθja] *nf* oddness; outlandishness; **extravagante** *adj* (*excéntrico*) eccentric; (*estrafalario*) outlandish
extraviado, a [ekstra'βjaðo, a] *adj* lost, missing
extraviar [ekstra'βjar] *vt* (*persona: desorientar*) to mislead, misdirect; (*perder*) to lose, misplace; **~se** *vr* to lose one's way, get lost; **extravío** *nm* loss; (*fig*) deviation
extremar [ekstre'mar] *vt* to carry to extremes; **~se** *vr* to do one's utmost,

make every effort
extremaunción [ekstremaun'θjon] *nf* extreme unction
extremidad [ekstremi'ðað] *nf* (*punta*) extremity; **~es** *nfpl* (ANAT) extremities
extremo, a [eks'tremo, a] *adj* extreme; (*último*) last ♦ *nm* end; (*límite, grado sumo*) extreme; **en último ~** as a last resort
extrovertido, a [ekstroβer'tiðo, a] *adj, nm/f* extrovert
exuberancia [eksuβe'ranθja] *nf* exuberance; **exuberante** *adj* exuberant; (*fig*) luxuriant, lush
eyacular [ejaku'lar] *vt, vi* to ejaculate

F, f

f.a.b. *abr* (= *franco a bordo*) f.o.b.
fabada [fa'βaða] *nf* bean and sausage stew
fábrica ['faβrika] *nf* factory; **marca de ~** trademark; **precio de ~** factory price
fabricación [faβrika'θjon] *nf* (*manufactura*) manufacture; (*producción*) production; **de ~ casera** home-made; **~ en serie** mass production
fabricante [faβri'kante] *nm/f* manufacturer
fabricar [faβri'kar] *vt* (*manufacturar*) to manufacture, make; (*construir*) to build; (*cuento*) to fabricate, devise
fábula ['faβula] *nf* (*cuento*) fable; (*chisme*) rumour; (*mentira*) fib
fabuloso, a [faβu'loso, a] *adj* (*oportunidad, tiempo*) fabulous, great
facción [fak'θjon] *nf* (POL) faction; **facciones** *nfpl* (*del rostro*) features
faceta [fa'θeta] *nf* facet
facha ['fatʃa] *nf* (*fam*) (*aspecto*) look; (*cara*) face
fachada [fa'tʃaða] *nf* (ARQ) façade, front
fácil ['faθil] *adj* (*simple*) easy; (*probable*) likely
facilidad [faθili'ðað] *nf* (*capacidad*) ease; (*sencillez*) simplicity; (*de palabra*) fluency; **~es** *nfpl* facilities

facilitar [faθili'tar] vt (hacer fácil) to make easy; (proporcionar) to provide

fácilmente ['faθilmente] adv easily

facsímil [fak'simil] nm facsimile, fax

factible [fak'tiβle] adj feasible

factor [fak'tor] nm factor

factura [fak'tura] nf (cuenta) bill; **facturación** nf (de equipaje) check-in; **facturar** vt (COM) to invoice, charge for; (equipaje) to check in

facultad [fakul'taθ] nf (aptitud, ESCOL etc) faculty; (poder) power

faena [fa'ena] nf (trabajo) work; (quehacer) task, job

faisán [fai'san] nm pheasant

faja ['faxa] nf (para la cintura) sash; (de mujer) corset; (de tierra) strip

fajo ['faxo] nm (de papeles) bundle; (de billetes) wad

falacia [fa'laθja] nf fallacy

falda ['falda] nf (prenda de vestir) skirt

falla ['faʎa] nf (defecto) fault, flaw

fallar [fa'ʎar] vt (JUR) to pronounce sentence on ♦ vi (memoria) to fail; (motor) to miss

---

Fallas

i In the week of 19 March (the feast of San José), Valencia honours its patron saint with a spectacular fiesta called **Las Fallas**. The **Fallas** are huge papier-mâché, cardboard and wooden sculptures which are built by competing teams throughout the year. They depict politicians and well-known public figures and are thrown onto bonfires and set alight once a jury has judged them - only the best sculpture escapes the flames.

---

fallecer [faʎe'θer] vi to pass away, die; **fallecimiento** nm decease, demise

fallido, a [fa'ʎiðo, a] adj (gen) frustrated, unsuccessful

fallo ['faʎo] nm (JUR) verdict, ruling; (fracaso) failure; ~ **cardíaco** heart failure

falsedad [false'ðaθ] nf falseness; (hipocresía) hypocrisy; (mentira) falsehood

falsificar [falsifi'kar] vt (firma etc) to forge; (moneda) to counterfeit

falso, a ['falso, a] adj false; (documento, moneda etc) fake; **en ~** falsely

falta ['falta] nf (defecto) fault, flaw; (privación) lack, want; (ausencia) absence; (carencia) shortage; (equivocación) mistake; (DEPORTE) foul; **echar en ~** to miss; **hacer ~ hacer algo** to be necessary to do sth; **me hace ~ una pluma** I need a pen; **~ de educación** bad manners pl

faltar [fal'tar] vi (escasear) to be lacking, be wanting; (ausentarse) to be absent, be missing; **faltan 2 horas para llegar** there are 2 hours to go till arrival; **~ al respeto a uno** to be disrespectful to sb; **¡no faltaba más!** (no hay de qué) don't mention it

fama ['fama] nf (renombre) fame; (reputación) reputation

famélico, a [fa'meliko, a] adj starving

familia [fa'milja] nf family; **~ política** in-laws pl

familiar [fami'ljar] adj (relativo a la familia) family cpd; (conocido, informal) familiar ♦ nm relative, relation; **~idad** nf (gen) familiarity; (informalidad) homeliness; **~izarse** vr: **~izarse con** to familiarize o.s. with

famoso, a [fa'moso, a] adj (renombrado) famous

fanático, a [fa'natiko, a] adj fanatical ♦ nm/f fanatic; (CINE, DEPORTE) fan; **fanatismo** nm fanaticism

fanfarrón, ona [fanfa'rron, ona] adj boastful

fango ['fango] nm mud; **~so, a** adj muddy

fantasía [fanta'sia] nf fantasy, imagination; **joyas de ~** imitation jewellery sg

fantasma [fan'tasma] nm (espectro) ghost, apparition; (fanfarrón) show-off

fantástico, a [fan'tastiko, a] adj fantastic

farmacéutico, a [farma'θeutiko, a] adj pharmaceutical ♦ nm/f chemist (BRIT), pharmacist

farmacia [far'maθja] nf chemist's (shop)

(*BRIT*), pharmacy; ~ **de turno** duty chemist; ~ **de guardia** all-night chemist

fármaco ['farmako] *nm* drug

faro ['faro] *nm* (*NAUT*: *torre*) lighthouse; (*AUTO*) headlamp; ~**s antiniebla** fog lamps; ~**s delanteros/traseros** headlights/rear lights

farol [fa'rol] *nm* lantern, lamp

farola [fa'rola] *nf* street lamp (*BRIT*) *o* light (*US*)

farsa ['farsa] *nf* (*gen*) farce

farsante [far'sante] *nm/f* fraud, fake

fascículo [fas'θikulo] *nm* (*de revista*) part, instalment

fascinar [fasθi'nar] *vt* (*gen*) to fascinate

fascismo [fas'θismo] *nm* fascism; **fascista** *adj*, *nm/f* fascist

fase ['fase] *nf* phase

fastidiar [fasti'ðjar] *vt* (*molestar*) to annoy, bother; (*estropear*) to spoil; ~**se** *vr*: **¡que se fastidie!** (*fam*) he'll just have to put up with it!

fastidio [fas'tiðjo] *nm* (*molestia*) annoyance; ~**so, a** *adj* (*molesto*) annoying

fastuoso, a [fas'twoso, a] *adj* (*banquete*, *boda*) lavish; (*acto*) pompous

fatal [fa'tal] *adj* (*gen*) fatal; (*desgraciado*) ill-fated; (*fam*: *malo*, *pésimo*) awful; ~**idad** *nf* (*destino*) fate; (*mala suerte*) misfortune

fatiga [fa'tixa] *nf* (*cansancio*) fatigue, weariness

fatigar [fati'xar] *vt* to tire, weary; ~**se** *vr* to get tired

fatigoso, a [fati'xoso, a] *adj* (*cansador*) tiring

fatuo, a ['fatwo, a] *adj* (*vano*) fatuous; (*presuntuoso*) conceited

favor [fa'ßor] *nm* favour; **estar a ~ de** to be in favour of; **haga el ~ de...** would you be so good as to..., kindly...; **por ~** please; ~**able** *adj* favourable

favorecer [faßore'θer] *vt* to favour; (*vestido etc*) to become, flatter; **este peinado le favorece** this hairstyle suits him

favorito, a [faßo'rito, a] *adj*, *nm/f* favourite

fax [faks] *nm inv* fax; **mandar por ~** to fax

faz [faθ] *nf* face; **la ~ de la tierra** the face of the earth

fe [fe] *nf* (*REL*) faith; (*documento*) certificate; **prestar ~ a** to believe, credit; **actuar con buena/mala ~** to act in good/bad faith; **dar ~ de** to bear witness to

fealdad [feal'dað] *nf* ugliness

febrero [fe'ßrero] *nm* February

febril [fe'ßril] *adj* (*fig*: *actividad*) hectic; (*mente*, *mirada*) feverish

fecha ['fetʃa] *nf* date; ~ **de caducidad** (*de producto alimenticio*) sell-by date; (*de contrato etc*) expiry date; **con ~ adelantada** postdated; **en ~ próxima** soon; **hasta la ~** to date, so far; **poner ~** to date; **fechar** *vt* to date

fecundar [fekun'dar] *vt* (*generar*) to fertilize, make fertile; **fecundo, a** *adj* (*fértil*) fertile; (*fig*) prolific; (*productivo*) productive

federación [feðera'θjon] *nf* federation

felicidad [feliθi'ðað] *nf* happiness; ~**es** *nfpl* (*felicitaciones*) best wishes, congratulations

felicitación [feliθita'θjon] *nf*: **¡felicitaciones!** congratulations!

felicitar [feliθi'tar] *vt* to congratulate

feligrés, esa [feli'ɣres, esa] *nm/f* parishioner

feliz [fe'liθ] *adj* happy

felpudo [fel'puðo] *nm* doormat

femenino, a [feme'nino, a] *adj*, *nm* feminine

feminista [femi'nista] *adj*, *nm/f* feminist

fenómeno [fe'nomeno] *nm* phenomenon; (*fig*) freak, accident ♦ *adj* great ♦ *excl* great!, marvellous!; **fenomenal** *adj* = **fenómeno**

feo, a ['feo, a] *adj* (*gen*) ugly; (*desagradable*) bad, nasty

féretro ['feretro] *nm* (*ataúd*) coffin; (*sarcófago*) bier

feria ['ferja] *nf* (*gen*) fair; (*descanso*) holiday, rest day; (*AM*: *mercado*) village market; (: *cambio*) loose *o* small change

fermentar [fermen'tar] *vi* to ferment
ferocidad [feroθi'ðað] *nf* fierceness, ferocity
feroz [fe'roθ] *adj* (*cruel*) cruel; (*salvaje*) fierce
férreo, a ['ferreo, a] *adj* iron
ferretería [ferrete'ria] *nf* (*tienda*) ironmonger's (shop) (*BRIT*), hardware store
ferrocarril [ferroka'rril] *nm* railway
ferroviario, a [ferro'ßjarjo, a] *adj* rail *cpd*
fértil ['fertil] *adj* (*productivo*) fertile; (*rico*) rich; **fertilidad** *nf* (*gen*) fertility; (*productividad*) fruitfulness
ferviente [fer'ßjente] *adj* fervent
fervor [fer'ßor] *nm* fervour; **~oso, a** *adj* fervent
festejar [feste'xar] *vt* (*celebrar*) to celebrate
festejo [fes'texo] *nm* celebration; **festejos** *nmpl* (*fiestas*) festivals
festín [fes'tin] *nm* feast, banquet
festival [festi'ßal] *nm* festival
festividad [festißi'ðað] *nf* festivity
festivo, a [fes'tißo, a] *adj* (*de fiesta*) festive; (*CINE, LITERATURA*) humorous; **día ~** holiday
fétido, a ['fetiðo, a] *adj* foul-smelling
feto ['feto] *nm* foetus
fiable ['fjaßle] *adj* (*persona*) trustworthy; (*máquina*) reliable
fiador, a [fia'ðor, a] *nm/f* (*JUR*) surety, guarantor; (*COM*) backer; **salir ~ por uno** to stand bail for sb
fiambre ['fjambre] *nm* cold meat
fianza ['fianθa] *nf* surety; (*JUR*): **libertad bajo ~** release on bail
fiar [fi'ar] *vt* (*salir garante de*) to guarantee; (*vender a crédito*) to sell on credit; (*secreto*): **~ a** to confide (to) ♦ *vi* to trust; **~se** *vr* to trust (in), rely on; **~se de uno** to rely on sb
fibra ['fißra] *nf* fibre; **~ óptica** optical fibre
ficción [fik'θjon] *nf* fiction
ficha ['fitʃa] *nf* (*TEL*) token; (*en juegos*) counter, marker; (*tarjeta*) (index) card; **fichar** *vt* (*archivar*) to file, index; (*DEPORTE*) to sign; **estar fichado** to have

a record; **fichero** *nm* box file; (*INFORM*) file
ficticio, a [fik'tiθjo, a] *adj* (*imaginario*) fictitious; (*falso*) fabricated
fidelidad [fiðeli'ðað] *nf* (*lealtad*) fidelity, loyalty; **alta ~** high fidelity, hi-fi
fideos [fi'ðeos] *nmpl* noodles
fiebre ['fjeßre] *nf* (*MED*) fever; (*fig*) fever, excitement; **~ amarilla/del heno** yellow/hay fever; **~ palúdica** malaria; **tener ~** to have a temperature
fiel [fjel] *adj* (*leal*) faithful, loyal; (*fiable*) reliable; (*exacto*) accurate, faithful ♦ *nm*: **los ~es** the faithful
fieltro ['fjeltro] *nm* felt
fiera ['fjera] *nf* (*animal feroz*) wild animal *o* beast; (*fig*) dragon; *ver tb* **fiero**
fiero, a ['fjero, a] *adj* (*cruel*) cruel; (*feroz*) fierce; (*duro*) harsh
fiesta ['fjesta] *nf* party; (*de pueblo*) festival; (*vacaciones, tb*: **~s**) holiday *sg*; (*REL*): **~ de guardar** day of obligation

---

Fiestas

Fiestas can be official public holidays or holidays set by each autonomous region, many of which coincide with religious festivals. There are also many **fiestas** all over Spain for a local patron saint or the Virgin Mary. These often last several days and can include religious processions, carnival parades, bullfights and dancing.

---

figura [fi'ɣura] *nf* (*gen*) figure; (*forma, imagen*) shape, form; (*NAIPES*) face card
figurar [fiɣu'rar] *vt* (*representar*) to represent; (*fingir*) to figure ♦ *vi* to figure; **~se** *vr* (*imaginarse*) to imagine; (*suponer*) to suppose
fijador [fixa'ðor] *nm* (*FOTO etc*) fixative; (*de pelo*) gel
fijar [fi'xar] *vt* (*gen*) to fix; (*estampilla*) to affix, stick (on); **~se** *vr*: **~se en** to notice
fijo, a ['fixo, a] *adj* (*gen*) fixed; (*firme*) firm; (*permanente*) permanent ♦ *adv*: **mirar ~** to stare

fila ['fila] *nf* row; (*MIL*) rank; **ponerse en ~** to line up, get into line

filántropo, a [fi'lantropo, a] *nm/f* philanthropist

filatelia [fila'telja] *nf* philately, stamp collecting

filete [fi'lete] *nm* (*carne*) fillet steak; (*pescado*) fillet

filiación [filja'θjon] *nf* (*POL*) affiliation

filial [fi'ljal] *adj* filial ♦ *nf* subsidiary

Filipinas [fili'pinas] *nfpl*: **las ~** the Philippines; **filipino, a** *adj, nm/f* Philippine

filmar [fil'mar] *vt* to film, shoot

filo ['filo] *nm* (*gen*) edge; **sacar ~ a** to sharpen; **al ~ del mediodía** at about midday; **de doble ~** double-edged

filón [fi'lon] *nm* (*MINERÍA*) vein, lode; (*fig*) goldmine

filosofía [filoso'fia] *nf* philosophy; **filósofo, a** *nm/f* philosopher

filtrar [fil'trar] *vt, vi* to filter, strain; **~se** *vr* to filter; **filtro** *nm* (*TEC, utensilio*) filter

fin [fin] *nm* end; (*objetivo*) aim, purpose; **al ~ y al cabo** when all's said and done; **a ~ de** in order to; **por ~** finally; **en ~** in short; **~ de semana** weekend

final [fi'nal] *adj* final ♦ *nm* end, conclusion ♦ *nf* final; **~idad** *nf* (*propósito*) purpose, intention; **~ista** *nm/f* finalist; **~izar** *vt* to end, finish; (*INFORM*) to log out o off ♦ *vi* to end, come to an end

financiar [finan'θjar] *vt* to finance; **financiero, a** *adj* financial ♦ *nm/f* financier

finca ['finka] *nf* (*bien inmueble*) property, land; (*casa de campo*) country house; (*AM*) farm

fingir [fin'xir] *vt* (*simular*) to simulate, feign ♦ *vi* (*aparentar*) to pretend

finlandés, esa [finlan'des, esa] *adj* Finnish ♦ *nm/f* Finn ♦ *nm* (*LING*) Finnish

Finlandia [fin'landja] *nf* Finland

fino, a ['fino, a] *adj* fine; (*delgado*) slender; (*de buenas maneras*) polite, refined; (*jerez*) fino, dry

firma ['firma] *nf* signature; (*COM*) firm, company

firmamento [firma'mento] *nm* firmament

firmar [fir'mar] *vt* to sign

firme ['firme] *adj* firm; (*estable*) stable; (*sólido*) solid; (*constante*) steady; (*decidido*) resolute ♦ *nm* road (surface); **~mente** *adv* firmly; **~za** *nf* firmness; (*constancia*) steadiness; (*solidez*) solidity

fiscal [fis'kal] *adj* fiscal ♦ *nm/f* public prosecutor; **año ~** tax o fiscal year

fisco ['fisko] *nm* (*hacienda*) treasury, exchequer (*BRIT*)

fisgar [fis'var] *vt* to pry into

fisgonear [fisvone'ar] *vt* to poke one's nose into ♦ *vi* to pry, spy

física ['fisika] *nf* physics *sg*; *ver tb* **físico**

físico, a ['fisiko, a] *adj* physical ♦ *nm* physique ♦ *nm/f* physicist

fisura [fi'sura] *nf* crack; (*MED*) fracture

flác(c)ido, a ['fla(k)θido, a] *adj* flabby

flaco, a ['flako, a] *adj* (*muy delgado*) skinny, thin; (*débil*) weak, feeble

flagrante [fla'xrante] *adj* flagrant

flamante [fla'mante] (*fam*) *adj* brilliant; (*nuevo*) brand-new

flamenco, a [fla'menko, a] *adj* (*de Flandes*) Flemish; (*baile, música*) flamenco ♦ *nm* (*baile, música*) flamenco

flan [flan] *nm* creme caramel

flaqueza [fla'keθa] *nf* (*delgadez*) thinness, leanness; (*fig*) weakness

flash [flaʃ] (*pl* **~s** o **~es**) *nm* (*FOTO*) flash

flauta ['flauta] *nf* (*MUS*) flute

flecha ['fletʃa] *nf* arrow

flechazo [fle'tʃaθo] *nm* love at first sight

fleco ['fleko] *nm* fringe

flema ['flema] *nm* phlegm

flequillo [fle'kiʎo] *nm* (*pelo*) fringe

flexible [flek'sißle] *adj* flexible

flexión [flek'sjon] *nf* press-up

flexo ['flekso] *nm* adjustable table-lamp

flojera [flo'xera] (*AM: fam*) *nf*: **me da ~** I can't be bothered

flojo, a ['floxo, a] *adj* (*gen*) loose; (*sin fuerzas*) limp; (*débil*) weak

flor [flor] *nf* flower; **a ~ de** on the surface of; **~ecer** *vi* (*BOT*) to flower, bloom; (*fig*) to flourish; **~eciente** *adj* (*BOT*) in flower, flowering; (*fig*) thriving; **~ero** *nm* vase; **~istería** *nf* florist's (shop)

flota ['flota] *nf* fleet

flotador [flota'ðor] *nm* (*gen*) float; (*para nadar*) rubber ring

flotar [flo'tar] *vi* (*gen*) to float; **flote** *nm*: **a flote** afloat; **salir a flote** (*fig*) to get back on one's feet

fluctuar [fluk'twar] *vi* (*oscilar*) to fluctuate

fluidez [flui'ðeθ] *nf* fluidity; (*fig*) fluency

flúido, a ['fluiðo, a] *adj, nm* fluid

fluir [flu'ir] *vi* to flow

flujo ['fluxo] *nm* flow; **~ y reflujo** ebb and flow

flúor ['fluor] *nm* fluoride

fluvial [flußi'al] *adj* (*navegación, cuenca*) fluvial, river *cpd*

foca ['foka] *nf* seal

foco ['foko] *nm* focus; (*ELEC*) floodlight; (*AM*) (light) bulb

fofo, a ['fofo, a] *adj* soft, spongy; (*carnes*) flabby

fogata [fo'vata] *nf* bonfire

fogón [fo'von] *nm* (*de cocina*) ring, burner

fogoso, a [fo'xoso, a] *adj* spirited

folio ['foljo] *nm* folio, page

follaje [fo'ʎaxe] *nm* foliage

folletín [foʎe'tin] *nm* newspaper serial

folleto [fo'ʎeto] *nm* (*POL*) pamphlet

follón [fo'ʎon] (*fam*) *nm* (*lío*) mess; (*conmoción*) fuss; **armar un ~** to kick up a row

fomentar [fomen'tar] *vt* (*MED*) to foment; **fomento** *nm* (*promoción*) promotion

fonda ['fonda] *nf* inn

fondo ['fondo] *nm* (*de mar*) bottom; (*de coche, sala*) back; (*ARTE etc*) background; (*reserva*) fund; **~s** *nmpl* (*COM*) funds, resources; **una investigación a ~** a thorough investigation; **en el ~** at bottom, deep down

fontanería [fontane'ria] *nf* plumbing; **fontanero, a** *nm/f* plumber

footing ['futɪn] *nm* jogging; **hacer ~** to jog, go jogging

forastero, a [foras'tero, a] *nm/f* stranger

forcejear [forθexe'ar] *vi* (*luchar*) to struggle

forense [fo'rense] *nm/f* pathologist

forjar [for'xar] *vt* to forge

forma ['forma] *nf* (*figura*) form, shape; (*MED*) fitness; (*método*) way, means; **las ~s** the conventions; **estar en ~** to be fit

formación [forma'θjon] *nf* (*gen*) formation; (*educación*) education; **~ profesional** vocational training

formal [for'mal] *adj* (*gen*) formal; (*fig: serio*) serious; (: *de fiar*) reliable; **~idad** *nf* formality; seriousness; **~izar** *vt* (*JUR*) to formalize; (*situación*) to put in order, regularize; **~izarse** *vr* (*situación*) to be put in order, be regularized

formar [for'mar] *vt* (*componer*) to form, shape; (*constituir*) to make up, constitute; (*ESCOL*) to train, educate; **~se** *vr* (*ESCOL*) to be trained, educated; (*cobrar forma*) to form, take form; (*desarrollarse*) to develop

formatear [formate'ar] *vt* to format

formativo, a [forma'tiβo, a] *adj* (*lecturas, años*) formative

formato [for'mato] *nm* format

formidable [formi'ðaβle] *adj* (*temible*) formidable; (*estupendo*) tremendous

fórmula ['formula] *nf* formula

formular [formu'lar] *vt* (*queja*) to make, lodge; (*petición*) to draw up; (*pregunta*) to pose

formulario [formu'larjo] *nm* form

fornido, a [for'niðo, a] *adj* well-built

forrar [fo'rrar] *vt* (*abrigo*) to line; (*libro*) to cover; **forro** *nm* (*de cuaderno*) cover; (*COSTURA*) lining; (*de sillón*) upholstery

fortalecer [fortale'θer] *vt* to strengthen

fortaleza [forta'leθa] *nf* (*MIL*) fortress, stronghold; (*fuerza*) strength; (*determinación*) resolution

fortuito, a [for'twito, a] *adj* accidental

fortuna [for'tuna] *nf* (*suerte*) fortune, (good) luck; (*riqueza*) fortune, wealth

forzar [for'θar] *vt* (*puerta*) to force (open); (*compeler*) to compel

forzoso, a [for'θoso, a] *adj* necessary

fosa ['fosa] *nf* (*sepultura*) grave; (*en tierra*)

pit; **~s nasales** nostrils
fósforo ['fosforo] *nm* (*QUÍM*) phosphorus;
  (*cerilla*) match
foso ['foso] *nm* ditch; (*TEATRO*) pit; (*AUTO*):
  ~ de reconocimiento inspection pit
foto ['foto] *nf* photo, snap(shot); **sacar
  una ~** to take a photo *o* picture
fotocopia [foto'kopja] *nf* photocopy;
  fotocopiadora *nf* photocopier;
  fotocopiar *vt* to photocopy
fotografía [fotoɣra'fia] *nf* (*ARTE*)
  photography; (*una ~*) photograph;
  fotografiar *vt* to photograph
fotógrafo, a [fo'toɣrafo, a] *nm/f*
  photographer
fracasar [fraka'sar] *vi* (*gen*) to fail
fracaso [fra'kaso] *nm* failure
fracción [frak'θjon] *nf* fraction;
  fraccionamiento (*AM*) *nm* housing
  estate
fractura [frak'tura] *nf* fracture, break
fragancia [fra'ɣanθja] *nf* (*olor*) fragrance,
  perfume
frágil ['fraxil] *adj* (*débil*) fragile; (*COM*)
  breakable
fragmento [fraɣ'mento] *nm* (*pedazo*)
  fragment
fragua ['fraɣwa] *nf* forge; **fraguar** *vt* to
  forge; (*fig*) to concoct ♦ *vi* to harden
fraile ['fraile] *nm* (*REL*) friar; (: *monje*)
  monk
frambuesa [fram'bwesa] *nf* raspberry
francamente [franka'mente] *adv* (*hablar,
  decir*) frankly; (*realmente*) really
francés, esa [fran'θes, esa] *adj* French
  ♦ *nm/f* Frenchman/woman ♦ *nm* (*LING*)
  French
Francia ['franθja] *nf* France
franco, a ['franko, a] *adj* (*cándido*) frank,
  open; (*COM: exento*) free ♦ *nm* (*moneda*)
  franc
francotirador, a [frankotira'ðor, a] *nm/f*
  sniper
franela [fra'nela] *nf* flannel
franja ['franxa] *nf* fringe
franquear [franke'ar] *vt* (*camino*) to clear;
  (*carta, paquete postal*) to frank, stamp;

(*obstáculo*) to overcome
franqueo [fran'keo] *nm* postage
franqueza [fran'keθa] *nf* (*candor*)
  frankness
frasco ['frasko] *nm* bottle, flask; **~ al vacío**
  (vacuum) flask
frase ['frase] *nf* sentence; **~ hecha** set
  phrase; (*pey*) stock phrase
fraterno, a [fra'terno, a] *adj* brotherly,
  fraternal
fraude ['frauðe] *nm* (*cualidad*) dishonesty;
  (*acto*) fraud; **fraudulento, a** *adj*
  fraudulent
frazada [fra'saða] (*AM*) *nf* blanket
frecuencia [fre'kwenθja] *nf* frequency;
  con ~ frequently, often
frecuentar [frekwen'tar] *vt* to frequent
fregadero [freɣa'ðero] *nm* (kitchen) sink
fregar [fre'ɣar] *vt* (*frotar*) to scrub; (*platos*)
  to wash (up); (*AM*) to annoy
fregona [fre'ɣona] *nf* mop
freír [fre'ir] *vt* to fry
frenar [fre'nar] *vt* to brake; (*fig*) to check
frenazo [fre'naθo] *nm*: **dar un ~** to brake
  sharply
frenesí [frene'si] *nm* frenzy; **frenético, a**
  adj frantic
freno ['freno] *nm* (*TEC, AUTO*) brake; (*de
  cabalgadura*) bit; (*fig*) check
frente ['frente] *nm* (*ARQ, POL*) front; (*de
  objeto*) front part ♦ *nf* forehead, brow; **~
  a** in front of; (*en situación opuesta de*)
  opposite; **al ~ de** (*fig*) at the head of;
  chocar de ~ to crash head-on; **hacer ~ a**
  to face up to
fresa ['fresa] (*ESP*) *nf* strawberry
fresco, a ['fresko, a] *adj* (*nuevo*) fresh;
  (*frío*) cool; (*descarado*) cheeky ♦ *nm* (*aire*)
  fresh air; (*ARTE*) fresco; (*AM: jugo*) fruit
  drink ♦ *nm/f* (*fam*): **ser un ~** to have a
  nerve; **tomar el ~** to get some fresh air;
  frescura *nf* freshness; (*descaro*) cheek,
  nerve
frialdad [frial'dað] *nf* (*gen*) coldness;
  (*indiferencia*) indifference
fricción [frik'θjon] *nf* (*gen*) friction; (*acto*)
  rub(bing); (*MED*) massage

frigidez [frixi'ðeθ] *nf* frigidity

frigorífico [friɣo'rifiko] *nm* refrigerator

frijol [fri'xol] *nm* kidney bean

frío, a *etc* ['frio, a] *vb ver* **freír ♦** *adj* cold; (*indiferente*) indifferent ♦ *nm* cold; indifference; **hace ~** it's cold; **tener ~** to be cold

frito, a ['frito, a] *adj* fried; **me trae ~ ese hombre** I'm sick and tired of that man; **fritos** *nmpl* fried food

frívolo, a ['friβolo, a] *adj* frivolous

frontal [fron'tal] *adj* frontal; **choque ~** head-on collision

frontera [fron'tera] *nf* frontier; **fronterizo, a** *adj* frontier *cpd*; (*contiguo*) bordering

frontón [fron'ton] *nm* (*DEPORTE: cancha*) pelota court; (: *juego*) pelota

frotar [fro'tar] *vt* to rub; **~se** *vr*: **~se las manos** to rub one's hands

fructífero, a [fruk'tifero, a] *adj* fruitful

fruncir [frun'θir] *vt* to pucker; (*COSTURA*) to pleat; **~ el ceño** to knit one's brow

frustrar [frus'trar] *vt* to frustrate

fruta ['fruta] *nf* fruit; **frutería** *nf* fruit shop; **frutero, a** *adj* fruit *cpd* ♦ *nm/f* fruiterer ♦ *nm* fruit bowl

frutilla [fru'tiʎa] (*AM*) *nf* strawberry

fruto ['fruto] *nm* fruit; (*fig: resultado*) result; (: *beneficio*) benefit; **~s secos** nuts; (*pasas etc*) dried fruit *sg*

fue *vb ver* **ser, ir**

fuego ['fweɣo] *nm* (*gen*) fire; **a ~ lento** on a low heat; **¿tienes ~?** have you (got) a light?; **~s artificiales** *o* **de artificio** fireworks

fuente ['fwente] *nf* fountain; (*manantial, fig*) spring; (*origen*) source; (*plato*) large dish

fuera *etc* ['fwera] *vb ver* **ser, ir ♦** *adv* out(side); (*en otra parte*) away; (*excepto, salvo*) except, save ♦ *prep*: **~ de** outside; (*fig*) besides; **~ de sí** beside o.s.; **por ~** (on the) outside

fuera-borda [fwera'βorða] *nm* speedboat

fuerte ['fwerte] *adj* strong; (*golpe*) hard; (*ruido*) loud; (*comida*) rich; (*lluvia*) heavy;

(*dolor*) intense ♦ *adv* strongly; hard; loud(ly)

fuerza *etc* ['fwerθa] *vb ver* **forzar ♦** *nf* (*fortaleza*) strength; (*TEC, ELEC*) power; (*coacción*) force; (*MIL: tb:* **~s**) forces *pl*; **a ~ de** by dint of; **cobrar ~s** to recover one's strength; **tener ~s para** to have the strength to; **a la ~** forcibly, by force; **por ~** of necessity; **~ de voluntad** willpower

fuga ['fuɣa] *nf* (*huida*) flight, escape; (*de gas etc*) leak

fugarse [fu'ɣarse] *vr* to flee, escape

fugaz [fu'ɣaθ] *adj* fleeting

fugitivo, a [fuxi'tiβo, a] *adj, nm/f* fugitive

fui *vb ver* **ser; ir**

fulano, a [fu'lano, a] *nm/f* so-and-so, what's-his-name/what's-her-name

fulminante [fulmi'nante] *adj* (*fig: mirada*) fierce; (*MED: enfermedad, ataque*) sudden; (*fam: éxito, golpe*) sudden

fumador, a [fuma'ðor, a] *nm/f* smoker

fumar [fu'mar] *vt, vi* to smoke; **~ en pipa** to smoke a pipe

función [fun'θjon] *nf* function; (*en trabajo*) duties *pl*; (*espectáculo*) show; **entrar en funciones** to take up one's duties

funcionar [funθjo'nar] *vi* (*gen*) to function; (*máquina*) to work; **"no funciona"** "out of order"

funcionario, a [funθjo'narjo, a] *nm/f* civil servant

funda ['funda] *nf* (*gen*) cover; (*de almohada*) pillowcase

fundación [funda'θjon] *nf* foundation

fundamental [fundamen'tal] *adj* fundamental, basic

fundamentar [fundamen'tar] *vt* (*poner base*) to lay the foundations of; (*establecer*) to found; (*fig*) to base; **fundamento** *nm* (*base*) foundation

fundar [fun'dar] *vt* to found; **~se** *vr*: **~se en** to be founded on

fundición [fundi'θjon] *nf* fusing; (*fábrica*) foundry

fundir [fun'dir] *vt* (*gen*) to fuse; (*metal*) to smelt, melt down; (*nieve etc*) to melt; (*COM*) to merge; (*estatua*) to cast; **~se** *vr* (*colores etc*) to merge, blend; (*unirse*) to fuse together; (*ELEC: fusible, lámpara etc*) to fuse, blow; (*nieve etc*) to melt

fúnebre ['funeßre] *adj* funeral *cpd*, funereal

funeral [fune'ral] *nm* funeral; **funeraria** *nf* undertaker's

funesto, a [fu'nesto, a] *adj* (*día*) ill-fated; (*decisión*) fatal

furgón [fur'ɣon] *nm* wagon; **furgoneta** *nf* (*AUTO, COM*) (transit) van (*BRIT*), pick-up (truck) (*US*)

furia ['furja] *nf* (*ira*) fury; (*violencia*) violence; **furibundo, a** *adj* furious; **furioso, a** *adj* (*iracundo*) furious; (*violento*) violent; **furor** *nm* (*cólera*) rage

furtivo, a [fur'tißo, a] *adj* furtive ♦ *nm* poacher

fusible [fu'sißle] *nm* fuse

fusil [fu'sil] *nm* rifle; **~ar** *vt* to shoot

fusión [fu'sjon] *nf* (*gen*) melting; (*unión*) fusion; (*COM*) merger

fútbol ['futßol] *nm* football; **futbolín** *nm* table football; **futbolista** *nm* footballer

futuro, a [fu'turo, a] *adj*, *nm* future

G, g

gabardina [gaßar'ðina] *nf* raincoat, gabardine

gabinete [gaßi'nete] *nm* (*POL*) cabinet; (*estudio*) study; (*de abogados etc*) office

gaceta [ga'θeta] *nf* gazette

gachas ['gatʃas] *nfpl* porridge *sg*

gafas ['gafas] *nfpl* glasses; **~ de sol** sunglasses

gafe ['gafe] *nm* jinx

gaita ['gaita] *nf* bagpipes *pl*

gajes ['gaxes] *nmpl*: **los ~ del oficio** occupational hazards

gajo ['gaxo] *nm* (*de naranja*) segment

gala ['gala] *nf* (*traje de etiqueta*) full dress; **~s** *nfpl* (*ropa*) finery *sg*; **estar de ~** to be in one's best clothes; **hacer ~ de** to display

galante [ga'lante] *adj* gallant; **galantería**

nf (*caballerosidad*) gallantry; (*cumplido*) politeness; (*comentario*) compliment

galápago [ga'lapaɣo] *nm* (*ZOOL*) turtle

galardón [galar'ðon] *nm* award, prize

galaxia [ga'laksja] *nf* galaxy

galera [ga'lera] *nf* (*nave*) galley; (*carro*) wagon; (*IMPRENTA*) galley

galería [gale'ria] *nf* (*gen*) gallery; (*balcón*) veranda(h); (*pasillo*) corridor

Gales ['gales] *nm* (*tb*: **País de ~**) Wales; **galés, esa** *adj* Welsh ♦ *nm/f* Welshman/woman ♦ *nm* (*LING*) Welsh

galgo, a ['galɣo, a] *nm/f* greyhound

galimatías [galima'tias] *nmpl* (*lenguaje*) gibberish *sg*, nonsense *sg*

gallardía [gaʎar'ðia] *nf* (*valor*) bravery

gallego, a [ga'ʎeɣo, a] *adj*, *nm/f* Galician

galleta [ga'ʎeta] *nf* biscuit (*BRIT*), cookie (*US*)

gallina [ga'ʎina] *nf* hen ♦ *nm/f* (*fam*: *cobarde*) chicken; **gallinero** *nm* henhouse; (*TEATRO*) top gallery

gallo ['gaʎo] *nm* cock, rooster

galón [ga'lon] *nm* (*MIL*) stripe; (*COSTURA*) braid; (*medida*) gallon

galopar [galo'par] *vi* to gallop

gama ['gama] *nf* (*fig*) range

gamba ['gamba] *nf* prawn (*BRIT*), shrimp (*US*)

gamberro, a [gam'berro, a] *nm/f* hooligan, lout

gamuza [ga'muθa] *nf* chamois

gana ['gana] *nf* (*deseo*) desire, wish; (*apetito*) appetite; (*voluntad*) will; (*añoranza*) longing; **de buena ~** willingly; **de mala ~** reluctantly; **me da ~s de** I feel like, I want to; **no me da la ~** I don't feel like it; **tener ~s de** to feel like

ganadería [ganaðe'ria] *nf* (*ganado*) livestock; (*ganado vacuno*) cattle *pl*; (*cría*, *comercio*) cattle raising

ganado [ga'naðo] *nm* livestock; **~ lanar** sheep *pl*; **~ mayor** cattle *pl*; **~ porcino** pigs *pl*

ganador, a [gana'ðor, a] *adj* winning ♦ *nm/f* winner

ganancia [ga'nanθja] *nf* (*lo ganado*) gain;

(*aumento*) increase; (*beneficio*) profit; **~s** *nfpl* (*ingresos*) earnings; (*beneficios*) profit *sg*, winnings

ganar [ga'nar] *vt* (*obtener*) to get, obtain; (*sacar ventaja*) to gain; (*salario etc*) to earn; (*DEPORTE, premio*) to win; (*derrotar a*) to beat; (*alcanzar*) to reach ♦ *vi* (*DEPORTE*) to win; **~se** *vr*: **~se la vida** to earn one's living

ganchillo [gan'tʃiʎo] *nm* crochet

gancho ['gantʃo] *nm* (*gen*) hook; (*colgador*) hanger

gandul, a [gan'dul, a] *adj*, *nm/f* good-for-nothing, layabout

ganga ['ganga] *nf* bargain

gangrena [gan'grena] *nf* gangrene

ganso, a ['ganso, a] *nm/f* (*ZOOL*) goose; (*fam*) idiot

ganzúa [gan'θua] *nf* skeleton key

garabatear [garaβate'ar] *vi*, *vt* (*al escribir*) to scribble, scrawl

garabato [gara'βato] *nm* (*escritura*) scrawl, scribble

garaje [ga'raxe] *nm* garage

garante [ga'rante] *adj* responsible ♦ *nm/f* guarantor

garantía [garan'tia] *nf* guarantee

garantizar [garanti'θar] *vt* to guarantee

garbanzo [gar'βanθo] *nm* chickpea (*BRIT*), garbanzo (*US*)

garbo ['garβo] *nm* grace, elegance

garfio ['garfjo] *nm* grappling iron

garganta [gar'vanta] *nf* (*ANAT*) throat; (*de botella*) neck; **gargantilla** *nf* necklace

gárgaras ['garvaras] *nfpl*: **hacer ~** to gargle

garita [ga'rita] *nf* cabin, hut; (*MIL*) sentry box

garra ['garra] *nf* (*de gato, TEC*) claw; (*de ave*) talon; (*fam: mano*) hand, paw

garrafa [ga'rrafa] *nf* carafe, decanter

garrapata [garra'pata] *nf* tick

garrote [ga'rrote] *nm* (*palo*) stick; (*porra*) cudgel; (*suplicio*) garrotte

garza ['garθa] *nf* heron

gas [gas] *nm* gas

gasa ['gasa] *nf* gauze

gaseosa [gase'osa] *nf* lemonade

gaseoso, a [gase'oso, a] *adj* gassy, fizzy

gasoil [ga'soil] *nm* diesel (oil)

gasóleo [ga'soleo] *nm* = **gasoil**

gasolina [gaso'lina] *nf* petrol, gas(oline) (*US*); **gasolinera** *nf* petrol (*BRIT*) *o* gas (*US*) station

gastado, a [gas'taðo, a] *adj* (*dinero*) spent; (*ropa*) worn out; (*usado: frase etc*) trite

gastar [gas'tar] *vt* (*dinero, tiempo*) to spend; (*fuerzas*) to use up; (*desperdiciar*) to waste; (*llevar*) to wear; **~se** *vr* to wear out; (*estropearse*) to waste; **~ en** to spend on; **~ bromas** to crack jokes; **¿qué número gastas?** what size (shoe) do you take?

gasto ['gasto] *nm* (*desembolso*) expenditure, spending; (*consumo, uso*) use; **~s** *nmpl* (*desembolsos*) expenses; (*cargos*) charges, costs

gastronomía [gastrono'mia] *nf* gastronomy

gatear [gate'ar] *vi* (*andar a gatas*) to go on all fours

gatillo [ga'tiʎo] *nm* (*de arma de fuego*) trigger; (*de dentista*) forceps

gato, a ['gato, a] *nm/f* cat ♦ *nm* (*TEC*) jack; **andar a gatas** to go on all fours

gaviota [ga'βjota] *nf* seagull

gay [ge] *adj inv*, *nm* gay, homosexual

gazpacho [gaθ'patʃo] *nm* gazpacho

gel [xel] *nm* (*tb*: **~ de baño/ducha**) gel

gelatina [xela'tina] *nf* jelly; (*polvos etc*) gelatine

gema ['xema] *nf* gem

gemelo, a [xe'melo, a] *adj*, *nm/f* twin; **~s** *nmpl* (*de camisa*) cufflinks; (*prismáticos*) field glasses, binoculars

gemido [xe'miðo] *nm* (*quejido*) moan, groan; (*aullido*) howl

Géminis ['xeminis] *nm* Gemini

gemir [xe'mir] *vi* (*quejarse*) to moan, groan; (*aullar*) to howl

generación [xenera'θjon] *nf* generation

general [xene'ral] *adj* general ♦ *nm* general; **por lo** *o* **en ~** in general; **G~itat** *nf* Catalan parliament; **~izar** *vt* to

generalize; **~izarse** *vr* to become
generalized, spread; **~mente** *adv*
generally

generar [xene'rar] *vt* to generate

género ['xenero] *nm* (*clase*) kind, sort;
(*tipo*) type; (*BIO*) genus; (*LING*) gender;
(*COM*) material; **~ humano** human race

generosidad [xenerosi'ðað] *nf* generosity;
generoso, a *adj* generous

genial [xe'njal] *adj* inspired; (*idea*) brilliant;
(*afable*) genial

genio ['xenjo] *nm* (*carácter*) nature,
disposition; (*humor*) temper; (*facultad
creadora*) genius; **de mal ~** bad-tempered

genital [xeni'tal] *adj* genital; **genitales**
nmpl genitals

gente ['xente] *nf* (*personas*) people *pl*;
(*parientes*) relatives *pl*

gentil [xen'til] *adj* (*elegante*) graceful;
(*encantador*) charming; **~eza** *nf* grace;
charm; (*cortesía*) courtesy

gentío [xen'tio] *nm* crowd, throng

genuino, a [xe'nwino, a] *adj* genuine

geografía [xeoγra'fia] *nf* geography

geología [xeolo'xia] *nf* geology

geometría [xeome'tria] *nf* geometry

gerencia [xe'renθja] *nf* management;
gerente *nm/f* (*supervisor*) manager; (*jefe*)
director

geriatría [xeria'tria] *nf* (*MED*) geriatrics *sg*

germen ['xermen] *nm* germ

germinar [xermi'nar] *vi* to germinate

gesticular [xestiku'lar] *vi* to gesticulate;
(*hacer muecas*) to grimace;
gesticulación *nf* gesticulation; (*mueca*)
grimace

gestión [xes'tjon] *nf* management;
(*diligencia, acción*) negotiation;
gestionar *vt* (*lograr*) to try to arrange;
(*dirigir*) to manage

gesto ['xesto] *nm* (*mueca*) grimace;
(*ademán*) gesture

Gibraltar [xiβral'tar] *nm* Gibraltar;
gibraltareño, a *adj, nm/f* Gibraltarian

gigante [xi'γante] *adj, nm/f* giant;
gigantesco, a *adj* gigantic

gilipollas [xili'poʎas] (*fam*) *adj inv* daft

♦ *nm/f inv* wally

gimnasia [xim'nasja] *nf* gymnastics *pl*;
gimnasio *nm* gymnasium; **gimnasta**
nm/f gymnast

gimotear [ximote'ar] *vi* to whine,
whimper

ginebra [xi'neβra] *nf* gin

ginecólogo, a [xine'kolovo, a] *nm/f*
gynaecologist

gira ['xira] *nf* tour, trip

girar [xi'rar] *vt* (*dar la vuelta*) to turn
(around); (: *rápidamente*) to spin; (*COM:
giro postal*) to draw; (: *letra de cambio*) to
issue ♦ *vi* to turn (round); (*rápido*) to spin

girasol [xira'sol] *nm* sunflower

giratorio, a [xira'torjo, a] *adj* revolving

giro ['xiro] *nm* (*movimiento*) turn,
revolution; (*LING*) expression; (*COM*) draft;
~ bancario / postal bank giro/postal order

gis [xis] (*AM*) *nm* chalk

gitano, a [xi'tano, a] *adj, nm/f* gypsy

glacial [gla'θjal] *adj* icy, freezing

glaciar [gla'θjar] *nm* glacier

glándula ['glandula] *nf* gland

global [glo'βal] *adj* global

globo ['gloβo] *nm* (*esfera*) globe, sphere;
(*aerostato, juguete*) balloon

glóbulo ['gloβulo] *nm* globule; (*ANAT*)
corpuscle

gloria ['glorja] *nf* glory

glorieta [glo'rjeta] *nf* (*de jardín*) bower,
arbour; (*plazoleta*) roundabout (*BRIT*),
traffic circle (*US*)

glorificar [glorifi'kar] *vt* (*enaltecer*) to
glorify, praise

glorioso, a [glo'rjoso, a] *adj* glorious

glotón, ona [glo'ton, ona] *adj* gluttonous,
greedy ♦ *nm/f* glutton

glucosa [glu'kosa] *nf* glucose

gobernador, a [goβerna'ðor, a] *adj*
governing ♦ *nm/f* governor;
gobernante *adj* governing

gobernar [goβer'nar] *vt* (*dirigir*) to guide,
direct; (*POL*) to rule, govern ♦ *vi* to
govern; (*NAUT*) to steer

gobierno *etc* [go'βjerno] *vb ver* **gobernar**
♦ *nm* (*POL*) government; (*dirección*)

guidance, direction; (NAUT) steering

goce etc ['goθe] vb ver **gozar** ♦ nm enjoyment

gol [gol] nm goal

golf [golf] nm golf

golfa ['golfa] (fam!) nf (mujer) slut, whore

golfo, a ['golfo, a] nm (GEO) gulf ♦ nm/f (fam: niño) urchin; (gamberro) lout

golondrina [golon'drina] nf swallow

golosina [golo'sina] nf (dulce) sweet; **goloso, a** adj sweet-toothed

golpe ['golpe] nm blow; (de puño) punch; (de mano) smack; (de remo) stroke; (fig: choque) clash; **no dar ~** to be bone idle; **de un ~** with one blow; **de ~** suddenly; **~ (de estado)** coup (d'état); **golpear** vt, vi to strike, knock; (asestar) to beat; (de puño) to punch; (golpetear) to tap

goma ['goma] nf (caucho) rubber; (elástico) elastic; (una ~) elastic band; **~ espuma** foam rubber; **~ de pegar** gum, glue; **~ de borrar** eraser, rubber (BRIT)

gomina [go'mina] nf hair gel

gordo, a ['gorðo, a] adj (gen) fat; (fam) enormous; **el (premio) ~** (en lotería) first prize; **gordura** nf fat; (corpulencia) fatness, stoutness

gorila [go'rila] nm gorilla

gorjear [gorxe'ar] vi to twitter, chirp

gorra ['gorra] nf cap; (de niño) bonnet; (militar) bearskin; **entrar de ~** (fam) to gatecrash; **ir de ~** to sponge

gorrión [go'rrjon] nm sparrow

gorro ['gorro] nm (gen) cap; (de niño, mujer) bonnet

gorrón, ona [go'rron, ona] nm/f scrounger; **gorronear** (fam) vi to scrounge

gota ['gota] nf (gen) drop; (de sudor) bead; (MED) gout; **gotear** vi to drip; (lloviznar) to drizzle; **gotera** nf leak

gozar [go'θar] vi to enjoy o.s.; **~ de** (disfrutar) to enjoy; (poseer) to possess

gozne ['goθne] nm hinge

gozo ['goθo] nm (alegría) joy; (placer) pleasure

gr. abr (= gramo, gramos) g

grabación [graβa'θjon] nf recording

grabado [gra'βaðo] nm print, engraving

grabadora [graβa'ðora] nf tape-recorder

grabar [gra'βar] vt to engrave; (discos, cintas) to record

gracia ['graθja] nf (encanto) grace, gracefulness; (humor) humour, wit; **¡(muchas) ~s!** thanks (very much)!; **~s a** thanks to; **tener ~** (chiste etc) to be funny; **no me hace ~** I am not keen; **gracioso, a** adj (divertido) funny, amusing; (cómico) comical ♦ nm/f (TEATRO) comic character

grada ['graða] nf (de escalera) step; (de anfiteatro) tier, row; **~s** nfpl (DEPORTE: de estadio) terraces

gradería [graðe'ria] nf (gradas) (flight of) steps pl; (de anfiteatro) tiers pl, rows pl; (DEPORTE: de estadio) terraces pl; **~ cubierta** covered stand

grado ['graðo] nm degree; (de aceite, vino) grade; (grada) step; (MIL) rank; **de buen ~** willingly

graduación [graðwa'θjon] nf (del alcohol) proof, strength; (ESCOL) graduation; (MIL) rank

gradual [gra'ðwal] adj gradual

graduar [gra'ðwar] vt (gen) to graduate; (MIL) to commission; **~se** vr to graduate; **~se la vista** to have one's eyes tested

gráfica ['grafika] nf graph

gráfico, a ['grafiko, a] adj graphic ♦ nm diagram; **~s** nmpl (INFORM) graphics

grajo ['graxo] nm rook

Gral abr (= General) Gen.

gramática [gra'matika] nf grammar

gramo ['gramo] nm gramme (BRIT), gram (US)

gran [gran] adj ver **grande**

grana ['grana] nf (color, tela) scarlet

granada [gra'naða] nf pomegranate; (MIL) grenade

granate [gra'nate] adj deep red

Gran Bretaña [-bre'taɲa] nf Great Britain

grande ['grande] (antes de nmsg: **gran**) adj (de tamaño) big, large; (alto) tall; (distinguido) great; (impresionante) grand

◆ *nm* grandee; **grandeza** *nf* greatness
grandioso, a [gran'djoso, a] *adj*
magnificent, grand
granel [gra'nel]: **a ~** *adv* (COM) in bulk
granero [gra'nero] *nm* granary, barn
granito [gra'nito] *nm* (AGR) small grain;
(*roca*) granite
granizado [grani'θaðo] *nm* iced drink
granizar [grani'θar] *vi* to hail; **granizo**
nm hail
granja ['granxa] *nf* (*gen*) farm; **granjear**
vt to win, gain; **granjearse** *vr* to win,
gain; **granjero, a** *nm/f* farmer
grano ['grano] *nm* grain; (*semilla*) seed; (*de
café*) bean; (MED) pimple, spot
granuja [gra'nuxa] *nm/f* rogue; (*golfillo*)
urchin
grapa ['grapa] *nf* staple; (TEC) clamp;
grapadora *nf* stapler
grasa ['grasa] *nf* (*gen*) grease; (*de cocinar*)
fat, lard; (*sebo*) suet; (*mugre*) filth;
grasiento, a *adj* greasy; (*de aceite*) oily;
graso, a *adj* (*leche, queso, carne*) fatty;
(*pelo, piel*) greasy
gratificación [gratifika'θjon] *nf* (*bono*)
bonus; (*recompensa*) reward
gratificar [gratifi'kar] *vt* to reward
gratinar [grati'nar] *vt* to cook au gratin
gratis ['gratis] *adv* free
gratitud [grati'tuð] *nf* gratitude
grato, a ['grato, a] *adj* (*agradable*)
pleasant, agreeable
gratuito, a [gra'twito, a] *adj* (*gratis*) free;
(*sin razón*) gratuitous
gravamen [gra'ßamen] *nm* (*impuesto*) tax
gravar [gra'ßar] *vt* to tax
grave ['graße] *adj* heavy; (*serio*) grave,
serious; **~dad** *nf* gravity
gravilla [gra'ßiʎa] *nf* gravel
gravitar [graßi'tar] *vi* to gravitate; **~ sobre**
to rest on
graznar [graθ'nar] *vi* (*cuervo*) to squawk;
(*pato*) to quack; (*hablar ronco*) to croak
Grecia ['greθja] *nf* Greece
gremio ['gremjo] *nm* trade, industry
greña ['greɲa] *nf* (*cabellos*) shock of hair
gresca ['greska] *nf* uproar

griego, a ['grjexo, a] *adj, nm/f* Greek
grieta ['grjeta] *nf* crack
grifo ['grifo] *nm* tap; (AM: AUTO) petrol
(BRIT) o gas (US) station
grilletes [gri'ʎetes] *nmpl* fetters
grillo ['griʎo] *nm* (ZOOL) cricket
gripe ['gripe] *nf* flu, influenza
gris [gris] *adj* (*color*) grey
gritar [gri'tar] *vt, vi* to shout, yell; **grito**
nm shout, yell; (*de horror*) scream
grosella [gro'seʎa] *nf* (red)currant; **~**
negra blackcurrant
grosería [grose'ria] *nf* (*actitud*) rudeness;
(*comentario*) vulgar comment; **grosero,**
a *adj* (*poco cortés*) rude, bad-mannered;
(*ordinario*) vulgar, crude
grosor [gro'sor] *nm* thickness
grotesco, a [gro'tesko, a] *adj* grotesque
grúa ['grua] *nf* (TEC) crane; (*de petróleo*)
derrick
grueso, a ['grweso, a] *adj* thick; (*persona*)
stout ◆ *nm* bulk; **el ~ de** the bulk of
grulla ['gruʎa] *nf* crane
grumo ['grumo] *nm* clot, lump
gruñido [gru'ɲiðo] *nm* grunt; (*de persona*)
grumble
gruñir [gru'ɲir] *vi* (*animal*) to growl;
(*persona*) to grumble
grupa ['grupa] *nf* (ZOOL) rump
grupo ['grupo] *nm* group; (TEC) unit, set
gruta ['gruta] *nf* grotto
guadaña [gwa'ðaɲa] *nf* scythe
guagua [gwa'xwa] (AM) *nf* (*niño*) baby;
(*bus*) bus
guante ['gwante] *nm* glove; **~ra** *nf* glove
compartment
guapo, a ['gwapo, a] *adj* good-looking,
attractive; (*elegante*) smart
guarda ['gwarða] *nm/f* (*persona*) guard,
keeper ◆ *nf* (*acto*) guarding; (*custodia*)
custody; **~bosques** *nm inv*
gamekeeper; **~costas** *nm inv*
coastguard vessel ◆ *nm/f* guardian,
protector; **~espaldas** *nm/f inv*
bodyguard; **~meta** *nm/f* goalkeeper;
guardar *vt* (*gen*) to keep; (*vigilar*) to
guard, watch over; (*dinero: ahorrar*) to

save; **guardarse** vr (preservarse) to
protect o.s.; (evitar) to avoid; **guardar
cama** to stay in bed; **~rropa** nm
(armario) wardrobe; (en establecimiento
público) cloakroom
guardería [gwarðe'ria] nf nursery
guardia ['gwarðja] nf (MIL) guard;
(cuidado) care, custody ♦ nm/f guard;
(policía) policeman/woman; **estar de ~** to
be on guard; **montar ~** to mount guard;
G~ Civil Civil Guard; **G~ Nacional**
National Guard
guardián, ana [gwar'ðjan, ana] nm/f
(gen) guardian, keeper
guarecer [gware'θer] vt (proteger) to
protect; (abrigar) to shelter; **~se** vr to
take refuge
guarida [gwa'riða] nf (de animal) den, lair;
(refugio) refuge
guarnecer [gwarne'θer] vt (equipar) to
provide; (adornar) to adorn; (TEC) to
reinforce; **guarnición** nf (de vestimenta)
trimming; (de piedra) mount; (CULIN)
garnish; (arneses) harness; (MIL) garrison
guarro, a ['gwarro, a] nm/f pig
guasa ['gwasa] nf joke; **guasón, ona** adj
(bromista) joking ♦ nm/f wit; joker
Guatemala [gwate'mala] nf Guatemala
guay [gwai] (fam) adj super, great
gubernativo, a [guβerna'tiβo, a] adj
governmental
guerra ['gerra] nf war; **~ civil** civil war; **~
fría** cold war; **dar ~** to annoy; **guerrear**
vi to wage war; **guerrero, a** adj
fighting; (carácter) warlike ♦ nm/f warrior
guerrilla [ge'rriʎa] nf guerrilla warfare;
(tropas) guerrilla band o group
guía etc ['gia] vb ver **guiar** ♦ nm/f
(persona) guide ♦ nm (libro) guidebook; **~
de ferrocarriles** railway timetable; **~
telefónica** telephone directory
guiar [gi'ar] vt to guide, direct; (AUTO) to
steer; **~se** vr: **~se por** to be guided by
guijarro [gi'xarro] nm pebble
guillotina [giʎo'tina] nf guillotine
guinda ['ginda] nf morello cherry
guindilla [gin'diʎa] nf chilli pepper

guiñapo [gi'ɲapo] nm (harapo) rag;
(persona) reprobate, rogue
guiñar [gi'ɲar] vt to wink
guión [gi'on] nm (LING) hyphen, dash;
(CINE) script; **guionista** nm/f scriptwriter
guiri ['giri] (fam: pey) nm/f foreigner
guirnalda [gir'nalda] nf garland
guisado [gi'saðo] nm stew
guisante [gi'sante] nm pea
guisar [gi'sar] vt, vi to cook; **guiso** nm
cooked dish
guitarra [gi'tarra] nf guitar
gula ['gula] nf gluttony, greed
gusano [gu'sano] nm worm; (lombriz)
earthworm
gustar [gus'tar] vt to taste, sample ♦ vi to
please, be pleasing; **~ de algo** to like o
enjoy sth; **me gustan las uvas** I like
grapes; **le gusta nadar** she likes o enjoys
swimming
gusto ['gusto] nm (sentido, sabor) taste;
(placer) pleasure; **tiene ~ a menta** it
tastes of mint; **tener buen ~** to have
good taste; **sentirse a ~** to feel at ease;
mucho ~ (en conocerle) pleased to meet
you; **el ~ es mío** the pleasure is mine;
con ~ willingly, gladly; **~so, a** adj
(sabroso) tasty; (agradable) pleasant

H, h

ha vb ver **haber**
haba ['aβa] nf bean
Habana [a'βana] nf: **la ~** Havana
habano [a'βano] nm Havana cigar
habéis vb ver **haber**

PALABRA CLAVE

haber [a'βer] vb aux 1 (tiempos
compuestos) to have; **había comido** I had
eaten; **antes/después de ~lo visto**
before seeing/after seeing o having seen
it
2: **¡~lo dicho antes!** you should have
said so before!
3: **~ de: he de hacerlo** I have to do it;

ha de llegar mañana it should arrive tomorrow

♦ *vb impers* **1** (*existencia*: *sg*) there is; (: *pl*) there are; **hay un hermano/dos hermanos** there is one brother/there are two brothers; **¿cuánto hay de aquí a Sucre?** how far is it from here to Sucre? **2** (*obligación*): **hay que hacer algo** something must be done; **hay que apuntarlo para acordarse** you have to write it down to remember **3**: **¡hay que ver!** well I never! **4**: **¡no hay de** o **por** (*AM*) **qué!** don't mention it!, not at all! **5**: **¿qué hay?** (*¿qué pasa?*) what's up?, what's the matter?; (*¿qué tal?*) how's it going?

♦ **~se** *vr*: **habérselas con uno** to have it out with sb

♦ *vt*: **he aquí unas sugerencias** here are some suggestions; **no hay cintas blancas pero sí las hay rojas** there aren't any white ribbons but there are some red ones

♦ *nm* (*en cuenta*) credit side; **~es** *nmpl* assets; **¿cuánto tengo en el ~?** how much do I have in my account?; **tiene varias novelas en su ~** he has several novels to his credit

habichuela [aßiˈtʃwela] *nf* kidney bean
hábil [ˈaßil] *adj* (*listo*) clever, smart; (*capaz*) fit, capable; (*experto*) expert; **día ~** working day; **habilidad** *nf* skill, ability
habilitar [aßiliˈtar] *vt* (*capacitar*) to enable; (*dar instrumentos*) to equip; (*financiar*) to finance
hábilmente [aßilˈmente] *adv* skilfully, expertly
habitación [aßitaˈθjon] *nf* (*cuarto*) room; (*BIO*: *morada*) habitat; **~ sencilla** o **individual** single room; **~ doble** o **de matrimonio** double room
habitante [aßiˈtante] *nm/f* inhabitant
habitar [aßiˈtar] *vt* (*residir en*) to inhabit; (*ocupar*) to occupy ♦ *vi* to live
hábito [ˈaßito] *nm* habit

habitual [aßiˈtwal] *adj* usual
habituar [aßiˈtwar] *vt* to accustom; **~se** *vr*: **~se a** to get used to
habla [ˈaßla] *nf* (*capacidad de hablar*) speech; (*idioma*) language; (*dialecto*) dialect; **perder el ~** to become speechless; **de ~ francesa** French-speaking; **estar al ~** to be in contact; (*TEL*) to be on the line; **¡González al ~!** (*TEL*) González speaking!
hablador, a [aßlaˈðor, a] *adj* talkative ♦ *nm/f* chatterbox
habladuría [aßlaðuˈria] *nf* rumour; **~s** *nfpl* gossip *sg*
hablante [aˈßlante] *adj* speaking ♦ *nm/f* speaker
hablar [aˈßlar] *vt* to speak, talk ♦ *vi* to speak; **~se** *vr* to speak to each other; **~ con** to speak to; **~ de** to speak of o about; **"se habla inglés"** "English spoken here"; **¡ni ~!** it's out of the question!
habré *etc vb ver* **haber**
hacendoso, a [aθenˈdoso, a] *adj* industrious

PALABRA CLAVE

hacer [aˈθer] *vt* **1** (*fabricar, producir*) to make; (*construir*) to build; **~ una película/un ruido** to make a film/noise; **el guisado lo hice yo** I made o cooked the stew

2 (*ejecutar*: *trabajo etc*) to do; **~ la colada** to do the washing; **~ la comida** to do the cooking; **¿qué haces?** what are you doing?; **~ el malo** o **el papel del malo** (*TEATRO*) to play the villain

3 (*estudios, algunos deportes*) to do; **~ español/económicas** to do o study Spanish/economics; **~ yoga/gimnasia** to do yoga/go to gym

4 (*transformar, incidir en*): **esto lo hará más difícil** this will make it more difficult; **salir te hará sentir mejor** going out will make you feel better

5 (*cálculo*): **2 y 2 hacen 4** 2 and 2 make 4; **éste hace 100** this one makes 100

6 (+*subjun*): **esto hará que ganemos** this will make us win; **harás que no quiera venir** you'll stop him wanting to come
7 (*como sustituto de vb*) to do; **él bebió y yo hice lo mismo** he drank and I did likewise
8: no hace más que criticar all he does is criticize
♦ *vb semi-aux*: **hacer +infin 1** (*directo*): **les hice venir** I made *o* had them come; **~ trabajar a los demás** to get others to work
2 (*por intermedio de otros*): **~ reparar algo** to get sth repaired
♦ *vi* **1: haz como que no lo sabes** act as if you don't know
2 (*ser apropiado*): **si os hace** if it's alright with you
3: ~ de: ~ de madre para uno to be like a mother to sb; (*TEATRO*): **~ de Otelo** to play Othello
♦ *vb impers* **1: hace calor/frío** it's hot/cold; *ver tb* **bueno; sol; tiempo**
2 (*tiempo*): **hace 3 años** 3 years ago; **hace un mes que voy/no voy** I've been going/I haven't been for a month
3: ¿cómo has hecho para llegar tan rápido? how did you manage to get here so quickly?
♦ **~se** *vr* **1** (*volverse*) to become; **se hicieron amigos** they became friends
2 (*acostumbrarse*): **~se a** to get used to
3: se hace con huevos y leche it's made out of eggs and milk; **eso no se hace** that's not done
4 (*obtener*): **~se de** *o* **con algo** to get hold of sth
5 (*fingirse*): **~se el sueco** to turn a deaf ear

hacha [ˈatʃa] *nf* axe; (*antorcha*) torch
hachís [aˈtʃis] *nm* hashish
hacia [ˈaθja] *prep* (*en dirección de*) towards; (*cerca de*) near; (*actitud*) towards; **~ arriba/abajo** up(wards)/down(wards); **~ mediodía** about noon
hacienda [aˈθjenda] *nf* (*propiedad*)

property; (*finca*) farm; (*AM*) ranch; **~ pública** public finance; **(Ministerio de) H~** Exchequer (*BRIT*), Treasury Department (*US*)
hada [ˈaða] *nf* fairy
hago *etc vb ver* **hacer**
Haití [aiˈti] *nm* Haiti
halagar [alaˈɣar] *vt* to flatter
halago [aˈlaɣo] *nm* flattery; **halagüeño, a** *adj* flattering
halcón [alˈkon] *nm* falcon, hawk
hallar [aˈʎar] *vt* (*gen*) to find; (*descubrir*) to discover; (*toparse con*) to run into; **~se** *vr* to be (situated); **hallazgo** *nm* discovery; (*cosa*) find
halterofilia [alteroˈfilja] *nf* weightlifting
hamaca [aˈmaka] *nf* hammock
hambre [ˈambre] *nf* hunger; (*plaga*) famine; (*deseo*) longing; **tener ~** to be hungry; **hambriento, a** *adj* hungry, starving
hamburguesa [amburˈɣesa] *nf* hamburger; **hamburguesería** *nf* burger bar
han *vb ver* **haber**
harapiento, a [araˈpjento, a] *adj* tattered, in rags
harapos [aˈrapos] *nmpl* rags
haré *etc vb ver* **hacer**
harina [aˈrina] *nf* flour
hartar [arˈtar] *vt* to satiate, glut; (*fig*) to tire, sicken; **~se** *vr* (*de comida*) to fill o.s., gorge o.s.; (*cansarse*) to get fed up (*de* with); **hartazgo** *nm* surfeit, glut; **harto, a** *adj* (*lleno*) full; (*cansado*) fed up ♦ *adv* (*bastante*) enough; (*muy*) very; **estar harto de** to be fed up with
has *vb ver* **haber**
hasta [ˈasta] *adv* even ♦ *prep* (*alcanzando a*) as far as; up to; down to; (*de tiempo: a tal hora*) till, until; (*antes de*) before ♦ *conj*: **~ que** until; **~ luego/el sábado** see you soon/on Saturday
hastiar [asˈtjar] *vt* (*gen*) to weary; (*aburrir*) to bore; **~se** *vr*: **~se de** to get fed up with; **hastío** *nm* weariness; boredom
hatillo [aˈtiʎo] *nm* belongings *pl*, kit;

(*montón*) bundle, heap
hay *vb ver* **haber**
Haya ['aja] *nf:* **la ~** The Hague
haya *etc* ['aja] *vb ver* **haber** ♦ *nf* beech tree
haz [aθ] *vb ver* **hacer** ♦ *nm* (*de luz*) beam
hazaña [a'θaɲa] *nf* feat, exploit
hazmerreír [aθmerre'ir] *nm inv* laughing stock
he *vb ver* **haber**
hebilla [e'ßiʎa] *nf* buckle, clasp
hebra ['eßra] *nf* thread; (*BOT: fibra*) fibre, grain
hebreo, a [e'ßreo, a] *adj, nm/f* Hebrew ♦ *nm* (*LING*) Hebrew
hechizar [etʃi'θar] *vt* to cast a spell on, bewitch
hechizo [e'tʃiθo] *nm* witchcraft, magic; (*acto de magía*) spell, charm
hecho, a [e'tʃo, a] *pp de* **hacer** ♦ *adj* (*carne*) done; (*COSTURA*) ready-to-wear ♦ *nm* deed, act; (*dato*) fact; (*cuestión*) matter; (*suceso*) event ♦ *excl* agreed!, done!; **¡bien ~!** well done!; **de ~** in fact, as a matter of fact
hechura [e'tʃura] *nf* (*forma*) form, shape; (*de persona*) build
hectárea [ek'tarea] *nf* hectare
heder [e'ðer] *vi* to stink, smell
hediondo, a [e'ðjondo, a] *adj* stinking
hedor [e'ðor] *nm* stench
helada [e'laða] *nf* frost
heladera [ela'ðera] (*AM*) *nf* (*refrigerador*) refrigerator
helado, a [e'laðo, a] *adj* frozen; (*glacial*) icy; (*fig*) chilly, cold ♦ *nm* ice cream
helar [e'lar] *vt* to freeze, ice (up); (*dejar atónito*) to amaze; (*desalentar*) to discourage ♦ *vi* to freeze; **~se** *vr* to freeze
helecho [e'letʃo] *nm* fern
hélice ['eliθe] *nf* (*TEC*) propeller
helicóptero [eli'koptero] *nm* helicopter
hembra ['embra] *nf* (*BOT, ZOOL*) female; (*mujer*) woman; (*TEC*) nut
hemorragia [emo'rraxja] *nf* haemorrhage
hemorroides [emo'rroiðes] *nfpl* haemorrhoids, piles

hemos *vb ver* **haber**
hendidura [endi'ðura] *nf* crack, split
heno ['eno] *nm* hay
herbicida [erßi'θiða] *nm* weedkiller
heredad [ere'ðað] *nf* landed property; (*granja*) farm
heredar [ere'ðar] *vt* to inherit; **heredero, a** *nm/f* heir(ess)
hereje [e'rexe] *nm/f* heretic
herencia [e'renθja] *nf* inheritance
herida [e'riða] *nf* wound, injury; *ver tb* **herido**
herido, a [e'riðo, a] *adj* injured, wounded ♦ *nm/f* casualty
herir [e'rir] *vt* to wound, injure; (*fig*) to offend
hermanastro, a [erma'nastro, a] *nm/f* stepbrother/sister
hermandad [erman'dað] *nf* brotherhood
hermano, a [er'mano, a] *nm/f* brother/sister; **~ gemelo** twin brother; **hermana gemela** twin sister; **~ político** brother-in-law; **hermana política** sister-in-law
hermético, a [er'metiko, a] *adj* hermetic; (*fig*) watertight
hermoso, a [er'moso, a] *adj* beautiful, lovely; (*estupendo*) splendid; (*guapo*) handsome; **hermosura** *nf* beauty
hernia ['ernja] *nf* hernia
héroe ['eroe] *nm* hero
heroína [ero'ina] *nf* (*mujer*) heroine; (*droga*) heroin
heroísmo [ero'ismo] *nm* heroism
herradura [erra'ðura] *nf* horseshoe
herramienta [erra'mjenta] *nf* tool
herrero [e'rrero] *nm* blacksmith
herrumbre [e'rrumbre] *nf* rust
hervidero [erßi'ðero] *nm* (*fig*) swarm; (*POL etc*) hotbed
hervir [er'ßir] *vi* to boil; (*burbujear*) to bubble; (*fig*): **~ de** to teem with; **~ a fuego lento** to simmer; **hervor** *nm* boiling; (*fig*) ardour, fervour
heterosexual [eterosek'swal] *adj* heterosexual
hice *etc vb ver* **hacer**
hidratante [iðra'tante] *adj:* **crema ~**

moisturizing cream, moisturizer; **hidratar** vt (piel) to moisturize; **hidrato** nm: **hidratos de carbono** carbohydrates

hidráulica [i'ðraulika] nf hydraulics sg

hidráulico, a [i'ðrauliko, a] adj hydraulic

hidro... [iðro] prefijo hydro..., water-...; **~eléctrico, a** adj hydroelectric; **~fobia** nf hydrophobia, rabies; **hidrógeno** nm hydrogen

hiedra ['jeðra] nf ivy

hiel [jel] nf gall, bile; (fig) bitterness

hiela etc vb ver **helar**

hielo ['jelo] nm (gen) ice; (escarcha) frost; (fig) coldness, reserve

hiena ['jena] nf hyena

hierba ['jerßa] nf (pasto) grass; (CULIN, MED: planta) herb; **mala ~** weed; (fig) evil influence; **~buena** nf mint

hierro ['jerro] nm (metal) iron; (objeto) iron object

hígado ['iɣaðo] nm liver

higiene [i'xjene] nf hygiene; **higiénico, a** adj hygienic

higo ['iɣo] nm fig; **higuera** nf fig tree

hijastro, a [i'xastro, a] nm/f stepson/daughter

hijo, a ['ixo, a] nm/f son/daughter, child; **~s** nmpl children, sons and daughters; **~ de papá/mamá** daddy's/mummy's boy; **~ de puta** (fam!) bastard (!), son of a bitch (!)

hilar [i'lar] vt to spin; **~ fino** to split hairs

hilera [i'lera] nf row, file

hilo ['ilo] nm thread; (BOT) fibre; (metal) wire; (de agua) trickle, thin stream

hilvanar [ilßa'nar] vt (COSTURA) to tack (BRIT), baste (US); (fig) to do hurriedly

himno ['imno] nm hymn; **~ nacional** national anthem

hincapié [inka'pje] nm: **hacer ~ en** to emphasize

hincar [in'kar] vt to drive (in), thrust (in); **~se** vr: **~se de rodillas** to kneel down

hincha ['intʃa] (fam) nm/f fan

hinchado, a [in'tʃaðo, a] adj (gen) swollen; (persona) pompous

hinchar [in'tʃar] vt (gen) to swell; (inflar)

to blow up, inflate; (fig) to exaggerate; **~se** vr (inflarse) to swell up; (fam: de comer) to stuff o.s.; **hinchazón** nf (MED) swelling; (altivez) arrogance

hinojo [i'noxo] nm fennel

hipermercado [ipermer'kaðo] nm hypermarket, superstore

hípico, a ['ipiko, a] adj horse cpd

hipnotismo [ipno'tismo] nm hypnotism; **hipnotizar** vt to hypnotize

hipo ['ipo] nm hiccups pl

hipocresía [ipokre'sia] nf hypocrisy; **hipócrita** adj hypocritical ♦ nm/f hypocrite

hipódromo [i'poðromo] nm racetrack

hipopótamo [ipo'potamo] nm hippopotamus

hipoteca [ipo'teka] nf mortgage

hipótesis [i'potesis] nf inv hypothesis

hiriente [i'rjente] adj offensive, wounding

hispánico, a [is'paniko, a] adj Hispanic

hispano, a [is'pano, a] adj Hispanic, Spanish, Hispano- ♦ nm/f Spaniard; **H~américa** nf Latin America; **~americano, a** adj, nm/f Latin American

histeria [is'terja] nf hysteria

historia [is'torja] nf history; (cuento) story, tale; **~s** nfpl (chismes) gossip sg; **dejarse de ~s** to come to the point; **pasar a la ~** to go down in history; **~dor, a** nm/f historian; **historial** nm (profesional) curriculum vitae, C.V.; (MED) case history; **histórico, a** adj historical; (memorable) historic

historieta [isto'rjeta] nf tale, anecdote; (dibujos) comic strip

hito ['ito] nm (fig) landmark

hizo vb ver **hacer**

Hnos abr (= Hermanos) Bros.

hocico [o'θiko] nm snout

hockey ['xoki] nm hockey; **~ sobre hielo** ice hockey

hogar [o'ɣar] nm fireplace, hearth; (casa) home; (vida familiar) home life; **~eño, a** adj home cpd; (persona) home-loving

hoguera [o'ɣera] nf (gen) bonfire

hoja ['oxa] *nf* (*gen*) leaf; (*de flor*) petal; (*de papel*) sheet; (*página*) page; **~ de afeitar** razor blade

hojalata [oxa'lata] *nf* tin(plate)

hojaldre [o'xaldre] *nm* (*CULIN*) puff pastry

hojear [oxe'ar] *vt* to leaf through, turn the pages of

hola ['ola] *excl* hello!

Holanda [o'landa] *nf* Holland; **holandés, esa** *adj* Dutch ♦ *nm/f* Dutchman/woman ♦ *nm* (*LING*) Dutch

holgado, a [ol'ɣaðo, a] *adj* (*ropa*) loose, baggy; (*rico*) comfortable

holgar [ol'ɣar] *vi* (*descansar*) to rest; (*sobrar*) to be superfluous; **huelga decir que** it goes without saying that

holgazán, ana [olɣa'θan, ana] *adj* idle, lazy ♦ *nm/f* loafer

holgura [ol'ɣura] *nf* looseness, bagginess; (*TEC*) play, free movement; (*vida*) comfortable living

hollín [o'ʎin] *nm* soot

hombre ['ombre] *nm* (*gen*) man; (*raza humana*): **el ~** man(kind) ♦ *excl*: **¡sí ~!** (*claro*) of course!; (*para énfasis*) man, old boy; **~ de negocios** businessman; **~ de pro** honest man; **~-rana** frogman

hombrera [om'brera] *nf* shoulder strap

hombro ['ombro] *nm* shoulder

hombruno, a [om'bruno, a] *adj* mannish

homenaje [ome'naxe] *nm* (*tributo*) homage; (*tributo*) tribute

homicida [omi'θiða] *adj* homicidal ♦ *nm/f* murderer; **homicidio** *nm* murder, homicide

homologar [omolo'ɣar] *vt* (*COM: productos, tamaños*) to standardize; **homólogo, a** *nm/f*: **su** *etc* **homólogo** his *etc* counterpart *o* opposite number

homosexual [omosek'swal] *adj, nm/f* homosexual

hondo, a ['ondo, a] *adj* deep; **lo ~** the depth(s) (*pl*), the bottom; **~nada** *nf* hollow, depression; (*cañón*) ravine

Honduras [on'duras] *nf* Honduras

hondureño, a [ondu'reɲo, a] *adj, nm/f* Honduran

honestidad [onesti'ðað] *nf* purity, chastity; (*decencia*) decency; **honesto, a** *adj* chaste; decent, honest; (*justo*) just

hongo ['ongo] *nm* (*BOT: gen*) fungus; (: *comestible*) mushroom; (: *venenoso*) toadstool

honor [o'nor] *nm* (*gen*) honour; **en ~ a la verdad** to be fair; **~able** *adj* honourable

honorario, a [ono'rarjo, a] *adj* honorary; **~s** *nmpl* fees

honra ['onra] *nf* (*gen*) honour; (*renombre*) good name; **~dez** *nf* honesty; (*de persona*) integrity; **~do, a** *adj* honest, upright

honrar [on'rar] *vt* to honour; **~se** *vr*: **~se con algo/de hacer algo** to be honoured by sth/to do sth

honroso, a [on'roso, a] *adj* (*honrado*) honourable; (*respetado*) respectable

hora ['ora] *nf* (*una ~*) hour; (*tiempo*) time; **¿qué ~ es?** what time is it?; **¿a qué ~?** at what time?; **media ~** half an hour; **a la ~ de recreo** at playtime; **a primera ~** first thing (in the morning); **a última ~** at the last moment; **a altas ~s** in the small hours; **¡a buena ~!** about time, too!; **dar la ~** to strike the hour; **~s de oficina/de trabajo** office/working hours; **~s de visita** visiting times; **~s extras** *o* **extraordinarias** overtime *sg*; **~s punta** rush hours

horadar [ora'ðar] *vt* to drill, bore

horario, a [o'rarjo, a] *adj* hourly, hour *cpd* ♦ *nm* timetable; **~ comercial** business hours *pl*

horca ['orka] *nf* gallows *sg*

horcajadas [orka'xaðas]: **a ~** *adv* astride

horchata [or'tʃata] *nf* cold drink made from tiger nuts and water, tiger nut milk

horizontal [oriθon'tal] *adj* horizontal

horizonte [ori'θonte] *nm* horizon

horma ['orma] *nf* mould

hormiga [or'miɣa] *nf* ant; **~s** *nfpl* (*MED*) pins and needles

hormigón [ormi'ɣon] *nm* concrete; **~ armado/pretensado** reinforced/prestressed concrete

hormigueo [ormi'ɣeo] *nm* (*comezón*) itch

hormona [or'mona] *nf* hormone

hornada [or'naða] *nf* batch (of loaves *etc*)

hornillo [or'niʎo] *nm* (*cocina*) portable stove

horno ['orno] *nm* (CULIN) oven; (TEC) furnace; **alto ~** blast furnace

horóscopo [o'roskopo] *nm* horoscope

horquilla [or'kiʎa] *nf* hairpin; (AGR) pitchfork

horrendo, a [o'rrendo, a] *adj* horrendous, frightful

horrible [o'rriβle] *adj* horrible, dreadful

horripilante [orripi'lante] *adj* hair-raising, horrifying

horror [o'rror] *nm* horror, dread; (*atrocidad*) atrocity; **¡qué ~!** (*fam*) how awful!; **~izar** *vt* to horrify, frighten; **~izarse** *vr* to be horrified; **~oso, a** *adj* horrifying, ghastly

hortaliza [orta'liθa] *nf* vegetable

hortelano, a [orte'lano, a] *nm/f* (market) gardener

hortera [or'tera] (*fam*) *adj* tacky

hosco, a ['osko, a] *adj* sullen, gloomy

hospedar [ospe'ðar] *vt* to put up; **~se** *vr* to stay, lodge

hospital [ospi'tal] *nm* hospital

hospitalario, a [ospita'larjo, a] *adj* (*acogedor*) hospitable; **hospitalidad** *nf* hospitality

hostal [os'tal] *nm* small hotel

hostelería [ostele'ria] *nf* hotel business *o* trade

hostia ['ostja] *nf* (REL) host, consecrated wafer; (*fam!: golpe*) whack, punch ♦ *excl* (*fam!*): **¡~(s)!** damn!

hostigar [osti'ɣar] *vt* to whip; (*fig*) to harass, pester

hostil [os'til] *adj* hostile; **~idad** *nf* hostility

hotel [o'tel] *nm* hotel; **~ero, a** *adj* hotel *cpd* ♦ *nm/f* hotelier

hotel

In Spain you can choose from the following categories of accommodation, in descending order of quality and price:

hotel (*from 5 stars to 1*), **hostal, pensión, casa de huéspedes, fonda.** *The State also runs luxury hotels called* **paradores,** *which are usually sited in places of particular historical interest and are often historic buildings themselves.*

hoy [oi] *adv* (*este día*) today; (*la actualidad*) now(adays) ♦ *nm* present time; **~ (en) día** now(adays)

hoyo ['ojo] *nm* hole, pit; **hoyuelo** *nm* dimple

hoz [oθ] *nf* sickle

hube *etc vb ver* **haber**

hucha ['utʃa] *nf* money box

hueco, a ['weko, a] *adj* (*vacío*) hollow, empty; (*resonante*) booming ♦ *nm* hollow, cavity

huelga *etc* ['welɣa] *vb ver* **holgar** ♦ *nf* strike; **declararse en ~** to go on strike, come out on strike; **~ de hambre** hunger strike

huelguista [wel'ɣista] *nm/f* striker

huella ['weʎa] *nf* (*pisada*) tread; (*marca del paso*) footprint, footstep; (: *de animal, máquina*) track; **~ digital** fingerprint

huelo *etc vb ver* **oler**

huérfano, a ['werfano, a] *adj* orphan(ed) ♦ *nm/f* orphan

huerta ['werta] *nf* market garden; (*en Murcia y Valencia*) irrigated region

huerto ['werto] *nm* kitchen garden; (*de árboles frutales*) orchard

hueso ['weso] *nm* (ANAT) bone; (*de fruta*) stone

huésped, a ['wespeð, a] *nm/f* guest

huesudo, a [we'suðo, a] *adj* bony, big-boned

hueva ['weβa] *nf* roe

huevera [we'βera] *nf* eggcup

huevo ['weβo] *nm* egg; **~ duro/ escalfado/frito** (ESP) *o* **estrellado** (AM)/ **pasado por agua** hard-boiled/poached/ fried/soft-boiled egg; **~s revueltos** scrambled eggs

huida [u'iða] *nf* escape, flight

huidizo, a [ui'ðiθo, a] *adj* shy

huir [u'ir] *vi* (*escapar*) to flee, escape; (*evitar*) to avoid; **~se** *vr* (*escaparse*) to escape

hule ['ule] *nm* oilskin

humanidad [umani'ðað] *nf* (*género humano*) man(kind); (*cualidad*) humanity

humanitario, a [umani'tarjo, a] *adj* humanitarian

humano, a [u'mano, a] *adj* (*gen*) human; (*humanitario*) humane ♦ *nm* human; **ser ~** human being

humareda [uma'reða] *nf* cloud of smoke

humedad [ume'ðað] *nf* (*del clima*) humidity; (*de pared etc*) dampness; **a prueba de ~** damp-proof; **humedecer** *vt* to moisten, wet; **humedecerse** *vr* to get wet

húmedo, a ['umeðo, a] *adj* (*mojado*) damp, wet; (*tiempo etc*) humid

humildad [umil'dað] *nf* humility, humbleness; **humilde** *adj* humble, modest

humillación [umiʎa'θjon] *nf* humiliation; **humillante** *adj* humiliating

humillar [umi'ʎar] *vt* to humiliate; **~se** *vr* to humble o.s., grovel

humo ['umo] *nm* (*de fuego*) smoke; (*gas nocivo*) fumes *pl*; (*vapor*) steam, vapour; **~s** *nmpl* (*fig*) conceit *sg*

humor [u'mor] *nm* (*disposición*) mood, temper; (*lo que divierte*) humour; **de buen/mal ~** in a good/bad mood; **~ista** *nm/f* comic; **~ístico, a** *adj* funny, humorous

hundimiento [undi'mjento] *nm* (*gen*) sinking; (*colapso*) collapse

hundir [un'dir] *vt* to sink; (*edificio, plan*) to ruin, destroy; **~se** *vr* to sink, collapse

húngaro, a ['ungaro, a] *adj, nm/f* Hungarian

Hungría [un'gria] *nf* Hungary

huracán [ura'kan] *nm* hurricane

huraño, a [u'raɲo, a] *adj* (*antisocial*) unsociable

hurgar [ur'xar] *vt* to poke, jab; (*remover*) to stir (up); **~se** *vr*: **~se (las narices)** to pick one's nose

hurón, ona [u'ron, ona] *nm* (*ZOOL*) ferret

hurtadillas [urta'ðiʎas]: **a ~** *adv* stealthily, on the sly

hurtar [ur'tar] *vt* to steal; **hurto** *nm* theft, stealing

husmear [usme'ar] *vt* (*oler*) to sniff out, scent; (*fam*) to pry into

huyo *etc vb ver* **huir**

I, i

iba *etc vb ver* **ir**

ibérico, a [i'ßeriko, a] *adj* Iberian

iberoamericano, a [ißeroameri'kano, a] *adj, nm/f* Latin American

Ibiza [i'ßiθa] *nf* Ibiza

iceberg [iθe'ßer] *nm* iceberg

icono [i'kono] *nm* ikon, icon

iconoclasta [ikono'klasta] *adj* iconoclastic ♦ *nm/f* iconoclast

ictericia [ikte'riθja] *nf* jaundice

I + D *abr* (= *Investigación y Desarrollo*) R & D

ida ['iða] *nf* going, departure; **~ y vuelta** round trip, return

idea [i'ðea] *nf* idea; **no tengo la menor ~** I haven't a clue

ideal [iðe'al] *adj, nm* ideal; **~ista** *nm/f* idealist; **~izar** *vt* to idealize

idear [iðe'ar] *vt* to think up; (*aparato*) to invent; (*viaje*) to plan

ídem ['iðem] *pron* ditto

idéntico, a [i'ðentiko, a] *adj* identical

identidad [iðenti'ðað] *nf* identity

identificación [iðentifika'θjon] *nf* identification

identificar [iðentifi'kar] *vt* to identify; **~se** *vr*: **~se con** to identify with

ideología [iðeolo'xia] *nf* ideology

idilio [i'ðiljo] *nm* love-affair

idioma [i'ðjoma] *nm* (*gen*) language

idiota [i'ðjota] *adj* idiotic ♦ *nm/f* idiot; **idiotez** *nf* idiocy

ídolo ['iðolo] *nm* (*tb fig*) idol

idóneo, a [i'ðoneo, a] *adj* suitable

iglesia [i'xlesja] *nf* church

ignorancia [iɣnoˈranθja] *nf* ignorance;
ignorante *adj* ignorant, uninformed
♦ *nm/f* ignoramus

ignorar [iɣnoˈrar] *vt* not to know, be
ignorant of; (*no hacer caso a*) to ignore

igual [iˈɣwal] *adj* (*gen*) equal; (*similar*) like,
similar; (*mismo*) (the) same; (*constante*)
constant; (*temperatura*) even ♦ *nm/f*
equal; **~ que** like, the same as; **me da** *o*
es ~ I don't care; **son ~es** they're the
same; **al ~ que** *prep, conj* like, just like

igualada [iɣwaˈlaða] *nf* equaliser

igualar [iɣwaˈlar] *vt* (*gen*) to equalize,
make equal; (*allanar, nivelar*) to level (off),
even (out); **~se** *vr* (*platos de balanza*) to
balance out

igualdad [iɣwalˈdað] *nf* equality;
(*similaridad*) sameness; (*uniformidad*)
uniformity

igualmente [iɣwalˈmente] *adv* equally;
(*también*) also, likewise ♦ *excl* the same
to you!

ikurriña [ikuˈrriɲa] *nf* Basque flag

ilegal [ileˈɣal] *adj* illegal

ilegítimo, a [ileˈxitimo, a] *adj* illegitimate

ileso, a [iˈleso, a] *adj* unhurt

ilícito, a [iˈliθito, a] *adj* illicit

ilimitado, a [ilimiˈtaðo, a] *adj* unlimited

ilógico, a [iˈloxiko, a] *adj* illogical

iluminación [iluminaˈθjon] *nf*
illumination; (*alumbrado*) lighting

iluminar [ilumiˈnar] *vt* to illuminate, light
(up); (*fig*) to enlighten

ilusión [iluˈsjon] *nf* illusion; (*quimera*)
delusion; (*esperanza*) hope; **hacerse
ilusiones** to build up one's hopes;
ilusionado, a *adj* excited; **ilusionar**
vi: **le ilusiona ir de vacaciones** he's
looking forward to going on holiday;
ilusionarse *vr*: **ilusionarse (con)** to get
excited (about)

ilusionista [ilusjoˈnista] *nm/f* conjurer

iluso, a [iˈluso, a] *adj* easily deceived
♦ *nm/f* dreamer

ilusorio, a [iluˈsorjo, a] *adj* (*de ilusión*)
illusory, deceptive; (*esperanza*) vain

ilustración [ilustraˈθjon] *nf* illustration;
(*saber*) learning, erudition; **la I~** the
Enlightenment; **ilustrado, a** *adj*
illustrated; learned

ilustrar [ilusˈtrar] *vt* to illustrate; (*instruir*)
to instruct; (*explicar*) to explain, make
clear; **~se** *vr* to acquire knowledge

ilustre [iˈlustre] *adj* famous, illustrious

imagen [iˈmaxen] *nf* (*gen*) image; (*dibujo*)
picture

imaginación [imaxinaˈθjon] *nf*
imagination

imaginar [imaxiˈnar] *vt* (*gen*) to imagine;
(*idear*) to think up; (*suponer*) to suppose;
~se *vr* to imagine; **~io, a** *adj* imaginary;
imaginativo, a *adj* imaginative

imán [iˈman] *nm* magnet

imbécil [imˈbeθil] *nm/f* imbecile, idiot

imitación [imitaˈθjon] *nf* imitation

imitar [imiˈtar] *vt* to imitate; (*parodiar,
remedar*) to mimic, ape

impaciencia [impaˈθjenθja] *nf*
impatience; **impaciente** *adj* impatient;
(*nervioso*) anxious

impacto [imˈpakto] *nm* impact

impar [imˈpar] *adj* odd

imparcial [imparˈθjal] *adj* impartial, fair

impartir [imparˈtir] *vt* to impart, give

impasible [impaˈsiβle] *adj* impassive

impecable [impeˈkaβle] *adj* impeccable

impedimento [impeðiˈmento] *nm*
impediment, obstacle

impedir [impeˈðir] *vt* (*obstruir*) to impede,
obstruct; (*estorbar*) to prevent

impenetrable [impeneˈtraβle] *adj*
impenetrable; (*fig*) incomprehensible

imperar [impeˈrar] *vi* (*reinar*) to rule,
reign; (*fig*) to prevail, reign; (*precio*) to be
current

imperativo, a [imperaˈtiβo, a] *adj*
(*urgente, LING*) imperative

imperceptible [imperθepˈtiβle] *adj*
imperceptible

imperdible [imperˈðiβle] *nm* safety pin

imperdonable [imperðoˈnaβle] *adj*
unforgivable, inexcusable

imperfección [imperfekˈθjon] *nf*
imperfection

imperfecto, a [imper'fekto, a] *adj* imperfect

imperial [impe'rjal] *adj* imperial; **~ismo** *nm* imperialism

imperio [im'perjo] *nm* empire; (*autoridad*) rule, authority; (*fig*) pride, haughtiness; **~so, a** *adj* imperious; (*urgente*) urgent; (*imperativo*) imperative

impermeable [imperme'aβle] *adj* waterproof ♦ *nm* raincoat, mac (*BRIT*)

impersonal [imperso'nal] *adj* impersonal

impertinencia [imperti'nenθja] *nf* impertinence; **impertinente** *adj* impertinent

imperturbable [impertur'βaβle] *adj* imperturbable

ímpetu ['impetu] *nm* (*impulso*) impetus, impulse; (*impetuosidad*) impetuosity; (*violencia*) violence

impetuoso, a [impe'twoso, a] *adj* impetuous; (*río*) rushing; (*acto*) hasty

impío, a [im'pio, a] *adj* impious, ungodly

implacable [impla'kaβle] *adj* implacable

implantar [implan'tar] *vt* to introduce

implicar [impli'kar] *vt* to involve; (*entrañar*) to imply

implícito, a [im'pliθito, a] *adj* (*tácito*) implicit; (*sobreentendido*) implied

implorar [implo'rar] *vt* to beg, implore

imponente [impo'nente] *adj* (*impresionante*) impressive, imposing; (*solemne*) grand

imponer [impo'ner] *vt* (*gen*) to impose; (*exigir*) to exact; **~se** *vr* to assert o.s.; (*prevalecer*) to prevail; **imponible** *adj* (*COM*) taxable

impopular [impopu'lar] *adj* unpopular

importación [importa'θjon] *nf* (*acto*) importing; (*mercancías*) imports *pl*

importancia [impor'tanθja] *nf* importance; (*valor*) value, significance; (*extensión*) size, magnitude; **importante** *adj* important; valuable, significant

importar [impor'tar] *vt* (*del extranjero*) to import; (*costar*) to amount to ♦ *vi* to be important, matter; **me importa un rábano** I couldn't care less; **no importa** it

doesn't matter; **¿le importa que fume?** do you mind if I smoke?

importe [im'porte] *nm* (*total*) amount; (*valor*) value

importunar [importu'nar] *vt* to bother, pester

imposibilidad [imposiβili'ðað] *nf* impossibility; **imposibilitar** *vt* to make impossible, prevent

imposible [impo'siβle] *adj* (*gen*) impossible; (*insoportable*) unbearable, intolerable

imposición [imposi'θjon] *nf* imposition; (*COM: impuesto*) tax; (: *inversión*) deposit

impostor, a [impos'tor, a] *nm/f* impostor

impotencia [impo'tenθja] *nf* impotence; **impotente** *adj* impotent

impracticable [imprakti'kaβle] *adj* (*irrealizable*) impracticable; (*intransitable*) impassable

impreciso, a [impre'θiso, a] *adj* imprecise, vague

impregnar [impreɣ'nar] *vt* to impregnate; **~se** *vr* to become impregnated

imprenta [im'prenta] *nf* (*acto*) printing; (*aparato*) press; (*casa*) printer's; (*letra*) print

imprescindible [impresθin'diβle] *adj* essential, vital

impresión [impre'sjon] *nf* (*gen*) impression; (*IMPRENTA*) printing; (*edición*) edition; (*FOTO*) print; (*marca*) imprint; **~ digital** fingerprint

impresionable [impresjo'naβle] *adj* (*sensible*) impressionable

impresionante [impresjo'nante] *adj* impressive; (*tremendo*) tremendous; (*maravilloso*) great, marvellous

impresionar [impresjo'nar] *vt* (*conmover*) to move; (*afectar*) to impress, strike; (*película fotográfica*) to expose; **~se** *vr* to be impressed; (*conmoverse*) to be moved

impreso, a [im'preso, a] *pp de* **imprimir** ♦ *adj* printed; **~s** *nmpl* printed matter; **impresora** *nf* printer

imprevisto, a [impre'βisto, a] *adj* (*gen*) unforeseen; (*inesperado*) unexpected

imprimir [impri'mir] *vt* to imprint, impress, stamp; (*textos*) to print; (*INFORM*) to output, print out

improbable [impro'βaβle] *adj* improbable; (*inverosímil*) unlikely

improcedente [improθe'ðente] *adj* inappropriate

improductivo, a [improðuk'tiβo, a] *adj* unproductive

improperio [impro'perjo] *nm* insult

impropio, a [im'propjo, a] *adj* improper

improvisado, a [improβi'saðo, a] *adj* improvised

improvisar [improβi'sar] *vt* to improvise

improviso, a [impro'βiso, a] *adj*: **de ~** unexpectedly, suddenly

imprudencia [impru'ðenθja] *nf* imprudence; (*indiscreción*) indiscretion; (*descuido*) carelessness; **imprudente** *adj* unwise, imprudent; (*indiscreto*) indiscreet

impúdico, a [im'puðiko, a] *adj* shameless; (*lujurioso*) lecherous

impuesto, a [im'pwesto, a] *adj* imposed ♦ *nm* tax; **~ sobre el valor añadido** value added tax

impugnar [impuɣ'nar] *vt* to oppose, contest; (*refutar*) to refute, impugn

impulsar [impul'sar] *vt* to drive; (*promover*) to promote, stimulate

impulsivo, a [impul'siβo, a] *adj* impulsive; **impulso** *nm* impulse; (*fuerza, empuje*) thrust, drive; (*fig: sentimiento*) urge, impulse

impune [im'pune] *adj* unpunished

impureza [impu're θa] *nf* impurity; **impuro, a** *adj* impure

imputar [impu'tar] *vt* to attribute

inacabable [inaka'βaβle] *adj* (*infinito*) endless; (*interminable*) interminable

inaccesible [inakθe'siβle] *adj* inaccessible

inacción [inak'θjon] *nf* inactivity

inaceptable [inaθep'taβle] *adj* unacceptable

inactividad [inaktiβi'ðað] *nf* inactivity; (*COM*) dullness; **inactivo, a** *adj* inactive

inadecuado, a [inaðe'kwaðo, a] *adj* (*insuficiente*) inadequate; (*inapto*) unsuitable

inadmisible [inaðmi'siβle] *adj* inadmissible

inadvertido, a [inaðβer'tiðo, a] *adj* (*no visto*) unnoticed

inagotable [inaɣo'taβle] *adj* inexhaustible

inaguantable [inaɣwan'taβle] *adj* unbearable

inalterable [inalte'raβle] *adj* immutable, unchangeable

inanición [inani'θjon] *nf* starvation

inanimado, a [inani'maðo, a] *adj* inanimate

inapreciable [inapre'θjaβle] *adj* (*cantidad, diferencia*) imperceptible; (*ayuda, servicio*) invaluable

inaudito, a [inau'ðito, a] *adj* unheard-of

inauguración [inauɣura'θjon] *nf* inauguration; opening

inaugurar [inauɣu'rar] *vt* to inaugurate; (*exposición*) to open

inca ['inka] *nm/f* Inca

incalculable [inkalku'laβle] *adj* incalculable

incandescente [inkandes'θente] *adj* incandescent

incansable [inkan'saβle] *adj* tireless, untiring

incapacidad [inkapaθi'ðað] *nf* incapacity; (*incompetencia*) incompetence; **~ física / mental** physical/mental disability

incapacitar [inkapaθi'tar] *vt* (*inhabilitar*) to incapacitate, render unfit; (*descalificar*) to disqualify

incapaz [inka'paθ] *adj* incapable

incautación [inkauta'θjon] *nf* confiscation

incautarse [inkau'tarse] *vr*: **~ de** to seize, confiscate

incauto, a [in'kauto, a] *adj* (*imprudente*) incautious, unwary

incendiar [inθen'djar] *vt* to set fire to; (*fig*) to inflame; **~se** *vr* to catch fire; **~io, a** *adj* incendiary

incendio [in'θendjo] *nm* fire

incentivo [inθen'tiβo] *nm* incentive

incertidumbre [inθerti'ðumbre] *nf* (*inseguridad*) uncertainty; (*duda*) doubt

incesante [inθe'sante] *adj* incessant
incesto [in'θesto] *nm* incest
incidencia [inθi'ðenθja] *nf* (*MAT*) incidence
incidente [inθi'ðente] *nm* incident
incidir [inθi'ðir] *vi* (*influir*) to influence; (*afectar*) to affect; **~ en un error** to fall into error
incienso [in'θjenso] *nm* incense
incierto, a [in'θjerto, a] *adj* uncertain
incineración [inθinera'θjon] *nf* incineration; (*de cadáveres*) cremation
incinerar [inθine'rar] *vt* to burn; (*cadáveres*) to cremate
incipiente [inθi'pjente] *adj* incipient
incisión [inθi'sjon] *nf* incision
incisivo, a [inθi'siβo, a] *adj* sharp, cutting; (*fig*) incisive
incitar [inθi'tar] *vt* to incite, rouse
inclemencia [inkle'menθja] *nf* (*severidad*) harshness, severity; (*del tiempo*) inclemency
inclinación [inklina'θjon] *nf* (*gen*) inclination; (*de tierras*) slope, incline; (*de cabeza*) nod, bow; (*fig*) leaning, bent
inclinar [inkli'nar] *vt* to incline; (*cabeza*) to nod, bow ♦ *vi* to lean, slope; **~se** *vr* to bow; (*encorvarse*) to stoop; **~se a** (*parecerse que*) to take after, resemble; **~se ante** to bow down to; **me inclino a pensar que** I'm inclined to think that
incluir [inklu'ir] *vt* to include; (*incorporar*) to incorporate; (*meter*) to enclose
inclusive [inklu'siβe] *adv* inclusive ♦ *prep* including
incluso [in'kluso] *adv* even
incógnita [in'koɣnita] *nf* (*MAT*) unknown quantity
incógnito [in'koɣnito] *nm*: **de ~** incognito
incoherente [inkoe'rente] *adj* incoherent
incoloro, a [inko'loro, a] *adj* colourless
incólume [in'kolume] *adj* unhurt, unharmed
incomodar [inkomo'ðar] *vt* to inconvenience; (*molestar*) to bother, trouble; (*fastidiar*) to annoy; **~se** *vr* to put o.s. out; (*fastidiarse*) to get annoyed

incomodidad [inkomoði'ðað] *nf* inconvenience; (*fastidio, enojo*) annoyance; (*de vivienda*) discomfort
incómodo, a [in'komoðo, a] *adj* (*inconfortable*) uncomfortable; (*molesto*) annoying; (*inconveniente*) inconvenient
incomparable [inkompa'raβle] *adj* incomparable
incompatible [inkompa'tiβle] *adj* incompatible
incompetencia [inkompe'tenθja] *nf* incompetence; **incompetente** *adj* incompetent
incompleto, a [inkom'pleto, a] *adj* incomplete, unfinished
incomprensible [inkompren'siβle] *adj* incomprehensible
incomunicado, a [inkomuni'kaðo, a] *adj* (*aislado*) cut off, isolated; (*confinado*) in solitary confinement
inconcebible [inkonθe'βiβle] *adj* inconceivable
incondicional [inkondiθjo'nal] *adj* unconditional; (*apoyo*) wholehearted; (*partidario*) staunch
inconexo, a [inko'nekso, a] *adj* (*gen*) unconnected; (*desunido*) disconnected
inconfundible [inkonfun'diβle] *adj* unmistakable
incongruente [inkon'ɣrwente] *adj* incongruous
inconsciencia [inkons'θjenθja] *nf* unconsciousness; (*fig*) thoughtlessness; **inconsciente** *adj* unconscious; thoughtless
inconsecuente [inkonse'kwente] *adj* inconsistent
inconsiderado, a [inkonside'raðo, a] *adj* inconsiderate
inconsistente [inkonsis'tente] *adj* weak; (*tela*) flimsy
inconstancia [inkons'tanθja] *nf* inconstancy; (*inestabilidad*) unsteadiness; **inconstante** *adj* inconstant
incontable [inkon'taβle] *adj* countless, innumerable
incontestable [inkontes'taβle] *adj*

unanswerable; (*innegable*) undeniable
incontinencia [inkonti'nenθja] *nf*
incontinence
inconveniencia [inkombe'njenθja] *nf*
unsuitability, inappropriateness;
(*descortesía*) impoliteness;
inconveniente *adj* unsuitable; impolite
♦ *nm* obstacle; (*desventaja*) disadvantage;
el inconveniente es que ... the trouble
is that ...
incordiar [inkor'ðjar] (*fam*) *vt* to bug,
annoy
incorporación [inkorpora'θjon] *nf*
incorporation
incorporar [inkorpo'rar] *vt* to incorporate;
~se *vr* to sit up
incorrección [inkorrek'θjon] *nf* (*gen*)
incorrectness, inaccuracy; (*descortesía*)
bad-mannered behaviour; **incorrecto, a**
adj (*gen*) incorrect, wrong;
(*comportamiento*) bad-mannered
incorregible [inkorre'xiβle] *adj*
incorrigible
incredulidad [inkreðuli'ðað] *nf*
incredulity; (*escepticismo*) scepticism;
incrédulo, a *adj* incredulous,
unbelieving; sceptical
increíble [inkre'iβle] *adj* incredible
incremento [inkre'mento] *nm* increment;
(*aumento*) rise, increase
increpar [inkre'par] *vt* to reprimand
incruento, a [in'krwento, a] *adj* bloodless
incrustar [inkrus'tar] *vt* to incrust;
(*piedras: en joya*) to inlay
incubar [inku'βar] *vt* to incubate
inculcar [inkul'kar] *vt* to inculcate
inculpar [inkul'par] *vt* (*acusar*) to accuse;
(*achacar, atribuir*) to charge, blame
inculto, a [in'kulto, a] *adj* (*persona*)
uneducated; (*grosero*) uncouth ♦ *nm/f*
ignoramus
incumplimiento [inkumpli'mjento] *nm*
non-fulfilment; **~ de contrato** breach of
contract
incurrir [inku'rrir] *vi*: **~ en** to incur;
(*crimen*) to commit; **~ en un error** to
make a mistake

indagación [indaɣa'θjon] *nf* investigation;
(*búsqueda*) search; (*JUR*) inquest
indagar [inda'ɣar] *vt* to investigate; to
search; (*averiguar*) to ascertain
indecente [inde'θente] *adj* indecent,
improper; (*lascivo*) obscene
indecible [inde'θiβle] *adj* unspeakable;
(*indescriptible*) indescribable
indeciso, a [inde'θiso, a] *adj* (*por decidir*)
undecided; (*vacilante*) hesitant
indefenso, a [inde'fenso, a] *adj*
defenceless
indefinido, a [indefi'niðo, a] *adj*
indefinite; (*vago*) vague, undefined
indeleble [inde'leβle] *adj* indelible
indemne [in'demne] *adj* (*objeto*)
undamaged; (*persona*) unharmed, unhurt
indemnizar [indemni'θar] *vt* to indemnify;
(*compensar*) to compensate
independencia [indepen'denθja] *nf*
independence
independiente [indepen'djente] *adj*
(*libre*) independent; (*autónomo*) self-
sufficient
indeterminado, a [indetermi'naðo, a] *adj*
indefinite; (*desconocido*) indeterminate
India ['indja] *nf*: **la ~** India
indicación [indika'θjon] *nf* indication;
(*señal*) sign; (*sugerencia*) suggestion, hint
indicado, a [indi'kaðo, a] *adj* (*momento,
método*) right; (*tratamiento*) appropriate;
(*solución*) likely
indicador [indika'ðor] *nm* indicator; (*TEC*)
gauge, meter
indicar [indi'kar] *vt* (*mostrar*) to indicate,
show; (*termómetro etc*) to read, register;
(*señalar*) to point to
índice ['indiθe] *nm* index; (*catálogo*)
catalogue; (*ANAT*) index finger, forefinger
indicio [in'diθjo] *nm* indication, sign; (*en
pesquisa etc*) clue
indiferencia [indife'renθja] *nf*
indifference; (*apatía*) apathy;
indiferente *adj* indifferent
indígena [in'dixena] *adj* indigenous,
native ♦ *nm/f* native
indigencia [indi'xenθja] *nf* poverty, need

indigestión [indixes'tjon] *nf* indigestion
indigesto, a [indi'xesto, a] *adj* (*alimento*)
indigestible; (*fig*) turgid
indignación [indiɣna'θjon] *nf* indignation
indignar [indiɣ'nar] *vt* to anger, make
indignant; ~**se** *vr:* ~**se por** to get
indignant about
indigno, a [in'diɣno, a] *adj* (*despreciable*)
low, contemptible; (*inmerecido*) unworthy
indio, a ['indjo, a] *adj, nm/f* Indian
indirecta [indi'rekta] *nf* insinuation,
innuendo; (*sugerencia*) hint
indirecto, a [indi'rekto, a] *adj* indirect
indiscreción [indiskre'θjon] *nf*
(*imprudencia*) indiscretion; (*irreflexión*)
tactlessness; (*acto*) gaffe, faux pas
indiscreto, a [indis'kreto, a] *adj* indiscreet
indiscriminado, a [indiskrimi'naðo, a]
adj indiscriminate
indiscutible [indisku'tiβle] *adj*
indisputable, unquestionable
indispensable [indispen'saβle] *adj*
indispensable, essential
indisponer [indispo'ner] *vt* to spoil,
upset; (*salud*) to make ill; ~**se** *vr* to fall ill;
~**se con uno** to fall out with sb
indisposición [indisposi'θjon] *nf*
indisposition
indispuesto, a [indis'pwesto, a] *adj*
(*enfermo*) unwell, indisposed
indistinto, a [indis'tinto, a] *adj* indistinct;
(*vago*) vague
individual [indiβi'ðwal] *adj* individual;
(*habitación*) single ♦ *nm* (DEPORTE) singles
sg
individuo, a [indi'βiðwo, a] *adj, nm*
individual
índole ['indole] *nf* (*naturaleza*) nature;
(*clase*) sort, kind
indómito, a [in'domito, a] *adj*
indomitable
inducir [indu'θir] *vt* to induce; (*inferir*) to
infer; (*persuadir*) to persuade
indudable [indu'ðaβle] *adj* undoubted;
(*incuestionable*) unquestionable
indulgencia [indul'xenθja] *nf* indulgence
indultar [indul'tar] *vt* (*perdonar*) to

pardon, reprieve; (*librar de pago*) to
exempt; **indulto** *nm* pardon; exemption
industria [in'dustrja] *nf* industry;
(*habilidad*) skill; **industrial** *adj* industrial
♦ *nm* industrialist
inédito, a [in'eðito, a] *adj* (*texto*)
unpublished; (*nuevo*) new
inefable [ine'faβle] *adj* ineffable,
indescribable
ineficaz [inefi'kaθ] *adj* (*inútil*) ineffective;
(*ineficiente*) inefficient
ineludible [inelu'ðiβle] *adj* inescapable,
unavoidable
ineptitud [inepti'tuð] *nf* ineptitude,
incompetence; **inepto, a** *adj* inept,
incompetent
inequívoco, a [ine'kiβoko, a] *adj*
unequivocal; (*inconfundible*) unmistakable
inercia [in'erθja] *nf* inertia; (*pasividad*)
passivity
inerme [in'erme] *adj* (*sin armas*) unarmed;
(*indefenso*) defenceless
inerte [in'erte] *adj* inert; (*inmóvil*)
motionless
inesperado, a [inespe'raðo, a] *adj*
unexpected, unforeseen
inestable [ines'taβle] *adj* unstable
inevitable [ineβi'taβle] *adj* inevitable
inexactitud [ineksakti'tuð] *nf* inaccuracy;
inexacto, a *adj* inaccurate; (*falso*)
untrue
inexperto, a [inek'sperto, a] *adj* (*novato*)
inexperienced
infalible [infa'liβle] *adj* infallible; (*plan*)
foolproof
infame [in'fame] *adj* infamous; (*horrible*)
dreadful; **infamia** *nf* infamy; (*deshonra*)
disgrace
infancia [in'fanθja] *nf* infancy, childhood
infantería [infante'ria] *nf* infantry
infantil [infan'til] *adj* (*pueril, aniñado*)
infantile; (*cándido*) childlike; (*literatura,
ropa etc*) children's
infarto [in'farto] *nm* (*tb:* ~ **de miocardio**)
heart attack
infatigable [infati'xaβle] *adj* tireless,
untiring

infección [infek'θjon] *nf* infection;
infeccioso, a *adj* infectious
infectar [infek'tar] *vt* to infect; **~se** *vr* to
become infected
infeliz [infe'liθ] *adj* unhappy, wretched
♦ *nm/f* wretch
inferior [infe'rjor] *adj* inferior; *(situación)*
lower ♦ *nm/f* inferior, subordinate
inferir [infe'rir] *vt (deducir)* to infer,
deduce; *(causar)* to cause
infestar [infes'tar] *vt* to infest
infidelidad [infiðeli'ðað] *nf (gen)*
infidelity, unfaithfulness
infiel [in'fjel] *adj* unfaithful, disloyal;
(erróneo) inaccurate ♦ *nm/f* infidel,
unbeliever
infierno [in'fjerno] *nm* hell
infiltrarse [infil'trarse] *vr*: **~ en** to infiltrate
in(to); *(persona)* to work one's way in(to)
ínfimo, a ['infimo, a] *adj (más bajo)*
lowest; *(despreciable)* vile, mean
infinidad [infini'ðað] *nf* infinity;
(abundancia) great quantity
infinito, a [infi'nito, a] *adj, nm* infinite
inflación [infla'θjon] *nf (hinchazón)*
swelling; *(monetaria)* inflation; *(fig)*
conceit; **inflacionario, a** *adj* inflationary
inflamar [infla'mar] *vt (MED, fig)* to
inflame; **~se** *vr* to catch fire; to become
inflamed
inflar [in'flar] *vt (hinchar)* to inflate, blow
up; *(fig)* to exaggerate; **~se** *vr* to swell
(up); *(fig)* to get conceited
inflexible [inflek'siβle] *adj* inflexible; *(fig)*
unbending
infligir [infli'xir] *vt* to inflict
influencia [influ'enθja] *nf* influence;
influenciar *vt* to influence
influir [influ'ir] *vt* to influence
influjo [in'fluxo] *nm* influence
influya *etc vb ver* **influir**
influyente [influ'jente] *adj* influential
información [informa'θjon] *nf*
information; *(noticias)* news *sg*; *(JUR)*
inquiry; **I~** *(oficina)* Information Office;
(mostrador) Information Desk; *(TEL)*
Directory Enquiries

informal [infor'mal] *adj (gen)* informal
informar [infor'mar] *vt (gen)* to inform;
(revelar) to reveal, make known ♦ *vi (JUR)*
to plead; *(denunciar)* to inform; *(dar
cuenta de)* to report on; **~se** *vr* to find
out; **~se de** to inquire into
informática [infor'matika] *nf* computer
science, information technology
informe [in'forme] *adj* shapeless ♦ *nm*
report
infortunio [infor'tunjo] *nm* misfortune
infracción [infrak'θjon] *nf* infraction,
infringement
infranqueable [infranke'aβle] *adj*
impassable; *(fig)* insurmountable
infravalorar [infrabalo'rar] *vt* to
undervalue, underestimate
infringir [infrin'xir] *vt* to infringe,
contravene
infructuoso, a [infruk'twoso, a] *adj*
fruitless, unsuccessful
infundado, a [infun'dado, a] *adj*
groundless, unfounded
infundir [infun'dir] *vt* to infuse, instil
infusión [infu'sjon] *nf* infusion; **~ de
manzanilla** camomile tea
ingeniar [inxe'njar] *vt* to think up, devise;
~se *vr*: **~se para** to manage to
ingeniería [inxenje'ria] *nf* engineering; **~
genética** genetic engineering;
ingeniero, a *nm/f* engineer; **ingeniero
de caminos / de sonido** civil engineer/
sound engineer
ingenio [in'xenjo] *nm (talento)* talent;
(agudeza) wit; *(habilidad)* ingenuity,
inventiveness; **~ azucarero** *(AM)* sugar
refinery
ingenioso, a [inxe'njoso, a] *adj*
ingenious, clever; *(divertido)* witty
ingenuidad [inxenwi'ðað] *nf*
ingenuousness; *(sencillez)* simplicity;
ingenuo, a *adj* ingenuous
ingerir [inxe'rir] *vt* to ingest; *(tragar)* to
swallow; *(consumir)* to consume
Inglaterra [ingla'terra] *nf* England
ingle ['ingle] *nf* groin
inglés, esa [in'gles, esa] *adj* English

♦ *nm/f* Englishman/woman ♦ *nm* (*LING*)
English
ingratitud [ingrati'tuð] *nf* ingratitude;
ingrato, a *adj* (*gen*) ungrateful
ingrediente [ingre'ðjente] *nm* ingredient
ingresar [ingre'sar] *vt* (*dinero*) to deposit
♦ *vi* to come in; ~ **en un club** to join a
club; ~ **en el hospital** to go into hospital
ingreso [in'greso] *nm* (*entrada*) entry;
(: *en hospital etc*) admission; ~**s** *nmpl*
(*dinero*) income *sg*; (: *COM*) takings *pl*
inhabitable [inaßi'taßle] *adj* uninhabitable
inhalar [ina'lar] *vt* to inhale
inherente [ine'rente] *adj* inherent
inhibir [ini'ßir] *vt* to inhibit
inhóspito, a [i'nospito, a] *adj* (*región,
paisaje*) inhospitable
inhumano, a [inu'mano, a] *adj* inhuman
inicial [ini'θjal] *adj, nf* initial
iniciar [ini'θjar] *vt* (*persona*) to initiate;
(*empezar*) to begin, commence;
(*conversación*) to start up
iniciativa [iniθja'tißa] *nf* initiative; **la ~
privada** private enterprise
ininterrumpido, a [ininterrum'piðo, a]
adj uninterrupted
injerencia [inxe'renθja] *nf* interference
injertar [inxer'tar] *vt* to graft; **injerto** *nm*
graft
injuria [in'xurja] *nf* (*agravio, ofensa*)
offence; (*insulto*) insult; **injuriar** *vt* to
insult; **injurioso, a** *adj* offensive;
insulting
injusticia [inxus'tiθja] *nf* injustice
injusto, a [in'xusto, a] *adj* unjust, unfair
inmadurez [inmaðu'reθ] *nf* immaturity
inmediaciones [inmeðja'θjones] *nfpl*
neighbourhood *sg*, environs
inmediato, a [inme'ðjato, a] *adj*
immediate; (*contiguo*) adjoining; (*rápido*)
prompt; (*próximo*) neighbouring, next; **de
~** immediately
inmejorable [inmexo'raßle] *adj*
unsurpassable; (*precio*) unbeatable
inmenso, a [in'menso, a] *adj* immense,
huge
inmerecido, a [inmere'θiðo, a] *adj*
undeserved
inmigración [inmiɣra'θjon] *nf*
immigration
inmiscuirse [inmisku'irse] *vr* to interfere,
meddle
inmobiliaria [inmoßi'ljarja] *nf* estate
agency
inmobiliario, a [inmoßi'ljarjo, a] *adj*
real-estate *cpd*, property *cpd*
inmolar [inmo'lar] *vt* to immolate,
sacrifice
inmoral [inmo'ral] *adj* immoral
inmortal [inmor'tal] *adj* immortal; ~**izar**
vt to immortalize
inmóvil [in'moßil] *adj* immobile
inmueble [in'mweßle] *adj*: **bienes ~s** real
estate, landed property ♦ *nm* property
inmundicia [inmun'diθja] *nf* filth;
inmundo, a *adj* filthy
inmune [in'mune] *adj*: ~ **(a)** (*MED*)
immune (to)
inmunidad [inmuni'ðað] *nf* immunity
inmutarse [inmu'tarse] *vr* to turn pale; **no
se inmutó** he didn't turn a hair
innato, a [in'nato, a] *adj* innate
innecesario, a [inneθe'sarjo, a] *adj*
unnecessary
innoble [in'noßle] *adj* ignoble
innovación [innoßa'θjon] *nf* innovation
innovar [inno'ßar] *vt* to introduce
inocencia [ino'θenθja] *nf* innocence
inocentada [inoθen'taða] *nf* practical joke
inocente [ino'θente] *adj* (*ingenuo*) naive,
innocent; (*inculpable*) innocent; (*sin
malicia*) harmless ♦ *nm/f* simpleton

Día de los Santos Inocentes

🛈 The 28th December, **el día de los
(Santos) Inocentes**, *is when the
Church commemorates the story of Herod's
slaughter of the innocent children of
Judaea. On this day Spaniards play*
inocentadas *(practical jokes) on each
other, much like our April Fool's Day
pranks.*

---

inodoro [ino'ðoro] *nm* toilet, lavatory

(*BRIT*)

inofensivo, a [inofen'siβo, a] *adj* inoffensive, harmless

inolvidable [inolβi'ðaβle] *adj* unforgettable

inopinado, a [inopi'naðo, a] *adj* unexpected

inoportuno, a [inopor'tuno, a] *adj* untimely; (*molesto*) inconvenient

inoxidable [inoksi'ðaβle] *adj*: **acero ~** stainless steel

inquebrantable [inkeβran'taβle] *adj* unbreakable

inquietar [inkje'tar] *vt* to worry, trouble; **~se** *vr* to worry, get upset; **inquieto, a** *adj* anxious, worried; **inquietud** *nf* anxiety, worry

inquilino, a [inki'lino, a] *nm/f* tenant

inquirir [inki'rir] *vt* to enquire into, investigate

insaciable [insa'θjaβle] *adj* insatiable

insalubre [insa'luβre] *adj* unhealthy

inscribir [inskri'βir] *vt* to inscribe; **~ a uno en** (*lista*) to put sb on; (*censo*) to register sb on

inscripción [inskrip'θjon] *nf* inscription; (*ESCOL etc*) enrolment; (*censo*) registration

insecticida [insekti'θiða] *nm* insecticide

insecto [in'sekto] *nm* insect

inseguridad [insexuri'ðað] *nf* insecurity

inseguro, a [inse'xuro, a] *adj* insecure; (*inconstante*) unsteady; (*incierto*) uncertain

insensato, a [insen'sato, a] *adj* foolish, stupid

insensibilidad [insensiβili'ðað] *nf* (*gen*) insensitivity; (*dureza de corazón*) callousness

insensible [insen'siβle] *adj* (*gen*) insensitive; (*movimiento*) imperceptible; (*sin sentido*) numb

insertar [inser'tar] *vt* to insert

inservible [inser'βiβle] *adj* useless

insidioso, a [insi'ðjoso, a] *adj* insidious

insignia [in'siɣnja] *nf* (*señal distintiva*) badge; (*estandarte*) flag

insignificante [insiɣnifi'kante] *adj* insignificant

insinuar [insi'nwar] *vt* to insinuate, imply

insípido, a [in'sipiðo, a] *adj* insipid

insistencia [insis'tenθja] *nf* insistence

insistir [insis'tir] *vi* to insist; **~ en algo** to insist on sth; (*enfatizar*) to stress sth

insolación [insola'θjon] *nf* (*MED*) sunstroke

insolencia [inso'lenθja] *nf* insolence; **insolente** *adj* insolent

insólito, a [in'solito, a] *adj* unusual

insoluble [inso'luβle] *adj* insoluble

insolvencia [insol'βenθja] *nf* insolvency

insomnio [in'somnjo] *nm* insomnia

insondable [inson'daβle] *adj* bottomless; (*fig*) impenetrable

insonorizado, a [insonori'θaðo, a] *adj* (*cuarto etc*) soundproof

insoportable [insopor'taβle] *adj* unbearable

insospechado, a [insospe'tʃaðo, a] *adj* (*inesperado*) unexpected

inspección [inspek'θjon] *nf* inspection, check; **inspeccionar** (*examinar*) to inspect, examine; (*controlar*) to check

inspector, a [inspek'tor, a] *nm/f* inspector

inspiración [inspira'θjon] *nf* inspiration

inspirar [inspi'rar] *vt* to inspire; (*MED*) to inhale; **~se** *vr*: **~se en** to be inspired by

instalación [instala'θjon] *nf* (*equipo*) fittings *pl*, equipment; **~ eléctrica** wiring

instalar [insta'lar] *vt* (*establecer*) to instal; (*erguir*) to set up, erect; **~se** *vr* to establish o.s.; (*en una vivienda*) to move into

instancia [ins'tanθja] *nf* (*JUR*) petition; (*ruego*) request; **en última ~** as a last resort

instantánea [instan'tanea] *nf* snap(shot)

instantáneo, a [instan'taneo, a] *adj* instantaneous; **café ~** instant coffee

instante [ins'tante] *nm* instant, moment

instar [ins'tar] *vt* to press, urge

instaurar [instau'rar] *vt* (*costumbre*) to establish; (*normas, sistema*) to bring in, introduce; (*gobierno*) to instal

instigar [insti'xar] *vt* to instigate

instinto [ins'tinto] *nm* instinct; **por ~**

instinctively

institución [institu'θjon] *nf* institution, establishment

instituir [institu'ir] *vt* to establish; (*fundar*) to found; **instituto** *nm* (*gen*) institute; (*ESP: ESCOL*) ≈ comprehensive (*BRIT*) o high (*US*) school

institutriz [institu'triθ] *nf* governess

instrucción [instruk'θjon] *nf* instruction

instructivo, a [instruk'tiβo, a] *adj* instructive

instruir [instru'ir] *vt* (*gen*) to instruct; (*enseñar*) to teach, educate

instrumento [instru'mento] *nm* (*gen*) instrument; (*herramienta*) tool, implement

insubordinarse [insuβorði'narse] *vr* to rebel

insuficiencia [insufi'θjenθja] *nf* (*carencia*) lack; (*inadecuación*) inadequacy; **insuficiente** *adj* (*gen*) insufficient; (*ESCOL: calificación*) unsatisfactory

insufrible [insu'friβle] *adj* insufferable

insular [insu'lar] *adj* insular

insultar [insul'tar] *vt* to insult; **insulto** *nm* insult

insumiso, a [insu'miso, a] *nm/f* (*POL*) person who refuses to do military service or its substitute, community service

insuperable [insupe'raβle] *adj* (*excelente*) unsurpassable; (*problema etc*) insurmountable

insurgente [insur'xente] *adj, nm/f* insurgent

insurrección [insurrek'θjon] *nf* insurrection, rebellion

intachable [inta'tʃaβle] *adj* irreproachable

intacto, a [in'takto, a] *adj* intact

integral [inte'xral] *adj* integral; (*completo*) complete; **pan ~** wholemeal (*BRIT*) o wholewheat (*US*) bread

integrar [inte'xrar] *vt* to make up, compose; (*MAT, fig*) to integrate

integridad [intexri'ðað] *nf* wholeness; (*carácter*) integrity; **íntegro, a** *adj* whole, entire; (*honrado*) honest

intelectual [intelek'twal] *adj, nm/f* intellectual

inteligencia [inteli'xenθja] *nf* intelligence; (*ingenio*) ability; **inteligente** *adj* intelligent

inteligible [inteli'xiβle] *adj* intelligible

intemperie [intem'perje] *nf*: **a la ~** out in the open, exposed to the elements

intempestivo, a [intempes'tiβo, a] *adj* untimely

intención [inten'θjon] *nf* (*gen*) intention, purpose; **con segundas intenciones** maliciously; **con ~** deliberately

intencionado, a [intenθjo'naðo, a] *adj* deliberate; **bien ~** well-meaning; **mal ~** ill-disposed, hostile

intensidad [intensi'ðað] *nf* (*gen*) intensity; (*ELEC, TEC*) strength; **llover con ~** to rain hard

intenso, a [in'tenso, a] *adj* intense; (*sentimiento*) profound, deep

intentar [inten'tar] *vt* (*tratar*) to try, attempt; **intento** *nm* attempt

interactivo, a [interak'tiβo, a] *adj* (*INFORM*) interactive

intercalar [interka'lar] *vt* to insert

intercambio [inter'kambjo] *nm* exchange, swap

interceder [interθe'ðer] *vi* to intercede

interceptar [interθep'tar] *vt* to intercept

intercesión [interθe'sjon] *nf* intercession

interés [inte'res] *nm* (*gen*) interest; (*parte*) share, part; (*pey*) self-interest; **intereses creados** vested interests

interesado, a [intere'saðo, a] *adj* interested; (*prejuiciado*) prejudiced; (*pey*) mercenary, self-seeking

interesante [intere'sante] *adj* interesting

interesar [intere'sar] *vt, vi* to interest, be of interest to; **~se** *vr*: **~se en** o **por** to take an interest in

interferir [interfe'rir] *vt* to interfere with; (*TEL*) to jam ♦ *vi* to interfere

interfono [inter'fono] *nm* intercom

interino, a [inte'rino, a] *adj* temporary ♦ *nm/f* temporary holder of a post; (*MED*) locum; (*ESCOL*) supply teacher

interior [inte'rjor] *adj* inner, inside; (*COM*) domestic, internal ♦ *nm* interior, inside;

(fig) soul, mind; **Ministerio del I~** ≈ Home Office *(BRIT)*, ≈ Department of the Interior *(US)*

interjección [interxek'θjon] *nf* interjection

interlocutor, a [interloku'tor, a] *nm/f* speaker

intermediario, a [interme'δjarjo, a] *nm/f* intermediary

intermedio, a [inter'meδjo, a] *adj* intermediate ♦ *nm* interval

interminable [intermi'naβle] *adj* endless

intermitente [intermi'tente] *adj* intermittent ♦ *nm* (AUTO) indicator

internacional [internaθjo'nal] *adj* international

internado [inter'naδo] *nm* boarding school

internar [inter'nar] *vt* to intern; *(en un manicomio)* to commit; **~se** *vr (penetrar)* to penetrate

interno, a [in'terno, a] *adj* internal, interior; *(POL etc)* domestic ♦ *nm/f (alumno)* boarder

interponer [interpo'ner] *vt* to interpose, put in; **~se** *vr* to intervene

interpretación [interpreta'θjon] *nf* interpretation

interpretar [interpre'tar] *vt* to interpret; *(TEATRO, MUS)* to perform, play; **intérprete** *nm/f (LING)* interpreter, translator; *(MUS, TEATRO)* performer, artist(e)

interrogación [interroxa'θjon] *nf* interrogation; *(LING: tb:* **signo de ~**) question mark

interrogar [interro'var] *vt* to interrogate, question

interrumpir [interrum'pir] *vt* to interrupt

interrupción [interrup'θjon] *nf* interruption

interruptor [interrup'tor] *nm (ELEC)* switch

intersección [intersek'θjon] *nf* intersection

interurbano, a [interur'βano, a] *adj:* **llamada interurbana** long-distance call

intervalo [inter'βalo] *nm* interval; *(descanso)* break; **a ~s** at intervals, every

now and then

intervenir [interβe'nir] *vt (controlar)* to control, supervise; *(MED)* to operate on ♦ *vi (participar)* to take part, participate; *(mediar)* to intervene

interventor, a [interβen'tor, a] *nm/f* inspector; *(COM)* auditor

intestino [intes'tino] *nm* intestine

intimar [inti'mar] *vi* to become friendly

intimidad [intimi'δaδ] *nf* intimacy; *(familiaridad)* familiarity; *(vida privada)* private life; *(JUR)* privacy

íntimo, a ['intimo, a] *adj* intimate

intolerable [intole'raβle] *adj* intolerable, unbearable

intoxicación [intoksika'θjon] *nf* poisoning

intranquilizarse [intrankili'θarse] *vr* to get worried *o* anxious; **intranquilo, a** *adj* worried

intransigente [intransi'xente] *adj* intransigent

intransitable [intransi'taβle] *adj* impassable

intrépido, a [in'trepiδo, a] *adj* intrepid

intriga [in'triva] *nf* intrigue; *(plan)* plot; **intrigar** *vt, vi* to intrigue

intrincado, a [intrin'kaδo, a] *adj* intricate

intrínseco, a [in'trinseko, a] *adj* intrinsic

introducción [introδuk'θjon] *nf* introduction

introducir [introδu'θir] *vt (gen)* to introduce; *(moneda etc)* to insert; *(INFORM)* to input, enter

intromisión [intromi'sjon] *nf* interference, meddling

introvertido, a [introβer'tiδo, a] *adj, nm/f* introvert

intruso, a [in'truso, a] *adj* intrusive ♦ *nm/f* intruder

intuición [intwi'θjon] *nf* intuition

inundación [inunda'θjon] *nf* flood(ing); **inundar** *vt* to flood; *(fig)* to swamp, inundate

inusitado, a [inusi'taδo, a] *adj* unusual, rare

inútil [in'util] *adj* useless; *(esfuerzo)* vain, fruitless; **inutilidad** *nf* uselessness

inutilizar [inutili'θar] *vt* to make *o* render useless; **~se** *vr* to become useless

invadir [imba'ðir] *vt* to invade

inválido, a [im'baliðo, a] *adj* invalid ♦ *nm/f* invalid

invariable [imba'rjaßle] *adj* invariable

invasión [imba'sjon] *nf* invasion

invasor, a [imba'sor, a] *adj* invading ♦ *nm/f* invader

invención [imben'θjon] *nf* invention

inventar [imben'tar] *vt* to invent

inventario [imben'tarjo] *nm* inventory

inventiva [imben'tißa] *nf* inventiveness

invento [im'bento] *nm* invention

inventor, a [imben'tor, a] *nm/f* inventor

invernadero [imberna'ðero] *nm* greenhouse

inverosímil [imbero'simil] *adj* implausible

inversión [imber'sjon] *nf* (COM) investment

inverso, a [im'berso, a] *adj* inverse, opposite; **en el orden ~** in reverse order; **a la inversa** inversely, the other way round

inversor, a [imber'sor, a] *nm/f* (COM) investor

invertir [imber'tir] *vt* (COM) to invest; (*volcar*) to turn upside down; (*tiempo etc*) to spend

investigación [imbestiva'θjon] *nf* investigation; (ESCOL) research; **~ de mercado** market research

investigar [imbesti'var] *vt* to investigate; (ESCOL) to do research into

invierno [im'bjerno] *nm* winter

invisible [imbi'sißle] *adj* invisible

invitado, a [imbi'taðo, a] *nm/f* guest

invitar [imbi'tar] *vt* to invite; (*incitar*) to entice; (*pagar*) to pay, pay for

invocar [imbo'kar] *vt* to invoke, call on

involucrar [imbolu'krar] *vt:* **~ en** to involve in; **~se** *vr* (*persona*): **~ en** to get mixed up in

involuntario, a [imbolun'tarjo, a] *adj* (*movimiento, gesto*) involuntary; (*error*) unintentional

inyección [injek'θjon] *nf* injection

inyectar [injek'tar] *vt* to inject

┌─────────────────┐
│ *PALABRA CLAVE* │
└─────────────────┘

ir [ir] *vi* **1** to go; (*a pie*) to walk; (*viajar*) to travel; **~ caminando** to walk; **fui en tren** I went *o* travelled by train; **¡(ahora) voy!** (I'm just) coming!

2: **~ (a) por:** **~ (a) por el médico** to fetch the doctor

3 (*progresar: persona, cosa*) to go; **el trabajo va muy bien** work is going very well; **¿cómo te va?** how are things going?; **me va muy bien** I'm getting on very well; **le fue fatal** it went awfully badly for him

4 (*funcionar*): **el coche no va muy bien** the car isn't running very well

5: **te va estupendamente ese color** that colour suits you fantastically well

6 (*locuciones*): **¿vino? - ¡que va!** did he come? - of course not!; **vamos, no llores** come on, don't cry; **¡vaya coche!** what a car!, that's some car!

7: **no vaya a ser: tienes que correr, no vaya a ser que pierdas el tren** you'll have to run so as not to miss the train

8 (+*pp*): **iba vestido muy bien** he was very well dressed

9: **no me** *etc* **va ni me viene** I *etc* don't care

♦ *vb aux* **1:** **~ a:** **voy/iba a hacerlo hoy** I am/was going to do it today

2 (+*gerundio*): **iba anocheciendo** it was getting dark; **todo se me iba aclarando** everything was gradually becoming clearer to me

3 (+*pp = pasivo*): **van vendidos 300 ejemplares** 300 copies have been sold so far

♦ **~se** *vr* **1:** **¿por dónde se va al zoológico?** which is the way to the zoo?

2 (*marcharse*) to leave; **ya se habrán ido** they must already have left *o* gone

ira ['ira] *nf* anger, rage

Irak [i'rak] *nm* = **Iraq**

Irán [i'ran] *nm* Iran; **iraní** *adj, nm/f*

Iranian

Iraq [i'rak] *nm* Iraq; **iraquí** *adj, nm/f* Iraqui

iris ['iris] *nm inv* (*tb*: **arco ~**) rainbow; (*ANAT*) iris

Irlanda [ir'landa] *nf* Ireland; **irlandés, esa** *adj* Irish ♦ *nm/f* Irishman/woman; **los irlandeses** the Irish

ironía [iro'nia] *nf* irony; **irónico, a** *adj* ironic(al)

IRPF ['i 'erre 'pe 'efe] *nm abr* (=*Impuesto sobre la Renta de las Personas Físicas*) (personal) income tax

irreal [irre'al] *adj* unreal

irrecuperable [irrekupe'raβle] *adj* irrecoverable, irretrievable

irreflexión [irreflek'sjon] *nf* thoughtlessness

irregular [irreɣu'lar] *adj* (*gen*) irregular; (*situación*) abnormal

irremediable [irreme'ðjaβle] *adj* irremediable; (*vicio*) incurable

irreparable [irrepa'raβle] *adj* (*daños*) irreparable; (*pérdida*) irrecoverable

irresoluto, a [irreso'luto, a] *adj* irresolute, hesitant

irrespetuoso, a [irrespe'twoso, a] *adj* disrespectful

irresponsable [irrespon'saβle] *adj* irresponsible

irreversible [irreβer'sible] *adj* irreversible

irrigar [irri'ɣar] *vt* to irrigate

irrisorio, a [irri'sorjo, a] *adj* derisory, ridiculous

irritar [irri'tar] *vt* to irritate, annoy

irrupción [irrup'θjon] *nf* irruption; (*invasión*) invasion

isla ['isla] *nf* island

islandés, esa [islan'des, esa] *adj* Icelandic ♦ *nm/f* Icelander

Islandia [is'landja] *nf* Iceland

isleño, a [is'leɲo, a] *adj* island *cpd* ♦ *nm/f* islander

Israel [isra'el] *nm* Israel; **israelí** *adj, nm/f* Israeli

istmo ['istmo] *nm* isthmus

Italia [i'talja] *nf* Italy; **italiano, a** *adj*, *nm/f* Italian

itinerario [itine'rarjo] *nm* itinerary, route

IVA ['iβa] *nm abr* (= *impuesto sobre el valor añadido*) VAT

izar [i'θar] *vt* to hoist

izdo, a *abr* (= *izquierdo, a*) l.

izquierda [iθ'kjerda] *nf* left; (*POL*) left (wing); **a la ~** (*estar*) on the left; (*torcer etc*) (to the) left

izquierdista [iθkjer'ðista] *nm/f* left-winger, leftist

izquierdo, a [iθ'kjerðo, a] *adj* left

J, j

jabalí [xaβa'li] *nm* wild boar

jabalina [xaβa'lina] *nf* javelin

jabón [xa'βon] *nm* soap; **jabonar** *vt* to soap

jaca ['xaka] *nf* pony

jacinto [xa'θinto] *nm* hyacinth

jactarse [xak'tarse] *vr* to boast, brag

jadear [xaðe'ar] *vi* to pant, gasp for breath; **jadeo** *nm* panting, gasping

jaguar [xa'ɣwar] *nm* jaguar

jalea [xa'lea] *nf* jelly

jaleo [xa'leo] *nm* racket, uproar; **armar un ~** to kick up a racket

jalón [xa'lon] (*AM*) *nm* tug

jamás [xa'mas] *adv* never

jamón [xa'mon] *nm* ham; **~ dulce**, **~ de York** cooked ham; **~ serrano** cured ham

Japón [xa'pon] *nm*: **el ~** Japan; **japonés, esa** *adj, nm/f* Japanese ♦ *nm* (*LING*) Japanese

jaque ['xake] *nm*: **~ mate** checkmate

jaqueca [xa'keka] *nf* (very bad) headache, migraine

jarabe [xa'raβe] *nm* syrup

jarcia ['xarθja] *nf* (*NAUT*) ropes *pl*, rigging

jardín [xar'ðin] *nm* garden; **~ de infancia** (*ESP*) *o* **de niños** (*AM*) nursery (school); **jardinería** *nf* gardening; **jardinero, a** *nm/f* gardener

jarra ['xarra] *nf* jar; (*jarro*) jug

jarro ['xarro] *nm* jug

jarrón [xaˈrron] *nm* vase

jaula [ˈxaula] *nf* cage

jauría [xauˈria] *nf* pack of hounds

jazmín [xaθˈmin] *nm* jasmine

J. C. *abr* (= *Jesucristo*) J.C.

jefa [ˈxefa] *nf ver* **jefe**

jefatura [xefaˈtura] *nf*: ~ **de policía** police headquarters *sg*

jefe, a [ˈxefe, a] *nm/f* (*gen*) chief, head; (*patrón*) boss; ~ **de cocina** chef; ~ **de estación** stationmaster; ~ **de estado** head of state

jengibre [xenˈxiβre] *nm* ginger

jeque [ˈxeke] *nm* sheik

jerarquía [xerarˈkia] *nf* (*orden*) hierarchy; (*rango*) rank; **jerárquico, a** *adj* hierarchic(al)

jerez [xeˈreθ] *nm* sherry

jerga [ˈxerɣa] *nf* jargon

jeringa [xeˈrinɣa] *nf* syringe; (*AM*) annoyance, bother; ~ **de engrase** grease gun; **jeringar** *vt* (*fam*) to annoy, bother; **jeringuilla** *nf* syringe

jeroglífico [xeroˈɣlifiko] *nm* hieroglyphic

jersey [xerˈsei] (*pl* ~**s**) *nm* jersey, pullover, jumper

Jerusalén [xerusaˈlen] *n* Jerusalem

Jesucristo [xesuˈkristo] *nm* Jesus Christ

jesuita [xeˈswita] *adj, nm* Jesuit

Jesús [xeˈsus] *nm* Jesus; ¡~! good heavens!; (*al estornudar*) bless you!

jinete, a [xiˈnete, a] *nm/f* horseman/ woman, rider

jipijapa [xipiˈxapa] (*AM*) *nm* straw hat

jirafa [xiˈrafa] *nf* giraffe

jirón [xiˈron] *nm* rag, shred

jocoso, a [xoˈkoso, a] *adj* humorous, jocular

joder [xoˈðer] (*fam!*) *vt, vi* to fuck(*!*)

jofaina [xoˈfaina] *nf* washbasin

jornada [xorˈnaða] *nf* (*viaje de un día*) day's journey; (*camino o viaje entero*) journey; (*día de trabajo*) working day

jornal [xorˈnal] *nm* (day's) wage; ~**ero** *nm* (day) labourer

joroba [xoˈroβa] *nf* hump, hunched back; ~**do, a** *adj* hunchbacked ♦ *nm/f* hunchback

jota [ˈxota] *nf* (the letter) J; (*danza*) Aragonese dance; **no saber ni** ~ to have no idea

joven [ˈxoβen] (*pl* **jóvenes**) *adj* young ♦ *nm* young man, youth ♦ *nf* young woman, girl

jovial [xoˈβjal] *adj* cheerful, jolly

joya [ˈxoja] *nf* jewel, gem; (*fig: persona*) gem; **joyería** *nf* (*joyas*) jewellery; (*tienda*) jeweller's (shop); **joyero** *nm* (*persona*) jeweller; (*caja*) jewel case

juanete [xwaˈnete] *nm* (*del pie*) bunion

jubilación [xuβilaˈθjon] *nf* (*retiro*) retirement

jubilado, a [xuβiˈlaðo, a] *adj* retired ♦ *nm/f* pensioner (*BRIT*), senior citizen

jubilar [xuβiˈlar] *vt* to pension off, retire; (*fam*) to discard; ~**se** *vr* to retire

júbilo [ˈxuβilo] *nm* joy, rejoicing; **jubiloso, a** *adj* jubilant

judía [xuˈðia] *nf* (*CULIN*) bean; ~ **verde** French bean; *ver tb* **judío**

judicial [xuðiˈθjal] *adj* judicial

judío, a [xuˈðio, a] *adj* Jewish ♦ *nm/f* Jew(ess)

judo [ˈjuðo] *nm* judo

juego *etc* [ˈxwexo] *vb ver* **jugar** ♦ *nm* (*gen*) play; (*pasatiempo, partido*) game; (*en casino*) gambling; (*conjunto*) set; **fuera de** ~ (*DEPORTE: persona*) offside; (*: pelota*) out of play; **J~s Olímpicos** Olympic Games

juerga [ˈxwerɣa] *nf* binge, (*fiesta*) party; **ir de** ~ to go out on a binge

jueves [ˈxweβes] *nm inv* Thursday

juez [xweθ] *nm/f* judge; ~ **de línea** linesman; ~ **de salida** starter

jugada [xuˈɣaða] *nf* play; **buena** ~ good move/shot/stroke *etc*

jugador, a [xuɣaˈðor, a] *nm/f* player; (*en casino*) gambler

jugar [xuˈɣar] *vt, vi* to play; (*en casino*) to gamble; (*apostar*) to bet; ~ **al fútbol** to play football

juglar [xuˈɣlar] *nm* minstrel

jugo [ˈxuɣo] *nm* (*BOT*) juice; (*fig*) essence, substance; ~ **de fruta** (*AM*) fruit juice;

~so, a adj juicy; (fig) substantial, important
juguete [xu'ɣete] nm toy; **~ar** vi to play; **~ría** nf toyshop
juguetón, ona [xuɣe'ton, ona] adj playful
juicio ['xwiθjo] nm judgement; (razón) sanity, reason; (opinión) opinion; **~so, a** adj wise, sensible
julio ['xuljo] nm July
junco ['xunko] nm rush, reed
jungla ['xungla] nf jungle
junio ['xunjo] nm June
junta ['xunta] nf (asamblea) meeting, assembly; (comité, consejo) board, council, committee; (TEC) joint
juntar [xun'tar] vt to join, unite; (maquinaria) to assemble, put together; (dinero) to collect; **~se** vr to join, meet; (reunirse: personas) to meet, assemble; (arrimarse) to approach, draw closer; **~se con uno** to join sb
junto, a ['xunto, a] adj joined; (unido) united; (anexo) near, close; (contiguo, próximo) next, adjacent ♦ adv: **todo ~** all at once; **~s** together; **~ a** near (to), next to
jurado [xu'raðo] nm (JUR: individuo) juror; (: grupo) jury; (de concurso: grupo) panel (of judges); (: individuo) member of a panel
juramento [xura'mento] nm oath; (maldición) oath, curse; **prestar ~** to take the oath; **tomar ~ a** to swear in, administer the oath to
jurar [xu'rar] vt, vi to swear; **~ en falso** to commit perjury; **jurárselas a uno** to have it in for sb
jurídico, a [xu'riðiko, a] adj legal
jurisdicción [xurisðik'θjon] nf (poder, autoridad) jurisdiction; (territorio) district
jurisprudencia [xurispru'ðenθja] nf jurisprudence
jurista [xu'rista] nm/f jurist
justamente [xusta'mente] adv justly, fairly; (precisamente) just, exactly
justicia [xus'tiθja] nf justice; (equidad) fairness, justice; **justiciero, a** adj just,

righteous
justificación [xustifika'θjon] nf justification; **justificar** vt to justify
justo, a ['xusto, a] adj (equitativo) just, fair, right; (preciso) exact, correct; (ajustado) tight ♦ adv (precisamente) exactly, precisely; (AM: apenas a tiempo) just in time
juvenil [xuβe'nil] adj youthful
juventud [xuβen'tuð] nf (adolescencia) youth; (jóvenes) young people pl
juzgado [xuθ'ɣaðo] nm tribunal; (JUR) court
juzgar [xuθ'ɣar] vt to judge; **a ~ por ...** to judge by ..., judging by ...

K, k

kg abr (= kilogramo) kg
kilo ['kilo] nm kilo ♦ pref: **~gramo** nm kilogramme; **~metraje** nm distance in kilometres, ≈ mileage; **kilómetro** nm kilometre; **~vatio** nm kilowatt
kiosco ['kjosko] nm = **quiosco**
km abr (= kilómetro) km
kv abr (= kilovatio) kw

L, l

l abr (= litro) l
la [la] art def the ♦ pron her; (Ud.) you; (cosa) it ♦ nm (MUS) la; **~ del sombrero rojo** the girl in the red hat; tb ver **el**
laberinto [laβe'rinto] nm labyrinth
labia ['laβja] nf fluency; (pey) glib tongue
labio ['laβjo] nm lip
labor [la'βor] nf labour; (AGR) farm work; (tarea) job, task; (COSTURA) needlework; **~able** adj (AGR) workable; **día ~able** working day; **~al** adj (accidente) at work; (jornada) working
laboratorio [laβora'torjo] nm laboratory
laborioso, a [laβo'rjoso, a] adj (persona) hard-working; (trabajo) tough
laborista [laβo'rista] adj: **Partido L~**

Labour Party

labrado, a [la'ßraðo, a] *adj* worked; (*madera*) carved; (*metal*) wrought

labrador, a [laßra'ðor, a] *adj* farming *cpd* ♦ *nm/f* farmer

labranza [la'ßranθa] *nf* (AGR) cultivation

labrar [la'ßrar] *vt* (*gen*) to work; (*madera etc*) to carve; (*fig*) to cause, bring about

labriego, a [la'ßrjeɣo, a] *nm/f* peasant

laca ['laka] *nf* lacquer

lacayo [la'kajo] *nm* lackey

lacio, a ['laθjo, a] *adj* (*pelo*) lank, straight

lacón [la'kon] *nm* shoulder of pork

lacónico, a [la'koniko, a] *adj* laconic

lacra ['lakra] *nf* (*fig*) blot; **lacrar** *vt* (*cerrar*) to seal (with sealing wax); **lacre** *nm* sealing wax

lactancia [lak'tanθja] *nf* lactation

lactar [lak'tar] *vt, vi* to suckle

lácteo, a ['lakteo, a] *adj*: **productos ~s** dairy products

ladear [laðe'ar] *vt* to tip, tilt ♦ *vi* to tilt; **~se** *vr* to lean

ladera [la'ðera] *nf* slope

lado ['laðo] *nm* (*gen*) side; (*fig*) protection; (*MIL*) flank; **al ~ de** beside; **poner de ~** to put on its side; **poner a un ~** to put aside; **por todos ~s** on all sides, all round (BRIT)

ladrar [la'ðrar] *vi* to bark; **ladrido** *nm* bark, barking

ladrillo [la'ðriʎo] *nm* (*gen*) brick; (*azulejo*) tile

ladrón, ona [la'ðron, ona] *nm/f* thief

lagartija [laɣar'tixa] *nf* (ZOOL) (small) lizard

lagarto [la'ɣarto] *nm* (ZOOL) lizard

lago ['laɣo] *nm* lake

lágrima ['laɣrima] *nf* tear

laguna [la'ɣuna] *nf* (*lago*) lagoon; (*hueco*) gap

laico, a ['laiko, a] *adj* lay

lamentable [lamen'taßle] *adj* lamentable, regrettable; (*miserable*) pitiful

lamentar [lamen'tar] *vt* (*sentir*) to regret; (*deplorar*) to lament; **lo lamento mucho** I'm very sorry; **~se** *vr* to lament;

lamento *nm* lament

lamer [la'mer] *vt* to lick

lámina ['lamina] *nf* (*plancha delgada*) sheet; (*para estampar, estampa*) plate

lámpara ['lampara] *nf* lamp; **~ de alcohol/gas** spirit/gas lamp; **~ de pie** standard lamp

lamparón [lampa'ron] *nm* grease spot

lana ['lana] *nf* wool

lancha ['lantʃa] *nf* launch; **~ de pesca** fishing boat; **~ salvavidas/torpedera** lifeboat/torpedo boat

langosta [lan'gosta] *nf* (*crustáceo*) lobster; (: *de río*) crayfish; **langostino** *nm* Dublin Bay prawn

languidecer [langiðe'θer] *vi* to languish; **languidez** *nf* languor; **lánguido, a** *adj* (*gen*) languid; (*sin energía*) listless

lanilla [la'niʎa] *nf* nap

lanza ['lanθa] *nf* (*arma*) lance, spear

lanzamiento [lanθa'mjento] *nm* (*gen*) throwing; (NAUT, COM) launch, launching; **~ de peso** putting the shot

lanzar [lan'θar] *vt* (*gen*) to throw; (DEPORTE: *pelota*) to bowl; (NAUT, COM) to launch; (JUR) to evict; **~se** *vr* to throw o.s.

lapa ['lapa] *nf* limpet

lapicero [lapi'θero] *nm* pencil; (AM: *bolígrafo*) Biro ®

lápida ['lapiða] *nf* stone; **~ mortuoria** headstone; **~ conmemorativa** memorial stone; **lapidario, a** *adj*, *nm* lapidary

lápiz ['lapiθ] *nm* pencil; **~ de color** coloured pencil; **~ de labios** lipstick

lapón, ona [la'pon, ona] *nm/f* Laplander, Lapp

lapso ['lapso] *nm* (*de tiempo*) interval; (*error*) error

lapsus ['lapsus] *nm inv* error, mistake

largar [lar'ɣar] *vt* (*soltar*) to release; (*aflojar*) to loosen; (*lanzar*) to launch; (*fam*) to let fly; (*velas*) to unfurl; (*fam*) to throw; **~se** *vr* (*fam*) to beat it; **~se a** (AM) to start to

largo, a ['larɣo, a] *adj* (*longitud*) long; (*tiempo*) lengthy; (*fig*) generous ♦ *nm* length; (MUS) largo; **dos años ~s** two

long years; tiene 9 metros de ~ it is 9
metres long; **a lo ~ de** along; (*tiempo*) all
through, throughout; **~metraje** *nm*
feature film

laringe [laˈrinxe] *nf* larynx; **laringitis** *nf*
laryngitis

larva [ˈlarβa] *nf* larva

las [las] *art def* the ♦ *pron* them; **~ que
cantan** the ones/women/girls who sing;
tb ver **el**

lascivo, a [lasˈθiβo, a] *adj* lewd

láser [ˈlaser] *nm* laser

lástima [ˈlastima] *nf* (*pena*) pity; **dar ~** to
be pitiful; **es una ~ que** it's a pity that;
¡qué ~! what a pity!; **ella está hecha
una ~** she looks pitiful

lastimar [lastiˈmar] *vt* (*herir*) to wound;
(*ofender*) to offend; **~se** *vr* to hurt o.s.;
lastimero, a *adj* pitiful, pathetic

lastre [ˈlastre] *nm* (*TEC, NAUT*) ballast; (*fig*)
dead weight

lata [ˈlata] *nf* (*metal*) tin; (*caja*) tin (*BRIT*),
can; (*fam*) nuisance; **en ~** tinned (*BRIT*),
canned; **dar (la) ~** to be a nuisance

latente [laˈtente] *adj* latent

lateral [lateˈral] *adj* side *cpd*, lateral ♦ *nm*
(*TEATRO*) wings

latido [laˈtiðo] *nm* (*del corazón*) beat

latifundio [latiˈfundjo] *nm* large estate;
latifundista *nm/f* owner of a large
estate

latigazo [latiˈɣaθo] *nm* (*golpe*) lash;
(*sonido*) crack

látigo [ˈlatiɣo] *nm* whip

latín [laˈtin] *nm* Latin

latino, a [laˈtino, a] *adj* Latin;
~americano, a *adj, nm/f* Latin-
American

latir [laˈtir] *vi* (*corazón, pulso*) to beat

latitud [latiˈtuð] *nf* (*GEO*) latitude

latón [laˈton] *nm* brass

latoso, a [laˈtoso, a] *adj* (*molesto*)
annoying; (*aburrido*) boring

laúd [laˈuð] *nm* lute

laurel [lauˈrel] *nm* (*BOT*) laurel; (*CULIN*) bay

lava [ˈlaβa] *nf* lava

lavabo [laˈβaβo] *nm* (*pila*) washbasin; (*tb:*

~s) toilet

lavado [laˈβaðo] *nm* washing; (*de ropa*)
laundry; (*ARTE*) wash; **~ de cerebro**
brainwashing; **~ en seco** dry-cleaning

lavadora [laβaˈðora] *nf* washing machine

lavanda [laˈβanda] *nf* lavender

lavandería [laβandeˈria] *nf* laundry;
(*automática*) launderette

lavaplatos [laβaˈplatos] *nm inv*
dishwasher

lavar [laˈβar] *vt* to wash; (*borrar*) to wipe
away; **~se** *vr* to wash o.s.; **~se las
manos** to wash one's hands; **~se los
dientes** to brush one's teeth; **~ y marcar**
(*pelo*) to shampoo and set; **~ en seco** to
dry-clean; **~ los platos** to wash the dishes

lavavajillas [laβaβaˈxiʎas] *nm inv*
dishwasher

laxante [lakˈsante] *nm* laxative

lazada [laˈθaða] *nf* bow

lazarillo [laθaˈriʎo] *nm*: **perro ~** guide dog

lazo [ˈlaθo] *nm* knot; (*lazada*) bow; (*para
animales*) lasso; (*trampa*) snare; (*vínculo*)
tie

le [le] *pron* (*directo*) him (*o* her); (: *usted*)
you; (*indirecto*) to him (*o* her *o* it);
(: *usted*) to you

leal [leˈal] *adj* loyal; **~tad** *nf* loyalty

lección [lekˈθjon] *nf* lesson

leche [ˈletʃe] *nf* milk; **tiene mala ~** (*fam!*)
he's a swine (*!*); **~ condensada/en polvo**
condensed/powdered milk; **~ desnatada**
skimmed milk; **~ra** *nf* (*vendedora*)
milkmaid; (*recipiente*) (milk) churn; (*AM*)
cow; **~ro, a** *adj* dairy

lecho [ˈletʃo] *nm* (*cama, de río*) bed; (*GEO*)
layer

lechón [leˈtʃon] *nm* sucking (*BRIT*) *o*
suckling (*US*) pig

lechoso, a [leˈtʃoso, a] *adj* milky

lechuga [leˈtʃuɣa] *nf* lettuce

lechuza [leˈtʃuθa] *nf* owl

lector, a [lekˈtor, a] *nm/f* reader ♦ *nm*: **~
de discos compactos** CD player

lectura [lekˈtura] *nf* reading

leer [leˈer] *vt* to read

legado [leˈɣaðo] *nm* (*don*) bequest;

(*herencia*) legacy; (*enviado*) legate
legajo [le'xaxo] *nm* file
legal [le'xal] *adj* (*gen*) legal; (*persona*) trustworthy; **~idad** *nf* legality
legalizar [lexali'θar] *vt* to legalize; (*documento*) to authenticate
legaña [le'xaŋa] *nf* sleep (*in eyes*)
legar [le'xar] *vt* to bequeath, leave
legendario, a [lexen'darjo, a] *adj* legendary
legión [le'xjon] *nf* legion; **legionario, a** *adj* legionary ♦ *nm* legionnaire
legislación [lexisla'θjon] *nf* legislation
legislar [lexis'lar] *vi* to legislate
legislatura [lexisla'tura] *nf* (*POL*) period of office
legitimar [lexiti'mar] *vt* to legitimize; **legítimo, a** *adj* (*genuino*) authentic; (*legal*) legitimate
lego, a [lexo, a] *adj* (*REL*) secular; (*ignorante*) ignorant ♦ *nm* layman
legua [lexwa] *nf* league
legumbres [le'xumbres] *nfpl* pulses
leído, a [le'iðo, a] *adj* well-read
lejanía [lexa'nia] *nf* distance; **lejano, a** *adj* far-off; (*en el tiempo*) distant; (*fig*) remote
lejía [le'xia] *nf* bleach
lejos ['lexos] *adv* far, far away; **a lo ~** in the distance; **de** *o* **desde ~** from afar; **~ de** far from
lelo, a ['lelo, a] *adj* silly ♦ *nm/f* idiot
lema ['lema] *nm* motto; (*POL*) slogan
lencería [lenθe'ria] *nf* linen, drapery
lengua ['lengwa] *nf* tongue; (*LING*) language; **morderse la ~** to hold one's tongue
lenguado [len'gwaðo] *nm* sole
lenguaje [len'gwaxe] *nm* language
lengüeta [len'gweta] *nf* (*ANAT*) epiglottis; (*zapatos*) tongue, (*MUS*) reed
lente ['lente] *nf/m* lens; (*lupa*) magnifying glass; **~s** *nfpl* (*gafas*) glasses; **~s de contacto** contact lenses
lenteja [len'texa] *nf* lentil; **lentejuela** *nf* sequin
lentilla [len'tiʎa] *nf* contact lens

lentitud [lenti'tuð] *nf* slowness; **con ~** slowly
lento, a ['lento, a] *adj* slow
leña ['leŋa] *nf* firewood; **~dor, a** *nm/f* woodcutter
leño ['leŋo] *nm* (*trozo de árbol*) log; (*madera*) timber; (*fig*) blockhead
Leo ['leo] *nm* Leo
león [le'on] *nm* lion; **~ marino** sea lion
leopardo [leo'parðo] *nm* leopard
leotardos [leo'tarðos] *nmpl* tights
lepra ['lepra] *nf* leprosy; **leproso, a** *nm/f* leper
lerdo, a ['lerðo, a] *adj* (*lento*) slow; (*patoso*) clumsy
les [les] *pron* (*directo*) them; (: *ustedes*) you; (*indirecto*) to them; (: *ustedes*) to you
lesbiana [les'βjana] *adj*, *nf* lesbian
lesión [le'sjon] *nf* wound, lesion; (*DEPORTE*) injury; **lesionado, a** *adj* injured ♦ *nm/f* injured person
letal [le'tal] *adj* lethal
letanía [leta'nia] *nf* litany
letargo [le'tarxo] *nm* lethargy
letra ['letra] *nf* letter; (*escritura*) handwriting; (*MUS*) lyrics *pl*; **~ de cambio** bill of exchange; **~ de imprenta** print; **~do, a** *adj* learned ♦ *nm/f* lawyer; **letrero** *nm* (*cartel*) sign; (*etiqueta*) label
letrina [le'trina] *nf* latrine
leucemia [leu'θemja] *nf* leukaemia
levadizo [leβa'ðiθo] *adj*: **puente ~** drawbridge
levadura [leβa'ðura] *nf* (*para el pan*) yeast; (*de la cerveza*) brewer's yeast
levantamiento [leβanta'mjento] *nm* raising, lifting; (*rebelión*) revolt, uprising; **~ de pesos** weight-lifting
levantar [leβan'tar] *vt* (*gen*) to raise; (*del suelo*) to pick up; (*hacia arriba*) to lift (up); (*plan*) to make, draw up; (*mesa*) to clear; (*campamento*) to strike; (*fig*) to cheer up, hearten; **~se** *vr* to get up; (*enderezarse*) to straighten up; (*rebelarse*) to rebel; **~ el ánimo** to cheer up
levante [le'βante] *nm* east coast; **el L~** *region of Spain extending from Castellón*

to Murcia

levar [le'ßar] *vt* to weigh

leve ['leße] *adj* light; (*fig*) trivial; **~dad** *nf* lightness

levita [le'ßita] *nf* frock coat

léxico ['leksiko] *nm* (*vocabulario*) vocabulary

ley [lei] *nf* (*gen*) law; (*metal*) standard

leyenda [le'jenda] *nf* legend

leyó *etc vb ver* **leer**

liar [li'ar] *vt* to tie (up); (*unir*) to bind; (*envolver*) to wrap (up); (*enredar*) to confuse; (*cigarrillo*) to roll; **~se** *vr* (*fam*) to get involved; **~se a palos** to get involved in a fight

Líbano ['lißano] *nm*: **el ~** (the) Lebanon

libelo [li'ßelo] *nm* satire, lampoon

libélula [li'ßelula] *nf* dragonfly

liberación [lißera'θjon] *nf* liberation; (*de la cárcel*) release

liberal [liße'ral] *adj, nm/f* liberal; **~idad** *nf* liberality, generosity

liberar [liße'rar] *vt* to liberate

libertad [lißer'tað] *nf* liberty, freedom; **~ de culto/de prensa/de comercio** freedom of worship/of the press/of trade; **~ condicional** probation; **~ bajo palabra** parole; **~ bajo fianza** bail

libertar [lißer'tar] *vt* (*preso*) to set free; (*de una obligación*) to release; (*eximir*) to exempt

libertino, a [lißer'tino, a] *adj* permissive ♦ *nm/f* permissive person

libra ['lißra] *nf* pound; (*ASTROLOGÍA*): **L~** Libra; **~ esterlina** pound sterling

librar [li'ßrar] *vt* (*de peligro*) to save; (*batalla*) to wage, fight; (*de impuestos*) to exempt; (*cheque*) to make out; (*JUR*) to exempt; **~se** *vr*: **~se de** to escape from, free o.s. from

libre ['lißre] *adj* free; (*lugar*) unoccupied; (*asiento*) vacant; (*de deudas*) free of debts; **~ de impuestos** free of tax; **tiro ~** free kick; **los 100 metros ~** the 100 metres free-style (race); **al aire ~** in the open air

librería [lißre'ria] *nf* (*tienda*) bookshop; **librero, a** *nm/f* bookseller

libreta [li'ßreta] *nf* notebook; **~ de ahorros** savings book

libro ['lißro] *nm* book; **~ de bolsillo** paperback; **~ de caja** cashbook; **~ de cheques** chequebook (*BRIT*), checkbook (*US*); **~ de texto** textbook

Lic. *abr* = **licenciado, a**

licencia [li'θenθja] *nf* (*gen*) licence; (*permiso*) permission; **~ por enfermedad** sick leave; **~ de caza** game licence; **~do, a** *adj* licensed ♦ *nm/f* graduate; **licenciar** *vt* (*empleado*) to dismiss; (*permitir*) to permit, allow; (*soldado*) to discharge; (*estudiante*) to confer a degree upon; **licenciarse** *vr*: **licenciarse en letras** to graduate in arts

licencioso, a [liθen'θjoso, a] *adj* licentious

licitar [liθi'tar] *vt* to bid for; (*AM*) to sell by auction

lícito, a ['liθito, a] *adj* (*legal*) lawful; (*justo*) fair, just; (*permisible*) permissible

licor [li'kor] *nm* spirits *pl* (*BRIT*), liquor (*US*); (*de frutas etc*) liqueur

licuadora [likwa'ðora] *nf* blender

licuar [li'kwar] *vt* to liquidize

líder ['liðer] *nm/f* leader; **liderato** *nm* leadership; **liderazgo** *nm* leadership

lidia ['liðja] *nf* bullfighting; (*una ~*) bullfight; **toros de ~** fighting bulls; **lidiar** *vt, vi* to fight

liebre ['ljeßre] *nf* hare

lienzo ['ljenθo] *nm* linen; (*ARTE*) canvas; (*ARQ*) wall

liga ['liɣa] *nf* (*de medias*) garter, suspender; (*AM: gomita*) rubber band; (*confederación*) league

ligadura [liɣa'ðura] *nf* bond, tie; (*MED, MUS*) ligature

ligamento [liɣa'mento] *nm* ligament

ligar [li'ɣar] *vt* (*atar*) to tie; (*unir*) to join; (*MED*) to bind up; (*MUS*) to slur ♦ *vi* to mix, blend; (*fam*): (**él**) **liga mucho** he pulls a lot of women; **~se** *vr* to commit o.s.

ligereza [lixe'reθa] *nf* lightness; (*rapidez*) swiftness; (*agilidad*) agility; (*superficialidad*) flippancy

ligero, a [li'xero, a] *adj (de peso)* light; *(tela)* thin; *(rápido)* swift, quick; *(ágil)* agile, nimble; *(de importancia)* slight; *(de carácter)* flippant, superficial ♦ *adv*: **a la ligera** superficially

liguero [li'vero] *nm* suspender *(BRIT)* o garter *(US)* belt

lija ['lixa] *nf (ZOOL)* dogfish; *(tb: papel de ~)* sandpaper

lila ['lila] *nf* lilac

lima ['lima] *nf* file; *(BOT)* lime; **~ de uñas** nailfile; **limar** *vt* to file

limitación [limita'θjon] *nf* limitation, limit; **~ de velocidad** speed limit

limitar [limi'tar] *vt* to limit; *(reducir)* to reduce, cut down ♦ *vi*: **~ con** to border on; **~se** *vr*: **~se a** to limit o.s. to

límite ['limite] *nm (gen)* limit; *(fin)* end; *(frontera)* border; **~ de velocidad** speed limit

limítrofe [li'mitrofe] *adj* neighbouring

limón [li'mon] *nm* lemon ♦ *adj*: **amarillo ~** lemon-yellow; **limonada** *nf* lemonade

limosna [li'mosna] *nf* alms *pl*; **vivir de ~** to live on charity

limpiaparabrisas [limpjapara'ßrisas] *nm inv* windscreen *(BRIT)* o windshield *(US)* wiper

limpiar [lim'pjar] *vt* to clean; *(con trapo)* to wipe; *(quitar)* to wipe away; *(zapatos)* to shine, polish; *(fig)* to clean up

limpieza [lim'pjeθa] *nf (estado)* cleanliness; *(acto)* cleaning; *(: de las calles)* cleansing; *(: de zapatos)* polishing; *(habilidad)* skill; *(fig: POLICÍA)* clean-up; *(pureza)* purity; *(MIL)*: **operación de ~** mopping-up operation; **~ en seco** dry cleaning

limpio, a ['limpjo, a] *adj* clean; *(moralmente)* pure; *(COM)* clear, net; *(fam)* honest ♦ *adv*: **jugar ~** to play fair; **pasar a** *(ESP)* o **en** *(AM)* **~** to make a clean copy

linaje [li'naxe] *nm* lineage, family

lince ['linθe] *nm* lynx

linchar [lin'tʃar] *vt* to lynch

lindar [lin'dar] *vi* to adjoin; **~ con** to

border on; **linde** *nm* o *f* boundary; **lindero, a** *adj* adjoining ♦ *nm* boundary

lindo, a ['lindo, a] *adj* pretty, lovely ♦ *adv*: **nos divertimos de lo ~** we had a marvellous time; **canta muy ~** *(AM)* he sings beautifully

línea ['linea] *nf (gen)* line; **en ~** *(INFORM)* on line; **~ aérea** airline; **~ de meta** goal line; *(de carrera)* finishing line; **~ recta** straight line

lingote [lin'gote] *nm* ingot

lingüista [lin'gwista] *nm/f* linguist; **lingüística** *nf* linguistics *sg*

lino ['lino] *nm* linen; *(BOT)* flax

linóleo [li'noleo] *nm* lino, linoleum

linterna [lin'terna] *nf* torch *(BRIT)*, flashlight *(US)*

lío ['lio] *nm* bundle; *(fam)* fuss; *(desorden)* muddle, mess; **armar un ~** to make a fuss

liquen ['liken] *nm* lichen

liquidación [likiða'θjon] *nf* liquidation; **venta de ~** clearance sale

liquidar [liki'ðar] *vt (mercancías)* to liquidate; *(deudas)* to pay off; *(empresa)* to wind up

líquido, a ['likiðo, a] *adj* liquid; *(ganancia)* net ♦ *nm* liquid; **~ imponible** net taxable income

lira ['lira] *nf (MUS)* lyre; *(moneda)* lira

lírico, a ['liriko, a] *adj* lyrical

lirio ['lirjo] *nm (BOT)* iris

lirón [li'ron] *nm (ZOOL)* dormouse; *(fig)* sleepyhead

Lisboa [lis'ßoa] *n* Lisbon

lisiado, a [li'sjaðo, a] *adj* injured ♦ *nm/f* cripple

lisiar [li'sjar] *vt* to maim; **~se** *vr* to injure o.s.

liso, a ['liso, a] *adj (terreno)* flat; *(cabello)* straight; *(superficie)* even; *(tela)* plain

lisonja [li'sonxa] *nf* flattery

lista ['lista] *nf* list; *(de alumnos)* school register; *(de libros)* catalogue; *(de platos)* menu; *(de precios)* price list; **pasar ~** to call the roll; **~ de correos** poste restante; **~ de espera** waiting list; **tela de ~s** striped material; **listín** *nm*: **~ (telefónico)**

telephone directory

listo, a ['listo, a] *adj* (*perspicaz*) smart, clever; (*preparado*) ready

listón [lis'ton] *nm* (*de madera, metal*) strip

litera [li'tera] *nf* (*en barco, tren*) berth; (*en dormitorio*) bunk, bunk bed

literal [lite'ral] *adj* literal

literario, a [lite'rarjo, a] *adj* literary

literato, a [lite'rato, a] *adj* literary ♦ *nm/f* writer

literatura [litera'tura] *nf* literature

litigar [liti'var] *vt* to fight ♦ *vi* (*JUR*) to go to law; (*fig*) to dispute, argue

litigio [li'tixjo] *nm* (*JUR*) lawsuit; (*fig*): **en ~ con** in dispute with

litografía [litovra'fia] *nf* lithography; (*una ~*) lithograph

litoral [lito'ral] *adj* coastal ♦ *nm* coast, seaboard

litro ['litro] *nm* litre

liviano, a [li'ßjano, a] *adj* (*cosa, objeto*) trivial

lívido, a ['lißiðo, a] *adj* livid

llaga ['ʎava] *nf* wound

llama ['ʎama] *nf* flame; (*ZOOL*) llama

llamada [ʎa'maða] *nf* call; **~ al orden** call to order; **~ a pie de página** reference note

llamamiento [ʎama'mjento] *nm* call

llamar [ʎa'mar] *vt* to call; (*atención*) to attract ♦ *vi* (*por teléfono*) to telephone; (*a la puerta*) to knock (*o* ring); (*por señas*) to beckon; (*MIL*) to call up; **~se** *vr* to be called, be named; **¿cómo se llama usted?** what's your name?

llamarada [ʎama'raða] *nf* (*llamas*) blaze; (*rubor*) flush

llamativo, a [ʎama'tißo, a] *adj* showy; (*color*) loud

llano, a ['ʎano, a] *adj* (*superficie*) flat; (*persona*) straightforward; (*estilo*) clear ♦ *nm* plain, flat ground

llanta ['ʎanta] *nf* (*wheel*) rim; (*AM*): **~ (de goma)** tyre; (: *cámara*) inner (tube)

llanto ['ʎanto] *nm* weeping

llanura [ʎa'nura] *nf* plain

llave ['ʎaße] *nf* key; (*del agua*) tap;

(*MECÁNICA*) spanner; (*de la luz*) switch; (*MUS*) key; **~ inglesa** monkey wrench; **~ maestra** master key; **~ de contacto** (*AUTO*) ignition key; **~ de paso** stopcock; **echar la ~ a** to lock up; **~ro** *nm* keyring

llegada [ʎe'vaða] *nf* arrival

llegar [ʎe'var] *vi* to arrive; (*alcanzar*) to reach; (*bastar*) to be enough; **~se** *vr*: **~se a** to approach; **~ a** to manage to, succeed in; **~ a saber** to find out; **~ a ser** to become; **~ a las manos de** to come into the hands of

llenar [ʎe'nar] *vt* to fill; (*espacio*) to cover; (*formulario*) to fill in *o* up; (*fig*) to heap

lleno, a ['ʎeno, a] *adj* full, filled; (*repleto*) full up ♦ *nm* (*TEATRO*) full house; **dar de ~ contra un muro** to hit a wall head-on

llevadero, a [ʎeßa'ðero, a] *adj* bearable, tolerable

llevar [ʎe'ßar] *vt* to take; (*ropa*) to wear; (*cargar*) to carry; (*quitar*) to take away; (*en coche*) to drive; (*transportar*) to transport; (*traer: dinero*) to carry; (*conducir*) to lead; (*MAT*) to carry ♦ *vi* (*suj: camino etc*): **~ a** to lead to; **~se** *vr* to carry off, take away; **llevamos dos días aquí** we have been here for two days; **él me lleva 2 años** he's 2 years older than me; (*COM*): **~ los libros** to keep the books; **~se bien** to get on well (together)

llorar [ʎo'rar] *vt*, *vi* to cry, weep; **~ de risa** to cry with laughter

lloriquear [ʎorike'ar] *vi* to snivel, whimper

lloro ['ʎoro] *nm* crying, weeping; **llorón, ona** *adj* tearful ♦ *nm/f* cry-baby; **~so, a** *adj* weeping, tearful; (*triste*) sad, sorrowful

llover [ʎo'ßer] *vi* to rain

llovizna [ʎo'ßiθna] *nf* drizzle; **lloviznar** *vi* to drizzle

llueve *etc vb ver* **llover**

lluvia ['ʎußja] *nf* rain; **~ radioactiva** (radioactive) fallout; **lluvioso, a** *adj* rainy

lo [lo] *art def*: **~ bello** the beautiful, what is beautiful, that which is beautiful ♦ *pron* (*persona*) him; (*cosa*) it; *tb ver* **el**

loable [lo'aβle] *adj* praiseworthy; **loar** *vt* to praise

lobo [ˈloβo] *nm* wolf; **~ de mar** (*fig*) sea dog; **~ marino** seal

lóbrego, a [ˈloβreɣo, a] *adj* dark; (*fig*) gloomy

lóbulo [ˈloβulo] *nm* lobe

local [loˈkal] *adj* local ♦ *nm* place, site; (*oficinas*) premises *pl*; **~idad** *nf* (*barrio*) locality; (*lugar*) location; (*TEATRO*) seat, ticket; **~izar** *vt* (*ubicar*) to locate, find; (*restringir*) to localize; (*situar*) to place

loción [loˈθjon] *nf* lotion

loco, a [ˈloko, a] *adj* mad ♦ *nm/f* lunatic, mad person

locomotora [lokomoˈtora] *nf* engine, locomotive

locuaz [loˈkwaθ] *adj* loquacious

locución [lokuˈθjon] *nf* expression

locura [loˈkura] *nf* madness; (*acto*) crazy act

locutor, a [lokuˈtor, a] *nm/f* (*RADIO*) announcer; (*comentarista*) commentator; (*TV*) newsreader

locutorio [lokuˈtorjo] *nm* (*en telefónica*) telephone booth

lodo [ˈloðo] *nm* mud

lógica [ˈloxika] *nf* logic

lógico, a [ˈloxiko, a] *adj* logical

logística [loˈxistika] *nf* logistics *sg*

logotipo [loɣoˈtipo] *nm* logo

logrado, a [loˈɣraðo, a] *adj* (*interpretación, reproducción*) polished, excellent

lograr [loˈɣrar] *vt* to achieve; (*obtener*) to get, obtain; **~ hacer** to manage to do; **~ que uno venga** to manage to get sb to come

logro [ˈloɣro] *nm* achievement, success

loma [ˈloma] *nf* hillock (*BRIT*), small hill

lombriz [lomˈbriθ] *nf* worm

lomo [ˈlomo] *nm* (*de animal*) back; (*CULIN: de cerdo*) pork loin; (: *de vaca*) rib steak; (*de libro*) spine

lona [ˈlona] *nf* canvas

loncha [ˈlontʃa] *nf* = **lonja**

lonche [ˈlontʃe] (*AM*) *nm* lunch; **~ría** (*AM*) *nf* snack bar, diner (*US*)

Londres [ˈlondres] *n* London

longaniza [longaˈniθa] *nf* pork sausage

longitud [lonxiˈtuð] *nf* length; (*GEO*) longitude; **tener 3 metros de ~** to be 3 metres long; **~ de onda** wavelength

lonja [ˈlonxa] *nf* slice; (*de tocino*) rasher; **~ de pescado** fish market

loro [ˈloro] *nm* parrot

los [los] *art def* the ♦ *pron* them; (*ustedes*) you; **mis libros y ~ tuyos** my books and yours; *tb ver* **el**

losa [ˈlosa] *nf* stone; **~ sepulcral** gravestone

lote [ˈlote] *nm* portion; (*COM*) lot

lotería [loteˈria] *nf* lottery; (*juego*) lotto

Lotería

i Millions of pounds are spent on lotteries each year in Spain, two of which are state-run: the **Lotería Primitiva** and the **Lotería Nacional**, with money raised going directly to the government. One of the most famous lotteries is run by the wealthy and influential society for the blind, "la ONCE".

---

loza [ˈloθa] *nf* crockery

lubina [luˈβina] *nf* sea bass

lubricante [luβriˈkante] *nm* lubricant

lubricar [luβriˈkar] *vt* to lubricate

lucha [ˈlutʃa] *nf* fight, struggle; **~ de clases** class struggle; **~ libre** wrestling; **luchar** *vi* to fight

lucidez [luθiˈðeθ] *nf* lucidity

lúcido, a [ˈluθiðo, a] *adj* (*persona*) lucid; (*mente*) logical; (*idea*) crystal-clear

luciérnaga [luˈθjernaɣa] *nf* glow-worm

lucir [luˈθir] *vt* to illuminate, light (up); (*ostentar*) to show off ♦ *vi* (*brillar*) to shine; **~se** *vr* (*irónico*) to make a fool of o.s.

lucro [ˈlukro] *nm* profit, gain

lúdico, a [ˈluðiko, a] *adj* (*aspecto, actividad*) play *cpd*

luego [ˈlweɣo] *adv* (*después*) next; (*más tarde*) later, afterwards

lugar [lu'ɣar] *nm* place; (*sitio*) spot; **en ~ de** instead of; **hacer ~** to make room; **fuera de ~** out of place; **tener ~** to take place; **~ común** commonplace

lugareño, a [luɣa'reɲo, a] *adj* village *cpd* ♦ *nm/f* villager

lugarteniente [luɣarte'njente] *nm* deputy

lúgubre ['luɣuβre] *adj* mournful

lujo ['luxo] *nm* luxury; (*fig*) profusion, abundance; **~so, a** *adj* luxurious

lujuria [lu'xurja] *nf* lust

lumbre ['lumbre] *nf* fire; (*para cigarrillo*) light

lumbrera [lum'brera] *nf* luminary

luminoso, a [lumi'noso, a] *adj* luminous, shining

luna ['luna] *nf* moon; (*de un espejo*) glass; (*de gafas*) lens; (*fig*) crescent; **~ llena/ nueva** full/new moon; **estar en la ~** to have one's head in the clouds; **~ de miel** honeymoon

lunar [lu'nar] *adj* lunar ♦ *nm* (*ANAT*) mole; **tela de ~es** spotted material

lunes ['lunes] *nm inv* Monday

lupa ['lupa] *nf* magnifying glass

lustrar [lus'trar] *vt* (*mueble*) to polish; (*zapatos*) to shine; **lustre** *nm* polish; (*fig*) lustre; **dar lustre a** to polish; **lustroso, a** *adj* shining

luto ['luto] *nm* mourning; **llevar el** *o* **vestirse de ~** to be in mourning

Luxemburgo [luksem'burɣo] *nm* Luxembourg

luz [luθ] (*pl* **luces**) *nf* light; **dar a ~ un niño** to give birth to a child; **sacar a la ~** to bring to light; **dar** *o* **encender** (*ESP*) *o* **prender** (*AM*)/**apagar la ~** to switch the light on/off; **a todas luces** by any reckoning; **tener pocas luces** to be dim *o* stupid; **~ roja/verde** red/green light; **~ de freno** brake light; **luces de tráfico** traffic lights; **traje de luces** bullfighter's costume

M, m

m *abr* (= *metro*) m; (= *minuto*) m

macarrones [maka'rrones] *nmpl* macaroni *sg*

macedonia [maθe'ðonja] *nf*: **~ de frutas** fruit salad

macerar [maθe'rar] *vt* to macerate

maceta [ma'θeta] *nf* (*de flores*) pot of flowers; (*para plantas*) flowerpot

machacar [matʃa'kar] *vt* to crush, pound ♦ *vi* (*insistir*) to go on, keep on

machete [ma'tʃete] (*AM*) *nm* machete, (large) knife

machismo [ma'tʃismo] *nm* male chauvinism; **machista** *adj, nm* sexist

macho ['matʃo] *adj* male; (*fig*) virile ♦ *nm* male; (*fig*) he-man

macizo, a [ma'θiθo, a] *adj* (*grande*) massive; (*fuerte, sólido*) solid ♦ *nm* mass, chunk

madeja [ma'ðexa] *nf* (*de lana*) skein, hank; (*de pelo*) mass, mop

madera [ma'ðera] *nf* wood; (*fig*) nature, character; **una ~** a piece of wood

madero [ma'ðero] *nm* beam

madrastra [ma'ðrastra] *nf* stepmother

madre ['maðre] *adj* mother *cpd*; (*AM*) tremendous ♦ *nf* mother; (*de vino etc*) dregs *pl*; **~ política/soltera** mother-in-law/unmarried mother

Madrid [ma'ðrið] *n* Madrid

madriguera [maðri'ɣera] *nf* burrow

madrileño, a [maðri'leɲo, a] *adj* of *o* from Madrid ♦ *nm/f* native of Madrid

madrina [ma'ðrina] *nf* godmother; (*ARQ*) prop, shore; (*TEC*) brace; (*de boda*) bridesmaid

madrugada [maðru'ɣaða] *nf* early morning; (*alba*) dawn, daybreak

madrugador, a [maðruɣa'ðor, a] *adj* early-rising

madrugar [maðru'ɣar] *vi* to get up early; (*fig*) to get ahead

madurar [maðu'rar] *vt, vi* (*fruta*) to ripen;

(fig) to mature; **madurez** nf ripeness; maturity; **maduro, a** adj ripe; mature

maestra [ma'estra] nf ver **maestro**

maestría [maes'tria] nf mastery; (habilidad) skill, expertise

maestro, a [ma'estro, a] adj masterly; (principal) main ♦ nm/f master/mistress; (profesor) teacher ♦ nm (autoridad) authority; (MUS) maestro; (AM) skilled workman; **~ albañil** master mason

magdalena [mayða'lena] nf fairy cake

magia ['maxja] nf magic; **mágico, a** adj magic(al) ♦ nm/f magician

magisterio [maxis'terjo] nm (enseñanza) teaching; (profesión) teaching profession; (maestros) teachers pl

magistrado [maxis'traðo] nm magistrate

magistral [maxis'tral] adj magisterial; (fig) masterly

magnánimo, a [may'nanimo, a] adj magnanimous

magnate [may'nate] nm magnate, tycoon

magnético, a [may'netiko, a] adj magnetic; **magnetizar** vt to magnetize

magnetofón [mayneto'fon] nm tape recorder; **magnetofónico, a** adj: **cinta magnetofónica** recording tape

magnetófono [mayne'tofono] nm = **magnetofón**

magnífico, a [may'nifiko, a] adj splendid, magnificent

magnitud [mayni'tuð] nf magnitude

mago, a ['mayo, a] nm/f magician; **los Reyes M~s** the Magi, the Three Wise Men

magro, a ['mayro, a] adj (carne) lean

maguey [ma'vei] nm agave

magullar [mayu'ʎar] vt (amoratar) to bruise; (dañar) to damage

mahometano, a [maome'tano, a] adj Mohammedan

mahonesa [mayu'nesa] nf mayonnaise

maíz [ma'iθ] nm maize (BRIT), corn (US); sweet corn

majadero, a [maxa'ðero, a] adj silly, stupid

majestad [maxes'taθ] nf majesty;

majestuoso, a adj majestic

majo, a ['maxo, a] adj nice; (guapo) attractive, good-looking; (elegante) smar

mal [mal] adv badly; (equivocadamente) wrongly ♦ adj = **malo** ♦ nm evil; (desgracia) misfortune; (daño) harm, damage; (MED) illness; **~ que bien** rightl or wrongly; **ir de ~ en peor** to get wors and worse

malabarismo [malaβa'rismo] nm juggling; **malabarista** nm/f juggler

malaria [ma'larja] nf malaria

malcriado, a [mal'krjaðo, a] adj spoiled

maldad [mal'daθ] nf evil, wickedness

maldecir [malde'θir] vt to curse ♦ vi: **~ d** to speak ill of

maldición [maldi'θjon] nf curse

maldito, a [mal'dito, a] adj (condenado) damned; (perverso) wicked; **¡~ sea!** damn it!

maleante [male'ante] nm/f criminal, croc

maledicencia [maleði'θenθja] nf slander scandal

maleducado, a [maleðu'kaðo, a] adj bad-mannered, rude

malentendido [malenten'diðo] nm misunderstanding

malestar [males'tar] nm (gen) discomfort (fig: inquietud) uneasiness; (POL) unrest

maleta [ma'leta] nf case, suitcase; (AUTO) boot (BRIT), trunk (US); **hacer las ~s** to pack; **maletera** (AM) nf, **maletero** nm (AUTO) boot (BRIT), trunk (US); **maletín** nm small case, bag

malévolo, a [ma'leβolo, a] adj malicious, spiteful

maleza [ma'leθa] nf (hierbas malas) weed pl; (arbustos) thicket

malgastar [malvas'tar] vt (tiempo, dinero) to waste; (salud) to ruin

malhechor, a [male'tʃor, a] nm/f delinquent

malhumorado, a [malumo'raðo, a] adj bad-tempered

malicia [ma'liθja] nf (maldad) wickedness; (astucia) slyness, guile; (mala intención) malice, spite; (carácter travieso) mischievousness; **malicioso, a** *adj* wicked, evil; sly, crafty; malicious, spiteful; mischievous

maligno, a [ma'liɣno, a] *adj* evil; (*malévolo*) malicious; (*MED*) malignant

malla ['maʎa] *nf* mesh; (*de baño*) swimsuit; (*de ballet, gimnasia*) leotard; **~s** *nfpl* tights; **~ de alambre** wire mesh

Mallorca [ma'ʎorka] *nf* Majorca

malo, a ['malo, a] *adj* bad; (*falso*) false ♦ *nm/f* villain; **estar ~** to be ill

malograr [malo'ɣrar] *vt* to spoil; (*plan*) to upset; (*ocasión*) to waste; **~se** *vr* (*plan etc*) to fail, come to grief; (*persona*) to die before one's time

malparado, a [malpa'raðo, a] *adj*: **salir ~** to come off badly

malpensado, a [malpen'saðo, a] *adj* nasty

malsano, a [mal'sano, a] *adj* unhealthy

malteada [malte'aða] (*AM*) *nf* milk shake

maltratar [maltra'tar] *vt* to ill-treat, mistreat

maltrecho, a [mal'tretʃo, a] *adj* battered, damaged

malvado, a [mal'ßaðo, a] *adj* evil, villainous

malversar [malßer'sar] *vt* to embezzle, misappropriate

Malvinas [mal'ßinas]: **Islas ~** *nfpl* Falkland Islands

malvivir [malßi'ßir] *vi* to live poorly

mama ['mama] *nf* (*de animal*) teat; (*de mujer*) breast

mamá [ma'ma] (*pl* **~s**) (*fam*) *nf* mum, mummy

mamar [ma'mar] *vt, vi* to suck

mamarracho [mama'rratʃo] *nm* sight, mess

mamífero [ma'mifero] *nm* mammal

mampara [mam'para] *nf* (*entre habitaciones*) partition; (*biombo*) screen

mampostería [mamposte'ria] *nf* masonry

manada [ma'naða] *nf* (*ZOOL*) herd; (: *de leones*) pride; (: *de lobos*) pack

manantial [manan'tjal] *nm* spring

manar [ma'nar] *vi* to run, flow

mancha ['mantʃa] *nf* stain, mark; (*ZOOL*) patch; **manchar** *vt* (*gen*) to stain, mark; (*ensuciar*) to soil, dirty

manchego, a [man'tʃeɣo, a] *adj* of *o* from La Mancha

manco, a ['manko, a] *adj* (*de un brazo*) one-armed; (*de una mano*) one-handed; (*fig*) defective, faulty

mancomunar [mankomu'nar] *vt* to unite, bring together; (*recursos*) to pool; (*JUR*) to make jointly responsible; **mancomunidad** *nf* union, association; (*comunidad*) community; (*JUR*) joint responsibility

mandamiento [manda'mjento] *nm* (*orden*) order, command; (*REL*) commandment; **~ judicial** warrant

mandar [man'dar] *vt* (*ordenar*) to order; (*dirigir*) to lead, command; (*enviar*) to send; (*pedir*) to order, ask for ♦ *vi* to be in charge; (*pey*) to be bossy; **¿mande?** pardon?, excuse me?; **~ hacer un traje** to have a suit made

mandarina [manda'rina] *nf* tangerine, mandarin (orange)

mandato [man'dato] *nm* (*orden*) order; (*POL: período*) term of office; (: *territorio*) mandate; **~ judicial** (*search*) warrant

mandíbula [man'dißula] *nf* jaw

mandil [man'dil] *nm* apron

mando ['mando] *nm* (*MIL*) command; (*de país*) rule; (*el primer lugar*) lead; (*POL*) term of office; (*TEC*) control; **~ a la izquierda** left-hand drive

mandón, ona [man'don, ona] *adj* bossy, domineering

manejable [mane'xaßle] *adj* manageable

manejar [mane'xar] *vt* to manage; (*máquina*) to work, operate; (*caballo etc*) to handle; (*casa*) to run, manage; (*AM: AUTO*) to drive; **~se** *vr* (*comportarse*) to act, behave; (*arreglárselas*) to manage; **manejo** *nm* management; handling; running; driving; (*facilidad de trato*) ease, confidence; **manejos** *nmpl* (*intrigas*) intrigues

manera [ma'nera] *nf* way, manner,

fashion; **~s** *nfpl* (*modales*) manners; **su ~ de ser** the way he is; (*aire*) his manner; **de ninguna ~** no way, by no means; **de otra ~** otherwise; **de todas ~s** at any rate; **no hay ~ de persuadirle** there's no way of convincing him

manga ['manga] *nf* (*de camisa*) sleeve; (*de riego*) hose

mangar [man'gar] (*fam*) *vt* to pinch, nick

mango ['mango] *nm* handle; (*BOT*) mango

mangonear [mangone'ar] *vi* (*meterse*) to meddle, interfere; (*ser mandón*) to boss people about

manguera [man'gera] *nf* hose

manía [ma'nia] *nf* (*MED*) mania; (*fig: moda*) rage, craze; (*disgusto*) dislike; (*malicia*) spite; **maníaco, a** *adj* maniac(al) ♦ *nm/f* maniac

maniatar [manja'tar] *vt* to tie the hands of

maniático, a [ma'njatiko, a] *adj* maniac(al) ♦ *nm/f* maniac

manicomio [mani'komjo] *nm* mental hospital (*BRIT*), insane asylum (*US*)

manifestación [manifesta'θjon] *nf* (*declaración*) statement, declaration; (*de emoción*) show, display; (*POL: desfile*) demonstration; (*: concentración*) mass meeting

manifestar [manifes'tar] *vt* to show, manifest; (*declarar*) to state, declare; **manifiesto, a** *adj* clear, manifest ♦ *nm* manifesto

manillar [mani'ʎar] *nm* handlebars *pl*

maniobra [ma'njoβra] *nf* manœuvre; **~s** *nfpl* (*MIL*) manœuvres; **maniobrar** *vt* to manœuvre

manipulación [manipula'θjon] *nf* manipulation

manipular [manipu'lar] *vt* to manipulate; (*manejar*) to handle

maniquí [mani'ki] *nm* dummy ♦ *nm/f* model

manirroto, a [mani'rroto, a] *adj* lavish, extravagant ♦ *nm/f* spendthrift

manivela [mani'βela] *nf* crank

manjar [man'xar] *nm* (tasty) dish

mano ['mano] *nf* hand; (*ZOOL*) foot, paw;

(*de pintura*) coat; (*serie*) lot, series; **a ~** by hand; **a ~ derecha/izquierda** on the right(-hand side)/left(-hand side); **de primera ~** (at) first hand; **de segunda ~** (at) second hand; **robo a ~ armada** armed robbery; **~ de obra** labour, manpower; **estrechar la ~ a uno** to shake sb's hand

manojo [ma'noxo] *nm* handful, bunch; **~ de llaves** bunch of keys

manopla [ma'nopla] *nf* mitten

manoseado, a [manose'aðo, a] *adj* well-worn

manosear [manose'ar] *vt* (*tocar*) to handle, touch; (*desordenar*) to mess up, rumple; (*insistir en*) to overwork; (*AM*) to caress, fondle

manotazo [mano'taθo] *nm* slap, smack

mansalva [man'salβa]: **a ~** *adv* indiscriminately

mansedumbre [manse'ðumbre] *nf* gentleness, meekness

mansión [man'sjon] *nf* mansion

manso, a ['manso, a] *adj* gentle, mild; (*animal*) tame

manta ['manta] *nf* blanket; (*AM: poncho*) poncho

manteca [man'teka] *nf* fat; (*AM*) butter; **~ de cacahuete/cacao** peanut/cocoa butter; **~ de cerdo** lard

mantecado [mante'kaðo] (*AM*) *nm* ice cream

mantel [man'tel] *nm* tablecloth

mantendré *etc vb ver* **mantener**

mantener [mante'ner] *vt* to support, maintain; (*alimentar*) to sustain; (*conservar*) to keep; (*TEC*) to maintain, service; **~se** *vr* (*seguir de pie*) to be still standing; (*no ceder*) to hold one's ground; (*subsistir*) to sustain o.s., keep going; **mantenimiento** *nm* maintenance; sustenance; (*sustento*) support

mantequilla [mante'kiʎa] *nf* butter

mantilla [man'tiʎa] *nf* mantilla; **~s** *nfpl* (*de bebé*) baby clothes

manto ['manto] *nm* (*capa*) cloak; (*de*

ceremonia) robe, gown

mantuve *etc vb ver* **mantener**

manual [ma'nwal] *adj* manual ♦ *nm*
manual, handbook

manufactura [manufak'tura] *nf*
manufacture; *(fábrica)* factory;
manufacturado, a *adj (producto)*
manufactured

manuscrito, a [manus'krito, a] *adj*
handwritten ♦ *nm* manuscript

manutención [manuten'θjon] *nf*
maintenance; *(sustento)* support

manzana [man'θana] *nf* apple; *(ARQ)*
block (of houses)

manzanilla [manθa'niʎa] *nf (planta)*
camomile; *(infusión)* camomile tea

manzano [man'θano] *nm* apple tree

maña ['maɲa] *nf (gen)* skill, dexterity; *(pey)*
guile; *(destreza)* trick, knack

mañana [ma'ɲana] *adv* tomorrow ♦ *nm*
future ♦ *nf* morning; **de** *o* **por la ~** in the
morning; **¡hasta ~!** see you tomorrow!; **~
por la ~** tomorrow morning

mañoso, a [ma'ɲoso, a] *adj (hábil)* skilful;
(astuto) smart, clever

mapa ['mapa] *nm* map

maqueta [ma'keta] *nf (scale)* model

maquillaje [maki'ʎaxe] *nm* make-up;
(acto) making up

maquillar [maki'ʎar] *vt* to make up; **~se**
vr to put on (some) make-up

máquina ['makina] *nf* machine; *(de tren)*
locomotive, engine; *(FOTO)* camera; *(AM:
coche)* car; *(fig)* machinery; **escrito a ~**
typewritten; **~ de escribir** typewriter; **~
de coser/lavar** sewing/washing machine

maquinación [makina'θjon] *nf*
machination, plot

maquinal [maki'nal] *adj (fig)* mechanical,
automatic

maquinaria [maki'narja] *nf (máquinas)*
machinery; *(mecanismo)* mechanism,
works *pl*

maquinilla [maki'niʎa] *nf:* **~ de afeitar**
razor

maquinista [maki'nista] *nm/f (de tren)*
engine driver; *(TEC)* operator; *(NAUT)*
engineer

mar [mar] *nm o f* sea; **~ adentro** *o* **afuera**
out at sea; **en alta ~** on the high seas; **la
~ de** *(fam)* lots of; **el M~ Negro/Báltico**
the Black/Baltic Sea

maraña [ma'raɲa] *nf (maleza)* thicket;
(confusión) tangle

maravilla [mara'βiʎa] *nf* marvel, wonder;
(BOT) marigold; **maravillar** *vt* to
astonish, amaze; **maravillarse** *vr* to be
astonished, be amazed; **maravilloso, a**
adj wonderful, marvellous

marca ['marka] *nf (gen)* mark; *(sello)*
stamp; *(COM)* make, brand; **de ~**
excellent, outstanding; **~ de fábrica**
trademark; **~ registrada** registered
trademark

marcado, a [mar'kaðo, a] *adj* marked,
strong

marcador [marka'ðor] *nm (DEPORTE)*
scoreboard; *(: persona)* scorer

marcapasos [marka'pasos] *nm inv*
pacemaker

marcar [mar'kar] *vt (gen)* to mark;
(número de teléfono) to dial; *(gol)* to
score; *(números)* to record, keep a tally of;
(pelo) to set ♦ *vi (DEPORTE)* to score; *(TEL)*
to dial

marcha ['martʃa] *nf* march; *(TEC)* running,
working; *(AUTO)* gear; *(velocidad)* speed;
(fig) progress; *(dirección)* course; **poner
en ~** to put into gear; *(fig)* to set in
motion, get going; **dar ~ atrás** to
reverse, put into reverse; **estar en ~** to be
under way, be in motion

marchar [mar'tʃar] *vi (ir)* to go; *(funcionar)*
to work, go; **~se** *vr* to go (away), leave

marchitar [martʃi'tar] *vt* to wither, dry up;
~se *vr (BOT)* to wither; *(fig)* to fade away;
marchito, a *adj* withered, faded; *(fig)* in
decline

marcial [mar'θjal] *adj* martial, military

marciano, a [mar'θjano, a] *adj, nm/f*
Martian

marco ['marko] *nm* frame; *(moneda)* mark;
(fig) framework

marea [ma'rea] *nf* tide

marear [mare'ar] *vt* (*fig*) to annoy, upset; (*MED*): ~ **a uno** to make sb feel sick; ~**se** *vr* (*tener náuseas*) to feel sick; (*desvanecerse*) to feel faint; (*aturdirse*) to feel dizzy; (*fam: emborracharse*) to get tipsy

maremoto [mare'moto] *nm* tidal wave

mareo [ma'reo] *nm* (*náusea*) sick feeling; (*en viaje*) travel sickness; (*aturdimiento*) dizziness; (*fam: lata*) nuisance

marfil [mar'fil] *nm* ivory

margarina [marɣa'rina] *nf* margarine

margarita [marɣa'rita] *nf* (*BOT*) daisy; (**rueda**) ~ daisywheel

margen ['marxen] *nm* (*borde*) edge, border; (*fig*) margin, space ♦ *nf* (*de río etc*) bank; **dar ~ para** to give an opportunity for; **mantenerse al ~** to keep out (of things)

marginar [marxi'nar] *vt* (*socialmente*) to marginalize, ostracize

marica [ma'rika] (*fam*) *nm* sissy

maricón [mari'kon] (*fam*) *nm* queer

marido [ma'riðo] *nm* husband

marihuana [mari'wana] *nf* marijuana, cannabis

marina [ma'rina] *nf* navy; ~ **mercante** merchant navy

marinero, a [mari'nero, a] *adj* sea *cpd* ♦ *nm* sailor, seaman

marino, a [ma'rino, a] *adj* sea *cpd*, marine ♦ *nm* sailor

marioneta [marjo'neta] *nf* puppet

mariposa [mari'posa] *nf* butterfly

mariquita [mari'kita] *nf* ladybird (*BRIT*), ladybug (*US*)

mariscos [ma'riskos] *nmpl* shellfish *inv*, seafood(s)

marítimo, a [ma'ritimo, a] *adj* sea *cpd*, maritime

mármol ['marmol] *nm* marble

marqués, esa [mar'kes, esa] *nm/f* marquis/marchioness

marrón [ma'rron] *adj* brown

marroquí [marro'ki] *adj, nm/f* Moroccan ♦ *nm* Morocco (leather)

Marruecos [ma'rrwekos] *nm* Morocco

martes ['martes] *nm inv* Tuesday

Martes y Trece

i According to Spanish superstition Tuesday is an unlucky day, even more so if it falls on the 13th of the month.

martillo [mar'tiʎo] *nm* hammer; ~ **neumático** pneumatic drill (*BRIT*), jackhammer

mártir ['martir] *nm/f* martyr; **martirio** *nm* martyrdom; (*fig*) torture, torment

marxismo [mark'sismo] *nm* Marxism; **marxista** *adj, nm/f* Marxist

marzo ['marθo] *nm* March

PALABRA CLAVE

más [mas] *adj, adv* **1**: ~ (**que/de**) (*compar*) more (than), ...+er (than); ~ **grande/inteligente** bigger/more intelligent; **trabaja ~ (que yo)** he works more (than me); *ver tb* **cada**

2 (*superl*): **el ~** the most, ...+est; **el ~ grande/inteligente (de)** the biggest/most intelligent (in)

3 (*negativo*): **no tengo ~ dinero** I haven't got any more money; **no viene ~ por aquí** he doesn't come round here any more

4 (*adicional*): **no le veo ~ solución que ...** I see no other solution than to ...; **¿quién ~?** anybody else?

5 (*+adj: valor intensivo*): **¡qué perro ~ sucio!** what a filthy dog!; **¡es ~ tonto!** he's so stupid!

6 (*locuciones*): ~ **o menos** more or less; **los ~** most people; **es ~** furthermore; ~ **bien** rather; **¡qué ~ da!** what does it matter!; *ver tb* **no**

7: **por ~**: **por ~ que te esfuerces** no matter how hard you try; **por ~ que quisiera ...** much as I should like to ...

8: **de ~**: **veo que aquí estoy de ~** I can see I'm not needed here; **tenemos uno de ~** we've got one extra

♦ *prep*: **2 ~ 2 son 4** 2 and o plus 2 are 4

♦ *nm inv*: **este trabajo tiene sus ~ y**

sus menos this job's got its good points and its bad points

mas [mas] *conj* but

masa ['masa] *nf (mezcla)* dough; *(volumen)* volume, mass; *(FÍSICA)* mass; **en ~** en masse; **las ~s** *(POL)* the masses

masacre [ma'sakre] *nf* massacre

masaje [ma'saxe] *nm* massage

máscara ['maskara] *nf* mask; **mascarilla** *nf (de belleza, MED)* mask

masculino, a [masku'lino, a] *adj* masculine; *(BIO)* male

masía [ma'sia] *nf* farmhouse

masificación [masifika'θjon] *nf* overcrowding

masivo, a [ma'sißo, a] *adj* mass *cpd*

masón [ma'son] *nm* (free)mason

masoquista [maso'kista] *nm/f* masochist

masticar [masti'kar] *vt* to chew

mástil ['mastil] *nm (de navío)* mast; *(de guitarra)* neck

mastín [mas'tin] *nm* mastiff

masturbación [masturßa'θjon] *nf* masturbation

masturbarse [mastur'ßarse] *vr* to masturbate

mata ['mata] *nf (arbusto)* bush, shrub; *(de hierba)* tuft

matadero [mata'ðero] *nm* slaughterhouse, abattoir

matador, a [mata'ðor, a] *adj* killing ♦ *nm/f* killer ♦ *nm (TAUR)* matador, bullfighter

matamoscas [mata'moskas] *nm inv (palo)* fly swat

matanza [ma'tanθa] *nf* slaughter

matar [ma'tar] *vt, vi* to kill; **~se** *vr (suicidarse)* to kill o.s., commit suicide; *(morir)* to be *o* get killed; **~ el hambre** to stave off hunger

matasellos [mata'seʎos] *nm inv* postmark

mate ['mate] *adj* matt ♦ *nm (en ajedrez)* (check)mate; *(AM: hierba)* maté; *(: vasija)* gourd

matemáticas [mate'matikas] *nfpl* mathematics; **matemático, a** *adj*

mathematical ♦ *nm/f* mathematician

materia [ma'terja] *nf (gen)* matter; *(TEC)* material; *(ESCOL)* subject; **en ~ de** on the subject of; **~ prima** raw material; **material** *adj* material ♦ *nm* material; *(TEC)* equipment; **materialismo** *nm* materialism; **materialista** *adj* materialist(ic); **materialmente** *adv* materially; *(fig)* absolutely

maternal [mater'nal] *adj* motherly, maternal

maternidad [materni'ðað] *nf* motherhood, maternity; **materno, a** *adj* maternal; *(lengua)* mother *cpd*

matinal [mati'nal] *adj* morning *cpd*

matiz [ma'tiθ] *nm* shade; **~ar** *vt (variar)* to vary; *(ARTE)* to blend; **~ar de** to tinge with

matón [ma'ton] *nm* bully

matorral [mato'rral] *nm* thicket

matraca [ma'traka] *nf* rattle

matrícula [ma'trikula] *nf (registro)* register; *(AUTO)* registration number; *(: placa)* number plate; **matricular** *vt* to register, enrol

matrimonial [matrimo'njal] *adj* matrimonial

matrimonio [matri'monjo] *nm (pareja)* (married) couple; *(unión)* marriage

matriz [ma'triθ] *nf (ANAT)* womb; *(TEC)* mould; **casa ~** *(COM)* head office

matrona [ma'trona] *nf (persona de edad)* matron; *(comadrona)* midwife

maullar [mau'ʎar] *vi* to mew, miaow

maxilar [maksi'lar] *nm* jaw(bone)

máxima ['maksima] *nf* maxim

máxime ['maksime] *adv* especially

máximo, a ['maksimo, a] *adj* maximum; *(más alto)* highest; *(más grande)* greatest ♦ *nm* maximum

mayo ['majo] *nm* May

mayonesa [majo'nesa] *nf* mayonnaise

mayor [ma'jor] *adj* main, chief; *(adulto)* adult; *(de edad avanzada)* elderly; *(MUS)* major; *(compar: de tamaño)* bigger; *(: de edad)* older; *(superl: de tamaño)* biggest; *(: de edad)* oldest ♦ *nm (adulto)* adult; **al**

por ~ wholesale; **~ de edad** adult; **~es** *nmpl* (*antepasados*) ancestors

mayoral [majo'ral] *nm* foreman

mayordomo [major'ðomo] *nm* butler

mayoría [majo'ria] *nf* majority, greater part

mayorista [majo'rista] *nm/f* wholesaler

mayoritario, a [majori'tarjo, a] *adj* majority *cpd*

mayúscula [ma'juskula] *nf* capital letter

mayúsculo, a [ma'juskulo, a] *adj* (*fig*) big, tremendous

mazapán [maθa'pan] *nm* marzipan

mazo ['maθo] *nm* (*martillo*) mallet; (*de flores*) bunch; (*DEPORTE*) bat

me [me] *pron* (*directo*) me; (*indirecto*) (to) me; (*reflexivo*) (to) myself; **¡dámelo!** give it to me!

mear [me'ar] (*fam*) *vi* to pee, piss (!)

mecánica [me'kanika] *nf* (*ESCOL*) mechanics *sg*; (*mecanismo*) mechanism; *ver tb* **mecánico**

mecánico, a [me'kaniko, a] *adj* mechanical ♦ *nm/f* mechanic

mecanismo [meka'nismo] *nm* mechanism; (*marcha*) gear

mecanografía [mekanoɤra'fia] *nf* typewriting; **mecanógrafo, a** *nm/f* typist

mecate [me'kate] (*AM*) *nm* rope

mecedora [meθe'ðora] *nf* rocking chair

mecer [me'θer] *vt* (*cuna*) to rock; **~se** *vr* to rock; (*ramo*) to sway

mecha ['metʃa] *nf* (*de vela*) wick; (*de bomba*) fuse

mechero [me'tʃero] *nm* (cigarette) lighter

mechón [me'tʃon] *nm* (*gen*) tuft; (*de pelo*) lock

medalla [me'ðaʎa] *nf* medal

media ['meðja] *nf* (*ESP*) stocking; (*AM*) sock; (*promedio*) average

mediado, a [me'ðjaðo, a] *adj* half-full; (*trabajo*) half-completed; **a ~s de** in the middle of, halfway through

mediano, a [me'ðjano, a] *adj* (*regular*) medium, average; (*mediocre*) mediocre

medianoche [meðja'notʃe] *nf* midnight

mediante [me'ðjante] *adv* by (means of), through

mediar [me'ðjar] *vi* (*interceder*) to mediate, intervene

medicación [meðika'θjon] *nf* medication, treatment

medicamento [meðika'mento] *nm* medicine, drug

medicina [meði'θina] *nf* medicine

medición [meði'θjon] *nf* measurement

médico, a ['meðiko, a] *adj* medical ♦ *nm/f* doctor

medida [me'ðiða] *nf* measure; (*medición*) measurement; (*prudencia*) moderation, prudence; **en cierta/gran ~** up to a point/to a great extent; **un traje a la ~** made-to-measure suit; **~ de cuello** collar size; **a ~ de** in proportion to; (*de acuerdo con*) in keeping with; **a ~ que** (*conforme*) as

medio, a ['meðjo, a] *adj* half (a); (*punto*) mid, middle; (*promedio*) average ♦ *adv* half ♦ *nm* (*centro*) middle, centre; (*promedio*) average; (*método*) means, way; (*ambiente*) environment; **~s** *nmpl* means, resources; **~ litro** half a litre; **las tres y media** half past three; **medio ambiente** environment; **M~ Oriente** Middle East; **~ terminar** half finished; **pagar a medias** to share the cost; **~ambiental** *adj* (*política, efectos*) environmental

mediocre [me'ðjokre] *adj* mediocre

mediodía [meðjo'ðia] *nm* midday, noon

medir [me'ðir] *vt, vi* (*gen*) to measure

meditar [meði'tar] *vt* to ponder, think over, meditate on; (*planear*) to think out

mediterráneo, a [meðite'rraneo, a] *adj* Mediterranean ♦ *nm*: **el M~** the Mediterranean (Sea)

médula ['meðula] *nf* (*ANAT*) marrow; **~ espinal** spinal cord

medusa [me'ðusa] (*ESP*) *nf* jellyfish

megafonía [meɣafo'nia] *nf* public address system, PA system; **megáfono** *nm* megaphone

megalómano, a [meɣa'lomano, a] *nm/f* megalomaniac

mejicano, a [mexiˈkano, a] *adj, nm/f*
Mexican
Méjico [ˈmexiko] *nm* Mexico
mejilla [meˈxiʎa] *nf* cheek
mejillón [mexiˈʎon] *nm* mussel
mejor [meˈxor] *adj, adv* (*compar*) better;
(*superl*) best; **a lo ~** probably; (*quizá*)
maybe; ◆ **dicho** rather; **tanto ~** so much
the better
mejora [meˈxora] *nf* improvement;
mejorar *vt* to improve, make better ◆ *vi*
to improve, get better; **mejorarse** *vr* to
improve, get better
melancólico, a [melanˈkoliko, a] *adj*
(*triste*) sad, melancholy; (*soñador*) dreamy
melena [meˈlena] *nf* (*de persona*) long
hair; (*ZOOL*) mane
mellizo, a [meˈʎiθo, a] *adj, nm/f* twin; **~s**
nmpl (*AM*) cufflinks
melocotón [melokoˈton] (*ESP*) *nm* peach
melodía [meloˈðia] *nf* melody, tune
melodrama [meloˈðrama] *nm* melodrama;
melodramático, a *adj* melodramatic
melón [meˈlon] *nm* melon
membrete [memˈbrete] *nm* letterhead
membrillo [memˈbriʎo] *nm* quince; **carne**
de ~ quince jelly
memorable [memoˈraβle] *adj* memorable
memoria [meˈmorja] *nf* (*gen*) memory; **~s**
nfpl (*de autor*) memoirs; **memorizar** *vt*
to memorize
menaje [meˈnaxe] *nm*: **~ de cocina**
kitchenware
mencionar [menθjoˈnar] *vt* to mention
mendigar [mendiˈɣar] *vt* to beg (for)
mendigo, a [menˈdiɣo, a] *nm/f* beggar
mendrugo [menˈdruɣo] *nm* crust
menear [meneˈar] *vt* to move; **~se** *vr* to
shake; (*balancearse*) to sway; (*moverse*) to
move; (*fig*) to get a move on
menestra [meˈnestra] *nf*: **~ de verduras**
vegetable stew
menguante [menˈɣwante] *adj* decreasing,
diminishing
menguar [menˈɣwar] *vt* to lessen,
diminish ◆ *vi* to diminish, decrease
menopausia [menoˈpausja] *nf*

menopause
menor [meˈnor] *adj* (*más pequeño:*
compar) smaller; (: *superl*) smallest; (*más*
joven: compar) younger; (: *superl*)
youngest; (*MUS*) minor ◆ *nm/f* (*joven*)
young person, juvenile; **no tengo la ~**
idea I haven't the faintest idea; **al por ~**
retail; **~ de edad** person under age
Menorca [meˈnorka] *nf* Minorca

PALABRA CLAVE

---

menos [menos] *adj* 1: **~ (que/de)**
(*compar: cantidad*) less (than); (: *número*)
fewer (than); **con ~ entusiasmo** with less
enthusiasm; **~ gente** fewer people; *ver tb*
cada

2 (*superl*): **es el que ~ culpa tiene** he is
the least to blame

◆ *adv* 1 (*compar*): **~ (que, de)** less (than);
me gusta ~ que el otro I like it less than
the other one

2 (*superl*): **es el ~ listo (de su clase)** he's
the least bright in his class; **de todas**
ellas es la que ~ me agrada out of all of
them she's the one I like least; **(por) lo ~**
at the (very) least

3 (*locuciones*): **no quiero verle y ~**
visitarle I don't want to see him let alone
visit him; **tenemos 7 de ~** we're seven
short

◆ *prep* except; (*cifras*) minus; **todos ~ él**
everyone except (for) him; **5 ~ 2** 5 minus
2

◆ *conj*: **a ~ que: a ~ que venga mañana**
unless he comes tomorrow

---

menospreciar [menospreˈθjar] *vt* to
underrate, undervalue; (*despreciar*) to
scorn, despise
mensaje [menˈsaxe] *nm* message; **~ro, a**
nm/f messenger
menstruación [menstruaˈθjon] *nf*
menstruation
menstruar [mensˈtrwar] *vi* to menstruate
mensual [menˈswal] *adj* monthly; **1000**
ptas ~es 1000 ptas a month; **~idad** *nf*
(*salario*) monthly salary; (*COM*) monthly

payment, monthly instalment

menta ['menta] *nf* mint

mental [men'tal] *adj* mental; ~**idad** *nf* mentality; ~**izar** *vt* (*sensibilizar*) to make aware; (*convencer*) to convince; (*padres*) to prepare (mentally); ~**izarse** *vr* (*concienciarse*) to become aware; ~**izarse (de)** to get used to the idea (of); ~**izarse de que ...** (*convencerse*) to get it into one's head that ...

mentar [men'tar] *vt* to mention, name

mente ['mente] *nf* mind

mentir [men'tir] *vi* to lie

mentira [men'tira] *nf* (*una ~*) lie; (*acto*) lying; (*invención*) fiction; **parece ~ que ...** it seems incredible that ..., I can't believe that ...

mentiroso, a [menti'roso, a] *adj* lying ♦ *nm/f* liar

menú [me'nu] (*pl* ~**s**) *nm* menu; (*AM*) set meal; ~ **del día** set menu

menudo, a [me'nuðo, a] *adj* (*pequeño*) small, tiny; (*sin importancia*) petty, insignificant; **¡~ negocio!** (*fam*) some deal!; **a ~** often, frequently

meñique [me'ɲike] *nm* little finger

meollo [me'oʎo] *nm* (*fig*) core

mercado [mer'kaðo] *nm* market

mercancía [merkan'θia] *nf* commodity; ~**s** *nfpl* goods, merchandise *sg*

mercantil [merkan'til] *adj* mercantile, commercial

mercenario, a [merθe'narjo, a] *adj*, *nm* mercenary

mercería [merθe'ria] *nf* haberdashery (*BRIT*), notions (*US*); (*tienda*) haberdasher's (*BRIT*), notions store (*US*); (*AM*) drapery

mercurio [mer'kurjo] *nm* mercury

merecer [mere'θer] *vt* to deserve, merit ♦ *vi* to be deserving, be worthy; **merece la pena** it's worthwhile; **merecido, a** *adj* (well) deserved; **llevar su merecido** to get one's deserts

merendar [meren'dar] *vt* to have for tea ♦ *vi* to have tea; (*en el campo*) to have a picnic; **merendero** *nm* open-air cafe

merengue [me'renge] *nm* meringue

meridiano [meri'ðjano] *nm* (*GEO*) meridian

merienda [me'rjenda] *nf* (light) tea, afternoon snack; (*de campo*) picnic

mérito ['merito] *nm* merit; (*valor*) worth, value

merluza [mer'luθa] *nf* hake

merma ['merma] *nf* decrease; (*pérdida*) wastage; **mermar** *vt* to reduce, lessen ♦ *vi* to decrease, dwindle

mermelada [merme'laða] *nf* jam

mero, a ['mero, a] *adj* mere; (*AM: fam*) very

merodear [meroðe'ar] *vi*: ~ **por** to prowl about

mes [mes] *nm* month

mesa ['mesa] *nf* table; (*de trabajo*) desk; (*GEO*) plateau; ~ **directiva** board; ~ **redonda** (*reunión*) round table; **poner/ quitar la ~** to lay/clear the table; **mesero, a** *nm/f* (*AM*) waiter/waitress

meseta [me'seta] *nf* (*GEO*) meseta, tableland

mesilla [me'siʎa] *nf*: ~ **(de noche)** bedside table

mesón [me'son] *nm* inn

mestizo, a [mes'tiθo, a] *adj* half-caste, of mixed race ♦ *nm/f* half-caste

mesura [me'sura] *nf* moderation, restraint

meta ['meta] *nf* goal; (*de carrera*) finish

metabolismo [metaßo'lismo] *nm* metabolism

metáfora [me'tafora] *nf* metaphor

metal [me'tal] *nm* (*materia*) metal; (*MUS*) brass; **metálico, a** *adj* metallic; (*de metal*) metal ♦ *nm* (*dinero contante*) cash

metalurgia [meta'lurxja] *nf* metallurgy

meteoro [mete'oro] *nm* meteor; ~**logía** *nf* meteorology

meter [me'ter] *vt* (*colocar*) to put, place; (*introducir*) to put in, insert; (*involucrar*) to involve; (*causar*) to make, cause; ~**se** *vr*: ~**se en** to go into, enter; (*fig*) to interfere in, meddle in; ~**se a** to start; ~**se a escritor** to become a writer; ~**se con uno** to provoke sb, pick a quarrel with sb

meticuloso, a [metiku'loso, a] *adj*

meticulous, thorough

metódico, a [me'toðiko, a] *adj* methodical

método ['metoðo] *nm* method

metralleta [metra'ʎeta] *nf* sub-machine-gun

métrico, a ['metriko, a] *adj* metric

metro ['metro] *nm* metre; (*tren*) underground (*BRIT*), subway (*US*)

México ['mexiko] *nm* Mexico; **Ciudad de ~** Mexico City

mezcla ['meθkla] *nf* mixture; **mezclar** *vt* to mix (up); **mezclarse** *vr* to mix, mingle; **mezclarse en** to get mixed up in, get involved in

mezquino, a [meθ'kino, a] *adj* mean

mezquita [meθ'kita] *nf* mosque

mg. *abr* (= *miligramo*) mg

mi [mi] *adj* my ♦ *nm* (*MUS*) E

mí [mi] *pron* me; myself

mía ['mia] *pron ver* **mío**

miaja ['mjaxa] *nf* crumb

michelín [mitʃe'lin] (*fam*) *nm* (*de grasa*) spare tyre

micro ['mikro] (*AM*) *nm* minibus

microbio [mi'kroβjo] *nm* microbe

micrófono [mi'krofono] *nm* microphone

microondas [mikro'ondas] *nm inv* (*tb*: **horno ~**) microwave (oven)

microscopio [mikro'skopjo] *nm* microscope

miedo ['mjeðo] *nm* fear; (*nerviosismo*) apprehension, nervousness; **tener ~** to be afraid; **de ~** wonderful, marvellous; **hace un frío de ~** (*fam*) it's terribly cold; **~so, a** *adj* fearful, timid

miel [mjel] *nf* honey

miembro ['mjembro] *nm* limb; (*socio*) member; **~ viril** penis

mientras ['mjentras] *conj* while; (*duración*) as long as ♦ *adv* meanwhile; **~ tanto** meanwhile; **~ más tiene, más quiere** the more he has, the more he wants

miércoles ['mjerkoles] *nm inv* Wednesday

mierda ['mjerða] (*fam!*) *nf* shit (!)

miga ['miɣa] *nf* crumb; (*fig*: *meollo*) essence; **hacer buenas ~s** (*fam*) to get

on well

migración [miɣra'θjon] *nf* migration

mil [mil] *num* thousand; **dos ~ libras** two thousand pounds

milagro [mi'laɣro] *nm* miracle; **~so, a** *adj* miraculous

milésima [mi'lesima] *nf* (*de segundo*) thousandth

mili ['mili] (*fam*) *nf*: **hacer la ~** to do one's military service

milicia [mi'liθja] *nf* militia; (*servicio militar*) military service

milímetro [mi'limetro] *nm* millimetre

militante [mili'tante] *adj* militant

militar [mili'tar] *adj* military ♦ *nm/f* soldier ♦ *vi* (*MIL*) to serve; (*en un partido*) to be a member

milla ['miʎa] *nf* mile

millar [mi'ʎar] *nm* thousand

millón [mi'ʎon] *num* million; **millonario, a** *nm/f* millionaire

mimar [mi'mar] *vt* to spoil, pamper

mimbre ['mimbre] *nm* wicker

mímica ['mimika] *nf* (*para comunicarse*) sign language; (*imitación*) mimicry

mimo ['mimo] *nm* (*caricia*) caress; (*de niño*) spoiling; (*TEATRO*) mime; (: *actor*) mime artist

mina ['mina] *nf* mine; **minar** *vt* to mine; (*fig*) to undermine

mineral [mine'ral] *adj* mineral ♦ *nm* (*GEO*) mineral; (*mena*) ore

minero, a [mi'nero, a] *adj* mining *cpd* ♦ *nm/f* miner

miniatura [minja'tura] *adj inv, nf* miniature

minifalda [mini'falda] *nf* miniskirt

mínimo, a ['minimo, a] *adj, nm* minimum

minino, a [mi'nino, a] (*fam*) *nm/f* puss, pussy

ministerio [minis'terjo] *nm* Ministry; **M~ de Hacienda/de Asuntos Exteriores** Treasury (*BRIT*), Treasury Department (*US*)/Foreign Office (*BRIT*), State Department (*US*)

ministro, a [mi'nistro, a] *nm/f* minister

minoría [mino'ria] *nf* minority

minucioso, a [minu'θjoso, a] *adj*
thorough, meticulous; (*prolijo*) very
detailed

minúscula [mi'nuskula] *nf* small letter

minúsculo, a [mi'nuskulo, a] *adj* tiny,
minute

minusválido, a [minus'βaliðo, a] *adj*
(physically) handicapped ♦ *nm/f*
(physically) handicapped person

minuta [mi'nuta] *nf* (*de comida*) menu

minutero [minu'tero] *nm* minute hand

minuto [mi'nuto] *nm* minute

mío, a ['mio, a] *pron*: **el ~/la mía** mine;
un amigo ~ a friend of mine; **lo ~** what is
mine

miope [mi'ope] *adj* short-sighted

mira ['mira] *nf* (*de arma*) sight(s) (*pl*); (*fig*)
aim, intention

mirada [mi'raða] *nf* look, glance;
(*expresión*) look, expression; **clavar la ~
en** to stare at; **echar una ~ a** to glance
at

mirado, a [mi'raðo, a] *adj* (*sensato*)
sensible; (*considerado*) considerate; **bien/
mal ~** well/not well thought of; **bien ~** all
things considered

mirador [mira'ðor] *nm* viewpoint, vantage
point

mirar [mi'rar] *vt* to look at; (*observar*) to
watch; (*considerar*) to consider, think
over; (*vigilar, cuidar*) to watch, look after
♦ *vi* to look; (*ARQ*) to face; **~se** *vr* (*dos
personas*) to look at each other; **~ bien/
mal** to think highly of/have a poor
opinion of; **~se al espejo** to look at o.s.
in the mirror

mirilla [mi'riʎa] *nf* spyhole, peephole

mirlo ['mirlo] *nm* blackbird

misa ['misa] *nf* mass

miserable [mise'raβle] *adj* (*avaro*) mean,
stingy; (*nimio*) miserable, paltry; (*lugar*)
squalid; (*fam*) vile, despicable ♦ *nm/f*
(*malvado*) rogue

miseria [mi'serja] *nf* (*pobreza*) poverty;
(*tacañería*) meanness, stinginess;
(*condiciones*) squalor; **una ~** a pittance

misericordia [miseri'korðja] *nf*

(*compasión*) compassion, pity; (*piedad*)
mercy

misil [mi'sil] *nm* missile

misión [mi'sjon] *nf* mission; **misionero,
a** *nm/f* missionary

mismo, a ['mismo, a] *adj* (*semejante*)
same; (*después de pron*) -self; (*para
enfásis*) very ♦ *adv*: **aquí/hoy ~** right
here/this very day; **ahora ~** right now
♦ *conj*: **lo ~ que** just like, just as; **el ~
traje** the same suit; **en ese ~ momento**
at that very moment; **vino el ~ Ministro**
the minister himself came; **yo ~ lo vi** I
saw it myself; **lo ~** the same (thing); **da
lo ~** it's all the same; **quedamos en las
mismas** we're no further forward; **por lo
~** for the same reason

misterio [mis'terjo] *nm* mystery; **~so, a**
adj mysterious

mitad [mi'tað] *nf* (*medio*) half; (*centro*)
middle; **a ~ de precio** (at) half-price; **en
o a ~ del camino** halfway along the road;
cortar por la ~ to cut through the
middle

mitigar [miti'var] *vt* to mitigate; (*dolor*) to
ease; (*sed*) to quench

mitin ['mitin] (*pl* **mítines**) *nm* meeting

mito ['mito] *nm* myth

mixto, a ['miksto, a] *adj* mixed

ml. *abr* (= *mililitro*) ml

mm. *abr* (= *milímetro*) mm

mobiliario [moβi'ljarjo] *nm* furniture

mochila [mo'tʃila] *nf* rucksack (*BRIT*),
back-pack

moción [mo'θjon] *nf* motion

moco ['moko] *nm* mucus; **~s** *nmpl* (*fam*)
snot; **limpiarse los ~s de la nariz** (*fam*)
to wipe one's nose

moda ['moða] *nf* fashion; (*estilo*) style; **a la
o de ~** in fashion, fashionable; **pasado de
~** out of fashion

modales [mo'ðales] *nmpl* manners

modalidad [moðali'ðað] *nf* kind, variety

modelar [moðe'lar] *vt* to model

modelo [mo'ðelo] *adj inv, nm/f* model

módem [mo'ðem] *nm* (*INFORM*) modem

moderado, a [moðe'raðo, a] *adj*

moderate

moderar [moðe'rar] vt to moderate;
(violencia) to restrain, control; (velocidad)
to reduce; **~se** vr to restrain o.s., control
o.s.

modernizar [moðerni'θar] vt to
modernize

moderno, a [mo'ðerno, a] adj modern;
(actual) present-day

modestia [mo'ðestja] nf modesty;
modesto, a adj modest

módico, a ['moðiko, a] adj moderate,
reasonable

modificar [moðifi'kar] vt to modify

modisto, a [mo'ðisto, a] nm/f (diseñador)
couturier, designer; (que confecciona)
dressmaker

modo ['moðo] nm way, manner; (MUS)
mode; **~s** nmpl manners; **de ningún ~** in
no way; **de todos ~s** at any rate; **~ de
empleo** directions pl (for use)

modorra [mo'ðorra] nf drowsiness

mofa ['mofa] nf: **hacer ~ de** to mock;
mofarse vr: **mofarse de** to mock, scoff
at

mogollón [moɣo'ʎon] (fam) adv a hell of
a lot

moho ['moo] nm mould, mildew; (en
metal) rust; **~so, a** adj mouldy; rusty

mojar [mo'xar] vt to wet; (humedecer) to
damp(en), moisten; (calar) to soak; **~se**
vr to get wet

mojón [mo'xon] nm boundary stone

molde ['molde] nm mould; (COSTURA)
pattern; (fig) model; **~ado** nm soft perm;
~ar vt to mould

mole ['mole] nf mass, bulk; (edificio) pile

moler [mo'ler] vt to grind, crush

molestar [moles'tar] vt to bother;
(fastidiar) to annoy; (incomodar) to
inconvenience, put out ♦ vi to be a
nuisance; **~se** vr to bother; (incomodarse)
to go to trouble; (ofenderse) to take
offence; **¿(no) te molesta si ...?** do you
mind if ...?

molestia [mo'lestja] nf bother, trouble;
(incomodidad) inconvenience; (MED)

discomfort; **es una ~** it's a nuisance;
molesto, a adj (que fastidia) annoying;
(incómodo) inconvenient; (inquieto)
uncomfortable, ill at ease; (enfadado)
annoyed

molido, a [mo'liðo, a] adj: **estar ~** (fig) to
be exhausted o dead beat

molinillo [moli'niʎo] nm: **~ de carne/
café** mincer/coffee grinder

molino [mo'lino] nm (edificio) mill;
(máquina) grinder

momentáneo, a [momen'taneo, a] adj
momentary

momento [mo'mento] nm moment; **de ~**
at the moment, for the moment

momia ['momja] nf mummy

monarca [mo'narka] nm/f monarch, ruler;
monarquía nf monarchy;
monárquico, a nm/f royalist,
monarchist

monasterio [monas'terjo] nm monastery

mondar [mon'dar] vt to peel; **~se** vr: **~se
de risa** (fam) to split one's sides laughing

moneda [mo'neða] nf (tipo de dinero)
currency, money; (pieza) coin; **una ~ de
5 pesetas** a 5 peseta piece; **monedero**
nm purse; **monetario, a** adj monetary,
financial

monitor, a [moni'tor, a] nm/f instructor,
coach ♦ nm (TV) set; (INFORM) monitor

monja ['monxa] nf nun

monje ['monxe] nm monk

mono, a ['mono, a] adj (bonito) lovely,
pretty; (gracioso) nice, charming ♦ nm/f
monkey, ape ♦ nm dungarees pl;
(overoles) overalls pl

monopatín [monopa'tin] nm skateboard

monopolio [mono'poljo] nm monopoly;
monopolizar vt to monopolize

monotonía [monoto'nia] nf (sonido)
monotone; (fig) monotony

monótono, a [mo'notono, a] adj
monotonous

monstruo ['monstrwo] nm monster ♦ adj
inv fantastic; **~so, a** adj monstrous

montaje [mon'taxe] nm assembly;
(TEATRO) décor; (CINE) montage

montaña [mon'taɲa] *nf* (*monte*) mountain; (*sierra*) mountains *pl*, mountainous area; (*AM*: *selva*) forest; ~ **rusa** roller coaster; **montañero, a** *nm/f* mountaineer; **montañés, esa** *nm/f* highlander; **montañismo** *nm* mountaineering

montar [mon'tar] *vt* (*subir a*) to mount, get on; (*TEC*) to assemble, put together; (*negocio*) to set up; (*arma*) to cock; (*colocar*) to lift on to; (*CULIN*) to beat ♦ *vi* to mount, get on; (*sobresalir*) to overlap; ~ **en cólera** to get angry; ~ **a caballo** to ride, go horseriding

monte ['monte] *nm* (*montaña*) mountain; (*bosque*) woodland; (*área sin cultivar*) wild area, wild country; **M~ de Piedad** pawnshop

montón [mon'ton] *nm* heap, pile; (*fig*): **un ~ de** heaps of, lots of

monumento [monu'mento] *nm* monument

monzón [mon'θon] *nm* monsoon

moño ['moɲo] *nm* bun

moqueta [mo'keta] *nf* fitted carpet

mora ['mora] *nf* blackberry; *ver tb* **moro**

morada [mo'raða] *nf* (*casa*) dwelling, abode

morado, a [mo'raðo, a] *adj* purple, violet ♦ *nm* bruise

moral [mo'ral] *adj* moral ♦ *nf* (*ética*) ethics *pl*; (*moralidad*) morals *pl*, morality; (*ánimo*) morale

moraleja [mora'lexa] *nf* moral

moralidad [morali'ðað] *nf* morals *pl*, morality

morboso, a [mor'ßoso, a] *adj* morbid

morcilla [mor'θiʎa] *nf* blood sausage, ≈ black pudding (*BRIT*)

mordaz [mor'ðaθ] *adj* (*crítica*) biting, scathing

mordaza [mor'ðaθa] *nf* (*para la boca*) gag; (*TEC*) clamp

morder [mor'ðer] *vt* to bite; (*fig: consumir*) to eat away, eat into; **mordisco** *nm* bite

moreno, a [mo'reno, a] *adj* (*color*) (*dark*) brown; (*de tez*) dark; (*de pelo ~*) dark-haired; (*negro*) black

morfina [mor'fina] *nf* morphine

moribundo, a [mori'ßundo, a] *adj* dying

morir [mo'rir] *vi* to die; (*fuego*) to die down; (*luz*) to go out; ~**se** *vr* to die; (*fig*) to be dying; **murió en un accidente** he was killed in an accident; ~**se por algo** to be dying for sth

moro, a ['moro, a] *adj* Moorish ♦ *nm/f* Moor

moroso, a [mo'roso, a] *nm/f* bad debtor, defaulter

morral [mo'rral] *nm* haversack

morro ['morro] *nm* (*ZOOL*) snout, nose; (*AUTO, AVIAT*) nose

morsa ['morsa] *nf* walrus

mortadela [morta'ðela] *nf* mortadella

mortaja [mor'taxa] *nf* shroud

mortal [mor'tal] *adj* mortal; (*golpe*) deadly; ~**idad** *nf* mortality

mortero [mor'tero] *nm* mortar

mortífero, a [mor'tifero, a] *adj* deadly, lethal

mortificar [mortifi'kar] *vt* to mortify

mosca ['moska] *nf* fly

Moscú [mos'ku] *n* Moscow

mosquearse [moske'arse] (*fam*) *vr* (*enojarse*) to get cross; (*ofenderse*) to take offence

mosquitero [moski'tero] *nm* mosquito net

mosquito [mos'kito] *nm* mosquito

mostaza [mos'taθa] *nf* mustard

mosto ['mosto] *nm* (unfermented) grape juice

mostrador [mostra'ðor] *nm* (*de tienda*) counter; (*de café*) bar

mostrar [mos'trar] *vt* to show; (*exhibir*) to display, exhibit; (*explicar*) to explain; ~**se** *vr*: ~**se amable** to be kind; to prove to be kind; **no se muestra muy inteligente** he doesn't seem (to be) very intelligent

mota ['mota] *nf* speck, tiny piece; (*en diseño*) dot

mote ['mote] *nm* nickname

motín [mo'tin] *nm* (*del pueblo*) revolt, rising; (*del ejército*) mutiny

motivar [moti'ßar] vt (causar) to cause,
motivate; (explicar) to explain, justify;
motivo nm motive, reason

moto ['moto] (fam) nf = **motocicleta**

motocicleta [motoθi'kleta] nf motorbike
(BRIT), motorcycle

motor [mo'tor] nm motor, engine; **~ a
chorro** o **de reacción/de explosión** jet
engine/internal combustion engine

motora [mo'tora] nf motorboat

movedizo, a [moße'ðiθo, a] adj ver **arena**

mover [mo'ßer] vt to move; (cabeza) to
shake; (accionar) to drive; (fig) to cause,
provoke; **~se** vr to move; (fig) to get a
move on

móvil ['moßil] adj mobile; (pieza de
máquina) moving; (mueble) movable
♦ nm motive; **movilidad** nf mobility;
movilizar vt to mobilize

movimiento [moßi'mjento] nm
movement; (TEC) motion; (actividad)
activity

mozo, a ['moθo, a] adj (joven) young
♦ nm/f youth, young man/girl

muchacho, a [mu'tʃatʃo, a] nm/f (niño)
boy/girl; (criado) servant; (criada) maid

muchedumbre [mutʃe'ðumbre] nf crowd

PALABRA CLAVE

mucho, a ['mutʃo, a] adj 1 (cantidad) a
lot of, much; (número) lots of, a lot of,
many; **~ dinero** a lot of money; **hace ~
calor** it's very hot; **muchas amigas** lots o
a lot of friends
2 (sg: grande): **ésta es mucha casa para
él** this house is much too big for him
♦ pron: **tengo ~ que hacer** I've got a lot
to do; **~s dicen que ...** a lot of people
say that ...; ver tb **tener**
♦ adv 1: **me gusta ~** I like it a lot; **lo
siento ~** I'm very sorry; **come ~** he eats a
lot; **¿te vas a quedar ~?** are you going
to be staying long?
2 (respuesta) very; **¿estás cansado? – ¡~!**
are you tired? – very!
3 (locuciones): **como ~** at (the) most; **con
~: el mejor con ~** by far the best; **ni ~**

menos: no es rico ni ~ menos he's far
from being rich
4: **por ~ que: por ~ que le creas** no
matter how o however much you believe
her

muda ['muða] nf change of clothes

mudanza [mu'ðanθa] nf (de casa) move

mudar [mu'ðar] vt to change; (ZOOL) to
shed ♦ vi to change; **~se** vr (la ropa) to
change; **~se de casa** to move house

mudo, a ['muðo, a] adj dumb; (callado,
CINE) silent

mueble ['mweßle] nm piece of furniture;
~s nmpl furniture sg

mueca ['mweka] nf face, grimace; **hacer
~s a** to make faces at

muela ['mwela] nf (back) tooth

muelle ['mweʎe] nm spring; (NAUT) wharf;
(malecón) pier

muero etc vb ver **morir**

muerte ['mwerte] nf death; (homicidio)
murder; **dar ~ a** to kill

muerto, a ['mwerto, a] pp de **morir** ♦ adj
dead ♦ nm/f dead man/woman; (difunto)
deceased; (cadáver) corpse; **estar ~ de
cansancio** to be dead tired

muestra ['mwestra] nf (señal) indication,
sign; (demostración) demonstration;
(prueba) proof; (estadística) sample;
(modelo) model, pattern; (testimonio)
token

muestreo [mwes'treo] nm sample,
sampling

muestro etc vb ver **mostrar**

muevo etc vb ver **mover**

mugir [mu'xir] vi (vaca) to moo

mugre ['muvre] nf dirt, filth; **mugriento,
a** adj dirty, filthy

mujer [mu'xer] nf woman; (esposa) wife;
~iego nm womanizer

mula ['mula] nf mule

muleta [mu'leta] nf (para andar) crutch;
(TAUR) stick with red cape attached

mullido, a [mu'ʎiðo, a] adj (cama) soft;
(hierba) soft, springy

multa ['multa] nf fine; **poner una ~ a** to

fine; **multar** *vt* to fine
multicines [multi'θines] *nmpl* multiscreen cinema
multinacional [multinaθjo'nal] *nf* multinational
múltiple ['multiple] *adj* multiple; (*pl*) many, numerous
multiplicar [multipli'kar] *vt* (*MAT*) to multiply; (*fig*) to increase; **~se** *vr* (*BIO*) to multiply; (*fig*) to be everywhere at once
multitud [multi'tuð] *nf* (*muchedumbre*) crowd; **~** de lots of
mundano, a [mun'dano, a] *adj* worldly
mundial [mun'djal] *adj* world-wide, universal; (*guerra, récord*) world *cpd*
mundo ['mundo] *nm* world; **todo el ~** everybody; **tener ~** to be experienced, know one's way around
munición [muni'θjon] *nf* ammunition
municipal [muniθi'pal] *adj* municipal, local
municipio [muni'θipjo] *nm* (*ayuntamiento*) town council, corporation; (*territorio administrativo*) town, municipality
muñeca [mu'ɲeka] *nf* (*ANAT*) wrist; (*juguete*) doll
muñeco [mu'ɲeko] *nm* (*figura*) figure; (*marioneta*) puppet; (*fig*) puppet, pawn
mural [mu'ral] *adj* mural, wall *cpd* ♦ *nm* mural
muralla [mu'raʎa] *nf* (city) wall(s) (*pl*)
murciélago [mur'θjelaɣo] *nm* bat
murmullo [mur'muʎo] *nm* murmur(ing); (*cuchicheo*) whispering
murmuración [murmura'θjon] *nf* gossip; **murmurar** *vi* to murmur, whisper; (*cotillear*) to gossip
muro ['muro] *nm* wall
muscular [musku'lar] *adj* muscular
músculo ['muskulo] *nm* muscle
museo [mu'seo] *nm* museum; **~** de arte art gallery
musgo ['musɣo] *nm* moss
música ['musika] *nf* music; *ver tb* **músico**
músico, a ['musiko, a] *adj* musical ♦ *nm/f* musician
muslo ['muslo] *nm* thigh

mustio, a ['mustjo, a] *adj* (*persona*) depressed, gloomy; (*planta*) faded, withered
musulmán, ana [musul'man, ana] *nm/f* Moslem
mutación [muta'θjon] *nf* (*BIO*) mutation; (*cambio*) (sudden) change
mutilar [muti'lar] *vt* to mutilate; (*a una persona*) to maim
mutismo [mu'tismo] *nm* (*de persona*) uncommunicativeness; (*de autoridades*) silence
mutuamente [mutwa'mente] *adv* mutually
mutuo, a ['mutwo, a] *adj* mutual
muy [mwi] *adv* very; (*demasiado*) too; **M~ Señor mío** Dear Sir; **~** de noche very late at night; **eso es ~** de él that's just like him

N, n

N *abr* (= *norte*) N
nabo ['naβo] *nm* turnip
nácar ['nakar] *nm* mother-of-pearl
nacer [na'θer] *vi* to be born; (*de huevo*) to hatch; (*vegetal*) to sprout; (*río*) to rise; **nací en Barcelona** I was born in Barcelona; **nació una sospecha en su mente** a suspicion formed in her mind; **nacido, a** *adj* born; **recién nacido** newborn; **naciente** *adj* new, emerging; (*sol*) rising; **nacimiento** *nm* birth; (*de Navidad*) Nativity; (*de río*) source
nación [na'θjon] *nf* nation; **nacional** *adj* national; **nacionalismo** *nm* nationalism; **nacionalista** *nm/f* nationalist; **nacionalizar** *vt* to nationalize; **nacionalizarse** *vr* (*persona*) to become naturalized
nada ['naða] *pron* nothing ♦ *adv* not at all, in no way; **no decir ~** to say nothing, not to say anything; **~** más nothing else; **de ~** don't mention it
nadador, a [naða'ðor, a] *nm/f* swimmer
nadar [na'ðar] *vi* to swim

nadie ['naðje] *pron* nobody, no-one; ~ **habló** nobody spoke; **no había ~** there was nobody there, there wasn't anybody there

nado ['naðo]: **a ~** *adv*: **pasar a ~** to swim across

nafta ['nafta] (*AM*) *nf* petrol (*BRIT*), gas (*US*)

naipe ['naipe] *nm* (playing) card; **~s** *nmpl* cards

nalgas ['nalɣas] *nfpl* buttocks

nana ['nana] *nf* lullaby

naranja [na'ranxa] *adj inv*, *nf* orange; **media ~** (*fam*) better half; **naranjada** *nf* orangeade; **naranjo** *nm* orange tree

narciso [nar'θiso] *nm* narcissus

narcótico, a [nar'kotiko, a] *adj*, *nm* narcotic; **narcotizar** *vt* to drug; **narcotráfico** *nm* drug trafficking *o* running

nardo ['narðo] *nm* lily

narigudo, a [narı'ɣuðo, a] *adj* big-nosed

nariz [na'riθ] *nf* nose

narración [narra'θjon] *nf* narration; **narrador, a** *nm/f* narrator

narrar [na'rrar] *vt* to narrate, recount; **narrativa** *nf* narrative

nata ['nata] *nf* cream

natación [nata'θjon] *nf* swimming

natal [na'tal] *adj*: **ciudad ~** home town; **~idad** *nf* birth rate

natillas [na'tiʎas] *nfpl* custard *sg*

nativo, a [na'tiβo, a] *adj*, *nm/f* native

nato, a ['nato, a] *adj* born; **un músico ~** a born musician

natural [natu'ral] *adj* natural; (*fruta etc*) fresh ♦ *nm/f* native ♦ *nm* (*disposición*) nature

naturaleza [natura'leθa] *nf* nature; (*género*) nature, kind; **~ muerta** still life

naturalidad [naturali'ðað] *nf* naturalness

naturalmente [natural'mente] *adv* (*de modo natural*) in a natural way; **¡~!** of course!

naufragar [naufra'ɣar] *vi* to sink; **naufragio** *nm* shipwreck; **náufrago, a** *nm/f* castaway, shipwrecked person

nauseabundo, a [nausea'ßundo, a] *adj* nauseating, sickening

náuseas ['nauseas] *nfpl* nausea *sg*; **me da ~** it makes me feel sick

náutico, a ['nautiko, a] *adj* nautical

navaja [na'ßaxa] *nf* knife; (*de barbero, peluquero*) razor

naval [na'ßal] *adj* naval

Navarra [na'ßarra] *n* Navarre

nave ['naße] *nf* (*barco*) ship, vessel; (*ARQ*) nave; **~ espacial** spaceship

navegación [naßeɣa'θjon] *nf* navigation; (*viaje*) sea journey; **~ aérea** air traffic; **~ costera** coastal shipping; **navegante** *nm/f* navigator; **navegar** *vi* (*barco*) to sail; (*avión*) to fly

Navidad [naßi'ðað] *nf* Christmas; **~es** *nfpl* Christmas time; **Feliz N~** Merry Christmas; **navideño, a** *adj* Christmas *cpd*

navío [na'ßio] *nm* ship

nazca *etc vb ver* **nacer**

nazi ['naθi] *adj*, *nm/f* Nazi

NE *abr* (= *nor(d)este*) NE

neblina [ne'ßlina] *nf* mist

nebulosa [neßu'losa] *nf* nebula

necesario, a [neθe'sarjo, a] *adj* necessary

neceser [neθe'ser] *nm* toilet bag; (*bolsa grande*) holdall

necesidad [neθesi'ðað] *nf* need; (*lo inevitable*) necessity; (*miseria*) poverty, need; **en caso de ~** in case of need *o* emergency; **hacer sus ~es** to relieve o.s.

necesitado, a [neθesi'taðo, a] *adj* needy, poor; **~ de** in need of

necesitar [neθesi'tar] *vt* to need, require

necio, a ['neθjo, a] *adj* foolish

necrópolis [ne'kropolis] *nf inv* cemetery

nectarina [nekta'rina] *nf* nectarine

nefasto, a [ne'fasto, a] *adj* ill-fated, unlucky

negación [neɣa'θjon] *nf* negation; (*rechazo*) refusal, denial

negar [ne'ɣar] *vt* (*renegar, rechazar*) to refuse; (*prohibir*) to refuse, deny; (*desmentir*) to deny; **~se** *vr*: **~se a** to refuse to

negativa [neɣa'tißa] *nf* negative; (*rechazo*)

refusal, denial

negativo, a [neɣa'tiβo, a] *adj, nm* negative

negligencia [neɣli'xenθja] *nf* negligence; **negligente** *adj* negligent

negociado [neɣo'θjaðo] *nm* department, section

negociante [neɣo'θjante] *nm/f* businessman/woman

negociar [neɣo'θjar] *vt, vi* to negotiate; ~ **en** to deal in, trade in

negocio [ne'ɣoθjo] *nm* (COM) business; (*asunto*) affair, business; (*operación comercial*) deal, transaction; (AM) firm; (*lugar*) place of business; **los ~s** business *sg*; **hacer ~** to do business

negra ['neɣra] *nf* (MUS) crotchet; *ver tb* **negro**

negro, a ['neɣro, a] *adj* black; (*suerte*) awful ♦ *nm* black ♦ *nm/f* black man/woman

nene, a ['nene, a] *nm/f* baby, small child

nenúfar [ne'nufar] *nm* water lily

neologismo [neolo'xismo] *nm* neologism

neón [ne'on] *nm*: **luces/lámpara de ~** neon lights/lamp

neoyorquino, a [neojor'kino, a] *adj* (of) New York

nervio ['nerβjo] *nm* nerve; **nerviosismo** *nm* nervousness, nerves *pl*; ~**so, a** *adj* nervous

neto, a ['neto, a] *adj* net

neumático, a [neu'matiko, a] *adj* pneumatic ♦ *nm* (ESP) tyre (BRIT), tire (US); ~ **de recambio** spare tyre

neurasténico, a [neuras'teniko, a] *adj* (*fig*) hysterical

neurólogo, a [neu'roloɣo, a] *nm/f* neurologist

neurona [neu'rona] *nf* nerve cell

neutral [neu'tral] *adj* neutral; ~**izar** *vt* to neutralize; (*contrarrestar*) to counteract

neutro, a ['neutro, a] *adj* (BIO, LING) neuter

neutrón [neu'tron] *nm* neutron

nevada [ne'βaða] *nf* snowstorm; (*caída de nieve*) snowfall

nevar [ne'βar] *vi* to snow

nevera [ne'βera] (ESP) *nf* refrigerator (BRIT), icebox (US)

nevería [neβe'ria] (AM) *nf* ice-cream parlour

nexo ['nekso] *nm* link, connection

ni [ni] *conj* nor, neither; (*tb*: ~ **siquiera**) not ... even; ~ **aunque que** not even if; ~ **blanco ~ negro** neither white nor black

Nicaragua [nika'raɣwa] *nf* Nicaragua; **nicaragüense** *adj, nm/f* Nicaraguan

nicho ['nitʃo] *nm* niche

nicotina [niko'tina] *nf* nicotine

nido ['niðo] *nm* nest

niebla ['njeβla] *nf* fog; (*neblina*) mist

niego *etc vb ver* **negar**

nieto, a ['njeto, a] *nm/f* grandson/daughter; ~**s** *nmpl* grandchildren

nieve *etc* ['njeβe] *vb ver* **nevar** ♦ *nf* snow; (AM) icecream

N.I.F. *nm abr* (= *Número de Identificación Fiscal*) *personal identification number used for financial and tax purposes*

nimiedad [nimje'ðað] *nf* triviality

nimio, a ['nimjo, a] *adj* trivial, insignificant

ninfa ['ninfa] *nf* nymph

ningún [nin'gun] *adj ver* **ninguno**

ninguno, a [nin'guno, a] (*delante de nm*: **ningún**) *adj* no ♦ *pron* (*nadie*) nobody; (*ni uno*) none, not one; (*ni uno ni otro*) neither; **de ninguna manera** by no means, not at all

niña ['nina] *nf* (ANAT) pupil; *ver tb* **niño**

niñera [ni'nera] *nf* nursemaid, nanny; **niñería** *nf* childish act

niñez [ni'neθ] *nf* childhood; (*infancia*) infancy

niño, a ['nino, a] *adj* (*joven*) young; (*inmaduro*) immature ♦ *nm/f* child, boy/girl

nipón, ona [ni'pon, ona] *adj, nm/f* Japanese

níquel ['nikel] *nm* nickel; **niquelar** *vt* (TEC) to nickel-plate

níspero ['nispero] *nm* medlar

nitidez [niti'ðeθ] *nf* (*claridad*) clarity; (: *de imagen*) sharpness; **nítido, a** *adj* clear;

sharp
nitrato [ni'trato] *nm* nitrate
nitrógeno [ni'troxeno] *nm* nitrogen
nivel [ni'ßel] *nm* (GEO) level; (*norma*) level,
standard; (*altura*) height; ~ **de aceite** oil
level; ~ **de aire** spirit level; ~ **de vida**
standard of living; **~ar** *vt* to level out;
(*fig*) to even up; (COM) to balance
NN. UU. *nfpl abr* (= *Naciones Unidas*)
UN *sg*
no [no] *adv* no; not; (*con verbo*) not ♦ *excl*
no!; ~ **tengo nada** I don't have anything,
I have nothing; ~ **es el mío** it's not mine;
ahora ~ not now; ¿~ **lo sabes?** don't
you know?; ~ **mucho** not much; ~ **bien
termine**, **le entregaré** as soon as I finish
I'll hand it over; ~ **más**: **ayer** ~ **más** just
yesterday; **¡pase** ~ **más!** come in!; **¡a que
** ~ **lo sabes!** I bet you don't know!;
¡cómo ~! of course!; **los países** ~
alineados the non-aligned countries; **la** ~
intervención non-intervention
noble [noßle] *adj*, *nm/f* noble; **~za** *nf*
nobility
noche ['notfe] *nf* night, night-time; (*la
tarde*) evening; **de** ~, **por la** ~ at night;
es de ~ it's dark

The **Noche de San Juan** *on the 24th
June is a* fiesta *coinciding with the
summer solstice and which has taken the
place of other ancient pagan festivals.
Traditionally fire plays a major part in
these festivities with celebrations and
dancing taking place around bonfires in
towns and villages across the country.*

nochebuena [notfe'ßwena] *nf* Christmas
Eve

*Traditional Christmas celebrations in
Spanish-speaking countries mainly take
place on the night of* **Nochebuena**,
*Christmas Eve. Families gather together for
a large meal and the more religiously*
*inclined attend Midnight Mass. While
presents are traditionally given by* **los
Reyes Magos** *on the 6th January, more
and more people are exchanging gifts on
Christmas Eve.*

nochevieja [notfe'ßjexa] *nf* New Year's
Eve
noción [no'θjon] *nf* notion
nocivo, a [no'θiβo, a] *adj* harmful
noctámbulo, a [nok'tambulo, a] *nm/f*
sleepwalker
nocturno, a [nok'turno, a] *adj* (*de la
noche*) nocturnal, night *cpd*; (*de la tarde*)
evening *cpd* ♦ *nm* nocturne
nodriza [no'ðriθa] *nf* wet nurse; **buque** *o*
nave ~ supply ship
nogal [no'val] *nm* walnut tree
nómada ['nomaða] *adj* nomadic ♦ *nm/f*
nomad
nombramiento [nombra'mjento] *nm*
naming; (*a un empleo*) appointment
nombrar [nom'brar] *vt* (*designar*) to name;
(*mencionar*) to mention; (*dar puesto a*) to
appoint
nombre ['nombre] *nm* name; (*sustantivo*)
noun; ~ **y apellidos** name in full; ~
común/propio common/proper noun; ~
de pila/de soltera Christian/maiden
name; **poner** ~ **a** to call, name
nómina ['nomina] *nf* (*lista*) payroll; (*hoja*)
payslip
nominal [nomi'nal] *adj* nominal
nominar [nomi'nar] *vt* to nominate
nominativo, a [nomina'tiβo, a] *adj*
(COM): **cheque** ~ **a X** cheque made out
to X
nono, a ['nono, a] *adj* ninth
nordeste [nor'ðeste] *adj* north-east,
north-eastern, north-easterly ♦ *nm* north-
east
nórdico, a ['norðiko, a] *adj* Nordic
noreste [no'reste] *adj*, *nm* = **nordeste**
noria ['norja] *nf* (AGR) waterwheel; (*de
carnaval*) big (BRIT) *o* Ferris (US) wheel
norma ['norma] *nf* rule (of thumb)
normal [nor'mal] *adj* (*corriente*) normal;

(habitual) usual, natural; **~idad** *nf* normality; **restablecer la ~idad** to restore order; **~izar** *vt (reglamentar)* to normalize; *(TEC)* to standardize; **~izarse** *vr* to return to normal; **~mente** *adv* normally

normando, a [nor'mando, a] *adj, nm/f* Norman

normativa [norma'tiβa] *nf* (set of) rules *pl*, regulations *pl*

noroeste [noro'este] *adj* north-west, north-western, north-westerly ♦ *nm* north-west

norte ['norte] *adj* north, northern, northerly ♦ *nm* north; *(fig)* guide

norteamericano, a [norteameri'kano, a] *adj, nm/f* (North) American

Noruega [no'rweɣa] *nf* Norway

noruego, a [no'rweɣo, a] *adj, nm/f* Norwegian

nos [nos] *pron (directo)* us; *(indirecto)* us; to us; for us; from us; *(reflexivo)* (to) ourselves; *(recíproco)* (to) each other; **~ levantamos a las 7** we get up at 7

nosotros, as [no'sotros, as] *pron (sujeto)* we; *(después de prep)* us

nostalgia [nos'talxja] *nf* nostalgia

nota ['nota] *nf* note; *(ESCOL)* mark

notable [no'taβle] *adj* notable; *(ESCOL)* outstanding

notar [no'tar] *vt* to notice, note; **~se** *vr* to be obvious; **se nota que ...** one observes that ...

notarial [nota'rjal] *adj*: **acta ~** affidavit

notario [no'tarjo] *nm* notary

noticia [no'tiθja] *nf (información)* piece of news; **las ~s** the news *sg*; **tener ~s de alguien** to hear from sb

noticiero [noti'θjero] *(AM) nm* news bulletin

notificación [notifika'θjon] *nf* notification; **notificar** *vt* to notify, inform

notoriedad [notorje'ðað] *nf* fame, renown; **notorio, a** *adj (público)* well-known; *(evidente)* obvious

novato, a [no'βato, a] *adj* inexperienced ♦ *nm/f* beginner, novice

novecientos, as [noβe'θjentos, as] *num* nine hundred

novedad [noβe'ðað] *nf (calidad de nuevo)* newness; *(noticia)* piece of news; *(cambio)* change, (new) development

novel [no'βel] *adj* new; *(inexperto)* inexperienced ♦ *nm/f* beginner

novela [no'βela] *nf* novel

noveno, a [no'βeno, a] *adj* ninth

noventa [no'βenta] *num* ninety

novia ['noβja] *nf ver* **novio**

noviazgo [no'βjaθvo] *nm* engagement

novicio, a [no'βiθjo, a] *nm/f* novice

noviembre [no'βjembre] *nm* November

novillada [noβi'ʎaða] *nf (TAUR)* bullfight with young bulls; **novillero** *nm* novice bullfighter; **novillo** *nm* young bull, bullock; **hacer novillos** *(fam)* to play truant

novio, a ['noβjo, a] *nm/f* boyfriend/ girlfriend; *(prometido)* fiancé/fiancée; *(recién casado)* bridegroom/bride; **los ~s** the newly-weds

nubarrón [nuβa'rron] *nm* storm cloud

nube ['nuβe] *nf* cloud

nublado, a [nu'βlaðo, a] *adj* cloudy; **nublarse** *vr* to grow dark

nubosidad [nuβosi'ðað] *nf* cloudiness; **había mucha ~** it was very cloudy

nuca ['nuka] *nf* nape of the neck

nuclear [nukle'ar] *adj* nuclear

núcleo ['nukleo] *nm (centro)* core; *(FÍSICA)* nucleus

nudillo [nu'ðiʎo] *nm* knuckle

nudista [nu'ðista] *adj* nudist

nudo ['nuðo] *nm* knot; **~so, a** *adj* knotty

nuera ['nwera] *nf* daughter-in-law

nuestro, a ['nwestro, a] *adj our* ♦ *pron* ours; **~ padre** our father; **un amigo ~** a friend of ours; **es el ~** it's ours

nueva ['nweβa] *nf* piece of news

nuevamente [nweβa'mente] *adv (otra vez)* again; *(de nuevo)* anew

Nueva York [-'jɔrk] *n* New York

Nueva Zelanda [-θe'landa] *nf* New Zealand

nueve ['nweβe] *num* nine

nuevo, a [ˈnweβo, a] adj (gen) new; **de ~** again

nuez [nweθ] nf walnut; **~ de Adán** Adam's apple; **~ moscada** nutmeg

nulidad [nuliˈðað] nf (incapacidad) incompetence; (abolición) nullity

nulo, a [ˈnulo, a] adj (inepto, torpe) useless; (inválido) (null and void); (DEPORTE) drawn, tied

núm. abr (= número) no

numeración [numeraˈθjon] nf (cifras) numbers pl; (arábiga, romana etc) numerals pl

numeral [numeˈral] nm numeral

numerar [numeˈrar] vt to number

número [ˈnumero] nm (gen) number; (tamaño: de zapato) size; (ejemplar: de diario) number, issue; **sin ~** numberless, unnumbered; **~ de matrícula/de teléfono** registration/telephone number; **~ atrasado** back number

numeroso, a [numeˈroso, a] adj numerous

nunca [ˈnunka] adv (jamás) never; **~ lo pensé** I never thought it; **no viene ~** he never comes; **~ más** never again; **más que ~** more than ever

nupcias [ˈnupθjas] nfpl wedding sg, nuptials

nutria [ˈnutrja] nf otter

nutrición [nutriˈθjon] nf nutrition

nutrido, a [nuˈtriðo, a] adj (alimentado) nourished; (fig: grande) large; (abundante) abundant

nutrir [nuˈtrir] vt (alimentar) to nourish; (dar de comer) to feed; (fig) to strengthen; **nutritivo, a** adj nourishing, nutritious

nylon [niˈlon] nm nylon

Ñ, ñ

ñato, a [ˈɲato, a] (AM) adj snub-nosed

ñoñería [ɲoɲeˈria] nf insipidness

ñoño, a [ˈɲoɲo, a] adj (AM: tonto) silly, stupid; (soso) insipid; (persona) spineless

O, o

O abr (= oeste) W

o [o] conj or

o/ abr (= orden) o.

oasis [oˈasis] nm inv oasis

obcecarse [oβθeˈkarse] vr to get o become stubborn

obedecer [oβeðeˈθer] vt to obey; **obediencia** nf obedience; **obediente** adj obedient

obertura [oβerˈtura] nf overture

obesidad [oβesiˈðað] nf obesity; **obeso, a** adj obese

obispo [oˈβispo] nm bishop

objeción [oβxeˈθjon] nf objection; **poner objeciones** to raise objections

objetar [oβxeˈtar] vt, vi to object

objetivo, a [oβxeˈtiβo, a] adj, nm objective

objeto [oβˈxeto] nm (cosa) object; (fin) aim

objetor, a [oβxeˈtor, a] nm/f objector

oblicuo, a [oˈβlikwo, a] adj (mirada) sidelong

obligación [oβliɣaˈθjon] nf obligation; (COM) bond

obligar [oβliˈɣar] vt to force; **~se** vr to bind o.s.; **obligatorio, a** adj compulsory, obligatory

oboe [oˈβoe] nm oboe

obra [ˈoβra] nf work; (ARQ) construction, building; (TEATRO) play; **~ maestra** masterpiece; **~s públicas** public works; **por ~ de** thanks to (the efforts of); **obrar** vt to work; (tener efecto) to have an effect on ♦ vi to act, behave; (tener efecto) to have an effect; **la carta obra en su poder** the letter is in his/her possession

obrero, a [oˈβrero, a] adj (clase) working; (movimiento) labour cpd ♦ nm/f (gen) worker; (sin oficio) labourer

obscenidad [oβsθeniˈðað] nf obscenity; **obsceno, a** adj obscene

obscu... = **oscu...**

obsequiar [oβse'kjar] *vt* (*ofrecer*) to present with; (*agasajar*) to make a fuss of, lavish attention on; **obsequio** *nm* (*regalo*) gift; (*cortesía*) courtesy, attention

observación [oβserβa'θjon] *nf* observation; (*reflexión*) remark

observador, a [oβserβa'ðor, a] *nm/f* observer

observar [oβser'βar] *vt* to observe; (*anotar*) to notice; **~se** *vr* to keep to, observe

obsesión [oβse'sjon] *nf* obsession; **obsesivo, a** *adj* obsessive

obsoleto, a [oβso'leto, a] *adj* obsolete

obstáculo [oβs'takulo] *nm* obstacle; (*impedimento*) hindrance, drawback

obstante [oβs'tante]: **no ~** *adv* nevertheless

obstinado, a [oβsti'naðo, a] *adj* obstinate, stubborn

obstinarse [oβsti'narse] *vr* to be obstinate; **~ en** to persist in

obstrucción [oβstruk'θjon] *nf* obstruction; **obstruir** *vt* to obstruct

obtener [oβte'ner] *vt* (*gen*) to obtain; (*premio*) to win

obturador [oβtura'ðor] *nm* (*FOTO*) shutter

obvio, a ['oβßjo, a] *adj* obvious

oca ['oka] *nf* (*animal*) goose; (*juego*) ≈ snakes and ladders

ocasión [oka'sjon] *nf* (*oportunidad*) opportunity, chance; (*momento*) occasion, time; (*causa*) cause; **de ~** secondhand; **ocasionar** *vt* to cause

ocaso [o'kaso] *nm* (*fig*) decline

occidente [okθi'ðente] *nm* west

OCDE *nf abr* (= *Organización de Cooperación y Desarrollo Económico*) OECD

océano [o'θeano] *nm* ocean; **el ~ Índico** the Indian Ocean

ochenta [o'tʃenta] *num* eighty

ocho ['otʃo] *num* eight; **~ días** a week

ocio ['oθjo] *nm* (*tiempo*) leisure; (*pey*) idleness; **~so, a** *adj* (*inactivo*) idle; (*inútil*) useless

octavilla [okta'viʎa] *nf* leaflet, pamphlet

octavo, a [ok'taβo, a] *adj* eighth

octubre [ok'tuβre] *nm* October

ocular [oku'lar] *adj* ocular, eye *cpd*; **testigo ~** eyewitness

oculista [oku'lista] *nm/f* oculist

ocultar [okul'tar] *vt* (*esconder*) to hide; (*callar*) to conceal; **oculto, a** *adj* hidden; (*fig*) secret

ocupación [okupa'θjon] *nf* occupation

ocupado, a [oku'paðo, a] *adj* (*persona*) busy; (*plaza*) occupied, taken; (*teléfono*) engaged; **ocupar** *vt* (*gen*) to occupy; **ocuparse** *vr*: **ocuparse de** *o* **en** (*gen*) to concern o.s. with; (*cuidar*) to look after

ocurrencia [oku'rrenθja] *nf* (*idea*) bright idea

ocurrir [oku'rrir] *vi* to happen; **~se** *vr*: **se me ocurrió que ...** it occurred to me that ...

odiar [o'ðjar] *vt* to hate; **odio** *nm* hate, hatred; **odioso, a** *adj* (*gen*) hateful; (*malo*) nasty

odontólogo, a [oðon'toloɣo, a] *nm/f* dentist, dental surgeon

OEA *nf abr* (= *Organización de Estados Americanos*) OAS

oeste [o'este] *nm* west; **una película del ~** a western

ofender [ofen'der] *vt* (*agraviar*) to offend; (*insultar*) to insult; **~se** *vr* to take offence; **ofensa** *nf* offence; **ofensiva** *nf* offensive; **ofensivo, a** *adj* offensive

oferta [o'ferta] *nf* offer; (*propuesta*) proposal; **la ~ y la demanda** supply and demand; **artículos en ~** goods on offer

oficial [ofi'θjal] *adj* official ♦ *nm* (*MIL*) officer

oficina [ofi'θina] *nf* office; **~ de correos** post office; **~ de turismo** tourist office; **oficinista** *nm/f* clerk

oficio [ofi'θjo] *nm* (*profesión*) profession; (*puesto*) post; (*REL*) service; **ser del ~** to be an old hand; **tener mucho ~** to have a lot of experience; **~ de difuntos** funeral service

oficioso, a [ofi'θjoso, a] *adj* (*pey*) officious; (*no oficial*) unofficial, informal

ofimática [ofi'matika] *nf* office

automation

ofrecer [ofre'θer] *vt* (*dar*) to offer; (*proponer*) to propose; **~se** *vr* (*persona*) to offer o.s., volunteer; (*situación*) to present itself; **¿qué se le ofrece?, ¿se le ofrece algo?** what can I do for you?, can I get you anything?

ofrecimiento [ofreθi'mjento] *nm* offer

oftalmólogo, a [oftal'moloɣo, a] *nm/f* ophthalmologist

ofuscar [ofus'kar] *vt* (*por pasión*) to blind; (*por luz*) to dazzle

oída [o'iða] *nf*: **de ~s** by hearsay

oído [o'iðo] *nm* (ANAT) ear; (*sentido*) hearing

oigo *etc vb ver* **oír**

oír [o'ir] *vt* (*gen*) to hear; (*atender a*) to listen to; **¡oiga!** listen!; **~ misa** to attend mass

OIT *nf abr* (= *Organización Internacional del Trabajo*) ILO

ojal [o'xal] *nm* buttonhole

ojalá [oxa'la] *excl* if only (it were so)!, some hope! ♦ *conj* if only ...!, would that ...!; **~ (que) venga hoy** I hope he comes today

ojeada [oxe'aða] *nf* glance

ojera [o'xera] *nf*: **tener ~s** to have bags under one's eyes

ojeriza [oxe'riθa] *nf* ill-will

ojeroso, a [oxe'roso, a] *adj* haggard

ojo [o'xo] *nm* eye; (*de puente*) span; (*de cerradura*) keyhole ♦ *excl* careful!; **tener ~ para** to have an eye for; **~ de buey** porthole

okupa [o'kupa] (*fam*) *nm/f* squatter

ola ['ola] *nf* wave

olé [o'le] *excl* bravo!, olé!

oleada [ole'aða] *nf* big wave, swell; (*fig*) wave

oleaje [ole'axe] *nm* swell

óleo ['oleo] *nm* oil; **oleoducto** *nm* (oil) pipeline

oler [o'ler] *vt* (*gen*) to smell; (*inquirir*) to pry into; (*fig: sospechar*) to sniff out ♦ *vi* to smell; **~ a** to smell of

olfatear [olfate'ar] *vt* to smell; (*inquirir*) to

pry into; **olfato** *nm* sense of smell

oligarquía [oliɣar'kia] *nf* oligarchy

olimpíada [olim'piaða] *nf*: **las O~s** the Olympics; **olímpico, a** [o'limpiko, a] *adj* Olympic

oliva [o'lißa] *nf* (*aceituna*) olive; **aceite de ~** olive oil; **olivo** *nm* olive tree

olla ['oʎa] *nf* pan; (*comida*) stew; **~ a presión** *o* **exprés** pressure cooker; **~ podrida** *type of Spanish stew*

olmo ['olmo] *nm* elm (tree)

olor [o'lor] *nm* smell; **~oso, a** *adj* scented

olvidar [olßi'ðar] *vt* to forget; (*omitir*) to omit; **~se** *vr* (*fig*) to forget o.s.; **se me olvidó** I forgot

olvido [ol'ßiðo] *nm* oblivion; (*despiste*) forgetfulness

ombligo [om'blivo] *nm* navel

omisión [omi'sjon] *nf* (*abstención*) omission; (*descuido*) neglect

omiso, a [o'miso, a] *adj*: **hacer caso ~ de** to ignore, pass over

omitir [omi'tir] *vt* to omit

omnipotente [omnipo'tente] *adj* omnipotent

omóplato [o'moplato] *nm* shoulder blade

OMS *nf abr* (= *Organización Mundial de la Salud*) WHO

once ['onθe] *num* eleven; **~s** (AM) *nfpl* tea break

onda ['onda] *nf* wave; **~ corta/larga/media** short/long/medium wave; **ondear** *vt, vi* to wave; (*tener ondas*) to be wavy; (*agua*) to ripple; **ondearse** *vr* to swing, sway

ondulación [ondula'θjon] *nf* undulation; **ondulado, a** *adj* wavy

ondular [ondu'lar] *vt* (*el pelo*) to wave ♦ *vi* to undulate; **~se** *vr* to undulate

ONG *nf abr* (= *organización no gubernamental*) NGO

ONU ['onu] *nf abr* (= *Organización de las Naciones Unidas*) UNO

opaco, a [o'pako, a] *adj* opaque

opción [op'θjon] *nf* (*gen*) option; (*derecho*) right, option

OPEP ['opep] *nf abr* (= *Organización de*

Países Exportadores de Petróleo) OPEC

ópera ['opera] *nf* opera; **~ bufa** *o* **cómica** comic opera

operación [opera'θjon] *nf* (*gen*) operation; (*COM*) transaction, deal

operador, a [opera'ðor, a] *nm/f* operator; (*CINE: proyección*) projectionist; (: *rodaje*) cameraman

operar [ope'rar] *vt* (*producir*) to produce, bring about; (*MED*) to operate on ♦ *vi* (*COM*) to operate, deal; **~se** *vr* to occur; (*MED*) to have an operation

opereta [ope'reta] *nf* operetta

opinar [opi'nar] *vt* to think ♦ *vi* to give one's opinion; **opinión** *nf* (*creencia*) belief; (*criterio*) opinion

opio ['opjo] *nm* opium

oponente [opo'nente] *nm/f* opponent

oponer [opo'ner] *vt* (*resistencia*) to put up, offer; **~se** *vr* (*objetar*) to object; (*estar frente a frente*) to be opposed; (*dos personas*) to oppose each other; **~ A a B** to set A against B; **me opongo a pensar que ...** I refuse to believe *o* think that **∴**.

oportunidad [oportuni'ðað] *nf* (*ocasión*) opportunity; (*posibilidad*) chance

oportuno, a [opor'tuno, a] *adj* (*en su tiempo*) opportune, timely; (*respuesta*) suitable; **en el momento ~** at the right moment

oposición [oposi'θjon] *nf* opposition; **oposiciones** *nfpl* (*ESCOL*) public examinations

opositor, a [oposi'tor, a] *nm/f* (*adversario*) opponent; (*candidato*): **~ (a)** candidate (for)

opresión [opre'sjon] *nf* oppression; **opresivo, a** *adj* oppressive; **opresor, a** *nm/f* oppressor

oprimir [opri'mir] *vt* to squeeze; (*fig*) to oppress

optar [op'tar] *vi* (*elegir*) to choose; **~ por** to opt for; **optativo, a** *adj* optional

óptico, a ['optiko, a] *adj* optic(al) ♦ *nm/f* optician; **óptica** *nf* optician's (shop); **desde esta óptica** from this point of view

optimismo [opti'mismo] *nm* optimism; **optimista** *nm/f* optimist

óptimo, a ['optimo, a] *adj* (*el mejor*) very best

opuesto, a [o'pwesto, a] *adj* (*contrario*) opposite; (*antagónico*) opposing

opulencia [opu'lenθja] *nf* opulence; **opulento, a** *adj* opulent

oración [ora'θjon] *nf* (*REL*) prayer; (*LING*) sentence

orador, a [ora'ðor, a] *nm/f* (*conferenciante*) speaker, orator

oral [o'ral] *adj* oral

orangután [orangu'tan] *nm* orangutan

orar [o'rar] *vi* to pray

oratoria [ora'torja] *nf* oratory

órbita ['orβita] *nf* orbit

orden ['orðen] *nm* (*gen*) order ♦ *nf* (*gen*) order; (*INFORM*) command; **~ del día** agenda; **de primer ~** first-rate; **en ~ de prioridad** in order of priority

ordenado, a [orðe'naðo, a] *adj* (*metódico*) methodical; (*arreglado*) orderly

ordenador [orðena'ðor] *nm* computer; **~ central** mainframe computer

ordenanza [orðe'nanθa] *nf* ordinance

ordenar [orðe'nar] *vt* (*mandar*) to order; (*poner orden*) to put in order, arrange; **~se** *vr* (*REL*) to be ordained

ordeñar [orðe'nar] *vt* to milk

ordinario, a [orði'narjo, a] *adj* (*común*) ordinary, usual; (*vulgar*) vulgar, common

orégano [o'reɣano] *nm* oregano

oreja [o'rexa] *nf* ear; (*MECÁNICA*) lug, flange

orfanato [orfa'nato] *nm* orphanage

orfandad [orfan'dað] *nf* orphanhood

orfebrería [orfeβre'ria] *nf* gold/silver work

orgánico, a [or'ɣaniko, a] *adj* organic

organigrama [orɣani'ɣrama] *nm* flow chart

organismo [orɣa'nismo] *nm* (*BIO*) organism; (*POL*) organization

organización [orɣaniθa'θjon] *nf* organization; **organizar** *vt* to organize

órgano ['orɣano] *nm* organ

orgasmo [or'ɣasmo] *nm* orgasm

orgía [or'xia] *nf* orgy

orgullo [or'ɣuʎo] *nm* pride; **orgulloso, a** *adj* (*gen*) proud; (*altanero*) haughty

orientación [orjenta'θjon] *nf* (*posición*) position; (*dirección*) direction

oriental [orjen'tal] *adj* eastern; (*del Lejano Oriente*) oriental

orientar [orjen'tar] *vt* (*situar*) to orientate; (*señalar*) to point; (*dirigir*) to direct; (*guiar*) to guide; **~se** *vr* to get one's bearings

oriente [o'rjente] *nm* east; **Cercano/Medio/Lejano O~** Near/Middle/Far East

origen [o'rixen] *nm* origin

original [orixi'nal] *adj* (*nuevo*) original; (*extraño*) odd, strange; **~idad** *nf* originality

originar [orixi'nar] *vt* to start, cause; **~se** *vr* to originate; **~io, a** *adj* original; **~io de** native of

orilla [o'riʎa] *nf* (*borde*) border; (*de río*) bank; (*de bosque, tela*) edge; (*de mar*) shore

orina [o'rina] *nf* urine; **orinal** *nm* (chamber) pot; **orinar** *vi* to urinate; **orinarse** *vr* to wet o.s.; **orines** *nmpl* urine

oriundo, a [o'rjundo, a] *adj*: **~ de** native of

ornitología [ornitolo'xia] *nf* ornithology, bird-watching

oro ['oro] *nm* gold; **~s** *nmpl* (*NAIPES*) hearts

oropel [oro'pel] *nm* tinsel

orquesta [or'kesta] *nf* orchestra; **~ de cámara/sinfónica** chamber/symphony orchestra

orquídea [or'kiðea] *nf* orchid

ortiga [or'tiɣa] *nf* nettle

ortodoxo, a [orto'ðokso, a] *adj* orthodox

ortografía [ortoɣra'fia] *nf* spelling

ortopedia [orto'peðja] *nf* orthopaedics *sg*; **ortopédico, a** *adj* orthopaedic

oruga [o'ruɣa] *nf* caterpillar

orzuelo [or'θwelo] *nm* stye

os [os] *pron* (*gen*) you; (*a vosotros*) to you

osa ['osa] *nf* (she-)bear; **O~ Mayor/Menor** Great/Little Bear

osadía [osa'ðia] *nf* daring

osar [o'sar] *vi* to dare

oscilación [osθila'θjon] *nf* (*movimiento*) oscillation; (*fluctuación*) fluctuation

oscilar [osθi'lar] *vi* to oscillate; to fluctuate

oscurecer [oskure'θer] *vt* to darken ♦ *vi* to grow dark; **~se** *vr* to grow o get dark

oscuridad [oskuri'ðað] *nf* obscurity; (*tinieblas*) darkness

oscuro, a [os'kuro, a] *adj* dark; (*fig*) obscure; **a oscuras** in the dark

óseo, a ['oseo, a] *adj* bone *cpd*

oso ['oso] *nm* bear; **~ de peluche** teddy bear; **~ hormiguero** anteater

ostentación [ostenta'θjon] *nf* (*gen*) ostentation; (*acto*) display

ostentar [osten'tar] *vt* (*gen*) to show; (*pey*) to flaunt, show off; (*poseer*) to have, possess

ostra ['ostra] *nf* oyster

OTAN ['otan] *nf abr* (= *Organización del Tratado del Atlántico Norte*) NATO

otear [ote'ar] *vt* to observe; (*fig*) to look into

otitis [o'titis] *nf* earache

otoñal [oto'ɲal] *adj* autumnal

otoño [o'toɲo] *nm* autumn

otorgar [otor'ɣar] *vt* (*conceder*) to concede; (*dar*) to grant

otorrino, a [oto'rrino, a], **otorrinola-ringólogo, a** [otorrinolarin'ɣoloɣo, a] *nm/f* ear, nose and throat specialist

┌─────────────────┐
│ **PALABRA CLAVE** │
└─────────────────┘

otro, a ['otro, a] *adj* **1** (*distinto: sg*) another; (: *pl*) other; **con ~s amigos** with other o different friends
2 (*adicional*): **tráigame ~ café (más), por favor** can I have another coffee please; **~s 10 días más** another ten days
♦ *pron* **1**: **el ~** the other one; **(los) ~s** (the) others; **de ~** somebody else's; **que lo haga ~** let somebody else do it
2 (*recíproco*): **se odian (la) una a (la) otra** they hate one another o each other
3: **~ tanto: comer ~ tanto** to eat the

same *o* as much again; **recibió una
decena de telegramas y otras tantas
llamadas** he got about ten telegrams
and as many calls

---

ovación [oβa'θjon] *nf* ovation

oval [o'βal] *adj* oval; **~ado, a** *adj* oval;
óvalo *nm* oval

ovario [o'βario] *nm* ovary

oveja [o'βexa] *nf* sheep

overol [oβe'rol] (*AM*) *nm* overalls *pl*

ovillo [o'βiʎo] *nm* (*de lana*) ball of wool;
hacerse un ~ to curl up

OVNI ['oβni] *nm abr* (= *objeto volante no
identificado*) UFO

ovulación [oβula'θjon] *nf* ovulation;
óvulo *nm* ovum

oxidación [oksiða'θjon] *nf* rusting

oxidar [oksi'ðar] *vt* to rust; **~se** *vr* to go
rusty

óxido ['oksiðo] *nm* oxide

oxigenado, a [oksixe'naðo, a] *adj* (*QUÍM*)
oxygenated; (*pelo*) bleached

oxígeno [ok'sixeno] *nm* oxygen

oyente [o'jente] *nm/f* listener, hearer

oyes *etc vb ver* **oír**

ozono [o'θono] *nm* ozone

P, p

P *abr* (= *padre*) Fr.

pabellón [paβe'ʎon] *nm* bell tent; (*ARQ*)
pavilion; (*de hospital etc*) block, section;
(*bandera*) flag

pacer [pa'θer] *vi* to graze

paciencia [pa'θjenθja] *nf* patience

paciente [pa'θjente] *adj, nm/f* patient

pacificación [paθifika'θjon] *nf*
pacification

pacificar [paθifi'kar] *vt* to pacify;
(*tranquilizar*) to calm

pacífico, a [pa'θifiko, a] *adj* (*persona*)
peaceable; (*existencia*) peaceful; **el
(océano) P~** the Pacific (Ocean)

pacifismo [paθi'fismo] *nm* pacifism;

pacifista *nm/f* pacifist

pacotilla [pako'tiʎa] *nf*: **de ~** (*actor,
escritor*) third-rate; (*mueble etc*) cheap

pactar [pak'tar] *vt* to agree to *o* on ♦ *vi* to
come to an agreement

pacto ['pakto] *nm* (*tratado*) pact; (*acuerdo*)
agreement

padecer [paðe'θer] *vt* (*sufrir*) to suffer;
(*soportar*) to endure, put up with;
padecimiento *nm* suffering

padrastro [pa'ðrastro] *nm* stepfather

padre ['paðre] *nm* father ♦ *adj* (*fam*): **un
éxito ~** a tremendous success; **~s** *nmpl*
parents

padrino [pa'ðrino] *nm* (*REL*) godfather; (*tb:
~ de boda*) best man; (*fig*) sponsor,
patron; **~s** *nmpl* godparents

padrón [pa'ðron] *nm* (*censo*) census, roll

paella [pa'eʎa] *nf* paella, *dish of rice with
meat, shellfish etc*

paga ['paxa] *nf* (*pago*) payment; (*sueldo*)
pay, wages *pl*

pagano, a [pa'ɣano, a] *adj, nm/f* pagan,
heathen

pagar [pa'ɣar] *vt* to pay; (*las compras,
crimen*) to pay for; (*fig: favor*) to repay
♦ *vi* to pay; **~ al contado/a plazos** to
pay (in) cash/in instalments

pagaré [paɣa're] *nm* I.O.U.

página ['paxina] *nf* page

pago ['paxo] *nm* (*dinero*) payment; **~
anticipado/a cuenta/contra
reembolso/en especie** advance
payment/payment on account/cash on
delivery/payment in kind; **en ~ de** in
return for

pág(s). *abr* (= *página(s)*) p(p).

pague *etc vb ver* **pagar**

país [pa'is] *nm* (*gen*) country; (*región*) land;
los P~es Bajos the Low Countries; **el P~
Vasco** the Basque Country

paisaje [pai'saxe] *nm* landscape, scenery

paisano, a [pai'sano, a] *adj* of the same
country ♦ *nm/f* (*compatriota*) fellow
countryman/woman; **vestir de ~**
(*soldado*) to be in civvies; (*guardia*) to be
in plain clothes

paja ['paxa] *nf* straw; (*fig*) rubbish (*BRIT*), trash (*US*)

pajarita [paxa'rita] *nf* (*corbata*) bow tie

pájaro ['paxaro] *nm* bird; **~ carpintero** woodpecker

pajita [pa'xita] *nf* (drinking) straw

pala ['pala] *nf* spade, shovel; (*raqueta etc*) bat; (: *de tenis*) racquet; (*CULIN*) slice; **~ matamoscas** fly swat

palabra [pa'laßra] *nf* word; (*facultad*) (power of) speech; (*derecho de hablar*) right to speak; **tomar la ~** (*en mitin*) to take the floor

palabrota [pala'brota] *nf* swearword

palacio [pa'laθjo] *nm* palace; (*mansión*) mansion, large house; **~ de justicia** courthouse; **~ municipal** town/city hall

paladar [pala'ðar] *nm* palate; **paladear** *vt* to taste

palanca [pa'lanka] *nf* lever; (*fig*) pull, influence

palangana [palan'gana] *nf* washbasin

palco ['palko] *nm* box

Palestina [pales'tina] *nf* Palestine; **palestino, a** *nm/f* Palestinian

paleta [pa'leta] *nf* (*de pintor*) palette; (*de albañil*) trowel; (*de ping-pong*) bat; (*AM*) ice lolly

paleto, a [pa'leto, a] (*fam*, *pey*) *nm/f* yokel

paliar [pa'ljar] *vt* (*mitigar*) to mitigate, alleviate; **paliativo** *nm* palliative

palidecer [paliðe'θer] *vi* to turn pale; **palidez** *nf* paleness; **pálido, a** *adj* pale

palillo [pa'liʎo] *nm* (*mondadientes*) toothpick; (*para comer*) chopstick

paliza [pa'liθa] *nf* beating, thrashing

palma ['palma] *nf* (*ANAT*) palm; (*árbol*) palm tree; **batir** *o* **dar ~s** to clap, applaud; **~da** *nf* slap; **~das** *nfpl* clapping *sg*, applause *sg*

palmar [pal'mar] (*fam*) *vi* (*tb*: **~la**) to die, kick the bucket

palmear [palme'ar] *vi* to clap

palmera [pal'mera] *nf* (*BOT*) palm tree

palmo ['palmo] *nm* (*medida*) span; (*fig*) small amount; **~ a ~** inch by inch

palo ['palo] *nm* stick; (*poste*) post; (*de

tienda de campaña) pole; (*mango*) handle, shaft; (*golpe*) blow, hit; (*de golf*) club; (*de béisbol*) bat; (*NAUT*) mast; (*NAIPES*) suit

paloma [pa'loma] *nf* dove, pigeon

palomitas [palo'mitas] *nfpl* popcorn *sg*

palpar [pal'par] *vt* to touch, feel

palpitación [palpita'θjon] *nf* palpitation

palpitante [palpi'tante] *adj* palpitating; (*fig*) burning

palpitar [palpi'tar] *vi* to palpitate; (*latir*) to beat

palta ['palta] (*AM*) *nf* avocado (pear)

paludismo [palu'ðismo] *nm* malaria

pamela [pa'mela] *nf* picture hat, sun hat

pampa ['pampa] (*AM*) *nf* pampas, prairie

pan [pan] *nm* bread; (*una barra*) loaf; **~ integral** wholemeal (*BRIT*) *o* wholewheat (*US*) bread; **~ rallado** breadcrumbs *pl*

pana ['pana] *nf* corduroy

panadería [panaðe'ria] *nf* baker's (shop); **panadero, a** *nm/f* baker

Panamá [pana'ma] *nm* Panama; **panameño, a** *adj* Panamanian

pancarta [pan'karta] *nf* placard, banner

panda ['panda] *nm* (*ZOOL*) panda

pandereta [pande'reta] *nf* tambourine

pandilla [pan'diʎa] *nf* set, group; (*de criminales*) gang; (*pey*: *camarilla*) clique

panecillo [pane'θiʎo] *nm* (bread) roll

panel [pa'nel] *nm* panel; **~ solar** solar panel

panfleto [pan'fleto] *nm* pamphlet

pánico ['paniko] *nm* panic

panorama [pano'rama] *nm* panorama; (*vista*) view

pantalla [pan'taʎa] *nf* (*de cine*) screen; (*de lámpara*) lampshade

pantalón [panta'lon] *nm* trousers; **pantalones** *nmpl* trousers

pantano [pan'tano] *nm* (*ciénaga*) marsh, swamp; (*depósito*: *de agua*) reservoir; (*fig*) jam, difficulty

panteón [pante'on] *nm*: **~ familiar** family tomb

pantera [pan'tera] *nf* panther

panti(e)s ['pantis] *nmpl* tights

pantomima [panto'mima] *nf* pantomime

pantorrilla [panto'rriʎa] *nf* calf (of the leg)

pantufla [pan'tufla] *nf* slipper

panty(s) ['panti(s)] *nm(pl)* tights

panza ['panθa] *nf* belly, paunch

pañal [pa'ɲal] *nm* nappy (*BRIT*), diaper (*US*); **~es** *nmpl* (*fig*) early stages, infancy *sg*

paño ['paɲo] *nm* (*tela*) cloth; (*pedazo de tela*) (piece of) cloth; (*trapo*) duster, rag; **~ higiénico** sanitary towel; **~s menores** underclothes

pañuelo [pa'ɲwelo] *nm* handkerchief, hanky (*fam*); (*para la cabeza*) (head)scarf

papa ['papa] *nm*: **el P~** the Pope ♦ *nf* (*AM*) potato

papá [pa'pa] (*pl* **~s**) (*fam*) *nm* dad(dy), pa (*US*)

papada [pa'paða] *nf* double chin

papagayo [papa'ɣajo] *nm* parrot

papanatas [papa'natas] (*fam*) *nm inv* simpleton

paparrucha [papa'rrutʃa] *nf* piece of nonsense

papaya [pa'paja] *nf* papaya

papear [pape'ar] (*fam*) *vt*, *vi* to scoff

papel [pa'pel] *nm* paper; (*hoja de ~*) sheet of paper; (*TEATRO*, *fig*) role; **~ de calco/carbón/de cartas** tracing paper/carbon paper/stationery; **~ de envolver/pintado** wrapping paper/wallpaper; **~ de aluminio/higiénico** aluminium (*BRIT*) *o* aluminum (*US*) foil/toilet paper; **~ de estaño** *o* **plata** tinfoil; **~ de lija** sandpaper; **~ moneda** paper money; **~ secante** blotting paper

papeleo [pape'leo] *nm* red tape

papelera [pape'lera] *nf* wastepaper basket; (*en la calle*) litter bin

papelería [papele'ria] *nf* stationer's (shop)

papeleta [pape'leta] *nf* (*POL*) ballot paper; (*ESCOL*) report

paperas [pa'peras] *nfpl* mumps *sg*

papilla [pa'piʎa] *nf* (*para niños*) baby food

paquete [pa'kete] *nm* (*de cigarrillos etc*) packet; (*CORREOS etc*) parcel; (*AM*) package tour; (: *fam*) nuisance

par [par] *adj* (*igual*) like, equal; (*MAT*) even ♦ *nm* equal; (*de guantes*) pair; (*de veces*) couple; (*POL*) peer; (*GOLF*, *COM*) par; **abrir de ~ en ~** to open wide

para ['para] *prep* for; **no es ~ comer** it's not for eating; **decir ~ sí** to say to o.s.; **¿~ qué lo quieres?** what do you want it for?; **se casaron ~ separarse otra vez** they married only to separate again; **lo tendré ~ mañana** I'll have it (for) tomorrow; **ir ~ casa** to go home, head for home; **~ profesor es muy estúpido** he's very stupid for a teacher; **¿quién es usted ~ gritar así?** who are you to shout like that?; **tengo bastante ~ vivir** I have enough to live on; *ver tb* **con**

parabién [para'βjen] *nm* congratulations *pl*

parábola [pa'raβola] *nf* parable; (*MAT*) parabola; **parabólica** *nf* (*tb*: **antena ~**) satellite dish

parabrisas [para'βrisas] *nm inv* windscreen (*BRIT*), windshield (*US*)

paracaídas [paraka'iðas] *nm inv* parachute; **paracaidista** *nm/f* parachutist; (*MIL*) paratrooper

parachoques [para'tʃokes] *nm inv* (*AUTO*) bumper; (*MECÁNICA etc*) shock absorber

parada [pa'raða] *nf* stop; (*acto*) stopping; (*de industria*) shutdown, stoppage; (*lugar*) stopping place; **~ de autobús** bus stop

paradero [para'ðero] *nm* stopping-place; (*situación*) whereabouts

parado, a [pa'raðo, a] *adj* (*persona*) motionless, standing still; (*fábrica*) closed, at a standstill; (*coche*) stopped; (*AM*) standing (up); (*sin empleo*) unemployed, idle

paradoja [para'ðoxa] *nf* paradox

parador [para'ðor] *nm* parador, state-run hotel

paráfrasis [pa'rafrasis] *nf inv* paraphrase

paraguas [pa'raɣwas] *nm inv* umbrella

Paraguay [para'ɣwai] *nm*: **el ~** Paraguay; **paraguayo, a** *adj*, *nm/f* Paraguayan

paraíso [para'iso] *nm* paradise, heaven

paraje [pa'raxe] *nm* place, spot

paralelo, a [para'lelo, a] *adj* parallel

parálisis [pa'ralisis] *nf inv* paralysis; **paralítico, a** *adj, nm/f* paralytic

paralizar [parali'θar] *vt* to paralyse; **~se** *vr* to become paralysed; (*fig*) to come to a standstill

paramilitar [paramili'tar] *adj* paramilitary

páramo ['paramo] *nm* bleak plateau

parangón [paran'gon] *nm*: **sin ~** incomparable

paranoico, a [para'noiko, a] *nm/f* paranoiac

parapente [para'pente] *nm* (*deporte*) paragliding; (*aparato*) paraglider

parapléjico, a [para'plexiko, a] *adj, nm/f* paraplegic

parar [pa'rar] *vt* to stop; (*golpe*) to ward off ♦ *vi* to stop; **~se** *vr* to stop; (*AM*) to stand up; **ha parado de llover** it has stopped raining; **van a ir a ~ a comisaría** they're going to end up in the police station; **~se en** to pay attention to

pararrayos [para'rrajos] *nm inv* lightning conductor

parásito, a [pa'rasito, a] *nm/f* parasite

parcela [par'θela] *nf* plot, piece of ground

parche ['partʃe] *nm* (*gen*) patch

parchís [par'tʃis] *nm* ludo

parcial [par'θjal] *adj* (*pago*) part-; (*eclipse*) partial; (*JUR*) prejudiced, biased; (*POL*) partisan; **~idad** *nf* prejudice, bias

pardillo, a [par'ðiʎo, a] (*pey*) *adj* yokel

parecer [pare'θer] *nm* (*opinión*) opinion, view; (*aspecto*) looks *pl* ♦ *vi* (*tener apariencia*) to seem, look; (*asemejarse*) to look *o* seem like; (*aparecer, llegar*) to appear; **~se** *vr* to look alike, resemble each other; **~se a** to look like, resemble; **según parece** evidently, apparently; **me parece que** I think (that), it seems to me that

parecido, a [pare'θiðo, a] *adj* similar ♦ *nm* similarity, likeness, resemblance; **bien ~** good-looking, nice-looking

pared [pa'reð] *nf* wall

pareja [pa'rexa] *nf* (*par*) pair; (*dos personas*) couple; (*otro: de un par*) other

one (of a pair); (*persona*) partner

parentela [paren'tela] *nf* relations *pl*

parentesco [paren'tesko] *nm* relationship

paréntesis [pa'rentesis] *nm inv* parenthesis; (*en escrito*) bracket

parezco *etc vb ver* **parecer**

pariente, a [pa'rjente, a] *nm/f* relative, relation

parir [pa'rir] *vt* to give birth to ♦ *vi* (*mujer*) to give birth, have a baby

París [pa'ris] *n* Paris

parking ['parkin] *nm* car park (*BRIT*), parking lot (*US*)

parlamentar [parlamen'tar] *vi* to parley

parlamentario, a [parlamen'tarjo, a] *adj* parliamentary ♦ *nm/f* member of parliament

parlamento [parla'mento] *nm* parliament

parlanchín, ina [parlan'tʃin, ina] *adj* indiscreet ♦ *nm/f* chatterbox

parlar [par'lar] *vi* to chatter (away)

paro ['paro] *nm* (*huelga*) stoppage (of work), strike; (*desempleo*) unemployment; **subsidio de ~** unemployment benefit

parodia [pa'roðja] *nf* parody; **parodiar** *vt* to parody

parpadear [parpaðe'ar] *vi* (*ojos*) to blink; (*luz*) to flicker

párpado ['parpaðo] *nm* eyelid

parque ['parke] *nm* (*lugar verde*) park; **~ de atracciones/infantil/zoológico** fairground/playground/zoo

parqué [par'ke] *nm* parquet (flooring)

parquímetro [par'kimetro] *nm* parking meter

parra ['parra] *nf* (*grape*)vine

párrafo ['parrafo] *nm* paragraph; **echar un ~** (*fam*) to have a chat

parranda [pa'rranda] (*fam*) *nf* spree, binge

parrilla [pa'rriʎa] *nf* (*CULIN*) grill; (*de coche*) grille; **(carne a la) ~** barbecue; **~da** *nf* barbecue

párroco ['parroko] *nm* parish priest

parroquia [pa'rrokja] *nf* parish; (*iglesia*) parish church; (*COM*) clientele, customers *pl*; **~no, a** *nm/f* parishioner; client, customer

parsimonia [parsi'monja] *nf* calmness, level-headedness

parte ['parte] *nm* message; (*informe*) report ♦ *nf* part; (*lado, cara*) side; (*de reparto*) share; (*JUR*) party; **en alguna ~ de Europa** somewhere in Europe; **en/por todas ~s** everywhere; **en gran ~** to a large extent; **la mayor ~ de los españoles** most Spaniards; **de un tiempo a esta ~** for some time past; **de ~ de alguien** on sb's behalf; **¿de ~ de quién?** (*TEL*) who is speaking?; **por ~ de** on the part of; **yo por mi ~** I for my part; **por otra ~** on the other hand; **dar ~ to** inform; **tomar ~** to take part

partición [parti'θjon] *nf* division, sharing-out; (*POL*) partition

participación [partiθipa'θjon] *nf* (*acto*) participation, taking part; (*parte, COM*) share; (*de lotería*) shared prize; (*aviso*) notice, notification

participante [partiθi'pante] *nm/f* participant

participar [partiθi'par] *vt* to notify, inform ♦ *vi* to take part, participate

partícipe [par'tiθipe] *nm/f* participant

particular [partiku'lar] *adj* (*especial*) particular, special; (*individual, personal*) private, personal ♦ *nm* (*punto, asunto*) particular, point; (*individuo*) individual; **tiene coche ~** he has a car of his own

partida [par'tiða] *nf* (*salida*) departure; (*COM*) entry, item; (*juego*) game; (*grupo de personas*) band, group; **mala ~** dirty trick; **~ de nacimiento / matrimonio / defunción** birth/marriage/death certificate

partidario, a [parti'ðarjo, a] *adj* partisan ♦ *nm/f* supporter, follower

partido [par'tiðo] *nm* (*POL*) party; (*DEPORTE*) game, match; **sacar ~ de** to profit *o* benefit from; **tomar ~** to take sides

partir [par'tir] *vt* (*dividir*) to split, divide; (*compartir, distribuir*) to share (out), distribute; (*romper*) to break open, split open; (*rebanada*) to cut (off) ♦ *vi* (*ponerse*

en camino) to set off *o* out; (*comenzar*) to start (off *o* out); **~se** *vr* to crack *o* split *o* break (in two *etc*); **a ~ de** (starting) from

partitura [parti'tura] *nf* (*MUS*) score

parto ['parto] *nm* birth; (*fig*) product, creation; **estar de ~** to be in labour

pasa ['pasa] *nf* raisin; **~ de Corinto / de Esmirna** currant/sultana

pasada [pa'saða] *nf* passing, passage; **de ~** in passing, incidentally; **una mala ~** a dirty trick

pasadizo [pasa'ðiθo] *nm* (*pasillo*) passage, corridor; (*callejuela*) alley

pasado, a [pa'saðo, a] *adj* past; (*malo: comida, fruta*) bad; (*muy cocido*) overdone; (*anticuado*) out of date ♦ *nm* past; **~ mañana** the day after tomorrow; **el mes ~** last month

pasador [pasa'ðor] *nm* (*cerrojo*) bolt; (*de pelo*) hair slide; (*horquilla*) grip

pasaje [pa'saxe] *nm* passage; (*pago de viaje*) fare; (*los pasajeros*) passengers *pl*; (*pasillo*) passageway

pasajero, a [pasa'xero, a] *adj* passing; (*situación, estado*) temporary; (*amor, enfermedad*) brief ♦ *nm/f* passenger

pasamontañas [pasamon'tañas] *nm inv* balaclava helmet

pasaporte [pasa'porte] *nm* passport

pasar [pa'sar] *vt* to pass; (*tiempo*) to spend; (*desgracias*) to suffer, endure; (*noticia*) to give, pass on; (*río*) to cross; (*barrera*) to pass through; (*falta*) to overlook, tolerate; (*contrincante*) to surpass, do better than; (*coche*) to overtake; (*CINE*) to show; (*enfermedad*) to give, infect with ♦ *vi* (*gen*) to pass; (*terminarse*) to be over; (*ocurrir*) to happen; **~se** *vr* (*flores*) to fade; (*comida*) to go bad *o* off; (*fig*) to overdo it, go too far; **~ de** to go beyond, exceed; **~ por** (*AM*) to fetch; **~lo bien/mal** to have a good/bad time; **¡pasa!** come in!; **hacer** to show in; **~se al enemigo** to go over to the enemy; **se me pasó** I forgot; **no se le pasa nada** he misses nothing; **pa lo que pase** come what may; **¿qué**

pasa? what's going on?, what's up?;
¿qué te pasa? what's wrong?

pasarela [pasaˈrela] *nf* footbridge; (*en
barco*) gangway

pasatiempo [pasaˈtjempo] *nm* pastime,
hobby

Pascua [ˈpaskwa] *nf*: **~ (de Resurrección)**
Easter; **~ de Navidad** Christmas; **~s** *nfpl*
Christmas (time); **¡felices ~s!** Merry
Christmas!

pase [ˈpase] *nm* pass; (*CINE*) performance,
showing

pasear [paseˈar] *vt* to take for a walk;
(*exhibir*) to parade, show off ♦ *vi* to walk,
go for a walk; **~se** *vr* to walk, go for a
walk; **~ en coche** to go for a drive;
paseo *nm* (*avenida*) avenue; (*distancia
corta*) walk, stroll; **dar un** *o* **ir de paseo**
to go for a walk

pasillo [paˈsiʎo] *nm* passage, corridor

pasión [paˈsjon] *nf* passion

pasivo, a [paˈsiβo, a] *adj* passive;
(*inactivo*) inactive ♦ *nm* (*COM*) liabilities
pl, debts *pl*

pasmar [pasˈmar] *vt* (*asombrar*) to amaze,
astonish; **pasmo** *nm* amazement,
astonishment; (*resfriado*) chill; (*fig*)
wonder, marvel; **pasmoso, a** *adj*
amazing, astonishing

paso, a [ˈpaso, a] *adj* dried ♦ *nm* step;
(*modo de andar*) walk; (*huella*) footprint;
(*rapidez*) speed, pace, rate; (*camino
accesible*) way through, passage; (*cruce*)
crossing; (*pasaje*) passing, passage; (*GEO*)
pass; (*estrecho*) strait; **~ a nivel** (*FERRO*)
level-crossing; **~ de peatones** pedestrian
crossing; **a ese ~** (*fig*) at that rate; **salir
al ~ de** *o* **a** to waylay; **estar de ~** to be
passing through; **~ elevado** flyover;
prohibido el ~ no entry; **ceda el ~** give
way

pasota [paˈsota] (*fam*) *adj, nm/f*
≈ dropout; **ser un (tipo) ~** to be a bit of
a dropout; (*ser indiferente*) not to care
about anything

pasta [ˈpasta] *nf* paste; (*CULIN: masa*)
dough; (: *de bizcochos etc*) pastry; (*fam*)

dough; **~s** *nfpl* (*bizcochos*) pastries, small
cakes; (*fideos, espaguetis etc*) pasta; **~ de
dientes** *o* **dentífrica** toothpaste

pastar [pasˈtar] *vt, vi* to graze

pastel [pasˈtel] *nm* (*dulce*) cake; (*ARTE*)
pastel; **~ de carne** meat pie; **~ería** *nf*
cake shop

pasteurizado, a [pasteuriˈθaðo, a] *adj*
pasteurized

pastilla [pasˈtiʎa] *nf* (*de jabón, chocolate*)
bar; (*píldora*) tablet, pill

pasto [ˈpasto] *nm* (*hierba*) grass; (*lugar*)
pasture, field

pastor, a [pasˈtor, a] *nm/f* shepherd/ess
♦ *nm* (*REL*) clergyman, pastor; **~ alemán**
Alsatian

pata [ˈpata] *nf* (*pierna*) leg; (*pie*) foot; (*de
muebles*) leg; **~s arriba** upside down;
metedura de ~ (*fam*) gaffe; **meter la ~**
(*fam*) to put one's foot in it; (*TEC*): **~ de
cabra** crowbar; **tener buena/mala ~** to
be lucky/unlucky; **~da** *nf* kick; (*en el
suelo*) stamp

patalear [patalaˈar] *vi* (*en el suelo*) to
stamp one's feet

patata [paˈtata] *nf* potato; **~s fritas** chips,
French fries; (*de bolsa*) crisps

paté [paˈte] *nm* pâté

patear [pateˈar] *vt* (*pisar*) to stamp on,
trample (on); (*pegar con el pie*) to kick
♦ *vi* to stamp (with rage), stamp one's
feet

patentar [patenˈtar] *vt* to patent

patente [paˈtente] *adj* obvious, evident;
(*COM*) patent ♦ *nf* patent

paternal [paterˈnal] *adj* fatherly, paternal;
paterno, a *adj* paternal

patético, a [paˈtetiko, a] *adj* pathetic,
moving

patilla [paˈtiʎa] *nf* (*de gafas*) side(piece);
~s *nfpl* sideburns

patín [paˈtin] *nm* skate; (*de trineo*) runner;
patinaje *nm* skating; **patinar** *vi* to
skate; (*resbalarse*) to skid, slip; (*fam*) to
slip up, blunder

patio [ˈpatjo] *nm* (*de casa*) patio,
courtyard; **~ de recreo** playground

pato ['pato] *nm* duck; **pagar el ~** (*fam*) to take the blame, carry the can

patológico, a [pato'loxiko, a] *adj* pathological

patoso, a [pa'toso, a] (*fam*) *adj* clumsy

patraña [pa'traɲa] *nf* story, fib

patria ['patrja] *nf* native land, mother country

patrimonio [patri'monjo] *nm* inheritance; (*fig*) heritage

patriota [pa'trjota] *nm/f* patriot; **patriotismo** *nm* patriotism

patrocinar [patroθi'nar] *vt* to sponsor; **patrocinio** *nm* sponsorship

patrón, ona [pa'tron, ona] *nm/f* (*jefe*) boss, chief, master/mistress; (*propietario*) landlord/lady; (*REL*) patron saint ♦ *nm* (*TEC, COSTURA*) pattern

patronal [patro'nal] *adj*: **la clase ~** management

patronato [patro'nato] *nm* sponsorship; (*acto*) patronage; (*fundación benéfica*) trust, foundation

patrulla [pa'truʎa] *nf* patrol

pausa ['pausa] *nf* pause, break

pausado, a [pau'saðo, a] *adj* slow, deliberate

pauta ['pauta] *nf* line, guide line

pavimento [paβi'mento] *nm* (*con losas*) pavement, paving

pavo ['paβo] *nm* turkey; **~ real** peacock

pavor [pa'βor] *nm* dread, terror

payaso, a [pa'jaso, a] *nm/f* clown

payo, a ['pajo, a] *nm/f* non-gipsy

paz [paθ] *nf* peace; (*tranquilidad*) peacefulness, tranquillity; **hacer las paces** to make peace; (*fig*) to make up

pazo ['paθo] *nm* country house

P.D. *abr* (= *posdata*) P.S., p.s.

peaje [pe'axe] *nm* toll

peatón [pea'ton] *nm* pedestrian

peca ['peka] *nf* freckle

pecado [pe'kaðo] *nm* sin; **pecador, a** *adj* sinful ♦ *nm/f* sinner

pecaminoso, a [pekami'noso, a] *adj* sinful

pecar [pe'kar] *vi* (*REL*) to sin; **peca de generoso** he is generous to a fault

pecera [pe'θera] *nf* fish tank; (*redondo*) goldfish bowl

pecho ['petʃo] *nm* (*ANAT*) chest; (*de mujer*) breast; **dar el ~ a** to breast-feed; **tomar algo a ~** to take sth to heart

pechuga [pe'tʃuɣa] *nf* breast

peculiar [peku'ljar] *adj* special, peculiar; (*característico*) typical, characteristic; **~idad** *nf* peculiarity; special feature, characteristic

pedal [pe'ðal] *nm* pedal; **~ear** *vi* to pedal

pedante [pe'ðante] *adj* pedantic ♦ *nm/f* pedant; **~ría** *nf* pedantry

pedazo [pe'ðaθo] *nm* piece, bit; **hacerse ~s** to smash, shatter

pedernal [peðer'nal] *nm* flint

pediatra [pe'ðjatra] *nm/f* paediatrician

pedido [pe'ðiðo] *nm* (*COM*) order; (*petición*) request

pedir [pe'ðir] *vt* to ask for, request; (*comida, COM: mandar*) to order; (*necesitar*) to need, demand, require ♦ *vi* to ask; **me pidió que cerrara la puerta** he asked me to shut the door; **¿cuánto piden por el coche?** how much are they asking for the car?

pedo ['peðo] (*fam!*) *nm* fart

pega ['peɣa] *nf* snag; **poner ~s (a)** to complain (about)

pegadizo, a [peɣa'ðiθo, a] *adj* (*MUS*) catchy

pegajoso, a [peɣa'xoso, a] *adj* sticky, adhesive

pegamento [peɣa'mento] *nm* gum, glue

pegar [pe'ɣar] *vt* (*papel, sellos*) to stick (on); (*cartel*) to stick up; (*coser*) to sew (on); (*unir: partes*) to join, fix together; (*MED*) to give, infect with; (*dar: golpe*) to give, deal ♦ *vi* (*adherirse*) to stick, adhere; (*ir juntos: colores*) to match, go together; (*golpear*) to hit; (*quemar: el sol*) to strike hot, burn (*fig*); **~se** *vr* (*gen*) to stick; (*dos personas*) to hit each other, fight; (*fam*): **~ un grito** to let out a yell; **~ un salto** to jump (with fright); **~ en** to touch; **~se un tiro** to shoot o.s.

pegatina [pexa'tina] nf sticker

pegote [pe'xote] (fam) nm eyesore, sight

peinado [pei'naðo] nm hairstyle

peinar [pei'nar] vt to comb; (hacer estilo) to style; **~se** vr to comb one's hair

peine ['peine] nm comb; **~ta** nf ornamental comb

p.ej. abr (= por ejemplo) e.g.

Pekín [pe'kin] n Pekin(g)

pelado, a [pe'laðo, a] adj (fruta, patata etc) peeled; (cabeza) shorn; (campo, fig) bare; (fam: sin dinero) broke

pelaje [pe'laxe] nm (ZOOL) fur, coat; (fig) appearance

pelar [pe'lar] vt (fruta, patatas etc) to peel; (cortar el pelo a) to cut the hair of; (quitar la piel: animal) to skin; **~se** vr (la piel) to peel off; **voy a ~me** I'm going to get my hair cut

peldaño [pel'daño] nm step

pelea [pe'lea] nf (lucha) fight; (discusión) quarrel, row

peleado, a [pele'aðo, a] adj: **estar ~ (con uno)** to have fallen out (with sb)

pelear [pele'ar] vi to fight; **~se** vr to fight; (reñirse) to fall out, quarrel

peletería [pelete'ria] nf furrier's, fur shop

pelícano [pe'likano] nm pelican

película [pe'likula] nf film; (cobertura ligera) thin covering; (FOTO: rollo) roll o reel of film

peligro [pe'lixro] nm danger; (riesgo) risk; **correr ~ de** to run the risk of; **~so, a** adj dangerous; risky

pelirrojo, a [peli'rroxo, a] adj red-haired, red-headed ♦ nm/f redhead

pellejo [pe'ʎexo] nm (de animal) skin, hide

pellizcar [peʎiθ'kar] vt to pinch, nip

pelma ['pelma] (fam) nm/f pain (in the neck)

pelmazo [pel'maθo] (fam) nm = **pelma**

pelo ['pelo] nm (cabellos) hair; (de barba, bigote) whisker; (de animal: pellejo) hair, fur, coat; **al ~** just right; **venir al ~** to be exactly what one needs; **un hombre de ~ en pecho** a brave man; **por los ~s** by the skin of one's teeth; **no tener ~s en la**

lengua to be outspoken, not mince words; **tomar el ~ a uno** to pull sb's leg

pelota [pe'lota] nf ball; **en ~** stark naked; **hacer la ~ (a uno)** (fam) to creep (to sb); **~ vasca** pelota

pelotari [pelo'tari] nm pelota player

pelotón [pelo'ton] nm (MIL) squad, detachment

peluca [pe'luka] nf wig

peluche [pe'lutʃe] nm: **oso/muñeco de ~** teddy bear/soft toy

peludo, a [pe'luðo, a] adj hairy, shaggy

peluquería [peluke'ria] nf hairdresser's; **peluquero, a** nm/f hairdresser

pelusa [pe'lusa] nf (BOT) down; (en tela) fluff

pena ['pena] nf (congoja) grief, sadness; (remordimiento) regret; (dificultad) trouble; (dolor) pain; (JUR) sentence; **merecer o valer la ~** to be worthwhile; **a duras ~s** with great difficulty; **~ de muerte** death penalty; **~ pecuniaria** fine; **¡qué ~!** what a shame!

penal [pe'nal] adj penal ♦ nm (cárcel) prison

penalidad [penali'ðað] nf (problema, dificultad) trouble, hardship; (JUR) penalty, punishment; **~es** nfpl trouble, hardship

penalti, penalty [pe'nalti] (pl **~s** o **~es**) nm penalty (kick)

pendiente [pen'djente] adj pending, unsettled ♦ nm earring ♦ nf hill, slope

pene ['pene] nm penis

penetración [penetra'θjon] nf (acto) penetration; (agudeza) sharpness, insight

penetrante [pene'trante] adj (herida) deep; (persona, arma) sharp; (sonido) penetrating, piercing; (mirada) searching; (viento, ironía) biting

penetrar [pene'trar] vt to penetrate, pierce; (entender) to grasp ♦ vi to penetrate, go in; (entrar) to enter, go in; (líquido) to soak in; (fig) to pierce

penicilina [peniθi'lina] nf penicillin

península [pe'ninsula] nf peninsula; **peninsular** adj peninsular

penique [pe'nike] nm penny

penitencia [peni'tenθja] *nf* penance

penoso, a [pe'noso, a] *adj* (*lamentable*) distressing; (*difícil*) arduous, difficult

pensador, a [pensa'ðor, a] *nm/f* thinker

pensamiento [pensa'mjento] *nm* thought; (*mente*) mind; (*idea*) idea

pensar [pen'sar] *vt* to think; (*considerar*) to think over, think out; (*proponerse*) to intend, plan; (*imaginarse*) to think up, invent ♦ *vi* to think; ~ **en** to aim at, aspire to; **pensativo, a** *adj* thoughtful, pensive

pensión [pen'sjon] *nf* (*casa*) boarding *o* guest house; (*dinero*) pension; (*cama y comida*) board and lodging; ~ **completa** full board; **media** ~ half-board; **pensionista** *nm/f* (*jubilado*) (old-age) pensioner; (*huésped*) lodger

penúltimo, a [pe'nultimo, a] *adj* penultimate, last but one

penumbra [pe'numbra] *nf* half-light

penuria [pe'nurja] *nf* shortage, want

peña ['peɲa] *nf* (*roca*) rock; (*cuesta*) cliff, crag; (*grupo*) group, circle; (*AM: club*) folk club

peñasco [pe'ɲasko] *nm* large rock, boulder

peñón [pe'ɲon] *nm* wall of rock; **el P~** the Rock (of Gibraltar)

peón [pe'on] *nm* labourer; (*AM*) farm labourer, farmhand; (*AJEDREZ*) pawn

peonza [pe'onθa] *nf* spinning top

peor [pe'or] *adj* (*comparativo*) worse; (*superlativo*) worst ♦ *adv* worse; worst; **de mal en ~** from bad to worse

pepinillo [pepi'niʎo] *nm* gherkin

pepino [pe'pino] *nm* cucumber; **(no) me importa un ~** I don't care one bit

pepita [pe'pita] *nf* (*BOT*) pip; (*MINERÍA*) nugget

pepito [pe'pito] *nm*: ~ **(de ternera)** steak sandwich

pequeñez [peke'ɲeθ] *nf* smallness, littleness; (*trivialidad*) trifle, triviality

pequeño, a [pe'keɲo, a] *adj* small, little

pera ['pera] *nf* pear; **peral** *nm* pear tree

percance [per'kanθe] *nm* setback, misfortune

percatarse [perka'tarse] *vr*: ~ **de** to notice, take note of

percebe [per'θeße] *nm* barnacle

percepción [perθep'θjon] *nf* (*vista*) perception; (*idea*) notion, idea

percha ['pertʃa] *nf* (coat)hanger; (*ganchos*) coat hooks *pl*; (*de ave*) perch

percibir [perθi'ßir] *vt* to perceive, notice; (*COM*) to earn, get

percusión [perku'sjon] *nf* percussion

perdedor, a [perðe'ðor, a] *adj* losing ♦ *nm/f* loser

perder [per'ðer] *vt* to lose; (*tiempo, palabras*) to waste; (*oportunidad*) to lose, miss; (*tren*) to miss ♦ *vi* to lose; ~**se** *vr* (*extraviarse*) to get lost; (*desaparecer*) to disappear, be lost to view; (*arruinarse*) to be ruined; **echar a ~** (*comida*) to spoil, ruin; (*oportunidad*) to waste

perdición [perði'θjon] *nf* perdition, ruin

pérdida ['perðiða] *nf* loss; (*de tiempo*) waste; ~**s** *nfpl* (*COM*) losses

perdido, a [per'ðiðo, a] *adj* lost

perdiz [per'ðiθ] *nf* partridge

perdón [per'ðon] *nm* (*disculpa*) pardon, forgiveness; (*clemencia*) mercy; **¡~!** sorry!, I beg your pardon!; **perdonar** *vt* to pardon, forgive; (*la vida*) to spare; (*excusar*) to exempt, excuse; **¡perdone (usted)!** sorry!, I beg your pardon!

perdurar [perdu'rar] *vi* (*resistir*) to last, endure; (*seguir existiendo*) to stand, still exist

perecedero, a [pereθe'ðero, a] *adj* perishable

perecer [pere'θer] *vi* to perish, die

peregrinación [perexrina'θjon] *nf* (*REL*) pilgrimage

peregrino, a [pere'xrino, a] *adj* (*idea*) strange, absurd ♦ *nm/f* pilgrim

perejil [pere'xil] *nm* parsley

perenne [pe'renne] *adj* everlasting, perennial

pereza [pe'reθa] *nf* laziness, idleness; **perezoso, a** *adj* lazy, idle

perfección [perfek'θjon] *nf* perfection;

perfeccionar vt to perfect; (mejorar) to improve; (acabar) to complete, finish

perfectamente [perfekta'mente] adv perfectly

perfecto, a [per'fekto, a] adj perfect; (total) complete

perfil [per'fil] nm profile; (contorno) silhouette, outline; (ARQ) (cross) section; **~es** nmpl features; **~ar** vt (trazar) to outline; (fig) to shape, give character to

perforación [perfora'θjon] nf perforation; (con taladro) drilling; **perforadora** nf punch

perforar [perfo'rar] vt to perforate; (agujero) to drill, bore; (papel) to punch a hole in ♦ vi to drill, bore

perfume [per'fume] nm perfume, scent

pericia [pe'riθja] nf skill, expertise

periferia [peri'ferja] nf periphery; (de ciudad) outskirts pl

periférico [peri'feriko] (AM) nm ring road (BRIT), beltway (US)

perímetro [pe'rimetro] nm perimeter

periódico, a [pe'rjoðiko, a] adj periodic(al) ♦ nm newspaper

periodismo [perjo'ðismo] nm journalism; **periodista** nm/f journalist

periodo [pe'rjoðo] nm period

período [pe'rioðo] nm = **periodo**

periquito [peri'kito] nm budgerigar, budgie

perito, a [pe'rito, a] adj (experto) expert; (diestro) skilled, skilful ♦ nm/f expert; skilled worker; (técnico) technician

perjudicar [perxuði'kar] vt (gen) to damage, harm; **perjudicial** adj damaging, harmful; (en detrimento) detrimental; **perjuicio** nm damage, harm

perjurar [perxu'rar] vi to commit perjury

perla ['perla] nf pearl; **me viene de ~s** it suits me fine

permanecer [permane'θer] vi (quedarse) to stay, remain; (seguir) to continue to be

permanencia [perma'nenθja] nf permanence; (estancia) stay

permanente [perma'nente] adj permanent, constant ♦ nf perm

permiso [per'miso] nm permission; (licencia) permit, licence; **con ~** excuse me; **estar de ~** (MIL) to be on leave; **~ de conducir** driving licence (BRIT), driver's license (US)

permitir [permi'tir] vt to permit, allow

pernera [per'nera] nf trouser leg

pernicioso, a [perni'θjoso, a] adj pernicious

pero ['pero] conj but; (aún) yet ♦ nm (defecto) flaw, defect; (reparo) objection

perpendicular [perpendiku'lar] adj perpendicular

perpetrar [perpe'trar] vt to perpetrate

perpetuar [perpe'twar] vt to perpetuate; **perpetuo, a** adj perpetual

perplejo, a [per'plexo, a] adj perplexed, bewildered

perra ['perra] nf (ZOOL) bitch; **estar sin una ~** to be flat broke

perrera [pe'rrera] nf kennel

perrito [pe'rrito] nm: **~ caliente** hot dog

perro ['perro] nm dog

persa ['persa] adj, nm/f Persian

persecución [perseku'θjon] nf pursuit, chase; (REL, POL) persecution

perseguir [perse'xir] vt to pursue, hunt; (cortejar) to chase after; (molestar) to pester, annoy; (REL, POL) to persecute

perseverante [perseβe'rante] adj persevering, persistent

perseverar [perseβe'rar] vi to persevere, persist

persiana [per'sjana] nf (Venetian) blind

persignarse [persix'narse] vr to cross o.s.

persistente [persis'tente] adj persistent

persistir [persis'tir] vi to persist

persona [per'sona] nf person; **~ mayor** elderly person

personaje [perso'naxe] nm important person, celebrity; (TEATRO etc) character

personal [perso'nal] adj (particular) personal; (para una persona) single, for one person ♦ nm personnel, staff; **~idad** nf personality

personarse [perso'narse] vr to appear in

person

personificar [personifiˈkar] *vt* to personify

perspectiva [perspekˈtiβa] *nf* perspective; (*vista, panorama*) view, panorama; (*posibilidad futura*) outlook, prospect

perspicacia [perspiˈkaθja] *nf* discernment, perspicacity

perspicaz [perspiˈkaθ] *adj* shrewd

persuadir [perswaˈðir] *vt* (*gen*) to persuade; (*convencer*) to convince; **~se** *vr* to become convinced; **persuasión** *nf* persuasion; **persuasivo, a** *adj* persuasive; convincing

pertenecer [perteneˈθer] *vi* to belong; (*fig*) to concern; **perteneciente** *adj*: **perteneciente a** belonging to; **pertenencia** *nf* ownership; **pertenencias** *nfpl* (*bienes*) possessions, property *sg*

pertenezca *etc vb ver* **pertenecer**

pértiga [ˈpertiɣa] *nf*: **salto de ~** pole vault

pertinente [pertiˈnente] *adj* relevant, pertinent; (*apropiado*) appropriate; **~ a** concerning, relevant to

perturbación [perturβaˈθjon] *nf* (*POL*) disturbance; (*MED*) upset, disturbance

perturbado, a [perturˈβaðo, a] *adj* mentally unbalanced

perturbar [perturˈβar] *vt* (*el orden*) to disturb; (*MED*) to upset, disturb; (*mentalmente*) to perturb

Perú [peˈru] *nm*: **el ~** Peru; **peruano, a** *adj, nm/f* Peruvian

perversión [perβerˈsjon] *nf* perversion; **perverso, a** *adj* perverse; (*depravado*) depraved

pervertido, a [perβerˈtiðo, a] *adj* perverted ♦ *nm/f* pervert

pervertir [perβerˈtir] *vt* to pervert, corrupt

pesa [ˈpesa] *nf* weight; (*DEPORTE*) shot

pesadez [pesaˈðeθ] *nf* (*peso*) heaviness; (*lentitud*) slowness; (*aburrimiento*) tediousness

pesadilla [pesaˈðiʎa] *nf* nightmare, bad dream

pesado, a [peˈsaðo, a] *adj* heavy; (*lento*) slow; (*difícil, duro*) tough, hard; (*aburrido*) boring, tedious; (*tiempo*) sultry

pésame [ˈpesame] *nm* expression of condolence, message of sympathy; **dar el ~** to express one's condolences

pesar [peˈsar] *vt* to weigh ♦ *vi* to weigh; (*ser pesado*) to weigh a lot, be heavy; (*fig: opinión*) to carry weight; **no pesa mucho** it is not very heavy ♦ *nm* (*arrepentimiento*) regret; (*pena*) grief, sorrow; **a ~ de** *o* **pese a (que)** in spite of, despite

pesca [ˈpeska] *nf* (*acto*) fishing; (*lo pescado*) catch; **ir de ~** to go fishing

pescadería [peskaðeˈria] *nf* fish shop, fishmonger's (*BRIT*)

pescadilla [peskaˈðiʎa] *nf* whiting

pescado [pesˈkaðo] *nm* fish

pescador, a [peskaˈðor, a] *nm/f* fisherman/woman

pescar [pesˈkar] *vt* (*tomar*) to catch; (*intentar tomar*) to fish for; (*conseguir: trabajo*) to manage to get ♦ *vi* to fish, go fishing

pescuezo [pesˈkweθo] *nm* neck

pesebre [peˈseβre] *nm* manger

peseta [peˈseta] *nf* peseta

pesimista [pesiˈmista] *adj* pessimistic ♦ *nm/f* pessimist

pésimo, a [ˈpesimo, a] *adj* awful, dreadful

peso [ˈpeso] *nm* weight; (*balanza*) scales *pl*; (*moneda*) peso; **~ bruto/neto** gross/ net weight; **vender al ~** to sell by weight

pesquero, a [pesˈkero, a] *adj* fishing *cpd*

pesquisa [pesˈkisa] *nf* inquiry, investigation

pestaña [pesˈtaɲa] *nf* (*ANAT*) eyelash; (*borde*) rim; **pestañear** *vi* to blink

peste [ˈpeste] *nf* plague; (*mal olor*) stink, stench

pesticida [pestiˈθiða] *nm* pesticide

pestillo [pesˈtiʎo] *nm* (*cerrojo*) bolt; (*picaporte*) doorhandle

petaca [peˈtaka] *nf* (*de cigarros*) cigarette case; (*de pipa*) tobacco pouch; (*AM: maleta*) suitcase

pétalo [ˈpetalo] *nm* petal

petardo [peˈtardo] *nm* firework, firecracker

petición [peti'θjon] nf (pedido) request, plea; (memorial) petition; (JUR) plea

petrificar [petrifi'kar] vt to petrify

petróleo [pe'troleo] nm oil, petroleum; **petrolero, a** adj petroleum cpd ♦ nm (oil) tanker

peyorativo, a [pejora'tiβo, a] adj pejorative

pez [peθ] nm fish

pezón [pe'θon] nm teat, nipple

pezuña [pe'θuɲa] nf hoof

piadoso, a [pja'ðoso, a] adj (devoto) pious, devout; (misericordioso) kind, merciful

pianista [pja'nista] nm/f pianist

piano ['pjano] nm piano

piar [pjar] vi to cheep

pibe, a ['piße, a] (AM) nm/f boy/girl

picadero [pika'ðero] nm riding school

picadillo [pika'ðiʎo] nm mince, minced meat

picado, a [pi'kaðo, a] adj pricked, punctured; (CULIN) minced, chopped; (mar) choppy; (diente) bad; (tabaco) cut; (enfadado) cross

picador [pika'ðor] nm (TAUR) picador; (minero) faceworker

picadura [pika'ðura] nf (pinchazo) puncture; (de abeja) sting; (de mosquito) bite; (tabaco picado) cut tobacco

picante [pi'kante] adj hot; (comentario) racy, spicy

picaporte [pika'porte] nm (manija) doorhandle; (pestillo) latch

picar [pi'kar] vt (agujerear, perforar) to prick, puncture; (abeja) to sting; (mosquito, serpiente) to bite; (CULIN) to mince, chop; (incitar) to incite, goad; (dañar, irritar) to annoy, bother; (quemar: lengua) to burn, sting ♦ vi (pez) to bite, take the bait; (sol) to burn, scorch; (abeja, MED) to sting; (mosquito) to bite; **~se** (agriarse) to turn sour, go off; (ofenderse) to take offence

picardía [pikar'ðia] nf villainy; (astucia) slyness, craftiness; (una ~) dirty trick; (palabra) rude/bad word o expression

pícaro, a ['pikaro, a] adj (malicioso) villainous; (travieso) mischievous ♦ nm (astuto) crafty sort; (sinvergüenza) rascal, scoundrel

pichón [pi'tʃon] nm young pigeon

pico ['piko] nm (de ave) beak; (punta) sharp point; (TEC) pick, pickaxe; (GEO) peak, summit; **y ~** and a bit

picor [pi'kor] nm itch

picotear [pikote'ar] vt to peck ♦ vi to nibble, pick

picudo, a [pi'kuðo, a] adj pointed, with a point

pidió etc vb ver **pedir**

pido etc vb ver **pedir**

pie [pje] (pl ~s) nm foot; (fig: motivo) motive, basis; (: fundamento) foothold; **ir a ~** to go on foot, walk; **estar de ~** to be standing (up); **ponerse de ~** to stand up; **de ~s a cabeza** from top to bottom; **al ~ de la letra** (citar) literally, verbatim; (copiar) exactly, word for word; **en ~ de guerra** on a war footing; **dar ~ a** to give cause for; **hacer ~** (en el agua) to touch (the) bottom

piedad [pje'ðað] nf (lástima) pity, compassion; (clemencia) mercy; (devoción) piety, devotion

piedra ['pjeðra] nf stone; (roca) rock; (de mechero) flint; (METEOROLOGÍA) hailstone

piel [pjel] nf (ANAT) skin; (ZOOL) skin, hide, fur; (cuero) leather; (BOT) skin, peel

pienso etc vb ver **pensar**

pierdo etc vb ver **perder**

pierna ['pjerna] nf leg

pieza ['pjeθa] nf piece; (habitación) room; **~ de recambio** o **repuesto** spare (part)

pigmeo, a [pix'meo, a] adj, nm/f pigmy

pijama [pi'xama] nm pyjamas pl

pila ['pila] nf (ELEC) battery; (montón) heap, pile; (lavabo) sink

píldora ['pildora] nf pill; **la ~ (anticonceptiva)** the (contraceptive) pill

pileta [pi'leta] nf basin, bowl; (AM) swimming pool

pillaje [pi'ʎaxe] nm pillage, plunder

pillar [pi'ʎar] vt (saquear) to pillage,

plunder; (*fam: coger*) to catch; (: *agarrar*) to grasp, seize; (: *entender*) to grasp, catch on to; **~se** *vr*: **~se un dedo con la puerta** to catch one's finger in the door

pillo, a ['piʎo, a] *adj* villainous; (*astuto*) sly, crafty ♦ *nm/f* rascal, rogue, scoundrel

piloto [pi'loto] *nm* pilot; (*de aparato*) (pilot) light; (*AUTO: luz*) tail *o* rear light; (: *conductor*) driver

pimentón [pimen'ton] *nm* paprika

pimienta [pi'mjenta] *nf* pepper

pimiento [pi'mjento] *nm* pepper, pimiento

pin [pin] (*pl* **pins**) *nm* badge

pinacoteca [pinako'teka] *nf* art gallery

pinar [pi'nar] *nm* pine forest (*BRIT*), pine grove (*US*)

pincel [pin'θel] *nm* paintbrush

pinchadiscos [pintʃa'ðiskos] *nm/f inv* disc-jockey, DJ

pinchar [pin'tʃar] *vt* (*perforar*) to prick, pierce; (*neumático*) to puncture; (*fig*) to prod

pinchazo [pin'tʃaθo] *nm* (*perforación*) prick; (*de neumático*) puncture; (*fig*) prod

pincho ['pintʃo] *nm* savoury (snack); **~ moruno** shish kebab; **~ de tortilla** small slice of omelette

ping-pong ['pin'pon] *nm* table tennis

pingüino [pin'gwino] *nm* penguin

pino ['pino] *nm* pine (tree)

pinta ['pinta] *nf* spot; (*de líquidos*) spot, drop; (*aspecto*) appearance, look(s) (*pl*); **~do, a** *adj* spotted; (*de colores*) colourful; **~das** *nfpl* graffiti *sg*

pintar [pin'tar] *vt* to paint ♦ *vi* to paint; (*fam*) to count, be important; **~se** *vr* to put on make-up

pintor, a [pin'tor, a] *nm/f* painter

pintoresco, a [pinto'resko, a] *adj* picturesque

pintura [pin'tura] *nf* painting; **~ a la acuarela** watercolour; **~ al óleo** oil painting

pinza ['pinθa] *nf* (*ZOOL*) claw; (*para colgar ropa*) clothes peg; (*TEC*) pincers *pl*; **~s** *nfpl* (*para depilar etc*) tweezers *pl*

piña ['pina] *nf* (*fruto del pino*) pine cone; (*fruta*) pineapple; (*fig*) group

piñón [pi'non] *nm* (*fruto*) pine nut; (*TEC*) pinion

pío, a ['pio, a] *adj* (*devoto*) pious, devout; (*misericordioso*) merciful

piojo ['pjoxo] *nm* louse

pionero, a [pjo'nero, a] *adj* pioneering ♦ *nm/f* pioneer

pipa ['pipa] *nf* pipe; **~s** *nfpl* (*BOT*) (edible) sunflower seeds

pipí [pi'pi] (*fam*) *nm*: **hacer ~** to have a wee(-wee) (*BRIT*), have to go (wee-wee) (*US*)

pique ['pike] *nm* (*resentimiento*) pique, resentment; (*rivalidad*) rivalry, competition; **irse a ~** to sink; (*esperanza, familia*) to be ruined

piqueta [pi'keta] *nf* pick(axe)

piquete [pi'kete] *nm* (*MIL*) squad, party; (*de obreros*) picket

pirado, a [pi'raðo, a] (*fam*) *adj* round the bend ♦ *nm/f* nutter

piragua [pi'raɣwa] *nf* canoe; **piragüismo** *nm* canoeing

pirámide [pi'ramiðe] *nf* pyramid

pirata [pi'rata] *adj, nm* pirate ♦ *nm/f*: **~ informático/a** hacker

Pirineo(s) [piri'neo(s)] *nm(pl)* Pyrenees *pl*

pirómano, a [pi'romano, a] *nm/f* (*MED, JUR*) arsonist

piropo [pi'ropo] *nm* compliment, (piece of) flattery

pirueta [pi'rweta] *nf* pirouette

pis [pis] (*fam*) *nm* pee, piss; **hacer ~** to have a pee; (*para niños*) to wee-wee

pisada [pi'saða] *nf* (*paso*) footstep; (*huella*) footprint

pisar [pi'sar] *vt* (*caminar sobre*) to walk on, tread on; (*apretar con el pie*) to press; (*fig*) to trample on, walk all over ♦ *vi* to tread, step, walk

piscina [pis'θina] *nf* swimming pool

Piscis ['pisθis] *nm* Pisces

piso ['piso] *nm* (*suelo, planta*) floor; (*apartamento*) flat (*BRIT*), apartment; **primer ~** (*ESP*) first floor; (*AM*) ground floor

pisotear [pisote'ar] *vt* to trample (on *o* underfoot)

pista ['pista] *nf* track, trail; (*indicio*) clue; ~ **de aterrizaje** runway; ~ **de baile** dance floor; ~ **de hielo** ice rink; ~ **de tenis** tennis court

pistola [pis'tola] *nf* pistol; (*TEC*) spray-gun; **pistolero, a** *nm/f* gunman/woman, gangster

pistón [pis'ton] *nm* (*TEC*) piston; (*MUS*) key

pitar [pi'tar] *vt* (*silbato*) to blow; (*rechiflar*) to whistle at, boo ♦ *vi* to whistle; (*AUTO*) to sound *o* toot one's horn; (*AM*) to smoke

pitillo [pi'tiʎo] *nm* cigarette

pito ['pito] *nm* whistle; (*de coche*) horn

pitón [pi'ton] *nm* (*ZOOL*) python

pitonisa [pito'nisa] *nf* fortune-teller

pitorreo [pito'rreo] *nm* joke; **estar de ~** to be joking

pizarra [pi'θarra] *nf* (*piedra*) slate; (*encerado*) blackboard

pizca ['piθka] *nf* pinch, spot; (*fig*) spot, speck; **ni ~** not a bit

placa ['plaka] *nf* plate; (*distintivo*) badge, insignia; ~ **de matrícula** number plate

placentero, a [plaθen'tero, a] *adj* pleasant, agreeable

placer [pla'θer] *nm* pleasure ♦ *vt* to please

plácido, a ['plaθiðo, a] *adj* placid

plaga ['plaγa] *nf* pest; (*MED*) plague; (*abundancia*) abundance; **plagar** *vt* to infest, plague; (*llenar*) to fill

plagio ['plaxjo] *nm* plagiarism

plan [plan] *nm* (*esquema, proyecto*) plan; (*idea, intento*) idea, intention; **tener ~** (*fam*) to have a date; **tener un ~** (*fam*) to have an affair; **en ~ económico** (*fam*) on the cheap; **vamos en ~ de turismo** we're going as tourists; **si te pones en ese ~** ... if that's your attitude ...

plana ['plana] *nf* sheet (of paper), page; (*TEC*) trowel; **en primera ~** on the front page; ~ **mayor** staff

plancha ['plantʃa] *nf* (*para planchar*) iron; (*rótulo*) plate, sheet; (*NAUT*) gangway; **a la** ~ (*CULIN*) grilled; ~**do** *nm* ironing; **planchar** *vt* to iron ♦ *vi* to do the ironing

planeador [planea'ðor] *nm* glider

planear [plane'ar] *vt* to plan ♦ *vi* to glide

planeta [pla'neta] *nm* planet

planicie [pla'niθje] *nf* plain

planificación [planifika'θjon] *nf* planning; ~ **familiar** family planning

plano, a ['plano, a] *adj* flat, level, even ♦ *nm* (*MAT, TEC*) plane; (*FOTO*) shot; (*ARQ*) plan; (*GEO*) map; (*de ciudad*) map, street plan; **primer ~** close-up; **caer de ~** to fall flat

planta ['planta] *nf* (*BOT, TEC*) plant; (*ANAT*) sole of the foot, foot; (*piso*) floor; (*AM: personal*) staff; ~ **baja** ground floor

plantación [planta'θjon] *nf* (*AGR*) plantation; (*acto*) planting

plantar [plan'tar] *vt* (*BOT*) to plant; (*levantar*) to erect, set up; ~**se** *vr* to stand firm; ~ **a uno en la calle** to throw sb out; **dejar plantado a uno** (*fam*) to stand sb up

plantear [plante'ar] *vt* (*problema*) to pose; (*dificultad*) to raise

plantilla [plan'tiʎa] *nf* (*de zapato*) insole; (*personal*) personnel; **ser de ~** to be on the staff

plantón [plan'ton] *nm* (*MIL*) guard, sentry; (*fam*) long wait; **dar (un) ~ a uno** to stand sb up

plasmar [plas'mar] *vt* (*dar forma*) to mould, shape; (*representar*) to represent; ~**se** *vr*: ~**se en** to take the form of

plasta ['plasta] (*fam*) *adj inv* boring ♦ *nm/f* bore

plástico, a ['plastiko, a] *adj* plastic ♦ *nm* plastic

Plastilina ® [plasti'lina] *nf* Plasticine ®

plata ['plata] *nf* (*metal*) silver; (*cosas hechas de* ~) silverware; (*AM*) cash, dough; **hablar en ~** to speak bluntly *o* frankly

plataforma [plata'forma] *nf* platform; ~ **de lanzamiento/perforación** launch(ing) pad/drilling rig

plátano ['platano] *nm* (*fruta*) banana;

(*árbol*) plane tree; banana tree

platea [pla'tea] *nf* (*TEATRO*) pit

plateado, a [plate'aðo, a] *adj* silver; (*TEC*) silver-plated

plática ['platika] *nf* talk, chat; **platicar** *vi* to talk, chat

platillo [pla'tiʎo] *nm* saucer; ~**s** *nmpl* (*MUS*) cymbals; ~ **volador** *o* **volante** flying saucer

platino [pla'tino] *nm* platinum; ~**s** *nmpl* (*AUTO*) contact points

plato ['plato] *nm* plate, dish; (*parte de comida*) course; (*comida*) dish; ~ **combinado** set main course (*served on one plate*); ~ **fuerte** main course; **primer** ~ first course

playa ['plaja] *nf* beach; (*costa*) seaside; ~ **de estacionamiento** (*AM*) car park

playera [pla'jera] *nf* (*AM: camiseta*) T-shirt; ~**s** *nfpl* (*zapatos*) canvas shoes

plaza ['plaθa] *nf* square; (*mercado*) market(place); (*sitio*) room, space; (*en vehículo*) seat, place; (*colocación*) post, job; ~ **de toros** bullring

plazo ['plaθo] *nm* (*lapso de tiempo*) time, period; (*fecha de vencimiento*) expiry date; (*pago parcial*) instalment; **a corto/largo** ~ short-/long-term; **comprar algo a** ~**s** to buy sth on hire purchase (*BRIT*) *o* on time (*US*)

plazoleta [plaθo'leta] *nf* small square

pleamar [plea'mar] *nf* high tide

plebe ['pleβe] *nf*: **la** ~ the common people *pl*, the masses *pl*; (*pey*) the plebs *pl*; ~**yo, a** *nf* plebeian; (*pey*) coarse, common

plebiscito [pleβis'θito] *nm* plebiscite

plegable [ple'βaβle] *adj* collapsible; (*silla*) folding

plegar [ple'var] *vt* (*doblar*) to fold, bend; (*COSTURA*) to pleat; ~**se** *vr* to yield, submit

pleito ['pleito] *nm* (*JUR*) lawsuit, case; (*fig*) dispute, feud

plenilunio [pleni'lunjo] *nm* full moon

plenitud [pleni'tuð] *nf* plenitude, fullness; (*abundancia*) abundance

pleno, a ['pleno, a] *adj* full; (*completo*) complete ♦ *nm* plenum; **en** ~ **día** in broad daylight; **en** ~ **verano** at the height of summer; **en plena cara** full in the face

pliego *etc* ['pljexo] *vb ver* **plegar** ♦ *nm* (*hoja*) sheet (of paper); (*carta*) sealed letter/document; ~ **de condiciones** details *pl*, specifications *pl*

pliegue *etc* ['pljexe] *vb ver* **plegar** ♦ *nm* fold, crease; (*de vestido*) pleat

plomero [plo'mero] *nm* (*AM*) plumber

plomo ['plomo] *nm* (*metal*) lead; (*ELEC*) fuse; **sin** ~ unleaded

pluma ['pluma] *nf* feather; (*para escribir*): ~ (**estilográfica**) ink pen; ~ **fuente** (*AM*) fountain pen

plumero [plu'mero] *nm* (*para el polvo*) feather duster

plumón [plu'mon] *nm* (*de ave*) down; (*AM: fino*) felt-tip pen; (: *ancho*) marker

plural [plu'ral] *adj* plural; ~**idad** *nf* plurality

pluriempleo [pluriem'pleo] *nm* having more than one job

plus [plus] *nm* bonus; ~**valía** *nf* (*COM*) appreciation

población [poβla'θjon] *nf* population; (*pueblo, ciudad*) town, city

poblado, a [po'βlaðo, a] *adj* inhabited ♦ *nm* (*aldea*) village; (*pueblo*) (small) town; **densamente** ~ densely populated

poblador, a [poβla'ðor, a] *nm/f* settler, colonist

poblar [po'βlar] *vt* (*colonizar*) to colonize; (*fundar*) to found; (*habitar*) to inhabit

pobre ['poβre] *adj* poor ♦ *nm/f* poor person; ~**za** *nf* poverty

pocilga [po'θilva] *nf* pigsty

pócima ['poθima] *nf* potion

PALABRA CLAVE

poco, a ['poko, a] *adj* **1** (*sg*) little, not much; ~ **tiempo** little *o* not much time; **de** ~ **interés** of little interest, not very interesting; **poca cosa** not much

2 (*pl*) few, not many; **unos** ~**s** a few, some; ~**s niños comen lo que les**

conviene few children eat what they should
♦ *adv* **1** little, not much; **cuesta ~** it doesn't cost much
2 (+*adj*: *= negativo, antónimo*): **~ amable/inteligente** not very nice/intelligent
3: por ~ me caigo I almost fell
4: a ~: a ~ de haberse casado shortly after getting married
5: ~ a ~ little by little
♦ *nm* a little, a bit; **un ~ triste/de dinero** a little sad/money

podar [po'ðar] *vt* to prune

PALABRA CLAVE

poder [po'ðer] *vi* **1** (*capacidad*) can, be able to; **no puedo hacerlo** I can't do it, I'm unable to do it
2 (*permiso*) can, may, be allowed to; **¿se puede?** may I (*o* we)?; **puedes irte ahora** you may go now; **no se puede fumar en este hospital** smoking is not allowed in this hospital
3 (*posibilidad*) may, might, could; **puede llegar mañana** he may *o* might arrive tomorrow; **pudiste haberte hecho daño** you might *o* could have hurt yourself; **¡podías habérmelo dicho antes!** you might have told me before!
4: puede ser: puede ser perhaps; **puede ser que lo sepa Tomás** Tomás may *o* might know
5: ¡no puedo más! I've had enough!; **no pude menos que dejarlo** I couldn't help but leave it; **es tonto a más no ~** he's as stupid as they come
6: ~ con: no puedo con este crío this kid's too much for me
♦ *nm* power; **~ adquisitivo** purchasing power; **detentar** *o* **ocupar** *o* **estar en el ~** to be in power

poderoso, a [poðe'roso, a] *adj* (*político, país*) powerful
podio ['poðjo] *nm* (*DEPORTE*) podium

podium ['poðjum] = **podio**
podrido, a [po'ðriðo, a] *adj* rotten, bad; (*fig*) rotten, corrupt
podrir [po'ðrir] = **pudrir**
poema [po'ema] *nm* poem
poesía [poe'sia] *nf* poetry
poeta [po'eta] *nm/f* poet; **poético, a** *adj* poetic(al)
poetisa [poe'tisa] *nf* (woman) poet
póker ['poker] *nm* poker
polaco, a [po'lako, a] *adj* Polish ♦ *nm/f* Pole
polar [po'lar] *adj* polar; **~idad** *nf* polarity; **~izarse** *vr* to polarize
polea [po'lea] *nf* pulley
polémica [po'lemika] *nf* polemics *sg*; (*una ~*) controversy, polemic
polen ['polen] *nm* pollen
policía [poli'θia] *nm/f* policeman/woman
♦ *nf* police; **~co, a** *adj* police *cpd*; **novela policíaca** detective story; **policial** *adj* police *cpd*
polideportivo [poliðepor'tiβo] *nm* sports centre *o* complex
poligamia [poli'ɣamja] *nf* polygamy
polígono [po'liɣono] *nm* (*MAT*) polygon; **~ industrial** industrial estate
polilla [po'liʎa] *nf* moth
polio ['poljo] *nf* polio
política [po'litika] *nf* politics *sg*; (*económica, agraria etc*) policy; *ver tb* **político**
político, a [po'litiko, a] *adj* political; (*discreto*) tactful; (*de familia*) -in-law
♦ *nm/f* politician; **padre ~** father-in-law
póliza ['poliθa] *nf* certificate, voucher; (*impuesto*) tax stamp; **~ de seguros** insurance policy
polizón [poli'θon] *nm* stowaway
pollera [po'ʎera] (*AM*) *nf* skirt
pollería [poʎe'ria] *nf* poulterer's (shop)
pollo ['poʎo] *nm* chicken
polo ['polo] *nm* (*GEO, ELEC*) pole; (*helado*) ice lolly; (*DEPORTE*) polo; (*suéter*) polo-neck; **~ Norte/Sur** North/South Pole
Polonia [po'lonja] *nf* Poland
poltrona [pol'trona] *nf* easy chair

polución [polu'θjon] *nf* pollution

polvera [pol'ßera] *nf* powder compact

polvo ['polßo] *nm* dust; (*QUÍM, CULIN, MED*) powder; **~s** *nmpl* (*maquillaje*) powder *sg*; **quitar el ~** to dust; **~ de talco** talcum powder; **estar hecho ~** (*fam*) to be worn out *o* exhausted

pólvora ['polßora] *nf* gunpowder; (*fuegos artificiales*) fireworks *pl*

polvoriento, a [polßo'rjento, a] *adj* (*superficie*) dusty; (*sustancia*) powdery

pomada [po'maða] *nf* cream, ointment

pomelo [po'melo] *nm* grapefruit

pómez ['pomeθ] *nf*: **piedra ~** pumice stone

pomo ['pomo] *nm* doorknob

pompa ['pompa] *nf* (*burbuja*) bubble; (*bomba*) pump; (*esplendor*) pomp, splendour; **pomposo, a** *adj* splendid, magnificent; (*pey*) pompous

pómulo ['pomulo] *nm* cheekbone

pon [pon] *vb ver* **poner**

ponche ['pontʃe] *nm* punch

poncho ['pontʃo] *nm* poncho

ponderar [ponde'rar] *vt* (*considerar*) to weigh up, consider; (*elogiar*) to praise highly, speak in praise of

pondré *etc vb ver* **poner**

PALABRA CLAVE

poner [po'ner] *vt* 1 (*colocar*) to put; (*telegrama*) to send; (*obra de teatro*) to put on; (*película*) to show; **ponlo más fuerte** turn it up; **¿qué ponen en el Excelsior?** what's on at the Excelsior?

2 (*tienda*) to open; (*instalar: gas etc*) to put in; (*radio, TV*) to switch *o* turn on

3 (*suponer*): **pongamos que ...** let's suppose that ...

4 (*contribuir*): **el gobierno ha puesto otro millón** the government has contributed another million

5 (*TELEC*): **póngame con el Sr. López** can you put me through to Mr. López?

6: **~ de**: **le han puesto de director general** they've appointed him general manager

7 (*+adj*) to make; **me estás poniendo nerviosa** you're making me nervous

8 (*dar nombre*): **al hijo le pusieron Diego** they called their son Diego

♦ *vi* (*gallina*) to lay

♦ **~se** *vr* 1 (*colocarse*): **se puso a mi lado** he came and stood beside me; **tú ponte en esa silla** you go and sit on that chair

2 (*vestido, cosméticos*) to put on; **¿por qué no te pones el vestido nuevo?** why don't you put on *o* wear your new dress?

3 (*+adj*) to get, become; **se puso muy serio** he got very serious; **después de lavarla la tela se puso azul** after washing it the material turned blue

4: **~se a**: **se puso a llorar** he started to cry; **tienes que ~te a estudiar** you must get down to studying

5: **~se a bien con uno** to make it up with sb; **~se a mal con uno** to get on the wrong side of sb

---

pongo *etc vb ver* **poner**

poniente [po'njente] *nm* (*occidente*) west; (*viento*) west wind

pontífice [pon'tifiθe] *nm* pope, pontiff

popa ['popa] *nf* stern

popular [popu'lar] *adj* popular; (*cultura*) of the people, folk *cpd*; **~idad** *nf* popularity; **~izarse** *vr* to become popular

---

PALABRA CLAVE

por [por] *prep* 1 (*objetivo*) for; **luchar ~ la patria** to fight for one's country

2 (*+infin*): **~ no llegar tarde** so as not to arrive late; **~ citar unos ejemplos** to give a few examples

3 (*causa*) out of, because of; **~ escasez de fondos** through *o* for lack of funds

4 (*tiempo*): **~ la mañana/noche** in the morning/at night; **se queda ~ una semana** she's staying for a week

5 (*lugar*): **pasar ~ Madrid** to pass through Madrid; **ir a Guayaquil ~ Quito** to go to Guayaquil via Quito; **caminar ~ la calle** to walk along the street; *ver tb*

todo

6 (*cambio, precio*): **te doy uno nuevo ~ el que tienes** I'll give you a new one (in return) for the one you've got

7 (*valor distributivo*): **550 pesetas ~ hora/cabeza** 550 pesetas an *o* per hour/a *o* per head

8 (*modo, medio*) by; **~ correo/avión** by post/air; **día ~ día** day by day; **entrar ~ la entrada principal** to go in through the main entrance

9: ~ 10 son 100 10 times 10 is 100

10 (*en lugar de*): **vino él ~ su jefe** he came instead of his boss

11: ~ mí que revienten as far as I'm concerned they can drop dead

12: ¿~ qué? why?; **¿~ qué no?** why not?

porcelana [porθe'lana] *nf* porcelain; (*china*) china

porcentaje [porθen'taxe] *nm* percentage

porción [por'θjon] *nf* (*parte*) portion, share; (*cantidad*) quantity, amount

pordiosero, a [porðjo'sero, a] *nm/f* beggar

porfiar [por'fjar] *vi* to persist, insist; (*disputar*) to argue stubbornly

pormenor [porme'nor] *nm* detail, particular

pornografía [pornoɣra'fia] *nf* pornography

poro ['poro] *nm* pore; **~so, a** *adj* porous

porque ['porke] *conj* (*a causa de*) because; (*ya que*) since; (*con el fin de*) so that, in order that

porqué [por'ke] *nm* reason, cause

porquería [porke'ria] *nf* (*suciedad*) filth, dirt; (*acción*) dirty trick; (*objeto*) small thing, trifle; (*fig*) rubbish

porra ['porra] *nf* (*arma*) stick, club

porrazo [po'rraθo] *nm* blow, bump

porro ['porro] (*fam*) *nm* (*droga*) joint (*fam*)

porrón [po'rron] *nm* glass wine jar with a long spout

portaaviones [porta'(a)ßjones] *nm inv* aircraft carrier

portada [por'taða] *nf* (*de revista*) cover

portador, a [porta'ðor, a] *nm/f* carrier, bearer; (*COM*) bearer, payee

portaequipajes [portaeki'paxes] *nm inv* (*AUTO: maletero*) boot; (: *baca*) luggage rack

portal [por'tal] *nm* (*entrada*) vestibule, hall; (*portada*) porch, doorway; (*puerta de entrada*) main door

portamaletas [portama'letas] *nm inv* (*AUTO: maletero*) boot; (: *baca*) roof rack

portarse [por'tarse] *vr* to behave, conduct o.s.

portátil [por'tatil] *adj* portable

portavoz [porta'ßoθ] *nm/f* spokesman/woman

portazo [por'taθo] *nm*: **dar un ~** to slam the door

porte ['porte] *nm* (*COM*) transport; (*precio*) transport charges *pl*

portento [por'tento] *nm* marvel, wonder; **~so, a** *adj* marvellous, extraordinary

porteño, a [por'teɲo, a] *adj* of *o* from Buenos Aires

portería [porte'ria] *nf* (*oficina*) porter's office; (*DEPORTE*) goal

portero, a [por'tero, a] *nm/f* porter; (*conserje*) caretaker; (*ujier*) doorman; (*DEPORTE*) goalkeeper; **~ automático** intercom

pórtico ['portiko] *nm* (*patio*) portico, porch; (*fig*) gateway; (*arcada*) arcade

portorriqueño, a [portorri'keɲo, a] *adj* Puerto Rican

Portugal [portu'ɣal] *nm* Portugal; **portugués, esa** *adj, nm/f* Portuguese ♦ *nm* (*LING*) Portuguese

porvenir [porße'nir] *nm* future

pos [pos] *prep*: **en ~ de** after, in pursuit of

posada [po'saða] *nf* (*refugio*) shelter, lodging; (*mesón*) guest house; **dar ~ a** to give shelter to, take in

posaderas [posa'ðeras] *nfpl* backside *sg*, buttocks

posar [po'sar] *vt* (*en el suelo*) to lay down, put down; (*la mano*) to place, put gently ♦ *vi* (*modelo*) to sit, pose; **~se** *vr* to settle; (*pájaro*) to perch; (*avión*) to land, come down

posavasos [posa'βasos] *nm inv* coaster; (*para cerveza*) beermat

posdata [pos'ðata] *nf* postscript

pose ['pose] *nf* pose

poseedor, a [posee'ðor, a] *nm/f* owner, possessor; (*de récord, puesto*) holder

poseer [pose'er] *vt* to possess, own; (*ventaja*) to enjoy; (*récord, puesto*) to hold

posesión [pose'sjon] *nf* possession; **posesionarse** *vr*: **posesionarse de** to take possession of, take over

posesivo, a [pose'siβo, a] *adj* possessive

posgrado [pos'graðo] *nm*: **curso de ~** postgraduate course

posibilidad [posiβili'ðað] *nf* possibility; (*oportunidad*) chance; **posibilitar** *vt* to make possible; (*hacer realizable*) to make feasible

posible [po'siβle] *adj* possible; (*realizable*) feasible; **de ser ~** if possible; **en lo ~** as far as possible

posición [posi'θjon] *nf* position; (*rango social*) status

positivo, a [posi'tiβo, a] *adj* positive

poso ['poso] *nm* sediment; (*heces*) dregs *pl*

posponer [pospo'ner] *vt* (*relegar*) to put behind/below; (*aplazar*) to postpone

posta ['posta] *nf*: **a ~** deliberately, on purpose

postal [pos'tal] *adj* postal ♦ *nf* postcard

poste ['poste] *nm* (*de telégrafos etc*) post, pole; (*columna*) pillar

póster ['poster] (*pl* **pósteres, pósters**) *nm* poster

postergar [poster'var] *vt* to postpone, delay

posteridad [posteri'ðað] *nf* posterity

posterior [poste'rjor] *adj* back, rear; (*siguiente*) following, subsequent; (*más tarde*) later; **~idad** *nf*: **con ~idad** later, subsequently

postgrado [post'graðo] *nm* = **posgrado**

postizo, a [pos'tiθo, a] *adj* false, artificial ♦ *nm* hairpiece

postor, a [pos'tor, a] *nm/f* bidder

postre ['postre] *nm* sweet, dessert

postrero, a [pos'trero, a] (*delante de nmsg*: **postrer**) *adj* (*último*) last; (*que viene detrás*) rear

postulado [postu'laðo] *nm* postulate

póstumo, a ['postumo, a] *adj* posthumous

postura [pos'tura] *nf* (*del cuerpo*) posture, position; (*fig*) attitude, position

potable [po'taβle] *adj* drinkable; **agua ~** drinking water

potaje [po'taxe] *nm* thick vegetable soup

pote ['pote] *nm* pot, jar

potencia [po'tenθja] *nf* power; **~l** [poten'θjal] *adj, nm* potential; **~r** *vt* to boost

potente [po'tente] *adj* powerful

potro, a ['potro, a] *nm/f* (*ZOOL*) colt/filly ♦ *nm* (*de gimnasia*) vaulting horse

pozo ['poθo] *nm* well; (*de río*) deep pool; (*de mina*) shaft

P.P. *abr* (= *porte pagado*) CP

práctica ['praktika] *nf* practice; (*método*) method; (*arte, capacidad*) skill; **en la ~ in** practice

practicable [prakti'kaβle] *adj* practicable; (*camino*) passable

practicante [prakti'kante] *nm/f* (*MED*: *ayudante de doctor*) medical assistant; (: *enfermero*) nurse; (*quien practica algo*) practitioner ♦ *adj* practising

practicar [prakti'kar] *vt* to practise; (*DEPORTE*) to play; (*realizar*) to carry out, perform

práctico, a ['praktiko, a] *adj* practical; (*instruído*: *persona*) skilled, expert

practique *etc vb ver* **practicar**

pradera [pra'ðera] *nf* meadow; (*US etc*) prairie

prado ['praðo] *nm* (*campo*) meadow, field; (*pastizal*) pasture

Praga ['praxa] *n* Prague

pragmático, a [prav'matiko, a] *adj* pragmatic

preámbulo [pre'ambulo] *nm* preamble, introduction

precario, a [pre'karjo, a] *adj* precarious

precaución [prekau'θjon] *nf* (*medida preventiva*) preventive measure, precaution; (*prudencia*) caution, wariness

precaver [preka'ßer] *vt* to guard against; (*impedir*) to forestall; **~se** *vr*: **~ de** *o* **contra algo** to (be on one's) guard against sth; **precavido, a** *adj* cautious, wary

precedente [preθe'ðente] *adj* preceding; (*anterior*) former ♦ *nm* precedent

preceder [preθe'ðer] *vt, vi* to precede, go before, come before

precepto [pre'θepto] *nm* precept

preciado, a [pre'θjaðo, a] *adj* (*estimado*) esteemed, valuable

preciarse [pre'θjarse] *vr* to boast; **~se de** to pride o.s. on, boast of being

precinto [pre'θinto] *nm* (*tb*: **~ de garantía**) seal

precio ['preθjo] *nm* price; (*costo*) cost; (*valor*) value, worth; (*de viaje*) fare; **~ al contado/de coste/de oportunidad** cash/cost/bargain price; **~ al detalle** *o* **al por menor** retail price; **~ tope** top price

preciosidad [preθjosi'ðað] *nf* (*valor*) (high) value, (great) worth; (*encanto*) charm; (*cosa bonita*) beautiful thing; **es una ~** it's lovely, it's really beautiful

precioso, a [pre'θjoso, a] *adj* precious; (*de mucho valor*) valuable; (*fam*) lovely, beautiful

precipicio [preθi'piθjo] *nm* cliff, precipice; (*fig*) abyss

precipitación [preθipita'θjon] *nf* haste; (*lluvia*) rainfall

precipitado, a [preθipi'taðo, a] *adj* (*conducta*) hasty, rash; (*salida*) hasty, sudden

precipitar [preθipi'tar] *vt* (*arrojar*) to hurl down, throw; (*apresurar*) to hasten; (*acelerar*) to speed up, accelerate; **~se** *vr* to throw o.s.; (*apresurarse*) to rush; (*actuar sin pensar*) to act rashly

precisamente [preθisa'mente] *adv* precisely; (*exactamente*) precisely, exactly

precisar [preθi'sar] *vt* (*necesitar*) to need, require; (*fijar*) to determine exactly, fix;

(*especificar*) to specify

precisión [preθi'sjon] *nf* (*exactitud*) precision

preciso, a [pre'θiso, a] *adj* (*exacto*) precise; (*necesario*) necessary, essential

preconcebido, a [prekonθe'ßiðo, a] *adj* preconceived

precoz [pre'koθ] *adj* (*persona*) precocious; (*calvicie etc*) premature

precursor, a [prekur'sor, a] *nm/f* predecessor, forerunner

predecir [preðe'θir] *vt* to predict, forecast

predestinado, a [preðesti'naðo, a] *adj* predestined

predicar [preði'kar] *vt, vi* to preach

predicción [preðik'θjon] *nf* prediction

predilecto, a [preði'lekto, a] *adj* favourite

predisponer [preðispo'ner] *vt* to predispose; (*pey*) to prejudice; **predisposición** *nf* inclination; prejudice, bias

predominante [preðomi'nante] *adj* predominant

predominar [preðomi'nar] *vt* to dominate ♦ *vi* to predominate; (*prevalecer*) to prevail; **predominio** *nm* predominance; prevalence

preescolar [pre(e)sko'lar] *adj* preschool

prefabricado, a [prefaßri'kaðo, a] *adj* prefabricated

prefacio [pre'faθjo] *nm* preface

preferencia [prefe'renθja] *nf* preference; **de ~** preferably, for preference

preferible [prefe'rißle] *adj* preferable

preferir [prefe'rir] *vt* to prefer

prefiero *etc vb ver* **preferir**

prefijo [pre'fixo] *nm* (*TELEC*) (dialling) code

pregonar [preⴳo'nar] *vt* to proclaim, announce

pregunta [pre'ⴳunta] *nf* question; **hacer una ~** to ask a question

preguntar [preⴳun'tar] *vt* to ask; (*cuestionar*) to question ♦ *vi* to ask; **~se** *vr* to wonder; **~ por alguien** to ask for sb

preguntón, ona [preⴳun'ton, ona] *adj* inquisitive

prehistórico, a [preis'toriko, a] *adj*

prehistoric

prejuicio [pre'xwiθjo] *nm* (*acto*) prejudgement; (*idea preconcebida*) preconception; (*parcialidad*) prejudice, bias

preliminar [prelimi'nar] *adj* preliminary

preludio [pre'luðjo] *nm* prelude

prematuro, a [prema'turo, a] *adj* premature

premeditación [premeðita'θjon] *nf* premeditation

premeditar [premeði'tar] *vt* to premeditate

premiar [pre'mjar] *vt* to reward; (*en un concurso*) to give a prize to

premio ['premjo] *nm* reward; prize; (*COM*) premium

premonición [premoni'θjon] *nf* premonition

prenatal [prena'tal] *adj* antenatal, prenatal

prenda ['prenda] *nf* (*ropa*) garment, article of clothing; (*garantía*) pledge; **~s** *nfpl* (*talentos*) talents, gifts

prendedor [prende'ðor] *nm* brooch

prender [pren'der] *vt* (*captar*) to catch, capture; (*detener*) to arrest; (*COSTURA*) to pin, attach; (*sujetar*) to fasten ♦ *vi* to catch; (*arraigar*) to take root; **~se** *vr* (*encenderse*) to catch fire

prendido, a [pren'diðo, a] (*AM*) *adj* (*luz etc*) on

prensa ['prensa] *nf* press; **la ~** the press; **prensar** *vt* to press

preñado, a [pre'ɲaðo, a] *adj* pregnant; **~ de** pregnant with, full of

preocupación [preokupa'θjon] *nf* worry, concern; (*ansiedad*) anxiety

preocupado, a [preoku'paðo, a] *adj* worried, concerned; (*ansioso*) anxious

preocupar [preoku'par] *vt* to worry; **~se** *vr* to worry; **~se de algo** (*hacerse cargo*) to take care of sth

preparación [prepara'θjon] *nf* (*acto*) preparation; (*estado*) readiness; (*entrenamiento*) training

preparado, a [prepa'raðo, a] *adj* (*dispuesto*) prepared; (*CULIN*) ready (to

serve) ♦ *nm* preparation

preparar [prepa'rar] *vt* (*disponer*) to prepare, get ready; (*TEC: tratar*) to prepare, process; (*entrenar*) to teach, train; **~se** *vr*: **~se a** *o* **para** to prepare to *o* for, get ready to *o* for; **preparativo, a** *adj* preparatory, preliminary; **preparativos** *nmpl* preparations; **preparatoria** (*AM*) *nf* sixth-form college (*BRIT*), senior high school (*US*)

prerrogativa [prerroɣa'tißa] *nf* prerogative, privilege

presa ['presa] *nf* (*cosa apresada*) catch; (*víctima*) victim; (*de animal*) prey; (*de agua*) dam

presagiar [presa'xjar] *vt* to presage, forebode; **presagio** *nm* omen

prescindir [presθin'dir] *vi*: **~ de** (*privarse de*) to do without, go without; (*descartar*) to dispense with

prescribir [preskri'ßir] *vt* to prescribe; **prescripción** *nf* prescription

presencia [pre'senθja] *nf* presence; **presencial** *adj*: **testigo presencial** eyewitness; **presenciar** *vt* to be present at; (*asistir a*) to attend; (*ver*) to see, witness

presentación [presenta'θjon] *nf* presentation; (*introducción*) introduction

presentador, a [presenta'ðor, a] *nm/f* presenter, compère

presentar [presen'tar] *vt* to present; (*ofrecer*) to offer; (*mostrar*) to show, display; (*a una persona*) to introduce; **~se** *vr* (*llegar inesperadamente*) to appear, turn up; (*ofrecerse como candidato*) to run, stand; (*aparecer*) to show, appear; (*solicitar empleo*) to apply

presente [pre'sente] *adj* present ♦ *nm* present; **hacer ~** to state, declare; **tener ~** to remember, bear in mind

presentimiento [presenti'mjento] *nm* premonition, presentiment

presentir [presen'tir] *vt* to have a premonition of

preservación [preserßa'θjon] *nf* protection, preservation

preservar [preser'ßar] *vt* to protect, preserve; **preservativo** *nm* sheath, condom

presidencia [presi'ðenθja] *nf* presidency; (*de comité*) chairmanship

presidente [presi'ðente] *nm/f* president; (*de comité*) chairman/woman

presidiario [presi'ðjarjo] *nm* convict

presidio [pre'sidjo] *nm* prison, penitentiary

presidir [presi'ðir] *vt* (*dirigir*) to preside at, preside over; (: *comité*) to take the chair at; (*dominar*) to dominate, rule ♦ *vi* to preside; to take the chair

presión [pre'sjon] *nf* pressure; **presionar** *vt* to press; (*fig*) to press, put pressure on ♦ *vi*: **presionar para** to press for

preso, a ['preso, a] *nm/f* prisoner; **tomar** *o* **llevar ~ a uno** to arrest sb, take sb prisoner

prestación [presta'θjon] *nf* service; (*subsidio*) benefit; **prestaciones** *nfpl* (*TEC, AUT*) performance features

prestado, a [pres'taðo, a] *adj* on loan; **pedir ~** to borrow

prestamista [presta'mista] *nm/f* moneylender

préstamo ['prestamo] *nm* loan; **~ hipotecario** mortgage

prestar [pres'tar] *vt* to lend, loan; (*atención*) to pay; (*ayuda*) to give

presteza [pres'teθa] *nf* speed, promptness

prestigio [pres'tixjo] *nm* prestige; **~so, a** *adj* (*honorable*) prestigious; (*famoso, renombrado*) renowned, famous

presto, a ['presto, a] *adj* (*rápido*) quick, prompt; (*dispuesto*) ready ♦ *adv* at once, right away

presumido, a [presu'miðo, a] *adj* (*persona*) vain

presumir [presu'mir] *vt* to presume ♦ *vi* (*tener aires*) to be conceited; **según cabe ~** as may be presumed, presumably; **presunción** *nf* presumption; **presunto, a** *adj* (*supuesto*) supposed, presumed; (*así llamado*) so-called; **presuntuoso, a** *adj* conceited, presumptuous

presuponer [presupo'ner] *vt* to presuppose

presupuesto [presu'pwesto] *pp de* **presuponer** ♦ *nm* (*FINANZAS*) budget; (*estimación: de costo*) estimate

pretencioso, a [preten'θjoso, a] *adj* pretentious

pretender [preten'der] *vt* (*intentar*) to try to, seek to; (*reivindicar*) to claim; (*buscar*) to seek, try for; (*cortejar*) to woo, court; **~ que** to expect that; **pretendiente** *nm/f* (*amante*) suitor; (*al trono*) pretender; **pretensión** *nf* (*aspiración*) aspiration; (*reivindicación*) claim; (*orgullo*) pretension

pretexto [pre'teksto] *nm* pretext; (*excusa*) excuse

prevalecer [preßale'θer] *vi* to prevail

prevención [preßen'θjon] *nf* prevention; (*precaución*) precaution

prevenido, a [preße'niðo, a] *adj* prepared, ready; (*cauteloso*) cautious

prevenir [preße'nir] *vt* (*impedir*) to prevent; (*predisponer*) to prejudice, bias; (*avisar*) to warn; (*preparar*) to prepare, get ready; **~se** *vr* to get ready, prepare; **~se contra** to take precautions against; **preventivo, a** *adj* preventive, precautionary

prever [pre'ßer] *vt* to foresee

previo, a ['preßjo, a] *adj* (*anterior*) previous; (*preliminar*) preliminary ♦ *prep*: **~ acuerdo de los otros** subject to the agreement of the others

previsión [preßi'sjon] *nf* (*perspicacia*) foresight; (*predicción*) forecast; **previsto, a** *adj* anticipated, forecast

prima ['prima] *nf* (*COM*) bonus; **~ de seguro** insurance premium; *ver tb* **primo**

primacía [prima'θia] *nf* primacy

primario, a [pri'marjo, a] *adj* primary

primavera [prima'ßera] *nf* spring(-time)

primera [pri'mera] *nf* (*AUTO*) first gear; (*FERRO: tb*: **~ clase**) first class; **de ~** (*fam*) first-class, first-rate

primero, a [pri'mero, a] (*delante de nmsg*: **primer**) *adj* first; (*principal*) prime ♦ *adv* first; (*más bien*) sooner, rather; **primera plana** front page

primicia [pri'miθja] *nf* (*tb*: ~ **informativa**) scoop

primitivo, a [primi'tiβo, a] *adj* primitive; (*original*) original

primo, a ['primo, a] *adj* prime ♦ *nm/f* cousin; (*fam*) fool, idiot; ~ **hermano** first cousin; **materias primas** raw materials

primogénito, a [primo'xenito, a] *adj* first-born

primordial [primor'ðjal] *adj* basic, fundamental

primoroso, a [primo'roso, a] *adj* exquisite, delicate

princesa [prin'θesa] *nf* princess

principal [prinθi'pal] *adj* principal, main ♦ *nm* (*jefe*) chief, principal

príncipe ['prinθipe] *nm* prince

principiante [prinθi'pjante] *nm/f* beginner

principio [prin'θipjo] *nm* (*comienzo*) beginning, start; (*origen*) origin; (*primera etapa*) rudiment, basic idea; (*moral*) principle; **a ~s de** at the beginning of

pringoso, a [prin'xoso, a] *adj* (*grasiento*) greasy; (*pegajoso*) sticky

pringue ['pringe] *nm* (*grasa*) grease, fat, dripping

prioridad [priori'ðað] *nf* priority

prisa ['prisa] *nf* (*apresuramiento*) hurry, haste; (*rapidez*) speed; (*urgencia*) (sense of) urgency; **a** *o* **de** ~ quickly; **correr** ~ to be urgent; **darse** ~ to hurry up; **estar de** *o* **tener** ~ to be in a hurry

prisión [pri'sjon] *nf* (*cárcel*) prison; (*período de cárcel*) imprisonment; **prisionero, a** *nm/f* prisoner

prismáticos [pris'matikos] *nmpl* binoculars

privación [priβa'θjon] *nf* deprivation; (*falta*) want, privation

privado, a [pri'βaðo, a] *adj* private

privar [pri'βar] *vt* to deprive; **privativo, a** *adj* exclusive

privilegiado, a [priβile'xjaðo, a] *adj* privileged; (*memoria*) very good

privilegiar [priβile'xjar] *vt* to grant a privilege to; (*favorecer*) to favour

privilegio [priβi'lexjo] *nm* privilege; (*concesión*) concession

pro [pro] *nm o f* profit, advantage ♦ *prep*: **asociación** ~ **ciegos** association for the blind ♦ *prefijo*: ~ **soviético/americano** pro-Soviet/American; **en** ~ **de** on behalf of, for; **los ~s y los contras** the pros and cons

proa ['proa] *nf* bow, prow; **de** ~ bow *cpd*, fore

probabilidad [proβaβili'ðað] *nf* probability, likelihood; (*oportunidad, posibilidad*) chance, prospect; **probable** *adj* probable, likely

probador [proβa'ðor] *nm* (*en tienda*) fitting room

probar [pro'βar] *vt* (*demostrar*) to prove; (*someter a prueba*) to test, try out; (*ropa*) to try on; (*comida*) to taste ♦ *vi* to try; **~se un traje** to try on a suit

probeta [pro'βeta] *nf* test tube

problema [pro'βlema] *nm* problem

procedente [proθe'ðente] *adj* (*razonable*) reasonable; (*conforme a derecho*) proper, fitting; ~ **de** coming from, originating in

proceder [proθe'ðer] *vi* (*avanzar*) to proceed; (*actuar*) to act; (*ser correcto*) to be right (and proper), be fitting ♦ *nm* (*comportamiento*) behaviour, conduct; ~ **de** to come from, originate in; **procedimiento** *nm* procedure; (*proceso*) process; (*método*) means *pl*, method

procesado, a [proθe'saðo, a] *nm/f* accused

procesador [proθesa'ðor] *nm*: ~ **de textos** word processor

procesar [proθe'sar] *vt* to try, put on trial

procesión [proθe'sjon] *nf* procession

proceso [pro'θeso] *nm* process; (*JUR*) trial

proclamar [prokla'mar] *vt* to proclaim

procreación [prokrea'θjon] *nf* procreation

procrear [prokre'ar] *vt*, *vi* to procreate

procurador, a [prokura'ðor, a] *nm/f* attorney

procurar [proku'rar] vt (*intentar*) to try, endeavour; (*conseguir*) to get, obtain; (*asegurar*) to secure; (*producir*) to produce

prodigio [pro'ðixjo] nm prodigy; (*milagro*) wonder, marvel; **~so, a** adj prodigious, marvellous

pródigo, a ['proðiɣo, a] adj: **hijo ~** prodigal son

producción [proðuk'θjon] nf (*gen*) production; (*producto*) output; **~ en serie** mass production

producir [proðu'θir] vt to produce; (*causar*) to cause, bring about; **~se** vr (*cambio*) to come about; (*accidente*) to take place; (*problema etc*) to arise; (*hacerse*) to be produced, be made; (*estallar*) to break out

productividad [proðuktiβi'ðað] nf productivity; **productivo, a** adj productive; (*provechoso*) profitable

producto [pro'ðukto] nm product

productor, a [proðuk'tor, a] adj productive, producing ♦ nm/f producer

proeza [pro'eθa] nf exploit, feat

profanar [profa'nar] vt to desecrate, profane; **profano, a** adj profane ♦ nm/f layman/woman

profecía [profe'θia] nf prophecy

proferir [profe'rir] vt (*palabra, sonido*) to utter; (*injuria*) to hurl, let fly

profesión [profe'sjon] nf profession; **profesional** adj professional

profesor, a [profe'sor, a] nm/f teacher; **~ado** nm teaching profession

profeta [pro'feta] nm/f prophet; **profetizar** vt, vi to prophesy

prófugo, a ['profuɣo, a] nm/f fugitive; (*MIL: desertor*) deserter

profundidad [profundi'ðað] nf depth; **profundizar** vi: **profundizar en** to go deeply into; **profundo, a** adj deep; (*misterio, pensador*) profound

progenitor [proxeni'tor] nm ancestor; **~es** nmpl (*padres*) parents

programa [pro'xrama] nm programme (*BRIT*), program (*US*); **~ción** nf programming; **~dor, a** nm/f

programmer; **programar** vt to program

progresar [proɣre'sar] vi to progress, make progress; **progresista** adj, nm/f progressive; **progresivo, a** adj progressive; (*gradual*) gradual; (*continuo*) continuous; **progreso** nm progress

prohibición [proiβi'θjon] nf prohibition, ban

prohibir [proi'βir] vt to prohibit, ban, forbid; **se prohibe fumar, prohibido fumar** no smoking; **"prohibido el paso"** "no entry"

prójimo, a ['proximo, a] nm/f fellow man; (*vecino*) neighbour

proletariado [proleta'rjaðo] nm proletariat

proletario, a [prole'tarjo, a] adj, nm/f proletarian

proliferación [prolifera'θjon] nf proliferation

proliferar [prolife'rar] vi to proliferate; **prolífico, a** adj prolific

prólogo ['proloɣo] nm prologue

prolongación [prolonga'θjon] nf extension; **prolongado, a** adj (*largo*) long; (*alargado*) lengthy

prolongar [prolon'var] vt to extend; (*reunión etc*) to prolong; (*calle, tubo*) to extend

promedio [pro'meðjo] nm average; (*de distancia*) middle, mid-point

promesa [pro'mesa] nf promise

prometer [prome'ter] vt to promise ♦ vi to show promise; **~se** vr (*novios*) to get engaged; **prometido, a** adj promised; engaged ♦ nm/f fiancé/fiancée

prominente [promi'nente] adj prominent

promiscuo, a [pro'miskwo, a] adj promiscuous

promoción [promo'θjon] nf promotion

promotor [promo'tor] nm promoter; (*instigador*) instigator

promover [promo'βer] vt to promote; (*causar*) to cause; (*instigar*) to instigate, stir up

promulgar [promul'var] vt to promulgate; (*anunciar*) to proclaim

pronombre [pro'nombre] nm pronoun

pronosticar [pronosti'kar] vt to predict, foretell, forecast; **pronóstico** nm prediction, forecast; **pronóstico del tiempo** weather forecast

pronto, a ['pronto, a] adj (rápido) prompt, quick; (preparado) ready ♦ adv quickly, promptly; (en seguida) at once, right away; (dentro de poco) soon; (temprano) early ♦ nm: **tener ~s de enojo** to be quick-tempered; **de ~** suddenly; **por lo ~** meanwhile, for the present

pronunciación [pronunθja'θjon] nf pronunciation

pronunciar [pronun'θjar] vt to pronounce; (discurso) to make, deliver; **~se** vr to revolt, rebel; (declararse) to declare o.s.

propagación [propaɣa'θjon] nf propagation

propaganda [propa'ɣanda] nf (política) propaganda; (comercial) advertising

propagar [propa'ɣar] vt to propagate

propensión [propen'sjon] nf inclination, propensity; **propenso, a** adj inclined to; **ser propenso a** to be inclined to, have a tendency to

propicio, a [pro'piθjo, a] adj favourable, propitious

propiedad [propje'ðað] nf property; (posesión) possession, ownership; **~ particular** private property

propietario, a [propje'tarjo, a] nm/f owner, proprietor

propina [pro'pina] nf tip

propio, a ['propjo, a] adj own, of one's own; (característico) characteristic, typical; (debido) proper; (mismo) selfsame, very; **el ~ ministro** the minister himself; **¿tienes casa propia?** have you a house of your own?

proponer [propo'ner] vt to propose, put forward; (problema) to pose; **~se** vr to propose, intend

proporción [propor'θjon] nf proportion; (MAT) ratio; **proporciones** nfpl (dimensiones) dimensions; (fig) size sg; **proporcionado, a** adj proportionate; (regular) medium, middling; (justo) just right; **proporcionar** vt (dar) to give, supply, provide

proposición [proposi'θjon] nf proposition; (propuesta) proposal

propósito [pro'posito] nm purpose; (intento) aim, intention ♦ adv: **a ~** by the way, incidentally; (a posta) on purpose, deliberately; **a ~ de** about, with regard to

propuesta [pro'pwesta] vb ver **proponer** ♦ nf proposal

propulsar [propul'sar] vt to drive, propel; (fig) to promote, encourage; **propulsión** nf propulsion; **propulsión a chorro** o **por reacción** jet propulsion

prórroga ['prorroɣa] nf extension; (JUR) stay; (COM) deferment; (DEPORTE) extra time; **prorrogar** vt (período) to extend; (decisión) to defer, postpone

prorrumpir [prorrum'pir] vi to burst forth, break out

prosa ['prosa] nf prose

proscrito, a [pro'skrito, a] adj banned

proseguir [prose'ɣir] vt to continue, carry on ♦ vi to continue, go on

prospección [prospek'θjon] nf exploration; (del oro) prospecting

prospecto [pros'pekto] nm prospectus

prosperar [prospe'rar] vi to prosper, thrive, flourish; **prosperidad** nf prosperity; (éxito) success; **próspero, a** adj prosperous, flourishing; (que tiene éxito) successful

prostíbulo [pros'tiβulo] nm brothel (BRIT), house of prostitution (US)

prostitución [prostitu'θjon] nf prostitution

prostituir [prosti'twir] vt to prostitute; **~se** vr to prostitute o.s., become a prostitute

prostituta [prosti'tuta] nf prostitute

protagonista [protaɣo'nista] nm/f protagonist

protagonizar [protaɣoni'θar] vt to take the chief rôle in

protección [protek'θjon] nf protection

protector, a [protek'tor, a] adj protective, protecting ♦ nm/f protector

proteger [prote'xer] *vt* to protect;
   protegido, a *nm/f* protégé/protégée
proteína [prote'ina] *nf* protein
protesta [pro'testa] *nf* protest;
   (declaración) protestation
protestante [protes'tante] *adj* Protestant
protestar [protes'tar] *vt* to protest, declare
   ♦ *vi* to protest
protocolo [proto'kolo] *nm* protocol
prototipo [proto'tipo] *nm* prototype
prov. *abr* (= *provincia*) prov
provecho [pro'βetʃo] *nm* advantage,
   benefit; *(FINANZAS)* profit; **¡buen ~!** bon
   appétit!; **en ~ de** to the benefit of; **sacar**
   ~ de to benefit from, profit by
proveer [proβe'er] *vt* to provide, supply
   ♦ *vi*: **~ a** to provide for
provenir [proβe'nir] *vi*: **~ de** to come
   from, stem from
proverbio [pro'βerβjo] *nm* proverb
providencia [proβi'ðenθja] *nf* providence
provincia [pro'βinθja] *nf* province; **~no,**
   a *adj* provincial; *(del campo)* country *cpd*
provisión [proβi'sjon] *nf* provision;
   (abastecimiento) provision, supply;
   (medida) measure, step
provisional [proβisjo'nal] *adj* provisional
provocación [proβoka'θjon] *nf*
   provocation
provocar [proβo'kar] *vt* to provoke;
   (alentar) to tempt, invite; *(causar)* to
   bring about, lead to; *(promover)* to
   promote; *(estimular)* to rouse, stimulate;
   ¿te provoca un café? *(AM)* would you
   like a coffee?; **provocativo, a** *adj*
   provocative
próximamente [proksima'mente] *adv*
   shortly, soon
proximidad [proksimi'ðað] *nf* closeness,
   proximity; **próximo, a** *adj* near, close;
   (vecino) neighbouring; *(siguiente)* next
proyectar [projek'tar] *vt* (*objeto*) to hurl,
   throw; *(luz)* to cast, shed; *(CINE)* to
   screen, show; *(planear)* to plan
proyectil [projek'til] *nm* projectile, missile
proyecto [pro'jekto] *nm* plan; *(estimación*
   de costo) detailed estimate

proyector [projek'tor] *nm* (*CINE*) projector
prudencia [pru'ðenθja] *nf* (*sabiduría*)
   wisdom; *(cuidado)* care; **prudente** *adj*
   sensible, wise; *(conductor)* careful
prueba *etc* ['prweβa] *vb ver* **probar** ♦ *nf*
   proof; *(ensayo)* test, trial; *(degustación)*
   tasting, sampling; *(de ropa)* fitting; **a ~** on
   trial; **a ~ de** proof against; **a ~ de agua/**
   fuego waterproof/fireproof; **someter a ~**
   to put to the test
prurito [pru'rito] *nm* itch; *(de bebé)* nappy
   (*BRIT*) o diaper (*US*) rash
psico... [siko] *prefijo* psycho...; **~análisis**
   nm inv psychoanalysis; **~logía** *nf*
   psychology; **~lógico, a** *adj*
   psychological; **psicólogo, a** *nm/f*
   psychologist; **psicópata** *nm/f*
   psychopath; **~sis** *nf inv* psychosis
psiquiatra [si'kjatra] *nm/f* psychiatrist;
   psiquiátrico, a *adj* psychiatric
psíquico, a ['sikiko, a] *adj* psychic(al)
PSOE [pe'soe] *nm abr* = **Partido**
   Socialista Obrero Español
pta(s) *abr* = **peseta(s)**
pts *abr* = **pesetas**
púa ['pua] *nf* (*BOT, ZOOL*) prickle, spine;
   (para guitarra) plectrum (*BRIT*), pick (*US*);
   alambre de ~ barbed wire
pubertad [puβer'tað] *nf* puberty
publicación [puβlika'θjon] *nf* publication
publicar [puβli'kar] *vt* (*editar*) to publish;
   (hacer público) to publicize; *(divulgar)* to
   make public, divulge
publicidad [puβliði'ðað] *nf* publicity;
   (COM: propaganda) advertising;
   publicitario, a *adj* publicity *cpd*;
   advertising *cpd*
público, a ['puβliko, a] *adj* public ♦ *nm*
   public; *(TEATRO etc)* audience
puchero [pu'tʃero] *nm* (*CULIN: guiso*) stew;
   (: *olla*) cooking pot; **hacer ~s** to pout
pude *etc vb ver* **poder**
púdico, a ['puðiko, a] *adj* modest
pudiente [pu'ðjente] *adj* (*rico*) wealthy,
   well-to-do
pudiera *etc vb ver* **poder**
pudor [pu'ðor] *nm* modesty

pudrir [pu'ðrir] *vt* to rot; **~se** *vr* to rot, decay

pueblo ['pweβlo] *nm* people; (*nación*) nation; (*aldea*) village

puedo *etc vb ver* **poder**

puente ['pwente] *nm* bridge; **hacer ~** (*inf*) to take extra days off work between 2 public holidays; to take a long weekend; **~ aéreo** shuttle service; **~ colgante** suspension bridge

---
hacer puente

When a public holiday in Spain falls on a Tuesday or Thursday it is common practice for employers to make the Monday or Friday a holiday as well and to give everyone a four-day weekend. This is known as **hacer puente**. *When a named public holiday such as the* **Día de la Constitución** *falls on a Tuesday or Thursday, people refer to the whole holiday period as e.g. the* **puente de la Constitución**.

---

puerco, a ['pwerko, a] *nm/f* pig/sow ♦ *adj* (*sucio*) dirty, filthy; (*obsceno*) disgusting; **~ de mar** porpoise; **~ marino** dolphin

pueril [pwe'ril] *adj* childish

puerro ['pwerro] *nm* leek

puerta ['pwerta] *nf* door; (*de jardín*) gate; (*portal*) doorway; (*fig*) gateway; (*portería*) goal; **a la ~** at the door; **a ~ cerrada** behind closed doors; **~ giratoria** revolving door

puerto ['pwerto] *nm* port; (*paso*) pass; (*fig*) haven, refuge

Puerto Rico [pwerto'riko] *nm* Puerto Rico; **puertorriqueño, a** *adj, nm/f* Puerto Rican

pues [pwes] *adv* (*entonces*) then; (*bueno*) well, well then; (*así que*) so ♦ *conj* (*ya que*) since; **¡~!** (*sí*) yes!, certainly!

puesta ['pwesta] *nf* (*apuesta*) bet, stake; **~ en marcha** starting; **~ del sol** sunset

puesto, a ['pwesto, a] *pp de* **poner** ♦ *adj*: **tener algo ~** to have sth on, be wearing sth ♦ *nm* (*lugar, posición*) place; (*trabajo*) post, job; (*COM*) stall ♦ *conj*: **~ que** since, as

púgil ['puxil] *nm* boxer

pugna ['puɣna] *nf* battle, conflict; **pugnar** *vi* (*luchar*) to struggle, fight; (*pelear*) to fight

pujar [pu'xar] *vi* (*en subasta*) to bid; (*esforzarse*) to struggle, strain

pulcro, a ['pulkro, a] *adj* neat, tidy

pulga ['pulɣa] *nf* flea

pulgada [pul'ɣaða] *nf* inch

pulgar [pul'ɣar] *nm* thumb

pulir [pu'lir] *vt* to polish; (*alisar*) to smooth; (*fig*) to polish up, touch up

pulla ['puʎa] *nf* cutting remark

pulmón [pul'mon] *nm* lung; **pulmonía** *nf* pneumonia

pulpa ['pulpa] *nf* pulp; (*de fruta*) flesh, soft part

pulpería [pulpe'ria] (*AM*) *nf* (*tienda*) small grocery store

púlpito ['pulpito] *nm* pulpit

pulpo ['pulpo] *nm* octopus

pulsación [pulsa'θjon] *nf* beat; **pulsaciones** pulse rate

pulsar [pul'sar] *vt* (*tecla*) to touch, tap; (*MUS*) to play; (*botón*) to press, push ♦ *vi* to pulsate; (*latir*) to beat, throb; (*MED*): **~ a uno** to take sb's pulse

pulsera [pul'sera] *nf* bracelet

pulso ['pulso] *nm* (*ANAT*) pulse; (*fuerza*) strength; (*firmeza*) steadiness, steady hand

pulverizador [pulβeriθa'ðor] *nm* spray, spray gun

pulverizar [pulβeri'θar] *vt* to pulverize; (*líquido*) to spray

puna ['puna] (*AM*) *nf* mountain sickness

punitivo, a [puni'tiβo, a] *adj* punitive

punta ['punta] *nf* point, tip; (*extremidad*) end; (*fig*) touch, trace; **horas ~s** peak hours, rush hours; **sacar ~ a** to sharpen

puntada [pun'taða] *nf* (*COSTURA*) stitch

puntal [pun'tal] *nm* prop, support

puntapié [punta'pje] *nm* kick

puntear [punte'ar] *vt* to tick, mark

puntería [punte'ria] *nf* (*de arma*) aim,

aiming; (*destreza*) marksmanship
puntero, a [pun'tero, a] *adj* leading ♦ *nm*
(*palo*) pointer
puntiagudo, a [puntja'ɣuðo, a] *adj* sharp,
pointed
puntilla [pun'tiʎa] *nf* (*encaje*) lace edging
o trim; **(andar) de ~s** (to walk) on tiptoe
punto ['punto] *nm* (*gen*) point; (*señal
diminuta*) spot, dot; (*COSTURA, MED*) stitch;
(*lugar*) spot, place; (*momento*) point,
moment; **a ~** ready; **estar a ~ de** to be
on the point of *o* about to; **en ~** on the
dot; **~ muerto** dead centre; (*AUTO*)
neutral (gear); **~ final** full stop (*BRIT*),
period (*US*); **~ y coma** semicolon; **~ de
interrogación** question mark; **~ de vista**
point of view, viewpoint; **hacer ~** (*tejer*)
to knit
puntuación [puntwa'θjon] *nf* punctuation;
(*puntos: en examen*) mark(s) (*pl*);
(: *DEPORTE*) score
puntual [pun'twal] *adj* (*a tiempo*)
punctual; (*exacto*) exact, accurate; **~idad**
nf punctuality; exactness, accuracy; **~izar**
vt to fix, specify
puntuar [pun'twar] *vi* (*DEPORTE*) to score,
count
punzada [pun'θaða] *nf* (*de dolor*) twinge
punzante [pun'θante] *adj* (*dolor*) shooting,
sharp; (*herramienta*) sharp; **punzar** *vt* to
prick, pierce ♦ *vi* to shoot, stab
puñado [pu'ɲaðo] *nm* handful
puñal [pu'ɲal] *nm* dagger; **~ada** *nf* stab
puñetazo [puɲe'taθo] *nm* punch
puño ['puɲo] *nm* (*ANAT*) fist; (*cantidad*)
fistful, handful; (*COSTURA*) cuff; (*de
herramienta*) handle
pupila [pu'pila] *nf* pupil
pupitre [pu'pitre] *nm* desk
puré [pu're] *nm* puree; (*sopa*) (thick) soup;
~ de patatas mashed potatoes
pureza [pu'reθa] *nf* purity
purga ['purɣa] *nf* purge; **purgante** *adj*,
nm purgative; **purgar** *vt* to purge
purgatorio [purɣa'torjo] *nm* purgatory
purificar [purifi'kar] *vt* to purify; (*refinar*)
to refine

puritano, a [puri'tano, a] *adj* (*actitud*)
puritanical; (*iglesia, tradición*) puritan
♦ *nm/f* puritan
puro, a ['puro, a] *adj* pure; (*verdad*)
simple, plain ♦ *adv*: **de ~ cansado** out of
sheer tiredness ♦ *nm* cigar
púrpura ['purpura] *nf* purple; **purpúreo,
a** *adj* purple
pus [pus] *nm* pus
puse *etc vb ver* **poner**
pusiera *etc vb ver* **poner**
pústula ['pustula] *nf* pimple, sore
puta ['puta] (*fam!*) *nf* whore, prostitute
putrefacción [putrefak'θjon] *nf* rotting,
putrefaction
PVP *abr* (*ESP*: = *precio venta al público*)
RRP
pyme, PYME ['pime] *nf abr* (= *Pequeña
y Mediana Empresa*) SME

Q, q

que [ke] *conj* **1** (*con oración subordinada*:
muchas veces no se traduce) that; **dijo ~
vendría** he said (that) he would come;
espero ~ lo encuentres I hope (that)
you find it; *ver tb* **el**
2 (*en oración independiente*): **¡~ entre!**
send him in; **¡~ se mejore tu padre!** I
hope your father gets better
3 (*enfático*): **¿me quieres? – ¡~ sí!** do
you love me? – of course!
4 (*consecutivo: muchas veces no se
traduce*) that; **es tan grande ~ no lo
puedo levantar** it's so big (that) I can't
lift it
5 (*comparaciones*) than; **yo ~ tú/él** if I
were you/him; *ver tb* **más; menos;
mismo**
6 (*valor disyuntivo*): **~ le guste o no**
whether he likes it or not; **~ venga o ~
no venga** whether he comes or not
7 (*porque*): **no puedo, ~ tengo ~
quedarme en casa** I can't, I've got to

stay in
♦ *pron* **1** (*cosa*) that, which; (+*prep*) which; **el sombrero ~ te compraste** the hat (that o which) you bought; **la cama en ~ dormí** the bed (that o which) I slept in
2 (*persona: suj*) that, who; (: *objeto*) that, whom; **el amigo ~ me acompañó al museo** the friend that o who went to the museum with me; **la chica ~ invité** the girl (that o whom) I invited

qué [ke] *adj* what?, which? ♦ *pron* what?; **¡~ divertido!** how funny!; **¿~ edad tienes?** how old are you?; **¿de ~ me hablas?** what are you saying to me?; **¿~ tal?** how are you?, how are things?; **¿~ hay (de nuevo)?** what's new?

quebradizo, a [keßra'ðiθo, a] *adj* fragile; (*persona*) frail

quebrado, a [ke'ßraðo, a] *adj* (*roto*) broken ♦ *nm/f* bankrupt ♦ *nm* (*MAT*) fraction

quebrantar [keßran'tar] *vt* (*infringir*) to violate, transgress; **~se** *vr* (*persona*) to fail in health

quebranto [ke'ßranto] *nm* damage, harm; (*dolor*) grief, pain

quebrar [ke'ßrar] *vt* to break, smash ♦ *vi* to go bankrupt; **~se** *vr* to break, get broken; (*MED*) to be ruptured

quedar [ke'ðar] *vi* to stay, remain; (*encontrarse: sitio*) to be; (*haber aún*) to remain, be left; (*~se* *vr* to remain, stay (behind); **~se (con) algo** to keep sth; **~ en** (*acordar*) to agree on/to; **~ en nada** to come to nothing; **~ por hacer** to be still to be done; **~ ciego/mudo** to be left blind/dumb; **no te queda bien ese vestido** that dress doesn't suit you; **eso queda muy lejos** that's a long way (away); **quedamos a las seis** we agreed to meet at six

quedo, a ['keðo, a] *adj* still ♦ *adv* softly, gently

quehacer [kea'θer] *nm* task, job; **~es (domésticos)** *nmpl* household chores

queja ['kexa] *nf* complaint; **quejarse** *vr* (*enfermo*) to moan, groan; (*protestar*) to complain; **quejarse de que** to complain (about the fact); **quejido** *nm* moan

quemado, a [ke'maðo, a] *adj* burnt

quemadura [kema'ðura] *nf* burn, scald

quemar [ke'mar] *vt* to burn; (*fig: malgastar*) to burn up, squander ♦ *vi* to be burning hot; **~se** *vr* (*consumirse*) to burn (up); (*del sol*) to get sunburnt

quemarropa [kema'rropa]: **a ~** *adv* point-blank

quepo *etc vb ver* **caber**

querella [ke'reʎa] *nf* (*JUR*) charge; (*disputa*) dispute; **~rse** *vr* (*JUR*) to file a complaint

---
PALABRA CLAVE
---

querer [ke'rer] *vt* **1** (*desear*) to want; **quiero más dinero** I want more money; **quisiera** o **querría un té** I'd like a tea; **sin ~** unintentionally; **quiero ayudar/que vayas** I want to help/you to go
2 (*preguntas: para pedir algo*): **¿quiere abrir la ventana?** could you open the window?; **¿quieres echarme una mano?** can you give me a hand?
3 (*amar*) to love; (*tener cariño a*) to be fond of; **quiere mucho a sus hijos** he's very fond of his children
4 (*requerir*): **esta planta quiere más luz** this plant needs more light
5: **le pedí que me dejara ir pero no quiso** I asked him to let me go but he refused

---

querido, a [ke'riðo, a] *adj* dear ♦ *nm/f* darling; (*amante*) lover

queso ['keso] *nm* cheese

quicio ['kiθjo] *nm* hinge; **sacar a uno de ~** to get on sb's nerves

quiebra ['kjeßra] *nf* break, split; (*COM*) bankruptcy; (*ECON*) slump

quiebro ['kjeßro] *nm* (*del cuerpo*) swerve

quien [kjen] *pron* who; **hay ~ piensa que** there are those who think that; **no hay ~ lo haga** no-one will do it

quién [kjen] *pron* who, whom; **¿~ es?** who's there?

quienquiera [kjen'kjera] (*pl* **quienesquiera**) *pron* whoever

quiero *etc vb ver* **querer**

quieto, a ['kjeto, a] *adj* still; (*carácter*) placid; **quietud** *nf* stillness

quilate [ki'late] *nm* carat

quilla ['kiʎa] *nf* keel

quimera [ki'mera] *nf* chimera; **quimérico, a** *adj* fantastic

químico, a ['kimiko, a] *adj* chemical ♦ *nm/f* chemist ♦ *nf* chemistry

quincalla [kin'kaʎa] *nf* hardware, ironmongery (*BRIT*)

quince ['kinθe] *num* fifteen; **~ días** a fortnight; **~añero, a** *nm/f* teenager; **~na** *nf* fortnight; (*pago*) fortnightly pay; **~nal** *adj* fortnightly

quiniela [ki'njela] *nf* football pools *pl*; **~s** *nfpl* (*impreso*) pools coupon *sg*

quinientos, as [ki'njentos, as] *adj, num* five hundred

quinina [ki'nina] *nf* quinine

quinto, a ['kinto, a] *adj* fifth ♦ *nf* country house; (*MIL*) call-up, draft

quiosco ['kjosko] *nm* (*de música*) bandstand; (*de periódicos*) news stand

quirófano [ki'rofano] *nm* operating theatre

quirúrgico, a [ki'rurxiko, a] *adj* surgical

quise *etc vb ver* **querer**

quisiera *etc vb ver* **querer**

quisquilloso, a [kiski'ʎoso, a] *adj* (*susceptible*) touchy; (*meticuloso*) pernickety

quiste ['kiste] *nm* cyst

quitaesmalte [kitaes'malte] *nm* nail-polish remover

quitamanchas [kita'mantʃas] *nm inv* stain remover

quitanieves [kita'njeβes] *nm inv* snowplough (*BRIT*), snowplow (*US*)

quitar [ki'tar] *vt* to remove, take away; (*ropa*) to take off; (*dolor*) to relieve; **¡quita de ahí!** get away!; **~se** *vr* to withdraw; (*ropa*) to take off; **se quitó el sombrero** he took off his hat

quite ['kite] *nm* (*esgrima*) parry; (*evasión*) dodge

Quito ['kito] *n* Quito

quizá(s) [ki'θa(s)] *adv* perhaps, maybe

R, r

rábano ['raβano] *nm* radish; **me importa un ~** I don't give a damn

rabia ['raβja] *nf* (*MED*) rabies *sg*; (*ira*) fury, rage; **rabiar** *vi* to have rabies; to rage, be furious; **rabiar por algo** to long for sth

rabieta [ra'βjeta] *nf* tantrum, fit of temper

rabino [ra'βino] *nm* rabbi

rabioso, a [ra'βjoso, a] *adj* rabid; (*fig*) furious

rabo ['raβo] *nm* tail

racha ['ratʃa] *nf* gust of wind; **buena/mala ~** spell of good/bad luck

racial [ra'θjal] *adj* racial, race *cpd*

racimo [ra'θimo] *nm* bunch

raciocinio [raθjo'θinjo] *nm* reason

ración [ra'θjon] *nf* portion; **raciones** *nfpl* rations

racional [raθjo'nal] *adj* (*razonable*) reasonable; (*lógico*) rational; **~izar** *vt* to rationalize

racionar [raθjo'nar] *vt* to ration (out)

racismo [ra'θismo] *nm* racism; **racista** *adj, nm/f* racist

radar [ra'ðar] *nm* radar

radiactivo, a [raðiak'tiβo, a] *adj* = **radioactivo**

radiador [raðja'ðor] *nm* radiator

radiante [ra'ðjante] *adj* radiant

radical [raði'kal] *adj, nm/f* radical

radicar [raði'kar] *vi*: **~ en** (*dificultad, problema*) to lie in; (*solución*) to consist in; **~se** *vr* to establish o.s., put down (one's) roots

radio ['raðjo] *nf* radio; (*aparato*) radio (set) ♦ *nm* (*MAT*) radius; (*QUÍM*) radium; **~actividad** *nf* radioactivity; **~activo, a** *adj* radioactive; **~difusión** *nf* broadcasting; **~emisora** *nf* transmitter,

radio station; **~escucha** *nm/f* listener;
~grafía *nf* X-ray; **~grafiar** *vt* to X-ray;
~terapia *nf* radiotherapy; **~yente** *nm/f*
listener

ráfaga [ˈrafaɣa] *nf* gust; (*de luz*) flash; (*de tiros*) burst

raído, a [raˈiðo, a] *adj* (*ropa*) threadbare

raigambre [raiˈɣambre] *nf* (*BOT*) roots *pl*; (*fig*) tradition

raíz [raˈiθ] *nf* root; **~ cuadrada** square root; **a ~ de** as a result of

raja [ˈraxa] *nf* (*de melón etc*) slice; (*grieta*) crack; **rajar** *vt* to split; (*fam*) to slash; **rajarse** *vr* to split, crack; **rajarse de** to back out of

rajatabla [raxaˈtaβla]: **a ~** *adv* (*estrictamente*) strictly, to the letter

rallador [raʎaˈðor] *nm* grater

rallar [raˈʎar] *vt* to grate

rama [ˈrama] *nf* branch; **~je** *nm* branches *pl*, foliage; **ramal** *nm* (*de cuerda*) strand; (*FERRO*) branch line (*BRIT*); (*AUTO*) branch (road) (*BRIT*)

rambla [ˈrambla] *nf* (*avenida*) avenue

ramificación [ramifikaˈθjon] *nf* ramification

ramificarse [ramifiˈkarse] *vr* to branch out

ramillete [ramiˈʎete] *nm* bouquet

ramo [ˈramo] *nm* branch; (*sección*) department, section

rampa [ˈrampa] *nf* ramp

ramplón, ona [ramˈplon, ona] *adj* uncouth, coarse

rana [ˈrana] *nf* frog; **salto de ~** leapfrog

ranchero [ranˈtʃero] *nm* (*AM*) rancher; smallholder

rancho [ˈrantʃo] *nm* (*grande*) ranch; (*pequeño*) small farm

rancio, a [ˈranθjo, a] *adj* (*comestibles*) rancid; (*vino*) aged, mellow; (*fig*) ancient

rango [ˈrango] *nm* rank, standing

ranura [raˈnura] *nf* (*de teléfono etc*) slot

rapar [raˈpar] *vt* to shave; (*los cabellos*) to crop

rapaz [raˈpaθ] (*nf*: **rapaza**) *nm/f* young

boy/girl ♦ *adj* (*ZOOL*) predatory

rape [ˈrape] *nm* (*pez*) monkfish; **al ~** cropped

rapé [raˈpe] *nm* snuff

rapidez [rapiˈðeθ] *nf* speed, rapidity; **rápido, a** *adj* fast, quick ♦ *adv* quickly ♦ *nm* (*FERRO*) express; **rápidos** *nmpl* rapids

rapiña [raˈpiɲa] *nm* robbery; **ave de ~** bird of prey

raptar [rapˈtar] *vt* to kidnap; **rapto** *nm* kidnapping; (*impulso*) sudden impulse; (*éxtasis*) ecstasy, rapture

raqueta [raˈketa] *nf* racquet

raquítico, a [raˈkitiko, a] *adj* stunted; (*fig*) poor, inadequate; **raquitismo** *nm* rickets *sg*

rareza [raˈreθa] *nf* rarity; (*fig*) eccentricity

raro, a [ˈraro, a] *adj* (*poco común*) rare; (*extraño*) odd, strange; (*excepcional*) remarkable

ras [ras] *nm*: **a ~ de** level with; **a ~ de tierra** at ground level

rasar [raˈsar] *vt* (*igualar*) to level

rascacielos [raskaˈθjelos] *nm inv* skyscraper

rascar [rasˈkar] *vt* (*con las uñas etc*) to scratch; (*raspar*) to scrape; **~se** *vr* to scratch (o.s.)

rasgar [rasˈɣar] *vt* to tear, rip (up)

rasgo [ˈrasɣo] *nm* (*con pluma*) stroke; **~s** *nmpl* (*facciones*) features, characteristics; **a grandes ~s** in outline, broadly

rasguñar [rasɣuˈɲar] *vt* to scratch; **rasguño** *nm* scratch

raso, a [ˈraso, a] *adj* (*liso*) flat, level; (*a baja altura*) very low ♦ *nm* satin; **cielo ~** clear sky

raspadura [raspaˈðura] *nf* (*acto*) scrape, scraping; (*marca*) scratch; **~s** *nfpl* (*de papel etc*) scrapings

raspar [rasˈpar] *vt* to scrape; (*arañar*) to scratch; (*limar*) to file

rastra [ˈrastra] *nf* (*AGR*) rake; **a ~s** by dragging; (*fig*) unwillingly

rastreador [rastreaˈðor] *nm* tracker; **~ de minas** minesweeper

rastrear [rastre'ar] *vt* (*seguir*) to track
rastrero, a [ras'trero, a] *adj* (*BOT, ZOOL*) creeping; (*fig*) despicable, mean
rastrillo [ras'triʎo] *nm* rake
rastro ['rastro] *nm* (*AGR*) rake; (*pista*) track, trail; (*vestigio*) trace; **el R~** the Madrid fleamarket
rastrojo [ras'troxo] *nm* stubble
rasurador [rasura'ðor] (*AM*) *nm* electric shaver
rasuradora [rasura'ðora] (*AM*) *nf* = **rasurador**
rasurarse [rasu'rarse] *vr* to shave
rata ['rata] *nf* rat
ratear [rate'ar] *vt* (*robar*) to steal
ratero, a [ra'tero, a] *adj* light-fingered ♦ *nm/f* (*carterista*) pickpocket; (*AM: de casas*) burglar
ratificar [ratifi'kar] *vt* to ratify
rato ['rato] *nm* while, short time; **a ~s** from time to time; **hay para ~** there's still a long way to go; **al poco ~** soon afterwards; **pasar el ~** to kill time; **pasar un buen/mal ~** to have a good/rough time; **en mis ~s libres** in my spare time
ratón [ra'ton] *nm* mouse; **ratonera** *nf* mousetrap
raudal [rau'ðal] *nm* torrent; **a ~es** in abundance
raya ['raja] *nf* line; (*marca*) scratch; (*en tela*) stripe; (*de pelo*) parting; (*límite*) boundary; (*pez*) ray; (*puntuación*) dash; **a ~s** striped; **pasarse de la ~** to go too far: **tener a ~** to keep in check; **rayar** *vt* to line; to scratch; (*subrayar*) to underline ♦ *vi*: **rayar en** *o* **con** to border on
rayo ['rajo] *nm* (*del sol*) ray, beam; (*de luz*) shaft; (*en una tormenta*) (flash of) lightning; **~s X** X-rays
raza ['raθa] *nf* race; **~ humana** human race
razón [ra'θon] *nf* reason; (*justicia*) right, justice; (*razonamiento*) reasoning; (*motivo*) reason, motive; (*MAT*) ratio; **a ~ de 10 cada día** at the rate of 10 a day; **"~: ..."** "inquiries to ..."; **en ~ de** with regard to; **dar ~ a uno** to agree that sb is right; **tener ~** to be right; **~ directa/inversa** direct/inverse proportion; **~ de ser** raison d'être; **razonable** *adj* reasonable; (*justo, moderado*) fair; **razonamiento** *nm* (*juicio*) judg(e)ment; (*argumento*) reasoning; **razonar** *vt, vi* to reason, argue

reacción [reak'θjon] *nf* reaction; **avión a ~** jet plane; **~ en cadena** chain reaction; **reaccionar** *vi* to react; **reaccionario, a** *adj* reactionary
reacio, a [re'aθjo, a] *adj* stubborn
reactivar [reakti'ßar] *vt* to revitalize
reactor [reak'tor] *nm* reactor
readaptación [reaðapta'θjon] *nf*: **~ profesional** industrial retraining
reajuste [rea'xuste] *nm* readjustment
real [re'al] *adj* real; (*del rey, fig*) royal
realce [re'alθe] *nm* (*lustre, fig*) splendour; **poner de ~** to emphasize
realidad [reali'ðað] *nf* reality, fact; (*verdad*) truth
realista [rea'lista] *nm/f* realist
realización [realiθa'θjon] *nf* fulfilment
realizador, a [realiθa'ðor, a] *nm/f* filmmaker
realizar [reali'θar] *vt* (*objetivo*) to achieve; (*plan*) to carry out; (*viaje*) to make, undertake; **~se** *vr* to come true, come true
realmente [real'mente] *adv* really, actually
realquilar [realki'lar] *vt* to sublet
realzar [real'θar] *vt* to enhance; (*acentuar*) to highlight
reanimar [reani'mar] *vt* to revive; (*alentar*) to encourage; **~se** *vr* to revive
reanudar [reanu'ðar] *vt* (*renovar*) to renew; (*historia, viaje*) to resume
reaparición [reapari'θjon] *nf* reappearance
rearme [re'arme] *nm* rearmament
rebaja [re'ßaxa] *nf* (*COM*) reduction; (: *descuento*) discount; **~s** *nfpl* (*COM*) sale; **rebajar** *vt* (*bajar*) to lower; (*reducir*) to reduce; (*disminuir*) to lessen; (*humillar*) to humble
rebanada [reßa'naða] *nf* slice
rebañar [reßa'ɲar] *vt* (*comida*) to scrape

up; (*plato*) to scrape clean

rebaño [re'ßaɲo] *nm* herd; (*de ovejas*) flock

rebasar [reßa'sar] *vt* (*tb:* **~ de**) to exceed

rebatir [reßa'tir] *vt* to refute

rebeca [re'ßeka] *nf* cardigan

rebelarse [reße'larse] *vr* to rebel, revolt

rebelde [re'ßelde] *adj* rebellious; (*niño*) unruly ♦ *nm/f* rebel; **rebeldía** *nf* rebelliousness; (*desobediencia*) disobedience

rebelión [reße'ljon] *nf* rebellion

reblandecer [reßlande'θer] *vt* to soften

rebobinar [reßoßi'nar] *vt* (*cinta, película de video*) to rewind

rebosante [reßo'sante] *adj* overflowing

rebosar [reßo'sar] *vi* (*líquido, recipiente*) to overflow; (*abundar*) to abound, be plentiful

rebotar [reßo'tar] *vt* to bounce; (*rechazar*) to repel ♦ *vi* (*pelota*) to bounce; (*bala*) to ricochet; **rebote** *nm* rebound; **de rebote** on the rebound

rebozado, a [reßo'θaðo, a] *adj* fried in batter *o* breadcrumbs

rebozar [reßo'θar] *vt* to wrap up; (*CULIN*) to fry in batter *o* breadcrumbs

rebuscado, a [reßus'kaðo, a] *adj* (*amanerado*) affected; (*palabra*) recherché; (*idea*) far-fetched

rebuscar [reßus'kar] *vi:* **~ (en/por)** to search carefully (in/for)

rebuznar [reßuθ'nar] *vi* to bray

recado [re'kaðo] *nm* (*mensaje*) message; (*encargo*) errand; **tomar un ~** (*TEL*) to take a message

recaer [reka'er] *vi* to relapse; **~ en** to fall to *o* on; (*criminal etc*) to fall back into, relapse into; **recaída** *nf* relapse

recalcar [rekal'kar] *vt* (*fig*) to stress, emphasize

recalcitrante [rekalθi'trante] *adj* recalcitrant

recalentar [rekalen'tar] *vt* (*volver a calentar*) to reheat; (*calentar demasiado*) to overheat

recámara [re'kamara] (*AM*) *nf* bedroom

recambio [re'kambjo] *nm* spare; (*de pluma*) refill

recapacitar [rekapaθi'tar] *vi* to reflect

recargado, a [rekar'ɣaðo, a] *adj* overloaded

recargar [rekar'ɣar] *vt* to overload; (*batería*) to recharge; **recargo** *nm* surcharge; (*aumento*) increase

recatado, a [reka'taðo, a] *adj* (*modesto*) modest, demure; (*prudente*) cautious

recato [re'kato] *nm* (*modestia*) modesty, demureness; (*cautela*) caution

recaudación [rekauða'θjon] *nf* (*acción*) collection; (*cantidad*) takings *pl*; (*en deporte*) gate; **recaudador, a** *nm/f* tax collector

recelar [reθe'lar] *vt:* **~ que** (*sospechar*) to suspect that; (*temer*) to fear that ♦ *vi:* **~ de** to distrust; **recelo** *nm* distrust, suspicion; **receloso, a** *adj* distrustful, suspicious

recepción [reθep'θjon] *nf* reception; **recepcionista** *nm/f* receptionist

receptáculo [reθep'takulo] *nm* receptacle

receptivo, a [reθep'tißo, a] *adj* receptive

receptor, a [reθep'tor, a] *nm/f* recipient ♦ *nm* (*TEL*) receiver

recesión [reθe'sjon] *nf* (*COM*) recession

receta [re'θeta] *nf* (*CULIN*) recipe; (*MED*) prescription

rechazar [retʃa'θar] *vt* to reject; (*oferta*) to turn down; (*ataque*) to repel

rechazo [re'tʃaðo] *nm* rejection

rechifla [re'tʃifla] *nf* hissing, booing; (*fig*) derision

rechinar [retʃi'nar] *vi* to creak; (*dientes*) to grind

rechistar [retʃis'tar] *vi:* **sin ~** without a murmur

rechoncho, a [re'tʃontʃo, a] (*fam*) *adj* thickset (*BRIT*), heavy-set (*US*)

rechupete [retʃu'pete]: **de ~** (*comida*) delicious, scrumptious

recibidor, a [reθißi'ðor, a] *nm* entrance hall

recibimiento [reθißi'mjento] *nm* reception, welcome

recibir [reθi'ßir] *vt* to receive; (*dar la bienvenida*) to welcome ♦ *vi* to entertain; **~se** *vr*: **~se de** to qualify as; **recibo** *nm* receipt

reciclar [reθi'klar] *vt* to recycle

recién [re'θjen] *adv* recently, newly; **los ~ casados** the newly-weds; **el ~ llegado** the newcomer; **el ~ nacido** the newborn child

reciente [re'θjente] *adj* recent; (*fresco*) fresh; **~mente** *adv* recently

recinto [re'θinto] *nm* enclosure; (*área*) area, place

recio, a ['reθjo, a] *adj* strong, tough; (*voz*) loud ♦ *adv* hard; loud(ly)

recipiente [reθi'pjente] *nm* receptacle

reciprocidad [reθiproθi'ðað] *nf* reciprocity; **recíproco, a** *adj* reciprocal

recital [reθi'tal] *nm* (*MUS*) recital; (*LITERATURA*) reading

recitar [reθi'tar] *vt* to recite

reclamación [reklama'θjon] *nf* claim, demand; (*queja*) complaint

reclamar [rekla'mar] *vt* to claim, demand ♦ *vi*: **~ contra** to complain about; **~ a uno en justicia** to take sb to court; **reclamo** *nm* (*anuncio*) advertisement; (*tentación*) attraction

reclinar [rekli'nar] *vt* to recline, lean; **~se** *vr* to lean back

recluir [reklu'ir] *vt* to intern, confine

reclusión [reklu'sjon] *nf* (*prisión*) prison; (*refugio*) seclusion; **~ perpetua** life imprisonment

recluta [re'kluta] *nm/f* recruit ♦ *nf* recruitment; **reclutar** *vt* (*datos*) to collect; (*dinero*) to collect up; **~miento** [rekluta'mjento] *nm* recruitment

recobrar [reko'ßrar] *vt* (*salud*) to recover; (*rescatar*) to get back; **~se** *vr* to recover

recodo [re'koðo] *nm* (*de río, camino*) bend

recogedor [rekoxe'ðor] *nm* dustpan

recoger [reko'xer] *vt* to collect; (*AGR*) to harvest; (*levantar*) to pick up; (*juntar*) to gather; (*pasar a buscar*) to come for, get; (*dar asilo*) to give shelter to; (*faldas*) to gather up; (*pelo*) to put up; **~se** *vr*

(*retirarse*) to retire; **recogido, a** *adj* (*lugar*) quiet, secluded; (*pequeño*) small ♦ *nf* (*CORREOS*) collection; (*AGR*) harvest

recolección [rekolek'θjon] *nf* (*AGR*) harvesting; (*colecta*) collection

recomendación [rekomenda'θjon] *nf* (*sugerencia*) suggestion, recommendation; (*referencia*) reference

recomendar [rekomen'dar] *vt* to suggest, recommend; (*confiar*) to entrust

recompensa [rekom'pensa] *nf* reward, recompense; **recompensar** *vt* to reward, recompense

recomponer [rekompo'ner] *vt* to mend

reconciliación [rekonθilja'θjon] *nf* reconciliation

reconciliar [rekonθi'ljar] *vt* to reconcile; **~se** *vr* to become reconciled

recóndito, a [re'kondito, a] *adj* (*lugar*) hidden, secret

reconfortar [rekonfor'tar] *vt* to comfort

reconocer [rekono'θer] *vt* to recognize; (*registrar*) to search; (*MED*) to examine; **reconocido, a** *adj* recognized; (*agradecido*) grateful; **reconocimiento** *nm* recognition; search; examination; gratitude; (*confesión*) admission

reconquista [rekon'kista] *nf* reconquest; **la R~** the Reconquest (of Spain)

reconstituyente [rekonstitu'jente] *nm* tonic

reconstruir [rekonstru'ir] *vt* to reconstruct

reconversión [rekonßer'sjon] *nf*: **~ industrial** industrial rationalization

recopilación [rekopila'θjon] *nf* (*resumen*) summary; (*compilación*) compilation; **recopilar** *vt* to compile

récord ['rekorð] (*pl* **~s**) *adj inv, nm* record

recordar [rekor'ðar] *vt* (*acordarse de*) to remember; (*acordar a otro*) to remind ♦ *vi* to remember

recorrer [reko'rrer] *vt* (*país*) to cross, travel through; (*distancia*) to cover; (*registrar*) to search; (*repasar*) to look over; **recorrido** *nm* run, journey; **tren de largo recorrido** main-line train

recortado, a [rekor'taðo, a] *adj* uneven,

irregular

recortar [rekor'tar] *vt* to cut out; **recorte** *nm* (*acción, de prensa*) cutting; (*de telas, chapas*) trimming; **recorte presupuestario** budget cut

recostado, a [rekos'taðo, a] *adj* leaning; **estar ~** to be lying down

recostar [rekos'tar] *vt* to lean; **~se** *vr* to lie down

recoveco [reko'βeko] *nm* (*de camino, río etc*) bend; (*en casa*) cubby hole

recreación [rekrea'θjon] *nf* recreation

recrear [rekre'ar] *vt* (*entretener*) to entertain; (*volver a crear*) to recreate; **recreativo, a** *adj* recreational; **recreo** *nm* recreation; (*ESCOL*) break, playtime

recriminar [rekrimi'nar] *vt* to reproach ♦ *vi* to recriminate; **~se** *vr* to reproach each other

recrudecer [rekruðe'θer] *vt, vi* to worsen; **~se** *vr* to worsen

recrudecimiento [rekruðeθi'mjento] *nm* upsurge

recta ['rekta] *nf* straight line

rectángulo, a [rek'tangulo, a] *adj* rectangular ♦ *nm* rectangle

rectificar [rektifi'kar] *vt* to rectify; (*volverse recto*) to straighten ♦ *vi* to correct o.s.

rectitud [rekti'tuð] *nf* straightness; (*fig*) rectitude

recto, a ['rekto, a] *adj* straight; (*persona*) honest, upright ♦ *nm* rectum

rector, a [rek'tor, a] *adj* governing

recuadro [re'kwaðro] *nm* box; (*TIPOGRAFÍA*) inset

recubrir [reku'βrir] *vt*: **~ (con)** (*pintura, crema*) to cover (with)

recuento [re'kwento] *nm* inventory; **hacer el ~ de** to count *o* reckon up

recuerdo [re'kwerðo] *nm* souvenir; **~s** *nmpl* (*memorias*) memories; **¡~s a tu madre!** give my regards to your mother!

recular [reku'lar] *vi* to back down

recuperable [rekupe'raβle] *adj* recoverable

recuperación [rekupera'θjon] *nf* recovery

recuperar [rekupe'rar] *vt* to recover;

(*tiempo*) to make up; **~se** *vr* to recuperate

recurrir [reku'rrir] *vi* (*JUR*) to appeal; **~ a** to resort to; (*persona*) to turn to; **recurso** *nm* resort; (*medios*) means *pl*, resources *pl*; (*JUR*) appeal

recusar [reku'sar] *vt* to reject, refuse

red [reð] *nf* net, mesh; (*FERRO etc*) network; (*trampa*) trap

redacción [reðak'θjon] *nf* (*acción*) editing; (*personal*) editorial staff; (*ESCOL*) essay, composition

redactar [reðak'tar] *vt* to draw up, draft; (*periódico*) to edit

redactor, a [reðak'tor, a] *nm/f* editor

redada [re'ðaða] *nf*: **~ policial** police raid, round-up

rededor [reðe'ðor] *nm*: **al** *o* **en ~** around, round about

redención [reðen'θjon] *nf* redemption

redicho, a [re'ðitʃo, a] *adj* affected

redil [re'ðil] *nm* sheepfold

redimir [reði'mir] *vt* to redeem

rédito ['reðito] *nm* interest, yield

redoblar [reðo'βlar] *vt* to redouble ♦ *vi* (*tambor*) to roll

redomado, a [reðo'maðo, a] *adj* (*astuto*) sly, crafty; (*perfecto*) utter

redonda [re'ðonda] *nf*: **a la ~** around, round about

redondear [reðonde'ar] *vt* to round, round off

redondel [reðon'del] *nm* (*círculo*) circle; (*TAUR*) bullring, arena

redondo, a [re'ðondo, a] *adj* (*circular*) round; (*completo*) complete

reducción [reðuk'θjon] *nf* reduction

reducido, a [reðu'θiðo, a] *adj* reduced; (*limitado*) limited; (*pequeño*) small

reducir [reðu'θir] *vt* to reduce; to limit; **~se** *vr* to diminish

redundancia [reðun'danθja] *nf* redundancy

reembolsar [re(e)mbol'sar] *vt* (*persona*) to reimburse; (*dinero*) to repay, pay back; (*depósito*) to refund; **reembolso** *nm* reimbursement; refund

reemplazar [re(e)mpla'θar] *vt* to replace;

reemplazo *nm* replacement; **de reemplazo** (*MIL*) reserve

reencuentro [re(e)nˈkwentro] *nm* reunion

referencia [refeˈrenθja] *nf* reference; **con ~ a** with reference to

referéndum [refeˈrendum] (*pl* **~s**) *nm* referendum

referente [refeˈrente] *adj*: **~ a** concerning, relating to

referir [refeˈrir] *vt* (*contar*) to tell, recount; (*relacionar*) to refer, relate; **~se** *vr*: **~se a** to refer to

refilón [refiˈlon]: **de ~** *adv* obliquely

refinado, a [refiˈnaðo, a] *adj* refined

refinamiento [refinaˈmjento] *nm* refinement

refinar [refiˈnar] *vt* to refine; **refinería** *nf* refinery

reflejar [refleˈxar] *vt* to reflect; **reflejo, a** *adj* reflected; (*movimiento*) reflex ♦ *nm* reflection; (*ANAT*) reflex

reflexión [reflekˈsjon] *nf* reflection; **reflexionar** *vt* to reflect on ♦ *vi* to reflect; (*detenerse*) to pause (to think)

reflexivo, a [reflekˈsiβo, a] *adj* thoughtful; (*LING*) reflexive

reflujo [reˈfluxo] *nm* ebb

reforma [reˈforma] *nf* reform; (*ARQ etc*) repair; **~ agraria** agrarian reform

reformar [reforˈmar] *vt* to reform; (*modificar*) to change, alter; (*ARQ*) to repair; **~se** *vr* to mend one's ways

reformatorio [reformaˈtorjo] *nm* reformatory

reforzar [reforˈθar] *vt* to strengthen; (*ARQ*) to reinforce; (*fig*) to encourage

refractario, a [refrakˈtarjo, a] *adj* (*TEC*) heat-resistant

refrán [reˈfran] *nm* proverb, saying

refregar [refreˈɣar] *vt* to scrub

refrenar [refreˈnar] *vt* to check, restrain

refrendar [refrenˈdar] *vt* (*firma*) to endorse, countersign; (*ley*) to approve

refrescante [refresˈkante] *adj* refreshing, cooling

refrescar [refresˈkar] *vt* to refresh ♦ *vi* to cool down; **~se** *vr* to get cooler; (*tomar*

aire fresco) to go out for a breath of fresh air; (*beber*) to have a drink

refresco [reˈfresko] *nm* soft drink, cool drink; **"~s"** "refreshments"

refriega [reˈfrjeɣa] *nf* scuffle, brawl

refrigeración [refrixeraˈθjon] *nf* refrigeration; (*de sala*) air-conditioning

refrigerador [refrixeraˈðor] *nm* refrigerator (*BRIT*), icebox (*US*)

refrigerar [refrixeˈrar] *vt* to refrigerate; (*sala*) to air-condition

refuerzo [reˈfwerθo] *nm* reinforcement; (*TEC*) support

refugiado, a [refuˈxjaðo, a] *nm/f* refugee

refugiarse [refuˈxjarse] *vr* to take refuge, shelter

refugio [reˈfuxjo] *nm* refuge; (*protección*) shelter

refunfuñar [refunfuˈɲar] *vi* to grunt, growl; (*quejarse*) to grumble

refutar [refuˈtar] *vt* to refute

regadera [reɣaˈðera] *nf* watering can

regadío [reɣaˈðio] *nm* irrigated land

regalado, a [reɣaˈlaðo, a] *adj* comfortable, luxurious; (*gratis*) free, for nothing

regalar [reɣaˈlar] *vt* (*dar*) to give (as a present); (*entregar*) to give away; (*mimar*) to pamper, make a fuss of

regaliz [reɣaˈliθ] *nm* liquorice

regalo [reˈɣalo] *nm* (*obsequio*) gift, present; (*gusto*) pleasure

regañadientes [reɣaɲaˈðjentes]: **a ~** *adv* reluctantly

regañar [reɣaˈɲar] *vt* to scold ♦ *vi* to grumble; **regañón, ona** *adj* nagging

regar [reˈɣar] *vt* to water, irrigate; (*fig*) to scatter, sprinkle

regatear [reɣateˈar] *vt* (*COM*) to bargain over; (*escatimar*) to be mean with ♦ *vi* to bargain, haggle; (*DEPORTE*) to dribble; **regateo** *nm* bargaining; dribbling; (*del cuerpo*) swerve, dodge

regazo [reˈɣaθo] *nm* lap

regeneración [rexeneraˈθjon] *nf* regeneration

regenerar [rexeneˈrar] *vt* to regenerate

regentar [rexen'tar] *vt* to direct, manage;
  regente *nm* (*COM*) manager; (*POL*)
  regent
régimen ['reximen] (*pl* **regímenes**) *nm*
  regime; (*MED*) diet
regimiento [rexi'mjento] *nm* regiment
regio, a ['rexjo, a] *adj* royal, regal; (*fig:
  suntuoso*) splendid; (*AM: fam*) great,
  terrific
región [re'xjon] *nf* region
regir [re'xir] *vt* to govern, rule; (*dirigir*) to
  manage, run ♦ *vi* to apply, be in force
registrar [rexis'trar] *vt* (*buscar*) to search;
  (: *en cajón*) to look through; (*inspeccionar*)
  to inspect; (*anotar*) to register, record;
  (*INFORM*) to log; **~se** *vr* to register;
  (*ocurrir*) to happen
registro [re'xistro] *nm* (*acto*) registration;
  (*MUS, libro*) register; (*inspección*)
  inspection, search; **~ civil** registry office
regla ['rexla] *nf* (*ley*) rule, regulation; (*de
  medir*) ruler; (*MED: período*) period
reglamentación [rexlamenta'θjon] *nf*
  (*acto*) regulation; (*lista*) rules *pl*
reglamentar [rexlamen'tar] *vt* to regulate;
  reglamentario, a *adj* statutory;
  reglamento *nm* rules *pl*, regulations *pl*
regocijarse [rexoθi'xarse] *vr*: **~ de** to
  rejoice at, be happy about; **regocijo** *nm*
  joy, happiness
regodearse [rexoðe'arse] *vr* to be glad,
  be delighted; **regodeo** *nm* delight
regresar [rexre'sar] *vi* to come back, go
  back, return; **regresivo, a** *adj*
  backward; (*fig*) regressive; **regreso** *nm*
  return
reguero [re'xero] *nm* (*de sangre etc*)
  trickle; (*de humo*) trail
regulador [rexula'ðor] *nm* regulator; (*de
  radio etc*) knob, control
regular [rexu'lar] *adj* regular; (*normal*)
  normal, usual; (*común*) ordinary;
  (*organizado*) regular, orderly; (*mediano*)
  average; (*fam*) not bad, so-so ♦ *adv* soso, alright ♦ *vt* (*controlar*) to control,
  regulate; (*TEC*) to adjust; **por lo ~** as a
  rule; **~idad** *nf* regularity; **~izar** *vt* to

regularize
regusto [re'xusto] *nm* aftertaste
rehabilitación [reaßilita'θjon] *nf*
  rehabilitation; (*ARQ*) restoration
rehabilitar [reaßili'tar] *vt* to rehabilitate;
  (*ARQ*) to restore; (*reintegrar*) to reinstate
rehacer [rea'θer] *vt* (*reparar*) to mend,
  repair; (*volver a hacer*) to redo, repeat;
  ~se *vr* (*MED*) to recover
rehén [re'en] *nm* hostage
rehuir [reu'ir] *vt* to avoid, shun
rehusar [reu'sar] *vt, vi* to refuse
reina ['reina] *nf* queen; **~do** *nm* reign
reinante [rei'nante] *adj* (*fig*) prevailing
reinar [rei'nar] *vi* to reign
reincidir [reinθi'ðir] *vi* to relapse
reincorporarse [reinkorpo'rarse] *vr*: **~ a**
  to rejoin
reino ['reino] *nm* kingdom; **el R~ Unido**
  the United Kingdom
reintegrar [reinte'xrar] *vt* (*reconstituir*) to
  reconstruct; (*persona*) to reinstate; (*dinero*)
  to refund, pay back; **~se** *vr*: **~se a** to
  return to
reír [re'ir] *vi* to laugh; **~se** *vr* to laugh; **~se
  de** to laugh at
reiterar [reite'rar] *vt* to reiterate
reivindicación [reißindika'θjon] *nf*
  (*demanda*) claim, demand; (*justificación*)
  vindication
reivindicar [reißindi'kar] *vt* to claim
reja ['rexa] *nf* (*de ventana*) grille, bars *pl*;
  (*en la calle*) grating
rejilla [re'xiʎa] *nf* grating, grille; (*muebles*)
  wickerwork; (*de ventilación*) vent; (*de
  coche etc*) luggage rack
rejoneador [rexonea'ðor] *nm* mounted
  bullfighter
rejuvenecer [rexußene'θer] *vt, vi* to
  rejuvenate
relación [rela'θjon] *nf* relation,
  relationship; (*MAT*) ratio; (*narración*)
  report; **relaciones públicas** public
  relations; **con ~ a, en ~ con** in relation
  to; **relacionar** *vt* to relate, connect;
  relacionarse *vr* to be connected, be
  linked

relajación [relaxa'θjon] *nf* relaxation
relajado, a [rela'xaðo, a] *adj* (*disoluto*)
  loose; (*cómodo*) relaxed; (*MED*) ruptured
relajar [rela'xar] *vt* to relax; **~se** *vr* to relax
relamerse [rela'merse] *vr* to lick one's lips
relamido, a [rela'miðo, a] *adj* (*pulcro*)
  overdressed; (*afectado*) affected
relámpago [re'lampaxo] *nm* flash of
  lightning; **visita/huelga ~** lightning visit/
  strike; **relampaguear** *vi* to flash
relatar [rela'tar] *vt* to tell, relate
relativo, a [rela'tiβo, a] *adj* relative; **en lo**
  ~ a concerning
relato [re'lato] *nm* (*narración*) story, tale
relegar [rele'xar] *vt* to relegate
relevante [rele'ßante] *adj* eminent,
  outstanding
relevar [rele'ßar] *vt* (*sustituir*) to relieve;
  ~se *vr* to relay; **~ a uno de un cargo** to
  relieve sb of his post
relevo [re'leßo] *nm* relief; **carrera de ~s**
  relay race
relieve [re'ljeße] *nm* (*ARTE, TEC*) relief; (*fig*)
  prominence, importance; **bajo ~** bas-relief
religión [reli'xjon] *nf* religion; **religioso,**
  a *adj* religious ♦ *nm/f* monk/nun
relinchar [relin'tʃar] *vi* to neigh; **relincho**
  nm neigh; (*acto*) neighing
reliquia [re'likja] *nf* relic; **~ de familia**
  heirloom
rellano [re'ʎano] *nm* (*ARQ*) landing
rellenar [reʎe'nar] *vt* (*llenar*) to fill up;
  (*CULIN*) to stuff; (*COSTURA*) to pad;
  relleno, a *adj* full up; stuffed ♦ *nm*
  stuffing; (*de tapicería*) padding
reloj [re'lo(x)] *nm* clock; **~ (de pulsera)**
  wristwatch; **~ despertador** alarm (clock);
  poner el ~ to set one's watch (o the
  clock); **~ero, a** *nm/f* clockmaker;
  watchmaker
reluciente [relu'θjente] *adj* brilliant,
  shining
relucir [relu'θir] *vi* to shine; (*fig*) to excel
relumbrar [relum'brar] *vi* to dazzle, shine
  brilliantly
remachar [rema'tʃar] *vt* to rivet; (*fig*) to
  hammer home, drive home; **remache**

nm rivet
remanente [rema'nente] *nm* remainder;
  (*COM*) balance; (*de producto*) surplus
remangar [reman'gar] *vt* to roll up
remanso [re'manso] *nm* pool
remar [re'mar] *vi* to row
rematado, a [rema'taðo, a] *adj* complete,
  utter
rematar [rema'tar] *vt* to finish off; (*COM*)
  to sell off cheap ♦ *vi* to end, finish off;
  (*DEPORTE*) to shoot
remate [re'mate] *nm* end, finish; (*punta*)
  tip; (*DEPORTE*) shot; (*ARQ*) top; **de *o* para**
  ~ to crown it all (*BRIT*), to top it off
remedar [reme'ðar] *vt* to imitate
remediar [reme'ðjar] *vt* to remedy;
  (*subsanar*) to make good, repair; (*evitar*)
  to avoid
remedio [re'meðjo] *nm* remedy; (*alivio*)
  relief, help; (*JUR*) recourse, remedy; **poner**
  ~ a to correct, stop; **no tener más ~** to
  have no alternative; **¡qué ~!** there's no
  choice!; **sin ~** hopeless
remedo [re'meðo] *nm* imitation; (*pey*)
  parody
remendar [remen'dar] *vt* to repair; (*con*
  parche) to patch
remesa [re'mesa] *nf* remittance; (*COM*)
  shipment
remiendo [re'mjendo] *nm* mend; (*con*
  parche) patch; (*cosido*) darn
remilgado, a [remil'xaðo, a] *adj* prim;
  (*afectado*) affected
remilgo [re'milxo] *nm* primness;
  (*afectación*) affectation
reminiscencia [reminis'θenθja] *nf*
  reminiscence
remiso, a [re'miso, a] *adj* slack, slow
remite [re'mite] *nm* (*en sobre*) name and
  address of sender
remitir [remi'tir] *vt* to remit, send ♦ *vi* to
  slacken; (*en carta*): **remite: X** sender: X;
  remitente *nm/f* sender
remo ['remo] *nm* (*de barco*) oar; (*DEPORTE*)
  rowing
remojar [remo'xar] *vt* to steep, soak;
  (*galleta etc*) to dip, dunk

remojo [re'moxo] *nm*: **dejar la ropa en ~** to leave clothes to soak

remolacha [remo'latʃa] *nf* beet, beetroot

remolcador [remolka'ðor] *nm* (*NAUT*) tug; (*AUTO*) breakdown lorry

remolcar [remol'kar] *vt* to tow

remolino [remo'lino] *nm* eddy; (*de agua*) whirlpool; (*de viento*) whirlwind; (*de gente*) crowd

remolque [re'molke] *nm* tow, towing; (*cuerda*) towrope; **llevar a ~** to tow

remontar [remon'tar] *vt* to mend; **~se** *vr* to soar; **~se a** (*COM*) to amount to; **~ el vuelo** to soar

remorder [remor'ðer] *vt* to distress, disturb; **~le la conciencia a uno** to have a guilty conscience; **remordimiento** *nm* remorse

remoto, a [re'moto, a] *adj* remote

remover [remo'ßer] *vt* to stir; (*tierra*) to turn over; (*objetos*) to move round

remozar [remo'θar] *vt* (*ARQ*) to refurbish

remuneración [remunera'θjon] *nf* remuneration

remunerar [remune'rar] *vt* to remunerate; (*premiar*) to reward

renacer [rena'θer] *vi* to be reborn; (*fig*) to revive; **renacimiento** *nm* rebirth; **el Renacimiento** the Renaissance

renacuajo [rena'kwaxo] *nm* (*ZOOL*) tadpole

renal [re'nal] *adj* renal, kidney *cpd*

rencilla [ren'θiʎa] *nf* quarrel

rencor [ren'kor] *nm* rancour, bitterness; **~oso, a** *adj* spiteful

rendición [rendi'θjon] *nf* surrender

rendido, a [ren'diðo, a] *adj* (*sumiso*) submissive; (*cansado*) worn-out, exhausted

rendija [ren'dixa] *nf* (*hendedura*) crack, cleft

rendimiento [rendi'mjento] *nm* (*producción*) output; (*TEC*, *COM*) efficiency

rendir [ren'dir] *vt* (*vencer*) to defeat; (*producir*) to produce; (*dar beneficio*) to yield; (*agotar*) to exhaust ♦ *vi* to pay; **~se** *vr* (*someterse*) to surrender; (*cansarse*) to

wear o.s. out; **~ homenaje** *o* **culto a** to pay homage to

renegar [rene'var] *vi* (*renunciar*) to renounce; (*blasfemar*) to blaspheme; (*quejarse*) to complain

RENFE ['renfe] *nf abr* (= *Red Nacional de los Ferrocarriles Españoles*) ≈ BR (*BRIT*)

renglón [ren'glon] *nm* (*línea*) line; (*COM*) item, article; **a ~ seguido** immediately after

renombrado, a [renom'braðo, a] *adj* renowned

renombre [re'nombre] *nm* renown

renovación [renoßa'θjon] *nf* (*de contrato*) renewal; (*ARQ*) renovation

renovar [reno'ßar] *vt* to renew; (*ARQ*) to renovate

renta ['renta] *nf* (*ingresos*) income; (*beneficio*) profit; (*alquiler*) rent; **~ vitalicia** annuity; **rentable** *adj* profitable; **rentar** *vt* to produce, yield

renuncia [re'nunθja] *nf* resignation

renunciar [renun'θjar] *vt* to renounce; (*tabaco, alcohol etc*): **~ a** to give up; (*oferta, oportunidad*) to turn down; (*puesto*) to resign ♦ *vi* to resign

reñido, a [re'niðo, a] *adj* (*batalla*) bitter, hard-fought; **estar ~ con uno** to be on bad terms with sb

reñir [re'nir] *vt* (*regañar*) to scold ♦ *vi* (*estar peleado*) to quarrel, fall out; (*combatir*) to fight

reo ['reo] *nm/f* culprit, offender; **~ de muerte** prisoner condemned to death

reojo [re'oxo]: **de ~** *adv* out of the corner of one's eye

reparación [repara'θjon] *nf* (*acto*) mending, repairing; (*TEC*) repair; (*fig*) amends, reparation

reparar [repa'rar] *vt* to repair; (*fig*) to make amends for; (*observar*) to observe ♦ *vi*: **~ en** (*darse cuenta de*) to notice; (*prestar atención a*) to pay attention to

reparo [re'paro] *nm* (*advertencia*) observation; (*duda*) doubt; (*dificultad*) difficulty; **poner ~s (a)** to raise objections (to)

repartición [reparti'θjon] *nf* distribution; (*división*) division; **repartidor, a** *nm/f* distributor

repartir [repar'tir] *vt* to distribute, share out; (*CORREOS*) to deliver; **reparto** *nm* distribution; delivery; (*TEATRO, CINE*) cast; (*AM: urbanización*) housing estate (*BRIT*), real estate development (*US*)

repasar [repa'sar] *vt* (*ESCOL*) to revise; (*MECÁNICA*) to check, overhaul; (*COSTURA*) to mend; **repaso** *nm* revision; overhaul, checkup; mending

repatriar [repa'trjar] *vt* to repatriate

repecho [re'petʃo] *nm* steep incline

repelente [repe'lente] *adj* repellent, repulsive

repeler [repe'ler] *vt* to repel

repensar [repen'sar] *vt* to reconsider

repente [re'pente] *nm*: **de ~** suddenly; **~ de ira** fit of anger

repentino, a [repen'tino, a] *adj* sudden

repercusión [reperku'sjon] *nf* repercussion

repercutir [reperku'tir] *vi* (*objeto*) to rebound; (*sonido*) to echo; **~ en** (*fig*) to have repercussions on

repertorio [reper'torjo] *nm* list; (*TEATRO*) repertoire

repetición [repeti'θjon] *nf* repetition

repetir [repe'tir] *vt* to repeat; (*plato*) to have a second helping of ♦ *vi* to repeat; (*sabor*) to come back; **~se** *vr* (*volver sobre un tema*) to repeat o.s.

repetitivo, a [repeti'tiβo, a] *adj* repetitive, repetitious

repicar [repi'kar] *vt* (*campanas*) to ring

repique [re'pike] *nm* pealing, ringing; **~teo** *nm* pealing; (*de tambor*) drumming

repisa [re'pisa] *nf* ledge, shelf; (*de ventana*) windowsill; **~ de chimenea** mantelpiece

repito *etc vb ver* **repetir**

replantearse [replante'arse] *vr*: **~ un problema** to reconsider a problem

replegarse [reple'xarse] *vr* to fall back, retreat

repleto, a [re'pleto, a] *adj* replete, full up

réplica ['replika] *nf* answer; (*ARTE*) replica

replicar [repli'kar] *vi* to answer; (*objetar*) to argue, answer back

repliegue [re'pljeɣe] *nm* (*MIL*) withdrawal

repoblación [repoβla'θjon] *nf* repopulation; (*de río*) restocking; **~ forestal** reafforestation

repoblar [repo'βlar] *vt* to repopulate; (*con árboles*) to reafforest

repollo [re'poʎo] *nm* cabbage

reponer [repo'ner] *vt* to replace, put back; (*TEATRO*) to revive; **~se** *vr* to recover; **~ que** to reply that

reportaje [repor'taxe] *nm* report, article

reportero, a [repor'tero, a] *nm/f* reporter

reposacabezas [reposaka'βeθas] *nm inv* headrest

reposado, a [repo'saðo, a] *adj* (*descansado*) restful; (*tranquilo*) calm

reposar [repo'sar] *vi* to rest, repose

reposición [reposi'θjon] *nf* replacement; (*CINE*) remake

reposo [re'poso] *nm* rest

repostar [repos'tar] *vt* to replenish; (*AUTO*) to fill up (with petrol (*BRIT*) o gasoline (*US*))

repostería [reposte'ria] *nf* confectioner's (shop); **repostero, a** *nm/f* confectioner

reprender [repren'der] *vt* to reprimand

represa [re'presa] *nf* dam; (*lago artificial*) lake, pool

represalia [repre'salja] *nf* reprisal

representación [representa'θjon] *nf* representation; (*TEATRO*) performance; **representante** *nm/f* representative; performer

representar [represen'tar] *vt* to represent; (*TEATRO*) to perform; (*edad*) to look; **~se** *vr* to imagine; **representativo, a** *adj* representative

represión [repre'sjon] *nf* repression

reprimenda [repri'menda] *nf* reprimand, rebuke

reprimir [repri'mir] *vt* to repress

reprobar [repro'βar] *vt* to censure, reprove

reprochar [repro'tʃar] *vt* to reproach; **reproche** *nm* reproach

reproducción [reproðuk'θjon] *nf* reproduction

reproducir [reproðu'θir] *vt* to reproduce; **~se** *vr* to breed; (*situación*) to recur

reproductor, a [reproðuk'tor, a] *adj* reproductive

reptil [rep'til] *nm* reptile

república [re'puβlika] *nf* republic; **R~ Dominicana** Dominican Republic; **republicano, a** *adj, nm/f* republican

repudiar [repu'ðjar] *vt* to repudiate; (*fe*) to renounce

repuesto [re'pwesto] *nm* (*pieza de recambio*) spare (part); (*abastecimiento*) supply; **rueda de ~** spare wheel

repugnancia [repuɣ'nanθja] *nf* repugnance; **repugnante** *adj* repugnant, repulsive

repugnar [repuɣ'nar] *vt* to disgust

repulsa [re'pulsa] *nf* rebuff

repulsión [repul'sjon] *nf* repulsion, aversion; **repulsivo, a** *adj* repulsive

reputación [reputa'θjon] *nf* reputation

requemado, a [reke'maðo, a] *adj* (*quemado*) scorched; (*bronceado*) tanned

requerimiento [rekeri'mjento] *nm* request; (*JUR*) summons

requerir [reke'rir] *vt* (*pedir*) to ask, request; (*exigir*) to require; (*llamar*) to send for, summon

requesón [reke'son] *nm* cottage cheese

requete... [re'kete] *prefijo* extremely

réquiem ['rekjem] (*pl* **~s**) *nm* requiem

requisito [reki'sito] *nm* requirement, requisite

res [res] *nf* beast, animal

resaca [re'saka] *nf* (*en el mar*) undertow, undercurrent; (*fam*) hangover

resaltar [resal'tar] *vi* to project, stick out; (*fig*) to stand out

resarcir [resar'θir] *vt* to compensate; **~se** *vr* to make up for

resbaladizo, a [resβala'ðiθo, a] *adj* slippery

resbalar [resβa'lar] *vi* to slip, slide; (*fig*) to slip (up); **~se** *vr* to slip, slide; to slip (up); **resbalón** *nm* (*acción*) slip

rescatar [reska'tar] *vt* (*salvar*) to save, rescue; (*objeto*) to get back, recover; (*cautivos*) to ransom

rescate [res'kate] *nm* rescue; (*de objeto*) recovery; **pagar un ~** to pay a ransom

rescindir [resθin'dir] *vt* to rescind

rescisión [resθi'sjon] *nf* cancellation

rescoldo [res'koldo] *nm* embers *pl*

resecar [rese'kar] *vt* to dry thoroughly; (*MED*) to cut out, remove; **~se** *vr* to dry up

reseco, a [re'seko, a] *adj* very dry; (*fig*) skinny

resentido, a [resen'tiðo, a] *adj* resentful

resentimiento [resenti'mjento] *nm* resentment, bitterness

resentirse [resen'tirse] *vr* (*debilitarse*: *persona*) to suffer; **~ de** (*consecuencias*) to feel the effects of; **~ de** (*o por*) **algo** to resent sth, be bitter about sth

reseña [re'seɲa] *nf* (*cuenta*) account; (*informe*) report; (*LITERATURA*) review

reseñar [rese'ɲar] *vt* to describe; (*LITERATURA*) to review

reserva [re'serβa] *nf* reserve; (*reservación*) reservation; **a ~ de que ...** unless ...; **con toda ~** in strictest confidence

reservado, a [reser'βaðo, a] *adj* reserved; (*retraído*) cold, distant ♦ *nm* private room

reservar [reser'βar] *vt* (*guardar*) to keep; (*habitación, entrada*) to reserve; **~se** *vr* to save o.s.; (*callar*) to keep to o.s.

resfriado [resfri'aðo] *nm* cold; **resfriarse** *vr* to cool; (*MED*) to catch (a) cold

resguardar [resɣwar'ðar] *vt* to protect, shield; **~se** *vr*: **~se de** to guard against; **resguardo** *nm* defence; (*vale*) voucher; (*recibo*) receipt, slip

residencia [resi'ðenθja] *nf* residence; **~l** *nf* (*urbanización*) housing estate

residente [resi'ðente] *adj, nm/f* resident

residir [resi'ðir] *vi* to reside, live; **~ en** to reside in, lie in

residuo [re'siðwo] *nm* residue

resignación [resiɣna'θjon] *nf* resignation; **resignarse** *vr*: **resignarse a** *o* **con** to resign o.s. to, be resigned to

resina [re'sina] *nf* resin
resistencia [resis'tenθja] *nf* (*dureza*)
  endurance, strength; (*oposición, ELEC*)
  resistance; **resistente** *adj* strong, hardy;
  resistant
resistir [resis'tir] *vt* (*soportar*) to bear;
  (*oponerse a*) to resist, oppose; (*aguantar*)
  to put up with ♦ *vi* to resist; (*aguantar*)
  to last, endure; **~se** *vr:* **~se a** to refuse
  to, resist
resolución [resolu'θjon] *nf* resolution;
  (*decisión*) decision; **resoluto, a** *adj*
  resolute
resolver [resol'ßer] *vt* to resolve;
  (*solucionar*) to solve, resolve; (*decidir*) to
  decide, settle; **~se** *vr* to make up one's
  mind
resonancia [reso'nanθja] *nf* (*del sonido*)
  resonance; (*repercusión*) repercussion
resonar [reso'nar] *vi* to ring, echo
resoplar [reso'plar] *vi* to snort; **resoplido**
  nm heavy breathing
resorte [re'sorte] *nm* spring; (*fig*) lever
respaldar [respal'dar] *vt* to back (up),
  support; **~se** *vr* to lean back; **~se con** *o*
  en (*fig*) to take one's stand on;
  respaldo *nm* (*de sillón*) back; (*fig*)
  support, backing
respectivo, a [respek'tißo, a] *adj*
  respective; **en lo ~ a** with regard to
respecto [res'pekto] *nm:* **al ~** on this
  matter; **con ~ a, ~ de** with regard to, in
  relation to
respetable [respe'taßle] *adj* respectable
respetar [respe'tar] *vt* to respect;
  respeto *nm* respect; (*acatamiento*)
  deference; **respetos** *nmpl* respects;
  respetuoso, a *adj* respectful
respingo [res'pingo] *nm* start, jump
respiración [respira'θjon] *nf* breathing;
  (*MED*) respiration; (*ventilación*) ventilation
respirar [respi'rar] *vi* to breathe;
  respiratorio, a *adj* respiratory; **respiro**
  nm breathing; (*fig: descanso*) respite
resplandecer [resplande'θer] *vi* to shine;
  resplandeciente *adj* resplendent,
  shining; **resplandor** *nm* brilliance,

brightness; (*de luz, fuego*) blaze
responder [respon'der] *vt* to answer ♦ *vi*
  to answer; (*fig*) to respond; (*pey*) to
  answer back; **~ de** *o* **por** to answer for;
  respondón, ona *adj* cheeky
responsabilidad [responsaßili'ðað] *nf*
  responsibility
responsabilizarse [responsaßili'θarse] *vr*
  to make o.s. responsible, take charge
responsable [respon'saßle] *adj*
  responsible
respuesta [res'pwesta] *nf* answer, reply
resquebrajar [reskeßra'xar] *vt* to crack,
  split; **~se** *vr* to crack, split
resquemor [reske'mor] *nm* resentment
resquicio [res'kiθjo] *nm* chink;
  (*hendedura*) crack
resta ['resta] *nf* (*MAT*) remainder
restablecer [restaßle'θer] *vt* to re-
  establish, restore; **~se** *vr* to recover
restallar [resta'ʎar] *vi* to crack
restante [res'tante] *adj* remaining; **lo ~**
  the remainder
restar [res'tar] *vt* (*MAT*) to subtract; (*fig*) to
  take away ♦ *vi* to remain, be left
restauración [restaura'θjon] *nf* restoration
restaurante [restau'rante] *nm* restaurant
restaurar [restau'rar] *vt* to restore
restitución [restitu'θjon] *nf* return,
  restitution
restituir [restitu'ir] *vt* (*devolver*) to return,
  give back; (*rehabilitar*) to restore
resto ['resto] *nm* (*residuo*) rest, remainder;
  (*apuesta*) stake; **~s** *nmpl* remains
restregar [restre'xar] *vt* to scrub, rub
restricción [restrik'θjon] *nf* restriction
restrictivo, a [restrik'tißo, a] *adj*
  restrictive
restringir [restrin'xir] *vt* to restrict, limit
resucitar [resuθi'tar] *vt, vi* to resuscitate,
  revive
resuello [re'sweʎo] *nm* (*aliento*) breath;
  estar sin ~ to be breathless
resuelto, a [re'swelto, a] *pp de* **resolver**
  ♦ *adj* resolute, determined
resultado [resul'taðo] *nm* result;
  (*conclusión*) outcome; **resultante** *adj*

resulting, resultant

resultar [resul'tar] *vi* (*ser*) to be; (*llegar a ser*) to turn out to be; (*salir bien*) to turn out well; (*COM*) to amount to; ~ **de** to stem from; **me resulta difícil hacerlo** it's difficult for me to do it

resumen [re'sumen] (*pl* **resúmenes**) *nm* summary, résumé; **en ~** in short

resumir [resu'mir] *vt* to sum up; (*cortar*) to abridge, cut down; (*condensar*) to summarize

resurgir [resur'xir] *vi* (*reaparecer*) to reappear

resurrección [resurre(k)'θjon] *nf* resurrection

retablo [re'taβlo] *nm* altarpiece

retaguardia [reta'ɣwarðja] *nf* rearguard

retahíla [reta'ila] *nf* series, string

retal [re'tal] *nm* remnant

retar [re'tar] *vt* to challenge; (*desafiar*) to defy, dare

retardar [retar'ðar] *vt* (*demorar*) to delay; (*hacer más lento*) to slow down; (*retener*) to hold back

retazo [re'taθo] *nm* snippet (*BRIT*), fragment

retener [rete'ner] *vt* (*intereses*) to withhold

reticente [reti'θente] *adj* (*tono*) insinuating; (*postura*) reluctant; **ser ~ a hacer algo** to be reluctant *o* unwilling to do sth

retina [re'tina] *nf* retina

retintín [retin'tin] *nm* jangle, jingle

retirada [reti'raða] *nf* (*MIL, refugio*) retreat; (*de dinero*) withdrawal; (*de embajador*) recall; **retirado, a** *adj* (*lugar*) remote; (*vida*) quiet; (*jubilado*) retired

retirar [reti'rar] *vt* to withdraw; (*quitar*) to remove; (*jubilar*) to retire, pension off; **~se** *vr* to retreat, withdraw; to retire; (*acostarse*) to retire, go to bed; **retiro** *nm* retreat; retirement; (*pago*) pension

reto ['reto] *nm* dare, challenge

retocar [reto'kar] *vt* (*fotografía*) to touch up, retouch

retoño [re'toɲo] *nm* sprout, shoot; (*fig*) offspring, child

retoque [re'toke] *nm* retouching

retorcer [retor'θer] *vt* to twist; (*manos, lavado*) to wring; **~se** *vr* to become twisted; (*mover el cuerpo*) to writhe

retorcido, a [retor'θiðo, a] *adj* (*persona*) devious

retórica [re'torika] *nf* rhetoric; (*pey*) affectedness; **retórico, a** *adj* rhetorical

retornar [retor'nar] *vt* to return, give back ♦ *vi* to return, go/come back; **retorno** *nm* return

retortijón [retorti'xon] *nm* twist, twisting

retozar [reto'θar] *vi* (*juguetear*) to frolic, romp; (*saltar*) to gambol; **retozón, ona** *adj* playful

retracción [retrak'θjon] *nf* retraction

retractarse [retrak'tarse] *vr* to retract; **me retracto** I take that back

retraerse [retra'erse] *vr* to retreat, withdraw; **retraído, a** *adj* shy, retiring; **retraimiento** *nm* retirement; (*timidez*) shyness

retransmisión [retransmi'sjon] *nf* repeat (broadcast)

retransmitir [retransmi'tir] *vt* (*mensaje*) to relay; (*TV etc*) to repeat, retransmit; (: *en vivo*) to broadcast live

retrasado, a [retra'saðo, a] *adj* late; (*MED*) mentally retarded; (*país etc*) backward, underdeveloped

retrasar [retra'sar] *vt* (*demorar*) to postpone, put off; (*retardar*) to slow down ♦ *vi* (*atrasarse*) to be late; (*reloj*) to be slow; (*producción*) to fall (off); (*quedarse atrás*) to lag behind; **~se** *vr* to be late; to be slow; to fall (off); to lag behind

retraso [re'traso] *nm* (*demora*) delay; (*lentitud*) slowness; (*tardanza*) lateness; (*atraso*) backwardness; **~s** (*FINANZAS*) *nmpl* arrears; **llegar con ~** to arrive late; **~ mental** mental deficiency

retratar [retra'tar] *vt* (*ARTE*) to paint the portrait of; (*fotografiar*) to photograph; (*fig*) to depict, describe; **~se** *vr* to have one's portrait painted; to have one's photograph taken; **retrato** *nm* portrait;

(*fig*) likeness; **retrato-robot** *nm* Identikit
® picture

retreta [re'treta] *nf* retreat

retrete [re'trete] *nm* toilet

retribución [retriβu'θjon] *nf* (*recompensa*)
reward; (*pago*) pay, payment

retribuir [retri'βwir] *vt* (*recompensar*) to
reward; (*pagar*) to pay

retro... ['retro] *prefijo* retro...

retroactivo, a [retroak'tiβo, a] *adj*
retroactive, retrospective

retroceder [retroθe'ðer] *vi* (*echarse atrás*)
to move back(wards); (*fig*) to back down

retroceso [retro'θeso] *nm* backward
movement; (*MED*) relapse; (*fig*) backing
down

retrógrado, a [re'troɣraðo, a] *adj*
retrograde, retrogressive; (*POL*) reactionary

retrospectivo, a [retrospek'tiβo, a] *adj*
retrospective

retrovisor [retroβi'sor] *nm* (*tb:* **espejo ~**)
rear-view mirror

retumbar [retum'bar] *vi* to echo, resound

reúma [re'uma], **reuma** ['reuma] *nm*
rheumatism

reumatismo [reuma'tismo] *nm* = **reúma**

reunificar [reunifi'kar] *vt* to reunify

reunión [reu'njon] *nf* (*asamblea*) meeting;
(*fiesta*) party

reunir [reu'nir] *vt* (*juntar*) to reunite, join
(together); (*recoger*) to gather (together);
(*personas*) to get together; (*cualidades*) to
combine; **~se** *vr* (*personas: en asamblea*)
to meet, gather

revalidar [reβali'ðar] *vt* (*ratificar*) to
confirm, ratify

revalorizar [reβalori'θar] *vt* to revalue,
reassess

revancha [re'βantʃa] *nf* revenge

revelación [reβela'θjon] *nf* revelation

revelado [reβe'laðo] *nm* developing

revelar [reβe'lar] *vt* to reveal; (*FOTO*) to
develop

reventa [re'βenta] *nf* (*de entradas: para
concierto*) touting

reventar [reβen'tar] *vt* to burst, explode

reventón [reβen'ton] *nm* (*AUTO*) blow-out

(*BRIT*), flat (*US*)

reverencia [reβe'renθja] *nf* reverence;
reverenciar *vt* to revere

reverendo, a [reβe'rendo, a] *adj* reverend

reverente [reβe'rente] *adj* reverent

reversible [reβer'siβle] *adj* (*prenda*)
reversible

reverso [re'βerso] *nm* back, other side; (*de
moneda*) reverse

revertir [reβer'tir] *vi* to revert

revés [re'βes] *nm* back, wrong side; (*fig*)
reverse, setback; (*DEPORTE*) backhand; **al ~**
the wrong way round; (*de arriba abajo*)
upside down; (*ropa*) inside out; **volver
algo del ~** to turn sth round; (*ropa*) to
turn sth inside out

revestir [reβes'tir] *vt* (*cubrir*) to cover, coat

revisar [reβi'sar] *vt* (*examinar*) to check;
(*texto etc*) to revise; **revisión** *nf* revision

revisor, a [reβi'sor, a] *nm/f* inspector;
(*FERRO*) ticket collector

revista [re'βista] *nf* magazine, review;
(*TEATRO*) revue; (*inspección*) inspection;
pasar ~ a to review, inspect

revivir [reβi'βir] *vi* to revive

revocación [reβoka'θjon] *nf* repeal

revocar [reβo'kar] *vt* to revoke

revolcarse [reβol'karse] *vr* to roll about

revolotear [reβolote'ar] *vi* to flutter

revoltijo [reβol'tixo] *nm* mess, jumble

revoltoso, a [reβol'toso, a] *adj* (*travieso*)
naughty, unruly

revolución [reβolu'θjon] *nf* revolution;
revolucionar *vt* to revolutionize;
revolucionario, a *adj, nm/f*
revolutionary

revolver [reβol'βer] *vt* (*desordenar*) to
disturb, mess up; (*mover*) to move about
♦ *vi*: **~ en** to go through, rummage
(about) in; **~se** *vr* (*volver contra*) to turn
on *o* against

revólver [re'βolβer] *nm* revolver

revuelo [re'βwelo] *nm* fluttering; (*fig*)
commotion

revuelta [re'βwelta] *nf* (*motín*) revolt;
(*agitación*) commotion

revuelto, a [re'βwelto, a] *pp de* **revolver**

♦ *adj* (*mezclado*) mixed-up, in disorder
rey [rei] *nm* king; **Día de R~es** Twelfth
Night

Reyes Magos
---

i On the night before the 6th January
(the Epiphany), children go to bed
expecting **los Reyes Magos** (the Three
Wise Men) to bring them presents. Twelfth
Night processions, known as **cabalgatas**,
take place that evening when 3 people
dressed as **los Reyes Magos** arrive in the
town by land or sea to the delight of the
children.

---

reyerta [re'jerta] *nf* quarrel, brawl
rezagado, a [reθa'ɣaðo, a] *nm/f* straggler
rezagar [reθa'ɣar] *vt* (*dejar atrás*) to leave
behind; (*retrasar*) to delay, postpone
rezar [re'θar] *vi* to pray; **~ con** (*fam*) to
concern, have to do with; **rezo** *nm*
prayer
rezongar [reθon'gar] *vi* to grumble
rezumar [reθu'mar] *vt* to ooze
ría ['ria] *nf* estuary
riada [ri'aða] *nf* flood
ribera [ri'ßera] *nf* (*de río*) bank; (: *área*)
riverside
ribete [ri'ßete] *nm* (*de vestido*) border; (*fig*)
addition; **~ar** *vt* to edge, border
ricino [ri'θino] *nm*: **aceite de ~** castor oil
rico, a ['riko, a] *adj* rich; (*adinerado*)
wealthy, rich; (*lujoso*) luxurious; (*comida*)
delicious; (*niño*) lovely, cute ♦ *nm/f* rich
person
rictus ['riktus] *nm* (*mueca*) sneer, grin
ridiculez [riðiku'leθ] *nf* absurdity
ridiculizar [riðikuli'θar] *vt* to ridicule
ridículo, a [ri'ðikulo, a] *adj* ridiculous;
hacer el ~ to make a fool of o.s.; **poner
a uno en ~** to make a fool of sb
riego ['rjeɣo] *nm* (*aspersión*) watering;
(*irrigación*) irrigation
riel [rjel] *nm* rail
rienda ['rjenda] *nf* rein; **dar ~ suelta a** to
give free rein to
riesgo ['rjesɣo] *nm* risk; **correr el ~ de** to

run the risk of
rifa ['rifa] *nf* (*lotería*) raffle; **rifar** *vt* to raffle
rifle ['rifle] *nm* rifle
rigidez [rixi'ðeθ] *nf* rigidity, stiffness; (*fig*)
strictness; **rígido, a** *adj* rigid, stiff; strict,
inflexible
rigor [ri'ɣor] *nm* strictness, rigour;
(*inclemencia*) harshness; **de ~** de rigueur,
essential; **riguroso, a** *adj* rigorous;
harsh; (*severo*) severe
rimar [ri'mar] *vi* to rhyme
rimbombante [rimbom'bante] *adj*
pompous
rímel ['rimel] *nm* mascara
rímmel ['rimel] *nm* = **rímel**
rincón [rin'kon] *nm* corner (*inside*)
rinoceronte [rinoθe'ronte] *nm* rhinoceros
riña ['riɲa] *nf* (*disputa*) argument; (*pelea*)
brawl
riñón [ri'ɲon] *nm* kidney
río *etc* ['rio] *vb ver* **reír** ♦ *nm* river; (*fig*)
torrent, stream; **~ abajo/arriba**
downstream/upstream; **~ de la Plata**
River Plate
rioja [ri'oxa] *nm* (*vino*) rioja (wine)
rioplatense [riopla'tense] *adj* of o from
the River Plate region
riqueza [ri'keθa] *nf* wealth, riches *pl*;
(*cualidad*) richness
risa ['risa] *nf* laughter; (*una ~*) laugh; **¡qué
~!** what a laugh!
risco ['risko] *nm* crag, cliff
risible [ri'sißle] *adj* ludicrous, laughable
risotada [riso'taða] *nf* guffaw, loud laugh
ristra ['ristra] *nf* string
risueño, a [ri'sweɲo, a] *adj* (*sonriente*)
smiling; (*contento*) cheerful
ritmo ['ritmo] *nm* rhythm; **a ~ lento**
slowly; **trabajar a ~ lento** to go slow
rito ['rito] *nm* rite
ritual [ri'twal] *adj, nm* ritual
rival [ri'ßal] *adj, nm/f* rival; **~idad** *nf*
rivalry; **~izar** *vi*: **~izar con** to rival, vie
with
rizado, a [ri'θaðo, a] *adj* curly ♦ *nm* curls
pl
rizar [ri'θar] *vt* to curl; **~se** *vr* (*pelo*) to

curl; (*agua*) to ripple; **rizo** *nm* curl; ripple

RNE *nf abr* = **Radio Nacional de España**

robar [ro'βar] *vt* to rob; (*objeto*) to steal; (*casa etc*) to break into; (*NAIPES*) to draw

roble ['roβle] *nm* oak; **~dal** *nm* oakwood

robo ['roβo] *nm* robbery, theft

robot [ro'βot] *nm* robot; **~ (de cocina)** food processor

robustecer [roβuste'θer] *vt* to strengthen

robusto, a [ro'βusto, a] *adj* robust, strong

roca ['roka] *nf* rock

roce ['roθe] *nm* (*caricia*) brush; (*TEC*) friction; (*en la piel*) graze; **tener ~ con** to be in close contact with

rociar [ro'θjar] *vt* to spray

rocín [ro'θin] *nm* nag, hack

rocío [ro'θio] *nm* dew

rocoso, a [ro'koso, a] *adj* rocky

rodaballo [roða'βaʎo] *nm* turbot

rodado, a [ro'ðaðo, a] *adj* (*con ruedas*) wheeled

rodaja [ro'ðaxa] *nf* slice

rodaje [ro'ðaxe] *nm* (*CINE*) shooting, filming; (*AUTO*): **en ~** running in

rodar [ro'ðar] *vt* (*vehículo*) to wheel (along); (*escalera*) to roll down; (*viajar por*) to travel (over) ♦ *vi* to roll; (*coche*) to go, run; (*CINE*) to shoot, film

rodear [roðe'ar] *vt* to surround ♦ *vi* to go round; **~se** *vr*: **~se de amigos** to surround o.s. with friends

rodeo [ro'ðeo] *nm* (*ruta indirecta*) detour; (*evasión*) evasion; (*AM*) rodeo; **hablar sin ~s** to come to the point, speak plainly

rodilla [ro'ðiʎa] *nf* knee; **de ~s** kneeling; **ponerse de ~s** to kneel (down)

rodillo [ro'ðiʎo] *nm* roller; (*CULIN*) rolling-pin

roedor, a [roe'ðor, a] *adj* gnawing ♦ *nm* rodent

roer [ro'er] *vt* (*masticar*) to gnaw; (*corroer, fig*) to corrode

rogar [ro'xar] *vt, vi* (*pedir*) to ask for; (*suplicar*) to beg, plead; **se ruega no fumar** please do not smoke

rojizo, a [ro'xiθo, a] *adj* reddish

rojo, a ['roxo, a] *adj, nm* red; **al ~ vivo** red-hot

rol [rol] *nm* list, roll; (*papel*) role

rollito [ro'ʎito] *nm*: **~ de primavera** spring roll

rollizo, a [ro'ʎiθo, a] *adj* (*objeto*) cylindrical; (*persona*) plump

rollo ['roʎo] *nm* roll; (*de cuerda*) coil; (*madera*) log; (*fam*) bore; **¡qué ~!** what a carry-on!

Roma ['roma] *n* Rome

romance [ro'manθe] *nm* (*amoroso*) romance; (*LITERATURA*) ballad

romano, a [ro'mano, a] *adj, nm/f* Roman; **a la romana** in batter

romanticismo [romanti'θismo] *nm* romanticism

romántico, a [ro'mantiko, a] *adj* romantic

rombo ['rombo] *nm* (*GEOM*) rhombus

romería [rome'ria] *nf* (*REL*) pilgrimage; (*excursión*) trip, outing

---

Romería

i Originally a pilgrimage to a shrine or church to express devotion to the Virgin Mary or a local Saint, the **romería** has also become a rural festival which accompanies the pilgrimage. People come from all over to attend, bringing their own food and drink, and spend the day in celebration.

---

romero, a [ro'mero, a] *nm/f* pilgrim ♦ *nm* rosemary

romo, a ['romo, a] *adj* blunt; (*fig*) dull

rompecabezas [rompeka'βeθas] *nm inv* riddle, puzzle; (*juego*) jigsaw (puzzle)

rompeolas [rompe'olas] *nm inv* breakwater

romper [rom'per] *vt* to break; (*hacer pedazos*) to smash; (*papel, tela etc*) to tear, rip ♦ *vi* (*olas*) to break; (*sol, diente*) to break through; **~ un contrato** to break a contract; **~ a** (*empezar a*) to start (suddenly) to; **~ a llorar** to burst into tears; **~ con uno** to fall out with sb

ron [ron] *nm* rum

roncar [ron'kar] *vi* to snore

ronco, a ['ronko, a] *adj* (*afónico*) hoarse; (*áspero*) raucous

ronda ['ronda] *nf* (*gen*) round; (*patrulla*) patrol; **rondar** *vt* to patrol ♦ *vi* to patrol; (*fig*) to prowl round

ronquido [ron'kiðo] *nm* snore, snoring

ronronear [ronrone'ar] *vi* to purr; **ronroneo** *nm* purr

roña ['roɲa] *nf* (*VETERINARIA*) mange; (*mugre*) dirt, grime; (*óxido*) rust

roñoso, a [ro'ɲoso, a] *adj* (*mugriento*) filthy; (*tacaño*) mean

ropa ['ropa] *nf* clothes *pl*, clothing; **~ blanca** linen; **~ de cama** bed linen; **~ interior** underwear; **~ para lavar** washing; **~je** *nm* gown, robes *pl*

ropero [ro'pero] *nm* linen cupboard; (*guardarropa*) wardrobe

rosa ['rosa] *adj* pink ♦ *nf* rose; **~ de los vientos** the compass

rosado, a [ro'saðo, a] *adj* pink ♦ *nm* rosé

rosal [ro'sal] *nm* rosebush

rosario [ro'sarjo] *nm* (*REL*) rosary; **rezar el ~** to say the rosary

rosca ['roska] *nf* (*de tornillo*) thread; (*de humo*) coil, spiral; (*pan, postre*) ring-shaped roll/pastry

rosetón [rose'ton] *nm* rosette; (*ARQ*) rose window

rosquilla [ros'kiʎa] *nf* doughnut-shaped fritter

rostro ['rostro] *nm* (*cara*) face

rotación [rota'θjon] *nf* rotation; **~ de cultivos** crop rotation

rotativo, a [rota'tiβo, a] *adj* rotary

roto, a ['roto, a] *pp de* **romper** ♦ *adj* broken

rotonda [ro'tonda] *nf* roundabout

rótula ['rotula] *nf* kneecap; (*TEC*) ball-and-socket joint

rotulador [rotula'ðor] *nm* felt-tip pen

rotular [rotu'lar] *vt* (*carta, documento*) to head, entitle; (*objeto*) to label; **rótulo** *nm* heading, title; label; (*letrero*) sign

rotundamente [rotunda'mente] *adv* (*negar*) flatly; (*responder, afirmar*) emphatically; **rotundo, a** *adj* round;

(*enfático*) emphatic

rotura [ro'tura] *nf* (*acto*) breaking; (*MED*) fracture

roturar [rotu'rar] *vt* to plough

rozadura [roθa'ðura] *nf* abrasion, graze

rozar [ro'θar] *vt* (*frotar*) to rub; (*arañar*) to scratch; (*tocar ligeramente*) to shave, touch lightly; **~se** *vr* to rub (together); **~se con** (*fam*) to rub shoulders with

rte. *abr* (= *remite, remitente*) sender

RTVE *nf abr* = **Radiotelevisión Española**

rubí [ru'βi] *nm* ruby; (*de reloj*) jewel

rubio, a [ru'βjo, a] *adj* fair-haired, blond(e) ♦ *nm/f* blond/blonde; **tabaco ~** Virginia tobacco

rubor [ru'βor] *nm* (*sonrojo*) blush; (*timidez*) bashfulness; **~izarse** *vr* to blush

rúbrica ['ruβrika] *nf* (*de la firma*) flourish; **rubricar** *vt* (*firmar*) to sign with a flourish; (*concluir*) to sign and seal

rudimentario, a [ruðimen'tarjo, a] *adj* rudimentary; **rudimento** *nm* rudiment

rudo, a ['ruðo, a] *adj* (*sin pulir*) unpolished; (*grosero*) coarse; (*violento*) violent; (*sencillo*) simple

rueda ['rweða] *nf* wheel; (*círculo*) ring, circle; (*rodaja*) slice, round; **~ delantera/trasera/de repuesto** front/back/spare wheel; **~ de prensa** press conference

ruedo ['rweðo] *nm* (*círculo*) circle; (*TAUR*) arena, bullring

ruego *etc* ['rweɣo] *vb ver* **rogar** ♦ *nm* request

rufián [ru'fjan] *nm* scoundrel

rugby ['ruɣβi] *nm* rugby

rugido [ru'xiðo] *nm* roar

rugir [ru'xir] *vi* to roar

rugoso, a [ru'ɣoso, a] *adj* (*arrugado*) wrinkled; (*áspero*) rough; (*desigual*) ridged

ruido [ru'iðo] *nm* noise; (*sonido*) sound; (*alboroto*) racket, row; (*escándalo*) commotion, rumpus; **~so, a** *adj* noisy, loud; (*fig*) sensational •

ruin [rwin] *adj* contemptible, mean

ruina ['rwina] *nf* ruin; (*colapso*) collapse; (*de persona*) ruin, downfall

ruindad [rwin'dað] *nf* lowness, meanness;

(*acto*) low o mean act

ruinoso, a [rwi'noso, a] *adj* ruinous; (*destartalado*) dilapidated, tumbledown; (*COM*) disastrous

ruiseñor [rwise'ɲor] *nm* nightingale

ruleta [ru'leta] *nf* roulette

rulo ['rulo] *nm* (*para el pelo*) curler

Rumanía [ruma'nia] *nf* Rumania

rumba ['rumba] *nf* rumba

rumbo ['rumbo] *nm* (*ruta*) route, direction; (*ángulo de dirección*) course, bearing; (*fig*) course of events; **ir con ~ a** to be heading for

rumboso, a [rum'boso, a] *adj* generous

rumiante [ru'mjante] *nm* ruminant

rumiar [ru'mjar] *vt* to chew; (*fig*) to chew over ♦ *vi* to chew the cud

rumor [ru'mor] *nm* (*ruido sordo*) low sound; (*murmuración*) murmur, buzz

rumorearse [rumore'arse] *vr*: **se rumorea que** it is rumoured that

runrún [run'run] *nm* (*voces*) murmur, sound of voices; (*fig*) rumour

rupestre [ru'pestre] *adj* rock *cpd*

ruptura [rup'tura] *nf* rupture

rural [ru'ral] *adj* rural

Rusia ['rusja] *nf* Russia; **ruso, a** *adj, nm/f* Russian

rústica ['rustika] *nf*: **libro en ~** paperback (book); *ver tb* **rústico**

rústico, a ['rustiko, a] *adj* rustic; (*ordinario*) coarse, uncouth ♦ *nm/f* yokel

ruta ['ruta] *nf* route

rutina [ru'tina] *nf* routine; **~rio, a** *adj* routine

S, s

S *abr* (= *santo, a*) St; (= *sur*) S

s. *abr* (= *siglo*) C.; (= *siguiente*) foll

S.A. *abr* (= *Sociedad Anónima*) Ltd. (*BRIT*), Inc. (*US*)

sábado ['saßaðo] *nm* Saturday

sábana ['saßana] *nf* sheet

sabandija [saßan'dixa] *nf* bug, insect

sabañón [saßa'ɲon] *nm* chilblain

saber [sa'ßer] *vt* to know; (*llegar a conocer*) to find out, learn; (*tener capacidad de*) to know how to ♦ *vi*: **~ a** to taste of, taste like ♦ *nm* knowledge, learning; **a ~** namely; **¿sabes conducir/nadar?** can you drive/swim?; **¿sabes francés?** do you speak French?; **~ de memoria** to know by heart; **hacer ~ algo a uno** to inform sb of sth, let sb know sth

sabiduría [saßiðu'ria] *nf* (*conocimientos*) wisdom; (*instrucción*) learning

sabiendas [sa'ßjendas]: **a ~** *adv* knowingly

sabio, a ['saßjo, a] *adj* (*docto*) learned; (*prudente*) wise, sensible

sabor [sa'ßor] *nm* taste, flavour; **~ear** *vt* to taste, savour; (*fig*) to relish

sabotaje [saßo'taxe] *nm* sabotage

saboteador, a [saßotea'ðor, a] *nm/f* saboteur

sabotear [saßote'ar] *vt* to sabotage

sabré *etc vb ver* **saber**

sabroso, a [sa'ßroso, a] *adj* tasty; (*fig: fam*) racy, salty

sacacorchos [saka'kortʃos] *nm inv* corkscrew

sacapuntas [saka'puntas] *nm inv* pencil sharpener

sacar [sa'kar] *vt* to take out; (*fig: extraer*) to get (out); (*quitar*) to remove, get out; (*hacer salir*) to bring out; (*conclusión*) to draw; (*novela etc*) to publish, bring out; (*ropa*) to take off; (*obra*) to make; (*premio*) to receive; (*entradas*) to get; (*TENIS*) to serve; **~ adelante** (*niño*) to bring up; (*negocio*) to carry on, go on with; **~ a uno a bailar** to get sb up to dance; **~ una foto** to take a photo; **~ la lengua** to stick out one's tongue; **~ buenas/malas notas** to get good/bad marks

sacarina [saka'rina] *nf* saccharin(e)

sacerdote [saθer'ðote] *nm* priest

saciar [sa'θjar] *vt* (*hambre, sed*) to satisfy; **~se** *vr* (*de comida*) to get full up; **comer hasta ~se** to eat one's fill

saco ['sako] *nm* bag; (*grande*) sack; (*su*

contenido) bagful; (*AM*) jacket; **~ de
dormir** sleeping bag
sacramento [sakra'mento] *nm* sacrament
sacrificar [sakrifi'kar] *vt* to sacrifice;
  sacrificio *nm* sacrifice
sacrilegio [sakri'lexjo] *nm* sacrilege;
  sacrílego, a *adj* sacrilegious
sacristía [sakris'tia] *nf* sacristy
sacro, a ['sakro, a] *adj* sacred
sacudida [saku'ðiða] *nf* (*agitación*) shake,
  shaking; (*sacudimiento*) jolt, bump; **~
  eléctrica** electric shock
sacudir [saku'ðir] *vt* to shake; (*golpear*) to
  hit
sádico, a ['saðiko, a] *adj* sadistic ♦ *nm/f*
  sadist; **sadismo** *nm* sadism
saeta [sa'eta] *nf* (*flecha*) arrow
sagacidad [savaθi'ðað] *nf* shrewdness,
  cleverness; **sagaz** *adj* shrewd, clever
sagitario [saxi'tarjo] *nm* Sagittarius
sagrado, a [sa'xraðo, a] *adj* sacred, holy
Sáhara ['saara] *nm*: **el ~** the Sahara
  (desert)
sal [sal] *vb ver* **salir** ♦ *nf* salt
sala ['sala] *nf* room; (*~ de estar*) living
  room; (*TEATRO*) house, auditorium; (*de
  hospital*) ward; **~ de apelación** court; **~
  de espera** waiting room; **~ de estar**
  living room; **~ de fiestas** dance hall
salado, a [sa'laðo, a] *adj* salty; (*fig*) witty,
  amusing; **agua salada** salt water
salar [sa'lar] *vt* to salt, add salt to
salarial [sala'rjal] *adj* (*aumento, revisión*)
  wage *cpd*, salary *cpd*
salario [sa'larjo] *nm* wage, pay
salchicha [sal'tʃitʃa] *nf* (*pork*) sausage;
  salchichón *nm* (salami-type) sausage
saldar [sal'dar] *vt* to pay; (*vender*) to sell
  off; (*fig*) to settle, resolve; **saldo** *nm*
  (*pago*) settlement; (*de una cuenta*)
  balance; (*lo restante*) remnant(s) (*pl*),
  remainder; **saldos** *nmpl* (*en tienda*) sale
saldré *etc vb ver* **salir**
salero [sa'lero] *nm* salt cellar
salgo *etc vb ver* **salir**
salida [sa'liða] *nf* (*puerta etc*) exit, way
  out; (*acto*) leaving, going out; (*de tren*,

AVIAT) departure; (*TEC*) output, production; (*fig*) way out; (*COM*) opening;
(*GEO, válvula*) outlet; (*de gas*) leak; **calle
sin ~** cul-de-sac; **~ de incendios** fire
escape
saliente [sa'ljente] *adj* (*ARQ*) projecting;
  (*sol*) rising; (*fig*) outstanding

┌─────────────────────┐
│ *PALABRA CLAVE* │
└─────────────────────┘

salir [sa'lir] *vi* **1** (*partir: tb:* **~ de**) to leave;
  Juan ha salido Juan is out; **salió de la
  cocina** he came out of the kitchen
  2 (*aparecer*) to appear; (*disco, libro*) to
  come out; **anoche salió en la tele** she
  appeared *o* was on TV last night; **salió en
  todos los periódicos** it was in all the
  papers
  3 (*resultar*): **la muchacha nos salió muy
  trabajadora** the girl turned out to be a
  very hard worker; **la comida te ha salido
  exquisita** the food was delicious; **sale
  muy caro** it's very expensive
  4: **~le a uno algo: la entrevista que
  hice me salió bien/mal** the interview I
  did went *o* turned out well/badly
  5: **~ adelante: no sé como haré para ~
  adelante** I don't know how I'll get by
  ♦ **~se** *vr* (*líquido*) to spill; (*animal*) to
  escape

saliva [sa'liβa] *nf* saliva
salmo ['salmo] *nm* psalm
salmón [sal'mon] *nm* salmon
salmonete [salmo'nete] *nm* red mullet
salmuera [sal'mwera] *nf* pickle, brine
salón [sa'lon] *nm* (*de casa*) living room,
  lounge; (*muebles*) lounge suite; **~ de
  belleza** beauty parlour; **~ de baile** dance
  hall
salpicadero [salpika'ðero] *nm* (*AUTO*)
  dashboard
salpicar [salpi'kar] *vt* (*rociar*) to sprinkle,
  spatter; (*esparcir*) to scatter
salpicón [salpi'kon] *nm*: **~ de mariscos**
  seafood salad
salsa ['salsa] *nf* sauce; (*con carne asada*)
  gravy; (*fig*) spice

saltamontes [salta'montes] *nm inv*
grasshopper

saltar [sal'tar] *vt* to jump (over), leap
(over); (*dejar de lado*) to skip, miss out
♦ *vi* to jump, leap; (*pelota*) to bounce; (*al
aire*) to fly up; (*quebrarse*) to break; (*al
agua*) to dive; (*fig*) to explode, blow up

salto ['salto] *nm* jump, leap; (*al agua*)
dive; **~ de agua** waterfall; **~ de altura**
high jump

saltón, ona [sal'ton, ona] *adj* (*ojos*)
bulging, popping; (*dientes*) protruding

salud [sa'luð] *nf* health; **¡(a su) ~!** cheers!,
good health!; **~able** *adj* (*de buena ~*)
healthy; (*provechoso*) good, beneficial

saludar [salu'ðar] *vt* to greet; (*MIL*) to
salute; **saludo** *nm* greeting; **"saludos"**
(*en carta*) "best wishes", "regards"

salva ['salßa] *nf*: **~ de aplausos** ovation

salvación [salßa'θjon] *nf* salvation;
(*rescate*) rescue

salvado [sal'ßaðo] *nm* bran

salvaguardar [salßaɣwar'ðar] *vt* to
safeguard

salvajada [salßa'xaða] *nf* atrocity

salvaje [sal'ßaxe] *adj* wild; (*tribu*) savage;
salvajismo *nm* savagery

salvamento [salßa'mento] *nm* rescue

salvar [sal'ßar] *vt* (*rescatar*) to save, rescue;
(*resolver*) to overcome, resolve; (*cubrir
distancias*) to cover, travel; (*hacer
excepción*) to except, exclude; (*barco*) to
salvage

salvavidas [salßa'ßiðas] *adj inv*: **bote /
chaleco / cinturón ~** lifeboat/life jacket/life
belt

salvo, a ['salßo, a] *adj* safe ♦ *adv* except
(for), save; **a ~** out of danger; **~ que**
unless; **~conducto** *nm* safe-conduct

san [san] *adj* saint; **S~ Juan** St John

sanar [sa'nar] *vt* (*herida*) to heal; (*persona*)
to cure ♦ *vi* (*persona*) to get well,
recover; (*herida*) to heal

sanatorio [sana'torjo] *nm* sanatorium

sanción [san'θjon] *nf* sanction;
sancionar *vt* to sanction

sandalia [san'dalja] *nf* sandal

sandez [san'deθ] *nf* foolishness

sandía [san'dia] *nf* watermelon

sandwich ['sandwitʃ] (*pl* **~s, ~es**) *nm*
sandwich

saneamiento [sanea'mjento] *nm*
sanitation

sanear [sane'ar] *vt* to clean up; (*terreno*)
to drain

Sanfermines

i The **Sanfermines** is a week-long
festival in Pamplona made famous by
Ernest Hemingway. From the 7th July, the
feast of "San Fermín", crowds of mainly
young people take to the streets drinking,
singing and dancing. Early in the morning
bulls are released along the narrow streets
leading to the bullring, and young men
risk serious injury to show their bravery by
running out in front of them, a custom
which is also typical of many Spanish
villages.

---

sangrar [san'grar] *vt, vi* to bleed; **sangre**
nf blood

sangría [san'gria] *nf* sangria, sweetened
drink of red wine with fruit

sangriento, a [san'grjento, a] *adj* bloody

sanguijuela [sangi'xwela] *nf* (*ZOOL, fig*)
leech

sanguinario, a [sangi'narjo, a] *adj*
bloodthirsty

sanguíneo, a [san'gineo, a] *adj* blood *cpd*

sanidad [sani'ðað] *nf*: **~ (pública)** public
health

San Isidro

i **San Isidro** is the patron saint of
Madrid, and gives his name to the
week-long festivities which take place
around the 15th May. Originally an
18th-century trade fair, the **San Isidro**
celebrations now include music, dance, a
famous **romería**, theatre and bullfighting.

---

sanitario, a [sani'tarjo, a] *adj* health *cpd*;
~s *nmpl* toilets (*BRIT*), washroom (*US*)

sano, a ['sano, a] *adj* healthy; (*sin daños*) sound; (*comida*) wholesome; (*entero*) whole, intact; ~ **y salvo** safe and sound

Santiago [san'tjaɣo] *nm*: ~ **(de Chile)** Santiago

santiamén [santja'men] *nm*: **en un** ~ in no time at all

santidad [santi'ðað] *nf* holiness, sanctity

santiguarse [santi'ɣwarse] *vr* to make the sign of the cross

santo, a ['santo, a] *adj* holy; (*fig*) wonderful, miraculous ♦ *nm/f* saint ♦ *nm* saint's day; ~ **y seña** password

santuario [san'twarjo] *nm* sanctuary, shrine

saña ['saɲa] *nf* rage, fury

sapo ['sapo] *nm* toad

saque ['sake] *nm* (*TENIS*) service, serve; (*FÚTBOL*) throw-in; ~ **de esquina** corner (kick)

saquear [sake'ar] *vt* (*MIL*) to sack; (*robar*) to loot, plunder; (*fig*) to ransack; **saqueo** *nm* sacking; looting, plundering; ransacking

sarampión [saram'pjon] *nm* measles *sg*

sarcasmo [sar'kasmo] *nm* sarcasm; **sarcástico, a** *adj* sarcastic

sardina [sar'ðina] *nf* sardine

sargento [sar'xento] *nm* sergeant

sarmiento [sar'mjento] *nm* (*BOT*) vine shoot

sarna ['sarna] *nf* itch; (*MED*) scabies

sarpullido [sarpu'ʎiðo] *nm* (*MED*) rash

sarro ['sarro] *nm* (*en dientes*) tartar, plaque

sartén [sar'ten] *nf* frying pan

sastre ['sastre] *nm* tailor; ~**ría** *nf* (*arte*) tailoring; (*tienda*) tailor's (shop)

Satanás [sata'nas] *nm* Satan

satélite [sa'telite] *nm* satellite

sátira ['satira] *nf* satire

satisfacción [satisfak'θjon] *nf* satisfaction

satisfacer [satisfa'θer] *vt* to satisfy; (*gastos*) to meet; (*pérdida*) to make good; ~**se** *vr* to satisfy o.s., be satisfied; (*vengarse*) to take revenge; **satisfecho, a** *adj* satisfied; (*contento*) content(ed), happy; (*tb*: **satisfecho de sí mismo**)

self-satisfied, smug

saturar [satu'rar] *vt* to saturate; ~**se** *vr* (*mercado, aeropuerto*) to reach saturation point

sauce ['sauθe] *nm* willow; ~ **llorón** weeping willow

sauna ['sauna] *nf* sauna

savia ['saßja] *nf* sap

saxofón [sakso'fon] *nm* saxophone

sazonar [saθo'nar] *vt* to ripen; (*CULIN*) to flavour, season

SE *abr* (= *sudeste*) SE

| PALABRA CLAVE |

se [se] *pron* **1** (*reflexivo: sg: m*) himself; (: *f*) herself; (: *pl*) themselves; (: *cosa*) itself; (: *de Vd*) yourself; (: *de Vds*) yourselves; ~ **está preparando** she's preparing herself; *para usos léxicos del pron ver el vb en cuestión, p.ej.* **arrepentirse**

2 (*con complemento indirecto*) to him; to her; to them; to it; to you; **a usted** ~ **lo dije ayer** I told you yesterday; ~ **compró un sombrero** he bought himself a hat; ~ **rompió la pierna** he broke his leg

3 (*uso recíproco*) each other, one another; ~ **miraron (el uno al otro)** they looked at each other *o* one another

4 (*en oraciones pasivas*): **se han vendido muchos libros** a lot of books have been sold

5 (*impers*): ~ **dice que** people say that, it is said that; **allí** ~ **come muy bien** the food there is very good, you can eat very well

---

sé *vb ver* **saber; ser**

sea *etc vb ver* **ser**

sebo ['seßo] *nm* fat, grease

secador [seka'ðor] *nm*: ~ **de pelo** hair-dryer

secadora [seka'ðora] *nf* tumble dryer

secar [se'kar] *vt* to dry; ~**se** *vr* to dry (off); (*río, planta*) to dry up

sección [sek'θjon] *nf* section

seco, a ['seko, a] *adj* dry; (*carácter*) cold; (*respuesta*) sharp, curt; **habrá pan a**

secas there will be just bread; **decir algo a secas** to say sth curtly; **parar en ~** to stop dead

secretaría [sekreta'ria] *nf* secretariat

secretario, a [sekre'tarjo, a] *nm/f* secretary

secreto, a [se'kreto, a] *adj* secret; (*persona*) secretive ♦ *nm* secret; (*calidad*) secrecy

secta ['sekta] *nf* sect; **~rio, a** *adj* sectarian

sector [sek'tor] *nm* sector

secuela [se'kwela] *nf* consequence

secuencia [se'kwenθja] *nf* sequence

secuestrar [sekwes'trar] *vt* to kidnap; (*bienes*) to seize, confiscate; **secuestro** *nm* kidnapping; seizure, confiscation

secular [seku'lar] *adj* secular

secundar [sekun'dar] *vt* to second, support

secundario, a [sekun'darjo, a] *adj* secondary

sed [seð] *nf* thirst; **tener ~** to be thirsty

seda ['seða] *nf* silk

sedal [se'ðal] *nm* fishing line

sedante [se'ðante] *nm* sedative

sede ['seðe] *nf* (*de gobierno*) seat; (*de compañía*) headquarters *pl*; **Santa S~** Holy See

sedentario, a [seðen'tarjo, a] *adj* sedentary

sediento, a [se'ðjento, a] *adj* thirsty

sedimento [seði'mento] *nm* sediment

sedoso, a [se'ðoso, a] *adj* silky, silken

seducción [seðuk'θjon] *nf* seduction

seducir [seðu'θir] *vt* to seduce; (*cautivar*) to charm, fascinate; (*atraer*) to attract; **seductor, a** *adj* seductive; charming, fascinating; attractive ♦ *nm/f* seducer

segar [se'ɣar] *vt* (*mies*) to reap, cut; (*hierba*) to mow, cut

seglar [se'ɣlar] *adj* secular, lay

segregación [seɣreɣa'θjon] *nf* segregation. **~ racial** racial segregation

segregar [seɣre'ɣar] *vt* to segregate, separate

seguida [se'ɣiða] *nf*: **en ~** at once, right away

seguido, a [se'ɣiðo, a] *adj* (*continuo*) continuous, unbroken; (*recto*) straight ♦ *adv* (*directo*) straight (on); (*después*) after; (*AM: a menudo*) often; **~s** consecutive, successive; **5 días ~s** 5 days running, 5 days in a row

seguimiento [seɣi'mjento] *nm* chase, pursuit; (*continuación*) continuation

seguir [se'ɣir] *vt* to follow; (*venir después*) to follow on, come after; (*proseguir*) to continue; (*perseguir*) to chase, pursue ♦ *vi* (*gen*) to follow; (*continuar*) to continue, carry *o* go on; **~se** *vr* to follow; **sigo sin comprender** I still don't understand; **sigue lloviendo** it's still raining

según [se'ɣun] *prep* according to ♦ *adv*: **¿irás? – ~** are you going? — it all depends ♦ *conj* as; **~ caminamos** while we walk

segundo, a [se'ɣundo, a] *adj* second ♦ *nm* second ♦ *nf* second meaning; **de segunda mano** second-hand; **segunda (clase)** second class; **segunda enseñanza** secondary education; **segunda (marcha)** (*AUT*) second (gear)

seguramente [seɣura'mente] *adv* surely; (*con certeza*) for sure, with certainty

seguridad [seɣuri'ðað] *nf* safety; (*del estado, de casa etc*) security; (*certidumbre*) certainty; (*confianza*) confidence; (*estabilidad*) stability; **~ social** social security

seguro, a [se'ɣuro, a] *adj* (*cierto*) sure, certain; (*fiel*) trustworthy; (*libre de peligro*) safe; (*bien defendido, firme*) secure ♦ *adv* for sure, certainly ♦ *nm* (*COM*) insurance; **~ contra terceros / a todo riesgo** third party/comprehensive insurance; **~s sociales** social security *sg*

seis [seis] *num* six

seísmo [se'ismo] *nm* tremor, earthquake

selección [selek'θjon] *nf* selection; **seleccionar** *vt* to pick, choose, select

selectividad [selektiβi'ðað] (*ESP*) *nf* university entrance examination

selecto, a [se'lekto, a] *adj* select, choice; (*escogido*) selected

sellar [se'ʎar] *vt* (*documento oficial*) to seal; (*pasaporte, visado*) to stamp

sello ['seʎo] *nm* stamp; (*precinto*) seal

selva ['selβa] *nf* (*bosque*) forest, woods *pl*; (*jungla*) jungle

semáforo [se'maforo] *nm* (*AUTO*) traffic lights *pl*; (*FERRO*) signal

semana [se'mana] *nf* week; **entre ~** during the week; **S~ Santa** Holy Week; **semanal** *adj* weekly; **~rio** *nm* weekly magazine

---
| Semana Santa |

In Spain celebrations for **Semana Santa** (*Holy Week*) *are often spectacular. "Viernes Santo", "Sábado Santo" and "Domingo de Resurrección" (Good Friday, Holy Saturday, Easter Sunday) are all national public holidays, with additional days being given as local holidays. There are fabulous* **procesiones** *all over the country, with members of "cofradías" (brotherhoods) dressing in hooded robes and parading their "pasos" (religious floats and sculptures) through the streets. Seville has the most famous Holy Week processions.*

---

semblante [sem'blante] *nm* face; (*fig*) look

sembrar [sem'brar] *vt* to sow; (*objetos*) to sprinkle, scatter about; (*noticias etc*) to spread

semejante [seme'xante] *adj* (*parecido*) similar ♦ *nm* fellow man, fellow creature; **~s** alike, similar; **nunca hizo cosa ~** he never did any such thing; **semejanza** *nf* similarity, resemblance

semejar [seme'xar] *vi* to seem like, resemble; **~se** *vr* to look alike, be similar

semen ['semen] *nm* semen

semestral [semes'tral] *adj* half-yearly, bi-annual

semicírculo [semi'θirkulo] *nm* semicircle

semidesnatado, a [semiðesna'taðo, a] *adj* semi-skimmed

semifinal [semifi'nal] *nf* semifinal

semilla [se'miʎa] *nf* seed

seminario [semi'narjo] *nm* (*REL*) seminary; (*ESCOL*) seminar

sémola ['semola] *nf* semolina

Sena ['sena] *nm*: **el ~** the (river) Seine

senado [se'naðo] *nm* senate; **senador, a** *nm/f* senator

sencillez [senθi'ʎeθ] *nf* simplicity; (*de persona*) naturalness; **sencillo, a** *adj* simple; natural, unaffected

senda ['senda] *nf* path, track

senderismo [sende'rismo] *nm* hiking

sendero [sen'dero] *nm* path, track

sendos, as ['sendos, as] *adj pl*: **les dio ~ golpes** he hit both of them

senil [se'nil] *adj* senile

seno ['seno] *nm* (*ANAT*) bosom, bust; (*fig*) bosom; **~s** breasts

sensación [sensa'θjon] *nf* sensation; (*sentido*) sense; (*sentimiento*) feeling; **sensacional** *adj* sensational

sensato, a [sen'sato, a] *adj* sensible

sensible [sen'sible] *adj* sensitive; (*apreciable*) perceptible, appreciable; (*pérdida*) considerable; **~ro, a** *adj* sentimental

sensitivo, a [sensi'tiβo, a] *adj* sense *cpd*

sensorial [senso'rjal] *adj* sensory

sensual [sen'swal] *adj* sensual

sentada [sen'taða] *nf* sitting; (*protesta*) sit-in

sentado, a [sen'taðo, a] *adj*: **estar ~** to sit, be sitting (down); **dar por ~** to take for granted, assume

sentar [sen'tar] *vt* to sit, seat; (*fig*) to establish ♦ *vi* (*vestido*) to suit; (*alimento*): **~ bien/mal a** to agree/disagree with; **~se** *vr* (*persona*) to sit, sit down; (*los depósitos*) to settle

sentencia [sen'tenθja] *nf* (*máxima*) maxim, saying; (*JUR*) sentence; **sentenciar** *vt* to sentence

sentido, a [sen'tiðo, a] *adj* (*pérdida*) regrettable; (*carácter*) sensitive ♦ *nm* sense; (*sentimiento*) feeling; (*significado*) sense, meaning; (*dirección*) direction; **mi más ~ pésame** my deepest sympathy; **~**

del humor sense of humour; **~ único** one-way (street); **tener ~** to make sense

sentimental [sentimen'tal] *adj* sentimental; **vida ~** love life

sentimiento [senti'mjento] *nm* feeling

sentir [sen'tir] *vt* to feel; (*percibir*) to perceive, sense; (*lamentar*) to regret, be sorry for ♦ *vi* (*tener la sensación*) to feel; (*lamentarse*) to feel sorry ♦ *nm* opinion, judgement; **~se bien/mal** to feel well/ill; **lo siento** I'm sorry

seña ['sena] *nf* sign; (*MIL*) password; **~s** *nfpl* (*dirección*) address *sg*; **~s personales** personal description *sg*

señal [se'nal] *nf* sign; (*síntoma*) symptom; (*FERRO, TELEC*) signal; (*marca*) mark; (*COM*) deposit; **en ~ de** as a token of, as a sign of; **~ar** *vt* to mark; (*indicar*) to point out, indicate

señor [se'nor] *nm* (*hombre*) man; (*caballero*) gentleman; (*dueño*) owner, master; (*trato: antes de nombre propio*) Mr; (: *hablando directamente*) sir; **muy ~ mío** Dear Sir; **el ~ alcalde/presidente** the mayor/president

señora [se'nora] *nf* (*dama*) lady; (*trato: antes de nombre propio*) Mrs; (: *hablando directamente*) madam; (*esposa*) wife; **Nuestra S~** Our Lady

señorita [seno'rita] *nf* (*con nombre y/o apellido*) Miss; (*mujer joven*) young lady

señorito [seno'rito] *nm* young gentleman; (*pey*) rich kid

señuelo [se'nwelo] *nm* decoy

sepa *etc vb ver* **saber**

separación [separa'θjon] *nf* separation; (*división*) division; (*hueco*) gap

separar [sepa'rar] *vt* to separate; (*dividir*) to divide; **en ~se** *vr* (*parte*) to come away; (*partes*) to come apart; (*persona*) to leave, go away; (*matrimonio*) to separate; **separatismo** *nm* separatism

sepia ['sepja] *nf* cuttlefish

septentrional [septentrjo'nal] *adj* northern

septiembre [sep'tjembre] *nm* September

séptimo, a ['septimo, a] *adj, nm* seventh

sepulcral [sepul'kral] *adj* (*fig: silencio, atmósfera*) deadly; **sepulcro** *nm* tomb, grave

sepultar [sepul'tar] *vt* to bury; **sepultura** *nf* (*acto*) burial; (*tumba*) grave, tomb

sequedad [seke'ðað] *nf* dryness; (*fig*) brusqueness, curtness

sequía [se'kia] *nf* drought

séquito ['sekito] *nm* (*de rey etc*) retinue; (*seguidores*) followers *pl*

PALABRA CLAVE

ser [ser] *vi* **1** (*descripción*) to be; **es médica/muy alta** she's a doctor/very tall; **la familia es de Cuzco** his (*o* her *etc*) family is from Cuzco; **soy Ana** (*TELEC*) Ana speaking *o* here

2 (*propiedad*): **es de Joaquín** it's Joaquín's, it belongs to Joaquín

3 (*horas, fechas, números*): **es la una** it's one o'clock; **son las seis y media** it's half-past six; **es el 1 de junio** it's the first of June; **somos/son seis** there are six of us/them

4 (*en oraciones pasivas*): **ha sido descubierto ya** it's already been discovered

5: **es de esperar que ...** it is to be hoped *o* I *etc* hope that ...

6 (*locuciones con sub*): **o sea** that is to say; **sea él sea su hermana** either him or his sister

7: **a no ~ por él ...** but for him ...

8: **a no ~ que: a no ~ que tenga uno ya** unless he's got one already

♦ *nm* being; **~ humano** human being

---

serenarse [sere'narse] *vr* to calm down

sereno, a [se'reno, a] *adj* (*persona*) calm, unruffled; (*el tiempo*) fine, settled; (*ambiente*) calm, peaceful ♦ *nm* night watchman

serial [ser'jal] *nm* serial

serie ['serje] *nf* series; (*cadena*) sequence, succession; **fuera de ~** out of order; (*fig*) special, out of the ordinary; **fabricación en ~** mass production

seriedad [serje'ðað] *nf* seriousness; (*formalidad*) reliability; **serio, a** *adj* serious; reliable, dependable; grave, serious; **en serio** *adv* seriously

serigrafía [seriɣra'fia] *nf* silk-screen printing

sermón [ser'mon] *nm* (*REL*) sermon

seropositivo, a [seroposi'tiβo, a] *adj* HIV positive

serpentear [serpente'ar] *vi* to wriggle; (*camino, río*) to wind, snake

serpentina [serpen'tina] *nf* streamer

serpiente [ser'pjente] *nf* snake; **~ de cascabel** rattlesnake

serranía [serra'nia] *nf* mountainous area

serrar [se'rrar] *vt* = **aserrar**

serrín [se'rrin] *nm* = **aserrín**

serrucho [se'rrutʃo] *nm* saw

servicio [ser'ßiθjo] *nm* service; **~s** *nmpl* toilet(s); **~ incluido** service charge included; **~ militar** military service

servidumbre [serßi'ðumbre] *nf* (*sujeción*) servitude; (*criados*) servants *pl*, staff

servil [ser'ßil] *adj* servile

servilleta [serßi'ʎeta] *nf* serviette, napkin

servir [ser'ßir] *vt* to serve ♦ *vi* to serve; (*tener utilidad*) to be of use, be serving; **~se** *vr* to serve o help o.s.; **~se de algo** to make use of sth, use sth; **sírvase pasar** please come in

sesenta [se'senta] *num* sixty

sesgo [sesɣo] *nm* slant; (*fig*) slant, twist

sesión [se'sjon] *nf* (*POL*) session, sitting; (*CINE*) showing

seso [seso] *nm* brain; **sesudo, a** *adj* sensible, wise

seta [seta] *nf* mushroom; **~ venenosa** toadstool

setecientos, as [sete'θjentos, as] *adj*, *num* seven hundred

setenta [se'tenta] *num* seventy

seto [seto] *nm* hedge

seudónimo [seu'ðonimo] *nm* pseudonym

severidad [seßeri'ðað] *nf* severity; **severo, a** *adj* severe

Sevilla [se'ßiʎa] *n* Seville; **sevillano, a** *adj* o from Seville ♦ *nm/f* native o

inhabitant of Seville

sexo ['sekso] *nm* sex

sexto, a ['seksto, a] *adj*, *nm* sixth

sexual [sek'swal] *adj* sexual; **vida ~** sex life

si [si] *conj* if; **me pregunto ~ ...** I wonder if o whether ...

sí [si] *adv* yes ♦ *nm* consent ♦ *pron* (*uso impersonal*) oneself; (*sg: m*) himself; (*: f*) herself; (*: de cosa*) itself; (*de usted*) yourself; (*pl*) themselves; (*de ustedes*) yourselves; (*recíproco*) each other; **él no quiere pero yo ~** he doesn't want to but I do; **ella ~ vendrá** she will certainly come, she is sure to come; **claro que ~** of course; **creo que ~** I think so

siamés, esa [sja'mes, esa] *adj*, *nm/f* Siamese

SIDA ['siða] *nm abr* (= *Síndrome de Inmunodeficiencia Adquirida*) AIDS

siderúrgico, a [siðe'rurxico, a] *adj* iron and steel *cpd*

sidra ['siðra] *nf* cider

siembra ['sjembra] *nf* sowing

siempre ['sjempre] *adv* always; (*todo el tiempo*) all the time; **~ que** (*cada vez*) whenever; (*dado que*) provided that; **como ~** as usual; **para ~** for ever

sien [sjen] *nf* temple

siento *etc vb ver* **sentar**; **sentir**

sierra ['sjerra] *nf* (*TEC*) saw; (*cadena de montañas*) mountain range

siervo, a ['sjerßo, a] *nm/f* slave

siesta ['sjesta] *nf* siesta, nap; **echar la ~** to have an afternoon nap o a siesta

siete ['sjete] *num* seven

sífilis ['sifilis] *nf* syphilis

sifón [si'fon] *nm* syphon; **whisky con ~** whisky and soda

sigla ['siɣla] *nf* abbreviation; acronym

siglo ['siɣlo] *nm* century; (*fig*) age

significación [siɣnifika'θjon] *nf* significance

significado [siɣnifi'kaðo] *nm* (*de palabra etc*) meaning

significar [siɣnifi'kar] *vt* to mean, signify; (*notificar*) to make known, express; **significativo, a** *adj* significant

signo ['siɣno] nm sign; ~ **de admiración** o **exclamación** exclamation mark; ~ **de interrogación** question mark

sigo etc vb ver **seguir**

siguiente [si'ɣjente] adj next, following

siguió etc vb ver **seguir**

sílaba ['silaβa] nf syllable

silbar [sil'βar] vt, vi to whistle; **silbato** nm whistle; **silbido** nm whistle, whistling

silenciador [silenθja'ðor] nm silencer

silenciar [silen'θjar] vt (persona) to silence; (escándalo) to hush up; **silencio** nm silence, quiet; **silencioso, a** adj silent, quiet

silla ['siʎa] nf (asiento) chair; (tb: ~ **de montar**) saddle; ~ **de ruedas** wheelchair

sillón [si'ʎon] nm armchair, easy chair

silueta [si'lweta] nf silhouette; (de edificio) outline; (figura) figure

silvestre [sil'βestre] adj wild

simbólico, a [sim'boliko, a] adj symbolic(al)

simbolizar [simboli'θar] vt to symbolize

símbolo ['simbolo] nm symbol

simetría [sime'tria] nf symmetry

simiente [si'mjente] nf seed

similar [simi'lar] adj similar

simio ['simjo] nm ape

simpatía [simpa'tia] nf liking; (afecto) affection; (amabilidad) kindness; **simpático, a** adj nice, pleasant; kind

simpatizante [simpati'θante] nm/f sympathizer

simpatizar [simpati'θar] vi: ~ **con** to get on well with

simple ['simple] adj simple; (elemental) simple, easy; (mero) mere; (puro) pure, sheer ♦ nm/f simpleton; ~**za** nf simpleness; (necedad) silly thing; **simplificar** vt to simplify

simposio [sim'posjo] nm symposium

simular [simu'lar] vt to simulate

simultáneo, a [simul'taneo, a] adj simultaneous

sin [sin] prep without; **la ropa está ~ lavar** the clothes are unwashed; ~ **que** without;

~ **embargo** however, still

sinagoga [sina'ɣoɣa] nf synagogue

sinceridad [sinθeri'ðað] nf sincerity; **sincero, a** adj sincere

sincronizar [sinkroni'θar] vt to synchronize

sindical [sindi'kal] adj union cpd, trade-union cpd; ~**ista** adj, nm/f trade unionist

sindicato [sindi'kato] nm (de trabajadores) trade(s) union; (de negociantes) syndicate

síndrome ['sindrome] nm (MED) syndrome; ~ **de abstinencia** (MED) withdrawal symptoms

sinfín [sin'fin] nm: **un ~ de** a great many, no end of

sinfonía [sinfo'nia] nf symphony

singular [singu'lar] adj singular; (fig) outstanding, exceptional; (raro) peculiar, odd; ~**idad** nf singularity, peculiarity; ~**izarse** vr to distinguish o.s., stand out

siniestro, a [si'njestro, a] adj sinister ♦ nm (accidente) accident

sinnúmero [sin'numero] nm = **sinfín**

sino ['sino] nm fate, destiny ♦ conj (pero) but; (salvo) except, save

sinónimo, a [si'nonimo, a] adj synonymous ♦ nm synonym

síntesis ['sintesis] nf synthesis; **sintético, a** adj synthetic

sintetizar [sinteti'θar] vt to synthesize

sintió vb ver **sentir**

síntoma ['sintoma] nm symptom

sintonía [sinto'nia] nf (RADIO, MUS: de programa) tuning; **sintonizar** vt (RADIO: emisora) to tune (in)

sinvergüenza [simber'xwenθa] nm/f rogue, scoundrel; **¡es un ~!** he's got a nerve!

siquiera [si'kjera] conj even if, even though ♦ adv at least; **ni ~** not even

sirena [si'rena] nf siren

Siria ['sirja] nf Syria

sirviente, a [sir'βjente, a] nm/f servant

sirvo etc vb ver **servir**

sisear [sise'ar] vt, vi to hiss

sistema [sis'tema] nm system; (método) method; **sistemático, a** adj systematic

---

sistema educativo

ⓘ The reform of the Spanish **sistema educativo** (education system) begun in the early 90s has replaced the courses **EGB**, **BUP** and **COU** with the following: "Primaria" a compulsory 6 years; "Secundaria" a compulsory 4 years and "Bachillerato" an optional 2-year secondary school course, essential for those wishing to go on to higher education.

---

sitiar [si'tjar] vt to besiege, lay siege to
sitio ['sitjo] nm (lugar) place; (espacio) room, space; (MIL) siege
situación [sitwa'θjon] nf situation, position; (estatus) position, standing
situado, a [situ'aðo] adj situated, placed
situar [si'twar] vt to place, put; (edificio) to locate, situate
slip [slip] nm pants pl, briefs pl
smoking ['smokin, es'mokin] (pl ~s) nm dinner jacket (BRIT), tuxedo (US)
snob [es'nob] = **esnob**
SO abr (= suroeste) SW
sobaco [so'βako] nm armpit
sobar [so'βar] vt (ropa) to rumple; (comida) to play around with
soberanía [soβera'nia] nf sovereignty; **soberano, a** adj sovereign; (fig) supreme ♦ nm/f sovereign
soberbia [so'βerβja] nf pride; haughtiness, arrogance; magnificence
soberbio, a [so'βerβjo, a] adj (orgulloso) proud; (altivo) haughty, arrogant; (estupendo) magnificent, superb
sobornar [soβor'nar] vt to bribe; **soborno** nm bribe
sobra [so'βra] nf excess, surplus; **~s** nfpl left-overs, scraps; **de ~** surplus, extra; **tengo de ~** I've more than enough; **~do, a** adj (más que suficiente) more than enough; (superfluo) excessive; **sobrante** adj remaining, extra ♦ nm surplus, remainder
sobrar [so'βrar] vt to exceed, surpass ♦ vi (tener de más) to be more than enough;

(quedar) to remain, be left (over)
sobrasada [soβra'saða] nf pork sausage spread
sobre ['soβre] prep (gen) on; (encima) on (top of); (por encima de, arriba de) over, above; (más que) more than; (además) in addition to, besides; (alrededor de) about ♦ nm envelope; **~ todo** above all
sobrecama [soβre'kama] nf bedspread
sobrecargar [soβrekar'var] vt (camión) to overload; (COM) to surcharge
sobredosis [soβre'ðosis] nf inv overdose
sobreentender [soβre(e)nten'der] vt to deduce, infer; **~se** vr: **se sobreentiende que ...** it is implied that ...
sobrehumano, a [soβreu'mano, a] adj superhuman
sobrellevar [soβreʎe'βar] vt to bear, endure
sobremesa [soβre'mesa] nf: **durante la ~** after dinner; **ordenador de ~** desktop computer
sobrenatural [soβrenatu'ral] adj supernatural
sobrenombre [soβre'nombre] nm nickname
sobrepasar [soβrepa'sar] vt to exceed, surpass
sobreponerse [soβrepo'nerse] vr: **~ a** to overcome
sobresaliente [soβresa'ljente] adj outstanding, excellent
sobresalir [soβresa'lir] vi to project, jut out; (fig) to stand out, excel
sobresaltar [soβresal'tar] vt (asustar) to scare, frighten; (sobrecoger) to startle; **sobresalto** nm (movimiento) start; (susto) scare; (turbación) sudden shock
sobretodo [soβre'toðo] nm overcoat
sobrevenir [soβreβe'nir] vi (ocurrir) to happen (unexpectedly); (resultar) to follow, ensue
sobreviviente [soβreβi'βjente] adj surviving ♦ nm/f survivor
sobrevivir [soβreβi'βir] vi to survive
sobrevolar [soβreβo'lar] vt to fly over
sobriedad [soβrje'ðað] nf sobriety,

soberness; (*moderación*) moderation, restraint

sobrino, a [so'ßrino, a] *nm/f* nephew/ niece

sobrio, a ['soßrjo, a] *adj* sober; (*moderado*) moderate, restrained

socarrón, ona [soka'rron, ona] *adj* (*sarcástico*) sarcastic, ironic(al)

socavar [soka'ßar] *vt* (*tb fig*) to undermine

socavón [soka'ßon] *nm* (*hoyo*) hole

sociable [so'θjaßle] *adj* (*persona*) sociable, friendly; (*animal*) social

social [so'θjal] *adj* social; (COM) company *cpd*

socialdemócrata [soθjalde'mokrata] *nm/f* social democrat

socialista [soθja'lista] *adj, nm/f* socialist

socializar [soθjali'θar] *vt* to socialize

sociedad [soθje'ðað] *nf* society; (COM) company; **~ anónima** limited company; **~ de consumo** consumer society

socio, a ['soθjo, a] *nm/f* (*miembro*) member; (COM) partner

sociología [soθjolo'xia] *nf* sociology; **sociólogo, a** *nm/f* sociologist

socorrer [soko'rrer] *vt* to help; **socorrista** *nm/f* first aider; (*en piscina, playa*) lifeguard; **socorro** *nm* (*ayuda*) help, aid; (MIL) relief; **¡socorro!** help!

soda ['soða] *nf* (*sosa*) soda; (*bebida*) soda (water)

sofá [so'fa] (*pl* **~s**) *nm* sofa, settee; **~-cama** *nm* studio couch; sofa bed

sofisticación [sofistika'θjon] *nf* sophistication

sofocar [sofo'kar] *vt* to suffocate; (*apagar*) to smother, put out; **~se** *vr* to suffocate; (*fig*) to blush, feel embarrassed; **sofoco** *nm* suffocation; embarrassment

sofreír [sofre'ir] *vt* (CULIN) to fry lightly

soga ['soxa] *nf* rope

sois *vb ver* **ser**

soja ['soxa] *nf* soya

sol [sol] *nm* sun; (*luz*) sunshine, sunlight; **hace ~** it is sunny

solamente [sola'mente] *adv* only, just

solapa [so'lapa] *nf* (*de chaqueta*) lapel; (*de libro*) jacket

solapado, a [sola'paðo, a] *adj* (*intenciones*) underhand; (*gestos, movimiento*) sly

solar [so'lar] *adj* solar, sun *cpd*

solaz [so'laθ] *nm* recreation, relaxation; **~ar** *vt* (*divertir*) to amuse

soldado [sol'daðo] *nm* soldier; **~ raso** private

soldador [solda'ðor] *nm* soldering iron; (*persona*) welder

soldar [sol'dar] *vt* to solder, weld

soleado, a [sole'aðo, a] *adj* sunny

soledad [sole'ðað] *nf* solitude; (*estado infeliz*) loneliness

solemne [so'lemne] *adj* solemn; **solemnidad** *nf* solemnity

soler [so'ler] *vi* to be in the habit of, be accustomed to; **suele salir a las ocho** she usually goes out at 8 o'clock

solfeo [sol'feo] *nm* solfa

solicitar [soliθi'tar] *vt* (*permiso*) to ask for, seek; (*puesto*) to apply for; (*votos*) to canvass for; (*atención*) to attract

solícito, a [so'liθito, a] *adj* (*diligente*) diligent; (*cuidadoso*) careful; **solicitud** *nf* (*calidad*) great care; (*petición*) request; (*a un puesto*) application

solidaridad [soliðari'ðað] *nf* solidarity; **solidario, a** *adj* (*participación*) joint, common; (*compromiso*) mutually binding

solidez [soli'ðeθ] *nf* solidity; **sólido, a** *adj* solid

soliloquio [soli'lokjo] *nm* soliloquy

solista [so'lista] *nm/f* soloist

solitario, a [soli'tarjo, a] *adj* (*persona*) lonely, solitary; (*lugar*) lonely, desolate ♦ *nm/f* (*reclusa*) recluse; (*en la sociedad*) loner ♦ *nm* solitaire

sollozar [soʎo'θar] *vi* to sob; **sollozo** *nm* sob

solo, a ['solo, a] *adj* (*único*) single, sole; (*sin compañía*) alone; (*solitario*) lonely; **hay una sola dificultad** there is just one difficulty; **a solas** alone, by oneself

sólo ['solo] *adv* only, just

solomillo [solo'miʎo] *nm* sirloin

soltar [sol'tar] *vt (dejar ir)* to let go of; *(desprender)* to unfasten, loosen; *(librar)* to release, set free; *(risa etc)* to let out

soltero, a [sol'tero, a] *adj* single, unmarried ♦ *nm/f* bachelor/single woman; **solterón, ona** *nm/f* old bachelor/spinster

soltura [sol'tura] *nf* looseness, slackness; *(de los miembros)* agility, ease of movement; *(en el hablar)* fluency, ease

soluble [so'luβle] *adj (QUÍM)* soluble; *(problema)* solvable; ~ **en agua** soluble in water

solución [solu'θjon] *nf* solution; **solucionar** *vt (problema)* to solve; *(asunto)* to settle, resolve

solventar [solβen'tar] *vt (pagar)* to settle, pay; *(resolver)* to resolve; **solvente** *adj (ECON: empresa, persona)* solvent

sombra ['sombra] *nf* shadow; *(como protección)* shade; **~s** *nfpl (oscuridad)* darkness *sg*, shadows; **tener buena/mala ~** to be lucky/unlucky

sombrero [som'brero] *nm* hat

sombrilla [som'briʎa] *nf* parasol, sunshade

sombrío, a [som'brio, a] *adj (oscuro)* dark; *(triste)* sombre, sad; *(persona)* gloomy

somero, a [so'mero, a] *adj* superficial

someter [some'ter] *vt (país)* to conquer; *(persona)* to subject to one's will; *(informe)* to present, submit; **~se** *vr* to give in, yield, submit; **~ a** to subject to

somier [so'mjer] *(pl* **somiers)** *n* spring mattress

somnífero [som'nifero] *nm* sleeping pill

somnolencia [somno'lenθja] *nf* sleepiness, drowsiness

somos [son] *vb ver* **ser**

son [son] *vb ver* **ser** ♦ *nm* sound; **en ~ de broma** as a joke

sonajero [sona'xero] *nm* (baby's) rattle

sonambulismo [sonambu'lismo] *nm* sleepwalking; **sonámbulo, a** *nm/f* sleepwalker

sonar [so'nar] *vt* to ring ♦ *vi* to sound; *(hacer ruido)* to make a noise; *(pronunciarse)* to be sounded, be pronounced; *(ser conocido)* to sound familiar; *(campana)* to ring; *(reloj)* to strike, chime; **~se** *vr:* **~se (las narices)** to blow one's nose; **me suena ese nombre** that name rings a bell

sonda ['sonda] *nf (NAUT)* sounding; *(TEC)* bore, drill; *(MED)* probe

sondear [sonde'ar] *vt* to sound; to bore (into), drill; to probe, sound; *(fig)* to sound out; **sondeo** *nm* sounding; boring, drilling; *(fig)* poll, enquiry

sonido [so'niðo] *nm* sound

sonoro, a [so'noro, a] *adj* sonorous; *(resonante)* loud, resonant

sonreír [sonre'ir] *vi* to smile; **~se** *vr* to smile; **sonriente** *adj* smiling; **sonrisa** *nf* smile

sonrojarse [sonro'xarse] *vr* to blush, go red; **sonrojo** *nm* blush

soñador, a [soɲa'ðor, a] *nm/f* dreamer

soñar [so'ɲar] *vt, vi* to dream; **~ con** to dream about *o* of

soñoliento, a [soɲo'ljento, a] *adj* sleepy, drowsy

sopa ['sopa] *nf* soup

sopesar [sope'sar] *vt* to consider, weigh up

soplar [so'plar] *vt (polvo)* to blow away, blow off; *(inflar)* to blow up; *(vela)* to blow out ♦ *vi* to blow; **soplo** *nm* blow, puff; *(de viento)* puff, gust

soplón, ona [so'plon, ona] *(fam)* *nm/f (niño)* telltale; *(de policía)* grass *(fam)*

sopor [so'por] *nm* drowsiness

soporífero [sopo'rifero] *nm* sleeping pill

soportable [sopor'taβle] *adj* bearable

soportar [sopor'tar] *vt* to bear, carry; *(fig)* to bear, put up with; **soporte** *nm* support; *(fig)* pillar, support

soprano [so'prano] *nf* soprano

sorber [sor'βer] *vt (chupar)* to sip; *(absorber)* to soak up, absorb

sorbete [sor'βete] *nm* iced fruit drink

sorbo ['sorβo] *nm (trago: grande)* gulp, swallow; *(: pequeño)* sip

sordera [sor'ðera] *nf* deafness

sórdido, a [sor'ðiðo, a] *adj* dirty, squalid

sordo, a ['sorðo, a] *adj (persona)* deaf
♦ *nm/f* deaf person; **~mudo, a** *adj* deaf
and dumb

sorna ['sorna] *nf* sarcastic tone

soroche [so'rotʃe] *(AM) nm* mountain
sickness

sorprendente [sorpren'dente] *adj*
surprising

sorprender [sorpren'der] *vt* to surprise;
sorpresa *nf* surprise

sortear [sorte'ar] *vt* to draw lots for; *(rifar)*
to raffle; *(dificultad)* to avoid; **sorteo** *nm*
(en lotería) draw; *(rifa)* raffle

sortija [sor'tixa] *nf* ring; *(rizo)* ringlet, curl

sosegado, a [sose'xaðo, a] *adj* quiet,
calm

sosegar [sose'xar] *vt* to quieten, calm; *(el
ánimo)* to reassure ♦ *vi* to rest; **sosiego**
nm quiet(ness), calm(ness)

soslayo [sos'lajo]: **de ~** *adv* obliquely,
sideways

soso, a ['soso, a] *adj (CULIN)* tasteless;
(aburrido) dull, uninteresting

sospecha [sos'petʃa] *nf* suspicion;
sospechar *vt* to suspect;
sospechoso, a *adj* suspicious;
(testimonio, opinión) suspect ♦ *nm/f*
suspect

sostén [sos'ten] *nm (apoyo)* support;
(sujetador) bra; *(alimentación)* sustenance,
food

sostener [soste'ner] *vt* to support;
(mantener) to keep up, maintain;
(alimentar) to sustain, keep going; **~se** *vr*
to support o.s.; *(seguir)* to continue,
remain; **sostenido, a** *adj* continuous,
sustained; *(prolongado)* prolonged

sotana [so'tana] *nf (REL)* cassock

sótano ['sotano] *nm* basement

soviético, a [so'βjetiko, a] *adj* Soviet; **los
~s** the Soviets

soy *vb ver* **ser**

Sr. *abr* (= *Señor*) Mr

Sra. *abr* (= *Señora*) Mrs

S.R.C. *abr* (= *se ruega contestación*)
R.S.V.P.

Sres. *abr* (= *Señores*) Messrs

Srta. *abr* (= *Señorita*) Miss

Sta. *abr* (= *Santa*) St

status ['status, e'status] *nm inv* status

Sto. *abr* (= *Santo*) St

su [su] *pron (de él)* his; *(de ella)* her; *(de
una cosa)* its; *(de ellos, ellas)* their; *(de
usted, ustedes)* your

suave ['swaβe] *adj* gentle; *(superficie)*
smooth; *(trabajo)* easy; *(música, voz)* soft,
sweet; **suavidad** *nf* gentleness;
smoothness; softness, sweetness;
suavizante *nm (de ropa)* softener; *(del
pelo)* conditioner; **suavizar** *vt* to soften;
(quitar la aspereza) to smooth (out)

subalimentado, a [suβalimen'taðo, a]
adj undernourished

subasta [su'βasta] *nf* auction; **subastar**
vt to auction (off)

subcampeón, ona [suβkampe'on, ona]
nm/f runner-up

subconsciente [suβkon'sθjente] *adj, nm*
subconscious

subdesarrollado, a [suβðesarro'ʎaðo, a]
adj underdeveloped

subdesarrollo [suβðesa'rroʎo] *nm*
underdevelopment

subdirector, a [suβðirek'tor, a] *nm/f*
assistant director

súbdito, a ['suβðito, a] *nm/f* subject

subestimar [suβesti'mar] *vt* to
underestimate, underrate

subida [su'βiða] *nf (de montaña etc)*
ascent, climb; *(de precio)* rise, increase;
(pendiente) slope, hill

subir [su'βir] *vt (objeto)* to raise, lift up;
(cuesta, calle) to go up; *(colina, montaña)*
to climb; *(precio)* to raise, put up ♦ *vi* to
go up, come up; *(a un coche)* to get in;
(a un autobús, tren o avión) to get on,
board; *(precio)* to rise, go up; *(río, marea)*
to rise; **~se** *vr* to get up, climb

súbito, a ['suβito, a] *adj (repentino)*
sudden; *(imprevisto)* unexpected

subjetivo, a [suβxe'tiβo, a] *adj* subjective

sublevación [suβleβa'θjon] *nf* revolt,
rising

sublevar [suβle'βar] *vt* to rouse to revolt;

~se *vr* to revolt, rise
sublime [su'βlime] *adj* sublime
submarinismo [sußmari'nismo] *nm* scuba diving
submarino, a [sußma'rino, a] *adj* underwater ♦ *nm* submarine
subnormal [sußnor'mal] *adj* subnormal ♦ *nm/f* subnormal person
subordinado, a [sußorδi'naδo, a] *adj*, *nm/f* subordinate
subrayar [sußra'jar] *vt* to underline
subsanar [sußsa'nar] *vt* to recitify
subscribir [sußskri'βir] *vt* = **suscribir**
subsidio [suß'siδjo] *nm* (*ayuda*) aid, financial help; (*subvención*) subsidy, grant; (*de enfermedad, paro etc*) benefit, allowance
subsistencia [sußsis'tenθja] *nf* subsistence
subsistir [sußsis'tir] *vi* to subsist; (*sobrevivir*) to survive, endure
subterráneo, a [sußte'rraneo, a] *adj* underground, subterranean ♦ *nm* underpass, underground passage
subtítulo [suß'titulo] *nm* (*CINE*) subtitle
suburbano, a [sußur'βano, a] *adj* suburban
suburbio [su'βurßjo] *nm* (*barrio*) slum quarter
subvención [sußßen'θjon] *nf* (*ECON*) subsidy, grant; **subvencionar** *vt* to subsidize
subversión [sußßer'sjon] *nf* subversion; **subversivo, a** *adj* subversive
subyugar [sußju'var] *vt* (*país*) to subjugate, subdue; (*enemigo*) to overpower; (*voluntad*) to dominate
sucedáneo, a [suθe'δaneo, a] *adj* substitute ♦ *nm* substitute (food)
suceder [suθe'δer] *vt*, *vi* to happen; (*seguir*) to succeed, follow; **lo que sucede es que ...** the fact is that ...; **sucesión** *nf* succession; (*serie*) sequence, series
sucesivamente [suθesißa'mente] *adv*: **y así ~** and so on
sucesivo, a [suθe'sißo, a] *adj* successive,

following; **en lo ~** in future, from now on
suceso [su'θeso] *nm* (*hecho*) event, happening; (*incidente*) incident
suciedad [suθje'δaδ] *nf* (*estado*) dirtiness; (*mugre*) dirt, filth
sucinto, a [su'θinto, a] *adj* (*conciso*) succinct, concise
sucio, a ['suθjo, a] *adj* dirty
suculento, a [suku'lento, a] *adj* succulent
sucumbir [sukum'bir] *vi* to succumb
sucursal [sukur'sal] *nf* branch (office)
sudadera [suδa'δera] *nf* sweatshirt
Sudáfrica [suδ'afrika] *nf* South Africa
Sudamérica [suδa'merika] *nf* South America; **sudamericano, a** *adj*, *nm/f* South American
sudar [su'δar] *vt*, *vi* to sweat
sudeste [su'δeste] *nm* south-east
sudoeste [suδo'este] *nm* south-west
sudor [su'δor] *nm* sweat; **~oso, a** *adj* sweaty, sweating
Suecia ['sweθja] *nf* Sweden; **sueco, a** *adj* Swedish ♦ *nm/f* Swede
suegro, a ['swevro, a] *nm/f* father-/ mother-in-law
suela ['swela] *nf* sole
sueldo ['sweldo] *nm* pay, wage(s) (*pl*)
suele *etc vb ver* **soler**
suelo ['swelo] *nm* (*tierra*) ground; (*de casa*) floor
suelto, a ['swelto, a] *adj* loose; (*libre*) free; (*separado*) detached; (*ágil*) quick, agile ♦ *nm* (*loose*) change, small change
sueño *etc* ['sweɲo] *vb ver* **soñar** ♦ *nm* sleep; (*somnolencia*) sleepiness, drowsiness; (*lo soñado, fig*) dream; **tener ~** to be sleepy
suero ['swero] *nm* (*MED*) serum; (*de leche*) whey
suerte ['swerte] *nf* (*fortuna*) luck; (*azar*) chance; (*destino*) fate, destiny; (*especie*) sort, kind; **tener ~** to be lucky; **de otra ~** otherwise, if not; **de ~ que** so that, in such a way that
suéter ['sweter] *nm* sweater
suficiente [sufi'θjente] *adj* enough, sufficient ♦ *nm* (*ESCOL*) pass

sufragio [suˈfraxjo] *nm* (*voto*) vote; (*derecho de voto*) suffrage

sufrido, a [suˈfriðo, a] *adj* (*persona*) tough; (*paciente*) long-suffering, patient

sufrimiento [sufriˈmjento] *nm* (*dolor*) suffering

sufrir [suˈfrir] *vt* (*padecer*) to suffer; (*soportar*) to bear, put up with; (*apoyar*) to hold up, support ♦ *vi* to suffer

sugerencia [suxeˈrenθja] *nf* suggestion

sugerir [suxeˈrir] *vt* to suggest; (*sutilmente*) to hint

sugestión [suxesˈtjon] *nf* suggestion; (*sutil*) hint; **sugestionar** *vt* to influence

sugestivo, a [suxesˈtiβo, a] *adj* stimulating; (*fascinante*) fascinating

suicida [suiˈθiða] *adj* suicidal ♦ *nm/f* suicidal person; (*muerto*) suicide, person who has committed suicide; **suicidarse** *vr* to commit suicide, kill o.s.; **suicidio** *nm* suicide

Suiza [ˈswiθa] *nf* Switzerland; **suizo, a** *adj, nm/f* Swiss

sujeción [suxeˈθjon] *nf* subjection

sujetador [suxetaˈðor] *nm* (*sostén*) bra

sujetar [suxeˈtar] *vt* (*fijar*) to fasten; (*detener*) to hold down; **~se** *vr* to subject o.s.; **sujeto, a** *adj* fastened, secure ♦ *nm* subject; (*individuo*) individual; **sujeto a** subject to

suma [ˈsuma] *nf* (*cantidad*) total, sum; (*de dinero*) sum; (*acto*) adding (up), addition; **en ~** in short

sumamente [sumaˈmente] *adv* extremely, exceedingly

sumar [suˈmar] *vt* to add (up) ♦ *vi* to add up

sumario, a [suˈmarjo, a] *adj* brief, concise ♦ *nm* summary

sumergir [sumerˈxir] *vt* to submerge; (*hundir*) to sink

suministrar [suminisˈtrar] *vt* to supply, provide; **suministro** *nm* supply, (*acto*) supplying, providing

sumir [suˈmir] *vt* to sink, submerge; (*fig*) to plunge

sumisión [sumiˈsjon] *nf* (*acto*) submission;

(*calidad*) submissiveness, docility; **sumiso, a** *adj* submissive, docile

sumo, a [ˈsumo, a] *adj* great, extreme; (*autoridad*) highest, supreme

suntuoso, a [sunˈtwoso, a] *adj* sumptuous, magnificent

supe *etc vb ver* **saber**

supeditar [supeðiˈtar] *vt*: **~ algo a algo** to subordinate sth to sth

super... [super] *prefijo* super..., over...; **~bueno** *adj* great, fantastic

súper [ˈsuper] *nf* (*gasolina*) three-star (petrol)

superar [supeˈrar] *vt* (*sobreponerse a*) to overcome; (*rebasar*) to surpass, do better than; (*pasar*) to go beyond; **~se** *vr* to excel o.s.

superávit [supeˈraβit] *nm inv* surplus

superficial [superfiˈθjal] *adj* superficial; (*medida*) surface *cpd*, of the surface

superficie [superˈfiθje] *nf* surface; (*área*) area

superfluo, a [suˈperflwo, a] *adj* superfluous

superior [supeˈrjor] *adj* (*piso, clase*) upper; (*temperatura, número, nivel*) higher; (*mejor: calidad, producto*) superior, better ♦ *nm/f* superior; **~idad** *nf* superiority

supermercado [supermerˈkaðo] *nm* supermarket

superponer [superpoˈner] *vt* to superimpose

supersónico, a [superˈsoniko, a] *adj* supersonic

superstición [superstiˈθjon] *nf* superstition; **supersticioso, a** *adj* superstitious

supervisar [superβiˈsar] *vt* to supervise

supervivencia [superβiˈβenθja] *nf* survival

superviviente [superβiˈβjente] *adj* surviving

supiera *etc vb ver* **saber**

suplantar [suplanˈtar] *vt* to supplant

suplemento [supleˈmento] *nm* supplement

suplente [suˈplente] *adj, nm/f* substitute

supletorio, a [supleˈtorjo, a] *adj*

supplementary ♦ *nm* supplement;
teléfono ~ extension
súplica ['suplika] *nf* request; (*JUR*) petition
suplicar [supli'kar] *vt* (*cosa*) to beg (for),
plead for; (*persona*) to beg, plead with
suplicio [su'pliθjo] *nm* torture
suplir [su'plir] *vt* (*compensar*) to make
good, make up for; (*reemplazar*) to
replace, substitute ♦ *vi*: **~ a** to take the
place of, substitute for
supo *etc vb ver* **saber**
suponer [supo'ner] *vt* to suppose;
suposición *nf* supposition
supremacía [suprema'θia] *nf* supremacy
supremo, a [su'premo, a] *adj* supreme
supresión [supre'sjon] *nf* suppression; (*de
derecho*) abolition; (*de palabra etc*)
deletion; (*de restricción*) cancellation,
lifting
suprimir [supri'mir] *vt* to suppress;
(*derecho, costumbre*) to abolish; (*palabra
etc*) to delete; (*restricción*) to cancel, lift
supuesto, a [su'pwesto, a] *pp de* **suponer**
♦ *adj* (*hipotético*) supposed ♦ *nm*
assumption, hypothesis; **~ que** since; **por
~** of course
sur [sur] *nm* south
surcar [sur'kar] *vt* to plough; **surco** *nm*
(*en metal, disco*) groove; (*AGR*) furrow
surgir [sur'xir] *vi* to arise, emerge;
(*dificultad*) to come up, crop up
suroeste [suro'este] *nm* south-west
surtido, a [sur'tiðo, a] *adj* mixed, assorted
♦ *nm* (*selección*) selection, assortment;
(*abastecimiento*) supply, stock; **~r** *nm* (*tb:*
~r de gasolina) petrol pump (*BRIT*), gas
pump (*US*)
surtir [sur'tir] *vt* to supply, provide ♦ *vi* to
spout, spurt
susceptible [susθep'tißle] *adj* susceptible;
(*sensible*) sensitive; **~ de** capable of
suscitar [susθi'tar] *vt* to cause, provoke;
(*interés, sospechas*) to arouse
suscribir [suskri'ßir] *vt* (*firmar*) to sign;
(*respaldar*) to subscribe to, endorse; **~se**
vr to subscribe; **suscripción** *nf*
subscription

susodicho, a [suso'ðitʃo, a] *adj* above-
mentioned
suspender [suspen'der] *vt* (*objeto*) to
hang (up), suspend; (*trabajo*) to stop,
suspend; (*ESCOL*) to fail; (*interrumpir*) to
adjourn; (*atrasar*) to postpone;
suspensión *nf* suspension; (*fig*)
stoppage, suspension
suspenso, a [sus'penso, a] *adj* hanging,
suspended; (*ESCOL*) failed ♦ *nm* (*ESCOL*)
fail; **quedar** *o* **estar en ~** to be pending
suspicacia [suspi'kaθja] *nf* suspicion,
mistrust; **suspicaz** *adj* suspicious,
distrustful
suspirar [suspi'rar] *vi* to sigh; **suspiro**
nm sigh
sustancia [sus'tanθja] *nf* substance
sustentar [susten'tar] *vt* (*alimentar*) to
sustain, nourish; (*objeto*) to hold up,
support; (*idea, teoría*) to maintain,
uphold; (*fig*) to sustain, keep going;
sustento *nm* support; (*alimento*)
sustenance, food
sustituir [sustitu'ir] *vt* to substitute,
replace; **sustituto, a** *nm/f* substitute,
replacement
susto ['susto] *nm* fright, scare
sustraer [sustra'er] *vt* to remove, take
away; (*MAT*) to subtract
susurrar [susu'rrar] *vi* to whisper;
susurro *nm* whisper
sutil [su'til] *adj* (*aroma, diferencia*) subtle;
(*tenue*) thin; (*inteligencia, persona*) sharp;
~eza *nf* subtlety; thinness
suyo, a ['sujo, a] (*con artículo o después
del verbo* **ser**) *adj* (*de él*) his; (*de ella*)
hers; (*de ellos, ellas*) theirs; (*de Ud, Uds*)
yours; **un amigo ~** a friend of his (*o* hers
o theirs *o* yours)

T, t

tabacalera [taßaka'lera] *nf*: **T~** *Spanish state tobacco monopoly*

tabaco [ta'ßako] *nm* tobacco; (*fam*) cigarettes *pl*

taberna [ta'ßerna] *nf* bar, pub (*BRIT*)

tabique [ta'ßike] *nm* partition (wall)

tabla ['taßla] *nf* (*de madera*) plank; (*estante*) shelf; (*de vestido*) pleat; (*ARTE*) panel; **~s** *nfpl*: **estar** *o* **quedar en ~s** to draw; **~do** *nm* (*plataforma*) platform; (*TEATRO*) stage

tablao [ta'ßlao] *nm* (*tb*: **~ flamenco**) flamenco show

tablero [ta'ßlero] *nm* (*de madera*) plank, board; (*de ajedrez, damas*) board; **~ de anuncios** notice (*BRIT*) *o* bulletin (*US*) board

tableta [ta'ßleta] *nf* (*MED*) tablet; (*de chocolate*) bar

tablón [ta'ßlon] *nm* (*de suelo*) plank; (*de techo*) beam; **~ de anuncios** notice board (*BRIT*), bulletin board (*US*)

tabú [ta'ßu] *nm* taboo

tabular [taßu'lar] *vt* to tabulate

taburete [taßu'rete] *nm* stool

tacaño, a [ta'kaɲo, a] *adj* mean

tacha ['tatʃa] *nf* flaw; (*TEC*) stud; **tachar** *vt* (*borrar*) to cross out; **tachar de** to accuse of

tácito, a ['taθito, a] *adj* tacit

taciturno, a [taθi'turno, a] *adj* silent

taco ['tako] *nm* (*BILLAR*) cue; (*libro de billetes*) book; (*AM*: *de zapato*) heel; (*tarugo*) peg; (*palabrota*) swear word

tacón [ta'kon] *nm* heel; **de ~ alto** high-heeled; **taconeo** *nm* (heel) stamping

táctica ['taktika] *nf* tactics *pl*

táctico, a ['taktiko, a] *adj* tactical

tacto ['takto] *nm* touch; (*fig*) tact

taimado, a [tai'maðo, a] *adj* (*astuto*) sly

tajada [ta'xaða] *nf* slice

tajante [ta'xante] *adj* sharp

tajo ['taxo] *nm* (*corte*) cut; (*GEO*) cleft

tal [tal] *adj* such; **~ vez** perhaps ♦ *pron* (*persona*) someone, such a one; (*cosa*) something, such a thing; **~ como** such as; **~ para cual** (*dos iguales*) two of a kind ♦ *adv*: **~ como** (*igual*) just as; **~ cual** (*como es*) just as it is; **¿qué ~?** how are things?; **¿qué ~ te gusta?** how do you like it? ♦ *conj*: **con ~ de que** provided that

taladrar [tala'ðrar] *vt* to drill; **taladro** *nm* drill

talante [ta'lante] *nm* (*humor*) mood; (*voluntad*) will, willingness

talar [ta'lar] *vt* to fell, cut down; (*devastar*) to devastate

talco ['talko] *nm* (*polvos*) talcum powder

talego [ta'lexo] *nm* sack

talento [ta'lento] *nm* talent; (*capacidad*) ability

TALGO ['talvo] (*ESP*) *nm abr* (= *tren articulado ligero Goicoechea-Oriol*) ≈ HST (*BRIT*)

talismán [talis'man] *nm* talisman

talla ['taʎa] *nf* (*estatura, fig, MED*) height, stature; (*palo*) measuring rod; (*ARTE*) carving; (*medida*) size

tallado, a [ta'ʎaðo, a] *adj* carved ♦ *nm* carving

tallar [ta'ʎar] *vt* (*madera*) to carve; (*metal etc*) to engrave; (*medir*) to measure

tallarines [taʎa'rines] *nmpl* noodles

talle ['taʎe] *nm* (*ANAT*) waist; (*fig*) appearance

taller [ta'ʎer] *nm* (*TEC*) workshop; (*de artista*) studio

tallo ['taʎo] *nm* (*de planta*) stem; (*de hierba*) blade; (*brote*) shoot

talón [ta'lon] *nm* (*ANAT*) heel; (*COM*) counterfoil; (*cheque*) cheque (*BRIT*), check (*US*)

talonario [talo'narjo] *nm* (*de cheques*) chequebook (*BRIT*), checkbook (*US*); (*de recibos*) receipt book

tamaño, a [ta'maɲo, a] *adj* (*tan grande*) such a big; (*tan pequeño*) such a small ♦ *nm* size; **de ~ natural** full-size

tamarindo [tama'rindo] *nm* tamarind

tambalearse [tambale'arse] *vr* (*persona*)
to stagger; (*vehículo*) to sway
también [tam'bjen] *adv* (*igualmente*) also,
too, as well; (*además*) besides
tambor [tam'bor] *nm* drum; (*ANAT*)
eardrum; **~ del freno** brake drum
tamiz [ta'miθ] *nm* sieve; **~ar** *vt* to sieve
tampoco [tam'poko] *adv* nor, neither; **yo
~ lo compré** I didn't buy it either
tampón [tam'pon] *nm* tampon
tan [tan] *adv* so; **~ es así que ...** so much
so that ....
tanda ['tanda] *nf* (*gen*) series; (*turno*) shift
tangente [tan'xente] *nf* tangent
Tánger ['tanxer] *n* Tangier(s)
tangible [tan'xiβle] *adj* tangible
tanque ['tanke] *nm* (*cisterna, MIL*) tank;
(*AUTO*) tanker
tantear [tante'ar] *vt* (*calcular*) to reckon
(up); (*medir*) to take the measure of;
(*probar*) to test, try out; (*tomar la medida:
persona*) to take the measurements of;
(*situación*) to weigh up; (*persona: opinión*)
to sound out ♦ *vi* (*DEPORTE*) to score;
tanteo *nm* (*cálculo*) (rough) calculation;
(*prueba*) test, trial; (*DEPORTE*) scoring
tanto, a ['tanto, a] *adj* (*cantidad*) so much,
as much; **~s** so many, as many; **20 y ~s**
20-odd ♦ *adv* (*cantidad*) so much, as
much; (*tiempo*) so long, as long ♦ *conj*:
en ~ que while; **hasta ~ (que)** until such
time as ♦ *nm* (*suma*) certain amount;
(*proporción*) so much; (*punto*) point; (*gol*)
goal; **un ~ perezoso** somewhat lazy
♦ *pron*: **cada uno paga ~** each one pays
so much; **~ tú como yo** both you and I;
~ como eso as much as that; **~ más ...
cuanto que** all the more ... because; **~
mejor/peor** so much the better/the
worse; **~ si viene como si va** whether he
comes or whether he goes; **~ es así que**
so much so that; **por o por lo ~**
therefore; **me he vuelto ronco de o con
~ hablar** I have become hoarse with so
much talking; **a ~s de agosto** on such
and such a day in August
tapa ['tapa] *nf* (*de caja, olla*) lid; (*de*

botella) top; (*de libro*) cover; (*comida*)
snack
tapadera [tapa'ðera] *nf* lid, cover
tapar [ta'par] *vt* (*cubrir*) to cover; (*envolver*)
to wrap o cover up; (*la vista*) to obstruct;
(*persona, falta*) to conceal; (*AM*) to fill;
~se *vr* to wrap o.s. up
taparrabo [tapa'rraβo] *nm* loincloth
tapete [ta'pete] *nm* table cover
tapia ['tapja] *nf* (*garden*) wall; **tapiar** *vt* to
wall in
tapicería [tapiθe'ria] *nf* tapestry; (*para
muebles*) upholstery; (*tienda*) upholsterer's
(shop)
tapiz [ta'piθ] *nm* (*alfombra*) carpet; (*tela
tejida*) tapestry; **~ar** *vt* (*muebles*) to
upholster
tapón [ta'pon] *nm* (*de botella*) top; (*de
lavabo*) plug; **~ de rosca** screw-top
taquigrafía [takiɣra'fia] *nf* shorthand;
taquígrafo, a *nm/f* shorthand writer,
stenographer
taquilla [ta'kiʎa] *nf* (*donde se compra*)
booking office; (*suma recogida*) takings *pl*;
taquillero, a *adj*: **función taquillera**
box office success ♦ *nm/f* ticket clerk
tara ['tara] *nf* (*defecto*) defect; (*COM*) tare
tarántula [ta'rantula] *nf* tarantula
tararear [tarare'ar] *vi* to hum
tardar [tar'ðar] *vi* (*tomar tiempo*) to take a
long time; (*llegar tarde*) to be late;
(*demorar*) to delay; **¿tarda mucho el
tren?** does the train take (very) long?; **a
más ~** at the latest; **no tardes en venir**
come soon
tarde ['tarðe] *adv* late ♦ *nf* (*de día*)
afternoon; (*al anochecer*) evening; **de ~
en ~** from time to time; **¡buenas ~s!**
good afternoon!; **a o por la ~** in the
afternoon; in the evening
tardío, a [tar'ðio, a] *adj* (*retrasado*) late;
(*lento*) slow (to arrive)
tarea [ta'rea] *nf* task; (*faena*) chore; (*ESCOL*)
homework
tarifa [ta'rifa] *nf* (*lista de precios*) price list;
(*precio*) tariff
tarima [ta'rima] *nf* (*plataforma*) platform

tarjeta [tar'xeta] *nf* card; ~ **postal/de crédito/de Navidad** postcard/credit card/Christmas card

tarro ['tarro] *nm* jar, pot

tarta ['tarta] *nf* (*pastel*) cake; (*de base dura*) tart

tartamudear [tartamuðe'ar] *vi* to stammer; **tartamudo, a** *adj* stammering ♦ *nm/f* stammerer

tártaro, a ['tartaro, a] *adj*: **salsa tártara** tartar(e) sauce

tasa ['tasa] *nf* (*precio*) (fixed) price, rate; (*valoración*) valuation; (*medida, norma*) measure, standard; ~ **de cambio/interés** exchange/interest rate; ~**s universitarias** university fees; ~**s de aeropuerto** airport tax; ~**ción** *nf* valuation; ~**dor, a** *nm/f* valuer

tasar [ta'sar] *vt* (*arreglar el precio*) to fix a price for; (*valorar*) to value, assess

tasca ['taska] (*fam*) *nf* pub

tatarabuelo, a [tatara'ßwelo, a] *nm/f* great-great-grandfather/mother

tatuaje [ta'twaxe] *nm* (*dibujo*) tattoo; (*acto*) tattooing

tatuar [ta'twar] *vt* to tattoo

taurino, a [tau'rino, a] *adj* bullfighting *cpd*

Tauro ['tauro] *nm* Taurus

tauromaquia [tauro'makja] *nf* tauromachy, (art of) bullfighting

taxi ['taksi] *nm* taxi

taxista [tak'sista] *nm/f* taxi driver

taza ['taθa] *nf* cup; (*de retrete*) bowl; ~ **para café** coffee cup; **tazón** *nm* (*taza grande*) mug, large cup; (*de fuente*) basin

te [te] *pron* (*complemento de objeto*) you; (*complemento indirecto*) (to) you; (*reflexivo*) (to) yourself; ¿~ **duele mucho el brazo?** does your arm hurt a lot?; ~ **equivocas** you're wrong; ¡**cálma~!** calm down!

té [te] *nm* tea

tea ['tea] *nf* torch

teatral [tea'tral] *adj* theatre *cpd*; (*fig*) theatrical

teatro [te'atro] *nm* theatre; (*LITERATURA*) plays *pl*, drama

tebeo [te'ßeo] *nm* comic

techo ['tetʃo] *nm* (*externo*) roof; (*interno*) ceiling; ~ **corredizo** sunroof

tecla ['tekla] *nf* key; ~**do** *nm* keyboard; **teclear** *vi* (*MUS*) to strum; (*con los dedos*) to tap ♦ *vt* (*INFORM*) to key in

técnica ['teknika] *nf* technique; (*tecnología*) technology; *ver tb* **técnico**

técnico, a ['tekniko, a] *adj* technical ♦ *nm/f* technician; (*experto*) expert

tecnología [teknolo'xia] *nf* technology; **tecnológico, a** *adj* technological

tedio ['teðjo] *nm* boredom, tedium; ~**so, a** *adj* boring, tedious

teja ['texa] *nf* tile; (*BOT*) lime (tree); ~**do** *nm* (tiled) roof

tejemaneje [texema'nexe] *nm* (*lío*) fuss; (*intriga*) intrigue

tejer [te'xer] *vt* to weave; (*hacer punto*) to knit; (*fig*) to fabricate; **tejido** *nm* (*tela*) material, fabric; (*telaraña*) web; (*ANAT*) tissue

tel [tel] *abr* (= *teléfono*) tel

tela ['tela] *nf* (*tejido*) material; (*telaraña*) web; (*en líquido*) skin; **telar** *nm* (*máquina*) loom

telaraña [tela'rapa] *nf* cobweb

tele ['tele] (*fam*) *nf* telly (*BRIT*), tube (*US*)

tele... ['tele] *prefijo* tele...; ~**comunicación** *nf* telecommunication; ~**control** *nm* remote control; ~**diario** *nm* television news; ~**difusión** *nf* (television) broadcast; ~**dirigido, a** *adj* remote-controlled

teléf *abr* (= *teléfono*) tel

teleférico [tele'feriko] *nm* (*de esquí*) ski-lift

telefonear [telefone'ar] *vi* to telephone

telefónico, a [tele'foniko, a] *adj* telephone *cpd*

telefonillo [telefo'niʎo] *nm* (*de puerta*) intercom

telefonista [telefo'nista] *nm/f* telephonist

teléfono [te'lefono] *nm* (tele)phone; **estar hablando al** ~ to be on the phone; **llamar a uno por** ~ to ring sb (up) *o* phone sb (up); ~ **móvil** car phone; ~ **portátil** mobile phone

telegrafía [teleɣra'fia] *nf* telegraphy

telégrafo [te'leɣrafo] *nm* telegraph

telegrama [tele'ɣrama] *nm* telegram

tele: ~**impresor** *nm* teleprinter (*BRIT*), teletype (*US*); ~**novela** *nf* soap (opera); ~**objetivo** *nm* telephoto lens; ~**patía** *nf* telepathy; ~**pático, a** *adj* telepathic; ~**scópico, a** *adj* telescopic; ~**scopio** *nm* telescope; ~**silla** *nm* chairlift; ~**spectador, a** *nm/f* viewer; ~**squí** *nm* ski-lift; ~**tarjeta** *nf* phonecard; ~**tipo** *nm* teletype

televidente [teleßi'ðente] *nm/f* viewer

televisar [teleßi'sar] *vt* to televise

televisión [teleßi'sjon] *nf* television; ~ **en colores** colour television

televisor [teleßi'sor] *nm* television set

télex ['teleks] *nm inv* telex

telón [te'lon] *nm* curtain; ~ **de acero** (*POL*) iron curtain; ~ **de fondo** backcloth, background

tema ['tema] *nm* (*asunto*) subject, topic; (*MUS*) theme; **temática** *nf* (*social, histórica, artística*) range of topics; **temático, a** *adj* thematic

temblar [tem'blar] *vi* to shake, tremble; (*de frío*) to shiver; **temblón, ona** *adj* shaking; **temblor** *nm* trembling; (*de tierra*) earthquake; **tembloroso, a** *adj* trembling

temer [te'mer] *vt* to fear ♦ *vi* to be afraid; **temo que llegue tarde** I am afraid he may be late

temerario, a [teme'rarjo, a] *adj* (*descuidado*) reckless; (*irreflexivo*) hasty; **temeridad** *nf* (*imprudencia*) rashness; (*audacia*) boldness

temeroso, a [teme'roso, a] *adj* (*miedoso*) fearful; (*que inspira temor*) frightful

temible [te'mißle] *adj* fearsome

temor [te'mor] *nm* (*miedo*) fear; (*duda*) suspicion

témpano ['tempano] *nm:* ~ **de hielo** ice-floe

temperamento [tempera'mento] *nm* temperament

temperatura [tempera'tura] *nf* temperature

tempestad [tempes'tað] *nf* storm; **tempestuoso, a** *adj* stormy

templado, a [tem'plaðo, a] *adj* (*moderado*) moderate; (*frugal*) frugal; (*agua*) lukewarm; (*clima*) mild; (*MUS*) well-tuned; **templanza** *nf* moderation; mildness

templar [tem'plar] *vt* (*moderar*) to moderate; (*furia*) to restrain; (*calor*) to reduce; (*afinar*) to tune (up); (*acero*) to temper; (*tuerca*) to tighten up; **temple** *nm* (*ajuste*) tempering; (*afinación*) tuning; (*pintura*) tempera

templo ['templo] *nm* (*iglesia*) church; (*pagano etc*) temple

temporada [tempo'raða] *nf* time, period; (*estación*) season

temporal [tempo'ral] *adj* (*no permanente*) temporary; (*REL*) temporal ♦ *nm* storm

tempranero, a [tempra'nero, a] *adj* (*BOT*) early; (*persona*) early-rising

temprano, a [tem'prano, a] *adj* early; (*demasiado pronto*) too soon, too early

ten *vb ver* **tener**

tenaces [te'naθes] *adj pl ver* **tenaz**

tenacidad [tenaθi'ðað] *nf* tenacity; (*dureza*) toughness; (*terquedad*) stubbornness

tenacillas [tena'θiʎas] *nfpl* tongs; (*para el pelo*) curling tongs (*BRIT*) o iron *sg* (*US*); (*MED*) forceps

tenaz [te'naθ] *adj* (*material*) tough; (*persona*) tenacious; (*creencia, resistencia*) stubborn

tenaza(s) [te'naθa(s)] *nf(pl)* (*MED*) forceps, (*TEC*) pliers; (*ZOOL*) pincers

tendedero [tende'ðero] *nm* (*para ropa*) drying place; (*cuerda*) clothes line

tendencia [ten'denθja] *nf* tendency; **tene** ~ **a** to tend to, have a tendency to; **tendencioso, a** *adj* tendentious

tender [ten'der] *vt* (*extender*) to spread out; (*colgar*) to hang out; (*vía férrea, cable*) to lay; (*estirar*) to stretch ♦ *vi:* ~ **a** to tend to, have a tendency towards; ~**se** *vr* to lie down; ~ **la cama/la mesa** (*AM*)

to make the bed/lay (BRIT) o set (US) the
table
tenderete [tende'rete] nm (puesto) stall;
(exposición) display of goods
tendero, a [ten'dero, a] nm/f shopkeeper
tendido, a [ten'diðo, a] adj (acostado)
lying down, flat; (colgado) hanging ♦ nm
(TAUR) front rows of seats; **a galope ~** flat
out
tendón [ten'don] nm tendon
tendré etc vb ver **tener**
tenebroso, a [tene'ßroso, a] adj (oscuro)
dark; (fig) gloomy
tenedor [tene'ðor] nm (CULIN) fork; **~ de
libros** book-keeper
tenencia [te'nenθja] nf (de casa) tenancy;
(de oficio) tenure; (de propiedad)
possession

PALABRA CLAVE

tener [te'ner] vt **1** (poseer, gen) to have;
(en la mano) to hold; **¿tienes un boli?**
have you got a pen?; **va a ~ un niño**
she's going to have a baby; **¡ten (o
tenga)!, ¡aquí tienes (o tiene)!** here you
are!
2 (edad, medidas) to be; **tiene 7 años**
she's 7 (years old); **tiene 15 cm de largo**
it's 15 cm long; ver **calor; hambre** etc
3 (considerar): **lo tengo por brillante** I
consider him to be brilliant; **~ en mucho
a uno** to think very highly of sb
4 (+pp: = pretérito): **tengo terminada ya
la mitad del trabajo** I've done half the
work already
5: **~ que hacer algo** to have to do sth;
tengo que acabar este trabajo hoy I
have to finish this job today
6: **¿qué tienes, estás enfermo?** what's
the matter with you, are you ill?
♦ **~se** vr **1**: **~se en pie** to stand up
2: **~se por** to think o.s.; **se tiene por
muy listo** he thinks himself very clever

-engo etc vb ver **tener**
-enia ['tenja] nf tapeworm
-eniente [te'njente] nm (rango) lieutenant;

(ayudante) deputy
tenis ['tenis] nm tennis; **~ de mesa** table
tennis; **~ta** nm/f tennis player
tenor [te'nor] nm (sentido) meaning; (MUS)
tenor; **a ~ de** on the lines of
tensar [ten'sar] vt to tighten; (arco) to
draw
tensión [ten'sjon] nf tension; (TEC) stress;
(MED): **~ arterial** blood pressure; **tener la
~ alta** to have high blood pressure
tenso, a ['tenso, a] adj tense
tentación [tenta'θjon] nf temptation
tentáculo [ten'takulo] nm tentacle
tentador, a [tenta'ðor, a] adj tempting
tentar [ten'tar] vt (seducir) to tempt;
(atraer) to attract; **tentativa** nf attempt;
tentativa de asesinato attempted
murder
tentempié [tentem'pje] nm snack
tenue ['tenwe] adj (delgado) thin, slender;
(neblina) light; (lazo, vínculo) slight
teñir [te'ɲir] vt to dye; (fig) to tinge; **~se**
vr to dye; **~se el pelo** to dye one's hair
teología [teolo'xia] nf theology
teoría [teo'ria] nf theory; **en ~** in theory;
teóricamente adv theoretically;
teórico, a adj theoretic(al) ♦ nm/f
theoretician, theorist; **teorizar** vi to
theorize
terapéutico, a [tera'peutiko, a] adj
therapeutic
terapia [te'rapja] nf therapy
tercer [ter'θer] adj ver **tercero**
tercermundista [terθermun'dista] adj
Third World cpd
tercero, a [ter'θero, a] adj (delante de
nmsg: **tercer**) third ♦ nm (JUR) third party
terceto [ter'θeto] nm trio
terciar [ter'θjar] vi (participar) to take part;
(hacer de árbitro) to mediate; **~se** vr to
come up; **~io, a** adj tertiary
tercio ['terθjo] nm third
terciopelo [terθjo'pelo] nm velvet
terco, a ['terko, a] adj obstinate
tergal ® [ter'xal] nm type of polyester
tergiversar [terxißer'sar] vt to distort
termal [ter'mal] adj thermal

termas ['termas] *nfpl* hot springs
térmico, a ['termiko, a] *adj* thermal
terminación [termina'θjon] *nf* (*final*) end; (*conclusión*) conclusion, ending
terminal [termi'nal] *adj, nm, nf* terminal
terminante [termi'nante] *adj* (*final*) final, definitive; (*tajante*) categorical; **~mente** *adv*: **~mente prohibido** strictly forbidden
terminar [termi'nar] *vt* (*completar*) to complete, finish; (*concluir*) to end ♦ *vi* (*llegar a su fin*) to end; (*parar*) to stop; (*acabar*) to finish; **~se** *vr* to come to an end; **~ por hacer algo** to end up (by) doing sth
término ['termino] *nm* end, conclusion; (*parada*) terminus; (*límite*) boundary; **~ medio** average; (*fig*) middle way; **en último ~** (*a fin de cuentas*) in the last analysis; (*como último recurso*) as a last resort
terminología [terminolo'xia] *nf* terminology
termodinámico, a [termoði'namiko, a] *adj* thermodynamic
termómetro [ter'mometro] *nm* thermometer
termonuclear [termonukle'ar] *adj* thermonuclear
termo(s) ® ['termo(s)] *nm* Thermos ® (flask)
termostato [termo'stato] *nm* thermostat
ternero, a [ter'nero, a] *nm/f* (*animal*) calf ♦ *nf* (*carne*) veal
ternura [ter'nura] *nf* (*trato*) tenderness; (*palabra*) endearment; (*cariño*) fondness
terquedad [terke'ðað] *nf* obstinacy
terrado [te'rraðo] *nm* terrace
terraplén [terra'plen] *nm* embankment
terrateniente [terrate'njente] *nm/f* landowner
terraza [te'rraθa] *nf* (*balcón*) balcony; (*tejado*) (flat) roof; (*AGR*) terrace
terremoto [terre'moto] *nm* earthquake
terrenal [terre'nal] *adj* earthly
terreno [te'rreno] *nm* (*tierra*) land; (*parcela*) plot; (*suelo*) soil; (*fig*) field; **un ~** a piece of land

terrestre [te'rrestre] *adj* terrestrial; (*ruta*) land *cpd*
terrible [te'rriβle] *adj* terrible, awful
territorio [terri'torjo] *nm* territory
terrón [te'rron] *nm* (*de azúcar*) lump; (*de tierra*) clod, lump
terror [te'rror] *nm* terror; **~ífico, a** *adj* terrifying; **~ista** *adj, nm/f* terrorist
terso, a ['terso, a] *adj* (*liso*) smooth; (*pulido*) polished; **tersura** *nf* smoothness
tertulia [ter'tulja] *nf* (*reunión informal*) social gathering; (*grupo*) group, circle
tesis ['tesis] *nf inv* thesis
tesón [te'son] *nm* (*firmeza*) firmness; (*tenacidad*) tenacity
tesorero, a [teso'rero, a] *nm/f* treasurer
tesoro [te'soro] *nm* treasure; (*COM, POL*) treasury
testaferro [testa'ferro] *nm* figurehead
testamentario, a [testamen'tarjo, a] *adj* testamentary ♦ *nm/f* executor/executrix
testamento [testa'mento] *nm* will
testar [tes'tar] *vi* to make a will
testarudo, a [testa'ruðo, a] *adj* stubborn
testículo [tes'tikulo] *nm* testicle
testificar [testifi'kar] *vt* to testify; (*fig*) to attest ♦ *vi* to give evidence
testigo [tes'tivo] *nm/f* witness; **~ de cargo/descargo** witness for the prosecution/defence; **~ ocular** eye witness
testimoniar [testimo'njar] *vt* to testify to; (*fig*) to show; **testimonio** *nm* testimony
teta ['teta] *nf* (*de biberón*) teat; (*ANAT: fam*) breast
tétanos ['tetanos] *nm* tetanus
tetera [te'tera] *nf* teapot
tétrico, a ['tetriko, a] *adj* gloomy, dismal
textil [teks'til] *adj* textile
texto ['teksto] *nm* text; **textual** *adj* textual
textura [teks'tura] *nf* (*de tejido*) texture
tez [teθ] *nf* (*cutis*) complexion
ti [ti] *pron* you; (*reflexivo*) yourself
tía ['tia] *nf* (*pariente*) aunt; (*fam*) chick, bird
tibieza [ti'βjeθa] *nf* (*temperatura*) tepidness; (*actitud*) coolness; **tibio, a** *adj* lukewarm
tiburón [tiβu'ron] *nm* shark

tic [tik] nm (ruido) click; (de reloj) tick; (MED): ~ **nervioso** nervous tic

tictac [tik'tak] nm (de reloj) tick tock

tiempo ['tjempo] nm time; (época, período) age, period; (METEOROLOGÍA) weather; (LING) tense; (DEPORTE) half; **a ~** in time; **a un** o **al mismo ~** at the same time; **al poco ~** very soon (after); **se quedó poco ~** he didn't stay very long; **hace poco ~** not long ago; **mucho ~** a long time; **de en ~** from time to time; **hace buen/mal ~** the weather is fine/bad; **estar a ~** to be in time; **hace ~** some time ago; **hacer ~** to while away the time; **motor de 2 ~s** two-stroke engine; **primer ~** first half

tienda ['tjenda] nf shop, store; ~ **(de campaña)** tent; ~ **de alimentación** o **comestibles** grocer's (BRIT), grocery store (US)

tienes etc vb ver **tener**

tienta etc ['tjenta] vb ver **tentar** ♦ nf: **andar a ~s** to grope one's way along

tiento ['tjento] vb ver **tentar** ♦ nm (tacto) touch; (precaución) wariness

tierno, a ['tjerno, a] adj (blando) tender; (fresco) fresh; (amable) sweet

tierra ['tjerra] nf earth; (suelo) soil; (mundo) earth, world; (país) country, land; ~ **adentro** inland

tieso, a ['tjeso, a] adj (rígido) rigid; (duro) stiff; (fam: orgulloso) conceited

tiesto ['tjesto] nm flowerpot

tifoidea [tifoi'ðea] nf typhoid

tifón [ti'fon] nm typhoon

tifus ['tifus] nm typhus

tigre ['tiɣre] nm tiger

tijera [ti'xera] nf scissors pl; (ZOOL) claw; ~**s** nfpl scissors; (para plantas) shears

tijeretear [tixerete'ar] vt to snip

tila ['tila] nf lime blossom tea

tildar [til'dar] vt: ~ **de** to brand as

tilde ['tilde] nf (TIP) tilde

tilín [ti'lin] nm tinkle

tilo ['tilo] nm lime tree

timar [ti'mar] vt (estafar) to swindle

timbal [tim'bal] nm small drum

timbrar [tim'brar] vt to stamp

timbre ['timbre] nm (sello) stamp; (campanilla) bell; (tono) timbre; (COM) stamp duty

timidez [timi'ðeθ] nf shyness; **tímido, a** adj shy

timo ['timo] nm swindle

timón [ti'mon] nm helm, rudder; **timonel** nm helmsman

tímpano ['timpano] nm (ANAT) eardrum; (MUS) small drum

tina ['tina] nf tub; (baño) bath(tub); **tinaja** nf large jar

tinglado [tin'glaðo] nm (cobertizo) shed; (fig: truco) trick; (intriga) intrigue

tinieblas [ti'njeßlas] nfpl darkness sg; (sombras) shadows

tino ['tino] nm (habilidad) skill; (juicio) insight

tinta ['tinta] nf ink; (TEC) dye; (ARTE) colour

tinte ['tinte] nm dye

tintero [tin'tero] nm inkwell

tintinear [tintine'ar] vt to tinkle

tinto ['tinto] nm red wine

tintorería [tintore'ria] nf dry cleaner's

tintura [tin'tura] nf (QUÍM) dye; (farmacéutico) tincture

tío ['tio] nm (pariente) uncle; (fam: individuo) bloke (BRIT), guy

tiovivo [tio'ßißo] nm merry-go-round

típico, a ['tipiko, a] adj typical

tipo ['tipo] nm (clase) type, kind; (hombre) fellow; (ANAT: de hombre) build; (: de mujer) figure; (IMPRENTA) type; ~ **bancario/de descuento/de interés/de cambio** bank/discount/interest/exchange rate

tipografía [tipoɣra'fia] nf printing cpd; **tipográfico, a** adj printing cpd

tíquet ['tiket] (pl ~**s**) nm ticket; (en tienda) cash slip

tiquismiquis [tikis'mikis] nm inv fussy person ♦ nmpl (querellas) squabbling sg; (escrúpulos) silly scruples

tira ['tira] nf strip; (fig) abundance; ~ **y afloja** give and take

tirabuzón [tiraßu'θon] nm (rizo) curl

tirachinas [tira'tʃinas] nm inv catapult

tirada [ti'raða] nf (acto) cast, throw; (serie) series; (TIP) printing, edition; **de una ~** at one go

tirado, a [ti'raðo, a] adj (barato) dirt-cheap; (fam: fácil) very easy

tirador [tira'ðor] nm (mango) handle

tiranía [tira'nia] nf tyranny; **tirano, a** adj tyrannical ♦ nm/f tyrant

tirante [ti'rante] adj (cuerda etc) tight, taut; (relaciones) strained ♦ nm (ARQ) brace; (TEC) stay; **~s** nmpl (de pantalón) braces (BRIT), suspenders (US); **tirantez** nf tightness; (fig) tension

tirar [ti'rar] vt to throw; (dejar caer) to drop; (volcar) to upset; (derribar) to knock down o over; (desechar) to throw out o away; (dinero) to squander; (imprimir) to print ♦ vi (disparar) to shoot; (de la puerta etc) to pull; (fam: andar) to go; (tender a, buscar realizar) to tend to; (DEPORTE) to shoot; **~se** vr to throw o.s.; **~ abajo** to bring down, destroy; **tira más a su padre** he takes more after his father; **ir tirando** to manage; **a todo ~** at the most

tirita [ti'rita] nf (sticking) plaster (BRIT), bandaid (US)

tiritar [tiri'tar] vi to shiver

tiro ['tiro] nm (lanzamiento) throw; (disparo) shot; (DEPORTE) shot; (GOLF, TENIS) drive; (alcance) range; **~ al blanco** target practice; **caballo de ~** cart-horse; **andar de ~s largos** to be all dressed up; **al ~** (AM) at once

tirón [ti'ron] nm (sacudida) pull, tug; **de un ~** in one go, all at once

tiroteo [tiro'teo] nm exchange of shots, shooting

tísico, a ['tisiko, a] adj consumptive

tisis ['tisis] nf inv consumption, tuberculosis

títere ['titere] nm puppet

titiritero, a [titiri'tero, a] nm/f puppeteer

titubeante [titußi'ante] adj (al andar) shaky, tottering; (al hablar) stammering; (dudoso) hesitant

titubear [titußi'ar] vi to stagger; to stammer; (fig) to hesitate; **titubeo** nm staggering; stammering; hesitation

titulado, a [titu'laðo, a] adj (libro) entitled; (persona) titled

titular [titu'lar] adj titular ♦ nm/f holder ♦ nm headline ♦ vt to title; **~se** vr to be entitled; **título** nm title; (de diario) headline; (certificado) professional qualification; (universitario) (university) degree; **a título de** in the capacity of

tiza ['tiθa] nf chalk

tiznar [tiθ'nar] vt to blacken

tizón [ti'θon] nm brand

toalla [to'aʎa] nf towel

tobillo [to'ßiʎo] nm ankle

tobogán [toßo'van] nm (montaña rusa) roller-coaster; (de niños) chute, slide

tocadiscos [toka'ðiskos] nm inv record player

tocado, a [to'kaðo, a] adj (fam) touched ♦ nm headdress

tocador [toka'ðor] nm (mueble) dressing table; (cuarto) boudoir; (fam) ladies' toilet (BRIT) o room (US)

tocante [to'kante]: **~ a** prep with regard to

tocar [to'kar] vt to touch; (MUS) to play; (referirse a) to allude to; (timbre) to ring ♦ vi (a la puerta) to knock (on o at the door); (ser de turno) to fall to, be the turn of; (ser hora) to be due; **~se** vr (cubrirse la cabeza) to cover one's head; (tener contacto) to touch (each other); **por lo que a mí me toca** as far as I am concerned; **te toca a tí** it's your turn

tocayo, a [to'kajo, a] nm/f namesake

tocino [to'θino] nm bacon

todavía [toða'ßia] adv (aun) even; (aún) still, yet; **~ más** yet more; **~ no** not yet

┌─────────────────────┐
│ PALABRA CLAVE   │
└─────────────────────┘

todo, a ['toðo, a] adj 1 (con artículo sg) all; **toda la carne** all the meat; **toda la noche** all night, the whole night; **~ el libro** the whole book; **toda una botella** a whole bottle; **~ lo contrario** quite the opposite; **está toda sucia** she's all dirty; **por ~ el país** throughout the whole country

2 (*con artículo pl*) all; every; **~s los libros** all the books; **todas las noches** every night; **~s los que quieran salir** all those who want to leave

♦ *pron* **1** everything, all; **~s** everyone, everybody; **lo sabemos ~** we know everything; **~s querían más tiempo** everybody *o* everyone wanted more time; **nos marchamos ~s** all of us left

2: con ~: con ~ él me sigue gustando even so I still like him

♦ *adv* all; **vaya ~ seguido** keep straight on *o* ahead

♦ *nm*: **como un ~** as a whole; **del ~: no me agrada del ~** I don't entirely like it

todopoderoso, a [toðopoðe'roso, a] *adj* all powerful; (*REL*) almighty

toga ['toχa] *nf* toga; (*ESCOL*) gown

Tokio ['tokjo] *n* Tokyo

toldo ['toldo] *nm* (*para el sol*) sunshade (*BRIT*), parasol; (*tienda*) marquee

tolerancia [tole'ranθja] *nf* tolerance; **tolerante** *adj* (*sociedad*) liberal; (*persona*) open-minded

tolerar [tole'rar] *vt* to tolerate; (*resistir*) to endure

toma ['toma] *nf* (*acto*) taking; (*MED*) dose; **~ (de corriente)** socket

tomar [to'mar] *vt* to take; (*aspecto*) to take on; (*beber*) to drink ♦ *vi* to take; (*AM*) to drink; **~se** *vr* to take; **~se por** to consider o.s. to be; **~ a bien/a mal** to take well/badly; **~ en serio** to take seriously; **~ el pelo a alguien** to pull sb's leg; **~la con uno** to pick a quarrel with sb; **¡tome!** here you are!; **~ el sol** to sunbathe

tomate [to'mate] *nm* tomato

tomillo [to'miʎo] *nm* thyme

tomo ['tomo] *nm* (*libro*) volume

ton [ton] *abr* = **tonelada** ♦ *nm*: **sin ~ ni son** without rhyme or reason

tonada [to'naða] *nf* tune

tonalidad [tonali'ðað] *nf* tone

tonel [to'nel] *nm* barrel

tonelada [tone'laða] *nf* ton; **tonelaje** *nm*

tonnage

tónica ['tonika] *nf* (*MUS*) tonic; (*fig*) keynote

tónico, a ['toniko, a] *adj* tonic ♦ *nm* (*MED*) tonic

tonificar [tonifi'kar] *vt* to tone up

tono ['tono] *nm* tone; **fuera de ~** inappropriate; **darse ~** to put on airs

tontería [tonte'ria] *nf* (*estupidez*) foolishness; (*cosa*) stupid thing; (*acto*) foolish act; **~s** *nfpl* (*disparates*) rubbish *sg*, nonsense *sg*

tonto, a ['tonto, a] *adj* stupid, silly ♦ *nm/f* fool

topar [to'par] *vi*: **~ contra** *o* **en** to run into; **~ con** to run up against

tope ['tope] *adj* maximum ♦ *nm* (*fin*) end; (*límite*) limit; (*FERRO*) buffer; (*AUTO*) bumper; **al ~** end to end

tópico, a ['topiko, a] *adj* topical ♦ *nm* platitude

topo ['topo] *nm* (*ZOOL*) mole; (*fig*) blunderer

topografía [topoχra'fia] *nf* topography; **topógrafo, a** *nm/f* topographer

toque *etc* ['toke] *vb ver* **tocar** ♦ *nm* touch; (*MUS*) beat; (*de campana*) peal; **dar un ~** a to warn; **~ de queda** curfew

toqué *vb ver* **tocar**

toquetear [tokete'ar] *vt* to finger

toquilla [to'kiʎa] *nf* (*pañuelo*) headscarf; (*chal*) shawl

tórax ['toraks] *nm* thorax

torbellino [torbe'ʎino] *nm* whirlwind; (*fig*) whirl

torcedura [torθe'ðura] *nf* twist; (*MED*) sprain

torcer [tor'θer] *vt* to twist; (*la esquina*) to turn; (*MED*) to sprain ♦ *vi* (*desviar*) to turn off; **~se** *vr* (*ladearse*) to bend; (*desviarse*) to go astray; (*fracasar*) to go wrong; **torcido, a** *adj* twisted; (*fig*) crooked ♦ *nm* curl

tordo, a ['torðo, a] *adj* dappled ♦ *nm* thrush

torear [tore'ar] *vt* (*fig: evadir*) to avoid; (*jugar con*) to tease ♦ *vi* to fight bulls;

toreo *nm* bullfighting; **torero, a** *nm/f* bullfighter

tormenta [tor'menta] *nf* storm; (*fig: confusión*) turmoil

tormento [tor'mento] *nm* torture; (*fig*) anguish

tornar [tor'nar] *vt* (*devolver*) to return, give back; (*transformar*) to transform ♦ *vi* to go back; **~se** *vr* (*ponerse*) to become

tornasolado, a [tornaso'laðo, a] *adj* (*brillante*) iridescent; (*reluciente*) shimmering

torneo [tor'neo] *nm* tournament

tornillo [tor'niʎo] *nm* screw

torniquete [torni'kete] *nm* (*MED*) tourniquet

torno ['torno] *nm* (*TEC*) winch; (*tambor*) drum; **en ~ (a)** round, about

toro ['toro] *nm* bull; (*fam*) he-man; **los ~s** bullfighting

toronja [to'ronxa] *nf* grapefruit

torpe ['torpe] *adj* (*poco hábil*) clumsy, awkward; (*necio*) dim; (*lento*) slow

torpedo [tor'peðo] *nm* torpedo

torpeza [tor'peθa] *nf* (*falta de agilidad*) clumsiness; (*lentitud*) slowness; (*error*) mistake

torre ['torre] *nf* tower; (*de petróleo*) derrick

torrefacto, a [torre'facto, a] *adj* roasted

torrente [to'rrente] *nm* torrent

tórrido, a ['torriðo, a] *adj* torrid

torrija [to'rrixa] *nf* French toast

torsión [tor'sjon] *nf* twisting

torso ['torso] *nm* torso

torta ['torta] *nf* cake; (*fam*) slap

tortícolis [tor'tikolis] *nm inv* stiff neck

tortilla [tor'tiʎa] *nf* omelette; (*AM*) maize pancake; **~ francesa/española** plain/potato omelette

tórtola ['tortola] *nf* turtledove

tortuga [tor'tuɣa] *nf* tortoise

tortuoso, a [tor'twoso, a] *adj* winding

tortura [tor'tura] *nf* torture; **torturar** *vt* to torture

tos [tos] *nf* cough; **~ ferina** whooping cough

tosco, a ['tosko, a] *adj* coarse

toser [to'ser] *vi* to cough

tostada [tos'taða] *nf* piece of toast; **tostado, a** *adj* toasted; (*por el sol*) dark brown; (*piel*) tanned

tostador [tosta'ðor] *nm* toaster

tostar [tos'tar] *vt* to toast; (*café*) to roast; (*persona*) to tan; **~se** *vr* to get brown

total [to'tal] *adj* total ♦ *adv* in short; (*al fin y al cabo*) when all is said and done ♦ *nm* total; **~ que** to cut (*BRIT*) o make (*US*) a long story short

totalidad [totali'ðað] *nf* whole

totalitario, a [totali'tarjo, a] *adj* totalitarian

tóxico, a ['toksiko, a] *adj* toxic ♦ *nm* poison; **toxicómano, a** *nm/f* drug addict

toxina [to'ksina] *nf* toxin

tozudo, a [to'θuðo, a] *adj* obstinate

traba ['traßa] *nf* bond, tie; (*cadena*) shackle

trabajador, a [traßaxa'ðor, a] *adj* hard-working ♦ *nm/f* worker

trabajar [traßa'xar] *vt* to work; (*AGR*) to till; (*empeñarse en*) to work at; (*convencer*) to persuade ♦ *vi* to work; (*esforzarse*) to strive; **trabajo** *nm* work; (*tarea*) task; (*POL*) labour; (*fig*) effort; **tomarse el trabajo de** to take the trouble to; **trabajo por turno/a destajo** shift work/piecework; **trabajoso, a** *adj* hard

trabalenguas [traßa'lengwas] *nm inv* tongue twister

trabar [tra'ßar] *vt* (*juntar*) to join, unite; (*atar*) to tie down, fetter; (*agarrar*) to seize; (*amistad*) to strike up; **~se** *vr* to become entangled; **trabársele a uno la lengua** to be tongue-tied

tracción [trak'θjon] *nf* traction; **~ delantera/trasera** front-wheel/rear-wheel drive

tractor [trak'tor] *nm* tractor

tradición [traði'θjon] *nf* tradition; **tradicional** *adj* traditional

traducción [traðuk'θjon] *nf* translation

traducir [traðu'θir] *vt* to translate; **traductor, a** *nm/f* translator

traer [tra'er] vt to bring; (*llevar*) to carry; (*llevar puesto*) to wear; (*incluir*) to carry; (*causar*) to cause; **~se** vr: **~se algo** to be up to sth

traficar [trafi'kar] vi to trade

tráfico ['trafiko] nm (COM) trade; (AUTO) traffic

tragaluz [traɣa'luθ] nm skylight

tragaperras [traɣa'perras] nm o f inv slot machine

tragar [tra'ɣar] vt to swallow; (*devorar*) to devour, bolt down; **~se** vr to swallow

tragedia [tra'xeðja] nf tragedy; **trágico, a** adj tragic

trago ['traɣo] nm (*líquido*) drink; (*bocado*) gulp; (fam: *de bebida*) swig; (*desgracia*) blow

traición [trai'θjon] nf treachery; (JUR) treason; (*una ~*) act of treachery; **traicionar** vt to betray

traicionero, a [traiθjo'nero, a] adj treacherous

traidor, a [trai'ðor, a] adj treacherous ♦ nm/f traitor

traigo etc vb ver **traer**

traje ['traxe] vb ver **traer** ♦ nm (*de hombre*) suit; (*de mujer*) dress; (*vestido típico*) costume; **~ de baño** swimsuit; **~ de luces** bullfighter's costume

trajera etc vb ver **traer**

trajín [tra'xin] nm (fam: *movimiento*) bustle; **trajinar** vi (*moverse*) to bustle about

trama ['trama] nf (*intriga*) plot; (*de tejido*) weft (BRIT), woof (US); **tramar** vt to plot; (TEC) to weave

tramitar [trami'tar] vt (*asunto*) to transact; (*negociar*) to negotiate

trámite ['tramite] nm (*paso*) step; (JUR) transaction; **~s** nmpl (*burocracia*) procedure sg; (JUR) proceedings

tramo ['tramo] nm (*de tierra*) plot; (*de escalera*) flight; (*de vía*) section

tramoya [tra'moja] nf (TEATRO) piece of stage machinery; **tramoyista** nm/f scene shifter; (fig) trickster

trampa ['trampa] nf trap; (*en el suelo*)

trapdoor; (*truco*) trick; (*engaño*) fiddle; **trampear** vt, vi to cheat

trampolín [trampo'lin] nm (*de piscina etc*) diving board

tramposo, a [tram'poso, a] adj crooked, cheating ♦ nm/f crook, cheat

tranca ['tranka] nf (*palo*) stick; (*de puerta, ventana*) bar; **trancar** vt to bar

trance ['tranθe] nm (*momento difícil*) difficult moment o juncture; (*estado hipnotizado*) trance

tranquilidad [trankili'ðað] nf (*calma*) calmness, stillness; (*paz*) peacefulness

tranquilizar [trankili'θar] vt (*calmar*) to calm (down); (*asegurar*) to reassure; **~se** vr to calm down; **tranquilo, a** adj (*calmado*) calm; (*apacible*) peaceful; (*mar*) calm; (*mente*) untroubled

transacción [transak'θjon] nf transaction

transbordador [transβorða'ðor] nm ferry

transbordar [transβor'ðar] vt to transfer; **transbordo** nm transfer; **hacer transbordo** to change (trains etc)

transcurrir [transku'rrir] vi (*tiempo*) to pass; (*hecho*) to take place

transcurso [trans'kurso] nm: **~ del tiempo** lapse (of time)

transeúnte [transe'unte] nm/f passer-by

transferencia [transfe'renθja] nf transference; (COM) transfer

transferir [transfe'rir] vt to transfer

transformador [transforma'ðor] nm (ELEC) transformer

transformar [transfor'mar] vt to transform; (*convertir*) to convert

tránsfuga ['transfuɣa] nm/f (MIL) deserter; (POL) turncoat

transfusión [transfu'sjon] nf transfusion

transición [transi'θjon] nf transition

transigir [transi'xir] vi to compromise, make concessions

transistor [transis'tor] nm transistor

transitar [transi'tar] vi to go (from place to place); **tránsito** nm transit; (AUTO) traffic; **transitorio, a** adj transitory

transmisión [transmi'sjon] nf (TEC) transmission; (*transferencia*) transfer; **~ en**

directo/exterior live/outside broadcast

transmitir [transmi'tir] *vt* to transmit; (*RADIO, TV*) to broadcast

transparencia [transpa'renθja] *nf* transparency; (*claridad*) clearness, clarity; (*foto*) slide

transparentar [transparen'tar] *vt* to reveal ♦ *vi* to be transparent; **transparente** *adj* transparent; (*claro*) clear

transpirar [transpi'rar] *vi* to perspire

transportar [transpor'tar] *vt* to transport; (*llevar*) to carry; **transporte** *nm* transport; (*COM*) haulage

transversal [transβer'sal] *adj* transverse, cross

tranvía [tram'bia] *nm* tram

trapecio [tra'peθjo] *nm* trapeze; **trapecista** *nm/f* trapeze artist

trapero, a [tra'pero, a] *nm/f* ragman

trapicheo [trapi'tʃeo] (*fam*) *nm* scheme, fiddle

trapo ['trapo] *nm* (*tela*) rag; (*de cocina*) cloth

tráquea ['trakea] *nf* windpipe

traqueteo [trake'teo] *nm* rattling

tras [tras] *prep* (*detrás*) behind; (*después*) after

trasatlántico [trasat'lantiko] *nm* (*barco*) (cabin) cruiser

trascendencia [trasθen'denθja] *nf* (*importancia*) importance; (*FILOSOFÍA*) transcendence

trascendental [trasθenden'tal] *adj* important; (*FILOSOFÍA*) transcendental

trascender [trasθen'der] *vi* (*noticias*) to come out; (*suceso*) to have a wide effect

trasero, a [tra'sero, a] *adj* back, rear ♦ *nm* (*ANAT*) bottom

trasfondo [tras'fondo] *nm* background

trasgredir [trasxre'ðir] *vt* to contravene

trashumante [trasu'mante] *adj* (*animales*) migrating

trasladar [trasla'ðar] *vt* to move; (*persona*) to transfer; (*postergar*) to postpone; (*copiar*) to copy; **~se** *vr* (*mudarse*) to move; **traslado** *nm* move; (*mudanza*) move, removal

traslucir [traslu'θir] *vt* to show; **~se** *vr* to be translucent; (*fig*) to be revealed

trasluz [tras'luθ] *nm* reflected light; **al ~** against *o* up to the light

trasnochador, a [trasnotʃa'ðor, a] *nm/f* night owl

trasnochar [trasno'tʃar] *vi* (*acostarse tarde*) to stay up late

traspapelar [traspape'lar] *vt* (*document, carta*) to mislay, misplace

traspasar [traspa'sar] *vt* (*suj: bala etc*) to pierce, go through; (*propiedad*) to sell, transfer; (*calle*) to cross over; (*límites*) to go beyond; (*ley*) to break; **traspaso** *nm* (*venta*) transfer, sale

traspié [tras'pje] *nm* (*tropezón*) trip; (*error*) blunder

trasplantar [trasplan'tar] *vt* to transplant

traste ['traste] *nm* (*MUS*) fret; **dar al ~ con algo** to ruin sth

trastero [tras'tero] *nm* storage room

trastienda [tras'tjenda] *nf* back of shop

trasto ['trasto] (*pey*) *nm* (*cosa*) piece of junk; (*persona*) dead loss

trastornado, a [trastor'naðo, a] *adj* (*loco*) mad, crazy

trastornar [trastor'nar] *vt* (*fig: planes*) to disrupt; (: *nervios*) to shatter; (: *persona*) to drive crazy; **~se** *vr* (*volverse loco*) to go mad *o* crazy; **trastorno** *nm* (*acto*) overturning; (*confusión*) confusion

tratable [tra'taßle] *adj* friendly

tratado [tra'taðo] *nm* (*POL*) treaty; (*COM*) agreement

tratamiento [trata'mjento] *nm* treatment; **~ de textos** (*INFORM*) word processing *cpd*

tratar [tra'tar] *vt* (*ocuparse de*) to treat; (*manejar, TEC*) to handle; (*MED*) to treat; (*dirigirse a: persona*) to address ♦ *vi*: **~ de** (*hablar sobre*) to deal with, be about; (*intentar*) to try to; **~se** *vr* to treat each other; **~ con** (*COM*) to trade in; (*negociar*) to negotiate with; (*tener contactos*) to have dealings with; **¿de qué se trata?** what's it about?; **trato** *nm* dealings *pl*; (*relaciones*) relationship; (*comportamiento*)

manner; (COM) agreement
trauma ['trauma] nm trauma
través [tra'ßes] nm (fig) reverse; **al ~**
across, crossways; **a ~ de** across; (sobre)
over; (por) through
travesaño [traße'saɲo] nm (ARQ)
crossbeam; (DEPORTE) crossbar
travesía [traße'sia] nf (calle) cross-street;
(NAUT) crossing
travesura [traße'sura] nf (broma) prank;
(ingenio) wit
traviesa [tra'ßjesa] nf (ARQ) crossbeam
travieso, a [tra'ßjeso, a] adj (niño)
naughty
trayecto [tra'jekto] nm (ruta) road, way;
(viaje) journey; (tramo) stretch; **~ria** nf
trajectory; (fig) path
traza ['traθa] nf (aspecto) looks pl; (señal)
sign; **~do, a** adj: **bien ~do** shapely,
well-formed ♦ nm (ARQ) plan, design; (fig)
outline
trazar [tra'θar] vt (ARQ) to plan; (ARTE) to
sketch; (fig) to trace; (plan) to draw up;
trazo nm (línea) line; (bosquejo) sketch
trébol ['treßol] nm (BOT) clover
trece ['treθe] num thirteen
trecho ['tretʃo] nm (distancia) distance; (de
tiempo) while; **de ~ en ~** at intervals
tregua ['treɣwa] nf (MIL) truce; (fig) respite
treinta ['treinta] num thirty
tremendo, a [tre'mendo, a] adj (terrible)
terrible; (imponente: cosa) imposing; (fam:
fabuloso) tremendous
trémulo, a ['tremulo, a] adj quivering
tren [tren] nm train; **~ de aterrizaje**
undercarriage
trenca ['trenka] nf duffel coat
trenza ['trenθa] nf (de pelo) plait (BRIT),
braid (US); **trenzar** vt (pelo) to plait,
braid; **trenzarse** vr (AM) to become
involved
trepadora [trepa'ðora] nf (BOT) climber
trepar [tre'par] vt, vi to climb
trepidante [trepi'ðante] adj (acción) fast;
(ritmo) hectic
tres [tres] num three
tresillo [tre'siʎo] nm three-piece suite;

(MUS) triplet
treta ['treta] nf trick
triángulo ['trjangulo] nm triangle
tribu ['trißu] nf tribe
tribuna [tri'ßuna] nf (plataforma) platform;
(DEPORTE) (grand)stand
tribunal [trißu'nal] nm (JUR) court;
(comisión, fig) tribunal
tributar [trißu'tar] vt (gen) to pay; **tributo**
nm (COM) tax
tricotar [triko'tar] vi to knit
trigal [tri'ɣal] nm wheat field
trigo ['triɣo] nm wheat
trigueño, a [tri'ɣeɲo, a] adj (pelo) corn-
coloured
trillado, a [tri'ʎaðo, a] adj threshed;
(asunto) trite, hackneyed; **trilladora** nf
threshing machine
trillar [tri'ʎar] vt (AGR) to thresh
trimestral [trimes'tral] adj quarterly;
(ESCOL) termly
trimestre [tri'mestre] nm (ESCOL) term
trinar [tri'nar] vi (pájaros) to sing; (rabiar)
to fume, be angry
trinchar [trin'tʃar] vt to carve
trinchera [trin'tʃera] nf (fosa) trench
trineo [tri'neo] nm sledge
trinidad [trini'ðað] nf trio; (REL): **la T~** the
Trinity
trino ['trino] nm trill
tripa ['tripa] nf (ANAT) intestine; (fam: tb:
~s) insides pl
triple ['triple] adj triple
triplicado, a [tripli'kaðo, a] adj: **por ~** in
triplicate
tripulación [tripula'θjon] nf crew
tripulante [tripu'lante] nm/f crewman/
woman
tripular [tripu'lar] vt (barco) to man;
(AUTO) to drive
triquiñuela [triki'ɲwela] nf trick
tris [tris] nm inv crack; **en un ~** in an
instant
triste ['triste] adj sad; (lamentable) sorry,
miserable; **~za** nf (aflicción) sadness;
(melancolía) melancholy
triturar [tritu'rar] vt (moler) to grind;

(*mascar*) to chew

triunfar [trjun'far] *vi* (*tener éxito*) to triumph; (*ganar*) to win; **triunfo** *nm* triumph

trivial [tri'βjal] *adj* trivial; **~izar** *vt* to minimize, play down

triza ['triθa] *nf*: **hacer ~s** to smash to bits; (*papel*) to tear to shreds

trocar [tro'kar] *vt* to exchange

trocear [troθe'ar] *vt* (*carne, manzana*) to cut up, cut into pieces

trocha ['trotʃa] *nf* short cut

troche ['trotʃe]: **a ~ y moche** *adv* helter-skelter, pell-mell

trofeo [tro'feo] *nm* (*premio*) trophy; (*éxito*) success

tromba ['tromba] *nf* downpour

trombón [trom'bon] *nm* trombone

trombosis [trom'bosis] *nf inv* thrombosis

trompa ['trompa] *nf* horn; (*trompo*) humming top; (*hocico*) snout; (*fam*): **cogerse una ~** to get tight

trompazo [trom'paθo] *nm* bump, bang

trompeta [trom'peta] *nf* trumpet; (*clarín*) bugle

trompicón [trompi'kon]: **a ~es** *adv* in fits and starts

trompo ['trompo] *nm* spinning top

trompón [trom'pon] *nm* bump

tronar [tro'nar] *vt* (*AM*) to shoot ♦ *vi* to thunder; (*fig*) to rage

tronchar [tron'tʃar] *vt* (*árbol*) to chop down; (*fig: vida*) to cut short; (*: esperanza*) to shatter; (*persona*) to tire out; **~se** *vr* to fall down

tronco ['tronko] *nm* (*de árbol, ANAT*) trunk

trono ['trono] *nm* throne

tropa ['tropa] *nf* (*MIL*) troop; (*soldados*) soldiers *pl*

tropel [tro'pel] *nm* (*muchedumbre*) crowd

tropezar [trope'θar] *vi* to trip, stumble; (*error*) to slip up; **~ con** to run into; (*topar con*) to bump into; **tropezón** *nm* trip; (*fig*) blunder

tropical [tropi'kal] *adj* tropical

trópico ['tropiko] *nm* tropic

tropiezo [tro'pjeθo] *vb ver* **tropezar** ♦ *nm*

(*error*) slip, blunder; (*desgracia*) misfortune; (*obstáculo*) snag

trotamundos [trota'mundos] *nm inv* globetrotter

trotar [tro'tar] *vi* to trot; **trote** *nm* trot; (*fam*) travelling; **de mucho trote** hard-wearing

trozo ['troθo] *nm* bit, piece

trucha ['trutʃa] *nf* trout

truco ['truko] *nm* (*habilidad*) knack; (*engaño*) trick

trueno ['trweno] *nm* thunder; (*estampido*) bang

trueque *etc* ['trweke] *vb ver* **trocar** ♦ *nm* exchange; (*COM*) barter

trufa ['trufa] *nf* (*BOT*) truffle

truhán, ana [tru'an, ana] *nm/f* rogue

truncar [trun'kar] *vt* (*cortar*) to truncate; (*fig: la vida etc*) to cut short; (*: el desarrollo*) to stunt

tu [tu] *adj* your

tú [tu] *pron* you

tubérculo [tu'βerkulo] *nm* (*BOT*) tuber

tuberculosis [tuβerku'losis] *nf inv* tuberculosis

tubería [tuβe'ria] *nf* pipes *pl*; (*conducto*) pipeline

tubo ['tuβo] *nm* tube, pipe; **~ de ensayo** test tube; **~ de escape** exhaust (pipe)

tuerca ['twerka] *nf* nut

tuerto, a ['twerto, a] *adj* blind in one eye ♦ *nm/f* one-eyed person

tuerza *etc vb ver* **torcer**

tuétano ['twetano] *nm* marrow; (*BOT*) pith

tufo ['tufo] *nm* (*hedor*) stench

tul [tul] *nm* tulle

tulipán [tuli'pan] *nm* tulip

tullido, a [tu'ʎiðo, a] *adj* crippled

tumba ['tumba] *nf* (*sepultura*) tomb

tumbar [tum'bar] *vt* to knock down; **~se** *vr* (*echarse*) to lie down; (*extenderse*) to stretch out

tumbo ['tumbo] *nm*: **dar ~s** to stagger

tumbona [tum'bona] *nf* (*butaca*) easy chair; (*de playa*) deckchair (*BRIT*), beach chair (*US*)

tumor [tu'mor] *nm* tumour

tumulto [tu'multo] *nm* turmoil
tuna ['tuna] *nf* (*MUS*) student music group; *ver tb* **tuno**

---
tuna
---

i A **tuna** *is a musical group made up of university students or former students who dress up in costumes from the "Edad de Oro", the Spanish Golden Age. These groups go through the town playing their guitars, lutes and tambourines and serenade the young ladies in the halls of residence or make impromptu appearances at weddings or parties singing traditional Spanish songs for a few* **pesetas**.

---

tunante [tu'nante] *nm/f* rascal
tunda ['tunda] *nf* (*golpeo*) beating
túnel ['tunel] *nm* tunnel
Túnez ['tuneθ] *nm* Tunisia; (*ciudad*) Tunis
tuno, a ['tuno, a] *nm/f* (*fam*) rogue ♦ *nm* member of student music group
tupido, a [tu'piðo, a] *adj* (*denso*) dense; (*tela*) close-woven
turba ['turβa] *nf* crowd
turbante [tur'βante] *nm* turban
turbar [tur'βar] *vt* (*molestar*) to disturb; (*incomodar*) to upset; **~se** *vr* to be disturbed
turbina [tur'βina] *nf* turbine
turbio, a ['turβjo, a] *adj* cloudy; (*tema etc*) confused
turbulencia [turβu'lenθja] *nf* turbulence; (*fig*) restlessness; **turbulento, a** *adj* turbulent; (*fig: intranquilo*) restless; (: *ruidoso*) noisy
turco, a ['turko, a] *adj* Turkish ♦ *nm/f* Turk
turismo [tu'rismo] *nm* tourism; (*coche*) car; **turista** *nm/f* tourist; **turístico, a** *adj* tourist *cpd*
turnar [tur'nar] *vi* to take (it in) turns; **~se** *vr* to take (it in) turns; **turno** *nm* (*de trabajo*) shift; (*juegos etc*) turn
turquesa [tur'kesa] *nf* turquoise
Turquía [tur'kia] *nf* Turkey
turrón [tu'rron] *nm* (*dulce*) nougat

tutear [tute'ar] *vt* to address as familiar "tú"; **~se** *vr* to be on familiar terms
tutela [tu'tela] *nf* (*legal*) guardianship; **tutelar** *adj* tutelary ♦ *vt* to protect
tutor, a [tu'tor, a] *nm/f* (*legal*) guardian; (*ESCOL*) tutor
tuve *etc vb ver* **tener**
tuviera *etc vb ver* **tener**
tuyo, a ['tujo, a] *adj* yours, of yours ♦ *pron* yours; **un amigo ~** a friend of yours; **los ~s** (*fam*) your relations, your family
TV ['te'βe] *nf abr* (= *televisión*) TV
TVE *nf abr* = **Televisión Española**

U, u

u [u] *conj* or
ubicar [uβi'kar] *vt* to place, situate; (*AM: encontrar*) to find; **~se** *vr* to lie, be located
ubre ['uβre] *nf* udder
UCI *nf abr* (= *Unidad de Cuidados Intensivos*) ICU
Ud(s) *abr* = **usted(es)**
UE *nf abr* (= *Unión Europea*) EU
ufanarse [ufa'narse] *vr* to boast; **~ de** to pride o.s. on; **ufano, a** *adj* (*arrogante*) arrogant; (*presumido*) conceited
UGT *nf abr* = **Unión General de Trabajadores**
ujier [u'xjer] *nm* usher; (*portero*) doorkeeper
úlcera ['ulθera] *nf* ulcer
ulcerar [ulθe'rar] *vt* to make sore; **~se** *vr* to ulcerate
ulterior [ulte'rjor] *adj* (*más allá*) farther, further; (*subsecuente, siguiente*) subsequent
últimamente ['ultimamente] *adv* (*recientemente*) lately, recently
ultimar [ulti'mar] *vt* to finish; (*finalizar*) to finalize; (*AM: rematar*) to finish off
ultimátum [ulti'matum] (*pl* **~s**) ultimatum
último, a ['ultimo, a] *adj* last; (*más reciente*) latest, most recent; (*más bajo*) bottom; (*más alto*) top; **en las últimas**

on one's last legs; **por ~** finally
ultra ['ultra] *adj* ultra ♦ *nm/f* extreme
right-winger
ultrajar [ultra'xar] *vt* (*ofender*) to outrage;
(*insultar*) to insult, abuse; **ultraje** *nm*
outrage; insult
ultramar [ultra'mar] *nm:* **de** *o* **en ~**
abroad, overseas
ultramarinos [ultrama'rinos] *nmpl*
groceries; **tienda de ~** grocer's (shop)
ultranza [ul'tranθa]: **a ~** *adv* (*a todo*
trance) at all costs; (*completo*) outright
ultratumba [ultra'tumba] *nf:* **la vida de ~**
the next life
umbral [um'bral] *nm* (*gen*) threshold
umbrío, a [um'brio, a] *adj* shady

PALABRA CLAVE

un, una [un, 'una] *art indef* a; (*antes de*
vocal) an; **una mujer/naranja** a woman/
an orange
♦ *adj:* **unos** (*o* **unas**): **hay unos regalos**
para ti there are some presents for you;
hay unas cervezas en la nevera there
are some beers in the fridge

---

unánime [u'nanime] *adj* unanimous;
unanimidad *nf* unanimity
undécimo, a [un'deθimo, a] *adj* eleventh
ungir [un'xir] *vt* to anoint
ungüento [un'gwento] *nm* ointment
únicamente ['unikamente] *adv* solely,
only
único, a ['uniko, a] *adj* only, sole; (*sin par*)
unique
unidad [uni'ðað] *nf* unity; (*COM, TEC etc*)
unit
unido, a [u'niðo, a] *adj* joined, linked; (*fig*)
united
unificar [unifi'kar] *vt* to unite, unify
uniformar [unifor'mar] *vt* to make
uniform, level up; (*persona*) to put into
uniform
uniforme [uni'forme] *adj* uniform, equal;
(*superficie*) even ♦ *nm* uniform;
uniformidad *nf* uniformity; (*de terreno*)
levelness, evenness

unilateral [unilate'ral] *adj* unilateral
unión [u'njon] *nf* union; (*acto*) uniting,
joining; (*unidad*) unity; (*TEC*) joint; **la U~**
Europea the European Union; **la U~**
Soviética the Soviet Union
unir [u'nir] *vt* (*juntar*) to join, unite; (*atar*)
to tie, fasten; (*combinar*) to combine; **~se**
vr to join together, unite; (*empresas*) to
merge
unísono [u'nisono] *nm:* **al ~** in unison
universal [uniβer'sal] *adj* universal;
(*mundial*) world *cpd*
universidad [uniβersi'ðað] *nf* university
universitario, a [uniβersi'tarjo, a] *adj*
university *cpd* ♦ *nm/f* (*profesor*) lecturer;
(*estudiante*) (university) student;
(*graduado*) graduate
universo [uni'βerso] *nm* universe

PALABRA CLAVE

uno, a ['uno, a] *adj* one; **es todo ~** it's all
one and the same; **~s pocos** a few; **~s**
cien about a hundred
♦ *pron* 1 one; **quiero sólo ~** I only want
one; **~ de ellos** one of them
2 (*alguien*) somebody, someone; **conozco**
a ~ que se te parece I know somebody
o someone who looks like you; **~ mismo**
oneself; **~s querían quedarse** some
(people) wanted to stay
3: **(los) ~s ... (los) otros ...** some ...
others; **una y otra son muy agradables**
they're both very nice
♦ *nf* one; **es la una** it's one o'clock
♦ *nm* (*number*) one

---

untar [un'tar] *vt* (*mantequilla*) to spread;
(*engrasar*) to grease, oil
uña ['uɲa] *nf* (*ANAT*) nail; (*garra*) claw;
(*casco*) hoof; (*arrancaclavos*) claw
uranio [u'ranjo] *nm* uranium
urbanidad [urβani'ðað] *nf* courtesy,
politeness
urbanismo [urβa'nismo] *nm* town
planning
urbanización [urβaniθa'θjon] *nf* (*barrio,*
colonia) housing estate

urbanizar [urßani'θar] vt (zona) to develop, urbanize
urbano, a [ur'ßano, a] adj (de ciudad) urban; (cortés) courteous, polite
urbe ['urße] nf large city
urdimbre [ur'ðimbre] nf (de tejido) warp; (intriga) intrigue
urdir [ur'ðir] vt to warp; (complot) to plot, contrive
urgencia [ur'xenθja] nf urgency; (prisa) haste, rush; (emergencia) emergency; **servicios de ~** emergency services; **"Urgencias"** "Casualty"; **urgente** adj urgent
urgir [ur'xir] vi to be urgent; **me urge** I'm in a hurry for it
urinario, a [uri'narjo, a] adj urinary ♦ nm urinal
urna ['urna] nf urn; (POL) ballot box
urraca [u'rraka] nf magpie
URSS nf: **la ~** the USSR
Uruguay [uru'ɣwai] nm: **el ~** Uruguay; **uruguayo, a** adj, nm/f Uruguayan
usado, a [u'saðo, a] adj used; (de segunda mano) secondhand
usar [u'sar] vt to use; (ropa) to wear; (tener costumbre) to be in the habit of; **~se** vr to be used; **uso** nm use; wear; (costumbre) usage, custom; (moda) fashion; **al uso** in keeping with custom; **al uso de** in the style of
usted [us'teð] pron (sg) you sg; (pl): **~es** you pl
usual [u'swal] adj usual
usuario, a [usu'arjo, a] nm/f user
usura [u'sura] nf usury; **usurero, a** nm/f usurer
usurpar [usur'par] vt to usurp
utensilio [uten'siljo] nm tool; (CULIN) utensil
útero ['utero] nm uterus, womb
útil ['util] adj useful ♦ nm tool; **utilidad** nf usefulness; (COM) profit; **utilizar** vt to use, utilize
utopía [uto'pia] nf Utopia; **utópico, a** adj Utopian
uva ['ußa] nf grape

---

las uvas

ⓘ In Spain **las uvas** play a big part on New Year's Eve (**Nochevieja**), when on the stroke of midnight people gather at home, in restaurants or in the **plaza mayor** and eat a grape for each stroke of the clock of the **Puerta del Sol** in Madrid. It is said to bring luck for the following year.

V, v

v abr (= voltio) v
va vb ver **ir**
vaca ['baka] nf (animal) cow; **carne de ~** beef
vacaciones [baka'θjones] nfpl holidays
vacante [ba'kante] adj vacant, empty ♦ nf vacancy
vaciar [ba'θjar] vt to empty out; (ahuecar) to hollow out; (moldear) to cast; **~se** vr to empty
vacilante [baθi'lante] adj unsteady; (habla) faltering; (dudoso) hesitant
vacilar [baθi'lar] vi to be unsteady; (al hablar) to falter; (dudar) to hesitate, waver; (memoria) to fail
vacío, a [ba'θio, a] adj empty; (puesto) vacant; (desocupado) idle; (vano) vain ♦ nm emptiness; (FÍSICA) vacuum; (un ~) (empty) space
vacuna [ba'kuna] nf vaccine; **vacunar** vt to vaccinate
vacuno, a [ba'kuno, a] adj cow cpd; **ganado ~** cattle
vacuo, a ['bakwo, a] adj empty
vadear [baðe'ar] vt (río) to ford; **vado** nm ford
vagabundo, a [baɣa'ßundo, a] adj wandering ♦ nm tramp
vagamente [baɣa'mente] adv vaguely
vagancia [ba'ɣanθja] nf (pereza) idleness, laziness
vagar [ba'ɣar] vi to wander; (no hacer

nada) to idle

vagina [ba'xina] *nf* vagina

vago, a ['baɣo, a] *adj* vague; (*perezoso*) lazy ♦ *nm/f* (*vagabundo*) tramp; (*flojo*) lazybones *sg*, idler

vagón [ba'ɣon] *nm* (*FERRO: de pasajeros*) carriage; (: *de mercancías*) wagon

vaguedad [baɣe'ðað] *nf* vagueness

vaho ['bao] *nm* (*vapor*) vapour, steam; (*respiración*) breath

vaina ['baina] *nf* sheath

vainilla [bai'niʎa] *nf* vanilla

vainita [bai'nita] (*AM*) *nf* green *o* French bean

vais *vb ver* **ir**

vaivén [bai'ßen] *nm* to-and-fro movement; (*de tránsito*) coming and going; **vaivenes** *nmpl* (*fig*) ups and downs

vajilla [ba'xiʎa] *nf* crockery, dishes *pl*; **lavar la ~** to do the washing-up (*BRIT*), wash the dishes (*US*)

valdré *etc vb ver* **valer**

vale ['bale] *nm* voucher; (*recibo*) receipt; (*pagaré*) IOU

valedero, a [bale'ðero, a] *adj* valid

valenciano, a [balen'θjano, a] *adj* Valencian

valentía [balen'tia] *nf* courage, bravery

valer [ba'ler] *vt* to be worth; (*MAT*) to equal; (*costar*) to cost ♦ *vi* (*ser útil*) to be useful; (*ser válido*) to be valid; **~se** *vr* to take care of oneself; **~se de** to make use of, take advantage of; **~ la pena** to be worthwhile; **¿vale?** (*ESP*) OK?

valeroso, a [bale'roso, a] *adj* brave, valiant

valgo *etc vb ver* **valer**

valía [ba'lia] *nf* worth, value

validar [bali'ðar] *vt* to validate; **validez** *nf* validity; **válido, a** *adj* valid

valiente [ba'ljente] *adj* brave, valiant ♦ *nm* hero

valioso, a [ba'ljoso, a] *adj* valuable

valla ['baʎa] *nf* fence; (*DEPORTE*) hurdle; **~ publicitaria** hoarding; **vallar** *vt* to fence in

valle ['baʎe] *nm* valley

valor [ba'lor] *nm* value, worth; (*precio*) price; (*valentía*) valour, courage; (*importancia*) importance; **~es** *nmpl* (*COM*) securities; **~ar** *vt* to value

vals [bals] *nm inv* waltz

válvula ['balßula] *nf* valve

vamos *vb ver* **ir**

vampiro, resa [bam'piro, 'resa] *nm/f* vampire

van *vb ver* **ir**

vanagloriarse [banaɣlo'rjarse] *vr* to boast

vandalismo [banda'lismo] *nm* vandalism; **vándalo, a** *nm/f* vandal

vanguardia [ban'gwarðja] *nf* vanguard; (*ARTE etc*) avant-garde

vanidad [bani'ðað] *nf* vanity; **vanidoso, a** *adj* vain, conceited

vano, a ['bano, a] *adj* vain

vapor [ba'por] *nm* vapour; (*vaho*) steam; **al ~** (*CULIN*) steamed; **~izador** *nm* atomizer; **~izar** *vt* to vaporize; **~oso, a** *adj* vaporous

vapulear [bapule'ar] *vt* to beat, thrash

vaquero, a [ba'kero, a] *adj* cattle *cpd* ♦ *nm* cowboy; **~s** *nmpl* (*pantalones*) jeans

vaquilla [ba'kiʎa] *nf* (*ZOOL*) heifer

vara ['bara] *nf* stick; (*TEC*) rod; **~ mágica** magic wand

variable [ba'rjaßle] *adj, nf* variable

variación [barja'θjon] *nf* variation

variar [bar'jar] *vt* to vary; (*modificar*) to modify; (*cambiar de posición*) to switch around ♦ *vi* to vary

varicela [bari'θela] *nf* chickenpox

varices [ba'riθes] *nfpl* varicose veins

variedad [barje'ðað] *nf* variety

varilla [ba'riʎa] *nf* stick; (*BOT*) twig; (*TEC*) rod; (*de rueda*) spoke

vario, a ['barjo, a] *adj* varied; **~s** various, several

varita [ba'rita] *nf*: **~ mágica** magic wand

varón [ba'ron] *nm* male, man; **varonil** *adj* manly, virile

Varsovia [bar'soßja] *n* Warsaw

vas *vb ver* **ir**

vasco, a ['basko, a] *adj, nm/f* Basque

vascongado, a [baskon'gaðo, a] *adj*
Basque; **las Vascongadas** the Basque
Country
vascuence [bas'kwenθe] *adj*
= **vascongado**
vaselina [base'lina] *nf* Vaseline ®
vasija [ba'sixa] *nf* container, vessel
vaso ['baso] *nm* glass, tumbler; (*ANAT*)
vessel
vástago ['bastaxo] *nm* (*BOT*) shoot; (*TEC*)
rod; (*fig*) offspring
vasto, a ['basto, a] *adj* vast, huge
Vaticano [bati'kano] *nm*: **el ~** the Vatican
vatio ['batjo] *nm* (*ELEC*) watt
vaya *etc vb ver* **ir**
Vd(s) *abr* = **usted(es)**
ve *vb ver* **ir**; **ver**
vecindad [beθin'daδ] *nf* neighbourhood;
(*habitantes*) residents *pl*
vecindario [beθin'darjo] *nm*
neighbourhood; residents *pl*
vecino, a [be'θino, a] *adj* neighbouring
♦ *nm/f* neighbour; (*residente*) resident
veda ['beða] *nf* prohibition
vedar [be'ðar] *vt* (*prohibir*) to ban,
prohibit; (*impedir*) to stop, prevent
vegetación [bexeta'θjon] *nf* vegetation
vegetal [bexe'tal] *adj, nm* vegetable
vegetariano, a [bexeta'rjano, a] *adj, nm/f*
vegetarian
vehemencia [be(e)'menθja] *nf*
vehemence; **vehemente** *adj* vehement
vehículo [be'ikulo] *nm* vehicle; (*MED*)
carrier
veía *etc vb ver* **ver**
veinte ['beinte] *num* twenty
vejación [bexa'θjon] *nf* vexation;
(*humillación*) humiliation
vejar [be'xar] *vt* (*irritar*) to annoy, vex;
(*humillar*) to humiliate
vejez [be'xeθ] *nf* old age
vejiga [be'xixa] *nf* (*ANAT*) bladder
vela ['bela] *nf* (*de cera*) candle; (*NAUT*) sail;
(*insomnio*) sleeplessness; (*vigilia*) vigil;
(*MIL*) sentry duty; **estar a dos ~s** (*fam:
sin dinero*) to be skint
velado, a [be'laðo, a] *adj* veiled; (*sonido*)

muffled; (*FOTO*) blurred ♦ *nf* soirée
velar [be'lar] *vt* (*vigilar*) to keep watch over
♦ *vi* to stay awake; **~ por** to watch over,
look after
velatorio [bela'torjo] *nm* (*funeral*) wake
veleidad [belei'ðaδ] *nf* (*ligereza*) fickleness;
(*capricho*) whim
velero [be'lero] *nm* (*NAUT*) sailing ship;
(*AVIAT*) glider
veleta [be'leta] *nf* weather vane
veliz [be'lis] (*AM*) *nm* suitcase
vello ['beʎo] *nm* down, fuzz
velo ['belo] *nm* veil
velocidad [beloθi'ðaδ] *nf* speed; (*TEC,
AUTO*) gear
velocímetro [belo'θimetro] *nm*
speedometer
veloz [be'loθ] *adj* fast
ven *vb ver* **venir**
vena ['bena] *nf* vein
venado [be'naðo] *nm* deer
vencedor, a [benθe'ðor, a] *adj* victorious
♦ *nm/f* victor, winner
vencer [ben'θer] *vt* (*dominar*) to defeat,
beat; (*derrotar*) to vanquish; (*superar,
controlar*) to overcome, master ♦ *vi*
(*triunfar*) to win (through), triumph;
(*plazo*) to expire; **vencido, a** *adj*
(*derrotado*) defeated, beaten; (*COM*) due
♦ *adv*: **pagar vencido** to pay in arrears;
vencimiento *nm* (*COM*) maturity
venda ['benda] *nf* bandage; **vendaje** *nm*
bandage, dressing; **vendar** *vt* to
bandage; **vendar los ojos** to blindfold
vendaval [benda'βal] *nm* (*viento*) gale
vendedor, a [bende'ðor, a] *nm/f* seller
vender [ben'der] *vt* to sell; **~ al contado/
al por mayor/al por menor** to sell for
cash/wholesale/retail
vendimia [ben'dimja] *nf* grape harvest
vendré *etc vb ver* **venir**
veneno [be'neno] *nm* poison; (*de
serpiente*) venom; **~so, a** *adj* poisonous;
venomous
venerable [bene'raβle] *adj* venerable;
venerar *vt* (*respetar*) to revere; (*adorar*)
to worship

venéreo, a [be'nereo, a] *adj*: **enfermedad venérea** venereal disease
venezolano, a [beneθo'lano, a] *adj* Venezuelan
Venezuela [bene'θwela] *nf* Venezuela
venganza [ben'ganθa] *nf* vengeance, revenge; **vengar** *vt* to avenge; **vengarse** *vr* to take revenge; **vengativo, a** *adj* (*persona*) vindictive
vengo *etc vb ver* **venir**
venia ['benja] *nf* (*perdón*) pardon; (*permiso*) consent
venial [be'njal] *adj* venial
venida [be'niða] *nf* (*llegada*) arrival; (*regreso*) return
venidero, a [beni'ðero, a] *adj* coming, future
venir [be'nir] *vi* to come; (*llegar*) to arrive; (*ocurrir*) to happen; (*fig*): **~ de** to stem from; **~ bien/mal** to be suitable/unsuitable; **el año que viene** next year; **~se abajo** to collapse
venta ['benta] *nf* (COM) sale; **~ a plazos** hire purchase; **~ al contado/al por mayor/al por menor** *o* **al detalle** cash sale/wholesale/retail; **~ con derecho a retorno** sale or return; **"en ~"** "for sale"
ventaja [ben'taxa] *nf* advantage; **ventajoso, a** *adj* advantageous
ventana [ben'tana] *nf* window; **ventanilla** *nf* (*de taquilla*) window (*of booking office etc*)
ventilación [bentila'θjon] *nf* ventilation; (*corriente*) draught
ventilador [bentila'ðor] *nm* fan
ventilar [benti'lar] *vt* to ventilate; (*para secar*) to put out to dry; (*asunto*) to air, discuss
ventisca [ben'tiska] *nf* blizzard
ventrílocuo, a [ben'trilokwo, a] *nm/f* ventriloquist
ventura [ben'tura] *nf* (*felicidad*) happiness; (*buena suerte*) luck; (*destino*) fortune; **a la (buena) ~** at random; **venturoso, a** *adj* happy; (*afortunado*) lucky, fortunate
veo *etc vb ver* **ver**
ver [ber] *vt* to see; (*mirar*) to look at,

watch; (*entender*) to understand; (*investigar*) to look into; ♦ *vi* to see; to understand; **~se** *vr* (*encontrarse*) to meet; (*dejarse ~*) to be seen; (*hallarse: en un apuro*) to find o.s., be; **a ~** let's see; **no tener nada que ~ con** to have nothing to do with; **a mi modo de ~** as I see it
vera ['bera] *nf* edge, verge; (*de río*) bank
veracidad [beraθi'ðað] *nf* truthfulness
veranear [berane'ar] *vi* to spend the summer; **veraneo** *nm* summer holiday; **veraniego, a** *adj* summer *cpd*
verano [be'rano] *nm* summer
veras ['beras] *nfpl* truth *sg*; **de ~** really, truly
veraz [be'raθ] *adj* truthful
verbal [ber'ßal] *adj* verbal
verbena [ber'ßena] *nf* (*baile*) open-air dance
verbo ['berßo] *nm* verb; **~so, a** *adj* verbose
verdad [ber'ðað] *nf* truth; (*fiabilidad*) reliability; **de ~** real, proper; **a decir ~** to tell the truth; **~ero, a** *adj* (*veraz*) true, truthful; (*fiable*) reliable; (*fig*) real
verde ['berðe] *adj* green; (*chiste*) blue, dirty ♦ *nm* green; **viejo ~** dirty old man; **~ar** *vi* to turn green; **verdor** *nm* greenness
verdugo [ber'ðuxo] *nm* executioner
verdulero, a [berðu'lero, a] *nm/f* greengrocer
verduras [ber'ðuras] *nfpl* (CULIN) greens
vereda [be'reða] *nf* path; (AM) pavement (BRIT), sidewalk (US)
veredicto [bere'ðikto] *nm* verdict
vergonzoso, a [berɣon'θoso, a] *adj* shameful; (*tímido*) timid, bashful
vergüenza [ber'ɣwenθa] *nf* shame, sense of shame; (*timidez*) bashfulness; (*pudor*) modesty; **me da ~** I'm ashamed
verídico, a [be'riðiko, a] *adj* true, truthful
verificar [berifi'kar] *vt* to check; (*corroborar*) to verify; (*llevar a cabo*) to carry out; **~se** *vr* (*predicción*) to prove to be true
verja ['berxa] *nf* (*cancela*) iron gate; (*valla*)

iron railings *pl*; (*de ventana*) grille
vermut [ber'mut] (*pl* **~s**) *nm* vermouth
verosímil [bero'simil] *adj* likely, probable;
   (*relato*) credible
verruga [be'rruxa] *nf* wart
versado, a [ber'saðo, a] *adj*: **~ en** versed
   in
versátil [ber'satil] *adj* versatile
versión [ber'sjon] *nf* version
verso ['berso] *nm* verse; **un ~** a line of
   poetry
vértebra ['berteßra] *nf* vertebra
verter [ber'ter] *vt* (*líquido: adrede*) to
   empty, pour (out); (: *sin querer*) to spill;
   (*basura*) to dump ♦ *vi* to flow
vertical [berti'kal] *adj* vertical
vértice ['bertiθe] *nm* vertex, apex
vertidos [ber'tiðos] *nmpl* waste *sg*
vertiente [ber'tjente] *nf* slope; (*fig*) aspect
vertiginoso, a [bertixi'noso, a] *adj* giddy,
   dizzy
vértigo ['bertiɣo] *nm* vertigo; (*mareo*)
   dizziness
vesícula [be'sikula] *nf* blister
vespino ® [bes'pino] *nm o nf* moped
vestíbulo [bes'tißulo] *nm* hall; (*de teatro*)
   foyer
vestido [bes'tiðo] *pp de* **vestir**; **~ de**
   azul/marinero dressed in blue/as a sailor
   ♦ *nm* (*ropa*) clothes *pl*, clothing; (*de*
   mujer) dress, frock
vestigio [bes'tixjo] *nm* (*huella*) trace; **~s**
   nmpl (*restos*) remains
vestimenta [besti'menta] *nf* clothing
vestir [bes'tir] *vt* (*poner: ropa*) to put on;
   (*llevar: ropa*) to wear; (*proveer de ropa a*)
   to clothe; (*suj: sastre*) to make clothes for
   ♦ *vi* to dress; (*verse bien*) to look good;
   ~se *vr* to get dressed, dress o.s.
vestuario [bes'twarjo] *nm* clothes *pl*,
   wardrobe; (*TEATRO: cuarto*) dressing room;
   (*DEPORTE*) changing room
veta ['beta] *nf* (*vena*) vein, seam; (*en carne*)
   streak; (*de madera*) grain
vetar [be'tar] *vt* to veto
veterano, a [bete'rano, a] *adj, nm* veteran
veterinaria [beteri'narja] *nf* veterinary

science; *ver tb* **veterinario**
veterinario, a [beteri'narjo, a] *nm/f*
   vet(erinary surgeon)
veto ['beto] *nm* veto
vez [beθ] *nf* time; (*turno*) turn; **a la ~ que**
   at the same time as; **a su ~** in its turn;
   otra ~ again; **una ~** once; **de una ~** in
   one go; **de una ~ para siempre** once
   and for all; **en ~ de** instead of; **a o**
   algunas veces sometimes; **una y otra ~**
   repeatedly; **de ~ en cuando** from time to
   time; **7 veces 9** 7 times 9; **hacer las**
   veces de to stand in for; **tal ~** perhaps
vía ['bia] *nf* track, route; (*FERRO*) line; (*fig*)
   way; (*ANAT*) passage, tube ♦ *prep* via, by
   way of; **por ~ judicial** by legal means;
   por ~ oficial through official channels; **en**
   ~s de in the process of; **~ aérea** airway;
   V~ Láctea Milky Way; **~ pública** public
   road *o* thoroughfare
viable ['bjaßle] *adj* (*solución, plan,*
   alternativa) feasible
viaducto [bja'ðukto] *nm* viaduct
viajante [bja'xante] *nm* commercial
   traveller
viajar [bja'xar] *vi* to travel; **viaje** *nm*
   journey; (*gira*) tour; (*NAUT*) voyage; **estar**
   de viaje to be on a trip; **viaje de ida y**
   vuelta round trip; **viaje de novios**
   honeymoon; **viajero, a** *adj* travelling;
   (*ZOOL*) migratory ♦ *nm/f* (*quien viaja*)
   traveller; (*pasajero*) passenger
vial [bjal] *adj* road *cpd*, traffic *cpd*
víbora ['bißora] *nf* viper; (*AM*) poisonous
   snake
vibración [bißra'θjon] *nf* vibration
vibrar [bi'ßrar] *vt, vi* to vibrate
vicario [bi'karjo] *nm* curate
vicepresidente [biθepresi'ðente] *nm/f*
   vice-president
viceversa [biθe'ßersa] *adv* vice versa
viciado, a [bi'θjaðo, a] *adj* (*corrompido*)
   corrupt; (*contaminado*) foul,
   contaminated; **viciar** *vt* (*pervertir*) to
   pervert; (*JUR*) to nullify; (*estropear*) to
   spoil; **viciarse** *vr* to become corrupted
vicio ['biθjo] *nm* vice; (*mala costumbre*)

bad habit; **~so, a** adj (muy malo)
vicious; (corrompido) depraved ♦ nm/f
depraved person
vicisitud [biθisi'tuð] nf vicissitude
víctima ['biktima] nf victim
victoria [bik'torja] nf victory; **victorioso,**
a adj victorious
vid [bið] nf vine
vida ['biða] nf (gen) life; (duración) lifetime;
de por ~ for life; **en la/mi ~** never; **estar**
con ~ to be still alive; **ganarse la ~** to
earn one's living
vídeo ['biðeo] nm video ♦ adj inv:
película ~ video film; **videocámara** nf
camcorder; **videocasete** nm video cassette, videotape; **videoclub** nm video
club; **videojuego** nm video game
vidriero, a [bi'ðrjero, a] nm/f glazier ♦ nf
(ventana) stained-glass window; (AM: de
tienda) shop window; (puerta) glass door
vidrio ['biðrjo] nm glass
vieira ['bjeira] nf scallop
viejo, a ['bjexo, a] adj old ♦ nm/f old
man/woman; **hacerse ~** to get old
Viena ['bjena] n Vienna
vienes etc vb ver **venir**
vienés, esa [bje'nes, esa] adj Viennese
viento ['bjento] nm wind; **hacer ~** to be
windy
vientre ['bjentre] nm belly; (matriz) womb
viernes ['bjernes] nm inv Friday; **V~**
Santo Good Friday
Vietnam [bjet'nam] nm: **el ~** Vietnam;
vietnamita adj Vietnamese
viga ['biɣa] nf beam, rafter; (de metal)
girder
vigencia [bi'xenθja] nf validity; **estar en ~**
to be in force; **vigente** adj valid, in
force; (imperante) prevailing
vigésimo, a [bi'xesimo, a] adj twentieth
vigía [bi'xia] nm look-out
vigilancia [bixi'lanθja] nf: **tener a uno**
bajo ~ to keep watch on sb
vigilar [bixi'lar] vt to watch over ♦ vi (gen)
to be vigilant; (hacer guardia) to keep
watch; **~ por** to take care of
vigilia [vi'xilja] nf wakefulness, being

awake; (REL) fast
vigor [bi'ɣor] nm vigour, vitality; **en ~** in
force; **entrar/poner en ~** to come/put
into effect; **~oso, a** adj vigorous
VIH nm abr (= virus de la
inmunodeficiencia humana) HIV; **~**
positivo/negativo HIV-positive/-negative
vil [bil] adj vile, low; **~eza** nf vileness;
(acto) base deed
vilipendiar [bilipen'djar] vt to vilify, revile
villa ['biʎa] nf (casa) villa; (pueblo) small
town; (municipalidad) municipality; **~**
miseria (AM) shantytown
villancico [biʎan'θiko] nm (Christmas)
carol
villorrio [bi'ʎorrjo] nm shantytown
vilo ['bilo]: **en ~** adv in the air, suspended;
(fig) on tenterhooks, in suspense
vinagre [bi'naɣre] nm vinegar
vinagreta [bina'ɣreta] nf vinaigrette,
French dressing
vinculación [binkula'θjon] nf (lazo) link,
bond; (acción) linking
vincular [binku'lar] vt to link, bind;
vínculo nm link, bond
vine etc vb ver **venir**
vinicultura [binikul'tura] nf wine growing
viniera etc vb ver **venir**
vino ['bino] vb ver **venir** ♦ nm wine; **~**
blanco/tinto white/red wine
viña ['biɲa] nf vineyard; **viñedo** nm
vineyard
viola ['bjola] nf viola
violación [bjola'θjon] nf violation; **~**
(sexual) rape
violar [bjo'lar] vt to violate; (sexualmente)
to rape
violencia [bjo'lenθja] nf violence, force;
(incomodidad) embarrassment; (acto
injusto) unjust act; **violentar** vt to force;
(casa) to break into; (agredir) to assault;
(violar) to violate; **violento, a** adj
violent; (furioso) furious; (situación)
embarrassing; (acto) forced, unnatural
violeta [bjo'leta] nf violet
violín [bjo'lin] nm violin
violón [bjo'lon] nm double bass

viraje [biˈraxe] *nm* turn; (*de vehículo*) swerve; (*fig*) change of direction; **virar** *vi* to change direction

virgen [ˈbirxen] *adj, nf* virgin

Virgo [ˈbirɣo] *nm* Virgo

viril [biˈril] *adj* virile; **~idad** *nf* virility

virtud [birˈtuð] *nf* virtue; **en ~ de** by virtue of; **virtuoso, a** *adj* virtuous ♦ *nm/f* virtuoso

viruela [biˈrwela] *nf* smallpox

virulento, a [biruˈlento, a] *adj* virulent

virus [ˈbirus] *nm inv* virus

visa [ˈbisa] (*AM*) *nf* = **visado**

visado [biˈsaðo] *nm* visa

víscera [ˈbisθera] *nf* (*ANAT, ZOOL*) gut, bowel; **~s** *nfpl* entrails

visceral [bisθeˈral] *adj* (*odio*) intense; **reacción ~** gut reaction

viscoso, a [bisˈkoso, a] *adj* viscous

visera [biˈsera] *nf* visor

visibilidad [bisiβiliˈðað] *nf* visibility; **visible** *adj* visible; (*fig*) obvious

visillos [biˈsiʎos] *nmpl* lace curtains

visión [biˈsjon] *nf* (*ANAT*) vision, (*eye*)sight; (*fantasía*) vision, fantasy

visita [biˈsita] *nf* call, visit; (*persona*) visitor; **hacer una ~** to pay a visit

visitar [bisiˈtar] *vt* to visit, call on

vislumbrar [bislumˈbrar] *vt* to glimpse, catch a glimpse of

viso [ˈbiso] *nm* (*del metal*) glint, gleam; (*de tela*) sheen; (*aspecto*) appearance

visón [biˈson] *nm* mink

visor [biˈsor] *nm* (*FOTO*) viewfinder

víspera [ˈbispera] *nf*: **la ~ de ...** the day before ...

vista [ˈbista] *nf* sight, vision; (*capacidad de ver*) (*eye*)sight; (*mirada*) look(s) (*pl*); **a primera ~** at first glance; **hacer la ~ gorda** to turn a blind eye; **volver la ~** to look back; **está a la ~ que** it's obvious that; **en ~ de** in view of; **en ~ de que** in view of the fact that; **¡hasta la ~!** so long!, see you!; **con ~s a** with a view to; **~zo** *nm* glance; **dar** *o* **echar un ~zo a** to glance at

visto, a [ˈbisto, a] *pp de* **ver** ♦ *vb ver tb*

vestir ♦ *adj* seen; (*considerado*) considered ♦ *nm*: **~ bueno** approval; **"~ bueno"** "approved"; **por lo ~** apparently; **está ~ que** it's clear that; **está bien/mal ~** it's acceptable/unacceptable; **~ que** since, considering that

vistoso, a [bisˈtoso, a] *adj* colourful

visual [biˈswal] *adj* visual

vital [biˈtal] *adj* life *cpd*, living *cpd*; (*fig*) vital; (*persona*) lively, vivacious; **~icio, a** *adj* for life; **~idad** *nf* (*de persona, negocio*) energy; (*de ciudad*) liveliness

vitamina [bitaˈmina] *nf* vitamin

viticultor, a [bitikulˈtor, a] *nm/f* wine grower; **viticultura** *nf* wine growing

vitorear [bitoreˈar] *vt* to cheer, acclaim

vitrina [biˈtrina] *nf* show case; (*AM*) shop window

viudez *nf* widowhood

viudo, a [ˈbjuðo, a] *nm/f* widower/widow

viva [ˈbiβa] *excl* hurrah!: **¡~ el rey!** long live the king!

vivacidad [biβaθiˈðað] *nf* (*vigor*) vigour; (*vida*) liveliness

vivaracho, a [biβaˈratʃo, a] *adj* jaunty, lively; (*ojos*) bright, twinkling

vivaz [biˈβaθ] *adj* lively

víveres [ˈbiβeres] *nmpl* provisions

vivero [biˈβero] *nm* (*para plantas*) nursery; (*para peces*) fish farm; (*fig*) hotbed

viveza [biˈβeθa] *nf* liveliness; (*agudeza: mental*) sharpness

vivienda [biˈβjenda] *nf* housing; (*una ~*) house; (*piso*) flat (*BRIT*), apartment (*US*)

viviente [biˈβjente] *adj* living

vivir [biˈβir] *vt, vi* to live ♦ *nm* life, living

vivo, a [ˈbiβo, a] *adj* living, alive; (*fig: descripción*) vivid; (*persona: astuto*) smart, clever; **en ~** (*transmisión etc*) live

vocablo [boˈkaβlo] *nm* (*palabra*) word; (*término*) term

vocabulario [bokaβuˈlarjo] *nm* vocabulary

vocación [bokaˈθjon] *nf* vocation; **vocacional** (*AM*) *nf* ≈ technical college

vocal [boˈkal] *adj* vocal ♦ *nf* vowel; **~izar** *vt* to vocalize

vocear [boθeˈar] *vt* (*para vender*) to cry;

(*aclamar*) to acclaim; (*fig*) to proclaim ♦ *vi* to yell; **vocerío** *nm* shouting

vocero [boˈθero] *nm/f* spokesman/woman

voces [ˈboθes] *pl de* **voz**

vociferar [boθifeˈrar] *vt* to shout ♦ *vi* to yell

vodka [ˈboðka] *nm o f* vodka

vol *abr* = **volumen**

volador, a [bolaˈðor, a] *adj* flying

volandas [boˈlandas]: **en ~** *adv* in the air

volante [boˈlante] *adj* flying ♦ *nm* (*de coche*) steering wheel; (*de reloj*) balance

volar [boˈlar] *vt* (*edificio*) to blow up ♦ *vi* to fly

volátil [boˈlatil] *adj* volatile

volcán [bolˈkan] *nm* volcano; **~ico, a** *adj* volcanic

volcar [bolˈkar] *vt* to upset, overturn; (*tumbar, derribar*) to knock over; (*vaciar*) to empty out ♦ *vi* to overturn; **~se** *vr* to tip over

voleibol [boleiˈβol] *nm* volleyball

volqué *etc vb ver* **volcar**

voltaje [bolˈtaxe] *nm* voltage

voltear [bolteˈar] *vt* to turn over; (*volcar*) to turn upside down

voltereta [bolteˈreta] *nf* somersault

voltio [ˈboltjo] *nm* volt

voluble [boˈluβle] *adj* fickle

volumen [boˈlumen] (*pl* **volúmenes**) *nm* volume; **voluminoso, a** *adj* voluminous; (*enorme*) massive

voluntad [bolunˈtað] *nf* will; (*resolución*) willpower; (*deseo*) desire, wish

voluntario, a [bolunˈtarjo, a] *adj* voluntary ♦ *nm/f* volunteer

voluntarioso, a [boluntaˈrjoso, a] *adj* headstrong

voluptuoso, a [bolupˈtwoso, a] *adj* voluptuous

volver [bolˈβer] *vt* (*gen*) to turn; (*dar vuelta a*) to turn (over); (*voltear*) to turn round, turn upside down; (*poner al revés*) to turn inside out; (*devolver*) to return ♦ *vi* to return, go back, come back; **~se** *vr* to turn round; **~ la espalda** to turn one's back; **~ triste** *etc* **a uno** to make sb

sad *etc*; **~ a hacer** to do again; **~ en sí** to come to; **~se insoportable/muy caro** to get *o* become unbearable/very expensive; **~se loco** to go mad

vomitar [bomiˈtar] *vt, vi* to vomit; **vómito** *nm* vomit

voraz [boˈraθ] *adj* voracious

vos [bos] (*AM*) *pron* you

vosotros, as [boˈsotros, as] *pron* you; (*reflexivo*) **entre/para ~** among/for yourselves

votación [botaˈθjon] *nf* (*acto*) voting; (*voto*) vote

votar [boˈtar] *vi* to vote; **voto** *nm* vote; (*promesa*) vow; **votos** (good) wishes

voy *vb ver* **ir**

voz [boθ] *nf* voice; (*grito*) shout; (*rumor*) rumour; (*LING*) word; **dar voces** to shout, yell; **a media ~** in a low voice; **a ~ en cuello** *o* **en grito** at the top of one's voice; **de viva ~** verbally; **en ~ alta** aloud; **~ de mando** command

vuelco [ˈbwelko] *vb ver* **volcar** ♦ *nm* spill, overturning

vuelo [ˈbwelo] *vb ver* **volar** ♦ *nm* flight; (*encaje*) lace, frill; **coger al ~** to catch in flight; **~ charter/regular** charter/scheduled flight; **~ libre** (*DEPORTE*) hanggliding

vuelque *etc vb ver* **volcar**

vuelta [ˈbwelta] *nf* (*gen*) turn; (*curva*) bend, curve; (*regreso*) return; (*revolución*) revolution; (*de circuito*) lap; (*de papel, tela*) reverse; (*cambio*) change; **a la ~** on one's return; **a ~ de correo** by return of post; **dar ~s** (*suj: cabeza*) to spin; **dar ~s a una idea** to turn over an idea (in one's head); **estar de ~** to be back; **dar una ~** to go for a walk; (*en coche*) to go for a drive; **~ ciclista** (*DEPORTE*) (cycle) tour

vuelto *pp de* **volver**

vuelvo *etc vb ver* **volver**

vuestro, a [ˈbwestro, a] *adj* your; **un amigo ~** a friend of yours ♦ *pron*: **el ~/la vuestra, los ~s/las vuestras** yours

vulgar [bulˈɣar] *adj* (*ordinario*) vulgar; (*común*) common; **~idad** *nf*

commonness; (*acto*) vulgarity; (*expresión*) coarse expression; **~izar** *vt* to popularize
vulgo ['bulɣo] *nm* common people
vulnerable [bulne'raßle] *adj* vulnerable
vulnerar [bulne'rar] *vt* (*ley, acuerdo*) to violate, breach; (*derechos, intimidad*) to violate; (*reputación*) to damage

W, w

Walkman ® [wak'man] *nm* Walkman ®
wáter ['bater] *nm* toilet
whisky ['wiski] *nm* whisky, whiskey

X, x

xenofobia [kseno'foßja] *nf* xenophobia
xilófono [ksi'lofono] *nm* xylophone

Y, y

y [i] *conj* and
ya [ja] *adv* (*gen*) already; (*ahora*) now; (*en seguida*) at once; (*pronto*) soon ♦ *excl* all right! ♦ *conj* (*ahora que*) now that; **~ lo sé** I know; **~ que** since
yacer [ja'θer] *vi* to lie
yacimiento [jaθi'mjento] *nm* (*de mineral*) deposit; (*arqueológico*) site
yanqui ['janki] *adj, nm/f* Yankee
yate ['jate] *nm* yacht
yazco *etc vb ver* **yacer**
yedra ['jeðra] *nf* ivy
yegua ['jeɣwa] *nf* mare
yema ['jema] *nf* (*del huevo*) yoke; (*BOT*) leaf bud; (*fig*) best part; **~ del dedo** fingertip
yergo *etc vb ver* **erguir**
yermo, a ['jermo, a] *adj* (*estéril, fig*) barren ♦ *nm* wasteland
yerno ['jerno] *nm* son-in-law
yerro *etc vb ver* **errar**
yeso ['jeso] *nm* plaster
yo [jo] *pron* I; **soy ~** it's me, it is I

yodo ['joðo] *nm* iodine
yoga ['joɣa] *nm* yoga
yogur(t) [jo'ɣur(t)] *nm* yoghurt
yugo ['juɣo] *nm* yoke
Yugoslavia [juɣos'laßja] *nf* Yugoslavia
yugular [juɣu'lar] *adj* jugular
yunque ['junke] *nm* anvil
yunta ['junta] *nf* yoke
yuxtaponer [jukstapo'ner] *vt* to juxtapose; **yuxtaposición** *nf* juxtaposition

Z, z

zafar [θa'far] *vt* (*soltar*) to untie; (*superficie*) to clear; **~se** *vr* (*escaparse*) to escape; (*TEC*) to slip off
zafio, a ['θafjo, a] *adj* coarse
zafiro [θa'firo] *nm* sapphire
zaga ['θaɣa] *nf*: **a la ~** behind, in the rear
zaguán [θa'ɣwan] *nm* hallway
zaherir [θae'rir] *vt* (*criticar*) to criticize
zaino, a ['θaino, a] *adj* (*caballo*) chestnut
zalamería [θalame'ria] *nf* flattery; **zalamero, a** *adj* flattering; (*cobista*) suave
zamarra [θa'marra] *nf* (*chaqueta*) sheepskin jacket
zambullirse [θambu'ʎirse] *vr* to dive
zampar [θam'par] *vt* to gobble down
zanahoria [θana'orja] *nf* carrot
zancada [θan'kaða] *nf* stride
zancadilla [θanka'ðiʎa] *nf* trip
zanco ['θanko] *nm* stilt
zancudo, a [θan'kuðo, a] *adj* long-legged ♦ *nm* (*AM*) mosquito
zángano ['θanɣano] *nm* drone
zanja ['θanxa] *nf* ditch; **zanjar** *vt* (*resolver*) to resolve
zapata [θa'pata] *nf* (*MECÁNICA*) shoe
zapatear [θapate'ar] *vi* to tap with one's feet
zapatería [θapate'ria] *nf* (*oficio*) shoemaking; (*tienda*) shoe shop; (*fábrica*) shoe factory; **zapatero, a** *nm/f*

shoemaker

zapatilla [θapa'tiʎa] *nf* slipper; **~ de deporte** training shoe

zapato [θa'pato] *nm* shoe

zapping ['θapin] *nm* channel-hopping; **hacer ~** to flick through the channels

zar [θar] *nm* tsar, czar

zarandear [θarande'ar] (*fam*) *vt* to shake vigorously

zarpa ['θarpa] *nf* (*garra*) claw

zarpar [θar'par] *vi* to weigh anchor

zarza ['θarθa] *nf* (*BOT*) bramble; **zarzal** *nm* (*matorral*) bramble patch

zarzamora [θarθa'mora] *nf* blackberry

zarzuela [θar'θwela] *nf* Spanish light opera

zigzag [θiɣ'θaɣ] *nm* zigzag; **zigzaguear** *vi* to zigzag

zinc [θink] *nm* zinc

zócalo ['θokalo] *nm* (*ARQ*) plinth, base

zodíaco [θo'ðiako] *nm* (*ASTRO*) zodiac

zona ['θona] *nf* zone; **~ fronteriza** border area

zoo ['θoo] *nm* zoo

zoología [θoolo'xia] *nf* zoology; **zoológico, a** *adj* zoological ♦ *nm* (*tb*: **parque ~**) zoo; **zoólogo, a** *nm/f* zoologist

zoom [θum] *nm* zoom lens

zopilote [θopi'lote] (*AM*) *nm* buzzard

zoquete [θo'kete] *nm* (*fam*) blockhead

zorro, a ['θorro, a] *adj* crafty ♦ *nm/f* fox/vixen

zozobra [θo'θoßra] *nf* (*fig*) anxiety; **zozobrar** *vi* (*hundirse*) to capsize; (*fig*) to fail

zueco ['θweko] *nm* clog

zumbar [θum'bar] *vt* (*golpear*) to hit ♦ *vi* to buzz; **zumbido** *nm* buzzing

zumo ['θumo] *nm* juice

zurcir [θur'θir] *vt* (*coser*) to darn

zurdo, a ['θurðo, a] *adj* (*persona*) left-handed

zurrar [θu'rrar] (*fam*) *vt* to wallop

USING YOUR COLLINS POCKET DICTIONARY

Supplement by
Roy Simon
reproduced by kind permission of
Tayside Region Education Department

USING YOUR COLLINS POCKET DICTIONARY

Introduction

We are delighted that you have decided to invest in this Collins Pocket Dictionary! Whether you intend to use it in school, at home, on holiday or at work, we are sure that you will find it very useful.

The purpose of this supplement is to help you become aware of the wealth of vocabulary and grammatical information your dictionary contains, to explain how this information is presented and also to point out some of the traps one can fall into when using a Spanish-English English-Spanish dictionary.

In the pages which follow you will find explanations and wordgames (not too difficult!) designed to give you practice in exploring the dictionary's contents and in retrieving information for a variety of purposes. Answers are provided at the end. If you spend a little time on these pages you should be able to use your dictionary more efficiently and effectively. Have fun!

Contents

i

HOW INFORMATION IS PRESENTED IN YOUR DICTIONARY

A great deal of information is packed into your Collins Pocket Dictionary using colour, various typefaces, sizes of type, symbols, abbreviations and brackets. The purpose of this section is to acquaint you with the conventions used in presenting information.

Headwords

A headword is the word you look up in a dictionary. Headwords are listed in alphabetical order throughout the dictionary. They are printed in colour so that they stand out clearly from all the other words on the dictionary page.

Note that at the top of each page two headwords appear. These tell you which is the first and last word dealt with on the page in question. They are there to help you scan through the dictionary more quickly.

The Spanish alphabet consists of 27 letters: the same 26 letters as the English alphabet, in the same order, plus 'ñ', which comes after letter 'n'. You will need to remember that words containing this letter will be listed slightly differently from what you would expect according to English alphabetical order: thus 'caña' does not come immediately after 'cana', but follows the last word beginning with 'can-' in the list, namely 'canuto'.

Where two Spanish words are distinguished only by an accent, the accented form follows the unaccented, e.g. 'de', 'dé'.

A dictionary entry

An entry is made up of a headword and all the information about that headword. Entries will be short or long depending on how frequently a word is used in either English or Spanish and how many meanings it has. Inevitably, the fuller the dictionary entry the more care is needed in sifting through it to find the information you require.

Meanings

The translations of a headword are given in ordinary type. Where there is more than one meaning or usage, a semi-colon separates one from the other.

completo, a [kom'pleto, a] *adj* complete;
(*perfecto*) perfect; (*lleno*) full ♦ *nm* full
complement
complicado, a [kompli'kaðo, a] *adj*
complicated; **estar ~ en** to be mixed up
in
cómplice ['kompliθe] *nm/f* accomplice
complot [kom'plo(t)] (*pl* **~s**) *nm* plot

aiming; (*destreza*) marksmanship
puntero, a [pun'tero, a] *adj* leading ♦ *nm*
(*palo*) pointer
puntiagudo, a [puntja'ɣuðo, a] *adj* sharp,
pointed
puntilla [pun'tiʎa] *nf* (*encaje*) lace edging

puritano, a [puri'tano, a] *adj* (*actitud*)
puritanical; (*iglesia, tradición*) puritan
♦ *nm/f* puritan
puro, a ['puro, a] *adj* pure; (*verdad*)
simple, plain ♦ *adv*: **de ~ cansado** out of
sheer tiredness ♦ *nm* cigar

nevar [ne'ßar] *vi* to snow

cuenta *etc* ['kwenta] *vb ver* **contar** ♦ *nf*
(*cálculo*) count, counting; (*en café,
restaurante*) bill (*BRIT*), check (*US*); (*COM*)
account; (*de collar*) bead; **a fin de ~s** in
the end; **caer en la ~** to catch on; **darse
~ de** to realize; **tener en ~** to bear in
mind; **echar ~s** to take stock; **~
corriente/de ahorros** current/savings
account; **~ atrás** countdown;
~kilómetros *nm inv* ≈ milometer; (*de
velocidad*) speedometer

titubear [tituße'ar] *vi* to stagger; to
stammer; (*fig*) to hesitate; **titubeo** *nm*
staggering; stammering; hesitation

In addition, you will often find other words appearing in *italics* in brackets before the translations. These either give some notion of the contexts in which the headword might appear (as with 'lane' opposite – 'lane in the country', 'lane in a race', etc.) or else they provide synonyms (as with 'hit' opposite – 'strike', 'reach', etc.).

Phonetic spellings

The phonetic spelling of each headword – i.e. its pronunciation – is given in square brackets immediately after it. The phonetic transcription of Spanish and English vowels and consonants is given on pages viii to xi at the front of your dictionary.

Additional information about headwords

Information about the usage or form of certain headwords is given in brackets between the phonetics and the translation or translations. Have a look at the entries for 'COU', 'cuenca', 'mast', 'R.S.V.P.' and 'burro' opposite.

This information is usually given in abbreviated form. A helpful list of abbreviations is given on pages vi and vii at the front of your dictionary.

You should be particularly careful with colloquial words or phrases. Words labelled (*fam*) would not normally be used in formal speech, while those labelled (*fam!*) would be considered offensive.

Careful consideration of such style labels will help indicate the degree of formality and appropriateness of a word and could help you avoid many an embarrassing situation when using Spanish!

Expressions in which the headword appears

An entry will often feature certain common expressions in which the headword appears. These expressions are in **bold** type, but in black as opposed to colour. A swung dash (~) is used instead of repeating a headword in an entry. 'Tono' and 'mano' opposite illustrate this point.

Related words

In the Pocket Dictionary words related to certain headwords are sometimes given at the end of an entry, as with 'ambición' and 'accept' opposite. These are easily picked out as they are also in colour. To help you find these words, they are placed in alphabetical order after the headword to which they belong: cf. 'accept', 'general' opposite.

lane [leɪn] n (in country) camino; (AUT) carril m; (in race) calle f

embrollar [embro'ʎar] vt (el asunto) to confuse, complicate; (implicar) to involve, embroil; **~se** vr (confundirse) to get into a muddle o mess

COU [kou] (ESP) nm abr (= Curso de Orientación Universitaria) 1 year course leading to final school-leaving certificate and university entrance examinations

cuenca ['kwenka] nf (ANAT) eye socket; (GEO) bowl, deep valley

menudo, a [me'nuðo, a] adj (pequeño) small, tiny; (sin importancia) petty, insignificant; **¡~ negocio!** (fam) some deal!; **a ~** often, frequently

tono ['tono] nm tone; **fuera de ~** inappropriate; **darse ~** to put on airs

ambición [ambi'θjon] nf ambition; **ambicionar** vt to aspire to; **ambicioso, a** adj ambitious

accept [ək'sept] vt aceptar; (responsibility, blame) admitir; **~able** adj acceptable; **~ance** n aceptación f

hit [hɪt] (pt, pp **hit**) vt (strike) golpear, pegar; (reach: target) alcanzar; (collide with: car) chocar contra; (fig: affect) afectar ♦ n golpe m; (success) éxito; **to ~ it off with sb** llevarse bien con uno; **~-and-run driver** n conductor(a) que atropella y huye

repoblación [repoβla'θjon] nf repopulation; (de río) restocking; **~ forestal** reafforestation

mast [maːst] n (NAUT) mástil m; (RADIO etc) torre f

R.S.V.P. abbr (= répondez s'il vous plaît) SRC

burro, a ['burro, a] nm/f donkey/she-donkey; (fig) ass, idiot

bocazas [bo'kaθas] (fam) nm inv bigmouth

cabrón [ka'ßron] nm cuckold; (fam!) bastard (!)

mano ['mano] nf hand; (ZOOL) foot, paw; (de pintura) coat; (serie) lot, series; **a ~** by hand; **a ~ derecha/izquierda** on the right(-hand side)/left(-hand side); **de primera ~** (at) first hand; **de segunda ~** (at) second hand; **robo a ~ armada** armed robbery; **~ de obra** labour, manpower; **estrechar la ~ a uno** to shake sb's hand

general [xene'ral] adj general ♦ nm general; **por lo o en ~** in general; **G~itat** nf Catalan parliament; **~izar** vt to generalize; **~izarse** vr to become generalized, spread; **~mente** adv generally

v

'Key' words

Your Collins Pocket Dictionary gives special status to certain Spanish and English words which can be looked on as 'key' words in each language. These are words which have many different usages. 'Poder', 'menos' and 'se' opposite are typical examples in Spanish. You are likely to become familiar with them in your day-to-day language studies.

There will be occasions, however, when you want to check on a particular usage. Your dictionary can be very helpful here. Note how with 'poder', for example, different parts of speech and different usages are clearly indicated by a combination of lozenges - ♦ - and numbers. In addition, further guides to usage are given in the language of the user who needs them. These are bracketed and in italics.

poder [po'ðer] *vi* **1** (*capacidad*) can, be able to; **no puedo hacerlo** I can't do it, I'm unable to do it

2 (*permiso*) can, may, be allowed to; **¿se puede?** may I (*o* we)?; **puedes irte ahora** you may go now; **no se puede fumar en este hospital** smoking is not allowed in this hospital

3 (*posibilidad*) may, might, could; **puede llegar mañana** he may *o* might arrive tomorrow; **pudiste haberte hecho daño** you might *o* could have hurt yourself; **¡podías habérmelo dicho antes!** you might have told me before!

4: **puede ser: puede ser** perhaps; **puede ser que lo sepa Tomás** Tomás may *o* might know

5: **¡no puedo más!** I've had enough!; **no pude menos que dejarlo** I couldn't help but leave it; **es tonto a más no ~** he's as stupid as they come

6: **~ con: no puedo con este crío** this kid's too much for me

♦ *nm* power; **~ adquisitivo** purchasing power; **detentar** *o* **ocupar** *o* **estar en el ~** to be in power

se [se] *pron* **1** (*reflexivo: sg: m*) himself; (: *f*) herself; (: *pl*) themselves; (: *cosa*) itself; (: *de Vd*) yourself; (: *de Vds*) yourselves; **~ está preparando** she's preparing herself; *para usos léxicos del pron ver el vb en cuestión, p.ej.* **arrepentirse**

2 (*con complemento indirecto*) to him; to her; to them; to it; to you; **a usted ~ lo dije ayer** I told you yesterday; **~ compró un sombrero** he bought himself a hat; **~ rompió la pierna** he broke his leg

3 (*uso recíproco*) each other, one another; **~ miraron (el uno al otro)** they looked at each other *o* one another

4 (*en oraciones pasivas*): **se han vendido muchos libros** a lot of books have been sold

5 (*impers*): **~ dice que** people say that, it is said that; **allí ~ come muy bien** the food there is very good, you can eat very well there

menos [menos] *adj* **1**: **~ (que/de)** (*compar: cantidad*) less (than); (: *número*) fewer (than); **con ~ entusiasmo** with less enthusiasm; **~ gente** fewer people; *ver tb* **cada**

2 (*superl*): **es el que ~ culpa tiene** he is the least to blame

♦ *adv* **1** (*compar*): **~ (que, de)** less (than); **me gusta ~ que el otro** I like it less than the other one

2 (*superl*): **es el ~ listo (de su clase)** he's the least bright in his class; **de todas ellas es la que ~ me agrada** out of all of them she's the one I like least; **(por) lo ~** at (the very) least

3 (*locuciones*): **no quiero verle y ~ visitarle** I don't want to see him let alone visit him; **tenemos 7 de ~** we're seven short

♦ *prep* except; (*cifras*) minus; **todos ~ él** everyone except (for) him; **5 ~ 2** 5 minus 2

♦ *conj*: **a ~ que: a ~ que venga mañana** unless he comes tomorrow

WORDGAME 1

HEADWORDS

Study the following sentences. In each sentence a wrong word spelt very similarly to the correct word has deliberately been put in and the sentence doesn't make sense. This word is shaded each time. Write out each sentence again, putting in the correct word which you will find in your dictionary near the wrong word.

> Example: Aparcar aquí no es delirio.

> ['Delirio' (= delirium) is the wrong word and
>   should be replaced by 'delito' (= offence)]

1. El mecánico se negó a arrebatarme el coche.

2. El baúl estaba cubierto de pólvora.

3. Es muy caro reventar las fotos en esa tienda.

4. Les gusta mucho dar pasillos a caballo.

5. Para ayunar a su madre pone la mesa todos los días.

6. La ballesta es el animal más grande del mundo.

7. Mientras esquiábamos nos cayó una nevera tremenda.

8. No me gustó el último capota del libro.

9. Tuvimos un pincho y hubo que parar el coche.

10. Hay que cerrar la puerta con candidato.

WORDGAME 2

DICTIONARY ENTRIES

Complete the crossword below by looking up the English words in the list and finding the correct Spanish translations. There is a slight catch, however! All the English words can be translated several ways into Spanish, but only one translation will fit correctly into each part of the crossword. So look carefully through the entries in the English-Spanish section of your dictionary.

1. HORN
2. THROW
3. REMEMBER
4. PERFORMANCE
5. SPEECH
6. WHOLE

7. AMUSE
8. OLD
9. BELL
10. MATERIAL
11. ENDING
12. PART

WORDGAME 3

FINDING MEANINGS

In this list there are eight pairs of words that have some sort of connection with each other. For example, '**curso**' (= 'course') and '**estudiante**' (= 'student') are linked. Find the other pairs by looking up the words in your dictionary.

1. bata
2. nido
3. cuero
4. zapatillas
5. campanario
6. estudiante
7. libro
8. bolso
9. pasarela
10. aleta
11. curso
12. estante
13. urraca
14. barco
15. veleta
16. tiburón

WORDGAME 4

SYNONYMS

Complete the crossword by supplying SYNONYMS of the words below. You will sometimes find the synonym you are looking for in italics bracketed at the entries for the words listed below. Sometimes you will have to turn to the English-Spanish section for help.

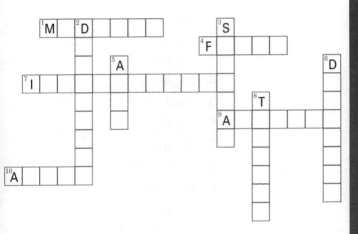

1. maneras
2. desilusión
3. exceder
4. incendio
5. cariño
6. vencer
7. inacabable
8. éxito
9. complacer
10. aeroplano

WORDGAME 5

SPELLING

You will often use your dictionary to check spellings. The person who has compiled this list of ten Spanish words has made <u>three</u> spelling mistakes. Find the three words which have been misspelt and write them out correctly.

1. pájaro
2. acienda
3. oleaje
4. gigante
5. avarrotar
6. peregil
7. ahora
8. velocidad
9. quinientos
10. abridor

WORDGAME 6

ANTONYMS

Complete the crossword by supplying ANTONYMS (i.e. opposites) in Spanish of the words below. Use your dictionary to help.

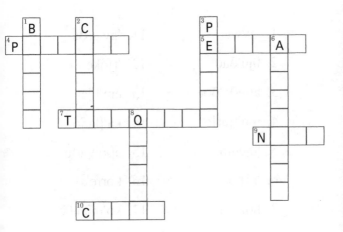

1. feo
2. abrir
3. ligero
4. riqueza
5. salir
6. engordar
7. inquieto
8. poner
9. todo
10. oscuro

WORDGAME 7

PHONETIC SPELLINGS

The phonetic transcriptions of twenty Spanish words are given below.
If you study pages viii and ix at the front of your dictionary you should be
able to work out what the words are.

1. 'aɣwa

2. θju'ðað

3. alreðe'ðor

4. mu'tʃatʃo

5. 'bjento

6. 'niɲo

7. bol'βer

8. 'kaʎe

9. θiɣ'θaɣ

10. 'xenjo

11. 'gwarða

12. 'tʃoke

13. em'bjar

14. ka'βaʎo

15. aβo'ɣaðo

16. korre'xir

17. ko'mjenθo

18. 'eʎos

19. xer'sei

20. i'ɣwal

WORDGAME 8

EXPRESSIONS IN WHICH THE HEADWORD APPEARS

If you look up the headword 'mismo' in the Spanish-English section of your dictionary you will find that the word can have many meanings. Study the entry carefully and translate the following sentences into English.

1. Ahora mismo se lo llevo.

2. A mí me da lo mismo.

3. Lo mismo que tú estudias francés yo estudio español.

4. En ese mismo momento llegó la policía.

5. Acudió el mismo Presidente.

6. Todos los domingos se ponía el mismo traje.

7. Lo hice yo mismo.

8. Era un hipócrita, y por lo mismo despreciado por todos.

9. Tenemos que empezar hoy mismo.

10. Lo vi aquí mismo.

WORDGAME 9

RELATED WORDS

Fill in the blanks in the pairs of sentences below. The missing words are
related to the headwords on the left. Choose the correct 'relative' each
time. You will find it in your dictionary near the headword provided.

HEADWORD	RELATED WORDS
estudiante	1. Realiza sus _____ en la Universidad. 2. Hay que _____ bien el texto.
pertenecer	3. Estos son los terrenos _____ al Ayuntamiento. 4. Recogió todas sus _____ y se fue.
empleo	5. Es _____ de banco. 6. Voy a _____ todos los medios a mi alcance.
atractivo	7. Esa perspectiva no me _____ nada. 8. Aquella mujer ejercía una gran _____ sobre él.
terminante	9. Al _____ de la reunión todos se fueron a tomar café. 10. No le dejaron _____ lo que estaba diciendo.
falsedad	11. Lo que estás diciendo es completamente _____ 12. Se dedicaban a _____ billetes de banco.

WORDGAME 10

'KEY' WORDS

Study carefully the entry **'hacer'** in your dictionary and find translations for the following:

1. it's cold

2. I made them come

3. to study Economics

4. this will make it more difficult

5. to do the cooking

6. they became friends

7. I've been going for a month

8. to turn a deaf ear

9. if it's alright with you

10. to get hold of something

THE DICTIONARY AND GRAMMAR

While it is true that a dictionary can never be a substitute for a detailed grammar reference book, it nevertheless provides a great deal of grammatical information. If you know how to extract this information you will be able to use Spanish more accurately both in speech and in writing.

The Collins Pocket Dictionary presents grammatical information as follows.

Parts of speech

Parts of speech are given in italics immediately after the phonetic spellings of headwords. Abbreviated forms are used. Abbreviations can be checked on pages vi and vii.

Changes in parts of speech within an entry – for example, from adjective to adverb to noun, or from noun to intransitive verb to transitive verb – are indicated by means of lozenges - ♦ - as with the Spanish 'derecho' and the English 'act' opposite.

Genders of Spanish nouns

The gender of each noun in the Spanish-English section of the dictionary is indicated in the following way:

> *nm* = nombre masculino
>
> *nf* = nombre femenino

You will occasionally see *nm/f* beside an entry. This indicates that a noun – 'habitante', for example – can be either masculine or feminine.

Feminine forms of nouns are shown, as with 'ministro' opposite: the feminine ending is substituted for the masculine, so that 'ministro' becomes 'ministra' in the feminine.

In the English-Spanish section of the dictionary, genders are not shown for masculine nouns ending in '-o' or feminine nouns ending in '-a'. Otherwise the gender immediately follows the translation. If a noun can be either masculine or feminine, this is shown by '*m/f*' if the form of the noun does not change, or by the feminine ending if it does change, as with 'graduate' and 'dentist' opposite. Note that when an ending is added on to a word rather than substituted for another ending it appears in brackets.

It is most important that you know the correct gender of a Spanish noun, since it is going to determine the form of both adjectives and past participles. If you are in any doubt as to the gender of a noun, it is always best to check it in your dictionary.

estría [es'tria] *nf* groove

tenue ['tenwe] *adj* (*delgado*) thin, slender; (*neblina*) light; (*lazo, vínculo*) slight

derecho, a [de'retʃo, a] *adj* right, right-hand ♦ *nm* (*privilegio*) right; (*lado*) right(-hand) side; (*leyes*) law ♦ *adv* straight, directly; **~s** *nmpl* (*de aduana*) duty *sg*; (*de autor*) royalties; **tener ~ a** to have a right to

act [ækt] *n* acto, acción *f*; (*of play*) acto; (*in music hall etc*) número; (*LAW*) decreto, ley *f* ♦ *vi* (*behave*) comportarse; (*have effect: drug, chemical*) hacer efecto; (*THEATRE*) actuar; (*pretend*) fingir; (*take action*) obrar ♦ *vt* (*part*) hacer el papel de; **in the ~ of**: **to catch sb in the ~ of ...** pillar a uno en el momento en que ...; **to ~ as** actuar *or* hacer de; **~ing** *adj* suplente ♦ *n* (*activity*) actuación *f*; (*profession*) profesión *f* de actor

criterio [kri'terjo] *nm* criterion; (*juicio*) judgement

manguera [man'gera] *nf* hose

habitante [aßi'tante] *nm/f* inhabitant

ministro, a [mi'nistro, a] *nm/f* minister

graduate [*n* 'grædjuɪt, *vb* 'grædjueɪt] *n* (*US: of high school*) graduado/a; (*of university*) licenciado/a ♦ *vi* graduarse; licenciarse; **graduation** [-'eɪʃən] *n* (*ceremony*) entrega del título

dentist ['dɛntɪst] *n* dentista *m/f*

Adjectives

Adjectives are given in both their masculine and feminine forms, where these are different. The usual rule is to drop the 'o' of the masculine form and add an 'a' to make an adjective feminine, as with 'negro' opposite.

Some adjectives have identical masculine and feminine forms. Where this occurs, there is no 'a' beside the basic masculine form.

Adverbs

The normal 'rule' for forming adverbs in Spanish is to add '-mente' to the feminine form of the adjective. Thus:

> seguro > segura > seguramente

The '-mente' ending is often the equivalent of the English '-ly':

> seguramente – surely
> lentamente – slowly

In your dictionary Spanish adverbs are not generally given, since the English translation can usually be derived from the relevant translation of the adjective headword. Usually the translation can be formed by adding '-ly' to the relevant adjective translation: e.g.

> fiel – faithful
> fielmente – faithfully

In cases where the basic translation for the adverb cannot be derived from those for the adjective, the adverb is likely to be listed as a headword in alphabetical order. This means it may not be immediately adjacent to the adjective headword: see 'actual' and 'actualmente' opposite.

Information about verbs

A major problem facing language learners is that the form of a verb will change according to the subject and/or the tense being used. A typical Spanish verb can take many different forms – too many to list in a dictionary entry.

negro, a ['neɣro, a] *adj* black; *(suerte)* awful ♦ *nm* black ♦ *nm/f* black man/woman

valiente [ba'ljente] *adj* brave, valiant ♦ *nm* hero

seguramente [seɣura'mente] *adv* surely; *(con certeza)* for sure, with certainty

actual [ak'twal] *adj* present(-day), current; **~idad** *nf* present; **~idades** *nfpl* *(noticias)* news *sg*; **en la ~idad** at present; *(hoy día)* nowadays
actualizar [aktwali'θar] *vt* to update, modernize
actualmente [aktwal'mente] *adv* at present; *(hoy día)* nowadays

Yet, although verbs are listed in your dictionary in their infinitive forms only, this does not mean that the dictionary is of limited value when it comes to handling the verb system of the Spanish language. On the contrary, it contains much valuable information.

First of all, your dictionary will help you with the meanings of unfamiliar verbs. If you came across the word 'decidió' in a text and looked it up in your dictionary you wouldn't find it. What you must do is assume that it is part of a verb and look for the infinitive form. Thus you will deduce that 'decidió' is a form of the verb 'decidir'. You now have the basic meaning of the word you are concerned with – something to do with English verb 'decide' – and this should be enough to help you understand the text you are reading.

It is usually an easy task to make the connection between the form of a verb and the infinitive. For example, 'decidieran', 'decidirá', 'decidimos' and 'decidido' are all recognisable as parts of the infinitive 'decidir'. However, sometimes it is less obvious – for example, 'pueda', 'podrán' and 'pude' are all parts of 'poder'. The only real solution to this problem is to learn the various forms of the main Spanish regular and irregular verbs.

And this is the second source of help offered by your dictionary as far as verbs are concerned. The verb tables on page xii of the Collins Pocket Dictionary provide a summary of some of the main forms of the main tenses of regular and irregular verbs. Consider the verb 'poder' below where the following information is given:

1 pudiendo	– Present Participle
2 puede	– Imperative
3 puedo, puedes, puede, pueden	– Present Tense forms
4 pude, pudiste, pudo, pudimos, pudisteis, pudieron	– Preterite forms
5 podré *etc*	– 1st Person Singular of the Future Tense
6 pueda, puedas, pueda, puedan	– Present Subjunctive forms
7 pudiera *etc*	– 1st Person Singular of the Imperfect Subjunctive

The regular '-ar', '-er', and '-ir' verbs – 'hablar', 'comer' and 'vivir' – are presented in greater detail. The main tenses and the different endings are given in full. This information can be transferred and applied to all verbs in the list. In addition, the main parts of the most common irregular verbs are listed in the body of the dictionary.

HABLAR

1 hablando
2 habla, hablad
3 hablo, hablas, habla, hablamos, habláis, hablan
4 hablé, hablaste, habló, hablamos, hablasteis, hablaron
5 hablaré, hablarás, hablará, hablaremos, hablaréis, hablarán
6 hable, hables, hable, hablemos, habléis, hablen
7 hablara, hablaras, hablara, habláramos, hablarais, hablaran
8 hablado
9 hablaba, hablabas, hablaba, hablábamos, hablabais, hablaban

In order to make maximum use of the information contained in these pages, a good working knowledge of the various rules affecting Spanish verbs is required. You will acquire this in the course of your Spanish studies and your Collins dictionary will serve as a useful reminder. If you happen to forget how to form the second person singular form of the Future Tense of 'poder' (i.e. how to translate 'you will be able to'), there will be no need to panic – your dictionary contains the information!

WORDGAME 11

PARTS OF SPEECH

In each sentence below a word has been shaded. Put a tick in the appropriate box to indicate the <u>part of speech</u> each time.

SENTENCE	Noun	Adj	Adv	Verb
1. Es estudiante de derecho.				
2. No hables tan alto.				
3. No tiene mucho dinero en su haber.				
4. Es un escrito muy largo.				
5. Vaya todo seguido.				
6. Es un dicho muy frecuente.				
7. Llegamos a casa muy tarde.				
8. Le gusta mucho andar por el campo.				
9. Lo hacemos por tu bien.				
10. A mi parecer es una buena película.				

WORDGAME 12

MEANING CHANGING WITH GENDER

Some Spanish nouns change meaning according to their gender, i.e. according to whether they are masculine or feminine. Look at the pairs of sentences below and fill in the blanks with either 'un', 'una', 'el' or 'la'. Use your dictionary to help.

1. No podía comprender _____ cólera de su padre.

   _____ cólera hace estragos en las regiones tropicales.

2. Perdí _____ pendiente en su casa.

   El coche no podía subir por _____ pendiente.

3. Los niños jugaban con _____ cometa.

   Dicen que en abril caerá _____ cometa.

4. Vimos _____ policía dentro de su coche.

   _____ policía ha descubierto una red de traficantes de droga.

5. Hay que cambiar _____ order de los números.

   En cuanto recibió _____ orden se puso en camino.

6. ¿Ha llegado _____ parte de la policía?

   _____ parte de atrás de la casa es muy sombría.

7. Pasó dos días en _____ coma profundo.

   Tienes que poner _____ coma ahí.

8. Los soldados están todavía en _____ frente.

   El pelo le cubría _____ frente.

WORDGAME 13

ADVERBS

Translate the following Spanish adverbs into English (generally by adding **-ly** to the adjective).

1. recientemente
2. lamentablemente
3. constantemente
4. mensualmente
5. pesadamente
6. inconscientemente
7. inmediatamente
8. ampliamente
9. tenazmente
10. brillantemente

WORDGAME 14

VERB TENSES

Use your dictionary to help you fill in the blanks in the table below. (Remember the important pages at the front of your dictionary.)

INFINITIVE	PRESENT SUBJUNCTIVE	PRETERITE	FUTURE
tener		yo	
hacer			yo
poder			yo
decir		yo	
agradecer	yo		
saber			yo
reír	yo		
querer		yo	
caber	yo		
ir	yo		
salir			yo
ser		yo	

WORDGAME 15

IRREGULAR VERBS

Use your dictionary to find the <u>first person</u> present indicative of these verbs.

INFINITIVE	PRESENT INDICATIVE
conocer	
saber	
estar	
ofrecer	
poder	
ser	
poner	
divertir	
traer	
decir	
preferir	
negar	
dar	
instruir	

WORDGAME 16

IDENTIFYING INFINITIVES

In the sentences below you will see various Spanish verbs shaded. Use your dictionary to help you find the **infinitive** form of each verb.

1. Cuando erá pequeño dormía en la misma habitación que mi hermano.

2. Mis amigos vienen conmigo.

3. No cupieron todos los libros en el estante.

4. ¿Es que no veías lo que pasaba?

5. El sábado saldremos todos juntos.

6. Ya hemos visto la casa.

7. ¿Quieres que lo ponga aquí?

8. Le dije que viniera a las ocho.

9. Nos han escrito tres cartas ya.

10. No sabían qué hacer.

11. Tuvimos que salir temprano.

12. En cuanto supe lo de su padre la llamé por teléfono.

13. ¿Por qué no trajiste el dinero?

14. Prefiero quedarme en casa.

15. Quiero que conozcas a mi padre.

MORE ABOUT MEANING

In this section we will consider some of the problems associated with using a bilingual dictionary.

Overdependence on your dictionary

That the dictionary is an invaluable tool for the language learner is beyond dispute. Nevertheless, it is possible to become overdependent on your dictionary, turning to it in an almost automatic fashion every time you come up against a new word or phrase in a Spanish text. Tackling an unfamiliar text in this way will turn reading in Spanish into an extremely tedious activity. It is possible to argue that if you stop to look up every new word you may actually be *hindering* your ability to read in Spanish – you are so concerned with the individual words that you pay no attention to the text as a whole and to the context which gives them meaning. It is therefore important to develop appropriate reading skills – using clues such as titles, headlines, illustrations, etc., understanding relations within a sentence, etc. to predict or infer what a text is about.

A detailed study of the development of reading skills is not within the scope of this supplement; we are concerned with knowing how to use a dictionary, which is only one of several important skills involved in reading. Nevertheless, it may be instructive to look at one example. You see the following text in a Spanish newspaper and are interested in working out what it is about.

Contextual clues here include the heading in large type, which indicates that this is some sort of announcement, and the names. The verb 'recibir' is very much like the English 'receive' and you will also know 'form' words such as 'una', 'y' and so forth from your general studies in Spanish, as well as essential vocabulary such as 'niña', 'hijos', 'nombre'. Given that this extract appeared in a newspaper,

> ### Natalicios
> La señora de García Rodríguez (don Alfonso), de soltera Laura Montes de la Torre, ha dado a luz una niña, cuarta de sus hijos, que recibirá el nombre de Beatriz y tendrá como padrinos a doña Mercedes Sánchez Serrano y don Felipe Gómez Morales.

you will probably have worked out by now that this is an announcement placed in the 'Personal Column'.

So you have used contextual and word-formation clues to get you to the point where you have understood that this notice has been placed in the personal column because something has happened to señora de García Rodríguez and that somebody is going to be given the name of 'Beatriz'. And you have reached this point *without* opening your dictionary once. Common sense and your knowledge of newspaper contents in this country will suggest that this must be an announcement of someone's birth or death. Thus 'dar a luz' ('to give birth') and 'padrinos' ('godparents') become the only words that you need to look up in order to confirm that this is indeed a birth announcement.

When learning Spanish we are helped considerably by the fact that many Spanish and English words look and sound alike and have exactly the same meaning. Such words are called 'COGNATES'. Many words which look similar in Spanish and English come from a common Latin root. Other words are the same or nearly the same in both languages because the Spanish language has borrowed a word from English or vice versa. The dictionary will often not be necessary where cognates are concerned – provided you know the English word that the Spanish word resembles!

Words with more than one meaning

The need to examine with care *all* the information contained in a dictionary entry must be stressed. This is particularly important with the many Spanish words which have more than one meaning. For example, the Spanish 'destino' can mean 'destiny' as well as 'destination'. How you translated the word would depend on the context in which you found it.

Similarly, if you were trying to translate a phrase such as 'sigo sin saber', you would have to look through the whole entry for 'seguir' to get the right translation. If you restricted your search to the first line of the entry and saw that the first meaning given is 'to follow', you might be tempted to assume that the phrase meant 'I follow without knowing'. But if you examined the entry closely you would see that 'seguir sin . . .' means 'to still do . . . or 'to still be . . .'. So 'sigo sin saber' means 'I still don't know'.

The same need for care applies when you are using the English-Spanish section of your dictionary to translate a word from English into Spanish. Watch out in particular for the lozenges indicating changes in parts of speech.

The noun 'sink' is 'fregadero', while the verb is 'hundir'. If you don't watch what you are doing, you could end up with ridiculous non-Spanish e.g. 'Dejó los platos en el hundir'!

Phrasal verbs

Another potential source of difficulty is English phrasal verbs. These consist of a common verb ('make', 'get', etc.) plus an adverb and/or a preposition to give English expressions such as 'to make out', 'to get on', etc. Entries for such verbs tend to be fairly full, so close examination of the contents is required. Note how these verbs appear in colour within the entry.

sink [sɪŋk] (*pt* **sank,** *pp* **sunk**) *n* fregadero
♦ *vt* (*ship*) hundir, echar a pique; (*foundations*) excavar; ♦ *vi* (*gen*) hundirse; **to ~ sth into** hundir algo en; **~ in** *vi* (*fig*) penetrar, calar

make [meɪk] (*pt, pp* **made**) *vt* hacer; (*manufacture*) fabricar; (*mistake*) cometer; (*speech*) pronunciar; (*cause to be*): **to ~ sb sad** poner triste a alguien; (*force*): **to ~ sb do sth** obligar a alguien a hacer algo; (*earn*) ganar; (*equal*): **2 and 2 ~ 4** 2 y 2 son 4 ♦ *n* marca; **to ~ the bed** hacer la cama; **to ~ a fool of sb** poner a alguien en ridículo; **to ~ a profit/loss** obtener ganancias/sufrir pérdidas; **to ~ it** (*arrive*) llegar; (*achieve sth*) tener éxito; **what time do you ~ it?** ¿qué hora tienes?; **to ~ do with** contentarse con; **~ for** *vt fus* (*place*) dirigirse a; **~ out** *vt* (*decipher*) descifrar; (*understand*) entender; (*see*) distinguir; (*cheque*) extender; **~ up** *vt* (*invent*) inventar; (*prepare*) hacer; (*constitute*) constituir ♦ *vi* reconciliarse;

Falsos amigos

We noted above that many Spanish and English words have similar forms *and* meanings. There are, however, many Spanish words which *look* like English words but have a completely *different* meaning. For example, 'la carpeta' means 'the folder'; 'sensible' means 'sensitive'. This can easily lead to serious mistranslations.

Sometimes the meaning of the Spanish word is quite close to the English. For example, 'la moneda' means 'coin' rather than 'money'; 'simpático' means 'nice' rather than 'sympathetic'. But some Spanish words which look similar to English words have two meanings, one the same as the English, the other completely different! 'El plato' can mean 'course' (in a meal) as well as 'plate'; 'la cámara' can mean 'camera', but also 'chamber'.

Such words are often referred to as FALSOS AMIGOS ('false friends'). You will have to look at the context in which they appear to arrive at the correct meaning. If they seem to fit in with the sense of the passage as a whole, you will probably not need to look them up. If they don't make sense, however, you may well be dealing with 'falsos amigos'.

WORDGAME 17

WORDS IN CONTEXT

Study the sentences below. Translations of the shaded words are given at the bottom. Match the number of the sentence and the letter of the translation correctly each time.

1. Tendremos que atarlo con una cuerda.
2. La cuerda del reloj se ha roto.
3. Iremos al cine para entretener a los niños.
4. No me entretengas, que llegaré tarde.
5. Le dieron una patada en la espinilla.
6. Tenía una espinilla enorme en la nariz.
7. Siempre le da mucho sueño después de comer.
8. Anoche me desperté sobresaltada por un mal sueño.
9. El niño tocaba todo lo que veía.
10. Su padre tocaba muy bien la guitarra.
11. Tuvo un acceso de tos.
12. Todas las vías de acceso estaban cerradas.
13. Me gustaría estudiar la carrera de Derecho.
14. Todos querían participar en la carrera.
15. He quebrado el plato sin darme cuenta.
16. No sabían que esa empresa había quebrado.

a. touched   e. fit   i. rope   m. gone bankrupt
b. shin(bone)   f. course   j. hold up   n. played
c. entertain   g. sleepiness k. entry   o. dream
d. spring   h. blackhead l. race   p. broken

WORDGAME 18

WORDS WITH MORE THAN ONE MEANING

Look at the advertisements below. The words which are shaded can have more than one meaning. Use your dictionary to help you work out the correct translation in the context.

1

El Pescador
RESTAURANTE

Mariscos de viveros propios
Teléfono 406 12 80 – MADRID 6

P FÁCIL
APARCAMIENTO

2

Restaurante
LOS CEREZOS

ALTA COCINA REGIONAL
Para amantes de lo tradicional
RESERVAS: 574 34 11/12

3

INTERLANGUE
ANUNCIA CURSO MASTER DE
INGLÉS JURÍDICO PARA
PROFESIONALES DEL DERECHO
Inicio: 20 de octubre

4

¡¡¡BUTACAS PIEL A MEDIDA!!!

APROVECHE GRANDES REBAJAS EN OCTUBRE

¡En fábrica, más calidad y menor precio!

Horario continuado de 9,30 a 20,30 –
incluso sábados

5

GRANDES ALMACENES
"EL CONDOR"
IMPORTANTES REBAJAS DE FIN
DE TEMPORADA

6

Guía   **TELEVISION**
JUEVES, 19
19.00. – Partido adelantado de la
JORNADA DE LIGA de PRIMERA DIVISION:
Atlético de Madrid – Barcelona (TV-2)

7

Bar-restaurante **"La Ballena"**

platos combinados desde 300 ptas.
helados, postres nuestra especialidad

8

ULTIMAS VIVIENDAS
de 2 y 3 dormitorios con
plaza de garaje opcional
Lunes a Viernes mañanas de 11 a 13,30.
Tardes de 16,30 a 19,30.

9

Calle de
ISABEL LA CATOLICA
N.ºs 50 - 56

PISOS EXTERIORES
DE 80 m^2

FINANCIACION A 11 AÑOS
13 Y 13,5% CON LA CAJA DE BARCELONA

WORDGAME 19

FALSE FRIENDS

Look at the advertisements below. The words which are shaded resemble English words but have different meanings here. Find a correct translation for each word in the context.

1
LA MAYOR COLECCION DE
**ALFOMBRAS
PERSAS Y
ORIENTALES**
*¡¡¡VENTA DE LIQUIDACION
POR CAMBIO DE DOMICILIO!!!*

2
Teatro Nacional:
**"El Alcalde de Zalamea"
Localidades en venta a partir de mañana**

3
PRODUCTOS BENGOLEA
**¡NO RECURRA A
LA COMPETENCIA!**
Visite nuestro local en Castellana 500

4
OFERTA ESPECIAL
cubiertos de acero inoxidable de
primerísima calidad en planta baja

HAVE FUN WITH YOUR DICTIONARY

Here are some word games for you to try. You will find your dictionary helpful as you attempt the activities.

WORDGAME 20

CODED WORDS

In the boxes below the letters of eight Spanish words have been replaced by numbers. A number represents the same letter each time (though an accent may be required sometimes).

Try to crack the code and find the eight words. If you need help, use your dictionary.

Here is a clue: all the words you are looking for have something to do with TRANSPORT.

1. | C¹ | A² | M³ | 4 | 5 | 6 |

2. | 2 | 7 | 8 | 5 | 9 | 7 | 10 |

3. | 1 | 5 | 1 | 11 | 12 |

4. | 9 | 4 | 1 | 4 | 1 | 13 | 12 | 8 | 2 |

5. | 8 | 14 | 12 | 6 |

6. | 11 | 12 | 13 | 4 | 1 | 5 | 15 | 8 | 12 | 14 | 5 |

7. | 2 | 3 | 9 | 7 | 13 | 2 | 6 | 1 | 4 | 2 |

8. | 3 | 5 | 8 | 5 |

WORDGAME 21

BEHEADED WORDS

If you 'behead' certain Spanish words, i.e. take away their first letter, you are left with another Spanish word. For example, if you behead **'aplomo'** (= 'self-assurance'), you get **'plomo'** (= 'lead'), and **'bala'** (= 'bullet') gives **'ala'** (= 'wing').

The following words have their heads chopped off, i.e. the first letter has been removed. Use your dictionary to help you form a new Spanish word by adding one letter to the start of each word below. You will find that some of them can have more than one answer. Write down the new Spanish word and its meaning.

1. bajo (= low)
2. oler (= to smell)
3. año (= year)
4. oro (= gold)
5. reparar (= to repair)
6. ama (= owner)
7. rendido (= worn-out)
8. cuerdo (= sane)
9. ave (= bird)
10. batir (= to beat)
11. resto (= rest)
12. precio (= price)
13. cera (= wax)
14. hora (= hour)
15. pinar (= pine forest)

WORDGAME 22

PALABRAS CRUZADAS

Complete this crossword by looking up the words listed below in the English-Spanish section of your dictionary. Remember to read through the entry carefully to find the word that will fit.

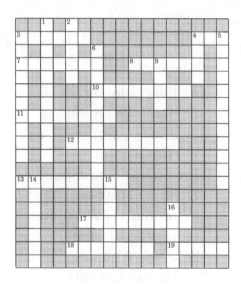

ACROSS
3. to bark
4. wing
7. lie
8. above
10. to work out
11. to lighten
12. to need
13. usual
17. cornet
18. to stink
19. radius

DOWN
1. to identify
2. to go out
3. regrettable
4. to love
5. streamlined
6. heating
9. expensive
14. to oblige
15. tricks
16. now

WORDGAME 23

There are twelve Spanish words hidden in the grid below. Each word is made up of five letters but has been split into two parts.

Find the Spanish words. Each group of letters can only be used once.

Use your dictionary to help you.

bla	lir	bu	ma	que	go
gor	ar	ver	vi	asi	jor
cal	me	ha	jo	lar	so
bo	jía	lo	vol	sa	eno

WORDGAME 24

Here is a list of Spanish words for things you will find in the kitchen. Unfortunately, they have all been jumbled up. Try to work out what each word is and put the word in the boxes on the right. You will see that there are seven shaded boxes below. With the seven letters in the shaded boxes make up <u>another</u> Spanish word for an object you can find in the kitchen.

1. azta   ¿Quieres una _____ de café?

2. eanevr   ¡Mete la mantequilla en la _____!

3. asme   ¡La comida está en la _____!

4. zoac   Su madre está calentando la leche en el _____

5. roegcanldo   ¡No saques el helado del _____ todavía!

6. uclclohi   ¿Dónde has puesto el _____ del queso?

7. rgoif   ¿Puedes cerrar ya el _____ del agua caliente?

The word you are looking for is:

WORDGAME 25

PALABRAS CRUZADAS

Take the four letters given each time and put them in the four empty boxes in the centre of each grid. Arrange them in such a way that you form four six-letter words. Use your dictionary to check the words.

| T | P | O | A |

	1 T	2 P	
	R	A	
3 C	R			E	R
4 R	E			S	O
		O	S	
T R I E		S	O		C N I T

	1 V	2 A	
	A	B	
3 A	R			O	S
4 Q	U			A	R
	A	O	
	R	S	

	1 P	2 G	
	I	R	
3 C	E			Z	A
4 P	A			O	S
	H	A	
	O	R	

ANSWERS

WORDGAME 1

1	arreglarme	6	ballena
2	polvo	7	nevada
3	revelar	8	capítulo
4	paseos	9	pinchazo
5	ayudar	10	candado

WORDGAME 2

1	cuerno	7	entretener
2	echar	8	antiguo
3	recordar	9	timbre
4	actuación	10	tela
5	habla	11	terminación
6	entero	12	parte

WORDGAME 3

bata + zapatillas
nido + urraca
cuero + bolso
campanario + veleta
estudiante + curso
libro + estante
pasarela + barco
aleta + tiburón

WORDGAME 4

1	modales	6	derrotar
2	decepción	7	interminable
3	superar	8	triunfo
4	fuego	9	agradar
5	amor	10	avión

WORDGAME 5

2	hacienda
5	abalorios
6	perejil

WORDGAME 6

1	bonito	6	adelgazar
2	cerrar	7	tranquilo
3	pesado	8	quitar
4	pobreza	9	nada
5	entrar	10	claro

WORDGAME 7

agua, ciudad, alrededor,
muchacho, viento, niño,
volver, calle, zigzag,
genio, guarda, choque,
enviar, caballo, abogado,
corregir, comienzo, ellos,
jersey, igual

WORDGAME 9

1	estudios	7	atrae
2	estudiar	8	atracción
3	pertenecientes	9	término
4	pertenencias	10	terminar
5	empleado	11	falso
6	emplear	12	falsificar

WORDGAME 11

1 n 2 adv 3 n 4 n 5 adv
6 n 7 adv 8 v 9 n 10 n

WORDGAME 12

1	la; El	5	el; la
2	el; la	6	el; La
3	una; un	7	un; una
4	un; La	8	el; la

WORDGAME 14

tuve	ría
haré	quise
podré	quepa
dije	vaya
agradezca	saldré
sabré	fui

WORDGAME 15

conozco	divierto
sé	traigo
estoy	digo
ofrezco	prefiero
puedo	niego
soy	doy
pongo	instruyo

WORDGAME 16

1	dormir	9	escribir
2	venir	10	saber
3	caber	11	tener
4	ver	12	saber
5	salir	13	traer
6	ver	14	preferir
7	poner	15	conocer
8	venir		

WORDGAME 17

1	i	5	b	9	a	13	f
2	d	6	h	10	n	14	l
3	c	7	g	11	e	15	p
4	j	8	o	12	k	16	m

WORDGAME 18

1 fish farm
2 cuisine
3 law
4 leather
5 significant
6 league
7 set main course
8 space
9 savings bank

WORDGAME 19

1 clearance sale;
  home (Here: address)
2 tickets
3 competition
4 cutlery
5 retirement
6 small hotel; rooms
7 guest house
8 premises
9 address

WORDGAME 20

1	camión	5	tren
2	autobús	6	helicóptero
3	coche	7	ambulancia
4	bicicleta	8	moto

WORDGAME 21

1	abajo	7	prendido
2	doler; moler;	8	acuerdo
	soler	9	nave
3	baño; paño;	10	abatir
	daño; caño	11	presto
4	coro; loro;	12	aprecio
	moro; poro	13	acera
5	preparar	14	ahora
6	cama; dama;	15	opinar
	fama; gama;		
	mama; rama		

WORDGAME 22

ACROSS:
3 ladrar
4 ala
7 mentira
8 encima
10 elaborar
11 aligerar
12 necesitar
13 corriente
17 cucurucho
18 apestar
19 radio

DOWN:
1 identificar
2 salir
3 lamentable
4 amar
5 aerodinámico
6 calefacción
9 caro
14 obligar
15 trucos
16 ahora

WORDGAME 23

enojo	verbo
queso	calma
salir	asilo
volar	largo
vigor	mejor
bujía	habla

WORDGAME 24

1	taza	5	congelador
2	nevera	6	cuchillo
3	mesa	7	grifo
4	cazo		

Missing word – ARMARIO

WORDGAME 25

1)	1	trapos	2	patoso
	3	cráter	4	reposo
2)	1	variar	2	abetos
	3	arreos	4	quitar
3)	1	pincho	2	gritar
	3	ceniza	4	pactos

ENGLISH - SPANISH
INGLÉS - ESPAÑOL

A, a

A [eɪ] n (MUS) la m

a [ə] indef art (before vowel or silent h: an)
1 un(a); ~ **book** un libro; **an apple** una manzana; **she's ~ doctor** (ella) es médica
2 (instead of the number "one") un(a); ~ **year ago** hace un año; ~ **hundred/ thousand** etc **pounds** cien/mil etc libras
3 (in expressing ratios, prices etc): **3 ~ day/week** 3 al día/a la semana; **10 km an hour** 10 km por hora; **£5 ~ person** £5 por persona; **30p ~ kilo** 30p el kilo

A.A. n abbr (= Automobile Association: BRIT) ≈ RACE m (SP); (= Alcoholics Anonymous) Alcohólicos Anónimos

A.A.A. (US) n abbr (= American Automobile Association) ≈ RACE m (SP)

aback [əˈbæk] adv: **to be taken ~** quedar desconcertado

abandon [əˈbændən] vt abandonar; (give up) renunciar a

abate [əˈbeɪt] vi (storm) amainar; (anger) aplacarse; (terror) disminuir

abattoir [ˈæbətwɑː*] (BRIT) n matadero

abbey [ˈæbɪ] n abadía

abbot [ˈæbət] n abad m

abbreviation [əˈbriːvɪˈeɪʃən] n abreviatura

abdicate [ˈæbdɪkeɪt] vt renunciar a ♦ vi abdicar

abdomen [ˈæbdəmən] n abdomen m

abduct [æbˈdʌkt] vt raptar, secuestrar

abeyance [əˈbeɪəns] n: **in ~** (law) en desuso; (matter) en suspenso

abide [əˈbaɪd] vt: **I can't ~ it/him** no lo/le puedo ver; ~ **by** vt fus atenerse a

ability [əˈbɪlɪtɪ] n habilidad f, capacidad f; (talent) talento

abject [ˈæbdʒekt] adj (poverty) miserable; (apology) rastrero

ablaze [əˈbleɪz] adj en llamas, ardiendo

able [ˈeɪbl] adj capaz; (skilled) hábil; **to be ~ to do sth** poder hacer algo; ~**-bodied** adj sano; **ably** adv hábilmente

abnormal [æbˈnɔːməl] adj anormal

aboard [əˈbɔːd] adv a bordo ♦ prep a bordo de

abode [əˈbəud] n: **of no fixed ~** sin domicilio fijo

abolish [əˈbɔlɪʃ] vt suprimir, abolir

aborigine [æbəˈrɪdʒɪnɪ] n aborigen m/f

abort [əˈbɔːt] vt, vi abortar; ~**ion** [əˈbɔːʃən] n aborto; **to have an ~ion** abortar, hacerse abortar; ~**ive** adj malogrado

about [əˈbaut] adv 1 (approximately) más o menos, aproximadamente; ~ **a hundred/thousand** etc unos(unas) cien/ mil etc; **it takes ~ 10 hours** se tarda unas or más o menos 10 horas; **at ~ 2 o'clock** sobre las dos; **I've just ~ finished** casi he terminado
2 (referring to place) por todas partes; **to leave things lying ~** dejar las cosas (tiradas) por ahí; **to run ~** correr por todas partes; **to walk ~** pasearse, ir y venir
3: **to be ~ to do sth** estar a punto de hacer algo
♦ prep 1 (relating to) de, sobre, acerca de; **a book ~ London** un libro sobre or acerca de Londres; **what is it ~?** ¿de qué se trata?, ¿qué pasa?; **we talked ~ it** hablamos de eso or ello; **what** or **how ~ doing this?** ¿qué tal si hacemos esto?
2 (referring to place) por; **to walk ~ the town** caminar por la ciudad

above [ə'bʌv] *adv* encima, por encima, arriba ♦ *prep* más de; (*greater than: in number*) más de; (*: in rank*) superior a; **mentioned ~** susodicho; **~ all** sobre todo; **~ board** *adj* legítimo

abrasive [ə'breɪzɪv] *adj* abrasivo; (*manner*) brusco

abreast [ə'brest] *adv* de frente; **to keep ~ of** (*fig*) mantenerse al corriente de

abroad [ə'brɔːd] *adv* (*to be*) en el extranjero; (*to go*) al extranjero

abrupt [ə'brʌpt] *adj* (*sudden*) brusco; (*curt*) áspero

abruptly [ə'brʌptlɪ] *adv* (*leave*) repentinamente; (*speak*) bruscamente

abscess ['æbsɪs] *n* absceso

abscond [əb'skɔnd] *vi* (*thief*): **to ~ with** fugarse con; (*prisoner*): **to ~ (from)** escaparse (de)

absence ['æbsəns] *n* ausencia

absent ['æbsənt] *adj* ausente; **~ee** [-'tiː] *n* ausente *m/f*; **~-minded** *adj* distraído

absolute ['æbsəluːt] *adj* absoluto; **~ly** [-'luːtlɪ] *adv* (*totally*) totalmente; (*certainly!*) ¡por supuesto (que sí)!

absolve [əb'zɔlv] *vt*: **to ~ sb (from)** absolver a alguien (de)

absorb [əb'zɔːb] *vt* absorber; **to be ~ed in a book** estar absorto en un libro; **~ent cotton** (*US*) *n* algodón *m* hidrófilo; **~ing** *adj* absorbente

absorption [əb'zɔːpʃən] *n* absorción *f*

abstain [əb'steɪn] *vi*: **to ~ (from)** abstenerse (de)

abstinence ['æbstɪnəns] *n* abstinencia

abstract ['æbstrækt] *adj* abstracto

absurd [əb'sɜːd] *adj* absurdo

abundance [ə'bʌndəns] *n* abundancia

abuse [*n* ə'bjuːs, *vb* ə'bjuːz] *n* (*insults*) insultos *mpl*, injurias *fpl*; (*ill-treatment*) malos tratos *mpl*; (*misuse*) abuso ♦ *vt* insultar; maltratar; abusar de; **abusive** *adj* ofensivo

abysmal [ə'bɪzməl] *adj* pésimo; (*failure*) garrafal; (*ignorance*) supino

abyss [ə'bɪs] *n* abismo

AC *abbr* (= *alternating current*) corriente *f* alterna

academic [ækə'demɪk] *adj* académico, universitario; (*pej: issue*) puramente teórico ♦ *n* estudioso/a; profesor(a) *m/f* universitario/a

academy [ə'kædəmɪ] *n* (*learned body*) academia; (*school*) instituto, colegio; **~ of music** conservatorio

accelerate [æk'seləreɪt] *vt, vi* acelerar; **accelerator** (*BRIT*) *n* acelerador *m*

accent ['æksənt] *n* acento; (*fig*) énfasis *m*

accept [ək'sept] *vt* aceptar; (*responsibility, blame*) admitir; **~able** *adj* aceptable; **~ance** *n* aceptación *f*

access ['ækses] *n* acceso; **to have ~ to** tener libre acceso a; **~ible** [-'sesəbl] *adj* (*place, person*) accesible; (*knowledge etc*) asequible

accessory [æk'sesərɪ] *n* accesorio; (*LAW*): **~ to** cómplice de

accident ['æksɪdənt] *n* accidente *m*; (*chance event*) casualidad *f*; **by ~** (*unintentionally*) sin querer; (*by chance*) por casualidad; **~al** [-'dentl] *adj* accidental, fortuito; **~ally** [-'dentəlɪ] *adv* sin querer; por casualidad; **~ insurance** *n* seguro contra accidentes; **~-prone** *adj* propenso a los accidentes

acclaim [ə'kleɪm] *vt* aclamar, aplaudir ♦ *n* aclamación *f*, aplausos *mpl*

acclimatize [ə'klaɪmətaɪz] (*US* **acclimate**) *vt*: **to become ~d** aclimatarse

accommodate [ə'kɔmədeɪt] *vt* (*subj: person*) alojar, hospedar; (*: car, hotel etc*) tener cabida para; (*oblige, help*) complacer; **accommodating** *adj* servicial, complaciente

accommodation [əkɔmə'deɪʃən] *n* (*US* **accommodations** *npl*) alojamiento

accompany [ə'kʌmpənɪ] *vt* acompañar

accomplice [ə'kʌmplɪs] *n* cómplice *m/f*

accomplish [ə'kʌmplɪʃ] *vt* (*finish*) concluir; (*achieve*) lograr; **~ed** *adj* experto, hábil; **~ment** *n* (*skill: gen pl*) talento; (*completion*) realización *f*

accord [ə'kɔːd] *n* acuerdo ♦ *vt* conceder;

of his own ~ espontáneamente; **~ance** *n*: **in ~ance with** de acuerdo con; **~ing**: **~ing to** *prep* según; (*in accordance with*) conforme a; **~ingly** *adv* (*appropriately*) de acuerdo con esto; (*as a result*) en consecuencia

accordion [əˈkɔːdɪən] *n* acordeón *m*

accost [əˈkɔst] *vt* abordar, dirigirse a

account [əˈkaunt] *n* (*COMM*) cuenta; (*report*) informe *m*; **~s** *npl* (*COMM*) cuentas *fpl*; **of no ~** de ninguna importancia; **on ~** a cuenta; **on no ~** bajo ningún concepto; **on ~ of** a causa de, por motivo de; **to take into ~, take ~ of** tener en cuenta; **~ for** *vt fus* (*explain*) explicar; (*represent*) representar; **~able** *adj*: **~able (to)** responsable (ante); **~ancy** *n* contabilidad *f*; **~ant** *n* contable *m/f*, contador(a) *m/f*; **~ number** *n* (*at bank etc*) número de cuenta

accrued interest [əˈkruːd-] *n* interés *m* acumulado

accumulate [əˈkjuːmjuleɪt] *vt* acumular ♦ *vi* acumularse

accuracy [ˈækjurəsɪ] *n* (*of total*) exactitud *f*; (*of description etc*) precisión *f*

accurate [ˈækjurɪt] *adj* (*total*) exacto; (*description*) preciso; (*person*) cuidadoso; (*device*) de precisión; **~ly** *adv* con precisión

accusation [ækjuˈzeɪʃən] *n* acusación *f*

accuse [əˈkjuːz] *vt*: **to ~ sb (of sth)** acusar a uno (de algo); **~d** *n* (*LAW*) acusado/a

accustom [əˈkʌstəm] *vt* acostumbrar; **~ed** *adj*: **~ed to** acostumbrado a

ace [eɪs] *n* as *m*

ache [eɪk] *n* dolor *m* ♦ *vi* doler; **my head ~s** me duele la cabeza

achieve [əˈtʃiːv] *vt* (*aim, result*) alcanzar; (*success*) lograr, conseguir; **~ment** *n* (*completion*) realización *f*; (*success*) éxito

acid [ˈæsɪd] *adj* ácido; (*taste*) agrio ♦ *n* (*CHEM, inf: LSD*) ácido; **~ rain** *n* lluvia ácida

acknowledge [əkˈnɒlɪdʒ] *vt* (*letter: also*: **~ receipt of**) acusar recibo de; (*fact, situation, person*) reconocer; **~ment** *n*

acuse *m* de recibo

acne [ˈæknɪ] *n* acné *m*

acorn [ˈeɪkɔːn] *n* bellota

acoustic [əˈkuːstɪk] *adj* acústico; **~s** *n, npl* acústica *sg*

acquaint [əˈkweɪnt] *vt*: **to ~ sb with sth** (*inform*) poner a uno al corriente de algo; **to be ~ed with** conocer; **~ance** *n* (*person*) conocido/a; (*with person, subject*) conocimiento

acquire [əˈkwaɪə*] *vt* adquirir; **acquisition** [ækwɪˈzɪʃən] *n* adquisición *f*

acquit [əˈkwɪt] *vt* absolver, exculpar; **to ~ o.s. well** salir con éxito

acre [ˈeɪkə*] *n* acre *m*

acrid [ˈækrɪd] *adj* acre

acrobat [ˈækrəbæt] *n* acróbata *m/f*

across [əˈkrɒs] *prep* (*on the other side of*) al otro lado de, del otro lado de; (*crosswise*) a través de ♦ *adv* de un lado a otro, de una parte a otra; a través, al través; (*measurement*): **the road is 10m ~** la carretera tiene 10m de ancho; **to run/ swim ~** atravesar corriendo/nadando; **~ from** enfrente de

acrylic [əˈkrɪlɪk] *adj* acrílico ♦ *n* acrílica

act [ækt] *n* acto, acción *f*; (*of play*) acto; (*in music hall etc*) número; (*LAW*) decreto, ley *f* ♦ *vi* (*behave*) comportarse; (*have effect*: *drug, chemical*) hacer efecto; (*THEATRE*) actuar; (*pretend*) fingir; (*take action*) obrar ♦ *vt* (*part*) hacer el papel de; **in the ~ of**: **to catch sb in the ~ of ...** pillar a uno en el momento en que ...; **to ~ as** actuar *or* hacer de; **~ing** *adj* suplente ♦ *n* (*activity*) actuación *f*; (*profession*) profesión *f* de actor

action [ˈækʃən] *n* acción *f*, acto; (*MIL*) acción *f*, batalla; (*LAW*) proceso, demanda; **out of ~** (*person*) fuera de combate; (*thing*) estropeado; **to take ~** tomar medidas; **~ replay** *n* (*TV*) repetición *f*

activate [ˈæktɪveɪt] *vt* activar

active [ˈæktɪv] *adj* activo, enérgico; (*volcano*) en actividad; **~ly** *adv* (*participate*) activamente; (*discourage,* *dislike*) enérgicamente; **activity** [-'tɪvɪtɪ] *n* actividad *f*; **activity holiday** *n* *vacaciones fpl con actividades organizadas*

actor ['æktə*] *n* actor *m*

actress ['æktrɪs] *n* actriz *f*

actual ['æktjuəl] *adj* verdadero, real; (*emphatic use*) propiamente dicho; **~ly** *adv* realmente, en realidad; (*even*) incluso

acumen ['ækjumən] *n* perspicacia

acute [ə'kjuːt] *adj* agudo

ad [æd] *n abbr* = **advertisement**

A.D. *adv abbr* (= *anno Domini*) A.C.

adamant ['ædəmənt] *adj* firme, inflexible

adapt [ə'dæpt] *vt* adaptar ♦ *vi*: **to ~ (to)** adaptarse (a), ajustarse (a); **~able** *adj* adaptable; **~er, ~or** *n* (*ELEC*) adaptador *m*

add [æd] *vt* añadir, agregar; (*figures: also*: ~ *up*) sumar ♦ *vi*: **to ~ to** (*increase*) aumentar, acrecentar; **it doesn't ~ up** (*fig*) no tiene sentido

adder ['ædə*] *n* víbora

addict ['ædɪkt] *n* adicto/a; (*enthusiast*) entusiasta *m/f*; **~ed** [ə'dɪktɪd] *adj*: **to be ~ed to** ser adicto a; (*football etc*) ser fanático de; **~ion** [ə'dɪkʃən] *n* (*to drugs etc*) adicción *f*; **~ive** [ə'dɪktɪv] *adj* que causa adicción

addition [ə'dɪʃən] *n* (*adding up*) adición *f*; (*thing added*) añadidura, añadido; **in ~** además, por añadidura; **in ~ to** además de; **~al** *adj* adicional

additive ['ædɪtɪv] *n* aditivo

address [ə'dres] *n* dirección *f*, señas *fpl*; (*speech*) discurso ♦ *vt* (*letter*) dirigir; (*speak to*) dirigirse a, dirigir la palabra a; (*problem*) tratar

adept ['ædept] *adj*: **~ at** experto *or* hábil en

adequate ['ædɪkwɪt] *adj* (*satisfactory*) adecuado; (*enough*) suficiente

adhere [əd'hɪə*] *vi*: **to ~ to** (*stick to*) pegarse a; (*fig: abide by*) observar; (: *belief etc*) ser partidario de

adhesive [əd'hiːzɪv] *n* adhesivo; **~ tape** *n* (*BRIT*) cinta adhesiva; (*US: MED*) esparadrapo

ad hoc [æd'hɔk] *adj* ad hoc

adjacent [ə'dʒeɪsənt] *adj*: **~ to** contiguo a, inmediato a

adjective ['ædʒektɪv] *n* adjetivo

adjoining [ə'dʒɔɪnɪŋ] *adj* contiguo, vecino

adjourn [ə'dʒəːn] *vt* aplazar ♦ *vi* suspender

adjudicate [ə'dʒuːdɪkeɪt] *vi* sentenciar

adjust [ə'dʒʌst] *vt* (*change*) modificar; (*clothing*) arreglar; (*machine*) ajustar ♦ *vi*: **to ~ (to)** adaptarse (a); **~able** *adj* ajustable; **~ment** *n* adaptación *f*; (*to machine, prices*) ajuste *m*

ad-lib [æd'lɪb] *vt, vi* improvisar; **ad lib** *adv* de forma improvisada

administer [əd'mɪnɪstə*] *vt* administrar; **administration** [-'treɪʃən] *n* (*management*) administración *f*; (*government*) gobierno; **administrative** [-trətɪv] *adj* administrativo

admiral ['ædmərəl] *n* almirante *m*; **A~ty** (*BRIT*) *n* Ministerio de Marina, Almirantazgo

admiration [ædmə'reɪʃən] *n* admiración *f*

admire [əd'maɪə*] *vt* admirar; **~r** *n* (*fan*) admirador(a) *m/f*

admission [əd'mɪʃən] *n* (*to university, club*) ingreso; (*entry fee*) entrada; (*confession*) confesión *f*

admit [əd'mɪt] *vt* (*confess*) confesar; (*permit to enter*) dejar entrar, dar entrada a; (*to club, organization*) admitir; (*accept: defeat*) reconocer; **to be ~ted to hospital** ingresar en el hospital; **~ to** *vt fus* confesarse culpable de; **~tance** *n* entrada; **~tedly** *adv* es cierto *or* verdad que

admonish [əd'mɔnɪʃ] *vt* amonestar

ad nauseam [æd'nɔːsɪæm] *adv* hasta el cansancio

ado [ə'duː] *n*: **without (any) more ~** sin más (ni más)

adolescent [ædəu'lesnt] *adj, n* adolescente *m/f*

adopt [ə'dɔpt] *vt* adoptar; **~ed** *adj* adoptivo; **~ion** [ə'dɔpʃən] *n* adopción *f*

adore [əˈdɔːʳ] vt adorar
Adriatic [eɪdrɪˈætɪk] n: **the ~ (Sea)** el (Mar) Adriático
adrift [əˈdrɪft] adv a la deriva
adult [ˈædʌlt] n adulto/a ♦ adj (grown-up) adulto; (for adults) para adultos
adultery [əˈdʌltərɪ] n adulterio
advance [ədˈvɑːns] n (progress) adelanto, progreso; (money) anticipo, préstamo; (MIL) avance m ♦ adj: **~ booking** venta anticipada; **~ notice, ~ warning** previo aviso ♦ vt (money) anticipar; (theory, idea) proponer (para la discusión) ♦ vi avanzar, adelantarse; **to make ~s (to sb)** hacer proposiciones (a alguien); **in ~** por adelantado; **~d** adj avanzado; (SCOL: studies) adelantado
advantage [ədˈvɑːntɪdʒ] n (also TENNIS) ventaja; **to take ~ of** (person) aprovecharse de; (opportunity) aprovechar
Advent [ˈædvənt] n (REL) Adviento
adventure [ədˈventʃəʳ] n aventura; **adventurous** [-tʃərəs] adj atrevido, aventurero
adverb [ˈædvəːb] n adverbio
adverse [ˈædvəːs] adj adverso, contrario
adversity [ədˈvəːsɪtɪ] n infortunio
advert [ˈædvəːt] (BRIT) n abbr = advertisement
advertise [ˈædvətaɪz] vi (in newspaper etc) anunciar, hacer publicidad; **to ~ for** (staff, accommodation etc) buscar por medio de anuncios ♦ vt anunciar; **~ment** [ədˈvəːtɪsmənt] n (COMM) anuncio; **~r** n anunciante m/f; **advertising** n publicidad f, anuncios mpl; (industry) industria publicitaria
advice [ədˈvaɪs] n consejo, consejos mpl; (notification) aviso; **a piece of ~** un consejo; **to take legal ~** consultar con un abogado
advisable [ədˈvaɪzəbl] adj aconsejable, conveniente
advise [ədˈvaɪz] vt aconsejar; (inform): **to ~ sb of sth** informar a uno de algo; **to ~ sb against sth/doing sth** desaconsejar algo a uno/aconsejar a uno que no haga algo;

~dly [ədˈvaɪzɪdlɪ] adv (deliberately) deliberadamente; **~r** n = advisor;
advisor n consejero/a; (consultant) asesor(a) m/f; **advisory** adj consultivo
advocate [ˈædvəkeɪt] vt abogar por ♦ n [-kɪt] (lawyer) abogado/a; (supporter): **~ of** defensor(a) m/f de
Aegean [iːˈdʒiːən] n: **the ~ (Sea)** el (Mar) Egeo
aerial [ˈɛərɪəl] n antena ♦ adj aéreo
aerobics [ɛəˈrəubɪks] n aerobic m
aeroplane [ˈɛərəpleɪn] (BRIT) n avión m
aerosol [ˈɛərəsɔl] n aerosol m
aesthetic [iːsˈθetɪk] adj estético
afar [əˈfɑːʳ] adv: **from ~** desde lejos
affair [əˈfɛəʳ] n asunto; (also: **love ~**) aventura (amorosa)
affect [əˈfekt] vt (influence) afectar, influir en; (afflict, concern) afectar; (move) conmover; **~ed** adj afectado
affection [əˈfekʃən] n afecto, cariño; **~ate** adj afectuoso, cariñoso
affinity [əˈfɪnɪtɪ] n (bond, rapport): **to feel an ~ with** sentirse identificado con; (resemblance) afinidad f
afflict [əˈflɪkt] vt afligir
affluence [ˈæfluəns] n opulencia, riqueza
affluent [ˈæfluənt] adj (wealthy) acomodado; **the ~ society** la sociedad opulenta
afford [əˈfɔːd] vt (provide) proporcionar; **can we ~ (to buy) it?** ¿tenemos bastante dinero para comprarlo?
Afghanistan [æfˈgænɪstæn] n Afganistán m
afield [əˈfiːld] adv: **far ~** muy lejos
afloat [əˈfləut] adv (floating) a flote
afoot [əˈfut] adv: **there is something ~** algo se está tramando
afraid [əˈfreɪd] adj: **to be ~ of** (person) tener miedo a; (thing) tener miedo de; **to be ~ to** tener miedo de, temer; **I am ~ that** me temo que; **I am ~ not/so** lo siento, pero no/es así
afresh [əˈfreʃ] adv de nuevo, otra vez
Africa [ˈæfrɪkə] n África; **~n** adj, n africano/a m/f

after ['ɑːftə*] *prep (time)* después de; *(place, order)* detrás de, tras ♦ *adv* después ♦ *conj* después (de) que; **what/ who are you ~?** ¿qué/a quién busca usted?; **~ having done/he left** después de haber hecho/después de que se marchó; **to name sb ~ sb** llamar a uno por uno; **it's twenty ~ eight** *(US)* son las ocho y veinte; **to ask ~ sb** preguntar por alguien; **~ all** después de todo, al fin y al cabo; **~ you!** ¡pase usted!; **~-effects** *npl* consecuencias *fpl*, efectos *mpl*; **~math** *n* consecuencias *fpl*, resultados *mpl*; **~noon** *n* tarde *f*; **~s** *(inf) n (dessert)* postre *m*; **~-sales service** *(BRIT) n* servicio de asistencia pos-venta; **~-shave (lotion)** *n* aftershave *m*; **~sun (lotion/cream)** *n* loción *f*/crema para después del sol, aftersun *m*; **~thought** *n* ocurrencia (tardía); **~wards** *(US ~ward) adv* después, más tarde

again [ə'gen] *adv* otra vez, de nuevo; **to do sth ~** volver a hacer algo; **~ and ~** una y otra vez

against [ə'genst] *prep (in opposition to)* en contra de; *(leaning on, touching)* contra, junto a

age [eɪdʒ] *n* edad *f; (period)* época ♦ *vi* envejecer(se) ♦ *vt* envejecer; **she is 20 years of ~** tiene 20 años; **to come of ~** llegar a la mayoría de edad; **it's been ~s since I saw you** hace siglos que no te veo; **~d 10** de 10 años de edad; **the ~d** ['eɪdʒɪd] *npl* los ancianos; **~ group** *n:* **to be in the same ~ group** tener la misma edad; **~ limit** *n* edad *f* mínima (or máxima)

agency ['eɪdʒənsɪ] *n* agencia

agenda [ə'dʒɛndə] *n* orden *m* del día

agent ['eɪdʒənt] *n* agente *m/f; (COMM: holding concession)* representante *m/f*, delegado/a; *(CHEM, fig)* agente *m*

aggravate ['ægrəveɪt] *vt (situation)* agravar; *(person)* irritar

aggregate ['ægrɪgeɪt] *n* conjunto

aggressive [ə'gresɪv] *adj (belligerent)* agresivo; *(assertive)* enérgico

aggrieved [ə'griːvd] *adj* ofendido, agraviado

aghast [ə'gɑːst] *adj* horrorizado

agile ['ædʒaɪl] *adj* ágil

agitate ['ædʒɪteɪt] *vt (trouble)* inquietar ♦ *vi:* **to ~ for/against** hacer campaña pro *or* en favor de/en contra de

AGM *n abbr* (= *annual general meeting*) asamblea anual

ago [ə'gəʊ] *adv:* **2 days ~** hace 2 días; **not long ~** hace poco; **how long ~?** ¿hace cuánto tiempo?

agog [ə'gɒg] *adj (eager)* ansioso; *(excited)* emocionado

agonizing ['ægənaɪzɪŋ] *adj (pain)* atroz; *(decision, wait)* angustioso

agony ['ægənɪ] *n (pain)* dolor *m* agudo; *(distress)* angustia; **to be in ~** retorcerse de dolor

agree [ə'griː] *vt (price, date)* acordar, quedar en ♦ *vi (have same opinion):* **to ~ (with/that)** estar de acuerdo (con/que); *(correspond)* coincidir, concordar; *(consent)* acceder; **to ~ with** *(subj: person)* estar de acuerdo con, ponerse de acuerdo con; *(: food)* sentar bien a; *(LING)* concordar con; **to ~ to sth/to do sth** consentir en algo/aceptar hacer algo; **to ~ that** *(admit)* estar de acuerdo en que; **~able** *adj (sensation)* agradable; *(person)* simpático; *(willing)* de acuerdo, conforme; **~d** *adj (time, place)* convenido; **~ment** *n* acuerdo; *(contract)* contrato; **in ~ment** de acuerdo, conforme

agricultural [ægrɪ'kʌltʃərəl] *adj* agrícola

agriculture ['ægrɪkʌltʃə*] *n* agricultura

aground [ə'graund] *adv:* **to run ~** *(NAUT)* encallar, embarrancar

ahead [ə'hed] *adv (in front)* delante; *(into the future):* **she had no time to think ~** no tenía tiempo de hacer planes para el futuro; **~ of** delante de; *(in advance of)* antes de; **~ of time** antes de la hora; **go right** *or* **straight ~** *(direction)* siga adelante; *(permission)* hazlo (or hágalo)

aid [eɪd] *n* ayuda, auxilio; *(device)* aparato ♦ *vt* ayudar, auxiliar; **in ~ of** a beneficio

de
aide [eɪd] n (person, also MIL) ayudante m/f

AIDS [eɪdz] n abbr (= acquired immune deficiency syndrome) SIDA m

ailment ['eɪlmənt] n enfermedad f, achaque m

aim [eɪm] vt (gun, camera) apuntar; (missile, remark) dirigir; (blow) asestar ♦ vi (also: **take ~**) apuntar ♦ n (in shooting: skill) puntería; (objective) propósito, meta; **to ~ at** (with weapon) apuntar a; (objective) aspirar a, pretender; **to ~ to do** tener la intención de hacer; **~less** adj sin propósito, sin objeto

ain't [eɪnt] (inf) = **am not**; **aren't**; **isn't**

air [ɛə*] n aire m; (appearance) aspecto ♦ vt (room) ventilar; (clothes, ideas) airear ♦ cpd aéreo; **to throw sth into the ~** (ball etc) lanzar algo al aire; **by ~** (travel) en avión; **to be on the ~** (RADIO, TV) estar en antena; **~bed** (BRIT) n colchón m neumático; **~-conditioned** adj climatizado; **~ conditioning** n aire acondicionado; **~craft** n inv avión m; **~craft carrier** n porta(a)viones m inv; **~field** n campo de aviación; **A~ Force** n fuerzas fpl aéreas, aviación f; **~ freshener** n ambientador m; **~gun** n escopeta de aire comprimido; **~ hostess** (BRIT) n azafata; **~ letter** (BRIT) n carta aérea; **~lift** n puente m aéreo; **~line** n línea aérea; **~liner** n avión m de pasajeros; **~mail** n: **by ~mail** por avión; **~plane** (US) n avión m; **~port** n aeropuerto; **~ raid** n ataque m aéreo; **~sick** adj: **to be ~sick** marearse (en avión); **~space** n espacio aéreo; **~tight** adj hermético; **~-traffic controller** n controlador(a) m/f aéreo/a; **~y** adj (room) bien ventilado; (fig: manner) desenfadado

aisle [aɪl] n (of church) nave f; (of theatre, supermarket) pasillo; **~ seat** n (on plane) asiento de pasillo

ajar [ə'dʒɑː*] adj entreabierto

alarm [ə'lɑːm] n (in shop, bank) alarma; (anxiety) inquietud f ♦ vt asustar,

inquietar; **~ call** n (in hotel etc) alarma; **~ clock** n despertador m

alas [ə'læs] adv desgraciadamente

albeit [ɔːl'biːɪt] conj aunque

album ['ælbəm] n álbum m; (L.P.) elepé m

alcohol ['ælkəhɔl] n alcohol m; **~ic** [-'hɔlɪk] adj, n alcohólico/a m/f

ale [eɪl] n cerveza

alert [ə'lɜːt] adj (attentive) atento; (to danger, opportunity) alerta ♦ n alerta m, alarma ♦ vt poner sobre aviso; **to be on the ~** (also MIL) estar alerta or sobre aviso

algebra ['ældʒɪbrə] n álgebra

Algeria [æl'dʒɪərɪə] n Argelia

alias ['eɪlɪəs] adv alias, conocido por ♦ n (of criminal) apodo; (of writer) seudónimo

alibi ['ælɪbaɪ] n coartada

alien ['eɪlɪən] n (foreigner) extranjero/a; (extraterrestrial) extraterrestre m/f ♦ adj: **~ to** ajeno a; **~ate** vt enajenar, alejar

alight [ə'laɪt] adj ardiendo; (eyes) brillante ♦ vi (person) apearse, bajar; (bird) posarse

align [ə'laɪn] vt alinear

alike [ə'laɪk] adj semejantes, iguales ♦ adv igualmente, del mismo modo; **to look ~** parecerse

alimony ['ælɪmənɪ] n manutención f

alive [ə'laɪv] adj vivo; (lively) alegre

KEYWORD

all [ɔːl] adj (sg) todo/a; (pl) todos/as; **~ day** todo el día; **~ night** toda la noche; **~ men** todos los hombres; **~ five came** vinieron los cinco; **~ the books** todos los libros; **~ his life** toda su vida
♦ pron 1 todo; **I ate it ~**, **I ate ~ of it** me lo comí todo; **~ of us went** fuimos todos; **~ the boys went** fueron todos los chicos; **is that ~?** ¿eso es todo?, ¿algo más?; (in shop) ¿algo más?, ¿alguna cosa más?
2 (in phrases): **above ~** sobre todo; por encima de todo; **after ~** después de todo; **at ~**: **not at ~** (in answer to question) en absoluto; (in answer to thanks) ¡de nada!, ¡no hay de qué!; **I'm not at ~ tired** no estoy nada cansado/a; **anything at ~ will do** cualquier cosa viene bien; **~ in ~** a fin

de cuentas
♦ *adv*: ~ **alone** completamente solo/a;
it's not as hard as ~ that no es tan
difícil como lo pintas; ~ **the more/the**
better tanto más/mejor; ~ **but** casi; **the**
score is 2 ~ están empatados a 2

all clear *n* (*after attack etc*) fin *m* de la
alerta; (*fig*) luz *f* verde
allege [ə'lɛdʒ] *vt* pretender; ~**dly**
[ə'lɛdʒɪdlɪ] *adv* supuestamente, según se
afirma
allegiance [ə'liːdʒəns] *n* lealtad *f*
allergy ['ælədʒɪ] *n* alergia
alleviate [ə'liːvɪeɪt] *vt* aliviar
alley ['ælɪ] *n* callejuela
alliance [ə'laɪəns] *n* alianza
allied ['ælaɪd] *adj* aliado
alligator ['ælɪgeɪtə*] *n* (*ZOOL*) caimán *m*
all-in (*BRIT*) *adj*, *adv* (*charge*) todo incluido
all-night *adj* (*café, shop*) abierto toda la
noche; (*party*) que dura toda la noche
allocate ['æləkeɪt] *vt* (*money etc*) asignar
allot [ə'lɔt] *vt* asignar; ~**ment** *n* ración *f*;
(*garden*) parcela
all-out *adj* (*effort etc*) supremo; **all out**
adv con todas las fuerzas
allow [ə'lau] *vt* permitir, dejar; (*a claim*)
admitir; (*sum, time etc*) dar, conceder;
(*concede*): **to ~ that** reconocer que; **to ~**
sb to do permitir a alguien hacer; **he is**
~ed to ... se le permite ...; ~ **for** *vt fus*
tener en cuenta; ~**ance** *n* subvención *f*;
(*welfare payment*) subsidio, pensión *f*;
(*pocket money*) dinero de bolsillo; (*tax*
~ance) desgravación *f*; **to make ~ances**
for (*person*) disculpar a; (*thing*) tener en
cuenta
alloy ['ælɔɪ] *n* mezcla
all: ~ **right** *adv* bien; (*as answer*)
¡conforme!, ¡está bien!; ~-**rounder** *n*:
he's a good ~-rounder se le da bien
todo; ~-**time** *adj* (*record*) de todos los
tiempos
alluring [ə'ljuərɪŋ] *adj* atractivo,
tentador(a)
ally ['ælaɪ] *n* aliado/a ♦ *vt*: **to ~ o.s. with**

aliarse con
almighty [ɔːl'maɪtɪ] *adj* todopoderoso;
(*row etc*) imponente
almond ['ɑːmənd] *n* almendra
almost ['ɔːlməust] *adv* casi
alone [ə'ləun] *adj, adv* solo; **to leave sb ~**
dejar a uno en paz; **to leave sth ~** no
tocar algo, dejar algo sin tocar; **let ~ ...** y
mucho menos ...
along [ə'lɔŋ] *prep* a lo largo de, por ♦ *adv*:
is he coming ~ with us? ¿viene con
nosotros?; **he was limping ~** iba
cojeando; ~ **with** junto con; **all ~** (*all the*
time) desde el principio; ~**side** *prep* al
lado de ♦ *adv* al lado
aloof [ə'luːf] *adj* reservado ♦ *adv*: **to stand**
~ mantenerse apartado
aloud [ə'laud] *adv* en voz alta
alphabet ['ælfəbɛt] *n* alfabeto
Alps [ælps] *npl*: **the ~** los Alpes
already [ɔːl'rɛdɪ] *adv* ya
alright ['ɔːl'raɪt] (*BRIT*) *adv* = **all right**
Alsatian [æl'seɪʃən] *n* (*dog*) pastor *m*
alemán
also ['ɔːlsəu] *adv* también, además
altar ['ɔltə*] *n* altar *m*
alter ['ɔltə*] *vt* cambiar, modificar ♦ *vi*
cambiar; ~**ation** [ɔltə'reɪʃən] *n* cambio; (*to*
clothes) arreglo; (*to building*) arreglos *mpl*
alternate [*adj* ɔl'tɜːnɪt, *vb* 'ɔltɜːneɪt] *adj*
(*actions etc*) alternativo; (*events*) alterno;
(*US*) = **alternative** ♦ *vi*: **to ~ (with)**
alternar (con); **on ~ days** un día sí y otro
no; **alternating current** [-neɪtɪŋ] *n*
corriente *f* alterna
alternative [ɔl'tɜːnətɪv] *adj* alternativo ♦ *n*
alternativa; ~ **medicine** medicina
alternativa; ~**ly** *adv*: ~**ly one could ...**
por otra parte se podría ...
although [ɔːl'ðəu] *conj* aunque
altitude ['æltɪtjuːd] *n* altura
alto ['æltəu] *n* (*female*) contralto *f*; (*male*)
alto
altogether [ɔːltə'gɛðə*] *adv*
completamente, del todo; (*on the whole*)
en total, en conjunto
aluminium [ælju'mɪnɪəm] (*BRIT*),

aluminum [ə'lu:mɪnəm] (*US*) *n* aluminio
always ['ɔːlweɪz] *adv* siempre
Alzheimer's (disease) ['æltshaɪməz-] *n* enfermedad *f* de Alzheimer
am [æm] *vb see* **be**
a.m. *adv abbr* (= *ante meridiem*) de la mañana
amalgamate [ə'mælgəmeɪt] *vi* amalgamar ♦ *vt* amalgamar, unir
amateur ['æmətə*] *n* aficionado/a, amateur *m/f*; **~ish** *adj* inexperto, superficial
amaze [ə'meɪz] *vt* asombrar, pasmar; **to be ~d (at)** quedar pasmado (de); **~ment** *n* asombro, sorpresa; **amazing** *adj* extraordinario; (*fantastic*) increíble
Amazon ['æməzən] *n* (*GEO*) Amazonas *m*
ambassador [æm'bæsədə*] *n* embajador(a) *m/f*
amber ['æmbə*] *n* ámbar *m*; **at ~** (*BRIT: AUT*) en el amarillo
ambiguous [æm'bɪgjuəs] *adj* ambiguo
ambition [æm'bɪʃən] *n* ambición *f*; **ambitious** [-[əs] *adj* ambicioso
ambulance ['æmbjuləns] *n* ambulancia
ambush ['æmbuʃ] *n* emboscada ♦ *vt* tender una emboscada a
amenable [ə'mi:nəbl] *adj*: **to be ~ to** dejarse influir por
amend [ə'mend] *vt* enmendar; **to make ~s** dar cumplida satisfacción
amenities [ə'mi:nɪtɪz] *npl* comodidades *fpl*
America [ə'merɪkə] *n* (*USA*) Estados *mpl* Unidos; **~n** *adj*, *n* norteamericano/a *m/f*; estadounidense *m/f*
amiable ['eɪmɪəbl] *adj* amable, simpático
amicable ['æmɪkəbl] *adj* amistoso, amigable
amid(st) [ə'mɪd(st)] *prep* entre, en medio de
amiss [ə'mɪs] *adv*: **to take sth ~** tomar algo a mal; **there's something ~** pasa algo
ammonia [ə'məunɪə] *n* amoníaco
ammunition [æmju'nɪʃən] *n* municiones *fpl*

amnesty ['æmnɪstɪ] *n* amnistía
amok [ə'mɔk] *adv*: **to run ~** enloquecerse, desbocarse
among(st) [ə'mʌŋ(st)] *prep* entre, en medio de
amorous ['æmərəs] *adj* amoroso
amount [ə'maunt] *n* (*gen*) cantidad *f*; (*of bill etc*) suma, importe *m* ♦ *vi*: **to ~ to** sumar; (*be same as*) equivaler a, significar
amp(ère) ['æmp(eə*)] *n* amperio
ample ['æmpl] *adj* (*large*) grande; (*abundant*) abundante; (*enough*) bastante, suficiente
amplifier ['æmplɪfaɪə*] *n* amplificador *m*
amuse [ə'mju:z] *vt* divertir; (*distract*) distraer, entretener; **~ment** *n* diversión *f*; (*pastime*) pasatiempo; (*laughter*) risa; **~ment arcade** *n* salón *m* de juegos; **~ment park** *n* parque *m* de atracciones
an [æn] *indef art see* **a**
anaemic [ə'ni:mɪk] (*US* **anemic**) *adj* anémico; (*fig*) soso, insípido
anaesthetic [ænɪs'θetɪk] *n* (*US* **anesthetic**) anestesia
analog(ue) ['ænəlɔg] *adj* (*computer, watch*) analógico
analyse ['ænəlaɪz] (*US* **analyze**) *vt* analizar; **analysis** [ə'næləsɪs] (*pl* **analyses**) *n* análisis *m inv*; **analyst** [-lɪst] *n* (*political analyst, psychoanalyst*) analista *m/f*
analyze ['ænəlaɪz] (*US*) *vt* = **analyse**
anarchist ['ænəkɪst] *n* anarquista *m/f*
anatomy [ə'nætəmɪ] *n* anatomía
ancestor ['ænsɪstə*] *n* antepasado
anchor ['æŋkə*] *n* ancla, áncora ♦ *vi* (*also*: **to drop ~**) anclar ♦ *vt* anclar; **to weigh ~** levar anclas
anchovy ['æntʃəvɪ] *n* anchoa
ancient ['eɪnʃənt] *adj* antiguo
ancillary [æn'sɪlərɪ] *adj* auxiliar
and [ænd] *conj* y; (*before i-, hi- +consonant*) e; **men ~ women** hombres y mujeres; **father ~ son** padre e hijo; **trees ~ grass** árboles y hierba; **~ so on** etcétera, y así sucesivamente; **try ~ come** procura venir; **he talked ~ talked** habló sin parar; **better ~ better** cada vez mejor

Andes ['ændi:z] npl: **the ~** los Andes

anemic etc [ə'ni:mɪk] (US) = **anaemic** etc

anesthetic etc [ænɪs'θetɪk] (US) = **anaesthetic** etc

anew [ə'nju:] adv de nuevo, otra vez

angel ['eɪndʒəl] n ángel m

anger ['æŋgə*] n cólera

angina [æn'dʒaɪnə] n angina (del pecho)

angle ['æŋgl] n ángulo; **from their ~** desde su punto de vista

angler ['æŋglə*] n pescador(a) m/f (de caña)

Anglican ['æŋglɪkən] adj, n anglicano/a m/f

angling ['æŋglɪŋ] n pesca con caña

Anglo... [æŋgləu] prefix anglo...

angrily ['æŋgrɪlɪ] adv coléricamente, airadamente

angry ['æŋgrɪ] adj enfadado, airado; (wound) inflamado; **to be ~ with sb/at sth** estar enfadado con alguien/por algo; **to get ~** enfadarse, enojarse

anguish ['æŋgwɪʃ] n (physical) tormentos mpl; (mental) angustia

animal ['ænɪməl] n animal m; (pej: person) bestia ♦ adj animal

animate ['ænɪmɪt] adj vivo; **~d** [-meɪtɪd] adj animado

aniseed ['ænɪsi:d] n anís m

ankle ['æŋkl] n tobillo m; **~ sock** n calcetín m corto

annex [n 'æneks, vb æ'neks] n (also: BRIT: annexe) (building) edificio anexo ♦ vt (territory) anexionar

annihilate [ə'naɪəleɪt] vt aniquilar

anniversary [ænɪ'vɜ:sərɪ] n aniversario

announce [ə'nauns] vt anunciar; **~ment** n anuncio; (official) declaración f; **~r** n (RADIO) locutor(a) m/f; (TV) presentador(a) m/f

annoy [ə'nɔɪ] vt molestar, fastidiar; **don't get ~ed!** ¡no se enfade!; **~ance** n enojo; **~ing** adj molesto, fastidioso; (person) pesado

annual ['ænjuəl] adj anual ♦ n (BOT) anual m; (book) anuario; **~ly** adv anualmente, cada año

annul [ə'nʌl] vt anular

annum ['ænəm] n see **per**

anonymous [ə'nɔnɪməs] adj anónimo

anorak ['ænəræk] n anorak m

anorexia [ænə'reksɪə] n (MED: also: ~ nervosa) anorexia

another [ə'nʌðə*] adj (one more, a different one) otro ♦ pron otro; see **one**

answer ['ɑ:nsə*] n contestación f, respuesta; (to problem) solución f ♦ vi contestar, responder ♦ vt (reply to) contestar a, responder a; (problem) resolver; (prayer) escuchar; **in ~ to your letter** contestando or en contestación a su carta; **to ~ the phone** contestar or coger el teléfono; **to ~ the bell** or **the door** acudir a la puerta; **~ back** vi replicar, ser respondón/ona; **~ for** vt fus responder de or por; **~ to** vt fus (description) corresponder a; **~able** adj: **~able to sb for sth** responsable ante uno de algo; **~ing machine** n contestador m automático

ant [ænt] n hormiga

antagonism [æn'tægənɪzm] n antagonismo, hostilidad f

antagonize [æn'tægənaɪz] vt provocar la enemistad de

Antarctic [ænt'ɑːktɪk] n: **the ~** el Antártico

antelope ['æntɪləup] n antílope m

antenatal ['æntɪ'neɪtl] adj antenatal, prenatal; **~ clinic** n clínica prenatal

anthem ['ænθəm] n: **national ~** himno nacional

anthropology [ænθrə'pɔlədʒɪ] n antropología

anti... [æntɪ] prefix anti...; **~-aircraft** [-'eəkrɑːft] adj antiaéreo; **~biotic** [-baɪ'ɔtɪk] n antibiótico; **~body** ['æntɪbɔdɪ] n anticuerpo

anticipate [æn'tɪsɪpeɪt] vt prever; (expect) esperar, contar con; (look forward to) esperar con ilusión; (do first) anticiparse a, adelantarse a; **anticipation** [-'peɪʃən] n (expectation) previsión f; (eagerness) ilusión f, expectación f

anticlimax [æntɪ'klaɪmæks] n decepción f

anticlockwise [æntɪˈklɔkwaɪz] (*BRIT*) *adv* en dirección contraria a la de las agujas del reloj

antics [ˈæntɪks] *npl* gracias *fpl*

anticyclone [æntɪˈsaɪkləun] *n* anticiclón *m*

antidote [ˈæntɪdəut] *n* antídoto

antifreeze [ˈæntɪfriːz] *n* anticongelante *m*

antihistamine [æntɪˈhɪstəmiːn] *n* antihistamínico

antiquated [ˈæntɪkweɪtɪd] *adj* anticuado

antique [ænˈtiːk] *n* antigüedad *f* ♦ *adj* antiguo; ~ **dealer** *n* anticuario/a; ~ **shop** *n* tienda de antigüedades

antiquity [ænˈtɪkwɪtɪ] *n* antigüedad *f*

anti-Semitism [æntɪˈsemɪtɪzm] *n* antisemitismo

antiseptic [æntɪˈseptɪk] *adj, n* antiséptico

antlers [ˈæntləz] *npl* cuernas *fpl*, cornamenta *sg*

anus [ˈeɪnəs] *n* ano

anvil [ˈænvɪl] *n* yunque *m*

anxiety [ænˈzaɪətɪ] *n* inquietud *f*; (*MED*) ansiedad *f*; ~ **to do** deseo de hacer

anxious [ˈæŋkʃəs] *adj* inquieto, preocupado; (*worrying*) preocupante; (*keen*): **to be ~ to do** tener muchas ganas de hacer

---
KEYWORD
---

any [ˈenɪ] *adj* **1** (*in questions etc*) algún/ alguna; **have you ~ butter/children?** ¿tienes mantequilla/hijos?; **if there are ~ tickets left** si quedan billetes, si queda algún billete

2 (*with negative*): **I haven't ~ money/ books** no tengo dinero/libros

3 (*no matter which*) cualquier; ~ **excuse will do** valdrá *or* servirá cualquier excusa; **choose ~ book you like** escoge el libro que quieras; ~ **teacher you ask will tell you** cualquier profesor al que preguntes te lo dirá

4 (*in phrases*): **in ~ case** de todas formas, en cualquier caso; ~ **day now** cualquier día (de estos); **at ~ moment** en cualquier momento, de un momento a otro; **at ~ rate** en todo caso; ~ **time: come (at) ~**

time ven cuando quieras; **he might come (at) ~ time** podría llegar de un momento a otro

♦ *pron* **1** (*in questions etc*): **have you got ~?** ¿tienes alguno(s)/a(s)?; **can ~ of you sing?** ¿sabe cantar alguno de vosotros/ ustedes?

2 (*with negative*): **I haven't ~ (of them)** no tengo ninguno

3 (*no matter which one(s)*): **take ~ of those books (you like)** toma el libro que quieras de ésos

♦ *adv* **1** (*in questions etc*): **do you want ~ more soup/sandwiches?** ¿quieres más sopa/bocadillos?; **are you feeling ~ better?** ¿te sientes algo mejor?

2 (*with negative*): **I can't hear him ~ more** ya no le oigo; **don't wait ~ longer** no esperes más

---

anybody [ˈenɪbɔdɪ] *pron* cualquiera; (*in interrogative sentences*) alguien; (*in negative sentences*): **I don't see ~** no veo a nadie; **if ~ should phone ...** si llama alguien ...

anyhow [ˈenɪhau] *adv* (*at any rate*) de todos modos, de todas formas; (*haphazard*): **do it ~ you like** hazlo como quieras; **she leaves things just ~** deja las cosas como quiera *or* de cualquier modo; **I shall go ~** de todos modos iré

anyone [ˈenɪwʌn] *pron* = **anybody**

anything [ˈenɪθɪŋ] *pron* (*in questions etc*) algo, alguna cosa; (*with negative*) nada; **can you see ~?** ¿ves algo?; **if ~ happens to me ...** si algo me ocurre ...; (*no matter what*): **you can say ~ you like** puedes decir lo que quieras; ~ **will do** vale todo *or* cualquier cosa; **he'll eat ~** come de todo *or* lo que sea

anyway [ˈenɪweɪ] *adv* (*at any rate*) de todos modos, de todas formas; **I shall go ~** iré de todos modos; (*besides*): **~, I couldn't come even if I wanted to** además, no podría venir aunque quisiera; **why are you phoning, ~?** ¿entonces, por qué llamas?, ¿por qué llamas, pues?

anywhere ['ɛnɪwɛə*] *adv* (*in questions etc*): **can you see him ~?** ¿le ves por algún lado?; **are you going ~?** ¿vas a algún sitio?; (*with negative*): **I can't see him ~** no le veo por ninguna parte; **~ in the world** (*no matter where*) en cualquier parte (del mundo); **put the books down ~** deja los libros donde quieras

apart [ə'pɑːt] *adv* (*aside*) aparte; (*situation*): **~ (from)** separado (de); (*movement*): **to pull ~** separar; **10 miles ~** separados por 10 millas; **to take ~** desmontar; **~ from** *prep* aparte de

apartheid [ə'pɑːteɪt] *n* apartheid *m*

apartment [ə'pɑːtmənt] *n* (*US*) piso (*SP*), departamento (*AM*), apartamento; (*room*) cuarto; **~ building** (*US*) *n* edificio de apartamentos

apathetic [æpə'θɛtɪk] *adj* apático, indiferente

ape [eɪp] *n* mono ♦ *vt* imitar, remedar

aperitif [ə'pɛrɪtɪf] *n* aperitivo

aperture ['æpətʃuə*] *n* rendija, resquicio; (*PHOT*) abertura

APEX ['eɪpɛks] *n abbr* (= *Advanced Purchase Excursion Fare*) tarifa APEX *f*

apex *n* ápice *m*; (*fig*) cumbre *f*

apiece [ə'piːs] *adv* cada uno

aplomb [ə'plɔm] *n* aplomo

apologetic [əpɔlə'dʒɛtɪk] *adj* de disculpa; (*person*) arrepentido

apologize [ə'pɔlədʒaɪz] *vi*: **to ~ (for sth to sb)** disculparse (con alguien de algo)

apology [ə'pɔlədʒɪ] *n* disculpa, excusa

apostrophe [ə'pɔstrəfɪ] *n* apóstrofo *m*

appal [ə'pɔːl] *vt* horrorizar, espantar; **~ling** *adj* espantoso; (*awful*) pésimo

apparatus [æpə'reɪtəs] *n* (*equipment*) equipo; (*organization*) aparato; (*in gymnasium*) aparatos *mpl*

apparel [ə'pærl] (*US*) *n* ropa

apparent [ə'pærənt] *adj* aparente; (*obvious*) evidente; **~ly** *adv* por lo visto, al parecer

appeal [ə'piːl] *vi* (*LAW*) apelar ♦ *n* (*LAW*) apelación *f*; (*request*) llamamiento; (*plea*) petición *f*; (*charm*) atractivo; **to ~ for**

reclamar; **to ~ to** (*be attractive to*) atraer; **it doesn't ~ to me** no me atrae, no me llama la atención; **~ing** *adj* (*attractive*) atractivo

appear [ə'pɪə*] *vi* aparecer, presentarse; (*LAW*) comparecer; (*publication*) salir (a luz), publicarse; (*seem*) parecer; **to ~ on TV/in "Hamlet"** salir por la tele/hacer un papel en "Hamlet"; **it would ~ that** parecería que; **~ance** *n* aparición *f*; (*look*) apariencia, aspecto

appease [ə'piːz] *vt* (*pacify*) apaciguar; (*satisfy*) satisfacer

appendices [ə'pɛndɪsiːz] *npl of* **appendix**

appendicitis [əpɛndɪ'saɪtɪs] *n* apendicitis *f*

appendix [ə'pɛndɪks] (*pl* **appendices**) *n* apéndice *m*

appetite ['æpɪtaɪt] *n* apetito; (*fig*) deseo, anhelo

appetizer ['æpɪtaɪzə*] *n* (*drink*) aperitivo; (*food*) tapas *fpl* (*SP*)

applaud [ə'plɔːd] *vt, vi* aplaudir

applause [ə'plɔːz] *n* aplausos *mpl*

apple ['æpl] *n* manzana; **~ tree** *n* manzano

appliance [ə'plaɪəns] *n* aparato

applicable [ə'plɪkəbl] *adj* (*relevant*): **to be ~ (to)** referirse (a)

applicant ['æplɪkənt] *n* candidato/a; solicitante *m/f*

application [æplɪ'keɪʃən] *n* aplicación *f*; (*for a job etc*) solicitud *f*, petición *f*; **~ form** *n* solicitud *f*

applied [ə'plaɪd] *adj* aplicado

apply [ə'plaɪ] *vt* (*paint etc*) poner; (*law etc: put into practice*) poner en vigor ♦ *vi*: **to ~ to** (*ask*) dirigirse a; (*be applicable*) ser aplicable a; **to ~ for** (*permit, grant, job*) solicitar; **to ~ o.s. to** aplicarse a, dedicarse a

appoint [ə'pɔɪnt] *vt* (*to post*) nombrar; **~ed** *adj*: **at the ~ed time** a la hora señalada; **~ment** *n* (*with client*) cita; (*act*) nombramiento; (*post*) puesto; (*at hairdresser etc*): **to have an ~ment** tener hora; **to make an ~ment (with sb)** citarse (con uno)

appraisal [ə'preɪzl] n valoración f
appreciate [ə'priːʃɪeɪt] vt apreciar, tener
  en mucho; (be grateful for) agradecer; (be
  aware of) comprender ♦ vi (COMM)
  aumentar(se) en valor; **appreciation**
  [-'eɪʃən] n apreciación f; (gratitude)
  reconocimiento, agradecimiento; (COMM)
  aumento en valor
appreciative [ə'priːʃɪətɪv] adj apreciativo;
  (comment) agradecido
apprehensive [æprɪ'hɛnsɪv] adj aprensivo
apprentice [ə'prɛntɪs] n aprendiz/a m/f;
  ~ship n aprendizaje m
approach [ə'prəʊtʃ] vi acercarse ♦ vt
  acercarse a; (ask, apply to) dirigirse a;
  (situation, problem) abordar ♦ n
  acercamiento; (access) acceso; (to
  problem, situation): ~ (to) actitud f (ante);
  ~able adj (person) abordable; (place)
  accesible
appropriate [adj ə'prəʊprɪɪt, vb
  ə'prəʊprɪeɪt] adj apropiado, conveniente
  ♦ vt (take) apropiarse de
approval [ə'pruːvəl] n aprobación f, visto
  bueno; (permission) consentimiento; **on ~**
  (COMM) a prueba
approve [ə'pruːv] vt aprobar; **~ of** vt fus
  (thing) aprobar; (person): **they don't ~ of
  her** (ella) no les parece bien
approximate [ə'prɒksɪmɪt] adj
  aproximado; **~ly** adv aproximadamente,
  más o menos
apricot ['eɪprɪkɒt] n albaricoque m (SP),
  damasco (AM)
April ['eɪprəl] n abril m; **~ Fools' Day** n
  el primero de abril; ≈ día m de los
  Inocentes (28 December)
apron ['eɪprən] n delantal m
apt [æpt] adj acertado, apropiado; (likely):
  ~ to do propenso a hacer
aquarium [ə'kwɛərɪəm] n acuario
Aquarius [ə'kwɛərɪəs] n Acuario
Arab ['ærəb] adj, n árabe m/f
Arabian [ə'reɪbɪən] adj árabe
Arabic ['ærəbɪk] adj árabe; (numerals)
  arábigo ♦ n árabe m
arable ['ærəbl] adj cultivable

Aragon ['ærəgən] n Aragón m
arbitrary ['ɑːbɪtrərɪ] adj arbitrario
arbitration [ɑːbɪ'treɪʃən] n arbitraje m
arcade [ɑː'keɪd] n (round a square)
  soportales mpl; (shopping mall) galería
  comercial
arch [ɑːtʃ] n arco; (of foot) arco del pie
  ♦ vt arquear
archaeologist [ɑːkɪ'ɔlədʒɪst] (US
  archeologist) n arqueólogo/a
archaeology [ɑːkɪ'ɔlədʒɪ] (US **archeology**)
  n arqueología
archbishop [ɑːtʃ'bɪʃəp] n arzobispo
archeology etc [ɑːkɪ'ɔlədʒɪ] (US)
  = **archaeology** etc
archery ['ɑːtʃərɪ] n tiro al arco
architect ['ɑːkɪtɛkt] n arquitecto/a; **~ure**
  n arquitectura
archives ['ɑːkaɪvz] npl archivo
Arctic ['ɑːktɪk] adj ártico ♦ n: **the ~** el
  Ártico
ardent ['ɑːdənt] adj ardiente, apasionado
arduous ['ɑːdjuəs] adj (task) arduo;
  (journey) agotador(a)
are [ɑː*] vb see **be**
area ['ɛərɪə] n área, región f; (part of place)
  zona; (MATH etc) área, superficie f; (in
  room: e.g. dining ~) parte f; (of knowledge,
  experience) campo
arena [ə'riːnə] n estadio; (of circus) pista
aren't [ɑːnt] = **are not**
Argentina [ɑːdʒən'tiːnə] n Argentina;
  Argentinian [-'tɪnɪən] adj, n argentino/a
  m/f
arguably ['ɑːgjuəblɪ] adv posiblemente
argue ['ɑːgjuː] vi (quarrel) discutir,
  pelearse; (reason) razonar, argumentar; **to
  ~ that** sostener que
argument ['ɑːgjumənt] n discusión f,
  pelea; (reasons) argumento; **~ative**
  [-'mɛntətɪv] adj discutidor(a)
Aries ['ɛərɪz] n Aries m
arise [ə'raɪz] (pt arose, pp arisen) vi
  surgir, presentarse
arisen [ə'rɪzn] pp of **arise**
aristocrat ['ærɪstəkræt] n aristócrata m/f
arithmetic [ə'rɪθmətɪk] n aritmética

ark [ɑːk] *n*: Noah's A~ el Arca *f* de Noé

arm [ɑːm] *n* brazo ♦ *vt* armar; **~s** *npl* armas *fpl*; **~ in ~** cogidos del brazo

armaments [ˈɑːməmənts] *npl* armamento

armchair [ˈɑːmtʃɛəʳ] *n* sillón *m*, butaca

armed [ɑːmd] *adj* armado; **~ robbery** *n* robo a mano armada

armour (*US* **armor**) [ˈɑːməʳ] *n* armadura; (*MIL: tanks*) blindaje *m*; **~ed car** *n* coche *m* (*SP*) *or* carro (*AM*) blindado

armpit [ˈɑːmpɪt] *n* sobaco, axila

armrest [ˈɑːmrest] *n* apoyabrazos *m inv*

army [ˈɑːmɪ] *n* ejército, (*fig*) multitud *f*

aroma [əˈrəumə] *n* aroma *m*, fragancia; **~therapy** *n* aromaterapia

arose [əˈrəuz] *pt of* **arise**

around [əˈraund] *adv* alrededor; (*in the area*): **there is no one else ~** no hay nadie más por aquí ♦ *prep* alrededor de

arouse [əˈrauz] *vt* despertar; (*anger*) provocar

arrange [əˈreɪndʒ] *vt* arreglar, ordenar; (*organize*) organizar; **to ~ to do sth** quedar en hacer algo; **~ment** *n* arreglo; (*agreement*) acuerdo; **~ments** *npl* (*preparations*) preparativos *mpl*

array [əˈreɪ] *n*: **~ of** (*things*) serie *f* de; (*people*) conjunto de

arrears [əˈrɪəz] *npl* atrasos *mpl*; **to be in ~ with one's rent** estar retrasado en el pago del alquiler

arrest [əˈrest] *vt* detener; (*sb's attention*) llamar ♦ *n* detención *f*; **under ~** detenido

arrival [əˈraɪvəl] *n* llegada; **new ~** recién llegado/a; (*baby*) recién nacido

arrive [əˈraɪv] *vi* llegar; (*baby*) nacer

arrogant [ˈærəgənt] *adj* arrogante

arrow [ˈærəu] *n* flecha

arse [ɑːs] (*BRIT: inf!*) *n* culo, trasero

arson [ˈɑːsn] *n* incendio premeditado

art [ɑːt] *n* arte *m*; (*skill*) destreza; **A~s** *npl* (*SCOL*) Letras *fpl*

artery [ˈɑːtərɪ] *n* arteria

art gallery *n* pinacoteca; (*saleroom*) galería de arte

arthritis [ɑːˈθraɪtɪs] *n* artritis *f*

artichoke [ˈɑːtɪtʃəuk] *n* alcachofa;

Jerusalem ~ aguaturma

article [ˈɑːtɪkl] *n* artículo; (*BRIT: LAW: training*): **~s** *npl* contrato de aprendizaje; **~ of clothing** prenda de vestir

articulate [*adj* ɑːˈtɪkjulɪt, *vb* ɑːˈtɪkjuleɪt] *adj* claro, bien expresado ♦ *vt* expresar; **~d lorry** (*BRIT*) *n* trailer *m*

artificial [ɑːtɪˈfɪʃl] *adj* artificial; (*affected*) afectado

artillery [ɑːˈtɪlərɪ] *n* artillería

artisan [ˈɑːtɪzæn] *n* artesano

artist [ˈɑːtɪst] *n* artista *m/f*; (*MUS*) intérprete *m/f*; **~ic** [ɑːˈtɪstɪk] *adj* artístico; **~ry** *n* arte *m*, habilidad *f* (artística)

art school *n* escuela de bellas artes

| KEYWORD |

as [æz] *conj* **1** (*referring to time*) cuando, mientras; a medida que; **~ the years went by** con el paso de los años; **he came in ~ I was leaving** entró cuando me marchaba; **~ from tomorrow** desde *or* a partir de mañana

2 (*in comparisons*): **~ big ~** tan grande como; **twice ~ big ~** el doble de grande que; **~ much money/many books ~** tanto dinero/tantos libros como; **~ soon ~** en cuanto

3 (*since, because*) como, ya que; **he left early ~ he had to be home by 10** se fue temprano ya que tenía que estar en casa a las 10

4 (*referring to manner, way*): **do ~ you wish** haz lo que quieras; **~ she said** como dijo; **he gave it to me ~ a present** me lo dio de regalo

5 (*in the capacity of*): **he works ~ a barman** trabaja de barman; **~ chairman of the company, he ...** como presidente de la compañía, ...

6 (*concerning*): **~ for** *or* **to that** por *or* en lo que respecta a eso

7: **~ if** *or* **though** como si; **he looked ~ if he was ill** parecía como si estuviera enfermo, tenía aspecto de enfermo; *see also* **long**; **such**; **well**

a.s.a.p. *abbr* (= *as soon as possible*) cuanto antes

asbestos [æz'bestəs] *n* asbesto, amianto

ascend [ə'sɛnd] *vt* subir; (*throne*) ascender *or* subir a

ascent [ə'sɛnt] *n* subida; (*slope*) cuesta, pendiente *f*

ascertain [æsə'teɪn] *vt* averiguar

ash [æʃ] *n* ceniza; (*tree*) fresno

ashamed [ə'ʃeɪmd] *adj* avergonzado, apenado (*AM*); **to be ~ of** avergonzarse de

ashore [ə'ʃɔː*] *adv* en tierra; (*swim etc*) a tierra

ashtray ['æʃtreɪ] *n* cenicero

Ash Wednesday *n* miércoles *m* de Ceniza

Asia ['eɪʃə] *n* Asia; **~n** *adj, n* asiático/a *m/f*

aside [ə'saɪd] *adv* a un lado ♦ *n* aparte *m*

ask [ɑːsk] *vt* (*question*) preguntar; (*invite*) invitar; **to ~ sb sth/to do sth** preguntar algo a alguien/pedir a alguien que haga algo; **to ~ sb about sth** preguntar algo a alguien; **to ~ (sb) a question** hacer una pregunta (a alguien); **to ~ sb out to dinner** invitar a cenar a uno; **~ after** *vt fus* preguntar por; **~ for** *vt fus* pedir; (*trouble*) buscar

asking price *n* precio inicial

asleep [ə'sliːp] *adj* dormido; **to fall ~** dormirse, quedarse dormido

asparagus [əs'pærəgəs] *n* (*plant*) espárrago; (*food*) espárragos *mpl*

aspect ['æspɛkt] *n* aspecto, apariencia; (*direction in which a building etc faces*) orientación *f*

aspersions [əs'pəːʃənz] *npl*: **to cast ~ on** difamar a, calumniar a

asphyxiation [æsfɪksɪ'eɪʃən] *n* asfixia

aspire [əs'paɪə*] *vi*: **to ~ to** aspirar a, ambicionar

aspirin ['æsprɪn] *n* aspirina

ass [æs] *n* asno, burro; (*inf: idiot*) imbécil *m/f*, (*US: inf!*) culo, trasero

assailant [ə'seɪlənt] *n* asaltador(a) *m/f*, agresor(a) *m/f*

assassinate [ə'sæsɪneɪt] *vt* asesinar;

assassination [əsæsɪ'neɪʃən] *n* asesinato

assault [ə'sɔːlt] *n* asalto; (*LAW*) agresión *f* ♦ *vt* asaltar, atacar; (*sexually*) violar

assemble [ə'sɛmbl] *vt* reunir, juntar; (*TECH*) montar ♦ *vi* reunirse, juntarse

assembly [ə'sɛmblɪ] *n* reunión *f*, asamblea; (*parliament*) parlamento *m*; (*construction*) montaje *m*; **~ line** *n* cadena de montaje

assent [ə'sɛnt] *n* asentimiento, aprobación *f*

assert [ə'səːt] *vt* afirmar; (*authority*) hacer valer; **~ion** [-ʃən] *n* afirmación *f*

assess [ə'sɛs] *vt* valorar, calcular; (*tax, damages*) fijar; (*for tax*) gravar; **~ment** *n* valoración *f*; (*for tax*) gravamen *m*; **~or** *n* asesor(a) *m/f*

asset ['æsɛt] *n* ventaja; **~s** *npl* (*COMM*) activo; (*property, funds*) fondos *mpl*

assign [ə'saɪn] *vt*: **to ~ (to)** (*date*) fijar (para); (*task*) asignar (a); (*resources*) destinar (a); **~ment** *n* tarea

assist [ə'sɪst] *vt* ayudar; **~ance** *n* ayuda, auxilio; **~ant** *n* ayudante *m/f*; (*BRIT: also:* **shop ~ant**) dependiente/a *m/f*

associate [*adj, n* ə'səʊʃɪt, *vb* ə'səʊʃɪeɪt] *adj* asociado ♦ *n* (*at work*) colega *m/f* ♦ *vt* asociar; (*ideas*) relacionar ♦ *vi*: **to ~ with sb** tratar con alguien

association [əsəʊsɪ'eɪʃən] *n* asociación *f*

assorted [ə'sɔːtɪd] *adj* surtido, variado

assortment [ə'sɔːtmənt] *n* (*of shapes, colours*) surtido; (*of books*) colección *f*; (*of people*) mezcla

assume [ə'sjuːm] *vt* suponer; (*responsibilities*) asumir; (*attitude*) adoptar, tomar

assumption [ə'sʌmpʃən] *n* suposición *f*, presunción *f*; (*of power etc*) toma

assurance [ə'ʃʊərəns] *n* garantía, promesa; (*confidence*) confianza, aplomo; (*insurance*) seguro

assure [ə'ʃʊə*] *vt* asegurar

asthma ['æsmə] *n* asma

astonish [ə'stɒnɪʃ] *vt* asombrar, pasmar; **~ment** *n* asombro, sorpresa

astound [ə'staʊnd] *vt* asombrar, pasmar

astray [ə'streɪ] *adv*: **to go ~** extraviarse; **to lead ~** (*morally*) llevar por mal camino

astride [ə'straɪd] *prep* a caballo *or* horcajadas sobre

astrology [æs'trɔlədʒɪ] *n* astrología

astronaut ['æstrɔnɔ:t] *n* astronauta *m/f*

astronomy [æs'trɔnəmɪ] *n* astronomía

asylum [ə'saɪləm] *n* (*refuge*) asilo; (*mental hospital*) manicomio

---
KEYWORD
---

at [æt] *prep* **1** (*referring to position*) en; (*direction*) a; **~ the top** en lo alto; **~ home/school** en casa/la escuela; **to look ~ sth/sb** mirar algo/a uno
2 (*referring to time*): **~ 4 o'clock** a las 4; **~ night** por la noche; **~ Christmas** en Navidad; **~ times** a veces
3 (*referring to rates, speed etc*): **~ £1 a kilo** a una libra el kilo; **two ~ a time** de dos en dos; **~ 50 km/h** a 50 km/h
4 (*referring to manner*): **~ a stroke** de un golpe; **~ peace** en paz
5 (*referring to activity*): **to be ~ work** estar trabajando; (*in the office etc*) estar en el trabajo; **to play ~ cowboys** jugar a los vaqueros; **to be good ~ sth** ser bueno en algo
6 (*referring to cause*): **shocked/ surprised/annoyed ~ sth** asombrado/ sorprendido/fastidiado por algo; **I went ~ his suggestion** fui a instancias suyas

---

ate [eɪt] *pt of* **eat**

atheist ['eɪθɪɪst] *n* ateo/a

Athens ['æθɪnz] *n* Atenas

athlete ['æθli:t] *n* atleta *m/f*

athletic [æθ'letɪk] *adj* atlético; **~s** *n* atletismo

Atlantic [ət'læntɪk] *adj* atlántico ♦ *n*: **the ~ (Ocean)** el (Océano) Atlántico

atlas ['ætləs] *n* atlas *m*

A.T.M. *n abbr* (= *automated telling machine*) cajero automático

atmosphere ['ætməsfɪə*] *n* atmósfera; (*of place*) ambiente *m*

atom ['ætəm] *n* átomo; **~ic** [ə'tɔmɪk] *adj*

atómico; **~(ic) bomb** *n* bomba atómica; **~izer** ['ætəmaɪzə*] *n* atomizador *m*

atone [ə'təun] *vi*: **to ~ for** expiar

atrocious [ə'trəuʃəs] *adj* atroz

attach [ə'tætʃ] *vt* (*fasten*) atar; (*join*) unir, sujetar; (*document, letter*) adjuntar; (*importance etc*) dar, conceder; **to be ~ed to sb/sth** (*to like*) tener cariño a alguien/ algo

attaché case [ə'tæʃeɪ-] *n* maletín *m*

attachment [ə'tætʃmənt] *n* (*tool*) accesorio; (*love*): **~ (to)** apego (a)

attack [ə'tæk] *vt* (*MIL*) atacar; (*subj: criminal*) agredir, asaltar; (*criticize*) criticar; (*task*) emprender ♦ *n* ataque *m*, asalto; (*on sb's life*) atentado; (*fig: criticism*) crítica; (*of illness*) ataque *m*; **heart ~** infarto (de miocardio); **~er** *n* agresor(a) *m/f*, asaltante *m/f*

attain [ə'teɪn] *vt* (*also*: **~ to**) alcanzar; (*achieve*) lograr, conseguir

attempt [ə'tempt] *n* tentativa, intento; (*attack*) atentado ♦ *vt* intentar; **~ed** *adj*: **~ed burglary/murder/suicide** tentativa *or* intento de robo/asesinato/suicidio

attend [ə'tend] *vt* asistir a; (*patient*) atender; **~ to** *vt fus* ocuparse de; (*customer, patient*) atender a; **~ance** *n* asistencia, presencia; (*people present*) concurrencia; **~ant** *n* ayudante *m/f*; (*in garage etc*) encargado/a ♦ *adj* (*dangers*) concomitante

attention [ə'tenʃən] *n* atención *f*; (*care*) atenciones *fpl* ♦ *excl* (*MIL*) ¡firme(s)!; **for the ~ of ...** (*ADMIN*) atención ...

attentive [ə'tentɪv] *adj* atento

attic ['ætɪk] *n* desván *m*

attitude ['ætɪtju:d] *n* actitud *f*; (*disposition*) disposición *f*

attorney [ə'tɔ:nɪ] *n* (*lawyer*) abogado/a; **A~ General** *n* (*BRIT*) ≈ Presidente *m* del Consejo del Poder Judicial (*SP*); (*US*) ≈ ministro de justicia

attract [ə'trækt] *vt* atraer; (*sb's attention*) llamar; **~ion** [ə'trækʃən] *n* encanto; (*gen pl: amusements*) diversiones *fpl*; (*PHYSICS*) atracción *f*; (*fig: towards sb, sth*) atractivo;

~ive *adj* guapo; (*interesting*) atrayente

attribute [*n* 'ætrɪbjuːt, *vb* ə'trɪbjuːt] *n* atributo ♦ *vt*: **to ~ sth to** atribuir algo a

attrition [ə'trɪʃən] *n*: **war of ~** guerra de agotamiento

aubergine ['əʊbəʒiːn] (*BRIT*) *n* berenjena; (*colour*) morado

auburn ['ɔːbən] *adj* color castaño rojizo

auction ['ɔːkʃən] *n* (*also: sale by ~*) subasta ♦ *vt* subastar; **~eer** [-'nɪə*] *n* subastador(a) *m/f*

audible ['ɔːdɪbl] *adj* audible, que se puede oír

audience ['ɔːdɪəns] *n* público; (*RADIO*) radioescuchas *mpl*; (*TV*) telespectadores *mpl*; (*interview*) audiencia

audio-visual [ɔːdɪəʊ'vɪzjuəl] *adj* audiovisual; **~ aid** *n* ayuda audiovisual

audit ['ɔːdɪt] *vt* revisar, intervenir

audition [ɔː'dɪʃən] *n* audición *f*

auditor ['ɔːdɪtə*] *n* interventor(a) *m/f*, censor(a) *m/f* de cuentas

augment [ɔːg'ment] *vt* aumentar

augur ['ɔːgə*] *vi*: **it ~s well** es un buen augurio

August ['ɔːgəst] *n* agosto

aunt [ɑːnt] *n* tía; **~ie** *n diminutive of* **aunt**; **~y** *n diminutive of* **aunt**

au pair ['əʊ'pɛə*] *n* (*also: ~ girl*) (chica) au pair *f*

auspicious [ɔːs'pɪʃəs] *adj* propicio, de buen augurio

Australia [ɔs'treɪlɪə] *n* Australia; **~n** *adj*, *n* australiano/a *m/f*

Austria ['ɔstrɪə] *n* Austria; **~n** *adj*, *n* austríaco/a *m/f*

authentic [ɔː'θentɪk] *adj* auténtico

author ['ɔːθə*] *n* autor(a) *m/f*

authoritarian [ɔːθɒrɪ'tɛərɪən] *adj* autoritario

authoritative [ɔː'θɒrɪtətɪv] *adj* autorizado; (*manner*) autoritario

authority [ɔː'θɒrɪtɪ] *n* autoridad *f*; (*official permission*) autorización *f*; **the authorities** *npl* las autoridades

authorize ['ɔːθəraɪz] *vt* autorizar

auto ['ɔːtəʊ] (*US*) *n* coche *m* (*SP*), carro

(*AM*), automóvil *m*

auto: ~biography [ɔːtəbaɪ'ɒgrəfɪ] *n* autobiografía; **~graph** ['ɔːtəgrɑːf] *n* autógrafo ♦ *vt* (*photo etc*) dedicar; (*programme*) firmar; **~mated** ['ɔːtəmeɪtɪd] *adj* automatizado; **~matic** [ɔːtə'mætɪk] *adj* automático ♦ *n* (*gun*) pistola automática; (*car*) coche *m* automático; **~matically** *adv* automáticamente; **~mation** [ɔːtə'meɪʃən] *n* reconversión *f*; **~mobile** ['ɔːtəməbiːl] (*US*) *n* coche *m* (*SP*), carro (*AM*), automóvil *m*; **~nomy** [ɔː'tɒnəmɪ] *n* autonomía

autumn ['ɔːtəm] *n* otoño

auxiliary [ɔːg'zɪlɪərɪ] *adj*, *n* auxiliar *m/f*

avail [ə'veɪl] *vt*: **to ~ o.s. of** aprovechar(se) de ♦ *n*: **to no ~** en vano, sin resultado

available [ə'veɪləbl] *adj* disponible; (*unoccupied*) libre; (*person: unattached*) soltero y sin compromiso

avalanche ['ævəlɑːnʃ] *n* alud *m*, avalancha

avant-garde ['ævãŋ'gɑːd] *adj* de vanguardia

Ave. *abbr* = **avenue**

avenge [ə'vendʒ] *vt* vengar

avenue ['ævɪnjuː] *n* avenida; (*fig*) camino

average ['ævərɪdʒ] *n* promedio, término medio ♦ *adj* medio, de término medio; (*ordinary*) regular, corriente ♦ *vt* sacar un promedio de; **on ~** por regla general; **~ out** *vi*: **to ~ out at** salir en un promedio de

averse [ə'vɜːs] *adj*: **to be ~ to sth/doing** sentir aversión *or* antipatía por algo/por hacer

avert [ə'vɜːt] *vt* prevenir; (*blow*) desviar; (*one's eyes*) apartar

aviary ['eɪvɪərɪ] *n* pajarera, avería

avocado [ævə'kɑːdəʊ] *n* (*also: BRIT: ~ pear*) aguacate *m* (*SP*), palta (*AM*)

avoid [ə'vɔɪd] *vt* evitar, eludir

await [ə'weɪt] *vt* esperar, aguardar

awake [ə'weɪk] (*pt* **awoke**, *pp* **awoken** *or* **awaked**) *adj* despierto ♦ *vt* despertar ♦ *vi* despertarse; **to be ~** estar despierto; **~ning** *n* el despertar

award [ə'wɔːd] n premio; (LAW: damages) indemnización f ♦ vt otorgar, conceder; (LAW: damages) adjudicar

aware [ə'weə*] adj: ~ **(of)** consciente (de); **to become ~ of/that** (realize) darse cuenta de/de que; (learn) enterarse de/de que; **~ness** n conciencia; (knowledge) conocimiento

away [ə'weɪ] adv fuera; (movement): **she went ~** se marchó; (far ~) lejos; **two kilometres ~** a dos kilómetros de distancia; **two hours ~ by car** a dos horas en coche; **the holiday was two weeks ~** faltaban dos semanas para las vacaciones; **he's ~ for a week** estará ausente una semana; **to take ~ (from)** quitar (a); (subtract) substraer (de); **to work/pedal ~** seguir trabajando/pedaleando; **to fade ~** (colour) desvanecerse; (sound) apagarse; **~ game** n (SPORT) partido de fuera

awe [ɔː] n admiración f respetuosa; **~-inspiring** adj imponente

awful ['ɔːfəl] adj horroroso; (quantity): **an ~ lot (of)** cantidad (de); **~ly** adv (very) terriblemente

awkward ['ɔːkwəd] adj desmañado, torpe; (shape) incómodo; (embarrassing) delicado, difícil

awning ['ɔːnɪŋ] n (of tent, caravan, shop) toldo

awoke [ə'wəuk] pt of **awake**

awoken [ə'wəukən] pp of **awake**

awry [ə'raɪ] adv: **to be ~** estar descolocado or mal puesto

axe [æks] (US **ax**) n hacha ♦ vt (project) cortar; (jobs) reducir

axes ['æksiːz] npl of **axis**

axis ['æksɪs] (pl **axes**) n eje m

axle ['æksl] n eje m, árbol m

ay(e) [aɪ] excl sí

B, b

B [biː] n (MUS) si m

B.A. abbr = **Bachelor of Arts**

baby ['beɪbɪ] n bebé m/f; (US: inf: darling) mi amor; **~ carriage** (US) n cochecito; **~-sit** vi hacer de canguro; **~-sitter** n canguro/a; **~ wipe** n toallita húmeda (para bebés)

bachelor ['bætʃələ*] n soltero; **B~ of Arts/Science** licenciado/a en Filosofía y Letras/Ciencias

back [bæk] n (of person) espalda; (of animal) lomo; (of hand) dorso; (as opposed to front) parte f de atrás; (of chair) respaldo; (of page) reverso; (of book) final m; (FOOTBALL) defensa m; (of crowd): **the ones at the ~** los del fondo ♦ vt (candidate: also: ~ **up**) respaldar, apoyar; (horse: at races) apostar a; (car) dar marcha atrás a or con ♦ vi (car etc) ir (or salir or entrar) marcha atrás ♦ adj (payment, rent) atrasado; (seats, wheels) de atrás ♦ adv (not forward) (hacia) atrás; (returned): **he's ~** está de vuelta, ha vuelto; **he ran ~** volvió corriendo; (restitution): **throw the ball ~** devuelve la pelota; **can I have it ~?** ¿me lo devuelve?; (again): **he called ~** llamó de nuevo; **~ down** vi echarse atrás; **~ out** vi (of promise) volverse atrás; **~ up** vt (person) apoyar, respaldar; (theory) defender; (COMPUT) hacer una copia preventiva or de reserva; **~bencher** (BRIT) n miembro del parlamento sin cargo relevante; **~bone** n columna vertebral; **~date** vt (pay rise) dar efecto retroactivo a; (letter) poner fecha atrasada a; **~drop** n telón m de fondo; **~fire** vi (AUT) petardear; (plans) fallar, salir mal; **~ground** n fondo; (of events) antecedentes mpl; (basic knowledge) bases fpl; (experience) conocimientos mpl, educación f; **family ~ground** origen m, antecedentes mpl; **~hand** n (TENNIS:

also: **~hand stroke**) revés *m*; **~hander** (*BRIT*) *n* (*bribe*) soborno; **~ing** *n* (*fig*) apoyo, respaldo; **~lash** *n* reacción *f*; **~log** *n*: **~log of work** trabajo atrasado; **~number** *n* (*of magazine etc*) número atrasado; **~pack** *n* mochila; **~packer** *n* mochilero/a; **~ pay** *n* pago atrasado; **~side** (*inf*) *n* trasero, culo; **~stage** *adv* entre bastidores; **~stroke** *n* espalda; **~up** *adj* suplementario; (*COMPUT*) de reserva ♦ *n* (*support*) apoyo; (*also*: **~-up file**) copia preventiva *or* de reserva; **~ward** *adj* (*person, country*) atrasado; **~wards** *adv* hacia atrás; (*read a list*) al revés; (*fall*) de espaldas; **~yard** *n* traspatio

bacon ['beɪkən] *n* tocino, beicon *m*

bad [bæd] *adj* malo; (*mistake, accident*) grave; (*food*) podrido, pasado; **his ~ leg** su pierna lisiada; **to go ~** (*food*) pasarse

badge [bædʒ] *n* insignia; (*policeman's*) chapa, placa

badger ['bædʒər] *n* tejón *m*

badly ['bædlɪ] *adv* mal; **to reflect ~ on sb** influir negativamente en la reputación de uno; **~ wounded** gravemente herido; **he needs it ~** le hace gran falta; **to be ~ off (for money)** andar mal de dinero

badminton ['bædmɪntən] *n* bádminton *m*

bad-tempered *adj* de mal genio *or* carácter; (*temporarily*) de mal humor

bag [bæg] *n* bolsa; (*handbag*) bolso; (*satchel*) mochila; (*case*) maleta; **~s of** (*inf*) un montón de; **~gage** *n* equipaje *m*; **~gage allowance** *n* límite *m* de equipaje; **~gage reclaim** *n* recogida de equipajes; **~gy** *adj* amplio; **~pipes** *npl* gaita

Bahamas [bə'hɑːməz] *npl*: **the ~** las Islas Bahamas

bail [beɪl] *n* fianza ♦ *vt* (*prisoner: gen: grant ~ to*) poner en libertad bajo fianza; (*boat: also*: **~ out**) achicar; **on ~** (*prisoner*) bajo fianza; **to ~ sb out** obtener la libertad de uno bajo fianza; *see also* **bale**

bailiff ['beɪlɪf] *n* alguacil *m*

bait [beɪt] *n* cebo ♦ *vt* poner cebo en; (*tease*) tomar el pelo a

bake [beɪk] *vt* cocer (al horno) ♦ *vi* cocerse; **~d beans** *npl* judías *fpl* en salsa de tomate; **~d potato** *n* patata al horno; **~r** *n* panadero; **~ry** *n* panadería; (*for cakes*) pastelería; **baking** *n* (*act*) amasar *m*; (*batch*) hornada; **baking powder** *n* levadura (en polvo)

balance ['bæləns] *n* equilibrio; (*COMM: sum*) balance *m*; (*remainder*) resto; (*scales*) balanza ♦ *vt* equilibrar; (*budget*) nivelar; (*account*) saldar; (*make equal*) equilibrar; **~ of trade/payments** balanza de comercio/pagos; **~d** *adj* (*personality, diet*) equilibrado; (*report*) objetivo; **~ sheet** *n* balance *m*

balcony ['bælkənɪ] *n* (*open*) balcón *m*; (*closed*) galería; (*in theatre*) anfiteatro

bald [bɔːld] *adj* calvo; (*tyre*) liso

bale [beɪl] *n* (*AGR*) paca, fardo; (*of papers etc*) fajo; **~ out** *vi* lanzarse en paracaídas

Balearics [bælɪ'ærɪks] *npl*: **the ~** las Baleares

ball [bɔːl] *n* pelota; (*football*) balón *m*; (*of wool, string*) ovillo; (*dance*) baile *m*; **to play ~** (*fig*) cooperar

ballast ['bæləst] *n* lastre *m*

ball bearings *npl* cojinetes *mpl* de bolas

ballerina [bælə'riːnə] *n* bailarina

ballet ['bæleɪ] *n* ballet *m*; **~ dancer** *n* bailarín/ina *m/f*

balloon [bə'luːn] *n* globo

ballot ['bælət] *n* votación *f*; **~ paper** *n* papeleta (para votar)

ballpoint (pen) ['bɔːlpɔɪnt-] *n* bolígrafo

ballroom ['bɔːlrum] *n* salón *m* de baile

Baltic ['bɔːltɪk] *n*: **the ~ (Sea)** el (Mar) Báltico

ban [bæn] *n* prohibición *f*, proscripción *f* ♦ *vt* prohibir, proscribir

banal [bə'nɑːl] *adj* banal, vulgar

banana [bə'nɑːnə] *n* plátano (*SP*), banana (*AM*)

band [bænd] *n* grupo; (*strip*) faja, tira; (*stripe*) lista; (*MUS: jazz*) orquesta; (*: rock*) grupo; (*: MIL*) banda; **~ together** *vi* juntarse, asociarse

bandage ['bændɪdʒ] *n* venda, vendaje *m*
♦ *vt* vendar
Bandaid ® ['bændeɪd] (*US*) *n* tirita
bandit ['bændɪt] *n* bandido
bandy-legged ['bændɪ'legd] *adj* estevado
bang [bæŋ] *n* (*of gun, exhaust*) estallido,
detonación *f*; (*of door*) portazo; (*blow*)
golpe *m* ♦ *vt* (*door*) cerrar de golpe;
(*one's head*) golpear ♦ *vi* estallar; (*door*)
cerrar de golpe
Bangladesh [bɑːŋglə'deʃ] *n* Bangladesh *m*
bangs [bæŋz] (*US*) *npl* flequillo
banish ['bænɪʃ] *vt* desterrar
banister(s) ['bænɪstə(z)] *n(pl)* barandilla,
pasamanos *m inv*
bank [bæŋk] *n* (*COMM*) banco; (*of river,
lake*) ribera, orilla; (*of earth*) terraplén *m*
♦ *vi* (*AVIAT*) ladearse; ~ **on** *vt fus* contar
con; ~ **account** *n* cuenta de banco; ~
card *n* tarjeta bancaria; ~**er** *n* banquero;
~**er's card** (*BRIT*) *n* = ~ **card**; **B~
holiday** (*BRIT*) *n* día *m* festivo; ~**ing** *n*
banca; ~**note** *n* billete *m* de banco; ~
rate *n* tipo de interés bancario

---
bank holiday

🛈 *El término* **bank holiday** *se aplica en
el Reino Unido a todo día festivo
oficial en el que cierran bancos y
comercios. Los más importantes son en
Navidad, Semana Santa, finales de mayo
y finales de agosto y, al contrario que en
los países de tradición católica, no
coincide necesariamente con una
celebración religiosa.*

---

bankrupt ['bæŋkrʌpt] *adj* quebrado,
insolvente; **to go ~** hacer bancarrota; **to
be ~** estar en quiebra; ~**cy** *n* quiebra
bank statement *n* balance *m* or detalle
m de cuenta
banner ['bænə*] *n* pancarta
bannister(s) ['bænɪstə(z)] *n(pl)*
= **banister(s)**
baptism ['bæptɪzəm] *n* bautismo; (*act*)
bautizo
bar [bɑː*] *n* (*pub*) bar *m*; (*counter*)

mostrador *m*; (*rod*) barra; (*of window,
cage*) reja; (*of soap*) pastilla; (*of chocolate*)
tableta; (*fig: hindrance*) obstáculo;
(*prohibition*) proscripción *f*; (*MUS*) barra
♦ *vt* (*road*) obstruir; (*person*) excluir;
(*activity*) prohibir; **the B~** (*LAW*) la
abogacía; **behind ~s** entre rejas; ~ **none**
sin excepción
barbaric [bɑː'bærɪk] *adj* bárbaro
barbecue ['bɑːbɪkjuː] *n* barbacoa
barbed wire ['bɑːbd-] *n* alambre *m* de
púas
barber ['bɑːbə*] *n* peluquero, barbero
bar code *n* código de barras
bare [beə*] *adj* desnudo; (*trees*) sin hojas;
(*necessities etc*) básico ♦ *vt* desnudar;
(*teeth*) enseñar; ~**back** *adv* a pelo, sin
silla; ~**faced** *adj* descarado; ~**foot** *adj,
adv* descalzo; ~**ly** *adv* apenas
bargain ['bɑːgɪn] *n* pacto, negocio; (*good
buy*) ganga ♦ *vi* negociar; (*haggle*)
regatear; **into the ~** además, por
añadidura; ~ **for** *vt fus*: **he got more
than he ~ed for** le resultó peor de lo que
esperaba
barge [bɑːdʒ] *n* barcaza; ~ **in** *vi* irrumpir;
(*interrupt: conversation*) interrumpir
bark [bɑːk] *n* (*of tree*) corteza; (*of dog*)
ladrido ♦ *vi* ladrar
barley ['bɑːlɪ] *n* cebada
barmaid ['bɑːmeɪd] *n* camarera
barman ['bɑːmən] *n* camarero, barman *m*
barn [bɑːn] *n* granero
barometer [bə'rɒmɪtə*] *n* barómetro
baron ['bærən] *n* barón *m*; (*press ~ etc*)
magnate *m*; ~**ess** *n* baronesa
barracks ['bærəks] *npl* cuartel *m*
barrage ['bærɑːʒ] *n* (*MIL*) descarga,
bombardeo; (*dam*) presa; (*of criticism*)
lluvia, aluvión *m*
barrel ['bærəl] *n* barril *m*; (*of gun*) cañón
m
barren ['bærən] *adj* estéril
barricade [bærɪ'keɪd] *n* barricada
barrier ['bærɪə*] *n* barrera
barring ['bɑːrɪŋ] *prep* excepto, salvo
barrister ['bærɪstə*] (*BRIT*) *n* abogado/a

barrow ['bærəu] n (cart) carretilla (de mano)

bartender ['bɑːtɛndəʳ] (US) n camarero, barman m

barter ['bɑːtəʳ] vt: **to ~ sth for sth** trocar algo por algo

base [beɪs] n base f ♦ vt: **to ~ sth on** basar or fundar algo en ♦ adj bajo, infame

baseball ['beɪsbɔːl] n béisbol m

basement ['beɪsmənt] n sótano

bases[1] ['beɪsiːz] npl of **basis**

bases[2] ['beɪsɪz] npl of **base**

bash [bæʃ] (inf) vt golpear

bashful ['bæʃful] adj tímido, vergonzoso

basic ['beɪsɪk] adj básico; **~ally** adv fundamentalmente, en el fondo; (simply) sencillamente; **~s** npl: **the ~s** los fundamentos

basil ['bæzl] n albahaca

basin ['beɪsn] n cuenco, tazón m; (GEO) cuenca; (also: **wash~**) lavabo

basis ['beɪsɪs] (pl **bases**) n base f; **on a part-time/trial ~** a tiempo parcial/a prueba

bask [bɑːsk] vi: **to ~ in the sun** tomar el sol

basket ['bɑːskɪt] n cesta, cesto; canasta; **~ball** n baloncesto

Basque [bæsk] adj, n vasco/a m/f; **~ Country** n Euskadi m, País m Vasco

bass [beɪs] n (MUS: instrument) bajo; (double ~) contrabajo; (singer) bajo

bassoon [bə'suːn] n fagot m

bastard ['bɑːstəd] n bastardo; (inf!) hijo de puta (!)

bat [bæt] n (ZOOL) murciélago; (for ball games) palo; (BRIT: for table tennis) pala ♦ vt: **he didn't ~ an eyelid** ni pestañeó

batch [bætʃ] n (of bread) hornada; (of letters etc) lote m

bated ['beɪtɪd] adj: **with ~ breath** sin respirar

bath [bɑːθ, pl bɑːðz] n (action) baño; (~tub) baño (SP), bañera (SP), tina (AM) ♦ vt bañar; **to have a ~** bañarse, tomar un baño; see also **baths**

bathe [beɪð] vi bañarse ♦ vt (wound) lavar; **~r** n bañista m/f

bathing ['beɪðɪŋ] n el bañarse; **~ costume** (US **~ suit**) n traje m de baño

bath: **~robe** n (man's) batín m; (woman's) bata; **~room** n (cuarto de) baño; **~s** [bɑːðz] npl (also: **swimming ~s**) piscina; **~ towel** n toalla de baño

baton ['bætən] n (MUS) batuta; (ATHLETICS) testigo; (weapon) porra

batter ['bætəʳ] vt maltratar; (subj: rain etc) azotar ♦ n masa (para rebozar); **~ed** adj (hat, pan) estropeado

battery ['bætərɪ] n (AUT) batería; (of torch) pila

battle ['bætl] n batalla; (fig) lucha ♦ vi luchar; **~ship** n acorazado

bawl [bɔːl] vi chillar, gritar; (child) berrear

bay [beɪ] n (GEO) bahía; **B~ of Biscay** ≈ mar Cantábrico; **to hold sb at ~** mantener a alguien a raya; **~ leaf** n hoja de laurel

bay window n ventana salediza

bazaar [bə'zɑːʳ] n bazar m; (fete) venta con fines benéficos

B. & B. n abbr (= bed and breakfast) cama y desayuno

BBC n abbr (= British Broadcasting Corporation) cadena de radio y televisión estatal británica

B.C. adv abbr (= before Christ) a. de C.

KEYWORD

---

be [biː] (pt **was**, **were**, pp **been**) aux vb **1** (with present participle: forming continuous tenses): **what are you doing?** ¿qué estás haciendo?, ¿qué haces?; **they're coming tomorrow** vienen mañana; **I've been waiting for you for hours** llevo horas esperándote

2 (with pp: forming passives) ser (but often replaced by active or reflective constructions); **to ~ murdered** ser asesinado; **the box had been opened** habían abierto la caja; **the thief was nowhere to ~ seen** no se veía al ladrón por ninguna parte

3 (*in tag questions*): **it was fun, wasn't it?** fue divertido, ¿no? *or* ¿verdad?; **he's good-looking, isn't he?** es guapo, ¿no te parece?; **she's back again, is she?** entonces, ¿ha vuelto?
4 (*+to +infin*): **the house is to ~ sold** (*necessity*) hay que vender la casa; (*future*) van a vender la casa; **he's not to open it** no tiene que abrirlo
♦ *vb +complement* 1 (*with n or num complement, but see also* 3, 4, 5 *and impers vb below*) ser; **he's a doctor** es médico; **2 and 2 are 4** 2 y 2 son 4
2 (*with adj complement: expressing permanent or inherent quality*) ser; (*: expressing state seen as temporary or reversible*) estar; **I'm English** soy inglés/ esa; **she's tall/pretty** es alta/bonita; **he's young** es joven; **~ careful/good/quiet** ten cuidado/pórtate bien/cállate; **I'm tired** estoy cansado/a; **it's dirty** está sucio/a
3 (*of health*) estar; **how are you?** ¿cómo estás?; **he's very ill** está muy enfermo; **I'm better now** ya estoy mejor
4 (*of age*) tener; **how old are you?** ¿cuántos años tienes?; **I'm sixteen (years old)** tengo dieciséis años
5 (*cost*) costar; ser; **how much was the meal?** ¿cuánto fue *or* costó la comida?; **that'll ~ £5.75, please** son £5.75, por favor; **this shirt is £17** esta camisa cuesta £17
♦ *vi* 1 (*exist, occur etc*) existir, haber; **the best singer that ever was** el mejor cantante que existió jamás; **is there a God?** ¿hay un Dios?, ¿existe Dios?; **~ that as it may** sea como sea; **so ~ it** así sea
2 (*referring to place*) estar; **I won't ~ here tomorrow** no estaré aquí mañana
3 (*referring to movement*): **where have you been?** ¿dónde has estado?
♦ *impers vb* 1 (*referring to time*): **it's 5 o'clock** son las 5; **it's the 28th of April** estamos a 28 de abril
2 (*referring to distance*): **it's 10 km to the village** el pueblo está a 10 km

3 (*referring to the weather*): **it's too hot/ cold** hace demasiado calor/frío; **it's windy today** hace viento hoy
4 (*emphatic*): **it's me** soy yo; **it was Maria who paid the bill** fue María la que pagó la cuenta

beach [biːtʃ] *n* playa ♦ *vt* varar
beacon ['biːkən] *n* (*lighthouse*) faro; (*marker*) guía
bead [biːd] *n* cuenta; (*of sweat etc*) gota
beak [biːk] *n* pico
beaker ['biːkə*] *n* vaso de plástico
beam [biːm] *n* (ARCH) viga, travesaño; (*of light*) rayo, haz *m* de luz ♦ *vi* brillar; (*smile*) sonreír
bean [biːn] *n* judía; **runner/broad ~** habichuela/haba; **coffee ~** grano de café; **~sprouts** *npl* brotes *mpl* de soja
bear [bɛə*] (*pt* **bore**, *pp* **borne**) *n* oso ♦ *vt* (*weight etc*) llevar; (*cost*) pagar; (*responsibility*) tener; (*endure*) soportar, aguantar; (*children*) parir, tener; (*fruit*) dar ♦ *vi*: **to ~ right/left** torcer a la derecha/ izquierda; **~ out** *vt* (*suspicions*) corroborar, confirmar; (*person*) dar la razón a; **~ up** *vi* (*remain cheerful*) mantenerse animado
beard [bɪəd] *n* barba; **~ed** *adj* con barba, barbudo
bearer ['bɛərə*] *n* portador(a) *m/f*
bearing ['bɛərɪŋ] *n* porte *m*, comportamiento; (*connection*) relación *f*; **~s** *npl* (*also*: **ball ~s**) cojinetes *mpl* a bolas; **to take a ~** tomar marcaciones; **to find one's ~s** orientarse
beast [biːst] *n* bestia; (*inf*) bruto, salvaje *m*; **~ly** *adj* horrible
beat [biːt] (*pt* **beat**, *pp* **beaten**) *n* (*of heart*) latido; (MUS) ritmo, compás *m*; (*of policeman*) ronda ♦ *vt* pegar, golpear; (*eggs*) batir; (*defeat: opponent*) vencer, derrotar; (*: record*) sobrepasar ♦ *vi* (*heart*) latir; (*drum*) redoblar; (*rain, wind*) azotar; **off the ~en track** aislado; **to ~ it** (*inf*) largarse; **~ off** *vt* rechazar; **~ up** *vt* (*attack*) dar una paliza a; **~ing** *n* paliza

beautiful ['bju:tiful] *adj* precioso, hermoso, bello; **~ly** *adv* maravillosamente

beauty ['bju:ti] *n* belleza; **~ salon** *n* salón *m* de belleza; **~ spot** *n* (*TOURISM*) lugar *m* pintoresco

beaver ['bi:və*] *n* castor *m*

became [bɪ'keɪm] *pt of* **become**

because [bɪ'kɔz] *conj* porque; **~ of** debido a, a causa de

beckon ['bekən] *vt* (*also:* **~ to**) llamar con señas

become [bɪ'kʌm] (*irreg: like* **come**) *vt* (*suit*) favorecer, sentar bien a ♦ *vi* (+*n*) hacerse, llegar a ser; (+*adj*) ponerse, volverse; **to ~ fat** engordar

becoming [bɪ'kʌmɪŋ] *adj* (*behaviour*) decoroso; (*clothes*) favorecedor(a)

bed [bed] *n* cama; (*of flowers*) macizo; (*of coal, clay*) capa; (*of river*) lecho; (*of sea*) fondo; **to go to ~** acostarse; **~ and breakfast** *n* (*place*) pensión *f*; (*terms*) cama y desayuno; **~clothes** *npl* ropa de cama; **~ding** *n* ropa de cama

bed and breakfast

i Se llama **bed and breakfast** a una forma de alojamiento, en el campo o la ciudad, que ofrece cama y desayuno a precios inferiores a los de un hotel. El servicio se suele anunciar con carteles en los que a menudo se usa únicamente la abreviatura **B. & B.**

bedraggled [bɪ'drægld] *adj* (*untidy: person*) desastrado; (*clothes, hair*) desordenado

bed: **~ridden** *adj* postrado (en cama); **~room** *n* dormitorio; **~side** *n*: **at the ~side of** a la cabecera de; **~sit(ter)** (*BRIT*) *n* estudio (*SP*), suite *m* (*AM*); **~spread** *n* cubrecama *m*, colcha; **~time** *n* hora de acostarse

bee [bi:] *n* abeja

beech [bi:tʃ] *n* haya

beef [bi:f] *n* carne *f* de vaca; **roast ~** rosbif *m*; **~burger** *n* hamburguesa; **B~eater** *n* alabardero de la Torre de Londres

beehive ['bi:haɪv] *n* colmena

beeline ['bi:laɪn] *n*: **to make a ~ for** ir derecho a

been [bi:n] *pp of* **be**

beer [bɪə*] *n* cerveza

beet [bi:t] (*US*) *n* (*also:* **red ~**) remolacha

beetle ['bi:tl] *n* escarabajo

beetroot ['bi:tru:t] (*BRIT*) *n* remolacha

before [bɪ'fɔ:*] *prep* (*of time*) antes de; (*of space*) delante de ♦ *conj* antes (de) que ♦ *adv* antes, anteriormente; delante, adelante; **~ going** antes de marcharse; **~ she goes** antes de que se vaya; **the week ~** la semana anterior; **I've never seen it ~** no lo he visto nunca; **~hand** *adv* de antemano, con anticipación

beg [beg] *vi* pedir limosna ♦ *vt* pedir, rogar; (*entreat*) suplicar; **to ~ sb to do sth** rogar a uno que haga algo; *see also* **pardon**

began [bɪ'gæn] *pt of* **begin**

beggar ['begə*] *n* mendigo/a

begin [bɪ'gɪn] (*pt* **began**, *pp* **begun**) *vt, vi* empezar, comenzar; **to ~ doing** *or* **to do sth** empezar a hacer algo; **~ner** *n* principiante *m/f*; **~ning** *n* principio, comienzo

begun [bɪ'gʌn] *pp of* **begin**

behalf [bɪ'hɑ:f] *n*: **on ~ of** en nombre de, por; (*for benefit of*) en beneficio de; **on my/his ~** por mí/él

behave [bɪ'heɪv] *vi* (*person*) portarse, comportarse; (*well: also:* **~ o.s.**) portarse bien; **behaviour** (*US* **behavior**) *n* comportamiento, conducta

behind [bɪ'haɪnd] *prep* detrás de; (*supporting*): **to be ~ sb** apoyar a alguien ♦ *adv* detrás, por detrás, atrás ♦ *n* trasero; **to be ~ (schedule)** ir retrasado; **~ the scenes** (*fig*) entre bastidores

behold [bɪ'həuld] (*irreg: like* **hold**) *vt* contemplar

beige [beɪʒ] *adj* color beige

Beijing ['beɪ'dʒɪŋ] *n* Pekín *m*

being ['bi:ɪŋ] *n* ser *m*; (*existence*): **in ~** existente; **to come into ~** aparecer

Beirut [beɪ'ru:t] *n* Beirut *m*

Belarus [belə'rus] *n* Bielorrusia

belated [bɪ'leɪtɪd] *adj* atrasado, tardío

belch [beltʃ] *vi* eructar ♦ *vt* (*gen*: ~ **out**: *smoke etc*) arrojar

Belgian ['beldʒən] *adj, n* belga *m/f*

Belgium ['beldʒəm] *n* Bélgica

belief [bɪ'liːf] *n* opinión *f*; (*faith*) fe *f*

believe [bɪ'liːv] *vt, vi* creer; **to ~ in** creer en; **~r** *n* partidario/a; (*REL*) creyente *m/f*, fiel *m/f*

belittle [bɪ'lɪtl] *vt* quitar importancia a

bell [bel] *n* campana; (*small*) campanilla; (*on door*) timbre *m*

belligerent [bɪ'lɪdʒərənt] *adj* agresivo

bellow ['beləʊ] *vi* bramar; (*person*) rugir

belly ['belɪ] *n* barriga, panza

belong [bɪ'lɒŋ] *vi*: **to ~ to** pertenecer a; (*club etc*) ser socio de; **this book ~s here** este libro va aquí; **~ings** *npl* pertenencias *fpl*

beloved [bɪ'lʌvɪd] *adj* querido/a

below [bɪ'ləʊ] *prep* bajo, debajo de; (*less than*) inferior a ♦ *adv* abajo, (por) debajo; **see ~** véase más abajo

belt [belt] *n* cinturón *m*; (*TECH*) correa, cinta ♦ *vt* (*thrash*) pegar con correa; **~way** (*US*) *n* (*AUT*) carretera de circunvalación

bench [bentʃ] *n* banco; (*BRIT*: *POL*): **the Government / Opposition ~es** (los asientos de) los miembros del Gobierno/de la Oposición; **the B~** (*LAW*: *judges*) magistratura

bend [bend] (*pt, pp* **bent**) *vt* doblar ♦ *vi* inclinarse ♦ *n* (*BRIT*: *in road, river*) curva; (*in pipe*) codo; **~ down** *vi* inclinarse, doblarse; **~ over** *vi* inclinarse

beneath [bɪ'niːθ] *prep* bajo, debajo de; (*unworthy of*) indigno de ♦ *adv* abajo, (por) debajo

benefactor ['benɪfæktə*] *n* bienhechor *m*

beneficial [benɪ'fɪʃəl] *adj* beneficioso

benefit ['benɪfɪt] *n* beneficio; (*allowance of money*) subsidio ♦ *vt* beneficiar ♦ *vi*: **he'll ~ from it** le sacará provecho

benevolent [bɪ'nevələnt] *adj* (*person*) benévolo

benign [bɪ'naɪn] *adj* benigno; (*smile*) afable

bent [bent] *pt, pp of* **bend** ♦ *n* inclinación *f* ♦ *adj*: **to be ~ on** estar empeñado en

bequest [bɪ'kwest] *n* legado

bereaved [bɪ'riːvd] *npl*: **the ~** *los íntimos de una persona afligidos por su muerte*

beret ['bereɪ] *n* boina

Berlin [bəː'lɪn] *n* Berlín

berm [bəːm] *n* (*US*) (*AUT*) arcén *m*

Bermuda [bəː'mjuːdə] *n* las Bermudas

berry ['berɪ] *n* baya

berserk [bə'səːk] *adj*: **to go ~** perder los estribos

berth [bəːθ] *n* (*bed*) litera; (*cabin*) camarote *m*; (*for ship*) amarradero ♦ *vi* atracar, amarrar

beseech [bɪ'siːtʃ] (*pt, pp* **besought**) *vt* suplicar

beset [bɪ'set] (*pt, pp* **beset**) *vt* (*person*) acosar

beside [bɪ'saɪd] *prep* junto a, al lado de; **to be ~ o.s. with anger** estar fuera de sí; **that's ~ the point** eso no tiene nada que ver; **~s** *adv* además ♦ *prep* además de

besiege [bɪ'siːdʒ] *vt* sitiar; (*fig*) asediar

best [best] *adj* (el/la) mejor ♦ *adv* (lo) mejor; **the ~ part of** (*quantity*) la mayor parte de; **at ~** en el mejor de los casos; **to make the ~ of sth** sacar el mejor partido de algo; **to do one's ~** hacer todo lo posible; **to the ~ of my knowledge** que yo sepa; **to the ~ of my ability** como mejor puedo; **~-before date** *n* fecha de consumo preferente; **~ man** *n* padrino de boda

bestow [bɪ'stəʊ] *vt* (*title*) otorgar

bestseller ['best'selə*] *n* éxito de librería, bestseller *m*

bet [bet] (*pt, pp* **bet** *or* **betted**) *n* apuesta ♦ *vt*: **to ~ money on** apostar dinero por; **to ~ sb sth** apostar algo a uno ♦ *vi* apostar

betray [bɪ'treɪ] *vt* traicionar; (*trust*) faltar a; **~al** *n* traición *f*

better ['betə*] *adj, adv* mejor ♦ *vt* superar ♦ *n*: **to get the ~ of sb** quedar por encima de alguien; **you had ~ do it** más vale que lo hagas; **he thought ~ of it** cambió de parecer; **to get ~** (*MED*) mejorar(se); **~ off** *adj* mejor; (*wealthier*) más acomodado

betting ['bɛtɪŋ] *n* juego, el apostar; **~ shop** (*BRIT*) *n* agencia de apuestas

between [bɪ'twiːn] *prep* entre ♦ *adv* (*time*) mientras tanto; (*place*) en medio

beverage ['bɛvərɪdʒ] *n* bebida

beware [bɪ'wɛə*] *vi*: **to ~ (of)** tener cuidado (con); **"~ of the dog"** "perro peligroso"

bewildered [bɪ'wɪldəd] *adj* aturdido, perplejo

beyond [bɪ'jɔnd] *prep* más allá de; (*past: understanding*) fuera de; (*after: date*) después de, más allá de; (*above*) superior a ♦ *adv* (*in space*) más allá; (*in time*) posteriormente; **~ doubt** fuera de toda duda; **~ repair** irreparable

bias ['baɪəs] *n* (*prejudice*) prejuicio, pasión *f*; (*preference*) predisposición *f*; **~(s)ed** *adj* parcial

bib [bɪb] *n* babero

Bible ['baɪbl] *n* Biblia

bicarbonate of soda [baɪ'kɑːbənɪt-] *n* bicarbonato sódico

bicker ['bɪkə*] *vi* pelearse

bicycle ['baɪsɪkl] *n* bicicleta

bid [bɪd] (*pt* **bade** *or* **bid**, *pp* **bidden** *or* **bid**) *n* oferta, postura; (*in tender*) licitación *f*; (*attempt*) tentativa, conato ♦ *vi* hacer una oferta ♦ *vt* (*offer*) ofrecer; **to ~ sb good day** dar a uno los buenos días; **~der** *n*: **the highest ~der** el mejor postor; **~ding** *n* (*at auction*) ofertas *fpl*

bide [baɪd] *vt*: **to ~ one's time** esperar el momento adecuado

bifocals [baɪ'fəʊklz] *npl* gafas *fpl* (*SP*) *or* anteojos *mpl* (*AM*) bifocales

big [bɪg] *adj* grande; (*brother, sister*) mayor

bigheaded ['bɪg'hɛdɪd] *adj* engreído

bigot ['bɪgət] *n* fanático/a, intolerante *m/f*; **~ed** *adj* fanático, intolerante; **~ry** *n* fanatismo, intolerancia

big top *n* (*at circus*) carpa

bike [baɪk] *n* bici *f*

bikini [bɪ'kiːnɪ] *n* bikini *m*

bilingual [baɪ'lɪŋgwəl] *adj* bilingüe

bill [bɪl] *n* cuenta; (*invoice*) factura; (*POL*) proyecto de ley; (*US: banknote*) billete *m*; (*of show*) programa *m*; (*of bird*) pico; **"post no ~s"** "prohibido fijar carteles"; **to fit** *or* **fill the ~** (*fig*) cumplir con los requisitos; **~board** (*US*) *n* cartelera

billet ['bɪlɪt] *n* alojamiento

billfold ['bɪlfəʊld] (*US*) *n* cartera

billiards ['bɪljədz] *n* billar *m*

billion ['bɪljən] *n* (*BRIT*) billón *m* (*millón de millones*); (*US*) mil millones *mpl*

bimbo ['bɪmbəʊ] (*inf*) *n* tía buena sin seso

bin [bɪn] *n* (*for rubbish*) cubo (*SP*) *or* bote *m* (*AM*) de la basura; (*container*) recipiente *m*

bind [baɪnd] (*pt, pp* **bound**) *vt* atar; (*book*) encuadernar; (*oblige*) obligar ♦ *n* (*inf: nuisance*) lata; **~ing** *adj* (*contract*) obligatorio

binge [bɪndʒ] (*inf*) *n*: **to go on a ~** ir de juerga

bingo ['bɪŋgəʊ] *n* bingo *m*

binoculars [bɪ'nɔkjuləz] *npl* prismáticos *mpl*

bio... [baɪə*] *prefix*: **~chemistry** *n* bioquímica; **~degradable** [baɪəʊdɪ'greɪdəbl] *adj* biodegradable; **~graphy** [baɪ'ɔgrəfɪ] *n* biografía; **~logical** *adj* biológico; **~logy** [baɪ'ɔlədʒɪ] *n* biología

birch [bəːtʃ] *n* (*tree*) abedul *m*

bird [bəːd] *n* ave *f*, pájaro; (*BRIT: inf: girl*) chica; **~'s eye view** *n* (*aerial view*) vista de pájaro; (*overview*) visión *f* de conjunto; **~ watcher** *n* ornitólogo/a

Biro ® ['baɪrəʊ] *n* bolígrafo

birth [bəːθ] *n* nacimiento; **to give ~ to** parir, dar a luz; **~ certificate** *n* partida de nacimiento; **~ control** *n* (*policy*) control *m* de natalidad; (*methods*) métodos *mpl* anticonceptivos; **~day** *n* cumpleaños *m inv* ♦ *cpd* (*cake, card etc*) de cumpleaños; **~place** *n* lugar *m* de nacimiento; **~ rate** *n* (tasa de) natalidad *f*

biscuit ['bɪskɪt] (*BRIT*) *n* galleta, bizcocho (*AM*)

bisect [baɪ'sɛkt] *vt* bisecar

bishop ['bɪʃəp] *n* obispo; (*CHESS*) alfil *m*

bit [bɪt] *pt of* **bite** ♦ *n* trozo, pedazo, pedacito; (*COMPUT*) bit *m*, bitio; (*for horse*) freno, bocado; **a ~ of** un poco de; **a ~ mad** un poco loco; **~ by ~** poco a poco

bitch [bɪtʃ] *n* perra; (*inf!: woman*) zorra (!)

bite [baɪt] (*pt* **bit**, *pp* **bitten**) *vt*, *vi* morder; (*insect etc*) picar ♦ *n* (*insect ~*) picadura; (*mouthful*) bocado; **to ~ one's nails** comerse las uñas; **let's have a ~ (to eat)** (*inf*) vamos a comer algo

bitter ['bɪtə*] *adj* amargo; (*wind*) cortante, penetrante; (*battle*) encarnizado ♦ *n* (*BRIT: beer*) cerveza típica británica a base de lúpulos; **~ness** *n* lo amargo, amargura; (*anger*) rencor *m*

bizarre [bɪ'zɑ:*] *adj* raro, extraño

black [blæk] *adj* negro; (*tea, coffee*) solo ♦ *n* color *m* negro; (*person*): **B~** negro/a ♦ *vt* (*BRIT: INDUSTRY*) boicotear; **to give sb a ~ eye** ponerle a uno el ojo morado; **~ and blue** (*bruised*) amoratado; **to be in the ~** (*bank account*) estar en números negros; **~berry** *n* zarzamora; **~bird** *n* mirlo; **~board** *n* pizarra; **~ coffee** *n* café *m* solo; **~currant** *n* grosella negra; **~en** *vt* (*fig*) desacreditar; **~ ice** *n* hielo invisible en la carretera; **~leg** (*BRIT*) *n* esquirol *m*, rompehuelgas *m inv*; **~list** *n* lista negra; **~mail** *n* chantaje *m* ♦ *vt* chantajear; **~ market** *n* mercado negro; **~out** *n* (*MIL*) oscurecimiento; (*power cut*) apagón *m*; (*TV, RADIO*) interrupción *f* de programas; (*fainting*) desvanecimiento; **B~ Sea** *n*: **the B~ Sea** el Mar Negro; **~ sheep** *n* (*fig*) oveja negra; **~smith** *n* herrero; **~ spot** *n* (*AUT*) lugar *m* peligroso; (*for unemployment etc*) punto negro

bladder ['blædə*] *n* vejiga

blade [bleɪd] *n* hoja; (*of propeller*) paleta; **a ~ of grass** una brizna de hierba

blame [bleɪm] *n* culpa ♦ *vt*: **to ~ sb for sth** echar a uno la culpa de algo; **to be to ~** tener la culpa de

bland [blænd] *adj* (*music, taste*) soso

blank [blæŋk] *adj* en blanco; (*look*) sin expresión ♦ *n* (*of memory*): **my mind is a ~** no puedo recordar nada; (*on form*) blanco, espacio en blanco; (*cartridge*) cartucho sin bala *or* de fogueo; **~ cheque** *n* cheque *m* en blanco

blanket ['blæŋkɪt] *n* manta (*SP*), cobija (*AM*); (*of snow*) capa; (*of fog*) manto

blare [blɛə*] *vi* sonar estrepitosamente

blasé ['blɑːzeɪ] *adj* hastiado

blast [blɑːst] *n* (*of wind*) ráfaga, soplo; (*of explosive*) explosión *f* ♦ *vt* (*blow up*) volar; **~-off** *n* (*SPACE*) lanzamiento

blatant ['bleɪtənt] *adj* descarado

blaze [bleɪz] *n* (*fire*) fuego; (*fig: of colour*) despliegue *m*; (: *of glory*) esplendor *m* ♦ *vi* arder en llamas; (*fig*) brillar ♦ *vt*: **to ~ a trail** (*fig*) abrir (un) camino; **in a ~ of publicity** con gran publicidad

blazer ['bleɪzə*] *n* chaqueta de uniforme de colegial *o* de socio de club

bleach [bliːtʃ] *n* (*also*: **household ~**) lejía ♦ *vt* blanquear; **~ed** *adj* (*hair*) teñido (de rubio); **~ers** (*US*) *npl* (*SPORT*) gradas *fpl* al sol

bleak [bliːk] *adj* (*countryside*) desierto; (*prospect*) poco prometedor(a); (*weather*) crudo; (*smile*) triste

bleat [bliːt] *vi* balar

bleed [bliːd] (*pt*, *pp* **bled**) *vt*, *vi* sangrar; **my nose is ~ing** me está sangrando la nariz

bleeper ['bliːpə*] *n* busca *m*

blemish ['blɛmɪʃ] *n* marca, mancha; (*on reputation*) tacha

blend [blɛnd] *n* mezcla ♦ *vt* mezclar; (*colours etc*) combinar, mezclar ♦ *vi* (*colours etc: also*: **~ in**) combinarse, mezclarse

bless [blɛs] (*pt*, *pp* **blessed** *or* **blest**) *vt* bendecir; **~ you!** (*after sneeze*) ¡Jesús!; **~ing** *n* (*approval*) aprobación *f*; (*godsend*) don *m* del cielo, bendición *f*; (*advantage*) beneficio, ventaja

blew [bluː] *pt of* **blow**

blind [blaɪnd] *adj* ciego; (*fig*): **~ (to)** ciego (a) ♦ *n* (*for window*) persiana ♦ *vt* cegar; (*dazzle*) deslumbrar; (*deceive*): **to ~ sb to ...** cegar a uno a ...; **the ~** *npl* los ciegos; **~ alley** *n* callejón *m* sin salida; **~ corner** (BRIT) *n* esquina escondida; **~fold** *n* venda ♦ *adv* con los ojos vendados ♦ *vt* vendar los ojos a; **~ly** *adv* a ciegas, ciegamente; **~ness** *n* ceguera; **~ spot** *n* (AUT) ángulo ciego

blink [blɪŋk] *vi* parpadear, pestañear; (*light*) oscilar; **~ers** *npl* anteojeras *fpl*

bliss [blɪs] *n* felicidad *f*

blister [ˈblɪstə*] *n* ampolla ♦ *vi* (*paint*) ampollarse

blizzard [ˈblɪzəd] *n* ventisca

bloated [ˈbləʊtɪd] *adj* hinchado; (*person: full*) ahíto

blob [blɔb] *n* (*drop*) gota; (*indistinct object*) bulto

bloc [blɔk] *n* (POL) bloque *m*

block [blɔk] *n* bloque *m*; (*in pipes*) obstáculo; (*of buildings*) manzana (SP), cuadra (AM) ♦ *vt* obstruir, cerrar; (*progress*) estorbar; **~ of flats** (BRIT) bloque *m* de pisos; **mental ~** bloqueo mental; **~ade** [-ˈkeɪd] *n* bloqueo ♦ *vt* bloquear; **~age** *n* estorbo, obstrucción *f*; **~buster** *n* (*book*) bestseller *m*; (*film*) éxito de público; **~ letters** *npl* letras *fpl* de molde

bloke [bləʊk] (BRIT: *inf*) *n* tipo, tío

blond(e) [blɔnd] *adj, n* rubio/a *m/f*

blood [blʌd] *n* sangre *f*; **~ donor** *n* donante *m/f* de sangre; **~ group** *n* grupo sanguíneo; **~hound** *n* sabueso; **~ poisoning** *n* envenenamiento de la sangre; **~ pressure** *n* presión *f* sanguínea; **~shed** *n* derramamiento de sangre; **~shot** *adj* inyectado en sangre; **~stream** *n* corriente *f* sanguínea; **~ test** *n* análisis *m inv* de sangre; **~thirsty** *adj* sanguinario; **~ vessel** *n* vaso sanguíneo; **~y** *adj* sangriento; (*nose etc*) lleno de sangre; (BRIT: *inf!*): **this ~y...** este

condenado *o* puñetero ... (!) ♦ *adv*: **~y strong/good** (BRIT: *inf!*) terriblemente fuerte/bueno; **~y-minded** (BRIT: *inf*) *adj* puñetero (!)

bloom [bluːm] *n* flor *f* ♦ *vi* florecer

blossom [ˈblɔsəm] *n* flor *f* ♦ *vi* (*also fig*) florecer

blot [blɔt] *n* borrón *m*; (*fig*) mancha ♦ *vt* (*stain*) manchar; **~ out** *vt* (*view*) tapar

blotchy [ˈblɔtʃi] *adj* (*complexion*) lleno de manchas

blotting paper [ˈblɔtɪŋ-] *n* papel *m* secante

blouse [blauz] *n* blusa

blow [bləʊ] (*pt* **blew**, *pp* **blown**) *n* golpe *m*; (*with sword*) espadazo ♦ *vi* soplar; (*dust, sand etc*) volar; (*fuse*) fundirse ♦ *vt* (*subj: wind*) llevarse; (*fuse*) quemar; (*instrument*) tocar; **to ~ one's nose** sonarse; **~ away** *vt* llevarse, arrancar; **~ down** *vt* derribar; **~ off** *vt* arrebatar; **~ out** *vi* apagarse; **~ over** *vi* amainar; **~ up** *vi* estallar ♦ *vt* volar; (*tyre*) inflar; (PHOT) ampliar; **~-dry** *n* moldeado (con secador); **~lamp** (BRIT) *n* soplete *m*, lámpara de soldar; **~-out** *n* (*of tyre*) pinchazo; **~torch** *n* = **~lamp**

blue [bluː] *adj* azul; (*depressed*) deprimido; **~ film/joke** película/chiste *m* verde; **out of the ~** (*fig*) de repente; **~bell** *n* campanilla, campánula azul; **~bottle** *n* moscarda, mosca azul; **~print** *n* (*fig*) anteproyecto

bluff [blʌf] *vi* tirarse un farol, farolear ♦ *n* farol *m*; **to call sb's ~** coger a uno la palabra

blunder [ˈblʌndə*] *n* patinazo, metedura de pata ♦ *vi* cometer un error, meter la pata

blunt [blʌnt] *adj* (*pencil*) despuntado; (*knife*) desafilado, romo; (*person*) franco, directo

blur [bləː*] *n* (*shape*): **to become a ~** hacerse borroso ♦ *vt* (*vision*) enturbiar; (*distinction*) borrar

blush [blʌʃ] *vi* ruborizarse, ponerse colorado ♦ *n* rubor *m*

blustery ['blʌstərɪ] *adj* (*weather*) tempestuoso, tormentoso

boar [bɔ:*] *n* verraco, cerdo

board [bɔ:d] *n* (*card~*) cartón *m*; (*wooden*) tabla, tablero; (*on wall*) tablón *m*; (*for chess etc*) tablero; (*committee*) junta, consejo; (*in firm*) mesa *or* junta directiva; (*NAUT, AVIAT*): **on ~** a bordo ♦ *vt* (*ship*) embarcarse en; (*train*) subir a; **full ~** (*BRIT*) pensión completa; **half ~** (*BRIT*) media pensión; **to go by the ~** (*fig*) ser abandonado *or* olvidado; **~ up** *vt* (*door*) tapiar; **~ and lodging** *n* casa y comida; **~er** *n* (*SCOL*) interno/a; **~ing card** (*BRIT*) *n* tarjeta de embarque; **~ing house** *n* casa de huéspedes; **~ing pass** (*US*) *n* = **~ing card**; **~ing school** *n* internado; **~ room** *n* sala de juntas

boast [bəust] *vi*: **to ~** (**about** *or* **of**) alardear (de)

boat [bəut] *n* barco, buque *m*; (*small*) barca, bote *m*

bob [bɔb] *vi* (*also*: **~ up and down**) menearse, balancearse; **~ up** *vi* (re)aparecer de repente

bobby ['bɔbɪ] (*BRIT: inf*) *n* poli *m*

bobsleigh ['bɔbsleɪ] *n* bob *m*

bode [bəud] *vi*: **to ~ well/ill (for)** ser prometedor/poco prometedor (para)

bodily ['bɔdɪlɪ] *adj* corporal ♦ *adv* (*move: person*) en peso

body ['bɔdɪ] *n* cuerpo; (*corpse*) cadáver *m*; (*of car*) caja, carrocería; (*fig: group*) grupo; (: *organization*) organismo; **~-building** *n* culturismo; **~guard** *n* guardaespaldas *m inv*; **~work** *n* carrocería

bog [bɔg] *n* pantano, ciénaga ♦ *vt*: **to get ~ged down** (*fig*) empantanarse, atascarse

bogus ['bəugəs] *adj* falso, fraudulento

boil [bɔɪl] *vt* (*water*) hervir; (*eggs*) pasar por agua, cocer ♦ *vi* hervir; (*fig: with anger*) estar furioso; (: *with heat*) asfixiarse ♦ *n* (*MED*) furúnculo, divieso; **to come to the ~, to come to a ~** (*US*) comenzar a hervir; **to ~ down to** (*fig*) reducirse a; **~ over** *vi* salirse, rebosar; (*anger etc*) llegar al colmo; **~ed egg** *n* huevo cocido (*SP*)

or pasado (*AM*); **~ed potatoes** *npl* patatas *fpl* (*SP*) *or* papas *fpl* (*AM*) hervidas; **~er** *n* caldera; **~er suit** (*BRIT*) *n* mono; **~ing point** *n* punto de ebullición

boisterous ['bɔɪstərəs] *adj* (*noisy*) bullicioso; (*excitable*) exuberante; (*crowd*) tumultuoso

bold [bəuld] *adj* valiente, audaz; (*pej*) descarado; (*colour*) llamativo

Bolivia [bə'lɪvɪə] *n* Bolivia; **~n** *adj, n* boliviano/a *m/f*

bollard ['bɔləd] (*BRIT*) *n* (*AUT*) poste *m*

bolt [bəult] *n* (*lock*) cerrojo; (*with nut*) perno, tornillo ♦ *adv*: **~ upright** rígido, erguido ♦ *vt* (*door*) echar el cerrojo a; (*also*: **~ together**) sujetar con tornillos; (*food*) engullir ♦ *vi* fugarse; (*horse*) desbocarse

bomb [bɔm] *n* bomba ♦ *vt* bombardear; **~ disposal** *n* desmontaje *m* de explosivos; **~er** *n* (*AVIAT*) bombardero; **~shell** *n* (*fig*) bomba

bond [bɔnd] *n* (*promise*) fianza; (*FINANCE*) bono; (*link*) vínculo, lazo; (*COMM*): **in ~** en depósito bajo fianza

bondage ['bɔndɪdʒ] *n* esclavitud *f*

bone [bəun] *n* hueso; (*of fish*) espina ♦ *vt* deshuesar; quitar las espinas a; **~ idle** *adj* gandul; **~ marrow** *n* médula

bonfire ['bɔnfaɪə*] *n* hoguera, fogata

bonnet ['bɔnɪt] *n* gorra; (*BRIT: of car*) capó *m*

bonus ['bəunəs] *n* (*payment*) paga extraordinaria, plus *m*; (*fig*) bendición *f*

bony ['bəunɪ] *adj* (*arm, face*) huesudo; (*MED: tissue*) óseo; (*meat*) lleno de huesos; (*fish*) lleno de espinas

boo [bu:] *excl* ¡uh! ♦ *vt* abuchear, rechiflar

booby trap ['bu:bɪ-] *n* trampa explosiva

book [buk] *n* libro; (*of tickets*) taco; (*of stamps etc*) librito ♦ *vt* (*ticket*) sacar; (*seat, room*) reservar; **~s** *npl* (*COMM*) cuentas *fpl*, contabilidad *f*; **~case** *n* librería, estante *m* para libros; **~ing office** *n* (*BRIT: RAIL*) despacho de billetes (*SP*) *or* boletos (*AM*); (*THEATRE*) taquilla (*SP*), boletería (*AM*); **~-keeping** *n* contabilidad

f; **~let** n folleto; **~maker** n corredor m
de apuestas; **~seller** n librero; **~shop, ~
store** n librería

boom [buːm] n (noise) trueno, estampido;
(in prices etc) alza rápida; (ECON, in
population) boom m ♦ vi (cannon) hacer
gran estruendo, retumbar; (ECON) estar en
alza

boon [buːn] n favor m, beneficio

boost [buːst] n estímulo, empuje m ♦ vt
estimular, empujar; **~er** n (MED)
reinyección f

boot [buːt] n bota; (BRIT: of car) maleta,
maletero ♦ vt (COMPUT) arrancar; **to ~** (in
addition) además, por añadidura

booth [buːð] n (telephone ~, voting ~)
cabina

booze [buːz] (inf) n bebida

border [ˈbɔːdə*] n borde m, margen m; (of
a country) frontera; (for flowers) arriate m
♦ vt (road) bordear; (another country:
also: **~ on**) lindar con; **B~s** n: **the B~s**
región fronteriza entre Escocia e
Inglaterra; **~ on** vt fus (insanity etc) rayar
en; **~line** n: **on the ~line** en el límite;
~line case n caso dudoso

bore [bɔː*] pt of **bear** ♦ vt (hole) hacer un
agujero en; (well) perforar; (person)
aburrir ♦ n (person) pelmazo, pesado; (of
gun) calibre m; **to be ~d** estar aburrido;
~dom n aburrimiento

boring [ˈbɔːrɪŋ] adj aburrido

born [bɔːn] adj: **to be ~** nacer; **I was ~ in
1960** nací en 1960

borne [bɔːn] pp of **bear**

borough [ˈbʌrə] n municipio

borrow [ˈbɔrəu] vt: **to ~ sth (from sb)**
tomar algo prestado (a alguien)

Bosnia(-Herzegovina)
[ˈbɔːsnɪə(herzəˈgəuviːnə)] n Bosnia
(-Herzegovina)

bosom [ˈbuzəm] n pecho

boss [bɔs] n jefe m ♦ vt (also: **~ about** or
around) mangonear; **~y** adj mandón/ona

bosun [ˈbəusn] n contramaestre m

botany [ˈbɔtənɪ] n botánica

botch [bɔtʃ] vt (also: **~ up**) arruinar,
estropear

both [bəuθ] adj, pron ambos/as, los/las
dos; **~ of us went, we ~ went** fuimos los
dos, ambos fuimos ♦ adv: **~ A and B**
tanto A como B

bother [ˈbɔðə*] vt (worry) preocupar;
(disturb) molestar, fastidiar ♦ vi (also: **~
o.s.**) molestarse ♦ n (trouble) dificultad f;
(nuisance) molestia, lata; **to ~ doing**
tomarse la molestia de hacer

bottle [ˈbɔtl] n botella; (small) frasco;
(baby's) biberón m ♦ vt embotellar; **~ up**
vt suprimir; **~ bank** n contenedor m de
vidrio; **~neck** n (AUT) embotellamiento;
(in supply) obstáculo; **~-opener** n
abrebotellas m inv

bottom [ˈbɔtəm] n (of box, sea) fondo;
(buttocks) trasero, culo; (of page) pie m;
(of list) final m; (of class) último/a ♦ adj
(lowest) más bajo; (last) último

bough [bau] n rama

bought [bɔːt] pt, pp of **buy**

boulder [ˈbəuldə*] n canto rodado

bounce [bauns] vi (ball) (re)botar;
(cheque) ser rechazado ♦ vt hacer
(re)botar ♦ n (rebound) (re)bote m; **~r**
(inf) n gorila m (que echa a los
alborotadores de un bar, club etc)

bound [baund] pt, pp of **bind** ♦ n (leap)
salto; (gen pl: limit) límite m ♦ vi (leap)
saltar ♦ vt (border) rodear ♦ adj: **~ by**
rodeado de; **to be ~ to do sth** (obliged)
tener el deber de hacer algo; **he's ~ to
come** es seguro que vendrá; **out of ~s**
prohibido el paso; **~ for** con destino a

boundary [ˈbaundrɪ] n límite m

bouquet [ˈbukeɪ] n (of flowers) ramo

bourgeois [ˈbuəʒwɑː] adj burgués/esa m/f

bout [baut] n (of malaria etc) ataque m; (of
activity) período; (BOXING etc) combate m,
encuentro

bow¹ [bəu] n (knot) lazo; (weapon, MUS)
arco

bow² [bau] n (of the head) reverencia;
(NAUT: also: **~s**) proa ♦ vi inclinarse, hacer
una reverencia; (yield): **to ~ to** or **before**
ceder ante, someterse a

bowels [ˈbauəlz] *npl* intestinos *mpl*, vientre *m*; (*fig*) entrañas *fpl*

bowl [bəul] *n* tazón *m*, cuenco; (*ball*) bola ♦ *vi* (*CRICKET*) arrojar la pelota; *see also* **bowls**

bow-legged [ˈbəuˈlegɪd] *adj* estevado

bowler [ˈbəuləˤ] *n* (*CRICKET*) lanzador *m* (de la pelota); (*BRIT: also:* ~ **hat**) hongo, bombín *m*

bowling [ˈbəulɪŋ] *n* (*game*) bochas *fpl*, bolos *mpl*; ~ **alley** *n* bolera; ~ **green** *n* pista para bochas

bowls [bəulz] *n* juego de las bochas, bolos *mpl*

bow tie [ˈbəu-] *n* corbata de lazo, pajarita

box [bɒks] *n* (*also:* **cardboard** ~) caja, cajón *m*; (*THEATRE*) palco ♦ *vt* encajonar ♦ *vi* (*SPORT*) boxear; ~**er** [ˈbɒksəˤ] *n* (*person*) boxeador *m*; ~**ing** [ˈbɒksɪŋ] *n* (*SPORT*) boxeo; **B~ing Day** (*BRIT*) *n* día en que se dan los aguinaldos, 26 de diciembre; ~**ing gloves** *npl* guantes *mpl* de boxeo; ~**ing ring** *n* ring *m*, cuadrilátero; ~ **office** *n* taquilla (*SP*), boletería (*AM*); ~**room** *n* trastero

---
Boxing Day

El día 26 de diciembre se conoce como **Boxing Day** *y es día festivo en todo el Reino Unido. En el siglo XIX era tradición entregar "Christmas boxes" (aguinaldos) a empleados, carteros y otros proveedores en este día, y de ahí el nombre.*

---

boy [bɔɪ] *n* (*young*) niño; (*older*) muchacho, chico; (*son*) hijo

boycott [ˈbɔɪkɔt] *n* boicot *m* ♦ *vt* boicotear

boyfriend [ˈbɔɪfrend] *n* novio

boyish [ˈbɔɪʃ] *adj* juvenil; (*girl*) con aspecto de muchacho

B.R. *n abbr* (*formerly* = *British Rail*) ≈ RENFE *f* (*SP*)

bra [brɑː] *n* sostén *m*, sujetador *m*

brace [breɪs] *n* (*BRIT: also:* ~**s:** *on teeth*) corrector *m*, aparato; (*tool*) berbiquí *m*

♦ *vt* (*knees, shoulders*) tensionar; ~**s** *npl* (*BRIT*) tirantes *mpl*; **to** ~ **o.s.** (*fig*) prepararse

bracelet [ˈbreɪslɪt] *n* pulsera, brazalete *m*

bracing [ˈbreɪsɪŋ] *adj* vigorizante, tónico

bracket [ˈbrækɪt] *n* (*TECH*) soporte *m*, puntal *m*; (*group*) clase *f*, categoría; (*also:* **brace** ~) soporte *m*, abrazadera; (*also:* **round** ~) paréntesis *m inv*; (*also:* **square** ~) corchete *m* ♦ *vt* (*word etc*) poner entre paréntesis

brag [bræg] *vi* jactarse

braid [breɪd] *n* (*trimming*) galón *m*; (*of hair*) trenza

brain [breɪn] *n* cerebro; ~**s** *npl* sesos *mpl*; **she's got** ~**s** es muy lista; ~**wash** *vt* lavar el cerebro; ~**wave** *n* idea luminosa; ~**y** *adj* muy inteligente

braise [breɪz] *vt* cocer a fuego lento

brake [breɪk] *n* (*on vehicle*) freno ♦ *vi* frenar; ~ **light** *n* luz *f* de frenado

bran [bræn] *n* salvado

branch [brɑːntʃ] *n* rama; (*COMM*) sucursal *f*; ~ **out** *vi* (*fig*) extenderse

brand [brænd] *n* marca; (*fig: type*) tipo ♦ *vt* (*cattle*) marcar con hierro candente; ~-**new** *adj* flamante, completamente nuevo

brandy [ˈbrændɪ] *n* coñac *m*

brash [bræʃ] *adj* (*forward*) descarado

brass [brɑːs] *n* latón *m*; **the** ~ (*MUS*) los cobres; ~ **band** *n* banda de metal

brat [bræt] (*pej*) *n* mocoso/a

brave [breɪv] *adj* valiente, valeroso ♦ *vt* (*face up to*) desafiar; ~**ry** *n* valor *m*, valentía

brawl [brɔːl] *n* pelea, reyerta

brazen [ˈbreɪzn] *adj* descarado, cínico ♦ *vt*: **to** ~ **it out** echarle cara

Brazil [brəˈzɪl] *n* (el) Brasil; ~**ian** *adj, n* brasileño/a *m/f*

breach [briːtʃ] *vt* abrir brecha en ♦ *n* (*gap*) brecha; (*breaking*): ~ **of contract** infracción *f* de contrato; ~ **of the peace** perturbación *f* del orden público

bread [bred] *n* pan *m*; ~ **and butter** *n* pan con mantequilla; (*fig*) pan (de cada día); **~bin** n panera; **~crumbs** npl migajas fpl; (CULIN) pan rallado; **~line** n: **on the ~line** en la miseria

breadth [brɛtθ] n anchura; (fig) amplitud f

breadwinner ['brɛdwɪnə*] n sustento m de la familia

break [breɪk] (pt **broke**, pp **broken**) vt romper; (promise) faltar a; (law) violar, infringir; (record) batir ♦ vi romperse, quebrarse; (storm) estallar; (weather) cambiar; (dawn) despuntar; (news etc) darse a conocer ♦ n (gap) abertura; (fracture) fractura; (time) intervalo m; (: at school) (período de) recreo; (chance) oportunidad f; **to ~ the news to sb** comunicar la noticia a uno; **~ down** vt (figures, data) analizar, descomponer ♦ vi (machine) estropearse; (AUT) averiarse; (person) romper a llorar; (talks) fracasar; **~ even** vi cubrir los gastos; **~ free** or **loose** vi escaparse; **~ in** vt (horse etc) domar ♦ vi (burglar) forzar una entrada; (interrupt) interrumpir; **~ into** vt fus (house) forzar; **~ off** vi (speaker) pararse, detenerse; (branch) partir; **~ open** vt (door etc) abrir por la fuerza, forzar; **~ out** vi estallar; (prisoner) escaparse; **to ~ out in spots** salirle a uno granos; **~ up** vi (ship) hacerse pedazos; (crowd, meeting) disolverse; (marriage) deshacerse; (SCOL) terminar (el curso) ♦ vt (rocks etc) partir; (journey) partir; (fight etc) acabar con; **~age** n rotura; **~down** n (AUT) avería; (in communications) interrupción f; (MED: also: **nervous ~down**) colapso, crisis f nerviosa; (of marriage, talks) fracaso; (of statistics) análisis m inv; **~down van** (BRIT) n (camión m) grúa; **~er** n (ola) rompiente f

breakfast ['brɛkfəst] n desayuno

break: **~-in** n robo con allanamiento de morada; **~ing and entering** n (LAW) violación f de domicilio, allanamiento de morada; **~through** n (also fig) avance m; **~water** n rompeolas m inv

breast [brɛst] n (of woman) pecho, seno; (chest) pecho; (of bird) pechuga; **~~feed**

(irreg: like **feed**) vt, vi amamantar, criar a los pechos; **~~stroke** n braza (de pecho)

breath [brɛθ] n aliento, respiración f; **to take a deep ~** respirar hondo; **out of ~** sin aliento, sofocado

Breathalyser ® ['brɛθəlaɪzə*] (BRIT) n alcoholímetro m

breathe [briːð] vt, vi respirar; **~ in** vt, vi aspirar; **~ out** vt, vi espirar; **~r** n respiro; **breathing** n respiración f

breath: **~less** adj sin aliento, jadeante; **~taking** adj imponente, pasmoso

breed [briːd] (pt, pp **bred**) vt criar ♦ vi reproducirse, procrear ♦ n (ZOOL) raza, casta; (type) tipo; **~ing** n (of person) educación f

breeze [briːz] n brisa

breezy ['briːzɪ] adj de mucho viento, ventoso; (person) despreocupado

brevity ['brɛvɪtɪ] n brevedad f

brew [bruː] vt (tea) hacer; (beer) elaborar ♦ vi (fig: trouble) prepararse; (storm) amenazar; **~ery** n fábrica de cerveza, cervecería

bribe [braɪb] n soborno ♦ vt sobornar, cohechar; **~ry** n soborno, cohecho

bric-a-brac ['brɪkəbræk] n inv baratijas fpl

brick [brɪk] n ladrillo; **~layer** n albañil m

bridal ['braɪdl] adj nupcial

bride [braɪd] n novia; **~groom** n novio; **~smaid** n dama de honor

bridge [brɪdʒ] n puente m; (NAUT) puente m de mando; (of nose) caballete m; (CARDS) bridge m ♦ vt (fig): **to ~ a gap** llenar un vacío

bridle ['braɪdl] n brida, freno; **~ path** n camino de herradura

brief [briːf] adj breve, corto ♦ n (LAW) escrito; (task) cometido, encargo ♦ vt informar; **~s** npl (for men) calzoncillos mpl; (for women) bragas fpl; **~case** n cartera (SP), portafolio (AM); **~ing** n (PRESS) informe m; **~ly** adv (glance) fugazmente; (say) en pocas palabras

brigadier [brɪgə'dɪə*] n general m de brigada

bright [braɪt] adj brillante; (room)

luminoso; (*day*) de sol; (*person: clever*)
listo, inteligente; (: *lively*) alegre; (*colour*)
vivo; (*future*) prometedor(a); **~en** (*also:*
~en up) *vt* (*room*) hacer más alegre;
(*event*) alegrar ♦ *vi* (*weather*) despejarse;
(*person*) animarse, alegrarse; (*prospects*)
mejorar

brilliance ['brɪljəns] *n* brillo, brillantez *f*;
(*of talent etc*) brillantez

brilliant ['brɪljənt] *adj* brillante; (*inf*)
fenomenal

brim [brɪm] *n* borde *m*; (*of hat*) ala

brine [braɪn] *n* (*CULIN*) salmuera

bring [brɪŋ] (*pt, pp* **brought**) *vt* (*thing,
person: with you*) traer; (: *to sb*) llevar,
conducir; (*trouble, satisfaction*) causar; **~
about** *vt* ocasionar, producir; **~ back**
volver a traer; (*return*) devolver; **~ down**
vt (*government, plane*) derribar; (*price*)
rebajar; **~ forward** *vt* adelantar; **~ off** *vt*
(*task, plan*) lograr, conseguir; **~ out** *vt*
sacar; (*book etc*) publicar; (*meaning*)
subrayar; **~ round** *vt* (*unconscious
person*) hacer volver en sí; **~ up** *vt* subir;
(*person*) educar, criar; (*question*) sacar a
colación; (*food: vomit*) devolver, vomitar

brink [brɪŋk] *n* borde *m*

brisk [brɪsk] *adj* (*abrupt: tone*) brusco;
(*person*) enérgico, vigoroso; (*pace*) rápido;
(*trade*) activo

bristle ['brɪsl] *n* cerda ♦ *vi*: **to ~ in anger**
temblar de rabia

Britain ['brɪtən] *n* (*also:* **Great ~**) Gran
Bretaña

British ['brɪtɪʃ] *adj* británico ♦ *npl*: **the ~**
los británicos; **~ Isles** *npl*: **the ~ Isles** las
Islas Británicas; **~ Rail** *n* ≈ RENFE *f* (*SP*)

Briton ['brɪtən] *n* británico/a

brittle ['brɪtl] *adj* quebradizo, frágil

broach [brəutʃ] *vt* (*subject*) abordar

broad [brɔːd] *adj* ancho; (*range*) amplio;
(*smile*) abierto; (*general: outlines etc*)
general; (*accent*) cerrado; **in ~ daylight** en
pleno día; **~cast** (*irreg: like* **cast**) *n*
emisión *f* ♦ *vt* (*RADIO*) emitir; (*TV*)
transmitir ♦ *vi* emitir; transmitir; **~en** *vt*
ampliar ♦ *vi* ensancharse; **to ~en one's**

mind hacer más tolerante a uno; **~ly** *adv*
en general; **~-minded** *adj* tolerante,
liberal

broccoli ['brɒkəlɪ] *n* brécol *m*

brochure ['brəuʃjuə*] *n* folleto

broil [brɔɪl] *vt* (*CULIN*) asar a la parrilla

broke [brəuk] *pt of* **break** ♦ *adj* (*inf*)
pelado, sin blanca

broken ['brəukən] *pp of* **break** ♦ *adj* roto;
(*machine: also:* **~ down**) averiado; **~ leg**
pierna rota; **in ~ English** en un inglés
imperfecto; **~-hearted** *adj* con el
corazón partido

broker ['brəukə*] *n* agente *m/f*, bolsista
m/f; (*insurance ~*) agente de seguros

brolly ['brɒlɪ] (*BRIT: inf*) *n* paraguas *m inv*

bronchitis [brɒŋ'kaɪtɪs] *n* bronquitis *f*

bronze [brɒnz] *n* bronce *m*

brooch [brəutʃ] *n* prendedor *m*, broche *m*

brood [bruːd] *n* camada, cría ♦ *vi* (*person*)
dejarse obsesionar

broom [brum] *n* escoba; (*BOT*) retama

Bros. *abbr* (= **Brothers**) Hnos

broth [brɒθ] *n* caldo

brothel ['brɒθl] *n* burdel *m*

brother ['brʌðə*] *n* hermano; **~-in-law** *n*
cuñado

brought [brɔːt] *pt, pp of* **bring**

brow [brau] *n* (*forehead*) frente *m*; (*eye~*)
ceja; (*of hill*) cumbre *f*

brown [braun] *adj* (*colour*) marrón; (*hair*)
castaño; (*tanned*) bronceado, moreno ♦ *n*
(*colour*) color *m* marrón *or* pardo ♦ *vt*
(*CULIN*) dorar; **~ bread** *n* pan integral

Brownie ['braunɪ] *n* niña exploradora; **b~**
(*US: cake*) pastel de chocolate con nueces

brown paper *n* papel *m* de estraza

brown sugar *n* azúcar *m* terciado

browse [brauz] *vi* (*through book*) hojear;
(*in shop*) mirar

bruise [bruːz] *n* cardenal *m* (*SP*), moretón
m (*AM*) ♦ *vt* magullar

brunch [brʌntʃ] *n* desayuno-almuerzo

brunette [bruː'net] *n* morena

brunt [brʌnt] *n*: **to bear the ~ of** llevar el
peso de

brush [brʌʃ] *n* cepillo; (*for painting,*

shaving etc) brocha; (artist's) pincel m;
(with police etc) roce m ♦ vt (sweep)
barrer; (groom) cepillar; (also: ~ against)
rozar al pasar; ~ aside vt rechazar, no
hacer caso a; ~ up vt (knowledge)
repasar, refrescar; ~wood n (sticks) leña

Brussels ['brʌslz] n Bruselas; ~ **sprout** n
col f de Bruselas

brute [bruːt] n bruto; (person) bestia ♦ adj:
by ~ force a fuerza bruta

B.Sc. abbr (= Bachelor of Science)
licenciado en Ciencias

BSE n abbr (= bovine spongiform
encephalopathy) encefalopatía
espongiforme bovina

bubble ['bʌbl] n burbuja ♦ vi burbujear,
borbotar; ~ **bath** n espuma para el
baño; ~ **gum** n chicle m de globo

buck [bʌk] n (rabbit) conejo macho; (deer)
gamo; (US: inf) dólar m ♦ vi corcovear; **to
pass the ~ (to sb)** echar (a uno) el
muerto; ~ **up** vi (cheer up) animarse,
cobrar ánimo

Buckingham Palace

i **Buckingham Palace** es la residencia
oficial del monarca británico en
Londres. El palacio se concluyó en 1703 y
fue residencia del Duque de Buckingham
hasta que, en 1762, pasó a manos de
Jorge III. Fue reconstruido en el siglo XIX
y posteriormente reformado a principios de
este siglo. Una parte del palacio está
actualmente abierta al público.

---

bucket ['bʌkɪt] n cubo, balde m

buckle ['bʌkl] n hebilla ♦ vt abrochar con
hebilla ♦ vi combarse

bud [bʌd] n (of plant) brote m, yema; (of
flower) capullo ♦ vi brotar, echar brotes

Buddhism ['budɪzm] n Budismo

budding ['bʌdɪŋ] adj en ciernes, en
embrión

buddy ['bʌdɪ] (US) n compañero,
compinche m

budge [bʌdʒ] vt mover; (fig) hacer ceder
♦ vi moverse, ceder

budgerigar ['bʌdʒərɪgɑː*] n periquito

budget ['bʌdʒɪt] n presupuesto ♦ vi: **to ~
for sth** presupuestar algo

budgie ['bʌdʒɪ] n = **budgerigar**

buff [bʌf] adj (colour) color de ante ♦ n
(inf: enthusiast) entusiasta m/f

buffalo ['bʌfələu] (pl ~ or ~es) n (BRIT)
búfalo; (US: bison) bisonte m

buffer ['bʌfə*] n (COMPUT) memoria
intermedia; (RAIL) tope m

buffet[1] ['bufeɪ] n (BRIT: in station) bar m,
cafetería; (food) buffet m; ~ **car** (BRIT) n
(RAIL) coche-comedor m

buffet[2] ['bʌfɪt] vt golpear

bug [bʌg] n (esp US: insect) bicho,
sabandija; (COMPUT) error m; (germ)
microbio, bacilo; (spy device) micrófono
oculto ♦ vt (inf: annoy) fastidiar; (room)
poner micrófono oculto en

buggy ['bʌgɪ] n cochecito de niño

bugle ['bjuːgl] n corneta, clarín m

build [bɪld] (pt, pp **built**) n (of person) tipo
♦ vt construir, edificar; ~ **up** vt (morale,
forces, production) acrecentar; (stocks)
acumular; ~**er** n (contractor) contratista
m/f; ~**ing** n construcción f; (structure)
edificio; ~**ing society** (BRIT) n sociedad f
inmobiliaria, cooperativa de
construcciones

built [bɪlt] pt, pp of **build** ♦ adj: ~**-in**
(wardrobe etc) empotrado; ~**-up area** n
zona urbanizada

bulb [bʌlb] n (BOT) bulbo; (ELEC) bombilla
(SP), foco (AM)

Bulgaria [bʌl'geərɪə] n Bulgaria; ~**n** adj, n
búlgaro/a m/f

bulge [bʌldʒ] n bulto, protuberancia ♦ vi
bombearse, pandearse; (pocket etc): **to ~
(with)** rebosar (de)

bulk [bʌlk] n masa, mole f; **in ~** (COMM) a
granel; **the ~ of** la mayor parte de; ~**y**
adj voluminoso, abultado

bull [bul] n toro; (male elephant, whale)
macho; ~**dog** n dogo

bulldozer ['buldəuzə*] n bulldozer m

bullet ['bulɪt] n bala

bulletin ['bulɪtɪn] n anuncio, parte m;

(*journal*) boletín m
bulletproof ['bulɪtpruːf] *adj* a prueba de balas
bullfight ['bulfaɪt] *n* corrida de toros; ~**er** *n* torero; ~**ing** *n* los toros, el toreo
bullion ['buljən] *n* oro (*or* plata) en barras
bullock ['bulək] *n* novillo
bullring ['bulrɪŋ] *n* plaza de toros
bull's-eye *n* centro del blanco
bully ['bulɪ] *n* valentón m, matón m ♦ *vt* intimidar, tiranizar
bum [bʌm] *n* (*inf: backside*) culo; (*esp US: tramp*) vagabundo
bumblebee ['bʌmblbiː] *n* abejorro
bump [bʌmp] *n* (*blow*) tope m, choque m; (*jolt*) sacudida; (*on road etc*) bache m; (*on head etc*) chichón m ♦ *vt* (*strike*) chocar contra; ~ **into** *vt fus* chocar contra, tropezar con; (*person*) topar con; ~**er** *n* (*AUT*) parachoques m inv ♦ *adj*: ~**er crop/harvest** cosecha abundante; ~**er cars** *npl* coches *mpl* de choque; ~**y** *adj* (*road*) lleno de baches
bun [bʌn] *n* (*BRIT: cake*) pastel m; (*US: bread*) bollo; (*of hair*) moño
bunch [bʌntʃ] *n* (*of flowers*) ramo; (*of keys*) manojo; (*of bananas*) piña; (*of people*) grupo; (*pej*) pandilla; ~**es** *npl* (*in hair*) coletas *fpl*
bundle ['bʌndl] *n* bulto, fardo; (*of sticks*) haz m; (*of papers*) legajo ♦ *vt* (*also*: ~ **up**) atar, envolver; **to** ~ **sth/sb into** meter algo/a alguien precipitadamente en
bungalow ['bʌŋɡələu] *n* bungalow m, chalé m
bungle ['bʌŋɡl] *vt* hacer mal
bunion ['bʌnjən] *n* juanete m
bunk [bʌŋk] *n* litera; ~ **beds** *npl* literas *fpl*
bunker ['bʌŋkə*] *n* (*coal store*) carbonera; (*MIL*) refugio; (*GOLF*) bunker m
bunny ['bʌnɪ] *n* (*also*: ~ **rabbit**) conejito
buoy [bɔɪ] *n* boya; ~**ant** *adj* (*ship*) capaz de flotar; (*economy*) boyante; (*person*) optimista
burden ['bəːdn] *n* carga ♦ *vt* cargar
bureau [bjuə'rəu] (*pl* **bureaux**) *n* (*BRIT:*

writing desk) escritorio, buró m; (*US: chest of drawers*) cómoda; (*office*) oficina, agencia
bureaucracy [bjuə'rɔkrəsɪ] *n* burocracia
burglar ['bəːɡlə*] *n* ladrón/ona m/f; ~ **alarm** *n* alarma f antirrobo; ~**y** *n* robo con allanamiento, robo de una casa
burial ['bɛrɪəl] *n* entierro
burly ['bəːlɪ] *adj* fornido, membrudo
Burma ['bəːmə] *n* Birmania
burn [bəːn] (*pt, pp* **burned** *or* **burnt**) *vt* quemar; (*house*) incendiar ♦ *vi* quemarse, arder; incendiarse; (*sting*) escocer ♦ *n* quemadura; ~ **down** *vt* incendiar; ~**er** *n* (*on cooker etc*) quemador m; ~**ing** *adj* (*building etc*) en llamas; (*hot: sand etc*) abrasador(a); (*ambition*) ardiente
burrow ['bʌrəu] *n* madriguera ♦ *vi* hacer una madriguera; (*rummage*) hurgar
bursary ['bəːsərɪ] (*BRIT*) *n* beca
burst [bəːst] (*pt, pp* **burst**) *vt* reventar; (*subj: river: banks etc*) romper ♦ *vi* reventarse; (*tyre*) pincharse ♦ *n* (*of gunfire*) ráfaga; (*also*: ~ **pipe**) reventón m; **a** ~ **of energy/speed/enthusiasm** una explosión de energía/un ímpetu de velocidad/un arranque de entusiasmo; **to** ~ **into flames** estallar en llamas; **to** ~ **into tears** deshacerse en lágrimas; **to** ~ **out laughing** soltar la carcajada; **to** ~ **open** abrirse de golpe; **to be** ~**ing with** (*subj: container*) estar lleno a rebosar de; (*person*) reventar por *or* de; ~ **into** *vt fus* (*room etc*) irrumpir en
bury ['bɛrɪ] *vt* enterrar; (*body*) enterrar, sepultar
bus [bʌs] (*pl* ~**es**) *n* autobús m
bush [buʃ] *n* arbusto; (*scrub land*) monte m; **to beat about the** ~ andar(se) con rodeos
bushy [buʃɪ] *adj* (*thick*) espeso, poblado
busily ['bɪzɪlɪ] *adv* afanosamente
business ['bɪznɪs] *n* (*matter*) asunto; (*trading*) comercio, negocios *mpl*; (*firm*) empresa, casa; (*occupation*) oficio; **to be away on** ~ estar en viaje de negocios; **it's my** ~ **to ...** me toca *or* corresponde ...;

it's none of my ~ yo no tengo nada que
ver; **he means ~** habla en serio; **~like**
adj eficiente; **~man** *n* hombre *m* de
negocios; **~ trip** *n* viaje *m* de negocios;
~woman *n* mujer *f* de negocios
busker ['bʌskə*] (*BRIT*) *n* músico/a
ambulante
bus: ~ shelter *n* parada cubierta; **~
station** *n* estación *f* de autobuses; **~-
stop** *n* parada de autobús
bust [bʌst] *n* (*ANAT*) pecho; (*sculpture*)
busto ♦ *adj* (*inf: broken*) roto, estropeado;
to go ~ quebrar
bustle ['bʌsl] *n* bullicio, movimiento ♦ *vi*
menearse, apresurarse; **bustling** *adj*
(*town*) animado, bullicioso
busy ['bɪzɪ] *adj* ocupado, atareado; (*shop,
street*) concurrido, animado; (*TEL: line*)
comunicando ♦ *vt:* **to ~ o.s. with**
ocuparse en; **~body** *n* entrometido/a; **~
signal** (*US*) *n* (*TEL*) señal *f* de
comunicando

but [bʌt] *conj* **1** pero; **he's not very
bright, ~ he's hard-working** no es muy
inteligente, ~ es trabajador
2 (*in direct contradiction*) sino; **he's not
English ~ French** no es inglés sino
francés; **he didn't sing ~ he shouted** no
cantó sino que gritó
3 (*showing disagreement, surprise etc*): **~
that's far too expensive!** ¡pero eso es
carísimo!; **~ it does work!** ¡(pero) sí que
funciona!
♦ *prep* (*apart from, except*) menos, salvo;
we've had nothing ~ trouble no hemos
tenido más que problemas; **no-one ~ him
can do it** nadie más que él puede
hacerlo; **who ~ a lunatic would do such
a thing?** ¡sólo un loco haría una cosa así!;
~ for you/your help si no fuera por ti/tu
ayuda; **anything ~ that** cualquier cosa
menos eso
♦ *adv* (*just, only*): **she's ~ a child** no es
más que una niña; **had I ~ known** si lo
hubiera sabido; **I can ~ try** al menos lo

puedo intentar; **it's all ~ finished** está
casi acabado

butcher ['bʊtʃə*] *n* carnicero ♦ *vt* hacer
una carnicería con; (*cattle etc*) matar; **~'s
(shop)** *n* carnicería
butler ['bʌtlə*] *n* mayordomo
butt [bʌt] *n* (*barrel*) tonel *m*; (*of gun*)
culata; (*of cigarette*) colilla; (*BRIT: fig:
target*) blanco ♦ *vt* dar cabezadas contra,
top(et)ar; **~ in** *vi* (*interrupt*) interrumpir
butter ['bʌtə*] *n* mantequilla ♦ *vt* untar
con mantequilla; **~cup** *n* botón *m* de
oro
butterfly ['bʌtəflaɪ] *n* mariposa;
(*SWIMMING: also: ~ stroke*) braza de
mariposa
buttocks ['bʌtəks] *npl* nalgas *fpl*
button ['bʌtn] *n* botón *m*; (*US*) placa,
chapa ♦ *vt* (*also: ~ up*) abotonar,
abrochar ♦ *vi* abrocharse
buttress ['bʌtrɪs] *n* contrafuerte *m*
buy [baɪ] (*pt, pp bought*) *vt* comprar ♦ *n*
compra; **to ~ sb sth/sth from sb**
comprarle algo a alguien; **to ~ sb a drink**
invitar a alguien a tomar algo; **~er** *n*
comprador(a) *m/f*
buzz [bʌz] *n* zumbido; (*inf: phone call*)
llamada (por teléfono) ♦ *vi* zumbar; **~er**
n timbre *m*; **~ word** *n* palabra que está
de moda

by [baɪ] *prep* **1** (*referring to cause, agent*)
por; de; **killed ~ lightning** muerto por un
relámpago; **a painting ~ Picasso** un
cuadro de Picasso
2 (*referring to method, manner, means*): **~
bus/car/train** en autobús/coche/tren; **to
pay ~ cheque** pagar con un cheque; **~
moonlight/candlelight** a la luz de la
luna/una vela; **~ saving hard, he ...**
ahorrando, ...
3 (*via, through*) por; **we came ~ Dover**
vinimos por Dover
4 (*close to, past*): **the house ~ the river**
la casa junto al río; **she rushed ~ me**

pasó a mi lado como una exhalación; **I go ~ the post office every day** paso por delante de Correos todos los días

5 (*time: not later than*) para; (: *during*): **~ daylight** de día; **~ 4 o'clock** para las cuatro; **~ this time tomorrow** mañana a estas horas; **~ the time I got here it was too late** cuando llegué ya era demasiado tarde

6 (*amount*): **~ the metre/kilo** por metro/kilo; **paid ~ the hour** pagado por hora

7 (MATH, *measure*): **to divide/multiply ~ 3** dividir/multiplicar por 3; **a room 3 metres ~ 4** una habitación de 3 metros por 4; **it's broader ~ a metre** es un metro más ancho

8 (*according to*) según, de acuerdo con; **it's 3 o'clock ~ my watch** según mi reloj, son las tres; **it's all right ~ me** por mí, está bien

9: (all) **~ oneself** *etc* todo solo; **he did it (all) ~ himself** lo hizo él solo; **he was standing (all) ~ himself in a corner** estaba de pie solo en un rincón

10: **~ the way** a propósito, por cierto; **this wasn't my idea, ~ the way** pues, no fue idea mía

♦ *adv* **1** *see* **go; pass** *etc*

2: **~ and ~** finalmente; **they'll come back ~ and ~** acabarán volviendo; **~ and large** en líneas generales, en general

---

bye(-bye) [ˈbaɪˈbaɪ] *excl* adiós, hasta luego

by(e)-law *n* ordenanza municipal

by: **~-election** (BRIT) *n* elección *f* parcial; **~gone** [ˈbaɪɡɔn] *adj* pasado, del pasado ♦ *n*: **let ~gones be ~gones** lo pasado, pasado está; **~pass** [ˈbaɪpɑːs] *n* carretera de circunvalación; (MED) (operación *f* de) by-pass *m* ♦ *vt* evitar; **~-product** *n* subproducto, derivado; (*of situation*) consecuencia; **~stander** [ˈbaɪstændə*] *n* espectador(a) *m/f*

byte [baɪt] *n* (COMPUT) byte *m*, octeto

byword [ˈbaɪwɜːd] *n*: **to be a ~ for** ser conocidísimo por

---

C, c

C [siː] *n* (MUS) do *m*

C. *abbr* (= *centigrade*) C.

C.A. *abbr* = **chartered accountant**

cab [kæb] *n* taxi *m*; (*of truck*) cabina

cabbage [ˈkæbɪdʒ] *n* col *f*, berza

cabin [ˈkæbɪn] *n* cabaña; (*on ship*) camarote *m*; (*on plane*) cabina; **~ crew** *n* tripulación *f* de cabina; **~ cruiser** *n* yate *m* de motor

cabinet [ˈkæbɪnɪt] *n* (POL) consejo de ministros; (*furniture*) armario; (*also*: **display ~**) vitrina

cable [ˈkeɪbl] *n* cable *m* ♦ *vt* cablegrafiar; **~-car** *n* teleférico; **~ television** *n* televisión *f* por cable

cache [kæʃ] *n* (*of arms, drugs etc*) alijo

cackle [ˈkækl] *vi* lanzar risotadas; (*hen*) cacarear

cactus [ˈkæktəs] (*pl* **cacti**) *n* cacto

cadge [kædʒ] (*inf*) *vt* gorronear

Caesarean [siːˈzɛərɪən] *adj*: **~ (section)** cesárea

café [ˈkæfeɪ] *n* café *m*

cafeteria [kæfɪˈtɪərɪə] *n* cafetería

cage [keɪdʒ] *n* jaula

cagey [ˈkeɪdʒɪ] (*inf*) *adj* cauteloso, reservado

cagoule [kəˈɡuːl] *n* chubasquero

cajole [kəˈdʒəʊl] *vt* engatusar

cake [keɪk] *n* (CULIN: *large*) tarta; (: *small*) pastel *m*; (*of soap*) pastilla; **~d** *adj*: **~d with** cubierto de

calculate [ˈkælkjuleɪt] *vt* calcular; **calculation** [-ˈleɪʃən] *n* cálculo, cómputo; **calculator** *n* calculadora

calendar [ˈkæləndə*] *n* calendario; **~ month/year** *n* mes *m*/año civil

calf [kɑːf] (*pl* **calves**) *n* (*of cow*) ternero, becerro; (*of other animals*) cría; (*also*: **~skin**) piel *f* de becerro; (ANAT) pantorrilla

calibre [ˈkælɪbə*] (US **caliber**) *n* calibre *m*

call [kɔːl] *vt* llamar; (*meeting*) convocar

♦ vi (shout) llamar; (TEL) llamar (por teléfono), telefonear (esp AM); (visit: also: ~ in, ~ round) hacer una visita ♦ n llamada; (of bird) canto; to be ~ed llamarse; on ~ (nurse, doctor etc) de guardia; ~ back vi (return) volver; (TEL) volver a llamar; ~ for vt fus (demand) pedir, exigir; (fetch) venir por (SP), pasar por (AM); ~ off vt (cancel: meeting, race) cancelar; (: deal) anular; (: strike) desconvocar; ~ on vt fus (visit) visitar; (turn to) acudir a; ~ out vi gritar, dar voces; ~ up vt (MIL) llamar al servicio militar; (TEL) llamar; ~box (BRIT) n cabina telefónica; ~er n visita; (TEL) usuario/a; ~ girl n prostituta; ~-in (US) n (programa m) coloquio (por teléfono); ~ing n vocación f; (occupation) profesión f; ~ing card (US) n tarjeta comercial or de visita

callous ['kæləs] adj insensible, cruel

calm [kɑːm] adj tranquilo; (sea) liso, en calma ♦ n calma, tranquilidad f ♦ vt calmar, tranquilizar; ~ down vi calmarse, tranquilizarse ♦ vt calmar, tranquilizar

Calor gas ® ['kælə*-] n butano

calorie ['kælərɪ] n caloría

calves [kɑːvz] npl of calf

Cambodia [kæm'bəudjə] n Camboya

camcorder ['kæmkɔːdə*] n videocámara

came [keɪm] pt of come

camel ['kæməl] n camello

camera ['kæmərə] n máquina fotográfica; (CINEMA, TV) cámara; in ~ (LAW) a puerta cerrada; ~man n cámara m

camouflage ['kæmɒflɑːʒ] n camuflaje m ♦ vt camuflar

camp [kæmp] n campamento, camping m; (MIL) campamento; (for prisoners) campo; (fig: faction) bando ♦ vi acampar ♦ adj afectado, afeminado

campaign [kæm'peɪn] n (MIL, POL etc) campaña ♦ vi hacer campaña

camp: ~bed (BRIT) n cama de campaña; ~er n campista m/f; (vehicle) caravana; ~ing n camping m; to go ~ing hacer camping; ~site n camping m

campus ['kæmpəs] n ciudad f universitaria

can¹ [kæn] n (of oil, water) bidón m; (tin) lata, bote m ♦ vt enlatar

KEYWORD

can² [kæn] (negative cannot, can't; conditional and pt could) aux vb 1 (be able to) poder; you ~ do it if you try puedes hacerlo si lo intentas; I ~'t see you no te veo

2 (know how to) saber; I ~ swim/play tennis/drive sé nadar/jugar al tenis/conducir; ~ you speak French? ¿hablas or sabes hablar francés?

3 (may) poder; ~ I use your phone? ¿me dejas or puedo usar tu teléfono?

4 (expressing disbelief, puzzlement etc): it ~'t be true! ¡no puede ser (verdad)!; what CAN he want? ¿qué querrá?

5 (expressing possibility, suggestion etc): he could be in the library podría estar en la biblioteca; she could have been delayed pudo haberse retrasado

Canada ['kænədə] n (el) Canadá; Canadian [kə'neɪdɪən] adj, n canadiense m/f

canal [kə'næl] n canal m

canary [kə'neərɪ] n canario; the C~ Islands npl las (Islas) Canarias

cancel ['kænsəl] vt cancelar; (train) suprimir; (cross out) tachar, borrar; ~lation [-'leɪʃən] n cancelación f; supresión f

cancer ['kænsə*] n cáncer m; C~ (ASTROLOGY) Cáncer m

candid ['kændɪd] adj franco, abierto

candidate ['kændɪdeɪt] n candidato/a

candle ['kændl] n vela; (in church) cirio; ~light n: by ~light a la luz de una vela; ~stick n (single) candelero; (low) palmatoria; (bigger, ornate) candelabro

candour ['kændə*] (US candor) n franqueza

candy ['kændɪ] n azúcar m cande; (US) caramelo; ~floss (BRIT) n algodón m (azucarado)

cane [keɪn] n (BOT) caña; (stick) vara,

palmeta; (*for furniture*) mimbre *f* ♦ (*BRIT*) *vt* (*SCOL*) castigar (con vara)
canister ['kænɪstə*] *n* bote *m*, lata; (*of gas*) bombona
cannabis ['kænəbɪs] *n* marijuana
canned [kænd] *adj* en lata, de lata
cannon ['kænən] (*pl* ~ *or* ~**s**) *n* cañón *m*
cannot ['kænɔt] = **can not**
canoe [kə'nu:] *n* canoa; (*SPORT*) piragua; ~**ing** *n* piragüismo
canon ['kænən] *n* (*clergyman*) canónigo; (*standard*) canon *m*
can-opener *n* abrelatas *m inv*
canopy ['kænəpɪ] *n* dosel *m*; toldo
can't [kænt] = **can not**
canteen [kæn'ti:n] *n* (*eating place*) cantina; (*BRIT: of cutlery*) juego
canter ['kæntə*] *vi* ir a medio galope
canvas ['kænvəs] *n* (*material*) lona; (*painting*) lienzo; (*NAUT*) velas *fpl*
canvass ['kænvəs] *vi* (*POL*): **to** ~ **for** solicitar votos por ♦ *vt* (*COMM*) sondear
canyon ['kænjən] *n* cañón *m*
cap [kæp] *n* (*hat*) gorra; (*of pen*) capuchón *m*; (*of bottle*) tapa, tapón *m*; (*contraceptive*) diafragma *m*; (*for toy gun*) cápsula ♦ *vt* (*outdo*) superar; (*limit*) recortar
capability [keɪpə'bɪlɪtɪ] *n* capacidad *f*
capable ['keɪpəbl] *adj* capaz
capacity [kə'pæsɪtɪ] *n* capacidad *f*; (*position*) calidad *f*
cape [keɪp] *n* capa; (*GEO*) cabo
caper ['keɪpə*] *n* (*CULIN: gen:* ~**s**) alcaparra; (*prank*) broma
capital ['kæpɪtl] *n* (*also:* ~ **city**) capital *f*; (*money*) capital *m*; (*also:* ~ **letter**) mayúscula; ~ **gains tax** *n* impuesto sobre las ganancias de capital; ~**ism** *n* capitalismo; ~**ist** *adj*, *n* capitalista *m/f*; ~**ize on** *vt fus* aprovechar; ~ **punishment** *n* pena de muerte

Capricorn ['kæprɪkɔ:n] *n* (*ASTROLOGY*) Capricornio
capsize [kæp'saɪz] *vt* volcar, hacer zozobrar ♦ *vi* volcarse, zozobrar
capsule ['kæpsju:l] *n* cápsula
captain ['kæptɪn] *n* capitán *m*
caption ['kæpʃən] *n* (*heading*) título; (*to picture*) leyenda
captive ['kæptɪv] *adj*, *n* cautivo/a *m/f*
capture ['kæptʃə*] *vt* prender, apresar; (*animal, COMPUT*) capturar; (*place*) tomar; (*attention*) captar, llamar ♦ *n* apresamiento; captura; toma; (*data* ~) formulación *f* de datos
car [kɑ:*] *n* coche *m*, carro (*AM*), automóvil *m*; (*US: RAIL*) vagón *m*
carafe [kə'ræf] *n* jarra
carat ['kærət] *n* quilate *m*
caravan ['kærəvæn] *n* (*BRIT*) caravana, ruló *f*; (*in desert*) caravana; ~**ning** *n*: **to go** ~**ning** ir de vacaciones en caravana, viajar en caravana; ~ **site** (*BRIT*) *n* camping *m* para caravanas
carbohydrate [kɑ:bəʊ'haɪdreɪt] *n* hidrato de carbono; (*food*) fécula
carbon ['kɑ:bən] *n* carbono; ~ **paper** *n* papel *m* carbón
car boot sale *n* mercadillo organizado en un aparcamiento, en el que se exponen las mercancías en el maletero del coche
carburettor [kɑ:bju'retə*] (*US* **carburetor**) *n* carburador *m*
card [kɑ:d] *n* (*material*) cartulina; (*index* ~ *etc*) ficha; (*playing* ~) carta, naipe *m*; (*visiting* ~, *greetings* ~ *etc*) tarjeta; ~**board** *n* cartón *m*
cardiac ['kɑ:dɪæk] *adj* cardíaco
cardigan ['kɑ:dɪgən] *n* rebeca
cardinal ['kɑ:dɪnl] *adj* cardinal; (*importance, principal*) esencial ♦ *n* cardenal *m*

card index *n* fichero
care [kɛəʳ] *n* cuidado; (*worry*) inquietud *f*; (*charge*) cargo, custodia ♦ *vi*: **to ~ about** (*person, animal*) tener cariño a; (*thing, idea*) preocuparse por; **~ of** en casa de, al cuidado de; **in sb's ~** a cargo de uno; **to take ~ to** cuidarse de, tener cuidado de; **to take ~ of** cuidar; (*problem etc*) ocuparse de; **I don't ~** no me importa; **I couldn't ~ less** eso me trae sin cuidado; **~ for** *vt fus* cuidar a; (*like*) querer
career [kəˈrɪəʳ] *n* profesión *f*; (*in work, school*) carrera ♦ *vi* (*also*: **~ along**) correr a toda velocidad; **~ woman** *n* mujer *f* dedicada a su profesión
care: ~free *adj* despreocupado; **~ful** *adj* cuidadoso; (*cautious*) cauteloso; **(be) ~ful!** ¡tenga cuidado!; **~fully** *adv* con cuidado, cuidadosamente; con cautela; **~less** *adj* descuidado; (*heedless*) poco atento; **~lessness** *n* descuido; falta de atención; **~r** [ˈkɛərəʳ] *n* enfermero/a *m/f* (*official*); (*unpaid*) persona que cuida a un pariente o vecino
caress [kəˈrɛs] *n* caricia ♦ *vt* acariciar
caretaker [ˈkɛəteɪkəʳ] *n* portero/a, conserje *m/f*
car-ferry *n* transbordador *m* para coches
cargo [ˈkɑːgəu] *n* (*pl* **~es**) *n* cargamento, carga
car hire *n* alquiler *m* de automóviles
Caribbean [kærɪˈbiːən] *n*: **the ~ (Sea)** el (Mar) Caribe
caring [ˈkɛərɪŋ] *adj* humanitario; (*behaviour*) afectuoso
carnation [kɑːˈneɪʃən] *n* clavel *m*
carnival [ˈkɑːnɪvəl] *n* carnaval *m*; (*US: funfair*) parque *m* de atracciones
carol [ˈkærəl] *n*: **(Christmas) ~** villancico
carp [kɑːp] *n* (*fish*) carpa
car park (*BRIT*) *n* aparcamiento, parking *m*
carpenter [ˈkɑːpɪntəʳ] *n* carpintero/a
carpet [ˈkɑːpɪt] *n* alfombra; (*fitted*) moqueta ♦ *vt* alfombrar
car phone *n* teléfono movil
car rental (*US*) *n* alquiler *m* de coches

carriage [ˈkærɪdʒ] *n* (*BRIT: RAIL*) vagón *m*; (*horse-drawn*) coche *m*; (*of goods*) transporte *m*; (*: cost*) porte *m*, flete *m*; **~way** (*BRIT*) *n* (*part of road*) calzada
carrier [ˈkærɪəʳ] *n* (*transport company*) transportista, empresa de transportes; (*MED*) portador *m*; **~ bag** (*BRIT*) *n* bolsa de papel *or* plástico
carrot [ˈkærət] *n* zanahoria
carry [ˈkærɪ] *vt* (*subj: person*) llevar; (*transport*) transportar; (*involve: responsibilities etc*) entrañar, implicar; (*MED*) ser portador de ♦ *vi* (*sound*) oírse; **to get carried away** (*fig*) entusiasmarse; **~ on** *vi* (*continue*) seguir (adelante), continuar ♦ *vt* proseguir, continuar; **~ out** *vt* (*orders*) cumplir; (*investigation*) llevar a cabo, realizar; **~ cot** (*BRIT*) *n* cuna portátil; **~-on** (*inf*) *n* (*fuss*) lío
cart [kɑːt] *n* carro, carreta ♦ *vt* (*inf: transport*) acarrear
carton [ˈkɑːtən] *n* (*box*) caja (de cartón); (*of milk etc*) bote *m*; (*of yogurt*) tarrina
cartoon [kɑːˈtuːn] *n* (*PRESS*) caricatura; (*comic strip*) tira cómica; (*film*) dibujos *mpl* animados
cartridge [ˈkɑːtrɪdʒ] *n* cartucho; (*of pen*) recambio; (*of record player*) cápsula
carve [kɑːv] *vt* (*meat*) trinchar; (*wood, stone*) cincelar, esculpir; (*initials etc*) grabar; **~ up** *vt* dividir, repartir; **carving** *n* (*object*) escultura; (*design*) talla; (*art*) tallado; **carving knife** *n* trinchante *m*
car wash *n* lavado de coches
case [keɪs] *n* (*container*) caja; (*MED*) caso; (*for jewels etc*) estuche *m*; (*LAW*) causa, proceso; (*BRIT: also*: **suit~**) maleta; **in ~ of** en caso de; **in any ~** en todo caso; **just in ~** por si acaso
cash [kæʃ] *n* dinero en efectivo, dinero contante ♦ *vt* cobrar, hacer efectivo; **to pay (in) ~** pagar al contado; **~ on delivery** cóbrese al entregar; **~book** *n* libro de caja; **~ card** *n* tarjeta *f* dinero; **~ desk** (*BRIT*) *n* caja; **~ dispenser** *n* cajero automático
cashew [kæˈʃuː] *n* (*also*: **~ nut**) anacardo

cash flow *n* flujo de fondos, cash-flow *m*
cashier [kæ'ʃɪə*] *n* cajero/a
cashmere ['kæʃmɪə*] *n* cachemira
cash register *n* caja
casing ['keɪsɪŋ] *n* revestimiento
casino [kə'siːnəu] *n* casino
casket ['kɑːskɪt] *n* cofre *m*, estuche *m*; (*US*: *coffin*) ataúd *m*
casserole ['kæsərəul] *n* (*food, pot*) cazuela
cassette [kæ'set] *n* cassette *f*; ~ **player / recorder** *n* tocacassettes *m inv*, cassette *m*
cast [kɑːst] (*pt, pp* **cast**) *vt* (*throw*) echar, arrojar, lanzar; (*glance, eyes*) dirigir; (*THEATRE*): **to ~ sb as Othello** dar a uno el papel de Otelo ♦ *vi* (*FISHING*) lanzar ♦ *n* (*THEATRE*) reparto; (*also*: **plaster ~**) vaciado; **to ~ one's vote** votar; **to ~ doubt on** suscitar dudas acerca de; ~ **off** *vi* (*NAUT*) desamarrar; (*KNITTING*) cerrar (los puntos); ~ **on** *vi* (*KNITTING*) poner los puntos
castanets [kæstə'nets] *npl* castañuelas *fpl*
castaway ['kɑːstəwəɪ] *n* náufrago/a
caster sugar ['kɑːstə*-] (*BRIT*) *n* azúcar *m* extrafino
Castile [kæs'tiːl] *n* Castilla; **Castilian** *adj, n* castellano/a *m/f*
casting vote ['kɑːstɪŋ-] (*BRIT*) *n* voto decisivo
cast iron *n* hierro fundido
castle ['kɑːsl] *n* castillo; (*CHESS*) torre *f*
castor oil ['kɑːstə*-] *n* aceite *m* de ricino
casual ['kæʒjul] *adj* fortuito, (*irregular: work etc*) eventual, temporero; (*unconcerned*) despreocupado; (*clothes*) de sport; ~**ly** *adv* de manera despreocupada; (*dress*) de sport
casualty ['kæʒjultɪ] *n* víctima, herido; (*dead*) muerto; (*MED: department*) urgencias *fpl*
cat [kæt] *n* gato; (*big* ~) felino
Catalan ['kætəlæn] *adj, n* catalán/ana *m/f*
catalogue ['kætəlɒg] (*US* **catalog**) *n* catálogo ♦ *vt* catalogar
Catalonia [kætə'ləunɪə] *n* Cataluña
catalyst ['kætəlɪst] *n* catalizador *m*
catalytic convertor [kætə'lɪtɪk kən'vɜːtə*]
n catalizador *m*
catapult ['kætəpʌlt] *n* tirachinas *m inv*
catarrh [kə'tɑː*] *n* catarro
catastrophe [kə'tæstrəfɪ] *n* catástrofe *f*
catch [kætʃ] (*pt, pp* **caught**) *vt* (*throw*) coger (*SP*), agarrar (*AM*); (*arrest*) detener; (*grasp*) asir; (*breath*) contener; (*surprise: person*) sorprender; (*attract: attention*) captar; (*hear*) oír; (*MED*) contagiarse de, coger; (*also*: ~ **up**) alcanzar ♦ *vi* (*fire*) encenderse; (*in branches etc*) enredarse ♦ *n* (*fish etc*) pesca; (*act of catching*) cogida; (*hidden problem*) dificultad *f*; (*game*) pilla-pilla; (*of lock*) pestillo, cerradura; **to ~ fire** encenderse; **to ~ sight of** divisar; ~ **on** *vi* (*understand*) caer en la cuenta; (*grow popular*) hacerse popular; ~ **up** *vi* (*fig*) ponerse al día; ~**ing** ['kætʃɪŋ] *adj* (*MED*) contagioso; ~**ment area** ['kætʃmənt-] (*BRIT*) *n* zona de captación; ~**phrase** ['kætʃfreɪz] *n* lema *m*, eslogan *m*; ~**y** ['kætʃɪ] *adj* (*tune*) pegadizo
category ['kætɪgərɪ] *n* categoría, clase *f*
cater ['keɪtə*] *vi*: **to ~ for** (*BRIT*) abastecer a; (*needs*) atender a; (*COMM: parties etc*) proveer comida a; (*COMM: parties etc*) hacerse cargo; ~**er** *n* abastecedor(a) *m/f*, proveedor(a) *m/f*; ~**ing** *n* (*trade*) hostelería
caterpillar ['kætəpɪlə*] *n* oruga, gusano
cathedral [kə'θiːdrəl] *n* catedral *f*
catholic ['kæθəlɪk] *adj* (*tastes etc*) amplio; **C~** *adj*, *n* (*REL*) católico/a *m/f*
CAT scan [kæt-] *n* TAC *f*, tomografía
Catseye ® ['kæts'aɪ] (*BRIT*) *n* (*AUT*) catafoto
cattle ['kætl] *npl* ganado
catty ['kætɪ] *adj* malicioso, rencoroso
caucus ['kɔːkəs] *n* (*POL*) camarilla política; (*: US: to elect candidates*) comité *m* electoral
caught [kɔːt] *pt, pp of* **catch**
cauliflower ['kɔlɪflauə*] *n* coliflor *f*
cause [kɔːz] *n* causa, motivo, razón *f*; (*principle: also: POL*) causa ♦ *vt* causar
caution ['kɔːʃən] *n* cautela, prudencia; (*warning*) advertencia, amonestación *f*

♦ *vt* amonestar; **cautious** *adj* cauteloso, prudente, precavido

cavalry ['kævəlrı] *n* caballería

cave [keɪv] *n* cueva, caverna; **~ in** *vi* (*roof etc*) derrumbarse, hundirse

caviar(e) ['kævɪɑ:*] *n* caviar *m*

CB *n abbr* (= *Citizens' Band (Radio)*) banda ciudadana

CBI *n abbr* (= *Confederation of British Industry*) ≈ C.E.O.E. *f* (*SP*)

cc *abbr* = **cubic centimetres**; = **carbon copy**

CD *n abbr* (= *compact disc*) DC *m*; (*player*) (reproductor *m* de) disco compacto; **~ player** *n* lector *m* de compact disc, reproductor *m* de disco compacto; **~-ROM** [si:di:'rɔm] *n abbr* CD-ROM *m*

cease [si:s] *vt, vi* cesar; **~fire** *n* alto *m* el fuego; **~less** *adj* incesante

cedar ['si:də*] *n* cedro

ceiling ['si:lɪŋ] *n* techo; (*fig*) límite *m*

celebrate ['selɪbreɪt] *vt* celebrar ♦ *vi* divertirse; **~d** *adj* célebre; **celebration** [-'breɪʃən] *n* fiesta, celebración *f*

celery ['selərı] *n* apio

cell [sel] *n* celda; (*BIOL*) célula; (*ELEC*) elemento

cellar ['selə*] *n* sótano; (*for wine*) bodega

cello ['tʃeləu] *n* violoncelo

Cellophane ® ['seləfeɪn] *n* celofán *m*

cellphone ['selfəun] *n* teléfono celular

Celt [kelt, selt] *adj, n* celta *m/f*; **~ic** *adj* celta

cement [sə'ment] *n* cemento; **~ mixer** *n* hormigonera

cemetery ['semɪtrı] *n* cementerio

censor ['sensə*] *n* censor *m* ♦ *vt* (*cut*) censurar; **~ship** *n* censura

censure ['senʃə*] *vt* censurar

census ['sensəs] *n* censo

cent [sent] *n* (*US*) (*coin*) centavo, céntimo; *see also* **per**

centenary [sen'ti:nərı] *n* centenario

center ['sentə*] (*US*) = **centre**

centi... [sentı] *prefix*: **~grade** *adj* centígrado; **~litre** (*US* **~liter**) *n* centilitro; **~metre** (*US* **~meter**) *n* centímetro

centipede ['sentɪpi:d] *n* ciempiés *m inv*

central ['sentrəl] *adj* central; (*of house etc*) céntrico; **C~ America** *n* Centroamérica; **~ heating** *n* calefacción *f* central; **~ize** *vt* centralizar

centre ['sentə*] (*US* **center**) *n* centro; (*fig*) núcleo ♦ *vt* centrar; **~-forward** *n* (*SPORT*) delantero centro; **~-half** *n* (*SPORT*) medio centro

century ['sentjurı] *n* siglo; **20th ~** siglo veinte

ceramic [sɪ'ræmɪk] *adj* cerámico; **~s** *n* cerámica

cereal ['si:rɪəl] *n* cereal *m*

ceremony ['serɪmənı] *n* ceremonia; **to stand on ~** hacer ceremonias, estar de cumplido

certain ['sə:tən] *adj* seguro, (*person*): **a ~ Mr Smith** un tal Sr Smith; (*particular, some*) cierto; **for ~** a ciencia cierta; **~ly** *adv* (*undoubtedly*) ciertamente; (*of course*) desde luego, por supuesto; **~ty** *n* certeza, certidumbre *f*, seguridad *f*; (*inevitability*) certeza

certificate [sə'tıfıkıt] *n* certificado

certified ['sə:tıfaıd]: **~ mail** (*US*) *n* correo certificado; **~ public accountant** (*US*) *n* contable *m/f* diplomado/a

certify ['sə:tıfaı] *vt* certificar; (*award diploma to*) conceder un diploma a; (*declare insane*) declarar loco

cervical ['sə:vɪkl] *adj* cervical

cervix ['sə:vɪks] *n* cuello del útero

cf. *abbr* (= *compare*) cfr

CFC *n abbr* (= *chlorofluorocarbon*) CFC *m*

ch. *abbr* (= *chapter*) cap

chain [tʃeɪn] *n* cadena; (*of mountains*) cordillera; (*of events*) sucesión *f* ♦ *vt* (*also:* **~ up**) encadenar; **~ reaction** *n* reacción *f* en cadena; **~-smoke** *vi* fumar un cigarrillo tras otro; **~ store** *n* tienda de una cadena, ≈ gran almacén

chair [tʃeə*] *n* silla; (*armchair*) sillón *m*, butaca; (*of university*) cátedra; (*of meeting etc*) presidencia ♦ *vt* (*meeting*) presidir; **~lift** *n* telesilla; **~man** *n* presidente *m*

chalk [tʃɔ:k] *n* (*GEO*) creta; (*for writing*) tiza

(*SP*), gis *m* (*AM*)

challenge [ˈtʃælɪndʒ] *n* desafío, reto ♦ *vt* desafiar, retar; (*statement, right*) poner en duda; **to ~ sb to do sth** retar a uno a que haga algo; **challenging** *adj* exigente; (*tone*) de desafío

chamber [ˈtʃeɪmbə*] *n* cámara, sala; (*POL*) cámara; (*BRIT: LAW: gen pl*) despacho; **~ of commerce** cámara de comercio; **~maid** *n* camarera; **~ music** *n* música de cámara

chamois [ˈʃæmwɑː] *n* gamuza

champagne [ʃæmˈpeɪn] *n* champaña *m*, champán *m*

champion [ˈtʃæmpɪən] *n* campeón/ona *m/f*; (*of cause*) defensor(a) *m/f*; **~ship** *n* campeonato

chance [tʃɑːns] *n* (*opportunity*) ocasión *f*, oportunidad *f*; (*likelihood*) posibilidad *f*; (*risk*) riesgo ♦ *vt* arriesgar, probar ♦ *adj* fortuito, casual; **to ~ it** arriesgarse, intentarlo; **to take a ~** arriesgarse; **by ~** por casualidad

chancellor [ˈtʃɑːnsələ*] *n* canciller *m*; **C~ of the Exchequer** (*BRIT*) *n* Ministro de Hacienda

chandelier [ʃændəˈlɪə*] *n* araña (de luces)

change [tʃeɪndʒ] *vt* cambiar; (*replace*) cambiar, reemplazar; (*gear, clothes, job*) cambiar de; (*transform*) transformar ♦ *vi* cambiar(se); (*trains*) hacer transbordo; (*traffic lights*) cambiar de color; (*be transformed*): **to ~ into** transformarse en ♦ *n* cambio; (*alteration*) modificación *f*, transformación *f*; (*of clothes*) muda; (*coins*) suelto, sencillo; (*money returned*) vuelta; **to ~ gear** (*AUT*) cambiar de marcha; **to ~ one's mind** cambiar de opinión o idea; **for a ~** para variar; **~able** *adj* (*weather*) cambiable; **~ machine** *n* máquina de cambio; **~over** *n* (*to new system*) cambio; **changing** *adj* cambiante; **changing room** (*BRIT*) *n* vestuario

channel [ˈtʃænl] *n* (*TV*) canal *m*; (*of river*) cauce *m*; (*groove*) conducto; (*fig: medium*) medio ♦ *vt* (*river etc*) encauzar; **the**

(**English**) **C~** el Canal (de la Mancha); **the C~ Islands** las Islas Normandas; **the C~ Tunnel** el túnel del Canal de la Mancha, el Eurotúnel; **~-hopping** *n* (*TV*) zapping *m*

chant [tʃɑːnt] *n* (*of crowd*) gritos *mpl*; (*REL*) canto ♦ *vt* (*slogan, word*) repetir a gritos

chaos [ˈkeɪɒs] *n* caos *m*

chap [tʃæp] (*BRIT: inf*) *n* (*man*) tío, tipo

chapel [ˈtʃæpəl] *n* capilla

chaperone [ˈʃæpərəun] *n* carabina

chaplain [ˈtʃæplɪn] *n* capellán *m*

chapped [tʃæpt] *adj* agrietado

chapter [ˈtʃæptə*] *n* capítulo

char [tʃɑː*] *vt* (*burn*) carbonizar, chamuscar

character [ˈkærɪktə*] *n* carácter *m*, naturaleza, índole *f*; (*moral strength, personality*) carácter; (*in novel, film*) personaje *m*; **~istic** [-ˈrɪstɪk] *adj* característico ♦ *n* característica

charcoal [ˈtʃɑːkəul] *n* carbón *m* vegetal; (*ART*) carboncillo

charge [tʃɑːdʒ] *n* (*LAW*) cargo, acusación *f*; (*cost*) precio, coste *m*; (*responsibility*) cargo ♦ *vt* (*LAW*): **to ~ (with)** acusar (de); (*battery*) cargar; (*price*) pedir; (*customer*) cobrar ♦ *vi* precipitarse; (*MIL*) cargar, atacar; **~s** *npl*: **to reverse the ~s** (*BRIT: TEL*) revertir el cobro; **to take ~ of** hacerse cargo de, encargarse de; **to be in ~ of** estar encargado de; (*business*) mandar; **how much do you ~?** ¿cuánto cobra usted?; **to ~ an expense (up) to sb's account** cargar algo a cuenta de alguien; **~ card** *n* tarjeta de cuenta

charity [ˈtʃærɪtɪ] *n* caridad *f*; (*organization*) sociedad *f* benéfica; (*money, gifts*) limosnas *fpl*

charm [tʃɑːm] *n* encanto, atractivo; (*talisman*) hechizo; (*on bracelet*) dije *m* ♦ *vt* encantar; **~ing** *adj* encantador(a)

chart [tʃɑːt] *n* (*diagram*) cuadro; (*graph*) gráfica; (*map*) carta de navegación ♦ *vt* (*course*) trazar; (*progress*) seguir; **~s** *npl* (*Top 40*): **the ~s** ≈ los 40 principales (*SP*)

charter [ˈtʃɑːtə*] *vt* (*plane*) alquilar; (*ship*) fletar ♦ *n* (*document*) carta; (*of university,*

company) estatutos *mpl*; **~ed
accountant** (*BRIT*) *n* contable *m/f*
diplomado/a; **~ flight** *n* vuelo chárter
chase [tʃeɪs] *vt* (*pursue*) perseguir; (*also*: **~
away**) ahuyentar ♦ *n* persecución *f*
chasm [ˈkæzəm] *n* sima
chassis [ˈʃæsɪ] *n* chasis *m*
chat [tʃæt] *vi* (*also*: **have a ~**) charlar ♦ *n*
charla; **~ show** (*BRIT*) *n* programa *m* de
entrevistas
chatter [ˈtʃætə*] *vi* (*person*) charlar; (*teeth*)
castañetear ♦ *n* (*of birds*) parloteo; (*of
people*) charla, cháchara; **~box** (*inf*) *n*
parlanchín/ina *m/f*
chatty [ˈtʃætɪ] *adj* (*style*) informal; (*person*)
hablador(a)
chauffeur [ˈʃəufə*] *n* chófer *m*
chauvinist [ˈʃəuvɪnɪst] *n* (*male ~*) machista
m; (*nationalist*) chovinista *m/f*
cheap [tʃiːp] *adj* barato; (*joke*) de mal
gusto; (*poor quality*) de mala calidad
♦ *adv* barato; **~ day return** *n* billete *m*
de ida y vuelta el mismo día; **~er** *adj*
más barato; **~ly** *adv* barato, a bajo
precio
cheat [tʃiːt] *vi* hacer trampa ♦ *vt*: **to ~ sb
(out of sth)** estafar (algo) a uno ♦ *n*
(*person*) tramposo/a
check [tʃek] *vt* (*examine*) controlar; (*facts*)
comprobar; (*halt*) parar, detener;
(*restrain*) refrenar, restringir ♦ *n*
(*inspection*) control *m*, inspección *f*; (*curb*)
freno; (*US*: *bill*) nota, cuenta; (*US*)
= **cheque**; (*pattern*: *gen pl*) cuadro ♦ *adj*
(*also*: **~ed**: *pattern*, *cloth*) a cuadros; **~ in**
vi (*at hotel*) firmar el registro; (*at airport*)
facturar el equipaje ♦ *vt* (*luggage*)
facturar; **~ out** *vi* (*of hotel*) marcharse; **~
up** *vi*: **to ~ up on sth** comprobar algo; **to
~ up on sb** investigar a alguien; **~ered**
(*US*) *adj* = **check; chequered**; **~ers** (*US*)
n juego de damas; **~-in** (**desk**) *n*
mostrador *m* de facturación; **~ing
account** (*US*) *n* cuenta corriente; **~mate**
n jaque *m* mate; **~out** *n* caja; **~point** *n*
(punto de) control *m*; **~room** (*US*) *n*
consigna; **~up** *n* (*MED*) reconocimiento

general
cheek [tʃiːk] *n* mejilla; (*impudence*)
descaro; **what a ~!** ¡qué cara!; **~bone** *n*
pómulo; **~y** *adj* fresco, descarado
cheep [tʃiːp] *vi* piar
cheer [tʃɪə*] *vt* vitorear, aplaudir; (*gladden*)
alegrar, animar ♦ *vi* dar vivas ♦ *n* viva *m*;
~s *npl* aplausos *mpl*; **~s!** ¡salud!; **~ up** *vi*
animarse ♦ *vt* alegrar, animar; **~ful** *adj*
alegre
cheerio [tʃɪərɪˈəu] (*BRIT*) *excl* ¡hasta luego!
cheese [tʃiːz] *n* queso; **~board** *n* tabla
de quesos
cheetah [ˈtʃiːtə] *n* leopardo cazador
chef [ʃef] *n* jefe/a *m/f* de cocina
chemical [ˈkemɪkəl] *adj* químico ♦ *n*
producto químico
chemist [ˈkemɪst] *n* (*BRIT*: *pharmacist*)
farmacéutico/a; (*scientist*) químico/a; **~ry**
n química; **~'s (shop)** (*BRIT*) *n* farmacia
cheque [tʃek] (*US* **check**) *n* cheque *m*;
~book *n* talonario de cheques (*SP*),
chequera (*AM*); **~ card** *n* tarjeta de
cheque
chequered [ˈtʃekəd] (*US* **checkered**) *adj*
(*fig*) accidentado
cherish [ˈtʃerɪʃ] *vt* (*love*) querer, apreciar;
(*protect*) cuidar; (*hope etc*) abrigar
cherry [ˈtʃerɪ] *n* cereza; (*also*: **~ tree**)
cerezo
chess [tʃes] *n* ajedrez *m*; **~board** *n*
tablero (de ajedrez)
chest [tʃest] *n* (*ANAT*) pecho; (*box*) cofre
m, cajón *m*; **~ of drawers** *n* cómoda
chestnut [ˈtʃesnʌt] *n* castaña; **~ (tree)** *n*
castaño
chew [tʃuː] *vt* mascar, masticar; **~ing
gum** *n* chicle *m*
chic [ʃiːk] *adj* elegante
chick [tʃɪk] *n* pollito, polluelo; (*inf*: *girl*)
chica
chicken [ˈtʃɪkɪn] *n* gallina, pollo; (*food*)
pollo; (*inf*: *coward*) gallina *m/f*; **~ out**
(*inf*) *vi* rajarse; **~pox** *n* varicela
chicory [ˈtʃɪkərɪ] *n* (*for coffee*) achicoria;
(*salad*) escarola
chief [tʃiːf] *n* jefe/a *m/f* ♦ *adj* principal; **~**

executive n director(a) m/f general; **~ly** adv principalmente

chilblain ['tʃɪlbleɪn] n sabañón m

child [tʃaɪld] (pl **children**) n niño/a; (offspring) hijo/a; **~birth** n parto; **~hood** n niñez f, infancia; **~ish** adj pueril, aniñado; **~like** adj de niño; **~ minder** (BRIT) n madre f de día; **~ren** ['tʃɪldrən] npl of **child**

Chile ['tʃɪlɪ] n Chile m; **~an** adj, n chileno/a m/f

chill [tʃɪl] n frío; (MED) resfriado ♦ vt enfriar; (CULIN) congelar

chil(l)i ['tʃɪlɪ] (BRIT) n chile m (SP), ají m (AM)

chilly ['tʃɪlɪ] adj frío

chime [tʃaɪm] n repique m; (of clock) campanada ♦ vi repicar; sonar

chimney ['tʃɪmnɪ] n chimenea; **~ sweep** n deshollinador m

chimpanzee [tʃɪmpæn'zi:] n chimpancé m

chin [tʃɪn] n mentón m, barbilla

china ['tʃaɪnə] n porcelana; (crockery) loza

China ['tʃaɪnə] n China; **Chinese** [tʃaɪ'ni:z] adj chino ♦ n inv chino/a; (LING) chino

chink [tʃɪŋk] n (opening) grieta, hendedura; (noise) tintineo

chip [tʃɪp] n (gen pl: CULIN: BRIT) patata (SP) or papa (AM) frita; (: US: also: **potato ~**) patata or papa frita; (of wood) astilla; (of glass, stone) lasca; (at poker) ficha; (COMPUT) chip m ♦ vt (cup, plate) desconchar

> **chip shop**
>
> *i* Se denomina **chip shop** o "fish-and-chip shop" a un establecimiento en el que se sirven algunas especialidades de comida rápida, muy populares entre los británicos, sobre todo pescado rebozado y patatas fritas.

chiropodist [kɪ'rɔpədɪst] (BRIT) n pedicuro/a, callista m/f

chirp [tʃə:p] vi (bird) gorjear, piar

chisel ['tʃɪzl] n (for wood) escoplo; (for stone) cincel m

chit [tʃɪt] n nota

chitchat ['tʃɪttʃæt] n chismes mpl, habladurías fpl

chivalry ['ʃɪvəlrɪ] n caballerosidad f

chives [tʃaɪvz] npl cebollinos mpl

chlorine ['klɔ:ri:n] n cloro

chock-a-block ['tʃɔkə'blɔk] adj atestado

chock-full ['tʃɔk'ful] adj atestado

chocolate ['tʃɔklɪt] n chocolate m; (sweet) bombón m

choice [tʃɔɪs] n elección f, selección f; (option) opción f; (preference) preferencia ♦ adj escogido

choir ['kwaɪə*] n coro; **~boy** n niño de coro

choke [tʃəuk] vi ahogarse; (on food) atragantarse ♦ vt estrangular, ahogar; (block): **to be ~d with** estar atascado de ♦ n (AUT) estárter m

cholesterol [kə'lestərɔl] n colesterol m

choose [tʃu:z] (pt **chose**, pp **chosen**) vt escoger, elegir; (team) seleccionar; **to ~ to do sth** optar por hacer algo

choosy ['tʃu:zɪ] adj delicado

chop [tʃɔp] vt (wood) cortar, tajar; (CULIN: also: **~ up**) picar ♦ n (CULIN) chuleta; **~s** npl (jaws) boca, labios mpl

chopper ['tʃɔpə*] n (helicopter) helicóptero

choppy ['tʃɔpɪ] adj (sea) picado, agitado

chopsticks ['tʃɔpstɪks] npl palillos mpl

chord [kɔ:d] n (MUS) acorde m

chore [tʃɔ:*] n faena, tarea; (routine task) trabajo rutinario

chorus ['kɔ:rəs] n coro; (repeated part of song) estribillo

chose [tʃəuz] pt of **choose**

chosen ['tʃəuzn] pp of **choose**

chowder ['tʃaudə*] n (esp US) sopa de pescado

Christ [kraɪst] n Cristo

christen ['krɪsn] vt bautizar

Christian ['krɪstɪən] adj, n cristiano/a m/f; **~ity** [-'ænɪtɪ] n cristianismo; **~ name** n nombre m de pila

Christmas ['krɪsməs] n Navidad f; **Merry ~!** ¡Felices Pascuas!; **~ card** n crismas m inv, tarjeta de Navidad; **~ Day** n día m de Navidad; **~ Eve** n Nochebuena; **~ tree** n árbol m de Navidad

chrome [krəum] n cromo

chronic ['krɒnɪk] adj crónico

chronological [krɒnə'lɒdʒɪkəl] adj cronológico

chubby ['tʃʌbɪ] adj regordete

chuck [tʃʌk] (inf) vt lanzar, arrojar; (BRIT: also: **~ up**) abandonar; **~ out** vt (person) echar (fuera); (rubbish etc) tirar

chuckle ['tʃʌkl] vi reírse entre dientes

chug [tʃʌg] vi resoplar; (car, boat: also: **~ along**) avanzar traqueteando

chum [tʃʌm] n compañero/a

chunk [tʃʌŋk] n pedazo, trozo

church [tʃɜːtʃ] n iglesia; **~yard** n cementerio

churn [tʃɜːn] n (for butter) mantequera; (for milk) lechera; **~ out** vt producir en serie

chute [ʃuːt] n (also: **rubbish ~**) vertedero; (for coal etc) rampa de caída

chutney ['tʃʌtnɪ] n condimento a base de frutas de la India

CIA (US) n abbr (= Central Intelligence Agency) CIA f

CID (BRIT) n abbr (= Criminal Investigation Department) ≈ B.I.C. f (SP)

cider ['saɪdə*] n sidra

cigar [sɪ'gɑ:*] n puro

cigarette [sɪgə'ret] n cigarrillo (SP), cigarro (AM); pitillo; **~ case** n pitillera; **~ end** n colilla

Cinderella [sɪndə'relə] n Cenicienta

cinders ['sɪndəz] npl cenizas fpl

cine camera ['sɪnɪ-] (BRIT) n cámara cinematográfica

cinema ['sɪnəmə] n cine m

cinnamon ['sɪnəmən] n canela

circle ['sɜːkl] n círculo; (in theatre) anfiteatro ♦ vi dar vueltas ♦ vt (surround) rodear, cercar; (move round) dar la vuelta a

circuit ['sɜːkɪt] n circuito; (tour) gira; (track) pista; (lap) vuelta; **~ous** [sɜː'kjuɪtəs] adj indirecto

circular ['sɜːkjulə*] adj circular ♦ n circular f

circulate ['sɜːkjuleɪt] vi circular; (person: at party etc) hablar con los invitados ♦ vt poner en circulación; **circulation** [-'leɪʃən] n circulación f; (of newspaper) tirada

circumstances ['sɜːkəmstənsɪz] npl circunstancias fpl; (financial condition) situación f económica

circus ['sɜːkəs] n circo

CIS n abbr (= Commonwealth of Independent States) CEI f

cistern ['sɪstən] n tanque m, depósito; (in toilet) cisterna

citizen ['sɪtɪzn] n (POL) ciudadano/a; (of city) vecino/a, habitante m/f; **~ship** n ciudadanía

citrus fruits ['sɪtrəs-] npl agrios mpl

city ['sɪtɪ] n ciudad f; **the C~** centro financiero de Londres

civic ['sɪvɪk] adj cívico; (authorities) municipal; **~ centre** (BRIT) n centro público

civil ['sɪvɪl] adj civil; (polite) atento, cortés; **~ engineer** n ingeniero de caminos(, canales y puertos); **~ian** [sɪ'vɪlɪən] adj civil (no militar) ♦ n civil m/f, paisano/a

civilization [sɪvɪlaɪ'zeɪʃən] n civilización f

civilized ['sɪvɪlaɪzd] adj civilizado

civil: ~ law n derecho civil; **~ servant** n funcionario/a del Estado; **C~ Service** n administración f pública; **~ war** n guerra civil

claim [kleɪm] vt exigir, reclamar; (rights etc) reivindicar; (assert) pretender ♦ vi (for insurance) reclamar ♦ n reclamación f; pretensión f; **~ant** n demandante m/f

clairvoyant [kleə'vɔɪənt] n clarividente m/f

clam [klæm] n almeja

clamber ['klæmbə*] vi trepar

clammy ['klæmɪ] adj frío y húmedo

clamour ['klæmə*] (US **clamor**) vi: **to ~ for** clamar por, pedir a voces

clamp [klæmp] n abrazadera, grapa ♦ vt (2 things together) cerrar fuertemente; (one thing on another) afianzar (con abrazadera); (AUT: wheel) poner el cepo a;

~ **down on** vt fus (subj: government, police) reforzar la lucha contra

clang [klæŋ] vi sonar, hacer estruendo

clap [klæp] vi aplaudir; ~**ping** n aplausos mpl

claret ['klærət] n burdeos m inv

clarify ['klærɪfaɪ] vt aclarar

clarinet [klærɪ'nɛt] n clarinete m

clash [klæʃ] n enfrentamiento; choque m; desacuerdo; estruendo ♦ vi (fight) enfrentarse; (beliefs) chocar; (disagree) estar en desacuerdo; (colours) desentonar; (two events) coincidir

clasp [klɑːsp] n (hold) apretón m; (of necklace, bag) cierre m ♦ vt apretar; abrazar

class [klɑːs] n clase f ♦ vt clasificar

classic ['klæsɪk] adj, n clásico; ~**al** adj clásico

classified ['klæsɪfaɪd] adj (information) reservado; ~ **advertisement** n anuncio por palabras

classmate ['klɑːsmeɪt] n compañero/a de clase

classroom ['klɑːsrum] n aula

clatter ['klætə*] n estrépito ♦ vi hacer ruido or estrépito

clause [klɔːz] n cláusula; (LING) oración f

claw [klɔː] n (of cat) uña; (of bird of prey) garra; (of lobster) pinza

clay [kleɪ] n arcilla

clean [kliːn] adj limpio; (record, reputation) bueno, intachable; (joke) decente ♦ vt limpiar; (hands etc) lavar; ~ **out** vt limpiar; ~ **up** vt limpiar, asear; ~~**cut** adj (person) bien parecido; ~**er** n (person) asistenta; (substance) producto para la limpieza; ~**er's** n tintorería; ~**ing** n limpieza; ~**liness** ['klɛnlɪnɪs] n limpieza

cleanse [klɛnz] vt limpiar; ~**r** n (for face) crema limpiadora

clean-shaven adj sin barba, afeitado

cleansing department (BRIT) n departamento de limpieza

clear [klɪə*] adj claro; (road, way) libre; (conscience) limpio, tranquilo; (skin) terso; (sky) despejado ♦ vt (space) despejar,

limpiar; (LAW: suspect) absolver; (obstacle) salvar, saltar por encima de; (cheque) aceptar ♦ vi (fog etc) despejarse ♦ adv: ~ **of** a distancia de; **to ~ the table** recoger or levantar la mesa; ~ **up** vt limpiar; (mystery) aclarar, resolver; ~**ance** n (removal) despeje m; (permission) acreditación f; ~~**cut** adj bien definido, nítido; ~**ing** n (in wood) claro; ~**ing bank** (BRIT) n cámara de compensación; ~**ly** adv claramente; (evidently) sin duda; ~**way** (BRIT) n carretera donde no se puede parar

clef [klɛf] n (MUS) clave f

cleft [klɛft] n (in rock) grieta, hendedura

clench [klɛntʃ] vt apretar, cerrar

clergy ['klɜːdʒɪ] n clero; ~**man** n clérigo

clerical ['klɛrɪkəl] adj de oficina; (REL) clerical

clerk [klɑːk, (US) klɜːrk] n (BRIT) oficinista m/f; (US) dependiente/a m/f, vendedor(a) m/f

clever ['klɛvə*] adj (intelligent) inteligente, listo; (skilful) hábil; (device, arrangement) ingenioso

click [klɪk] vt (tongue) chasquear; (heels) taconear

client ['klaɪənt] n cliente m/f

cliff [klɪf] n acantilado

climate ['klaɪmɪt] n clima m

climax ['klaɪmæks] n (of battle, career) apogeo; (of film, book) punto culminante; (sexual) orgasmo

climb [klaɪm] vi subir; (plant) trepar; (move with effort): **to ~ over a wall/into a car** trepar a una tapia/subir a un coche ♦ vt (stairs) subir; (tree) trepar a; (mountain) escalar ♦ n subida; ~~**down** n vuelta atrás; ~**er** n alpinista m/f (SP), andinista m/f (AM); ~**ing** n alpinismo (SP), andinismo (AM)

clinch [klɪntʃ] vt (deal) cerrar; (argument) remachar

cling [klɪŋ] (pt, pp **clung**) vi: **to ~ to** agarrarse a; (clothes) pegarse a

clinic ['klɪnɪk] n clínica; ~**al** adj clínico; (fig) frío

clink [klɪŋk] *vi* tintinar

clip [klɪp] *n* (*for hair*) horquilla; (*also:* **paper ~**) sujetapapeles *m inv*, clip *m*; (*TV, CINEMA*) fragmento ♦ *vt* (*cut*) cortar; (*also:* **~ together**) unir; **~pers** *npl* (*for gardening*) tijeras *fpl*; **~ping** *n* (*newspaper*) recorte *m*

clique [kliːk] *n* camarilla

cloak [kləuk] *n* capa, manto ♦ *vt* (*fig*) encubrir, disimular; **~room** *n* guardarropa; (*BRIT: WC*) lavabo (*SP*), aseos *mpl* (*SP*), baño (*AM*)

clock [klɔk] *n* reloj *m*; **~ in** *or* **on** *vi* fichar, picar; **~ off** *or* **out** *vi* fichar *or* picar la salida; **~wise** *adv* en el sentido de las agujas del reloj; **~work** *n* aparato de relojería ♦ *adj* (*toy*) de cuerda

clog [klɔg] *n* zueco, chanclo ♦ *vt* atascar ♦ *vi* (*also:* **~ up**) atascarse

cloister [ˈklɔɪstəʳ] *n* claustro

close¹ [kləus] *adj* (*near*): **~ (to)** cerca (de); (*friend*) íntimo; (*connection*) estrecho; (*examination*) detallado, minucioso; (*weather*) bochornoso; **to have a ~ shave** (*fig*) escaparse por un pelo ♦ *adv* cerca; **~ by, ~ at hand** muy cerca; **~ to** *prep* cerca de

close² [kləuz] *vt* (*shut*) cerrar; (*end*) concluir, terminar ♦ *vi* (*shop etc*) cerrarse; (*end*) concluirse, terminarse ♦ *n* (*end*) fin *m*, final *m*, conclusión *f*; **~ down** *vi* cerrarse definitivamente; **~d** *adj* (*shop etc*) cerrado; **~d shop** *n* taller *m* gremial

close-knit [kləusˈnɪt] *adj* (*fig*) muy unido

closely [ˈkləuslɪ] *adv* (*study*) con detalle; (*watch*) de cerca; (*resemble*) estrechamente

closet [ˈklɔzɪt] *n* armario

close-up [ˈkləusʌp] *n* primer plano

closure [ˈkləuʒəʳ] *n* cierre *m*

clot [klɔt] *n* (*gen:* **blood ~**) coágulo; (*inf:* *idiot*) imbécil *m/f* ♦ *vi* (*blood*) coagularse

cloth [klɔθ] *n* (*material*) tela, paño; (*rag*) trapo

clothe [kləuð] *vt* vestir; **~s** *npl* ropa; **~s brush** *n* cepillo (para la ropa); **~s line** *n* cuerda (para tender la ropa); **~s peg** (*US*

~s pin) *n* pinza

clothing [ˈkləuðɪŋ] *n* = **clothes**

cloud [klaud] *n* nube *f*; **~burst** *n* aguacero; **~y** *adj* nublado, nubloso; (*liquid*) turbio

clout [klaut] *vt* dar un tortazo a

clove [kləuv] *n* clavo; **~ of garlic** diente de ajo

clover [ˈkləuvəʳ] *n* trébol *m*

clown [klaun] *n* payaso ♦ *vi* (*also:* **~ about, ~ around**) hacer el payaso

cloying [ˈklɔɪɪŋ] *adj* empalagoso

club [klʌb] *n* (*society*) club *m*; (*weapon*) porra, cachiporra; (*also:* **golf ~**) palo ♦ *vt* aporrear ♦ *vi*: **to ~ together** (*for gift*) comprar entre todos; **~s** *npl* (*CARDS*) tréboles *mpl*; **~ class** *n* (*AVIAT*) clase *f* preferente; **~house** *n* local social, sobre todo en clubs deportivos

cluck [klʌk] *vi* cloquear

clue [kluː] *n* pista; (*in crosswords*) indicación *f*; **I haven't a ~** no tengo ni idea

clump [klʌmp] *n* (*of trees*) grupo

clumsy [ˈklʌmzɪ] *adj* (*person*) torpe, desmañado; (*tool*) difícil de manejar; (*movement*) desgarbado

clung [klʌŋ] *pt, pp of* **cling**

cluster [ˈklʌstəʳ] *n* grupo ♦ *vi* agruparse, apiñarse

clutch [klʌtʃ] *n* (*AUT*) embrague *m*; (*grasp*): **~es** garras *fpl* ♦ *vt* asir; agarrar

clutter [ˈklʌtəʳ] *vt* atestar

cm *abbr* (= *centimetre*) cm

CND *n abbr* (= *Campaign for Nuclear Disarmament*) plataforma pro desarme nuclear

Co. *abbr* = **county; company**

c/o *abbr* (= *care of*) c/a, a/c

coach [kəutʃ] *n* autocar *m* (*SP*), coche *m* de línea; (*horse-drawn*) coche *m*; (*of train*) vagón *m*, coche *m*; (*SPORT*) entrenador(a) *m/f*, instructor(a) *m/f*; (*tutor*) profesor(a) *m/f* particular ♦ *vt* (*SPORT*) entrenar; (*student*) preparar, enseñar; **~ trip** *n* excursión *f* en autocar

coal [kəul] *n* carbón *m*; **~ face** *n* frente *m*

de carbón; **~field** *n* yacimiento de carbón

coalition [kəuə'lɪʃən] *n* coalición *f*

coalman ['kəulmən] (*irreg*) *n* carbonero

coalmine ['kəulmaɪn] *n* mina de carbón

coarse [kɔːs] *adj* basto, burdo; (*vulgar*) grosero, ordinario

coast [kəust] *n* costa, litoral *m* ♦ *vi* (*AUT*) ir en punto muerto; **~al** *adj* costero, costanero; **~guard** *n* guardacostas *m inv*; **~line** *n* litoral *m*

coat [kəut] *n* abrigo; (*of animal*) pelaje *m*, lana; (*of paint*) mano *f*, capa ♦ *vt* cubrir, revestir; **~ of arms** *n* escudo de armas; **~ hanger** *n* percha (*SP*), gancho (*AM*); **~ing** *n* capa, baño

coax [kəuks] *vt* engatusar

cobbler ['kɔblə] *n* zapatero (remendón)

cobbles ['kɔblz] *npl*, **cobblestones** ['kɔblstəunz] *npl* adoquines *mpl*

cobweb ['kɔbweb] *n* telaraña

cocaine [kə'keɪn] *n* cocaína

cock [kɔk] *n* (*rooster*) gallo; (*male bird*) macho ♦ *vt* (*gun*) amartillar; **~erel** *n* gallito

cockle ['kɔkl] *n* berberecho

cockney ['kɔknɪ] *n* habitante de ciertos barrios de Londres

cockpit ['kɔkpɪt] *n* cabina

cockroach ['kɔkrəutʃ] *n* cucaracha

cocktail ['kɔkteɪl] *n* coctel *m*, cóctel *m*; **~ cabinet** *n* mueble-bar *m*; **~ party** *n* coctel *m*, cóctel *m*

cocoa ['kəukəu] *n* cacao; (*drink*) chocolate *m*

coconut ['kəukənʌt] *n* coco

cod [kɔd] *n* bacalao

C.O.D. *abbr* (= *cash on delivery*) C.A.E.

code [kəud] *n* código; (*cipher*) clave *f*; (*dialling ~*) prefijo; (*post ~*) código postal

cod-liver oil ['kɔdlɪvər-] *n* aceite *m* de hígado de bacalao

coercion [kəu'əːʃən] *n* coacción *f*

coffee ['kɔfɪ] *n* café *m*; **~ bar** (*BRIT*) *n* cafetería; **~ bean** *n* grano de café; **~ break** *n* descanso (para tomar café); **~pot** *n* cafetera; **~ table** *n* mesita (para

servir el café)

coffin ['kɔfɪn] *n* ataúd *m*

cog [kɔg] *n* (*wheel*) rueda dentada; (*tooth*) diente *m*

cogent ['kəudʒənt] *adj* convincente

cognac ['kɔnjæk] *n* coñac *m*

coil [kɔɪl] *n* rollo; (*ELEC*) bobina, carrete *m*; (*contraceptive*) espiral *f* ♦ *vt* enrollar

coin [kɔɪn] *n* moneda ♦ *vt* (*word*) inventar, idear; **~age** *n* moneda; **~-box** (*BRIT*) *n* cabina telefónica

coincide [kəuɪn'saɪd] *vi* coincidir; (*agree*) estar de acuerdo; **coincidence** [kəu'ɪnsɪdəns] *n* casualidad *f*

Coke ® [kəuk] *n* Coca-Cola ®

coke [kəuk] *n* (*coal*) coque *m*

colander ['kɔləndə*] *vt* colador *m*, escurridor *m*

cold [kəuld] *adj* frío ♦ *n* frío; (*MED*) resfriado; **it's** ~ hace frío; **to be** ~ (*person*) tener frío; **to catch** ~ enfriarse; **to catch a** ~ resfriarse, acatarrarse; **in** ~ **blood** a sangre fría; **~-shoulder** *vt* dar *or* volver la espalda a; **~ sore** *n* herpes *mpl or fpl*

coleslaw ['kəulslɔː] *n* especie de ensalada de col

colic ['kɔlɪk] *n* cólico

collapse [kə'læps] *vi* hundirse, derrumbarse; (*MED*) sufrir un colapso ♦ *n* hundimiento, derrumbamiento; (*MED*) colapso; **collapsible** *adj* plegable

collar ['kɔlə*] *n* (*of coat, shirt*) cuello; (*of dog etc*) collar; **~bone** *n* clavícula

collateral [kɔ'lætərəl] *n* garantía colateral

colleague ['kɔliːg] *n* colega *m/f*; (*at work*) compañero, a

collect [kə'lekt] *vt* (*litter, mail etc*) recoger; (*as a hobby*) coleccionar; (*BRIT: call and pick up*) recoger; (*debts, subscriptions etc*) recaudar ♦ *vi* reunirse; (*dust*) acumularse; **to call** ~ (*US: TEL*) llamar a cobro revertido; **~ion** [kə'lekʃən] *n* colección *f*; (*of mail, for charity*) recogida; **~or** *n* coleccionista *m/f*

college ['kɔlɪdʒ] *n* colegio mayor; (*of agriculture, technology*) escuela universitaria

collide [kə'laɪd] *vi* chocar
colliery ['kɒlɪərɪ] (*BRIT*) *n* mina de carbón
collision [kə'lɪʒən] *n* choque *m*
colloquial [kə'ləʊkwɪəl] *adj* familiar, coloquial
Colombia [kə'lɒmbɪə] *n* Colombia; **~n** *adj, n* colombiano/a
colon ['kəʊlən] *n* (*sign*) dos puntos; (*MED*) colon *m*
colonel ['kɜːnl] *n* coronel *m*
colonial [kə'ləʊnɪəl] *adj* colonial
colony ['kɒlənɪ] *n* colonia
colour ['kʌlə*] (*US* **color**) *n* color *m* ♦ *vt* color(e)ar; (*dye*) teñir; (*fig: account*) adornar; (*: judgement*) distorsionar ♦ *vi* (*blush*) sonrojarse; **~s** *npl* (*of party, club*) colores *mpl*; **in ~** en color; **~ in** *vt* colorear; **~ bar** *n* segregación *f* racial; **~-blind** *adj* daltónico; **~ed** *adj* de color; (*photo*) en color; **~ film** *n* película en color; **~ful** *adj* lleno de color; (*story*) fantástico; (*person*) excéntrico; **~ing** *n* (*complexion*) tez *f*; (*in food*) colorante *m*; **~ scheme** *n* combinación *f* de colores; **~ television** *n* televisión *f* en color
colt [kəʊlt] *n* potro
column ['kɒləm] *n* columna; **~ist** ['kɒləmnɪst] *n* columnista *m/f*
coma ['kəʊmə] *n* coma *m*
comb [kəʊm] *n* peine *m*; (*ornamental*) peineta ♦ *vt* (*hair*) peinar; (*area*) registrar a fondo
combat ['kɒmbæt] *n* combate *m* ♦ *vt* combatir
combination [kɒmbɪ'neɪʃən] *n* combinación *f*
combine [*vb* kəm'baɪn, *n* 'kɒmbaɪn] *vt* combinar; (*qualities*) reunir ♦ *vi* combinarse ♦ *n* (*ECON*) cartel *m*; **~ (harvester)** *n* cosechadora

---

KEYWORD

---

come [kʌm] (*pt* **came**, *pp* **come**) *vi* **1** (*movement towards*) venir; **to ~ running** venir corriendo
2 (*arrive*) llegar; **he's ~ here to work** ha venido aquí para trabajar; **to ~ home**

volver a casa
3 (*reach*): **to ~ to** llegar a; **the bill came to £40** la cuenta ascendía a cuarenta libras
4 (*occur*): **an idea came to me** se me ocurrió una idea
5 (*be, become*): **to ~ loose/undone** *etc* aflojarse/desabrocharse, desatarse *etc*; **I've ~ to like him** por fin ha llegado a gustarme
come about *vi* suceder, ocurrir
come across *vt fus* (*person*) topar con; (*thing*) dar con
come away *vi* (*leave*) marcharse; (*become detached*) desprenderse
come back *vi* (*return*) volver
come by *vt fus* (*acquire*) conseguir
come down *vi* (*price*) bajar; (*tree, building*) ser derribado
come forward *vi* presentarse
come from *vt fus* (*place, source*) ser de
come in *vi* (*visitor*) entrar; (*train, report*) llegar; (*fashion*) ponerse de moda; (*on deal etc*) entrar
come in for *vt fus* (*criticism etc*) recibir
come into *vt fus* (*money*) heredar; (*be involved*) tener que ver con; **to ~ into fashion** ponerse de moda
come off *vi* (*button*) soltarse, desprenderse; (*attempt*) salir bien
come on *vi* (*pupil*) progresar; (*work, project*) desarrollarse; (*lights*) encenderse; (*electricity*) volver; **~ on!** ¡vamos!
come out *vi* (*fact*) salir a la luz; (*book, sun*) salir; (*stain*) quitarse
come round *vi* (*after faint, operation*) volver en sí
come to *vi* (*wake*) volver en sí
come up *vi* (*sun*) salir; (*problem*) surgir; (*event*) aproximarse; (*in conversation*) mencionarse
come up against *vt fus* (*resistance etc*) tropezar con
come up with *vt fus* (*idea*) sugerir; (*money*) conseguir
come upon *vt fus* (*find*) dar con

comeback ['kʌmbæk] n: **to make a ~** (THEATRE) volver a las tablas

comedian [kə'mi:dɪən] n cómico; **comedienne** [-'ɛn] n cómica

comedy ['kɒmɪdɪ] n comedia; (humour) comicidad f

comet ['kɒmɪt] n cometa m

comeuppance [kʌm'ʌpəns] n: **to get one's ~** llevar su merecido

comfort ['kʌmfət] n bienestar m; (relief) alivio ♦ vt consolar; **~s** npl (of home etc) comodidades fpl; **~able** adj cómodo; (financially) acomodado; (easy) fácil; **~ably** adv (sit) cómodamente; (live) holgadamente; **~ station** (US) n servicios mpl

comic ['kɒmɪk] adj (also: **~al**) cómico ♦ n (comedian) cómico; (BRIT: for children) tebeo; (BRIT: for adults) comic m; **~ strip** n tira cómica

coming ['kʌmɪŋ] n venida, llegada ♦ adj que viene; **~(s) and going(s)** n(pl) ir y venir m, ajetreo

comma ['kɒmə] n coma

command [kə'mɑːnd] n orden f, mandato; (MIL: authority) mando; (mastery) dominio ♦ vt (troops) mandar; (give orders to): **to ~ sb to do** mandar or ordenar a uno hacer; **~eer** [kɒmən'dɪə*] vt requisar; **~er** n (MIL) comandante m/f, jefe/a m/f

commemorate [kə'meməreɪt] vt conmemorar

commence [kə'mɛns] vt, vi comenzar, empezar

commend [kə'mɛnd] vt elogiar, alabar; (recommend) recomendar

commensurate [kə'mɛnsərɪt] adj: **~ with** en proporción a, que corresponde a

comment ['kɒment] n comentario ♦ vi: **to ~ on** hacer comentarios sobre; **"no ~"** (written) "sin comentarios"; (spoken) "no tengo nada que decir"; **~ary** ['kɒməntəri] n comentario; **~ator** ['kɒmənteɪtə*] n comentarista m/f

commerce ['kɒmə:s] n comercio

commercial [kə'mə:ʃəl] adj comercial ♦ n

(TV, RADIO) anuncio

commiserate [kə'mɪzəreɪt] vi: **to ~ with** compadecerse de, condolerse de

commission [kə'mɪʃən] n (committee, fee) comisión f ♦ vt (work of art) encargar; **out of ~** fuera de servicio; **~aire** [kəmɪʃə'nɛə*] (BRIT) n portero; **~er** n (POLICE) comisario de policía

commit [kə'mɪt] vt (act) cometer; (resources) dedicar; (to sb's care) entregar; **to ~ o.s. (to do)** comprometerse (a hacer); **to ~ suicide** suicidarse; **~ment** n compromiso; (to ideology etc) entrega

committee [kə'mɪtɪ] n comité m

commodity [kə'mɒdɪtɪ] n mercancía

common ['kɒmən] adj común; (pej) ordinario ♦ n campo común; **the C~s** npl (BRIT) (la Cámara de) los Comunes mpl; **in ~** en común; **~er** n plebeyo; **~ law** n ley f consuetudinaria; **~ly** adv comúnmente; **C~ Market** n Mercado Común; **~place** adj de lo más común; **~room** n sala común; **~ sense** n sentido común; **the C~wealth** n la Commonwealth

commotion [kə'məʊʃən] n tumulto, confusión f

commune [n 'kɒmju:n, vb kə'mju:n] n (group) comuna ♦ vi: **to ~ with** comulgar or conversar con

communicate [kə'mju:nɪkeɪt] vt comunicar ♦ vi: **to ~ (with)** comunicarse (con); (in writing) estar en contacto (con)

communication [kəmju:nɪ'keɪʃən] n comunicación f; **~ cord** (BRIT) n timbre m de alarma

communion [kə'mju:nɪən] n (also: **Holy C~**) comunión f

communiqué [kə'mju:nɪkeɪ] n comunicado, parte f

communism ['kɒmjunɪzəm] n comunismo; **communist** adj, n comunista m/f

community [kə'mju:nɪtɪ] n comunidad f; (large group) colectividad f; **~ centre** n centro social; **~ chest** (US) n arca comunitaria, fondo común

commutation ticket [kɔmju'teɪʃən-] (*US*) n billete m de abono

commute [kə'mju:t] vi viajar a diario de la casa al trabajo ♦ vt conmutar; **~r** n persona (que viaja ... *see vi*)

compact [*adj* kəm'pækt, *n* 'kɔmpækt] *adj* compacto ♦ n (*also:* **powder ~**) polvera; **~ disc** n compact disc m; **~ disc player** n reproductor m de disco compacto, compact disc m

companion [kəm'pænɪən] n compañero/a; **~ship** n compañerismo

company ['kʌmpənɪ] n compañía; (*COMM*) sociedad f, compañía; **to keep sb ~** acompañar a uno; **~ secretary** (*BRIT*) n secretario/a de compañía

comparative [kəm'pærətɪv] *adj* relativo; (*study*) comparativo; **~ly** *adv* (*relatively*) relativamente

compare [kəm'pɛə*] vt: **to ~ sth/sb with/to** comparar algo/a uno con ♦ vi: **to ~ (with)** compararse (con); **comparison** [-'pærɪsn] n comparación f

compartment [kəm'pɑ:tmənt] n (*also: RAIL*) compartim(i)ento

compass ['kʌmpəs] n brújula; **~es** *npl* (*MATH*) compás m

compassion [kəm'pæʃən] n compasión f; **~ate** *adj* compasivo

compatible [kəm'pætɪbl] *adj* compatible

compel [kəm'pɛl] vt obligar

compensate ['kɔmpənseɪt] vt compensar ♦ vi: **to ~ for** compensar; **compensation** [-'seɪʃən] n (*for loss*) indemnización f

compère ['kɔmpɛə*] n presentador m

compete [kəm'pi:t] vi (*take part*) tomar parte, concurrir; (*vie with*): **to ~ with** competir con, hacer competencia a

competent ['kɔmpɪtənt] *adj* competente, capaz

competition [kɔmpɪ'tɪʃən] n (*contest*) concurso; (*rivalry*) competencia

competitive [kəm'petɪtɪv] *adj* (*ECON, SPORT*) competitivo

competitor [kəm'petɪtə*] n (*rival*) competidor(a) m/f; (*participant*)

concursante m/f

complacency [kəm'pleɪsnsɪ] n autosatisfacción f

complacent [kəm'pleɪsənt] *adj* autocomplaciente

complain [kəm'pleɪn] vi quejarse; (*COMM*) reclamar; **~t** n queja; reclamación f; (*MED*) enfermedad f

complement [*n* 'kɔmplɪmənt, *vb* 'kɔmplɪmənt] n complemento; (*esp of ship's crew*) dotación f ♦ vt (*enhance*) complementar; **~ary** [kɔmplɪ'mentərɪ] *adj* complementario

complete [kəm'pli:t] *adj* (*full*) completo; (*finished*) acabado ♦ vt (*fulfil*) completar; (*finish*) acabar; (*a form*) llenar; **~ly** *adv* completamente; **completion** [-'pli:ʃən] n terminación f; (*of contract*) realización f

complex ['kɔmpleks] *adj, n* complejo

complexion [kəm'plekʃən] n (*of face*) tez f, cutis m

compliance [kəm'plaɪəns] n (*submission*) sumisión f; (*agreement*) conformidad f; **in ~ with** de acuerdo con

complicate ['kɔmplɪkeɪt] vt complicar; **~d** *adj* complicado; **complication** [-'keɪʃən] n complicación f

compliment ['kɔmplɪmənt] n (*formal*) cumplido ♦ vt felicitar; **~s** *npl* (*regards*) saludos *mpl*; **to pay sb a ~** hacer cumplidos a uno; **~ary** [-'mentərɪ] *adj* lisonjero; (*free*) de favor

comply [kəm'plaɪ] vi: **to ~ with** cumplir con

component [kəm'pəʊnənt] *adj* componente ♦ n (*TECH*) pieza

compose [kəm'pəʊz] vt: **to be ~d of** componerse de; (*music etc*) componer; **to ~ o.s.** tranquilizarse; **~d** *adj* sosegado; **~r** n (*MUS*) compositor(a) m/f; **composition** [kɔmpə'zɪʃən] n composición f

compost ['kɔmpɔst] n abono (vegetal)

composure [kəm'pəʊʒə*] n serenidad f, calma

compound ['kɔmpaʊnd] n (*CHEM*) compuesto; (*LING*) palabra compuesta;

(*enclosure*) recinto ♦ *adj* compuesto; (*fracture*) complicado

comprehend [kɔmprɪ'hend] *vt* comprender; **comprehension** [-'henʃən] *n* comprensión *f*

comprehensive [kɔmprɪ'hensɪv] *adj* exhaustivo; (*INSURANCE*) contra todo riesgo; **~ (school)** *n centro estatal de enseñanza secundaria;* ≈ Instituto Nacional de Bachillerato (*SP*)

compress [*vb* kəm'pres, *n* 'kɔmpres] *vt* comprimir; (*information*) condensar ♦ *n* (*MED*) compresa

comprise [kəm'praɪz] *vt* (*also*: **be ~d of**) comprender, constar de; (*constitute*) constituir

compromise ['kɔmprəmaɪz] *n* (*agreement*) arreglo ♦ *vt* comprometer ♦ *vi* transigir

compulsion [kəm'pʌlʃən] *n* compulsión *f*; (*force*) obligación *f*

compulsive [kəm'pʌlsɪv] *adj* compulsivo; (*viewing, reading*) obligado

compulsory [kəm'pʌlsərɪ] *adj* obligatorio

computer [kəm'pju:tə*] *n* ordenador *m*, computador *m*, computadora; **~ game** *n* juego para ordenador; **~-generated** *adj* realizado por ordenador, creado por ordenador; **~ize** *vt* (*data*) computerizar; (*system*) informatizar; **~ programmer** *n* programador(a) *m/f*; **~ programming** *n* programación *f*; **~ science** *n* informática; **computing** [kəm'pju:tɪŋ] *n* (*activity, science*) informática

comrade ['kɔmrɪd] *n* (*POL, MIL*) camarada; (*friend*) compañero/a; **~ship** *n* camaradería, compañerismo

con [kɔn] *vt* (*deceive*) engañar; (*cheat*) estafar ♦ *n* estafa

conceal [kən'si:l] *vt* ocultar

conceit [kən'si:t] *n* presunción *f*; **~ed** *adj* presumido

conceive [kən'si:v] *vt, vi* concebir

concentrate ['kɔnsəntreɪt] *vi* concentrarse ♦ *vt* concentrar

concentration [kɔnsən'treɪʃən] *n* concentración *f*

concept ['kɔnsept] *n* concepto

concern [kən'sə:n] *n* (*matter*) asunto; (*COMM*) empresa; (*anxiety*) preocupación *f* ♦ *vt* (*worry*) preocupar; (*involve*) afectar; (*relate to*) tener que ver con; **to be ~ed (about)** interesarse (por), preocuparse (por); **~ing** *prep* sobre, acerca de

concert ['kɔnsət] *n* concierto; **~ed** [kən'sə:təd] *adj* (*efforts etc*) concertado; **~ hall** *n* sala de conciertos

concerto [kən'tʃə:təʊ] *n* concierto

concession [kən'seʃən] *n* concesión *f*; **tax ~** privilegio fiscal

conclude [kən'klu:d] *vt* concluir; (*treaty etc*) firmar; (*agreement*) llegar a; (*decide*) llegar a la conclusión de; **conclusion** [-'klu:ʒən] *n* conclusión *f*; firma; **conclusive** [-'klu:sɪv] *adj* decisivo, concluyente

concoct [kən'kɔkt] *vt* confeccionar; (*plot*) tramar; **~ion** [-'kɔkʃən] *n* mezcla

concourse ['kɔŋkɔ:s] *n* vestíbulo

concrete ['kɔnkri:t] *n* hormigón *m* ♦ *adj* de hormigón; (*fig*) concreto

concur [kən'kə:*] *vi* estar de acuerdo, asentir

concurrently [kən'kʌrntlɪ] *adv* al mismo tiempo

concussion [kən'kʌʃən] *n* conmoción *f* cerebral

condemn [kən'dem] *vt* condenar; (*building*) declarar en ruina

condense [kən'dens] *vi* condensarse ♦ *vt* condensar, abreviar; **~d milk** *n* leche *f* condensada

condition [kən'dɪʃən] *n* condición *f*, estado; (*requirement*) condición *f* ♦ *vt* condicionar; **on ~ that** a condición (de) que; **~er** *n* suavizante

condolences [kən'dəʊlənsɪz] *npl* pésame *m*

condom ['kɔndəm] *n* condón *m*

condone [kən'dəʊn] *vt* condonar

conducive [kən'dju:sɪv] *adj*: **~ to** conducente a

conduct [*n* 'kɔndʌkt, *vb* kən'dʌkt] *n* conducta, comportamiento ♦ *vt* (*lead*) conducir; (*manage*) llevar a cabo, dirigir;

(MUS) dirigir; **to ~ o.s.** comportarse; **~ed tour** (BRIT) n visita acompañada; **~or** n (of orchestra) director m; (US: on train) revisor(a) m/f; (on bus) cobrador m; (ELEC) conductor m; **~ress** n (on bus) cobradora

cone [kəun] n cono; (pine ~) piña; (on road) pivote m; (for ice-cream) cucurucho

confectioner [kən'fekʃənə*] n repostero/a; **~'s (shop)** n confitería; **~y** n dulces mpl

confer [kən'fə:*] vt: **to ~ sth on** otorgar algo a ♦ vi conferenciar

conference ['kɔnfərns] n (meeting) reunión f; (convention) congreso

confess [kən'fes] vt confesar ♦ vi admitir; **~ion** [-'feʃən] n confesión f

confetti [kən'feti] n confeti m

confide [kən'faid] vi: **to ~ in** confiar en

confidence ['kɔnfidns] n (also: **self-~**) confianza; (secret) confidencia; **in ~** (speak, write) en confianza; **~ trick** n timo; **confident** adj seguro de sí mismo; (certain) seguro; **confidential** [kɔnfi'denʃəl] adj confidencial

confine [kən'fain] vt (limit) limitar; (shut up) encerrar; **~d** adj (space) reducido; **~ment** n (prison) prisión f; **~s** ['kɔnfainz] npl confines mpl

confirm [kən'fə:m] vt confirmar; **~ation** [kɔnfə'meiʃən] n confirmación f; **~ed** adj empedernido

confiscate ['kɔnfiskeit] vt confiscar

conflict [n 'kɔnflikt, vb kən'flikt] n conflicto ♦ vi (opinions) chocar; **~ing** adj contradictorio

conform [kən'fɔ:m] vi conformarse; **to ~ to** ajustarse a

confound [kən'faund] vt confundir

confront [kən'frʌnt] vt (problems) hacer frente a; (enemy, danger) enfrentarse con; **~ation** [kɔnfrən'teiʃən] n enfrentamiento

confuse [kən'fju:z] vt (perplex) aturdir, desconcertar; (mix up) confundir; (complicate) complicar; **~d** adj confuso; (person) perplejo; **confusing** adj confuso; **confusion** [-'fju:ʒən] n confusión f

congeal [kən'dʒi:l] vi (blood) coagularse; (sauce etc) cuajarse

congested [kən'dʒestid] adj congestionado; **congestion** n congestión f

congratulate [kən'grætjuleit] vt: **to ~ sb (on)** felicitar a uno (por); **congratulations** [-'leiʃənz] npl felicitaciones fpl; **congratulations!** ¡enhorabuena!

congregate ['kɔngrigeit] vi congregarse; **congregation** [-'geiʃən] n (of a church) feligreses mpl

congress ['kɔngres] n congreso; (US): **C~** Congreso; **C~man** (irreg) (US) n miembro del Congreso

conifer ['kɔnifə*] n conífera

conjunctivitis [kəndʒʌŋkti'vaitis] n conjuntivitis f

conjure ['kʌndʒə*] vi hacer juegos de manos; **~ up** vt (ghost, spirit) hacer aparecer; (memories) evocar; **~r** n ilusionista m/f

con man [kɔn-] n estafador m

connect [kə'nekt] vt juntar, unir; (ELEC) conectar; (TEL: subscriber) poner; (: caller) poner al habla; (fig) relacionar, asociar ♦ vi: **to ~ with** (train) enlazar con; **to be ~ed with** (associated) estar relacionado con; **~ion** [-ʃən] n juntura, unión f; (ELEC) conexión f; (RAIL) enlace m; (TEL) comunicación f; (fig) relación f

connive [kə'naiv] vi: **to ~ at** hacer la vista gorda a

connoisseur [kɔni'sə*] n experto/a, entendido/a

conquer ['kɔŋkə*] vt (territory) conquistar; (enemy, feelings) vencer; **~or** n conquistador m

conquest ['kɔŋkwest] n conquista

cons [kɔnz] npl see **convenience; pro**

conscience ['kɔnʃəns] n conciencia

conscientious [kɔnʃi'enʃəs] adj concienzudo; (objection) de conciencia

conscious ['kɔnʃəs] adj (deliberate) deliberado; (awake, aware) consciente; **~ness** n conciencia; (MED) conocimiento

conscript ['kɒnskrɪpt] n recluta m; **~ion** [kən'skrɪpʃən] n servicio militar (obligatorio)

consensus [kən'sɛnsəs] n consenso

consent [kən'sɛnt] n consentimiento ♦ vi: **to ~ (to)** consentir (en)

consequence ['kɒnsɪkwəns] n consecuencia; (*significance*) importancia

consequently ['kɒnsɪkwəntlɪ] adv por consiguiente

conservation [kɒnsə'veɪʃən] n conservación f

conservative [kən'sə:vətɪv] adj conservador(a); (*estimate etc*) cauteloso; **C~** (*BRIT*) adj, n (*POL*) conservador(a) m/f

conservatory [kən'sə:vətrɪ] n invernadero; (*MUS*) conservatorio

conserve [kən'sə:v] vt conservar ♦ n conserva

consider [kən'sɪdə*] vt considerar; (*take into account*) tener en cuenta; (*study*) estudiar, examinar; **to ~ doing sth** pensar en (la posibilidad de) hacer algo; **~able** adj considerable; **~ably** adv notablemente; **~ate** adj considerado; **consideration** [-'reɪʃən] n consideración f; (*factor*) factor m; **to give sth further consideration** estudiar algo más a fondo; **~ing** prep teniendo en cuenta

consign [kən'saɪn] vt: **to ~ to** (*sth unwanted*) relegar a; (*person*) destinar a; **~ment** n envío

consist [kən'sɪst] vi: **to ~ of** consistir en

consistency [kən'sɪstənsɪ] n (*of argument etc*) coherencia; consecuencia; (*thickness*) consistencia

consistent [kən'sɪstənt] adj (*person*) consecuente; (*argument etc*) coherente

consolation [kɒnsə'leɪʃən] n consuelo

console[1] [kən'səʊl] vt consolar

console[2] ['kɒnsəʊl] n consola

consonant ['kɒnsənənt] n consonante f

consortium [kən'sɔ:tɪəm] n consorcio

conspicuous [kən'spɪkjuəs] adj (*visible*) visible

conspiracy [kən'spɪrəsɪ] n conjura, complot m

constable ['kʌnstəbl] (*BRIT*) n policía m/f; **chief ~** ≈ jefe m de policía

constabulary [kən'stæbjulərɪ] n ≈ policía

constant ['kɒnstənt] adj constante; **~ly** adv constantemente

constipated ['kɒnstɪpeɪtəd] adj estreñido; **constipation** [kɒnstɪ'peɪʃən] n estreñimiento

constituency [kən'stɪtjuənsɪ] n (*POL: area*) distrito electoral; (: *electors*) electorado; **constituent** [-ənt] n (*POL*) elector(a) m/f; (*part*) componente m

constitution [kɒnstɪ'tju:ʃən] n constitución f; **~al** adj constitucional

constraint [kən'streɪnt] n obligación f; (*limit*) restricción f

construct [kən'strʌkt] vt construir; **~ion** [-ʃən] n construcción f; **~ive** adj constructivo

consul ['kɒnsl] n cónsul m/f; **~ate** ['kɒnsjulɪt] n consulado

consult [kən'sʌlt] vt consultar; **~ant** n (*BRIT: MED*) especialista m/f; (*other specialist*) asesor(a) m/f; **~ation** [kɒnsəl'teɪʃən] n consulta; **~ing room** (*BRIT*) n consultorio

consume [kən'sju:m] vt (*eat*) comerse; (*drink*) beberse; (*fire etc, COMM*) consumir; **~r** n consumidor(a) m/f; **~r goods** npl bienes mpl de consumo

consummate ['kɒnsʌmeɪt] vt consumar

consumption [kən'sʌmpʃən] n consumo

cont. abbr (= *continued*) sigue

contact ['kɒntækt] n contacto; (*person*) contacto; (: *pej*) enchufe m ♦ vt ponerse en contacto con; **~ lenses** npl lentes fpl de contacto

contagious [kən'teɪdʒəs] adj contagioso

contain [kən'teɪn] vt contener; **to ~ o.s.** contenerse; **~er** n recipiente m; (*for shipping etc*) contenedor m

contaminate [kən'tæmɪneɪt] vt contaminar

cont'd abbr (= *continued*) sigue

contemplate ['kɒntəmpleɪt] vt contemplar; (*reflect upon*) considerar

contemporary [kən'tɛmpərərɪ] adj, n

contemporáneo/a *m/f*
contempt [kən'tɛmpt] *n* desprecio; **~ of**
court (*LAW*) desacato (a los tribunales);
~ible *adj* despreciable; **~uous** *adj*
desdeñoso
contend [kən'tɛnd] *vt* (*argue*) afirmar ♦ *vi*:
to ~ with/for luchar contra/por; **~er** *n*
(*SPORT*) contendiente *m/f*
content [*adj, vb* kən'tɛnt, *n* 'kɔntɛnt] *adj*
(*happy*) contento; (*satisfied*) satisfecho
♦ *vt* contentar; satisfacer ♦ *n* contenido;
~s *npl* contenido; (**table of) ~s** índice *m*
de materias; **~ed** *adj* contento; satisfecho
contention [kən'tɛnʃən] *n* (*assertion*)
aseveración *f*; (*disagreement*) discusión *f*
contest [*n* 'kɔntɛst, *vb* kən'tɛst] *n* lucha;
(*competition*) concurso ♦ *vt* (*dispute*)
impugnar; (*POL*) presentarse como
candidato/a en; **~ant** [kən'tɛstənt] *n*
concursante *m/f*; (*in fight*) contendiente
m/f
context ['kɔntɛkst] *n* contexto
continent ['kɔntɪnənt] *n* continente *m*;
the C~ (*BRIT*) el continente europeo; **~al**
[-'nɛntl] *adj* continental; **~al breakfast** *n*
desayuno estilo europeo; **~al quilt** (*BRIT*)
n edredón *m*
contingency [kən'tɪndʒənsɪ] *n*
contingencia
continual [kən'tɪnjuəl] *adj* continuo; **~ly**
adv constantemente
continuation [kəntɪnjuˈeɪʃən] *n*
prolongación *f*; (*after interruption*)
reanudación *f*
continue [kən'tɪnjuː] *vi*, *vt* seguir,
continuar
continuous [kən'tɪnjuəs] *adj* continuo
contort [kən'tɔːt] *vt* retorcer
contour ['kɔntuə*] *n* contorno; (*also:* **~**
line) curva de nivel
contraband ['kɔntrəbænd] *n* contrabando
contraceptive [kɔntrə'sɛptɪv] *adj, n*
anticonceptivo
contract [*n* 'kɔntrækt, *vb* kən'trækt] *n*
contrato ♦ *vi* (*COMM*): **to ~ to do sth**
comprometerse por contrato a hacer
algo; (*become smaller*) contraerse,

encogerse ♦ *vt* contraer; **~ion**
[kən'trækʃən] *n* contracción *f*; **~or** *n*
contratista *m/f*
contradict [kɔntrə'dɪkt] *vt* contradecir;
~ion [-ʃən] *n* contradicción *f*
contraption [kən'træpʃən] (*pej*) *n* artilugio
m
contrary¹ ['kɔntrərɪ] *adj* contrario ♦ *n* lo
contrario; **on the ~** al contrario; **unless**
you hear to the ~ a no ser que le digan
lo contrario
contrary² [kən'trɛərɪ] *adj* (*perverse*) terco
contrast [*n* 'kɔntrɑːst, *vt* kən'trɑːst] *n*
contraste *m* ♦ *vt* comparar; **in ~ to** en
contraste con
contravene [kɔntrə'viːn] *vt* infringir
contribute [kən'trɪbjuːt] *vi* contribuir ♦ *vt*:
to ~ £10/an article to contribuir con 10
libras/un artículo a; **to ~ to** (*charity*) donar
a; (*newspaper*) escribir para; (*discussion*)
intervenir en; **contribution**
[kɔntrɪ'bjuːʃən] *n* (*donation*) donativo;
(*BRIT: for social security*) cotización *f*; (*to
debate*) intervención *f*; (*to journal*)
colaboración *f*; **contributor** *n*
contribuyente *m/f*; (*to newspaper*)
colaborador(a) *m/f*
contrive [kən'traɪv] *vt* (*invent*) idear ♦ *vi*:
to ~ to do lograr hacer
control [kən'trəul] *vt* controlar; (*process
etc*) dirigir; (*machinery*) manejar; (*temper*)
dominar; (*disease*) contener ♦ *n* control
m; **~s** *npl* (*of vehicle*) instrumentos *mpl*
de mando; (*of radio*) controles *mpl*;
(*governmental*) medidas *fpl* de control;
under ~ bajo control; **to be in ~ of** tener
el mando de; **the car went out of ~** se
perdió el control del coche; **~led**
substance *n* sustancia controlada; **~**
panel *n* tablero de instrumentos; **~**
room *n* sala de mando; **~ tower** *n*
(*AVIAT*) torre *f* de control
controversial [kɔntrə'vəːʃl] *adj* polémico
controversy ['kɔntrəvəːsɪ] *n* polémica
convalesce [kɔnvə'lɛs] *vi* convalecer
convector [kən'vɛktə*] *n* calentador *m* de
aire

convene [kən'viːn] *vt* convocar ♦ *vi* reunirse

convenience [kən'viːnɪəns] *n* (*easiness*) comodidad *f*; (*suitability*) idoneidad *f*; (*advantage*) ventaja; **at your ~** cuando le sea conveniente; **all modern ~s, all mod cons** (*BRIT*) todo confort

convenient [kən'viːnɪənt] *adj* (*useful*) útil; (*place, time*) conveniente

convent ['kɔnvənt] *n* convento

convention [kən'vɛnʃən] *n* convención *f*; (*meeting*) asamblea; (*agreement*) convenio; **~al** *adj* convencional

converge [kən'vəːdʒ] *vi* convergir; (*people*): **to ~ on** dirigirse todos a

conversant [kən'vəːsnt] *adj*: **to be ~ with** estar al tanto de

conversation [kɔnvə'seɪʃən] *n* conversación *f*; **~al** *adj* familiar; **~al skill** facilidad *f* de palabra

converse [*n* 'kɔnvəːs, *vb* kən'vəːs] *n* inversa ♦ *vi* conversar; **~ly** [-'vəːslɪ] *adv* a la inversa

conversion [kən'vəːʃən] *n* conversión *f*

convert [*vb* kən'vəːt, *n* 'kɔnvəːt] *vt* (*REL, COMM*) convertir; (*alter*): **to ~ sth into/to** transformar algo en/convertir algo a ♦ *n* converso/a; **~ible** *adj* convertible ♦ *n* descapotable *m*

convey [kən'veɪ] *vt* llevar; (*thanks*) comunicar; (*idea*) expresar; **~or belt** *n* cinta transportadora

convict [*vb* kən'vɪkt, *n* 'kɔnvɪkt] *vt* (*find guilty*) declarar culpable a ♦ *n* presidiario/a; **~ion** [-ʃən] *n* condena; (*belief, certainty*) convicción *f*

convince [kən'vɪns] *vt* convencer; **~d** *adj*: **~d of/that** convencido de/de que; **convincing** *adj* convincente

convoluted ['kɔnvəluːtɪd] *adj* (*argument etc*) enrevesado

convoy ['kɔnvɔɪ] *n* convoy *m*

convulse [kən'vʌls] *vt*: **to be ~d with laughter** desternillarse de risa; **convulsion** [-'vʌlʃən] *n* convulsión *f*

cook [kuk] *vt* (*stew etc*) guisar; (*meal*) preparar ♦ *vi* cocer; (*person*) cocinar ♦ *n*

cocinero/a; **~ book** *n* libro de cocina; **~er** *n* cocina; **~ery** *n* cocina; **~ery book** (*BRIT*) *n* = **~ book**; **~ie** (*US*) *n* galleta; **~ing** *n* cocina

cool [kuːl] *adj* fresco; (*not afraid*) tranquilo; (*unfriendly*) frío ♦ *vt* enfriar ♦ *vi* enfriarse; **~ness** *n* frescura; tranquilidad *f*; (*indifference*) falta de entusiasmo

coop [kuːp] *n* gallinero ♦ *vt*: **to ~ up** (*fig*) encerrar

cooperate [kəu'ɔpəreɪt] *vi* cooperar, colaborar; **cooperation** [-'reɪʃən] *n* cooperación *f*, colaboración *f*; **cooperative** [-rətɪv] *adj* (*business*) cooperativo; (*person*) servicial ♦ *n* cooperativa

coordinate [*vb* kəu'ɔːdɪneɪt, *n* kəu'ɔːdɪnət] *vt* coordinar ♦ *n* (*MATH*) coordenada; **~s** *npl* (*clothes*) coordinados *mpl*; **coordination** [-'neɪʃən] *n* coordinación *f*

co-ownership [kəu'əunəʃɪp] *n* co-propiedad *f*

cop [kɔp] (*inf*) *n* poli *m* (*SP*), tira *m* (*AM*)

cope [kəup] *vi*: **to ~ with** (*problem*) hacer frente a

copper ['kɔpə*] *n* (*metal*) cobre *m*; (*BRIT: inf*) poli *m*; **~s** *npl* (*money*) calderilla (*SP*), centavos *mpl* (*AM*)

copulate ['kɔpjuleɪt] *vi* copularse

copy ['kɔpɪ] *n* copia; (*of book etc*) ejemplar *m* ♦ *vt* copiar; **~right** *n* derechos *mpl* de autor

coral ['kɔrəl] *n* coral *m*

cord [kɔːd] *n* cuerda; (*ELEC*) cable *m*; (*fabric*) pana

cordial ['kɔːdɪəl] *adj* cordial ♦ *n* cordial *m*

cordon ['kɔːdn] *n* cordón *m*; **~ off** *vt* acordonar

corduroy ['kɔːdərɔɪ] *n* pana

core [kɔː*] *n* centro, núcleo; (*of fruit*) corazón *m*; (*of problem*) meollo ♦ *vt* quitar el corazón de

coriander [kɔrɪ'ændə*] *n* culantro

cork [kɔːk] *n* corcho; (*tree*) alcornoque *m*; **~screw** *n* sacacorchos *m inv*

corn [kɔːn] *n* (*BRIT: cereal crop*) trigo; (*US: maize*) maíz *m*; (*on foot*) callo; **~ on the**

cob (CULIN) maíz en la mazorca (SP), choclo (AM)

corned beef ['kɔːnd-] n carne f acecinada (en lata)

corner ['kɔːnə*] n (outside) esquina; (inside) rincón m; (in road) curva; (FOOTBALL) córner m; (BOXING) esquina ♦ vt (trap) arrinconar; (COMM) acaparar ♦ vi (in car) tomar las curvas; **~stone** n (also fig) piedra angular

cornet ['kɔːnɪt] n (MUS) corneta; (BRIT: of ice-cream) cucurucho

cornflakes ['kɔːnfleɪks] npl copos mpl de maíz, cornflakes mpl

cornflour ['kɔːnflauə*] (BRIT), **cornstarch** ['kɔːnstɑːtʃ] (US) n harina de maíz

Cornwall ['kɔːnwəl] n Cornualles m

corny ['kɔːnɪ] (inf) adj gastado

coronary ['kɔrənərɪ] n (also: ~ thrombosis) infarto

coronation [kɔrə'neɪʃən] n coronación f

coroner ['kɔrənə*] n juez m (de instrucción)

corporal ['kɔːpərl] n cabo ♦ adj: **~ punishment** castigo corporal

corporate ['kɔːpərɪt] adj (action, ownership) colectivo; (finance, image) corporativo

corporation [kɔːpə'reɪʃən] n (of town) ayuntamiento; (COMM) corporación f

corps [kɔː*, pl kɔːz] n inv cuerpo; **diplomatic ~** cuerpo diplomático; **press ~** gabinete m de prensa

corpse [kɔːps] n cadáver m

correct [kə'rɛkt] adj justo, exacto; (proper) correcto ♦ vt corregir; (exam) corregir, calificar; **~ion** [-ʃən] n (act) corrección f; (instance) rectificación f

correspond [kɔrɪs'pɔnd] vi (write): **to ~ (with)** escribirse (con); (be equivalent to): **to ~ (to)** corresponder (a); (be in accordance): **to ~ (with)** corresponder (con); **~ence** n correspondencia; **~ence course** n curso por correspondencia; **~ent** n corresponsal m/f

corridor ['kɔrɪdɔː*] n pasillo

corrode [kə'rəud] vt corroer ♦ vi corroerse

corrugated ['kɔrəgeɪtɪd] adj ondulado; **~ iron** n chapa ondulada

corrupt [kə'rʌpt] adj (person) corrupto; (COMPUT) corrompido ♦ vt corromper; (COMPUT) degradar

Corsica ['kɔːsɪkə] n Córcega

cosmetic [kɔz'mɛtɪk] adj, n cosmético

cosmopolitan [kɔzmə'pɔlɪtn] adj cosmopolita

cost [kɔst] (pt, pp cost) n (price) precio; **~s** npl (COMM) costes mpl; (LAW) costas fpl ♦ vi costar, valer ♦ vt preparar el presupuesto de; **how much does it ~?** ¿cuánto cuesta?; **to ~ sb time/effort** costarle a uno tiempo/esfuerzo; **it ~ him his life** le costó la vida; **at all ~s** cueste lo que cueste

co-star ['kəustɑː*] n coprotagonista m/f

Costa Rica ['kɔstə'riːkə] n Costa Rica; **~n** adj, n costarriqueño/a m/f

cost-effective [kɔstɪ'fɛktɪv] adj rentable

costly ['kɔstlɪ] adj costoso

cost-of-living [kɔstəv'lɪvɪŋ] adj: **~ allowance** plus m de carestía de vida; **~ index** índice m del costo de vida

cost price (BRIT) n precio de coste

costume ['kɔstjuːm] n traje m; (BRIT: also: **swimming ~**) traje de baño; **~ jewellery** n bisutería

cosy ['kəuzɪ] (US **cozy**) adj (person) cómodo; (room) acogedor/a

cot [kɔt] n (BRIT: child's) cuna; (US: campbed) cama de campaña

cottage ['kɔtɪdʒ] n casita de campo; (rustic) barraca; **~ cheese** n requesón m

cotton ['kɔtn] n algodón m; (thread) hilo; **~ on to** (inf) vt fus caer en la cuenta de; **~ candy** (US) n algodón m (azucarado); **~ wool** (BRIT) n algodón m (hidrófilo)

couch [kautʃ] n sofá m; (doctor's etc) diván m

couchette [kuː'ʃɛt] n litera

cough [kɔf] vi toser ♦ n tos f; **~ drop** n pastilla para la tos

could [kud] pt of **can²**; **~n't** = **could not**

council ['kaunsl] n consejo; **city** or **town ~** consejo municipal; **~ estate** (BRIT) n *urbanización f de viviendas municipales de alquiler;* **~ house** (BRIT) *n* vivienda municipal de alquiler; **~lor** *n* concejal(a) *m/f*

counsel ['kaunsl] *n* (*advice*) consejo; (*lawyer*) abogado/a ♦ *vt* aconsejar; **~lor** *n* consejero/a; **~or** (US) *n* abogado/a

count [kaunt] *vt* contar; (*include*) incluir ♦ *vi* contar ♦ *n* cuenta; (*of votes*) escrutinio; (*level*) nivel *m*; (*nobleman*) conde *m*; **~ on** *vt fus* contar con; **~down** *n* cuenta atrás

countenance ['kauntɪnəns] *n* semblante *m*, rostro ♦ *vt* (*tolerate*) aprobar, tolerar

counter ['kauntə*] *n* (*in shop*) mostrador *m*; (*in games*) ficha ♦ *vt* contrarrestar ♦ *adv*: **to run ~ to** ser contrario a, ir en contra de; **~act** *vt* contrarrestar

counterfeit ['kauntəfɪt] *n* falsificación f, simulación f ♦ *vt* falsificar ♦ *adj* falso, falsificado

counterfoil ['kauntəfɔɪl] *n* talón *m*

counterpart ['kauntəpɑ:t] *n* homólogo/a *m/f*

counter-productive [kauntəprə'dʌktɪv] *adj* contraproducente

countersign ['kauntəsaɪn] *vt* refrendar

countess ['kauntɪs] *n* condesa

countless ['kauntlɪs] *adj* innumerable

country ['kʌntrɪ] *n* país *m*; (*native land*) patria; (*as opposed to town*) campo; (*region*) región f, tierra; **~ dancing** (BRIT) *n* baile *m* regional; **~ house** *n* casa de campo; **~man** *n* (*irreg*) (*compatriot*) compatriota *m*; (*rural*) campesino, paisano; **~side** *n* campo

county ['kauntɪ] *n* condado

coup [ku:] (*pl* **~s**) *n* (*also*: **~ d'état**) golpe *m* (de estado); (*achievement*) éxito

couple ['kʌpl] *n* (*of things*) par *m*; (*of people*) pareja; (*married ~*) matrimonio; **a ~ of** un par de

coupon ['ku:pɔn] *n* cupón *m*; (*voucher*) valé *m*

courage ['kʌrɪdʒ] *n* valor *m*, valentía; **~ous** [kə'reɪdʒəs] *adj* valiente

courgette [kuə'ʒɛt] (BRIT) *n* calabacín *m* (SP), calabacita (AM)

courier ['kurɪə*] *n* mensajero/a; (*for tourists*) guía *m/f* (de turismo)

course [kɔ:s] *n* (*direction*) dirección f; (*of river*, SCOL) curso; (*process*) transcurso; (MED): **~ of treatment** tratamiento; (*of ship*) rumbo; (*part of meal*) plato; (GOLF) campo; **of ~** desde luego, naturalmente; **of ~!** ¡claro!

court [kɔ:t] *n* (*royal*) corte f; (LAW) tribunal *m*, juzgado; (TENNIS etc) pista, cancha ♦ *vt* (*woman*) cortejar a; **to take to ~** demandar

courteous ['kɜ:tɪəs] *adj* cortés

courtesy ['kɜ:təsɪ] *n* cortesía; **(by) ~ of** por cortesía de; **~ bus**, **~ coach** *n* autobús *m* gratuito

court-house ['kɔ:thaus] (US) *n* palacio de justicia

courtier ['kɔ:tɪə*] *n* cortesano

court-martial (*pl* **courts-martial**) *n* consejo de guerra

courtroom ['kɔ:trum] *n* sala de justicia

courtyard ['kɔ:tjɑ:d] *n* patio

cousin ['kʌzn] *n* primo/a; **first ~** primo/a carnal, primo/a hermano/a

cove [kəuv] *n* cala, ensenada

covenant ['kʌvənənt] *n* pacto

cover ['kʌvə*] *vt* cubrir; (*feelings, mistake*) ocultar; (*with lid*) tapar; (*book etc*) forrar; (*distance*) recorrer; (*include*) abarcar; (*protect*: *also*: INSURANCE) cubrir; (PRESS) investigar; (*discuss*) tratar ♦ *n* cubierta; (*lid*) tapa; (*for chair etc*) funda; (*envelope*) sobre *m*; (*for book*) forro; (*of magazine*) portada; (*shelter*) abrigo; (INSURANCE) cobertura; (*of spy*) cobertura; **~s** *npl* (*on bed*) sábanas; mantas; **to take ~** (*shelter*) protegerse, resguardarse; **under ~** (*indoors*) bajo techo; **under ~ of darkness** al amparo de la oscuridad; **under separate ~** (COMM) por separado; **~ up** *vi*: **to ~ up for sb** encubrir a uno; **~age** *n* (TV, PRESS) cobertura; **~alls** (US) *npl* mono; **~ charge** *n* precio del cubierto; **~ing** *n* capa; **~ing letter** (US = **letter**) *n* carta de explicación; **~ note** *n* (INSURANCE) póliza provisional

covert ['kʌuvət] *adj* secreto, encubierto

cover-up *n* encubrimiento

cow [kau] *n* vaca; (*infl: woman*) bruja ♦ *vt* intimidar

coward ['kauəd] *n* cobarde *m/f*; **~ice** [-ɪs] *n* cobardía; **~ly** *adj* cobarde

cowboy ['kaubɔɪ] *n* vaquero

cower ['kauə*] *vi* encogerse (de miedo)

coy [kɔɪ] *adj* tímido

cozy ['kəuzɪ] (*US*) *adj* = **cosy**

CPA (*US*) *n abbr* = **certified public accountant**

crab [kræb] *n* cangrejo; **~ apple** *n* manzana silvestre

crack [kræk] *n* grieta; (*noise*) crujido; (*drug*) crack *m* ♦ *vt* agrietar, romper; (*nut*) cascar; (*solve: problem*) resolver; (*: code*) descifrar; (*whip etc*) chasquear; (*knuckles*) crujir; (*joke*) contar ♦ *adj* (*expert*) de primera; **~ down on** *vt fus* adoptar fuertes medidas contra; **~ up** *vi* (*MED*) sufrir una crisis nerviosa; **~er** *n* (*biscuit*) crácker *m*; (*Christmas ~er*) petardo sorpresa

crackle ['krækl] *vi* crepitar

cradle ['kreɪdl] *n* cuna

craft [krɑːft] *n* (*skill*) arte *m*; (*trade*) oficio; (*cunning*) astucia; (*boat: pl inv*) barco; (*plane: pl inv*) avión *m*

craftsman ['krɑːftsmən] *n* artesano; **~ship** *n* (*quality*) destreza

crafty ['krɑːftɪ] *adj* astuto

crag [kræg] *n* peñasco

cram [kræm] *vt* (*fill*): **to ~ sth with** llenar algo (a reventar) de; (*put*): **to ~ sth into** meter algo a la fuerza en ♦ *vi* (*for exams*) empollar

cramp [kræmp] *n* (*MED*) calambre *m*; **~ed** *adj* apretado, estrecho

cranberry ['krænbərɪ] *n* arándano agrio

crane [kreɪn] *n* (*TECH*) grúa; (*bird*) grulla

crank [kræŋk] *n* manivela; (*person*) chiflado

cranny ['krænɪ] *n see* **nook**

crash [kræʃ] *n* (*noise*) estrépito; (*of cars etc*) choque *m*; (*of plane*) accidente *m* de aviación; (*COMM*) quiebra ♦ *vt* (*car, plane*) estrellar ♦ *vi* (*car, plane*) estrellarse; (*two*

cars) chocar; (*COMM*) quebrar; **~ course** *n* curso acelerado; **~ helmet** *n* casco (protector); **~ landing** *n* aterrizaje *m* forzado

crass [kræs] *adj* grosero, maleducado

crate [kreɪt] *n* cajón *m* de embalaje; (*for bottles*) caja

cravat(e) [krə'væt] *n* pañuelo

crave [kreɪv] *vt, vi*: **to ~ (for)** ansiar, anhelar

crawl [krɔːl] *vi* (*drag o.s.*) arrastrarse; (*child*) andar a gatas, gatear; (*vehicle*) avanzar (lentamente) ♦ *n* (*SWIMMING*) crol *m*

crayfish ['kreɪfɪʃ] *n inv* (*freshwater*) cangrejo de río; (*saltwater*) cigala

crayon ['kreɪən] *n* lápiz *m* de color

craze [kreɪz] *n* (*fashion*) moda

crazy ['kreɪzɪ] *adj* (*person*) loco; (*idea*) disparatado; (*inf: keen*): **~ about sb/sth** loco por uno/algo

creak [kriːk] *vi* (*floorboard*) crujir; (*hinge etc*) chirriar, rechinar

cream [kriːm] *n* (*of milk*) nata, crema; (*lotion*) crema; (*fig*) flor *f* y nata ♦ *adj* (*colour*) color crema; **~ cake** *n* pastel *m* de nata; **~ cheese** *n* queso blanco; **~y** *adj* cremoso; (*colour*) color crema

crease [kriːs] *n* (*fold*) pliegue *m*; (*in trousers*) raya; (*wrinkle*) arruga ♦ *vt* (*wrinkle*) arrugar ♦ *vi* (*wrinkle up*) arrugarse

create [kriː'eɪt] *vt* crear; **creation** [-ʃən] *n* creación *f*; **creative** *adj* creativo; **creator** *n* creador(a) *m/f*

creature ['kriːtʃə*] *n* (*animal*) animal *m*, bicho; (*person*) criatura

crèche [kreʃ] *n* guardería (infantil)

credence ['kriːdəns] *n*: **to lend** *or* **give ~ to** creer en, dar crédito a

credentials [krɪ'denʃlz] *npl* (*references*) referencias *fpl*; (*identity papers*) documentos *mpl* de identidad

credible ['kredɪbl] *adj* creíble; (*trustworthy*) digno de confianza

credit ['kredɪt] *n* crédito; (*merit*) honor *m*, mérito ♦ *vt* (*COMM*) abonar; (*believe: also:*

give ~ to) creer, prestar fe a ♦ *adj* crediticio; **~s** *npl* (*CINEMA*) fichas *fpl* técnicas; **to be in ~** (*person*) tener saldo a favor; **to ~ sb with** (*fig*) reconocer a uno el mérito de; **~ card** *n* tarjeta de crédito; **~or** *n* acreedor(a) *m/f*

creed [kriːd] *n* credo

creek [kriːk] *n* cala, ensenada; (*US*) riachuelo

creep [kriːp] (*pt, pp* **crept**) *vi* arrastrarse; **~er** *n* enredadera; **~y** *adj* (*frightening*) horripilante

cremate [krɪˈmeɪt] *vt* incinerar

crematorium [kremaˈtɔːriəm] (*pl* **crematoria**) *n* crematorio

crêpe [kreɪp] *n* (*fabric*) crespón *m*; (*also*: ~ **rubber**) crepé *m*; **~ bandage** (*BRIT*) *n* venda de crepé

crept [krept] *pt, pp of* **creep**

crescent [ˈkresnt] *n* media luna; (*street*) calle *f* (*en forma de semicírculo*)

cress [kres] *n* berro

crest [krest] *n* (*of bird*) cresta; (*of hill*) cima, cumbre *f*; (*of coat of arms*) blasón *m*; **~fallen** *adj* alicaído

crevice [ˈkrevɪs] *n* grieta, hendedura

crew [kruː] *n* (*of ship etc*) tripulación *f*; (*TV, CINEMA*) equipo; **~-cut** *n* corte *m* al rape; **~-neck** *n* cuello a la caja

crib [krɪb] *n* cuna ♦ *vt* (*inf*) plagiar

crick [krɪk] *n* (*in neck*) tortícolis *f*

cricket [ˈkrɪkɪt] *n* (*insect*) grillo; (*game*) críquet *m*

crime [kraɪm] *n* (*no pl: illegal activities*) crimen *m*; (*illegal action*) delito; **criminal** [ˈkrɪmɪnl] *n* criminal *m/f*, delincuente *m/f* ♦ *adj* criminal; (*illegal*) delictivo; (*law*) penal

crimson [ˈkrɪmzn] *adj* carmesí

cringe [krɪndʒ] *vi* agacharse, encogerse

crinkle [ˈkrɪŋkl] *vt* arrugar

cripple [ˈkrɪpl] *n* lisiado/a, cojo/a ♦ *vt* lisiar, mutilar

crisis [ˈkraɪsɪs] (*pl* **crises**) *n* crisis *f inv*

crisp [krɪsp] *adj* fresco; (*vegetables etc*) crujiente; (*manner*) seco; **~s** (*BRIT*) *npl* patatas *fpl* (*SP*) *or* papas *fpl* (*AM*) fritas

crisscross [ˈkrɪskrɔs] *adj* entrelazado

criterion [kraɪˈtɪəriən] (*pl* **criteria**) *n* criterio

critic [ˈkrɪtɪk] *n* crítico/a; **~al** *adj* crítico; (*illness*) grave; **~ally** *adv* (*speak etc*) en tono crítico; (*ill*) gravemente; **~ism** [ˈkrɪtɪsɪzm] *n* crítica; **~ize** [ˈkrɪtɪsaɪz] *vt* criticar

croak [krəuk] *vi* (*frog*) croar; (*raven*) graznar; (*person*) gruñir

Croatia [krəuˈeɪʃə] *n* Croacia

crochet [ˈkrəuʃeɪ] *n* ganchillo

crockery [ˈkrɔkərɪ] *n* loza, vajilla

crocodile [ˈkrɔkədaɪl] *n* cocodrilo

crocus [ˈkrəukəs] *n* croco, crocus *m*

croft [krɔft] *n* granja pequeña

crony [ˈkrəunɪ] (*inf: pej*) *n* compinche *m/f*

crook [kruk] *n* ladrón/ona *m/f*; (*of shepherd*) cayado; **~ed** [ˈkrukɪd] *adj* torcido; (*dishonest*) nada honrado

crop [krɔp] *n* (*produce*) cultivo; (*amount produced*) cosecha; (*riding ~*) látigo de montar ♦ *vt* cortar, recortar; **~ up** *vi* surgir, presentarse

cross [krɔs] *n* cruz *f*; (*hybrid*) cruce *m* ♦ *vt* (*street etc*) cruzar, atravesar ♦ *adj* de mal humor, enojado; **~ out** *vt* tachar; **~ over** *vi* cruzar; **~bar** *n* travesaño; **~country (race)** *n* carrera a campo traviesa, cross *m*; **~-examine** *vt* interrogar; **~-eyed** *adj* bizco; **~fire** *n* fuego cruzado; **~ing** *n* (*sea passage*) travesía; (*also*: **pedestrian ~ing**) paso para peatones; **~ing guard** (*US*) *n* persona encargada de ayudar a los niños a cruzar la calle; **~ purposes** *npl*: **to be at ~ purposes** no comprenderse uno a otro; **~-reference** *n* referencia, llamada; **~roads** *n* cruce *m*, encrucijada; **~ section** *n* corte *m* transversal; (*of population*) muestra (*representativa*); **~walk** (*US*) *n* paso de peatones; **~wind** *n* viento de costado; **~word** *n* crucigrama *m*

crotch [krɔtʃ] *n* (*ANAT, of garment*) entrepierna

crotchet [ˈkrɔtʃɪt] *n* (*MUS*) negra

crouch [krautʃ] *vi* agacharse, acurrucarse

crow → cupboard

crow [krəʊ] n (bird) cuervo; (of cock) canto, cacareo ♦ vi (cock) cantar

crowbar ['krəʊbɑː*] n palanca

crowd [kraud] n muchedumbre f, multitud f ♦ vt (fill) llenar ♦ vi (gather): **to ~ round** reunirse en torno a; (cram): **to ~ in** entrar en tropel; **~ed** adj (full) atestado; (densely populated) superpoblado

crown [kraun] n corona; (of head) coronilla; (for tooth) funda; (of hill) cumbre f ♦ vt coronar; (fig) completar, rematar; **~ jewels** npl joyas fpl reales; **~ prince** n príncipe m heredero

crow's feet npl patas fpl de gallo

crucial ['kruːʃl] adj decisivo

crucifix ['kruːsɪfɪks] n crucifijo; **~ion** [-'fɪkʃən] n crucifixión f

crude [kruːd] adj (materials) bruto; (fig: basic) tosco; (: vulgar) ordinario; **~ (oil)** n (petróleo) crudo

cruel ['kruəl] adj cruel; **~ty** n crueldad f

cruise [kruːz] n crucero ♦ vi (ship) hacer un crucero; (car) ir a velocidad de crucero; **~r** n (motorboat) yate m de motor; (warship) crucero

crumb [krʌm] n miga, migaja

crumble ['krʌmbl] vt desmenuzar ♦ vi (building, also fig) desmoronarse; **crumbly** adj que se desmigaja fácilmente

crumpet ['krʌmpɪt] n ≈ bollo para tostar

crumple ['krʌmpl] vt (paper) estrujar; (material) arrugar

crunch [krʌntʃ] vt (with teeth) mascar; (underfoot) hacer crujir ♦ n (fig) hora or momento de la verdad; **~y** adj crujiente

crusade [kruː'seɪd] n cruzada

crush [krʌʃ] n (crowd) aglomeración f; (infatuation): **to have a ~ on sb** estar loco por uno; (drink): **lemon ~** limonada ♦ vt aplastar; (paper) estrujar; (cloth) arrugar; (fruit) exprimir; (opposition) aplastar; (hopes) destruir

crust [krʌst] n corteza; (of snow, ice) costra

crutch [krʌtʃ] n muleta

crux [krʌks] n: **the ~ of** lo esencial de, el quid de

cry [kraɪ] vi llorar; (shout: also: ~ **out**) gritar ♦ n (shriek) chillido; (shout) grito; **~ off** vi echarse atrás

cryptic ['krɪptɪk] adj enigmático, secreto

crystal ['krɪstl] n cristal m; **~-clear** adj claro como el agua

cub [kʌb] n cachorro; (also: ~ **scout**) niño explorador

Cuba ['kjuːbə] n Cuba; **~n** adj, n cubano/a m/f

cube [kjuːb] n cubo ♦ vt (MATH) cubicar; **cubic** adj cúbico

cubicle ['kjuːbɪkl] n (at pool) caseta; (for bed) cubículo

cuckoo ['kʊkuː] n cuco; **~ clock** n reloj m de cucú

cucumber ['kjuːkʌmbə*] n pepino

cuddle ['kʌdl] vt abrazar ♦ vi abrazarse

cue [kjuː] n (snooker ~) taco; (THEATRE etc) señal f

cuff [kʌf] n (of sleeve) puño; (US: of trousers) vuelta; (blow) bofetada; **off the ~** adv de improviso; **~links** npl gemelos mpl

cuisine [kwɪ'ziːn] n cocina

cul-de-sac ['kʌldəsæk] n callejón m sin salida

cull [kʌl] vt (idea) sacar ♦ n (of animals) matanza selectiva

culminate ['kʌlmɪneɪt] vi: **to ~ in** terminar en; **culmination** [-'neɪʃən] n culminación f, colmo

culottes [kuː'lɒts] npl falda pantalón f

culprit ['kʌlprɪt] n culpable m/f

cult [kʌlt] n culto

cultivate ['kʌltɪveɪt] vt (also fig) cultivar; **~d** adj culto; **cultivation** [-'veɪʃən] n cultivo

cultural ['kʌltʃərəl] adj cultural

culture ['kʌltʃə*] n (also fig) cultura; (BIO) cultivo; **~d** adj culto

cumbersome ['kʌmbəsəm] adj de mucho bulto, voluminoso; (process) enrevesado

cunning ['kʌnɪŋ] n astucia ♦ adj astuto

cup [kʌp] n taza; (as prize) copa

cupboard ['kʌbəd] n armario; (kitchen) alacena

cup tie (*BRIT*) *n* partido de copa
curate ['kjuərɪt] *n* cura *m*
curator [kjuə'reɪtə*] *n* director(a) *m/f*
curb [kəːb] *vt* refrenar; (*person*) reprimir ♦ *n* freno; (*US*) bordillo
curdle ['kəːdl] *vi* cuajarse
cure [kjuə*] *vt* curar ♦ *n* cura, curación *f*; (*fig: solution*) remedio
curfew ['kəːfjuː] *n* toque *m* de queda
curiosity [kjuərɪ'ɔsɪtɪ] *n* curiosidad *f*
curious ['kjuərɪəs] *adj* curioso; (*person: interested*): **to be ~** sentir curiosidad
curl [kəːl] *n* rizo ♦ *vt* (*hair*) rizar ♦ *vi* rizarse; **~ up** *vi* (*person*) hacerse un ovillo; **~er** *n* rulo; **~y** *adj* rizado
currant ['kʌrnt] *n* pasa (de Corinto); (*black~, red~*) grosella
currency ['kʌrnsɪ] *n* moneda; **to gain ~** (*fig*) difundirse
current ['kʌrnt] *n* corriente *f* ♦ *adj* (*accepted*) corriente; (*present*) actual; **~ account** (*BRIT*) *n* cuenta corriente; **~ affairs** *npl* noticias *fpl* de actualidad; **~ly** *adv* actualmente
curriculum [kə'rɪkjuləm] (*pl* **~s** or **curricula**) *n* plan *m* de estudios; **~ vitae** *n* currículum *m*
curry ['kʌrɪ] *n* curry *m* ♦ *vt*: **to ~ favour with** buscar favores con; **~ powder** *n* curry *m* en polvo
curse [kəːs] *vi* soltar tacos ♦ *vt* maldecir ♦ *n* maldición *f*; (*swearword*) palabrota, taco
cursor ['kəːsə*] *n* (*COMPUT*) cursor *m*
cursory ['kəːsərɪ] *adj* rápido, superficial
curt [kəːt] *adj* corto, seco
curtail [kəː'teɪl] *vt* (*visit etc*) acortar; (*freedom*) restringir; (*expenses etc*) reducir
curtain ['kəːtn] *n* cortina; (*THEATRE*) telón *m*
curts(e)y ['kəːtsɪ] *vi* hacer una reverencia
curve [kəːv] *n* curva ♦ *vi* (*road*) hacer una curva; (*line etc*) curvarse
cushion ['kuʃən] *n* cojín *m*; (*of air*) colchón *m* ♦ *vt* (*shock*) amortiguar
custard ['kʌstəd] *n* natillas *fpl*
custody ['kʌstədɪ] *n* custodia; **to take into**

~ detener
custom ['kʌstəm] *n* costumbre *f*; (*COMM*) clientela; **~ary** *adj* acostumbrado
customer ['kʌstəmə*] *n* cliente *m/f*
customized ['kʌstəmaɪzd] *adj* (*car etc*) hecho a encargo
custom-made *adj* hecho a la medida
customs ['kʌstəmz] *npl* aduana; **~ officer** *n* aduanero/a
cut [kʌt] (*pt, pp* **cut**) *vt* cortar; (*price*) rebajar; (*text, programme*) acortar; (*reduce*) reducir ♦ *vi* cortar ♦ *n* (*of garment*) corte *m*; (*in skin*) cortadura; (*in salary etc*) rebaja; (*in spending*) reducción *f*, recorte *m*; (*slice of meat*) tajada; **to ~ a tooth** echar un diente; **~ down** *vt* (*tree*) derribar; (*reduce*) reducir; **~ off** *vt* (*person, place*) aislar; (*TEL*) desconectar; **~ out** *vt* (*shape*) recortar; (*stop: activity etc*) dejar; (*remove*) quitar; **~ up** *vt* cortar (en pedazos); **~back** *n* reducción *f*
cute [kjuːt] *adj* mono
cuticle ['kjuːtɪkl] *n* cutícula
cutlery ['kʌtlərɪ] *n* cubiertos *mpl*
cutlet ['kʌtlɪt] *n* chuleta; (*nut etc* ~) plato vegetariano hecho con nueces y verdura en forma de chuleta
cut-: **~out** *n* (*switch*) dispositivo de seguridad, disyuntor *m*; (*cardboard ~out*) recortable *m*; **~-price** (*US* **~-rate**) *adj* a precio reducido; **~throat** *n* asesino/a ♦ *adj* feroz
cutting ['kʌtɪŋ] *adj* (*remark*) mordaz ♦ *n* (*BRIT: from newspaper*) recorte *m*; (*from plant*) esqueje *m*
CV *n abbr* = **curriculum vitae**
cwt *abbr* = **hundredweight(s)**
cyanide ['saɪənaɪd] *n* cianuro
cycle ['saɪkl] *n* ciclo; (*bicycle*) bicicleta ♦ *vi* ir en bicicleta; **~ lane** *n* carril-bici *m*; **~ path** *n* carril-bici *m*; **cycling** *n* ciclismo; **cyclist** *n* ciclista *m/f*
cyclone ['saɪkləun] *n* ciclón *m*
cygnet ['sɪgnɪt] *n* pollo de cisne
cylinder ['sɪlɪndə*] *n* cilindro; (*of gas*) bombona; **~-head gasket** *n* junta de culata

cymbals ['sɪmblz] *npl* platillos *mpl*
cynic ['sɪnɪk] *n* cínico/a; **~al** *adj* cínico;
~ism ['sɪnɪsɪzəm] *n* cinismo
Cyprus ['saɪprəs] *n* Chipre *f*
cyst [sɪst] *n* quiste *m*; **~itis** [-'taɪtɪs] *n*
cistitis *f*
czar [zɑ:*] *n* zar *m*
Czech [tʃek] *adj, n* checo/a *m/f*; **~
Republic** *n* la República Checa

D, d

D [di:] *n* (MUS) re *m*
dab [dæb] *vt* (*eyes, wound*) tocar
(ligeramente); (*paint, cream*) poner un
poco de
dabble ['dæbl] *vi*: **to ~ in** ser algo
aficionado a
dad [dæd] *n* = **daddy**
daddy ['dædɪ] *n* papá *m*
daffodil ['dæfədɪl] *n* narciso
daft [dɑ:ft] *adj* tonto
dagger ['dægə*] *n* puñal *m*, daga
daily ['deɪlɪ] *adj* diario, cotidiano ♦ *adv*
todos los días, cada día
dainty ['deɪntɪ] *adj* delicado
dairy ['dɛərɪ] *n* (*shop*) lechería; (*on farm*)
vaquería; **~ farm** *n* granja; **~ products**
npl productos *mpl* lácteos; **~ store** (US)
n lechería
daisy ['deɪzɪ] *n* margarita
dale [deɪl] *n* valle *m*
dam [dæm] *n* presa ♦ *vt* construir una
presa para, represar
damage ['dæmɪdʒ] *n* lesión *f*; daño; (*dents
etc*) desperfectos *mpl*; (*fig*) perjuicio ♦ *vt*
dañar, perjudicar; (*spoil, break*) estropear;
~s *npl* (LAW) daños *mpl* y perjuicios
damn [dæm] *vt* condenar; (*curse*) maldecir
♦ *n* (*inf*): **I don't give a ~** me importa un
pito ♦ *adj* (*inf: also:* **~ed**) maldito; **~ (it)!**
¡maldito sea!; **~ing** *adj* (*evidence*)
irrecusable
damp [dæmp] *adj* húmedo, mojado ♦ *n*
humedad *f* ♦ *vt* (*also:* **~en**: *cloth, rag*)
mojar; (: *enthusiasm*) enfriar

damson ['dæmzən] *n* ciruela damascena
dance [dɑ:ns] *n* baile *m* ♦ *vi* bailar; **~ hall**
n salón *m* de baile; **~r** *n* bailador(a) *m/f*;
(*professional*) bailarín/ina *m/f*; **dancing** *n*
baile *m*
dandelion ['dændɪlaɪən] *n* diente *m* de
león
dandruff ['dændrəf] *n* caspa
Dane [deɪn] *n* danés/esa *m/f*
danger ['deɪndʒə*] *n* peligro; (*risk*) riesgo;
~! (*on sign*) ¡peligro de muerte!; **to be in
~ of** correr riesgo de; **~ous** *adj* peligroso;
~ously *adv* peligrosamente
dangle ['dæŋgl] *vt* colgar ♦ *vi* pender,
colgar
Danish ['deɪnɪʃ] *adj* danés/esa ♦ *n* (LING)
danés *m*
dare [dɛə*] *vt*: **to ~ sb to do** desafiar a
uno a hacer ♦ *vi*: **to ~ (to) do sth**
atreverse a hacer algo; **I ~ say** (*I suppose*)
puede ser (que); **daring** *adj* atrevido,
osado ♦ *n* atrevimiento, osadía
dark [dɑ:k] *adj* oscuro; (*hair, complexion*)
moreno ♦ *n*: **in the ~** a oscuras; **to be in
the ~ about** (*fig*) no saber nada de; **after
~** después del anochecer; **~en** *vt* (*colour*)
hacer más oscuro ♦ *vi* oscurecerse; **~
glasses** *npl* gafas *fpl* negras (SP),
anteojos *mpl* negros (AM); **~ness** *n*
oscuridad *f*; **~room** *n* cuarto oscuro
darling ['dɑ:lɪŋ] *adj, n* querido/a *m/f*
darn [dɑ:n] *vt* zurcir
dart [dɑ:t] *n* dardo; (*in sewing*) sisa ♦ *vi*
precipitarse; **~ away/along** *vi* salir/
marchar disparado; **~board** *n* diana; **~s**
n dardos *mpl*
dash [dæʃ] *n* (*small quantity: of liquid*)
gota, chorrito; (: *of solid*) pizca; (*sign*)
raya ♦ *vt* (*throw*) tirar; (*hopes*) defraudar
♦ *vi* precipitarse, ir de prisa; **~ away** *or*
off *vi* marcharse apresuradamente
dashboard ['dæʃbɔ:d] *n* (AUT) salpicadero
dashing ['dæʃɪŋ] *adj* gallardo
data ['deɪtə] *npl* datos *mpl*; **~base** *n* base
f de datos; **~ processing** *n* proceso de
datos
date [deɪt] *n* (*day*) fecha; (*with friend*) cita;

(*fruit*) dátil *m* ♦ *vt* fechar; (*person*) salir con; **~ of birth** fecha de nacimiento; **to ~** *adv* hasta la fecha; **~d** *adj* anticuado; **~ rape** *n* violación ocurrida durante una cita con un conocido

daub [dɔːb] *vt* embadurnar

daughter ['dɔːtə*] *n* hija; **~-in-law** *n* nuera, hija política

daunting ['dɔːntɪŋ] *adj* desalentador(a)

dawdle ['dɔːdl] *vi* (*go slowly*) andar muy despacio

dawn [dɔːn] *n* alba, amanecer *m*; (*fig*) nacimiento ♦ *vi* (*day*) amanecer; (*fig*): **it ~ed on him that ...** cayó en la cuenta de que ...

day [deɪ] *n* día *m*; (*working ~*) jornada; (*hey~*) tiempos *mpl*, días *mpl*; **the before/after** el día anterior/siguiente; **the ~ after tomorrow** pasado mañana; **the ~ before yesterday** anteayer; **the following ~** el día siguiente; **by ~** de día; **~break** *n* amanecer *m*; **~dream** *vi* soñar despierto; **~light** *n* luz *f* (del día); **~ return** (*BRIT*) *n* billete *m* de ida y vuelta (en un día); **~time** *n* día *m*; **~-to-~** *adj* cotidiano

daze [deɪz] *vt* (*stun*) aturdir ♦ *n*: **in a ~** aturdido

dazzle ['dæzl] *vt* deslumbrar

DC *abbr* (= *direct current*) corriente *f* continua

dead [dɛd] *adj* muerto; (*limb*) dormido; (*telephone*) cortado; (*battery*) agotado ♦ *adv* (*completely*) totalmente; (*exactly*) exactamente; **to shoot sb ~** matar a uno a tiros; **~ tired** muerto (de cansancio); **to stop ~** parar en seco; **the ~** *npl* los muertos; **to be a ~ loss** (*inf*: *person*) ser un inútil; **~en** *vt* (*blow, sound*) amortiguar; (*pain etc*) aliviar; **~ end** *n* callejón sin salida; **~ heat** *n* (*SPORT*) empate *m*; **~line** *n* fecha (*or* hora) tope; **~lock** *n*: **to reach ~lock** llegar a un punto muerto; **~ly** *adj* mortal, fatal; **~pan** *adj* sin expresión; **the D~ Sea** *n* el Mar Muerto

deaf [dɛf] *adj* sordo; **~en** *vt* ensordecer; **~ness** *n* sordera

deal [diːl] (*pt, pp* **dealt**) *n* (*agreement*) pacto, convenio; (*business ~*) trato ♦ *vt* dar; (*card*) repartir; **a great ~ (of)** bastante, mucho; **~ in** *vt fus* tratar en, comerciar en; **~ with** *vt fus* (*people*) tratar con; (*problem*) ocuparse de; (*subject*) tratar de; **~ings** *npl* (*COMM*) transacciones *fpl*; (*relations*) relaciones *fpl*

dealt [dɛlt] *pt, pp of* **deal**

dean [diːn] *n* (*REL*) deán *m*; (*SCOL*: *BRIT*) decano; (: *US*) decano; rector *m*

dear [dɪə*] *adj* querido; (*expensive*) caro ♦ *n*: **my ~** mi querido/a ♦ *excl*: **~ me!** ¡Dios mío!; **D~ Sir/Madam** (*in letter*) Muy Señor Mío, Estimado Señor/Estimada Señora; **D~ Mr/Mrs X** Estimado/a Señor(a) X; **~ly** *adv* (*love*) mucho; (*pay*) caro

death [dɛθ] *n* muerte *f*; **~ certificate** *n* partida de defunción; **~ly** *adj* (*white*) como un muerto; (*silence*) sepulcral; **~ penalty** *n* pena de muerte; **~ rate** *n* mortalidad *f*; **~ toll** *n* número de víctimas

debacle [deɪ'bɑːkl] *n* desastre *m*

debase [dɪ'beɪs] *vt* degradar

debatable [dɪ'beɪtəbl] *adj* discutible

debate [dɪ'beɪt] *n* debate *m* ♦ *vt* discutir

debit ['dɛbɪt] *n* debe *m* ♦ *vt*: **to ~ a sum to sb** *or* **to sb's account** cargar una suma en cuenta a alguien

debris ['dɛbriː] *n* escombros *mpl*

debt [dɛt] *n* deuda; **to be in ~** tener deudas; **~or** *n* deudor(a) *m/f*

début ['deɪbjuː] *n* presentación *f*

decade ['dɛkeɪd] *n* decenio, década

decadence ['dɛkədəns] *n* decadencia

decaff ['diːkæf] (*inf*) *n* descafeinado

decaffeinated [dɪ'kæfɪneɪtɪd] *adj* descafeinado

decanter [dɪ'kæntə*] *n* garrafa

decay [dɪ'keɪ] *n* (*of building*) desmoronamiento; (*of tooth*) caries *f inv* ♦ *vi* (*rot*) pudrirse

deceased [dɪ'siːst] *n*: **the ~** el/la difunto/a

deceit [dɪ'siːt] *n* engaño; **~ful** *adj* engañoso; **deceive** [dɪ'siːv] *vt* engañar

December [dɪ'sembə*] n diciembre m

decent ['di:sənt] adj (proper) decente; (person: kind) amable, bueno

deception [dɪ'sepʃən] n engaño

deceptive [dɪ'septɪv] adj engañoso

decibel ['desɪbel] n decibel(io) m

decide [dɪ'saɪd] vt (person) decidir; (question, argument) resolver ♦ vi decidir; **to ~ to do/that** decidir hacer/que; **to ~ on sth** decidirse por algo; **~d** adj (resolute) decidido; (clear, definite) indudable; **~dly** [-dɪdlɪ] adv decididamente; (emphatically) con resolución

deciduous [dɪ'sɪdjuəs] adj de hoja caduca

decimal ['desɪməl] adj decimal ♦ n decimal m; **~ point** n coma decimal

decipher [dɪ'saɪfə*] vt descifrar

decision [dɪ'sɪʒən] n decisión f

decisive [dɪ'saɪsɪv] adj decisivo; (person) decidido

deck [dek] n (NAUT) cubierta f; (of bus) piso; (record ~) platina f; (of cards) baraja; **~chair** n tumbona

declaration [dekləˈreɪʃən] n declaración f

declare [dɪ'kleə*] vt declarar

decline [dɪ'klaɪn] n disminución f, descenso ♦ vt rehusar ♦ vi (person, business) decaer; (strength) disminuir

decoder [di:ˈkəʊdə*] n (TV) decodificador m

décor ['deɪkɔ:*] n decoración f; (THEATRE) decorado

decorate ['dekəreɪt] vt (adorn): **to ~ (with)** adornar (de), decorar (de); (paint) pintar; (paper) empapelar; **decoration** [-'reɪʃən] n adorno; (act) decoración f; (medal) condecoración f; **decorator** n (workman) pintor m (decorador)

decorum [dɪ'kɔ:rəm] n decoro

decoy ['di:kɔɪ] n señuelo

decrease [n 'di:kri:s, vb dɪ'kri:s] n: **~ (in)** disminución f (de) ♦ vt disminuir, reducir ♦ vi reducirse

decree [dɪ'kri:] n decreto; **~ nisi** n sentencia provisional de divorcio

dedicate ['dedɪkeɪt] vt dedicar;

dedication [-'keɪʃən] n (devotion) dedicación f; (in book) dedicatoria

deduce [dɪ'dju:s] vt deducir

deduct [dɪ'dʌkt] vt restar; descontar; **~ion** [dɪ'dʌkʃən] n (amount deducted) descuento; (conclusion) deducción f, conclusión f

deed [di:d] n hecho, acto; (feat) hazaña; (LAW) escritura

deep [di:p] adj profundo; (expressing measurements) de profundidad; (voice) bajo; (breath) profundo; (colour) intenso ♦ adv: **the spectators stood 20 ~** los espectadores se formaron de 20 en fondo; **to be 4 metres ~** tener 4 metros de profundidad; **~en** vt ahondar, profundizar ♦ vi aumentar, crecer; **~-freeze** n congelador m; **~-fry** vt freír en aceite abundante; **~ly** adv (breathe) a pleno pulmón; (interested, moved, grateful) profundamente, hondamente; **~-sea diving** n buceo de altura; **~-seated** adj (beliefs) (profundamente) arraigado

deer [dɪə*] n inv ciervo

deface [dɪ'feɪs] vt (wall, surface) estropear, pintarrajear

default [dɪ'fɔ:lt] n: **by ~** (win) por incomparecencia ♦ adj (COMPUT) por defecto

defeat [dɪ'fi:t] n derrota ♦ vt derrotar, vencer; **~ist** adj, n derrotista m/f

defect [n 'di:fekt, vb dɪ'fekt] n defecto ♦ vi: **to ~ to the enemy** pasarse al enemigo; **~ive** [dɪ'fektɪv] adj defectuoso

defence [dɪ'fens] (US **defense**) n defensa; **~less** adj indefenso

defend [dɪ'fend] vt defender; **~ant** n acusado/a; (in civil case) demandado/a; **~er** n defensor(a) m/f; (SPORT) defensa m/f

defense [dɪ'fens] (US) n = **defence**

defensive [dɪ'fensɪv] adj defensivo ♦ n: **on the ~** a la defensiva

defer [dɪ'fə:*] vt aplazar

defiance [dɪ'faɪəns] n desafío; **in ~ of** en contra de; **defiant** [dɪ'faɪənt] adj (*challenging*) desafiante, retador(a)

deficiency [dɪˈfɪʃənsɪ] *n* (*lack*) falta; (*defect*) defecto; **deficient** [dɪˈfɪʃənt] *adj* deficiente

deficit [ˈdɛfɪsɪt] *n* déficit *m*

define [dɪˈfaɪn] *vt* (*word etc*) definir; (*limits etc*) determinar

definite [ˈdɛfɪnɪt] *adj* (*fixed*) determinado; (*obvious*) claro; (*certain*) indudable; **he was ~ about it** no dejó lugar a dudas (sobre ello); **~ly** *adv* desde luego, por supuesto

definition [dɛfɪˈnɪʃən] *n* definición *f*; (*clearness*) nitidez *f*

deflate [diːˈfleɪt] *vt* desinflar

deflect [dɪˈflɛkt] *vt* desviar

defraud [dɪˈfrɔːd] *vt*: **to ~ sb of sth** estafar algo a uno

defrost [diːˈfrɔst] *vt* descongelar; **~er** (*US*) *n* (*demister*) eliminador *m* de vaho

deft [dɛft] *adj* diestro, hábil

defunct [dɪˈfʌŋkt] *adj* difunto; (*organization etc*) ya que no existe

defuse [diːˈfjuːz] *vt* desactivar; (*situation*) calmar

defy [dɪˈfaɪ] *vt* (*resist*) oponerse a; (*challenge*) desafiar; (*fig*): **it defies description** resulta imposible describirlo

degenerate [*vb* dɪˈdʒɛnəreɪt, *adj* dɪˈdʒɛnərɪt] *vi* degenerar ♦ *adj* degenerado

degree [dɪˈɡriː] *n* grado; (*SCOL*) título; **to have a ~ in maths** tener una licenciatura en matemáticas; **by ~s** (*gradually*) poco a poco, por etapas; **to some ~** hasta cierto punto

dehydrated [diːhaɪˈdreɪtɪd] *adj* deshidratado; (*milk*) en polvo

de-ice [diːˈaɪs] *vt* deshelar

deign [deɪn] *vi*: **to ~ to do** dignarse hacer

dejected [dɪˈdʒɛktɪd] *adj* abatido, desanimado

delay [dɪˈleɪ] *vt* demorar, aplazar; (*person*) entretener; (*train*) retrasar ♦ *vi* tardar ♦ *n* demora, retraso; **to be ~ed** retrasarse; **without ~** en seguida, sin tardar

delectable [dɪˈlɛktəbl] *adj* (*person*)

encantador(a); (*food*) delicioso

delegate [*n* ˈdɛlɪɡɪt, *vb* ˈdɛlɪɡeɪt] *n* delegado/a ♦ *vt* (*person*) delegar en; (*task*) delegar

delete [dɪˈliːt] *vt* suprimir, tachar

deliberate [*adj* dɪˈlɪbərɪt, *vb* dɪˈlɪbəreɪt] *adj* (*intentional*) intencionado; (*slow*) pausado, lento ♦ *vi* deliberar; **~ly** *adv* (*on purpose*) a propósito

delicacy [ˈdɛlɪkəsɪ] *n* delicadeza; (*choice food*) manjar *m*

delicate [ˈdɛlɪkɪt] *adj* delicado; (*fragile*) frágil

delicatessen [dɛlɪkəˈtɛsn] *n* ultramarinos *mpl* finos

delicious [dɪˈlɪʃəs] *adj* delicioso

delight [dɪˈlaɪt] *n* (*feeling*) placer *m*, deleite *m*; (*person, experience etc*) encanto, delicia ♦ *vt* encantar, deleitar; **to take ~ in** deleitarse en; **~ed** *adj*: **~ed (at *or* with/ to do)** encantado (con/de hacer); **~ful** *adj* encantador(a), delicioso

delinquent [dɪˈlɪŋkwənt] *adj, n* delincuente *m/f*

delirious [dɪˈlɪrɪəs] *adj*: **to be ~** delirar, desvariar; **to be ~ with** estar loco de

deliver [dɪˈlɪvə*] *vt* (*distribute*) repartir; (*hand over*) entregar; (*message*) comunicar; (*speech*) pronunciar; (*MED*) asistir al parto de; **~y** *n* reparto; entrega; (*of speaker*) modo de expresarse; (*MED*) parto, alumbramiento; **to take ~y of** recibir

delude [dɪˈluːd] *vt* engañar

deluge [ˈdɛljuːdʒ] *n* diluvio

delusion [dɪˈluːʒən] *n* ilusión *f*, engaño

de luxe [dəˈlʌks] *adj* de lujo

demand [dɪˈmɑːnd] *vt* (*gen*) exigir; (*rights*) reclamar ♦ *n* exigencia; (*claim*) reclamación *f*; (*ECON*) demanda; **to be in ~** ser muy solicitado; **on ~** a solicitud; **~ing** *adj* (*boss*) exigente; (*work*) absorbente

demean [dɪˈmiːn] *vt*: **to ~ o.s.** rebajarse

demeanour [dɪˈmiːnə*] (*US* **demeanor**) *n* porte *m*, conducta

demented [dɪˈmɛntɪd] *adj* demente

demise [dɪˈmaɪz] n (death) fallecimiento

demister [diːˈmɪstə*] n (AUT) eliminador m de vaho

demo [ˈdɛməu] (inf) n abbr (= demonstration) manifestación f

democracy [dɪˈmɒkrəsɪ] n democracia; **democrat** [ˈdɛməkræt] n demócrata m/f; **democratic** [dɛməˈkrætɪk] adj democrático; (US) demócrata

demolish [dɪˈmɒlɪʃ] vt derribar, demoler; (fig: argument) destruir

demon [ˈdiːmən] n (evil spirit) demonio

demonstrate [ˈdɛmənstreɪt] vt demostrar; (skill, appliance) mostrar ♦ vi manifestarse; **demonstration** [-ˈstreɪʃən] n (POL) manifestación f; (proof, exhibition) demostración f; **demonstrator** n (POL) manifestante m/f; (COMM) demostrador(a) m/f; vendedor(a) m/f

demote [dɪˈməut] vt degradar

demure [dɪˈmjuə*] adj recatado

den [dɛn] n (of animal) guarida; (room) habitación f

denial [dɪˈnaɪəl] n (refusal) negativa; (of report etc) negación f

denim [ˈdɛnɪm] n tela vaquera; **~s** npl vaqueros mpl

Denmark [ˈdɛnmɑːk] n Dinamarca

denomination [dɪnɒmɪˈneɪʃən] n valor m; (REL) confesión f

denounce [dɪˈnauns] vt denunciar

dense [dɛns] adj (crowd) denso; (thick) espeso; (: foliage etc) tupido; (inf: stupid) torpe; **~ly** adv: **~ly populated** con una alta densidad de población

density [ˈdɛnsɪtɪ] n densidad f; **single/ double-~ disk** (COMPUT) disco de densidad sencilla/doble densidad

dent [dɛnt] n abolladura ♦ vt (also: **make a ~ in**) abollar

dental [ˈdɛntl] adj dental; **~ surgeon** n odontólogo/a

dentist [ˈdɛntɪst] n dentista m/f

dentures [ˈdɛntʃəz] npl dentadura (postiza)

deny [dɪˈnaɪ] vt negar; (charge) rechazar

deodorant [diːˈəudərənt] n desodorante m

depart [dɪˈpɑːt] vi irse, marcharse; (train) salir; **to ~ from** (fig: differ from) apartarse de

department [dɪˈpɑːtmənt] n (COMM) sección f; (SCOL) departamento; (POL) ministerio; **~ store** n gran almacén m

departure [dɪˈpɑːtʃə*] n partida, ida; (of train) salida; (of employee) marcha; **a new ~** un nuevo rumbo; **~ lounge** n (at airport) sala de embarque

depend [dɪˈpɛnd] vi: **to ~ on** depender de; (rely on) contar con; **it ~s** depende, según; **~ing on the result** según el resultado; **~able** adj (person) formal, serio; (watch) exacto; (car) seguro; **~ant** n dependiente m/f; **~ent** adj: **to be ~ent on** depender de ♦ n = **dependant**

depict [dɪˈpɪkt] vt (in picture) pintar; (describe) representar

depleted [dɪˈpliːtɪd] adj reducido

deploy [dɪˈplɔɪ] vt desplegar

deport [dɪˈpɔːt] vt deportar

deposit [dɪˈpɒzɪt] n depósito; (CHEM) sedimento; (of ore, oil) yacimiento ♦ vt (gen) depositar; **~ account** (BRIT) n cuenta de ahorros

depot [ˈdɛpəu] n (storehouse) depósito; (for vehicles) parque m; (US) estación f

depreciate [dɪˈpriːʃɪeɪt] vi depreciarse, perder valor

depress [dɪˈprɛs] vt deprimir; (wages etc) hacer bajar; (press down) apretar; **~ed** adj deprimido; **~ing** adj deprimente; **~ion** [dɪˈprɛʃən] n depresión f

deprivation [dɛprɪˈveɪʃən] n privación f

deprive [dɪˈpraɪv] vt: **to ~ sb of** privar a uno de; **~d** adj necesitado

depth [dɛpθ] n profundidad f; (of cupboard) fondo; **to be in the ~s of despair** sentir la mayor desesperación; **to be out of one's ~** (in water) no hacer pie; (fig) sentirse totalmente perdido

deputize [ˈdɛpjutaɪz] vi: **to ~ for sb** suplir a uno

deputy [ˈdɛpjutɪ] adj: **~ head** subdirector(a) m/f ♦ n sustituto/a, suplente m/f; (US: POL) diputado/a; (US:

also: **~ sheriff**) agente *m* (del sheriff)
derail [dɪ'reɪl] *vt*: **to be ~ed** descarrilarse
deranged [dɪ'reɪndʒd] *adj* trastornado
derby ['dɑːbɪ] (*US*) *n* (*hat*) hongo
derelict ['derɪlɪkt] *adj* abandonado
derisory [dɪ'raɪzərɪ] *adj* (*sum*) irrisorio
derive [dɪ'raɪv] *vt* (*benefit etc*) obtener
♦ *vi*: **to ~ from** derivarse de
derogatory [dɪ'rɒgətərɪ] *adj* despectivo
descend [dɪ'send] *vt, vi* descender, bajar;
to ~ from descender de; **to ~ to** rebajarse
a; **~ant** *n* descendiente *m/f*
descent [dɪ'sent] *n* descenso; (*origin*)
descendencia
describe [dɪs'kraɪb] *vt* describir;
description [-'krɪpʃən] *n* descripción *f*;
(*sort*) clase *f*, género
desecrate ['desɪkreɪt] *vt* profanar
desert [*n* 'dezət, *vb* dɪ'zɜːt] *n* desierto ♦ *vt*
abandonar ♦ *vi* (*MIL*) desertar; **~er**
[dɪ'zɜːtə*] *n* desertor(a) *m/f*; **~ion**
[dɪ'zɜːʃən] *n* deserción *f*; (*LAW*) abandono;
~ island *n* isla desierta; **~s** [dɪ'zɜːts] *npl*:
to get one's just ~s llevar su merecido
deserve [dɪ'zɜːv] *vt* merecer, ser digno de;
deserving *adj* (*person*) digno; (*action,
cause*) meritorio
design [dɪ'zaɪn] *n* (*sketch*) bosquejo;
(*layout, shape*) diseño; (*pattern*) dibujo;
(*intention*) intención *f* ♦ *vt* diseñar
designate [*vb* 'dezɪgneɪt, *adj* 'dezɪgnɪt] *vt*
(*appoint*) nombrar; (*destine*) designar
♦ *adj* designado
designer [dɪ'zaɪnə*] *n* diseñador(a) *m/f*;
(*fashion ~*) modisto/a, diseñador(a) *m/f*
de moda
desirable [dɪ'zaɪərəbl] *adj* (*proper*)
deseable; (*attractive*) atractivo
desire [dɪ'zaɪə*] *n* deseo ♦ *vt* desear
desk [desk] *n* (*in office*) escritorio; (*for
pupil*) pupitre *m*; (*in hotel, at airport*)
recepción *f*; (*BRIT: in shop, restaurant*) caja
desk-top publishing ['desktɒp-] *n*
autoedición *f*
desolate ['desəlɪt] *adj* (*place*) desierto;
(*person*) afligido
despair [dɪs'peə*] *n* desesperación *f* ♦ *vi*:

to ~ of perder la esperanza de
despatch [dɪs'pætʃ] *n*, *vt* = **dispatch**
desperate ['despərɪt] *adj* desesperado;
(*fugitive*) peligroso; **to be ~ for sth/to do**
necesitar urgentemente algo/hacer; **~ly**
adv desesperadamente; (*very*)
terriblemente, gravemente
desperation [despə'reɪʃən] *n*
desesperación *f*; **in (sheer) ~**
(*absolutamente*) desesperado
despicable [dɪs'pɪkəbl] *adj* vil,
despreciable
despise [dɪs'paɪz] *vt* despreciar
despite [dɪs'paɪt] *prep* a pesar de, pese a
despondent [dɪs'pɒndənt] *adj* deprimido,
abatido
dessert [dɪ'zɜːt] *n* postre *m*; **~spoon** *n*
cuchara (de postre)
destination [destɪ'neɪʃən] *n* destino
destiny ['destɪnɪ] *n* destino
destitute ['destɪtjuːt] *adj* desamparado,
indigente
destroy [dɪs'trɔɪ] *vt* destruir; (*animal*)
sacrificar; **~er** *n* (*NAUT*) destructor *m*
destruction [dɪs'trʌkʃən] *n* destrucción *f*
detach [dɪ'tætʃ] *vt* separar; (*unstick*)
despegar; **~ed** *adj* (*attitude*) objetivo,
imparcial; **~ed house** *n* ≈ chalé *m*,
≈ chalet *m*; **~ment** *n* (*aloofness*) frialdad
f; (*MIL*) destacamento
detail ['diːteɪl] *n* detalle *m*; (*no pl: in
picture etc*) detalles *mpl*; (*trifle*) pequeñez
f ♦ *vt* detallar; (*MIL*) destacar; **in ~**
detalladamente; **~ed** *adj* detallado
detain [dɪ'teɪn] *vt* retener; (*in captivity*)
detener
detect [dɪ'tekt] *vt* descubrir; (*MED, POLICE*)
identificar; (*MIL, RADAR, TECH*) detectar;
~ion [dɪ'tekʃən] *n* descubrimiento;
identificación *f*; **~ive** *n* detective *m/f*;
~ive story *n* novela policíaca; **~or** *n*
detector *m*
detention [dɪ'tenʃən] *n* detención *f*,
arresto; (*SCOL*) castigo
deter [dɪ'tɜː*] *vt* (*dissuade*) disuadir
detergent [dɪ'tɜːdʒənt] *n* detergente *m*
deteriorate [dɪ'tɪərɪəreɪt] *vi* deteriorarse;

deterioration [-'reɪʃən] n deterioro
determination [dɪtɜ:mɪ'neɪʃən] n
resolución f
determine [dɪ'tɜ:mɪn] vt determinar; ~d
adj (person) resuelto, decidido; ~d to do
resuelto a hacer
deterrent [dɪ'terənt] n (MIL) fuerza de
disuasión
detest [dɪ'test] vt aborrecer
detonate ['detəneɪt] vi estallar ♦ vt hacer
detonar
detour ['di:tuə*] n (gen, US: AUT)
desviación f
detract [dɪ'trækt] vt: to ~ from quitar
mérito a, desvirtuar
detriment ['detrɪmənt] n: to the ~ of en
perjuicio de; ~al [detrɪ'mentl] adj: ~al (to)
perjudicial (a)
devaluation [dɪvælju'eɪʃən] n devaluación
f
devalue [di:'vælju:] vt (currency) devaluar;
(fig) quitar mérito a
devastate ['devəsteɪt] vt devastar; (fig): to
be ~d by quedar destrozado por;
devastating adj devastador(a); (fig)
arrollador(a)
develop [dɪ'veləp] vt desarrollar; (PHOT)
revelar; (disease) coger; (habit) adquirir;
(fault) empezar a tener ♦ vi desarrollarse;
(advance) progresar; (facts, symptoms)
aparecer; ~er n promotor m; ~ing
country n país m en (vías de) desarrollo;
~ment n desarrollo; (advance) progreso;
(of affair, case) desenvolvimiento; (of land)
urbanización f
deviation [di:vɪ'eɪʃən] n desviación f
device [dɪ'vaɪs] n (apparatus) aparato,
mecanismo
devil ['devl] n diablo, demonio
devious ['di:vɪəs] adj taimado
devise [dɪ'vaɪz] vt idear, inventar
devoid [dɪ'vɔɪd] adj: ~ of desprovisto de
devolution [di:və'lu:ʃən] n (POL)
descentralización f
devote [dɪ'vəut] vt: to ~ sth to dedicar
algo a; ~d adj (loyal) leal, fiel; to be ~d
to sb querer con devoción a alguien; the

book is ~d to politics el libro trata de la
política; ~e [devəu'ti:] n entusiasta m/f;
(REL) devoto/a; **devotion** n dedicación f;
(REL) devoción f
devour [dɪ'vauə*] vt devorar
devout [dɪ'vaut] adj devoto
dew [dju:] n rocío
diabetes [daɪə'bi:ti:z] n diabetes f;
diabetic [-'betɪk] adj, n diabético/a m/f
diabolical [daɪə'bɒlɪkəl] (inf) adj (weather,
behaviour) pésimo
diagnosis [daɪəg'nəusɪs] (pl -ses) n
diagnóstico
diagonal [daɪ'ægənl] adj, n diagonal f
diagram ['daɪəgræm] n diagrama m,
esquema m
dial ['daɪəl] n esfera, cuadrante m, cara
(AM); (on radio etc) selector m; (of phone)
disco ♦ vt (number) marcar
dialling ['daɪəlɪŋ]: ~ **code** n prefijo; ~
tone (US **dial tone**) n (BRIT) señal f or
tono de marcar
dialogue ['daɪəlɔg] (US **dialog**) n diálogo
diameter [daɪ'æmɪtə*] n diámetro
diamond ['daɪəmənd] n diamante m;
(shape) rombo; ~s npl (CARDS) diamantes
mpl
diaper ['daɪəpə*] (US) n pañal m
diaphragm ['daɪəfræm] n diafragma m
diarrhoea [daɪə'ri:ə] (US **diarrhea**) n
diarrea
diary ['daɪərɪ] n (daily account) diario;
(book) agenda
dice [daɪs] n inv dados mpl ♦ vt (CULIN)
cortar en cuadritos
Dictaphone ® ['dɪktəfəun] n dictáfono ®
dictate [dɪk'teɪt] vt dictar; (conditions)
imponer; **dictation** [-'teɪʃən] n dictado;
(giving of orders) órdenes fpl
dictator [dɪk'teɪtə*] n dictador m; ~ship n
dictadura
dictionary ['dɪkʃənrɪ] n diccionario
did [dɪd] pt of **do**
didn't ['dɪdənt] = **did not**
die [daɪ] vi morir; (fig: fade) desvanecerse,
desaparecer; **to be dying for sth/to do
sth** morirse por algo/de ganas de hacer

algo; **~ away** vi (*sound, light*) perderse;
~ down vi apagarse; (*wind*) amainar; **~
out** vi desaparecer

diesel ['diːzəl] n vehículo con motor
Diesel; **~ engine** n motor m Diesel; **~
(oil)** n gasoil m

diet ['daɪət] n dieta; (*restricted food*)
régimen m ♦ vi (*also:* **be on a ~**) estar a
dieta, hacer régimen

differ ['dɪfə*] vi: **to ~ (from)** (*be different*)
ser distinto (a), diferenciarse (de);
(*disagree*) discrepar (de); **~ence** n
diferencia; (*disagreement*) desacuerdo;
~ent adj diferente, distinto; **~entiate**
[-'renʃieit] vi: **to ~entiate (between)**
distinguir (entre); **~ently** adv de otro
modo, en forma distinta

difficult ['dɪfɪkəlt] adj difícil; **~y** n
dificultad f

diffident ['dɪfɪdənt] adj tímido

dig [dɪg] (*pt, pp* **dug**) vt (*hole, ground*)
cavar ♦ n (*prod*) empujón m;
(*archaeological*) excavación f; (*remark*)
indirecta; **to ~ one's nails into** clavar las
uñas en; **~ into** vt fus (*savings*)
consumir; **~ up** vt (*information*)
desenterrar; (*plant*) desarraigar

digest [vb daɪ'dʒest, n 'daɪdʒest] vt (*food*)
digerir; (*facts*) asimilar ♦ n resumen m;
~ion [dɪ'dʒestʃən] n digestión f

digit ['dɪdʒɪt] n (*number*) dígito; (*finger*)
dedo; **~al** adj digital

dignified ['dɪgnɪfaɪd] adj grave, solemne

dignity ['dɪgnɪtɪ] n dignidad f

digress [daɪ'gres] vi: **to ~ from** apartarse
de

digs [dɪgz] (*BRIT: inf*) npl pensión f,
alojamiento

dilapidated [dɪ'læpɪdeɪtɪd] adj
desmoronado, ruinoso

dilemma [daɪ'lemə] n dilema m

diligent ['dɪlɪdʒənt] adj diligente

dilute [daɪ'luːt] vt diluir

dim [dɪm] adj (*light*) débil; (*outline*)
indistinto; (*room*) oscuro; (*inf: stupid*)
lerdo ♦ vt (*light*) bajar

dime [daɪm] (*US*) n moneda de diez

centavos

dimension [dɪ'menʃən] n dimensión f

diminish [dɪ'mɪnɪʃ] vt, vi disminuir

diminutive [dɪ'mɪnjutɪv] adj diminuto ♦ n
(*LING*) diminutivo

dimmers ['dɪməz] (*US*) npl (*AUT: dipped
headlights*) luces fpl cortas; (: *parking
lights*) luces fpl de posición

dimple ['dɪmpl] n hoyuelo

din [dɪn] n estruendo, estrépito

dine [daɪn] vi cenar; **~r** n (*person*)
comensal m/f; (*US*) restaurante m
económico

dinghy ['dɪŋgɪ] n bote m; (*also:* **rubber ~**)
lancha (neumática)

dingy ['dɪndʒɪ] adj (*room*) sombrío; (*colour*)
sucio

dining car ['daɪnɪŋ-] (*BRIT*) n (*RAIL*) coche-
comedor m

dining room n comedor m

dinner ['dɪnə*] n (*evening meal*) cena;
(*lunch*) comida; (*public*) cena, banquete
m; **~ jacket** n smoking m; **~ party** n
cena; **~ time** n (*evening*) hora de cenar;
(*midday*) hora de comer

dinosaur ['daɪnəsɔː*] n dinosaurio

diocese ['daɪəsɪs] n diócesis f inv

dip [dɪp] n (*slope*) pendiente m; (*in sea*)
baño; (*CULIN*) salsa ♦ vt (*in water*) mojar;
(*ladle etc*) meter; (*BRIT: AUT*): **to ~ one's
lights** poner luces de cruce ♦ vi (*road etc*)
descender, bajar

diploma [dɪ'pləumə] n diploma m

diplomacy [dɪ'pləuməsɪ] n diplomacia

diplomat ['dɪpləmæt] n diplomático/a; **~ic**
[dɪplə'mætɪk] adj diplomático

diprod ['dɪprɒd] (*US*) n = **dipstick**

dipstick ['dɪpstɪk] (*BRIT*) n (*AUT*) varilla de
nivel (del aceite)

dipswitch ['dɪpswɪtʃ] (*BRIT*) n (*AUT*)
interruptor m

dire [daɪə*] adj calamitoso

direct [daɪ'rekt] adj directo; (*challenge*)
claro; (*person*) franco ♦ vt dirigir; (*order*):
to ~ sb to do sth mandar a uno hacer
algo ♦ adv derecho; **can you ~ me to...?**
¿puede indicarme dónde está...?; **~ debit**

(*BRIT*) *n* domiciliación *f* bancaria de recibos

direction [dɪˈrekʃən] *n* dirección *f*; **sense of ~** sentido de la dirección; **~s** *npl* (*instructions*) instrucciones *fpl*; **~s for use** modo de empleo

directly [dɪˈrektlɪ] *adv* (*in straight line*) directamente; (*at once*) en seguida

director [dɪˈrektə*] *n* director(a) *m/f*

directory [dɪˈrektərɪ] *n* (*TEL*) guía (telefónica); (*COMPUT*) directorio; **~ enquiries**, **~ assistance** (*US*) *n* (servicio de) información *f*

dirt [dɜːt] *n* suciedad *f*; (*earth*) tierra; **~-cheap** *adj* baratísimo; **~y** *adj* sucio; (*joke*) verde (*SP*), colorado (*AM*) ♦ *vt* ensuciar; (*stain*) manchar; **~y trick** *n* juego sucio

disability [dɪsəˈbɪlɪtɪ] *n* incapacidad *f*

disabled [dɪsˈeɪbld] *adj*: **to be physically ~** ser minusválido/a; **to be mentally ~** ser deficiente mental

disadvantage [dɪsədˈvɑːntɪdʒ] *n* desventaja, inconveniente *m*

disagree [dɪsəˈgriː] *vi* (*differ*) discrepar; **to ~ (with)** no estar de acuerdo (con); **~able** *adj* desagradable; (*person*) antipático; **~ment** *n* desacuerdo

disallow [dɪsəˈlau] *vt* (*goal*) anular; (*claim*) rechazar

disappear [dɪsəˈpɪə*] *vi* desaparecer; **~ance** *n* desaparición *f*

disappoint [dɪsəˈpɔɪnt] *vt* decepcionar, defraudar; **~ed** *adj* decepcionado; **~ing** *adj* decepcionante; **~ment** *n* decepción *f*

disapproval [dɪsəˈpruːvəl] *n* desaprobación *f*

disapprove [dɪsəˈpruːv] *vi*: **to ~ of** ver mal

disarmament [dɪsˈɑːməmənt] *n* desarme *m*

disarray [dɪsəˈreɪ] *n*: **in ~** (*army*, *organization*) desorganizado; (*hair*, *clothes*) desarreglado

disaster [dɪˈzɑːstə*] *n* desastre *m*

disband [dɪsˈbænd] *vt* disolver ♦ *vi* desbandarse

disbelief [dɪsbəˈliːf] *n* incredulidad *f*

disc [dɪsk] *n* disco; (*COMPUT*) = **disk**

discard [dɪsˈkɑːd] *vt* (*old things*) tirar; (*fig*) descartar

discern [dɪˈsɜːn] *vt* percibir, discernir; (*understand*) comprender; **~ing** *adj* perspicaz

discharge [*vb* dɪsˈtʃɑːdʒ, *n* ˈdɪstʃɑːdʒ] *vt* (*task*, *duty*) cumplir; (*waste*) verter; (*patient*) dar de alta; (*employee*) despedir; (*soldier*) licenciar; (*defendant*) poner en libertad ♦ *n* (*ELEC*) descarga; (*MED*) supuración *f*; (*dismissal*) despedida; (*of duty*) desempeño; (*of debt*) pago, descargo

discipline [ˈdɪsɪplɪn] *n* disciplina ♦ *vt* disciplinar; (*punish*) castigar

disc jockey *n* pinchadiscos *m/f inv*

disclaim [dɪsˈkleɪm] *vt* negar

disclose [dɪsˈkləuz] *vt* revelar; **disclosure** [-ˈkləuʒə*] *n* revelación *f*

disco [ˈdɪskəu] *n abbr* = **discothèque**

discomfort [dɪsˈkʌmfət] *n* incomodidad *f*; (*unease*) inquietud *f*; (*physical*) malestar *m*

disconcert [dɪskənˈsɜːt] *vt* desconcertar

disconnect [dɪskəˈnekt] *vt* separar; (*ELEC etc*) desconectar

discontent [dɪskənˈtent] *n* descontento; **~ed** *adj* descontento

discontinue [dɪskənˈtɪnjuː] *vt* interrumpir; (*payments*) suspender; "**~d**" (*COMM*) "ya no se fabrica"

discord [ˈdɪskɔːd] *n* discordia; (*MUS*) disonancia

discothèque [ˈdɪskəutek] *n* discoteca

discount [*n* ˈdɪskaunt, *vb* dɪsˈkaunt] *n* descuento ♦ *vt* descontar

discourage [dɪsˈkʌrɪdʒ] *vt* desalentar; (*advise against*): **to ~ sb from doing** disuadir a uno de hacer

discover [dɪsˈkʌvə*] *vt* descubrir; (*error*) darse cuenta de; **~y** *n* descubrimiento

discredit [dɪsˈkredɪt] *vt* desacreditar

discreet [dɪˈskriːt] *adj* (*tactful*) discreto; (*careful*) circunspecto, prudente

discrepancy [dɪˈskrepənsɪ] *n* diferencia

discretion [dɪˈskreʃən] *n* (*tact*) discreción *f*

f; **at the ~ of** a criterio de

discriminate [dɪˈskrɪmɪneɪt] vi: **to ~ between** distinguir entre; **to ~ against** discriminar contra; **discriminating** adj entendido; **discrimination** [-ˈneɪʃən] n (*discernment*) perspicacia; (*bias*) discriminación f

discuss [dɪˈskʌs] vt discutir; (*a theme*) tratar; **~ion** [dɪˈskʌʃən] n discusión f

disdain [dɪsˈdeɪn] n desdén m

disease [dɪˈziːz] n enfermedad f

disembark [dɪsɪmˈbɑːk] vt, vi desembarcar

disentangle [dɪsɪnˈtæŋgl] vt soltar; (*wire, thread*) desenredar

disfigure [dɪsˈfɪgə*] vt (*person*) desfigurar; (*object*) afear

disgrace [dɪsˈgreɪs] n ignominia; (*shame*) vergüenza, escándalo ♦ vt deshonrar; **~ful** adj vergonzoso

disgruntled [dɪsˈgrʌntld] adj disgustado, descontento

disguise [dɪsˈgaɪz] n disfraz m ♦ vt disfrazar; **in ~** disfrazado

disgust [dɪsˈgʌst] n repugnancia ♦ vt repugnar, dar asco a; **~ing** adj repugnante, asqueroso; (*behaviour etc*) vergonzoso

dish [dɪʃ] n (*gen*) plato; **to do** or **wash the ~es** fregar los platos; **~ out** vt repartir; **~ up** vt servir; **~cloth** n estropajo

dishearten [dɪsˈhɑːtn] vt desalentar

dishevelled [dɪˈʃevəld] (*US* **disheveled**) adj (*hair*) despeinado; (*appearance*) desarreglado

dishonest [dɪsˈɒnɪst] adj (*person*) poco honrado, tramposo; (*means*) fraudulento; **~y** n falta de honradez

dishonour [dɪsˈɒnə*] (*US* **dishonor**) n deshonra; **~able** adj deshonroso

dishtowel [ˈdɪʃtaʊəl] (*US*) n estropajo

dishwasher [ˈdɪʃwɒʃə*] n lavaplatos m inv

disillusion [dɪsɪˈluːʒən] vt desilusionar

disinfect [dɪsɪnˈfekt] vt desinfectar; **~ant** n desinfectante m

disintegrate [dɪsˈɪntɪgreɪt] vi disgregarse, desintegrarse

disinterested [dɪsˈɪntrəstɪd] adj desinteresado

disjointed [dɪsˈdʒɔɪntɪd] adj inconexo

disk [dɪsk] n (*esp US*) = **disc**; (*COMPUT*) disco, disquete m; **single-/double-sided ~** disco de una cara/dos caras; **~ drive** n disc drive m; **~ette** n = **disk**

dislike [dɪsˈlaɪk] n antipatía, aversión f ♦ vt tener antipatía a

dislocate [ˈdɪsləkeɪt] vt dislocar

dislodge [dɪsˈlɒdʒ] vt sacar

disloyal [dɪsˈlɔɪəl] adj desleal

dismal [ˈdɪzml] adj (*gloomy*) deprimente, triste; (*very bad*) malísimo, fatal

dismantle [dɪsˈmæntl] vt desmontar, desarmar

dismay [dɪsˈmeɪ] n consternación f ♦ vt consternar

dismiss [dɪsˈmɪs] vt (*worker*) despedir; (*pupils*) dejar marchar; (*soldiers*) dar permiso para irse; (*idea, LAW*) rechazar; (*possibility*) descartar; **~al** n despido

dismount [dɪsˈmaʊnt] vi apearse

disobedient [dɪsəˈbiːdɪənt] adj desobediente

disobey [dɪsəˈbeɪ] vt desobedecer

disorder [dɪsˈɔːdə*] n desorden m; (*rioting*) disturbios mpl; (*MED*) trastorno; **~ly** adj desordenado; (*meeting*) alborotado; (*conduct*) escandaloso

disorientated [dɪsˈɔːrɪenteɪtəd] adj desorientado

disown [dɪsˈəʊn] vt (*action*) renegar de; (*person*) negar cualquier tipo de relación con

disparaging [dɪsˈpærɪdʒɪŋ] adj despreciativo

dispassionate [dɪsˈpæʃənɪt] adj (*unbiased*) imparcial

dispatch [dɪsˈpætʃ] vt enviar ♦ n (*sending*) envío; (*PRESS*) informe m; (*MIL*) parte m

dispel [dɪsˈpel] vt disipar

dispense [dɪsˈpens] vt (*medicines*) preparar; **~ with** vt fus prescindir de; **~r** n (*container*) distribuidor m automático; **dispensing chemist** (*BRIT*) n farmacia

disperse [dɪsˈpɜːs] vt dispersar ♦ vi dispersarse

dispirited [dɪˈspɪrɪtɪd] *adj* desanimado, desalentado

displace [dɪsˈpleɪs] *vt* desplazar, reemplazar; **~d person** *n* (*POL*) desplazado/a

display [dɪsˈpleɪ] *n* (*in shop window*) escaparate *m*; (*exhibition*) exposición *f*; (*COMPUT*) visualización *f*; (*of feeling*) manifestación *f* ♦ *vt* exponer; manifestar; (*ostentatiously*) lucir

displease [dɪsˈpliːz] *vt* (*offend*) ofender; (*annoy*) fastidiar; **~d** *adj*: **~d with** disgustado con; **displeasure** [-ˈpleʒə*] *n* disgusto

disposable [dɪsˈpəuzəbl] *adj* desechable; (*income*) disponible; **~ nappy** *n* pañal *m* desechable

disposal [dɪsˈpəuzl] *n* (*of rubbish*) destrucción *f*; **at one's ~** a su disposición

dispose [dɪsˈpəuz] *vi*: **to ~ of** (*unwanted goods*) deshacerse de; (*problem etc*) resolver; **~d** *adj*: **~d to do** dispuesto a hacer; **to be well-~d towards sb** estar bien dispuesto hacia uno; **disposition** [dɪspəˈzɪʃən] *n* (*nature*) temperamento; (*inclination*) propensión *f*

disprove [dɪsˈpruːv] *vt* refutar

dispute [dɪsˈpjuːt] *n* disputa; (*also:* **industrial ~**) conflicto (laboral) ♦ *vt* (*argue*) disputar, discutir; (*question*) cuestionar

disqualify [dɪsˈkwɔlɪfaɪ] *vt* (*SPORT*) desclasificar; **to ~ sb for sth/from doing sth** incapacitar a alguien para algo/hacer algo

disquiet [dɪsˈkwaɪət] *n* preocupación *f*, inquietud *f*

disregard [dɪsrɪˈɡɑːd] *vt* (*ignore*) no hacer caso de

disrepair [dɪsrɪˈpeə*] *n*: **to fall into ~** (*building*) desmoronarse

disreputable [dɪsˈrepjutəbl] *adj* (*person*) de mala fama; (*behaviour*) vergonzoso

disrespectful [dɪsrɪˈspektful] *adj* irrespetuoso

disrupt [dɪsˈrʌpt] *vt* (*plans*) desbaratar, trastornar; (*conversation*) interrumpir

dissatisfaction [dɪssætɪsˈfækʃən] *n* disgusto, descontento

dissect [dɪˈsekt] *vt* disecar

dissent [dɪˈsent] *n* disensión *f*

dissertation [dɪsəˈteɪʃən] *n* tesina

disservice [dɪsˈsəːvɪs] *n*: **to do sb a ~** perjudicar a alguien

dissimilar [dɪˈsɪmɪlə*] *adj* distinto

dissipate [ˈdɪsɪpeɪt] *vt* disipar; (*waste*) desperdiciar

dissolve [dɪˈzɔlv] *vt* disolver ♦ *vi* disolverse; **to ~ in(to) tears** deshacerse en lágrimas

dissuade [dɪˈsweɪd] *vt*: **to ~ sb (from)** disuadir a uno (de)

distance [ˈdɪstəns] *n* distancia; **in the ~** a lo lejos

distant [ˈdɪstənt] *adj* lejano; (*manner*) reservado, frío

distaste [dɪsˈteɪst] *n* repugnancia; **~ful** *adj* repugnante, desagradable

distended [dɪˈstendɪd] *adj* (*stomach*) hinchado

distil [dɪsˈtɪl] (*US* **distill**) *vt* destilar; **~lery** *n* destilería

distinct [dɪsˈtɪŋkt] *adj* (*different*) distinto; (*clear*) claro; (*unmistakeable*) inequívoco; **as ~ from** a diferencia de; **~ion** [dɪsˈtɪŋkʃən] *n* distinción *f*; (*honour*) honor *m*; (*in exam*) sobresaliente *m*; **~ive** *adj* distintivo

distinguish [dɪsˈtɪŋgwɪʃ] *vt* distinguir; **to ~ o.s.** destacarse; **~ed** *adj* (*eminent*) distinguido; **~ing** *adj* (*feature*) distintivo

distort [dɪsˈtɔːt] *vt* distorsionar; (*shape, image*) deformar; **~ion** [dɪsˈtɔːʃən] *n* distorsión *f*; deformación *f*

distract [dɪsˈtrækt] *vt* distraer; **~ed** *adj* distraído; **~ion** [dɪsˈtrækʃən] *n* distracción *f*; (*confusion*) aturdimiento

distraught [dɪsˈtrɔːt] *adj* loco de inquietud

distress [dɪsˈtres] *n* (*anguish*) angustia, aflicción *f* ♦ *vt* afligir; **~ing** *adj* angustioso; doloroso; **~ signal** *n* señal *f* de socorro

distribute [dɪsˈtrɪbjuːt] *vt* distribuir; (*share out*) repartir; **distribution** [-ˈbjuːʃən] *n*

distribución *f*, reparto; **distributor** *n*
(*AUT*) distribuidor *m*; (*COMM*) distribuidora
district ['dɪstrɪkt] *n* (*of country*) zona,
región *f*; (*of town*) barrio; (*ADMIN*) distrito;
~ **attorney** (*US*) *n* fiscal *m/f*; ~ **nurse**
(*BRIT*) *n* enfermera que atiende a pacientes
a domicilio
distrust [dɪs'trʌst] *n* desconfianza ♦ *vt*
desconfiar de
disturb [dɪs'təːb] *vt* (*person: bother,*
interrupt) molestar; (*: upset*) perturbar,
inquietar; (*disorganize*) alterar; ~**ance** *n*
(*upheaval*) perturbación *f*; (*political etc:*
gen pl) disturbio; (*of mind*) trastorno; ~**ed**
adj (*worried, upset*) preocupado,
angustiado; **emotionally ~ed** trastornado;
(*childhood*) inseguro; ~**ing** *adj*
inquietante, perturbador(a)
disuse [dɪs'juːs] *n*: **to fall into ~** caer en
desuso
disused [dɪs'juːzd] *adj* abandonado
ditch [dɪtʃ] *n* zanja; (*irrigation ~*) acequia
♦ *vt* (*inf: partner*) deshacerse de; (*: plan,*
car etc) abandonar
dither ['dɪðə*] (*pej*) *vi* vacilar
ditto ['dɪtəu] *adv* ídem, lo mismo
divan [dɪ'væn] *n* (*also*: ~ **bed**) cama turca
dive [daɪv] *n* (*from board*) salto;
(*underwater*) buceo; (*of submarine*)
sumersión *f* ♦ *vi* (*swimmer: into water*)
saltar; (*: under water*) zambullirse, bucear;
(*fish, submarine*) sumergirse; (*bird*)
lanzarse en picado; **to ~ into** (*bag etc*)
meter la mano en; (*place*) meterse de
prisa en; ~ *r n* (*underwater*) buzo
diverse [daɪ'vəːs] *adj* diversos/as, varios/as
diversion [daɪ'vəːʃən] *n* (*BRIT: AUT*)
desviación *f*; (*distraction, MIL*) diversión *f*;
(*of funds*) distracción *f*
divert [daɪ'vəːt] *vt* (*turn aside*) desviar
divide [dɪ'vaɪd] *vt* dividir; (*separate*)
separar ♦ *vi* dividirse; (*road*) bifurcarse;
~**d highway** (*US*) *n* carretera de doble
calzada
dividend ['dɪvɪdɛnd] *n* dividendo; (*fig*): **to**
pay ~s proporcionar beneficios
divine [dɪ'vaɪn] *adj* (*also fig*) divino

diving ['daɪvɪŋ] *n* (*SPORT*) salto;
(*underwater*) buceo; ~ **board** *n*
trampolín *m*
divinity [dɪ'vɪnɪtɪ] *n* divinidad *f*; (*SCOL*)
teología
division [dɪ'vɪʒən] *n* división *f*; (*sharing*
out) reparto; (*disagreement*) diferencias
fpl; (*COMM*) sección *f*
divorce [dɪ'vɔːs] *n* divorcio ♦ *vt* divorciarse
de; ~**d** *adj* divorciado; ~**e** [-'siː] *n*
divorciado/a
divulge [daɪ'vʌldʒ] *vt* divulgar, revelar
D.I.Y. (*BRIT*) *adj, n abbr* = **do-it- yourself**
dizzy ['dɪzɪ] *adj* (*spell*) de mareo; **to feel ~**
marearse
DJ *n abbr* = **disc jockey**

─────────────
KEYWORD
─────────────

do [duː] (*pt* **did**, *pp* **done**) *n* (*inf: party etc*):
we're having a little ~ on Saturday
damos una fiestecita el sábado; **it was**
rather a grand ~ fue un acontecimiento
a lo grande
♦ *aux vb* **1** (*in negative constructions: not*
translated) **I don't understand** no
entiendo
2 (*to form questions: not translated*) **didn't**
you know? ¿no lo sabías?; **what ~ you**
think? ¿qué opinas?
3 (*for emphasis, in polite expressions*):
people ~ make mistakes sometimes sí
que se cometen errores a veces; **she**
does seem rather late a mí también me
parece que se ha retrasado; **~ sit down/**
help yourself siéntase/sírvete por favor; **~**
take care! ¡ten cuidado(, te pido)!
4 (*used to avoid repeating vb*): **she sings**
better than I ~ canta mejor que yo; **~**
you agree? — yes, I ~/no, I don't ¿estás
de acuerdo? — sí (lo estoy)/no (lo estoy);
she lives in Glasgow — so ~ I vive en
Glasgow — yo también; **he didn't like it**
and neither did we no le gustó y a
nosotros tampoco; **who made this**
mess? — I did ¿quién hizo esta chapuza?
— yo; **he asked me to help him and I**
did me pidió que le ayudara y lo hice

5 (*in question tags*): **you like him, don't you?** te gusta, ¿verdad? *or* ¿no?; **I don't know him, ~ I?** creo que no le conozco
♦ *vt* **1** (*gen, carry out, perform etc*): **what are you ~ing tonight?** ¿qué haces esta noche?; **what can I ~ for you?** ¿en qué puedo servirle?; **to ~ the washing-up/cooking** fregar los platos/cocinar; **to ~ one's teeth/hair/nails** lavarse los dientes/arreglarse el pelo/arreglarse las uñas
2 (*AUT etc*): **the car was ~ing 100** el coche iba a 100; **we've done 200 km already** ya hemos hecho 200 km; **he can ~ 100 in that car** puede ir a 100 en ese coche
♦ *vi* **1** (*act, behave*) hacer; **~ as I ~** haz como yo
2 (*get on, fare*): **he's ~ing well/badly at school** va bien/mal en la escuela; **the firm is ~ing well** la empresa anda *or* va bien; **how ~ you ~?** mucho gusto; (*less formal*) ¿qué tal?
3 (*suit*): **will it ~?** ¿sirve?, ¿está *or* va bien?
4 (*be sufficient*) bastar; **will £10 ~?** ¿será bastante con £10?; **that'll ~** así está bien; **that'll ~!** (*in annoyance*) ¡ya está bien!, ¡basta ya!; **to make ~ (with)** arreglárselas (con)
do away with *vt fus* (*kill, disease*) eliminar; (*abolish: law etc*) abolir; (*withdraw*) retirar
do up *vt* (*laces*) atar; (*zip, dress, shirt*) abrochar; (*renovate: room, house*) renovar
do with *vt fus* (*need*): **I could ~ with a drink/some help** no me vendría mal un trago/un poco de ayuda; (*be connected*) tener que ver con; **what has it got to ~ with you?** ¿qué tiene que ver contigo?
do without *vi* pasar sin; **if you're late for tea then you'll ~ without** si llegas tarde tendrás que quedarte sin cenar ♦ *vt fus* pasar sin; **I can ~ without a car** puedo pasar sin coche

dock [dɔk] *n* (*NAUT*) muelle *m*; (*LAW*)

banquillo (de los acusados); **~s** *npl* (*NAUT*) muelles *mpl*, puerto *sg* ♦ *vi* (*enter ~*) atracar (la) muelle; (*SPACE*) acoplarse; **~er** *n* trabajador *m* portuario, estibador *m*; **~yard** *n* astillero
doctor [ˈdɔktə*] *n* médico/a; (*Ph.D. etc*) doctor(a) *m/f* ♦ *vt* (*drink etc*) adulterar; **D~ of Philosophy** *n* Doctor en Filosofía y Letras
document [ˈdɔkjumənt] *n* documento; **~ary** [-ˈmentərɪ] *adj* documental ♦ *n* documental *m*
dodge [dɔdʒ] *n* (*fig*) truco ♦ *vt* evadir; (*blow*) esquivar
dodgems [ˈdɔdʒəmz] (*BRIT*) *npl* coches *mpl* de choque
doe [dəu] *n* (*deer*) cierva, gama; (*rabbit*) coneja
does [dʌz] *vb see* **do**; **~n't = does not**
dog [dɔg] *n* perro ♦ *vt* seguir los pasos de; (*subj: bad luck*) perseguir; **~ collar** *n* collar *m* de perro; (*of clergyman*) alzacuellos *m inv*; **~-eared** *adj* sobado
dogged [ˈdɔgɪd] *adj* tenaz, obstinado
dogsbody [ˈdɔgzbɔdɪ] (*BRIT: inf*) *n* burro de carga
doings [ˈduɪŋz] *npl* (*activities*) actividades *fpl*
do-it-yourself *n* bricolaje *m*
doldrums [ˈdɔldrəmz] *npl*: **to be in the ~** (*person*) estar abatido; (*business*) estar estancado
dole [dəul] (*BRIT*) *n* (*payment*) subsidio de paro; **on the ~** parado; **~ out** *vt* repartir
doll [dɔl] *n* muñeca; (*US: inf: woman*) muñeca, gachí *f*
dollar [ˈdɔlə*] *n* dólar *m*
dolled up (*inf*) *adj* arreglado
dolphin [ˈdɔlfɪn] *n* delfín *m*
domain [dəˈmeɪn] *n* (*fig*) campo, competencia; (*land*) dominios *mpl*
dome [dəum] *n* (*ARCH*) cúpula
domestic [dəˈmestɪk] *adj* (*animal, duty*) doméstico; (*flight, policy*) nacional; **~ated** *adj* domesticado; (*home-loving*) casero, hogareño
dominate [ˈdɔmɪneɪt] *vt* dominar

domineering [dɔmɪ'nɪərɪŋ] *adj* dominante

dominion [də'mɪnɪən] *n* dominio

domino ['dɔmɪnəu] (*pl* **~es**) *n* ficha de dominó; **~es** *n* (*game*) dominó

don [dɔn] (*BRIT*) *n* profesor(a) *m/f* universitario/a

donate [də'neɪt] *vt* donar; **donation** [də'neɪʃən] *n* donativo

done [dʌn] *pp of* **do**

donkey ['dɔŋkɪ] *n* burro

donor ['dəunə*] *n* donante *m/f*; **~ card** *n* carnet *m* de donante de órganos

don't [dəunt] = **do not**

donut ['dəunʌt] (*US*) *n* = **doughnut**

doodle ['du:dl] *vi* hacer dibujitos *or* garabatos

doom [du:m] *n* (*fate*) suerte *f* ♦ *vt*: **to be ~ed to failure** estar condenado al fracaso

door [dɔ:*] *n* puerta; **~bell** *n* timbre *m*; **~ handle** *n* tirador *m*; (*of car*) manija; **~man** (*irreg*) *n* (*in hotel*) portero; **~mat** *n* felpudo, estera; **~step** *n* peldaño; **~-to-~** *adj* de puerta en puerta; **~way** *n* entrada, puerta

dope [dəup] *n* (*inf: illegal drug*) droga; (: *person*) imbécil *m/f* ♦ *vt* (*horse etc*) drogar

dormant ['dɔ:mənt] *adj* inactivo

dormitory ['dɔ:mɪtrɪ] *n* (*BRIT*) dormitorio; (*US*) colegio mayor

dormouse ['dɔ:maus] (*pl* **-mice**) *n* lirón *m*

DOS *n abbr* (= *disk operating system*) DOS *m*

dosage ['dəusɪdʒ] *n* dosis *f inv*

dose [dəus] *n* dósis *f inv*

doss house ['dɔss-] (*BRIT*) *n* pensión *f* de mala muerte

dossier ['dɔsɪeɪ] *n* expediente *m*, dosier *m*

dot [dɔt] *n* punto ♦ *vt*: **~ted with** salpicado de; **on the ~** *n* punto

double ['dʌbl] *adj* doble ♦ *adv* (*twice*): **to cost ~** costar el doble ♦ *n* doble *m* ♦ *vt* doblar ♦ *vi* doblarse; **on the ~**, **at the ~** (*BRIT*) corriendo; **~ bass** *n* contrabajo; **~ bed** *n* cama de matrimonio; **~ bend** (*BRIT*) *n* doble curva; **~-breasted** *adj* cruzado; **~cross** *vt* (*trick*) engañar;

(*betray*) traicionar; **~decker** *n* autobús *m* de dos pisos; **~ glazing** (*BRIT*) *n* doble acristalamiento; **~ room** *n* habitación *f* doble; **~s** *n* (*TENNIS*) juego de dobles; **doubly** *adv* doblemente

doubt [daut] *n* duda ♦ *vt* dudar; (*suspect*) dudar de; **to ~ that** dudar que; **~ful** *adj* dudoso; (*person*): **to be ~ful about sth** tener dudas sobre algo; **~less** *adv* sin duda

dough [dəu] *n* masa, pasta; **~nut** (*US* **donut**) *n* ≈ rosquilla

dove [dʌv] *n* paloma

dovetail ['dʌvteɪl] *vi* (*fig*) encajar

dowdy ['daudɪ] *adj* (*person*) mal vestido; (*clothes*) pasado de moda

down [daun] *n* (*feathers*) plumón *m*, flojel *m* ♦ *adv* (~wards) abajo, hacia abajo; (*on the ground*) por *or* en tierra ♦ *prep* abajo ♦ *vt* (*inf: drink*) beberse; **~ with X!** ¡abajo X!; **~-and-out** *n* vagabundo/a; **~-at-heel** *adj* venido a menos; (*appearance*): desaliñado; **~cast** *adj* abatido; **~fall** *n* caída, ruina; **~hearted** *adj* desanimado; **~hill** *adv*: **to go ~hill** (*also fig*) ir cuesta abajo; **~ payment** *n* entrada, pago al contado; **~pour** *n* aguacero; **~right** *adj* (*nonsense, lie*) manifiesto; (*refusal*) terminante; **~size** *vi* (*ECON: company*) reducir la plantilla de

---

Downing Street

ⓘ **Downing Street** es la calle de Londres en la que están las residencias oficiales del Presidente del Gobierno (Prime Minister), tradicionalmente en el No. 10, y del Ministro de Economía (Chancellor of the Exchequer). La calle está situada en el céntrico barrio londinense de Westminster y está cerrada al tráfico de peatones y vehículos. En lenguaje periodístico, se usa también **Downing Street** para referirse al primer ministro o al Gobierno.

Down's syndrome ['daunz-] *n* síndrome *m* de Down

down: **~stairs** *adv* (*below*) (en la casa de)

abajo; (~**wards**) escaleras abajo; **~stream** *adv* aguas or río abajo; **~-to-earth** *adj* práctico; **~town** *adv* en el centro de la ciudad; **~ under** *adv* en Australia (or Nueva Zelanda); **~ward** [-wəd] *adj, adv* hacia abajo; **~wards** [-wədz] *adv* hacia abajo

dowry ['dauri] *n* dote *f*

doz. *abbr* = **dozen**

doze [dəuz] *vi* dormitar; **~ off** *vi* quedarse medio dormido

dozen ['dʌzn] *n* docena; **a ~ books** una docena de libros; **~s of** cantidad de

Dr. *abbr* = **doctor; drive**

drab [dræb] *adj* gris, monótono

draft [drɑːft] *n* (*first copy*) borrador *m*; (*POL: of bill*) anteproyecto *m*; (*US: call-up*) quinta ♦ *vt* (*plan*) preparar; (*write roughly*) hacer un borrador de; *see also* **draught**

draftsman ['drɑːftsmən] (*US*) *n* = **draughtsman**

drag [dræg] *vt* arrastrar; (*river*) dragar, rastrear ♦ *vi* (*time*) pasar despacio; (*play, film etc*) hacerse pesado ♦ *n* (*inf*) lata; (*women's clothing*): **in ~** vestido de travesti; **~ on** *vi* ser interminable; **~ and drop** *vt* (*COMPUT*) arrastrar y soltar

dragon ['drægən] *n* dragón *m*

dragonfly ['drægənflaɪ] *n* libélula

drain [dreɪn] *n* desaguadero; (*in street*) sumidero; (*source of loss*): **to be a ~ on** consumir, agotar ♦ *vt* (*land, marshes*) desaguar; (*reservoir*) desecar; (*vegetables*) escurrir ♦ *vi* escurrirse; **~age** *n* (*act*) desagüe *m*; (*MED, AGR*) drenaje *m*; (*sewage*) alcantarillado; **~ing board** (*US* **~board**) *n* escurridera, escurridor *m*; **~pipe** *n* tubo de desagüe

drama ['drɑːmə] *n* (*art*) teatro; (*play*) drama *m*; (*excitement*) emoción *f*; **~tic** [drə'mætɪk] *adj* dramático; (*sudden, marked*) espectacular; **~tist** ['dræmətɪst] *n* dramaturgo/a; **~tize** ['dræmətaɪz] *vt* (*events*) dramatizar

drank [dræŋk] *pt of* **drink**

drape [dreɪp] *vt* (*cloth*) colocar; (*flag*) colgar; **~s** (*US*) *npl* cortinas *fpl*

drastic ['dræstɪk] *adj* (*measure*) severo; (*change*) radical, drástico

draught [drɑːft] (*US* **draft**) *n* (*of air*) corriente *f* de aire; (*NAUT*) calado; **on ~** (*beer*) de barril; **~ beer** *n* cerveza de barril; **~board** (*BRIT*) *n* tablero de damas; **~s** (*BRIT*) *n* (*game*) juego de damas

draughtsman ['drɑːftsmən] (*US* **draftsman**) (*irreg*) *n* delineante *m*

draw [drɔː] (*pt* **drew**, *pp* **drawn**) *vt* (*picture*) dibujar; (*cart*) tirar de; (*curtain*) correr; (*take out*) sacar; (*attract*) atraer; (*money*) retirar; (*wages*) cobrar ♦ *vi* (*SPORT*) empatar ♦ *n* (*SPORT*) empate *m*; (*lottery*) sorteo; **~ near** *vi* acercarse; **~ out** *vi* (*lengthen*) alargarse ♦ *vt* sacar; **~ up** *vi* (*stop*) pararse ♦ *vt* (*chair*) acercar; (*document*) redactar; **~back** *n* inconveniente *m*, desventaja; **~bridge** *n* puente *m* levadizo

drawer [drɔː*] *n* cajón *m*

drawing ['drɔːɪŋ] *n* dibujo; **~ board** *n* tablero (de dibujante); **~ pin** (*BRIT*) *n* chincheta; **~ room** *n* salón *m*

drawl [drɔːl] *n* habla lenta y cansina

drawn [drɔːn] *pp of* **draw**

dread [dred] *n* pavor *m*, terror *m* ♦ *vt* temer, tener miedo or pavor a; **~ful** *adj* horroroso

dream [driːm] (*pt, pp* **dreamed** or **dreamt**) *n* sueño ♦ *vt, vi* soñar; **~y** *adj* (*distracted*) soñador(a), distraído; (*music*) suave

dreary ['drɪərɪ] *adj* monótono

dredge [dredʒ] *vt* dragar

dregs [dregz] *npl* posos *mpl*; (*of humanity*) hez *f*

drench [drentʃ] *vt* empapar

dress [dres] *n* vestido; (*clothing*) ropa ♦ *vt* vestir; (*wound*) vendar ♦ *vi* vestirse; **to get ~ed** vestirse; **~ up** *vi* vestirse de etiqueta; (*in fancy dress*) disfrazarse; **~ circle** (*BRIT*) *n* principal *m*; **~er** *n* (*furniture*) aparador *m*; (: *US*) cómoda (con espejo); **~ing** *n* (*MED*) vendaje *m*; (*CULIN*) aliño; **~ing gown** (*BRIT*) *n* bata; **~ing room** *n* (*THEATRE*) camarín *m*;

(*SPORT*) vestuario; **~ing table** n tocador m; **~maker** n modista, costurera; **~ rehearsal** n ensayo general

drew [dru:] pt of **draw**

dribble ['drɪbl] vi (*baby*) babear ♦ vt (*ball*) regatear

dried [draɪd] adj (*fruit*) seco; (*milk*) en polvo

drier ['draɪə*] n = **dryer**

drift [drɪft] n (*of current etc*) flujo; (*of snow*) ventisquero; (*meaning*) significado ♦ vi (*boat*) ir a la deriva; (*sand, snow*) amontonarse; **~wood** n madera de deriva

drill [drɪl] n (*~ bit*) broca; (*tool for DIY etc*) taladro; (*of dentist*) fresa; (*for mining etc*) perforadora, barrena; (*MIL*) instrucción f ♦ vt perforar, taladrar; (*troops*) enseñar la instrucción a ♦ vi (*for oil*) perforar

drink [drɪŋk] (*pt* **drank**, *pp* **drunk**) n bebida; (*sip*) trago ♦ vt, vi beber; **to have a ~** tomar algo; tomar una copa *or* un trago; **a ~ of water** un trago de agua; **~er** n bebedor(a) m/f; **~ing water** n agua potable

drip [drɪp] n (*act*) goteo; (*one ~*) gota; (*MED*) gota a gota m ♦ vi gotear; **~-dry** adj (*shirt*) inarrugable; **~ping** n (*animal fat*) pringue m

drive [draɪv] (*pt* **drove**, *pp* **driven**) n (*journey*) viaje m (en coche); (*also*: **~way**) entrada; (*energy*) energía, vigor m; (*COMPUT: also*: **disk ~**) drive m ♦ vt (*car*) conducir (*SP*), manejar (*AM*); (*nail*) clavar; (*push*) empujar; (*TECH: motor*) impulsar ♦ vi (*AUT: at controls*) conducir; (*: travel*) pasearse en coche; **left-/right-hand ~** conducción f a la izquierda/derecha; **to ~ sb mad** volverle loco a uno

drivel ['drɪvl] (*inf*) n tonterías fpl

driven ['drɪvn] pp of **drive**

driver ['draɪvə*] n conductor(a) m/f (*SP*), chofer m (*AM*); (*of taxi, bus*) chofer; **~'s license** (*US*) n carnet m de conducir

driveway ['draɪvweɪ] n entrada

driving ['draɪvɪŋ] n el conducir (*SP*), el manejar (*AM*); **~ instructor** n

instructor(a) m/f de conducción *or* manejo; **~ lesson** n clase f de conducción *or* manejo; **~ licence** (*BRIT*) n permiso de conducir; **~ school** n autoescuela; **~ test** n examen m de conducción *or* manejo

drizzle ['drɪzl] n llovizna

drool [dru:l] vi babear

droop [dru:p] vi (*flower*) marchitarse; (*shoulders*) encorvarse; (*head*) inclinarse

drop [drɒp] n (*of water*) gota; (*lessening*) baja; (*fall*) caída ♦ vt dejar caer; (*voice, eyes, price*) bajar; (*passenger*) dejar; (*omit*) omitir ♦ vi (*object*) caer; (*wind*) amainar; **~s** npl (*MED*) gotas fpl; **~ off** vi (*sleep*) dormirse ♦ vt (*passenger*) dejar; **~ out** vi (*withdraw*) retirarse; **~out** n marginado/ a; (*SCOL*) estudiante que abandona los estudios; **~per** n cuentagotas m inv; **~pings** npl excremento

drought [draut] n sequía

drove [drəuv] pt of **drive**

drown [draun] vt ahogar ♦ vi ahogarse

drowsy ['drauzɪ] adj soñoliento; **to be ~** tener sueño

drug [drʌg] n medicamento; (*narcotic*) droga ♦ vt drogar; **to be on ~s** drogarse; **~ addict** n drogadicto/a; **~gist** (*US*) n farmacéutico; **~store** (*US*) n farmacia

drum [drʌm] n tambor m; (*for oil, petrol*) bidón m; **~s** npl batería; **~mer** n tambor m

drunk [drʌŋk] pp of **drink** ♦ adj borracho ♦ n (*also*: **~ard**) borracho/a; **~en** adj borracho; (*laughter, party*) de borrachos

dry [draɪ] adj seco; (*day*) sin lluvia; (*climate*) árido, seco ♦ vt secar; (*tears*) enjugarse ♦ vi secarse; **~ up** vi (*river*) secarse; **~ cleaner's** n tintorería; **~-cleaning** n lavado en seco; **~er** n (*for hair*) secador m; (*US: for clothes*) secadora; **~ rot** n putrefacción f fungoide

DSS n abbr = **Department of Social Security**

DTP n abbr (= *desk-top publishing*) autoedición f

dual ['djuəl] adj doble; **~ carriageway**

(*BRIT*) *n* carretera de doble calzada; **~-purpose** *adj* de doble uso
dubbed [dʌbd] *adj* (*CINEMA*) doblado
dubious ['djuːbɪəs] *adj* indeciso; (*reputation, company*) sospechoso
duchess ['dʌtʃɪs] *n* duquesa
duck [dʌk] *n* pato ♦ *vi* agacharse; **~ling** *n* patito
duct [dʌkt] *n* conducto, canal *m*
dud [dʌd] *n* (*object, tool*) engaño, engañifa ♦ *adj*: **~ cheque** (*BRIT*) cheque *m* sin fondos
due [djuː] *adj* (*owed*): **he is ~ £10** se le deben 10 libras; (*expected: event*): **the meeting is ~ on Wednesday** la reunión tendrá lugar el miércoles; (: *arrival*): **the train is ~ at 8am** el tren tiene su llegada para las 8; (*proper*) debido ♦ *n*: **to give sb his** (*or* **her**) **~** ser justo con alguien ♦ *adv*: **~ north** derecho al norte; **~s** *npl* (*for club, union*) cuota; (*in harbour*) derechos *mpl*; **in ~ course** a su debido tiempo; **~ to** debido a; **to be ~ to** deberse a
duet [djuː'et] *n* dúo
duffel bag ['dʌfəl] *n* bolsa de lona
duffel coat *n* trenca, abrigo de tres cuartos
dug [dʌg] *pt*, *pp of* **dig**
duke [djuːk] *n* duque *m*
dull [dʌl] *adj* (*light*) débil; (*stupid*) torpe; (*boring*) pesado; (*sound, pain*) sordo; (*weather, day*) gris ♦ *vt* (*pain, grief*) aliviar; (*mind, senses*) entorpecer
duly ['djuːlɪ] *adv* debidamente; (*on time*) a su debido tiempo
dumb [dʌm] *adj* mudo; (*pej: stupid*) estúpido; **~founded** [dʌm'faʊndɪd] *adj* pasmado
dummy ['dʌmɪ] *n* (*tailor's ~*) maniquí *m*; (*mock-up*) maqueta; (*BRIT: for baby*) chupete *m* ♦ *adj* falso, postizo
dump [dʌmp] *n* (*also*: **rubbish ~**) basurero, vertedero; (*inf: place*) cuchitril *m* ♦ *vt* (*put down*) dejar; (*get rid of*) deshacerse de; (*COMPUT: data*) transferir
dumpling ['dʌmplɪŋ] *n* bola de masa

hervida
dumpy ['dʌmpɪ] *adj* regordete/a
dunce [dʌns] *n* zopenco
dung [dʌŋ] *n* estiércol *m*
dungarees [dʌŋgə'riːz] *npl* mono
dungeon ['dʌndʒən] *n* calabozo
duplex ['djuːpleks] *n* dúplex *m*
duplicate [*n* 'djuːplɪkət, *vb* 'djuːplɪkeɪt] *n* duplicado ♦ *vt* duplicar; (*photocopy*) fotocopiar; (*repeat*) repetir; **in ~** por duplicado
durable ['djʊərəbl] *adj* duradero
duration [djʊə'reɪʃən] *n* duración *f*
during ['djʊərɪŋ] *prep* durante
dusk [dʌsk] *n* crepúsculo, anochecer *m*
dust [dʌst] *n* polvo ♦ *vt* quitar el polvo a, desempolvar; (*cake etc*): **to ~ with** espolvorear de; **~bin** (*BRIT*) *n* cubo de la basura (*SP*), balde *m* (*AM*); **~er** *n* paño, trapo; **~man** (*BRIT irreg*) *n* basurero; **~y** *adj* polvoriento
Dutch [dʌtʃ] *adj* holandés/esa ♦ *n* (*LING*) holandés *m*; **the ~** *npl* los holandeses; **to go ~** (*inf*) pagar cada uno lo suyo; **~man / woman** (*irreg*) *n* holandés/esa *m/f*
duty ['djuːtɪ] *n* deber *m*; (*tax*) derechos *mpl* de aduana; **on ~** de servicio; (*at night etc*) de guardia; **off ~** libre (de servicio); **~-free** *adj* libre de impuestos
duvet ['duːveɪ] (*BRIT*) *n* edredón *m*
dwarf [dwɔːf] (*pl* **dwarves**) *n* enano/a ♦ *vt* empequeñecer
dwell [dwel] (*pt*, *pp* **dwelt**) *vi* morar; **~ on** *vt fus* explayarse en
dwindle ['dwɪndl] *vi* menguar, disminuir
dye [daɪ] *n* tinte *m* ♦ *vt* teñir
dying ['daɪɪŋ] *adj* moribundo, agonizante
dyke [daɪk] (*BRIT*) *n* dique *m*
dynamic [daɪ'næmɪk] *adj* dinámico
dynamite ['daɪnəmaɪt] *n* dinamita
dynamo ['daɪnəməʊ] *n* dínamo *f*
dynasty ['dɪnəstɪ] *n* dinastía

E, e

E [iː] *n* (*MUS*) mi *m*

each [iːtʃ] *adj* cada *inv* ♦ *pron* cada uno;
~ **other** el uno al otro; **they hate ~ other**
se odian (entre ellos *or* mutuamente);
they have 2 books ~ tienen 2 libros por
persona

eager ['iːgəʳ] *adj* (*keen*) entusiasmado; **to
be ~ to do sth** tener muchas ganas de
hacer algo, impacientarse por hacer algo;
to be ~ for tener muchas ganas de

eagle ['iːgl] *n* águila

ear [ɪəʳ] *n* oreja; oído; (*of corn*) espiga;
~**ache** *n* dolor *m* de oídos; ~**drum** *n*
tímpano

earl [əːl] *n* conde *m*

earlier ['əːlɪəʳ] *adj* anterior ♦ *adv* antes

early ['əːlɪ] *adv* temprano; (*before time*)
con tiempo, con anticipación ♦ *adj*
temprano; (*settlers etc*) primitivo; (*death,
departure*) prematuro; (*reply*) pronto; **to
have an ~ night** acostarse temprano; **in
the ~** *or* **in the spring/19th century** a
principios de primavera/del siglo
diecinueve; ~ **retirement** *n* jubilación *f*
anticipada

earmark ['ɪəmɑːk] *vt*: **to ~ (for)** reservar
(para), destinar (a)

earn [əːn] *vt* (*salary*) percibir; (*interest*)
devengar; (*praise*) merecerse

earnest ['əːnɪst] *adj* (*wish*) fervoroso;
(*person*) serio, formal; **in ~** en serio

earnings ['əːnɪŋz] *npl* (*personal*) sueldo,
ingresos *mpl*; (*company*) ganancias *fpl*

ear: ~**phones** *npl* auriculares *mpl*; ~**ring**
n pendiente *m*, arete *m*; ~**shot** *n*: **within
~shot** al alcance del oído

earth [əːθ] *n* tierra; (*BRIT: ELEC*) cable *m* de
toma de tierra ♦ *vt* (*BRIT: ELEC*) conectar a
tierra; ~**enware** *n* loza (de barro);
~**quake** *n* terremoto; ~**y** *adj* (*fig: vulgar*)
grosero

ease [iːz] *n* facilidad *f*; (*comfort*)
comodidad *f* ♦ *vt* (*lessen: problem*)

mitigar; (: *pain*) aliviar; (: *tension*) reducir;
to ~ sth in/out meter/sacar algo con
cuidado; **at ~!** (*MIL*) ¡descansen!; ~ **off** *or*
up *vi* (*wind, rain*) amainar; (*slow down*)
aflojar la marcha

easel ['iːzl] *n* caballete *m*

easily ['iːzɪlɪ] *adv* fácilmente

east [iːst] *n* este *m* ♦ *adj* del este, oriental;
(*wind*) este ♦ *adv* al este, hacia el este;
the E~ el Oriente; (*POL*) los países del Este

Easter ['iːstəʳ] *n* Pascua (de Resurrección);
~ **egg** *n* huevo de Pascua

east: ~**erly** ['iːstəlɪ] *adj* (*to the east*) al
este; (*from the east*) del este; ~**ern**
['iːstən] *adj* del este, oriental; (*oriental*)
oriental; (*communist*) del este; ~**ward(s)**
['iːstwəd(z)] *adv* hacia el este

easy ['iːzɪ] *adj* fácil; (*simple*) sencillo;
(*comfortable*) holgado, cómodo; (*relaxed*)
tranquilo ♦ *adv*: **to take it** *or* **things ~**
(*not worry*) tomarlo con calma; (*rest*)
descansar; ~ **chair** *n* sillón *m*; ~**-going**
adj acomodadizo

eat [iːt] (*pt* **ate**, *pp* **eaten**) *vt* comer; ~
away *at vt fus* corroer; mermar; ~ **into**
vt fus corroer; (*savings*) mermar

eaves [iːvz] *npl* alero

eavesdrop ['iːvzdrɔp] *vi*: **to ~ (on)**
escuchar a escondidas

ebb [ɛb] *n* reflujo ♦ *vi* bajar; (*fig: also*: ~
away) decaer

ebony ['ɛbənɪ] *n* ébano

EC *n abbr* (= *European Community*) CE *f*

eccentric [ɪk'sɛntrɪk] *adj, n* excéntrico/a
m/f

echo ['ɛkəu] (*pl* ~**es**) *n* eco *m* ♦ *vt* (*sound*)
repetir ♦ *vi* resonar, hacer eco

éclair [ɪ'klɛəʳ] *n* pastelillo relleno de crema
y con chocolate por encima

eclipse [ɪ'klɪps] *n* eclipse *m*

ecology [ɪ'kɔlədʒɪ] *n* ecología

economic [iːkə'nɔmɪk] *adj* económico;
(*business etc*) rentable; ~**al** *adj*
económico; ~**s** *n* (*SCOL*) economía ♦ *npl*
(*of project etc*) rentabilidad *f*

economize [ɪ'kɔnəmaɪz] *vi* economizar,
ahorrar

economy [ɪ'kɔnəmɪ] n economía; ~ **class** n (AVIAT) clase f económica; ~ **size** n tamaño económico

ecstasy ['ekstəsɪ] n éxtasis m inv; (drug) éxtasis m inv; **ecstatic** [ɛks'tætɪk] adj extático

ECU ['eɪkjuː] n (= European Currency Unit) ECU m

Ecuador ['ekwədɔːr] n Ecuador m; ~**ian** adj, n ecuatoriano/a m/f

eczema ['eksɪmə] n eczema m

edge [edʒ] n (of knife etc) filo; (of object) borde m; (of lake etc) orilla ♦ vt (SEWING) ribetear; **on** ~ (fig) = **edgy**; **to** ~ **away from** alejarse poco a poco de; ~**ways** adv: **he couldn't get a word in** ~**ways** no pudo meter ni baza

edgy ['edʒɪ] adj nervioso, inquieto

edible ['edɪbl] adj comestible

Edinburgh ['edɪnbərə] n Edimburgo

edit ['edɪt] vt (be editor of) dirigir; (text, report) corregir, preparar; ~**ion** [ɪ'dɪʃən] n edición f; ~**or** n (of newspaper) director(a) m/f; (of column): **foreign / political** ~**or** encargado de la sección de extranjero/política; (of book) redactor(a) m/f; ~**orial** [-'tɔːrɪəl] adj editorial ♦ n editorial m

educate ['edjukeɪt] vt (gen) educar; (instruct) instruir

education [edju'keɪʃən] n educación f; (schooling) enseñanza; (SCOL) pedagogía; ~**al** adj (policy etc) educacional; (experience) docente; (toy) educativo

EEC n abbr (= European Economic Community) CEE f

eel [iːl] n anguila

eerie ['ɪərɪ] adj misterioso

effect [ɪ'fekt] n efecto ♦ vt efectuar, llevar a cabo; **to take** ~ (law) entrar en vigor or vigencia; (drug) surtir efecto; **in** ~ en realidad; ~**ive** adj eficaz; (actual) verdadero; ~**ively** adv eficazmente; (in reality) efectivamente; ~**iveness** n eficacia

effeminate [ɪ'femɪnɪt] adj afeminado

efficiency [ɪ'fɪʃənsɪ] n eficiencia; (of

rendimiento

efficient [ɪ'fɪʃənt] adj eficiente; (machine) de buen rendimiento

effort ['efət] n esfuerzo; ~**less** adj sin ningún esfuerzo; (style) natural

effusive [ɪ'fjuːsɪv] adj efusivo

e.g. adv abbr (= exempli gratia) p. ej.

egg [eg] n huevo; **hard-boiled / soft-boiled** ~ huevo duro/pasado por agua; ~ **on** vt incitar; ~**cup** n huevera; ~ **plant** (esp US) n berenjena; ~**shell** n cáscara de huevo

ego ['iːgəu] n ego; ~**tism** n egoísmo; ~**tist** n egoísta m/f

Egypt ['iːdʒɪpt] n Egipto; ~**ian** [ɪ'dʒɪpʃən] adj, n egipcio/a m/f

eiderdown ['aɪdədaun] n edredón m

eight [eɪt] num ocho; ~**een** num diez y ocho, dieciocho; **eighth** [eɪtθ] num octavo; ~**y** num ochenta

Eire ['ɛərə] n Eire m

either ['aɪðər] adj cualquiera de los dos; (both, each) cada ♦ pron: ~ **(of them)** cualquiera (de los dos) ♦ adv tampoco; **on** ~ **side** en ambos lados; **I don't like** ~ no me gusta ninguno/a de los/las dos; **no, I don't** ~ no, yo tampoco ♦ conj: ~ **yes or no** o sí o no

eject [ɪ'dʒekt] vt echar, expulsar; (tenant) desahuciar; ~**or seat** n asiento proyectable

elaborate [adj ɪ'læbərɪt, vb ɪ'læbəreɪt] adj (complex) complejo ♦ vt (expand) ampliar; (refine) refinar ♦ vi explicar con más detalles

elastic [ɪ'læstɪk] n elástico ♦ adj elástico; (fig) flexible; ~ **band** (BRIT) n gomita

elated [ɪ'leɪtɪd] adj: **to be** ~ regocijarse

elbow ['elbəu] n codo

elder ['eldər] adj mayor ♦ n (tree) saúco; (person) mayor; ~**ly** adj de edad, mayor ♦ npl: **the** ~**ly** los mayores

eldest ['eldɪst] adj, n el/la mayor

elect [ɪ'lekt] vt elegir ♦ adj: **the president** ~ el presidente electo; **to** ~ **to do** optar por hacer; ~**ion** [ɪ'lekʃən] n elección f; ~**ioneering** [ɪlekʃə'nɪərɪŋ] n campaña

electoral; **~or** n elector(a) m/f; **~oral** adj
electoral; **~orate** n electorado
electric [ɪ'lektrɪk] adj eléctrico; **~al** adj
eléctrico; **~ blanket** n manta eléctrica; **~
fire** n estufa eléctrica; **~ian** [ɪlek'trɪʃən] n
electricista m/f; **~ity** [ɪlek'trɪsɪtɪ] n
electricidad f; **electrify** [ɪ'lektrɪfaɪ] vt
(RAIL) electrificar; (fig: audience) electrizar
electronic [ɪlek'trɔnɪk] adj electrónico; **~
mail** n correo electrónico; **~s** n
electrónica
elegant ['elɪgənt] adj elegante
element ['elɪmənt] n elemento; (of kettle
etc) resistencia; **~ary** [-'mentərɪ] adj
elemental; (primitive) rudimentario;
(school) primario
elephant ['elɪfənt] n elefante m
elevation [elɪ'veɪʃən] n elevación f;
(height) altura
elevator ['elɪveɪtə*] n (US) ascensor m; (in
warehouse etc) montacargas m inv
eleven [ɪ'levn] num once; **~ses** (BRIT) npl
café m de las once; **~th** num undécimo
elicit [ɪ'lɪsɪt] vt: **to ~ (from)** sacar (de)
eligible ['elɪdʒəbl] adj: **an ~ young man/
woman** un buen partido; **to be ~ for sth**
llenar los requisitos para algo
elm [elm] n olmo
elongated ['iːlɔŋgeɪtɪd] adj alargado
elope [ɪ'ləup] vi fugarse (para casarse)
eloquent ['eləkwənt] adj elocuente
else [els] adv: **something ~** otra cosa;
somewhere ~ en otra parte; **everywhere
~** en todas partes menos aquí; **where ~?**
¿dónde más?, ¿en qué otra parte?; **there
was little ~ to do** apenas quedaba otra
cosa que hacer; **nobody ~ spoke** no
habló nadie más; **~where** adv (be) en
otra parte; (go) a otra parte
elude [ɪ'luːd] vt (subj: idea etc) escaparse a;
(capture) esquivar
elusive [ɪ'luːsɪv] adj esquivo; (quality)
difícil de encontrar
emaciated [ɪ'meɪsɪeɪtɪd] adj demacrado
E-mail, e-mail ['iːmeɪl] n abbr
(= electronic mail) correo electrónico, e-
mail m

emancipate [ɪ'mænsɪpeɪt] vt emancipar
embankment [ɪm'bæŋkmənt] n terraplén
m
embark [ɪm'bɑːk] vi embarcarse ♦ vt
embarcar; **to ~ on** (journey) emprender;
(course of action) lanzarse a; **~ation**
[embɑː'keɪʃən] n (people) embarco; (goods)
embarque m
embarrass [ɪm'bærəs] vt avergonzar;
(government etc) dejar en mal lugar; **~ed**
adj (laugh, silence) embarazoso; **~ing** adj
(situation) violento; (question)
embarazoso; **~ment** n (shame)
vergüenza; (problem): **to be an ~ment for
sb** poner en un aprieto a uno
embassy ['embəsɪ] n embajada
embedded [ɪm'bedɪd] adj (object)
empotrado; (thorn etc) clavado
embellish [ɪm'belɪʃ] vt embellecer; (story)
adornar
embers ['embəz] npl rescoldo, ascua
embezzle [ɪm'bezl] vt desfalcar, malversar
embitter [ɪm'bɪtə*] vt (fig: sour) amargar
embody [ɪm'bɔdɪ] vt (spirit) encarnar;
(include) incorporar
embossed [ɪm'bɔst] adj realzado
embrace [ɪm'breɪs] vt abrazar, dar un
abrazo a; (include) abarcar ♦ vi abrazarse
♦ n abrazo
embroider [ɪm'brɔɪdə*] vt bordar; **~y** n
bordado
embryo ['embrɪəu] n embrión m
emerald ['emərəld] n esmeralda
emerge [ɪ'məːdʒ] vi salir; (arise) surgir
emergency [ɪ'məːdʒənsɪ] n crisis f inv; **in
an ~** en caso de urgencia; **state of ~**
estado de emergencia; **~ cord** (US) n
timbre m de alarma; **~ exit** n salida de
emergencia; **~ landing** n aterrizaje m
forzoso; **~ services** npl (fire, police,
ambulance) servicios mpl de urgencia or
emergencia
emery board ['emərɪ-] n lima de uñas
emigrate ['emɪgreɪt] vi emigrar
emissions [ɪ'mɪʃənz] npl emisión f
emit [ɪ'mɪt] vt emitir; (smoke) arrojar;
(smell) despedir; (sound) producir

emotion [ɪ'məʊʃən] n emoción f; **~al** adj
(needs) emocional; (person) sentimental;
(scene) conmovedor(a), emocionante;
(speech) emocionado
emperor ['empərə*] n emperador m
emphasis ['emfəsɪs] (pl **-ses**) n énfasis m
inv
emphasize ['emfəsaɪz] vt (word, point)
subrayar, recalcar; (feature) hacer resaltar
emphatic [em'fætɪk] adj (reply) categórico;
(person) insistente
empire ['empaɪə*] n (also fig) imperio m
employ [ɪm'plɔɪ] vt emplear; **~ee** [-'iː] n
empleado/a; **~er** n patrón/ona m/f;
empresario; **~ment** n (work) trabajo;
~ment agency n agencia de
colocaciones
empower [ɪm'paʊə*] vt: **to ~ sb to do sth**
autorizar a uno para hacer algo
empress ['emprɪs] n emperatriz f
emptiness ['emptɪnɪs] n vacío m; (of life etc)
vaciedad f
empty ['emptɪ] adj vacío; (place) desierto;
(house) desocupado; (threat) vano ♦ vt
vaciar; (place) dejar vacío ♦ vi vaciarse;
(house etc) quedar desocupado; **~-
handed** adj con las manos vacías
EMU n abbr (= European Monetary Union)
UME f
emulate ['emjʊleɪt] vt emular
emulsion [ɪ'mʌlʃən] n emulsión f; (also: **~
paint**) pintura emulsión
enable [ɪ'neɪbl] vt: **to ~ sb to do sth**
permitir a uno hacer algo
enamel [ɪ'næməl] n esmalte m; (also: **~
paint**) pintura esmaltada
enchant [ɪn'tʃɑːnt] vt encantar; **~ing** adj
encantador(a)
encl. abbr (= enclosed) adj
enclose [ɪn'kləʊz] vt (land) cercar; (letter
etc) adjuntar; **please find ~d** le
mandamos adjunto
enclosure [ɪn'kləʊʒə*] n cercado, recinto
encompass [ɪn'kʌmpəs] vt abarcar
encore [ɔŋ'kɔː*] excl ¡otra!, ¡bis! ♦ n bis m
encounter [ɪn'kaʊntə*] n encuentro ♦ vt
encontrar, encontrarse con; (difficulty)

tropezar con
encourage [ɪn'kʌrɪdʒ] vt alentar, animar;
(activity) fomentar; (growth) estimular;
~ment n estímulo; (of industry) fomento
encroach [ɪn'krəʊtʃ] vi: **to ~ (up)on**
invadir; (rights) usurpar; (time) adueñarse
de
encyclop(a)edia [ensaɪkləʊ'piːdɪə] n
enciclopedia
end [end] n (gen, also aim) fin m; (of table)
extremo; (of street) final m; (SPORT) lado
♦ vt terminar, acabar; (also: **bring to an
~, put an ~ to**) acabar con ♦ vi terminar,
acabar; **in the ~** al fin; **on ~** (object) de
punta, de cabeza; **to stand on ~** (hair)
erizarse; **for hours on ~** hora tras hora; **~
up** vi: **to ~ up in** terminar en; (place) ir a
parar en
endanger [ɪn'deɪndʒə*] vt poner en
peligro; **an ~ed species** una especie en
peligro de extinción
endearing [ɪn'dɪərɪŋ] adj simpático,
atractivo
endeavour [ɪn'devə*] (US **endeavor**) n
esfuerzo; (attempt) tentativa ♦ vi: **to ~ to
do** esforzarse por hacer; (try) procurar
hacer
ending ['endɪŋ] n (of book) desenlace m;
(LING) terminación f
endive ['endaɪv] n (chicory) endibia; (curly)
escarola
endless ['endlɪs] adj interminable,
inacabable
endorse [ɪn'dɔːs] vt (cheque) endosar;
(approve) aprobar; **~ment** n (on driving
licence) nota de inhabilitación
endure [ɪn'djʊə*] vt (bear) aguantar,
soportar ♦ vi (last) durar
enemy ['enəmɪ] adj, n enemigo/a m/f
energetic [enə'dʒetɪk] adj enérgico
energy ['enədʒɪ] n energía
enforce [ɪn'fɔːs] vt (LAW) hacer cumplir
engage [ɪn'geɪdʒ] vt (attention) llamar;
(interest) ocupar; (in conversation)
abordar; (worker) contratar; (AUT): **to ~
the clutch** embragar ♦ vi (TECH)
engranar; **to ~ in** dedicarse a, ocuparse

en; **~d** *adj* (*BRIT: busy, in use*) ocupado; (*betrothed*) prometido; **to get ~d** prometerse; **~d tone** (*BRIT*) *n* (*TEL*) señal *f* de comunicando; **~ment** *n* (*appointment*) compromiso, cita; (*booking*) contratación *f*; (*to marry*) compromiso; (*period*) noviazgo; **~ment ring** *n* anillo de prometida

engaging [ɪnˈɡeɪdʒɪŋ] *adj* atractivo
engine [ˈendʒɪn] *n* (*AUT*) motor *m*; (*RAIL*) locomotora; **~ driver** *n* maquinista *m/f*
engineer [endʒɪˈnɪə*] *n* ingeniero; (*BRIT: for repairs*) mecánico; (*on ship, US: RAIL*) maquinista *m*; **~ing** *n* ingeniería
England [ˈɪŋɡlənd] *n* Inglaterra
English [ˈɪŋɡlɪʃ] *adj* inglés/esa ♦ *n* (*LING*) inglés *m*; **the ~** *npl* los ingleses *mpl*; **the ~ Channel** *n* (el Canal de) la Mancha; **~man/woman** (*irreg*) *n* inglés/esa *m/f*
engraving [ɪnˈɡreɪvɪŋ] *n* grabado
engrossed [ɪnˈɡrəʊst] *adj*: **~ in** absorto en
engulf [ɪnˈɡʌlf] *vt* (*subj: water*) sumergir, hundir; (: *fire*) prender; (: *fear*) apoderarse de
enhance [ɪnˈhɑːns] *vt* (*gen*) aumentar; (*beauty*) realzar
enjoy [ɪnˈdʒɔɪ] *vt* (*health, fortune*) disfrutar de, gozar de; (*like*) gustarle a uno; **to ~ o.s.** divertirse; **~able** *adj* agradable; (*amusing*) divertido; **~ment** *n* (*joy*) placer *m*; (*activity*) diversión *f*
enlarge [ɪnˈlɑːdʒ] *vt* aumentar; (*broaden*) extender; (*PHOT*) ampliar ♦ *vi*: **to ~ on** (*subject*) tratar con más detalles; **~ment** *n* (*PHOT*) ampliación *f*
enlighten [ɪnˈlaɪtn] *vt* (*inform*) informar; **~ed** *adj* comprensivo; **the E~ment** *n* (*HISTORY*) ≈ la Ilustración, ≈ el Siglo de las Luces
enlist [ɪnˈlɪst] *vt* alistar; (*support*) conseguir ♦ *vi* alistarse
enmity [ˈenmɪtɪ] *n* enemistad *f*
enormous [ɪˈnɔːməs] *adj* enorme
enough [ɪˈnʌf] *adj*: **~ time/books** bastante tiempo/bastantes libros ♦ *pron* bastante(s) ♦ *adv*: **big ~** bastante grande; **he has not worked ~** no ha trabajado

bastante; **have you got ~?** ¿tiene usted bastante(s)?; **~ to eat** (lo) suficiente or (lo) bastante para comer; **~!** ¡basta ya!; **that's ~, thanks** con eso basta, gracias; **I've had ~ of him** estoy harto de él; ... **which, funnily** or **oddly ~ ...** ... lo que, por extraño que parezca ...
enquire [ɪnˈkwaɪə*] *vt, vi* = **inquire**
enrage [ɪnˈreɪdʒ] *vt* enfurecer
enrol [ɪnˈrəʊl] (*US* **enroll**) *vt* (*members*) inscribir; (*SCOL*) matricular ♦ *vi* inscribirse; matricularse; **~ment** (*US* **enrollment**) *n* inscripción *f*; matriculación *f*
en route [ɒnˈruːt] *adv* durante el viaje
en suite [ɒnˈswiːt] *adj*: **with ~ bathroom** con baño
ensure [ɪnˈʃʊə*] *vt* asegurar
entail [ɪnˈteɪl] *vt* suponer
entangled [ɪnˈtæŋɡld] *adj*: **to become ~ (in)** quedarse enredado (en) or enmarañado (en)
enter [ˈentə*] *vt* (*room*) entrar en; (*club*) hacerse socio de; (*army*) alistarse en; (*sb for a competition*) inscribir; (*write down*) anotar, apuntar; (*COMPUT*) meter ♦ *vi* entrar; **~ for** *vt fus* presentarse para; **~ into** *vt fus* (*discussion etc*) entablar; (*agreement*) llegar a, firmar
enterprise [ˈentəpraɪz] *n* empresa; (*spirit*) iniciativa; **free ~** la libre empresa; **private ~** la iniciativa privada; **enterprising** *adj* emprendedor(a)
entertain [entəˈteɪn] *vt* (*amuse*) divertir; (*invite: guest*) invitar (a casa); (*idea*) abrigar; **~er** *n* artista *m/f*; **~ing** *adj* divertido, entretenido; **~ment** *n* (*amusement*) diversión *f*; (*show*) espectáculo
enthralled [ɪnˈθrɔːld] *adj* encantado
enthusiasm [ɪnˈθuːzɪæzəm] *n* entusiasmo
enthusiast [ɪnˈθuːzɪæst] *n* entusiasta *m/f*; **~ic** [-ˈæstɪk] *adj* entusiasta; **to be ~ic about** entusiasmarse por
entire [ɪnˈtaɪə*] *adj* entero; **~ly** *adv* totalmente; **~ty** [ɪnˈtaɪərətɪ] *n*: **in its ~ty** en su totalidad
entitle [ɪnˈtaɪtl] *vt*: **to ~ sb to sth** dar a

uno derecho a algo; **~d** *adj* (*book*)
titulado; **to be ~d to do** tener derecho a
hacer
entrance [*n* 'entrəns, *vb* ɪn'trɑːns] *n*
entrada ♦ *vt* encantar, hechizar; **to gain ~
to** (*university etc*) ingresar en; **~
examination** *n* examen *m* de ingreso;
~ fee *n* cuota; **~ ramp** (*US*) *n* (*AUT*)
rampa de acceso
entrant ['entrənt] *n* (*in race, competition*)
participante *m/f*; (*in examination*)
candidato/a
entrenched [ɛn'trɛntʃd] *adj* inamovible
entrepreneur [ɔntrəprə'nəː*] *n* empresario
entrust [ɪn'trʌst] *vt*: **to ~ sth to sb** confiar
algo a uno
entry ['entrɪ] *n* entrada; (*in competition*)
participación *f*; (*in register*) apunte *m*; (*in
account*) partida; (*in reference book*)
artículo; **"no ~"** "prohibido el paso";
(*AUT*) "dirección prohibida"; **~ form** *n*
hoja de inscripción; **~ phone** *n* portero
automático
envelop [ɪn'vɛləp] *vt* envolver
envelope ['ɛnvələup] *n* sobre *m*
envious ['ɛnvɪəs] *adj* envidioso; (*look*) de
envidia
environment [ɪn'vaɪərnmənt] *n*
(*surroundings*) entorno; (*natural world*):
the ~ el medio ambiente; **~al** [-'mɛntl]
adj ambiental; medioambiental; **~-
friendly** *adj* no perjudicial para el medio
ambiente
envisage [ɪn'vɪzɪdʒ] *vt* prever
envoy ['ɛnvɔɪ] *n* enviado
envy ['ɛnvɪ] *n* envidia ♦ *vt* tener envidia a;
to ~ sb sth envidiar algo a uno
epic ['ɛpɪk] *n* épica ♦ *adj* épico
epidemic [ɛpɪ'dɛmɪk] *n* epidemia
epilepsy ['ɛpɪlɛpsɪ] *n* epilepsia
episode ['ɛpɪsəud] *n* episodio
epitomize [ɪ'pɪtəmaɪz] *vt* epitomar,
resumir
equal ['iːkwl] *adj* igual; (*treatment*)
equitativo ♦ *n* igual *m/f* ♦ *vt* ser igual a;
(*fig*) igualar; **to be ~ to** (*task*) estar a la
altura de; **~ity** [iː'kwɔlɪtɪ] *n* igualdad *f*;

~ize *vi* (*SPORT*) empatar; **~ly** *adv*
igualmente; (*share etc*) a partes iguales
equate [ɪ'kweɪt] *vt*: **to ~ sth with**
equiparar algo con; **equation** [ɪ'kweɪʒən]
n (*MATH*) ecuación *f*
equator [ɪ'kweɪtə*] *n* ecuador *m*
equilibrium [iːkwɪ'lɪbrɪəm] *n* equilibrio
equip [ɪ'kwɪp] *vt* equipar; (*person*) proveer;
to be well ~ped estar bien equipado;
~ment *n* equipo; (*tools*) avíos *mpl*
equities ['ɛkwɪtɪz] (*BRIT*) *npl* (*COMM*)
derechos *mpl* sobre *or* en el activo
equivalent [ɪ'kwɪvələnt] *adj*: **~ (to)**
equivalente (a) ♦ *n* equivalente *m*
era ['ɪərə] *n* era, época
eradicate [ɪ'rædɪkeɪt] *vt* erradicar
erase [ɪ'reɪz] *vt* borrar; **~r** *n* goma de
borrar
erect [ɪ'rɛkt] *adj* erguido ♦ *vt* erigir,
levantar; (*assemble*) montar; **~ion** [-ʃən] *n*
construcción *f*; (*assembly*) montaje *m*;
(*PHYSIOL*) erección *f*
ERM *n abbr* (= *Exchange Rate Mechanism*)
tipo de cambio europeo
erode [ɪ'rəud] *vt* (*GEO*) erosionar; (*metal*)
corroer, desgastar; (*fig*) desgastar
erotic [ɪ'rɔtɪk] *adj* erótico
errand ['ɛrnd] *n* recado (*SP*), mandado
(*AM*)
erratic [ɪ'rætɪk] *adj* desigual, poco
uniforme
error ['ɛrə*] *n* error *m*, equivocación *f*
erupt [ɪ'rʌpt] *vi* entrar en erupción; (*fig*)
estallar; **~ion** [ɪ'rʌpʃən] *n* erupción *f*; (*of
war*) estallido
escalate ['ɛskəleɪt] *vi* extenderse,
intensificarse
escalator ['ɛskəleɪtə*] *n* escalera móvil
escapade [ɛskə'peɪd] *n* travesura
escape [ɪ'skeɪp] *n* fuga ♦ *vi* escaparse;
(*flee*) huir, evadirse; (*leak*) fugarse ♦ *vt*
(*responsibility etc*) evitar, eludir;
(*consequences*) escapar a; (*elude*): **his
name ~s me** no me sale su nombre; **to ~
from** (*place*) escaparse de; (*person*)
escaparse a
escort [*n* 'ɛskɔːt, *vb* ɪ'skɔːt] *n* acompañante

m/f; (MIL) escolta ♦ *vt* acompañar
Eskimo ['eskɪməu] *n* esquimal *m/f*
especially [ɪ'speʃlɪ] *adv* (*above all*) sobre
 todo; (*particularly*) en particular,
 especialmente
espionage ['espɪɒnɑːʒ] *n* espionaje *m*
esplanade [esplə'neɪd] *n* (*by sea*) paseo
 marítimo
Esquire [ɪ'skwaɪə] (*abbr* **Esq.**) *n*: **J.
 Brown, ~** Sr. D. J. Brown
essay ['eseɪ] *n* (LITERATURE) ensayo; (SCOL:
 short) redacción *f*; (: *long*) trabajo
essence ['esns] *n* esencia
essential [ɪ'senʃl] *adj* (*necessary*)
 imprescindible; (*basic*) esencial; **~s** *npl* lo
 imprescindible, lo esencial; **~ly** *adv*
 esencialmente
establish [ɪ'stæblɪʃ] *vt* establecer; (*prove*)
 demostrar; (*relations*) entablar;
 (*reputation*) ganarse; **~ed** *adj* (*business*)
 conocido; (*practice*) arraigado; **~ment** *n*
 establecimiento; **the E~ment** la clase
 dirigente
estate [ɪ'steɪt] *n* (*land*) finca, hacienda;
 (*inheritance*) herencia; (BRIT: *also*: **housing
 ~**) urbanización *f*; **~ agent** (BRIT) *n*
 agente *m/f* inmobiliario/a; **~ car** (BRIT) *n*
 furgoneta
esteem [ɪ'stiːm] *n*: **to hold sb in high ~**
 estimar en mucho a uno
esthetic [ɪs'θetɪk] (*US*) *adj* = **aesthetic**
estimate [*n* 'estɪmət, *vb* 'estɪmeɪt] *n*
 estimación *f*, apreciación *f*; (*assessment*)
 tasa, cálculo; (COMM) presupuesto ♦ *vt*
 estimar, tasar; calcular; **estimation**
 [-'meɪʃən] *n* opinión *f*, juicio; cálculo
estranged [ɪ'streɪndʒd] *adj* separado
estuary ['estjuərɪ] *n* estuario, ría
etc *abbr* (= *et cetera*) etc
eternal [ɪ'tɜːnl] *adj* eterno
eternity [ɪ'tɜːnɪtɪ] *n* eternidad *f*
ethical ['eθɪkl] *adj* ético; **ethics** ['eθɪks] *n*
 ética ♦ *npl* moralidad *f*
Ethiopia [iːθɪ'əupɪə] *n* Etiopía
ethnic ['eθnɪk] *adj* étnico; **~ minority** *n*
 minoría étnica
ethos ['iːθɒs] *n* genio, carácter *m*

etiquette ['etɪket] *n* etiqueta
EU *n abbr* (= *European Union*) UE *f*
euro ['juərəu] *n* euro
Eurocheque ['juərəutʃek] *n* Eurocheque
 m
Europe ['juərəp] *n* Europa; **~an** [-'piːən]
 adj, n europeo/a *m/f*; **~an Community**
 n Comunidad *f* Europea; **~an Union** *n*
 Unión *f* Europea
evacuate [ɪ'vækjueɪt] *vt* (*people*) evacuar;
 (*place*) desocupar
evade [ɪ'veɪd] *vt* evadir, eludir
evaporate [ɪ'væpəreɪt] *vi* evaporarse; (*fig*)
 desvanecerse; **~d milk** *n* leche *f*
 evaporada
evasion [ɪ'veɪʒən] *n* evasión *f*
eve [iːv] *n*: **on the ~ of** en vísperas de
even ['iːvn] *adj* (*level*) llano; (*smooth*) liso;
 (*speed, temperature*) uniforme; (*number*)
 par ♦ *adv* hasta, incluso; (*introducing a
 comparison*) aún, todavía; **~ if**, **~ though**
 aunque +*sub*; **~ more** aun más; **~ so** aun
 así; **not ~** ni siquiera; **~ he was there**
 hasta él estuvo allí; **~ on Sundays** incluso
 los domingos; **to get ~ with sb** ajustar
 cuentas con uno
evening ['iːvnɪŋ] *n* tarde *f*; (*late*) noche *f*;
 in the ~ por la tarde; **~ class** *n* clase *f*
 nocturna; **~ dress** *n* (*no pl: formal
 clothes*) traje *m* de etiqueta; (*woman's*)
 traje *m* de noche
event [ɪ'vent] *n* suceso, acontecimiento *m*;
 (SPORT) prueba; **in the ~ of** en caso
 de; **~ful** *adj* (*life*) activo; (*day*)
 ajetreado
eventual [ɪ'ventʃuəl] *adj* final; **~ity** [-'ælɪtɪ]
 n eventualidad *f*; **~ly** *adv* (*finally*)
 finalmente; (*in time*) con el tiempo
ever ['evə*] *adv* (*at any time*) nunca,
 jamás; (*at all times*) siempre; (*in question*):
 why ~ not? ¿y por qué no?; **the best ~**
 lo nunca visto; **have you ~ seen it?** ¿lo
 ha visto usted alguna vez?; **better than ~**
 mejor que nunca; **~ since** *adv* desde
 entonces ♦ *conj* después de que; **~green**
 n árbol *m* de hoja perenne; **~lasting** *adj*
 eterno, perpetuo

every ['ɛvrɪ] *adj* 1 (*each*) cada; ~ **one of them** (*persons*) todos ellos/as; (*objects*) cada uno de ellos/as; ~ **shop in the town was closed** todas las tiendas de la ciudad estaban cerradas
2 (*all possible*) todo/a; **I gave you ~ assistance** te di toda la ayuda posible; **I have ~ confidence in him** tiene toda mi confianza; **we wish you ~ success** te deseamos toda suerte de éxitos
3 (*showing recurrence*) todo/a; ~ **day/week** todos los días/todas las semanas; ~ **other car had been broken into** habían forzado uno de cada dos coches; **she visits me ~ other/third day** me visita cada dos/tres días; ~ **now and then** de vez en cuando

every: ~**body** *pron* = **everyone**; ~**day** *adj* (*daily*) cotidiano, de todos los días; (*usual*) acostumbrado; ~**one** *pron* todos/as, todo el mundo; ~**thing** *pron* todo; **this shop sells ~thing** esta tienda vende de todo; ~**where** *adv*: **I've been looking for you ~where** te he estado buscando por todas partes; ~**where you go you meet ...** en todas partes encuentras ...

evict [ɪ'vɪkt] *vt* desahuciar; ~**ion** [ɪ'vɪkʃən] *n* desahucio

evidence ['ɛvɪdəns] *n* (*proof*) prueba; (*of witness*) testimonio; (*sign*) indicios *mpl*; **to give ~** prestar declaración, dar testimonio

evident ['ɛvɪdənt] *adj* evidente, manifiesto; ~**ly** *adv* por lo visto

evil ['iːvl] *adj* malo; (*influence*) funesto ♦ *n* mal *m*

evoke [ɪ'vəuk] *vt* evocar

evolution [iːvə'luːʃən] *n* evolución *f*

evolve [ɪ'vɒlv] *vt* desarrollar ♦ *vi* evolucionar, desarrollarse

ewe [juː] *n* oveja

ex- [ɛks] *prefix* ex

exact [ɪg'zækt] *adj* exacto; (*person*) meticuloso ♦ *vt*: **to ~ sth (from)** exigir algo (de); ~**ing** *adj* exigente; (*conditions*) arduo; ~**ly** *adv* exactamente; (*indicating agreement*) exacto

exaggerate [ɪg'zædʒəreɪt] *vt, vi* exagerar; **exaggeration** [-'reɪʃən] *n* exageración *f*

exalted [ɪg'zɔːltɪd] *adj* eminente

exam [ɪg'zæm] *n abbr* (*SCOL*) = **examination**

examination [ɪgzæmɪ'neɪʃən] *n* examen *m*; (*MED*) reconocimiento

examine [ɪg'zæmɪn] *vt* examinar; (*inspect*) inspeccionar, escudriñar; (*MED*) reconocer; ~**r** *n* examinador(a) *m/f*

example [ɪg'zɑːmpl] *n* ejemplo; **for ~** por ejemplo

exasperate [ɪg'zɑːspəreɪt] *vt* exasperar, irritar; **exasperation** [-'ʃən] *n* exasperación *f*, irritación *f*

excavate ['ɛkskəveɪt] *vt* excavar

exceed [ɪk'siːd] *vt* (*amount*) exceder; (*number*) pasar de; (*speed limit*) sobrepasar; (*powers*) excederse en; (*hopes*) superar; ~**ingly** *adv* sumamente, sobremanera

excellent ['ɛksələnt] *adj* excelente

except [ɪk'sɛpt] *prep* (*also*: ~ **for**, ~**ing**) excepto, salvo ♦ *vt* exceptuar, excluir; ~ **if/when** excepto si/cuando; ~ **that** salvo que; ~**ion** [ɪk'sɛpʃən] *n* excepción *f*; **to take ~ion to** ofenderse por; ~**ional** [ɪk'sɛpʃənl] *adj* excepcional

excerpt ['ɛksəːpt] *n* extracto

excess [ɪk'sɛs] *n* exceso; ~**es** *npl* (*of cruelty etc*) atrocidades *fpl*; ~ **baggage** *n* exceso de equipaje; ~ **fare** *n* suplemento; ~**ive** *adj* excesivo

exchange [ɪks'tʃeɪndʒ] *n* intercambio; (*conversation*) diálogo; (*also*: **telephone ~**) central *f* (telefónica) ♦ *vt*: **to ~ (for)** cambiar (por); ~ **rate** *n* tipo de cambio

exchequer [ɪks'tʃɛkə*] (*BRIT*) *n*: **the E~** la Hacienda del Fisco

excise ['ɛksaɪz] *n* impuestos *mpl* sobre el alcohol y el tabaco

excite [ɪk'saɪt] *vt* (*stimulate*) estimular; (*arouse*) excitar; ~**d** *adj*: **to get ~d** emocionarse; ~**ment** *n* (*agitation*)

excitación *f*; (*exhilaration*) emoción *f*;
exciting *adj* emocionante
exclaim [ɪkˈskleɪm] *vi* exclamar;
exclamation [ɛkskləˈmeɪʃən] *n*
exclamación *f*; **exclamation mark** *n*
punto de admiración
exclude [ɪkˈskluːd] *vt* excluir; exceptuar
exclusive [ɪkˈskluːsɪv] *adj* exclusivo; (*club,
district*) selecto; **~ of tax** excluyendo
impuestos; **~ly** *adv* únicamente
excruciating [ɪkˈskruːʃɪeɪtɪŋ] *adj* (*pain*)
agudísimo, atroz; (*noise, embarrassment*)
horrible
excursion [ɪkˈskəːʃən] *n* (*tourist ~*)
excursión *f*
excuse [*n* ɪkˈskjuːs, *vb* ɪkˈskjuːz] *n* disculpa,
excusa; (*pretext*) pretexto ♦ *vt* (*justify*)
justificar; (*forgive*) disculpar, perdonar; **to
~ sb from doing sth** dispensar a uno de
hacer algo; **~ me!** (*attracting attention*)
¡por favor!; (*apologizing*) ¡perdón!; **if you
will ~ me** con su permiso
ex-directory [ˈɛksdɪˈrɛktərɪ] (*BRIT*) *adj* que
no consta en la guía
execute [ˈɛksɪkjuːt] *vt* (*plan*) realizar;
(*order*) cumplir; (*person*) ajusticiar,
ejecutar; **execution** [-ˈkjuːʃən] *n*
realización *f*; cumplimiento; ejecución *f*
executive [ɪɡˈzɛkjutɪv] *n* (*person,
committee*) ejecutivo; (*POL: committee*)
poder *m* ejecutivo ♦ *adj* ejecutivo
exemplify [ɪɡˈzɛmplɪfaɪ] *vt* ejemplificar;
(*illustrate*) ilustrar
exempt [ɪɡˈzɛmpt] *adj*: **~ from** exento de
♦ *vt*: **to ~ sb from** eximir a uno de; **~ion**
[-ʃən] *n* exención *f*
exercise [ˈɛksəsaɪz] *n* ejercicio ♦ *vt*
(*patience*) usar de; (*right*) valerse de; (*dog*)
llevar de paseo; (*mind*) preocupar ♦ *vi*
(*also: to take ~*) hacer ejercicio(s); **~ bike**
n ciclostátic ℝ *m*, bicicleta estática; **~
book** *n* cuaderno
exert [ɪɡˈzəːt] *vt* ejercer; **to ~ o.s.**
esforzarse; **~ion** [-ʃən] *n* esfuerzo
exhale [ɛksˈheɪl] *vt* despedir ♦ *vi* exhalar
exhaust [ɪɡˈzɔːst] *n* (*AUT: also:* **~ pipe**)
escape *m*; (: *fumes*) gases *mpl* de escape

♦ *vt* agotar; **~ed** *adj* agotado; **~ion**
[ɪɡˈzɔːstʃən] *n* agotamiento; **nervous ~ion**
postración *f* nerviosa; **~ive** *adj*
exhaustivo
exhibit [ɪɡˈzɪbɪt] *n* (*ART*) obra expuesta;
(*LAW*) objeto expuesto ♦ *vt* (*show:
emotions*) manifestar; (: *courage, skill*)
demostrar; (*paintings*) exponer; **~ion**
[ɛksɪˈbɪʃən] *n* exposición *f*; (*of talent etc*)
demostración *f*
exhilarating [ɪɡˈzɪləreɪtɪŋ] *adj* estimulante,
tónico
exile [ˈɛksaɪl] *n* exilio; (*person*) exiliado/a
♦ *vt* desterrar, exiliar
exist [ɪɡˈzɪst] *vi* existir; (*live*) vivir; **~ence** *n*
existencia; **~ing** *adj* existente, actual
exit [ˈɛksɪt] *n* salida ♦ *vi* (*THEATRE*) hacer
mutis; (*COMPUT*) salir (al sistema); **~ poll**
n encuesta a la salida de los colegios
electorales; **~ ramp** (*US*) *n* (*AUT*) vía de
acceso
exodus [ˈɛksədəs] *n* éxodo
exonerate [ɪɡˈzɔnəreɪt] *vt*: **to ~ from**
exculpar de
exotic [ɪɡˈzɔtɪk] *adj* exótico
expand [ɪkˈspænd] *vt* ampliar; (*number*)
aumentar ♦ *vi* (*population*) aumentar;
(*trade etc*) expandirse; (*gas, metal*)
dilatarse
expanse [ɪkˈspæns] *n* extensión *f*
expansion [ɪkˈspænʃən] *n* (*of population*)
aumento; (*of trade*) expansión *f*
expect [ɪkˈspɛkt] *vt* esperar; (*require*)
contar con; (*suppose*) suponer ♦ *vi*: **to be
~ing** (*pregnant woman*) estar embarazada;
~ancy (*anticipation*) esperanza; **life
~ancy** esperanza de vida; **~ant mother**
n futura madre *f*; **~ation** [ɛkspɛkˈteɪʃən] *n*
(*hope*) esperanza; (*belief*) expectativa
expedient [ɪkˈspiːdɪənt] *adj* conveniente,
oportuno ♦ *n* recurso, expediente *m*
expedition [ɛkspəˈdɪʃən] *n* expedición *f*
expel [ɪkˈspɛl] *vt* arrojar; (*from place*)
expulsar
expend [ɪkˈspɛnd] *vt* (*money*) gastar; (*time,
energy*) consumir; **~iture** *n* gastos *mpl*,
desembolso; consumo

expense [ɪk'spens] n gasto, gastos mpl; (high cost) costa; **~s** npl (COMM) gastos mpl; **at the ~ of** a costa de; **~ account** n cuenta de gastos

expensive [ɪk'spensɪv] adj caro, costoso

experience [ɪk'spɪərɪəns] n experiencia ♦ vt experimentar; (suffer) sufrir; **~d** adj experimentado

experiment [ɪk'sperɪmənt] n experimento ♦ vi hacer experimentos

expert ['ekspə:t] adj experto, perito ♦ n experto/a, perito/a; (specialist) especialista m/f; **~ise** [-'ti:z] n pericia

expire [ɪk'spaɪə*] vi caducar, vencer; **expiry** n vencimiento

explain [ɪk'spleɪn] vt explicar; **explanation** [eksplə'neɪʃən] n explicación f; **explanatory** [ɪk'splænətrɪ] adj explicativo; aclaratorio

explicit [ɪk'splɪsɪt] adj explícito

explode [ɪk'spləud] vi estallar, explotar; (population) crecer rápidamente; (with anger) reventar

exploit [n 'eksplɔɪt, vb ɪk'splɔɪt] n hazaña ♦ vt explotar; **~ation** [-'teɪʃən] n explotación f

exploratory [ɪk'splɔrətrɪ] adj de exploración; (fig: talks) exploratorio, preliminar

explore [ɪk'splɔ:*] vt explorar; (fig) examinar; investigar; **~r** n explorador(a) m/f

explosion [ɪk'spləuʒən] n (also fig) explosión f; **explosive** [ɪks'pləusɪv] adj, n explosivo

exponent [ɪk'spəunənt] n (of theory etc) partidario/a; (of skill etc) exponente m/f

export [vb ek'spɔ:t, n 'ekspɔ:t] vt exportar ♦ n (process) exportación f; (product) producto de exportación ♦ cpd de exportación; **~er** n exportador m

expose [ɪk'spəuz] vt exponer; (unmask) desenmascarar; **~d** adj expuesto

exposure [ɪk'spəuʒə*] n exposición f; (publicity) publicidad f; (PHOT: speed) velocidad f de obturación; (: shot) fotografía f; **to die from ~** (MED) morir de

frío; **~ meter** n fotómetro

express [ɪk'spres] adj (definite) expreso, explícito; (BRIT: letter etc) urgente ♦ n (train) rápido ♦ vt expresar; **~ion** [ɪk'spreʃən] n expresión f; (of actor etc) sentimiento; **~ly** adv expresamente; **~way** (US) n (urban motorway) autopista

exquisite [ek'skwɪzɪt] adj exquisito

extend [ɪk'stend] vt (visit, street) prolongar; (building) ampliar; (invitation) ofrecer ♦ vi (land) extenderse; (period of time) prolongarse

extension [ɪk'stenʃən] n extensión f; (building) ampliación f; (of time) prolongación f; (TEL: in private house) línea derivada; (: in office) extensión f

extensive [ɪk'stensɪv] adj extenso; (damage) importante; (knowledge) amplio; **~ly** adv: **he's travelled ~ly** ha viajado por muchos países

extent [ɪk'stent] n (breadth) extensión f; (scope) alcance m; **to some ~** hasta cierto punto; **to the ~ of...** hasta el punto de...; **to such an ~ that...** hasta tal punto que...; **to what ~?** ¿hasta qué punto?

extenuating [ɪk'stenjueɪtɪŋ] adj: **~ circumstances** circunstancias fpl atenuantes

exterior [ek'stɪərɪə*] adj exterior, externo ♦ n exterior m

external [ek'stə:nl] adj externo

extinct [ɪk'stɪŋkt] adj (volcano) extinguido; (race) extinto

extinguish [ɪk'stɪŋgwɪʃ] vt extinguir, apagar; **~er** n extintor m

extort [ɪk'stɔ:t] vt obtener por fuerza; **~ionate** adj excesivo, exorbitante

extra ['ekstrə] adj adicional ♦ adv (in addition) de más ♦ n (luxury, addition) extra m; (CINEMA, THEATRE) extra m/f, comparsa m/f

extra... ['ekstrə] prefix extra...

extract [vb ɪk'strækt, n 'ekstrækt] vt sacar; (tooth) extraer; (money, promise) obtener ♦ n extracto

extracurricular [ekstrəkə'rɪkjulə*] adj extraescolar, extra-académico

extradite ['ɛkstrədaɪt] *vt* extraditar
extra: ~**marital** *adj* extramatrimonial;
~**mural** [ɛkstrə'mjuərl] *adj* extraescolar;
~**ordinary** [ɪk'strɔːdnrɪ] *adj*
extraordinario; *(odd)* raro
extravagance [ɪk'strævəgəns] *n* derroche
m, despilfarro; *(thing bought)*
extravagancia
extravagant [ɪk'strævəgənt] *adj (lavish:
person)* pródigo; *(: gift)* (demasiado) caro;
(wasteful) despilfarrador(a)
extreme [ɪk'striːm] *adj* extremo,
extremado ♦ *n* extremo; ~**ly** *adv*
sumamente, extremadamente
extricate ['ɛkstrɪkeɪt] *vt:* **to ~ sth/sb from**
librar algo/a uno de
extrovert ['ɛkstrəvəːt] *n* extrovertido/a
eye [aɪ] *n* ojo ♦ *vt* mirar de soslayo, ojear;
to keep an ~ on vigilar; ~**bath** *n* ojera;
~**brow** *n* ceja; ~**drops** *npl* gotas *fpl*
para los ojos, colino; ~**lash** *n* pestaña;
~**lid** *n* párpado; ~**liner** *n* lápiz *m* de
ojos; ~-**opener** *n* revelación *f*, gran
sorpresa; ~**shadow** *n* sombreador *m* de
ojos; ~**sight** *n* vista; ~**sore** *n*
monstruosidad *f;* ~ **witness** *n* testigo
m/f presencial

F, f

F [ɛf] *n (MUS)* fa *m*
F. *abbr* = **Fahrenheit**
fable ['feɪbl] *n* fábula
fabric ['fæbrɪk] *n* tejido, tela
fabulous ['fæbjuləs] *adj* fabuloso
façade [fə'sɑːd] *n* fachada
face [feɪs] *n (ANAT)* cara, rostro; *(of clock)*
esfera *(SP)*, cara *(AM)*; *(of mountain)*
ladera; *(of building)* fachada ♦ *vt*
(direction) estar de cara a; *(situation)* hacer
frente a; *(facts)* aceptar; ~ **down** *(person,
card)* boca abajo; **to lose** or **pull a ~** hacer
muecas; **in the ~ of** *(difficulties etc)* ante;
on the ~ of it a primera vista; ~ **to ~** cara
a cara; ~ **up to** *vt fus* hacer frente a,

arrostrar; ~ **cloth** *(BRIT) n* manopla; ~
cream *n* crema (de belleza); ~ **lift** *n*
estirado facial; *(of building)* renovación *f;*
~ **powder** *n* polvos *mpl;* ~-**saving** *adj*
para salvar las apariencias; ~ **value** *n (of
stamp)* valor *m* nominal; **to take sth at ~
value** *(fig)* tomar algo en sentido literal
facilities [fə'sɪlɪtɪz] *npl (buildings)*
instalaciones *fpl; (equipment)* servicios
mpl; **credit ~** facilidades *fpl* de crédito
facing ['feɪsɪŋ] *prep* frente a
facsimile [fæk'sɪmɪlɪ] *n (replica)* facsímil(e)
m; (machine) telefax *m; (fax)* fax *m*
fact [fækt] *n* hecho; **in ~** en realidad
factor ['fæktə*] *n* factor *m*
factory ['fæktərɪ] *n* fábrica
factual ['fæktjuəl] *adj* basado en los
hechos
faculty ['fækəltɪ] *n* facultad *f; (US: teaching
staff)* personal *m* docente
fad [fæd] *n* novedad *f*, moda
fade [feɪd] *vi* desteñirse; *(sound, smile)*
desvanecerse; *(light)* apagarse; *(flower)*
marchitarse; *(hope, memory)* perderse
fag [fæg] *(BRIT: inf) n (cigarette)* pitillo *(SP)*,
cigarro
fail [feɪl] *vt (candidate)* suspender; *(exam)*
no aprobar *(SP)*, reprobar *(AM); (subj:
memory etc)* fallar a ♦ *vi* suspender; *(be
unsuccessful)* fracasar; *(strength, brakes)*
fallar; *(light)* acabarse; **to ~ to do sth**
(neglect) dejar de hacer algo; *(be unable)*
no poder hacer algo; **without ~** sin falta;
~**ing** *n* falta, defecto ♦ *prep* a falta de;
~**ure** ['feɪljə*] *n* fracaso; *(person)*
fracasado/a; *(mechanical etc)* fallo
faint [feɪnt] *adj* débil; *(recollection)* vago;
(mark) apenas visible ♦ *n* desmayo ♦ *vi*
desmayarse; **to feel ~** estar mareado,
marearse
fair [fɛə*] *adj* justo; *(hair, person)* rubio;
(weather) bueno; *(good enough)* regular;
(considerable) considerable ♦ *adv (play)*
limpio ♦ *n* feria; *(BRIT: funfair)* parque *m*
de atracciones; ~**ly** *adv (justly)* con
justicia; *(quite)* bastante; ~**ness** *n* justicia,
imparcialidad *f;* ~ **play** *n* juego limpio

fairy ['feərɪ] n hada; ~ tale n cuento de hadas

faith [feɪθ] n fe f; (trust) confianza; (sect) religión f; ~ful adj (loyal: troops etc) leal; (spouse) fiel; (account) exacto; ~fully adv fielmente; yours ~fully (BRIT: in letters) le saluda atentamente

fake [feɪk] n (painting etc) falsificación f; (person) impostor(a) m/f ♦ adj falso ♦ vt fingir; (painting etc) falsificar

falcon ['fɔːlkən] n halcón m

fall [fɔːl] (pt fell, pp fallen) n caída; (in price etc) descenso; (US) otoño ♦ vi caer(se); (price) bajar, descender; ~s npl (water~) cascada, salto de agua; to ~ flat (on one's face) caerse (boca abajo); (plan) fracasar; (joke, story) no hacer gracia; ~ back vi retroceder; ~ back on vt fus (remedy etc) recurrir a; ~ behind vi quedarse atrás; ~ down vi (person) caerse; (building, hopes) derrumbarse; ~ for vt fus (trick) dejarse engañar por; (person) enamorarse de; ~ in vi (roof) hundirse; (MIL) alinearse; ~ off vi caerse; (diminish) disminuir; ~ out vi (friends etc) reñir; (hair, teeth) caerse; ~ through vi (plan, project) fracasar

fallacy ['fæləsɪ] n error m

fallen ['fɔːlən] pp of fall

fallout ['fɔːlaut] n lluvia radioactiva

fallow ['fæləu] adj en barbecho

false [fɔːls] adj falso; under ~ pretences con engaños; ~ alarm n falsa alarma; ~ teeth (BRIT) npl dentadura postiza

falter ['fɔːltə*] vi vacilar; (engine) fallar

fame [feɪm] n fama

familiar [fə'mɪlɪə*] adj conocido, familiar; (tone) de confianza; to be ~ with (subject) conocer (bien)

family ['fæmɪlɪ] n familia; ~ business n negocio familiar; ~ doctor n médico/a de cabecera

famine ['fæmɪn] n hambre f, hambruna

famished ['fæmɪʃt] adj hambriento

famous ['feɪməs] adj famoso, célebre; ~ly adv (get on) estupendamente

fan [fæn] n abanico; (ELEC) ventilador m; (of pop star) fan m/f; (SPORT) hincha m/f ♦ vt abanicar; (fire, quarrel) atizar

fanatic [fə'nætɪk] n fanático/a

fan belt n correa del ventilador

fanciful ['fænsɪful] adj (design, name) fantástico

fancy ['fænsɪ] n (whim) capricho, antojo; (imagination) imaginación f ♦ adj (luxury) lujoso, de lujo ♦ vt (feel like, want) tener ganas de; (imagine) imaginarse; (think) creer; to take a ~ to sb tomar cariño a uno; he fancies her (inf) le gusta (ella) mucho; ~ dress n disfraz m; ~-dress ball n baile m de disfraces

fanfare ['fænfeə*] n fanfarria (de trompeta)

fang [fæŋ] n colmillo

fantastic [fæn'tæstɪk] adj (enormous) enorme; (strange, wonderful) fantástico

fantasy ['fæntəzɪ] n (dream) sueño; (unreality) fantasía

far [fɑː*] adj (distant) lejano ♦ adv lejos; (much, greatly) mucho; ~ away, ~ off (a lo) lejos; ~ better mucho mejor; ~ from lejos de; by ~ con mucho; go as ~ as the farm vaya hasta la granja; as ~ as I know que yo sepa; how ~? ¿hasta dónde?; (fig) ¿hasta qué punto?; ~away adj remoto; (look) distraído

farce [fɑːs] n farsa

fare [feə*] n (on trains, buses) precio (del billete); (in taxi: cost) tarifa; (food) comida; half ~ medio pasaje m; full ~ pasaje completo

Far East n: the ~ el Extremo Oriente

farewell [feə'wel] excl, n adiós m

farm [fɑːm] n granja (SP), finca (AM), estancia (AM) ♦ vt cultivar; ~er n granjero (SP), estanciero (AM); ~hand n peón m; ~house n granja, casa de hacienda (AM); ~ing n agricultura; (of crops) cultivo; (of animals) cría; ~land n tierra de cultivo; ~ worker n = ~hand; ~yard n corral m

far-reaching [fɑː'riːtʃɪŋ] adj (reform, effect) de gran alcance

fart [fɑːt] (inf!) vi tirarse un pedo (!)

farther ['fɑːðə*] adv más lejos, más allá

♦ *adj* más lejano

farthest ['fɑːðɪst] *superlative of* **far**

fascinate ['fæsɪneɪt] *vt* fascinar;
  fascination [-'neɪʃən] *n* fascinación *f*

fascism ['fæʃɪzəm] *n* fascismo

fashion ['fæʃən] *n* moda; (~ *industry*)
  industria de la moda; (*manner*) manera
  ♦ *vt* formar; **in ~** a la moda; **out of ~**
  pasado de moda; **~able** *adj* de moda; **~
  show** *n* desfile *m* de modelos

fast [fɑːst] *adj* rápido; (*dye, colour*)
  resistente; (*clock*): **to be ~** estar
  adelantado ♦ *adv* rápidamente, de prisa;
  (*stuck, held*) firmemente ♦ *n* ayuno ♦ *vi*
  ayunar; **~ asleep** profundamente
  dormido

fasten ['fɑːsn] *vt* atar, sujetar; (*coat, belt*)
  abrochar ♦ *vi* atarse; abrocharse; **~er,
  ~ing** *n* cierre *m*; (*of door etc*) cerrojo

fast food *n* comida rápida, platos *mpl*
  preparados

fastidious [fæs'tɪdɪəs] *adj* (*fussy*)
  quisquilloso

fat [fæt] *adj* gordo; (*book*) grueso; (*profit*)
  grande, pingüe ♦ *n* grasa; (*on person*)
  carnes *fpl*; (*lard*) manteca

fatal ['feɪtl] *adj* (*mistake*) fatal; (*injury*)
  mortal; **~ity** [fə'tælɪtɪ] *n* (*road death etc*)
  víctima; **~ly** *adv* fatalmente; mortalmente

fate [feɪt] *n* destino; (*of person*) suerte *f*;
  ~ful *adj* fatídico

father ['fɑːðə*] *n* padre *m*; **~-in-law** *n*
  suegro; **~ly** *adj* paternal

fathom ['fæðəm] *n* braza ♦ *vt* (*mystery*)
  desentrañar; (*understand*) lograr
  comprender

fatigue [fə'tiːg] *n* fatiga, cansancio

fatten ['fætn] *vt, vi* engordar

fatty ['fætɪ] *adj* (*food*) graso ♦ *n* (*inf*)
  gordito/a, gordinflón/ona *m/f*

fatuous ['fætjuəs] *adj* fatuo, necio

faucet ['fɔːsɪt] (*US*) *n* grifo (*SP*), llave *f* (*AM*)

fault [fɔːlt] *n* (*in blame*) culpa; (*defect: in
  person, machine*) defecto; (*GEO*) falla ♦ *vt*
  criticar; **it's my ~** es culpa mía; **to find ~
  with** criticar, poner peros a; **at ~** culpable;
  ~y *adj* defectuoso

fauna ['fɔːnə] *n* fauna

favour ['feɪvə*] (*US* **favor**) *n* favor *m*;
  (*approval*) aprobación *f* ♦ *vt* (*proposition*)
  estar a favor de, aprobar; (*assist*) ser
  propicio a; **to do sb a ~** hacer un favor a
  uno; **to find ~ with sb** caer en gracia a
  uno; **in ~ of** a favor de; **~able** *adj*
  favorable; **~ite** ['feɪvrɪt] *adj, n* favorito,
  preferido

fawn [fɔːn] *n* cervato ♦ *adj* (*also*: **~-
  coloured**) color de cervato, leonado ♦ *vi*:
  to ~ (up)on adular

fax [fæks] *n* (*document*) fax *m*; (*machine*)
  telefax *m* ♦ *vt* mandar por telefax

FBI (*US*) *n abbr* (= *Federal Bureau of
  Investigation*) ≈ BIC *f* (*SP*)

fear [fɪə*] *n* miedo, temor *m* ♦ *vt* tener
  miedo de, temer; **for ~ of** por si; **~ful** *adj*
  temeroso, miedoso; (*awful*) terrible;
  ~less *adj* audaz

feasible ['fiːzəbl] *adj* factible

feast [fiːst] *n* banquete *m*; (*REL: also*: **~
  day**) fiesta ♦ *vi* festejar

feat [fiːt] *n* hazaña

feather ['feðə*] *n* pluma

feature ['fiːtʃə*] *n* característica; (*article*)
  artículo de fondo ♦ *vt* (*subj: film*)
  presentar ♦ *vi*: **to ~ in** tener un papel
  destacado en; **~s** *npl* (*of face*) facciones
  fpl; **~ film** *n* largometraje *m*

February ['februərɪ] *n* febrero

fed [fed] *pt, pp of* **feed**

federal ['fedərəl] *adj* federal

fed up [fed'ʌp] *adj*: **to be ~ (with)** estar
  harto (de)

fee [fiː] *n* pago; (*professional*) derechos
  mpl, honorarios *mpl*; (*of club*) cuota;
  school ~s matrícula

feeble ['fiːbl] *adj* débil; (*joke*) flojo

feed [fiːd] (*pt, pp* **fed**) *n* comida; (*of
  animal*) pienso; (*on printer*) dispositivo de
  alimentación ♦ *vt* alimentar; (*BRIT: baby:
  breast~*) dar el pecho a; (*animal*) dar de
  comer a; (*data, information*): **to ~ into**
  meter en; **~ on** *vt fus* alimentarse de;
  ~back *n* reacción *f*, feedback *m*

feel [fiːl] (*pt, pp* **felt**) *n* (*sensation*)

sensación *f*; (*sense of touch*) tacto; (*impression*): **to have the ~ of** parecerse a ♦ *vt* tocar; (*pain etc*) sentir; (*think, believe*) creer; **to ~ hungry/cold** tener hambre/frío; **I don't ~ well** no me siento bien; **it ~s soft** es suave al tacto; **to ~ like** (*want*) tener ganas de; **~ about** *or* **around** *vi* tantear; **~er** *n* (*of insect*) antena; **~ing** *n* (*physical*) sensación *f*; (*foreboding*) presentimiento; (*emotion*) sentimiento

feet [fiːt] *npl of* **foot**

feign [feɪn] *vt* fingir

fell [fel] *pt of* **fall** ♦ *vt* (*tree*) talar

fellow ['feləu] *n* tipo, tío (*SP*); (*comrade*) compañero; (*of learned society*) socio/a ♦ *cpd*: **~ citizen** *n* conciudadano/a; **~ countryman** (*irreg*) *n* compatriota *m*; **~ men** *npl* semejantes *mpl*; **~ship** *n* compañerismo; (*grant*) beca

felony ['feləni] *n* crimen *m*

felt [felt] *pt, pp of* **feel** ♦ *n* fieltro; **~-tip pen** *n* rotulador *m*

female ['fiːmeɪl] *n* (*pej: woman*) mujer *f*, tía; (*ZOOL*) hembra ♦ *adj* femenino; hembra

feminine ['feminin] *adj* femenino

feminist ['feminist] *n* feminista

fence [fens] *n* valla, cerca ♦ *vt* (*also: ~ in*) cercar ♦ *vi* (*SPORT*) hacer esgrima; **fencing** *n* esgrima

fend [fend] *vi*: **to ~ for o.s.** valerse por sí mismo; **~ off** *vt* (*attack*) rechazar; (*questions*) evadir

fender ['fendə*] *n* guardafuego; (*US: AUT*) parachoques *m inv*

ferment [*vb* fə'mɛnt, *n* 'fəːmɛnt] *vi* fermentar ♦ *n* (*fig*) agitación *f*

fern [fəːn] *n* helecho

ferocious [fə'rəuʃəs] *adj* feroz

ferret ['ferit] *n* hurón *m*

ferry ['feri] *n* (*small*) barca (de pasaje), balsa; (*large: also: ~boat*) transbordador *m* (*SP*), embarcadero (*AM*) ♦ *vt* transportar

fertile ['fəːtaɪl] *adj* fértil; (*BIOL*) fecundo;

fertilize ['fəːtɪlaɪz] *vt* (*BIOL*) fecundar; (*AGR*) abonar; **fertilizer** *n* abono

fester ['festə*] *vi* ulcerarse

festival ['festɪvəl] *n* (*REL*) fiesta; (*ART, MUS*) festival *m*

festive ['festɪv] *adj* festivo; **the ~ season** (*BRIT: Christmas*) las Navidades

festivities [fes'tɪvɪtɪz] *npl* fiestas *fpl*

festoon [fes'tuːn] *vt*: **to ~ with** engalanar de

fetch [fetʃ] *vt* ir a buscar; (*sell for*) venderse por

fête [feɪt] *n* fiesta

fetus ['fiːtəs] (*US*) *n* = **foetus**

feud [fjuːd] *n* (*hostility*) enemistad *f*; (*quarrel*) disputa

fever ['fiːvə*] *n* fiebre *f*; **~ish** *adj* febril

few [fjuː] *adj* (*not many*) pocos ♦ *pron* pocos; algunos; **a ~** *adj* unos pocos, algunos; **~er** *adj* menos; **~est** *adj* los/las menos

fiancé [fɪ'ãːnseɪ] *n* novio, prometido; **~e** *n* novia, prometida

fib [fɪb] *n* mentirilla

fibre ['faɪbə*] (*US* **fiber**) *n* fibra; **~glass** (**Fiberglass** ® *US*) *n* fibra de vidrio

fickle ['fɪkl] *adj* inconstante

fiction ['fɪkʃən] *n* ficción *f*; **~al** *adj* novelesco; **fictitious** [fɪk'tɪʃəs] *adj* ficticio

fiddle ['fɪdl] *n* (*MUS*) violín *m*; (*cheating*) trampa ♦ *vt* (*BRIT: accounts*) falsificar; **~ with** *vt fus* juguetear con

fidget ['fɪdʒɪt] *vi* enredar; **stop ~ing!** ¡estáte quieto!

field [fiːld] *n* campo; (*fig*) campo, esfera; (*SPORT*) campo, cancha (*AM*); **~ marshal** *n* mariscal *m*; **~work** *n* trabajo de campo

fiend [fiːnd] *n* demonio

fierce [fɪəs] *adj* feroz; (*wind, heat*) fuerte; (*fighting, enemy*) encarnizado

fiery ['faɪərɪ] *adj* (*burning*) ardiente; (*temperament*) apasionado

fifteen [fɪf'tiːn] *num* quince

fifth [fɪfθ] *num* quinto

fifty ['fɪftɪ] *num* cincuenta; **~-~** *adj* (*deal, split*) a medias ♦ *adv* a medias, mitad por mitad

fig [fɪg] *n* higo

fight [faɪt] (*pt, pp* **fought**) *n* (*gen*) pelea; (*MIL*) combate *m*; (*struggle*) lucha ♦ *vt* luchar contra; (*cancer, alcoholism*) combatir; (*election*) intentar ganar; (*emotion*) resistir ♦ *vi* pelear, luchar; **~er** *n* combatiente *m/f*; (*plane*) caza *m*; **~ing** *n* combate *m*, pelea

figment ['fɪgmənt] *n*: **a ~ of the imagination** una quimera

figurative ['fɪgjurətɪv] *adj* (*meaning*) figurado; (*style*) figurativo

figure ['fɪgə*] *n* (*DRAWING, GEOM*) figura, dibujo; (*number, cipher*) cifra; (*body, outline*) tipo; (*personality*) figura ♦ *vt* (*esp US*) imaginar ♦ *vi* (*appear*) figurar; **~ out** *vt* (*work out*) resolver; **~head** *n* (*NAUT*) mascarón *m* de proa; (*pej: leader*) figura decorativa; **~ of speech** *n* figura retórica

file [faɪl] *n* (*tool*) lima; (*dossier*) expediente *m*; (*folder*) carpeta; (*COMPUT*) fichero; (*row*) fila ♦ *vt* limar; (*LAW: claim*) presentar; (*store*) archivar; **~ in / out** *vi* entrar/salir en fila; **filing cabinet** *n* fichero, archivador *m*

fill [fɪl] *vt* (*space*) **to ~ (with)** llenar (de); (*vacancy, need*) cubrir ♦ *n*: **to eat one's ~** llenarse; **~ in** *vt* rellenar; **~ up** *vt* llenar (hasta el borde) ♦ *vi* (*AUT*) poner gasolina

fillet [ˈfɪlɪt] *n* filete *m*; **~ steak** *n* filete *m* de ternera

filling ['fɪlɪŋ] *n* (*CULIN*) relleno; (*for tooth*) empaste *m*; **~ station** *n* estación *f* de servicio

film [fɪlm] *n* película ♦ *vt* (*scene*) filmar ♦ *vi* rodar (una película); **~ star** *n* astro, estrella de cine

filter ['fɪltə*] *n* filtro ♦ *vt* filtrar; **~ lane** (*BRIT*) *n* carril *m* de selección; **~-tipped** *adj* con filtro

filth [fɪlθ] *n* suciedad *f*; **~y** *adj* sucio; (*language*) obsceno

fin [fɪn] *n* (*gen*) aleta

final ['faɪnl] *adj* (*last*) final, último; (*definitive*) definitivo, terminante ♦ *n* (*BRIT: SPORT*) final *f*; **~s** *npl* (*SCOL*) examen *m*

final; (*US: SPORT*) final *f*

finale [fɪˈnɑːlɪ] *n* final *m*

final: ~ist *n* (*SPORT*) finalista *m/f*; **~ize** *vt* concluir, completar; **~ly** *adv* (*lastly*) por último, finalmente; (*eventually*) por fin

finance [faɪˈnæns] *n* (*money*) fondos *mpl*; **~s** *npl* finanzas *fpl*; (*personal ~s*) situación *f* económica ♦ *vt* financiar; **financial** [-ˈnænʃəl] *adj* financiero

find [faɪnd] (*pt, pp* **found**) *vt* encontrar, hallar; (*come upon*) descubrir ♦ *n* hallazgo; descubrimiento; **to ~ sb guilty** (*LAW*) declarar culpable a uno; **~ out** *vt* averiguar; (*truth, secret*) descubrir; **to ~ out about** (*subject*) informarse sobre; (*by chance*) enterarse de; **~ings** *npl* (*LAW*) veredicto, fallo; (*of report*) recomendaciones *fpl*

fine [faɪn] *adj* excelente; (*thin*) fino ♦ *adv* (*well*) bien ♦ *n* (*LAW*) multa ♦ *vt* (*LAW*) multar; **to be ~** (*person*) estar bien; (*weather*) hacer buen tiempo; **~ arts** *npl* bellas artes *fpl*

finery ['faɪnərɪ] *n* adornos *mpl*

finger ['fɪŋgə*] *n* dedo ♦ *vt* (*touch*) manosear; **little/index ~** (dedo) meñique *m*/índice *m*; **~nail** *n* uña; **~print** *n* huella dactilar; **~tip** *n* yema del dedo

finish ['fɪnɪʃ] *n* (*end*) fin *m*; (*SPORT*) meta; (*polish etc*) acabado ♦ *vt, vi* terminar; **to ~ doing sth** acabar de hacer algo; **to ~ third** llegar el tercero; **~ off** *vt* acabar, terminar; (*kill*) acabar con; **~ up** *vt* acabar, terminar ♦ *vi* ir a parar, terminar; **~ing line** *n* línea de llegada *or* meta

finite ['faɪnaɪt] *adj* finito; (*verb*) conjugado

Finland ['fɪnlənd] *n* Finlandia

Finn [fɪn] *n* finlandés/esa *m/f*; **~ish** *adj* finlandés/esa ♦ *n* (*LING*) finlandés *m*

fir [fəː*] *n* abeto

fire ['faɪə*] *n* fuego; (*in hearth*) lumbre *f*; (*accidental*) incendio; (*heater*) estufa ♦ *vt* (*gun*) disparar; (*interest*) despertar; (*inf: dismiss*) despedir ♦ *vi* (*shoot*) disparar; **on ~** ardiendo, en llamas; **~ alarm** *n* alarma de incendios; **~arm** *n* arma de fuego; **~ brigade** (*US* **~ department**) *n* (cuerpo de) bomberos *mpl*; ~ **engine** *n* coche *m* de bomberos; ~ **escape** *n* escalera de incendios; ~ **extinguisher** *n* extintor *m* (de incendios); ~**guard** *n* rejilla de protección; ~**man** (*irreg*) *n* bombero; ~**place** *n* chimenea; ~**side** *n*: **by the ~side** al lado de la chimenea; ~ **station** *n* parque *m* de bomberos; ~**wood** *n* leña; ~**works** *npl* fuegos *mpl* artificiales

firing squad ['faɪrɪŋ-] *n* pelotón *m* de ejecución

firm [fəːm] *adj* firme; (*look, voice*) resuelto ♦ *n* firma, empresa; ~**ly** *adv* firmemente; resueltamente

first [fəːst] *adj* primero ♦ *adv* (*before others*) primero; (*when listing reasons etc*) en primer lugar, primeramente ♦ *n* (*person: in race*) primero/a; (*AUT*) primera; (*BRIT: SCOL*) título de licenciado con calificación de sobresaliente; **at ~** al principio; ~ **of all** ante todo; ~ **aid** *n* primera ayuda, primeros auxilios *mpl*; ~- **aid kit** *n* botiquín *m*; ~-**class** *adj* (*excellent*) de primera (categoría); (*ticket etc*) de primera clase; ~-**hand** *adj* de primera mano; **F~ Lady** (*esp US*) *n* primera dama; ~**ly** *adv* en primer lugar; ~ **name** *n* nombre *m* (de pila); ~-**rate** *adj* estupendo

fish [fɪʃ] *n inv* pez *m*; (*food*) pescado ♦ *vt*, *vi* pescar; **to go ~ing** ir de pesca; ~**erman** (*irreg*) *n* pescador *m*; ~ **farm** *n* criadero de peces; ~ **fingers** (*BRIT*) *npl* croquetas *fpl* de pescado; ~**ing boat** *n* barca de pesca; ~**ing line** *n* sedal *m*; ~**ing rod** *n* caña (de pescar); ~**monger's (shop)** (*BRIT*) *n* pescadería; ~ **sticks** (*US*) *npl* = ~ **fingers**; ~**y** (*inf*) *adj* sospechoso

fist [fɪst] *n* puño

fit [fɪt] *adj* (*healthy*) en (buena) forma; (*proper*) adecuado, apropiado ♦ *vt* (*subj: clothes*) estar o sentar bien a; (*instal*) poner; (*equip*) proveer, dotar; (*facts*) cuadrar *or* corresponder con ♦ *vi* (*clothes*) sentar bien; (*in space, gap*) caber; (*facts*) coincidir ♦ *n* (*MED*) ataque *m*; ~ **to** (*ready*)

a punto de; ~ **for** apropiado para; **a ~ of anger / pride** un arranque de cólera/ orgullo; **this dress is a good ~** este vestido me sienta bien; **by ~s and starts** a rachas; ~ **in** *vi* (*fig: person*) llevarse bien (con todos); ~**ful** *adj* espasmódico, intermitente; ~**ment** *n* módulo adosable; ~**ness** *n* (*MED*) salud *f*; ~**ted carpet** *n* moqueta; ~**ted kitchen** *n* cocina amueblada; ~**ter** *n* ajustador *m*; ~**ting** *adj* apropiado ♦ *n* (*of dress*) prueba; (*of piece of equipment*) instalación *f*; ~**ting room** *n* probador *m*; ~**tings** *npl* instalaciones *fpl*

five [faɪv] *num* cinco; ~**r** (*inf*) *n* (*BRIT*) billete *m* de cinco libras; (*US*) billete *m* de cinco dólares

fix [fɪks] *vt* (*secure*) fijar, asegurar; (*mend*) arreglar; (*prepare*) preparar ♦ *n*: **to be in a ~** estar en un aprieto; ~ **up** *vt* (*meeting*) arreglar; **to ~ sb up with sth** proveer a uno de algo; ~**ation** [fɪk'seɪʃən] *n* obsesión *f*; ~**ed** *adj* (*prices etc*) fijo; ~**ture** *n* (*SPORT*) encuentro; ~**tures** *npl* (*cupboards etc*) instalaciones *fpl* fijas

fizzy ['fɪzɪ] *adj* (*drink*) gaseoso

fjord [fjɔːd] *n* fiordo

flabbergasted ['flæbəgɑːstɪd] *adj* pasmado, alucinado

flabby ['flæbɪ] *adj* gordo

flag [flæg] *n* bandera; (*stone*) losa ♦ *vi* decaer; **to ~ sb down** hacer señas a uno para que se pare; ~**pole** *n* asta de bandera; ~**ship** *n* buque *m* insignia; (*fig*) bandera

flair [fleə*] *n* aptitud *f* especial

flak [flæk] *n* (*MIL*) fuego antiaéreo; (*inf: criticism*) lluvia de críticas

flake [fleɪk] *n* (*of rust, paint*) escama; (*of snow, soap powder*) copo ♦ *vi* (*also:* ~ **off**) desconcharse

flamboyant [flæm'bɔɪənt] *adj* (*dress*) vistoso; (*person*) extravagante

flame [fleɪm] *n* llama

flamingo [flə'mɪŋgəu] *n* flamenco

flammable ['flæməbl] *adj* inflamable

flan [flæn] (*BRIT*) *n* tarta

flank [flæŋk] n (of animal) ijar m; (of army) flanco ♦ vt flanquear

flannel ['flænl] n (BRIT: also: **face ~**) manopla; (fabric) franela

flap [flæp] n (of pocket, envelope) solapa ♦ vt (wings, arms) agitar ♦ vi (sail, flag) ondear

flare [flɛə*] n llamarada; (MIL) bengala; (in skirt etc) vuelo; ~ **up** vi encenderse; (fig: person) encolerizarse; (: revolt) estallar

flash [flæʃ] n relámpago; (also: **news ~**) noticias fpl de última hora; (PHOT) flash m ♦ vt (light, headlights) lanzar un destello con; (news, message) transmitir; (smile) lanzar ♦ vi brillar; (hazard light etc) lanzar destellos; **in a ~** en un instante; **he ~ed by** or **past** pasó como un rayo; ~**back** n (CINEMA) flashback m; ~**bulb** n bombilla fusible; ~ **cube** n cubo de flash; ~**light** n linterna

flashy ['flæʃɪ] (pej) adj ostentoso

flask [flɑːsk] n frasco; (also: **vacuum ~**) termo

flat [flæt] adj llano; (smooth) liso; (tyre) desinflado; (battery) descargado; (beer) muerto; (refusal etc) rotundo; (MUS) desafinado; (rate) fijo ♦ n (BRIT: apartment) piso (SP), departamento (AM), apartamento; (AUT) pinchazo; (MUS) bemol m; **to work ~ out** trabajar a toda mecha; ~**ly** adv terminantemente, de plano; ~**ten** vt (also: ~**ten out**) allanar; (smooth out) alisar; (building, plants) arrasar

flatter ['flætə*] vt adular, halagar; ~**ing** adj halagüeño; (dress) que favorece; ~**y** n adulación f

flaunt [flɔːnt] vt ostentar, lucir

flavour ['fleɪvə*] (US **flavor**) n sabor m, gusto ♦ vt sazonar, condimentar; **strawberry-~ed** con sabor a fresa; ~**ing** n (in product) aromatizante m

flaw [flɔː] n defecto; ~**less** adj impecable

flax [flæks] n lino

flea [fliː] n pulga

fleck [flɛk] n (mark) mota

flee [fliː] (pt, pp **fled**) vt huir de ♦ vi huir, fugarse

fleece [fliːs] n vellón m; (wool) lana ♦ vt (inf) desplumar

fleet [fliːt] n flota; (of lorries etc) escuadra

fleeting ['fliːtɪŋ] adj fugaz

Flemish ['flɛmɪʃ] adj flamenco

flesh [flɛʃ] n carne f; (skin) piel f; (of fruit) pulpa; ~ **wound** n herida superficial

flew [fluː] pt of **fly**

flex [flɛks] n cordón m ♦ vt (muscles) tensar; ~**ible** adj flexible

flick [flɪk] n capirotazo; chasquido ♦ vt (with hand) dar un capirotazo a; (whip etc) chasquear; (switch) accionar; ~ **through** vt fus hojear

flicker ['flɪkə*] vi (light) parpadear; (flame) vacilar

flier ['flaɪə*] n aviador(a) m/f

flight [flaɪt] n vuelo; (escape) huida, fuga; (also: ~ **of steps**) tramo (de escaleras); ~ **attendant** (US) n camarero/azafata; ~ **deck** n (AVIAT) cabina de mandos; (NAUT) cubierta de aterrizaje

flimsy ['flɪmzɪ] adj (thin) muy ligero; (building) endeble; (excuse) flojo

flinch [flɪntʃ] vi encogerse; **to ~ from** retroceder ante

fling [flɪŋ] (pt, pp **flung**) vt arrojar

flint [flɪnt] n pedernal m; (in lighter) piedra

flip [flɪp] vt dar la vuelta a; (switch: turn on) encender; (: turn off) apagar; (coin) echar a cara o cruz

flippant ['flɪpənt] adj poco serio

flipper ['flɪpə*] n aleta

flirt [flɜːt] vi coquetear, flirtear ♦ n coqueta

float [fləut] n flotador m; (in procession) carroza; (money) reserva ♦ vi flotar; (swimmer) hacer la plancha

flock [flɒk] n (of sheep) rebaño; (of birds) bandada ♦ vi: **to ~ to** acudir en tropel a

flog [flɒg] vt azotar

flood [flʌd] n inundación f; (of letters, imports etc) avalancha ♦ vt inundar ♦ vi (place) inundarse; (people): **to ~ into** inundar; ~**ing** n inundaciones fpl; ~**light** n foco

floor [flɔː*] n suelo; (storey) piso; (of sea)

fondo ♦ vt (subj: question) dejar sin respuesta; (: blow) derribar; **ground ~**, **first ~** (US) planta baja; **first ~**, **second ~** (US) primer piso; **~board** n tabla; **~ show** n cabaret m

flop [flɔp] n fracaso ♦ vi (fail) fracasar; (fall) derrumbarse; **~py** adj flojo ♦ n (COMPUT: also: **~py disk**) floppy m

flora [ˈflɔːrə] n flora

floral [ˈflɔːrl] adj (pattern) floreado

florid [ˈflɔrɪd] adj florido; (complexion) rubicundo

florist [ˈflɔrɪst] n florista m/f; **~'s (shop)** n florería

flounder [ˈflaundə*] vi (swimmer) patalear; (fig: economy) estar en dificultades ♦ n (ZOOL) platija

flour [ˈflauə*] n harina

flourish [ˈflʌrɪʃ] vi florecer ♦ n ademán m, movimiento (ostentoso)

flout [flaut] vt burlarse de

flow [fləu] n (movement) flujo; (of traffic) circulación f; (tide) corriente f ♦ vi (river, blood) fluir; (traffic) circular; **~ chart** n organigrama m

flower [ˈflauə*] n flor f ♦ vi florecer; **~ bed** n macizo; **~pot** n tiesto; **~y** adj (fragrance) floral; (pattern) floreado; (speech) florido

flown [fləun] pp of **fly**

flu [fluː] n: **to have ~** tener la gripe

fluctuate [ˈflʌktjueɪt] vi fluctuar

fluent [ˈfluːənt] adj (linguist) que habla perfectamente; (speech) elocuente; **he speaks ~ French**, **he's ~ in French** domina el francés; **~ly** adv con fluidez

fluff [flʌf] n pelusa; **~y** adj de pelo suave

fluid [ˈfluːɪd] adj (movement) fluido, líquido; (situation) inestable ♦ n fluido, líquido

fluke [fluːk] (inf) n chiripa

flung [flʌŋ] pt, pp of **fling**

fluoride [ˈfluəraɪd] n fluoruro

flurry [ˈflʌrɪ] n (of snow) temporal m; **~ of activity** frenesí m de actividad

flush [flʌʃ] n rubor m; (fig: of youth etc) resplandor m ♦ vt limpiar con agua ♦ vi

ruborizarse ♦ adj: **~ with** a ras de; **to ~ the toilet** hacer funcionar la cisterna; **~ed** adj ruborizado

flustered [ˈflʌstəd] adj aturdido

flute [fluːt] n flauta

flutter [ˈflʌtə*] n (of wings) revoloteo, aleteo; **a ~ of panic/excitement** una oleada de pánico/excitación ♦ vi revolotear

flux [flʌks] n: **to be in a state of ~** estar continuamente cambiando

fly [flaɪ] (pt flew, pp flown) n mosca; (on trousers: also: **flies**) bragueta ♦ vt (plane) pilot(e)ar; (cargo) transportar (en avión); (distances) recorrer (en avión) ♦ vi volar; (passengers) ir en avión; (escape) evadirse; (flag) ondear; **~ away** or **off** vi emprender el vuelo; **~-drive** n: **~-drive holiday** vacaciones que incluyen vuelo y alquiler de coche; **~ing** n (activity) (el) volar; (action) vuelo ♦ adj: **~ing visit** visita relámpago; **with ~ing colours** con lucimiento; **~ing saucer** n platillo volante; **~ing start** n: **to get off to a ~ing start** empezar con buen pie; **~over** (BRIT) n paso a desnivel or superior; **~sheet** n (for tent) doble techo

foal [fəul] n potro

foam [fəum] n espuma ♦ vi hacer espuma; **~ rubber** n goma espuma

fob [fɔb] vt: **to ~ sb off with sth** despachar a uno con algo

focal point [ˈfəukl-] n (fig) centro de atención

focus [ˈfəukəs] (pl **~es**) n foco; (centre) centro ♦ vt (field glasses etc) enfocar ♦ vi: **to ~ (on)** enfocar (a); (issue etc) centrarse en; **in/out of ~** enfocado/desenfocado

fodder [ˈfɔdə*] n pienso

foetus [ˈfiːtəs] (US fetus) n feto

fog [fɔg] n niebla; **~gy** adj: **it's ~gy** hay niebla, está brumoso; **~ lamp** (US **~ light**) n (AUT) faro de niebla

foil [fɔɪl] vt frustrar ♦ n hoja; (kitchen ~) papel m (de) aluminio; (complement) complemento; (FENCING) florete m

fold [fəuld] n (bend, crease) pliegue m;

(*AGR*) redil *m* ♦ *vt* doblar; (*arms*) cruzar; ~
up *vi* plegarse, doblarse; (*business*)
quebrar ♦ *vt* (*map etc*) plegar; ~**er** *n* (*for
papers*) carpeta; ~**ing** *adj* (*chair, bed*)
plegable
foliage ['fəʊlɪdʒ] *n* follaje *m*
folk [fəʊk] *npl* gente *f* ♦ *adj* popular,
folklórico; ~**s** *npl* (*family*) familia *sg*,
parientes *mpl*; ~**lore** ['fəʊklɔ:*] *n* folklore
m; ~ **song** *n* canción *f* popular *or*
folklórica
follow ['fɒləʊ] *vt* seguir ♦ *vi* seguir; (*result*)
resultar; **to ~ suit** hacer lo mismo; ~ **up**
vt (*letter, offer*) responder a; (*case*)
investigar; ~**er** *n* (*of person, belief*)
partidario/a, partidarios *mpl*; ~**ing** *adj* siguiente ♦ *n*
afición *f*, partidarios *mpl*
folly ['fɒlɪ] *n* locura
fond [fɒnd] *adj* (*memory, smile etc*)
cariñoso; (*hopes*) ilusorio; **to be ~ of** tener
cariño a; (*pastime, food*) ser aficionado a
fondle ['fɒndl] *vt* acariciar
font [fɒnt] *n* pila bautismal; (*TYP*) fundición
f
food [fu:d] *n* comida; ~ **mixer** *n* batidora;
~ **poisoning** *n* intoxicación *f*
alimenticia; ~ **processor** *n* robot *m* de
cocina; ~**stuffs** *npl* comestibles *mpl*
fool [fu:l] *n* tonto/a; (*CULIN*) puré *m* de
frutas con nata ♦ *vt* engañar ♦ *vi* (*gen*: ~
around) bromear; ~**hardy** *adj* temerario;
~**ish** *adj* tonto; (*careless*) imprudente;
~**proof** *adj* (*plan etc*) infalible
foot [fut] (*pl* **feet**) *n* pie *m*; (*measure*) pie
m (= 304 *mm*); (*of animal*) pata ♦ *vt*
(*bill*) pagar; **on ~** a pie; ~**age** *n* (*CINEMA*)
imágenes *fpl*; ~**ball** *n* balón *m*; (*game*:
BRIT) fútbol *m*; (: *US*) fútbol *m* americano;
~**ball player** *n* (*BRIT*: *also*: ~**baller**)
futbolista *m*; (*US*) jugador *m* de fútbol
americano; ~**brake** *n* freno de pie;
~**bridge** *n* puente *m* para peatones;
~**hills** *npl* estribaciones *fpl*; ~**hold** *n* pie
m firme; ~**ing** *n* (*fig*) posición *f*; **to lose
one's ~ing** perder el pie; ~**lights** *npl*
candilejas *fpl*; ~**note** *n* nota (al pie de la
página); ~**path** *n* sendero; ~**print** *n*

huella, pisada; ~**step** *n* paso; ~**wear** *n*
calzado

KEYWORD

for [fɔ:] *prep* **1** (*indicating destination,
intention*) para; **the train ~ London** el
tren con destino a *or* de Londres; **he left
~ Rome** marchó por Roma; **he went ~
the paper** fue por el periódico; **is this ~
me?** ¿es esto para mí?; **it's time ~ lunch**
es la hora de comer
2 (*indicating purpose*) para; **what's it) ~?**
¿para qué (es)?; **to pray ~ peace** rezar
por la paz
3 (*on behalf of, representing*): **the MP ~
Hove** el diputado por Hove; **he works ~
the government/a local firm** trabaja
para el gobierno/en una empresa local;
I'll ask him ~ you se lo pediré por ti; **G ~
George** G de Gerona
4 (*because of*) por esta razón; ~ **fear of
being criticized** por temor a ser criticado
5 (*with regard to*) para; **it's cold ~ July**
hace frío para julio; **he has a gift ~
languages** tiene don de lenguas
6 (*in exchange for*) por; **I sold it ~ £5** lo
vendí por £5; **to pay 50 pence ~ a ticket**
pagar 50 peniques por un billete
7 (*in favour of*): **are you ~ or against us?**
¿estás con nosotros o contra nosotros?;
I'm all ~ it estoy totalmente a favor; **vote
~ X** vote (a) X
8 (*referring to distance*): **there are
roadworks ~ 5 km** hay obras en 5 km;
we walked ~ miles caminamos
kilómetros y kilómetros
9 (*referring to time*): **he was away ~ 2
years** estuvo fuera (durante) dos años; **it
hasn't rained ~ 3 weeks** no ha llovido
durante *or* en 3 semanas; **I have known
her ~ years** la conozco desde hace años;
can you do it ~ tomorrow? ¿lo podrás
hacer para mañana?
10 (*with infinitive clauses*): **it is not ~ me
to decide** la decisión no es cosa mía; **it
would be best ~ you to leave** sería
mejor que te fueras; **there is still time ~**

you to do it todavía te queda tiempo para hacerlo; **~ this to be possible ...** para que esto sea posible ... **11** (*in spite of*) a pesar de; **~ all his complaints** a pesar de sus quejas ♦ *conj* (*since, as: rather formal*) puesto que

forage ['fɔrɪdʒ] *vi* (*animal*) forrajear; (*person*): **to ~ for** hurgar en busca de

foray ['fɔreɪ] *n* incursión *f*

forbid [fə'bɪd] (*pt* **forbad(e)**, *pp* **forbidden**) *vt* prohibir; **to ~ sb to do sth** prohibir a uno hacer algo; **~ding** *adj* amenazador(a)

force [fɔːs] *n* fuerza ♦ *vt* forzar; (*push*) meter a la fuerza; **to ~ o.s. to do** hacer un esfuerzo por hacer; **the F~s** *npl* (*BRIT*) las Fuerzas Armadas; **~d** [fɔːst] *adj* forzado; **~-feed** *vt* alimentar a la fuerza; **~ful** *adj* enérgico

forcibly ['fɔːsəblɪ] *adv* a la fuerza; (*speak*) enérgicamente

ford [fɔːd] *n* vado

fore [fɔː*] *n*: **to come to the ~** empezar a destacar

fore: **~arm** *n* antebrazo; **~boding** *n* presentimiento; **~cast** *n* pronóstico ♦ *vt* (*irreg: like* **cast**) pronosticar; **~court** *n* patio; **~finger** *n* (dedo) índice *m*; **~front** *n*: **in the ~front of** en la vanguardia de

forego *vt* = **forgo**

foregone ['fɔːgɔn] *pp of* **forego** ♦ *adj*: **it's a ~ conclusion** es una conclusión evidente

foreground ['fɔːgraund] *n* primer plano

forehead ['fɔrɪd] *n* frente *f*

foreign ['fɔrɪn] *adj* extranjero; (*trade*) exterior; (*object*) extraño; **~er** *n* extranjero/a; **~ exchange** *n* divisas *fpl*; **F~ Office** (*BRIT*) *n* Ministerio de Asuntos Exteriores; **F~ Secretary** (*BRIT*) *n* Ministro de Asuntos Exteriores

fore: **~leg** *n* pata delantera; **~man** (*irreg*) *n* capataz *m*; (*in construction*) maestro de obras; **~most** *adj* principal ♦ *adv*: **first**

and ~most ante todo

forensic [fə'rensɪk] *adj* forense

fore: **~runner** *n* precursor(a) *m/f*; **~see** (*pt* **foresaw**, *pp* **foreseen**) *vt* prever; **~seeable** *adj* previsible; **~shadow** *vt* prefigurar, anunciar; **~sight** *n* previsión *f*

forest ['fɔrɪst] *n* bosque *m*

forestry ['fɔrɪstrɪ] *n* silvicultura

foretaste ['fɔːteɪst] *n* muestra

foretell [fɔː'tel] (*pt, pp* **foretold**) *vt* predecir, pronosticar

forever [fə'revə*] *adv* para siempre; (*endlessly*) constantemente

foreword ['fɔːwəːd] *n* prefacio

forfeit ['fɔːfɪt] *vt* perder

forgave [fə'geɪv] *pt of* **forgive**

forge [fɔːdʒ] *n* herrería ♦ *vt* (*signature, money*) falsificar; (*metal*) forjar; **~ ahead** *vi* avanzar mucho; **~ry** *n* falsificación *f*

forget [fə'get] (*pt* **forgot**, *pp* **forgotten**) *vt* olvidar ♦ *vi* olvidarse; **~ful** *adj* despistado; **~-me-not** *n* nomeolvides *f inv*

forgive [fə'gɪv] (*pt* **forgave**, *pp* **forgiven**) *vt* perdonar; **to ~ sb for sth** perdonar algo a uno; **~ness** *n* perdón *m*

forgo [fə'gəu] (*pt* **forwent**, *pp* **forgone**) *vt* (*give up*) renunciar a; (*go without*) privarse de

forgot [fə'gɔt] *pt of* **forget**

forgotten [fə'gɔtn] *pp of* **forget**

fork [fɔːk] *n* (*for eating*) tenedor *m*; (*for gardening*) horca; (*of roads*) bifurcación *f* ♦ *vi* (*road*) bifurcarse; **~ out** (*inf*) *vt* (*pay*) desembolsar; **~-lift truck** *n* máquina elevadora

forlorn [fə'lɔːn] *adj* (*person*) triste, melancólico; (*place*) abandonado; (*attempt, hope*) desesperado

form [fɔːm] *n* forma; (*BRIT: SCOL*) clase *f*; (*document*) formulario ♦ *vt* formar; (*idea*) concebir; (*habit*) adquirir; **in top ~** en plena forma; **to ~ a queue** hacer cola

formal ['fɔːməl] *adj* (*offer, receipt*) por escrito; (*person etc*) correcto; (*occasion, dinner*) de etiqueta; (*dress*) correcto; (*garden*) (de estilo) clásico; **~ity** [-'mælɪtɪ]

n (*procedure*) trámite *m*; corrección *f*; etiqueta; **~ly** *adv* oficialmente
format ['fɔːmæt] *n* formato ♦ *vt* (COMPUT) formatear
formative ['fɔːmətɪv] *adj* (*years*) de formación; (*influence*) formativo
former ['fɔːmə*] *adj* anterior; (*earlier*) antiguo; (*ex*) ex; **the ~ ... the latter ...** aquél ... éste ...; **~ly** *adv* antes
formula ['fɔːmjulə] *n* fórmula
forsake [fəˈseɪk] (*pt* **forsook**, *pp* **forsaken**) *vt* (*gen*) abandonar; (*plan*) renunciar a
fort [fɔːt] *n* fuerte *m*
forte ['fɔːtɪ] *n* fuerte *m*
forth [fɔːθ] *adv*: **back and ~** de acá para allá; **and so ~** y así sucesivamente; **~coming** *adj* próximo, venidero; (*help, information*) disponible; (*character*) comunicativo; **~right** *adj* franco; **~with** *adv* en el acto
fortify ['fɔːtɪfaɪ] *vt* (*city*) fortificar; (*person*) fortalecer
fortitude ['fɔːtɪtjuːd] *n* fortaleza
fortnight ['fɔːtnaɪt] (*BRIT*) *n* quince días *mpl*; quincena; **~ly** *adj* de cada quince días, quincenal ♦ *adv* cada quince días, quincenalmente
fortress ['fɔːtrɪs] *n* fortaleza
fortunate ['fɔːtʃənɪt] *adj* afortunado; **it is ~ that ...** (es una) suerte que ...; **~ly** *adv* afortunadamente
fortune ['fɔːtʃən] *n* suerte *f*; (*wealth*) fortuna; **~-teller** *n* adivino/a
forty ['fɔːtɪ] *num* cuarenta
forum ['fɔːrəm] *n* foro
forward ['fɔːwəd] *adj* (*movement, position*) avanzado; (*front*) delantero; (*in time*) adelantado; (*not shy*) atrevido ♦ *n* (SPORT) delantero ♦ *vt* (*letter*) remitir; (*career*) promocionar; **to move ~** avanzar; **~(s)** *adv* (hacia) adelante
fossil ['fɔsl] *n* fósil *m*
foster ['fɔstə*] *vt* (*child*) acoger en una familia; fomentar; **~ child** *n* hijo/a adoptivo/a
fought [fɔːt] *pt*, *pp* of **fight**
foul [faul] *adj* sucio, puerco; (*weather, smell etc*) asqueroso; (*language*) grosero; (*temper*) malísimo ♦ *n* (SPORT) falta ♦ *vt* (*dirty*) ensuciar; **~ play** *n* (LAW) muerte *f* violenta
found [faund] *pt*, *pp* of **find** ♦ *vt* fundar; **~ation** [-ˈdeɪʃən] *n* (*act*) fundación *f*; (*basis*) base *f*; (*also*: **~ation cream**) crema base; **~ations** *npl* (*of building*) cimientos *mpl*
founder ['faundə*] *n* fundador(a) *m/f* ♦ *vi* hundirse
foundry ['faundrɪ] *n* fundición *f*
fountain ['fauntɪn] *n* fuente *f*; **~ pen** *n* pluma (estilográfica) (SP), pluma-fuente *f* (AM)
four [fɔː*] *num* cuatro; **on all ~s** a gatas; **~-poster (bed)** *n* cama de dosel; **~teen** *num* catorce; **~th** *num* cuarto
fowl [faul] *n* ave *f* (de corral)
fox [fɔks] *n* zorro ♦ *vt* confundir
foyer ['fɔɪeɪ] *n* vestíbulo
fraction ['frækʃən] *n* fracción *f*
fracture ['fræktʃə*] *n* fractura
fragile ['frædʒaɪl] *adj* frágil
fragment ['frægmənt] *n* fragmento
fragrant ['freɪgrənt] *adj* fragante, oloroso
frail [freɪl] *adj* frágil; (*person*) débil
frame [freɪm] *n* (TECH) armazón *m*; (*of person*) cuerpo; (*of picture, door etc*) marco; (*of spectacles*: *also*: **~s**) montura ♦ *vt* enmarcar; **~ of mind** *n* estado de ánimo; **~work** *n* marco
France [frɑːns] *n* Francia
franchise ['fræntʃaɪz] *n* (POL) derecho de votar, sufragio; (COMM) licencia, concesión *f*
frank [fræŋk] *adj* franco ♦ *vt* (*letter*) franquear; **~ly** *adv* francamente
frantic ['fræntɪk] *adj* (*distraught*) desesperado; (*hectic*) frenético
fraternity [frəˈtɜːnɪtɪ] *n* (*feeling*) fraternidad *f*; (*group of people*) círculos *mpl*
fraud [frɔːd] *n* fraude *m*; (*person*) impostor(a) *m/f*
fraught [frɔːt] *adj*: **~ with** lleno de
fray [freɪ] *vi* deshilacharse
freak [friːk] *n* (*person*) fenómeno; (*event*)

suceso anormal

freckle ['frɛkl] n peca

free [fri:] adj libre; (gratis) gratuito ♦ vt (prisoner etc) poner en libertad; (jammed object) soltar; **~ (of charge), for ~** gratis; **~dom** ['fri:dəm] n libertad f; **F~fone** ® ['fri:fəun] n número gratuito; **~-for-all** n riña general; **~ gift** n prima; **~hold** n propiedad f vitalicia; **~ kick** n tiro libre; **~lance** adj independiente ♦ adv por cuenta propia; **~ly** adv libremente; (liberally) generosamente; **F~mason** n francmasón m; **F~post** ® n porte m pagado; **~-range** adj (hen, eggs) de granja; **~ trade** n libre comercio; **~way** (US) n autopista; **~ will** n libre albedrío; **of one's own ~ will** por su propia voluntad

freeze [fri:z] (pt **froze**, pp **frozen**) vi (weather) helar; (liquid, pipe, person) helarse, congelarse ♦ vt helar; (food, prices, salaries) congelar ♦ n helada; (on arms, wages) congelación f; **~-dried** adj liofilizado; **~r** n congelador m (SP), congeladora (AM)

freezing ['fri:zɪŋ] adj helado; **3 degrees below ~** tres grados bajo cero; **~ point** n punto de congelación

freight [freɪt] n (goods) carga; (money charged) flete m; **~ train** (US) n tren m de mercancías

French [frɛntʃ] adj francés/esa ♦ n (LING) francés m; **the ~** npl los franceses; **~ bean** n judía verde; **~ fried potatoes** npl patatas fpl (SP) or papas fpl (AM) fritas; **~ fries** (US) npl = **~ fried potatoes**; **~man/woman** (irreg) n francés/esa m/f; **~ window** n puerta de cristal

frenzy ['frɛnzɪ] n frenesí m

frequent [adj 'fri:kwənt, vb frɪ'kwɛnt] adj frecuente ♦ vt frecuentar; **~ly** [-əntlɪ] adv frecuentemente, a menudo

fresh [frɛʃ] adj fresco; (bread) tierno; (new) nuevo; **~en** vi (wind, air) soplar más recio; **~en up** vi (person) arreglarse, lavarse; **~er** (BRIT: inf) n (UNIV) estudiante

m/f de primer año; **~ly** adv (made, painted etc) recién; **~man** (US irreg) n = **~er**; **~ness** n frescura; **~water** adj (fish) de agua dulce

fret [frɛt] vi inquietarse

friar ['fraɪə*] n fraile m; (before name) fray m

friction ['frɪkʃən] n fricción f

Friday ['fraɪdɪ] n viernes m inv

fridge [frɪdʒ] (BRIT) n nevera (SP), refrigeradora (AM)

fried [fraɪd] adj frito

friend [frɛnd] n amigo/a; **~ly** adj simpático; (government) amigo; (place) acogedor(a); (match) amistoso; **~ly fire** fuego amigo, disparos mpl del propio bando; **~ship** n amistad f

frieze [fri:z] n friso

fright [fraɪt] n (terror) terror m; (scare) susto; **to take ~** asustarse; **~en** vt asustar; **~ened** adj asustado; **~ening** adj espantoso; **~ful** adj espantoso, horrible

frill [frɪl] n volante m

fringe [frɪndʒ] n (BRIT: of hair) flequillo; (on lampshade etc) flecos mpl; (of forest etc) borde m, margen m; **~ benefits** npl beneficios mpl marginales

frisk [frɪsk] vt cachear, registrar

frisky ['frɪskɪ] adj juguetón/ona

fritter ['frɪtə*] n buñuelo; **~ away** vt desperdiciar

frivolous ['frɪvələs] adj frívolo

frizzy ['frɪzɪ] adj rizado

fro [frəu] see **to**

frock [frɔk] n vestido

frog [frɔg] n rana; **~man** n hombre-rana m

frolic ['frɔlɪk] vi juguetear

KEYWORD

---

from [frɔm] prep **1** (indicating starting place) de, desde; **where do you come ~?** ¿de dónde eres?; **~ London to Glasgow** de Londres a Glasgow; **to escape ~ sth/ sb** escaparse de algo/alguien

2 (indicating origin etc) de; **a letter/ telephone call ~ my sister** una carta/

llamada de mi hermana; **tell him ~ me that ...** dígale de mi parte que ...
3 (*indicating time*): **~ one o'clock to** *or* **until** *or* **till two** de(sde) la una a *or* hasta las dos; **~ January (on)** a partir de enero
4 (*indicating distance*) de; **the hotel is 1 km ~ the beach** el hotel está a 1 km de la playa
5 (*indicating price, number etc*) de; **prices range ~ £10 to £50** los precios van desde £10 a *or* hasta £50; **the interest rate was increased ~ 9% to 10%** el tipo de interés fue incrementado de un 9% a un 10%
6 (*indicating difference*) de; **he can't tell red ~ green** no sabe distinguir el rojo del verde; **to be different ~ sb/sth** ser diferente a algo/alguien
7 (*because of, on the basis of*): **~ what he says** por lo que dice; **weak ~ hunger** debilitado por el hambre

front [frʌnt] *n* (*foremost part*) parte *f* delantera; (*of house*) fachada; (*of dress*) delantero; (*promenade: also:* **sea ~**) paseo marítimo; (*MIL, POL, METEOROLOGY*) frente *m*; (*fig: appearances*) apariencias *fpl* ♦ *adj* (*wheel, leg*) delantero; (*row, line*) primero; **in ~ (of)** delante (de); **~ door** *n* puerta principal; **~ier** ['frʌntɪə*] *n* frontera; **~ page** *n* primera plana; **~ room** (*BRIT*) *n* salón *m*, sala; **~-wheel drive** *n* tracción *f* delantera

frost [frɔst] *n* helada; (*also:* **hoar~**) escarcha; **~bite** *n* congelación *f*; **~ed** *adj* (*glass*) deslustrado; **~y** *adj* (*weather*) de helada; (*welcome etc*) glacial

froth [frɔθ] *n* espuma

frown [fraun] *vi* fruncir el ceño

froze [frəuz] *pt of* **freeze**

frozen ['frəuzn] *pp of* **freeze**

fruit [fruːt] *n inv* fruta; fruto; (*fig*) resultados *mpl*; **~erer** *n* frutero/a; **~erer's (shop)** *n* frutería; **~ful** *adj* provechoso; **~ion** [fruːˈɪʃən] *n*: **to come to ~ion** realizarse; **~ juice** *n* zumo (*SP*) *or* jugo (*AM*) de fruta; **~ machine** (*BRIT*) *n*

máquina *f* tragaperras; **~ salad** *n* macedonia (*SP*) *or* ensalada (*AM*) de frutas

frustrate [frʌsˈtreɪt] *vt* frustrar

fry [fraɪ] (*pt, pp* **fried**) *vt* freír; **small ~** gente *f* menuda; **~ing pan** *n* sartén *f*

ft. *abbr* = **foot; feet**

fudge [fʌdʒ] *n* (*CULIN*) caramelo blando

fuel [fjuəl] *n* (*for heating*) combustible *m*; (*coal*) carbón *m*; (*wood*) leña; (*for engine*) carburante *m*; **~ oil** *n* fuel oil *m*; **~ tank** *n* depósito (de combustible)

fugitive ['fjuːdʒɪtɪv] *n* fugitivo/a

fulfil [ful'fɪl] *vt* (*function*) cumplir con; (*condition*) satisfacer; (*wish, desire*) realizar; **~ment** (*US* **fulfillment**) *n* satisfacción *f*; (*of promise, desire*) realización *f*

full [ful] *adj* lleno; (*fig*) pleno; (*complete*) completo; (*maximum*) máximo; (*information*) detallado; (*price*) íntegro; (*skirt*) amplio ♦ *adv*: **to know ~ well that** saber perfectamente que; **I'm ~ (up)** no puedo más; **~ employment** pleno empleo; **a ~ two hours** dos horas completas; **at ~ speed** a máxima velocidad; **in ~** (*reproduce, quote*) íntegramente; **~-length** *adj* (*novel etc*) entero; (*coat*) largo; (*portrait*) de cuerpo entero; **~ moon** *n* luna llena; **~-scale** *adj* (*attack, war*) en gran escala; (*model*) de tamaño natural; **~ stop** *n* punto; **~-time** *adj* (*work*) de tiempo completo ♦ *adv*: **to work ~-time** trabajar a tiempo completo; **~y** *adv* completamente; (*at least*) por lo menos; **~y-fledged** *adj* (*teacher, barrister*) diplomado

fumble ['fʌmbl] *vi*: **to ~ with** manejar torpemente

fume [fjuːm] *vi* (*rage*) estar furioso; **~s** *npl* humo, gases *mpl*

fun [fʌn] *n* (*amusement*) diversión *f*; **to have ~** divertirse; **for ~** en broma; **to make ~ of** burlarse de

function ['fʌŋkʃən] *n* función *f* ♦ *vi* funcionar; **~al** *adj* (*operational*) en buen estado; (*practical*) funcional

fund [fʌnd] *n* fondo; (*reserve*) reserva; **~s** *npl* (*money*) fondos *mpl*

fundamental [fʌndə'mɛntl] *adj* fundamental

funeral ['fju:nərəl] *n* (*burial*) entierro; (*ceremony*) funerales *mpl*; **~ parlour** (*BRIT*) *n* funeraria; **~ service** *n* misa de difuntos, funeral *m*

funfair ['fʌnfɛə*] (*BRIT*) *n* parque *m* de atracciones

fungus ['fʌŋgəs] (*pl* **fungi**) *n* hongo; (*mould*) moho

funnel ['fʌnl] *n* embudo; (*of ship*) chimenea

funny ['fʌnɪ] *adj* gracioso, divertido; (*strange*) curioso, raro

fur [fə:*] *n* piel *f*; (*BRIT: in kettle etc*) sarro; **~ coat** *n* abrigo de pieles

furious ['fjuərɪəs] *adj* furioso; (*effort*) violento

furlong ['fə:lɔŋ] *n* octava parte de una milla, = 201.17 m

furnace ['fə:nɪs] *n* horno

furnish ['fə:nɪʃ] *vt* amueblar; (*supply*) suministrar; (*information*) facilitar; **~ings** *npl* muebles *mpl*

furniture ['fə:nɪtʃə*] *n* muebles *mpl*; **piece of ~** mueble *m*

furrow ['fʌrəu] *n* surco

furry ['fə:rɪ] *adj* peludo

further ['fə:ðə*] *adj* (*new*) nuevo, adicional ♦ *adv* más lejos; (*more*) más; (*moreover*) además ♦ *vt* promover, adelantar; **~ education** *n* educación *f* superior; **~more** [fə:ðə'mɔ:*] *adv* además

furthest ['fə:ðɪst] *superlative of* **far**

fury ['fjuərɪ] *n* furia

fuse [fju:z] (*US* **fuze**) *n* fusible *m*; (*for bomb etc*) mecha ♦ *vt* (*metal*) fundir; (*fig*) fusionar ♦ *vi* fundirse; fusionarse; (*BRIT: ELEC*): **to ~ the lights** fundir los plomos; **~ box** *n* caja de fusibles

fuss [fʌs] *n* (*excitement*) conmoción *f*; (*trouble*) alboroto; **to make a ~** armar un lío *or* jaleo; **to make a ~ of sb** mimar a uno; **~y** *adj* (*person*) exigente; (*too ornate*) recargado

futile ['fju:taɪl] *adj* vano

future ['fju:tʃə*] *adj* futuro; (*coming*)

venidero ♦ *n* futuro; (*prospects*) porvenir; **in ~** de ahora en adelante

fuze [fju:z] (*US*) = **fuse**

fuzzy ['fʌzɪ] *adj* (*PHOT*) borroso; (*hair*) muy rizado

G, g

G [dʒi:] *n* (*MUS*) sol *m*

g. *abbr* (= *gram(s)*) gr.

G7 *abbr* (= *Group of Seven*) el grupo de los 7

gabble ['gæbl] *vi* hablar atropelladamente

gable ['geɪbl] *n* aguilón *m*

gadget ['gædʒɪt] *n* aparato

Gaelic ['geɪlɪk] *adj, n* (*LING*) gaélico

gag [gæg] *n* (*on mouth*) mordaza; (*joke*) chiste *m* ♦ *vt* amordazar

gaiety ['geɪtɪ] *n* alegría

gaily ['geɪlɪ] *adv* alegremente

gain [geɪn] *n*: **~ (in)** aumento (de); (*profit*) ganancia ♦ *vt* ganar ♦ *vi* (*watch*) adelantarse; **to ~ from/by sth** sacar provecho de algo; **to ~ on sb** ganar terreno a uno; **to ~ 3 lbs (in weight)** engordar 3 libras

gal. *abbr* = **gallon**

gala ['gɑ:lə] *n* fiesta

gale [geɪl] *n* (*wind*) vendaval *m*

gallant ['gælənt] *adj* valiente; (*towards ladies*) atento

gall bladder ['gɔ:l-] *n* vesícula biliar

gallery ['gælərɪ] *n* (*also*: **art ~**: *public*) pinacoteca; (: *private*) galería de arte; (*for spectators*) tribuna

gallon ['gæln] *n* galón *m* (*BRIT* = 4,546 *litros*, *US* = 3,785 *litros*)

gallop ['gæləp] *n* galope *m* ♦ *vi* galopar

gallows ['gæləuz] *n* horca

gallstone ['gɔ:lstəun] *n* cálculo biliario

galore [gə'lɔ:*] *adv* en cantidad, en abundancia

gambit ['gæmbɪt] *n* (*fig*): **(opening) ~** estrategia (inicial)

gamble ['gæmbl] *n* (*risk*) riesgo ♦ *vt* jugar, apostar ♦ *vi* (*take a risk*) jugársela; (*bet*)

apostar; **to ~ on** apostar a; (*success etc*) contar con; **~r** n jugador(a) m/f;
gambling n juego

game [geɪm] n juego; (*match*) partido; (*of cards*) partida; (*HUNTING*) caza ♦ adj (*willing*): **to be ~ for anything** atreverse a todo; **big ~** caza mayor; **~keeper** n guardabosques m inv

gammon [ˈgæmən] n (*bacon*) tocino ahumado; (*ham*) jamón m ahumado

gamut [ˈgæmət] n gama

gang [gæŋ] n (*of criminals*) pandilla; (*of friends etc*) grupo; (*of workmen*) brigada; **~ up** vi: **to ~ up on sb** aliarse contra uno

gangster [ˈgæŋstə*] n gángster m

gangway [ˈgæŋweɪ] n (*on ship*) pasarela; (*BRIT: in theatre, bus etc*) pasillo

gaol [dʒeɪl] (*BRIT*) n, vt = **jail**

gap [gæp] n vacío, hueco (*AM*); (*in trees, traffic*) claro; (*in time*) intervalo; (*difference*): **~ (between)** diferencia (entre)

gape [geɪp] vi mirar boquiabierto; (*shirt etc*) abrirse (completamente); **gaping** adj (completamente) abierto

garage [ˈgærɑːʒ] n garaje m; (*for repairs*) taller m

garbage [ˈgɑːbɪdʒ] (*US*) n basura; (*inf: nonsense*) tonterías fpl; **~ can** n cubo (*SP*) or bote m (*AM*) de la basura

garbled [ˈgɑːbld] adj (*distorted*) falsificado, amañado

garden [ˈgɑːdn] n jardín m; **~s** npl (*park*) parque m; **~er** n jardinero/a; **~ing** n jardinería

gargle [ˈgɑːgl] vi hacer gárgaras, gargarear (*AM*)

garish [ˈgeərɪʃ] adj chillón/ona

garland [ˈgɑːlənd] n guirnalda

garlic [ˈgɑːlɪk] n ajo

garment [ˈgɑːmənt] n prenda (de vestir)

garnish [ˈgɑːnɪʃ] vt (*CULIN*) aderezar

garrison [ˈgærɪsn] n guarnición f

garter [ˈgɑːtə*] n (*for sock*) liga; (*US*) liguero

gas [gæs] n gas m; (*fuel*) combustible m; (*US: gasoline*) gasolina ♦ vt asfixiar con gas; **~ cooker** (*BRIT*) n cocina de gas; **~**

cylinder n bombona de gas; **~ fire** n estufa de gas

gash [gæʃ] n raja; (*wound*) cuchillada ♦ vt rajar; acuchillar

gasket [ˈgæskɪt] n (*AUT*) junta de culata

gas mask n careta antigás

gas meter n contador m de gas

gasoline [ˈgæsəliːn] (*US*) n gasolina

gasp [gɑːsp] n boqueada; (*of shock etc*) grito sofocado ♦ vi (*pant*) jadear

gas station (*US*) n gasolinera

gastric [ˈgæstrɪk] adj gástrico

gate [geɪt] n puerta; (*iron ~*) verja; **~crash** (*BRIT*) vt colarse en; **~way** n (*also fig*) puerta

gather [ˈgæðə*] vt (*flowers, fruit*) coger (*SP*), recoger (*assemble*) reunir; (*pick up*) recoger; (*SEWING*) fruncir; (*understand*) entender ♦ vi (*assemble*) reunirse; **to ~ speed** ganar velocidad; **~ing** n reunión f, asamblea

gaudy [ˈgɔːdɪ] adj chillón/ona

gauge [geɪdʒ] n (*instrument*) indicador m ♦ vt medir; (*fig*) juzgar

gaunt [gɔːnt] adj (*haggard*) demacrado; (*stark*) desolado

gauntlet [ˈgɔːntlɪt] n (*fig*): **to run the ~ of** exponerse a; **to throw down the ~** arrojar el guante

gauze [gɔːz] n gasa

gave [geɪv] pt of **give**

gay [geɪ] adj (*homosexual*) gay; (*joyful*) alegre; (*colour*) vivo

gaze [geɪz] n mirada fija ♦ vi: **to ~ at sth** mirar algo fijamente

gazelle [gəˈzel] n gacela

gazumping [gəˈzʌmpɪŋ] (*BRIT*) n *la subida del precio de una casa una vez que ya ha sido apalabrado*

GB abbr = **Great Britain**

GCE n abbr (*BRIT*) = *General Certificate of Education*

GCSE (*BRIT*) n abbr (= *General Certificate of Secondary Education*) *examen de reválida que se hace a los 16 años*

gear [gɪə*] n equipo, herramientas fpl; (*TECH*) engranaje m; (*AUT*) velocidad f,

marcha ♦ vt (fig: adapt): **to ~ sth to**
adaptar or ajustar algo a; **top** or **high**
(US)**/low ~** cuarta/primera velocidad; **in ~**
en marcha; **~ box** n caja de cambios; **~
shift** (US)
n = **~ lever**

eese [giːs] npl of **goose**

el [dʒɛl] n gel m

em [dʒɛm] n piedra preciosa

iemini ['dʒɛmɪnaɪ] n Géminis m, Gemelos
mpl

ender ['dʒɛndə*] n género

ene [dʒiːn] n gen(e) m

eneral ['dʒɛnərl] n general m ♦ adj
general; **in ~** en general; **~ delivery** (US)
n lista de correos; **~ election** n
elecciones fpl generales; **~ly** adv
generalmente, en general; **~
practitioner** n médico general

enerate ['dʒɛnəreɪt] vt (ELEC) generar;
(jobs, profits) producir

eneration [dʒɛnə'reɪʃən] n generación f

enerator ['dʒɛnəreɪtə*] n generador m

enerosity [dʒɛnə'rɔsɪtɪ] n generosidad f

enerous ['dʒɛnərəs] adj generoso

enetic [dʒɪ'nɛtɪk] adj: **~ engineering**
ingeniería genética; **~ fingerprinting**
identificación f genética

eneva [dʒɪ'niːvə] n Ginebra

enial [dʒiːnɪəl] adj afable, simpático

enitals ['dʒɛnɪtlz] npl (órganos mpl)
genitales mpl

enius [dʒiːnɪəs] n genio

enteel [dʒɛn'tiːl] adj fino, elegante

entle ['dʒɛntl] adj apacible, dulce;
(animal) manso; (breeze, curve etc) suave

entleman ['dʒɛntlmən] (irreg) n señor m;
(well-bred man) caballero

ently ['dʒɛntlɪ] adv dulcemente,
suavemente

entry ['dʒɛntrɪ] n alta burguesía

ents [dʒɛnts] n aseos mpl (de caballeros)

enuine ['dʒɛnjuɪn] adj auténtico; (person)
sincero

eography [dʒɪ'ɔgrəfɪ] n geografía

eology [dʒɪ'ɔlədʒɪ] n geología

eometric(al) [dʒɪə'mɛtrɪk(l)] adj

geométrico

geranium [dʒɪ'reɪnjəm] n geranio

geriatric [dʒɛrɪ'ætrɪk] adj, n geriátrico/a
m/f

germ [dʒəːm] n (microbe) microbio,
bacteria; (seed, fig) germen m

German ['dʒəːmən] adj alemán/ana ♦ n
alemán/ana m/f; (LING) alemán m; **~
measles** n rubéola

Germany ['dʒəːmənɪ] n Alemania

gesture ['dʒɛstjə*] n gesto; (symbol)
muestra

KEYWORD

---

get [gɛt] (pt, pp **got**, pp **gotten** (US)) vi 1
(become, be) ponerse, volverse; **to ~ old/
tired** envejecer/cansarse; **to ~ drunk**
emborracharse; **to ~ dirty** ensuciarse; **to ~
married** casarse; **when do I ~ paid?**
¿cuándo me pagan or se me paga?; **it's
~ting late** se está haciendo tarde
2 (go): **to ~ to/from** llegar a/de; **to ~
home** llegar a casa
3 (begin) empezar a; **to ~ to know sb**
(llegar a) conocer a uno; **I'm ~ting to like
him** me está empezando a gustar; **let's ~
going** or **started** ¡vamos (a empezar)!
4 (modal aux vb): **you've got to do it**
tienes que hacerlo
♦ vt 1: **to ~ sth done** (finish) terminar
algo; (have done) mandar hacer algo; **to ~
one's hair cut** cortarse el pelo; **to ~ the
car going** or **to go** arrancar el coche; **to
~ sb to do sth** conseguir or hacer que
alguien haga algo; **to ~ sth/sb ready**
preparar algo/a alguien
2 (obtain: money, permission, results)
conseguir; (find: job, flat) encontrar;
(fetch: person, doctor) buscar; (object) ir a
buscar, traer; **to ~ sth for sb** conseguir
algo para alguien; **~ me Mr Jones,
please** (TEL) póngame or comuníqueme
(AM) con el Sr. Jones, por favor; **can I ~
you a drink?** ¿quieres algo de beber?
3 (receive: present, letter) recibir; (acquire:
reputation) alcanzar; (: prize) ganar; **what
did you ~ for your birthday?** ¿qué te

regalaron por tu cumpleaños?; **how
much did you ~ for the painting?**
¿cuánto sacaste por el cuadro?
4 (*catch*) coger (*SP*), agarrar (*AM*); (*hit:
target etc*) dar en; **to ~ sb by the arm/
throat** coger *or* agarrar a uno por el
brazo/cuello; **~ him!** ¡cógelo! (*SP*),
¡atrápalo! (*AM*); **the bullet got him in the
leg** la bala le dio en la pierna
5 (*take, move*) llevar; **to ~ sth to sb** hacer
llegar algo a alguien; **do you think we'll
~ it through the door?** ¿crees que lo
podremos meter por la puerta?
6 (*catch, take: plane, bus etc*) coger (*SP*),
tomar (*AM*); **where do I ~ the train for
Birmingham?** ¿dónde se coge *or* se toma
el tren para Birmingham?
7 (*understand*) entender; (*hear*) oír; **I've
got it!** ¡ya lo tengo!, ¡eureka!; **I don't ~
your meaning** no te entiendo; **I'm sorry,
I didn't ~ your name** lo siento, no cogí
tu nombre
8 (*have, possess*): **to have got** tener
get about *vi* salir mucho; (*news*)
divulgarse
get along *vi* (*agree*) llevarse bien;
(*depart*) marcharse; (*manage*) = **get by**
get at *vt fus* (*attack*) atacar; (*reach*)
alcanzar
get away *vi* marcharse; (*escape*)
escaparse
get away with *vt fus* hacer
impunemente
get back *vi* (*return*) volver ♦ *vt* recobrar
get by *vi* (*pass*) lograr pasar; (*manage*)
arreglárselas
get down *vi* bajarse ♦ *vt fus* bajar ♦ *vt*
bajar; (*depress*) deprimir
get down to *vt fus* (*work*) ponerse a
get in *vi* entrar; (*train*) llegar; (*arrive
home*) volver a casa, regresar
get into *vt fus* entrar en; (*vehicle*) subir
a; **to ~ into a rage** enfadarse
get off *vi* (*from train etc*) bajar; (*depart:
person, car*) marcharse ♦ *vt* (*remove*)
quitar ♦ *vt fus* (*train, bus*) bajar de
get on *vi* (*at exam etc*): **how are you**

~ting on? ¿cómo te va?; (*agree*): **to ~ o
(with)** llevarse bien (con) ♦ *vt fus* subir
get out *vi* salir; (*of vehicle*) bajar ♦ *vt*
sacar
get out of *vt fus* salir de; (*duty etc*)
escaparse de
get over *vt fus* (*illness*) recobrarse de
get round *vt fus* rodear; (*fig: person*)
engatusar a
get through *vi* (*TEL*) lograr
comunicarse
get through to *vt fus* (*TEL*) comunicar
con
get together *vi* reunirse ♦ *vt* reunir,
juntar
get up *vi* (*rise*) levantarse ♦ *vt fus* subi
get up to *vt fus* (*reach*) llegar a; (*pran*
hacer

geyser [ˈgiːzə*] *n* (*water heater*) calentad
m de agua; (*GEO*) géiser *m*
ghastly [ˈgɑːstlɪ] *adj* horrible
gherkin [ˈgəːkɪn] *n* pepinillo
ghetto blaster [ˈgetəʊblɑːstə*] *n* cassett
m portátil de gran tamaño
ghost [gəʊst] *n* fantasma *m*
giant [ˈdʒaɪənt] *n* gigante *m/f* ♦ *adj*
gigantesco, gigante
gibberish [ˈdʒɪbərɪʃ] *n* galimatías *m*
giblets [ˈdʒɪblɪts] *npl* menudillos *mpl*
Gibraltar [dʒɪˈbrɔːltə*] *n* Gibraltar *m*
giddy [ˈgɪdɪ] *adj* mareado
gift [gɪft] *n* regalo; (*ability*) talento; **~ed**
adj dotado; **~ token** *or* **voucher** *n* va
m canjeable por un regalo
gigantic [dʒaɪˈgæntɪk] *adj* gigantesco
giggle [ˈgɪgl] *vi* reírse tontamente
gill [dʒɪl] *n* (*measure*) = 0.25 pints (*BRIT*
= 0.148l, *US* = 0.118l)
gills [gɪlz] *npl* (*of fish*) branquias *fpl*,
agallas *fpl*
gilt [gɪlt] *adj, n* dorado; **~-edged** *adj*
(*COMM*) de máxima garantía
gimmick [ˈgɪmɪk] *n* truco
gin [dʒɪn] *n* ginebra
ginger [ˈdʒɪndʒə*] *n* jengibre *m*; **~ ale** =
beer; **~ beer** (*BRIT*) *n* gaseosa de

jengibre; **~bread** n pan m (or galleta) de jengibre
gingerly ['dʒɪndʒəlɪ] adv con cautela
gipsy ['dʒɪpsɪ] n = **gypsy**
giraffe [dʒɪ'rɑːf] n jirafa
girder ['gəːdə•] n viga
girl [gəːl] n (small) niña; (young woman) chica, joven f, muchacha; (daughter) hija; **an English ~** una (chica) inglesa; **~friend** n (of girl) amiga; (of boy) novia; **~ish** adj de niña
giro ['dʒaɪərəu] n (BRIT: bank ~) giro bancario; (post office ~) giro postal; (state benefit) cheque quincenal del subsidio de desempleo
gist [dʒɪst] n lo esencial
give [gɪv] (pt **gave**, pp **given**) vt dar; (deliver) entregar; (as gift) regalar ♦ vi (break) romperse; (stretch: fabric) dar de sí; **to ~ sb sth, ~ sth to sb** dar algo a uno; **~ away** vt (give free) regalar; (betray) traicionar; (disclose) revelar; **~ back** vt devolver; **~ in** vi ceder ♦ vt entregar; **~ off** vt despedir; **~ out** vt distribuir; **~ up** vi rendirse, darse por vencido ♦ vt renunciar a; **to ~ up smoking** dejar de fumar; **to ~ o.s. up** entregarse; **~ way** vi ceder; (BRIT: AUT) ceder el paso
glacier ['glæsɪə•] n glaciar m
glad [glæd] adj contento
gladly ['glædlɪ] adv con mucho gusto
glamorous ['glæmərəs] adj encantador(a), atractivo; **glamour** ['glæmə•] n encanto, atractivo
glance [glɑːns] n ojeada, mirada ♦ vi: **to ~ at** echar una ojeada a; **glancing** adj (blow) oblicuo
gland [glænd] n glándula
glare [glɛə•] n (of anger) mirada feroz; (of light) deslumbramiento, brillo; **to be in the ~ of publicity** ser el foco de la atención pública ♦ vi deslumbrar; **to ~ at** mirar con odio a; **glaring** adj (mistake) manifiesto
glass [glɑːs] n vidrio, cristal m; (for drinking) vaso; (: with stem) copa; **~es** npl

(spectacles) gafas fpl; **~house** n invernadero; **~ware** n cristalería
glaze [gleɪz] vt (window) poner cristales a; (pottery) vidriar ♦ n vidriado; **glazier** ['gleɪzɪə•] n vidriero/a
gleam [gliːm] vi brillar
glean [gliːn] vt (information) recoger
glee [gliː] n alegría, regocijo
glen [glɛn] n cañada
glib [glɪb] adj de mucha labia; (promise, response) poco sincero
glide [glaɪd] vi deslizarse; (AVIAT, birds) planear; **~r** n (AVIAT) planeador m; **gliding** n (AVIAT) vuelo sin motor
glimmer ['glɪmə•] n luz f tenue; (of interest) muestra; (of hope) rayo
glimpse [glɪmps] n vislumbre m ♦ vt vislumbrar, entrever
glint [glɪnt] vi centellear
glisten ['glɪsn] vi relucir, brillar
glitter ['glɪtə•] vi relucir, brillar
gloat [gləut] vi: **to ~ over** recrearse en
global ['gləubl] adj mundial; **~ warming** (re)calentamiento global or de la tierra
globe [gləub] n globo; (model) globo terráqueo
gloom [gluːm] n tinieblas fpl, oscuridad f; (sadness) tristeza, melancolía; **~y** adj (dark) oscuro; (sad) triste; (pessimistic) pesimista
glorious ['glɔːrɪəs] adj glorioso; (weather etc) magnífico
glory ['glɔːrɪ] n gloria
gloss [glɔs] n (shine) brillo; (paint) pintura de aceite; **~ over** vt fus disimular
glossary ['glɔsərɪ] n glosario
glossy ['glɔsɪ] adj lustroso; (magazine) de lujo
glove [glʌv] n guante m; **~ compartment** n (AUT) guantera
glow [gləu] vi brillar
glower ['glauə•] vi: **to ~ at** mirar con ceño
glue [gluː] n goma (de pegar), cemento ♦ vt pegar
glum [glʌm] adj (person, tone) melancólico
glut [glʌt] n superabundancia
glutton ['glʌtn] n glotón/ona m/f; **a ~ for**

work un(a) trabajador(a) incansable

gnat [næt] *n* mosquito

gnaw [nɔː] *vt* roer

gnome [nəʊm] *n* gnomo

go [gəʊ] (*pt* **went**, *pp* **gone**; *pl* **~es**) *vi* ir; (*travel*) viajar; (*depart*) irse, marcharse; (*work*) funcionar, marchar; (*be sold*) venderse; (*time*) pasar; (*fit, suit*): **to ~ with** hacer juego con; (*become*) ponerse; (*break etc*) estropearse, romperse ♦ *n*: **to have a ~ (at)** probar suerte (con); **to be on the ~** no parar; **whose ~ is it?** ¿a quién le toca?; **he's going to do it** va a hacerlo; **to ~ for a walk** ir de paseo; **to ~ dancing** ir a bailar; **how did it ~?** ¿qué tal salió *or* resultó?, ¿cómo ha ido?; **to ~ round the back** pasar por detrás; **~ about** *vi* (*rumour*) propagarse ♦ *vt*: **how do I ~ about this?** ¿cómo me las arreglo para hacer esto?; **~ ahead** *vi* seguir adelante; **~ along** *vi* ir ♦ *vt fus* bordear; **to ~ along with** (*agree*) estar de acuerdo con; **~ away** *vi* irse, marcharse; **~ back** *vi* volver; **~ back on** *vt fus* (*promise*) faltar a; **~ by** *vi* (*time*) pasar ♦ *vt fus* guiarse por; **~ down** *vi* bajar; (*ship*) hundirse; (*sun*) ponerse ♦ *vt fus* bajar; **~ for** *vt fus* (*fetch*) ir por; (*like*) gustar; (*attack*) atacar; **~ in** *vi* entrar; **~ in for** *vt fus* (*competition*) presentarse a; **~ into** *vt fus* entrar en; (*investigate*) investigar; (*embark on*) dedicarse a; **~ off** *vi* irse, marcharse; (*food*) pasarse; (*explode*) estallar; (*event*) realizarse ♦ *vt fus* dejar de gustar; **I'm going off him/the idea** ya no me gusta tanto él/la idea; **~ on** *vi* (*continue*) seguir, continuar; (*happen*) pasar, ocurrir; **to ~ on doing sth** seguir haciendo algo; **~ out** *vi* salir; (*fire, light*) apagarse; **~ over** *vi* (*ship*) zozobrar ♦ *vt fus* (*check*) revisar; **~ through** *vt fus* (*town etc*) atravesar; **~ up** *vi, vt fus* subir; **~ without** *vt fus* pasarse sin

goad [gəʊd] *vt* aguijonear

go-ahead *adj* (*person*) dinámico; (*firm*) innovador(a) ♦ *n* luz *f* verde

goal [gəʊl] *n* meta; (*score*) gol *m*;

~keeper *n* portero; **~-post** *n* poste *m* (de la portería)

goat [gəʊt] *n* cabra

gobble ['gɒbl] *vt* (*also*: **~ down, ~ up**) tragarse, engullir

go-between *n* intermediario/a

god [gɒd] *n* dios *m*; **G~** *n* Dios *m*; **~child** *n* ahijado/a; **~daughter** *n* ahijada; **~dess** *n* diosa; **~father** *n* padrino; **~forsaken** *adj* dejado de la mano de Dios; **~mother** *n* madrina; **~send** *n* don *m* del cielo; **~son** *n* ahijado

goggles ['gɒglz] *npl* gafas *fpl*

going ['gəʊɪŋ] *n* (*conditions*) estado del terreno ♦ *adj*: **the ~ rate** la tarifa corriente *or* en vigor

gold [gəʊld] *n* oro ♦ *adj* de oro; **~en** *adj* (*made of ~*) de oro; (*~ in colour*) dorado; **~fish** *n* pez *m* de colores; **~mine** *n* (*also fig*) mina de oro; **~-plated** *adj* chapado en oro; **~smith** *n* orfebre *m/f*

golf [gɒlf] *n* golf *m*; **~ ball** *n* (*for game*) pelota de golf; (*on typewriter*) esfera; **~ club** *n* club *m* de golf; (*stick*) palo (de golf); **~ course** *n* campo de golf; **~er** *n* golfista *m/f*

gone [gɒn] *pp* de **go**

good [gʊd] *adj* bueno; (*pleasant*) agradable; (*kind*) bueno, amable; (*well-behaved*) educado ♦ *n* bien *m*, provecho; **~s** *npl* (*COMM*) mercancías *fpl*; **~!** ¡qué bien!; **to be ~ at** tener aptitud para; **to be ~ for** servir para; **it's ~ for you** te hace bien; **would you be ~ enough to ...?** ¿podría hacerme el favor de ...?, ¿sería tan amable de ...?; **a ~ deal (of)** mucho; **a ~ many** muchos; **to make ~** reparar; **it's no ~ complaining** no vale la pena (de) quejarse; **for ~** para siempre, definitivamente; **~ morning/afternoon** ¡buenos días/buenas tardes!; **~ evening!** ¡buenas noches!; **~ night!** ¡buenas noches!; **~bye!** ¡adiós!; **to say ~bye** despedirse; **G~ Friday** *n* Viernes *m* Santo; **~-looking** *adj* guapo; **~-nature** *adj* amable, simpático; **~ness** *n* (*of person*) bondad *f*; **for ~ness sake!** ¡por

Dios!; **~ness gracious!** ¡Dios mío!; **~s
train** (*BRIT*) *n* tren *m* de mercancías;
~will *n* buena voluntad *f*

goose [gu:s] (*pl* **geese**) *n* ganso, oca

gooseberry ['guzbəri] *n* grosella espinosa;
to play ~ hacer de carabina

gooseflesh ['gu:sfleʃ] *n* = **goose
pimples**

goose pimples *npl* carne *f* de gallina

gore [gɔ:*] *vt* cornear ♦ *n* sangre *f*

gorge [gɔ:dʒ] *n* barranco ♦ *vr*: **to ~ o.s.
(on)** atracarse (de)

gorgeous ['gɔ:dʒəs] *adj* (*thing*) precioso;
(*weather*) espléndido; (*person*) guapísimo

gorilla [gə'rɪlə] *n* gorila *m*

gorse [gɔ:s] *n* tojo

gory ['gɔ:rɪ] *adj* sangriento

go-slow (*BRIT*) *n* huelga de manos caídas

gospel ['gɔspl] *n* evangelio

gossip ['gɔsɪp] *n* (*scandal*) cotilleo,
chismes *mpl*; (*chat*) charla;
(*scandalmonger*) cotilla *m/f*, chismoso/a
♦ *vi* cotillear

got [gɔt] *pt, pp of* **get**; **~ten** (*US*) *pp of* **get**

gout [gaut] *n* gota

govern ['gʌvən] *vt* gobernar; (*influence*)
dominar; **~ess** *n* institutriz *f*; **~ment**
n gobierno; **~or** *n* gobernador(a) *m/f*; (*of
school etc*) miembro del consejo; (*of jail*)
director(a) *m/f*

gown [gaun] *n* traje *m*; (*of teacher, BRIT: of
judge*) toga

G.P. *n abbr* = **general practitioner**

grab [græb] *vt* coger (*SP*) *or* agarrar (*AM*),
arrebatar ♦ *vi*: **to ~ at** intentar agarrar

grace [greis] *n* gracia ♦ *vt* honrar; (*adorn*)
adornar; **5 days' ~** un plazo de 5 días;
~ful *adj* grácil, ágil; (*style, shape*)
elegante, gracioso; **gracious** ['greiʃəs] *adj*
amable

grade [greid] *n* (*quality*) clase *f*, calidad *f*;
(*in hierarchy*) grado; (*SCOL: mark*) nota;
(*US: school class*) curso ♦ *vt* clasificar; **~
crossing** (*US*) *n* paso a nivel; **~ school**
(*US*) *n* escuela primaria

gradient ['greidiənt] *n* pendiente *f*

gradual ['grædjuəl] *adj* paulatino; **~ly** *adv*

paulatinamente

graduate [*n* 'grædjuit, *vb* 'grædjueit] *n* (*US:
of high school*) graduado/a; (*of university*)
licenciado/a ♦ *vi* graduarse; licenciarse;
graduation [-'eiʃən] *n* (*ceremony*)
entrega del título

graffiti [grə'fi:ti] *n* pintadas *fpl*

graft [grɑ:ft] *n* (*AGR, MED*) injerto; (*BRIT: inf*)
trabajo duro; (*bribery*) corrupción *f* ♦ *vt*
injertar

grain [grein] *n* (*single particle*) grano;
(*corn*) granos *mpl*, cereales *mpl*; (*of wood*)
fibra

gram [græm] *n* gramo

grammar ['græmə*] *n* gramática; **~
school** (*BRIT*) *n* ≈ instituto de segunda
enseñanza, liceo (*SP*)

grammatical [grə'mætikl] *adj* gramatical

gramme [græm] *n* = **gram**

gramophone ['græməfəun] (*BRIT*) *n*
tocadiscos *m inv*

grand [grænd] *adj* magnífico, imponente;
(*wonderful*) estupendo; (*gesture etc*)
grandioso; **~children** *npl* nietos *mpl*;
~dad (*inf*) *n* yayo, abuelito; **~daughter**
n nieta; **~eur** ['grændjə*] *n* magnificencia,
lo grandioso; **~father** *n* abuelo; **~ma**
(*inf*) *n* yaya, abuelita; **~mother** *n* abuela;
~pa (*inf*) *n* = **~dad**; **~parents** *npl*
abuelos *mpl*; **~ piano** *n* piano de cola;
~son *n* nieto; **~stand** *n* (*SPORT*) tribuna

granite ['grænit] *n* granito

granny ['græni] (*inf*) *n* abuelita, yaya

grant [grɑ:nt] *vt* (*concede*) conceder;
(*admit*) reconocer ♦ *n* (*SCOL*) beca;
(*ADMIN*) subvención *f*; **to take sth/sb for
~ed** dar algo por sentado/no hacer
ningún caso a uno

granulated sugar ['grænju:leitid-] (*BRIT*)
n azúcar *m* blanquilla

grape [greip] *n* uva

grapefruit ['greipfru:t] *n* pomelo (*SP*),
toronja (*AM*)

graph [grɑ:f] *n* gráfica; **~ic** ['græfik] *adj*
gráfico; **~ics** *n* artes *fpl* gráficas ♦ *npl*
(*drawings*) dibujos *mpl*

grapple ['græpl] *vi*: **to ~ with sth/sb**

agarrar a algo/uno

grasp [grɑːsp] *vt* agarrar, asir; (*understand*) comprender ♦ *n* (*grip*) asimiento; (*understanding*) comprensión *f*; **~ing** *adj* (*mean*) avaro

grass [grɑːs] *n* hierba; (*lawn*) césped *m*; **~hopper** *n* saltamontes *m inv*; **~-roots** *adj* (*fig*) popular

grate [greɪt] *n* parrilla de chimenea ♦ *vi*: **to ~ (on)** chirriar (sobre) ♦ *vt* (*CULIN*) rallar

grateful [ˈɡreɪtfʊl] *adj* agradecido

grater [ˈɡreɪtə*] *n* rallador *m*

gratifying [ˈɡrætɪfaɪŋ] *adj* grato

grating [ˈɡreɪtɪŋ] *n* (*iron bars*) reja ♦ *adj* (*noise*) áspero

gratitude [ˈɡrætɪtjuːd] *n* agradecimiento

gratuity [ɡrəˈtjuːɪtɪ] *n* gratificación *f*

grave [ɡreɪv] *n* tumba ♦ *adj* serio, grave

gravel [ˈɡrævl] *n* grava

gravestone [ˈɡreɪvstəʊn] *n* lápida

graveyard [ˈɡreɪvjɑːd] *n* cementerio

gravity [ˈɡrævɪtɪ] *n* gravedad *f*

gravy [ˈɡreɪvɪ] *n* salsa de carne

gray [ɡreɪ] *adj* = **grey**

graze [ɡreɪz] *vi* pacer ♦ *vt* (*touch lightly*) rozar; (*scrape*) raspar ♦ *n* (*MED*) abrasión *f*

grease [ɡriːs] *n* (*fat*) grasa; (*lubricant*) lubricante *m* ♦ *vt* engrasar; lubrificar; **~proof paper** (*BRIT*) *n* papel *m* apergaminado; **greasy** *adj* grasiento

great [ɡreɪt] *adj* grande; (*inf*) magnífico, estupendo; **G~ Britain** *n* Gran Bretaña; **~-grandfather** *n* bisabuelo; **~-grandmother** *n* bisabuela; **~ly** *adv* muy; (*with verb*) mucho; **~ness** *n* grandeza

Greece [ɡriːs] *n* Grecia

greed [ɡriːd] *n* (*also*: **~iness**) codicia, avaricia; (*for food*) gula; (*for power etc*) avidez *f*; **~y** *adj* avaro; (*for food*) glotón/ona

Greek [ɡriːk] *adj* griego ♦ *n* griego/a; (*LING*) griego

green [ɡriːn] *adj* (*also POL*) verde; (*inexperienced*) novato ♦ *n* verde *m*; (*stretch of grass*) césped *m*; (*GOLF*) green

m; **~s** *npl* (*vegetables*) verduras *fpl*; **~ belt** *n* zona verde; **~ card** *n* (*AUT*) carta verde; (*US: work permit*) permiso de trabajo para los extranjeros en EE. UU.; **~ery** *n* verdura; **~grocer** (*BRIT*) *n* verdulero/a; **~house** *n* invernadero; **~house effect** *n* efecto invernadero; **~house gas** *n* gases *mpl* de invernadero; **~ish** *adj* verdoso

Greenland [ˈɡriːnlənd] *n* Groenlandia

greet [ɡriːt] *vt* (*welcome*) dar la bienvenida a; (*receive: news*) recibir; **~ing** *n* (*welcome*) bienvenida; **~ing(s) card** *n* tarjeta de felicitación

grenade [ɡrəˈneɪd] *n* granada

grew [ɡruː] *pt of* **grow**

grey [ɡreɪ] *adj* gris; (*weather*) sombrío; **~-haired** *adj* canoso; **~hound** *n* galgo

grid [ɡrɪd] *n* reja; (*ELEC*) red *f*; **~lock** *n* (*traffic jam*) retención *f*

grief [ɡriːf] *n* dolor *m*, pena

grievance [ˈɡriːvəns] *n* motivo de queja, agravio

grieve [ɡriːv] *vi* afligirse, acongojarse ♦ *vt* dar pena a; **to ~ for** llorar por

grievous [ˈɡriːvəs] *adj*: **~ bodily harm** (*LAW*) daños *mpl* corporales graves

grill [ɡrɪl] *n* (*on cooker*) parrilla; (*also*: **mixed ~**) parillada ♦ *vt* (*BRIT*) asar a la parrilla; (*inf: question*) interrogar

grille [ɡrɪl] *n* reja; (*AUT*) rejilla

grim [ɡrɪm] *adj* (*place*) sombrío; (*situation*) triste; (*person*) ceñudo

grimace [ɡrɪˈmeɪs] *n* mueca ♦ *vi* hacer muecas

grime [ɡraɪm] *n* mugre *f*, suciedad *f*

grin [ɡrɪn] *n* sonrisa abierta ♦ *vi* sonreír abiertamente

grind [ɡraɪnd] (*pt, pp* **ground**) *vt* (*coffee, pepper etc*) moler; (*US: meat*) picar; (*make sharp*) afilar ♦ *n* (*work*) rutina

grip [ɡrɪp] *n* (*hold*) asimiento; (*control*) control *m*, dominio; (*of tyre etc*): **to have a good/bad ~** agarrarse bien/mal; (*handle*) asidero; (*holdall*) maletín *m* ♦ *vt* agarrar; (*viewer, reader*) fascinar; **to get to ~s with** enfrentarse con; **~ping** *adj* absorbente

grisly ['grɪzlɪ] adj horripilante, horrible

gristle ['grɪsl] n ternilla

grit [grɪt] n gravilla; (courage) valor m ♦ vt (road) poner gravilla en; **to ~ one's teeth** apretar los dientes

groan [grəun] n gemido; quejido ♦ vi gemir; quejarse

grocer ['grəusə*] n tendero (de ultramarinos (SP)); **~ies** npl comestibles mpl; **~'s (shop)** n tienda de ultramarinos or de abarrotes (AM)

groin [grɔɪn] n ingle f

groom [gruːm] n mozo/a de cuadra; (also: **bride~**) novio ♦ vt (horse) almohazar; (fig): **to ~ sb for** preparar a uno para; **well-~ed** de buena presencia

groove [gruːv] n ranura, surco

grope [grəup]: **to ~ for** vt fus buscar a tientas

gross [grəus] adj (neglect, injustice) grave; (vulgar: behaviour) grosero; (: appearance) de mal gusto; (COMM) bruto; **~ly** adv (greatly) enormemente

grotto ['grɔtəu] n gruta

grotty ['grɔtɪ] (inf) adj horrible

ground [graund] pt, pp of **grind** ♦ n suelo, tierra; (SPORT) campo, terreno; (reason: gen pl) causa, razón f; (US: also: **~ wire**) tierra ♦ vt (plane) mantener en tierra; (US: ELEC) conectar con tierra; **~s** npl (of coffee etc) poso; (gardens etc) jardines mpl, parque m; **on the ~** en el suelo; **to the ~** al suelo; **to gain/lose ~** ganar/perder terreno; **~ cloth** (US) n =**sheet**; **~ing** n (in education) conocimientos mpl básicos; **~less** adj infundado; **~sheet** (BRIT) n tela impermeable; suelo; **~ staff** n personal m de tierra; **~work** n preparación f

group [gruːp] n grupo; (musical) conjunto ♦ vt (also: **~ together**) agrupar ♦ vi (also: **~ together**) agruparse

grouse [graus] n inv (bird) urogallo ♦ vi (complain) quejarse

grove [grəuv] n arboleda

grovel ['grɔvl] vi (fig): **to ~ before**

humillarse ante

grow [grəu] (pt **grew**, pp **grown**) vi crecer; (increase) aumentar; (expand) desarrollarse; (become) volverse; **to ~ rich/weak** enriquecerse/debilitarse ♦ vt cultivar; (hair, beard) dejar crecer; **~ up** vi crecer, hacerse hombre/mujer; **~er** n cultivador(a) m/f, productor(a) m/f; **~ing** adj creciente

growl [graul] vi gruñir

grown [grəun] pp of **grow**; **~-up** n adulto, mayor m/f

growth [grəuθ] n crecimiento, desarrollo; (what has grown) brote m; (MED) tumor m

grub [grʌb] n larva, gusano m; (inf: food) comida

grubby ['grʌbɪ] adj sucio, mugriento

grudge [grʌdʒ] n (motivo de) rencor m ♦ vt: **to ~ sb sth** dar algo a uno de mala gana; **to bear sb a ~** guardar rencor a uno

gruelling ['gruəlɪŋ] (US **grueling**) adj penoso, duro

gruesome ['gruːsəm] adj horrible

gruff [grʌf] adj (voice) ronco; (manner) brusco

grumble ['grʌmbl] vi refunfuñar, quejarse

grumpy ['grʌmpɪ] adj gruñón/ona

grunt [grʌnt] vi gruñir

G-string ['dʒiːstrɪŋ] n taparrabo

guarantee [gærən'tiː] n garantía ♦ vt garantizar

guard [gɑːd] n (squad) guardia; (one man) guardia m; (BRIT: RAIL) jefe m de tren; (on machine) dispositivo de seguridad; (also: **fire~**) rejilla de protección ♦ vt guardar; (prisoner) vigilar; **to be on one's ~** estar alerta; **~ against** vt fus (prevent) protegerse de; **~ed** adj (fig) cauteloso; **~ian** n guardián/ana m/f; (of minor) tutor(a) m/f; **~'s van** n (BRIT: RAIL) furgón m

Guatemala [gwætɪ'mɑːlə] n Guatemala; **~n** adj, n guatemalteco/a m/f

guerrilla [gə'rɪlə] n guerrillero/a

guess [ges] vi adivinar; (US) suponer ♦ vt

adivinar; suponer ♦ *n* suposición *f*, conjetura; **to take** *or* **have a ~** tratar de adivinar; **~work** *n* conjeturas *fpl*

guest [gest] *n* invitado/a; (*in hotel*) huésped(a) *m/f*; **~ house** *n* casa de huéspedes, pensión *f*; **~ room** *n* cuarto de huéspedes

guffaw [gʌ'fɔ:] *vi* reírse a carcajadas

guidance ['gaɪdəns] *n* (*advice*) consejos *mpl*

guide [gaɪd] *n* (*person*) guía *m/f*; (*book, fig*) guía *f*; (*round museum etc*) guiar; (*lead*) conducir; (*direct*) orientar; (*girl*) **~** *n* exploradora; **~book** *n* guía; **~ dog** *n* perro *m* guía; **~lines** *npl* (*advice*) directrices *fpl*

guild [gɪld] *n* gremio

guilt [gɪlt] *n* culpabilidad *f*; **~y** *adj* culpable

guinea pig ['gɪnɪ-] *n* cobaya; (*fig*) conejillo de Indias

guise [gaɪz] *n*: **in** *or* **under the ~ of** bajo apariencia de

guitar [gɪ'tɑ:*] *n* guitarra

gulf [gʌlf] *n* golfo; (*abyss*) abismo

gull [gʌl] *n* gaviota

gullible ['gʌlɪbl] *adj* crédulo

gully ['gʌlɪ] *n* barranco

gulp [gʌlp] *vi* tragar saliva ♦ *vt* (*also: ~ down*) tragarse

gum [gʌm] *n* (*ANAT*) encía; (*glue*) goma, cemento; (*sweet*) caramelo de goma; (*also: **chewing~**) chicle *m* ♦ *vt* pegar con goma; **~boots** (*BRIT*) *npl* botas *fpl* de goma

gun [gʌn] *n* (*small*) pistola, revólver *m*; (*shotgun*) escopeta; (*rifle*) fusil *m*; (*cannon*) cañón *m*; **~boat** *n* cañonero; **~fire** *n* disparos *mpl*; **~man** *n* pistolero; **~point** *n*: **at ~point** a mano armada; **~powder** *n* pólvora; **~shot** *n* escopetazo

gurgle ['gə:gl] *vi* (*baby*) gorgotear; (*water*) borbotear

gush [gʌʃ] *vi* salir a raudales; (*person*) deshacerse en efusiones

gust [gʌst] *n* (*of wind*) ráfaga

gusto ['gʌstəu] *n* entusiasmo

gut [gʌt] *n* intestino; **~s** *npl* (*ANAT*) tripas *fpl*; (*courage*) valor *m*

gutter ['gʌtə*] *n* (*of roof*) canalón *m*; (*in street*) cuneta

guy [gaɪ] *n* (*also:* **~rope**) cuerda; (*inf: man*) tío (*SP*), tipo; (*figure*) monigote *m*

Guy Fawkes' Night

La noche del cinco de noviembre, **Guy Fawkes' Night**, *se celebra en el Reino Unido el fracaso de la conspiración de la pólvora ("Gunpowder Plot"), un intento fallido de volar el parlamento de Jaime I en 1605. Esa noche se lanzan fuegos artificiales y se hacen hogueras en las que se queman unos muñecos de trapo que representan a* **Guy Fawkes**, *uno de los cabecillas de la revuelta. Días antes, los niños tienen por costumbre pedir a los transeúntes "a penny for the guy", dinero que emplean en comprar cohetes y petardos.*

---

guzzle ['gʌzl] *vi* tragar ♦ *vt* engullir

gym [dʒɪm] *n* (*also:* **gymnasium**) gimnasio; (*also:* **gymnastics**) gimnasia; **~nast** *n* gimnasta *m/f*; **~ shoes** *npl* zapatillas *fpl* (de deporte); **~ slip** (*BRIT*) *n* túnica de colegiala

gynaecologist [gaɪnɪ'kɔlədʒɪst] (*US* **gynecologist**) *n* ginecólogo/a

gypsy ['dʒɪpsɪ] *n* gitano/a

H, h

haberdashery [hæbə'dæʃərɪ] (*BRIT*) *n* mercería

habit ['hæbɪt] *n* hábito, costumbre *f*; (*drug ~*) adicción *f*; (*costume*) hábito

habitual [hə'bɪtjuəl] *adj* acostumbrado, habitual; (*drinker, liar*) empedernido

hack [hæk] *vt* (*cut*) cortar; (*slice*) tajar ♦ *n* (*pej: writer*) escritor(a) *m/f* a sueldo; **~er** *n* (*COMPUT*) pirata *m/f* informático/a

hackneyed ['hæknɪd] *adj* trillado

had [hæd] *pt, pp of* **have**
haddock ['hædək] (*pl* **~** *or* **~s**) *n especie de merluza*
hadn't ['hædnt] = **had not**
haemorrhage ['hemərɪdʒ] (*US* **hemorrhage**) *n* hemorragia
haemorrhoids ['hemərɔɪdz] (*US* **hemorrhoids**) *npl* hemorroides *fpl*
haggle ['hægl] *vi* regatear
Hague [heɪg] *n*: **The ~** La Haya
hail [heɪl] *n* granizo; (*fig*) lluvia ♦ *vt* saludar; (*taxi*) llamar a; (*acclaim*) aclamar ♦ *vi* granizar; **~stone** *n* (piedra de) granizo
hair [hɛə•] *n* pelo, cabellos *mpl*; (*one ~*) pelo, cabello; (*on legs etc*) vello; **to do one's ~** arreglarse el pelo; **to have grey ~** tener canas *fpl*; **~brush** *n* cepillo (para el pelo); **~cut** *n* corte *m* (de pelo); **~do** *n* peinado; **~dresser** *n* peluquero/a; **~dresser's** *n* peluquería; **~ dryer** *n* secador *m* de pelo; **~grip** *n* horquilla; **~net** *n* redecilla; **~piece** *n* postizo; **~pin** *n* horquilla; **~pin bend** (*US* **~pin curve**) *n* curva de horquilla; **~raising** *adj* espeluznante; **~ removing cream** *n* crema depilatoria; **~ spray** *n* laca; **~style** *n* peinado; **~y** *adj* peludo; velludo; (*inf: frightening*) espeluznante
hake [heɪk] (*pl inv or* **~s**) *n* merluza
half [hɑ:f] (*pl* **halves**) *n* mitad *f*; (*of beer*) ≈ caña (*SP*), media pinta; (*RAIL, BUS*) billete *m* de niño ♦ *adj* medio ♦ *adv* medio, a medias; **two and a ~** dos y media; **~ a dozen** media docena; **~ a pound** media libra; **to cut sth in ~** cortar algo por la mitad; **~-caste** ['hɑ:fkɑ:st] *n* mestizo/a; **~-hearted** *adj* indiferente, poco entusiasta; **~-hour** *n* media hora; **~-mast** *n*: **at ~-mast** (*flag*) a media asta; **~-price** *adj, adv* a mitad de precio; **~ term** (*BRIT*) *n* (*SCOL*) vacaciones de mediados del trimestre; **~-time** *n* descanso; **~way** *adv* a medio camino; (*in period of time*) a mitad de
hall [hɔ:l] *n* (for concerts) sala; (*entrance way*) hall *m*; vestíbulo; **~ of residence**

(*BRIT*) *n* residencia
hallmark ['hɔ:lmɑ:k] *n* sello
hallo [hə'ləʊ] *excl* = **hello**
Hallowe'en [hæləʊ'iːn] *n* víspera de Todos los Santos

Hallowe'en

i *La tradición anglosajona dice que en la noche del 31 de octubre, Hallowe'en, víspera de Todos los Santos, es posible ver a brujas y fantasmas. En este día los niños se disfrazan y van de puerta en puerta llevando un farol hecho con una calabaza en forma de cabeza humana. Cuando se les abre la puerta gritan "trick or treat", amenazando con gastar una broma a quien no les dé golosinas o algo de calderilla.*

---

hallucination [həluːsɪ'neɪʃən] *n* alucinación *f*
hallway ['hɔ:lweɪ] *n* vestíbulo
halo ['heɪləʊ] *n* (*of saint*) halo, aureola
halt [hɔ:lt] *n* (*stop*) alto, parada ♦ *vt* parar; interrumpir ♦ *vi* pararse
halve [hɑ:v] *vt* partir por la mitad
halves [hɑ:vz] *npl of* **half**
ham [hæm] *n* jamón *m* (cocido)
hamburger ['hæmbɜ:gə•] *n* hamburguesa
hamlet ['hæmlɪt] *n* aldea
hammer ['hæmə•] *n* martillo ♦ *vt* (*nail*) clavar; (*force*): **to ~ an idea into sb/a message across** meter una idea en la cabeza a uno/machacar una idea ♦ *vi* dar golpes
hammock ['hæmək] *n* hamaca
hamper ['hæmpə•] *vt* estorbar ♦ *n* cesto
hand [hænd] *n* mano *f*; (*of clock*) aguja; (*writing*) letra; (*worker*) obrero ♦ *vt* dar, pasar; **to give** *or* **lend sb a ~** echar una mano a uno, ayudar a uno; **at ~** a mano; **in ~** (*time*) libre; (*job etc*) entre manos; **on ~** (*person, services*) a mano, al alcance; **to ~** (*information etc*) a mano; **on the one ~ ..., on the other ~ ...** por una parte ... por otra (parte) ...; **~ in** *vt* entregar; **~ out** *vt* distribuir; **~ over** *vt* (*deliver*)

entregar; **~bag** *n* bolso (*SP*), cartera (*AM*); **~book** *n* manual *m*; **~brake** *n* freno de mano; **~cuffs** *npl* esposas *fpl*; **~ful** *n* puñado

handicap ['hændɪkæp] *n* minusvalía; (*disadvantage*) desventaja; (*SPORT*) handicap *m* ♦ *vt* estorbar; **mentally / physically ~ped** deficiente *m/f* (mental)/ minusválido/-a (físico/-a)

handicraft ['hændɪkrɑːft] *n* artesanía; (*object*) objeto de artesanía

handiwork ['hændɪwɜːk] *n* obra

handkerchief ['hæŋkətʃɪf] *n* pañuelo

handle ['hændl] *n* (*of door etc*) tirador *m*; (*of cup etc*) asa; (*of knife etc*) mango; (*for winding*) manivela ♦ *vt* (*touch*) tocar; (*deal with*) encargarse de; (*treat: people*) manejar; **"~ with care"** "(manéjese) con cuidado"; **to fly off the ~** perder los estribos; **~bar(s)** *n(pl)* manillar *m*

hand: **~ luggage** *n* equipaje *m* de mano; **~made** *adj* hecho a mano; **~out** *n* (*money etc*) limosna; (*leaflet*) folleto; **~rail** *n* pasamanos *m inv*; **~shake** *n* apretón *m* de manos

handsome ['hænsəm] *adj* guapo; (*building*) bello; (*fig: profit*) considerable

handwriting ['hændraɪtɪŋ] *n* letra

handy ['hændɪ] *adj* (*close at hand*) a la mano; (*tool etc*) práctico; (*skilful*) hábil, diestro

hang [hæŋ] (*pt, pp* **hung**) *vt* colgar; (*criminal: pt, pp* **hanged**) ahorcar ♦ *vi* (*painting, coat etc*) colgar; (*hair, drapery*) caer; **to get the ~ of sth** (*inf*) lograr dominar algo; **~ about** *or* **around** *vi* haraganear; **~ on** *vi* (*wait*) esperar; **~ up** *vi* (*TEL*) colgar ♦ *vt* colgar

hanger ['hæŋə*] *n* percha; **~-on** *n* parásito

hang: **~-gliding** ['-glaɪdɪŋ] *n* vuelo libre; **~over** *n* (*after drinking*) resaca; **~-up** *n* complejo

hanker ['hæŋkə*] *vi*: **to ~ after** añorar

hankie, **hanky** ['hæŋkɪ] *n abbr* = **handkerchief**

haphazard [hæp'hæzəd] *adj* fortuito

happen ['hæpən] *vi* suceder, ocurrir; (*chance*): **he ~ed to hear / see** dió la casualidad de que oyó/vió; **as it ~s** da la casualidad de que; **~ing** *n* suceso, acontecimiento

happily ['hæpɪlɪ] *adv* (*luckily*) afortunadamente; (*cheerfully*) alegremente

happiness ['hæpɪnɪs] *n* felicidad *f*; (*cheerfulness*) alegría

happy ['hæpɪ] *adj* feliz; (*cheerful*) alegre; **to be ~ (with)** estar contento (con); **to be ~ to do** estar encantado de hacer; **~ birthday!** ¡feliz cumpleaños!; **~-go-lucky** *adj* despreocupado; **~ hour** *n* horas *fpl* en las que la bebida es más barata, happy hour *f*

harass ['hærəs] *vt* acosar, hostigar; **~ment** *n* persecución *f*

harbour ['hɑːbə*] (*US* **harbor**) *n* puerto ♦ *vt* (*fugitive*) dar abrigo a; (*hope etc*) abrigar

hard [hɑːd] *adj* duro; (*difficult*) difícil; (*work*) arduo; (*person*) severo; (*fact*) innegable ♦ *adv* (*work*) mucho, duro; (*think*) profundamente; **to look ~ at** clavar los ojos en; **to try ~** esforzarse; **no ~ feelings!** ¡sin rencor(es)!; **to be ~ of hearing** ser duro de oído; **to be ~ done by** ser tratado injustamente; **~back** *n* libro en cartoné; **~ cash** *n* dinero contante; **~ disk** *n* (*COMPUT*) disco duro *or* rígido; **~en** *vt* endurecer; (*fig*) curtir ♦ *vi* endurecerse; curtirse; **~-headed** *adj* realista; **~ labour** *n* trabajos *mpl* forzados

hardly ['hɑːdlɪ] *adv* apenas; **~ ever** casi nunca

hard: **~ship** *n* privación *f*; **~ shoulder** (*BRIT*) *n* (*AUT*) arcén *m*; **~-up** (*inf*) *adj* sin un duro (*SP*), sin plata (*AM*); **~ware** *n* ferretería; (*COMPUT*) hardware *m*; (*MIL*) armamento; **~ware shop** *n* ferretería; **~-wearing** *adj* resistente, duradero; **~-working** *adj* trabajador(a)

hardy ['hɑːdɪ] *adj* fuerte; (*plant*) resistente

hare [heə*] *n* liebre *f*; **~-brained** *adj* descabellado

harm [hɑːm] n daño, mal m ♦ vt (person) hacer daño a; (health, interests) perjudicar; (thing) dañar; **out of ~'s way** a salvo; **~ful** adj dañino; **~less** adj (person) inofensivo; (joke etc) inocente

harmony [ˈhɑːmənɪ] n armonía

harness [ˈhɑːnɪs] n arreos mpl; (for child) arnés m; (safety ~) arneses mpl ♦ vt (horse) enjaezar; (resources) aprovechar

harp [hɑːp] n arpa ♦ vi: **to ~ on (about)** machacar (con)

harrowing [ˈhærəʊɪŋ] adj angustioso

harsh [hɑːʃ] adj (cruel) duro, cruel; (severe) severo; (sound) áspero; (light) deslumbrador(a)

harvest [ˈhɑːvɪst] n (~ time) siega; (of cereals etc) cosecha; (of grapes) vendimia ♦ vt cosechar

has [hæz] vb see **have**

hash [hæʃ] n (CULIN) picadillo; (fig: mess) lío

hashish [ˈhæʃɪʃ] n hachís m

hasn't [ˈhæznt] = **has not**

hassle [ˈhæsl] (inf) n lata

haste [heɪst] n prisa; **~n** [ˈheɪsn] vt acelerar ♦ vi darse prisa; **hastily** adv de prisa; precipitadamente; **hasty** adj apresurado; (rash) precipitado

hat [hæt] n sombrero

hatch [hætʃ] n (NAUT: also: **~way**) escotilla; (also: **service ~**) ventanilla ♦ vi (bird) salir del cascarón ♦ vt incubar; (plot) tramar; **5 eggs have ~ed** han salido 5 pollos

hatchback [ˈhætʃbæk] n (AUT) tres or cinco puertas m

hatchet [ˈhætʃɪt] n hacha

hate [heɪt] vt odiar, aborrecer ♦ n odio; **~ful** adj odioso; **hatred** [ˈheɪtrɪd] n odio

naughty [ˈhɔːtɪ] adj altanero

haul [hɔːl] vt tirar ♦ n (of fish) redada; (of stolen goods etc) botín m; **~age** (BRIT) n transporte m; (costs) gastos mpl de transporte; **~ier** (US **~er**) n transportista m/f

naunch [hɔːntʃ] n anca; (of meat) pierna

naunt [hɔːnt] vt (subj: ghost) aparecerse en; (obsess) obsesionar ♦ n guarida

---

have [hæv] (pt, pp **had**) aux vb 1 (gen) haber; **to ~ arrived/eaten** haber llegado/comido; **having finished** or **when he had finished, he left** cuando hubo acabado, se fue

2 (in tag questions): **you've done it, ~n't you?** lo has hecho, ¿verdad? or ¿no?

3 (in short answers and questions): **I ~n't** no; **so I ~** pues, es verdad; **we ~n't paid – yes we ~!** no hemos pagado — ¡sí que hemos pagado!; **I've been there before, ~ you?** he estado allí antes, ¿y tú?

♦ modal aux vb (be obliged): **to ~ (got) to do sth** tener que hacer algo; **you ~n't to tell her** no hay que or no debes decírselo

♦ vt 1 (possess): **he has (got) blue eyes/dark hair** tiene los ojos azules/el pelo negro

2 (referring to meals etc): **to ~ breakfast/ lunch/dinner** desayunar/comer/cenar; **to ~ a drink/a cigarette** tomar algo/fumar un cigarrillo

3 (receive) recibir; (obtain) obtener; **may I ~ your address?** ¿puedes darme tu dirección?; **you can ~ it for £5** te lo puedes quedar por £5; **I must ~ it by tomorrow** lo necesito para mañana; **to ~ a baby** tener un niño or bebé

4 (maintain, allow): **I won't ~ it/this nonsense!** ¡no lo permitiré!/¡no permitiré estas tonterías!; **we can't ~ that** no podemos permitir eso

5: **to ~ sth done** hacer or mandar hacer algo; **to ~ one's hair cut** cortarse el pelo; **to ~ sb do sth** hacer que alguien haga algo

6 (experience, suffer): **to ~ a cold/flu** tener un resfriado/la gripe; **she had her bag stolen/her arm broken** le robaron el bolso/se rompió un brazo; **to ~ an operation** operarse

7 (+noun): **to ~ a swim/walk/bath/rest** nadar/dar un paseo/darse un baño/ descansar; **let's ~ a look** vamos a ver; **to**

~ **a meeting / party** celebrar una reunión/una fiesta; **let me ~ a try** déjame intentarlo

have out *vt*: **to ~ it out with sb** (*settle a problem etc*) dejar las cosas en claro con alguien

haven ['heɪvn] *n* puerto; (*fig*) refugio
haven't ['hævnt] = **have not**
havoc ['hævək] *n* estragos *mpl*
hawk [hɔːk] *n* halcón *m*
hay [heɪ] *n* heno; ~ **fever** *n* fiebre *f* del heno; ~**stack** *n* almiar *m*
haywire ['heɪwaɪə*] (*inf*) *adj*: **to go ~** (*plan*) embrollarse
hazard ['hæzəd] *n* peligro ♦ *vt* aventurar; ~**ous** *adj* peligroso; ~ **warning lights** *npl* (*AUT*) señales *fpl* de emergencia
haze [heɪz] *n* neblina
hazelnut ['heɪzlnʌt] *n* avellana
hazy ['heɪzɪ] *adj* brumoso; (*idea*) vago
he [hiː] *pron* él; ~ **who ...** él que ..., quien ...
head [hed] *n* cabeza; (*leader*) jefe/a *m/f*; (*of school*) director(a) *m/f* ♦ *vt* (*list*) encabezar; (*group*) capitanear; (*company*) dirigir; ~**s (or tails)** cara (o cruz); ~ **first** de cabeza; ~ **over heels** (*in love*) perdidamente; **to ~ the ball** cabecear (la pelota); ~ **for** *vt fus* dirigirse a; (*disaster*) ir camino de; ~**ache** *n* dolor *m* de cabeza; ~**dress** *n* tocado; ~**ing** *n* título; ~**lamp** (*BRIT*) *n* = ~**light**; ~**land** *n* promontorio; ~**light** *n* faro; ~**line** *n* titular *m*; ~**long** *adv* (*fall*) de cabeza; (*rush*) precipitadamente; ~**master / mistress** *n* director(a) *m/f* (de escuela); ~ **office** *n* oficina central, central *f*; ~-**on** *adj* (*collision*) de frente; ~**phones** *npl* auriculares *mpl*; ~**quarters** *npl* sede *f* central; (*MIL*) cuartel *m* general; ~**rest** *n* reposa-cabezas *m inv*; ~**room** *n* (*in car*) altura interior; (*under bridge*) (límite *m* de) altura; ~**scarf** *n* pañuelo; ~**strong** *adj* testarudo; ~ **waiter** *n* maître *m*; ~**way** *n*: **to make ~way** (*fig*) hacer progresos; ~**wind** *n* viento contrario; ~**y** *adj*

(*experience, period*) apasionante; (*wine*) cabezón; (*atmosphere*) embriagador(a)
heal [hiːl] *vt* curar ♦ *vi* cicatrizarse
health [hɛlθ] *n* salud *f*; ~ **food** *n* alimentos *mpl* orgánicos; **the H~ Service** (*BRIT*) *n* el servicio de salud pública; ≈ el Insalud (*SP*); ~**y** *adj* sano, saludable
heap [hiːp] *n* montón *m* ♦ *vt*: **to ~ (up)** amontonar; **to ~ sth with** llenar algo hasta arriba de; ~**s of** un montón de
hear [hɪə*] (*pt, pp* **heard**) *vt* (*also LAW*) oír; (*news*) saber *vi* oír; **to ~ about** oír hablar de; **to ~ from sb** tener noticias de uno; ~**ing** *n* (*sense*) oído; (*LAW*) vista; ~**ing aid** *n* audífono; ~**say** *n* rumores *mpl*, hablillas *fpl*
hearse [hɜːs] *n* coche *m* fúnebre
heart [hɑːt] *n* corazón *m*; (*fig*) valor *m*; (*of lettuce*) cogollo; ~**s** *npl* (*CARDS*) corazones *mpl*; **to lose / take ~** descorazonarse/ cobrar ánimo; **at** ~ en el fondo; **by ~** (*learn, know*) de memoria; ~ **attack** *n* infarto (de miocardio); ~**beat** *n* latido (del corazón); ~**breaking** *adj* desgarrador(a); ~**broken** *adj*: **she was ~broken about it** esto le partió el corazón; ~**burn** *n* acedía; ~ **failure** *n* fallo cardíaco; ~**felt** *adj* (*deeply felt*) más sentido
hearth [hɑːθ] *n* (*fireplace*) chimenea
hearty ['hɑːtɪ] *adj* (*person*) campechano; (*laugh*) sano; (*dislike, support*) absoluto
heat [hiːt] *n* calor *m*; (*SPORT: also:* **qualifying ~**) prueba eliminatoria ♦ *vt* calentar; ~ **up** *vi* calentarse ♦ *vt* calentar; ~**ed** *adj* caliente; (*fig*) acalorado; ~**er** *n* estufa; (*in car*) calefacción *f*
heath [hiːθ] (*BRIT*) *n* brezal *m*
heather ['hɛðə*] *n* brezo
heating ['hiːtɪŋ] *n* calefacción *f*
heatstroke ['hiːtstrəʊk] *n* insolación *f*
heatwave ['hiːtweɪv] *n* ola de calor
heave [hiːv] *vt* (*pull*) tirar; (*push*) empujar con esfuerzo; (*lift*) levantar (con esfuerzo) ♦ *vi* (*chest*) palpitar; (*retch*) tener náuseas ♦ *n* tirón *m*; empujón *m*; **to ~ a sigh**

suspirar

heaven ['hɛvn] n cielo; (fig) una maravilla; **~ly** adj celestial; (fig) maravilloso

heavily ['hɛvɪlɪ] adv pesadamente; (drink, smoke) con exceso; (sleep, sigh) profundamente; (depend) mucho

heavy ['hɛvɪ] adj pesado; (work, blow) duro; (sea, rain, meal) fuerte; (drinker, smoker) grande; (responsibility) grave; (schedule) ocupado; (weather) bochornoso; **~ goods vehicle** n vehículo pesado; **~weight** n (SPORT) peso pesado

Hebrew ['hi:bru:] adj, n (LING) hebreo

heckle ['hɛkl] vt interrumpir

hectic ['hɛktɪk] adj agitado

he'd [hi:d] = **he would**; **he had**

hedge [hɛdʒ] n seto ♦ vi contestar con evasivas; **to ~ one's bets** (fig) cubrirse

hedgehog ['hɛdʒhɔg] n erizo

heed [hi:d] vt (also: **take ~ of**) (pay attention to) hacer caso de; **~less** adj: **to be ~less (of)** no hacer caso (de)

heel [hi:l] n talón m; (of shoe) tacón m ♦ vt (shoe) poner tacón a

hefty ['hɛftɪ] adj (person) fornido; (parcel, profit) gordo

heifer ['hɛfə*] n novilla, ternera

height [haɪt] n (of person) estatura; (of building) altura; (high ground) cerro; (altitude) altitud f; (fig: of season): **at the ~ of summer** en los días más calurosos del verano; (: of power etc) cúspide f; (: of stupidity etc) colmo; **~en** vt elevar; (fig) aumentar

heir [ɛə*] n heredero; **~ess** n heredera; **~loom** n reliquia de familia

held [hɛld] pt, pp of **hold**

helicopter ['hɛlɪkɔptə*] n helicóptero

hell [hɛl] n infierno; **~!** (inf) ¡demonios!

he'll [hi:l] = **he will**; **he shall**

hello [hə'ləu] excl ¡hola!; (to attract attention) ¡oiga!; (surprise) ¡caramba!

helm [hɛlm] n (NAUT) timón m

helmet ['hɛlmɪt] n casco

help [hɛlp] n ayuda; (cleaner etc) criada, asistenta ♦ vt ayudar; **~!** ¡socorro!; **~**

yourself sírvete; **he can't ~ it** no es culpa suya; **~er** n ayudante m/f; **~ful** adj útil; (person) servicial; (advice) útil; **~ing** n ración f; **~less** adj (incapable) incapaz; (defenceless) indefenso

hem [hɛm] n dobladillo ♦ vt poner or coser el dobladillo; **~ in** vt cercar

hemorrhage ['hɛmərɪdʒ] (US) n = **haemorrhage**

hemorrhoids ['hɛmərɔɪdz] (US) npl = **haemorrhoids**

hen [hɛn] n gallina; (female bird) hembra

hence [hɛns] adv (therefore) por lo tanto; **2 years ~** de aquí a 2 años; **~forth** adv de hoy en adelante

hepatitis [hɛpə'taɪtɪs] n hepatitis f

her [hə:*] pron (direct) la; (indirect) le; (stressed, after prep) ella ♦ adj su; see also **me**; **my**

herald ['hɛrəld] n heraldo ♦ vt anunciar; **~ry** n heráldica

herb [hə:b] n hierba

herd [hə:d] n rebaño

here [hɪə*] adv aquí; (at this point) en este punto; **~!** (present) ¡presente!; **~ is/are** aquí está/están; **~ she is** aquí está; **~after** adv en el futuro; **~by** adv (in letter) por la presente

heritage ['hɛrɪtɪdʒ] n patrimonio

hermit ['hə:mɪt] n ermitaño/a

hernia ['hə:nɪə] n hernia

hero ['hɪərəu] (pl **~es**) n héroe m; (in book, film) protagonista m

heroin ['hɛrəuɪn] n heroína

heroine ['hɛrəuɪn] n heroína; (in book, film) protagonista

heron ['hɛrən] n garza

herring ['hɛrɪŋ] n arenque m

hers [hə:z] pron (el) suyo/(la) suya etc; see also **mine**[1]

herself [hə:'sɛlf] pron (reflexive) se; (emphatic) ella misma; (after prep) sí (misma); see also **oneself**

he's [hi:z] = **he is**; **he has**

hesitant ['hɛzɪtənt] adj vacilante

hesitate ['hɛzɪteɪt] vi vacilar; (in speech) titubear; (be unwilling) resistirse a;

hesitation [ˌhɛzɪ'teɪʃən] n indecisión f;
titubeo; dudas fpl
heterosexual [hɛtərəu'sɛksjuəl] adj
heterosexual
heyday ['heɪdeɪ] n: **the ~ of** el apogeo de
HGV n abbr = **heavy goods vehicle**
hi [haɪ] excl ¡hola!; (to attract attention)
¡oiga!
hiatus [haɪ'eɪtəs] n vacío
hibernate ['haɪbəneɪt] vi invernar
hiccough ['hɪkʌp] = **hiccup**
hiccup ['hɪkʌp] vi hipar; **~s** npl hipo
hide [haɪd] (pt **hid**, pp **hidden**) n (skin)
piel f ♦ vt esconder, ocultar ♦ vi: **to ~
(from sb)** esconderse or ocultarse (de
uno); **~-and-seek** n escondite m
hideous ['hɪdɪəs] adj horrible
hiding ['haɪdɪŋ] n (beating) paliza; **to be in
~** (concealed) estar escondido
hierarchy ['haɪərɑːkɪ] n jerarquía
hi-fi ['haɪfaɪ] n estéreo, hifi m ♦ adj de alta
fidelidad
high [haɪ] adj alto; (speed, number) grande;
(price) elevado; (wind) fuerte; (voice)
agudo ♦ adv alto, a gran altura; **it is 20
m ~** tiene 20 m de altura; **~ in the air** en
las alturas; **~brow** adj intelectual;
~chair n silla alta; **~er education** n
educación f or enseñanza superior; **~-
handed** adj despótico; **~-heeled** adj
de tacón alto; **~ jump** n (SPORT) salto de
altura; **the H~lands** npl las tierras altas
de Escocia; **~light** n (fig: of event) punto
culminante; (in hair) reflejo ♦ vt subrayar;
~ly adv (paid) muy bien; (critical,
confidential) sumamente; (a lot): **to
speak/think ~ly of** hablar muy bien de/
tener en mucho a; **~ly strung** adj
hipertenso; **~ness** n altura; **Her or His
H~ness** Su Alteza; **~-pitched** adj agudo;
~-rise block n torre f de pisos; **~
school** n ≈ Instituto Nacional de
Bachillerato (SP); **~ season** (BRIT) n
temporada alta; **~ street** (BRIT) n calle f
mayor; **~way** n carretera, (US) carretera
nacional; autopista; **H~way Code** (BRIT)
n código de la circulación

hijack ['haɪdʒæk] vt secuestrar; **~er** n
secuestrador(a) m/f
hike [haɪk] vi (go walking) ir de excursión
(a pie) ♦ n caminata; **~r** n excursionista
m/f; **hiking** n senderismo
hilarious [hɪ'lɛərɪəs] adj divertidísimo
hill [hɪl] n colina; (high) montaña; (slope)
cuesta; **~side** n ladera; **~ walking** n
senderismo (de montaña); **~y** adj
montañoso
hilt [hɪlt] n (of sword) empuñadura; **to the
~** (fig: support) incondicionalmente
him [hɪm] pron (direct) le, lo; (indirect) le;
(stressed, after prep) él; see also **me**;
~self pron (reflexive) se; (emphatic) él
mismo; (after prep) sí (mismo); see also
oneself
hinder ['hɪndə*] vt estorbar, impedir;
hindrance ['hɪndrəns] n estorbo
hindsight ['haɪndsaɪt] n: **with ~** en
retrospectiva
Hindu ['hɪnduː] n hindú m/f
hinge [hɪndʒ] n bisagra, gozne m ♦ vi
(fig): **to ~ on** depender de
hint [hɪnt] n indirecta; (advice) consejo;
(sign) dejo ♦ vt: **to ~ that** insinuar que
♦ vi: **to ~ at** hacer alusión a
hip [hɪp] n cadera
hippopotamus [hɪpə'pɒtəməs] (pl **~es** or
hippopotami) n hipopótamo
hire ['haɪə*] vt (BRIT: car, equipment)
alquilar; (worker) contratar ♦ n alquiler m;
for ~ se alquila; (taxi) libre; **~(d) car**
(BRIT) n coche m de alquiler; **~
purchase** (BRIT) n compra a plazos
his [hɪz] pron (el) suyo/(la) suya etc ♦ adj
su; see also **mine**[1]; **my**
Hispanic [hɪs'pænɪk] adj hispánico
hiss [hɪs] vi silbar
historian [hɪ'stɔːrɪən] n historiador(a) m/f
historic(al) [hɪ'stɔrɪk(l)] adj histórico
history ['hɪstərɪ] n historia
hit [hɪt] (pt, pp **hit**) vt (strike) golpear,
pegar; (reach: target) alcanzar; (collide
with: car) chocar contra; (fig: affect)
afectar ♦ n golpe m; (success) éxito; **to ~
it off with sb** llevarse bien con uno; **~-**

and-run driver n conductor(a) que atropella y huye

hitch [hɪtʃ] vt (fasten) atar, amarrar; (also: ~ **up**) remangar ♦ n (difficulty) dificultad f; **to ~ a lift** hacer autostop

hitch-hike vi hacer autostop; **~hiking** n autostop m

hi-tech [haɪˈtek] adj de alta tecnología

hitherto [ˈhɪðəˈtuː] adv hasta ahora

HIV n abbr (= human immunodeficiency virus) VIH m; **~-negative/positive** adj VIH negativo/positivo

hive [haɪv] n colmena

HMS abbr = His (Her) Majesty's Ship

hoard [hɔːd] n (treasure) tesoro; (stockpile) provisión f ♦ vt acumular; (goods in short supply) acaparar; **~ing** n (for posters) cartelera

hoarse [hɔːs] adj ronco

hoax [həuks] n trampa

hob [hɔb] n quemador m

hobble [ˈhɔbl] vi cojear

hobby [ˈhɔbɪ] n pasatiempo, afición f

hobo [ˈhəubəu] (US) n vagabundo

hockey [ˈhɔkɪ] n hockey m

hog [hɔg] n cerdo, puerco ♦ vt (fig) acaparar; **to go the whole ~** poner toda la carne en el asador

hoist [hɔɪst] n (crane) grúa ♦ vt levantar, alzar; (flag, sail) izar

hold [həuld] (pt, pp held) vt sostener; (contain) contener; (have: power, qualification) tener; (keep back) retener; (believe) sostener; (consider) considerar; (keep in position): **to ~ one's head up** mantener la cabeza alta; (meeting) celebrar ♦ vi (withstand pressure) resistir; (be valid) valer ♦ n (grasp) asimiento; (fig) dominio; **~ the line!** (TEL) ¡no cuelgue!; **to ~ one's own** (fig) defenderse; **to catch** or **get (a) ~ of** agarrarse or asirse de; **~ back** vt retener; (secret) ocultar; **~ down** vt (person) sujetar; (job) mantener; **~ off** vt (enemy) rechazar; **~ on** vi agarrarse bien; (wait) esperar; **~ on!** (TEL) ¡(espere) un momento!; **~ on to** vt fus agarrarse a; (keep) guardar; **~ out** vt

ofrecer ♦ vi (resist) resistir; **~ up** vt (raise) levantar; (support) apoyar; (delay) retrasar; (rob) asaltar; **~all** (BRIT) n bolsa; **~er** n (container) receptáculo; (of ticket, record) poseedor(a) m/f; (of office, title etc) titular m/f; **~ing** n (share) interés m; (farmland) parcela; **~up** n (robbery) atraco; (delay) retraso; (BRIT: in traffic) embotellamiento

hole [həul] n agujero

holiday [ˈhɔlɪdɪ] n vacaciones fpl; (public ~) (día m de) fiesta, día m feriado; **on ~** de vacaciones; **~ camp** n (BRIT: also: ~ **centre**) centro de vacaciones; **~-maker** (BRIT) n turista m/f; **~ resort** n centro turístico

holiness [ˈhəulɪnɪs] n santidad f

Holland [ˈhɔlənd] n Holanda

hollow [ˈhɔləu] adj hueco; (claim) vacío; (eyes) hundido; (sound) sordo ♦ n hueco; (in ground) hoyo ♦ vt: **to ~ out** excavar

holly [ˈhɔlɪ] n acebo

holocaust [ˈhɔləkɔːst] n holocausto

holy [ˈhəulɪ] adj santo, sagrado; (water) bendito

homage [ˈhɔmɪdʒ] n homenaje m

home [həum] n casa; (country) patria; (institution) asilo ♦ cpd (domestic) casero, de casa; (ECON, POL) nacional ♦ adv (direction) a casa; (right in: nail etc) a fondo; **at ~** en casa; (in country) en el país; (fig) como pez en el agua; **to go/come ~** ir/volver a casa; **make yourself at ~** ¡estás en tu casa!; **~ address** n domicilio; **~land** n tierra natal; **~less** adj sin hogar, sin casa; **~ly** adj (simple) sencillo; **~-made** adj casero; **H~ Office** (BRIT) n Ministerio del Interior; **~ rule** n autonomía; **H~ Secretary** (BRIT) n Ministro del Interior; **~sick** adj: **to be ~sick** tener morriña, sentir nostalgia; **~ town** n ciudad f natal; **~ward** [ˈhəumwəd] adj (journey) hacia casa; **~work** n deberes mpl

homoeopathic [həumɪəˈpæθɪk] (US **homeopathic**) adj homeopático

homosexual [hɔməuˈseksjuəl] adj, n homosexual m/f

Honduran [hɔnˈdjuərən] *adj, n*
hondureño/a *m/f*

Honduras [hɔnˈdjuərəs] *n* Honduras *f*

honest [ˈɔnɪst] *adj* honrado; (*sincere*)
franco, sincero; ~**ly** *adv* honradamente;
francamente; ~**y** *n* honradez *f*

honey [ˈhʌnɪ] *n* miel *f*; ~**comb** *n* panal
m; ~**moon** *n* luna de miel; ~**suckle** *n*
madreselva

honk [hɔŋk] *vi* (*AUT*) tocar el pito, pitar

honorary [ˈɔnərərɪ] *adj* (*member, president*)
de honor; (*title*) honorífico; ~ **degree**
doctorado honoris causa

honour [ˈɔnə*] (*US* **honor**) *vt* honrar;
(*commitment, promise*) cumplir con ♦ *n*
honor *m*, honra; ~**able** *adj* honorable;
~**s degree** *n* (*SCOL*) título de licenciado
con calificación alta

hood [hud] *n* capucha; (*BRIT: AUT*) capota;
(*US: AUT*) capó *m*; (*of cooker*) campana de
humos

hoof [huːf] (*pl* **hooves**) *n* pezuña

hook [huk] *n* gancho; (*on dress*) corchete
m, broche *m*; (*for fishing*) anzuelo ♦ *vt*
enganchar; (*fish*) pescar

hooligan [ˈhuːlɪgən] *n* gamberro

hoop [huːp] *n* aro

hooray [huːˈreɪ] *excl* = **hurray**

hoot [huːt] (*BRIT*) *vi* (*AUT*) tocar el pito,
pitar; (*siren*) sonar la sirena; (*owl*) ulular;
~**er** (*BRIT*) *n* (*AUT*) pito, claxon *m*; (*NAUT*)
sirena

Hoover ® [ˈhuːvə*] (*BRIT*) *n* aspiradora
♦ *vt*: **h~** pasar la aspiradora por

hooves [huːvz] *npl* of **hoof**

hop [hɔp] *vi* saltar, brincar; (*on one foot*)
saltar con un pie

hope [həup] *vt, vi* esperar ♦ *n* esperanza; **I
~ so/not** espero que sí/no; ~**ful** *adj*
(*person*) optimista; (*situation*)
prometedor(a); ~**fully** *adv* con
esperanza; (*one hopes*) ~**fully he will
recover** esperamos que se recupere;
~**less** *adj* desesperado; (*person*): **to be
~less** ser un desastre

hops [hɔps] *npl* lúpulo

horizon [həˈraɪzn] *n* horizonte *m*; ~**tal**

[hɔrɪˈzɔntl] *adj* horizontal

hormone [ˈhɔːməun] *n* hormona

horn [hɔːn] *n* cuerno; (*MUS: also*: **French
~**) trompa; (*AUT*) pito, claxon *m*

hornet [ˈhɔːnɪt] *n* avispón *m*

horoscope [ˈhɔrəskəup] *n* horóscopo

horrible [ˈhɔrɪbl] *adj* horrible

horrid [ˈhɔrɪd] *adj* horrible, horroroso

horrify [ˈhɔrɪfaɪ] *vt* horrorizar

horror [ˈhɔrə*] *n* horror *m*; ~ **film** *n*
película de horror

hors d'œuvre [ɔːˈdɜːvrə] *n* entremeses
mpl

horse [hɔːs] *n* caballo; ~**back** *n*: **on
~back** a caballo; ~ **chestnut** *n* (*tree*)
castaño de Indias; (*nut*) castaña de Indias;
~**man/woman** (*irreg*) *n* jinete/a *m/f*;
~**power** *n* caballo (de fuerza); ~**racing**
n carreras *fpl* de caballos; ~**radish** *n*
rábano picante; ~**shoe** *n* herradura

hose [həuz] *n* (*also*: ~**pipe**) manguera

hospitable [hɔsˈpɪtəbl] *adj* hospitalario

hospital [ˈhɔspɪtl] *n* hospital *m*

hospitality [hɔspɪˈtælɪtɪ] *n* hospitalidad *f*

host [həust] *n* anfitrión *m*; (*TV, RADIO*)
presentador *m*; (*REL*) hostia; (*large
number*): **a ~ of** multitud de

hostage [ˈhɔstɪdʒ] *n* rehén *m*

hostel [ˈhɔstl] *n* hostal *m*; (**youth**) ~
albergue *m* juvenil

hostess [ˈhəustɪs] *n* anfitriona; (*BRIT*: **air ~**)
azafata; (*TV, RADIO*) presentadora

hostile [ˈhɔstaɪl] *adj* hostil

hot [hɔt] *adj* caliente; (*weather*) caluroso,
de calor; (*as opposed to warm*) muy
caliente; (*spicy*) picante; **to be ~** (*person*)
tener calor; (*object*) estar caliente;
(*weather*) hacer calor; ~**bed** *n* (*fig*)
semillero; ~ **dog** *n* perro caliente

hotel [həuˈtɛl] *n* hotel *m*

hot: ~**house** *n* invernadero; ~ **line** *n*
(*POL*) teléfono rojo; ~**ly** *adv* con pasión,
apasionadamente; ~**water bottle** *n*
bolsa de agua caliente

hound [haund] *vt* acosar ♦ *n* perro (de
caza)

hour [ˈauə*] *n* hora; ~**ly** *adj* (de) cada hora

house [n haus, pl 'hauzız, vb hauz] n (gen, firm) casa; (POL) cámara; (THEATRE) sala ♦ vt (person) alojar; (collection) albergar; **on the ~** (fig) la casa invita; **~ arrest** n arresto domiciliario; **~boat** n casa flotante; **~bound** adj confinado en casa; **~breaking** n allanamiento de morada; **~hold** n familia; (home) casa; **~keeper** n ama de llaves; **~keeping** n (work) trabajos mpl domésticos; **~keeping (money)** n dinero para gastos domésticos; **~warming party** n fiesta de estreno de una casa; **~wife** (irreg) n ama de casa; **~work** n faenas fpl (de la casa)

housing ['hauzıŋ] n (act) alojamiento; (houses) viviendas fpl; **~ development** n urbanización f; **~ estate** (BRIT) n = **~ development**

hovel ['hɔvl] n casucha

hover ['hɔvə*] vi flotar (en el aire); **~craft** n aerodeslizador m

how [hau] adv: **~ are you?** (in what way) cómo; **~ are you?** ¿cómo estás?; **~ much milk/many people?** ¿cuánta leche/gente?; **~ much does it cost?** ¿cuánto cuesta?; **~ long have you been here?** ¿cuánto hace que estás aquí?; **~ old are you?** ¿cuántos años tienes?; **~ tall is he?** ¿cómo es de alto?; **~ is school?** ¿cómo (te) va en la escuela?; **~ was the film?** ¿qué tal la película?; **~ lovely/awful!** ¡qué bonito/horror!

however [hau'ɛvə*] adv: **~ I do it** lo haga como lo haga; **~ cold it is** por mucho frío que haga; **~ fast he runs** por muy rápido que corra; **~ did you do it?** ¿cómo lo hiciste? ♦ conj sin embargo, no obstante

howl [haul] n aullido ♦ vi aullar; (person) dar alaridos; (wind) ulular

H.P. n abbr = **hire purchase**

h.p. abbr = **horse power**

HQ n abbr = **headquarters**

hub [hʌb] n (of wheel) cubo m; (fig) centro

hubcap ['hʌbkæp] n tapacubos m inv

huddle ['hʌdl] vi: **to ~ together** acurrucarse

hue [hju:] n color m, matiz m

huff [hʌf] n: **in a ~** enojado

hug [hʌg] vt abrazar; (thing) apretar con los brazos

huge [hju:dʒ] adj enorme

hull [hʌl] n (of ship) casco

hullo [hə'ləu] excl = **hello**

hum [hʌm] vt tararear, canturrear ♦ vi tararear, canturrear; (insect) zumbar

human ['hju:mən] adj, n humano; **~e** [hju:'meın] adj humano, humanitario; **~itarian** [hju:mænı'teəriən] adj humanitario; **~ity** [hju:'mænıtı] n humanidad f

humble ['hʌmbl] adj humilde

humdrum ['hʌmdrʌm] adj (boring) monótono, aburrido

humid ['hju:mıd] adj húmedo

humiliate [hju:'mılıeıt] vt humillar

humorous ['hju:mərəs] adj gracioso, divertido

humour ['hju:mə*] (US **humor**) n humorismo, sentido del humor; (mood) humor m ♦ vt (person) complacer

hump [hʌmp] n (in ground) montículo; (camel's) giba

hunch [hʌntʃ] n (premonition) presentimiento; **~back** n joroba m/f; **~ed** adj jorobado

hundred ['hʌndrəd] num ciento; (before n) cien; **~s of** centenares de, cientos de; **~weight** n (BRIT) = 50.8 kg; 112 lb; (US) = 45.3 kg; 100 lb

hung [hʌŋ] pt, pp of **hang**

Hungarian [hʌŋ'geəriən] adj, n húngaro/a m/f

Hungary ['hʌŋgəri] n Hungría

hunger ['hʌŋgə*] n hambre f ♦ vi: **to ~ for** (fig) tener hambre de, anhelar; **~ strike** n huelga de hambre

hungry ['hʌŋgrı] adj: **~ (for)** hambriento (de); **to be ~** tener hambre

hunk [hʌŋk] n (of bread etc) trozo, pedazo

hunt [hʌnt] vt (seek) buscar; (SPORT) cazar ♦ vi (search): **to ~ (for)** buscar; (SPORT) cazar ♦ n búsqueda; caza, cacería; **~er** n cazador(a) m/f; **~ing** n caza

hurdle ['hɜːdl] n (SPORT) valla; (fig)
obstáculo

hurl [hɜːl] vt lanzar, arrojar

hurrah [huːˈrɑː] excl = **hurray**

hurray [huːˈreɪ] excl ¡viva!

hurricane ['hʌrɪkən] n huracán m

hurried ['hʌrɪd] adj (rushed) hecho de
prisa; **~ly** adv con prisa, apresuradamente

hurry ['hʌrɪ] n prisa ♦ vi (also: ~ up)
apresurarse, darse prisa ♦ vt (also: ~ up:
person) dar prisa a; (: work) apresurar,
hacer de prisa; **to be in a ~** tener prisa

hurt [hɜːt] (pt, pp hurt) vt hacer daño a
♦ vi doler ♦ adj lastimado; **~ful** adj
(remark etc) hiriente

hurtle ['hɜːtl] vi: **to ~ past** pasar como un
rayo; **to ~ down** ir a toda velocidad

husband ['hʌzbənd] n marido

hush [hʌʃ] n silencio ♦ vt hacer callar; **~!**
¡chitón!, ¡cállate!; **~ up** vt encubrir

husk [hʌsk] n (of wheat) cáscara

husky ['hʌskɪ] adj ronco ♦ n perro
esquimal

hustle ['hʌsl] vt (hurry) dar prisa a ♦ n: **~
and bustle** ajetreo

hut [hʌt] n cabaña; (shed) cobertizo

hutch [hʌtʃ] n conejera

hyacinth ['haɪəsɪnθ] n jacinto

hydrant ['haɪdrənt] n (also: **fire ~**) boca de
incendios

hydraulic [haɪˈdrɔːlɪk] adj hidráulico

hydroelectric [haɪdrəʊˈlektrɪk] adj
hidroeléctrico

hydrofoil ['haɪdrəfɔɪl] n aerodeslizador m

hydrogen ['haɪdrədʒən] n hidrógeno

hygiene ['haɪdʒiːn] n higiene f; **hygienic**
[-'dʒiːnɪk] adj higiénico

hymn [hɪm] n himno

hype [haɪp] (inf) n bombardeo publicitario

hypermarket ['haɪpəmɑːkɪt] n
hipermercado

hyphen ['haɪfn] n guión m

hypnotize ['hɪpnətaɪz] vt hipnotizar

hypocrisy [hɪˈpɒkrɪsɪ] n hipocresía;
hypocrite ['hɪpəkrɪt] n hipócrita m/f;
hypocritical [hɪpəˈkrɪtɪkl] adj hipócrita

hypothesis [haɪˈpɒθɪsɪs] (pl **hypotheses**)

n hipótesis f inv

hysteria [hɪˈstɪərɪə] n histeria; **hysterical**
[-'sterɪkl] adj histérico; (funny) para morirse
de risa; **hysterics** [-'sterɪks] npl histeria;
to be in hysterics (fig) morirse de risa

I, i

I [aɪ] pron yo

ice [aɪs] n hielo; (~ cream) helado ♦ vt
(cake) alcorzar ♦ vi (also: ~ **over**, ~ **up**)
helarse; **~berg** n iceberg m; **~box** n
(BRIT) congelador m; (US) nevera (SP),
refrigeradora (AM); ~ **cream** n helado; ~
cube n cubito de hielo; **~d** adj (cake)
escarchado; (drink) helado; ~ **hockey** n
hockey m sobre hielo

Iceland ['aɪslənd] n Islandia

ice: ~ **lolly** (BRIT) n polo; ~ **rink** n pista
de hielo; ~ **skating** n patinaje m sobre
hielo

icicle ['aɪsɪkl] n carámbano

icing ['aɪsɪŋ] n (CULIN) alcorza; ~ **sugar**
(BRIT) n azúcar m glas(eado)

icy ['aɪsɪ] adj helado

I'd [aɪd] = **I would**; **I had**

idea [aɪˈdɪə] n idea

ideal [aɪˈdɪəl] n ideal m ♦ adj ideal

identical [aɪˈdentɪkl] adj idéntico

identification [aɪdentɪfɪˈkeɪʃən] n
identificación f; **(means of) ~**
documentos mpl personales

identify [aɪˈdentɪfaɪ] vt identificar

Identikit ® [aɪˈdentɪkɪt] n: ~ **(picture)**
retrato-robot m

identity [aɪˈdentɪtɪ] n identidad f; ~ **card**
n carnet m de identidad

ideology [aɪdɪˈɒlədʒɪ] n ideología

idiom ['ɪdɪəm] n modismo; (style of
speaking) lenguaje m

idiosyncrasy [ɪdɪəʊˈsɪŋkrəsɪ] n
idiosincrasia

idiot ['ɪdɪət] n idiota m/f; **~ic** [-'ɒtɪk] adj
tonto

idle ['aɪdl] adj (inactive) ocioso; (lazy)
holgazán/ana; (unemployed) parado,

desocupado; (*machinery etc*) parado; (*talk etc*) frívolo ♦ *vi* (*machine*) marchar en vacío

idol ['aɪdl] *n* ídolo; **~ize** *vt* idolatrar

i.e. *abbr* (= *that is*) esto es

if [ɪf] *conj* si; **~ necessary** si fuera necesario, si hiciese falta; **~ I were you** yo en tu lugar; **~ so/not** de ser así/si no; **~ only I could!** ¡ojalá pudiera!; *see also* **as; even**

igloo ['ɪgluː] *n* iglú *m*

ignite [ɪg'naɪt] *vt* (*set fire to*) encender ♦ *vi* encenderse

ignition [ɪg'nɪʃən] *n* (*AUT: process*) ignición *f*; (*: mechanism*) encendido; **to switch on/off the ~** arrancar/apagar el motor; **~ key** *n* (*AUT*) llave *f* de contacto

ignorant ['ɪgnərənt] *adj* ignorante; **to be ~ of** ignorar

ignore [ɪg'nɔː*] *vt* (*person, advice*) no hacer caso de; (*fact*) pasar por alto

I'll [aɪl] = **I will; I shall**

ill [ɪl] *adj* enfermo, malo ♦ *n* mal *m* ♦ *adv* mal; **to be taken ~** ponerse enfermo; **~-advised** (*decision*) imprudente; **~-at-ease** *adj* incómodo

illegal [ɪ'liːgl] *adj* ilegal

illegible [ɪ'ledʒɪbl] *adj* ilegible

illegitimate [ɪlɪ'dʒɪtɪmət] *adj* ilegítimo

ill-fated *adj* malogrado

ill feeling *n* rencor *m*

illicit [ɪ'lɪsɪt] *adj* ilícito

illiterate [ɪ'lɪtərət] *adj* analfabeto

ill: ~-mannered *adj* mal educado; **~ness** *n* enfermedad *f*; **~-treat** *vt* maltratar

illuminate [ɪ'luːmɪneɪt] *vt* (*room, street*) iluminar, alumbrar; **illumination** [-'neɪʃən] *n* alumbrado; **illuminations** *npl* (*decorative lights*) iluminaciones *fpl*, luces *fpl*

illusion [ɪ'luːʒən] *n* ilusión *f*; (*trick*) truco

illustrate ['ɪləstreɪt] *vt* ilustrar

illustration [ɪlə'streɪʃən] *n* (*act of illustrating*) ilustración *f*; (*example*) ejemplo, ilustración *f*; (*in book*) lámina

illustrious [ɪ'lʌstrɪəs] *adj* ilustre

I'm [aɪm] = **I am**

image ['ɪmɪdʒ] *n* imagen *f*; **~ry** [-ərɪ] *n* imágenes *fpl*

imaginary [ɪ'mædʒɪnərɪ] *adj* imaginario

imagination [ɪmædʒɪ'neɪʃən] *n* imaginación *f*; (*inventiveness*) inventiva

imaginative [ɪ'mædʒɪnətɪv] *adj* imaginativo

imagine [ɪ'mædʒɪn] *vt* imaginarse

imbalance [ɪm'bæləns] *n* desequilibrio

imitate ['ɪmɪteɪt] *vt* imitar; **imitation** [ɪmɪ'teɪʃən] *n* imitación *f*; (*copy*) copia

immaculate [ɪ'mækjulət] *adj* inmaculado

immaterial [ɪmə'tɪərɪəl] *adj* (*unimportant*) sin importancia

immature [ɪmə'tjuə*] *adj* (*person*) inmaduro

immediate [ɪ'miːdɪət] *adj* inmediato; (*pressing*) urgente, apremiante; (*nearest: family*) próximo; (*: neighbourhood*) inmediato; **~ly** *adv* (*at once*) en seguida; (*directly*) inmediatamente; **~ly next to** muy junto a

immense [ɪ'mens] *adj* inmenso, enorme; (*importance*) enorme

immerse [ɪ'məːs] *vt* (*submerge*) sumergir; **to be ~d in** (*fig*) estar absorto en

immersion heater [ɪ'məːʃən-] (*BRIT*) *n* calentador *m* de inmersión

immigrant ['ɪmɪgrənt] *n* inmigrante *m/f*; **immigration** [ɪmɪ'greɪʃən] *n* inmigración *f*

imminent ['ɪmɪnənt] *adj* inminente

immobile [ɪ'məubaɪl] *adj* inmóvil

immoral [ɪ'mɔrl] *adj* inmoral

immortal [ɪ'mɔːtl] *adj* inmortal

immune [ɪ'mjuːn] *adj*: **~ (to)** inmune (a); **immunity** *n* (*MED, of diplomat*) inmunidad *f*

immunize ['ɪmjunaɪz] *vt* inmunizar

impact ['ɪmpækt] *n* impacto

impair [ɪm'peə*] *vt* perjudicar

impart [ɪm'pɑːt] *vt* comunicar; (*flavour*) proporcionar

impartial [ɪm'pɑːʃl] *adj* imparcial

impassable [ɪm'pɑːsəbl] *adj* (*barrier*) infranqueable; (*river, road*) intransitable

impassive [ɪm'pæsɪv] *adj* impasible
impatience [ɪm'peɪʃəns] *n* impaciencia
impatient [ɪm'peɪʃənt] *adj* impaciente; **to get** *or* **grow ~** impacientarse
impeccable [ɪm'pekəbl] *adj* impecable
impede [ɪm'piːd] *vt* estorbar
impediment [ɪm'pedɪmənt] *n* obstáculo, estorbo; *(also: **speech ~**)* defecto (del habla)
impending [ɪm'pendɪŋ] *adj* inminente
imperative [ɪm'perətɪv] *adj (tone)* imperioso; *(need)* imprescindible
imperfect [ɪm'pəːfɪkt] *adj (goods etc)* defectuoso ♦ *n (LING: also: **~ tense**)* imperfecto
imperial [ɪm'pɪərɪəl] *adj* imperial
impersonal [ɪm'pəːsənl] *adj* impersonal
impersonate [ɪm'pəːsəneɪt] *vt* hacerse pasar por; *(THEATRE)* imitar
impertinent [ɪm'pəːtɪnənt] *adj* impertinente, insolente
impervious [ɪm'pəːvɪəs] *adj* impermeable; *(fig)*: **~ to** insensible a
impetuous [ɪm'petjuəs] *adj* impetuoso
impetus ['ɪmpətəs] *n* ímpetu *m*; *(fig)* impulso
impinge [ɪm'pɪndʒ]: **to ~ on** *vt fus (affect)* afectar a
implement [*n* 'ɪmplɪmənt, *vb* 'ɪmplɪment] *n* herramienta; *(for cooking)* utensilio ♦ *vt (regulation)* hacer efectivo; *(plan)* realizar
implicit [ɪm'plɪsɪt] *adj* implícito; *(belief, trust)* absoluto
imply [ɪm'plaɪ] *vt (involve)* suponer; *(hint)* dar a entender que
impolite [ɪmpə'laɪt] *adj* mal educado
import [*vb* ɪm'pɔːt, *n* 'ɪmpɔːt] *vt* importar ♦ *n (COMM)* importación *f*; *(: article)* producto importado; *(meaning)* significado, sentido
importance [ɪm'pɔːtəns] *n* importancia
important [ɪm'pɔːtənt] *adj* importante; **it's not ~** no importa, no tiene importancia
importer [ɪm'pɔːtə*] *n* importador(a) *m/f*
impose [ɪm'pəuz] *vt* imponer ♦ *vi*: **to ~ on sb** abusar de uno; **imposing** *adj* imponente, impresionante

imposition [ɪmpə'zɪʃn] *n (of tax etc)* imposición *f*; **to be an ~ on** *(person)* molestar a
impossible [ɪm'pɔsɪbl] *adj* imposible; *(person)* insoportable
impotent ['ɪmpətənt] *adj* impotente
impound [ɪm'paund] *vt* embargar
impoverished [ɪm'pɔvərɪʃt] *adj* necesitado
impractical [ɪm'præktɪkl] *adj (person, plan)* poco práctico
imprecise [ɪmprɪ'saɪs] *adj* impreciso
impregnable [ɪm'pregnəbl] *adj (castle)* inexpugnable
impress [ɪm'pres] *vt* impresionar; *(mark)* estampar; **to ~ sth on sb** hacer entender algo a uno
impression [ɪm'preʃən] *n* impresión *f*; *(imitation)* imitación *f*; **to be under the ~ that** tener la impresión de que; **~ist** *n* impresionista *m/f*
impressive [ɪm'presɪv] *adj* impresionante
imprint ['ɪmprɪnt] *n (outline)* huella; *(PUBLISHING)* pie *m* de imprenta
imprison [ɪm'prɪzn] *vt* encarcelar; **~ment** *n* encarcelamiento; *(term of ~ment)* cárcel *f*
improbable [ɪm'prɔbəbl] *adj* improbable, inverosímil
improper [ɪm'prɔpə*] *adj (unsuitable: conduct etc)* incorrecto; *(: activities)* deshonesto
improve [ɪm'pruːv] *vt* mejorar; *(foreign language)* perfeccionar ♦ *vi* mejorarse; **~ment** *n* mejoramiento; perfección *f*; progreso
improvise ['ɪmprəvaɪz] *vt, vi* improvisar
impulse ['ɪmpʌls] *n* impulso; **to act on ~** obrar sin reflexión; **impulsive** [-'pʌlsɪv] *adj* irreflexivo
impure [ɪm'pjuə*] *adj (adulterated)* adulterado; *(morally)* impuro; **impurity** *n* impureza

---

KEYWORD

---

in [ɪn] *prep* **1** *(indicating place, position, with place names)* en; **~ the house/garden** en

(la) casa/el jardín; ~ **here/there** aquí/ahí
or allí dentro; ~ **London/England** en
Londres/Inglaterra
2 (*indicating time*) en; ~ **spring** en (la)
primavera; ~ **the afternoon** por la tarde;
at 4 o'clock ~ **the afternoon** a las 4 de
la tarde; **I did it** ~ **3 hours/days** lo hice
en 3 horas/días; **I'll see you** ~ **2 weeks**
or ~ **2 weeks' time** te veré dentro de 2
semanas
3 (*indicating manner etc*) en; ~ **a loud/
soft voice** en voz alta/baja; ~ **pencil/ink**
a lápiz/bolígrafo; **the boy** ~ **the blue
shirt** el chico de la camisa azul
4 (*indicating circumstances*): ~ **the sun/
shade/rain** al sol/a la sombra/bajo la
lluvia; **a change** ~ **policy** un cambio de
política
5 (*indicating mood, state*): ~ **tears** en
lágrimas, llorando; ~ **anger/despair**
enfadado/desesperado; **to live** ~ **luxury**
vivir lujosamente
6 (*with ratios, numbers*): **1** ~ **10
households, 1 household** ~ **10** una de
cada 10 familias; **20 pence** ~ **the pound**
20 peniques por libra; **they lined up** ~
twos se alinearon de dos en dos
7 (*referring to people, works*) en; entre;
the disease is common ~ **children** la
enfermedad es común entre los niños; ~
(the works of) Dickens en (las obras de)
Dickens
8 (*indicating profession etc*): **to be** ~
teaching estar en la enseñanza
9 (*after superlative*) de; **the best pupil** ~
the class el/la mejor alumno/a de la
clase
10 (*with present participle*): ~ **saying this**
al decir esto
♦ *adv*: **to be** ~ (*person: at home*) estar en
casa; (*work*) estar; (*train, ship, plane*)
haber llegado; (*in fashion*) estar de moda;
she'll be ~ **later today** llegará más tarde
hoy; **to ask sb** ~ hacer pasar a uno; **to
run/limp** *etc* ~ entrar corriendo/cojeando
etc
♦ *n*: **the** ~**s and outs** (*of proposal,*

situation *etc*) los detalles

in. *abbr* = **inch**
inability [ɪnə'bɪlɪtɪ] *n*: ~ **(to do)**
incapacidad *f* (de hacer)
inaccurate [ɪn'ækjurət] *adj* inexacto,
incorrecto
inadequate [ɪn'ædɪkwət] *adj* (*income,
reply etc*) insuficiente; (*person*) incapaz
inadvertently [ɪnəd'vɜːtntlɪ] *adv* por
descuido
inadvisable [ɪnəd'vaɪzəbl] *adj* poco
aconsejable
inane [ɪ'neɪn] *adj* necio, fatuo
inanimate [ɪn'ænɪmət] *adj* inanimado
inappropriate [ɪnə'prəuprɪət] *adj*
inadecuado, (*improper*) poco oportuno
inarticulate [ɪnɑː'tɪkjulət] *adj* (*person*)
incapaz de expresarse; (*speech*) mal
pronunciado
inasmuch as [ɪnəz'mʌtʃ-] *conj* puesto
que, ya que
inauguration [ɪnɔːgju'reɪʃən] *n* ceremonia
de apertura
inborn [ɪn'bɔːn] *adj* (*quality*) innato
inbred [ɪn'bred] *adj* innato; (*family*)
engendrado por endogamia
Inc. *abbr* (*US:* = *incorporated*) S.A.
incapable [ɪn'keɪpəbl] *adj* incapaz
incapacitate [ɪnkə'pæsɪteɪt] *vt*: **to** ~ **sb**
incapacitar a uno
incense [*n* 'ɪnsens, *vb* ɪn'sens] *n* incienso
♦ *vt* (*anger*) indignar, encolerizar
incentive [ɪn'sentɪv] *n* incentivo, estímulo
incessant [ɪn'sesnt] *adj* incesante,
continuo; ~**ly** *adv* constantemente
incest ['ɪnsest] *n* incesto
inch [ɪntʃ] *n* pulgada; **to be within an** ~ **of**
estar a dos dedos de; **he didn't give an** ~
no dio concesión alguna
incident ['ɪnsɪdnt] *n* incidente *m*
incidental [ɪnsɪ'dentl] *adj* accesorio; ~ **to**
relacionado con; ~**ly** [-'dentəlɪ] *adv* (*by the
way*) a propósito
incite [ɪn'saɪt] *vt* provocar
inclination [ɪnklɪ'neɪʃən] *n* (*tendency*)
tendencia, inclinación *f*; (*desire*) deseo;

(*disposition*) propensión *f*
incline [*n* ˈɪnklaɪn, *vb* ɪnˈklaɪn] *n* pendiente *m*, cuesta ♦ *vt* (*head*) poner de lado ♦ *vi* inclinarse; **to be ~d to** (*tend*) ser propenso a
include [ɪnˈkluːd] *vt* (*incorporate*) incluir; (*in letter*) adjuntar; **including** *prep* incluso, inclusive
inclusion [ɪnˈkluːʒən] *n* inclusión *f*
inclusive [ɪnˈkluːsɪv] *adj* inclusivo; **~ of tax** incluidos los impuestos
income [ˈɪŋkʌm] *n* (*earned*) ingresos *mpl*; (*from property etc*) renta; (*from investment etc*) rédito; **~ tax** *n* impuesto sobre la renta
incoming [ˈɪnkʌmɪŋ] *adj* (*flight, government etc*) entrante
incomparable [ɪnˈkɒmpərəbl] *adj* incomparable, sin par
incompatible [ɪnkəmˈpætɪbl] *adj* incompatible
incompetent [ɪnˈkɒmpɪtənt] *adj* incompetente
incomplete [ɪnkəmˈpliːt] *adj* (*partial: achievement etc*) incompleto; (*unfinished: painting etc*) inacabado
incongruous [ɪnˈkɒŋgruəs] *adj* (*strange*) discordante; (*inappropriate*) incongruente
inconsiderate [ɪnkənˈsɪdərət] *adj* desconsiderado
inconsistent [ɪnkənˈsɪstənt] *adj* inconsecuente; (*contradictory*) incongruente; **~ with** (que) no concuerda con
inconspicuous [ɪnkənˈspɪkjuəs] *adj* (*colour, building etc*) discreto; (*person*) que llama poco la atención
inconvenience [ɪnkənˈviːnjəns] *n* inconveniencies *mpl*; (*trouble*) molestia, incomodidad *f* ♦ *vt* incomodar
inconvenient [ɪnkənˈviːnjənt] *adj* incómodo, poco práctico; (*time, place, visitor*) inoportuno
incorporate [ɪnˈkɔːpəreɪt] *vt* incorporar; (*contain*) comprender; (*add*) agregar; **~d** *adj*: **~d company** (*US*) ≈ sociedad *f* anónima

incorrect [ɪnkəˈrekt] *adj* incorrecto
increase [*n* ˈɪnkriːs, *vb* ɪnˈkriːs] *n* aumento ♦ *vi* aumentar; (*grow*) crecer; (*price*) subir ♦ *vt* aumentar; (*price*) subir; **increasing** *adj* creciente; **increasingly** *adv* cada vez más, más y más
incredible [ɪnˈkredɪbl] *adj* increíble
incubator [ˈɪnkjubeɪtə*] *n* incubadora
incumbent [ɪnˈkʌmbənt] *adj*: **it is ~ on him to ...** le incumbe ...
incur [ɪnˈkɜː*] *vt* (*expenditure*) incurrir; (*loss*) sufrir; (*anger, disapproval*) provocar
indebted [ɪnˈdetɪd] *adj*: **to be ~ to sb** estar agradecido a uno
indecent [ɪnˈdiːsnt] *adj* indecente; **~ assault** (*BRIT*) *n* atentado contra el pudor; **~ exposure** *n* exhibicionismo
indecisive [ɪndɪˈsaɪsɪv] *adj* indeciso
indeed [ɪnˈdiːd] *adv* efectivamente, en realidad; (*in fact*) en efecto; (*furthermore*) es más; **yes ~!** ¡claro que sí!
indefinitely [ɪnˈdefɪnɪtlɪ] *adv* (*wait*) indefinidamente
indemnity [ɪnˈdemnɪtɪ] *n* (*insurance*) indemnidad *f*; (*compensation*) indemnización *f*
independence [ɪndɪˈpendns] *n* independencia

Independence Day

ⓘ *El cuatro de julio es* **Independence Day**, *la fiesta nacional de Estados Unidos, que se celebra en conmemoración de la Declaración de Independencia, escrita por Thomas Jefferson y aprobada en 1776. En ella se proclamaba la independencia total de Gran Bretaña de las trece colonias americanas que serían el origen de los Estados Unidos de América.*

---

independent [ɪndɪˈpendənt] *adj* independiente
index [ˈɪndeks] (*pl* **~es**) *n* (*in book*) índice *m*; (*: in library etc*) catálogo; (*pl* **indices**: *ratio, sign*) exponente *m*; **~ card** *n* ficha; **~ed** (*US*) *adj* = **~-linked**; **~ finger** *n* índice *m*; **~-linked** (*BRIT*) *adj* vinculado al

índice del coste de la vida

India ['ɪndɪə] n la India; **~n** adj, n indio/a m/f; **Red ~n** piel roja m/f; **~n Ocean** n: **the ~n Ocean** el Océano Índico

indicate ['ɪndɪkeɪt] vt indicar; **indication** [-'keɪʃən] n indicio, señal f; **indicative** [ɪn'dɪkətɪv] adj: **to be indicative of** indicar; **indicator** n indicador m; (AUT) intermitente m

indices ['ɪndɪsi:z] npl of **index**

indictment [ɪn'daɪtmənt] n acusación f

indifferent [ɪn'dɪfrənt] adj indiferente; (mediocre) regular

indigenous [ɪn'dɪdʒɪnəs] adj indígena

indigestion [ɪndɪ'dʒestʃən] n indigestión f

indignant [ɪn'dɪgnənt] adj: **to be ~ at sth/with sb** indignarse por algo/con uno

indigo ['ɪndɪgəʊ] adj de color añil ♦ n añil m

indirect [ɪndɪ'rɛkt] adj indirecto

indiscreet [ɪndɪ'skri:t] adj indiscreto, imprudente

indiscriminate [ɪndɪ'skrɪmɪnət] adj indiscriminado

indisputable [ɪndɪ'spju:təbl] adj incontestable

indistinct [ɪndɪ'stɪŋkt] adj (noise, memory etc) confuso

individual [ɪndɪ'vɪdjuəl] n individuo ♦ adj individual; (personal) personal; (particular) particular; **~ly** adv (singly) individualmente

indoctrinate [ɪn'dɔktrɪneɪt] vt adoctrinar

indoor ['ɪndɔ:*] adj (swimming pool) cubierto; (plant) de interior; (sport) bajo cubierta; **~s** [ɪn'dɔ:z] adv dentro

induce [ɪn'dju:s] vt inducir, persuadir; (bring about) producir; (birth) provocar; **~ment** n (incentive) incentivo; (pej: bribe) soborno

indulge [ɪn'dʌldʒ] vt (whim) satisfacer; (person) complacer; (child) mimar ♦ vi: **to ~ in** darse el gusto de; **~nce** n vicio; (leniency) indulgencia; **~nt** adj indulgente

industrial [ɪn'dʌstrɪəl] adj industrial; **~ action** n huelga; **~ estate** (BRIT) n polígono (SP) or zona (AM) industrial; **~ist**

n industrial m/f; **~ize** vt industrializar; **~ park** (US) n = **~ estate**

industrious [ɪn'dʌstrɪəs] adj trabajador(a); (student) aplicado

industry ['ɪndəstrɪ] n industria; (diligence) aplicación f

inebriated [ɪ'ni:brɪeɪtɪd] adj borracho

inedible [ɪn'ɛdɪbl] adj incomible; (poisonous) no comestible

ineffective [ɪnɪ'fɛktɪv] adj ineficaz, inútil

ineffectual [ɪnɪ'fɛktjuəl] adj = **ineffective**

inefficient [ɪnɪ'fɪʃənt] adj ineficaz, ineficiente

inept [ɪ'nɛpt] adj incompetente

inequality [ɪnɪ'kwɔlɪtɪ] n desigualdad f

inert [ɪ'nə:t] adj inerte, inactivo; (immobile) inmóvil

inescapable [ɪnɪ'skeɪpəbl] adj ineludible

inevitable [ɪn'ɛvɪtəbl] adj inevitable; **inevitably** adv inevitablemente

inexcusable [ɪnɪks'kju:zəbl] adj imperdonable

inexpensive [ɪnɪk'spɛnsɪv] adj económico

inexperienced [ɪnɪk'spɪərɪənst] adj inexperto

infallible [ɪn'fælɪbl] adj infalible

infamous ['ɪnfəməs] adj infame

infancy ['ɪnfənsɪ] n infancia

infant ['ɪnfənt] n niño/a; (baby) niño pequeño, bebé m; (pej) aniñado

infantry ['ɪnfəntrɪ] n infantería

infant school (BRIT) n parvulario

infatuated [ɪn'fætjueɪtɪd] adj: **~ with** (in love) loco por

infatuation [ɪnfætju'eɪʃən] n enamoramiento, pasión f

infect [ɪn'fɛkt] vt (wound) infectar; (food) contaminar; (person, animal) contagiar; **~ion** [ɪn'fɛkʃən] n infección f; (fig) contagio; **~ious** [ɪn'fɛkʃəs] adj (also fig) contagioso

infer [ɪn'fə:*] vt deducir, inferir

inferior [ɪn'fɪərɪə*] adj, n inferior m/f; **~ity** [-rɪ'ɔrətɪ] n inferioridad f

infertile [ɪn'fə:taɪl] adj estéril; (person) infecundo

infested [ɪn'fɛstɪd] adj: **~ with** plagado de

in-fighting n (fig) lucha(s) f(pl) interna(s)

infinite ['ɪnfɪnɪt] adj infinito

infinitive [ɪn'fɪnɪtɪv] n infinitivo

infinity [ɪn'fɪnɪtɪ] n infinito; (an ~) infinidad f

infirmary [ɪn'fɜ:mərɪ] n hospital m

inflamed [ɪn'fleɪmd] adj: **to become ~** inflamarse

inflammable [ɪn'flæməbl] adj inflamable

inflammation [ɪnflə'meɪʃən] n inflamación f

inflatable [ɪn'fleɪtəbl] adj (ball, boat) inflable

inflate [ɪn'fleɪt] vt (tyre, price etc) inflar; (fig) hinchar; **inflation** [ɪn'fleɪʃən] n (ECON) inflación f

inflexible [ɪn'fleksəbl] adj (rule) rígido; (person) inflexible

inflict [ɪn'flɪkt] vt: **to ~ sth on sb** infligir algo en uno

influence ['ɪnfluəns] n influencia ♦ vt influir en, influenciar; **under the ~ of alcohol** en estado de embriaguez; **influential** [-'enʃl] adj influyente

influenza [ɪnflu'enzə] n gripe f

influx ['ɪnflʌks] n afluencia

inform [ɪn'fɔ:m] vt: **to ~ sb of sth** informar a uno sobre or de algo ♦ vi: **to ~ on sb** delatar a uno

informal [ɪn'fɔ:məl] adj (manner, tone) familiar; (dress, interview, occasion) informal; (visit, meeting) extraoficial; **~ity** [-'mælɪtɪ] n informalidad f; sencillez f

informant [ɪn'fɔ:mənt] n informante m/f

information [ɪnfə'meɪʃən] n información f; (knowledge) conocimientos mpl; **a piece of ~** un dato; **~ desk** n (mostrador m de) información f; **~ office** n información f

informative [ɪn'fɔ:mətɪv] adj informativo

informer [ɪn'fɔ:mə*] n (also: **police ~**) soplón/ona m/f

infra-red [ɪnfrə'red] adj infrarrojo

infrastructure ['ɪnfrəstrʌktʃə*] n (of system etc) infraestructura

infringe [ɪn'frɪndʒ] vt infringir, violar ♦ vi: **to ~ on** abusar de; **~ment** n infracción f;

(of rights) usurpación f

infuriating [ɪn'fjuərɪeɪtɪŋ] adj (habit, noise) enloquecedor(a)

ingenious [ɪn'dʒi:nɪəs] adj ingenioso; **ingenuity** [-dʒɪ'nju:ɪtɪ] n ingeniosidad f

ingenuous [ɪn'dʒenjuəs] adj ingenuo

ingot ['ɪŋgət] n lingote m, barra

ingrained [ɪn'greɪnd] adj arraigado

ingratiate [ɪn'greɪʃɪeɪt] vt: **to ~ o.s. with** congraciarse con

ingredient [ɪn'gri:dɪənt] n ingrediente m

inhabit [ɪn'hæbɪt] vt vivir en; **~ant** n habitante m/f

inhale [ɪn'heɪl] vt inhalar ♦ vi (breathe in) aspirar; (in smoking) tragar

inherent [ɪn'hɪərənt] adj: **~ in** or **to** inherente a

inherit [ɪn'herɪt] vt heredar; **~ance** n herencia; (fig) patrimonio

inhibit [ɪn'hɪbɪt] vt inhibir, impedir; **~ed** adj (PSYCH) cohibido; **~ion** [-'bɪʃən] n cohibición f

inhospitable [ɪnhɔs'pɪtəbl] adj (person) inhospitalario; (place) inhóspito

inhuman [ɪn'hju:mən] adj inhumano

initial [ɪ'nɪʃl] adj primero ♦ n inicial f ♦ vt firmar con las iniciales; **~s** npl (as signature) iniciales fpl; (abbreviation) siglas fpl; **~ly** adv al principio

initiate [ɪ'nɪʃɪeɪt] vt iniciar; **to ~ proceedings against sb** (LAW) entablar proceso contra uno

initiative [ɪ'nɪʃətɪv] n iniciativa

inject [ɪn'dʒekt] vt inyectar; **to ~ sb with sth** inyectar algo a uno; **~ion** [ɪn'dʒekʃən] n inyección f

injunction [ɪn'dʒʌŋkʃən] n interdicto

injure ['ɪndʒə*] vt (hurt) herir, lastimar; (fig: reputation etc) perjudicar; **~d** adj (person, arm) herido, lastimado; **injury** n herida, lesión f; (wrong) perjuicio, daño; **injury time** n (SPORT) (tiempo de) descuento

injustice [ɪn'dʒʌstɪs] n injusticia

ink [ɪŋk] n tinta

inkling ['ɪŋklɪŋ] n sospecha; (idea) idea

inlaid ['ɪnleɪd] adj (with wood, gems etc) incrustado

inland [adj 'ɪnlənd, adv ɪn'lænd] adj
(waterway, port etc) interior ♦ adv tierra
adentro; **I~ Revenue** (BRIT) n
departamento de impuestos; ≈ Hacienda
(SP)

in-laws npl suegros mpl

inlet ['ɪnlɛt] n (GEO) ensenada, cala; (TECH)
admisión f, entrada

inmate ['ɪnmeɪt] n (in prison) preso/a;
presidiario/a; (in asylum) internado/a

inn [ɪn] n posada, mesón m

innate [ɪ'neɪt] adj innato

inner ['ɪnə*] adj (courtyard, calm) interior;
(feelings) íntimo; ~ **city** n barrios
deprimidos del centro de una ciudad; ~
tube n (of tyre) cámara (SP), llanta (AM)

innings ['ɪnɪŋz] n (CRICKET) entrada, turno

innocent ['ɪnəsnt] adj inocente

innocuous [ɪ'nɔkjuəs] adj inocuo

innovation [ɪnəu'veɪʃən] n novedad f

innuendo [ɪnju'ɛndəu] (pl **~es**) n indirecta

inoculation [ɪnɔkju'leɪʃən] n inoculación f

in-patient n paciente m/f interno/a

input ['ɪnput] n (of resources)
inversión f; (COMPUT) entrada de datos

inquest ['ɪnkwɛst] n (coroner's) encuesta
judicial

inquire [ɪn'kwaɪə*] vi preguntar ♦ vt: **to ~
whether** preguntar si; **to ~ about** (person)
preguntar por; (fact) informarse de; ~
into vt fus investigar, indagar; **inquiry** n
pregunta; (investigation) investigación f,
pesquisa; **"Inquiries"** "Información";
inquiry office (BRIT) n oficina de
información

inquisitive [ɪn'kwɪzɪtɪv] adj (curious)
curioso

ns. abbr = **inches**

insane [ɪn'seɪn] adj loco; (MED) demente

insanity [ɪn'sænɪtɪ] n demencia, locura

inscription [ɪn'skrɪpʃən] n inscripción f; (in
book) dedicatoria

inscrutable [ɪn'skru:təbl] adj inescrutable,
insondable

insect ['ɪnsɛkt] n insecto; **~icide**
[ɪn'sɛktɪsaɪd] n insecticida m; ~ **repellent**
n loción f contra insectos

insecure [ɪnsɪ'kjuə*] adj inseguro

insemination [ɪnsɛmɪ'neɪʃn] n: **artificial ~**
inseminación f artificial

insensitive [ɪn'sɛnsɪtɪv] adj insensible

insert [vb ɪn'sə:t, n 'ɪnsə:t] vt (into sth)
introducir ♦ n encarte m; **~ion** [ɪn'sə:ʃən]
n inserción f

in-service ['ɪnsə:vɪs] adj (training, course)
a cargo de la empresa

inshore [ɪn'ʃɔ:*] adj de bajura ♦ adv (be)
cerca de la orilla; (move) hacia la orilla

inside ['ɪn'saɪd] n interior m ♦ adj interior,
interno ♦ adv (be) (por) dentro; (go)
hacia dentro ♦ prep dentro de; (of time):
~ 10 minutes en menos de 10 minutos;
~s npl (inf: stomach) tripas fpl; ~
information n información f
confidencial; ~ **lane** n (AUT: in Britain)
carril m izquierdo; (: in US, Europe etc)
carril m derecho; ~ **out** adv (turn) al
revés; (know) a fondo

insider dealing, insider trading n
(STOCK EXCHANGE) abuso de información
privilegiada

insight ['ɪnsaɪt] n perspicacia

insignificant [ɪnsɪg'nɪfɪknt] adj
insignificante

insincere [ɪnsɪn'sɪə*] adj poco sincero

insinuate [ɪn'sɪnjueɪt] vt insinuar

insipid [ɪn'sɪpɪd] adj soso, insulso

insist [ɪn'sɪst] vi insistir; **to ~ on** insistir en;
to ~ that insistir en que; (claim) exigir
que; **~ent** adj insistente; (noise, action)
persistente

insole ['ɪnsəul] n plantilla

insolent ['ɪnsələnt] adj insolente,
descarado

insomnia [ɪn'sɔmnɪə] n insomnio

inspect [ɪn'spɛkt] vt inspeccionar,
examinar; (troops) pasar revista a; **~ion**
[ɪn'spɛkʃən] n inspección f, examen m; (of
troops) revista; **~or** n inspector(a) m/f;
(BRIT: on buses, trains) revisor(a) m/f

inspiration [ɪnspə'reɪʃən] n inspiración f;
inspire [ɪn'spaɪə*] vt inspirar

instability [ɪnstə'bɪlɪtɪ] n inestabilidad f

install [ɪn'stɔ:l] vt instalar; (official)

nombrar; **~ation** [ɪnstə'leɪʃən] *n*
instalación *f*
instalment [ɪn'stɔːlmənt] (*US* **installment**)
n plazo; (*of story*) entrega; (*of TV serial
etc*) capítulo; **in ~s** (*pay, receive*) a plazos
instance ['ɪnstəns] *n* ejemplo, caso; **for ~**
por ejemplo; **in the first ~** en primer
lugar
instant ['ɪnstənt] *n* instante *m*, momento
♦ *adj* inmediato; (*coffee etc*) instantáneo;
~ly *adv* en seguida
instead [ɪn'sted] *adv* en cambio; **~ of** en
lugar de, en vez de
instep ['ɪnstep] *n* empeine *m*
instil [ɪn'stɪl] *vt*: **to ~ sth into** inculcar algo
a
instinct ['ɪnstɪŋkt] *n* instinto
institute ['ɪnstɪtjuːt] *n* instituto;
(*professional body*) colegio ♦ *vt* (*begin*)
iniciar, empezar; (*proceedings*) entablar;
(*system, rule*) establecer
institution [ɪnstɪ'tjuːʃən] *n* institución *f*;
(*MED: home*) asilo; (: *asylum*) manicomio;
(*of system etc*) establecimiento; (*of
custom*) iniciación *f*
instruct [ɪn'strʌkt] *vt*: **to ~ sb in sth**
instruir a uno en *or* sobre algo; **to ~ sb to
do sth** dar instrucciones a uno de hacer
algo; **~ion** [ɪn'strʌkʃən] *n* (*teaching*)
instrucción *f*; **~ions** *npl* (*orders*) órdenes
fpl; **~ions (for use)** modo de empleo;
~or *n* instructor(a) *m/f*
instrument ['ɪnstrəmənt] *n* instrumento;
~al [-'mentl] *adj* (*MUS*) instrumental; **to
be ~al in** ser (el) artífice de; **~ panel** *n*
tablero (de instrumentos)
insufficient [ɪnsə'fɪʃənt] *adj* insuficiente
insular ['ɪnsjulə*] *adj* insular; (*person*)
estrecho de miras
insulate ['ɪnsjuleɪt] *vt* aislar; **insulation**
[-'leɪʃən] *n* aislamiento
insulin ['ɪnsjulɪn] *n* insulina
insult [*n* 'ɪnsʌlt, *vb* ɪn'sʌlt] *n* insulto ♦ *vt*
insultar; **~ing** *adj* insultante
insurance [ɪn'ʃuərəns] *n* seguro; **fire/life
~** seguro contra incendios/sobre la vida; **~
agent** *n* agente *m/f* de seguros; **~**

policy *n* póliza (de seguros)
insure [ɪn'ʃuə*] *vt* asegurar
intact [ɪn'tækt] *adj* íntegro; (*unharmed*)
intacto
intake ['ɪnteɪk] *n* (*of food*) ingestión *f*; (*of
air*) consumo; (*BRIT: SCOL*): **an ~ of 200 a
year** 200 matriculados al año
integral ['ɪntɪgrəl] *adj* (*whole*) íntegro; (*part*) integrante
integrate ['ɪntɪgreɪt] *vt* integrar ♦ *vi*
integrarse
integrity [ɪn'tegrɪtɪ] *n* honradez *f*, rectitud
f
intellect ['ɪntəlekt] *n* intelecto; **~ual**
[-'lektjuəl] *adj*, *n* intelectual *m/f*
intelligence [ɪn'telɪdʒəns] *n* inteligencia
intelligent [ɪn'telɪdʒənt] *adj* inteligente
intelligible [ɪn'telɪdʒɪbl] *adj* inteligible,
comprensible
intend [ɪn'tend] *vt* (*gift etc*): **to ~ sth for**
destinar algo a; **to ~ to do sth** tener
intención de *or* pensar hacer algo
intense [ɪn'tens] *adj* intenso; **~ly** *adv*
(*extremely*) sumamente
intensify [ɪn'tensɪfaɪ] *vt* intensificar;
(*increase*) aumentar
intensive [ɪn'tensɪv] *adj* intensivo; **~ care
unit** *n* unidad *f* de vigilancia intensiva
intent [ɪn'tent] *n* propósito; (*LAW*)
premeditación *f* ♦ *adj* (*absorbed*) absorto;
(*attentive*) atento; **to all ~s and purposes**
prácticamente; **to be ~ on doing sth**
estar resuelto a hacer algo
intention [ɪn'tenʃən] *n* intención *f*,
propósito; **~al** *adj* deliberado; **~ally** *adv*
a propósito
intently [ɪn'tentlɪ] *adv* atentamente,
fijamente
interact [ɪntər'ækt] *vi* influirse
mutuamente; **~ive** *adj* (*COMPUT*)
interactivo
interchange ['ɪntətʃeɪndʒ] *n* intercambio;
(*on motorway*) intersección *f*; **~able** *adj*
intercambiable
intercom ['ɪntəkɔm] *n* interfono
intercourse ['ɪntəkɔːs] *n* (*sexual*)
relaciones *fpl* sexuales

nterest ['ɪntrɪst] n (also COMM) interés m
♦ vt interesar; **to be ~ed in** interesarse
por; **~ing** adj interesante; **~ rate** n tipo
or tasa de interés

nterface ['ɪntəfeɪs] n (COMPUT) junción f

nterfere [ɪntə'fɪə*] vi: **to ~ in** (quarrel,
other people's business) entrometerse en;
to ~ with (hinder) estorbar; (damage)
estropear

nterference [ɪntə'fɪərəns] n intromisión f;
(RADIO, TV) interferencia

nterim ['ɪntərɪm] n: **in the ~** en el ínterin
♦ adj provisional

nterior [ɪn'tɪərɪə*] n interior m ♦ adj
interior; **~ designer** n interiorista m/f

nterjection [ɪntə'dʒekʃən] n interposición
f; (LING) interjección f

nterlock [ɪntə'lɔk] vi entrelazarse

nterlude ['ɪntəluːd] n intervalo; (THEATRE)
intermedio

ntermediate [ɪntə'miːdɪət] adj
intermedio

ntermission [ɪntə'mɪʃən] n intermisión f;
(THEATRE) descanso

ntern [vb ɪn'təːn, n 'ɪntəːn] vt internar ♦ n
(US) interno/a

nternal [ɪn'təːnl] adj (layout, pipes,
security) interior; (injury, structure, memo)
internal; **~ly** adv: "**not to be taken ~ly**"
"uso externo"; **I~ Revenue Service**
(US) n departamento de impuestos;
≈ Hacienda (SP)

nternational [ɪntə'næʃənl] adj
internacional ♦ n (BRIT: match) partido
internacional

nternet ['ɪntənet] n: **the ~** Internet m or f

nterplay ['ɪntəpleɪ] n interacción f

nterpret [ɪn'təːprɪt] vt interpretar;
(translate) traducir; (understand) entender
♦ vi hacer de intérprete; **~er** n intérprete
m/f

nterrelated [ɪntərɪ'leɪtɪd] adj
interrelacionado

nterrogate [ɪn'terəgeɪt] vt interrogar;
interrogation [-'geɪʃən] n interrogatorio

nterrupt [ɪntə'rʌpt] vt, vi interrumpir;
~ion [-'rʌpʃən] n interrupción f

intersect [ɪntə'sekt] vi (roads) cruzarse;
~ion [-'sekʃən] n (of roads) cruce m

intersperse [ɪntə'spəːs] vt: **to ~ with**
salpicar de

intertwine [ɪntə'twaɪn] vt entrelazarse

interval ['ɪntəvl] n intervalo; (BRIT: THEATRE,
SPORT) descanso; (: SCOL) recreo; **at ~s** a
ratos, de vez en cuando

intervene [ɪntə'viːn] vi intervenir; (event)
interponerse; (time) transcurrir;
intervention n intervención f

interview ['ɪntəvjuː] n entrevista ♦ vt
entrevistarse con; **~er** n entrevistador(a)
m/f

intestine [ɪn'testɪn] n intestino

intimacy ['ɪntɪməsɪ] n intimidad f

intimate [adj 'ɪntɪmət, vb 'ɪntɪmeɪt] adj
íntimo; (friendship) estrecho; (knowledge)
profundo ♦ vt dar a entender

into ['ɪntuː] prep en; (towards) a; (inside)
hacia el interior de; **~ 3 pieces/French**
en 3 pedazos/al francés

intolerable [ɪn'tɔlərəbl] adj intolerable,
insoportable

intolerant [ɪn'tɔlərənt] adj: **~ (of)**
intolerante (con or para)

intoxicated [ɪn'tɔksɪkeɪtɪd] adj
embriagado

intractable [ɪn'træktəbl] adj (person)
intratable; (problem) espinoso

intransitive [ɪn'trænsɪtɪv] adj intransitivo

intravenous [ɪntrə'viːnəs] adj intravenoso

in-tray n bandeja de entrada

intricate ['ɪntrɪkət] adj (design, pattern)
intrincado

intrigue [ɪn'triːg] n intriga ♦ vt fascinar;
intriguing adj fascinante

intrinsic [ɪn'trɪnsɪk] adj intrínseco

introduce [ɪntrə'djuːs] vt introducir,
meter; (speaker, TV show etc) presentar;
to ~ sb (to sb) presentar uno (a otro); **to
~ sb to** (pastime, technique) introducir a
uno a; **introduction** [-'dʌkʃən] n
introducción f; (of person) presentación f;
introductory [-'dʌktərɪ] adj
introductorio; (lesson, offer) de
introducción

introvert ['ɪntrəvəːt] n introvertido/a ♦ adj (also: **~ed**) introvertido

intrude [ɪn'truːd] vi (person) entrometerse; **to ~ on** estorbar; **~r** n intruso/a; **intrusion** [-ʒən] n invasión f

intuition [ɪntjuːˈɪʃən] n intuición f

inundate ['ɪnʌndeɪt] vt: **to ~ with** inundar de

invade [ɪn'veɪd] vt invadir

invalid [n 'ɪnvəlɪd, adj ɪn'vælɪd] n (MED) minusválido/a ♦ adj (not valid) inválido, nulo

invaluable [ɪn'væljuəbl] adj inestimable

invariable [ɪn'veərɪəbl] adj invariable

invent [ɪn'vɛnt] vt inventar; **~ion** [ɪn'vɛnʃən] n invento; (lie) ficción f, mentira; **~ive** adj inventivo; **~or** n inventor(a) m/f

inventory ['ɪnvəntrɪ] n inventario

invert [ɪn'vəːt] vt invertir

inverted commas (BRIT) npl comillas fpl

invest [ɪn'vɛst] vt invertir ♦ vi: **to ~ in** (company etc) invertir dinero en; (fig: sth useful) comprar

investigate [ɪn'vɛstɪgeɪt] vt investigar; **investigation** [-ˈgeɪʃən] n investigación f, pesquisa

investment [ɪn'vɛstmənt] n inversión f

investor [ɪn'vɛstə*] n inversionista m/f

invigilator [ɪn'vɪdʒɪleɪtə*] n persona que vigila en un examen

invigorating [ɪn'vɪgəreɪtɪŋ] adj vigorizante

invisible [ɪn'vɪzɪbl] adj invisible

invitation [ɪnvɪ'teɪʃən] n invitación f

invite [ɪn'vaɪt] vt invitar; (opinions etc) solicitar, pedir; **inviting** adj atractivo; (food) apetitoso

invoice ['ɪnvɔɪs] n factura ♦ vt facturar

involuntary [ɪn'vɔləntrɪ] adj involuntario

involve [ɪn'vɔlv] vt suponer, implicar; tener que ver con; (concern, affect) corresponder; **to ~ sb (in sth)** comprometer a uno (con algo); **~d** adj complicado; **to be ~d in** (take part) tomar parte en; (be engrossed) estar muy metido en; **~ment** n participación f; dedicación f

inward ['ɪnwəd] adj (movement) interior, interno; (thought, feeling) íntimo; **~(s)** adv hacia dentro

I/O abbr (COMPUT = input/output) entrada/salida

iodine ['aɪəudiːn] n yodo

ion ['aɪən] n ion m; **ioniser** ['aɪənaɪzə*] n ionizador m

iota [aɪ'əutə] n jota, ápice m

IOU n abbr (= I owe you) pagaré m

IQ n abbr (= intelligence quotient) cociente m intelectual

IRA n abbr (= Irish Republican Army) IRA m

Iran [ɪ'rɑːn] n Irán m; **~ian** [ɪ'reɪnɪən] adj, n iraní m/f

Iraq [ɪ'rɑːk] n Iraq; **~i** adj, n iraquí m/f

irate [aɪ'reɪt] adj enojado, airado

Ireland ['aɪələnd] n Irlanda

iris ['aɪrɪs] (pl **~es**) n (ANAT) iris m; (BOT) lirio

Irish ['aɪrɪʃ] adj irlandés/esa ♦ npl: **the ~** los irlandeses; **~man/woman** (irreg) n irlandés/esa m/f; **~ Sea** n: **the ~ Sea** el mar de Irlanda

iron ['aɪən] n hierro; (for clothes) plancha ♦ cpd de hierro ♦ vt (clothes) planchar; **~ out** vt (fig) allanar

ironic(al) [aɪ'rɔnɪk(l)] adj irónico

ironing ['aɪənɪŋ] n (activity) planchado; (clothes: ironed) ropa planchada; (: to be ironed) ropa por planchar; **~ board** n tabla de planchar

ironmonger's (shop) ['aɪənmʌŋgəz] (BRIT) n ferretería, quincallería

irony ['aɪrənɪ] n ironía

irrational [ɪ'ræʃənl] adj irracional

irreconcilable [ɪrekən'saɪləbl] adj (ideas) incompatible; (enemies) irreconciliable

irregular [ɪ'regjulə*] adj irregular; (surface) desigual; (action, event) anómalo; (behaviour) poco ortodoxo

irrelevant [ɪ'reləvənt] adj fuera de lugar, inoportuno

irresolute [ɪ'rezəluːt] adj indeciso

irrespective [ɪrɪ'spektɪv]: **~ of** prep sin tener en cuenta, no importa

irresponsible [ɪrɪ'spɔnsɪbl] *adj* (*act*) irresponsable; (*person*) poco serio

irrigate ['ɪrɪgeɪt] *vt* regar; **irrigation** [-'geɪʃən] *n* riego

irritable ['ɪrɪtəbl] *adj* (*person*) de mal humor

irritate ['ɪrɪteɪt] *vt* fastidiar; (*MED*) picar; **irritating** *adj* fastidioso; **irritation** [-'teɪʃən] *n* fastidio; irritación; picazón *f*, picor *m*

IRS (*US*) *n abbr* = **Internal Revenue Service**

is [ɪz] *vb see* **be**

Islam ['ɪzlɑːm] *n* Islam *m*; **~ic** [ɪz'læmɪk] *adj* islámico

island ['aɪlənd] *n* isla; **~er** *n* isleño/a

isle [aɪl] *n* isla

isn't ['ɪznt] = **is not**

isolate ['aɪsəleɪt] *vt* aislar; **~d** *adj* aislado; **isolation** [-'leɪʃən] *n* aislamiento

Israel ['ɪzreɪl] *n* Israel *m*; **~i** [ɪz'reɪlɪ] *adj*, *n* israelí *m/f*

issue ['ɪsjuː] *n* (*problem, subject, most important part*) cuestión *f*; (*outcome*) resultado; (*of banknotes etc*) emisión *f*; (*of newspaper etc*) edición *f* ♦ *vt* (*rations, equipment*) distribuir, repartir; (*orders*) dar; (*certificate, passport*) expedir; (*decree*) promulgar; (*magazine*) publicar; (*cheques*) extender; (*banknotes, stamps*) emitir; **at ~** en cuestión; **to take ~ with sb (over)** estar en desacuerdo con uno (sobre); **to make an ~ of sth** hacer una cuestión de algo

Istanbul [ɪstæn'buːl] *n* Estambul *m*

KEYWORD

it [ɪt] *pron* 1 (*specific: subject: not generally translated*) él/ella; (: *direct object*) lo, la; (: *indirect object*) le; (*after prep*) él/ella; (*abstract concept*) ello; **~'s on the table** está en la mesa; **I can't find ~** no lo (*or* la) encuentro; **give ~ to me** dámelo (*or* dámela); **I spoke to him about ~** le hablé del asunto; **what did you learn from ~?** ¿qué aprendiste de él (*or* ella)?; **did you go to ~?** (*party, concert etc*) ¿fuiste?

2 (*impersonal*): **~'s raining** llueve, está lloviendo; **~'s 6 o'clock/the 10th of August** son las 6/es el 10 de agosto; **how far is ~? - ~'s 10 miles/2 hours on the train** ¿a qué distancia está? — a 10 millas/2 horas en tren; **who is ~? - ~'s me** ¿quién es? — soy yo

---

Italian [ɪ'tæljən] *adj* italiano ♦ *n* italiano/a; (*LING*) italiano

italics [ɪ'tælɪks] *npl* cursiva

Italy ['ɪtəlɪ] *n* Italia

itch [ɪtʃ] *n* picazón *f* ♦ *vi* (*part of body*) picar; **to ~ to do sth** rabiar por hacer algo; **~y** *adj*: **my hand is ~y** me pica la mano

it'd ['ɪtd] = **it would**; **it had**

item ['aɪtəm] *n* artículo; (*on agenda*) asunto (a tratar); (*also*: **news ~**) noticia; **~ize** *vt* detallar

itinerary [aɪ'tɪnərərɪ] *n* itinerario

it'll ['ɪtl] = **it will**; **it shall**

its [ɪts] *adj* su; sus *pl*

it's [ɪts] = **it is**; **it has**

itself [ɪt'self] *pron* (*reflexive*) sí mismo/a; (*emphatic*) él mismo/ella misma

ITV *n abbr* (*BRIT*: = *Independent Television*) cadena de televisión comercial independiente del Estado

I.U.D. *n abbr* (= *intra-uterine device*) DIU *m*

I've [aɪv] = **I have**

ivory ['aɪvərɪ] *n* marfil *m*

ivy ['aɪvɪ] *n* (*BOT*) hiedra

J, j

jab [dʒæb] *vt*: **to ~ sth into sth** clavar algo en algo ♦ *n* (*inf*) (*MED*) pinchazo

jack [dʒæk] *n* (*AUT*) gato; (*CARDS*) sota; **~ up** *vt* (*AUT*) levantar con gato

jackal ['dʒækɔːl] *n* (*ZOOL*) chacal *m*

jacket ['dʒækɪt] *n* chaqueta, americana, saco (*AM*); (*of book*) sobrecubierta

jack: ~-knife *vi* colear; **~ plug** *n* (*ELEC*) enchufe *m* de clavija; **~pot** *n* premio gordo

jaded ['dʒeɪdɪd] *adj* (*tired*) cansado; (*fed-up*) hastiado

jagged ['dʒægɪd] *adj* dentado

jail [dʒeɪl] *n* cárcel f ♦ *vt* encarcelar

jam [dʒæm] *n* mermelada; (*also:* **traffic ~**) embotellamiento; (*inf: difficulty*) apuro ♦ *vt* (*passage etc*) obstruir; (*mechanism, drawer etc*) atascar; (*RADIO*) interferir ♦ *vi* atascarse, trabarse; **to ~ sth into sth** meter algo a la fuerza en algo

Jamaica [dʒə'meɪkə] *n* Jamaica

jangle ['dʒæŋgl] *vi* entrechocar (ruidosamente)

janitor ['dʒænɪtə*] *n* (*caretaker*) portero, conserje *m*

January ['dʒænjuərɪ] *n* enero

Japan [dʒə'pæn] *n* (el) Japón; **~ese** [dʒæpə'niːz] *adj* japonés/esa ♦ *n inv* japonés/esa *m/f*; (*LING*) japonés *m*

jar [dʒɑː*] *n* tarro, bote *m* ♦ *vi* (*sound*) chirriar; (*colours*) desentonar

jargon ['dʒɑːgən] *n* jerga

jasmine ['dʒæzmɪn] *n* jazmín *m*

jaundice ['dʒɔːndɪs] *n* icteria

jaunt [dʒɔːnt] *n* excursión f

javelin ['dʒævlɪn] *n* jabalina

jaw [dʒɔː] *n* mandíbula

jay [dʒeɪ] *n* (*ZOOL*) arrendajo

jaywalker ['dʒeɪwɔːkə*] *n* peatón/ona *m/f* imprudente

jazz [dʒæz] *n* jazz *m*; **~ up** *vt* (*liven up*) animar, avivar

jealous ['dʒeləs] *adj* celoso; (*envious*) envidioso; **~y** *n* celos *mpl*; envidia

jeans [dʒiːnz] *npl* vaqueros *mpl*, tejanos *mpl*

Jeep ® [dʒiːp] *n* jeep *m*

jeer [dʒɪə*] *vi*: **to ~ (at)** (*mock*) mofarse (de)

jelly ['dʒelɪ] *n* (*jam*) jalea; (*dessert etc*) gelatina; **~fish** *n inv* medusa (*SP*), aguaviva (*AM*)

jeopardy ['dʒepədɪ] *n*: **to be in ~** estar en peligro

jerk [dʒəːk] *n* (*jolt*) sacudida; (*wrench*) tirón *m*; (*inf*) imbécil *m/f* ♦ *vt* tirar

bruscamente de ♦ *vi* (*vehicle*) traquetear

jersey ['dʒəːzɪ] *n* jersey *m*; (*fabric*) (tejido de) punto

Jesus ['dʒiːzəs] *n* Jesús *m*

jet [dʒet] *n* (*of gas, liquid*) chorro; (*AVIAT*) avión m a reacción; **~-black** *adj* negro como el azabache; **~ engine** *n* motor *m* a reacción; **~ lag** *n* desorientación f después de un largo vuelo

jettison ['dʒetɪsn] *vt* desechar

jetty ['dʒetɪ] *n* muelle *m*, embarcadero

Jew [dʒuː] *n* judío

jewel ['dʒuːəl] *n* joya; (*in watch*) rubí *m*; **~ler** (*US* **~er**) *n* joyero/a; **~ler's (shop)** (*US* **~ry store**) *n* joyería; **~lery** (*US* **~ry**) *n* joyas *fpl*, alhajas *fpl*

Jewess ['dʒuːɪs] *n* judía

Jewish ['dʒuːɪʃ] *adj* judío

jibe [dʒaɪb] *n* mofa

jiffy ['dʒɪfɪ] (*inf*) *n*: **in a ~** en un santiamén

jigsaw ['dʒɪgsɔː] *n* (*also:* **~ puzzle**) rompecabezas *m inv*, puzle *m*

jilt [dʒɪlt] *vt* dejar plantado a

jingle ['dʒɪŋgl] *n* musiquilla ♦ *vi* tintinear

jinx [dʒɪŋks] *n*: **there's a ~ on it** está gafado

jitters ['dʒɪtəz] (*inf*) *npl*: **to get the ~** ponerse nervioso

job [dʒɔb] *n* (*task*) tarea; (*post*) empleo; **it's not my ~** no me incumbe a mí; **it's a good ~ that ...** menos mal que ...; **just the ~!** ¡estupendo!; **~ centre** (*BRIT*) *n* oficina estatal de colocaciones; **~less** *adj* sin trabajo

jockey ['dʒɔkɪ] *n* jockey *m/f* ♦ *vi*: **to ~ for position** maniobrar para conseguir una posición

jog [dʒɔg] *vt* empujar (ligeramente) ♦ *vi* (*run*) hacer footing; **to ~ sb's memory** refrescar la memoria a uno; **~ along** *vi* (*fig*) ir tirando; **~ging** *n* footing *m*

join [dʒɔɪn] *vt* (*things*) juntar, unir; (*club*) hacerse socio de; (*POL: party*) afiliarse a; (*queue*) ponerse en; (*meet: people*) reunirse con ♦ *vi* (*roads*) juntarse; (*rivers*) confluir ♦ *n* juntura; **~ in** *vi* tomar parte, participar ♦ *vt fus* tomar parte *or* participar en; **~ up** vi reunirse; (MIL) alistarse

oiner ['dʒɔɪnəʳ] (BRIT) n carpintero/a; **~y** n carpintería

oint [dʒɔɪnt] n (TECH) junta, unión f; (ANAT) articulación f; (BRIT: CULIN) pieza de carne (para asar); (inf: place) tugurio; (: of cannabis) porro ♦ adj (common) común; (combined) combinado; **~ account** (with bank etc) cuenta común

oke [dʒəʊk] n chiste m; (also: **practical ~**) broma ♦ vi bromear; **to play a ~ on** gastar una broma a; **~r** n (CARDS) comodín m

olly ['dʒɔlɪ] adj (merry) alegre; (enjoyable) divertido ♦ adv (BRIT: inf) muy, terriblemente

olt [dʒəʊlt] n (jerk) sacudida; (shock) susto ♦ vt (physically) sacudir; (emotionally) asustar

ostle ['dʒɔsl] vt dar empellones a, codear

ot [dʒɔt] n: **not one ~** ni jota, ni pizca; **~ down** vt apuntar; **~ter** (BRIT) n bloc m

ournal ['dʒɜːnl] n (magazine) revista; (diary) periódico, diario; **~ism** n periodismo; **~ist** n periodista m/f, reportero/a

ourney ['dʒɜːnɪ] n viaje m; (distance covered) trayecto

ovial ['dʒəʊvɪəl] adj risueño, jovial

oy [dʒɔɪ] n alegría; **~ful** adj alegre; **~ous** adj alegre; **~ ride** n (illegal) paseo en coche robado; **~rider** n gamberro que roba un coche para dar una vuelta y luego abandonarlo; **~ stick** n (AVIAT) palanca de mando; (COMPUT) palanca de control

P n abbr = **Justice of the Peace**

r abbr = **junior**

ubilant ['dʒuːbɪlnt] adj jubiloso

udge [dʒʌdʒ] n juez m/f; (fig: expert) perito ♦ vt juzgar; (consider) considerar; **judg(e)ment** n juicio

udiciary [dʒuːˈdɪʃɪərɪ] n poder m judicial

udicious [dʒuːˈdɪʃəs] adj juicioso

udo ['dʒuːdəʊ] n judo

ug [dʒʌg] n jarra

juggernaut ['dʒʌɡənɔːt] (BRIT) n (huge truck) trailer m

juggle ['dʒʌɡl] vi hacer juegos malabares; **~r** n malabarista m/f

juice [dʒuːs] n zumo, jugo (esp AM); **juicy** adj jugoso

jukebox ['dʒuːkbɔks] n máquina de discos

July [dʒuːˈlaɪ] n julio

jumble ['dʒʌmbl] n revoltijo ♦ vt (also: **~ up**) revolver; **~ sale** (BRIT) n venta de objetos usados con fines benéficos

---
jumble sale
---

i Los **jumble sales** son unos mercadillos que se organizan con fines benéficos en los locales de un colegio, iglesia u otro centro público. En ellos puede comprarse todo tipo de artículos baratos de segunda mano, sobre todo ropa, juguetes, libros, vajillas o muebles.

---

jumbo (jet) ['dʒʌmbəʊ-] n jumbo

jump [dʒʌmp] vi saltar, dar saltos; (with fear etc) pegar un bote; (increase) aumentar ♦ vt saltar ♦ n salto; aumento; **to ~ the queue** (BRIT) colarse

jumper ['dʒʌmpəʳ] n (BRIT: pullover) suéter m, jersey m; (US: dress) mandil m; **~ cables** (US) npl = **jump leads**

jump leads (BRIT) npl cables mpl puente de batería

jumpy ['dʒʌmpɪ] (inf) adj nervioso

Jun. abbr = **junior**

junction ['dʒʌŋkʃən] n (BRIT: of roads) cruce m; (RAIL) empalme m

juncture ['dʒʌŋktʃəʳ] n: **at this ~** en este momento, en esta coyuntura

June [dʒuːn] n junio

jungle ['dʒʌŋɡl] n selva, jungla

junior ['dʒuːnɪəʳ] adj (in age) menor, más joven; (brother/sister etc): **7 years her ~** siete años menor que ella; (position) subalterno ♦ n menor m/f, joven m/f; **~ school** (BRIT) n escuela primaria

junk [dʒʌŋk] n (cheap goods) baratijas fpl; (rubbish) basura; **~ food** n alimentos preparados y envasados de escaso valor *nutritivo*

junkie ['dʒʌŋkı] (*inf*) *n* drogadicto/a, yonqui *m/f*

junk mail *n* propaganda de buzón

junk shop *n* tienda de objetos usados

Junr *abbr* = **junior**

juror ['dʒuərə*] *n* jurado

jury ['dʒuərı] *n* jurado

just [dʒʌst] *adj* justo ♦ *adv* (*exactly*) exactamente; (*only*) sólo, solamente; **he's ~ done it/left** acaba de hacerlo/irse; **~ right** perfecto; **~ two o'clock** las dos en punto; **she's ~ as clever as you** es tan lista como tú; **~ as well that ...** menos mal que ...; **~ as he was leaving** en el momento en que se marchaba; **~ before/enough** justo antes/lo suficiente; **~ here** aquí mismo; **he ~ missed** ha fallado por poco; **~ listen to this** escucha esto un momento

justice ['dʒʌstıs] *n* justicia; (*US: judge*) juez *m*; **to do ~ to** (*fig*) hacer justicia a; **J~ of the Peace** *n* juez *m* de paz

justify ['dʒʌstıfaı] *vt* justificar; (*text*) alinear

jut [dʒʌt] *vi* (*also*: **~ out**) sobresalir

juvenile ['dʒuːvənaıl] *adj* (*court*) de menores; (*humour, mentality*) infantil ♦ *n* menor *m* de edad

K, k

K *abbr* (= *one thousand*) mil; (= *kilobyte*) kilobyte *m*, kilocteto

kangaroo [kæŋgə'ruː] *n* canguro

karate [kə'rɑːtı] *n* karate *m*

kebab [kə'bæb] *n* pincho moruno

keel [kiːl] *n* quilla; **on an even ~** (*fig*) en equilibrio

keen [kiːn] *adj* (*interest, desire*) grande, vivo; (*eye, intelligence*) agudo; (*competition*) reñido; (*edge*) afilado; (*eager*) entusiasta; **to be ~ to do** *or* **on doing sth** tener muchas ganas de hacer algo; **to be ~ on sth/sb** interesarse por algo/uno

keep [kiːp] (*pt, pp* **kept**) *vt* (*preserve, store*) guardar; (*hold back*) quedarse con; (*maintain*) mantener; (*detain*) detener; (*shop*) ser propietario de; (*feed: family etc*) mantener; (*promise*) cumplir; (*chickens, bees etc*) criar; (*accounts*) llevar; (*diary*) escribir; (*prevent*): **to ~ sb from doing sth** impedir a uno hacer algo ♦ *vi* (*food*) conservarse; (*remain*) seguir, continuar ♦ *n* (*of castle*) torreón *m*; (*food etc*) comida, subsistencia; (*inf*): **for ~s** para siempre; **to ~ doing sth** seguir haciendo algo; **to ~ sb happy** tener a uno contento; **to ~ a place tidy** mantener un lugar limpio; **to ~ sth to o.s.** guardar algo para sí mismo; **to ~ sth (back) from sb** ocultar algo a uno; **to ~ time** (*clock*) mantener la hora exacta; **~ on** *vi*: **to ~ on doing** seguir *or* continuar haciendo; **to ~ on (about sth)** no parar de hablar (de algo); **~ out** *vi* (*stay out*) permanecer fuera; **"~ out"** "prohibida la entrada"; **~ up** *vt* mantener, conservar ♦ *vi* no retrasarse; **to ~ up with** (*pace*) ir al paso de; (*level*) mantenerse a la altura de; **~er** *n* guardián/ana *m/f*; **~-fit** *n* gimnasia (para mantenerse en forma); **~ing** *n* (*care*) cuidado; **in ~ing with** de acuerdo con; **~sake** *n* recuerdo

kennel ['kɛnl] *n* perrera; **~s** *npl* residencia canina

Kenya ['kɛnjə] *n* Kenia

kept [kɛpt] *pt, pp of* **keep**

kerb [kəːb] (*BRIT*) *n* bordillo

kernel ['kəːnl] *n* (*nut*) almendra; (*fig*) meollo

ketchup ['kɛtʃəp] *n* salsa de tomate, catsup *m*

kettle ['kɛtl] *n* hervidor *m* de agua; **~ drum** *n* (*MUS*) timbal *m*

key [kiː] *n* llave *f*; (*MUS*) tono; (*of piano, typewriter*) tecla ♦ *adj* (*issue etc*) clave *in* ♦ *vt* (*also*: **~ in**) teclear; **~board** *n* teclado; **~ed up** *adj* (*person*) nervioso; **~hole** *n* ojo (de la cerradura); **~hole surgery** *n* cirugía cerrada, cirugía no invasiva; **~note** *n* (*MUS*) tónica; (*of speech*) punto principal *or* clave; **~ring** *n* llavero

khaki ['kɑːkɪ] n caqui

kick [kɪk] vt dar una patada or un puntapié a; (inf: habit) quitarse de ♦ vi (horse) dar coces ♦ n patada; puntapié m; (of animal) coz f; (thrill): **he does it for ~s** lo hace por pura diversión; **~ off** vi (SPORT) hacer el saque inicial

kid [kɪd] n (inf: child) chiquillo/a; (animal) cabrito; (leather) cabritilla ♦ vi (inf) bromear

kidnap ['kɪdnæp] vt secuestrar; **~per** n secuestrador(a) m/f; **~ping** n secuestro

kidney ['kɪdnɪ] n riñón m

kill [kɪl] vt matar; (murder) asesinar ♦ n matanza; **to ~ time** matar el tiempo; **~er** n asesino/a; **~ing** n (one) asesinato; (several) matanza; **to make a ~ing** (fig) hacer su agosto; **~joy** n (BRIT) aguafiestas m/f inv

kiln [kɪln] n horno

kilo ['kiːləʊ] n kilo; **~byte** n (COMPUT) kilobyte m, kilocteto; **~gram(me)** ['kɪləʊɡræm] n kilo, kilogramo; **~metre** ['kɪləmiːtə*] (US **~meter**) n kilómetro; **~watt** ['kɪləʊwɒt] n kilovatio

kilt [kɪlt] n falda escocesa

kin [kɪn] n see **next**

kind [kaɪnd] adj amable, atento ♦ n clase f, especie f; (species) género; **in ~** (COMM) en especie; **a ~ of** una especie de; **to be two of a ~** ser tal para cual

kindergarten ['kɪndəɡɑːtn] n jardín m de la infancia

kind-hearted adj bondadoso, de buen corazón

kindle ['kɪndl] vt encender; (arouse) despertar

kindly ['kaɪndlɪ] adj bondadoso; cariñoso ♦ adv bondadosamente, amablemente; **will you ~ ...** sea usted tan amable de ...

kindness ['kaɪndnɪs] n (quality) bondad f, amabilidad f; (act) favor m

king [kɪŋ] n rey m; **~dom** n reino; **~fisher** n martín m pescador; **~-size** adj de tamaño extra

kiosk ['kiːɒsk] n quiosco; (BRIT: TEL) cabina

kipper ['kɪpə*] n arenque m ahumado

kiss [kɪs] n beso ♦ vt besar; **to ~ (each other)** besarse; **~ of life** n respiración f boca a boca

kit [kɪt] n (equipment) equipo; (tools etc) (caja de) herramientas fpl; (assembly ~) juego de armar

kitchen ['kɪtʃɪn] n cocina; **~ sink** n fregadero

kite [kaɪt] n (toy) cometa

kitten ['kɪtn] n gatito/a

kitty ['kɪtɪ] n (pool of money) fondo común

km abbr (= kilometre) km

knack [næk] n: **to have the ~ of doing sth** tener el don de hacer algo

knapsack ['næpsæk] n mochila

knead [niːd] vt amasar

knee [niː] n rodilla; **~cap** n rótula

kneel [niːl] (pt, pp knelt) vi (also: ~ down) arrodillarse

knew [njuː] pt of **know**

knickers ['nɪkəz] (BRIT) npl bragas fpl

knife [naɪf] (pl knives) n cuchillo ♦ vt acuchillar

knight [naɪt] n caballero; (CHESS) caballo; **~hood** (BRIT) n (title): **to receive a ~hood** recibir el título de Sir

knit [nɪt] vt tejer, tricotar ♦ vi hacer punto, tricotar; (bones) soldarse; **to ~ one's brows** fruncir el ceño; **~ting** n labor f de punto; **~ting machine** n máquina de tricotar; **~ting needle** n aguja de hacer punto; **~wear** n prendas fpl de punto

knives [naɪvz] npl of **knife**

knob [nɒb] n (of door) tirador m; (of stick) puño; (on radio, TV) botón m

knock [nɒk] vt (strike) golpear; (bump into) chocar contra; (inf) criticar ♦ vi (at door etc): **to ~ at/on** llamar a ♦ n golpe m; (on door) llamada; **~ down** vt atropellar; **~ off** (inf) vi (finish) salir del trabajo ♦ vt (from price) descontar; (inf: steal) birlar; **~ out** vt dejar sin sentido; (BOXING) poner fuera de combate, dejar K.O.; (in competition) eliminar; **~ over** vt (object) tirar; (person) atropellar; **~er** n (on door) aldabón m; **~out** n (BOXING) K.O. m, knockout *m* ♦ *cpd* (*competition etc*) eliminatorio

knot [nɒt] *n* nudo ♦ *vt* anudar

know [nəu] (*pt* knew, *pp* known) *vt* (*facts*) saber; (*be acquainted with*) conocer; (*recognize*) reconocer, conocer; to ~ how to swim saber nadar; to ~ about *or* of sb/sth saber de uno/algo; ~-all *n* sabelotodo *m/f*; ~-how *n* conocimientos *mpl*; ~ing *adj* (*look*) de complicidad; ~ingly *adv* (*purposely*) adrede; (*smile, look*) con complicidad

knowledge ['nɒlɪdʒ] *n* conocimiento; (*learning*) saber *m*, conocimientos *mpl*; ~able *adj* entendido

knuckle ['nʌkl] *n* nudillo

Koran [kɔ'rɑːn] *n* Corán *m*

Korea [kə'rɪə] *n* Corea

kosher ['kəuʃə*] *adj* autorizado por la ley judía

L, l

L (*BRIT*) *abbr* = learner driver

l. *abbr* (= litre) l

lab [læb] *n abbr* = laboratory

label ['leɪbl] *n* etiqueta ♦ *vt* poner etiqueta a

labor *etc* ['leɪbə*] (*US*) = labour

laboratory [lə'bɒrətərɪ] *n* laboratorio

laborious [lə'bɔːrɪəs] *adj* penoso

labour ['leɪbə*] (*US* labor) *n* (*hard work*) trabajo; (~ *force*) mano *f* de obra; (*MED*): to be in ~ estar de parto ♦ *vi*: to ~ (at sth) trabajar (en algo) ♦ *vt*: to ~ a point insistir en un punto; L~, the L~ party (*BRIT*) el partido laborista, los laboristas *mpl*; ~ed *adj* (*breathing*) fatigoso; ~er *n* peón *m*; farm ~er peón *m*; (day ~er) jornalero

lace [leɪs] *n* encaje *m*; (*of shoe etc*) cordón *m* ♦ *vt* (*shoes: also:* ~ up) atarse (los zapatos)

lack [læk] *n* (*absence*) falta ♦ *vt* faltarle a uno, carecer de; through *or* for ~ of por falta de; to be ~ing faltar, no haber; to

be ~ing in sth faltarle a uno algo

lacquer ['lækə*] *n* laca

lad [læd] *n* muchacho, chico

ladder ['lædə*] *n* escalera (de mano); (*BRIT in tights*) carrera

laden ['leɪdn] *adj*: ~ (with) cargado (de)

ladle ['leɪdl] *n* cucharón *m*

lady ['leɪdɪ] *n* señora; (*dignified, graceful*) dama; "ladies and gentlemen ..." "señoras y caballeros ..."; young ~ señorita; the ladies' (room) los servicios de señoras; ~bird (*US* ~bug) *n* mariquita; ~like *adj* fino; L~ship *n*: your L~ship su Señoría

lag [læg] *n* retraso ♦ *vi* (*also:* ~ behind) retrasarse, quedarse atrás ♦ *vt* (*pipes*) revestir

lager ['lɑːgə*] *n* cerveza (rubia)

lagoon [lə'guːn] *n* laguna

laid [leɪd] *pt, pp of* lay; ~ back (*inf*) *adj* relajado; ~ up *adj*: to be ~ up (with) tener que guardar cama (a causa de)

lain [leɪn] *pp of* lie

lake [leɪk] *n* lago

lamb [læm] *n* cordero; (*meat*) (carne *f* de) cordero; ~ chop *n* chuleta de cordero; lambswool *n* lana de cordero

lame [leɪm] *adj* cojo; (*excuse*) poco convincente

lament [lə'mɛnt] *n* quejo ♦ *vt* lamentarse de

laminated ['læmɪneɪtɪd] *adj* (*metal*) laminado; (*wood*) contrachapado; (*surface*) plastificado

lamp [læmp] *n* lámpara; ~post (*BRIT*) *n* (poste *m* de) farol *m*; ~shade *n* pantalla

lance [lɑːns] *vt* (*MED*) abrir con lanceta

land [lænd] *n* tierra; (*country*) país *m*; (*piece of* ~) terreno; (*estate*) tierras *fpl*, finca ♦ *vi* (*from ship*) desembarcar; (*AVIAT*) aterrizar; (*fig: fall*) caer, terminar ♦ *vt* (*passengers, goods*) desembarcar; to ~ sb with sth (*inf*) hacer cargar a uno con algo; ~ up *vi*: to ~ up in/at ir a parar a/ en; ~fill site ['lændfɪl-] *n* vertedero; ~ing *n* aterrizaje *m*; (*of staircase*) rellano; ~ing gear *n* (*AVIAT*) tren *m* de aterrizaje;

~**lady** n (of rented house, pub etc) dueña; ~**lord** n propietario; (of pub etc) patrón m; ~**mark** n lugar m conocido; **to be a ~mark** (fig) marcar un hito histórico; ~**owner** n terrateniente m/f; ~**scape** n paisaje m; ~**scape gardener** n arquitecto de jardines; ~**slide** n (GEO) corrimiento de tierras; (fig: POL) victoria arrolladora

ane [leɪn] n (in country) camino; (AUT) carril m; (in race) calle f

anguage ['læŋgwɪdʒ] n lenguaje m; (national tongue) idioma m, lengua; **bad ~** palabrotas fpl; ~ **laboratory** n laboratorio de idiomas

ank [læŋk] adj (hair) lacio

anky ['læŋkɪ] adj larguirucho

antern ['læntn] n linterna, farol m

ap [læp] n (of track) vuelta; (of body) regazo; **to sit on sb's ~** sentarse en las rodillas de uno ♦ vt (also: ~ **up**) beber a lengüetadas ♦ vi (waves) chapotear; ~ **up** vt (fig) tragarse

apel [lə'pɛl] n solapa

apland ['læplænd] n Laponia

apse [læps] n fallo; (moral) desliz m; (of time) intervalo ♦ vi (expire) caducar; (time) pasar, transcurrir; **to ~ into bad habits** caer en malos hábitos

aptop (computer) ['læptɔp-] n (ordenador m) portátil m

arch [lɑːtʃ] n alerce m

ard [lɑːd] n manteca (de cerdo)

arder ['lɑːdə*] n despensa

arge [lɑːdʒ] adj grande; **at ~** (free) en libertad; (generally) en general; ~**ly** adv (mostly) en su mayor parte; (introducing reason) en gran parte; ~**-scale** adj (map) en gran escala; (fig) importante

ark [lɑːk] n (bird) alondra; (joke) broma

aryngitis [lærɪn'dʒaɪtɪs] n laringitis f

aser ['leɪzə*] n láser m; ~ **printer** n impresora (por) láser

ash [læʃ] n latigazo; (also: **eye~**) pestaña ♦ vt azotar; (tie): **to ~ to/together** atar a/atar; ~ **out** vi: **to ~ out (at sb)** (hit) arremeter (contra uno); **to ~ out against**

sb lanzar invectivas contra uno

lass [læs] (BRIT) n chica

lasso [læ'suː] n lazo

last [lɑːst] adj último; (end: of series etc) final ♦ adv (most recently) la última vez; (finally) por último ♦ vi durar; (continue) continuar, seguir; ~ **night** anoche; ~ **week** la semana pasada; **at ~** por fin; ~ **but one** penúltimo; ~**-ditch** adj (attempt) último, desesperado; ~**ing** adj duradero; ~**ly** adv por último, finalmente; ~**-minute** adj de última hora

latch [lætʃ] n pestillo

late [leɪt] adj último; (not on time) tarde, atrasado; (dead) fallecido ♦ adv tarde; (behind time, schedule) con retraso; **of ~** últimamente; ~ **at night** a última hora de la noche; **in ~ May** hacia fines de mayo; **the ~ Mr X** el difunto Sr X; ~**comer** n recién llegado/a; ~**ly** adv últimamente; ~**r** adj (date etc) posterior; (version etc) más reciente ♦ adv más tarde, después; ~**st** ['leɪtɪst] adj último; **at the ~st** a más tardar

lathe [leɪð] n torno

lather ['lɑːðə*] n espuma (de jabón) ♦ vt enjabonar

Latin ['lætɪn] n latín m ♦ adj latino; ~ **America** n América latina; ~-**American** adj, n latinoamericano/a

latitude ['lætɪtjuːd] n latitud f; (fig) libertad f

latter ['lætə*] adj último; (of two) segundo ♦ n: **the ~** el último, éste; ~**ly** adv últimamente

laudable ['lɔːdəbl] adj loable

laugh [lɑːf] n risa ♦ vi reír(se); **(to do sth) for a ~** (hacer algo) en broma; ~ **at** vt fus reírse de; ~ **off** vt tomar algo a risa; ~**able** adj ridículo; ~**ing stock** n: **the ~ing stock of** el hazmerreír de; ~**ter** n risa

launch [lɔːntʃ] n lanzamiento; (boat) lancha ♦ vt (ship) botar; (rocket etc) lanzar; (fig) comenzar; ~ **into** vt fus lanzarse a; ~**(ing) pad** n plataforma de lanzamiento

launder ['lɔːndə*] vt lavar

Launderette ® [lɔːn'drɛt] (*BRIT*) n lavandería (automática)

Laundromat ® ['lɔːndrəmæt] (*US*) n = **Launderette**

laundry ['lɔːndrɪ] n (*dirty*) ropa sucia; (*clean*) colada; (*room*) lavadero

lavatory ['lævətərɪ] n wáter m

lavender ['lævəndə*] n lavanda

lavish ['lævɪʃ] adj (*amount*) abundante; (*person*): ~ **with** pródigo en ♦ vt: **to ~ sth on sb** colmar a uno de algo

law [lɔː] n ley f; (*SCOL*) derecho; (*a rule*) regla; (*professions connected with* ~) jurisprudencia; **~-abiding** adj respetuoso de la ley; ~ **and order** n orden m público; ~ **court** n tribunal m (de justicia); **~ful** adj legítimo, lícito; **~less** adj (*action*) criminal

lawn [lɔːn] n césped m; **~mower** n cortacésped m; ~ **tennis** n tenis m sobre hierba

law school (*US*) n (*SCOL*) facultad f de derecho

lawsuit ['lɔːsuːt] n pleito

lawyer ['lɔːjə*] n abogado/a; (*for sales, wills etc*) notario/a

lax [læks] adj laxo

laxative ['læksətɪv] n laxante m

lay [leɪ] (*pt, pp* **laid**) *pt of* **lie** ♦ adj laico; (*not expert*) lego ♦ vt (*place*) colocar; (*eggs, table*) poner; (*cable*) tender; (*carpet*) extender; ~ **aside** *or* **by** vt dejar a un lado; ~ **down** vt (*pen etc*) dejar; (*rules etc*) establecer; **to ~ down the law** (*pej*) imponer las normas; ~ **off** vt (*workers*) despedir; ~ **on** vt (*meal, facilities*) proveer; ~ **out** vt (*spread out*) disponer, exponer; **~about** (*inf*) n vago/a; **~-by** n (*BRIT: AUT*) área de aparcamiento

layer ['leɪə*] n capa

layman ['leɪmən] (*irreg*) n lego

layout ['leɪaʊt] n (*design*) plan m, trazado; (*PRESS*) composición f

laze [leɪz] vi (*also:* ~ **about**) holgazanear

lazy ['leɪzɪ] adj perezoso, vago; (*movement*) lento

lb. *abbr* = **pound** (*weight*)

lead[1] [liːd] n (*pt, pp* **led**) n (*front position*) delantera; (*clue*) pista; (*ELEC*) cable m; (*for dog*) correa; (*THEATRE*) papel m principal ♦ vt (*walk etc in front of*) ir a la cabeza de; (*guide*): **to ~ sb somewhere** conducir a uno a algún sitio; (*be leader of*) dirigir; (*start, guide: activity*) protagonizar ♦ vi (*road, pipe etc*) conducir a; (*SPORT*) ir primero; **to be in the ~** (*SPORT*) llevar la delantera; (*fig*) ir a la cabeza; **to ~ the way** (*also fig*) llevar la delantera; ~ **away** vt llevar; ~ **back** vt (*person, route*) llevar de vuelta; ~ **on** vt (*tease*) engañar; ~ **to** vt *fus* producir, provocar; ~ **up to** vt *fus* (*events*) conducir a; (*in conversation*) preparar el terreno para

lead[2] [lɛd] n (*metal*) plomo; (*in pencil*) mina; **~ed petrol** n gasolina con plomo

leader ['liːdə*] n jefe/a m/f, líder m; (*SPORT*) líder m; **~ship** n dirección f; (*position*) mando; (*quality*) iniciativa

leading ['liːdɪŋ] adj (*main*) principal; (*first*) primero; (*front*) delantero; ~ **lady** n (*THEATRE*) primera actriz f; ~ **light** n (*person*) figura principal; ~ **man** (*irreg*) n (*THEATRE*) primer galán m

lead singer [liːd-] n cantante m/f

leaf [liːf] (*pl* **leaves**) n hoja ♦ vi: **to ~ through** hojear; **to turn over a new ~** reformarse

leaflet ['liːflɪt] n folleto

league [liːg] n sociedad f; (*FOOTBALL*) liga; **to be in ~ with** haberse confabulado con

leak [liːk] n (*of liquid, gas*) escape m, fuga; (*in pipe*) agujero; (*in roof*) gotera; (*in security*) filtración f ♦ vi (*shoes, ship*) hacer agua; (*pipe*) tener (un) escape; (*roof*) gotear; (*liquid, gas*) escaparse, fugarse; (*fig*) divulgarse ♦ vt (*fig*) filtrar

lean [liːn] (*pt, pp* **leaned** *or* **leant**) adj (*thin*) flaco; (*meat*) magro ♦ vt: **to ~ sth on sth** apoyar algo en algo ♦ vi (*slope*) inclinarse; **to ~ against** apoyarse contra; **to ~ on** apoyarse en; ~ **back/forward** vi inclinarse hacia atrás/adelante; ~ **out**

vi asomarse; ~ **over** *vi* inclinarse; ~**ing**
n: ~**ing (towards)** inclinación *f* (hacia);
leant [lɛnt] *pt, pp of* **lean**

leap [liːp] (*pt, pp* **leaped** *or* **leapt**) *n* salto
♦ *vi* saltar; ~**frog** *n* pídola; ~ **year** *n*
año bisiesto

learn [ləːn] (*pt, pp* **learned** *or* **learnt**) *vt*
aprender ♦ *vi* aprender; **to ~ about sth**
enterarse de algo; **to ~ to do sth**
aprender a hacer algo; ~**ed** ['ləːnɪd] *adj*
erudito; ~**er** *n* (*BRIT: also:* ~**er driver**)
principiante *m/f*; ~**ing** *n* el saber *m*,
conocimientos *mpl*

lease [liːs] *n* arriendo ♦ *vt* arrendar
leash [liːʃ] *n* correa
least [liːst] *adj*: **the ~** (*slightest*) el menor,
el más pequeño; (*smallest amount of*)
mínimo ♦ *adv* (+*vb*) menos; (+*adj*): **the ~
expensive** el/la menos costoso/a; **the ~
possible effort** el menor esfuerzo posible;
at ~ por lo menos, al menos; **you could
at ~ have written** por lo menos podías
haber escrito; **not in the ~** en absoluto
leather ['lɛðə*] *n* cuero

leave [liːv] (*pt, pp* **left**) *vt* dejar; (*go away
from*) abandonar; (*place etc: permanently*)
salir de ♦ *vi* irse; (*train etc*) salir ♦ *n*
permiso; **to ~ sth to sb** (*money etc*) legar
algo a uno; (*responsibility etc*) encargar a
uno de algo; **to be left** quedar, sobrar;
there's some milk left over sobra *or*
queda algo de leche; **on ~** de permiso; ~
behind *vt* (*on purpose*) dejar;
(*accidentally*) dejarse; ~ **out** *vt* omitir; ~
of absence *n* permiso de ausentarse
eaves [liːvz] *npl of* **leaf**
Lebanon ['lɛbənən] *n*: **the ~** el Líbano
echerous ['lɛtʃərəs] (*pej*) *adj* lascivo
ecture ['lɛktʃə*] *n* conferencia; (*SCOL*)
clase *f* ♦ *vi* dar una clase ♦ *vt* (*scold*): **to
~ sb on** *or* **about sth** echar una
reprimenda a uno por algo; **to give a ~
on** dar una conferencia sobre; ~**r** *n*
conferenciante *m/f*; (*BRIT: at university*)
profesor(a) *m/f*
ed [lɛd] *pt, pp of* **lead**
edge [lɛdʒ] *n* repisa; (*of window*) alféizar

m; (*of mountain*) saliente *m*
ledger ['lɛdʒə*] *n* libro mayor
leech [liːtʃ] *n* sanguijuela
leek [liːk] *n* puerro
leer [lɪə*] *vi*: **to ~ at sb** mirar de manera
lasciva a uno
leeway ['liːweɪ] *n* (*fig*): **to have some ~**
tener cierta libertad de acción
left [lɛft] *pt, pp of* **leave** ♦ *adj* izquierdo;
(*remaining*): **there are 2 ~** quedan dos
♦ *n* izquierda ♦ *adv* a la izquierda; **on** *or*
to the ~ a la izquierda; **the L~** (*POL*) la
izquierda; ~**-handed** *adj* zurdo; **the ~-
hand side** *n* la izquierda; ~**-luggage
(office)** (*BRIT*) *n* consigna; ~**-overs** *npl*
sobras *fpl*; ~**-wing** *adj* (*POL*) de
izquierdas, izquierdista
leg [lɛg] *n* pierna; (*of animal, chair*) pata;
(*trouser ~*) pernera; (*CULIN: of lamb*)
pierna; (*of chicken*) pata; (*of journey*)
etapa
legacy ['lɛgəsɪ] *n* herencia
legal ['liːgl] *adj* (*permitted by law*) lícito; (*of
law*) legal; ~ **holiday** (*US*) *n* fiesta oficial;
~**ize** *vt* legalizar; ~**ly** *adv* legalmente; ~
tender *n* moneda de curso legal
legend ['lɛdʒənd] *n* (*also fig: person*)
leyenda
legislation [lɛdʒɪs'leɪʃən] *n* legislación *f*
legislature ['lɛdʒɪslətʃə*] *n* cuerpo
legislativo
legitimate [lɪ'dʒɪtɪmət] *adj* legítimo
leg-room *n* espacio para las piernas
leisure ['lɛʒə*] *n* ocio, tiempo libre; **at ~**
con tranquilidad; ~ **centre** *n* centro de
recreo; ~**ly** *adj* sin prisa; lento
lemon ['lɛmən] *n* limón *m*; ~**ade** *n* (*fizzy*)
gaseosa; ~ **tea** *n* té *m* con limón
lend [lɛnd] (*pt, pp* **lent**) *vt*: **to ~ sth to sb**
prestar algo a alguien; ~**ing library** *n*
biblioteca de préstamo
length [lɛŋθ] *n* (*size*) largo, longitud *f*;
(*distance*): **the ~ of** todo lo largo de; (*of
swimming pool, cloth*) largo; (*of wood,
string*) trozo; (*amount of time*) duración *f*;
at ~ (*at last*) por fin, finalmente;
(*lengthily*) largamente; ~**en** *vt* alargar

♦ vi alargarse; **~ways** adv a lo largo; **~y**
adj largo, extenso
lenient ['liːnɪənt] adj indulgente
lens [lenz] n (of spectacles) lente f; (of
camera) objetivo
Lent [lent] n Cuaresma
lent [lent] pt, pp of **lend**
lentil ['lentl] n lenteja
Leo ['liːəu] n Leo
leotard ['liːətɑːd] n mallas fpl
leprosy ['leprəsɪ] n lepra
lesbian ['lezbɪən] n lesbiana
less [les] adj (in size, degree etc) menor; (in
quality) menos ♦ pron, adv menos ♦ prep:
~ tax/10% discount menos impuestos/el
10 por ciento de descuento; **~ than half**
menos de la mitad; **~ than ever** menos
que nunca; **~ and ~** cada vez menos; **the
~ he works ...** cuanto menos trabaja ...;
~en vi disminuir, reducirse ♦ vt
disminuir, reducir; **~er** ['lesə*] adj menor;
to a ~er extent en menor grado
lesson ['lesn] n clase f; (warning) lección f
let [let] (pt, pp **let**) vt (allow) dejar,
permitir; (BRIT: lease) alquilar; **to ~ sb do
sth** dejar que uno haga algo; **to ~ sb
know sth** comunicar algo a uno; **~'s go**
¡vamos!; **~ him come** que venga; **"to ~"**
"se alquila"; **~ down** vt (tyre) desinflar;
(disappoint) defraudar; **~ go** vi, vt soltar;
~ in vt dejar entrar; (visitor etc) hacer
pasar; **~ off** vt (culprit) dejar escapar;
(gun) disparar; (bomb) accionar; (firework)
hacer estallar; **~ on** (inf) vi divulgar; **~
out** vt dejar salir; (sound) soltar; **~ up** vi
amainar, disminuir
lethal ['liːθl] adj (weapon) mortífero;
(poison, wound) mortal
letter ['letə*] n (of alphabet) letra;
(correspondence) carta; **~ bomb** n carta-
bomba; **~box** (BRIT) n buzón m; **~ing** n
letras fpl
lettuce ['letɪs] n lechuga
let-up n disminución f
leukaemia [luːˈkiːmɪə] (US **leukemia**) n
leucemia
level ['levl] adj (flat) llano ♦ adv: **to draw**

~ with llegar a la altura de ♦ n nivel m;
(height) altura ♦ vt nivelar; allanar;
(destroy: building) derribar; (: forest)
arrasar; **to be ~ with** estar a nivel de;
"A" ~s (BRIT) npl ≈ exámenes mpl de
bachillerato superior, B.U.P.; **"O" ~s**
(BRIT) npl ≈ exámenes mpl de octavo de
básica; **on the ~** (fig: honest) serio; **~ off**
or **out** vi (prices etc) estabilizarse; **~
crossing** (BRIT) n paso a nivel; **~-
headed** adj sensato
lever ['liːvə*] n (also fig) palanca ♦ vt: **to ~
up** levantar con palanca; **~age** n (using
bar etc) apalancamiento; (fig: influence)
influencia
levy ['levɪ] n impuesto ♦ vt exigir, recaudar
lewd [luːd] adj lascivo; (joke) obsceno,
colorado (AM)
liability [laɪəˈbɪlɪtɪ] n (pej: person, thing)
estorbo, lastre m; (JUR: responsibility)
responsabilidad f; **liabilities** npl (COMM)
pasivo
liable ['laɪəbl] adj (subject): **~ to** sujeto a;
(responsible): **~ for** responsable de; (likely):
~ to do propenso a hacer
liaise [lɪˈeɪz] vi: **to ~ with** enlazar con;
liaison [liːˈeɪzɒn] n (coordination) enlace
m; (affair) relaciones fpl amorosas
liar ['laɪə*] n mentiroso/a
libel ['laɪbl] n calumnia ♦ vt calumniar
liberal ['lɪbərəl] adj liberal; (offer, amount
etc) generoso
liberate ['lɪbəreɪt] vt (people: from poverty
etc) librar; (prisoner) libertar; (country)
liberar
liberty ['lɪbətɪ] n libertad f; (criminal): **to
be at ~** estar en libertad; **to be at ~ to
do** estar libre para hacer; **to take the ~ of
doing sth** tomarse la libertad de hacer
algo
Libra ['liːbrə] n Libra
librarian [laɪˈbreərɪən] n bibliotecario/a
library ['laɪbrərɪ] n biblioteca
libretto [lɪˈbretəu] n libreto
Libya ['lɪbɪə] n Libia; **~n** adj, n libio/a m/f
lice [laɪs] npl of **louse**
licence ['laɪsəns] (US **license**) n licencia;

(*permit*) permiso; (*also:* **driving ~**, (*US*) **driver's ~**) carnet *m* de conducir (*SP*), permiso (*AM*)

license ['laɪsəns] *n* (*US*) = **licence** ♦ *vt* autorizar, dar permiso a; **~d** *adj* (*for alcohol*) autorizado para vender bebidas alcohólicas; (*car*) matriculado; **~ plate** (*US*) *n* placa (de matrícula)

lick [lɪk] *vt* lamer; (*inf: defeat*) dar una paliza a; **to ~ one's lips** relamerse

licorice ['lɪkərɪs] (*US*) *n* = **liquorice**

lid [lɪd] *n* (*of box, case*) tapa; (*of pan*) tapadera

lido ['laɪdəʊ] *n* (*BRIT*) piscina

lie [laɪ] (*pt* **lay**, *pp* **lain**) *vi* (*rest*) estar echado, estar acostado; (*of object: be situated*) estar, encontrarse; (*tell lies: pt, pp* **lied**) mentir ♦ *n* mentira; **to ~ low** (*fig*) mantenerse a escondidas; **~ about** *or* **around** *vi* (*things*) estar tirado; (*BRIT: people*) estar tumbado; **~-down** (*BRIT*) *n*: **to have a ~-down** echarse (una siesta); **~-in** (*BRIT*) *n*: **to have a ~-in** quedarse en la cama

lieu [luː]: **in ~ of** *prep* en lugar de

lieutenant [lef'tenənt, (*US*) luː'tenənt] *n* (*MIL*) teniente *m*

life [laɪf] (*pl* **lives**) *n* vida; **to come to ~** animarse; **~ assurance** (*BRIT*) *n* seguro de vida; **~belt** (*BRIT*) *n* salvavidas *m inv*; **~boat** *n* lancha de socorro; **~guard** *n* vigilante *m/f*, socorrista *m/f*; **~ insurance** *n* = **~ assurance**; **~ jacket** *n* chaleco salvavidas; **~less** *adj* sin vida; (*dull*) soso; **~like** *adj* (*model etc*) que parece vivo; (*realistic*) realista; **~long** *adj* de toda la vida; **~ preserver** (*US*) *n* cinturón *m*/chaleco salvavidas; **~ sentence** *n* cadena perpetua; **~-size** *adj* de tamaño natural; **~ span** *n* vida; **~style** *n* estilo de vida; **~ support system** *n* (*MED*) sistema *m* de respiración asistida; **~time** *n* (*of person*) vida; (*of thing*) período de vida

lift [lɪft] *vt* levantar; (*end: ban, rule*) levantar, suprimir ♦ *vi* (*fog*) disiparse ♦ *n* (*BRIT: machine*) ascensor *m*; **to give sb a**

~ (*BRIT*) llevar a uno en el coche; **~-off** *n* despegue *m*

light [laɪt] (*pt, pp* **lighted** *or* **lit**) *n* luz *f*; (*lamp*) luz *f*, lámpara; (*AUT*) faro; (*for cigarette etc*): **have you got a ~?** ¿tienes fuego? ♦ *vt* (*candle, cigarette, fire*) encender (*SP*), prender (*AM*); (*room*) alumbrar ♦ *adj* (*colour*) claro; (*not heavy, also fig*) ligero; (*room*) con mucha luz; (*gentle, graceful*) ágil; **~s** *npl* (*traffic ~s*) semáforos *mpl*; **to come to ~** salir a luz; **in the ~ of** (*new evidence etc*) a la luz de; **~ up** *vi* (*smoke*) encender un cigarrillo; (*face*) iluminarse ♦ *vt* (*illuminate*) iluminar, alumbrar; (*set fire to*) encender; **~ bulb** *n* bombilla (*SP*), foco (*AM*); **~en** *vt* (*make less heavy*) aligerar; **~er** *n* (*also:* **cigarette ~er**) encendedor *m*, mechero; **~-headed** *adj* (*dizzy*) mareado; (*excited*) exaltado; **~-hearted** *adj* (*person*) alegre; (*remark etc*) divertido; **~house** *n* faro; **~ing** *n* (*system*) alumbrado; **~ly** *adv* ligeramente; (*not seriously*) con poca seriedad; **to get off ~ly** ser castigado con poca severidad; **~ness** *n* (*in weight*) ligereza

lightning ['laɪtnɪŋ] *n* relámpago, rayo; **~ conductor** (*US* **~ rod**) *n* pararrayos *m inv*

light: ~ pen *n* lápiz *m* óptico; **~weight** *adj* (*suit*) ligero ♦ *n* (*BOXING*) peso ligero; **~ year** *n* año luz

like [laɪk] *vt* gustarle a uno ♦ *prep* como ♦ *adj* parecido, semejante ♦ *n*: **and the ~** y otros por el estilo; **his ~s and dislikes** sus gustos y aversiones; **I would ~, I'd ~** me gustaría; (*for purchase*) quisiera; **would you ~ a coffee?** ¿te apetece un café?; **I ~ swimming** me gusta nadar; **she ~s apples** le gustan las manzanas; **to be** *or* **look ~ sb/sth** parecerse a alguien/ algo; **what does it look/taste/sound ~?** ¿cómo es/a qué sabe/cómo suena?; **that's just ~ him** es muy de él, es característico de él; **do it ~ this** hazlo así; **it is nothing ~ ...** no tiene parecido alguno con ...; **~able** *adj* simpático, agradable

likelihood ['laɪklɪhud] *n* probabilidad *f*
likely ['laɪklɪ] *adj* probable; **he's ~ to
leave** es probable que se vaya; **not ~!** ¡ni
hablar!
likeness ['laɪknɪs] *n* semejanza, parecido;
that's a good ~ se parece mucho
likewise ['laɪkwaɪz] *adv* igualmente; **to do
~** hacer lo mismo
liking ['laɪkɪŋ] *n*: ~ **(for)** *(person)* cariño (a);
(thing) afición (a); **to be to sb's ~** ser del
gusto de uno
lilac ['laɪlək] *n (tree)* lilo; *(flower)* lila
lily ['lɪlɪ] *n* lirio, azucena; **~ of the valley** *n*
lirio de los valles
limb [lɪm] *n* miembro
limber ['lɪmbə*]: **to ~ up** *vi (SPORT)* hacer
ejercicios de calentamiento
limbo ['lɪmbəʊ] *n*: **to be in ~** *(fig)* quedar a
la expectativa
lime [laɪm] *n (tree)* limero; *(fruit)* lima;
(GEO) cal *f*
limelight ['laɪmlaɪt] *n*: **to be in the ~** *(fig)*
ser el centro de atención
limerick ['lɪmərɪk] *n especie de poema
humorístico*
limestone ['laɪmstəʊn] *n* piedra caliza
limit ['lɪmɪt] *n* límite *m* ♦ *vt* limitar; **~ed**
adj limitado; **to be ~ed to** limitarse a;
~ed (liability) company *(BRIT)* *n*
sociedad *f* anónima
limousine ['lɪməziːn] *n* limusina
limp [lɪmp] *n*: **to have a ~** tener cojera
♦ *vi* cojear ♦ *adj* flojo; *(material)* fláccido
limpet ['lɪmpɪt] *n* lapa
line [laɪn] *n* línea; *(rope)* cuerda; *(for
fishing)* sedal *m*; *(wire)* hilo; *(row, series)*
fila, hilera; *(of writing)* renglón *m*, línea;
(of song) verso; *(on face)* arruga; *(RAIL)* vía
♦ *vt (road etc)* llenar; *(SEWING)* forrar; **to ~
the streets** llenar las aceras; **in ~ with**
alineado con; *(according to)* de acuerdo
con; **~ up** *vi* hacer cola ♦ *vt* alinear;
(prepare) preparar; organizar
lined [laɪnd] *adj (face)* arrugado; *(paper)*
rayado
linen ['lɪnɪn] *n* ropa blanca; *(cloth)* lino
liner ['laɪnə*] *n* vapor *m* de línea,

transatlántico; *(for bin)* bolsa (de basura)
linesman ['laɪnzmən] *n (SPORT)* juez *m* de
línea
line-up *n (US: queue)* cola; *(SPORT)*
alineación *f*
linger ['lɪŋgə*] *vi* retrasarse, tardar en
marcharse; *(smell, tradition)* persistir
lingerie ['lænʒəriː] *n* lencería
linguist ['lɪŋgwɪst] *n* lingüista *m/f*; **~ics** *n*
lingüística
lining ['laɪnɪŋ] *n* forro; *(ANAT)* (membrana)
mucosa
link [lɪŋk] *n (of a chain)* eslabón *m*;
(relationship) relación *f*, vínculo ♦ *vt*
vincular, unir; *(associate)*: **to ~ with** *or* **to**
relacionar con; **~s** *npl (GOLF)* campo de
golf; **~ up** *vt* acoplar ♦ *vi* unirse
lino ['laɪnəʊ] *n* = **linoleum**
linoleum [lɪ'nəʊlɪəm] *n* linóleo
lion ['laɪən] *n* león *m*; **~ess** *n* leona
lip [lɪp] *n* labio
liposuction ['lɪpəʊsʌkʃən] *n* liposucción *f*
lip: **~read** *vi* leer los labios; **~ salve** *n*
crema protectora para labios; **~ service**
n: **to pay ~ service to sth** *(pej)* prometer
algo de boquilla; **~stick** *n* lápiz *m* de
labios, carmín *m*
liqueur [lɪ'kjʊə*] *n* licor *m*
liquid ['lɪkwɪd] *adj, n* líquido; **~ize** [-aɪz] *vt*
(CULIN) licuar; **~izer** [-aɪzə*] *n* licuadora
liquor ['lɪkə*] *n* licor *m*, bebidas *fpl*
alcohólicas
liquorice ['lɪkərɪs] *(BRIT)* *n* regaliz *m*
liquor store *(US)* *n* bodega, *tienda de
vinos y bebidas alcohólicas*
Lisbon ['lɪzbən] *n* Lisboa
lisp [lɪsp] *n* ceceo ♦ *vi* cecear
list [lɪst] *n* lista ♦ *vt (mention)* enumerar;
(put on a list) poner en una lista; **~ed
building** *(BRIT)* *n* monumento declarado
de interés histórico-artístico
listen ['lɪsn] *vi* escuchar, oír; **to ~ to sb/
sth** escuchar a uno/algo; **~er** *n* oyente
m/f; *(RADIO)* radioyente *m/f*
listless ['lɪstlɪs] *adj* apático, indiferente
lit [lɪt] *pt, pp of* **light**
liter ['liːtə*] *(US)* *n* = **litre**

literacy ['lɪtərəsɪ] *n* capacidad *f* de leer y escribir

literal ['lɪtərl] *adj* literal

literary ['lɪtərərɪ] *adj* literario

literate ['lɪtərət] *adj* que sabe leer y escribir; (*educated*) culto

literature ['lɪtərɪtʃə*] *n* literatura; (*brochures etc*) folletos *mpl*

lithe [laɪð] *adj* ágil

litigation [lɪtɪ'geɪʃən] *n* litigio

litre ['liːtə*] (*US* **liter**) *n* litro

litter ['lɪtə*] *n* (*rubbish*) basura; (*young animals*) camada, cría; (*BRIT*) *n* papelera; **~ed** *adj*: **~ed with** (*scattered*) lleno de

little ['lɪtl] *adj* (*small*) pequeño; (*not much*) poco ♦ *adv* poco; **a ~** un poco (de); **~ house/bird** casita/pajarito; **a ~ bit** un poquito; **~ by ~** poco a poco; **~ finger** *n* dedo meñique

live¹ [laɪv] *adj* (*animal*) vivo; (*wire*) conectado; (*broadcast*) en directo; (*shell*) cargado

live² [lɪv] *vi* vivir; **~ down** *vt* hacer olvidar; **~ on** *vt fus* (*food, salary*) vivir de; **~ together** *vi* vivir juntos; **~ up to** *vt fus* (*fulfil*) cumplir con

livelihood ['laɪvlɪhud] *n* sustento

lively ['laɪvlɪ] *adj* vivo; (*interesting: place, book etc*) animado

liven up ['laɪvn-] *vt* animar ♦ *vi* animarse

liver ['lɪvə*] *n* hígado

lives [laɪvz] *npl of* **life**

livestock ['laɪvstɔk] *n* ganado

livid ['lɪvɪd] *adj* lívido; (*furious*) furioso

living ['lɪvɪŋ] *adj* (*alive*) vivo ♦ *n*: **to earn** *or* **make a ~** ganarse la vida; **~ conditions** *npl* condiciones *fpl* de vida; **~ room** *n* sala (de estar); **~ standards** *npl* nivel *m* de vida; **~ wage** *n* jornal *m* suficiente para vivir

lizard ['lɪzəd] *n* lagarto; (*small*) lagartija

load [ləud] *n* carga; (*weight*) peso ♦ *vt* (*COMPUT*) cargar; (*also*: **~ up**): **to ~ (with)** cargar (con *or* de); **a ~ of rubbish** (*inf*) tonterías *fpl*; **a ~ of**, **~s of** (*fig*) (gran) cantidad de, montones de; **~ed** *adj*

(*vehicle*): **to be ~ed with** estar cargado de; (*question*) intencionado; (*inf: rich*) forrado (de dinero)

loaf [ləuf] (*pl* **loaves**) *n* (barra de) pan *m*

loan [ləun] *n* préstamo ♦ *vt* prestar; **on ~** prestado

loath [ləuθ] *adj*: **to be ~ to do sth** estar poco dispuesto a hacer algo

loathe [ləuð] *vt* aborrecer; (*person*) odiar; **loathing** *n* aversión *f*; odio

loaves [ləuvz] *npl of* **loaf**

lobby ['lɔbɪ] *n* vestíbulo, sala de espera; (*POL: pressure group*) grupo de presión ♦ *vt* presionar

lobster ['lɔbstə*] *n* langosta

local ['ləukl] *adj* local ♦ *n* (*pub*) bar *m*; **the ~s** los vecinos, los del lugar; **~ anaesthetic** *n* (*MED*) anestesia local; **~ authority** *n* municipio, ayuntamiento (*SP*); **~ call** *n* (*TEL*) llamada local; **~ government** *n* gobierno municipal; **~ity** [-'kælɪtɪ] *n* localidad *f*; **~ly** [-kəlɪ] *adv* en la vecindad; por aquí

locate [ləu'keɪt] *vt* (*find*) localizar; (*situate*): **to be ~d in** estar situado en

location [ləu'keɪʃən] *n* situación *f*; **on ~** (*CINEMA*) en exteriores

loch [lɔx] *n* lago

lock [lɔk] *n* (*of door, box*) cerradura; (*of canal*) esclusa; (*of hair*) mechón *m* ♦ *vt* (*with key*) cerrar (con llave) ♦ *vi* (*door etc*) cerrarse (con llave); (*wheels*) trabarse; **~ in** *vt* encerrar; **~ out** *vt* (*person*) cerrar la puerta a; **~ up** *vt* (*criminal*) meter en la cárcel; (*mental patient*) encerrar; (*house*) cerrar (con llave) ♦ *vi* echar la llave

locker ['lɔkə*] *n* casillero

locket ['lɔkɪt] *n* medallón *m*

locksmith ['lɔksmɪθ] *n* cerrajero/a

lockup ['lɔkʌp] *n* (*jail, cell*) cárcel *f*

locum ['ləukəm] *n* (*MED*) (médico/a) interino/a

locust ['ləukəst] *n* langosta

lodge [lɔdʒ] *n* casita (del guarda) ♦ *vi* (*person*): **to ~ (with)** alojarse (en casa de); (*bullet, bone*) incrustarse ♦ *vt* (*complaint*) presentar; **~r** *n* huésped(a) *m/f*

lodgings [ˈlɔdʒɪŋz] *npl* alojamiento
loft [lɔft] *n* desván *m*
lofty [ˈlɔftɪ] *adj* (*noble*) sublime; (*haughty*) altanero
log [lɔg] *n* (*of wood*) leño, tronco; (*written account*) diario ♦ *vt* anotar
logbook [ˈlɔgbuk] *n* (*NAUT*) diario de a bordo; (*AVIAT*) libro de vuelo; (*of car*) documentación *f* (del coche (*SP*) *or* carro (*AM*))
loggerheads [ˈlɔgəhedz] *npl*: **to be at ~ (with)** estar en desacuerdo (con)
logic [ˈlɔdʒɪk] *n* lógica; **~al** *adj* lógico
logo [ˈlaugəu] *n* logotipo
loin [lɔɪn] *n* (*CULIN*) lomo, solomillo
loiter [ˈlɔɪtə*] *vi* (*linger*) entretenerse
loll [lɔl] *vi* (*also*: **~ about**) repantigarse
lollipop [ˈlɔlɪpɔp] *n* chupa-chups ® *m inv*, pirulí *m*; **~ man/lady** (*BRIT irreg*) *n* persona encargada de ayudar a los niños a cruzar la calle

lollipop man/lollipop lady

> *En el Reino Unido, se llama* **lollipop man** *o* **lollipop lady** *a la persona que se ocupa de parar el tráfico en los alrededores de los colegios para que los niños crucen sin peligro. Suelen ser personas ya jubiladas, vestidas con una gabardina de color llamativo y llevan una señal de stop portátil, la cual recuerda por su forma a una piruleta, y de ahí su nombre.*

London [ˈlʌndən] *n* Londres; **~er** *n* londinense *m/f*
lone [ləun] *adj* solitario
loneliness [ˈləunlɪnɪs] *n* soledad *f*; aislamiento
lonely [ˈləunlɪ] *adj* (*situation*) solitario; (*person*) solo; (*place*) aislado
long [lɔŋ] *adj* largo ♦ *adv* mucho tiempo, largamente ♦ *vi*: **to ~ for sth** anhelar algo; **so** *or* **as ~ as** mientras, con tal que; **don't be ~!** ¡no tardes!, ¡vuelve pronto!; **how ~ is the street?** ¿cuánto tiene la calle de largo?; **how ~ is the lesson?**

¿cuánto dura la clase?; **6 metres ~** que mide 6 metros, de 6 metros de ancho; **6 months ~** que dura 6 meses, de 6 meses de duración; **all night ~** toda la noche; **he no ~er comes** ya no viene; **~ before** mucho antes; **before ~** (+*future*) dentro de poco; (+*past*) poco tiempo después; **at ~ last** al fin, por fin; **~-distance** *adj* (*race*) de larga distancia; (*call*) interurbano; **~-haired** *adj* de pelo largo; **~-hand** *n* escritura sin abreviaturas; **~ing** *n* anhelo, ansia; (*nostalgia*) nostalgia ♦ *adj* anhelante
longitude [ˈlɔŋgɪtjuːd] *n* longitud *f*
long: **~ jump** *n* salto de longitud; **~-life** *adj* (*batteries*) de larga duración; (*milk*) uperizado; **~-lost** *adj* desaparecido hace mucho tiempo; **~-range** *adj* (*plan*) de gran alcance; (*missile*) de largo alcance; **~-sighted** (*BRIT*) *adj* présbita; **~-standing** *adj* de mucho tiempo; **~-suffering** *adj* sufrido; **~-term** *adj* a largo plazo; **~ wave** *n* onda larga; **~-winded** *adj* prolijo
loo [luː] (*BRIT: inf*) *n* wáter *m*
look [luk] *vi* mirar; (*seem*) parecer; (*building etc*): **to ~ south/on to the sea** dar al sur/al mar ♦ *n* (*gen*): **to have a ~** mirar; (*glance*) mirada; (*appearance*) aire *m*, aspecto; **~s** *npl* (*good ~s*) belleza; **~ (here)!** (*expressing annoyance etc*) ¡oye!; **~!** (*expressing surprise*) ¡mira!; **~ after** *vt fus* (*care for*) cuidar a; (*deal with*) encargarse de; **~ at** *vt fus* mirar; (*read quickly*) echar un vistazo a; **~ back** *vi* mirar hacia atrás; **~ down on** *vt fus* (*fig*) despreciar, mirar con desprecio; **~ for** *vt fus* buscar; **~ forward to** *vt fus* esperar con ilusión; (*in letters*): **we ~ forward to hearing from you** quedamos a la espera de sus gratas noticias; **~ into** *vt* investigar; **~ on** *vi* mirar (como espectador); **~ out** *vi* (*beware*): **to ~ out (for)** tener cuidado (de); **~ out for** *vt fus* (*seek*) buscar; (*await*) esperar; **~ round** *vi* volver la cabeza; **~ through** *vt fus* (*examine*) examinar; **~ to** *vt fus* (*rely on*)

contar con; **~ up** *vi* mirar hacia arriba; (*improve*) mejorar ♦ *vt* (*word*) buscar; **~ up to** *vt fus* admirar; **~-out** *n* (*tower etc*) puesto de observación; (*person*) vigía *m/f*; **to be on the ~-out for sth** estar al acecho de algo

loom [luːm] *vi*: **~ (up)** (*threaten*) surgir, amenazar; (*event: approach*) aproximarse

loony ['luːnɪ] (*inf*) *n, adj* loco/a *m/f*

loop [luːp] *n* lazo ♦ *vt*: **to ~ sth round sth** pasar algo alrededor de algo; **~hole** *n* escapatoria

loose [luːs] *adj* suelto; (*clothes*) ancho; (*morals, discipline*) relajado; **to be on the ~** estar en libertad; **to be at a ~ end** *or* **at ~ ends** (*US*) no saber qué hacer; **~ change** *n* cambio; **~ chippings** *npl* (*on road*) gravilla suelta; **~ly** *adv* libremente, aproximadamente; **~n** *vt* aflojar

loot [luːt] *n* botín *m* ♦ *vt* saquear

lop off [lɔp-] *vt* (*branches*) podar

lop-sided *adj* torcido

lord [lɔːd] *n* señor *m*; **L~ Smith** Lord Smith; **the L~** el Señor; **my ~** (*to bishop*) Ilustrísima; (*to noble etc*) Señor; **good L~!** ¡Dios mío!; **the (House of) L~s** (*BRIT*) la Cámara de los Lores; **~ship** *n*: **your L~ship** su Señoría

lore [lɔː*] *n* tradiciones *fpl*

lorry ['lɔrɪ] (*BRIT*) *n* camión *m*; **~ driver** *n* camionero/a

lose [luːz] (*pt, pp* lost) *vt* perder ♦ *vi* perder, ser vencido; **to ~ (time)** (*clock*) atrasarse; **~r** *n* perdedor(a) *m/f*

loss [lɔs] *n* pérdida; **heavy ~es** (*MIL*) grandes pérdidas; **to be at a ~** no saber qué hacer; **to make a ~** sufrir pérdidas

lost [lɔst] *pt, pp of* **lose** ♦ *adj* perdido; **~ property** (*US* **~ and found**) *n* objetos *mpl* perdidos

lot [lɔt] *n* (*group: of things*) grupo; (*at auctions*) lote *m*; **the ~** el todo, todos; **a ~** (*large number: of books etc*) muchos; (*a great deal*) mucho, bastante; **a ~ of, ~s of** mucho(s) (*pl*); **I read a ~** leo bastante; **to draw ~s (for sth)** echar suertes (para decidir algo)

lotion ['ləʊʃən] *n* loción *f*

lottery ['lɔtərɪ] *n* lotería

loud [laud] *adj* (*voice, sound*) fuerte; (*laugh, shout*) estrepitoso; (*condemnation etc*) enérgico; (*gaudy*) chillón/ona ♦ *adv* (*speak etc*) fuerte; **out ~** en voz alta; **~hailer** (*BRIT*) *n* megáfono; **~ly** *adv* (*noisily*) fuerte; (*aloud*) en voz alta; **~speaker** *n* altavoz *m*

lounge [laundʒ] *n* salón *m*, sala (de estar); (*at airport etc*) sala; (*BRIT: also*: **~-bar**) salón-bar *m* ♦ *vi* (*also*: **~ about** *or* **around**) reposar, holgazanear

louse [laus] (*pl* lice) *n* piojo

lousy ['lauzɪ] (*inf*) *adj* (*bad quality*) malísimo, asqueroso; (*ill*) fatal

lout [laut] *n* gamberro/a

lovable ['lʌvəbl] *adj* amable, simpático

love [lʌv] *n* (*romantic, sexual*) amor *m*; (*kind, caring*) cariño ♦ *vt* amar, querer; (*thing, activity*) encantarle a uno; **"~ from Anne"** (*on letter*) "un abrazo (de) Anne"; **to ~ to do** encantarle a uno hacer; **to be/fall in ~ with** estar enamorado/ enamorarse de; **to make ~** hacer el amor; **for the ~ of** por amor de; **"15 ~"** (*TENNIS*) "15 a cero"; **I ~ paella** me encanta la paella; **~ affair** *n* aventura sentimental; **~ letter** *n* carta de amor; **~ life** *n* vida sentimental

lovely ['lʌvlɪ] *adj* (*delightful*) encantador(a); (*beautiful*) precioso

lover ['lʌvə*] *n* amante *m/f*; (*person in love*) enamorado; (*amateur*): **a ~ of** un(a) aficionado/a *or* un(a) amante de

loving ['lʌvɪŋ] *adj* amoroso, cariñoso; (*action*) tierno

low [ləu] *adj, adv* bajo ♦ *n* (*METEOROLOGY*) área de baja presión; **to be ~ on** (*supplies etc*) andar mal de; **to feel ~** sentirse deprimido; **to turn (down) ~** bajar; **~-alcohol** *adj* de bajo contenido en alcohol; **~-calorie** *adj* bajo en calorías; **~-cut** *adj* (*dress*) escotado

lower ['ləuə*] *adj* más bajo; (*less important*) menos importante ♦ *vt* bajar;

(*reduce*) reducir ♦ *vr*: **to ~ o.s. to** (*fig*) rebajarse a

low: **~-fat** *adj* (*milk, yoghurt*) desnatado; (*diet*) bajo en calorías; **~lands** *npl* (*GEO*) tierras *fpl* bajas; **~ly** *adj* humilde, inferior; **~ season** *n* la temporada baja

loyal ['lɔɪəl] *adj* leal; **~ty** *n* lealtad *f*

lozenge ['lɔzɪndʒ] *n* (*MED*) pastilla

L.P. *n abbr* (= *long-playing record*) elepé *m*

L-plates ['ɛl-] (*BRIT*) *npl* placas *fpl* de aprendiz de conductor

┌─────────────┐
│ **L-plates** │
└─────────────┘

ⓘ *En el Reino Unido las personas que están aprendiendo a conducir deben llevar en la parte delantera y trasera de su vehículo unas placas blancas con una L en rojo conocidas como* **L-plates** *(de* **learner***). No es necesario que asistan a clases teóricas sino que, desde el principio, se les entrega un carnet de conducir provisional ("provisional driving licence") para que realicen sus prácticas, aunque no pueden circular por las autopistas y deben ir siempre acompañadas por un conductor con carnet definitivo ("full driving licence").*

Ltd *abbr* (= *limited company*) S.A.

lubricate ['lu:brɪkeɪt] *vt* lubricar, engrasar

luck [lʌk] *n* suerte *f*; **bad ~** mala suerte; **good ~!** ¡que tengas suerte!, ¡suerte!; **bad or hard or tough ~!** ¡qué pena!; **~ily** *adv* afortunadamente; **~y** *adj* afortunado; (*at cards etc*) con suerte; (*object*) que trae suerte

ludicrous ['lu:dɪkrəs] *adj* absurdo

lug [lʌg] *vt* (*drag*) arrastrar

luggage ['lʌgɪdʒ] *n* equipaje *m*; **~ rack** *n* (*on car*) baca, portaequipajes *m inv*

lukewarm ['lu:kwɔ:m] *adj* tibio

lull [lʌl] *n* tregua ♦ *vt*: **to ~ sb to sleep** arrullar a uno; **to ~ sb into a false sense of security** dar a alguien una falsa sensación de seguridad

lullaby ['lʌləbaɪ] *n* nana

lumbago [lʌm'beɪgəu] *n* lumbago

lumber ['lʌmbə*] *n* (*junk*) trastos *mpl* viejos; (*wood*) maderos *mpl*; **~ with** *vt*: **to be ~ed with** tener que cargar con algo; **~jack** *n* maderero

luminous ['lu:mɪnəs] *adj* luminoso

lump [lʌmp] *n* terrón *m*; (*fragment*) trozo; (*swelling*) bulto ♦ *vt* (*also:* **~ together**) juntar; **~ sum** *n* suma global; **~y** *adj* (*sauce*) lleno de grumos; (*mattress*) lleno de bultos

lunatic ['lu:nətɪk] *adj* loco

lunch [lʌntʃ] *n* almuerzo, comida ♦ *vi* almorzar

luncheon ['lʌntʃən] *n* almuerzo; **~ voucher** (*BRIT*) *n* vale *m* de comida

lunch time *n* hora de comer

lung [lʌŋ] *n* pulmón *m*

lunge [lʌndʒ] *vi* (*also:* **~ forward**) abalanzarse; **to ~ at** arremeter contra

lurch [lə:tʃ] *vi* dar sacudidas ♦ *n* sacudida; **to leave sb in the ~** dejar a uno plantado

lure [luə*] *n* (*attraction*) atracción *f* ♦ *vt* tentar

lurid ['luərɪd] *adj* (*colour*) chillón/ona; (*account*) espeluznante

lurk [lə:k] *vi* (*person, animal*) estar al acecho; (*fig*) acechar

luscious ['lʌʃəs] *adj* (*attractive: person, thing*) precioso; (*food*) delicioso

lush [lʌʃ] *adj* exuberante

lust [lʌst] *n* lujuria; (*greed*) codicia

lustre ['lʌstə*] (*US* **luster**) *n* lustre *m*, brillo

lusty ['lʌstɪ] *adj* robusto, fuerte

Luxembourg ['lʌksəmbə:g] *n* Luxemburgo

luxuriant [lʌg'zjuərɪənt] *adj* exuberante

luxurious [lʌg'zjuərɪəs] *adj* lujoso

luxury ['lʌkʃərɪ] *n* lujo ♦ *cpd* de lujo

lying ['laɪɪŋ] *n* mentiras *fpl* ♦ *adj* mentiroso

lyrical ['lɪrɪkl] *adj* lírico

lyrics ['lɪrɪks] *npl* (*of song*) letra

M, m

m. *abbr* = **metre; mile; million**

M.A. *abbr* = **Master of Arts**

mac [mæk] (*BRIT*) *n* impermeable *m*

macaroni [mækə'rəuni] *n* macarrones *mpl*

machine [mə'ʃi:n] *n* máquina ♦ *vt* (*dress etc*) coser a máquina; (*TECH*) hacer a máquina; **~ gun** *n* ametralladora; **~ language** *n* (*COMPUT*) lenguaje *m* máquina; **~ry** *n* maquinaria; (*fig*) mecanismo

macho ['mætʃəu] *adj* machista

mackerel ['mækrl] *n inv* caballa

mackintosh ['mækɪntɔʃ] (*BRIT*) *n* impermeable *m*

mad [mæd] *adj* loco; (*idea*) disparatado; (*angry*) furioso; (*keen*): **to be ~ about sth** volverle loco a uno algo

madam ['mædəm] *n* señora

madden ['mædn] *vt* volver loco

made [meɪd] *pt, pp of* **make**

Madeira [mə'dɪərə] *n* (*GEO*) Madera; (*wine*) vino de Madera

made-to-measure (*BRIT*) *adj* hecho a la medida

madly ['mædlɪ] *adv* locamente

madman ['mædmən] (*irreg*) *n* loco

madness ['mædnɪs] *n* locura

Madrid [mə'drɪd] *n* Madrid

magazine [mægə'zi:n] *n* revista; (*RADIO, TV*) programa *m* magazina

maggot ['mægət] *n* gusano

magic ['mædʒɪk] *n* magia ♦ *adj* mágico; **~ian** [mə'dʒɪʃən] *n* mago/a; (*conjurer*) prestidigitador(a) *m/f*

magistrate ['mædʒɪstreɪt] *n* juez *m/f* (*municipal*)

magnet ['mægnɪt] *n* imán *m*; **~ic** [-'nɛtɪk] *adj* magnético; (*personality*) atrayente

magnificent [mæg'nɪfɪsənt] *adj* magnífico

magnify ['mægnɪfaɪ] *vt* (*object*) ampliar; (*sound*) aumentar; **~ing glass** *n* lupa

magpie ['mægpaɪ] *n* urraca

mahogany [mə'hɔgənɪ] *n* caoba

maid [meɪd] *n* criada; **old ~** (*pej*) solterona

maiden ['meɪdn] *n* doncella ♦ *adj* (*aunt etc*) solterona; (*speech, voyage*) inaugural; **~ name** *n* nombre *m* de soltera

mail [meɪl] *n* correo; (*letters*) cartas *fpl* ♦ *vt* echar al correo; **~box** (*US*) *n* buzón *m*; **~ing list** *n* lista de direcciones; **~-order** *n* pedido postal

maim [meɪm] *vt* mutilar, lisiar

main [meɪn] *adj* principal, mayor ♦ *n* (*pipe*) cañería maestra; (*US*) red *f* eléctrica; **the ~s** *npl* (*BRIT: ELEC*) la red eléctrica; **in the ~** en general; **~frame** *n* (*COMPUT*) ordenador *m* central; **~land** *n* tierra firme; **~ly** *adv* principalmente; **~ road** *n* carretera; **~stay** *n* (*fig*) pilar *m*; **~stream** *n* corriente *f* principal

maintain [meɪn'teɪn] *vt* mantener; **maintenance** ['meɪntənəns] *n* mantenimiento; (*LAW*) manutención *f*

maize [meɪz] (*BRIT*) *n* maíz *m* (*SP*), choclo (*AM*)

majestic [mə'dʒɛstɪk] *adj* majestuoso

majesty ['mædʒɪstɪ] *n* majestad *f*; (*title*): **Your M~** Su Majestad

major ['meɪdʒə*] *n* (*MIL*) comandante *m* ♦ *adj* principal; (*MUS*) mayor

Majorca [mə'jɔ:kə] *n* Mallorca

majority [mə'dʒɔrɪtɪ] *n* mayoría

make [meɪk] (*pt, pp* **made**) *vt* hacer; (*manufacture*) fabricar; (*mistake*) cometer; (*speech*) pronunciar; (*cause to be*): **to ~ sb sad** poner triste a alguien; (*force*): **to ~ sb do sth** obligar a alguien a hacer algo; (*earn*) ganar; (*equal*): **2 and 2 ~ 4** 2 y 2 son 4 ♦ *n* marca; **to ~ the bed** hacer la cama; **to ~ a fool of sb** poner a alguien en ridículo; **to ~ a profit/loss** obtener ganancias/sufrir pérdidas; **to ~ it** (*arrive*) llegar; (*achieve sth*) tener éxito; **what time do you ~ it?** ¿qué hora tienes?; **to ~ do with** contentarse con; **~ for** *vt fus* (*place*) dirigirse a; **~ out** *vt* (*decipher*) descifrar; (*understand*) entender; (*see*) distinguir; (*cheque*) extender; **~ up** *vt* (*invent*) inventar; (*prepare*) hacer; (*constitute*) constituir ♦ *vi* reconciliarse;

(*with cosmetics*) maquillarse; ~ **up for** *vt fus* compensar; **~-believe** *n* ficción *f*, invención *f*; **~r** *n* fabricante *m/f*; (*of film, programme*) autor(a) *m/f*; **~shift** *adj* improvisado; **~-up** *n* maquillaje *m*; **~-up remover** *n* desmaquillador *m*

making ['meɪkɪŋ] *n* (*fig*): **in the ~** en vías de formación; **to have the ~s of** (*person*) tener madera de

Malaysia [məˈleɪzɪə] *n* Malasia, Malaysia

male [meɪl] *n* (*BIOL*) macho ♦ *adj* (*sex, attitude*) masculino; (*child etc*) varón

malfunction [mælˈfʌŋkʃən] *n* mal funcionamiento

malice ['mælɪs] *n* malicia; **malicious** [məˈlɪʃəs] *adj* malicioso; rencoroso

malignant [məˈlɪgnənt] *adj* (*MED*) maligno

mall [mɔːl] (*US*) *n* (*also*: **shopping ~**) centro comercial

mallet ['mælɪt] *n* mazo

malnutrition [mælnjuːˈtrɪʃən] *n* desnutrición *f*

malpractice [mælˈpræktɪs] *n* negligencia profesional

malt [mɔːlt] *n* malta; (*whisky*) whisky *m* de malta

Malta ['mɔːltə] *n* Malta; **Maltese** [-'tiːz] *adj, n inv* maltés/esa *m/f*

mammal ['mæml] *n* mamífero

mammoth ['mæməθ] *n* mamut *m* ♦ *adj* gigantesco

man [mæn] (*pl* **men**) *n* hombre *m*; (*~kind*) el hombre ♦ *vt* (*NAUT*) tripular; (*MIL*) guarnecer; (*operate: machine*) manejar; **an old ~** un viejo; **~ and wife** marido y mujer

manage ['mænɪdʒ] *vi* arreglárselas, ir tirando ♦ *vt* (*be in charge of*) dirigir; (*control: person*) manejar; (: *ship*) gobernar; **~able** *adj* manejable; **~ment** *n* dirección *f*; **~r** *n* director(a) *m/f*; (*of pop star*) mánayer *m/f*; (*SPORT*) entrenador(a) *m/f*; **~ress** *n* directora; entrenadora; **~rial** [-əˈdʒɪərɪəl] *adj* directivo; **managing director** *n* director(a) *m/f* general

mandarin ['mændərɪn] *n* (*also*: **~ orange**)

mandarina; (*person*) mandarín *m*

mandatory ['mændətərɪ] *adj* obligatorio

mane [meɪn] *n* (*of horse*) crin *f*; (*of lion*) melena

maneuver [məˈnuːvə*] (*US*) = **manoeuvre**

manfully ['mænfəlɪ] *adv* valientemente

mangle ['mæŋgl] *vt* mutilar, destrozar

man: ~handle *vt* maltratar; **~hole** *n* agujero de acceso; **~hood** *n* edad *f* viril; (*state*) virilidad *f*; **~-hour** *n* hora-hombre *f*; **~hunt** *n* (*POLICE*) búsqueda y captura

mania ['meɪnɪə] *n* manía; **~c** ['meɪnɪæk] *n* maníaco/a; (*fig*) maniático

manic ['mænɪk] *adj* frenético; **~-depressive** *n* maníaco/a depresivo/a

manicure ['mænɪkjuə*] *n* manicura

manifest ['mænɪfɛst] *vt* manifestar, mostrar ♦ *adj* manifiesto

manifesto [mænɪˈfɛstəu] *n* manifiesto

manipulate [məˈnɪpjuleɪt] *vt* manipular

man: ~kind [mænˈkaɪnd] *n* humanidad *f*, género humano; **~ly** *adj* varonil; **~-made** *adj* artificial

manner ['mænə*] *n* manera, modo; (*behaviour*) conducta, manera de ser; (*type*): **all ~ of things** toda clase de cosas; **~s** *npl* (*behaviour*) modales *mpl*; **bad ~s** mala educación; **~ism** *n* peculiaridad *f* de lenguaje (*or* de comportamiento)

manoeuvre [məˈnuːvə*] (*US* **maneuver**) *vt, vi* maniobrar ♦ *n* maniobra

manor ['mænə*] *n* (*also*: **~ house**) casa solariega

manpower ['mænpauə*] *n* mano *f* de obra

mansion ['mænʃən] *n* palacio, casa grande

manslaughter ['mænslɔːtə*] *n* homicidio no premeditado

mantelpiece ['mæntlpiːs] *n* repisa, chimenea

manual ['mænjuəl] *adj* manual ♦ *n* manual *m*

manufacture [mænjuˈfæktʃə*] *vt* fabricar ♦ *n* fabricación *f*; **~r** *n* fabricante *m/f*

manure [məˈnjuə*] *n* estiércol *m*

manuscript ['mænjuskrɪpt] *n* manuscrito

many ['mɛnɪ] *adj, pron* muchos/as; **a**

great ~ muchísimos, un buen número de; ~ **a time** muchas veces
map [mæp] n mapa m; **to ~ out** vt proyectar
maple ['meɪpl] n arce m (SP), maple m (AM)
mar [mɑː*] vt estropear
marathon ['mærəθən] n maratón m
marble ['mɑːbl] n mármol m; (toy) canica
March [mɑːtʃ] n marzo
march [mɑːtʃ] vi (MIL) marchar; (demonstrators) manifestarse ♦ n marcha; (demonstration) manifestación f
mare [mɛə*] n yegua
margarine [mɑːdʒə'riːn] n margarina
margin ['mɑːdʒɪn] n margen m; (COMM: profit ~) margen m de beneficios; **~al** adj marginal; **~al seat** n (POL) escaño electoral difícil de asegurar
marigold ['mærɪɡəʊld] n caléndula
marijuana [mærɪ'wɑːnə] n marijuana
marina [mə'riːnə] n puerto deportivo
marinate ['mærɪneɪt] vt marinar
marine [mə'riːn] adj marino ♦ n soldado de marina
marital ['mærɪtl] adj matrimonial; ~ **status** estado civil
marjoram ['mɑːdʒərəm] n mejorana
mark [mɑːk] n marca, señal f; (in snow, mud etc) huella; (stain) mancha; (BRIT: SCOL) nota; (currency) marco ♦ vt marcar; manchar; (damage: furniture) rayar; (indicate: place etc) señalar; (BRIT: SCOL) calificar, corregir; **to ~ time** marcar el paso; (fig) marcar(se) un ritmo; **~ed** adj (obvious) marcado, acusado; **~er** n (sign) marcador m; (bookmark) señal f (de libro)
market ['mɑːkɪt] n mercado ♦ vt (COMM) comercializar; ~ **garden** (BRIT) n huerto; **~ing** n márketing m; **~place** n mercado; ~ **research** n análisis m inv de mercados
marksman ['mɑːksmən] n tirador m
marmalade ['mɑːməleɪd] n mermelada de naranja
maroon [mə'ruːn] vt: **to be ~ed** quedar aislado; (fig) quedar abandonado

marquee [mɑː'kiː] n entoldado
marriage ['mærɪdʒ] n (relationship, institution) matrimonio; (wedding) boda; (act) casamiento; ~ **certificate** n partida de casamiento
married ['mærɪd] adj casado; (life, love) conyugal
marrow ['mærəʊ] n médula; (vegetable) calabacín m
marry ['mærɪ] vt casarse con; (subj: father, priest etc) casar ♦ vi (also: **get married**) casarse
Mars [mɑːz] n Marte m
marsh [mɑːʃ] n pantano; (salt ~) marisma
marshal ['mɑːʃl] n (MIL) mariscal m; (at sports meeting etc) oficial m; (US: of police, fire department) jefe/a m/f ♦ vt (thoughts etc) ordenar; (soldiers) formar
marshy ['mɑːʃɪ] adj pantanoso
martial law ['mɑːʃl-] n ley f marcial
martyr ['mɑːtə*] n mártir m/f; **~dom** n martirio
marvel ['mɑːvl] n maravilla, prodigio ♦ vi: **to ~ (at)** maravillarse (de); **~lous** (US **~ous**) adj maravilloso
Marxist ['mɑːksɪst] adj, n marxista m/f
marzipan ['mɑːzɪpæn] n mazapán m
mascara [mæs'kɑːrə] n rímel m
masculine ['mæskjʊlɪn] adj masculino
mash [mæʃ] vt machacar; **~ed potatoes** npl puré m de patatas (SP) or papas (AM)
mask [mɑːsk] n máscara ♦ vt (cover): **to ~ one's face** ocultarse la cara; (hide: feelings) esconder
mason ['meɪsn] n (also: **stone~**) albañil m; (also: **free~**) masón m; **~ry** n (in building) mampostería
masquerade [mæskə'reɪd] vi: **to ~ as** disfrazarse de, hacerse pasar por
mass [mæs] n (people) muchedumbre f; (of air, liquid etc) masa; (of detail, hair etc) gran cantidad f; (REL) misa ♦ cpd masivo ♦ vi reunirse; concentrarse; **the ~es** npl las masas; **~es of** (inf) montones de
massacre ['mæsəkə*] n masacre f
massage ['mæsɑːʒ] n masaje m ♦ vt dar masaje en

masseur [mæ'sə:*] *n* masajista *m*

masseuse [mæ'sə:z] *n* masajista *f*

massive ['mæsɪv] *adj* enorme; (*support, changes*) masivo

mass media *npl* medios *mpl* de comunicación

mass production *n* fabricación *f* en serie

mast [mɑ:st] *n* (NAUT) mástil *m*; (RADIO etc) torre *f*

master ['mɑ:stə*] *n* (*of servant*) amo; (*of situation*) dueño, maestro; (*in primary school*) maestro; (*in secondary school*) profesor *m*; (*title for boys*): M~ X Señorito X ♦ *vt* dominar; M~ of Arts/Science *n* licenciatura superior en Letras/Ciencias; ~ly *adj* magistral; ~mind *n* inteligencia superior ♦ *vt* dirigir, planear; ~piece *n* obra maestra; ~y *n* maestría

mat [mæt] *n* estera; (*also:* door~) felpudo; (*also:* table ~) salvamanteles *m inv*, posavasos *m inv* ♦ *adj* = matt

match [mætʃ] *n* cerilla, fósforo; (*game*) partido; (*equal*) igual *m/f* ♦ *vt* (*go well with*) hacer juego con; (*equal*) igualar; (*correspond to*) corresponderse con; (*pair: also:* ~ up) casar con ♦ *vi* hacer juego; **to be a good ~** hacer juego; ~box *n* caja de cerillas; ~ing *adj* que hace juego

mate [meɪt] *n* (*work*~) colega *m/f*; (*inf: friend*) amigo/a; (*animal*) macho *m*/ hembra *f*; (*in merchant navy*) segundo a bordo ♦ *vi* acoplarse, aparearse ♦ *vt* aparear

material [mə'tɪərɪəl] *n* (*substance*) materia; (*information*) material *m*; (*cloth*) tela, tejido ♦ *adj* material; (*important*) esencial; ~s *npl* materiales *mpl*

maternal [mə'tə:nl] *adj* maternal

maternity [mə'tə:nɪtɪ] *n* maternidad *f*; ~ **dress** *n* vestido premamá

math [mæθ] (US) *n* = mathematics

mathematical [mæθə'mætɪkl] *adj* matemático

mathematician [mæθəmə'tɪʃən] *n* matemático/a

mathematics [mæθə'mætɪks] *n*

matemáticas *fpl*

maths [mæθs] (BRIT) *n* = mathematics

matinée ['mætɪneɪ] *n* sesión *f* de tarde

matrices ['meɪtrɪsi:z] *npl of* matrix

matriculation [mətrɪkju'leɪʃən] *n* (formalización *f* de) matrícula

matrimony ['mætrɪmənɪ] *n* matrimonio

matrix ['meɪtrɪks] (*pl* matrices) *n* matriz *f*

matron ['meɪtrən] *n* enfermera *f* jefe; (*in school*) ama de llaves

mat(t) [mæt] *adj* mate

matted ['mætɪd] *adj* enmarañado

matter ['mætə*] *n* cuestión *f*, asunto; (PHYSICS) sustancia, materia; (*reading* ~) material *m*; (MED: pus) pus *m* ♦ *vi* importar; ~s *npl* (*affairs*) asuntos *mpl*, temas *mpl*; **it doesn't** ~ no importa; **what's the** ~? ¿qué pasa?; **no** ~ **what** pase lo que pase; **as a** ~ **of course** por rutina; **as a** ~ **of fact** de hecho; ~-of-fact *adj* prosaico, práctico

mattress ['mætrɪs] *n* colchón *m*

mature [mə'tjuə*] *adj* maduro ♦ *vi* madurar; **maturity** *n* madurez *f*

maul [mɔ:l] *vt* magullar

mauve [məuv] *adj* de color malva (SP) or guinda (AM)

maximum ['mæksɪməm] (*pl* maxima) *adj* máximo ♦ *n* máximo

May [meɪ] *n* mayo

may [meɪ] (*conditional:* might) *vi* (*indicating possibility*): **he** ~ **come** puede que venga; (*be allowed to*): ~ **I smoke?** ¿puedo fumar?; (*wishes*): ~ **God bless you!** ¡que Dios le bendiga!; **you** ~ **as well go** bien puedes irte

maybe ['meɪbi:] *adv* quizá(s)

May Day *n* el primero de Mayo

mayhem ['meɪhem] *n* caos *m* total

mayonnaise [meɪə'neɪz] *n* mayonesa

mayor [mɛə*] *n* alcalde *m*; ~ess *n* alcaldesa

maze [meɪz] *n* laberinto

M.D. *abbr* = Doctor of Medicine

me [mi:] *pron* (*direct*) me; (*stressed, after pron*) mí; **can you hear** ~? ¿me oyes?; **he heard** *ME*! me oyó a mí; **it's** ~ soy yo;

give them to ~ dámelos/las; **with/
without** ~ conmigo/sin mí

meadow ['mɛdəʊ] n prado, pradera

meagre ['miːgəʳ] (US **meager**) adj escaso,
pobre

meal [miːl] n comida; (flour) harina;
~time n hora de comer

mean [miːn] (pt, pp **meant**) adj (with
money) tacaño; (unkind) mezquino, malo;
(shabby) humilde; (average) medio ♦ vt
(signify) querer decir, significar; (refer to)
referirse a; (intend): **to ~ to do sth** pensar
or pretender hacer algo ♦ n medio,
término medio; **~s** npl (way) medio,
manera; (money) recursos mpl, medios
mpl; **by ~s of** mediante, por medio de;
by all ~s! ¡naturalmente!, ¡claro que sí!;
do you ~ it? ¿lo dices en serio?; **what do
you ~?** ¿qué quiere decir?; **to be meant
for sb/sth** ser para uno/algo

meander [mɪ'ændəʳ] vi (river) serpentear

meaning ['miːnɪŋ] n significado, sentido;
(purpose) sentido, propósito; **~ful** adj
significativo; **~less** adj sin sentido

meanness ['miːnnɪs] n (with money)
tacañería; (unkindness) maldad f,
mezquindad f; (shabbiness) humildad f

meant [mɛnt] pt, pp of **mean**

meantime ['miːntaɪm] adv (also: **in the ~**)
mientras tanto

meanwhile ['miːnwaɪl] adv = **meantime**

measles ['miːzlz] n sarampión m

measure ['mɛʒəʳ] vt, vi medir ♦ n
medida; (ruler) regla; **~ments** npl
medidas fpl

meat [miːt] n carne f; **cold ~** fiambre m;
~ball n albóndiga; **~ pie** n pastel m de
carne

Mecca ['mɛkə] n La Meca

mechanic [mɪ'kænɪk] n mecánico/a; **~s** n
mecánica ♦ npl mecanismo; **~al** adj
mecánico

mechanism ['mɛkənɪzəm] n mecanismo

medal ['mɛdl] n medalla; **~lion** [mɪ'dæliən]
n medallón m; **~list** (US **~ist**) n (SPORT)
medallista m/f

meddle ['mɛdl] vi: **to ~ in** entrometerse

en; **to ~ with sth** manosear algo

media ['miːdɪə] npl medios mpl de
comunicación ♦ npl of **medium**

mediaeval [mɛdɪ'iːvl] adj = **medieval**

mediate ['miːdɪeɪt] vi mediar; **mediator**
n intermediario/a, mediador(a) m/f

Medicaid ® ['mɛdɪkeɪd] (US) n programa
de ayuda médica para los pobres

medical ['mɛdɪkl] adj médico ♦ n
reconocimiento médico

Medicare ® ['mɛdɪkeəʳ] (US) n programa
de ayuda médica para los ancianos

medication [mɛdɪ'keɪʃən] n medicación f

medicine ['mɛdsɪn] n medicina; (drug)
medicamento

medieval [mɛdɪ'iːvl] adj medieval

mediocre [miːdɪ'əʊkəʳ] adj mediocre

meditate ['mɛdɪteɪt] vi meditar

Mediterranean [mɛdɪtə'reɪnɪən] adj
mediterráneo; **the ~ (Sea)** el (Mar)
Mediterráneo

medium ['miːdɪəm] (pl **media**) adj
mediano, regular ♦ n (means) medio; (pl
mediums: person) médium m/f; **~ wave** n
onda media

meek [miːk] adj manso, sumiso

meet [miːt] (pt, pp **met**) vt encontrar;
(accidentally) encontrarse con, tropezar
con; (by arrangement) reunirse con; (for
the first time) conocer; (go and fetch) ir a
buscar; (opponent) enfrentarse con;
(obligations) cumplir; (encounter: problem)
hacer frente a; (need) satisfacer ♦ vi
encontrarse; (in session) reunirse; (join:
objects) unirse; (for the first time)
conocerse; **~ with** vt fus (difficulty)
tropezar con; **to ~ with success** tener
éxito; **~ing** n encuentro; (arranged) cita,
compromiso; (business ~ing) reunión f;
(POL) mitin m

megabyte ['mɛgəbaɪt] n (COMPUT)
megabyte m, megaocteto

megaphone ['mɛgəfəʊn] n megáfono

melancholy ['mɛlənkəlɪ] n melancolía
♦ adj melancólico

mellow ['mɛləʊ] adj (wine) añejo; (sound,
colour) suave ♦ vi (person) ablandar

melody ['mɛlədɪ] *n* melodía

melon ['mɛlən] *n* melón *m*

melt [mɛlt] *vi* (*metal*) fundirse; (*snow*) derretirse ♦ *vt* fundir; **~down** *n* (*in nuclear reactor*) fusión *f* de un reactor (nuclear); **~ing pot** *n* (*fig*) crisol *m*

member ['mɛmbə*] *n* (*gen, ANAT*) miembro; (*of club*) socio/a; **M~ of Parliament** (*BRIT*) diputado/a; **M~ of the European Parliament** (*BRIT*) eurodiputado/a; **~ship** *n* (*members*) número de miembros; (*state*) filiación *f*; **~ship card** *n* carnet *m* de socio

memento [mə'mɛntəu] *n* recuerdo

memo ['mɛməu] *n* apunte *m*, nota

memoirs ['mɛmwɑːz] *npl* memorias *fpl*

memorandum [mɛmə'rændəm] (*pl* **memoranda**) *n* apunte *m*, nota; (*official note*) acta

memorial [mɪ'mɔːrɪəl] *n* monumento conmemorativo ♦ *adj* conmemorativo

memorize ['mɛməraɪz] *vt* aprender de memoria

memory ['mɛmərɪ] *n* (*also: COMPUT*) memoria; (*instance*) recuerdo; (*of dead person*): **in ~ of** a la memoria de

men [mɛn] *npl of* **man**

menace ['mɛnəs] *n* amenaza ♦ *vt* amenazar; **menacing** *adj* amenazador(a)

mend [mɛnd] *vt* reparar, arreglar; (*darn*) zurcir ♦ *vi* reponerse ♦ *n* arreglo, reparación *f*; zurcido ♦ *n*: **to be on the ~** ir mejorando; **to ~ one's ways** enmendarse; **~ing** *n* reparación *f*; (*clothes*) ropa por remendar

meningitis [mɛnɪn'dʒaɪtɪs] *n* meningitis *f*

menopause ['mɛnəupɔːz] *n* menopausia

menstruation [mɛnstru'eɪʃən] *n* menstruación *f*

mental ['mɛntl] *adj* mental; **~ity** [-'tælɪtɪ] *n* mentalidad *f*

mention ['mɛnʃən] *n* mención *f* ♦ *vt* mencionar; (*speak of*) hablar de; **don't ~ it!** ¡de nada!

menu ['mɛnjuː] *n* (*set ~*) menú *m*; (*printed*) carta; (*COMPUT*) menú *m*

MEP *n abbr* = **Member of the European Parliament**

merchandise ['mɜːtʃəndaɪz] *n* mercancías *fpl*

merchant ['mɜːtʃənt] *n* comerciante *m/f*; **~ bank** (*BRIT*) *n* banco comercial; **~ navy** (*US* **~ marine**) *n* marina mercante

merciful ['mɜːsɪful] *adj* compasivo; (*fortunate*) afortunado

merciless ['mɜːsɪlɪs] *adj* despiadado

mercury ['mɜːkjurɪ] *n* mercurio

mercy ['mɜːsɪ] *n* compasión *f*; (*REL*) misericordia; **at the ~ of** a la merced de

merely ['mɪəlɪ] *adv* simplemente, sólo

merge [mɜːdʒ] *vt* (*join*) unir ♦ *vi* unirse; (*COMM*) fusionarse; (*colours etc*) fundirse; **~r** *n* (*COMM*) fusión *f*

meringue [mə'ræŋ] *n* merengue *m*

merit ['mɛrɪt] *n* mérito ♦ *vt* merecer

mermaid ['mɜːmeɪd] *n* sirena

merry ['mɛrɪ] *adj* alegre; **M~ Christmas!** ¡Felices Pascuas!; **~-go-round** *n* tiovivo

mesh [mɛʃ] *n* malla

mesmerize ['mɛzməraɪz] *vt* hipnotizar

mess [mɛs] *n* (*muddle: of situation*) confusión *f*; (*: of room*) revoltijo; (*dirt*) porquería; (*MIL*) comedor *m*; **~ about** or **around** (*inf*) *vi* perder el tiempo; (*pass the time*) entretenerse; **~ about** or **around with** (*inf*) *vt fus* divertirse con; **~ up** *vt* (*spoil*) estropear; (*dirty*) ensuciar

message ['mɛsɪdʒ] *n* recado, mensaje *m*

messenger ['mɛsɪndʒə*] *n* mensajero/a

Messrs *abbr* (*on letters*: = *Messieurs*) Sres

messy ['mɛsɪ] *adj* (*dirty*) sucio; (*untidy*) desordenado

met [mɛt] *pt, pp of* **meet**

metal ['mɛtl] *n* metal *m*; **~lic** [-'tælɪk] *adj* metálico

metaphor ['mɛtəfə*] *n* metáfora

meteor ['miːtɪə*] *n* meteoro; **~ite** [-aɪt] *n* meteorito

meteorology [miːtɪə'rɔlədʒɪ] *n* meteorología

meter ['miːtə*] *n* (*instrument*) contador *m*; (*US: unit*) = **metre** ♦ *vt* (*US: POST*) franquear

method ['mɛθəd] *n* método

meths [meθs] (*BRIT*) *n*, **methylated spirit** ['meθɪleɪtɪd-] (*BRIT*) *n* alcohol *m* metilado *or* desnaturalizado

metre ['mi:tə*] (*US* **meter**) *n* metro

metric ['metrɪk] *adj* métrico

metropolitan [metrə'pɒlɪtən] *adj* metropolitano; **the M~ Police** (*BRIT*) la policía londinense

mettle ['metl] *n*: **to be on one's ~** estar dispuesto a mostrar todo lo que uno vale

mew [mju:] *vi* (*cat*) maullar

mews [mju:z] *n*: **~ flat** (*BRIT*) piso *acondicionado en antiguos establos o cocheras*

Mexican ['meksɪkən] *adj*, *n* mejicano/a *m/f*, mexicano/a *m/f*

Mexico ['meksɪkəʊ] *n* Méjico (*SP*), México (*AM*); **~ City** *n* Ciudad *f* de Méjico *or* México

miaow [mi:'aʊ] *vi* maullar

mice [maɪs] *npl of* **mouse**

micro... [maɪkrəʊ] *prefix* micro...; **~chip** *n* microplaqueta; **~(computer)** *n* microordenador *m*; **~phone** *n* micrófono; **~processor** *n* microprocesador *m*; **~scope** *n* microscopio; **~wave** *n* (*also*: **~wave oven**) horno microondas

mid [mɪd] *adj*: **in ~ May** a mediados de mayo; **in ~ afternoon** a media tarde; **in ~ air** en el aire; **~day** *n* mediodía *m*

middle ['mɪdl] *n* centro; (*half-way point*) medio; (*waist*) cintura ♦ *adj* en medio; (*course, way*) intermedio; **in the ~ of the night** en plena noche; **~-aged** *adj* de mediana edad; **the M~ Ages** *npl* la Edad Media; **~-class** *adj* de clase media; **the ~ class(es)** *n(pl)* la clase media; **M~ East** *n* Oriente *m* Medio; **~man** *n* intermediario; **~ name** *n* segundo nombre; **~-of-the-road** *adj* moderado; **~weight** *n* (*BOXING*) peso medio

middling ['mɪdlɪŋ] *adj* mediano

midge [mɪdʒ] *n* mosquito

midget ['mɪdʒɪt] *n* enano/a

Midlands ['mɪdləndz] *npl*: **the ~** la región central de Inglaterra

midnight ['mɪdnaɪt] *n* medianoche *f*

midst [mɪdst] *n*: **in the ~ of** (*crowd*) en medio de; (*situation, action*) en mitad de

midsummer [mɪd'sʌmə*] *n*: **in ~** en pleno verano

midway [mɪd'weɪ] *adj*, *adv*: **~ (between)** a medio camino (entre); **~ through** a la mitad (de)

midweek [mɪd'wi:k] *adv* entre semana

midwife ['mɪdwaɪf] (*pl* **midwives**) *n* comadrona, partera

might [maɪt] *vb see* **may** ♦ *n* fuerza, poder *m*; **~y** *adj* fuerte, poderoso

migraine ['mi:greɪn] *n* jaqueca

migrant ['maɪgrənt] *n adj* (*bird*) migratorio; (*worker*) emigrante

migrate [maɪ'greɪt] *vi* emigrar

mike [maɪk] *n abbr* (= **microphone**) micro

mild [maɪld] *adj* (*person*) apacible; (*climate*) templado; (*slight*) ligero; (*taste*) suave; (*illness*) leve; **~ly** *adv* ligeramente; suavemente; **to put it ~ly** para no decir más

mile [maɪl] *n* milla; **~age** *n* número de millas, ≈ kilometraje *m*; **~ometer** [maɪ'lɒmɪtə*] *n* ≈ cuentakilómetros *m inv*; **~stone** *n* mojón *m*

militant ['mɪlɪtnt] *adj*, *n* militante *m/f*

military ['mɪlɪtəri] *adj* militar

militia [mɪ'lɪʃə] *n* milicia

milk [mɪlk] *n* leche *f* ♦ *vt* (*cow*) ordeñar; (*fig*) chupar; **~ chocolate** *n* chocolate *m* con leche; **~man** (*irreg*) *n* lechero; **~ shake** *n* batido, malteada (*AM*); **~y** *adj* lechoso; **M~y Way** *n* Vía Láctea

mill [mɪl] *n* (*windmill etc*) molino; (*coffee ~*) molinillo; (*factory*) fábrica ♦ *vt* moler ♦ *vi* (*also*: **~ about**) arremolinarse

millennium [mɪ'lenɪəm] (*pl* **~s** or **millennia**) *n* milenio, milenario

miller ['mɪlə*] *n* molinero

milli... ['mɪlɪ] *prefix*: **~gram(me)** *n* miligramo; **~metre** (*US* **~meter**) *n* milímetro

million ['mɪljən] *n* millón *m*; **a ~ times** un millón de veces; **~aire** [-jə'neə*] *n* millonario/a

milometer [maɪˈlɒmɪtə*] (*BRIT*) *n*
= **mileometer**

mime [maɪm] *n* mímica; (*actor*) mimo/a
♦ *vt* remedar ♦ *vi* actuar de mimo

mimic [ˈmɪmɪk] *n* imitador(a) *m/f* ♦ *adj*
mímico ♦ *vt* remedar, imitar

min. *abbr* = **minimum; minute(s)**

mince [mɪns] *vt* picar ♦ *n* (*BRIT: CULIN*)
carne *f* picada; **~meat** *n conserva de
fruta picada*; (*US: meat*) carne *f* picada; **~
pie** *n empanadilla rellena de fruta
picada*; **~r** *n* picadora de carne

mind [maɪnd] *n* mente *f*; (*intellect*)
intelecto; (*contrasted with matter*) espíritu
m ♦ *vt* (*attend to, look after*) ocuparse de,
cuidar; (*be careful of*) tener cuidado con;
(*object to*): **I don't ~ the noise** no me
molesta el ruido; **it is on my ~** me
preocupa; **to bear sth in ~** tomar *or*
tener algo en cuenta; **to make up one's
~** decidirse; **I don't ~** me es igual; **~ you,
...** te advierto que ...; **never ~!** ¡es igual!,
¡no importa!; (*don't worry*) ¡no te
preocupes!; **"~ the step"** "cuidado con
el escalón"; **~er** *n* guardaespaldas *m inv*;
(*child ~er*) ≈ niñera; **~ful** *adj*: **~ful of**
consciente de; **~less** *adj* (*crime*) sin
motivo; (*work*) de autómata

mine¹ [maɪn] *pron* el mío/la mía *etc*; **a
friend of ~** un(a) amigo/a mío/mía ♦ *adj*:
this book is ~ este libro es mío

mine² [maɪn] *n* mina ♦ *vt* (*coal*) extraer;
(*bomb: beach etc*) minar; **~field** *n* campo
de minas; **miner** *n* minero/a

mineral [ˈmɪnərəl] *adj* mineral ♦ *n* mineral
m; **~s** *npl* (*BRIT: soft drinks*) refrescos *mpl*;
~ water *n* agua mineral

mingle [ˈmɪŋgl] *vi*: **to ~ with** mezclarse
con

miniature [ˈmɪnətʃə*] *adj* (en) miniatura
♦ *n* miniatura

minibus [ˈmɪnɪbʌs] *n* microbús *m*

minimal [ˈmɪnɪml] *adj* mínimo

minimize [ˈmɪnɪmaɪz] *vt* minimizar; (*play
down*) empequeñecer

minimum [ˈmɪnɪməm] (*pl* **minima**) *n, adj*
mínimo

mining [ˈmaɪnɪŋ] *n* explotación *f* minera

miniskirt [ˈmɪnɪskə:t] *n* minifalda

minister [ˈmɪnɪstə*] *n* (*BRIT: POL*) ministro/a
(*SP*), secretario/a (*AM*); (*REL*) pastor *m*
♦ *vi*: **to ~ to** atender a

ministry [ˈmɪnɪstrɪ] *n* (*BRIT: POL*) ministerio
(*SP*), secretaria (*AM*); (*REL*) sacerdocio

mink [mɪŋk] *n* visón *m*

minnow [ˈmɪnəu] *n* pececillo (*de agua
dulce*)

minor [ˈmaɪnə*] *adj* (*repairs, injuries*) leve;
(*poet, planet*) menor; (*MUS*) menor ♦ *n*
(*LAW*) menor *m* de edad

Minorca [mɪˈnɔːkə] *n* Menorca

minority [maɪˈnɔrɪtɪ] *n* minoría

mint [mɪnt] *n* (*plant*) menta, hierbabuena;
(*sweet*) caramelo de menta ♦ *vt* (*coins*)
acuñar; **the (Royal) M~, the (US) M~** la
Casa de la Moneda; **in ~ condition** en
perfecto estado

minus [ˈmaɪnəs] *n* (*also*: **~ sign**) signo de
menos ♦ *prep* menos; **12 ~ 6 equals 6**
12 menos 6 son 6; **~ 24°C** menos 24
grados

minute¹ [ˈmɪnɪt] *n* minuto; (*fig*)
momento; **~s** *npl* (*of meeting*) actas *fpl*;
at the last ~ a última hora

minute² [maɪˈnjuːt] *adj* diminuto; (*search*)
minucioso

miracle [ˈmɪrəkl] *n* milagro

mirage [ˈmɪrɑːʒ] *n* espejismo

mirror [ˈmɪrə*] *n* espejo; (*in car*) retrovisor
m

mirth [mə:θ] *n* alegría

misadventure [mɪsədˈventʃə*] *n* desgracia

misapprehension [mɪsæprɪˈhenʃən] *n*
equivocación *f*

misappropriate [mɪsəˈprəuprɪeɪt] *vt*
malversar

misbehave [mɪsbɪˈheɪv] *vi* portarse mal

miscalculate [mɪsˈkælkjuleɪt] *vt* calcular
mal

miscarriage [ˈmɪskærɪdʒ] *n* (*MED*) aborto;
~ of justice error *m* judicial

miscellaneous [mɪsɪˈleɪnɪəs] *adj* varios/
as, diversos/as

mischief [ˈmɪstʃɪf] *n* travesuras *fpl*,

diabluras *fpl*; (*maliciousness*) malicia; **mischievous** [-ʃɪvəs] *adj* travieso

misconception [mɪskən'sepʃən] *n* idea equivocada; equivocación *f*

misconduct [mɪs'kɒndʌkt] *n* mala conducta; **professional ~** falta profesional

misdemeanour [mɪsdɪ'mi:nə*] (*US* **misdemeanor**) *n* delito, ofensa

miser ['maɪzə*] *n* avaro/a

miserable ['mɪzərəbl] *adj* (*unhappy*) triste, desgraciado; (*unpleasant, contemptible*) miserable

miserly ['maɪzəlɪ] *adj* avariento, tacaño

misery ['mɪzərɪ] *n* tristeza; (*wretchedness*) miseria, desdicha

misfire [mɪs'faɪə*] *vi* fallar

misfit ['mɪsfɪt] *n* inadaptado/a

misfortune [mɪs'fɔ:tʃən] *n* desgracia

misgiving [mɪs'gɪvɪŋ] *n* (*apprehension*) presentimiento; **to have ~s about sth** tener dudas acerca de algo

misguided [mɪs'gaɪdɪd] *adj* equivocado

mishandle [mɪs'hændl] *vt* (*mismanage*) manejar mal

mishap ['mɪshæp] *n* desgracia, contratiempo

misinform [mɪsɪn'fɔ:m] *vt* informar mal

misinterpret [mɪsɪn'tə:prɪt] *vt* interpretar mal

misjudge [mɪs'dʒʌdʒ] *vt* juzgar mal

mislay [mɪs'leɪ] (*irreg*) *vt* extraviar, perder

mislead [mɪs'li:d] (*irreg*) *vt* llevar a conclusiones erróneas; **~ing** *adj* engañoso

mismanage [mɪs'mænɪdʒ] *vt* administrar mal

misplace [mɪs'pleɪs] *vt* extraviar

misprint ['mɪsprɪnt] *n* errata, error *m* de imprenta

Miss [mɪs] *n* Señorita

miss [mɪs] *vt* (*train etc*) perder; (*fail to hit: target*) errar; (*regret the absence of*): **I ~ him** (yo) le echo de menos *or* a faltar; (*fail to see*): **you can't ~ it** no tiene pérdida ♦ *vi* fallar ♦ *n* (*shot*) tiro fallido *or* perdido; **~ out** (*BRIT*) *vt* omitir

misshapen [mɪs'ʃeɪpən] *adj* deforme

missile ['mɪsaɪl] *n* (*AVIAT*) mísil *m*; (*object thrown*) proyectil *m*

missing ['mɪsɪŋ] *adj* (*pupil*) ausente; (*thing*) perdido; (*MIL*): **~ in action** desaparecido en combate

mission ['mɪʃən] *n* misión *f*; (*official representation*) delegación *f*; **~ary** *n* misionero/a

mist [mɪst] *n* (*light*) neblina; (*heavy*) niebla; (*at sea*) bruma ♦ *vi* (*eyes: also*: **~ over, ~ up**) llenarse de lágrimas; (*BRIT: windows: also*: **~ over, ~ up**) empañarse

mistake [mɪs'teɪk] (*vt: irreg*) *n* error *m* ♦ *vt* entender mal; **by ~** por equivocación; **to make a ~** equivocarse; **to ~ A for B** confundir A con B; **mistaken** *pp of* **mistake** ♦ *adj* equivocado; **to be mistaken** equivocarse, engañarse

mister ['mɪstə*] (*inf*) *n* señor *m*; *see* **Mr**

mistletoe ['mɪsltəu] *n* muérdago

mistook [mɪs'tuk] *pt of* **mistake**

mistress ['mɪstrɪs] *n* (*lover*) amante *f*; (*of house*) señora (de la casa); (*BRIT: in primary school*) maestra; (*in secondary school*) profesora; (*of situation*) dueña

mistrust [mɪs'trʌst] *vt* desconfiar de

misty ['mɪstɪ] *adj* (*day*) de niebla; (*glasses etc*) empañado

misunderstand [mɪsʌndə'stænd] (*irreg*) *vt, vi* entender mal; **~ing** *n* malentendido

misuse [*n* mɪs'ju:s, *vb* mɪs'ju:z] *n* mal uso; (*of power*) abuso; (*of funds*) malversación *f* ♦ *vt* abusar de; malversar

mitt(en) ['mɪt(n)] *n* manopla

mix [mɪks] *vt* mezclar; (*combine*) unir ♦ *vi* mezclarse; (*people*) llevarse bien ♦ *n* mezcla; **~ up** *vt* mezclar; (*confuse*) confundir; **~ed** *adj* mixto; (*feelings etc*) encontrado; **~ed-up** *adj* (*confused*) confuso, revuelto; **~er** *n* (*for food*) licuadora; (*for drinks*) coctelera; (*person*): **he's a good ~er** tiene don de gentes; **~ture** *n* mezcla; (*also*: **cough ~ture**) jarabe *m*; **~-up** *n* confusión *f*

mm *abbr* (= *millimetre*) mm

moan [məun] n gemido ♦ vi gemir; (inf: complain): **to ~ (about)** quejarse (de)

moat [məut] n foso

mob [mɔb] n multitud f ♦ vt acosar

mobile ['məubaɪl] adj móvil ♦ n móvil m; **~ home** n caravana; **~ phone** n teléfono portátil

mock [mɔk] vt (ridicule) ridiculizar; (laugh at) burlarse de ♦ adj fingido; **~ exam** examen preparatorio antes de los exámenes oficiales; **~ery** n burla; **~-up** n maqueta

mod [mɔd] adj see **convenience**

mode [məud] n modo

model ['mɔdl] n modelo; (fashion ~, artist's ~) modelo m/f ♦ adj modelo ♦ vt (with clay etc) modelar (copy): **to ~ o.s. on** tomar como modelo a ♦ vi ser modelo; **to ~ clothes** pasar modelos, ser modelo; **~ railway** n ferrocarril m de juguete

modem ['məudəm] n modem m

moderate [adj 'mɔdərət, vb 'mɔdəreɪt] adj moderado/a ♦ vi moderarse, calmarse ♦ vt moderar

modern ['mɔdən] adj moderno; **~ize** vt modernizar

modest ['mɔdɪst] adj modesto; (small) módico; **~y** n modestia

modify ['mɔdɪfaɪ] vt modificar

mogul ['məugəl] n (fig) magnate m

mohair ['məuhɛə*] n mohair m

moist [mɔɪst] adj húmedo; **~en** ['mɔɪsn] vt humedecer; **~ure** ['mɔɪstʃə*] n humedad f; **~urizer** ['mɔɪstʃəraɪzə*] n crema hidratante

molar ['məulə*] n muela

mold [məuld] (US) n, vt = **mould**

mole [məul] n (animal, spy) topo; (spot) lunar m

molest [məu'lɛst] vt importunar; (assault sexually) abusar sexualmente de

mollycoddle ['mɔlɪkɔdl] vt mimar

molt [məult] (US) vi = **moult**

molten ['məultən] adj fundido; (lava) líquido

mom [mɔm] (US) n = **mum**

moment ['məumənt] n momento; **at the ~** de momento, por ahora; **~ary** adj momentáneo; **~ous** [-'mɛntəs] adj trascendental, importante

momentum [məu'mɛntəm] n momento; (fig) ímpetu m; **to gather ~** cobrar velocidad; (fig) ganar fuerza

mommy ['mɔmɪ] (US) n = **mummy**

Monaco ['mɔnəkəu] n Mónaco

monarch ['mɔnək] n monarca m/f; **~y** n monarquía

monastery ['mɔnəstəri] n monasterio

Monday ['mʌndɪ] n lunes m inv

monetary ['mʌnɪtəri] adj monetario

money ['mʌnɪ] n dinero; (currency) moneda; **to make ~** ganar dinero; **~ order** n giro; **~-spinner** (inf) n: **to be a ~-spinner** dar mucho dinero

mongrel ['mʌngrəl] n (dog) perro mestizo

monitor ['mɔnɪtə*] n (SCOL) monitor m; (also: **television ~**) receptor m de control; (of computer) monitor m ♦ vt controlar

monk [mʌŋk] n monje m

monkey ['mʌŋkɪ] n mono; **~ nut** (BRIT) n cacahuete m (SP), maní m (AM); **~ wrench** n llave f inglesa

monopoly [mə'nɔpəli] n monopolio

monotone ['mɔnətəun] n voz f (or tono) monocorde

monotonous [mə'nɔtənəs] adj monótono

monsoon [mɔn'su:n] n monzón m

monster ['mɔnstə*] n monstruo

monstrous ['mɔnstrəs] adj (huge) enorme; (atrocious, ugly) monstruoso

month [mʌnθ] n mes m; **~ly** adj mensual ♦ adv mensualmente

monument ['mɔnjumənt] n monumento

moo [mu:] vi mugir

mood [mu:d] n humor m; (of crowd, group) clima m; **to be in a good/bad ~** estar de buen/mal humor; **~y** adj (changeable) de humor variable; (sullen) malhumorado

moon [mu:n] n luna; **~light** n luz f de la luna; **~lighting** n pluriempleo; **~lit** adj: **a ~lit night** una noche de luna

Moor [muə*] n moro/a

moor [muə*] *n* páramo ♦ *vt* (*ship*) amarrar ♦ *vi* echar las amarras

Moorish ['muərɪʃ] *adj* moro; (*architecture*) árabe, morisco

moorland ['muələnd] *n* páramo, brezal *m*

moose [muːs] *n inv* alce *m*

mop [mɔp] *n* fregona, (*of hair*) greña, melena ♦ *vt* fregar; **~ up** *vt* limpiar

mope [məup] *vi* estar *or* andar deprimido

moped ['məupɛd] *n* ciclomotor *m*

moral ['mɔrl] *adj* moral ♦ *n* moraleja; **~s** *npl* moralidad *f*, moral *f*

morale [mɔ'raːl] *n* moral *f*

morality [mə'rælɪtɪ] *n* moralidad *f*

morass [mə'ræs] *n* pantano

KEYWORD

more [mɔː*] *adj* **1** (*greater in number etc*) más; **~ people/work than before** más gente/trabajo que antes

2 (*additional*) más; **do you want (some) ~ tea?** ¿quieres más té?; **is there any ~ wine?** ¿queda vino?; **it'll take a few ~ weeks** tardará unas semanas más; **it's 2 kms ~ to the house** faltan 2 kms para la casa; **~ time/letters than we expected** más tiempo del que/más cartas de las que esperábamos

♦ *pron* (*greater amount, additional amount*) más; **~ than 10** más de 10; **it cost ~ than the other one/than we expected** costó más que el otro/más de lo que esperábamos; **is there any ~?** ¿hay más?; **many/much ~** muchos(as)/mucho(a) más

♦ *adv* más; **~ dangerous/easily (than)** más peligroso/fácilmente (que); **~ and ~ expensive** cada vez más caro; **~ or less** más o menos; **~ than ever** más que nunca

moreover [mɔː'rəuvə*] *adv* además, por otra parte

morning ['mɔːnɪŋ] *n* mañana; (*early ~*) madrugada ♦ *cpd* matutino, de la mañana; **in the ~** por la mañana; **7 o'clock in the ~** las 7 de la mañana; **~ sickness** *n* náuseas *fpl* matutinas

Morocco [mə'rɔkəu] *n* Marruecos *m*

moron ['mɔːrɔn] (*inf*) *n* imbécil *m/f*

morphine ['mɔːfiːn] *n* morfina

Morse [mɔːs] *n* (*also:* **~ code**) (código) Morse

morsel ['mɔːsl] *n* (*of food*) bocado

mortar ['mɔːtə*] *n* argamasa

mortgage ['mɔːgɪdʒ] *n* hipoteca ♦ *vt* hipotecar; **~ company** (*US*) *n* ≈ banco hipotecario

mortuary ['mɔːtjuərɪ] *n* depósito de cadáveres

Moscow ['mɔskəu] *n* Moscú

Moslem ['mɔzləm] *adj, n* = **Muslim**

mosque [mɔsk] *n* mezquita

mosquito [mɔs'kiːtəu] (*pl* **~es**) *n* mosquito (*SP*), zancudo (*AM*)

moss [mɔs] *n* musgo

most [məust] *adj* la mayor parte de, la mayoría de ♦ *pron* la mayor parte, la mayoría ♦ *adv* el más; (*very*) muy; **the ~** (*also:* **+adj**) el más; **~ of them** la mayor parte de ellos; **I saw the ~** yo vi el que más; **at the (very) ~** a lo sumo, todo lo más; **to make the ~ of** aprovechar (al máximo); **a ~ interesting book** un libro interesantísimo; **~ly** *adv* en su mayor parte, principalmente

MOT (*BRIT*) *n abbr* (= *Ministry of Transport*): **the ~ (test)** inspección (anual) obligatoria de coches y camiones

motel [məu'tɛl] *n* motel *m*

moth [mɔθ] *n* mariposa nocturna; (*clothes ~*) polilla

mother ['mʌðə*] *n* madre *f* ♦ *adj* materno ♦ *vt* (*care for*) cuidar (como una madre); **~hood** *n* maternidad *f*; **~-in-law** *n* suegra; **~ly** *adj* maternal; **~-of-pearl** *n* nácar *m*; **~-to-be** *n* futura madre *f*; **~ tongue** *n* lengua materna

motion ['məuʃən] *n* movimiento; (*gesture*) ademán *m*, señal *f*; (*at meeting*) moción *f* ♦ *vt, vi*: **to ~ (to) sb to do sth** hacer señas a uno para que haga algo; **~less** *adj* inmóvil; **~ picture** *n* película

motivated ['məutɪveɪtɪd] *adj* motivado

motive ['məʊtɪv] n motivo

motley ['mɒtlɪ] adj variado

motor ['məʊtə*] n motor m; (BRIT: inf: vehicle) coche m (SP), carro (AM), automóvil m ♦ adj motor (f: motora or motriz); ~**bike** n moto f; ~**boat** n lancha motora; ~**car** (BRIT) n coche m, carro, automóvil m; ~**cycle** n motocicleta; ~**cycle racing** n motociclismo; ~**cyclist** n motociclista m/f; ~**ing** (BRIT) n automovilismo; ~**ist** n conductor(a) m/f, automovilista m/f; ~ **racing** (BRIT) n carreras fpl de coches, automovilismo; ~ **vehicle** n automóvil m; ~**way** (BRIT) n autopista

mottled ['mɒtld] adj abigarrado, multicolor

motto ['mɒtəʊ] (pl ~es) n lema m; (watchword) consigna

mould [məʊld] (US **mold**) n molde m; (mildew) moho ♦ vt moldear; (fig) formar; ~**y** adj enmohecido

moult [məʊlt] (US **molt**) vi mudar la piel (or las plumas)

mound [maʊnd] n montón m, montículo

mount [maʊnt] n monte m ♦ vt montar, subir a; (jewel) engarzar; (picture) enmarcar; (exhibition etc) organizar ♦ vi (increase) aumentar; ~ **up** vi aumentar

mountain ['maʊntɪn] n montaña ♦ cpd de montaña; ~ **bike** n bicicleta de montaña; ~**eer** [-'nɪə*] n montañero/a (SP), andinista m/f (AM); ~**eering** [-'nɪərɪŋ] n montañismo, andinismo; ~**ous** adj montañoso; ~ **rescue team** n equipo de rescate de montaña; ~**side** n ladera de la montaña

mourn [mɔːn] vt llorar, lamentar ♦ vi: **to ~ for** llorar la muerte de; ~**er** n doliente m/f; dolorido/a; ~**ing** n luto; **in ~ing** de luto

mouse [maʊs] (pl **mice**) n (ZOOL, COMPUT) ratón m; ~**trap** n ratonera

mousse [muːs] n (CULIN) crema batida; (for hair) espuma (moldeadora)

moustache [məs'tɑːʃ] (US **mustache**) n bigote m

mousy ['maʊsɪ] adj (hair) pardusco

mouth [maʊθ, pl maʊðz] n boca; (of river) desembocadura; ~**ful** n bocado; ~ **organ** n armónica; ~**piece** n (of musical instrument) boquilla; (spokesman) portavoz m/f; ~**wash** n enjuague m; ~-**watering** adj apetitoso

movable ['muːvəbl] adj movible

move [muːv] n (movement) movimiento; (in game) jugada; (: turn to play) turno; (change: of house) mudanza; (: of job) cambio de trabajo ♦ vt mover; (emotionally) conmover; (POL: resolution etc) proponer ♦ vi moverse; (traffic) circular; (also: ~ **house**) trasladarse, mudarse; **to ~ sb to do sth** mover a uno a hacer algo; **to get a ~ on** darse prisa; ~ **about** or **around** vi moverse; (travel) viajar; ~ **along** vi avanzar, adelantarse; ~ **away** vi alejarse; ~ **back** vi retroceder; ~ **forward** vi avanzar; ~ **in** vi (to a house) instalarse; (police, soldiers) intervenir; ~ **on** vi ponerse en camino; ~ **out** vi (of house) mudarse; ~ **over** vi apartarse, hacer sitio; ~ **up** vi (employee) ser ascendido

moveable ['muːvəbl] adj = **movable**

movement ['muːvmənt] n movimiento

movie ['muːvɪ] n película; **to go to the ~s** ir al cine

moving ['muːvɪŋ] adj (emotional) conmovedor(a); (that moves) móvil

mow [məʊ] (pt **mowed**, pp **mowed** or **mown**) vt (grass, corn) cortar, segar; ~ **down** vt (shoot) acribillar; ~**er** n (also: **lawn-er**) cortacéspedes m inv, segadora

MP n abbr = **Member of Parliament**

m.p.h. abbr = **miles per hour** (60 m.p.h. = 96 k.p.h.)

Mr ['mɪstə*] (US **Mr.**) n: ~ **Smith** (el) Sr. Smith

Mrs ['mɪsɪz] (US **Mrs.**) n: ~ **Smith** (la) Sra. Smith

Ms [mɪz] (US **Ms.**) n (= Miss or Mrs): ~ **Smith** (la) Sr(t)a. Smith

M.Sc. abbr = **Master of Science**

much [mʌtʃ] adj mucho ♦ adv mucho;

(before pp) muy ♦ n or pron mucho; **how ~ is it?** ¿cuánto es?, ¿cuánto cuesta?; **too ~** demasiado; **it's not ~** no es mucho; **as ~ as** tanto como; **however ~ he tries** por mucho que se esfuerce

muck [mʌk] n suciedad f; **~ about** or **around** (inf) vi perder el tiempo; (enjoy o.s.) entretenerse; **~ up** (inf) vt arruinar, estropear

mud [mʌd] n barro, lodo

muddle ['mʌdl] n desorden m, confusión f; (mix-up) embrollo, lío ♦ vt (also: ~ **up**) embrollar, confundir; **~ through** vi salir del paso

muddy ['mʌdɪ] adj fangoso, cubierto de lodo

mudguard ['mʌdgɑːd] n guardabarros m inv

muffin ['mʌfɪn] n panecillo dulce

muffle ['mʌfl] vt (sound) amortiguar; (against cold) embozar; **~d** adj (noise etc) amortiguado, apagado; **~r** (US) n (AUT) silenciador m

mug [mʌg] n taza grande (sin platillo); (for beer) jarra; (inf: face) jeta; (: fool) bobo ♦ vt (assault) asaltar; **~ging** n asalto

muggy ['mʌgɪ] adj bochornoso

mule [mjuːl] n mula

multi... [mʌltɪ] prefix multi...

multi-level [mʌltɪ'levl] (US) adj = **multistorey**

multiple ['mʌltɪpl] adj múltiple ♦ n múltiplo; **~ sclerosis** n esclerosis f múltiple

multiplex cinema ['mʌltɪpleks-] n multicines mpl

multiplication [mʌltɪplɪ'keɪʃən] n multiplicación f

multiply ['mʌltɪplaɪ] vt multiplicar ♦ vi multiplicarse

multistorey [mʌltɪ'stɔːrɪ] (BRIT) adj de muchos pisos

multitude ['mʌltɪtjuːd] n multitud f

mum [mʌm] (BRIT: inf) n mamá ♦ adj: **to keep ~** mantener la boca cerrada

mumble ['mʌmbl] vt, vi hablar entre dientes, refunfuñar

mummy ['mʌmɪ] n (BRIT: mother) mamá; (embalmed) momia

mumps [mʌmps] n paperas fpl

munch [mʌntʃ] vt, vi mascar

mundane [mʌn'deɪn] adj trivial

municipal [mjuː'nɪsɪpl] adj municipal

murder ['mɜːdə*] n asesinato; (in law) homicidio ♦ vt asesinar, matar; **~er/ess** n asesino/a; **~ous** adj homicida

murky ['mɜːkɪ] adj (water) turbio; (street, night) lóbrego

murmur ['mɜːmə*] n murmullo ♦ vt, vi murmurar

muscle ['mʌsl] n músculo; (fig: strength) garra, fuerza; **~ in** vi entrometerse; **muscular** ['mʌskjulə*] adj muscular; (person) musculoso

muse [mjuːz] vi meditar ♦ n musa

museum [mjuː'zɪəm] n museo

mushroom ['mʌʃrum] n seta, hongo; (CULIN) champiñón m ♦ vi crecer de la noche a la mañana

music ['mjuːzɪk] n música; **~al** adj musical; (sound) melodioso; (person) con talento musical ♦ n (show) comedia musical; **~al instrument** n instrumento musical; **~ hall** n teatro de variedades; **~ian** [-'zɪʃən] n músico/a

Muslim ['mʌzlɪm] adj, n musulmán/ana m/f

muslin ['mʌzlɪn] n muselina

mussel ['mʌsl] n mejillón m

must [mʌst] aux vb (obligation): **I ~ do it** debo hacerlo, tengo que hacerlo; (probability): **he ~ be there by now** ya debe (de) estar allí ♦ n: **it's a ~** es imprescindible

mustache ['mʌstæʃ] (US) n = **moustache**

mustard ['mʌstəd] n mostaza

muster ['mʌstə*] vt juntar, reunir

mustn't ['mʌsnt] = **must not**

mute [mjuːt] adj, n mudo/a m/f

muted ['mjuːtɪd] adj callado; (colour) apagado

mutiny ['mjuːtɪnɪ] n motín m ♦ vi amotinarse

mutter ['mʌtə*] vt, vi murmurar

mutton [ˈmʌtn] *n* carne *f* de cordero
mutual [ˈmjuːtʃʊəl] *adj* mutuo; (*interest*) común; **~ly** *adv* mutuamente
muzzle [ˈmʌzl] *n* hocico; (*for dog*) bozal *m*; (*of gun*) boca ♦ *vt* (*dog*) poner un bozal a
my [maɪ] *adj* mi(s); **~ house/brother/ sisters** mi casa/mi hermano/mis hermanas; **I've washed ~ hair/cut ~ finger** me he lavado el pelo/cortado un dedo; **is this ~ pen or yours?** ¿es este bolígrafo mío o tuyo?
myself [maɪˈself] *pron* (*reflexive*) me; (*emphatic*) yo mismo; (*after prep*) mí (mismo); *see also* **oneself**
mysterious [mɪsˈtɪərɪəs] *adj* misterioso
mystery [ˈmɪstərɪ] *n* misterio
mystify [ˈmɪstɪfaɪ] *vt* (*perplex*) dejar perplejo
myth [mɪθ] *n* mito

N, n

n/a *abbr* (= *not applicable*) no interesa
nag [næg] *vt* (*scold*) regañar; **~ging** *adj* (*doubt*) persistente; (*pain*) continuo
nail [neɪl] *n* (*human*) uña; (*metal*) clavo ♦ *vt* clavar; **to ~ sth to sth** clavar algo en algo; **to ~ sb down to doing sth** comprometer a uno a que haga algo; **~brush** *n* cepillo para las uñas; **~file** *n* lima para las uñas; **~ polish** *n* esmalte *m* or laca para las uñas; **~ polish remover** *n* quitaesmalte *m*; **~ scissors** *npl* tijeras *fpl* para las uñas; **~ varnish** (*BRIT*) *n* = **~ polish**
naïve [naɪˈiːv] *adj* ingenuo
naked [ˈneɪkɪd] *adj* (*nude*) desnudo; (*flame*) expuesto al aire
name [neɪm] *n* nombre *m*; (*surname*) apellido; (*reputation*) fama, renombre *m* ♦ *vt* (*child*) poner nombre a; (*criminal*) identificar; (*price, date etc*) fijar; **what's your ~?** ¿cómo se llama?; **by ~** de nombre; **in the ~ of** en nombre de; **to give one's ~ and address** dar sus señas;

~ly *adv* a saber; **~sake** *n* tocayo/a
nanny [ˈnænɪ] *n* niñera
nap [næp] *n* (*sleep*) sueñecito, siesta
nape [neɪp] *n*: **~ of the neck** nuca, cogote *m*
napkin [ˈnæpkɪn] *n* (*also*: **table ~**) servilleta
nappy [ˈnæpɪ] (*BRIT*) *n* pañal *m*; **~ rash** *n* prurito
narcotic [nɑːˈkɔtɪk] *adj, n* narcótico
narrow [ˈnærəʊ] *adj* estrecho, angosto; (*fig: majority etc*) corto; (: *ideas etc*) estrecho ♦ *vi* (*road*) estrecharse; (*diminish*) reducirse; **to have a ~ escape** escaparse por los pelos; **to ~ sth down** reducir algo; **~ly** *adv* (*miss*) por poco; **~-minded** *adj* de miras estrechas
nasty [ˈnɑːstɪ] *adj* (*remark*) feo; (*person*) antipático; (*revolting: taste, smell*) asqueroso; (*wound, disease etc*) peligroso, grave
nation [ˈneɪʃən] *n* nación *f*
national [ˈnæʃənl] *adj, n* nacional *m/f*; **~ dress** *n* vestido nacional; **N~ Health Service** (*BRIT*) *n* servicio nacional de salud pública; ≈ Insalud *m* (*SP*); **N~ Insurance** (*BRIT*) *n* seguro social nacional; **~ism** *n* nacionalismo; **~ist** *adj, n* nacionalista *m/f*; **~ity** [-ˈnælɪtɪ] *n* nacionalidad *f*; **~ize** *vt* nacionalizar; **~ly** *adv* (*nationwide*) en escala nacional; (*as a nation*) nacionalmente, como nación; **~ park** (*BRIT*) *n* parque *m* nacional
nationwide [ˈneɪʃənwaɪd] *adj* en escala *or* a nivel nacional
native [ˈneɪtɪv] *n* (*local inhabitant*) natural *m/f*, nacional *m/f* ♦ *adj* (*indigenous*) indígena; (*country*) natal; (*innate*) natural, innato; **a ~ of Russia** un(a) natural *m/f* de Rusia; **a ~ speaker of French** un hablante nativo de francés; **N~ American** *adj, n* americano/a indígena, amerindio/a; **~ language** *n* lengua materna
Nativity [nəˈtɪvɪtɪ] *n*: **the ~** Navidad *f*
NATO [ˈneɪtəʊ] *n abbr* (= *North Atlantic Treaty Organization*) OTAN *f*
natural [ˈnætʃrəl] *adj* natural; **~ly** *adv*

(*speak etc*) naturalmente; (*of course*) desde luego, por supuesto

nature ['neɪtʃə*] n (*also*: **N~**) naturaleza; (*group, sort*) género, clase f; (*character*) carácter m, genio; **by ~** por *or* de naturaleza

naught [nɔːt] n = **nought**

naughty ['nɔːtɪ] *adj* (*child*) travieso

nausea ['nɔːsɪə] n náuseas *fpl*

nautical ['nɔːtɪkl] *adj* náutico, marítimo; (*mile*) marino

naval ['neɪvl] *adj* naval, de marina; **~ officer** n oficial m/f de marina

nave [neɪv] n nave f

navel ['neɪvl] n ombligo

navigate ['nævɪgeɪt] *vt* gobernar ♦ *vi* navegar; (*AUT*) ir de copiloto; **navigation** [-'geɪʃən] n (*action*) navegación f; (*science*) náutica; **navigator** n navegador(a) m/f, navegante m/f; (*AUT*) copiloto m/f

navvy ['nævɪ] (*BRIT*) n peón m caminero

navy ['neɪvɪ] n marina de guerra; (*ships*) armada, flota; **~(-blue)** *adj* azul marino

Nazi ['nɑːtsɪ] n nazi m/f

NB *abbr* (= *nota bene*) nótese

near [nɪə*] *adj* (*place, relation*) cercano; (*time*) próximo ♦ *adv* cerca ♦ *prep* (*also*: **~ to**: *space*) cerca de, junto a; (: *time*) cerca de ♦ *vt* acercarse a, aproximarse a; **~by** [nɪə'baɪ] *adj* cercano, próximo ♦ *adv* cerca; **~ly** *adv* casi, por poco; **I ~ly fell** por poco me caigo; **~ miss** n tiro cercano; **~side** n (*AUT*: *in Britain*) lado izquierdo; (: *in US, Europe etc*) lado derecho; **~-sighted** *adj* miope, corto de vista

neat [niːt] *adj* (*place*) ordenado, bien cuidado; (*person*) pulcro; (*plan*) ingenioso; (*spirits*) solo; **~ly** *adv* (*tidily*) con esmero; (*skilfully*) ingeniosamente

necessarily ['nesɪsrɪlɪ] *adv* necesariamente

necessary ['nesɪsrɪ] *adj* necesario, preciso

necessitate [nɪ'sesɪteɪt] *vt* hacer necesario

necessity [nɪ'sesɪtɪ] n necesidad f; **necessities** *npl* artículos *mpl* de primera necesidad

neck [nek] n (*of person, garment, bottle*) cuello; (*of animal*) pescuezo ♦ *vi* (*inf*) besuquearse; **~ and ~** parejos; **~lace** ['neklɪs] n collar m; **~line** n escote m; **~tie** ['nektaɪ] n corbata

née [neɪ] *adj*: **~ Scott** de soltera Scott

need [niːd] n (*lack*) escasez f, falta; (*necessity*) necesidad f ♦ *vt* (*require*) necesitar; **I ~ to do it** tengo que *or* debo hacerlo; **you don't ~ to go** no hace falta que (te) vayas

needle ['niːdl] n aguja ♦ *vt* (*fig: inf*) picar, fastidiar

needless ['niːdlɪs] *adj* innecesario; **~ to say** huelga decir que

needlework ['niːdlwəːk] n (*activity*) costura, labor f de aguja

needn't ['niːdnt] = **need not**

needy ['niːdɪ] *adj* necesitado

negative ['negətɪv] n (*PHOT*) negativo; (*LING*) negación f ♦ *adj* negativo; **~ equity** n situación que se da cuando el valor de la vivienda es menor que el de la hipoteca que pesa sobre ella

neglect [nɪ'glekt] *vt* (*one's duty*) faltar a, no cumplir con; (*child*) descuidar, desatender ♦ n (*of house, garden etc*) abandono; (*of child*) desatención f; (*of duty*) incumplimiento

negligee ['neglɪʒeɪ] n (*nightgown*) salto de cama

negotiate [nɪ'gəʊʃɪeɪt] *vt* (*treaty, loan*) negociar; (*obstacle*) franquear; (*bend in road*) tomar ♦ *vi*: **to ~ (with)** negociar (con); **negotiation** [-'eɪʃən] n negociación f, gestión f

neigh [neɪ] *vi* relinchar

neighbour ['neɪbə*] (*US* **neighbor**) n vecino/a; **~hood** n (*place*) vecindad f, barrio; (*people*) vecindario; **~ing** *adj* vecino; **~ly** *adj* (*person*) amable; (*attitude*) de buen vecino

neither ['naɪðə*] *adj* ni ♦ *conj*: **I didn't move and ~ did John** no me he movido, ni Juan tampoco ♦ *pron* ninguno ♦ *adv*: **~ good nor bad** ni bueno ni malo; **~ is true** ninguno/a de los/las dos es cierto/a

neon [ˈniːɔn] *n* neón *m*; ~ **light** *n* lámpara de neón
nephew [ˈnɛvjuː] *n* sobrino
nerve [nɜːv] *n* (*ANAT*) nervio; (*courage*) valor *m*; (*impudence*) descaro, frescura; **a fit of ~s** un ataque de nervios; **~-racking** *adj* desquiciante
nervous [ˈnɜːvəs] *adj* (*anxious, ANAT*) nervioso; (*timid*) tímido, miedoso; ~ **breakdown** *n* crisis *f* nerviosa
nest [nɛst] *n* (*of bird*) nido; (*wasps' ~*) avispero ♦ *vi* anidar; ~ **egg** *n* (*fig*) ahorros *mpl*
nestle [ˈnɛsl] *vi*: **to ~ down** acurrucarse
net [nɛt] *n* (*gen*) red *f*; (*fabric*) tul *m* ♦ *adj* (*COMM*) neto, líquido ♦ *vt* coger (*SP*) or agarrar (*AM*) con red; (*SPORT*) marcar; ~**ball** *n* básquet *m*
Netherlands [ˈnɛðələndz] *npl*: **the ~** los Países Bajos
nett [nɛt] *adj* = **net**
netting [ˈnɛtɪŋ] *n* red *f*, redes *fpl*
nettle [ˈnɛtl] *n* ortiga
network [ˈnɛtwɜːk] *n* red *f*
neurotic [njuəˈrɔtɪk] *adj, n* neurótico/a *m/f*
neuter [ˈnjuːtə*] *adj* (*LING*) neutro ♦ *vt* castrar, capar
neutral [ˈnjuːtrəl] *adj* (*person*) neutral; (*colour etc, ELEC*) neutro ♦ *n* (*AUT*) punto muerto; ~**ize** *vt* neutralizar
never [ˈnɛvə*] *adv* nunca, jamás; **I ~ went** no fui nunca; ~ **in my life** jamás en la vida; *see also* **mind**; ~**-ending** *adj* interminable, sin fin; ~**theless** [nɛvəðəˈlɛs] *adv* sin embargo, no obstante
new [njuː] *adj* nuevo; (*brand new*) a estrenar; (*recent*) reciente; **N~ Age** *n* Nueva Era; ~**-born** *adj* recién nacido; ~**comer** [ˈnjuːkʌmə*] *n* recién venido/a *or* llegado/a; ~**-fangled** (*pej*) *adj* modernísimo; ~**-found** *adj* (*friend*) nuevo; (*enthusiasm*) recién adquirido; ~**ly** *adv* nuevamente, recién; ~**ly-weds** *npl* recién casados *mpl*
news [njuːz] *n* noticias *fpl*; **a piece of ~** una noticia; **the ~** (*RADIO, TV*) las noticias

fpl; ~ **agency** *n* agencia de noticias; ~**agent** (*BRIT*) *n* vendedor(a) *m/f* de periódicos; ~**caster** *n* presentador(a) *m/f*, locutor(a) *m/f*; ~ **flash** *n* noticia de última hora; ~**letter** *n* hoja informativa, boletín *m*; ~**paper** *n* periódico, diario; ~**print** *n* papel *m* de periódico; ~**reader** *n* = ~**caster**; ~**reel** *n* noticiario; ~ **stand** *n* quiosco *or* puesto de periódicos
newt [njuːt] *n* tritón *m*
New Year *n* Año Nuevo; ~**'s Day** *n* Día *m* de Año Nuevo; ~**'s Eve** *n* Nochevieja
New York [ˈnjuːˈjɔːk] *n* Nueva York
New Zealand [njuːˈziːlənd] *n* Nueva Zelanda; ~**er** *n* neozelandés/esa *m/f*
next [nɛkst] *adj* (*house, room*) vecino; (*bus stop, meeting*) próximo; (*following: page etc*) siguiente ♦ *adv* después; **the ~ day** el día siguiente; ~ **time** la próxima vez; ~ **year** el año próximo *or* que viene; ~ **to** junto a, al lado de; ~ **to nothing** casi nada; ~ **please!** ¡el siguiente! ~ **door** *adv* en la casa de al lado ♦ *adj* vecino, de al lado; ~**-of-kin** *n* pariente *m* más cercano
NHS *n abbr* = **National Health Service**
nib [nɪb] *n* plumilla
nibble [ˈnɪbl] *vt* mordisquear, mordiscar
Nicaragua [nɪkəˈrægjuə] *n* Nicaragua; ~**n** *adj, n* nicaragüense *m/f*
nice [naɪs] *adj* (*likeable*) simpático; (*kind*) amable; (*pleasant*) agradable; (*attractive*) bonito, mono, lindo (*AM*); ~**ly** *adv* amablemente; bien
nick [nɪk] *n* (*wound*) rasguño; (*cut, indentation*) mella, muesca ♦ *vt* (*inf*) birlar, robar; **in the ~ of time** justo a tiempo
nickel [ˈnɪkl] *n* níquel *m*; (*US*) moneda de 5 centavos
nickname [ˈnɪkneɪm] *n* apodo, mote *m* ♦ *vt* apodar
nicotine [ˈnɪkətiːn] *n* nicotina
niece [niːs] *n* sobrina
Nigeria [naɪˈdʒɪərɪə] *n* Nigeria; ~**n** *adj, n* nigeriano/a *m/f*
niggling [ˈnɪglɪŋ] *adj* (*trifling*) nimio,

insignificante; (*annoying*) molesto
night [naɪt] *n* noche *f*; (*evening*) tarde *f*;
the ~ before last anteanoche; **at ~, by ~**
de noche, por la noche; **~cap** *n* (*drink*)
bebida que se toma antes de acostarse; **~
club** *n* cabaret *m*; **~dress** (*BRIT*) *n*
camisón *m*; **~fall** *n* anochecer *m*;
~gown *n* = **~dress**; **~ie** ['naɪtɪ] *n*
= **~dress**
nightingale ['naɪtɪŋgeɪl] *n* ruiseñor *m*
night: **~life** *n* vida nocturna; **~ly** *adj* de
todas las noches ♦ *adv* todas las noches,
cada noche; **~mare** *n* pesadilla; **~
porter** *n* portero de noche; **~ school** *n*
clase(s) *f(pl)* nocturna(s); **~ shift** *n* turno
nocturno *or* de noche; **~time** *n* noche *f*;
~ watchman *n* vigilante *m* nocturno
nil [nɪl] (*BRIT*) *n* (*SPORT*) cero, nada
Nile [naɪl] *n*: **the ~** el Nilo
nimble ['nɪmbl] *adj* (*agile*) ágil, ligero;
(*skilful*) diestro
nine [naɪn] *num* nueve; **~teen** *num*
diecinueve, diez y nueve; **~ty** *num*
noventa
ninth [naɪnθ] *adj* noveno
nip [nɪp] *vt* (*pinch*) pellizcar; (*bite*) morder
nipple ['nɪpl] *n* (*ANAT*) pezón *m*
nitrogen ['naɪtrədʒən] *n* nitrógeno

---KEYWORD---

no [nəʊ] (*pl* **~es**) *adv* (*opposite of "yes"*)
no; **are you coming? – ~ (I'm not)**
¿vienes? — no; **would you like some
more? – ~ thank you** ¿quieres más? —
no gracias
♦ *adj* (*not any*): **I have ~ money/time/
books** no tengo dinero/tiempo/libros; **~
other man would have done it** ningún
otro lo hubiera hecho; **"~ entry"**
"prohibido el paso"; **"~ smoking"**
"prohibido fumar"
♦ *n* no *m*

nobility [nəʊ'bɪlɪtɪ] *n* nobleza
noble ['nəʊbl] *adj* noble
nobody ['nəʊbədɪ] *pron* nadie
nod [nɒd] *vi* saludar con la cabeza; (*in

agreement*) decir que sí con la cabeza;
(*doze*) dar cabezadas ♦ *vt*: **to ~ one's
head** inclinar la cabeza ♦ *n* inclinación *f*
de cabeza; **~ off** *vi* dar cabezadas
noise [nɔɪz] *n* ruido; (*din*) escándalo,
estrépito; **noisy** *adj* ruidoso; (*child*)
escandaloso
nominate ['nɒmɪneɪt] *vt* (*propose*)
proponer; (*appoint*) nombrar; **nominee**
[-'niː] *n* candidato/a
non... [nɒn] *prefix* no, des..., in...; **~
alcoholic** *adj* no alcohólico; **~chalant**
adj indiferente; **~committal** *adj*
evasivo; **~descript** *adj* soso
none [nʌn] *pron* ninguno/a ♦ *adv* de
ninguna manera; **~ of you** ninguno de
vosotros; **I've ~ left** no me queda
ninguno/a; **he's ~ the worse for it** no le
ha hecho ningún mal
nonentity [nɒ'nentɪtɪ] *n* cero a la
izquierda, nulidad *f*
nonetheless [nʌnðə'les] *adv* sin
embargo, no obstante
non-existent *adj* inexistente
non-fiction *n* literatura no novelesca
nonplussed [nɒn'plʌst] *adj* perplejo
nonsense ['nɒnsəns] *n* tonterías *fpl*,
disparates *fpl*; **~!** ¡qué tonterías!
non: **~smoker** *n* no fumador(a) *m/f*; **~
smoking** *adj* (de) no fumador; **~stick**
adj (*pan, surface*) antiadherente; **~stop**
adj continuo; (*RAIL*) directo ♦ *adv* sin
parar
noodles ['nuːdlz] *npl* tallarines *mpl*
nook [nuk] *n*: **~s and crannies** escondrijos
mpl
noon [nuːn] *n* mediodía *m*
no-one *pron* = **nobody**
noose [nuːs] *n* (*hangman's*) dogal *m*
nor [nɔː*] *conj* = **neither** ♦ *adv see* **neither**
norm [nɔːm] *n* norma
normal ['nɔːml] *adj* normal; **~ly** *adv*
normalmente
north [nɔːθ] *n* norte *m* ♦ *adj* del norte,
norteño ♦ *adv* al *or* hacia el norte; **N~
Africa** *n* África del Norte; **N~ America**
n América del Norte; **~east** *n* nor(d)este

m; **~erly** ['nɔːðəlɪ] adj (point, direction) norteño; **~ern** ['nɔːðən] adj norteño, del norte; **N~ern Ireland** n Irlanda del Norte; **N~ Pole** n Polo Norte; **N~ Sea** n Mar m del Norte; **~ward(s)** ['nɔːθwəd(z)] adv hacia el norte; **~-west** n nor(d)oeste m

Norway ['nɔːweɪ] n Noruega; **Norwegian** [-'wiːdʒən] adj noruego/a ♦ n noruego/a; (LING) noruego

nose [nəʊz] n (ANAT) nariz f; (ZOOL) hocico; (sense of smell) olfato m; **to ~ about** curiosear; **~bleed** n hemorragia nasal; **~-dive** n (of plane: deliberate) picado vertical; (: involuntary) caída en picado; **~y** (inf) adj curioso, fisgón/ona

nostalgia [nɔs'tældʒɪə] n nostalgia

nostril ['nɔstrɪl] n ventana de la nariz

nosy ['nəʊzɪ] (inf) adj = **nosey**

not [nɔt] adv no; **~ that ...** no es que ...; **it's too late, isn't it?** es demasiado tarde, ¿verdad or no?; **~ yet/now** todavía/ahora no; **why ~?** ¿por qué no?; see also **all**; **only**

notably ['nəʊtəblɪ] adv especialmente

notary ['nəʊtərɪ] n notario/a

notch [nɔtʃ] n muesca, corte m

note [nəʊt] n (MUS, record, letter) nota; (banknote) billete m; (tone) tono ♦ vt (observe) notar, observar; (write down) apuntar, anotar; **~book** n libreta, cuaderno; **~d** ['nəʊtɪd] adj célebre, conocido; **~pad** n bloc m; **~paper** n papel m para cartas

nothing ['nʌθɪŋ] n nada; (zero) cero; **he does ~** no hace nada; **~ new** nada nuevo; **~ much** no mucho; **for ~** (free) gratis, sin pago; (in vain) en balde

notice ['nəʊtɪs] n (announcement) anuncio; (warning) aviso; (dismissal) despido; (resignation) dimisión f; (period of time) plazo ♦ vt (observe) notar, observar; **to bring sth to sb's ~** (attention) llamar la atención de uno sobre algo; **to take ~ of** tomar nota de, prestar atención a; **at short ~** con poca anticipación; **until further ~** hasta nuevo aviso; **to hand in**

one's **~** dimitir; **~able** adj evidente, obvio; **~ board** (BRIT) n tablón m de anuncios

notify ['nəʊtɪfaɪ] vt: **to ~ sb (of sth)** comunicar (algo) a uno

notion ['nəʊʃən] n idea; (opinion) opinión f

notorious [nəʊ'tɔːrɪəs] adj notorio

nougat ['nuːgɑː] n turrón m

nought [nɔːt] n cero

noun [naʊn] n nombre m, sustantivo

nourish ['nʌrɪʃ] vt nutrir; (fig) alimentar; **~ing** adj nutritivo; **~ment** n alimento, sustento

novel ['nɔvl] n novela ♦ adj (new) nuevo, original; (unexpected) insólito; **~ist** n novelista m/f; **~ty** n novedad f

November [nəʊ'vɛmbə*] n noviembre m

novice ['nɔvɪs] n (REL) novicio/a

now [naʊ] adv (at the present time) ahora; (these days) actualmente, hoy día ♦ conj: **~ (that)** ya que, ahora que; **right ~** ahora mismo; **by ~** ya; **just ~** ahora mismo; **~ and then, ~ and again** de vez en cuando; **from ~ on** de ahora en adelante; **~adays** ['nauədeɪz] adv hoy (en) día, actualmente

nowhere ['nəʊwɛə*] adv (direction) a ninguna parte; (location) en ninguna parte

nozzle ['nɔzl] n boquilla

nuance ['njuːɑːns] n matiz m

nuclear ['njuːklɪə*] adj nuclear

nucleus ['njuːklɪəs] (pl **nuclei**) n núcleo

nude [njuːd] adj, n desnudo/a m/f; **in the ~** desnudo

nudge [nʌdʒ] vt dar un codazo a

nudist ['njuːdɪst] n nudista m/f

nuisance ['njuːsns] n molestia, fastidio; (person) pesado, latoso; **what a ~!** ¡qué lata!

null [nʌl] adj: **~ and void** nulo y sin efecto

numb [nʌm] adj: **~ with cold/fear** entumecido por el frío/paralizado de miedo

number ['nʌmbə*] n número; (quantity) cantidad f ♦ vt (pages etc) numerar, poner número a; (amount to) sumar,

ascender a; **to be ~ed among** figurar
entre; **a ~ of** varios, algunos; **they were
ten in ~** eran diez; **~ plate** (*BRIT*) *n*
matrícula, placa

numeral ['nju:mərəl] *n* número, cifra

numerate ['nju:mərɪt] *adj* competente en
la aritmética

numerous ['nju:mərəs] *adj* numeroso

nun [nʌn] *n* monja, religiosa

nurse [nɜ:s] *n* enfermero/a; (*also:* **~maid**)
niñera ♦ *vt* (*patient*) cuidar, atender

nursery ['nɜ:sərɪ] *n* (*institution*) guardería
infantil; (*room*) cuarto de los niños; (*for
plants*) criadero, semillero; **~ rhyme** *n*
canción *f* infantil; **~ school** *n* parvulario,
escuela de párvulos; **~ slope** (*BRIT*) *n*
(*SKI*) cuesta para principiantes

nursing ['nɜ:sɪŋ] *n* (*profession*) profesión *f*
de enfermera; (*care*) asistencia, cuidado;
~ home *n* clínica de reposo

nut [nʌt] *n* (*TECH*) tuerca; (*BOT*) nuez *f*;
~crackers *npl* cascanueces *m inv*

nutmeg ['nʌtmeg] *n* nuez *f* moscada

nutritious [nju:'trɪʃəs] *adj* nutritivo,
alimenticio

nuts [nʌts] (*inf*) *adj* loco

nutshell ['nʌtʃel] *n*: **in a ~** en resumidas
cuentas

nylon ['naɪlɔn] *n* nilón *m* ♦ *adj* de nilón

O, o

oak [əuk] *n* roble *m* ♦ *adj* de roble

O.A.P. (*BRIT*) *n abbr* = **old-age
pensioner**

oar [ɔ:*] *n* remo

oasis [əu'eɪsɪs] (*pl* **oases**) *n* oasis *m inv*

oath [əuθ] *n* juramento; (*swear word*)
palabrota; **on** (*BRIT*) *or* **under ~** bajo
juramento

oatmeal ['əutmi:l] *n* harina de avena

oats [əuts] *n* avena

obedience [ə'bi:dɪəns] *n* obediencia

obedient [ə'bi:dɪənt] *adj* obediente

obey [ə'beɪ] *vt* obedecer; (*instructions,
regulations*) cumplir

obituary [ə'bɪtjuərɪ] *n* necrología

object [*n* 'ɔbdʒɪkt, *vb* əb'dʒɛkt] *n* objeto;
(*purpose*) objeto, propósito; (*LING*)
complemento ♦ *vi*: **to ~ to** estar en
contra de; (*proposal*) oponerse a; **to ~
that** objetar que; **expense is no ~** no
importa cuánto cuesta; **I ~!** ¡yo protesto!;
~ion [əb'dʒekʃən] *n* protesta; **I have no
~ion to ...** no tengo inconveniente en
que ...; **~ionable** [əb'dʒekʃənəbl] *adj*
desagradable; (*conduct*) censurable; **~ive**
adj, n objetivo

obligation [ɔblɪ'geɪʃən] *n* obligación *f*;
(*debt*) deber *m*; **without ~** sin
compromiso

oblige [ə'blaɪdʒ] *vt* (*do a favour for*)
complacer, hacer un favor a; **to ~ sb to
do sth** forzar *or* obligar a uno a hacer
algo; **to be ~d to sb for sth** estarle
agradecido a uno por algo; **obliging** *adj*
servicial, atento

oblique [ə'bli:k] *adj* oblicuo; (*allusion*)
indirecto

obliterate [ə'blɪtəreɪt] *vt* borrar

oblivion [ə'blɪvɪən] *n* olvido; **oblivious**
[-ɪəs] *adj*: **oblivious of** inconsciente de

oblong ['ɔblɔŋ] *adj* rectangular ♦ *n*
rectángulo

obnoxious [əb'nɔkʃəs] *adj* odioso,
detestable; (*smell*) nauseabundo

oboe ['əubəu] *n* oboe *m*

obscene [əb'si:n] *adj* obsceno

obscure [əb'skjuə*] *adj* oscuro ♦ *vt*
oscurecer; (*hide: sun*) esconder

observant [əb'zɔ:vnt] *adj* observador(a)

observation [ɔbzə'veɪʃən] *n* observación *f*;
(*MED*) examen *m*

observe [əb'zɔ:v] *vt* observar; (*rule*)
cumplir; **~r** *n* observador(a) *m/f*

obsess [əb'ses] *vt* obsesionar; **~ive** *adj*
obsesivo; obsesionante

obsolete ['ɔbsəli:t] *adj*: **to be ~** estar en
desuso

obstacle ['ɔbstəkl] *n* obstáculo; (*nuisance*)
estorbo; **~ race** *n* carrera de obstáculos

obstinate ['ɔbstɪnɪt] *adj* terco, porfiado;
(*determined*) obstinado

obstruct [əb'strʌkt] vt obstruir; (*hinder*) estorbar, obstaculizar; **~ion** [əb'strʌkʃən] n (*action*) obstrucción f; (*object*) estorbo, obstáculo

obtain [əb'teɪn] vt obtener; (*achieve*) conseguir

obvious ['ɔbvɪəs] adj obvio, evidente; **~ly** adv evidentemente, naturalmente; **~ly not** por supuesto que no

occasion [ə'keɪʒən] n oportunidad f, ocasión f; (*event*) acontecimiento; **~al** adj poco frecuente, ocasional; **~ally** adv de vez en cuando

occupant ['ɔkjupənt] n (*of house*) inquilino/a; (*of car*) ocupante m/f

occupation [ɔkju'peɪʃən] n ocupación f; (*job*) trabajo; (*pastime*) ocupaciones fpl; **~al hazard** n riesgo profesional

occupier ['ɔkjupaɪə*] n inquilino/a

occupy ['ɔkjupaɪ] vt (*seat, post, time*) ocupar; (*house*) habitar; **to ~ o.s. in doing** pasar el tiempo haciendo

occur [ə'kə:*] vi pasar, suceder; **to ~ to sb** ocurrírsele a uno; **~rence** [ə'kʌrəns] n acontecimiento; (*existence*) existencia

ocean ['əuʃən] n océano

o'clock [ə'klɔk] adv: **it is 5 ~** son las 5

OCR n abbr = **optical character recognition/reader**

October [ɔk'təubə*] n octubre m

octopus ['ɔktəpəs] n pulpo

odd [ɔd] adj extraño, raro; (*number*) impar; (*sock, shoe etc*) suelto; **60-~** 60 y pico; **at ~ times** de vez en cuando; **to be the ~ one out** estar de más; **~ity** n rareza; (*person*) excéntrico; **~-job man** n chico para todo; **~ jobs** npl bricolaje m; **~ly** adv curiosamente, extrañamente; *see also* **enough**; **~ments** npl (COMM) retales mpl; **~s** npl (*in betting*) puntos mpl de ventaja; **it makes no ~s** da lo mismo; **at ~s** reñidos/as; **~s and ends** minucias fpl

odometer [ɔ'dɔmɪtə*] (US) n cuentakilómetros m inv

odour ['əudə*] (US **odor**) n olor m; (*unpleasant*) hedor m

---

of [ɔv, əv] prep **1** (*gen*) de; **a friend ~ ours** un amigo nuestro; **a boy ~ 10** un chico de 10 años; **that was kind ~ you** eso fue muy amable por or de tu parte

2 (*expressing quantity, amount, dates etc*) de; **a kilo ~ flour** un kilo de harina; **there were 3 ~ them** había tres; **3 ~ us went** tres de nosotros fuimos; **the 5th ~ July** el 5 de julio

3 (*from, out of*) de; **made ~ wood** (hecho) de madera

---

off [ɔf] adj, adv (*engine*) desconectado; (*light*) apagado; (*tap*) cerrado; (BRIT: *food*: *bad*) pasado, malo; (: *milk*) cortado; (*cancelled*) cancelado ♦ prep de; **to be ~** (*to leave*) irse, marcharse; **to be ~ sick** estar enfermo or de baja; **a day ~** un día libre or sin trabajar; **to have an ~ day** tener un día malo; **he had his coat ~** se había quitado el abrigo; **10% ~** (COMM) (con el) 10% de descuento; **5 km ~ (the road)** a 5 km (de la carretera); **~ the coast** frente a la costa; **I'm ~ meat** (*no longer eat/like it*) paso de la carne; **on the ~ chance** por si acaso; **~ and on** de vez en cuando

offal ['ɔfl] (BRIT) n (CULIN) menudencias fpl

off-colour [ɔf'kʌlə*] (BRIT) adj (*ill*) indispuesto

offence [ə'fens] (US **offense**) n (*crime*) delito; **to take ~ at** ofenderse por

offend [ə'fend] vt (*person*) ofender; **~er** n delincuente m/f

offensive [ə'fensɪv] adj ofensivo; (*smell etc*) repugnante ♦ n (MIL) ofensiva

offer ['ɔfə*] n oferta, ofrecimiento; (*proposal*) propuesta ♦ vt ofrecer; (*opportunity*) facilitar; **"on ~"** (COMM) "en oferta"; **~ing** n ofrenda

offhand [ɔf'hænd] adj informal ♦ adv de improviso

office ['ɔfɪs] n (*place*) oficina; (*room*) despacho; (*position*) carga, oficio; **doctor's ~** (US) consultorio; **to take ~**

entrar en funciones; **~ automation** *n* ofimática, buromática; **~ block** (*US* **~ building**) *n* bloque *m* de oficinas; **~ hours** *npl* horas *fpl* de oficina; (*US: MED*) horas *fpl* de consulta

fficer ['ɔfisə*] *n* (*MIL etc*) oficial *m/f*; (*also:* **police ~**) agente *m/f* de policía; (*of organization*) director(a) *m/f*

fice worker *n* oficinista *m/f*

fficial [ə'fiʃl] *adj* oficial, autorizado ♦ *n* funcionario, oficial *m*

fing ['ɔfiŋ] *n*: **in the ~** (*fig*) en perspectiva

ff: **~-licence** (*BRIT*) *n* (*shop*) bodega, tienda de vinos y bebidas alcohólicas; **~-line** *adj, adv* (*COMPUT*) fuera de línea; **~-peak** *adj* (*electricity*) de banda económica; (*ticket*) billete de precio reducido por viajar fuera de las horas punta; **~-putting** (*BRIT*) *adj* (*person*) asqueroso; (*remark*) desalentador(a); **~-season** *adj, adv* fuera de temporada

---
off-licence

En el Reino Unido la venta de bebidas alcohólicas está estrictamente regulada se necesita una licencia especial, con la ue cuentan los bares, restaurantes y los stablecimientos de **off-licence**, *los únicos ugares en donde se pueden adquirir ebidas alcohólicas para su consumo fuera el local, de donde viene su nombre. ambién venden bebidas no alcohólicas, abaco, chocolatinas, patatas fritas etc y a enudo forman parte de una cadena acional.*

---

fset ['ɔfset] (*irreg*) *vt* contrarrestar, compensar

fshoot ['ɔfʃu:t] *n* (*fig*) ramificación *f*

fshore [ɔf'ʃɔ:*] *adj* (*breeze, island*) costera; (*fishing*) de bajura

fside ['ɔf'said] *adj* (*SPORT*) fuera de juego; (*AUT: in UK*) del lado derecho; (*: in US, Europe etc*) del lado izquierdo

fspring ['ɔfspriŋ] *n inv* descendencia

f: **~stage** *adv* entre bastidores; **~-the-**

peg (*US* **~-the-rack**) *adv* confeccionado; **~-white** *adj* color crudo

often ['ɔfn] *adv* a menudo, con frecuencia; **how ~ do you go?** ¿cada cuánto vas?

oh [əu] *excl* ¡ah!

oil [ɔil] *n* aceite *m*; (*petroleum*) petróleo; (*for heating*) aceite *m* combustible ♦ *vt* engrasar; **~can** *n* lata de aceite; **~field** *n* campo petrolífero; **~ filter** *n* (*AUT*) filtro de aceite; **~ painting** *n* pintura al óleo; **~ rig** *n* torre *f* de perforación; **~ tanker** *n* petrolero; (*truck*) camión *m* cisterna; **~ well** *n* pozo (de petróleo); **~y** *adj* aceitoso; (*food*) grasiento

ointment ['ɔintmənt] *n* ungüento

O.K., okay ['əu'kei] *excl* O.K., ¡está bien!, ¡vale! (*SP*) ♦ *adj* bien ♦ *vt* dar el visto bueno a

old [əuld] *adj* viejo; (*former*) antiguo; **how ~ are you?** ¿cuántos años tienes?, ¿qué edad tienes?; **he's 10 years ~** tiene 10 años; **~er brother** hermano mayor; **~ age** *n* vejez *f*; **~-age pensioner** (*BRIT*) *n* jubilado/a; **~-fashioned** *adj* anticuado, pasado de moda

olive ['ɔliv] *n* (*fruit*) aceituna; (*tree*) olivo ♦ *adj* (*also:* **~-green**) verde oliva; **~ oil** *n* aceite *m* de oliva

Olympic [əu'limpik] *adj* olímpico; **the ~ Games**, **the ~s** las Olimpíadas

omelet(te) ['ɔmlit] *n* tortilla (*SP*), tortilla de huevo (*AM*)

omen ['əumen] *n* presagio

ominous ['ɔminəs] *adj* de mal agüero, amenazador(a)

omit [əu'mit] *vt* omitir

| KEYWORD |
---

on [ɔn] *prep* **1** (*indicating position*) en; sobre; **~ the wall** en la pared; **it's ~ the table** está sobre *or* en la mesa; **~ the left** a la izquierda
2 (*indicating means, method, condition etc*): **~ foot** a pie; **~ the train/plane** (*go*) en tren/avión; (*be*) en el tren/el avión; **~ the radio/television/telephone** por *or* en la radio/televisión/al teléfono; **to be ~**

drugs drogarse; (*MED*) estar a tratamiento; **to be ~ holiday/business** estar de vacaciones/en viaje de negocios 3 (*referring to time*): **~ Friday** el viernes; **~ Fridays** los viernes; **~ June 20th** el 20 de junio; **a week ~ Friday** del viernes en una semana; **~ arrival** al llegar; **~ seeing this** al ver esto 4 (*about, concerning*) sobre, acerca de; **a book ~ physics** un libro de *or* sobre física ♦ *adv* 1 (*referring to dress*): **to have one's coat ~** tener *or* llevar el abrigo puesto; **she put her gloves ~** se puso los guantes 2 (*referring to covering*): **"screw the lid ~ tightly"** "cerrar bien la tapa" 3 (*further, continuously*): **to walk** *etc* **~** seguir caminando *etc* ♦ *adj* 1 (*functioning, in operation*): *machine, radio, TV, light*) encendido/a (*SP*), prendido/a (*AM*); (: *tap*) abierto/a; (: *brakes*) echado/a, puesto/a; **is the meeting still ~?** (*in progress*) ¿todavía continúa la reunión?; (*not cancelled*) ¿va a haber reunión al fin?; **there's a good film ~ at the cinema** ponen una buena película en el cine 2: **that's not ~!** (*inf*: *not possible*) ¡eso ni hablar!; (: *not acceptable*) ¡eso no se hace!

once [wʌns] *adv* una vez; (*formerly*) antiguamente ♦ *conj* una vez que; **~ he had left/it was done** una vez que se había marchado/se hizo; **at ~** en seguida, inmediatamente; (*simultaneously*) a la vez; **~ a week** una vez por semana; **~ more** otra vez; **~ and for all** de una vez por todas; **~ upon a time** érase una vez

oncoming [ˈɒnkʌmɪŋ] *adj* (*traffic*) que viene de frente

KEYWORD

one [wʌn] *num* un(o)/una; **~ hundred and fifty** ciento cincuenta; **~ by ~** uno a uno ♦ *adj* 1 (*sole*) único; **the ~ book which** el único libro que; **the ~ man who** el único que

2 (*same*) mismo/a; **they came in the ~ car** vinieron en un solo coche ♦ *pron* 1: **this ~** éste/ésta; **that ~** ése/ésa (*more remote*) aquél/aquella; **I've already got (a red) ~** ya tengo uno/a (rojo/a); **~ by ~** uno/a por uno/a 2: **~ another** os (*SP*), se (+*el uno al otro, unos a otros etc*); **do you two ever see ~ another?** ¿vosotros dos os veis alguna vez? (*SP*), ¿se ven ustedes dos alguna vez?; **the boys didn't dare look at ~ another** los chicos no se atrevieron a mirarse (el uno al otro); **they all kissed another** se besaron unos a otros 3 (*impers*): **~ never knows** nunca se sab **to cut ~'s finger** cortarse el dedo; **~ needs to eat** hay que comer

one: **~-day excursion** (*US*) *n* billete *m* de ida y vuelta en un día; **~-man** *adj* (*business*) individual; **~-man band** *n* hombre-orquesta *m*; **~-off** (*BRIT*: *inf*) *n* (*event*) acontecimiento único

oneself [wʌnˈself] *pron* (*reflexive*) se; (*afte prep*) sí; (*emphatic*) uno/a mismo/a; **to hurt ~** hacerse daño; **to keep sth for ~** guardarse algo; **to talk to ~** hablar solo

one: **~-sided** *adj* (*argument*) parcial; **~-to-~** *adj* (*relationship*) de dos; **~-way** *a* (*street*) de sentido único

ongoing [ˈɒŋgəʊɪŋ] *adj* continuo

onion [ˈʌnjən] *n* cebolla

on-line *adj*, *adv* (*COMPUT*) en línea

onlooker [ˈɒnlʊkə*] *n* espectador(a) *m/f*

only [ˈəʊnlɪ] *adv* solamente, sólo ♦ *adj* único, solo ♦ *conj* solamente que, pero; **an ~ child** un hijo único; **not ~ ... but also ...** no sólo ... sino también ...

onset [ˈɒnset] *n* comienzo

onshore [ˈɒnʃɔː*] *adj* (*wind*) que sopla de mar hacia la tierra

onslaught [ˈɒnslɔːt] *n* ataque *m*, embestida

onto [ˈɒntu] *prep* = **on to**

onward(s) [ˈɒnwəd(z)] *adv* (*move*) (hacia adelante; **from that time ~** desde entonces en adelante

nyx ['ɒnɪks] n ónice m

oze [u:z] vi rezumar

paque [əu'peik] adj opaco

PEC ['əupek] n abbr (= Organization of Petroleum-Exporting Countries) OPEP f

pen ['əupn] adj abierto; (car) descubierto; (road, view) despejado; (meeting) público; (admiration) manifiesto ♦ vt abrir ♦ vi abrirse; (book etc: commence) comenzar; **in the ~** (air) al aire libre; **~ on to** vt fus (subj: room, door) dar a; **~ up** vt abrir; (blocked road) despejar ♦ vi abrirse, empezar; **~ing** n abertura; (start) comienzo; (opportunity) oportunidad f; **~ing hours** npl horario de apertura; **~ learning** n enseñanza flexible a tiempo parcial; **~ly** adv abiertamente; **~-minded** adj imparcial; **~-necked** adj (shirt) desabrochado; sin corbata; **~-plan** adj: **~-plan office** gran oficina sin particiones

---

Open University

La **Open University**, fundada en 1969, está especializada en impartir cursos a distancia que no exigen una dedicación exclusiva. Cuenta con sus propios materiales de apoyo, entre ellos programas de radio y televisión emitidos por la BBC y para conseguir los créditos de la licenciatura es necesaria la presentación de unos trabajos y la asistencia a los cursos de verano.

---

pera ['ɒpərə] n ópera f; **~ house** n teatro de la ópera

perate ['ɒpəreit] vt (machine) hacer funcionar; (company) dirigir ♦ vi funcionar; **to ~ on sb** (MED) operar a uno

peratic [ɒpə'rætɪk] adj de ópera

perating table ['ɒpəreitɪŋ-] n mesa de operaciones

perating theatre n sala de operaciones

peration [ɒpə'reɪʃən] n operación f; (of machine) funcionamiento; **to be in ~** estar funcionando or en funcionamiento; **to**

have an ~ (MED) ser operado; **~al** adj operacional, en buen estado

operative ['ɒpərətɪv] adj en vigor

operator ['ɒpəreitə*] n (of machine) maquinista m/f, operario/a; (TEL) operador(a) m/f, telefonista m/f

opinion [ə'pɪnɪən] n opinión f; **in my ~** en mi opinión, a mi juicio; **~ated** adj testarudo; **~ poll** n encuesta, sondeo

opponent [ə'pəunənt] n adversario/a, contrincante m/f

opportunity [ɒpə'tju:nɪtɪ] n oportunidad f; **to take the ~ of doing** aprovechar la ocasión para hacer

oppose [ə'pəuz] vt oponerse a; **to be ~d to sth** oponerse a algo; **as ~d to** a diferencia de; **opposing** adj opuesto, contrario

opposite ['ɒpəzɪt] adj opuesto, contrario a; (house etc) de enfrente ♦ adv en frente ♦ prep en frente de, frente a ♦ n lo contrario

opposition [ɒpə'zɪʃən] n oposición f

oppressive [ə'presɪv] adj opresivo; (weather) agobiante

opt [ɒpt] vi: **to ~ for** optar por; **to ~ to do** optar por hacer; **~ out** vi: **to ~ out of** optar por no hacer

optical ['ɒptɪkl] adj óptico

optician [ɒp'tɪʃən] n óptico m/f

optimist ['ɒptɪmɪst] n optimista m/f; **~ic** [-'mɪstɪk] adj optimista

option ['ɒpʃən] n opción f; **~al** adj facultativo, discrecional

or [ɔ:*] conj o; (before o, ho) u; (with negative): **he hasn't seen ~ heard anything** no ha visto ni oído nada; **~ else** si no

oral ['ɔ:rəl] adj oral ♦ n examen m oral

orange ['ɒrɪndʒ] n (fruit) naranja ♦ adj color naranja

orbit ['ɔ:bɪt] n órbita ♦ vt, vi orbitar

orchard ['ɔ:tʃəd] n huerto

orchestra ['ɔ:kɪstrə] n orquesta; (US: seating) platea

orchid ['ɔ:kɪd] n orquídea

ordain [ɔ:'deɪn] vt (REL) ordenar, decretar

ordeal [ɔː'diːl] *n* experiencia horrorosa
order ['ɔːdə*] *n* orden *m*; (*command*)
orden *f*; (*good ~*) buen estado; (*COMM*)
pedido ♦ *vt* (*also*: **put in ~**) arreglar,
poner en orden; (*COMM*) pedir;
(*command*) mandar, ordenar; **in ~** en
orden; (*of document*) en regla; **in
(working) ~** en funcionamiento; **in ~ to
do/that** para hacer/que; **on ~** (*COMM*)
pedido; **to be out of ~** estar
desordenado; (*not working*) no funcionar;
to ~ sb to do sth mandar a uno hacer
algo; **~ form** *n* hoja de pedido; **~ly**
(*MIL*) ordenanza *m*; (*MED*) enfermero/a
(auxiliar) ♦ *adj* ordenado
ordinary ['ɔːdnrɪ] *adj* corriente, normal;
(*pej*) común y corriente; **out of the ~**
fuera de lo común
Ordnance Survey ['ɔːdnəns-] (*BRIT*) *n*
servicio oficial de topografía
ore [ɔː*] *n* mineral *m*
organ ['ɔːgən] *n* órgano; **~ic** [ɔː'gænɪk] *adj*
orgánico; **~ism** *n* organismo
organization [ɔːgənaɪ'zeɪʃən] *n*
organización *f*
organize ['ɔːgənaɪz] *vt* organizar; **~r** *n*
organizador(a) *m/f*
orgasm ['ɔːgæzəm] *n* orgasmo
orgy ['ɔːdʒɪ] *n* orgía
Orient ['ɔːrɪənt] *n* Oriente *m*; **oriental**
[-'ɛntl] *adj* oriental
orientate ['ɔːrɪənteɪt] *vt*: **to ~ o.s.**
orientarse
origin ['ɔrɪdʒɪn] *n* origen *m*
original [ə'rɪdʒɪnl] *adj* original; (*first*)
primero; (*earlier*) primitivo ♦ *n* original *m*;
~ly *adv* al principio
originate [ə'rɪdʒɪneɪt] *vi*: **to ~ from, to ~
in** surgir de, tener su origen en
Orkney ['ɔːknɪ] *n* (*also*: **the Orkney
Islands**) las Orcadas
ornament ['ɔːnəmənt] *n* adorno; (*trinket*)
chuchería; **~al** [-'mɛntl] *adj* decorativo, de
adorno
ornate [ɔː'neɪt] *adj* muy ornado, vistoso
orphan ['ɔːfn] *n* huérfano/a
orthopaedic [ɔːθə'piːdɪk] (*US* **orthopedic**)

adj ortopédico
ostensibly [ɔs'tɛnsɪblɪ] *adv* aparentement
ostentatious [ɔstɛn'teɪʃəs] *adj* ostentoso
osteopath ['ɔstɪəpæθ] *n* osteópata *m/f*
ostracize ['ɔstrəsaɪz] *vt* hacer el vacío a
ostrich ['ɔstrɪtʃ] *n* avestruz *m*
other ['ʌðə*] *adj* otro ♦ *pron*: **the ~ (one)**
el/la otro/a ♦ *adv*: **~ than** aparte de; **~s**
(*~ people*) otros; **the ~ day** el otro día;
~wise *adv* de otra manera ♦ *conj* (*if not*
si no
otter ['ɔtə*] *n* nutria
ouch [autʃ] *excl* ¡ay!
ought [ɔːt] (*pt* **ought**) *aux vb*: **I ~ to do it**
debería hacerlo; **this ~ to have been
corrected** esto debiera haberse corregido
he ~ to win (*probability*) debe *or* debiera
ganar
ounce [auns] *n* onza (*28.35g*)
our ['auə*] *adj* nuestro; *see also* **my**; **~s**
pron (el) nuestro/(la) nuestra *etc*; *see also*
mine[1]; **~selves** *pron pl* (*reflexive, after
prep*) nosotros; (*emphatic*) nosotros
mismos; *see also* **oneself**
oust [aust] *vt* desalojar
out [aut] *adv* fuera, afuera; (*not at home*)
fuera (de casa); (*light, fire*) apagado; **~
there** allí (fuera); **he's ~** (*absent*) no está
ha salido; **to be ~ in one's calculations**
equivocarse (en sus cálculos); **to run ~**
salir corriendo; **~ loud** en alta voz; **~ of**
(*outside*) fuera de; (*because of: anger etc*)
por; **~ of petrol** sin gasolina; **"~ of order**
"no funciona"; **~-and-~** *adj* (*liar, thief
etc*) redomado, empedernido; **~back** *n*
interior *m*; **~board** *adj*: **~board motor**
(motor *m*) fuera borda *m*; **~break** *n* (*of
war*) comienzo; (*of disease*) epidemia; (*of
violence etc*) ola; **~burst** *n* explosión *f*,
arranque *m*; **~cast** *n* paria *m/f*; **~come**
n resultado; **~crop** *n* (*of rock*)
afloramiento; **~cry** *n* protestas *fpl*;
~dated *adj* anticuado, fuera de moda;
~do (*irreg*) *vt* superar; **~door** *adj*
exterior, de aire libre; (*clothes*) de calle;
~doors *adv* al aire libre
outer ['autə*] *adj* exterior, externo; **~**

space *n* espacio exterior
outfit ['autfɪt] *n* (*clothes*) conjunto
out: **~going** *adj* (*character*) extrovertido; (*retiring: president etc*) saliente; **~goings** (BRIT) *npl* gastos *mpl*; **~grow** (*irreg*) *vt*: **he has ~grown his clothes** su ropa le queda pequeña ya; **~house** *n* dependencia; **~ing** ['autɪŋ] *n* excursión *f*, paseo
out: **~law** *n* proscrito ♦ *vt* proscribir; **~lay** *n* inversión *f*; **~let** *n* salida; (*of pipe*) desagüe *m*; (US: ELEC) toma de corriente; (*also: retail* **~let**) punto de venta; **~line** *n* (*shape*) contorno, perfil *m*; (*sketch, plan*) esbozo ♦ *vt* (*plan etc*) esbozar; **in ~line** (*fig*) a grandes rasgos; **~live** *vt* sobrevivir a; **~look** *n* (*fig: prospects*) perspectivas *fpl*; (: *for weather*) pronóstico; **~lying** *adj* remoto, aislado; **~moded** *adj* anticuado, pasado de moda; **~number** *vt* superar en número; **~-of-date** *adj* (*passport*) caducado; (*clothes*) pasado de moda; **~-of-the-way** *adj* apartado; **~patient** *n* paciente *m/f* externo/a; **~post** *n* puesto avanzado; **~put** *n* (volumen *m* de) producción *f*, rendimiento; (COMPUT) salida
outrage ['autreɪdʒ] *n* escándalo *m*; (*atrocity*) atrocidad *f* ♦ *vt* ultrajar; **~ous** [-'reɪdʒəs] *adj* monstruoso
outright [*adv* aut'raɪt, *adj* 'autraɪt] *adv* (*ask, deny*) francamente; (*refuse*) rotundamente; (*win*) de manera absoluta; (*be killed*) en el acto ♦ *adj* franco; rotundo
outset ['autset] *n* principio
outside [aut'saɪd] *n* exterior *m* ♦ *adj* exterior, externo ♦ *adv* fuera ♦ *prep* fuera de; (*beyond*) más allá de; **at the ~** (*fig*) a lo sumo; **~ lane** *n* (AUT: *in Britain*) carril *m* de la derecha; (: *in US, Europe etc*) carril *m* de la izquierda; **~ line** *n* (TEL) línea (exterior); **~r** *n* (*stranger*) extraño, forastero
out: **~size** *adj* (*clothes*) de talla grande; **~skirts** *npl* alrededores *mpl*, afueras *fpl*; **~spoken** *adj* muy franco; **~standing**

adj excepcional, destacado; (*remaining*) pendiente; **~stay** *vt*: **to ~stay one's welcome** quedarse de más de la cuenta; **~stretched** *adj* (*hand*) extendido; **~strip** *vt* (*competitors, demand*) dejar atrás, aventajar; **~-tray** *n* bandeja de salida
outward ['autwəd] *adj* externo; (*journey*) de ida
outweigh [aut'weɪ] *vt* pesar más que
outwit [aut'wɪt] *vt* ser más listo que
oval ['əuvl] *adj* ovalado ♦ *n* óvalo
ovary ['əuvərɪ] *n* ovario
oven ['ʌvn] *n* horno; **~proof** *adj* resistente al horno
over ['əuvə•] *adv* encima, por encima ♦ *adj* (*or adv*) (*finished*) terminado; (*surplus*) de sobra ♦ *prep* (*por*) encima de; (*above*) sobre; (*on the other side of*) al otro lado de; (*more than*) más de; (*during*) durante; **~ here** (*por*) aquí; **~ there** (*por*) allí *or* allá; **all ~** (*everywhere*) por todas partes; **~ and ~ (again)** una y otra vez; **~ and above** además de; **to ask sb ~** invitar a uno a casa; **to bend ~** inclinarse
overall [*adj, n* 'əuvərɔ:l, *adv* əuvər'ɔ:l] *adj* (*length etc*) total; (*study*) de conjunto ♦ *adv* en conjunto ♦ *n* (BRIT) guardapolvo; **~s** *npl* mono (SP), overol *m* (AM)
over: **~awe** *vt*: **to be ~awed (by)** quedar impresionado (con); **~balance** *vi* perder el equilibrio; **~board** *adv* (NAUT) por la borda; **~book** [əuvə'buk] *vt* sobrereservar
overcast ['əuvəka:st] *adj* encapotado
overcharge [əuvə'tʃa:dʒ] *vt*: **to ~ sb** cobrar un precio excesivo a uno
overcoat ['əuvəkəut] *n* abrigo, sobretodo
overcome [əuvə'kʌm] (*irreg*) *vt* vencer; (*difficulty*) superar
over: **~crowded** *adj* atestado de gente; (*city, country*) superpoblado; **~do** (*irreg*) *vt* exagerar; (*overcook*) cocer demasiado; **to ~do it** (*work etc*) pasarse; **~dose** *n* sobredosis *f inv*; **~draft** *n* saldo deudor; **~drawn** *adj* (*account*) en descubierto;

~**due** adj retrasado; ~**estimate**
[əuvər'estimeit] vt sobreestimar
overflow [vb əuvə'fləu, n 'əuvəfləu] vi
desbordarse ♦ n (also: ~ **pipe**) (cañería
de) desagüe m
overgrown [əuvə'grəun] adj (garden)
invadido por la vegetación
overhaul [vb əuvə'hɔːl, n 'əuvəhɔːl] vt
revisar, repasar ♦ n revisión f
overhead [adv əuvə'hed, adj, n 'əuvəhed]
adv por arriba or encima ♦ adj (cable)
aéreo ♦ n (US) = ~**s**; ~**s** npl (expenses)
gastos mpl generales
over: ~**hear** (irreg) vt oír por casualidad;
~**heat** vi (engine) recalentarse; ~**joyed**
adj encantado, lleno de alegría
overland ['əuvəlænd] adj, adv por tierra
overlap [əuvə'læp] vi traslaparse
over: ~**leaf** adv al dorso; ~**load** vt
sobrecargar; ~**look** vt (have view of) dar
a, tener vistas a; (miss: by mistake) pasar
por alto; (excuse) perdonar
overnight [əuvə'nait] adv durante la
noche; (fig) de la noche a la mañana
♦ adj de noche; **to stay** ~ pasar la noche
overpass ['əuvəpaːs] (US) n paso superior
overpower [əuvə'pauə*] vt dominar; (fig)
embargar; ~**ing** adj (heat) agobiante;
(smell) penetrante
over: ~**rate** vt sobreestimar; ~**ride** (irreg)
vt no hacer caso de; ~**riding** adj
predominante; ~**rule** vt (decision) anular;
(claim) denegar; ~**run** (irreg) vt (country)
invadir; (time limit) rebasar, exceder
overseas [əuvə'siːz] adv (abroad: live) en
el extranjero; (: travel) al extranjero ♦ adj
(trade) exterior; (visitor) extranjero
overshadow [əuvə'fædəu] vt: **to be ~ed
by** estar a la sombra de
overshoot [əuvə'fuːt] (irreg) vt excederse
oversight ['əuvəsait] n descuido
oversleep [əuvə'sliːp] (irreg) vi quedarse
dormido
overstep [əuvə'step] vt: **to** ~ **the mark**
pasarse de la raya
overt [əu'vəːt] adj abierto
overtake [əuvə'teik] (irreg) vt sobrepasar;

(BRIT: AUT) adelantar
over: ~**throw** (irreg) vt (government)
derrocar; ~**time** n horas fpl
extraordinarias; ~**tone** n (fig) tono
overture ['əuvətfuə*] n (MUS) obertura;
(fig) preludio
over: ~**turn** vt volcar; (fig: plan)
desbaratar; (: government) derrocar ♦ vi
volcar; ~**weight** adj demasiado gordo or
pesado; ~**whelm** vt aplastar; (subj:
emotion) sobrecoger; ~**whelming** adj
(victory, defeat) arrollador(a); (feeling)
irresistible; ~**work** vi trabajar demasiado;
~**wrought** [əuvə'rɔːt] adj sobreexcitado
owe [əu] vt: **to** ~ **sb sth, to** ~ **sth to sb**
deber algo a uno; **owing to** prep debido
a, por causa de
owl [aul] n búho, lechuza
own [əun] vt tener, poseer ♦ adj propio; **a
room of my** ~ una habitación propia; **to
get one's** ~ **back** tomar revancha; **on
one's** ~ solo, a solas; ~ **up** vi confesar;
~**er** n dueño/a; ~**ership** n posesión f
ox [ɔks] (pl ~**en**) n buey m; ~**tail** n: ~**tail
soup** sopa de rabo de buey
oxygen ['ɔksidʒən] n oxígeno
oyster ['ɔistə*] n ostra
oz. abbr = **ounce(s)**
ozone ['əuzəun]: ~ **friendly** adj que no
daña la capa de ozono; ~ **hole** n agujero
m de/en la capa de ozono; ~ **layer** n
capa f de ozono

P, p

p [piː] abbr = **penny; pence**
P.A. n abbr = **personal assistant; public
address system**
p.a. abbr = **per annum**
pa [paː] (inf) n papá m
pace [peis] n paso ♦ vi: **to** ~ **up and down**
pasearse de un lado a otro; **to keep** ~
with llevar el mismo paso que; ~**maker**
n (MED) regulador m cardíaco,
marcapasos m inv; (SPORT: also: ~**setter**)
liebre f

Pacific [pə'sɪfɪk] n: **the ~ (Ocean)** el (Océano) Pacífico

pack [pæk] n (packet) paquete m; (of hounds) jauría; (of people) manada, bando; (of cards) baraja; (bundle) fardo; (US: of cigarettes) paquete m; (back ~) mochila ♦ vt (fill) llenar; (in suitcase etc) meter, poner; (cram) llenar, atestar; **to ~ (one's bags)** hacerse la maleta; **to ~ sb off** despachar a uno; **~ it in!** (inf) ¡déjalo!

package ['pækɪdʒ] n paquete m; (bulky) bulto; (also: ~ **deal**) acuerdo global; ~ **holiday** n vacaciones fpl organizadas; ~ **tour** n viaje m organizado

packed lunch n almuerzo frío

packet ['pækɪt] n paquete m

packing ['pækɪŋ] n embalaje m; ~ **case** n cajón m de embalaje

pact [pækt] n pacto

pad [pæd] n (of paper) bloc m; (cushion) cojinete m; (inf: home) casa ♦ vt rellenar; **~ding** n (material) relleno

paddle ['pædl] n (oar) canalete m; (US: for table tennis) paleta ♦ vt impulsar con canalete ♦ vi (with feet) chapotear; **paddling pool** (BRIT) n estanque m de juegos

paddock ['pædək] n corral m

padlock ['pædlɒk] n candado

paediatrics [piːdɪ'ætrɪks] (US **pediatrics**) n pediatría

pagan ['peɪɡən] adj, n pagano/a m/f

page [peɪdʒ] n (of book) página; (of newspaper) plana; (also: ~ **boy**) paje m ♦ vt (in hotel etc) llamar por altavoz a

pageant ['pædʒənt] n (procession) desfile m; (show) espectáculo; **~ry** n pompa

pager ['peɪdʒə*] n (TEL) busca m

paging device ['peɪdʒɪŋ-] n = **pager**

paid [peɪd] pt, pp of **pay** ♦ adj (work) remunerado; (holiday) pagado; (official etc) a sueldo; **to put ~ to** (BRIT) acabar con

pail [peɪl] n cubo, balde m

pain [peɪn] n dolor m; **to be in ~** sufrir; **to take ~s to do sth** tomarse grandes molestias en hacer algo; **~ed** adj

(expression) afligido; **~ful** adj doloroso; (difficult) penoso; (disagreeable) desagradable; **~fully** adv (fig: very) terriblemente; **~killer** n analgésico; **~less** adj que no causa dolor; **~staking** ['peɪnzteɪkɪŋ] adj (person) concienzudo, esmerado

paint [peɪnt] n pintura ♦ vt pintar; **to ~ the door blue** pintar la puerta de azul; **~brush** n (artist's) pincel m; (decorator's) brocha; **~er** n pintor(a) m/f; **~ing** n pintura; **~work** n pintura

pair [pɛə*] n (of shoes, gloves etc) par m; (of people) pareja; **a ~ of scissors** unas tijeras; **a ~ of trousers** unos pantalones, un pantalón

pajamas [pə'dʒɑːməz] (US) npl pijama m

Pakistan [pɑːkɪ'stɑːn] n Paquistán m; **~i** adj, n paquistaní m/f

pal [pæl] (inf) n compinche m/f, compañero/a

palace ['pæləs] n palacio

palatable ['pælɪtəbl] adj sabroso

palate ['pælɪt] n paladar m

pale [peɪl] adj (gen) pálido; (colour) claro ♦ n: **to be beyond the ~** pasarse de la raya

Palestine ['pælɪstaɪn] n Palestina; **Palestinian** [-'tɪnɪən] adj, n palestino/a m/f

palette ['pælɪt] n paleta

pall [pɔːl] vi perder el sabor

pallet ['pælɪt] n (for goods) pallet m

pallid ['pælɪd] adj pálido

palm [pɑːm] n (ANAT) palma; (also: ~ **tree**) palmera, palma ♦ vt: **to ~ sth off on sb** (inf) encajar algo a uno; **P~ Sunday** n Domingo de Ramos

paltry ['pɔːltrɪ] adj irrisorio

pamper ['pæmpə*] vt mimar

pamphlet ['pæmflət] n folleto

pan [pæn] n (also: **sauce~**) cacerola, cazuela, olla; (also: **frying ~**) sartén f

Panama ['pænəmɑː] n Panamá m; **the ~ Canal** el Canal de Panamá

pancake ['pænkeɪk] n crepe f

panda ['pændə] n panda m; ~ **car** (BRIT) n

coche *m* Z (*SP*)

pandemonium [pændɪˈməʊnɪəm] *n* jaleo

pander [ˈpændəʳ] *vi*: **to ~ to** complacer a

pane [peɪn] *n* cristal *m*

panel [ˈpænl] *n* (*of wood etc*) panel *m*; (*RADIO, TV*) panel *m* de invitados; **~ling** (*US* **~ing**) *n* paneles *mpl*

pang [pæŋ] *n*: **a ~ of regret** (una punzada de) remordimiento; **hunger ~s** dolores *mpl* del hambre

panic [ˈpænɪk] *n* (terror *m*) pánico ♦ *vi* dejarse llevar por el pánico; **~ky** *adj* (*person*) asustadizo; **~-stricken** *adj* preso de pánico

pansy [ˈpænzɪ] *n* (*BOT*) pensamiento; (*inf: pej*) maricón *m*

pant [pænt] *vi* jadear

panther [ˈpænθəʳ] *n* pantera

panties [ˈpæntɪz] *npl* bragas *fpl*, pantis *mpl*

pantihose [ˈpæntɪhəʊz] (*US*) *n* pantimedias *fpl*

pantomime [ˈpæntəmaɪm] (*BRIT*) *n* revista musical representada en Navidad, basada en cuentos de hadas

---

pantomime

🛈 En época navideña se ponen en escena en los teatros británicos las llamadas **pantomimes**, que son versiones libres de cuentos tradicionales como Aladino o El gato con botas. En ella nunca faltan personajes como la dama ("dame"), papel que siempre interpreta un actor, el protagonista joven ("principal boy"), normalmente interpretado por una actriz, y el malvado ("villain"). Es un espectáculo familiar en el que se anima al público a participar y aunque va dirigido principalmente a los niños, cuenta con grandes dosis de humor para adultos.

---

pantry [ˈpæntrɪ] *n* despensa

pants [pænts] *n* (*BRIT: underwear: woman's*) bragas *fpl*; (: *man's*) calzoncillos *mpl*; (*US: trousers*) pantalones *mpl*

paper [ˈpeɪpəʳ] *n* papel *m*; (*also:* **news~**) periódico, diario; (*academic essay*) ensayo; (*exam*) examen *m* ♦ *adj* de papel ♦ *vt* empapelar (*SP*), tapizar (*AM*); **~s** *npl* (*also:* **identity ~s**) papeles *mpl*, documentos *mpl*; **~back** *n* libro en rústica; **~ bag** *n* bolsa de papel; **~ clip** *n* clip *m*; **~ hankie** *n* pañuelo de papel; **~weight** *n* pisapapeles *m inv*; **~work** *n* trabajo administrativo

paprika [ˈpæprɪkə] *n* pimentón *m*

par [pɑːʳ] *n* par *f*; (*GOLF*) par *m*; **to be on a ~ with** estar a la par con

parachute [ˈpærəʃuːt] *n* paracaídas *m inv*

parade [pəˈreɪd] *n* desfile *m* ♦ *vt* (*show off*) hacer alarde de ♦ *vi* desfilar; (*MIL*) pasar revista

paradise [ˈpærədaɪs] *n* paraíso

paradox [ˈpærədɔks] *n* paradoja; **~ically** [-ˈdɔksɪklɪ] *adv* paradójicamente

paraffin [ˈpærəfɪn] (*BRIT*) *n* (*also:* **~ oil**) parafina

paragon [ˈpærəgən] *n* modelo

paragraph [ˈpærəgrɑːf] *n* párrafo

parallel [ˈpærəlɛl] *adj* en paralelo; (*fig*) semejante ♦ *n* (*line*) paralela; (*fig, GEO*) paralelo

paralyse [ˈpærəlaɪz] *vt* paralizar

paralysis [pəˈrælɪsɪs] *n* parálisis *f inv*

paralyze [ˈpærəlaɪz] (*US*) *vt* = **paralyse**

paramount [ˈpærəmaʊnt] *adj*: **of ~ importance** de suma importancia

paranoid [ˈpærənɔɪd] *adj* (*person, feeling*) paranoico

paraphernalia [pærəfəˈneɪlɪə] *n* (*gear*) avíos *mpl*

parasite [ˈpærəsaɪt] *n* parásito/a

parasol [ˈpærəsɔl] *n* sombrilla, quitasol *m*

paratrooper [ˈpærətruːpəʳ] *n* paracaidista *m/f*

parcel [ˈpɑːsl] *n* paquete *m* ♦ *vt* (*also:* **~ up**) empaquetar, embalar

parched [pɑːtʃt] *adj* (*person*) muerto de sed

parchment [ˈpɑːtʃmənt] *n* pergamino

pardon [ˈpɑːdn] *n* (*LAW*) indulto ♦ *vt* perdonar; **~ me!, I beg your ~!** (*I'm sorry!*) ¡perdone usted!; **(I beg your) ~?, ~**

me? (*US*) (*what did you say?*) ¿cómo?
parent ['peərənt] *n* (*mother*) madre *f*;
(*father*) padre *m*; **~s** *npl* padres *mpl*; **~al**
[pə'rentl] *adj* paternal/maternal
parenthesis [pə'renθɪsɪs] (*pl*
parentheses) *n* paréntesis *m inv*
Paris ['pærɪs] *n* París
parish ['pærɪʃ] *n* parroquia
Parisian [pə'rɪzɪən] *adj*, *n* parisiense *m/f*
park [pɑːk] *n* parque *m* ♦ *vt* aparcar,
estacionar ♦ *vi* aparcar, estacionarse
parking ['pɑːkɪŋ] *n* aparcamiento,
estacionamiento; **"no ~"** "prohibido
estacionarse"; **~ lot** (*US*) *n* parking *m*; **~
meter** *n* parquímetro; **~ ticket** *n* multa
de aparcamiento
parliament ['pɑːləmənt] *n* parlamento;
(*Spanish*) Cortes *fpl*; **~ary** [-'mentərɪ] *adj*
parlamentario

Parliament

El Parlamento británico (**Parliament**)
*tiene como sede el palacio de
Westminster, también llamado "Houses of
Parliament" y consta de dos cámaras. La
Cámara de los Comunes ("House of
Commons"), compuesta por 650 diputados
(**Members of Parliament**) elegidos por
sufragio universal en su respectiva
circunscripción electoral (**constituency**),
se reúne 175 días al año y sus sesiones
son moderadas por el Presidente de la
Cámara (**Speaker**). La cámara alta es la
Cámara de los Lores ("House of Lords") y
está formada por miembros que han sido
nombrados por el monarca o que han
heredado su escaño. Su poder es limitado,
aunque actúa como tribunal supremo de
apelación, excepto en Escocia.*

---

parlour ['pɑːlə*] (*US* **parlor**) *n* sala de
recibo, salón *m*, living *m* (*AM*)
parochial [pə'rəʊkɪəl] (*pej*) *adj* de miras
estrechas
parole [pə'rəʊl] *n*: **on ~** libre bajo palabra
parquet ['pɑːkeɪ] *n*: **~ floor(ing)** parquet
m

parrot ['pærət] *n* loro, papagayo
parry ['pærɪ] *vt* parar
parsley ['pɑːslɪ] *n* perejil *m*
parsnip ['pɑːsnɪp] *n* chirivía
parson ['pɑːsn] *n* cura *m*
part [pɑːt] *n* (*gen, MUS*) parte *f*; (*bit*) trozo;
(*of machine*) pieza; (*THEATRE etc*) papel *m*;
(*of serial*) entrega; (*US: in hair*) raya ♦ *adv*
= **partly** ♦ *vt* separar ♦ *vi* (*people*)
separarse; (*crowd*) apartarse; **to take ~ in**
tomar parte *or* participar en; **to take sth
in good ~** tomar algo en buena parte; **to
take sb's ~** defender a uno; **for my ~** por
mi parte; **for the most ~** en su mayor
parte; **to ~ one's hair** hacerse la raya; **~
with** *vt fus* ceder, entregar; (*money*)
pagar; **~ exchange** (*BRIT*) *n*: **in ~
exchange** como parte del pago
partial ['pɑːʃl] *adj* parcial; **to be ~ to** ser
aficionado a
participant [pɑː'tɪsɪpənt] *n* (*in competition*)
concursante *m/f*; (*in campaign etc*)
participante *m/f*
participate [pɑː'tɪsɪpeɪt] *vi*: **to ~ in**
participar en; **participation** [-'peɪʃən] *n*
participación *f*
participle ['pɑːtɪsɪpl] *n* participio
particle ['pɑːtɪkl] *n* partícula; (*of dust*)
grano
particular [pə'tɪkjulə*] *adj* (*special*)
particular; (*concrete*) concreto; (*given*)
determinado; (*fussy*) quisquilloso;
(*demanding*) exigente; **~s** *npl*
(*information*) datos *mpl*; (*details*)
pormenores *mpl*; **in ~** en particular; **~ly**
adv (*in particular*) sobre todo; (*difficult,
good etc*) especialmente
parting ['pɑːtɪŋ] *n* (*act of*) separación *f*;
(*farewell*) despedida; (*BRIT: in hair*) raya
♦ *adj* de despedida
partisan [pɑːtɪ'zæn] *adj* partidista ♦ *n*
partidario/a
partition [pɑː'tɪʃən] *n* (*POL*) división *f*;
(*wall*) tabique *m*
partly ['pɑːtlɪ] *adv* en parte
partner ['pɑːtnə*] *n* (*COMM*) socio/a;
(*SPORT, at dance*) pareja; (*spouse*) cónyuge

m/f; (lover) compañero/a; ~ship n asociación f; (COMM) sociedad f

partridge ['pɑːtrɪdʒ] n perdiz f

part-time adj, adv a tiempo parcial

party ['pɑːtɪ] n (POL) partido; (celebration) fiesta; (group) grupo; (LAW) parte f interesada ♦ cpd (POL) de partido; ~ **dress** n vestido de fiesta

pass [pɑːs] vt (time, object) pasar; (place) pasar por; (overtake) rebasar; (exam) aprobar; (approve) aprobar ♦ vi pasar; (SCOL) aprobar, ser aprobado ♦ n (permit) permiso; (membership card) carnet m; (in mountains) puerto, desfiladero; (SPORT) pase m; (SCOL: also: ~ **mark**): **to get a ~ in** aprobar en; **to ~ sth through sth** pasar algo por algo; **to make a ~ at sb** (inf) hacer proposiciones a uno; ~ **away** vi fallecer; ~ **by** vi pasar ♦ vt (ignore) pasar por alto; ~ **for** vt fus pasar por; ~ **on** vt transmitir; ~ **out** vi desmayarse; ~ **up** vt (opportunity) renunciar a; ~**able** adj (road) transitable; (tolerable) pasable

passage ['pæsɪdʒ] n (also ~**way**) pasillo; (act of passing) tránsito; (fare, in book) pasaje m; (by boat) travesía; (ANAT) tubo

passbook ['pɑːsbʊk] n libreta de banco

passenger ['pæsɪndʒə*] n pasajero/a, viajero/a

passer-by [pɑːsə'baɪ] n transeúnte m/f

passing ['pɑːsɪŋ] adj pasajero; **in** ~ de paso; ~ **place** n (AUT) apartadero

passion ['pæʃən] n pasión f; ~**ate** adj apasionado

passive ['pæsɪv] adj (gen, also LING) pasivo; ~ **smoking** n efectos del tabaco en fumadores pasivos

Passover ['pɑːsəuvə*] n Pascua (de los judíos)

passport ['pɑːspɔːt] n pasaporte m; ~ **control** n control m de pasaporte; ~ **office** n oficina de pasaportes

password ['pɑːswɜːd] n contraseña

past [pɑːst] prep (in front of) por delante de; (further than) más allá de; (later than) después de ♦ adj pasado; (president etc) antiguo ♦ n (time) pasado; (of person)

antecedentes mpl; **he's ~ forty** tiene más de cuarenta años; **ten/quarter ~ eight** las ocho y diez/cuarto; **for the ~ few/3 days** durante los últimos días/últimos 3 días; **to run ~ sb** pasar a uno corriendo

pasta ['pæstə] n pasta

paste [peɪst] n pasta; (glue) engrudo ♦ vt pegar

pasteurized ['pæstəraɪzd] adj pasteurizado

pastille ['pæstl] n pastilla

pastime ['pɑːstaɪm] n pasatiempo

pastry ['peɪstrɪ] n (dough) pasta; (cake) pastel m

pasture ['pɑːstʃə*] n pasto

pasty[1] ['pæstɪ] n empanada

pasty[2] ['peɪstɪ] adj (complexion) pálido

pat [pæt] vt dar una palmadita a; (dog etc) acariciar

patch [pætʃ] n (of material, eye ~) parche m; (mended part) remiendo; (of land) terreno ♦ vt remendar; **(to go through) a bad** ~ (pasar por) una mala racha; ~ **up** vt reparar; (quarrel) hacer las paces en; ~**work** n labor m de retazos; ~**y** adj desigual

pâté ['pæteɪ] n paté m

patent ['peɪtnt] n patente f ♦ vt patentar ♦ adj patente, evidente; ~ **leather** n charol m

paternal [pə'tɜːnl] adj paternal; (relation) paterno

path [pɑːθ] n camino, sendero; (trail, track) pista; (of missile) trayectoria

pathetic [pə'θetɪk] adj patético, lastimoso; (very bad) malísimo

pathological [pæθə'lɔdʒɪkəl] adj patológico

pathway ['pɑːθweɪ] n sendero, vereda

patience ['peɪʃns] n paciencia; (BRIT: CARDS) solitario

patient ['peɪʃnt] n paciente m/f ♦ adj paciente, sufrido

patio ['pætɪəu] n patio

patriot ['peɪtrɪət] n patriota m/f; ~**ic** [pætrɪ'ɔtɪk] adj patriótico

patrol [pə'trəul] n patrulla ♦ vt patrullar por; ~ **car** n coche m patrulla; ~**man**

(US irreg) n policía m

patron ['peɪtrən] n (in shop) cliente m/f; (of charity) patrocinador(a) m/f; **~ of the arts** mecenas m; **~ize** ['pætrənaɪz] vt (shop) ser cliente de; (artist etc) proteger; (look down on) condescender con; **~ saint** n santo/a patrón/ona m/f

patter ['pætə*] n golpeteo; (sales talk) labia ♦ vi (rain) tamborilear

pattern ['pætən] n (SEWING) patrón m; (design) dibujo

pauper ['pɔːpə*] n pobre m/f

pause [pɔːz] n pausa ♦ vi hacer una pausa

pave [peɪv] vt pavimentar; **to ~ the way for** preparar el terreno para

pavement ['peɪvmənt] n (BRIT) acera (SP), vereda (AM)

pavilion [pə'vɪlɪən] n (SPORT) caseta

paving ['peɪvɪŋ] n pavimento, enlosado; **~ stone** n losa

paw [pɔː] n pata

pawn [pɔːn] n (CHESS) peón m; (fig) instrumento ♦ vt empeñar; **~ broker** n prestamista m/f; **~shop** n monte m de piedad

pay [peɪ] (pt, pp **paid**) n (wage etc) sueldo, salario ♦ vt pagar ♦ vi (be profitable) rendir; **to ~ attention (to)** prestar atención (a); **to ~ sb a visit** hacer una visita a uno; **to ~ one's respects to sb** presentar sus respetos a uno; **~ back** vt (money) reembolsar; (person) pagar; **~ for** vt fus pagar; **~ in** vt ingresar; **~ off** vt saldar ♦ vi (scheme, decision) dar resultado; **~able** adj: **~able to** pagadero a; **~ day** n día m de paga; **~ee** n portador(a) m/f; **~ envelope** (US) n = **~ packet**; **~ment** n pago; **monthly ~ment** mensualidad f; **~ packet** (BRIT) n sobre m (de paga); **~ phone** n teléfono público; **~roll** n nómina; **~ slip** n recibo de sueldo; **~ television** n televisión f de pago

PC n abbr = **personal computer**; (BRIT) = **police constable** ♦ adj abbr = **politically correct**

p.c. abbr = **per cent**

pea [piː] n guisante m (SP), chícharo (AM), arveja (AM)

peace [piːs] n paz f; (calm) paz f, tranquilidad f; **~ful** adj (gentle) pacífico; (calm) tranquilo, sosegado

peach [piːtʃ] n melocotón m (SP), durazno (AM)

peacock ['piːkɔk] n pavo real

peak [piːk] n (of mountain) cumbre f, cima; (of cap) visera; (fig) cumbre f; **~ hours** npl, **~ period** n horas fpl punta

peal [piːl] n (of bells) repique m; **~ of laughter** carcajada

peanut ['piːnʌt] n cacahuete m (SP), maní m (AM); **~ butter** manteca de cacahuete or maní

pear [pɛə*] n pera

pearl [pəːl] n perla

peasant ['peznt] n campesino/a

peat [piːt] n turba

pebble ['pɛbl] n guijarro

peck [pɛk] vt (also: **~ at**) picotear ♦ n picotazo; (kiss) besito; **~ing order** n orden m de jerarquía; **~ish** (BRIT: inf) adj: **I feel ~ish** tengo ganas de picar algo

peculiar [pɪ'kjuːlɪə*] adj (odd) extraño, raro; (typical) propio, característico; **~ to** propio de

pedal ['pɛdl] n pedal m ♦ vi pedalear

pedantic [pɪ'dæntɪk] adj pedante

peddler ['pɛdlə*] n: **drug ~** traficante m/f; camello

pedestrian [pɪ'dɛstrɪən] n peatón/ona m/f ♦ adj pedestre; **~ crossing** (BRIT) n paso de peatones; **~ precinct** (BRIT), **~ zone** (US) n zona peatonal

pediatrics [piːdɪ'ætrɪks] (US) n = **paediatrics**

pedigree ['pɛdɪgriː] n genealogía; (of animal) raza, pedigrí m ♦ cpd (animal) de raza, de casta

pee [piː] (inf) vi mear

peek [piːk] vi mirar a hurtadillas

peel [piːl] n piel f; (of orange, lemon) cáscara; (: removed) peladuras fpl ♦ vt pelar ♦ vi (paint etc) desconcharse; (wallpaper) despegarse, desprenderse;

(*skin*) pelar
peep [piːp] *n* (*BRIT: look*) mirada furtiva; (*sound*) pío ♦ *vi* (*BRIT: look*) mirar furtivamente; ~ **out** *vi* salir (un poco); ~**hole** *n* mirilla
peer [pɪə*] *vi*: **to ~ at** esudriñar ♦ *n* (*noble*) par *m*; (*equal*) igual *m*; (*contemporary*) contemporáneo/a; ~**age** *n* nobleza
peeved [piːvd] *adj* enojado
peg [peg] *n* (*for coat etc*) gancho, colgadero; (*BRIT: also*: **clothes ~**) pinza
Pekingese [piːkɪˈniːz] *n* (*dog*) pequinés/esa *m/f*
pelican [ˈpelɪkən] *n* pelícano; ~ **crossing** (*BRIT*) *n* (*AUT*) paso de peatones señalizado
pellet [ˈpelɪt] *n* bolita; (*bullet*) perdigón *m*
pelt [pelt] *vt*: **to ~ sb with sth** arrojarle algo a uno ♦ *vi* (*rain*) llover a cántaros: (*inf: run*) correr ♦ *n* pellejo
pen [pen] *n* (*fountain ~*) pluma; (*ballpoint ~*) bolígrafo; (*for sheep*) redil *m*
penal [ˈpiːnl] *adj* penal; ~**ize** *vt* castigar
penalty [ˈpenltɪ] *n* (*gen*) pena; (*fine*) multa; ~ (**kick**) (*FOOTBALL*) penalty *m*; (*RUGBY*) golpe *m* de castigo
penance [ˈpenəns] *n* penitencia
pence [pens] *npl* of **penny**
pencil [ˈpensl] *n* lápiz *m*, lapicero (*AM*); ~ **case** *n* estuche *m*; ~ **sharpener** *n* sacapuntas *m inv*
pendant [ˈpendnt] *n* pendiente *m*
pending [ˈpendɪŋ] *prep* antes de ♦ *adj* pendiente
pendulum [ˈpendjuləm] *n* péndulo
penetrate [ˈpenɪtreɪt] *vt* penetrar
penfriend [ˈpenfrend] (*BRIT*) *n* amigo/a por carta
penguin [ˈpeŋgwɪn] *n* pingüino
penicillin [penɪˈsɪlɪn] *n* penicilina
peninsula [pəˈnɪnsjulə] *n* península
penis [ˈpiːnɪs] *n* pene *m*
penitentiary [penɪˈtenʃərɪ] (*US*) *n* cárcel *f*, presidio
penknife [ˈpennaɪf] *n* navaja
pen name *n* seudónimo
penniless [ˈpenɪlɪs] *adj* sin dinero

penny [ˈpenɪ] (*pl* **pennies** or (*BRIT*) **pence**) *n* penique *m*; (*US*) centavo
penpal [ˈpenpæl] *n* amigo/a por carta
pension [ˈpenʃən] *n* (*state benefit*) jubilación *f*; (*BRIT*) *n* jubilado/a; ~ **fund** *n* caja or fondo de pensiones
pentagon [ˈpentəgən] *n*: **the P~** (*US: POL*) el Pentágono

---
Pentagon
---

i Se conoce como **Pentagon** al edificio de planta pentagonal que acoge las dependencias del Ministerio de Defensa estadounidense (*"Department of Defense"*) en Arlington, Virginia. En lenguaje periodístico se aplica también a la dirección militar del país.

Pentecost [ˈpentɪkɔst] *n* Pentecostés *m*
penthouse [ˈpenthaus] *n* ático de lujo
pent-up [ˈpentʌp] *adj* reprimido
people [ˈpiːpl] *npl* gente *f*; (*citizens*) pueblo, ciudadanos *mpl*; (*POL*): **the ~** el pueblo ♦ *n* (*nation, race*) pueblo, nación *f*; **several ~ came** vinieron varias personas; ~ **say that ...** dice la gente que ...
pep [pep] (*inf*): ~ **up** *vt* animar
pepper [ˈpepə*] *n* (*spice*) pimienta; (*vegetable*) pimiento ♦ *vt*: **to ~ with** (*fig*) salpicar de; ~**mint** *n* (*sweet*) pastilla de menta
peptalk [ˈpeptɔːk] *n*: **to give sb a ~** darle a uno una inyección de ánimo
per [pəː*] *prep* por; ~ **day/person** por día/persona; ~ **annum** al año; ~ **capita** *adj, adv* per cápita
perceive [pəˈsiːv] *vt* percibir; (*realize*) darse cuenta de
per cent *n* por ciento
percentage [pəˈsentɪdʒ] *n* porcentaje *m*
perception [pəˈsepʃən] *n* percepción *f*; (*insight*) perspicacia; (*opinion etc*) opinión *f*; **perceptive** [-ˈseptɪv] *adj* perspicaz
perch [pəːtʃ] *n* (*fish*) perca; (*for bird*) percha ♦ *vi*: **to ~ (on**) (*bird*) posarse (en); (*person*) encaramarse (en)

percolator ['pɜːkəleɪtə*] n (also: **coffee ~**) cafetera de filtro

perennial [pə'renɪəl] adj perenne

perfect [adj, n 'pɜːfɪkt, vb pə'fekt] adj perfecto ♦ n (also: **~ tense**) perfecto ♦ vt perfeccionar; **~ly** ['pɜːfɪktlɪ] adv perfectamente

perforate ['pɜːfəreɪt] vt perforar

perform [pə'fɔːm] vt (carry out) realizar, llevar a cabo; (THEATRE) representar; (piece of music) interpretar ♦ vi (well, badly) funcionar; **~ance** n (of a play) representación f; (of actor, athlete etc) actuación f; (of car, engine, company) rendimiento; (of economy) resultados mpl; **~er** n (actor) actor m, actriz f

perfume ['pɜːfjuːm] n perfume m

perhaps [pə'hæps] adv quizá(s), tal vez

peril ['perɪl] n peligro, riesgo

perimeter [pə'rɪmɪtə*] n perímetro

period ['pɪərɪəd] n período; (SCOL) clase f; (full stop) punto; (MED) regla ♦ adj (costume, furniture) de época; **~ic(al)** [-'ɒdɪk(l)] adj periódico; **~ical** [-'ɒdɪkl] n periódico; **~ically** [-'ɒdɪklɪ] adv de vez en cuando, cada cierto tiempo

peripheral [pə'rɪfərəl] adj periférico ♦ n (COMPUT) periférico, unidad f periférica

perish ['perɪʃ] vi perecer; (decay) echarse a perder; **~able** adj perecedero

perjury ['pɜːdʒərɪ] n (LAW) perjurio

perk [pɜːk] n extra m; **~ up** vi (cheer up) animarse

perm [pɜːm] n permanente f

permanent ['pɜːmənənt] adj permanente

permeate ['pɜːmɪeɪt] vi penetrar, trascender ♦ vt penetrar, trascender a

permissible [pə'mɪsɪbl] adj permisible, lícito

permission [pə'mɪʃən] n permiso

permissive [pə'mɪsɪv] adj permisivo

permit [n 'pɜːmɪt, vt pə'mɪt] n permiso, licencia ♦ vt permitir

perplex [pə'pleks] vt dejar perplejo

persecute ['pɜːsɪkjuːt] vt perseguir

persevere [pɜːsɪ'vɪə*] vi persistir

Persian ['pɜːʃən] adj, n persa m/f; **the ~ Gulf** el Golfo Pérsico

persist [pə'sɪst] vi: **to ~ (in doing sth)** persistir (en hacer algo); **~ence** n empeño; **~ent** adj persistente; (determined) porfiado

person ['pɜːsn] n persona; **in ~** en persona; **~al** adj personal; individual; (visit) en persona; **~al assistant** n ayudante m/f personal; **~al column** n anuncios mpl personales; **~al computer** n ordenador m personal; **~ality** [-'nælɪtɪ] n personalidad f; **~ally** adv personalmente; (in person) en persona; **to take sth ~ally** tomarse algo a mal; **~al organizer** n agenda; **~al stereo** n Walkman ® m; **~ify** [-'sɒnɪfaɪ] vt encarnar

personnel [pɜːsə'nel] n personal m

perspective [pə'spektɪv] n perspectiva

Perspex ® ['pɜːspeks] n plexiglás ® m

perspiration [pɜːspɪ'reɪʃən] n transpiración f

persuade [pə'sweɪd] vt: **to ~ sb to do sth** persuadir a uno para que haga algo

Peru [pə'ruː] n el Perú; **Peruvian** adj, n peruano/a m/f

perverse [pə'vɜːs] adj perverso; (wayward) travieso

pervert [n 'pɜːvɜːt, vb pə'vɜːt] n pervertido/a ♦ vt pervertir; (truth, sb's words) tergiversar

pessimist ['pesɪmɪst] n pesimista m/f; **~ic** [-'mɪstɪk] adj pesimista

pest [pest] n (insect) insecto nocivo; (fig) lata, molestia

pester ['pestə*] vt molestar, acosar

pesticide ['pestɪsaɪd] n pesticida m

pet [pet] n animal m doméstico ♦ cpd favorito ♦ vt acariciar; **teacher's ~** favorito/a (del profesor); **~ hate** manía

petal ['petl] n pétalo

peter ['piːtə*]: **to ~ out** vi agotarse, acabarse

petite [pə'tiːt] adj chiquita

petition [pə'tɪʃən] n petición f

petrified ['petrɪfaɪd] adj horrorizado

petrol ['petrəl] n (BRIT) gasolina; **two/four-star ~** gasolina normal/súper; **~ can**

n bidón *m* de gasolina

petroleum [pəˈtrəʊlɪəm] *n* petróleo

petrol: ~ **pump** (BRIT) *n* (in garage) surtidor *m* de gasolina; ~ **station** (BRIT) *n* gasolinera; ~ **tank** (BRIT) *n* depósito (de gasolina)

petticoat [ˈpetɪkəʊt] *n* enaguas *fpl*

petty [ˈpetɪ] *adj* (mean) mezquino; (unimportant) insignificante; ~ **cash** *n* dinero para gastos menores; ~ **officer** *n* contramaestre *m*

petulant [ˈpetjulənt] *adj* malhumorado

pew [pju:] *n* banco

pewter [ˈpjuːtə*] *n* peltre *m*

phantom [ˈfæntəm] *n* fantasma *m*

pharmacist [ˈfɑːməsɪst] *n* farmacéutico/a

pharmacy [ˈfɑːməsɪ] *n* farmacia

phase [feɪz] *n* fase *f* ♦ *vt*: **to ~ sth in/out** introducir/retirar algo por etapas

Ph.D. *abbr* = **Doctor of Philosophy**

pheasant [ˈfeznt] *n* faisán *m*

phenomenon [fəˈnɔmɪnən] (*pl* **phenomena**) *n* fenómeno

philanthropist [fɪˈlænθrəpɪst] *n* filántropo/a

Philippines [ˈfɪlɪpiːnz] *npl*: **the ~** las Filipinas

philosopher [fɪˈlɔsəfə*] *n* filósofo/a

philosophy [fɪˈlɔsəfɪ] *n* filosofía

phobia [ˈfəʊbjə] *n* fobia

phone [fəʊn] *n* teléfono ♦ *vt* telefonear, llamar por teléfono; **to be on the ~** tener teléfono; (be calling) estar hablando por teléfono; ~ **back** *vt*, *vi* volver a llamar; ~ **up** *vt*, *vi* llamar por teléfono; ~ **book** *n* guía telefónica; ~ **booth** *n* cabina telefónica; ~ **box** (BRIT) *n* = ~ **booth**; ~ **call** *n* llamada (telefónica); ~**card** *n* teletarjeta; ~**-in** (BRIT) *n* (RADIO, TV) programa *m* de participación (telefónica)

phonetics [fəˈnetɪks] *n* fonética

phoney [ˈfəʊnɪ] *adj* falso

photo [ˈfəʊtəʊ] *n* foto *f*; ~**copier** *n* fotocopiadora; ~**copy** *n* fotocopia ♦ *vt* fotocopiar

photograph [ˈfəʊtəgrɑːf] *n* fotografía ♦ *vt* fotografiar; ~**er** [fəˈtɔgrəfə*] *n* fotógrafo;

~**y** [fəˈtɔgrəfɪ] *n* fotografía

phrase [freɪz] *n* frase *f* ♦ *vt* expresar; ~ **book** *n* libro de frases

physical [ˈfɪzɪkl] *adj* físico; ~ **education** *n* educación *f* física; ~**ly** *adv* físicamente

physician [fɪˈzɪʃən] *n* médico/a

physicist [ˈfɪzɪsɪst] *n* físico/a

physics [ˈfɪzɪks] *n* física

physiotherapy [fɪzɪəʊˈθerəpɪ] *n* fisioterapia

physique [fɪˈziːk] *n* físico

pianist [ˈpiːənɪst] *n* pianista *m/f*

piano [pɪˈænəʊ] *n* piano

pick [pɪk] *n* (tool: also: ~~**axe**) pico, piqueta ♦ *vt* (select) elegir, escoger; (gather) coger (SP), recoger; (remove, take out) sacar, quitar; (lock) abrir con ganzúa; **take your ~** escoja lo que quiera; **the ~ of** lo mejor de; **to ~ one's nose/teeth** hurgarse las narices/limpiarse los dientes; **to ~ a quarrel with sb** meterse con alguien; ~ **at** *vt fus*: **to ~ at one's food** comer con poco apetito; ~ **on** *vt fus* (person) meterse con; ~ **out** *vt* escoger; (distinguish) identificar; ~ **up** *vi* (improve: sales) ir mejor; (: patient) reponerse; (: FINANCE) recobrarse ♦ *vt* recoger; (learn) aprender; (POLICE: arrest) detener; (person: for sex) ligar; (RADIO) captar; **to ~ up speed** acelerarse; **to ~ o.s. up** levantarse

picket [ˈpɪkɪt] *n* piquete *m* ♦ *vt* piquetear

pickle [ˈpɪkl] *n* (also: ~**s**: as condiment) escabeche *m*; (fig: mess) apuro ♦ *vt* encurtir

pickpocket [ˈpɪkpɔkɪt] *n* carterista *m/f*

pickup [ˈpɪkʌp] *n* (small truck) furgoneta

picnic [ˈpɪknɪk] *n* merienda ♦ *vi* ir de merienda; ~ **area** *n* zona de picnic; (AUT) área de descanso

picture [ˈpɪktʃə*] *n* cuadro; (painting) pintura; (photograph) fotografía; (TV) imagen *f*; (film) película; (fig: description) descripción *f*; (: situation) situación *f* ♦ *vt* (imagine) imaginar; ~**s** *npl*: **the ~s** (BRIT) el cine; ~ **book** *n* libro de dibujos

picturesque [pɪktʃəˈresk] *adj* pintoresco

pie [pai] *n* pastel *m*; (*open*) tarta; (*small: of meat*) empanada

piece [pi:s] *n* pedazo, trozo; (*of cake*) trozo; (*item*): **a ~ of clothing/furniture/advice** una prenda (de vestir)/un mueble/un consejo ♦ *vt*: **to ~ together** juntar; (*TECH*) armar; **to take to ~s** desmontar; **~meal** *adv* poco a poco; **~work** *n* trabajo a destajo

pie chart *n* gráfico de sectores *or* tarta

pier [pɪə*] *n* muelle *m*, embarcadero

pierce [pɪəs] *vt* perforar

piercing [ˈpɪəsɪŋ] *adj* penetrante

pig [pɪg] *n* cerdo (*SP*), puerco (*SP*), chancho (*AM*); (*pej: unkind person*) asqueroso; (: *greedy person*) glotón/ona *m/f*

pigeon [ˈpɪdʒən] *n* paloma; (*as food*) pichón *m*; **~hole** *n* casilla

piggy bank [ˈpɪgɪ-] *n* hucha (*en forma de cerdito*)

pig: **~headed** [ˈpɪgˈhedɪd] *adj* terco, testarudo; **~let** [ˈpɪglɪt] *n* cochinillo; **~skin** *n* piel *f* de cerdo; **~sty** [ˈpɪgstaɪ] *n* pocilga; **~tail** *n* (*girl's*) trenza; (*Chinese, TAUR*) coleta

pike [paɪk] *n* (*fish*) lucio

pilchard [ˈpɪltʃəd] *n* sardina

pile [paɪl] *n* montón *m*; (*of carpet, cloth*) pelo ♦ *vt* (*also:* **~ up**) amontonar; (*fig*) acumular ♦ *vi* (*also:* **~ up**) amontonarse; acumularse; **~ into** *vt fus* (*car*) meterse en; **~s** [paɪlz] *npl* (*MED*) almorranas *fpl*, hemorroides *mpl*; **~-up** *n* (*AUT*) accidente *m* múltiple

pilfering [ˈpɪlfərɪŋ] *n* ratería

pilgrim [ˈpɪlgrɪm] *n* peregrino/a; **~age** *n* peregrinación *f*, romería

pill [pɪl] *n* píldora; **the ~** la píldora

pillage [ˈpɪlɪdʒ] *vt* pillar, saquear

pillar [ˈpɪlə*] *n* pilar *m*; **~ box** (*BRIT*) *n* buzón *m*

pillion [ˈpɪljən] *n* (*of motorcycle*) asiento trasero

pillow [ˈpɪləu] *n* almohada; **~case** *n* funda

pilot [ˈpaɪlət] *n* piloto ♦ *cpd* (*scheme etc*) piloto ♦ *vt* pilotar; **~ light** *n* piloto

pimp [pɪmp] *n* chulo (*SP*), cafiche *m* (*AM*)

pimple [ˈpɪmpl] *n* grano

PIN *n abbr* (= *personal identification number*) número personal

pin [pɪn] *n* alfiler *m* ♦ *vt* prender (con alfiler); **~s and needles** hormigueo; **to ~ sb down** (*fig*) hacer que uno concrete; **to ~ sth on sb** (*fig*) colgarle a uno el sambenito de algo

pinafore [ˈpɪnəfɔː*] *n* delantal *m*; **~ dress** (*BRIT*) *n* mandil *m*

pinball [ˈpɪnbɔːl] *n* mesa americana

pincers [ˈpɪnsəz] *npl* pinzas *fpl*, tenazas *fpl*

pinch [pɪntʃ] *n* (*of salt etc*) pizca ♦ *vt* pellizcar; (*inf: steal*) birlar; **at a ~** en caso de apuro

pincushion [ˈpɪnkuʃən] *n* acerico

pine [paɪn] *n* (*also:* **~ tree, wood**) pino ♦ *vi*: **to ~ for** suspirar por; **~ away** *vi* morirse de pena

pineapple [ˈpaɪnæpl] *n* piña, ananás *m*

ping [pɪŋ] *n* (*noise*) sonido agudo; **~-pong** ® *n* pingpong ® *m*

pink [pɪŋk] *adj* rosado, (color de) rosa ♦ *n* (*colour*) rosa; (*BOT*) clavel *m*, clavellina

pinpoint [ˈpɪnpɔɪnt] *vt* precisar

pint [paɪnt] *n* pinta (*BRIT = 568cc; US = 473cc*); (*BRIT: inf: of beer*) pinta de cerveza, ≈ jarra (*SP*)

pin-up *n* fotografía erótica

pioneer [paɪəˈnɪə*] *n* pionero/a

pious [ˈpaɪəs] *adj* piadoso, devoto

pip [pɪp] *n* (*seed*) pepita; **the ~s** (*BRIT*) la señal

pipe [paɪp] *n* tubo, caño; (*for smoking*) pipa ♦ *vt* conducir en cañerías; **~s** *npl* (*gen*) cañería; (*also:* **bag~s**) gaita; **~ cleaner** *n* limpiapipas *m inv*; **~ dream** *n* sueño imposible; **~line** *n* (*for oil*) oleoducto; (*for gas*) gasoducto; **~r** *n* gaitero/a

piping [ˈpaɪpɪŋ] *adv*: **to be ~ hot** estar que quema

piquant [ˈpiːkənt] *adj* picante; (*fig*) agudo

pique [piːk] *n* pique *m*, resentimiento

pirate [ˈpaɪərət] *n* pirata *m/f* ♦ *vt* (*cassette,*

book) piratear; ~ **radio** (*BRIT*) *n* emisora pirata

Pisces ['paɪsiːz] *n* Piscis *m*

piss [pɪs] (*inf!*) *vi* mear; **~ed** (*inf!*) *adj* (*drunk*) borracho

pistol ['pɪstl] *n* pistola

piston ['pɪstən] *n* pistón *m*, émbolo

pit [pɪt] *n* hoyo; (*also:* **coal ~**) mina; (*in garage*) foso de inspección; (*also:* **orchestra ~**) platea ♦ *vt:* **to ~ one's wits against sb** medir fuerzas con uno; **~s** *npl* (*AUT*) box *m*

pitch [pɪtʃ] *n* (*MUS*) tono; (*BRIT: SPORT*) campo, terreno; (*fig*) punto; (*tar*) brea ♦ *vt* (*throw*) arrojar, lanzar ♦ *vi* (*fall*) caer(se); **to ~ a tent** montar una tienda (de campaña); **~-black** *adj* negro como boca de lobo; **~ed battle** *n* batalla campal

pitfall ['pɪtfɔːl] *n* riesgo

pith [pɪθ] *n* (*of orange*) médula

pithy ['pɪθɪ] *adj* (*fig*) jugoso

pitiful ['pɪtɪful] *adj* (*touching*) lastimoso, conmovedor(a)

pitiless ['pɪtɪlɪs] *adj* despiadado

pittance ['pɪtns] *n* miseria

pity ['pɪtɪ] *n* compasión *f*, piedad *f* ♦ *vt* compadecer(se de); **what a ~!** ¡qué pena!

pizza ['piːtsə] *n* pizza

placard ['plækɑːd] *n* letrero; (*in march etc*) pancarta

placate [plə'keɪt] *vt* apaciguar

place [pleɪs] *n* lugar *m*, sitio; (*seat*) plaza, asiento; (*post*) puesto; (*home*): **at/to his ~** en/a su casa; (*role: in society etc*) papel *m* ♦ *vt* (*object*) poner, colocar; (*identify*) reconocer; **to take ~** tener lugar; **to be ~d** (*in race, exam*) colocarse; **out of ~** (*not suitable*) fuera de lugar; **in the first ~** en primer lugar; **to change ~s with sb** cambiarse de sitio con uno; **~ of birth** lugar *m* de nacimiento

placid ['plæsɪd] *adj* apacible

plague [pleɪg] *n* plaga; (*MED*) peste *f* ♦ *vt* (*fig*) acosar, atormentar

plaice [pleɪs] *n inv* platija

plaid [plæd] *n* (*material*) tartán *m*

plain [pleɪn] *adj* (*unpatterned*) liso; (*clear*) claro, evidente; (*simple*) sencillo; (*not handsome*) poco atractivo ♦ *adv* claramente ♦ *n* llano, llanura; ~ **chocolate** *n* chocolate *m* amargo; **~- clothes** *adj* (*police*) vestido de paisano; **~ly** *adv* claramente

plaintiff ['pleɪntɪf] *n* demandante *m/f*

plait [plæt] *n* trenza

plan [plæn] *n* (*drawing*) plano; (*scheme*) plan *m*, proyecto ♦ *vt* proyectar, planificar ♦ *vi* hacer proyectos; **to ~ to do** pensar hacer

plane [pleɪn] *n* (*AVIAT*) avión *m*; (*MATH, fig*) plano; (*also:* ~ **tree**) plátano; (*tool*) cepillo

planet ['plænɪt] *n* planeta *m*

plank [plæŋk] *n* tabla

planner ['plænə*] *n* planificador(a) *m/f*

planning ['plænɪŋ] *n* planificación *f*; **family ~** planificación familiar; ~ **permission** *n* permiso para realizar obras

plant [plɑːnt] *n* planta; (*machinery*) maquinaria; (*factory*) fábrica ♦ *vt* plantar; (*field*) sembrar; (*bomb*) colocar

plaster ['plɑːstə*] *n* (*for walls*) yeso; (*also:* ~ **of Paris**) yeso mate; (*BRIT: also:* **sticking** ~) tirita (*SP*), esparadrapo, curita (*AM*) ♦ *vt* enyesar; (*cover*) **to ~ with** llenar *or* cubrir de; **~ed** (*inf*) *adj* borracho; **~er** *n* yesero

plastic ['plæstɪk] *n* plástico ♦ *adj* de plástico; ~ **bag** *n* bolsa de plástico

Plasticine ® ['plæstɪsiːn] (*BRIT*) *n* plastilina ®

plastic surgery *n* cirugía plástica

plate [pleɪt] *n* (*dish*) plato; (*metal, in book*) lámina; (*dental* ~) placa de dentadura postiza

plateau ['plætəu] (*pl* ~s *or* ~x) *n* meseta, altiplanicie *f*

plateaux ['plætəuz] *npl of* **plateau**

plate glass *n* vidrio cilindrado

platform ['plætfɔːm] *n* (*RAIL*) andén *m*; (*stage, BRIT: on bus*) plataforma; (*at meeting*) tribuna; (*POL*) programa *m* (electoral)

platinum ['plætɪnəm] *adj, n* platino

latoon [plə'tu:n] n pelotón m

latter ['plætə*] n fuente f

lausible ['plɔ:zɪbl] adj verosímil; (person) convincente

lay [pleɪ] n (THEATRE) obra, comedia ♦ vt (game) jugar; (compete against) jugar contra; (instrument) tocar; (part: in play etc) hacer el papel de; (tape, record) poner ♦ vi jugar; (band) tocar; (tape, record) sonar; **to ~ safe** ir a lo seguro; **~ down** vt quitar importancia a; **~ up** vi (cause trouble to) dar guerra; **~boy** n playboy m; **~er** n jugador(a) m/f; (THEATRE) actor/actriz m/f; (MUS) músico/a; **~ful** adj juguetón/ona; **~ground** n (in school) patio de recreo; (in park) parque m infantil; **~group** n jardín m de niños; **~ing card** n naipe m, carta; **~ing field** n campo de deportes; **~mate** n compañero/a de juego; **~-off** n (SPORT) (partido de) desempate m; **~pen** n corral m; **~thing** n juguete m; **~time** n (SCOL) recreo; **~wright** n dramaturgo/a

lc abbr (= public limited company) ≈ S.A.

lea [pli:] n súplica, petición f; (LAW) alegato, defensa; **~ bargaining** n (LAW) acuerdo entre fiscal y defensor para agilizar los trámites judiciales

lead [pli:d] vt (LAW): **to ~ sb's case** defender a uno; (give as excuse) poner como pretexto ♦ vi (LAW) declararse; (beg): **to ~ with sb** suplicar or rogar a uno

leasant ['plɛznt] adj agradable; **~ries** npl cortesías fpl

lease [pli:z] excl ¡por favor! ♦ vt (give pleasure to) dar gusto a, agradar ♦ vi (think fit): **do as you ~** haz lo que quieras; **~ yourself!** (inf) ¡haz lo que quieras!, ¡como quieras!; **~d** adj (happy) alegre, contento; **~d (with)** satisfecho (de); **~d to meet you** ¡encantado!, ¡tanto gusto!; **pleasing** adj agradable, grato

leasure ['plɛʒə*] n placer m, gusto; **"it's a ~"** "el gusto es mío"

leat [pli:t] n pliegue m

ledge [plɛdʒ] n (promise) promesa, voto

♦ vt prometer

plentiful ['plɛntɪful] adj copioso, abundante

plenty ['plɛntɪ] n: **~ of** mucho(s)/a(s)

pliable ['plaɪəbl] adj flexible

pliers ['plaɪəz] npl alicates mpl, tenazas fpl

plight [plaɪt] n situación f difícil

plimsolls ['plɪmsəlz] (BRIT) npl zapatos mpl de tenis

plinth [plɪnθ] n plinto

plod [plɒd] vi caminar con paso pesado; (fig) trabajar laboriosamente

plonk [plɒŋk] (inf) n (BRIT: wine) vino peleón ♦ vt: **to ~ sth down** dejar caer algo

plot [plɒt] n (scheme) complot m, conjura; (of story, play) argumento; (of land) terreno, lote m (AM) ♦ vt (mark out) trazar; (conspire) tramar, urdir ♦ vi conspirar

plough [plau] (US **plow**) n arado ♦ vt (earth) arar; **to ~ money into** invertir dinero en; **~ through** vt fus (crowd) abrirse paso por la fuerza por; **~man's lunch** (BRIT) n almuerzo de pub a base de pan, queso y encurtidos

pluck [plʌk] vt (fruit) coger (SP), recoger (AM); (musical instrument) puntear; (bird) desplumar; (eyebrows) depilar; **to ~ up courage** hacer de tripas corazón

plug [plʌg] n tapón m; (ELEC) enchufe m, clavija; (AUT: also: **spark(ing) ~**) bujía ♦ vt (hole) tapar; (inf: advertise) dar publicidad a; **~ in** vt (ELEC) enchufar

plum [plʌm] n (fruit) ciruela

plumb [plʌm] vt: **to ~ the depths of** alcanzar los mayores extremos de

plumber ['plʌmə*] n fontanero/a (SP), plomero/a (AM)

plumbing ['plʌmɪŋ] n (trade) fontanería, plomería; (piping) cañería

plummet ['plʌmɪt] vi: **to ~ (down)** caer a plomo

plump [plʌmp] adj rechoncho, rollizo ♦ vi: **to ~ for** (inf: choose) optar por; **~ up** vt mullir

plunder ['plʌndə*] vt pillar, saquear

plunge [plʌndʒ] n zambullida ♦ vt
sumergir, hundir ♦ vi (fall) caer; (dive)
saltar; (person) arrojarse; **to take the ~**
lanzarse; **plunging** adj: **plunging
neckline** escote m pronunciado
pluperfect [pluː'pəːfɪkt] n
pluscuamperfecto
plural ['pluərl] adj plural ♦ n plural m
plus [plʌs] n (also: **~ sign**) signo más
♦ prep más, y, además de; **ten/twenty ~**
más de diez/veinte
plush [plʌʃ] adj lujoso
plutonium [pluː'təunɪəm] n plutonio
ply [plaɪ] vt (a trade) ejercer ♦ vi (ship) ir y
venir ♦ n (of wool, rope) cabo; **to ~ sb
with drink** insistir en ofrecer a uno
muchas copas; **~wood** n madera
contrachapada
P.M. n abbr = **Prime Minister**
p.m. adv abbr (= post meridiem) de la
tarde or noche
pneumatic [njuː'mætɪk] adj neumático; **~
drill** n martillo neumático
pneumonia [njuː'məunɪə] n pulmonía
poach [pəutʃ] vt (cook) escalfar; (steal)
cazar (or pescar) en vedado ♦ vi cazar (or
pescar) en vedado; **~ed** adj escalfado;
~er n cazador(a) m/f furtivo/a
P.O. Box n abbr = **Post Office Box**
pocket ['pɔkɪt] n bolsillo; (fig: small area)
bolsa ♦ vt meter en el bolsillo; (steal)
embolsar; **to be out of ~** (BRIT) salir
perdiendo; **~book** (US) n cartera; **~
calculator** n calculadora de bolsillo; **~
knife** n navaja; **~ money** n asignación f
pod [pɔd] n vaina
podgy ['pɔdʒɪ] adj gordinflón/ona
podiatrist [pɔ'diːətrɪst] (US) n pedicuro/a
poem ['pəuɪm] n poema m
poet ['pəuɪt] n poeta m/f; **~ic** [-'ɛtɪk] adj
poético; **~ry** n poesía
poignant ['pɔɪnjənt] adj conmovedor(a)
point [pɔɪnt] n punto; (tip) punta;
(purpose) fin m, propósito; (use) utilidad f;
(significant part) lo significativo; (moment)
momento; (ELEC) toma (de corriente);
(also: **decimal ~**): **2 ~ 3 (2.3)** dos coma

tres (2,3) ♦ vt señalar; (gun etc): **to ~ sth
at sb** apuntar algo a uno ♦ vi: **to ~ at**
señalar; **~s** npl (AUT) contactos mpl; (RAIL)
agujas fpl; **to be on the ~ of doing sth**
estar a punto de hacer algo; **to make a ~
of** poner empeño en; **to get/miss the ~**
comprender/no comprender; **to come to
the ~** ir al meollo; **there's no ~ (in
doing)** no tiene sentido (hacer); **~ out** vt
señalar; **~ to** vt fus (fig) indicar, señalar;
~-blank adv (say, refuse) sin más hablar;
(also: **at ~-blank range**) a quemarropa;
~ed adj (shape) puntiagudo, afilado;
(remark) intencionado; **~edly** adv
intencionadamente; **~er** n (needle) aguja,
indicador m; **~less** adj sin sentido; **~ of
view** n punto de vista
poise [pɔɪz] n aplomo, elegancia
poison ['pɔɪzn] n veneno ♦ vt envenenar;
~ing n envenenamiento; **~ous** adj
venenoso; (fumes etc) tóxico
poke [pəuk] vt (jab with finger, stick etc)
empujar; (put): **to ~ sth in(to)** introducir
algo en; **~ about** vi fisgonear
poker ['pəukə*] n atizador m; (CARDS)
póker m
poky ['pəukɪ] adj estrecho
Poland ['pəulənd] n Polonia
polar ['pəulə*] adj polar; **~ bear** n oso
polar
Pole [pəul] n polaco/a
pole [pəul] n palo; (fixed) poste m; (GEO)
polo; **~ bean** (US) n ≈ judía verde; **~
vault** n salto con pértiga
police [pə'liːs] n policía ♦ vt vigilar; **~ car**
n coche-patrulla m; **~man** (irreg) n
policía m, guardia m; **~ state** n estado
policial; **~ station** n comisaría;
~woman (irreg) n mujer f policía
policy ['pɔlɪsɪ] n política; (also: **insurance
~**) póliza
polio ['pəulɪəu] n polio f
Polish ['pəulɪʃ] adj polaco ♦ n (LING)
polaco
polish ['pɔlɪʃ] n (for shoes) betún m; (for
floor) cera (de lustrar); (shine) brillo, lustre
m; (fig: refinement) educación f ♦ vt

(shoes) limpiar; (make shiny) pulir, sacar brillo a; ~ **off** vt (food) despachar; ~**ed** adj (fig: person) elegante

polite [pə'laɪt] adj cortés, atento; ~**ness** n cortesía

political [pə'lɪtɪkl] adj político; ~**ly** adv políticamente; ~**ly correct** políticamente correcto

politician [pɒlɪ'tɪʃən] n político/a

politics ['pɒlɪtɪks] n política

poll [pəul] n (election) votación f; (also: **opinion** ~) sondeo, encuesta ♦ vt encuestar; (votes) obtener

pollen ['pɒlən] n polen m

polling day ['pəulɪŋ-] n día m de elecciones

polling station n centro electoral

pollute [pə'luːt] vt contaminar

pollution [pə'luːʃən] n polución f, contaminación f del medio ambiente

polo ['pəuləu] n (sport) polo; ~-**necked** adj de cuello vuelto; ~ **shirt** n polo, niqui m

polyester [pɒlɪ'estə*] n poliéster m

polystyrene [pɒlɪ'staɪriːn] n poliestireno

polythene ['pɒlɪθiːn] (BRIT) n politeno

pomegranate ['pɒmɪgrænɪt] n granada

pomp [pɒmp] n pompa

pompous ['pɒmpəs] adj pomposo

pond [pɒnd] n (natural) charca; (artificial) estanque m

ponder ['pɒndə*] vt meditar

ponderous ['pɒndərəs] adj pesado

pong [pɒŋ] (BRIT: inf) n hedor m

pony ['pəunɪ] n poney m, jaca, potro (AM); ~**tail** n cola de caballo; ~ **trekking** (BRIT) n excursión f a caballo

poodle ['puːdl] n caniche m

pool [puːl] n (natural) charca; (also: **swimming** ~) piscina (SP), alberca (AM); (fig: of light etc) charco; (SPORT) chapolín m ♦ vt juntar; ~**s** npl (football ~s) quinielas fpl; **typing** ~ servicio de mecanografía

poor [puə*] adj pobre; (bad) de mala calidad ♦ npl: **the** ~ los pobres; ~**ly** adj mal, enfermo ♦ adv mal

pop [pɒp] n (sound) ruido seco; (MUS) (música) pop m; (inf: father) papá m; (drink) gaseosa ♦ vt (put quickly) meter (de prisa) ♦ vi reventar; (cork) saltar; ~ **in/out** vi entrar/salir en un momento; ~ **up** vi aparecer inesperadamente; ~**corn** n palomitas fpl

pope [pəup] n papa m

poplar ['pɒplə*] n álamo

popper ['pɒpə*] (BRIT) n automático

poppy ['pɒpɪ] n amapola

Popsicle ® ['pɒpsɪkl] (US) n polo

pop star n estrella del pop

populace ['pɒpjuləs] n pueblo, plebe f

popular ['pɒpjulə*] adj popular

population [pɒpju'leɪʃən] n población f

porcelain ['pɔːslɪn] n porcelana

porch [pɔːtʃ] n pórtico, entrada; (US) veranda

porcupine ['pɔːkjupaɪn] n puerco m espín

pore [pɔː*] n poro ♦ vi: **to** ~ **over** engolfarse en

pork [pɔːk] n carne f de cerdo (SP) or chancho (AM)

pornography [pɔː'nɔgrəfɪ] n pornografía

porpoise ['pɔːpəs] n marsopa

porridge ['pɒrɪdʒ] n gachas fpl de avena

port [pɔːt] n puerto; (NAUT: left side) babor m; (wine) vino de Oporto; ~ **of call** puerto de escala

portable ['pɔːtəbl] adj portátil

porter ['pɔːtə*] n (for luggage) maletero; (doorkeeper) portero/a, conserje m/f

portfolio [pɔːt'fəuləu] n cartera

porthole ['pɔːthəul] n portilla

portion ['pɔːʃən] n porción f; (of food) ración f

portrait ['pɔːtreɪt] n retrato

portray [pɔː'treɪ] vt retratar; (subj: actor) representar

Portugal ['pɔːtjugl] n Portugal m

Portuguese [pɔːtju'giːz] adj portugués/esa ♦ n inv portugués/esa m/f; (LING) portugués m

pose [pəuz] n postura, actitud f ♦ vi (pretend): **to** ~ **as** hacerse pasar por ♦ vt (question) plantear; **to** ~ **for** posar para

posh [pɔʃ] (*inf*) *adj* elegante, de lujo
position [pə'zɪʃən] *n* posición *f*; (*job*) puesto; (*situation*) situación *f* ♦ *vt* colocar
positive ['pɔzɪtɪv] *adj* positivo; (*certain*) seguro; (*definite*) definitivo
possess [pə'zes] *vt* poseer; **~ion** [pə'zeʃən] *n* posesión *f*; **~ions** *npl* (*belongings*) pertenencias *fpl*
possibility [pɔsɪ'bɪlɪti] *n* posibilidad *f*
possible ['pɔsɪbl] *adj* posible; **as big as ~** lo más grande posible; **possibly** *adv* posiblemente; **I cannot possibly come** me es imposible venir
post [pəust] *n* (*BRIT: system*) correos *mpl*; (*BRIT: letters, delivery*) correo; (*job, situation*) puesto; (*pole*) poste *m* ♦ *vt* (*BRIT: send by post*) echar al correo; (*BRIT: appoint*): **to ~ to** enviar a; **~age** *n* porte *m*, franqueo; **~age stamp** *n* sello de correos; **~al** *adj* postal, de correos; **~al order** *n* giro postal; **~box** (*BRIT*) *n* buzón *m*; **~card** *n* tarjeta postal; **~code** (*BRIT*) *n* código postal
postdate [pəust'deɪt] *vt* (*cheque*) poner fecha adelantada a
poster ['pəustə*] *n* cartel *m*
poste restante [pəust'restɔ̃nt] (*BRIT*) *n* lista de correos
postgraduate ['pəust'grædjuət] *n* posgraduado/a
posthumous ['pɔstjuməs] *adj* póstumo
postman ['pəustmən] (*irreg*) *n* cartero
postmark ['pəustmɑːk] *n* matasellos *m inv*
post-mortem [-'mɔːtəm] *n* autopsia
post office *n* (*building*) (oficina de) correos *m*; (*organization*): **the Post Office** Administración *f* General de Correos; **Post Office Box** *n* apartado postal (*SP*), casilla de correos (*AM*)
postpone [pəs'pəun] *vt* aplazar
postscript ['pəustskrɪpt] *n* posdata
posture ['pɔstʃə*] *n* postura, actitud *f*
postwar [pəust'wɔː*] *adj* de la posguerra
posy ['pəuzi] *n* ramillete *m* (de flores)
pot [pɔt] *n* (*for cooking*) olla; (*tea~*) tetera; (*coffee~*) cafetera; (*for flowers*) maceta; (*for jam*) tarro, pote *m*; (*inf: marijuana*)

chocolate *m* ♦ *vt* (*plant*) poner en tiesto; **to go to ~** (*inf*) irse al traste
potato [pə'teɪtəu] (*pl* **~es**) *n* patata (*SP*), papa (*AM*); **~ peeler** *n* pelapatatas *m in*
potent ['pəutnt] *adj* potente, poderoso; (*drink*) fuerte
potential [pə'tenʃl] *adj* potencial, posible ♦ *n* potencial *m*; **~ly** *adv* en potencia
pothole ['pɔthəul] *n* (*in road*) bache *m*; (*BRIT: underground*) gruta; **potholing** (*BRIT*) *n*: **to go potholing** dedicarse a la espeleología
potluck [pɔt'lʌk] *n*: **to take ~** tomar lo que haya
potted ['pɔtɪd] *adj* (*food*) en conserva; (*plant*) en tiesto *or* maceta; (*shortened*) resumido
potter ['pɔtə*] *n* alfarero/a ♦ *vi*: **to ~ around**, **~ about** (*BRIT*) hacer trabajitos; **~y** *n* cerámica; (*factory*) alfarería
potty ['pɔti] *n* orinal *m* de niño
pouch [pautʃ] *n* (*ZOOL*) bolsa; (*for tobacco*) petaca
poultry ['pəultri] *n* aves *fpl* de corral; (*meat*) pollo
pounce [pauns] *vi*: **to ~ on** precipitarse sobre
pound [paund] *n* libra (*weight = 453g or 16oz; money = 100 pence*) ♦ *vt* (*beat*) golpear; (*crush*) machacar ♦ *vi* (*heart*) latir; **~ sterling** *n* libra esterlina
pour [pɔː*] *vt* echar; (*tea etc*) servir ♦ *vi* correr, fluir; **to ~ sb a drink** servirle a un una copa; **~ away** *or* **off** *vt* vaciar, verter; **~ in** *vi* (*people*) entrar en tropel; **out** *vi* salir en tropel ♦ *vt* (*drink*) echar, servir; (*fig*): **to ~ out one's feelings** desahogarse; **~ing** *adj*: **~ing rain** lluvia torrencial
pout [paut] *vi* hacer pucheros
poverty ['pɔvəti] *n* pobreza, miseria; **~-stricken** *adj* necesitado
powder ['paudə*] *n* polvo; (*face ~*) polvos *mpl* ♦ *vt* polvorear; **to ~ one's face** empolvarse la cara; **~ compact** *n* polvera; **~ed milk** *n* leche *f* en polvo; **~ room** *n* aseos *mpl*

power ['pauə*] n poder m; (strength) fuerza; (nation, TECH) potencia; (drive) empuje m; (ELEC) fuerza, energía ♦ vt impulsar; **to be in ~** (POL) estar en el poder; **~ cut** (BRIT) n apagón m; **~ed** adj: **~ed by** impulsado por; **~ failure** n = **~ cut**; **~ful** adj poderoso; (engine) potente; (speech etc) convincente; **~less** adj: **~less (to do)** incapaz (de hacer); **~ point** (BRIT) n enchufe m; **~ station** n central f eléctrica

p.p. abbr (= per procurationem): **~ J. Smith** p.p. (por poder de) J. Smith; (= pages) págs

PR n abbr = **public relations**

practical ['præktɪkl] adj práctico; **~ity** [-'kælɪtɪ] n factibilidad f; **~ joke** n broma pesada; **~ly** adv (almost) casi

practice ['præktɪs] n costumbre f; (exercise) práctica, ejercicio; (training) adiestramiento; (MED: of profession) práctica, ejercicio; (MED, LAW: business) consulta ♦ vt, vi (US) = **practise**; **in ~** (in reality) en la práctica; **out of ~** desentrenado

practise ['præktɪs] (US **practice**) vt (carry out) practicar; (profession) ejercer; (train at) practicar ♦ vi ejercer; (train) practicar; **practising** adj (Christian etc) practicante; (lawyer) en ejercicio

practitioner [præk'tɪʃənə*] n (MED) médico/a

prairie ['prɛərɪ] n pampa

praise [preɪz] n alabanza(s) f(pl), elogio(s) m(pl) ♦ vt alabar, elogiar; **~worthy** adj loable

pram [præm] (BRIT) n cochecito de niño

prank [præŋk] n travesura

prawn [prɔːn] n gamba; **~ cocktail** n cóctel m de gambas

pray [preɪ] vi rezar

prayer [prɛə*] n oración f, rezo; (entreaty) ruego, súplica

preach [priːtʃ] vi (also fig) predicar; **~er** n predicador(a) m/f

precaution [prɪ'kɔːʃən] n precaución f

precede [prɪ'siːd] vt, vi preceder

precedent ['presɪdənt] n precedente m

preceding [prɪ'siːdɪŋ] adj anterior

precinct ['priːsɪŋkt] n recinto; **~s** npl contornos mpl; **pedestrian ~** (BRIT) zona peatonal; **shopping ~** (BRIT) centro comercial

precious ['preʃəs] adj precioso

precipitate [prɪ'sɪpɪteɪt] vt precipitar

precise [prɪ'saɪs] adj preciso, exacto; **~ly** adv precisamente, exactamente

precocious [prɪ'kəʊʃəs] adj precoz

precondition [priːkən'dɪʃən] n condición f previa

predecessor ['priːdɪsesə*] n antecesor(a) m/f

predicament [prɪ'dɪkəmənt] n apuro

predict [prɪ'dɪkt] vt pronosticar; **~able** adj previsible; **~ion** [-'dɪkʃən] n predicción f

predominantly [prɪ'dɔmɪnəntlɪ] adv en su mayoría

pre-empt [priː'emt] vt adelantarse a

preen [priːn] vt: **to ~ itself** (bird) limpiarse (las plumas); **to ~ o.s.** pavonearse

preface ['prefəs] n prefacio

prefect ['priːfekt] (BRIT) n (in school) monitor(a) m/f

prefer [prɪ'fɜː*] vt preferir; **to ~ doing** or **to do** preferir hacer; **~able** ['prefrəbl] adj preferible; **~ably** ['prefrəblɪ] adv de preferencia; **~ence** ['prefrəns] n preferencia; (priority) prioridad f; **~ential** [prefə'renʃəl] adj preferente

prefix ['priːfɪks] n prefijo

pregnancy ['pregnənsɪ] n (of woman) embarazo; (of animal) preñez f

pregnant ['pregnənt] adj (woman) embarazada; (animal) preñada

prehistoric ['priːhɪs'tɔrɪk] adj prehistórico

prejudice ['predʒudɪs] n prejuicio; **~d** adj (person) predispuesto

premarital ['priː'mærɪtl] adj premarital

premature ['prɛmətʃuə*] adj prematuro

premier ['prɛmɪə*] adj primero, principal ♦ n (POL) primer(a) ministro/a

première ['prɛmɪeə*] n estreno

premise ['prɛmɪs] n premisa; **~s** npl (of business etc) local m; **on the ~s** en el lugar mismo

premium ['pri:mɪəm] n premio; (*insurance*) prima; **to be at a ~** ser muy solicitado; **~ bond** (*BRIT*) n bono del estado que participa en una lotería nacional

premonition [premə'nɪʃən] n presentimiento

preoccupied [pri:'ɔkjupaɪd] *adj* ensimismado

prep [prep] n (*SCOL: study*) deberes *mpl*

prepaid [pri:'peɪd] *adj* porte pagado

preparation [prepə'reɪʃən] n preparación f; **~s** *npl* preparativos *mpl*

preparatory [prɪ'pærətərɪ] *adj* preparatorio, preliminar; **~ school** n escuela preparatoria

prepare [prɪ'pɛə*] vt preparar, disponer; (*CULIN*) preparar ♦ vi: **to ~ for** (*action*) prepararse *or* disponerse para; (*event*) hacer preparativos para; **~d to** dispuesto a; **~d for** listo para

preposition [prepə'zɪʃən] n preposición f

preposterous [prɪ'pɔstərəs] *adj* absurdo, ridículo

prep school n = **preparatory school**

prerequisite [pri:'rekwɪzɪt] n requisito

Presbyterian [prezbɪ'tɪərɪən] *adj, n* presbiteriano/a *m/f*

preschool ['pri:'sku:l] *adj* preescolar

prescribe [prɪ'skraɪb] vt (*MED*) recetar

prescription [prɪ'skrɪpʃən] n (*MED*) receta

presence ['prezns] n presencia; **in sb's ~** en presencia de uno; **~ of mind** aplomo

present [*adj, n* 'preznt, *vb* prɪ'zent] *adj* (*in attendance*) presente; (*current*) actual ♦ n (*gift*) regalo; (*actuality*): **the ~** la actualidad, el presente ♦ vt (*introduce, describe*) presentar; (*expound*) exponer; (*give*) presentar, dar, ofrecer; (*THEATRE*) representar; **to give sb a ~** regalar algo a uno; **at ~** actualmente; **~able** [prɪ'zentəbl] *adj*: **to make o.s. ~able** arreglarse; **~ation** [-'teɪʃən] n presentación f; (*of report etc*) exposición f; (*formal ceremony*) entrega de un regalo; **~-day** *adj* actual; **~er** [prɪ'zentə*] n (*RADIO, TV*) locutor(a) *m/f*; **~ly** *adv* (*soon*) dentro de poco;

(*now*) ahora

preservative [prɪ'zə:vətɪv] n conservante *m*

preserve [prɪ'zə:v] vt (*keep safe*) preservar, proteger; (*maintain*) mantener; (*food*) conservar ♦ n (*for game*) coto, vedado; (*often pl: jam*) conserva, confitura

president ['prezɪdənt] n presidente *m/f*; **~ial** [-'denʃl] *adj* presidencial

press [pres] n (*newspapers*): **the P~** la prensa; (*printer's*) imprenta; (*of button*) pulsación f ♦ vt empujar; (*button etc*) apretar; (*clothes: iron*) planchar; (*put pressure on: person*) presionar; (*insist*): **to ~ sth on sb** insistir en que uno acepte algo ♦ vi (*squeeze*) apretar; (*pressurize*): **to ~ for** presionar por; **we are ~ed for time/money** estamos apurados de tiempo/dinero; **~ on** vi avanzar; (*hurry*) apretar el paso; **~ agency** n agencia de prensa; **~ conference** n rueda de prensa; **~ing** *adj* apremiante; **~ stud** (*BRIT*) n botón m de presión; **~-up** (*BRIT*) n plancha

pressure ['preʃə*] n presión f; **to put ~ on sb** presionar a uno; **~ cooker** n olla a presión; **~ gauge** n manómetro; **~ group** n grupo de presión

pressurized *adj* (*container*) a presión

prestige [pres'ti:ʒ] n prestigio

presumably [prɪ'zju:məblɪ] *adv* es de suponer que, cabe presumir que

presume [prɪ'zju:m] vt: **to ~ (that)** presumir (que), suponer (que)

pretence [prɪ'tens] (*US* **pretense**) n fingimiento; **under false ~s** con engaños

pretend [prɪ'tend] vt, vi (*feign*) fingir

pretentious [prɪ'tenʃəs] *adj* presumido; (*ostentatious*) ostentoso, aparatoso

pretext ['pri:tekst] n pretexto

pretty ['prɪtɪ] *adj* bonito, (*SP*), lindo (*AM*) ♦ *adv* bastante

prevail [prɪ'veɪl] vi (*gain mastery*) prevalecer; (*be current*) predominar; **~ing** *adj* (*dominant*) predominante

prevalent ['prevələnt] *adj* (*widespread*) extendido

prevent [prɪˈvent] *vt*: **to ~ sb from doing sth** impedir a uno hacer algo; **to ~ sth from happening** evitar que ocurra algo; **~ative** *adj* = **preventive**; **~ive** *adj* preventivo

preview [ˈpriːvjuː] *n* (*of film*) preestreno

previous [ˈpriːvɪəs] *adj* previo, anterior; **~ly** *adv* antes

prewar [priːˈwɔːˈ] *adj* de antes de la guerra

prey [preɪ] *n* presa ♦ *vi*: **to ~ on** (*feed on*) alimentarse de; **it was ~ing on his mind** le preocupaba, le obsesionaba

price [praɪs] *n* precio ♦ *vt* (*goods*) fijar el precio de; **~less** *adj* que no tiene precio; **~ list** *n* tarifa

prick [prɪk] *n* (*sting*) picadura ♦ *vt* pinchar; (*hurt*) picar; **to ~ up one's ears** aguzar el oído

prickle [ˈprɪkl] *n* (*sensation*) picor *m*; (*BOT*) espina; **prickly** *adj* espinoso; (*fig: person*) enojadizo; **prickly heat** *n* sarpullido causado por exceso de calor

pride [praɪd] *n* orgullo; (*pej*) soberbia ♦ *vt*: **to ~ o.s. on** enorgullecerse de

priest [priːst] *n* sacerdote *m*; **~hood** *n* sacerdocio

prim [prɪm] *adj* (*demure*) remilgado; (*prudish*) gazmoño

primarily [ˈpraɪmərɪlɪ] *adv* ante todo

primary [ˈpraɪmərɪ] *adj* (*first in importance*) principal ♦ *n* (*US: POL*) (elección *f*) primaria; **~ school** (*BRIT*) *n* escuela primaria

prime [praɪm] *adj* primero, principal; (*excellent*) selecto, de primera clase ♦ *n*: **in the ~ of life** en la flor de la vida ♦ *vt* (*wood, fig*) preparar; **~ example** ejemplo típico; **P~ Minister** *n* primer(a) ministro/a

primeval [praɪˈmiːvəl] *adj* primitivo

primitive [ˈprɪmɪtɪv] *adj* primitivo; (*crude*) rudimentario

primrose [ˈprɪmrəʊz] *n* primavera, prímula

Primus (stove) ® [ˈpraɪməs-] (*BRIT*) *n* hornillo de camping

prince [prɪns] *n* príncipe *m*

princess [prɪnˈses] *n* princesa

principal [ˈprɪnsɪpl] *adj* principal, mayor ♦ *n* director(a) *m/f*; **~ity** [-ˈpælɪtɪ] *n* principado

principle [ˈprɪnsɪpl] *n* principio; **in ~** en principio; **on ~** por principio

print [prɪnt] *n* (*foot~*) huella; (*finger~*) huella dactilar; (*letters*) letra de molde; (*fabric*) estampado; (*ART*) grabado; (*PHOT*) impresión *f* ♦ *vt* imprimir; (*cloth*) estampar; (*write in capitals*) escribir en letras de molde; **out of ~** agotado; **~ed matter** *n* impresos *mpl*; **~er** *n* (*person*) impresor(a) *m/f*; (*machine*) impresora; **~ing** *n* (*art*) imprenta; (*act*) impresión *f*; **~out** *n* (*COMPUT*) impresión *f*

prior [ˈpraɪəˈ] *adj* anterior, previo; (*more important*) más importante; **~ to** antes de

priority [praɪˈɒrɪtɪ] *n* prioridad *f*; **to have ~ (over)** tener prioridad (sobre)

prison [ˈprɪzn] *n* cárcel *f*, prisión *f* ♦ *cpd* carcelario; **~er** *n* (*in prison*) preso/a; (*captured person*) prisionero; **~er-of-war** *n* prisionero de guerra

privacy [ˈprɪvəsɪ] *n* intimidad *f*

private [ˈpraɪvɪt] *adj* (*personal*) particular; (*property, industry, discussion etc*) privado; (*person*) reservado; (*place*) tranquilo ♦ *n* soldado raso; **"~"** (*on envelope*) "confidencial"; (*on door*) "prohibido el paso"; **in ~** en privado; **~ enterprise** *n* empresa privada; **~ eye** *n* detective *m/f* privado/a; **~ property** *n* propiedad *f* privada; **~ school** *n* colegio particular

privet [ˈprɪvɪt] *n* alheña

privilege [ˈprɪvɪlɪdʒ] *n* privilegio; (*prerogative*) prerrogativa

privy [ˈprɪvɪ] *adj*: **to be ~ to** estar enterado de

prize [praɪz] *n* premio ♦ *adj* de primera clase ♦ *vt* apreciar, estimar; **~-giving** *n* distribución *f* de premios; **~winner** *n* premiado/a

pro [prəʊ] *n* (*SPORT*) profesional *m/f* ♦ *prep* a favor de; **the ~s and cons** los pros y los contras

probability [prɒbəˈbɪlɪtɪ] *n* probabilidad *f*;

in all ~ con toda probabilidad
probable ['prɔbəbl] *adj* probable
probably ['prɔbəblɪ] *adv* probablemente
probation [prə'beɪʃən] *n*: **on ~** (*employee*) a prueba; (*LAW*) en libertad condicional
probe [prəub] *n* (*MED, SPACE*) sonda; (*enquiry*) encuesta, investigación *f* ♦ *vt* sondar; (*investigate*) investigar
problem ['prɔbləm] *n* problema *m*
procedure [prə'si:dʒə*] *n* procedimiento; (*bureaucratic*) trámites *mpl*
proceed [prə'si:d] *vi* (*do afterwards*): **to ~ to do sth** proceder a hacer algo; (*continue*): **to ~ (with)** continuar *or* seguir (con); **~ings** *npl* acto(s) (*pl*); (*LAW*) proceso; **~s** ['prəusi:dz] *npl* (*money*) ganancias *fpl*, ingresos *mpl*
process ['prəuses] *n* proceso ♦ *vt* tratar, elaborar; **~ing** *n* tratamiento, elaboración *f*; (*PHOT*) revelado
procession [prə'seʃən] *n* desfile *m*; **funeral ~** cortejo fúnebre
pro-choice [prəu'tʃɔɪs] *adj* en favor del derecho a elegir de la madre
proclaim [prə'kleɪm] *vt* anunciar
procrastinate [prəu'kræstɪneɪt] *vi* demorarse
procure [prə'kjuə*] *vt* conseguir
prod [prɔd] *vt* empujar ♦ *n* empujón *m*
prodigy ['prɔdɪdʒɪ] *n* prodigio
produce [*n* 'prɔdju:s, *vb* prə'dju:s] *n* (*AGR*) productos *mpl* agrícolas ♦ *vt* producir; (*play, film, programme*) presentar; **~r** *n* productor(a) *m/f*; (*of film, programme*) director(a) *m/f*; (*of record*) productor(a) *m/f*
product ['prɔdʌkt] *n* producto
production [prə'dʌkʃən] *n* producción *f*; (*THEATRE*) presentación *f*; **~ line** *n* línea de producción
productivity [prɔdʌk'tɪvɪtɪ] *n* productividad *f*
profession [prə'feʃən] *n* profesión *f*; **~al** *adj* profesional ♦ *n* profesional *m/f*; (*skilled person*) perito
professor [prə'fesə*] *n* (*BRIT*) catedrático/a; (*US, Canada*) profesor(a) *m/f*

proficient [prə'fɪʃənt] *adj* experto, hábil
profile ['prəufaɪl] *n* perfil *m*
profit ['prɔfɪt] *n* (*COMM*) ganancia ♦ *vi*: **to ~ by** *or* **from** aprovechar *or* sacar provecho de; **~ability** [-ə'bɪlɪtɪ] *n* rentabilidad *f*; **~able** *adj* (*ECON*) rentable
profound [prə'faund] *adj* profundo
profusely [prə'fju:slɪ] *adv* profusamente
programme ['prəugræm] (*US* **program**) *n* programa *m* ♦ *vt* programar; **~r** (*US* **programer**) *n* programador(a) *m/f*; **programming** (*US* **programing**) *n* programación *f*
progress [*n* 'prəugres, *vi* prə'gres] *n* progreso; (*development*) desarrollo ♦ *vi* progresar, avanzar; **in ~** en curso; **~ive** [-'gresɪv] *adj* progresivo; (*person*) progresista
prohibit [prə'hɪbɪt] *vt* prohibir; **to ~ sb from doing sth** prohibir a uno hacer algo; **~ion** [-'bɪʃn] *n* prohibición *f*; (*US*): **P-ion** Ley *f* Seca
project [*n* 'prɔdʒekt, *vb* prə'dʒekt] *n* proyecto ♦ *vt* proyectar ♦ *vi* (*stick out*) salir, sobresalir; **~ion** [prə'dʒekʃən] *n* proyección *f*; (*overhang*) saliente *m*; **~or** [prə'dʒektə*] *n* proyector *m*
pro-life [prəu'laɪf] *adj* pro-vida
prolong [prə'lɔŋ] *vt* prolongar, extender
prom [prɔm] *n* *abbr* = **promenade**; (*US*: *ball*) baile *m* de gala

---
Prom

🛈 *El ciclo de conciertos de música clásica más conocido de Londres es el llamado* **the Proms** (*promenade concerts*), *que se celebra anualmente en el Royal Albert Hall. Su nombre se debe a que originalmente el público paseaba durante las actuaciones, costumbre que en la actualidad se mantiene de forma simbólica, permitiendo que parte de los asistentes permanezcan de pie. En Estados Unidos se llama* **prom** *a un baile de gala en un centro de educación secundaria o universitaria.*

promenade [prɔmə'nɑːd] *n* (*by sea*) paseo marítimo; **~ concert** (*BRIT*) *n* concierto (en que parte del público permanece de pie)

prominence ['prɔmɪnəns] *n* importancia

prominent ['prɔmɪnənt] *adj* (*standing out*) saliente; (*important*) eminente, importante

promiscuous [prə'mɪskjuəs] *adj* (*sexually*) promiscuo

promise ['prɔmɪs] *n* promesa ♦ *vt, vi* prometer; **promising** *adj* prometedor(a)

promote [prə'məut] *vt* (*employee*) ascender; (*product, pop star*) hacer propaganda por; (*ideas*) fomentar; **~r** *n* (*of event*) promotor(a) *m/f*; (*of cause etc*) impulsor(a) *m/f*; **promotion** [-'məuʃən] *n* (*advertising campaign*) campaña de promoción *f*; (*in rank*) ascenso

prompt [prɔmpt] *adj* rápido ♦ *adv*: **at 6 o'clock ~** a las seis en punto ♦ *n* (*COMPUT*) aviso ♦ *vt* (*urge*) mover, incitar; (*when talking*) instar; (*THEATRE*) apuntar; **to ~ sb to do sth** instar a uno a hacer algo; **~ly** *adv* rápidamente; (*exactly*) puntualmente

prone [prəun] *adj* (*lying*) postrado; **~ to** propenso a

prong [prɔŋ] *n* diente *m*, punta

pronoun ['prəunaun] *n* pronombre *m*

pronounce [prə'nauns] *vt* pronunciar; **~d** *adj* (*marked*) marcado

pronunciation [prənʌnsɪ'eɪʃən] *n* pronunciación *f*

proof [pruːf] *n* prueba ♦ *adj*: **~ against** a prueba de

prop [prɔp] *n* apoyo, (*fig*) sostén *m* ♦ *vt* (*also*: **~ up**) apoyar; (*lean*): **to ~ sth against** apoyar algo contra

propaganda [prɔpə'gændə] *n* propaganda

propel [prə'pel] *vt* impulsar, propulsar; **~ler** *n* hélice *f*

propensity [prə'pensɪtɪ] *n* propensión *f*

proper ['prɔpə*] *adj* (*suited, right*) propio; (*exact*) justo; (*seemly*) correcto, decente; (*authentic*) verdadero; (*referring to place*): **the village ~** el pueblo mismo; **~ly** *adv*

(*adequately*) correctamente; (*decently*) decentemente; **~ noun** *n* nombre *m* propio

property ['prɔpətɪ] *n* propiedad *f*; (*personal*) bienes *mpl* muebles; **~ owner** *n* dueño/a de propiedades

prophecy ['prɔfɪsɪ] *n* profecía

prophesy ['prɔfɪsaɪ] *vt* (*fig*) predecir

prophet ['prɔfɪt] *n* profeta *m*

proportion [prə'pɔːʃən] *n* proporción *f*; (*share*) parte *f*; **~al** *adj*: **~al to** en proporción (con); **~al representation** *n* representación *f* proporcional; **~ate** *adj*: **~ate (to)** en proporción (con)

proposal [prə'pəuzl] *n* (*offer of marriage*) oferta de matrimonio; (*plan*) proyecto

propose [prə'pəuz] *vt* proponer ♦ *vi* declararse; **to ~ to do** tener intención de hacer

proposition [prɔpə'zɪʃən] *n* propuesta

proprietor [prə'praɪətə*] *n* propietario/a, dueño/a

propriety [prə'praɪətɪ] *n* decoro

pro rata [-'rɑːtə] *adv* a prorrateo

prose [prəuz] *n* prosa

prosecute ['prɔsɪkjuːt] *vt* (*LAW*) procesar; **prosecution** [-'kjuːʃən] *n* proceso, causa; (*accusing side*) acusación *f*; **prosecutor** *n* acusador(a) *m/f*; (*also*: **public prosecutor**) fiscal *m*

prospect [*n* 'prɔspekt, *vb* prə'spekt] *n* (*possibility*) posibilidad *f*; (*outlook*) perspectiva ♦ *vi*: **to ~ for** buscar; **~s** *npl* (*for work etc*) perspectivas *fpl*; **~ing** *n* prospección *f*; **~ive** [prə'spektɪv] *adj* futuro

prospectus [prə'spektəs] *n* prospecto

prosper ['prɔspə*] *vi* prosperar; **~ity** [-'sperɪtɪ] *n* prosperidad *f*; **~ous** *adj* próspero

prostitute ['prɔstɪtjuːt] *n* prostituta; (*male*) *hombre que se dedica a la prostitución*

protect [prə'tekt] *vt* proteger; **~ion** [-'tekʃən] *n* protección *f*; **~ive** *adj* protector(a)

protein ['prəutiːn] *n* proteína

protest [*n* 'prəutest, *vb* prə'test] *n* protesta

♦ vi: **to ~ about** or **at/against** protestar
de/contra ♦ vt (insist): **to ~ (that)** insistir
en (que)

Protestant ['prɒtɪstənt] adj, n protestante
m/f

protester [prə'tɛstə*] n manifestante m/f

protracted [prə'træktɪd] adj prolongado

protrude [prə'truːd] vi salir, sobresalir

proud [praud] adj orgulloso; (pej)
soberbio, altanero

prove [pruːv] vt probar; (show) demostrar
♦ vi: **to ~ (to be) correct** resultar
correcto; **to ~ o.s.** probar su valía

proverb ['prɒvɜːb] n refrán m

provide [prə'vaɪd] vt proporcionar, dar; **to
~ sb with sth** proveer a uno de algo; **~d
(that)** conj con tal de que, a condición de
que; **~ for** vt fus (person) mantener a;
(problem etc) tener en cuenta; **providing**
[prə'vaɪdɪŋ] conj: **providing (that)** a
condición de que, con tal de que

province ['prɒvɪns] n provincia; (fig)
esfera; **provincial** [prə'vɪnʃəl] adj
provincial; (pej) provinciano

provision [prə'vɪʒən] n (supplying)
suministro, abastecimiento; (of contract
etc) disposición f; **~s** npl (food)
comestibles mpl; **~al** adj provisional

proviso [prə'vaɪzəu] n condición f,
estipulación f

provocative [prə'vɒkətɪv] adj provocativo

provoke [prə'vəuk] vt (cause) provocar,
incitar; (anger) enojar

prowess ['prauɪs] n destreza

prowl [praul] vi (also: **~ about, ~ around**)
merodear ♦ n: **on the ~** de merodeo;
~er n merodeador(a) m/f

proxy ['prɒksɪ] n: **by ~** por poderes

prudent ['pruːdənt] adj prudente

prune [pruːn] n ciruela pasa ♦ vt podar

pry [praɪ] vi: **to ~ (into)** entrometerse (en)

PS n abbr (= postscript) P.D.

psalm [sɑːm] n salmo

pseudonym ['sjuːdəunɪm] n seudónimo

psyche ['saɪkɪ] n psique f

psychiatric [saɪkɪ'ætrɪk] adj psiquiátrico

psychiatrist [saɪ'kaɪətrɪst] n psiquiatra m/f

psychic ['saɪkɪk] adj (also: **~al**) psíquico

psychoanalyse [saɪkəu'ænəlaɪz] vt
psicoanalizar; **psychoanalysis**
[-ə'nælɪsɪs] n psicoanálisis m inv

psychological [saɪkə'lɒdʒɪkl] adj
psicológico

psychologist [saɪ'kɒlədʒɪst] n psicólogo/a

psychology [saɪ'kɒlədʒɪ] n psicología

PTO abbr (= please turn over) sigue

pub [pʌb] n abbr (= public house) pub m,
bar m

---
pub

ℹ️ Un **pub** es un local público donde se
pueden consumir bebidas alcohólicas.
La estricta regulación sobre la venta de
alcohol prohíbe que se sirva a menores de
18 años y controla las horas de apertura,
aunque éstas son más flexibles desde hace
unos años. El **pub** es, además, un lugar
de encuentro donde se sirven comidas
ligeras o se juega a los dardos o al billar,
entre otras actividades.

---

puberty ['pjuːbətɪ] n pubertad f

public ['pʌblɪk] adj público ♦ n: **the ~** el
público; **in ~** en público; **to make ~** hacer
público; **~ address system** n
megafonía

publican ['pʌblɪkən] n tabernero/a

publication [pʌblɪ'keɪʃən] n publicación f

public: **~ company** n sociedad f
anónima; **~ convenience** (BRIT) n aseos
mpl públicos; (SP), sanitarios mpl (AM); **~
holiday** n día de fiesta (SP), (día) feriado
(AM); **~ house** (BRIT) n bar m, pub m

publicity [pʌb'lɪsɪtɪ] n publicidad f

publicize ['pʌblɪsaɪz] vt publicitar

publicly ['pʌblɪklɪ] adv públicamente, en
público

public: **~ opinion** n opinión f pública; **~
relations** n relaciones fpl públicas; **~
school** n (BRIT) escuela privada; (US)
instituto; **~-spirited** adj que tiene
sentido del deber ciudadano; **~
transport** n transporte m público

publish ['pʌblɪʃ] vt publicar; **~er** n

(*person*) editor(a) *m/f*; (*firm*) editorial *f*;
~**ing** *n* (*industry*) industria del libro
ub lunch *n* almuerzo que se sirve en un pub; **to go for a ~** almorzar o comer en un pub
ucker ['pʌkə*] *vt* (*pleat*) arrugar; (*brow etc*) fruncir
udding ['pudɪŋ] *n* pudín *m*; (*BRIT: dessert*) postre *m*; **black ~** morcilla
uddle ['pʌdl] *n* charco
uff [pʌf] *n* soplo; (*of smoke, air*) bocanada; (*of breathing*) resoplido ♦ *vt*: **to ~ one's pipe** chupar la pipa ♦ *vi* (*pant*) jadear; **~ out** *vt* hinchar; **~ pastry** *n* hojaldre *m*; **~y** *adj* hinchado
ull [pul] *n* (*tug*): **to give sth a ~** dar un tirón a algo ♦ *vt* tirar de; (*press: trigger*) apretar; (*haul*) tirar, arrastrar; (*close: curtain*) echar ♦ *vi* tirar; **to ~ to pieces** hacer pedazos; **to not ~ one's punches** no andarse con bromas; **to ~ one's weight** hacer su parte; **to ~ o.s. together** sobreponerse; **to ~ sb's leg** tomar el pelo a uno; **~ apart** *vt* (*break*) romper; **~ down** *vt* (*building*) derribar; **~ in** *vi* (*car etc*) parar (junto a la acera); (*train*) llegar a la estación; **~ off** *vt* (*deal etc*) cerrar; **~ out** *vi* (*car, train etc*) salir ♦ *vt* sacar, arrancar; **~ over** *vi* (*AUT*) hacerse a un lado; **~ through** *vi* (*MED*) reponerse; **~ up** *vi* (*stop*) parar ♦ *vt* (*raise*) levantar; (*uproot*) arrancar, desarraigar
ulley ['pulɪ] *n* polea
ullover ['puləuvə*] *n* jersey *m*, suéter *m*
ulp [pʌlp] *n* (*of fruit*) pulpa
ulpit ['pulpɪt] *n* púlpito
ulsate [pʌl'seɪt] *vi* pulsar, latir
ulse [pʌls] *n* (*ANAT*) pulso; (*rhythm*) pulsación *f*; (*BOT*) legumbre *f*
ump [pʌmp] *n* bomba; (*shoe*) zapatilla ♦ *vt* sacar con una bomba; **~ up** *vt* inflar
umpkin ['pʌmpkɪn] *n* calabaza
un [pʌn] *n* juego de palabras
unch [pʌntʃ] *n* (*blow*) golpe *m*, puñetazo; (*tool*) punzón *m*; (*drink*) ponche *m* ♦ *vt* (*hit*): **to ~ sb/sth** dar un puñetazo or golpear a uno/algo; **~line** *n* palabras que

rematan un chiste; **~-up** (*BRIT: inf*) *n* riña
punctual ['pʌŋktjuəl] *adj* puntual
punctuation [pʌŋktju'eɪʃən] *n* puntuación *f*
puncture ['pʌŋktʃə*] (*BRIT*) *n* pinchazo ♦ *vt* pinchar
pungent ['pʌndʒənt] *adj* acre
punish ['pʌnɪʃ] *vt* castigar; **~ment** *n* castigo
punk [pʌŋk] *n* (*also*: **~ rocker**) punki *m/f*; (*also*: **~ rock**) música punk; (*US: inf: hoodlum*) rufián *m*
punt [pʌnt] *n* (*boat*) batea
punter ['pʌntə*] (*BRIT*) *n* (*gambler*) jugador(a) *m/f*; (*inf*) cliente *m/f*
puny ['pju:nɪ] *adj* débil
pup [pʌp] *n* cachorro
pupil ['pju:pl] *n* alumno/a; (*of eye*) pupila
puppet ['pʌpɪt] *n* títere *m*
puppy ['pʌpɪ] *n* cachorro, perrito
purchase ['pə:tʃɪs] *n* compra ♦ *vt* comprar; **~r** *n* comprador(a) *m/f*
pure [pjuə*] *adj* puro
purée ['pjuəreɪ] *n* puré *m*
purely ['pjuəlɪ] *adv* puramente
purge [pə:dʒ] *n* (*MED, POL*) purga ♦ *vt* purgar
purify ['pjuərɪfaɪ] *vt* purificar, depurar
purple ['pə:pl] *adj* purpúreo; morado
purpose ['pə:pəs] *n* propósito; **on ~** a propósito, adrede; **~ful** *adj* resuelto, determinado
purr [pə:*] *vi* ronronear
purse [pə:s] *n* monedero; (*US*) bolsa (*SP*), cartera (*AM*) ♦ *vt* fruncir
pursue [pə'sju:] *vt* seguir; **~r** *n* perseguidor(a) *m/f*
pursuit [pə'sju:t] *n* (*chase*) caza; (*occupation*) actividad *f*
push [puʃ] *n* empuje *m*, empujón *m*; (*of button*) presión *f*; (*drive*) empuje *m* ♦ *vt* empujar; (*button*) apretar; (*promote*) promover ♦ *vi* empujar; (*demand*): **to ~ for** luchar por; **~ aside** *vt* apartar con la mano; **~ off** (*inf*) *vi* largarse; **~ on** *vi* seguir adelante; **~ through** *vi* (*crowd*) abrirse paso a empujones ♦ *vt* (*measure*)

despachar; **~ up** vt (total, prices) hacer subir; **~chair** (BRIT) n sillita de ruedas; **~er** n (drug ~er) traficante m/f de drogas; **~over** (inf) n: **it's a ~over** está tirado; **~-up** (US) n plancha; **~y** (pej) adj agresivo

puss [pus] (inf) n minino

pussy(-cat) ['pusɪ-] (inf) n = **puss**

put [put] (pt, pp **put**) vt (place) poner, colocar; (~ into) meter; (say) expresar; (a question) hacer; (estimate) estimar; **~ about** or **around** vt (rumour) diseminar; **~ across** vt (ideas etc) comunicar; **~ away** vt (store) guardar; **~ back** vt (replace) devolver a su lugar; (postpone) aplazar; **~ by** vt (money) guardar; **~ down** vt (on ground) poner en el suelo; (animal) sacrificar; (in writing) apuntar; (revolt etc) sofocar; (attribute): **to ~ sth down to** atribuir algo a; **~ forward** vt (ideas) presentar, proponer; **~ in** vt (complaint) presentar; (time) dedicar; **~ off** vt (postpone) aplazar; (discourage) desanimar; **~ on** vt ponerse; (light etc) encender; (play etc) presentar; (gain): **to ~ on weight** engordar; (brake) echar; (record, kettle etc) poner; (assume) adoptar; **~ out** vt (fire, light) apagar; (rubbish etc) sacar; (cat etc) echar; (one's hand) alargar; (inf: person): **to be ~ out** alterarse; **~ through** vt (TEL) poner; (plan etc) hacer aprobar; **~ up** vt (raise) levantar, alzar; (hang) colgar; (build) construir; (increase) aumentar; (accommodate) alojar; **~ up with** vt fus aguantar

putt [pʌt] n putt m, golpe m corto; **~ing green** n green m; minigolf m

putty ['pʌtɪ] n masilla

put-up ['putʌp] adj: **~ job** (BRIT) amaño

puzzle ['pʌzl] n rompecabezas m inv; (also: **crossword ~**) crucigrama m; (mystery) misterio ♦ vt dejar perplejo, confundir ♦ vi: **to ~ over sth** devanarse los sesos con algo; **puzzling** adj misterioso, extraño

pyjamas [pɪ'dʒɑːməz] (BRIT) npl pijama m

pylon ['paɪlən] n torre f de conducción eléctrica

pyramid ['pɪrəmɪd] n pirámide f

Pyrenees [pɪrə'niːz] npl: **the ~** los Pirineos

python ['paɪθən] n pitón m

Q, q

quack [kwæk] n graznido; (pej: doctor) curandero/a

quad [kwɔd] n abbr = **quadrangle**; **quadruplet**

quadrangle ['kwɔdræŋgl] n patio

quadruple [kwɔ'drupl] vt, vi cuadruplicar

quadruplets [kwɔ'druːplɪts] npl cuatrillizos/as

quail [kweɪl] n codorniz f ♦ vi: **to ~ at** or **before** amedrentarse ante

quaint [kweɪnt] adj extraño; (picturesque) pintoresco

quake [kweɪk] vi temblar ♦ n abbr = **earthquake**

Quaker ['kweɪkə*] n cuáquero/a

qualification [kwɔlɪfɪ'keɪʃən] n (ability) capacidad f; (often pl: diploma etc) título; (reservation) salvedad f

qualified ['kwɔlɪfaɪd] adj capacitado; (professionally) titulado; (limited) limitado

qualify ['kwɔlɪfaɪ] vt (make competent) capacitar; (modify) modificar ♦ vi (in competition): **to ~ (for)** calificarse (para); (pass examination(s)): **to ~ (as)** calificarse (de), graduarse (en); (be eligible): **to ~ (for)** reunir los requisitos (para)

quality ['kwɔlɪtɪ] n calidad f; (of person) cualidad f; **~ time** n tiempo dedicado a la familia y a los amigos

---

quality press

---

i La expresión **quality press** se refiere a los periódicos que dan un tratamiento serio de las noticias, ofreciendo información detallada sobre un amplio espectro de temas y un análisis en profundidad de la actualidad. Por su tamaño, considerablemente mayor que el *de los periódicos sensacionalistas, se les conoce también como "broadsheets".*

qualm [kwɑːm] *n* escrúpulo

quandary ['kwɒndrɪ] *n*: **to be in a ~** tener dudas

quantity ['kwɒntɪtɪ] *n* cantidad *f*; **in ~** en grandes cantidades; **~ surveyor** *n* aparejador(a) *m/f*

quarantine ['kwɒrntiːn] *n* cuarentena

quarrel ['kwɒrl] *n* riña, pelea ♦ *vi* reñir, pelearse

quarry ['kwɒrɪ] *n* cantera

quart [kwɔːt] *n* ≈ litro

quarter ['kwɔːtə*] *n* cuarto, cuarta parte *f*; (*US: coin*) moneda de 25 centavos; (*of year*) trimestre *m*; (*district*) barrio ♦ *vt* dividir en cuartos; (*MIL: lodge*) alojar; **~s** *npl* (*barracks*) cuartel *m*; (*living ~s*) alojamiento; **a ~ of an hour** un cuarto de hora; **~ final** *n* cuarto de final; **~ly** *adj* trimestral ♦ *adv* cada 3 meses, trimestralmente

quartet(te) [kwɔː'tet] *n* cuarteto

quartz [kwɔːts] *n* cuarzo

quash [kwɒʃ] *vt* (*verdict*) anular

quaver ['kweɪvə*] (*BRIT*) *n* (*MUS*) corchea ♦ *vi* temblar

quay [kiː] *n* (*also*: **~side**) muelle *m*

queasy ['kwiːzɪ] *adj*: **to feel ~** tener náuseas

queen [kwiːn] *n* reina; (*CARDS etc*) dama; **~ mother** *n* reina madre

queer [kwɪə*] *adj* raro, extraño ♦ *n* (*inf*: *highly offensive*) maricón *m*

quell [kwel] *vt* (*feeling*) calmar; (*rebellion etc*) sofocar

quench [kwentʃ] *vt*: **to ~ one's thirst** apagar la sed

query ['kwɪərɪ] *n* (*question*) pregunta ♦ *vt* dudar de

quest [kwest] *n* busca, búsqueda

question ['kwestʃən] *n* pregunta; (*doubt*) duda; (*matter*) asunto, cuestión *f* ♦ *vt* (*doubt*) dudar de; (*interrogate*) interrogar, hacer preguntas a; **beyond ~** fuera de toda duda; **out of the ~** imposible; ni

hablar; **~able** *adj* dudoso; **~ mark** *n* punto de interrogación; **~naire** [-'neə*] *n* cuestionario

queue [kjuː] (*BRIT*) *n* cola ♦ *vi* (*also*: **~ up**) hacer cola

quibble ['kwɪbl] *vi* sutilizar

quick [kwɪk] *adj* rápido; (*agile*) ágil; (*mind*) listo ♦ *n*: **cut to the ~** (*fig*) herido en lo vivo; **be ~!** ¡date prisa!; **~en** *vt* apresurar ♦ *vi* apresurarse, darse prisa; **~ly** *adv* rápidamente, de prisa; **~sand** *n* arenas *fpl* movedizas; **~-witted** *adj* perspicaz

quid [kwɪd] (*BRIT*: *inf*) *n inv* libra

quiet ['kwaɪət] *adj* (*voice, music etc*) bajo; (*person, place*) tranquilo; (*ceremony*) íntimo ♦ *n* silencio; (*calm*) tranquilidad *f* ♦ *vt*, *vi* (*US*) = **~en**; **~en** (*also*: **~en down**) *vi* calmarse; (*grow silent*) callarse ♦ *vt* calmar; hacer callar; **~ly** *adv* tranquilamente; (*silently*) silenciosamente; **~ness** *n* silencio; tranquilidad *f*

quilt [kwɪlt] *n* edredón *m*

quin [kwɪn] *n abbr* = **quintuplet**

quintet(te) [kwɪn'tet] *n* quinteto

quintuplets [kwɪn'tjuːplɪts] *npl* quintillizos/as

quip [kwɪp] *n* pulla

quirk [kwəːk] *n* peculiaridad *f*; (*accident*) capricho

quit [kwɪt] (*pt, pp* **quit** *or* **quitted**) *vt* dejar, abandonar; (*premises*) desocupar ♦ *vi* (*give up*) renunciar; (*resign*) dimitir

quite [kwaɪt] *adv* (*rather*) bastante; (*entirely*) completamente; **that's not ~ big enough** no acaba de ser lo bastante grande; **~ a few of them** un buen número de ellos; **~ (so)!** ¡así es!, ¡exactamente!

quits [kwɪts] *adj*: **~ (with)** en paz (con); **let's call it ~** dejémoslo en tablas

quiver ['kwɪvə*] *vi* estremecerse

quiz [kwɪz] *n* concurso ♦ *vt* interrogar; **~zical** *adj* burlón(ona)

quota ['kwəʊtə] *n* cuota

quotation [kwəʊ'teɪʃən] *n* cita; (*estimate*) presupuesto; **~ marks** *npl* comillas *fpl*

quote [kwəʊt] *n* cita; (*estimate*)

presupuesto ♦ *vt* citar; (*price*) cotizar ♦ *vi*: **to ~ from** citar de; **~s** *npl* (*inverted commas*) comillas *fpl*

R, r

rabbi ['ræbaɪ] *n* rabino
rabbit ['ræbɪt] *n* conejo; **~ hutch** *n* conejera
rabble ['ræbl] (*pej*) *n* chusma, populacho
rabies ['reɪbiːz] *n* rabia
RAC (*BRIT*) *n abbr* = **Royal Automobile Club**
rac(c)oon [rə'kuːn] *n* mapache *m*
race [reɪs] *n* carrera; (*species*) raza ♦ *vt* (*horse*) hacer correr; (*engine*) acelerar ♦ *vi* (*compete*) competir; (*run*) correr; (*pulse*) latir a ritmo acelerado; **~ car** (*US*) *n* = **racing car**; **~ car driver** (*US*) *n* = **racing driver**; **~course** *n* hipódromo; **~horse** *n* caballo de carreras; **~track** *n* pista; (*for cars*) autódromo
racial ['reɪʃl] *adj* racial
racing ['reɪsɪŋ] *n* carreras *fpl*; **~ car** (*BRIT*) *n* coche de carreras; **~ driver** (*BRIT*) *n* corredor(a) *m/f* de coches
racism ['reɪsɪzəm] *n* racismo; **racist** [-sɪst] *adj*, *n* racista *m/f*
rack [ræk] *n* (*also*: **luggage ~**) rejilla; (*shelf*) estante *m*; (*also*: **roof ~**) baca, portaequipajes *m inv*; (*dish ~*) escurreplatos *m inv*; (*clothes ~*) percha ♦ *vt* atormentar; **to ~ one's brains** devanarse los sesos
racket ['rækɪt] *n* (*for tennis*) raqueta; (*noise*) ruido, estrépito; (*swindle*) estafa, timo
racquet ['rækɪt] *n* raqueta
racy ['reɪsɪ] *adj* picante, salado
radar ['reɪdɑː*] *n* radar *m*
radiant ['reɪdɪənt] *adj* radiante (de felicidad)
radiate ['reɪdɪeɪt] *vt* (*heat*) radiar; (*emotion*) irradiar ♦ *vi* (*lines*) extenderse
radiation [reɪdɪ'eɪʃən] *n* radiación *f*
radiator ['reɪdɪeɪtə*] *n* radiador *m*

radical ['rædɪkl] *adj* radical
radii ['reɪdɪaɪ] *npl of* **radius**
radio ['reɪdɪəu] *n* radio *f*; **on the ~** por radio
radio... [reɪdɪəu] *prefix*: **~active** *adj* radioactivo; **~graphy** [reɪdɪ'ɔgrəfɪ] *n* radiografía; **~logy** [reɪdɪ'ɔlədʒɪ] *n* radiología
radio station *n* emisora
radiotherapy [-'θerəpɪ] *n* radioterapia
radish ['rædɪʃ] *n* rábano
radius ['reɪdɪəs] (*pl* **radii**) *n* radio
RAF *n abbr* = **Royal Air Force**
raffle ['ræfl] *n* rifa, sorteo
raft [rɑːft] *n* balsa; (*also*: **life ~**) balsa salvavidas
rafter ['rɑːftə*] *n* viga
rag [ræg] *n* (*piece of cloth*) trapo; (*torn cloth*) harapo; (*pej*: *newspaper*) periodicucho; (*for charity*) actividades estudiantiles benéficas; **~s** *npl* (*torn clothes*) harapos *mpl*; **~ doll** *n* muñeca de trapo
rage [reɪdʒ] *n* rabia, furor *m* ♦ *vi* (*person*) rabiar, estar furioso; (*storm*) bramar; **it's all the ~** (*very fashionable*) está muy de moda
ragged ['rægɪd] *adj* (*edge*) desigual, mellado; (*appearance*) andrajoso, harapiento
raid [reɪd] *n* (*MIL*) incursión *f*; (*criminal*) asalto; (*by police*) redada ♦ *vt* invadir, atacar; asaltar
rail [reɪl] *n* (*on stair*) barandilla, pasamanos *m inv*; (*on bridge, balcony*) pretil *m*; (*of ship*) barandilla; (*also*: **towel ~**) toallero; **~s** *npl* (*RAIL*) vía; **by ~** por ferrocarril; **~ing(s)** *n*(*pl*) vallado; **~road** (*US*) *n* = **~way**; **~way** (*BRIT*) *n* ferrocarril *m*, vía férrea; **~way line** (*BRIT*) *n* línea (de ferrocarril); **~wayman** (*BRIT irreg*) *n* ferroviario; **~way station** (*BRIT*) *n* estación *f* de ferrocarril
rain [reɪn] *n* lluvia ♦ *vi* llover; **in the ~** bajo la lluvia; **it's ~ing** llueve, está lloviendo; **~bow** *n* arco iris; **~coat** *n* impermeable *m*; **~drop** *n* gota de lluvia; **~fall** *n* lluvia

~forest n selvas fpl tropicales; ~y adj
lluvioso

raise [reɪz] n aumento ♦ vt levantar;
(increase) aumentar; (improve: morale)
subir; (: standards) mejorar; (doubts)
suscitar; (a question) plantear; (cattle,
family) criar; (crop) cultivar; (army)
reclutar; (loan) obtener; to ~ one's voice
alzar la voz

raisin ['reɪzn] n pasa de Corinto

rake [reɪk] n (tool) rastrillo; (person)
libertino ♦ vt (garden) rastrillar

rally ['rælɪ] n (POL etc) reunión f, mitin m;
(AUT) rallye m; (TENNIS) peloteo ♦ vt
reunir ♦ vi recuperarse; ~ round vt fus
(fig) dar apoyo a

RAM [ræm] n abbr (= random access
memory) RAM f

ram [ræm] n carnero; (also: battering ~)
ariete m ♦ vt (crash into) dar contra,
chocar con; (push: fist etc) empujar con
fuerza

ramble ['ræmbl] n caminata, excursión f
en el campo ♦ vi (pej: also: ~ on) divagar;
~r n excursionista m/f; (BOT) trepadora;
rambling adj (speech) inconexo; (house)
laberíntico; (BOT) trepador(a)

ramp [ræmp] n rampa; on/off ~ (US: AUT)
vía de acceso/salida

rampage [ræm'peɪdʒ] n: to be on the ~
desmandarse ♦ vi: they went rampaging
through the town recorrieron la ciudad
armando alboroto

rampant ['ræmpənt] adj (disease etc): to
be ~ estar extendiéndose mucho

ram raid vt atracar (rompiendo el
escaparate con un coche)

ramshackle ['ræmʃækl] adj destartalado

ran [ræn] pt of run

ranch [rɑːntʃ] n hacienda, estancia; ~er n
ganadero

rancid ['rænsɪd] adj rancio

rancour ['ræŋkə*] (US rancor) n rencor m

random ['rændəm] adj fortuito, sin orden;
(COMPUT, MATH) aleatorio ♦ n: at ~ al azar

randy ['rændɪ] (BRIT: inf) adj cachondo

rang [ræŋ] pt of ring

range [reɪndʒ] n (of mountains) cadena de
montañas, cordillera; (of missile) alcance
m; (of voice) registro; (series) serie f; (of
products) surtido; (MIL: also: shooting ~)
campo de tiro; (also: kitchen ~) fogón m
♦ vt (place) colocar; (arrange) arreglar
♦ vi: to ~ over (extend) extenderse por;
to ~ from ... to ... oscilar entre ... y ...

ranger ['reɪndʒə*] n guardabosques m inv

rank [ræŋk] n (row) fila; (MIL) rango;
(status) categoría; (BRIT: also: taxi ~)
parada de taxis ♦ vi: to ~ among figurar
entre ♦ adj fétido, rancio; the ~ and file
(fig) la base

ransack ['rænsæk] vt (search) registrar;
(plunder) saquear

ransom ['rænsəm] n rescate m; to hold to
~ (fig) hacer chantaje a

rant [rænt] vi divagar, desvariar

rap [ræp] vt golpear, dar un golpecito en
♦ n (music) rap m

rape [reɪp] n violación f; (BOT) colza ♦ vt
violar; ~ (seed) oil n aceite m de colza

rapid ['ræpɪd] adj rápido; ~ity [rə'pɪdɪtɪ] n
rapidez f; ~s npl (GEO) rápidos mpl

rapist ['reɪpɪst] n violador m

rapport [ræ'pɔː*] n simpatía

rapturous ['ræptʃərəs] adj extático

rare [reə*] adj raro, poco común; (CULIN:
steak) poco hecho

rarely ['reəlɪ] adv pocas veces

raring ['reərɪŋ] adj: to be ~ to go (inf)
tener muchas ganas de empezar

rascal ['rɑːskl] n pillo, pícaro

rash [ræʃ] adj imprudente, precipitado ♦ n
(MED) sarpullido, erupción f (cutánea); (of
events) serie f

rasher ['ræʃə*] n lonja

raspberry ['rɑːzbərɪ] n frambuesa

rasping ['rɑːspɪŋ] adj: a ~ noise un ruido
áspero

rat [ræt] n rata

rate [reɪt] n (ratio) razón f; (price) precio;
(: of hotel etc) tarifa; (of interest) tipo;
(speed) velocidad f ♦ vt (value) tasar;
(estimate) estimar; ~s npl (BRIT: property
tax) impuesto municipal; (fees) tarifa; to ~

sth/sb as considerar algo/a uno como; **~able value** *(BRIT)* n valor m impuesto; **~payer** *(BRIT)* n contribuyente m/f

rather ['rɑːðə*] adv: **it's ~ expensive** es algo caro; *(too much)* es demasiado caro; *(to some extent)* más bien; **there's ~ a lot** hay bastante; **I would** or **I'd ~ go** preferiría ir; **or ~** mejor dicho

rating ['reɪtɪŋ] n tasación f; *(score)* índice m; *(of ship)* clase f; **~s** npl *(RADIO, TV)* niveles mpl de audiencia

ratio ['reɪʃɪəʊ] n razón f; **in the ~ of 100 to 1** a razón de 100 a 1

ration ['ræʃən] n ración f ♦ vt racionar; **~s** npl víveres mpl

rational ['ræʃənl] adj *(solution, reasoning)* lógico, razonable; *(person)* cuerdo, sensato; **~e** [-'nɑːl] n razón f fundamental; **~ize** vt justificar

rat race n lucha incesante por la supervivencia

rattle ['rætl] n golpeteo; *(of train etc)* traqueteo; *(for baby)* sonaja, sonajero ♦ vi castañetear; *(car, bus)*: **to ~ along** traquetear ♦ vt hacer sonar agitando; **~snake** n serpiente f de cascabel

raucous ['rɔːkəs] adj estridente, ronco

ravage ['rævɪdʒ] vt hacer estragos en, destrozar; **~s** npl estragos mpl

rave [reɪv] vi *(in anger)* encolerizarse; *(with enthusiasm)* entusiasmarse; *(MED)* delirar, desvariar ♦ n *(inf: party)* rave m

raven ['reɪvən] n cuervo

ravenous ['rævənəs] adj hambriento

ravine [rə'viːn] n barranco

raving ['reɪvɪŋ] adj: **~ lunatic** loco/a de atar

ravishing ['rævɪʃɪŋ] adj encantador(a)

raw [rɔː] adj crudo; *(not processed)* bruto; *(sore)* vivo; *(inexperienced)* novato, inexperto; **~ deal** *(inf)* n injusticia; **~ material** n materia prima

ray [reɪ] n rayo; **~ of hope** (rayo de) esperanza

raze [reɪz] vt arrasar

razor ['reɪzə*] n *(open)* navaja; *(safety ~)* máquina de afeitar; *(electric ~)* máquina

(eléctrica) de afeitar; **~ blade** n hoja de afeitar

Rd abbr = **road**

re [riː] prep con referencia a

reach [riːtʃ] n alcance m; *(of river etc)* extensión f entre dos recodos ♦ vt alcanzar, llegar a; *(achieve)* lograr ♦ vi extenderse; **within ~** al alcance (de la mano); **out of ~** fuera del alcance; **~ out** vt *(hand)* tender ♦ vi: **to ~ out for sth** alargar or tender la mano para tomar algo

react [riː'ækt] vi reaccionar; **~ion** [-'ækʃən] n reacción f

reactor [riː'æktə*] n *(also:* **nuclear ~**) reactor m *(nuclear)*

read [riːd, pt, pp red] *(pt, pp* **read**) vi leer ♦ vt leer; *(understand)* entender; *(study)* estudiar; **~ out** vt leer en alta voz; **~able** adj *(writing)* legible; *(book)* leíble; **~er** n lector(a) m/f; *(BRIT: at university)* profesor(a) m/f adjunto/a; **~ership** n *(of paper etc)* (número de) lectores mpl

readily ['redɪlɪ] adv *(willingly)* de buena gana; *(easily)* fácilmente; *(quickly)* en seguida

readiness ['redɪnɪs] n buena voluntad f; *(preparedness)* preparación f; **in ~** *(prepared)* listo, preparado

reading ['riːdɪŋ] n lectura; *(on instrument)* indicación f

ready ['redɪ] adj listo, preparado; *(willing)* dispuesto; *(available)* disponible ♦ adv: **~-cooked** listo para comer ♦ n: **at the ~** *(MIL)* listo para tirar; **to get ~** vi prepararse ♦ vt preparar; **~-made** adj confeccionado; **~-to-wear** adj confeccionado

real [rɪəl] adj verdadero, auténtico; **in ~ terms** en términos reales; **~ estate** n bienes mpl raíces; **~istic** [-'lɪstɪk] adj realista

reality [riː'ælɪtɪ] n realidad f

realization [rɪəlaɪ'zeɪʃən] n comprensión f, *(fulfilment, COMM)* realización f

realize ['rɪəlaɪz] vt *(understand)* darse cuenta de

eally ['rɪəlɪ] *adv* realmente; *(for emphasis)* verdaderamente; *(actually)*: **what ~ happened** lo que pasó en realidad; **~?** ¿de veras?; **~!** *(annoyance)* ¡vamos!, ¡por favor!

ealm [rɛlm] *n* reino; *(fig)* esfera

ealtor ® ['rɪəltɔːʳ] *(US) n* corredor(a) *m/f* de bienes raíces

eap [riːp] *vt* segar; *(fig)* cosechar, recoger

eappear [riːə'pɪəʳ] *vi* reaparecer

ear [rɪəʳ] *adj* trasero ♦ *n* parte *f* trasera ♦ *vt (cattle, family)* criar ♦ *vi (also: ~ up) (animal)* encabritarse; **~guard** *n* retaguardia

earmament [riːˈɑːməmənt] *n* rearme *m*

earrange [riːə'reɪndʒ] *vt* ordenar *or* arreglar de nuevo

ear-view mirror *n (AUT)* (espejo) retrovisor *m*

eason ['riːzn] *n* razón *f* ♦ *vi*: **to ~ with sb** tratar de que uno entre en razón; **it stands to ~ that** es lógico que; **~able** *adj* razonable; *(sensible)* sensato; **~ably** *adv* razonablemente; **~ing** *n* razonamiento, argumentos *mpl*

eassurance [riːə'ʃuərəns] *n* consuelo

eassure [riːə'ʃuəʳ] *vt* tranquilizar, alentar; **to ~ sb that** tranquilizar a uno asegurando que

ebate ['riːbeɪt] *n (on tax etc)* desgravación *f*

ebel [*n* 'rɛbl, *vi* rɪ'bɛl] *n* rebelde *m/f* ♦ *vi* rebelarse, sublevarse; **~lious** [rɪ'bɛljəs] *adj* rebelde; *(child)* revoltoso

ebirth ['riːbɜːθ] *n* renacimiento

ebound [*vi* rɪ'baund, *n* 'riːbaund] *vi (ball)* rebotar ♦ *n* rebote *m*; **on the ~** *(also fig)* de rebote

ebuff [rɪ'bʌf] *n* desaire *m*, rechazo

ebuild [riː'bɪld] *(irreg) vt* reconstruir

ebuke [rɪ'bjuːk] *n* reprimenda ♦ *vt* reprender

ebut [rɪ'bʌt] *vt* rebatir

ecall [*vb* rɪ'kɔːl, *n* 'riːkɔl] *vt (remember)* recordar; *(ambassador etc)* retirar ♦ *n* recuerdo; retirada

ecap ['riːkæp], **recapitulate** [riːkə'pɪtjuleɪt] *vt, vi* recapitular

rec'd *abbr* (= *received*) rbdo

recede [rɪ'siːd] *vi (memory)* ir borrándose; *(hair)* retroceder; **receding** *adj (forehead, chin)* huidizo; **to have a receding hairline** tener entradas

receipt [rɪ'siːt] *n (document)* recibo; *(for parcel etc)* acuse *m* de recibo; *(act of receiving)* recepción *f*; **~s** *npl (COMM)* ingresos *mpl*

receive [rɪ'siːv] *vt* recibir; *(guest)* acoger; *(wound)* sufrir; **~r** *n (TEL)* auricular *m*; *(RADIO)* receptor *m*; *(of stolen goods)* perista *m/f*; *(COMM)* administrador *m* jurídico

recent ['riːsnt] *adj* reciente; **~ly** *adv* recientemente; **~ly arrived** recién llegado

receptacle [rɪ'sɛptɪkl] *n* receptáculo

reception [rɪ'sɛpʃən] *n* recepción *f*; *(welcome)* acogida; **~ desk** *n* recepción *f*; **~ist** *n* recepcionista *m/f*

recess [rɪ'sɛs] *n (in room)* hueco; *(for bed)* nicho; *(secret place)* escondrijo; *(POL etc: holiday)* clausura

recession [rɪ'sɛʃən] *n* recesión *f*

recipe ['rɛsɪpɪ] *n* receta; *(for disaster, success)* fórmula

recipient [rɪ'sɪpɪənt] *n* recibidor(a) *m/f*; *(of letter)* destinatario/a

recital [rɪ'saɪtl] *n* recital *m*

recite [rɪ'saɪt] *vt (poem)* recitar

reckless ['rɛkləs] *adj* temerario, imprudente; *(driving, driver)* peligroso; **~ly** *adv* imprudentemente; de modo peligroso

reckon ['rɛkən] *vt* calcular; *(consider)* considerar; *(think)*: **I ~ that ...** me parece que ...; **~ on** *vt fus* contar con; **~ing** *n* cálculo

reclaim [rɪ'kleɪm] *vt (land, waste)* recuperar; *(land: from sea)* rescatar; *(demand back)* reclamar

reclamation [rɛklə'meɪʃən] *n (of land)* acondicionamiento de tierras

recline [rɪ'klaɪn] *vi* reclinarse; **reclining** *adj (seat)* reclinable

recluse [rɪ'kluːs] *n* recluso/a

recognition [rekəg'nɪʃən] *n*
reconocimiento; **transformed beyond ~**
irreconocible

recognizable ['rekəgnaɪzəbl] *adj*: **~ (by)**
reconocible (por)

recognize ['rekəgnaɪz] *vt*: **to ~ (by/as)**
reconocer (por/como)

recoil [*vi* rɪ'kɔɪl, *n* 'ri:kɔɪl] *vi* (*person*): **to ~
from doing sth** retraerse de hacer algo
♦ *n* (*of gun*) retroceso

recollect [rekə'lekt] *vt* recordar, acordarse
de; **~ion** [-'lekʃən] *n* recuerdo

recommend [rekə'mend] *vt* recomendar

reconcile ['rekənsaɪl] *vt* (*two people*)
reconciliar; (*two facts*) compaginar; **to ~
o.s. to sth** conformarse a algo

recondition [ri:kən'dɪʃən] *vt* (*machine*)
reacondicionar

reconnoitre [rekə'nɔɪtə*] (*US* **reconnoiter**)
vt, vi (*MIL*) reconocer

reconsider [ri:kən'sɪdə*] *vt* repensar

reconstruct [ri:kən'strʌkt] *vt* reconstruir

record [*n* 'rekɔ:d, *vt* rɪ'kɔ:d] *n* (*MUS*) disco;
(*of meeting etc*) acta; (*register*) registro,
partida; (*file*) archivo; (*also*: **criminal ~**)
antecedentes *mpl*; (*written*) expediente *m*;
(*SPORT, COMPUT*) récord *m* ♦ *vt* registrar;
(*MUS: song etc*) grabar; **in ~ time** en un
tiempo récord; **off the ~** *adj* no oficial
♦ *adv* confidencialmente; **~ card** *n* (*in
file*) ficha; **~ed delivery** (*BRIT*) *n* (*POST*)
entrega con acuse de recibo; **~er** *n* (*MUS*)
flauta de pico; **~ holder** *n* (*SPORT*) actual
poseedor(a) *m/f* del récord; **~ing** *n* (*MUS*)
grabación *f*; **~ player** *n* tocadiscos *m
inv*

recount [rɪ'kaunt] *vt* contar

re-count ['ri:kaunt] *n* (*POL: of votes*)
segundo escrutinio

recoup [rɪ'ku:p] *vt*: **to ~ one's losses**
recuperar las pérdidas

recourse [rɪ'kɔ:s] *n*: **to have ~ to** recurrir
a

recover [rɪ'kʌvə*] *vt* recuperar ♦ *vi* (*from
illness, shock*) recuperarse; **~y** *n*
recuperación *f*

recreation [rekrɪ'eɪʃən] *n* recreo; **~al** *adj*

de recreo; **~al drug** droga recreativa

recruit [rɪ'kru:t] *n* recluta *m/f* ♦ *vt* recluta
(*staff*) contratar

rectangle ['rektæŋgl] *n* rectángulo;
rectangular [-'tæŋgjulə*] *adj* rectangula

rectify ['rektɪfaɪ] *vt* rectificar

rector ['rektə*] *n* (*REL*) párroco; **~y** *n* casa
del párroco

recuperate [rɪ'ku:pəreɪt] *vi* reponerse,
restablecerse

recur [rɪ'kə:*] *vi* repetirse; (*pain, illness*)
producirse de nuevo; **~rence** [rɪ'kʌrəns]
repetición *f*; **~rent** [rɪ'kʌrent] *adj* repetid

recycle [ri:'saɪkl] *vt* reciclar

red [red] *n* rojo ♦ *adj* rojo; (*hair*) pelirrojo;
(*wine*) tinto; **to be in the ~** (*account*) esta
en números rojos; (*business*) tener un
saldo negativo; **to give sb the ~ carpet
treatment** recibir a uno con todos los
honores; **R~ Cross** *n* Cruz *f* Roja;
~currant *n* grosella roja; **~den** *vt*
enrojecer ♦ *vi* enrojecerse

redeem [rɪ'di:m] *vt* redimir; (*promises*)
cumplir; (*sth in pawn*) desempeñar; (*fig,
also REL*) rescatar; **~ing** *adj*: **~ing feature**
rasgo bueno *or* favorable

redeploy [ri:dɪ'plɔɪ] *vt* (*resources*)
reorganizar

red: **~-haired** *adj* pelirrojo; **~-handed**
adj: **to be caught ~-handed** cogerse (*SP*)
or pillarse (*AM*) con las manos en la masa
~head *n* pelirrojo/a; **~ herring** *n* (*fig*)
pista falsa; **~-hot** *adj* candente

redirect [ri:daɪ'rekt] *vt* (*mail*) reexpedir

red light *n*: **to go through a ~** (*AUT*)
pasar la luz roja; **red-light district** *n*
barrio chino

redo [ri:'du:] (*irreg*) *vt* rehacer

redress [rɪ'dres] *vt* reparar

Red Sea *n*: **the ~** el mar Rojo

redskin ['redskɪn] *n* piel roja *m/f*

red tape *n* (*fig*) trámites *mpl*

reduce [rɪ'dju:s] *vt* reducir; **to ~ sb to
tears** hacer llorar a uno; **to be ~d to
begging** no quedarle a uno otro remedi
que pedir limosna; **"~ speed now"** (*AUT*
"reduzca la velocidad"; **at a ~d price** (*of*

goods) (a precio) rebajado; **reduction** [rɪ'dʌkʃən] *n* reducción *f*; (*of price*) rebaja; (*discount*) descuento; (*smaller-scale copy*) copia reducida

redundancy [rɪ'dʌndənsɪ] *n* (*dismissal*) despido; (*unemployment*) desempleo

redundant [rɪ'dʌndnt] *adj* (*BRIT: worker*) parado, sin trabajo; (*detail, object*) superfluo; **to be made ~** quedar(se) sin trabajo

reed [riːd] *n* (*BOT*) junco, caña; (*MUS*) lengüeta

reef [riːf] *n* (*at sea*) arrecife *m*

reek [riːk] *vi*: **to ~ (of)** apestar (a)

reel [riːl] *n* carrete *m*, bobina; (*of film*) rollo; (*dance*) baile *m* escocés ♦ *vt* (*also: ~ up*) devanar; (*also: ~ in*) sacar ♦ *vi* (*sway*) tambalear(se)

ref [ref] (*inf*) *n abbr* = **referee**

refectory [rɪ'fektərɪ] *n* comedor *m*

refer [rɪ'fɜː*] *vt* (*send: patient*) referir; (: *matter*) remitir ♦ *vi*: **to ~ to** (*allude to*) referirse a, aludir a; (*apply to*) relacionarse con; (*consult*) consultar

referee [refə'riː] *n* árbitro; (*BRIT: for job application*): **to be a ~ for sb** proporcionar referencias a uno ♦ *vt* (*match*) arbitrar en

reference ['refrəns] *n* referencia; (*for job application: letter*) carta de recomendación; **with ~ to** (*COMM: in letter*) me remito a; **~ book** *n* libro de consulta; **~ number** *n* número de referencia

refill [*vt* riː'fɪl, *n* 'riːfɪl] *vt* rellenar ♦ *n* repuesto, recambio

refine [rɪ'faɪn] *vt* refinar; **~d** *adj* (*person*) fino; **~ment** *n* cultura, educación *f*; (*of system*) refinamiento

reflect [rɪ'flekt] *vt* reflejar ♦ *vi* (*think*) reflexionar, pensar; **it ~s badly/well on him** le perjudica/le hace honor; **~ion** [-'flekʃən] *n* (*act*) reflexión *f*; (*image*) reflejo; (*criticism*) crítica; **on ~ion** pensándolo bien; **~or** *n* (*AUT*) captafaros *m inv*; (*of light, heat*) reflector *m*

reflex ['riːfleks] *adj, n* reflejo; **~ive**

[rɪ'fleksɪv] *adj* (*LING*) reflexivo

reform [rɪ'fɔːm] *n* reforma ♦ *vt* reformar; **~atory** (*US*) *n* reformatorio

refrain [rɪ'freɪn] *vi*: **to ~ from doing** abstenerse de hacer ♦ *n* estribillo

refresh [rɪ'freʃ] *vt* refrescar; **~er course** (*BRIT*) *n* curso de repaso; **~ing** *adj* refrescante; **~ments** *npl* refrescos *mpl*

refrigerator [rɪ'frɪdʒəreɪtə*] *n* nevera (*SP*), refrigeradora (*AM*)

refuel [riː'fjuəl] *vi* repostar (combustible)

refuge ['refjuːdʒ] *n* refugio, asilo; **to take ~ in** refugiarse en

refugee [refju'dʒiː] *n* refugiado/a

refund [*n* 'riːfʌnd, *vb* rɪ'fʌnd] *n* reembolso ♦ *vt* devolver, reembolsar

refurbish [riː'fɜːbɪʃ] *vt* restaurar, renovar

refusal [rɪ'fjuːzəl] *n* negativa; **to have first ~ on** tener la primera opción a

refuse¹ ['refjuːs] *n* basura; **~ collection** *n* recolección *f* de basuras

refuse² [rɪ'fjuːz] *vt* rechazar; (*invitation*) declinar; (*permission*) denegar ♦ *vi*: **to ~ to do sth** negarse a hacer algo; (*horse*) rehusar

regain [rɪ'geɪn] *vt* recobrar, recuperar

regal ['riːgl] *adj* regio, real

regard [rɪ'gɑːd] *n* mirada; (*esteem*) respeto; (*attention*) consideración *f* ♦ *vt* (*consider*) considerar; **to give one's ~s to** saludar de su parte a; **"with kindest ~s"** "con muchos recuerdos"; **~ing, as ~s, with ~ to** con respecto a, en cuanto a; **~less** *adv* a pesar de todo; **~less of** sin reparar en

régime [reɪ'ʒiːm] *n* régimen *m*

regiment ['redʒɪmənt] *n* regimiento; **~al** [-'mentl] *adj* militar

region ['riːdʒən] *n* región *f*; **in the ~ of** (*fig*) alrededor de; **~al** *adj* regional

register ['redʒɪstə*] *n* registro ♦ *vt* registrar; (*birth*) declarar; (*car*) matricular; (*letter*) certificar; (*subj: instrument*) marcar, indicar ♦ *vi* (*at hotel*) registrarse; (*as student*) matricularse; (*make impression*) producir impresión; **~ed** *adj* (*letter, parcel*) certificado; **~ed**

trademark *n* marca registrada

registrar ['redʒistrɑː*] *n* secretario/a (del registro civil)

registration [redʒis'treiʃən] *n* (*act*) declaración *f*; (*AUT: also:* ~ **number**) matrícula

registry ['redʒistri] *n* registro; ~ **office** (*BRIT*) *n* registro civil; **to get married in a** ~ **office** casarse por lo civil

regret [ri'gret] *n* sentimiento, pesar *m* ♦ *vt* sentir, lamentar; ~**fully** *adv* con pesar; ~**table** *adj* lamentable

regular ['regjulə*] *adj* regular; (*soldier*) profesional; (*usual*) habitual; (: *doctor*) de cabecera ♦ *n* (*client etc*) cliente/a *m/f* habitual; ~**ly** *adv* con regularidad; (*often*) repetidas veces

regulate ['regjuleit] *vt* controlar; **regulation** [-'leiʃən] *n* (*rule*) regla, reglamento

rehearsal [ri'həːsəl] *n* ensayo

rehearse [ri'həːs] *vt* ensayar

reign [rein] *n* reinado; (*fig*) predominio ♦ *vi* reinar; (*fig*) imperar

reimburse [riːim'bəːs] *vt* reembolsar

rein [rein] *n* (*for horse*) rienda

reindeer ['reindiə*] *n inv* reno

reinforce [riːin'fɔːs] *vt* reforzar; ~**d concrete** *n* hormigón *m* armado; ~**ments** *npl* (*MIL*) refuerzos *mpl*

reinstate [riːin'steit] *vt* reintegrar; (*tax, law*) reinstaurar

reiterate [riː'itəreit] *vt* reiterar, repetir

reject [*n* 'riːdʒekt, *vb* ri'dʒekt] *n* (*thing*) desecho ♦ *vt* rechazar; (*suggestion*) descartar; (*coin*) expulsar; ~**ion** [ri'dʒekʃən] *n* rechazo

rejoice [ri'dʒɔis] *vi*: **to** ~ **at** *or* **over** regocijarse *or* alegrarse de

rejuvenate [ri'dʒuːvəneit] *vt* rejuvenecer

relapse [ri'læps] *n* recaída

relate [ri'leit] *vt* (*tell*) contar, relatar; (*connect*) relacionar ♦ *vi* relacionarse; ~**d** *adj* afín; (*person*) emparentado; ~**d to** (*subject*) relacionado con; **relating to** *prep* referente a

relation [ri'leiʃən] *n* (*person*) familiar *m/f*,

pariente/a *m/f*; (*link*) relación *f*; ~**s** *npl* (*relatives*) familiares *mpl*; ~**ship** *n* relación *f*; (*personal*) relaciones *fpl*; (*also:* **family** ~**ship**) parentesco

relative ['relətiv] *n* pariente/a *m/f*, familiar *m/f* ♦ *adj* relativo; ~**ly** *adv* (*comparatively*) relativamente

relax [ri'læks] *vi* descansar; (*unwind*) relajarse ♦ *vt* (*one's grip*) soltar, aflojar; (*control*) relajar; (*mind, person*) descansar; ~**ation** [riːlæk'seiʃən] *n* descanso; (*of rule, control*) relajamiento; (*entertainment*) diversión *f*; ~**ed** *adj* relajado; (*tranquil*) tranquilo; ~**ing** *adj* relajante

relay ['riːlei] *n* (*race*) carrera de relevos ♦ *vt* (*RADIO, TV*) retransmitir

release [ri'liːs] *n* (*liberation*) liberación *f*; (*from prison*) puesta en libertad; (*of gas etc*) escape *m*; (*of film etc*) estreno; (*of record*) lanzamiento ♦ *vt* (*prisoner*) poner en libertad; (*gas*) despedir, arrojar; (*from wreckage*) soltar; (*catch, spring etc*) desenganchar; (*film*) estrenar; (*book*) publicar; (*news*) difundir

relegate ['reləgeit] *vt* relegar; (*BRIT: SPORT*): **to be** ~**d to** bajar a

relent [ri'lent] *vi* ablandarse; ~**less** *adj* implacable

relevant ['reləvənt] *adj* (*fact*) pertinente; ~ **to** relacionado con

reliable [ri'laiəbl] *adj* (*person, firm*) de confianza, de fiar; (*method, machine*) seguro; (*source*) fidedigno; **reliably** *adv*: **to be reliably informed that ...** saber de fuente fidedigna que ...

reliance [ri'laiəns] *n*: ~ **(on)** dependencia (de)

relic ['relik] *n* (*REL*) reliquia; (*of the past*) vestigio

relief [ri'liːf] *n* (*from pain, anxiety*) alivio; (*help, supplies*) socorro, ayuda; (*ART, GEO*) relieve *m*

relieve [ri'liːv] *vt* (*pain*) aliviar; (*bring help to*) ayudar, socorrer; (*take over from*) sustituir; (: *guard*) relevar; **to** ~ **sb of sth** quitar algo a uno; **to** ~ **o.s.** hacer sus necesidades

religion [rɪˈlɪdʒən] n religión f; **religious** adj religioso

relinquish [rɪˈlɪŋkwɪʃ] vt abandonar; (plan, habit) renunciar a

relish [ˈrelɪʃ] n (CULIN) salsa; (enjoyment) entusiasmo ♦ vt (food etc) saborear; (enjoy): **to ~ sth** hacerle mucha ilusión a uno algo

relocate [riːləʊˈkeɪt] vt cambiar de lugar, mudar ♦ vi mudarse

reluctance [rɪˈlʌktəns] n renuencia

reluctant [rɪˈlʌktənt] adj renuente; **~ly** adv de mala gana

rely on [rɪˈlaɪ-] vt fus depender de; (trust) contar con

remain [rɪˈmeɪn] vi (survive) quedar; (be left) sobrar; (continue) quedar(se), permanecer; **~der** n resto; **~ing** adj que queda(n); (surviving) restante(s); **~s** npl restos mpl

remand [rɪˈmɑːnd] n: **on ~** detenido (bajo custodia) ♦ vt: **to be ~ed in custody** quedar detenido bajo custodia; **~ home** (BRIT) n reformatorio

remark [rɪˈmɑːk] n comentario ♦ vt comentar; **~able** adj (outstanding) extraordinario

remarry [riːˈmærɪ] vi volver a casarse

remedial [rɪˈmiːdɪəl] adj de recuperación

remedy [ˈremədɪ] n remedio ♦ vt remediar, curar

remember [rɪˈmembə*] vt recordar, acordarse de; (bear in mind) tener presente; (send greetings to): **~ me to him** dale recuerdos de mi parte;

remembrance n recuerdo; **R~ Day** n ≈ día en el que se recuerda a los caídos en las dos guerras mundiales

Remembrance Day

ⓘ En el Reino Unido el domingo más próximo al 11 de noviembre se conoce como **Remembrance Sunday** o **Remembrance Day**, aniversario de la firma del armisticio de 1918 que puso fin a la Primera Guerra Mundial. Ese día, a las once de la mañana (hora en que se firmó el armisticio), se recuerda a los que murieron en las dos guerras mundiales con dos minutos de silencio ante los monumentos a los caídos. Allí se colocan coronas de amapolas, flor que también se suele llevar prendida en el pecho tras pagar un donativo destinado a los inválidos de guerra.

remind [rɪˈmaɪnd] vt: **to ~ sb to do sth** recordar a uno que haga algo; **to ~ sb of sth** (of fact) recordar algo a uno; **she ~s me of her mother** me recuerda a su madre; **~er** n notificación f; (memento) recuerdo

reminisce [remɪˈnɪs] vi recordar (viejas historias); **reminiscent** adj: **to be reminiscent of sth** recordar algo

remiss [rɪˈmɪs] adj descuidado; **it was ~ of him** fue un descuido de su parte

remission [rɪˈmɪʃən] n remisión f; (of prison sentence) disminución f de pena; (REL) perdón m

remit [rɪˈmɪt] vt (send: money) remitir, enviar; **~tance** n remesa, envío

remnant [ˈremnənt] n resto; (of cloth) retal m; **~s** npl (COMM) restos mpl de serie

remorse [rɪˈmɔːs] n remordimientos mpl; **~ful** adj arrepentido; **~less** adj (fig) implacable, inexorable

remote [rɪˈməʊt] adj (distant) lejano; (person) distante; **~ control** n telecontrol m; **~ly** adv remotamente; (slightly) levemente

remould [ˈriːməʊld] (BRIT) n (tyre) neumático or llanta (AM) recauchutado/a

removable [rɪˈmuːvəbl] adj (detachable) separable

removal [rɪˈmuːvəl] n (taking away) el quitar; (BRIT: from house) mudanza; (from office: dismissal) destitución f; (MED) extirpación f; **~ van** (BRIT) n camión m de mudanzas

remove [rɪˈmuːv] vt quitar; (employee) destituir; (name: from list) tachar, borrar; (doubt) disipar; (abuse) suprimir, acabar con; (MED) extirpar

Renaissance [rɪˈneɪsɑ̃ns] n: **the ~** el Renacimiento

render [ˈrɛndə*] vt (thanks) dar; (aid) proporcionar, prestar; (make): **to ~ sth useless** hacer algo inútil; **~ing** n (MUS etc) interpretación f

rendezvous [ˈrɔndɪvuː] n cita

renew [rɪˈnjuː] vt renovar; (resume) reanudar; (loan etc) prorrogar; **~able** adj renovable; **~al** n reanudación f; prórroga

renounce [rɪˈnauns] vt renunciar a; (right, inheritance) renunciar

renovate [ˈrɛnəveɪt] vt renovar

renown [rɪˈnaun] n renombre m; **~ed** adj renombrado

rent [rɛnt] n (for house) arriendo, renta ♦ vt alquilar; **~al** n (for television, car) alquiler m

rep [rɛp] n abbr = **representative**; **repertory**

repair [rɪˈpɛə*] n reparación f, compostura ♦ vt reparar, componer; (shoes) remendar; **in good/bad ~** en buen/mal estado; **~ kit** n caja de herramientas

repatriate [riːˈpætrɪeɪt] vt repatriar

repay [riːˈpeɪ] (irreg) vt (money) devolver, reembolsar; (person) pagar; (debt) liquidar; (sb's efforts) devolver, corresponder a; **~ment** n reembolso, devolución f; (sum of money) recompensa

repeal [rɪˈpiːl] n revocación f ♦ vt revocar

repeat [rɪˈpiːt] n (RADIO, TV) reposición f ♦ vt repetir ♦ vi repetirse; **~edly** adv repetidas veces

repel [rɪˈpɛl] vt (drive away) rechazar; (disgust) repugnar; **~lent** adj repugnante ♦ n: **insect ~lent** crema (or loción f) anti-insectos

repent [rɪˈpɛnt] vi: **to ~ (of)** arrepentirse (de); **~ance** n arrepentimiento

repercussions [riːpəˈkʌʃənz] npl consecuencias fpl

repertory [ˈrɛpətərɪ] n (also: **~ theatre**) teatro de repertorio

repetition [rɛpɪˈtɪʃən] n repetición f

repetitive [rɪˈpɛtɪtɪv] adj repetitivo

replace [rɪˈpleɪs] vt (put back) devolver a su sitio; (take the place of) reemplazar, sustituir; **~ment** n (act) reposición f; (thing) recambio; (person) suplente m/f

replay [ˈriːpleɪ] n (SPORT) desempate m; (of tape, film) repetición f

replenish [rɪˈplɛnɪʃ] vt rellenar; (stock etc) reponer

replica [ˈrɛplɪkə] n copia, reproducción f (exacta)

reply [rɪˈplaɪ] n respuesta, contestación f ♦ vi contestar, responder

report [rɪˈpɔːt] n informe m; (PRESS etc) reportaje m; (BRIT: also: **school ~**) boletín m escolar; (of gun) estallido ♦ vt informar de; (PRESS etc) hacer un reportaje sobre; (notify: accident, culprit) denunciar ♦ vi (make a report) presentar un informe; (present o.s.): **to ~ (to sb)** presentarse (ante uno); **~ card** n (US, Scottish) cartilla escolar; **~edly** adv según se dice; **~er** n periodista m/f

repose [rɪˈpəuz] n: **in ~** (face, mouth) en reposo

reprehensible [rɛprɪˈhɛnsɪbl] adj reprensible, censurable

represent [rɛprɪˈzɛnt] vt representar; (COMM) ser agente de; (describe): **to ~ sth as** describir algo como; **~ation** [-ˈteɪʃən] n representación f; **~ations** npl (protest) quejas fpl; **~ative** n representante m/f; (US: POL) diputado/a m/f ♦ adj representativo

repress [rɪˈprɛs] vt reprimir; **~ion** [-ˈprɛʃən] n represión f

reprieve [rɪˈpriːv] n (LAW) indulto; (fig) alivio

reprisals [rɪˈpraɪzlz] npl represalias fpl

reproach [rɪˈprəutʃ] n reproche m ♦ vt: **to ~ sb for sth** reprochar algo a uno; **~ful** adj de reproche, de acusación

reproduce [riːprəˈdjuːs] vt reproducir ♦ vi reproducirse; **reproduction** [-ˈdʌkʃən] n reproducción f

reprove [rɪˈpruːv] vt: **to ~ sb for sth** reprochar algo a uno

reptile [ˈrɛptaɪl] n reptil m

republic [rɪˈpʌblɪk] n república; **~an** adj,

n republicano/a *m/f*

repudiate [rɪ'pjuːdɪeɪt] *vt* rechazar; (*violence etc*) repudiar

repulsive [rɪ'pʌlsɪv] *adj* repulsivo

reputable ['repjutəbl] *adj* (*make etc*) de renombre

reputation [repju'teɪʃən] *n* reputación *f*

reputed [rɪ'pjuːtɪd] *adj* supuesto; **~ly** *adv* según dicen o se dice

request [rɪ'kwest] *n* petición *f*; (*formal*) solicitud *f* ♦ *vt*: **to ~ sth of** *or* **from sb** solicitar algo a uno; **~ stop** (*BRIT*) *n* parada discrecional

require [rɪ'kwaɪə*] *vt* (*need: subj: person*) necesitar, tener necesidad de; (: *thing, situation*) exigir; (*want*) pedir; **to ~ sb to do sth** pedir a uno que haga algo; **~ment** *n* requisito; (*need*) necesidad *f*

requisition [rekwɪ'zɪʃən] *n*: **~ (for)** solicitud *f* (de) ♦ *vt* (*MIL*) requisar

rescue ['reskjuː] *n* rescate *m* ♦ *vt* rescatar; **~ party** *n* expedición *f* de salvamento; **~r** *n* salvador(a) *m/f*

research [rɪ'səːtʃ] *n* investigaciones *fpl* ♦ *vt* investigar; **~er** *n* investigador(a) *m/f*

resemblance [rɪ'zembləns] *n* parecido

resemble [rɪ'zembl] *vt* parecerse a

resent [rɪ'zent] *vt* tomar a mal; **~ful** *adj* resentido; **~ment** *n* resentimiento

reservation [rezə'veɪʃən] *n* reserva

reserve [rɪ'zəːv] *n* reserva; (*SPORT*) suplente *m/f* ♦ *vt* (*seats etc*) reservar; **~s** *npl* (*MIL*) reserva; **in ~** de reserva; **~d** *adj* reservado

reshuffle [riː'ʃʌfl] *n*: **Cabinet ~** (*POL*) remodelación *f* del gabinete

residence ['rezɪdəns] *n* (*formal: home*) domicilio; (*length of stay*) permanencia; **~ permit** (*BRIT*) *n* permiso de permanencia

resident ['rezɪdənt] *n* (*of area*) vecino/a; (*in hotel*) huésped(a) *m/f* ♦ *adj* (*population*) permanente; (*doctor*) residente; **~ial** [-'denʃəl] *adj* residencial

residue ['rezɪdjuː] *n* resto

resign [rɪ'zaɪn] *vt* renunciar a ♦ *vi* dimitir; **to ~ o.s. to** (*situation*) resignarse a; **~ation** [rezɪg'neɪʃən] *n* dimisión *f*; (*state of*

mind) resignación *f*; **~ed** *adj* resignado

resilient [rɪ'zɪlɪənt] *adj* (*material*) elástico; (*person*) resistente

resist [rɪ'zɪst] *vt* resistir, oponerse a; **~ance** *n* resistencia

resolute ['rezəluːt] *adj* resuelto; (*refusal*) tajante

resolution [rezə'luːʃən] *n* (*gen*) resolución *f*

resolve [rɪ'zɒlv] *n* resolución *f* ♦ *vt* resolver ♦ *vi*: **to ~ to do** resolver hacer; **~d** *adj* resuelto

resort [rɪ'zɔːt] *n* (*town*) centro turístico; (*recourse*) recurso ♦ *vi*: **to ~ to** recurrir a; **in the last ~** como último recurso

resounding [rɪ'zaundɪŋ] *adj* sonoro; (*fig*) clamoroso

resource [rɪ'sɔːs] *n* recurso; **~s** *npl* recursos *mpl*; **~ful** *adj* despabilado, ingenioso

respect [rɪs'pekt] *n* respeto ♦ *vt* respetar; **~s** *npl* recuerdos *mpl*, saludos *mpl*; **with ~ to** con respecto a; **in this ~** en cuanto a eso; **~able** *adj* respetable; (*large: amount*) apreciable; (*passable*) tolerable; **~ful** *adj* respetuoso

respective [rɪs'pektɪv] *adj* respectivo; **~ly** *adv* respectivamente

respite ['respaɪt] *n* respiro

respond [rɪs'pɒnd] *vi* responder; (*react*) reaccionar; **response** [-'pɒns] *n* respuesta; reacción *f*

responsibility [rɪspɒnsɪ'bɪlɪtɪ] *n* responsabilidad *f*

responsible [rɪs'pɒnsɪbl] *adj* (*character*) serio, formal; (*job*) de confianza; (*liable*): **~ (for)** responsable (de)

responsive [rɪs'pɒnsɪv] *adj* sensible

rest [rest] *n* descanso, reposo; (*MUS, pause*) pausa, silencio; (*support*) apoyo; (*remainder*) resto ♦ *vi* descansar; (*be supported*): **to ~ on** descansar sobre ♦ *vt* (*lean*): **to ~ sth on/against** apoyar algo en o sobre/contra; **the ~ of them** (*people, objects*) los demás; **it ~s with him to ...** depende de él el que ...

restaurant ['restərɒn] *n* restaurante *m*; **~**

car (BRIT) n (RAIL) coche-comedor m
restful ['restful] adj descansado, tranquilo
rest home n residencia para jubilados
restive ['restiv] adj inquieto; (horse) rebelón(ona)
restless ['restlis] adj inquieto
restoration [restə'reɪʃən] n restauración f; devolución f
restore [rɪ'stɔ:*] vt (building) restaurar; (sth stolen) devolver; (health) restablecer; (to power) volver a poner a
restrain [rɪs'treɪn] vt (feeling) contener, refrenar; (person): **to ~ (from doing)** disuadir (de hacer); **~ed** adj reservado; **~t** n (restriction) restricción f; (moderation) moderación f; (of manner) reserva
restrict [rɪs'trɪkt] vt restringir, limitar; **~ion** [-kʃən] n restricción f, limitación f; **~ive** adj restrictivo
rest room (US) n aseos mpl
result [rɪ'zʌlt] n resultado ♦ vi: **to ~ in** terminar en, tener por resultado; **as a ~ of** a consecuencia de
resume [rɪ'zju:m] vt reanudar ♦ vi comenzar de nuevo
résumé ['reɪzju:meɪ] n resumen m; (US) currículum m
resumption [rɪ'zʌmpʃən] n reanudación f
resurgence [rɪ'sə:dʒəns] n resurgimiento m
resurrection [rezə'rekʃən] n resurrección f
resuscitate [rɪ'sʌsɪteɪt] vt (MED) resucitar
retail ['ri:teɪl] adj, adv al por menor; **~er** n detallista m/f; **~ price** n precio de venta al público
retain [rɪ'teɪn] vt (keep) retener, conservar; **~er** n (fee) anticipo
retaliate [rɪ'tælɪeɪt] vi: **to ~ (against)** tomar represalias (contra); **retaliation** [-'eɪʃən] n represalias fpl
retarded [rɪ'tɑ:dɪd] adj retrasado
retch [retʃ] vi dársele a uno arcadas
retentive [rɪ'tentɪv] adj (memory) retentivo
retire [rɪ'taɪə*] vi (give up work) jubilarse; (withdraw) retirarse; (go to bed) acostarse; **~d** adj (person) jubilado; **~ment** n (giving up work: state) retiro; (: act) jubilación f; **retiring** adj (leaving)

saliente; (shy) retraído
retort [rɪ'tɔ:t] vi contestar
retrace [ri:'treɪs] vt: **to ~ one's steps** volver sobre sus pasos, desandar lo andado
retract [rɪ'trækt] vt (statement) retirar; (claws) retraer; (undercarriage, aerial) replegar
retrain [ri:'treɪn] vt reciclar; **~ing** n readaptación f profesional
retread ['ri:tred] n neumático (SP) or llanta (AM) recauchutado/a
retreat [rɪ'tri:t] n (place) retiro; (MIL) retirada ♦ vi retirarse
retribution [retrɪ'bju:ʃən] n desquite m
retrieval [rɪ'tri:vəl] n recuperación f
retrieve [rɪ'tri:v] vt recobrar; (situation, honour) salvar; (COMPUT) recuperar; (error) reparar; **~r** n perro cobrador
retrospect ['retrəspekt] n: **in ~** retrospectivamente; **~ive** [-'spektɪv] adj retrospectivo; (law) retroactivo
return [rɪ'tə:n] n (going or coming back) vuelta, regreso; (of sth stolen etc) devolución f; (FINANCE: from land, shares) ganancia, ingresos mpl ♦ cpd (journey) de regreso; (BRIT: ticket) de ida y vuelta; (match) de vuelta ♦ vi (person etc: come or go back) volver, regresar; (symptoms etc) reaparecer; (regain): **to ~ to** recuperar ♦ vt devolver; (favour, love etc) corresponder a; (verdict) pronunciar; (POL: candidate) elegir; **~s** npl (COMM) ingresos mpl; **in ~ (for)** a cambio (de); **by ~ of post** a vuelta de correo; **many happy ~s (of the day)!** ¡feliz cumpleaños!
reunion [ri:'ju:nɪən] n (of family) reunión f; (of two people, school) reencuentro
reunite [ri:ju:'naɪt] vt reunir; (reconcile) reconciliar
rev [rev] (AUT) n abbr (= revolution) revolución f ♦ vt (also: **~ up**) acelerar
reveal [rɪ'vi:l] vt revelar; **~ing** adj revelador(a)
revel ['revl] vi: **to ~ in sth/in doing sth** gozar de algo/con hacer algo
revenge [rɪ'vendʒ] n venganza; **to take ~**

on vengarse de

revenue ['revǝnju:] n ingresos mpl, rentas fpl

reverberate [rɪ'vǝ:bǝreɪt] vi (sound) resonar, retumbar; (fig: shock) repercutir

reverence ['revǝrǝns] n reverencia

Reverend ['revǝrǝnd] adj (in titles): **the ~ John Smith** (Anglican) el Reverendo John Smith; (Catholic) el Padre John Smith; (Protestant) el Pastor John Smith

reversal [rɪ'vǝ:sl] n (of order) inversión f; (of direction, policy) cambio; (of decision) revocación f

reverse [rɪ'vǝ:s] n (opposite) contrario; (back: of cloth) revés m; (: of coin) reverso; (: of paper) dorso; (AUT: also: ~ gear) marcha atrás; (setback) revés m ♦ adj (order) inverso; (direction) contrario; (process) opuesto ♦ vt (decision, AUT) dar marcha atrás a; (position, function) invertir ♦ vi (BRIT: AUT) dar marcha atrás; **~-charge call** (BRIT) n llamada a cobro revertido; **reversing lights** (BRIT) npl (AUT) luces fpl de retroceso

revert [rɪ'vǝ:t] vi: **to ~ to** volver a

review [rɪ'vju:] n (magazine, MIL) revista; (of book, film) reseña; (US: examination) repaso, examen m ♦ vt repasar, examinar; (MIL) pasar revista a; (book, film) reseñar; **~er** n crítico/a

revise [rɪ'vaɪz] vt (manuscript) corregir; (opinion) modificar; (price, procedure) revisar ♦ vi (study) repasar; **revision** [rɪ'vɪʒǝn] n corrección f; modificación f; (for exam) repaso

revival [rɪ'vaɪvǝl] n (recovery) reanimación f; (of interest) renacimiento; (THEATRE) reestreno; (of faith) despertar m

revive [rɪ'vaɪv] vt resucitar; (custom) restablecer; (hope) despertar; (play) reestrenar ♦ vi (person) volver en sí; (business) reactivarse

revolt [rɪ'vǝult] n rebelión f ♦ vi rebelarse, sublevarse ♦ vt dar asco a, repugnar; **~ing** adj asqueroso, repugnante

revolution [revǝ'lu:ʃǝn] n revolución f; **~ary** adj, n revolucionario/a m/f; **~ize** vt

revolucionar

revolve [rɪ'vɒlv] vi dar vueltas, girar; (life, discussion): **to ~ (a)round** girar en torno a

revolver [rɪ'vɒlvǝ*] n revólver m

revolving [rɪ'vɒlvɪŋ] adj (chair, door etc) giratorio

revue [rɪ'vju:] n (THEATRE) revista

revulsion [rɪ'vʌlʃǝn] n asco, repugnancia

reward [rɪ'wɔ:d] n premio, recompensa ♦ vt: **to ~ (for)** recompensar or premiar (por); **~ing** adj (fig) valioso

rewind [ri:'waɪnd] (irreg) vt rebobinar

rewire [ri:'waɪǝ*] vt (house) renovar la instalación eléctrica de

rheumatism ['ru:mǝtɪzǝm] n reumatismo, reúma m

Rhine [raɪn] n: **the ~** el (río) Rin

rhinoceros [raɪ'nɒsǝrǝs] n rinoceronte m

rhododendron [rǝudǝ'dendrn] n rododendro

Rhone [rǝun] n: **the ~** el (río) Ródano

rhubarb ['ru:bɑ:b] n ruibarbo

rhyme [raɪm] n rima; (verse) poesía

rhythm ['rɪðm] n ritmo

rib [rɪb] n (ANAT) costilla ♦ vt (mock) tomar el pelo a

ribbon ['rɪbǝn] n cinta; **in ~s** (torn) hecho trizas

rice [raɪs] n arroz m; **~ pudding** n arroz m con leche

rich [rɪtʃ] adj rico; (soil) fértil; (food) pesado; (: sweet) empalagoso; (abundant): **~ in** (minerals etc) rico en; **the ~** npl los ricos; **~es** npl riqueza; **~ly** adv ricamente; (deserved, earned) bien

rickets ['rɪkɪts] n raquitismo

rid [rɪd] (pt, pp rid) vt: **to ~ sb of sth** librar a uno de algo; **to get ~ of** deshacerse or desembarazarse de

ridden ['rɪdn] pp of ride

riddle ['rɪdl] n (puzzle) acertijo; (mystery) enigma m, misterio ♦ vt: **to be ~d with** ser lleno or plagado de

ride [raɪd] (pt rode, pp ridden) n paseo; (distance covered) viaje m, recorrido ♦ vi (as sport) montar; (go somewhere: on horse, bicycle) dar un paseo, pasearse;

(*travel: on bicycle, motorcycle, bus*) viajar ♦ *vt* (*a horse*) montar a; (*a bicycle, motorcycle*) andar en; (*distance*) recorrer; **to take sb for a ~** (*fig*) engañar a uno; **~r** *n* (*on horse*) jinete/a *m/f*; (*on bicycle*) ciclista *m/f*; (*on motorcycle*) motociclista *m/f*

ridge [rɪdʒ] *n* (*of hill*) cresta; (*of roof*) caballete *m*; (*wrinkle*) arruga

ridicule [ˈrɪdɪkjuːl] *n* irrisión *f*, burla ♦ *vt* poner en ridículo, burlarse de; **ridiculous** [-ˈdɪkjuləs] *adj* ridículo

riding [ˈraɪdɪŋ] *n* equitación *f*; **I like ~** me gusta montar a caballo; **~ school** *n* escuela de equitación

rife [raɪf] *adj*: **to be ~** ser muy común; **to be ~ with** abundar en

riffraff [ˈrɪfræf] *n* gentuza

rifle [ˈraɪfl] *n* rifle *m*, fusil *m* ♦ *vt* saquear; **~ through** *vt* (*papers*) registrar; **~ range** *n* campo de tiro; (*at fair*) tiro al blanco

rift [rɪft] *n* (*in clouds*) claro *m*; (*fig: disagreement*) desavenencia

rig [rɪg] *n* (*also*: **oil ~**: *at sea*) plataforma petrolera ♦ *vt* (*election etc*) amañar; **~ out** (*BRIT*) *vt* disfrazar; **~ up** *vt* improvisar; **~ging** *n* (*NAUT*) aparejo

right [raɪt] *adj* (*correct*) correcto, exacto; (*suitable*) indicado, debido; (*proper*) apropiado; (*just*) justo; (*morally good*) bueno; (*not left*) derecho ♦ *n* bueno; (*title, claim*) derecho; (*not left*) derecha ♦ *adv* bien, correctamente; (*not left*) a la derecha; (*exactly*): **~ now** ahora mismo ♦ *vt* enderezar; (*correct*) corregir ♦ *excl* ¡bueno!, ¡está bien!; **to be ~** (*person*) tener razón; (*answer*) ser correcto; **is that the ~ time?** (*of clock*) ¿es esa la hora buena?; **by ~s** en justicia; **on the ~** a la derecha; **to be in the ~** tener razón; **~ away** en seguida; **~ in the middle** exactamente en el centro; **~ angle** *n* ángulo recto; **~eous** [ˈraɪtʃəs] *adj* justado, honrado; (*anger*) justificado; **~ful** *adj* legítimo; **~-handed** *adj* diestro; **~-hand man** *n* brazo derecho; **~-hand side** *n*

derecha; **~ly** *adv* correctamente, debidamente; (*with reason*) con razón; **~ of way** *n* (*on path etc*) derecho de paso; (*AUT*) prioridad *f*; **~-wing** *adj* (*POL*) derechista

rigid [ˈrɪdʒɪd] *adj* rígido; (*person, ideas*) inflexible

rigmarole [ˈrɪgmərəul] *n* galimatías *m inv*

rigorous [ˈrɪgərəs] *adj* riguroso

rile [raɪl] *vt* irritar

rim [rɪm] *n* borde *m*; (*of spectacles*) aro; (*of wheel*) llanta

rind [raɪnd] *n* (*of bacon*) corteza; (*of lemon etc*) cáscara; (*of cheese*) costra

ring [rɪŋ] (*pt* **rang**, *pp* **rung**) *n* (*of metal*) aro; (*on finger*) anillo; (*of people*) corro; (*of objects*) círculo; (*gang*) banda; (*for boxing*) cuadrilátero; (*of circus*) pista; (*bull ~*) ruedo, plaza; (*sound of bell*) toque *m* ♦ *vi* (*on telephone*) llamar por teléfono; (*bell*) repicar; (*doorbell, phone*) sonar; (*also*: **~ out**) sonar; (*ears*) zumbar ♦ *vt* (*BRIT: TEL*) llamar, telefonear; (*bell etc*) hacer sonar; (*doorbell*) tocar; **to give sb a ~** (*BRIT: TEL*) llamar *or* telefonear a alguien; **~ back** (*BRIT*) *vt, vi* (*TEL*) devolver la llamada; **~ off** (*BRIT*) *vi* (*TEL*) colgar, cortar la comunicación; **~ up** (*BRIT*) *vt* (*TEL*) llamar, telefonear; **~ing** *n* (*of bell*) repique *m*; (*of phone*) el sonar; (*in ears*) zumbido; **~ing tone** *n* (*TEL*) tono de llamada; **~leader** *n* (*of gang*) cabecilla *m*; **~lets** [ˈrɪŋlɪts] *npl* rizos *mpl*, bucles *mpl*; **~ road** (*BRIT*) *n* carretera periférica *or* de circunvalación

rink [rɪŋk] *n* (*also*: **ice ~**) pista de hielo

rinse [rɪns] *n* aclarado *m*; (*dye*) tinte *m* ♦ *vt* aclarar; (*mouth*) enjuagar

riot [ˈraɪət] *n* motín *m*, disturbio ♦ *vi* amotinarse; **to run ~** desmandarse; **~ous** *adj* alborotado; (*party*) bullicioso

rip [rɪp] *n* rasgón *m*, rasgadura ♦ *vt* rasgar, desgarrar ♦ *vi* rasgarse, desgarrarse; **~cord** *n* cabo de desgarre

ripe [raɪp] *adj* maduro; **~n** *vt* madurar; (*cheese*) curar ♦ *vi* madurar

ripple [ˈrɪpl] *n* onda, rizo; (*sound*)

murmullo ♦ vi rizarse

rise [raɪz] (pt **rose**, pp **risen**) n (slope) cuesta, pendiente f; (hill) altura; (BRIT: in wages) aumento; (in prices, temperature) subida; (in rank) ascenso ♦ vi subir; (waters) crecer; (sun, moon) salir; (person: from bed etc) levantarse; (also: ~ **up**: rebel) sublevarse; (in rank) ascender; **to give ~ to** dar lugar al origen a; **to ~ to the occasion** ponerse a la altura de las circunstancias; **risen** ['rɪzn] pp of **rise**; **rising** adj (increasing: number) creciente; (: prices) en aumento al alza; (tide) creciente; (sun, moon) naciente

risk [rɪsk] n riesgo, peligro ♦ vt arriesgar; (run the ~ of) exponerse a; **to take** or **run the ~ of doing** correr el riesgo de hacer; **at ~** en peligro; **at one's own ~** bajo su propia responsabilidad; **~y** adj arriesgado, peligroso

rissole ['rɪsəul] n croqueta

rite [raɪt] n rito; **last ~s** exequias fpl

ritual ['rɪtjuəl] adj ritual ♦ n ritual m, rito

rival ['raɪvl] n rival m/f; (in business) competidor(a) m/f ♦ adj rival, opuesto ♦ vt competir con; **~ry** n competencia

river ['rɪvə*] n río ♦ cpd (port) de río; (traffic) fluvial; **up/down** ~ río arriba/abajo; **~bank** n orilla (del río); **~bed** n lecho, cauce m

rivet ['rɪvɪt] n roblón m, remache m ♦ vt (fig) captar

Riviera [rɪvɪ'eərə] n: **the (French) ~** la Costa Azul (francesa)

road [rəud] n camino; (motorway etc) carretera; (in town) calle f ♦ cpd (accident) de tráfico; **major/minor** ~ carretera principal/secundaria; ~ **accident** n accidente m de tráfico; **~block** n barricada; **~hog** n loco/a del volante; ~ **map** n mapa m de carreteras; ~ **rage** n agresividad en la carretera; ~ **safety** n seguridad f vial; **~side** n borde m (del camino); **~sign** n señal f de tráfico; ~ **user** n usuario/a de la vía pública; **~way** n calzada; **~works** npl obras fpl; **~worthy** adj (car) en buen estado para

circular

roam [rəum] vi vagar

roar [rɔː*] n rugido; (of vehicle, storm) estruendo; (of laughter) carcajada ♦ vi rugir; hacer estruendo; **to ~ with laughter** reírse a carcajadas; **to do a ~ing trade** hacer buen negocio

roast [rəust] n carne f asada, asado ♦ vt asar; (coffee) tostar; ~ **beef** n rosbif m

rob [rɒb] vt robar; **to ~ sb of sth** robar algo a uno; (fig: deprive) quitar algo a uno; **~ber** n ladrón/ona m/f; **~bery** n robo

robe [rəub] n (for ceremony etc) toga; (also: **bath~**, US) albornoz m

robin ['rɒbɪn] n petirrojo

robot ['rəubɒt] n robot m

robust [rəu'bʌst] adj robusto, fuerte

rock [rɒk] n roca; (boulder) peña, peñasco; (US: small stone) piedrecita; (BRIT: sweet) ≈ pirulí ♦ vt (swing gently: cradle) balancear, mecer; (: child) arrullar; (shake) sacudir ♦ vi mecerse, balancearse; sacudirse; **on the ~s** (drink) con hielo; (marriage etc) en ruinas; ~ **and roll** n rocanrol m; **~-bottom** n (fig) punto más bajo; **~ery** n cuadro alpino

rocket ['rɒkɪt] n cohete m

rocking ['rɒkɪŋ]: ~ **chair** n mecedora; ~ **horse** n caballo de balancín

rocky ['rɒkɪ] adj rocoso

rod [rɒd] n vara, varilla; (also: **fishing ~**) caña

rode [rəud] pt of **ride**

rodent ['rəudnt] n roedor m

roe [rəu] n (species: also: ~ **deer**) corzo; (of fish): **hard/soft** ~ hueva/lecha

rogue [rəug] n pícaro, pillo

role [rəul] n papel m

roll [rəul] n rollo; (of bank notes) fajo; (also: **bread ~**) panecillo; (register, list) lista, nómina; (sound: of drums etc) redoble m ♦ vt hacer rodar; (also: ~ **up**: string) enrollar; (: sleeves) arremangar; (cigarette) liar; (also: ~ **out**: pastry) aplanar; (flatten: road, lawn) apisonar ♦ vi rodar; (drum) redoblar; (ship) balancearse; ~ **about** or

around vi (*person*) revolcarse; (*object*) rodar (por); ~ **by** vi (*time*) pasar; ~ **over** vi dar una vuelta; ~ **up** vi (*inf: arrive*) aparecer ♦ vt (*carpet*) arrollar; ~ **call** n: **to take a ~ call** pasar lista; **~er** n rodillo; (*wheel*) rueda; (*for road*) apisonadora; (*for hair*) rulo; **~erblade** n patín m (en línea); **~er coaster** n montaña rusa; **~er skates** npl patines mpl de rueda

rolling ['rəʊlɪŋ] adj (*landscape*) ondulado; ~ **pin** n rodillo (de cocina); ~ **stock** n (*RAIL*) material m rodante

ROM [rɔm] n abbr (*COMPUT*: = *read only memory*) ROM f

Roman ['rəʊmən] adj romano/a; ~ **Catholic** adj, n católico/a m/f (romano/a)

romance [rə'mæns] n (*love affair*) amor m; (*charm*) lo romántico; (*novel*) novela de amor

Romania [ruː'meɪnɪə] n = **Rumania**

Roman numeral n número romano

romantic [rə'mæntɪk] adj romántico

Rome [rəʊm] n Roma

romp [rɔmp] n retozo, juego ♦ vi (*also*: ~ **about**) jugar, brincar

rompers ['rɔmpəz] npl pelele m

roof [ruːf] (*pl* ~**s**) n (*gen*) techo; (*of house*) techo, tejado ♦ vt techar, poner techo a; **the ~ of the mouth** el paladar; **~ing** n techumbre f; ~ **rack** n (*AUT*) baca, portaequipajes m inv

rook [rʊk] n (*bird*) graja; (*CHESS*) torre f

room [ruːm] n cuarto, habitación f, pieza (*esp AM*); (*also*: **bed~**) dormitorio; (*in school etc*) sala; (*space, scope*) sitio, cabida; **~s** npl (*lodging*) alojamiento; "**~s to let**", "**~s for rent**" (*US*) "se alquilan cuartos"; **single/double** ~ habitación individual/doble *or* para dos personas; **~ing house** (*US*) n pensión f; **~mate** n compañero/a de cuarto; ~ **service** n servicio de habitaciones; **~y** adj espacioso; (*garment*) amplio

roost [ruːst] vi pasar la noche

rooster ['ruːstə*] n gallo

root [ruːt] n raíz f ♦ vi arraigarse; ~ **about**

vi (*fig*) buscar y rebuscar; ~ **for** vt fus (*support*) apoyar a; ~ **out** vt desarraigar

rope [rəʊp] n cuerda; (*NAUT*) cable m ♦ vt (*tie*) atar *or* amarrar con (una) cuerda; (*climbers*: *also*: ~ **together**) encordarse; (*an area*: *also*: ~ **off**) acordonar; **to know the ~s** (*fig*) conocer los trucos (del oficio); ~ **in** vt (*fig*): **to ~ sb in** persuadir a uno a tomar parte

rosary ['rəʊzərɪ] n rosario

rose [rəʊz] pt of **rise** ♦ n rosa; (*shrub*) rosal m; (*on watering can*) roseta

rosé ['rəʊzeɪ] n vino rosado

rosebud ['rəʊzbʌd] n capullo de rosa

rosebush ['rəʊzbʊʃ] n rosal m

rosemary ['rəʊzmərɪ] n romero

roster ['rɔstə*] n: **duty ~** lista de deberes

rostrum ['rɔstrəm] n tribuna

rosy ['rəʊzɪ] adj rosado, sonrosado; **a ~ future** un futuro prometedor

rot [rɔt] n podredumbre f; (*fig: pej*) tonterías fpl ♦ vt pudrir ♦ vi pudrirse

rota ['rəʊtə] n (sistema m de) turnos mpl

rotary ['rəʊtərɪ] adj rotativo

rotate [rəʊ'teɪt] vt (*revolve*) hacer girar, dar vueltas a; (*jobs*) alternar ♦ vi girar, dar vueltas; **rotating** adj rotativo; **rotation** [-'teɪʃən] n rotación f

rotten ['rɔtn] adj podrido; (*dishonest*) corrompido; (*inf: bad*) pocho; **to feel ~** (*ill*) sentirse fatal

rotund [rəʊ'tʌnd] adj regordete

rouble ['ruːbl] (*US* **ruble**) n rublo

rough [rʌf] adj (*skin, surface*) áspero; (*terrain*) quebrado; (*road*) desigual; (*voice*) bronco; (*person, manner*) tosco, grosero; (*weather*) borrascoso; (*treatment*) brutal; (*sea*) picado; (*town, area*) peligroso; (*cloth*) basto; (*plan*) preliminar; (*guess*) aproximado ♦ n (*GOLF*): **in the ~** en las hierbas altas; **to ~ it** vivir sin comodidades; **to sleep ~** (*BRIT*) pasar la noche al raso; **~age** n fibra(s) f(pl); **~-and-ready** adj improvisado; ~ **copy** n borrador m; ~ **draft** n = ~ **copy**; **~ly** adv (*handle*) torpemente; (*make*) toscamente; (*speak*) groseramente;

(*approximately*) aproximadamente; **~ness**
n (*of surface*) aspereza; (*of person*) rudeza
roulette [ru:'let] *n* ruleta
Roumania [ru:'meɪnɪə] *n* = **Rumania**
round [raund] *adj* redondo ♦ *n* círculo;
(*BRIT: of toast*) rebanada; (*of policeman*)
ronda; (*of milkman*) recorrido; (*of doctor*)
visitas *fpl*; (*game: of cards, in competition*)
partida; (*of ammunition*) cartucho;
(*BOXING*) asalto; (*of talks*) ronda ♦ *vt*
(*corner*) doblar ♦ *prep* alrededor de;
(*surrounding*): **~ his neck/the table** en su
cuello/alrededor de la mesa; (*in a circular
movement*): **to move ~ the room/sail ~
the world** dar una vuelta a la habitación/
circunnavegar el mundo; (*in various
directions*): **to move ~ a room/house**
moverse por toda la habitación/casa;
(*approximately*) alrededor de ♦ *adv*: **all ~**
por todos lados; **~ up** *vt* (*cattle*)
por todos lados; **the long way ~** por el
camino menos directo; **all the year ~**
durante todo el año; **it's just ~ the
corner** (*fig*) está a la vuelta de la esquina;
~ the clock *adv* las 24 horas; **to go ~ to
sb's (house)** ir a casa de uno; **to go ~
the back** pasar por atrás; **enough to go ~**
bastante (para todos); **a ~ of applause**
una salva de aplausos; **a ~ of drinks/
sandwiches** una ronda de bebidas/
bocadillos; **~ off** *vt* (*speech etc*) acabar,
poner término a; **~ up** *vt* (*cattle*)
acorralar; (*people*) reunir; (*price*)
redondear; **~about** (*BRIT*) *n* (*AUT*) isleta;
(*at fair*) tiovivo ♦ *adj* (*route, means*)
indirecto; **~ers** *n* (*game*) juego similar al
béisbol; **~ly** *adv* (*fig*) rotundamente; **~
trip** *n* viaje *m* de ida y vuelta; **~up** *n*
rodeo; (*of criminals*) redada; (*of news*)
resumen *m*

rouse [rauz] *vt* (*wake up*) despertar; (*stir
up*) suscitar; **rousing** *adj* (*cheer,
welcome*) caluroso

route [ru:t] *n* ruta, camino; (*of bus*)
recorrido; (*of shipping*) derrota

routine [ru:'ti:n] *adj* rutinario ♦ *n* rutina;
(*THEATRE*) número

rove [rəuv] *vt* vagar *or* errar por

row¹ [rəu] *n* (*line*) fila, hilera; (*KNITTING*)
pasada ♦ *vi* (*in boat*) remar ♦ *vt* conducir
remando; **4 days in a ~** 4 días seguidos
row² [rau] *n* (*racket*) escándalo; (*dispute*)
bronca, pelea; (*scolding*) regaño ♦ *vi*
pelear(se)
rowboat ['rəubəut] (*US*) *n* bote *m* de
remos
rowdy ['raudɪ] *adj* (*person: noisy*) ruidoso;
(*occasion*) alborotado
rowing ['rəuɪŋ] *n* remo; **~ boat** (*BRIT*) *n*
bote *m* de remos
royal ['rɔɪəl] *adj* real; **R~ Air Force** *n*
Fuerzas *fpl* Aéreas Británicas; **~ty** *n* (*~
persons*) familia real; (*payment to author*)
derechos *mpl* de autor
rpm *abbr* (= *revs per minute*) r.p.m.
R.S.V.P. *abbr* (= *répondez s'il vous plaît*)
SRC
Rt. Hon. *abbr* (*BRIT: = Right Honourable*)
título honorífico de diputado
rub [rʌb] *vt* frotar; (*scrub*) restregar ♦ *n*: **to
give sth a ~** frotar algo; **to ~ sb up** *or* **~
sb** (*US*) **the wrong way** entrarle uno por
mal ojo; **~ off** *vi* borrarse; **~ off on** *vt
fus* influir en; **~ out** *vt* borrar
rubber ['rʌbə*] *n* caucho, goma; (*BRIT:
eraser*) goma de borrar; **~ band** *n* goma,
gomita; **~ plant** *n* ficus *m*
rubbish ['rʌbɪʃ] *n* basura; (*waste*)
desperdicios *mpl*; (*fig: pej*) tonterías *fpl*;
(*junk*) pacotilla; **~ bin** (*BRIT*) *n* cubo (*SP*)
or bote *m* (*AM*) de la basura; **~ dump** *n*
vertedero, basurero
rubble ['rʌbl] *n* escombros *mpl*
ruble ['ru:bl] (*US*) *n* = **rouble**
ruby ['ru:bɪ] *n* rubí *m*
rucksack ['rʌksæk] *n* mochila
rudder ['rʌdə*] *n* timón *m*
ruddy ['rʌdɪ] *adj* (*face*) rubicundo; (*inf:
damned*) condenado
rude [ru:d] *adj* (*impolite: person*) mal
educado; (: *word, manners*) grosero;
(*crude*) crudo; (*indecent*) indecente;
~ness *n* descortesía
ruffle ['rʌfl] *vt* (*hair*) despeinar; (*clothes*)
arrugar; **to get ~d** (*fig: person*) alterarse

rug [rʌg] n alfombra; (*BRIT*: *blanket*) manta
rugby ['rʌgbɪ] n (*also*: ~ **football**) rugby m
rugged ['rʌgɪd] adj (*landscape*) accidentado; (*features*) robusto
ruin ['ruːɪn] n ruina ♦ vt arruinar; (*spoil*) estropear; **~s** npl ruinas fpl, restos mpl
rule [ruːl] n (*norm*) norma, costumbre f; (*regulation, ruler*) regla; (*government*) dominio ♦ vt (*country, person*) gobernar ♦ vi gobernar; (*LAW*) fallar; **as a ~** por regla general; **~ out** vt excluir; **~d** adj (*paper*) rayado; **~r** n (*sovereign*) soberano; (*for measuring*) regla; **ruling** adj (*party*) gobernante; (*class*) dirigente ♦ n (*LAW*) fallo, decisión f
rum [rʌm] n ron m
Rumania [ruːˈmeɪnɪə] n Rumanía; **~n** adj rumano/a ♦ n rumano/a m/f; (*LING*) rumano
rumble ['rʌmbl] n (*noise*) ruido sordo ♦ vi retumbar, hacer un ruido sordo; (*stomach, pipe*) sonar
rummage ['rʌmɪdʒ] vi (*search*) hurgar
rumour ['ruːmə*] (*US* **rumor**) n rumor m ♦ vt: **it is ~ed that ...** se rumorea que ...
rump [rʌmp] n (*of animal*) ancas fpl, grupa; **~ steak** n filete m de lomo
rumpus ['rʌmpəs] n lío, jaleo
run [rʌn] (*pt* **ran**, *pp* **run**) n (*fast pace*): **at a ~** corriendo; (*SPORT, in tights*) carrera; (*outing*) paseo, excursión f; (*distance travelled*) trayecto; (*series*) serie f; (*THEATRE*) temporada; (*SKI*) pista ♦ vt correr; (*operate: business*) dirigir; (: *competition, course*) organizar; (: *hotel, house*) administrar, llevar; (*COMPUT*) ejecutar; (*pass: hand*) pasar; (*PRESS: feature*) publicar ♦ vi correr; (*work: machine*) funcionar, marchar; (*bus, train: operate*) circular, ir; (: *travel*) ir; (*continue: play*) seguir; (: *contract*) ser válido; (*flow: river*) fluir; (*colours, washing*) desteñirse; (*in election*) ser candidato; **there was a ~ on** (*meat, tickets*) hubo mucha demanda de; **in the long ~** a la larga; **on the ~** en fuga; **I'll ~ you to the station** te llevaré a la estación (en coche); **to ~ a risk** correr

un riesgo; **to ~ a bath** llenar la bañera; **~ about** *or* **around** vi (*children*) correr por todos lados; **~ across** vt fus (*find*) dar *or* topar con; **~ away** vi huir; **~ down** vt (*production*) ir reduciendo; (*factory*) ir restringiendo la producción en; (*subj: car*) atropellar; (*criticize*) criticar; **to be ~ down** (*person: tired*) estar debilitado; **~ in** (*BRIT*) vt (*car*) rodar; **~ into** vt fus (*meet: person, trouble*) tropezar con; (*collide with*) chocar con; **~ off** vt (*water*) dejar correr; (*copies*) sacar ♦ vi huir corriendo; **~ out** vi (*person*) salir corriendo; (*liquid*) irse; (*lease*) caducar, vencer; (*money etc*) acabarse; **~ out of** vt fus quedar sin; **~ over** vt (*AUT*) atropellar ♦ vt fus (*revise*) repasar; **~ through** vt fus (*instructions*) repasar; **~ up** vt (*debt*) contraer; **to ~ up against** (*difficulties*) tropezar con; **~away** adj (*horse*) desbocado; (*truck*) sin frenos; (*child*) escapado de casa
rung [rʌŋ] pp of **ring** ♦ n (*of ladder*) escalón m, peldaño
runner ['rʌnə*] n (*in race: person*) corredor(a) m/f; (: *horse*) caballo; (*on sledge*) patín m; **~ bean** (*BRIT*) n ≈ judía verde; **~-up** n subcampeón/ona m/f
running ['rʌnɪŋ] n (*sport*) atletismo; (*business*) administración f ♦ adj (*water, costs*) corriente; (*commentary*) continuo; **to be in/out of the ~ for sth** tener/no tener posibilidades de ganar algo; **6 days ~** 6 días seguidos; **~ commentary** n (*TV, RADIO*) comentario en directo; (*on guided tour etc*) comentario detallado; **~ costs** npl gastos mpl corrientes
runny ['rʌnɪ] adj fluido; (*nose, eyes*) gastante
run-of-the-mill adj común y corriente
runt [rʌnt] n (*also pej*) redrojo, enano
run-up n: **~ to** (*election etc*) período previo a
runway ['rʌnweɪ] n (*AVIAT*) pista de aterrizaje
rural ['ruərl] adj rural
rush [rʌʃ] n ímpetu m; (*hurry*) prisa; (*COMM*) demanda repentina; (*current*)

corriente f fuerte; (of feeling) torrente;
(BOT) junco ♦ vt apresurar; (work) hacer
de prisa ♦ vi correr, precipitarse; ~ **hour**
n horas fpl punta

rusk [rʌsk] n bizcocho tostado

Russia ['rʌʃə] n Rusia; ~n adj ruso/a ♦ n
ruso/a m/f; (LING) ruso

rust [rʌst] n herrumbre f, moho m ♦ vi
oxidarse

rustic ['rʌstɪk] adj rústico

rustle ['rʌsl] vi susurrar ♦ vt (paper) hacer
crujir

rustproof ['rʌstpruːf] adj inoxidable

rusty ['rʌstɪ] adj oxidado

rut [rʌt] n surco; (ZOOL) celo; **to be in a ~**
ser esclavo de la rutina

ruthless ['ruːθlɪs] adj despiadado

rye [raɪ] n centeno

S, s

Sabbath ['sæbəθ] n domingo; (Jewish)
sábado

sabotage ['sæbətɑːʒ] n sabotaje m ♦ vt
sabotear

saccharin(e) ['sækərɪn] n sacarina

sachet ['sæʃeɪ] n sobrecito

sack [sæk] n (bag) saco, costal m ♦ vt
(dismiss) despedir; (plunder) saquear; **to**
get the ~ ser despedido; ~ing n despido;
(material) arpillera

sacred ['seɪkrɪd] adj sagrado, santo

sacrifice ['sækrɪfaɪs] n sacrificio ♦ vt
sacrificar

sad [sæd] adj (unhappy) triste; (deplorable)
lamentable

saddle ['sædl] n silla (de montar); (of
cycle) sillín m ♦ vt (horse) ensillar; **to be**
~d with sth (inf) quedar cargado con
algo; ~**bag** n alforja

sadistic [sə'dɪstɪk] adj sádico

sadly ['sædlɪ] adv lamentablemente; **to be**
~ lacking in estar por desgracia carente
de

sadness ['sædnɪs] n tristeza

s.a.e. abbr (= stamped addressed

envelope) sobre con las propias señas de
uno y con sello

safari [sə'fɑːrɪ] n safari m

safe [seɪf] adj (out of danger) fuera de
peligro; (not dangerous, sure) seguro;
(unharmed) ileso ♦ n caja de caudales,
caja fuerte; **~ and sound** sano y salvo;
(just) to be on the ~ side para mayor
seguridad; ~**-conduct** n salvoconducto;
~**-deposit** n (vault) cámara acorazada;
(box) caja de seguridad; ~**guard** n
protección f, garantía ♦ vt proteger,
defender; ~**keeping** n custodia; ~**ly** adv
seguramente, con seguridad; **to arrive**
~ly llegar bien; ~ **sex** n sexo seguro or
sin riesgo

safety ['seɪftɪ] n seguridad f; ~ **belt** n
cinturón m (de seguridad); ~ **pin** n
imperdible m (SP), seguro (AM); ~ **valve**
n válvula de seguridad

saffron ['sæfrən] n azafrán m

sag [sæg] vi aflojarse

sage [seɪdʒ] n (herb) salvia; (man) sabio

Sagittarius [sædʒɪ'tɛərɪəs] n Sagitario

Sahara [sə'hɑːrə] n: **the ~ (Desert)** el
(desierto del) Sáhara

said [sed] pt, pp of **say**

sail [seɪl] n (on boat) vela; (trip): **to go for**
a ~ dar un paseo en barco ♦ vt (boat)
gobernar ♦ vi (travel: ship) navegar;
(SPORT) hacer vela; (begin voyage) salir;
they ~ed into Copenhagen arribaron a
Copenhague; ~ **through** vt fus (exam)
aprobar sin ningún problema; ~**boat** (US)
n velero, barco de vela; ~**ing** n (SPORT)
vela; **to go ~ing** hacer vela; ~**ing boat** n
barco de vela; ~**ing ship** n velero, barco
de vela; ~**or** n marinero, marino

saint [seɪnt] n santo; ~**ly** adj santo

sake [seɪk] n: **for the ~ of** por

salad ['sæləd] n ensalada; ~ **bowl** n
ensaladera; ~ **cream** (BRIT) n (especie f
de) mayonesa; ~ **dressing** n aliño

salary ['sælərɪ] n sueldo

sale [seɪl] n venta; (at reduced prices)
liquidación f, saldo; (auction) subasta; ~**s**
npl (total amount sold) ventas fpl,

facturación f; **"for ~"** "se vende"; **on ~** en venta; **on ~ or return** (*goods*) venta por reposición; **~room** n sala de subastas; **~s assistant** (*US* **~s clerk**) n dependiente/a *m/f*; **salesman/woman** (*irreg*) n (*in shop*) dependiente/a *m/f*; (*representative*) viajante *m/f*

salmon ['sæmən] n *inv* salmón m

salon ['sælɔn] n (*hairdressing ~*) peluquería; (*beauty ~*) salón m de belleza

saloon [sə'luːn] n (*US*) bar m, taberna; (*BRIT: AUT*) (coche m de) turismo; (*ship's lounge*) cámara, salón m

salt [sɔlt] n sal f ♦ vt salar; (*put ~ on*) poner sal en; **~ cellar** n salero; **~water** *adj* de agua salada; **~y** *adj* salado

salute [sə'luːt] n saludo; (*of guns*) salva ♦ vt saludar

salvage ['sælvɪdʒ] n (*saving*) salvamento, recuperación f; (*things saved*) objetos *mpl* salvados ♦ vt salvar

salvation [sæl'veɪʃən] n salvación f; **S~ Army** n Ejército de Salvación

same [seɪm] *adj* mismo ♦ *pron*: **the ~** el/la mismo/a, los/las mismos/as; **the ~ book as** el mismo libro que; **at the ~ time** (*at the ~ moment*) al mismo tiempo; (*yet*) sin embargo; **all or just the ~** sin embargo, aun así; **to do the ~ (as sb)** hacer lo mismo (que uno); **the ~ to you!** ¡igualmente!

sample ['saːmpl] n muestra ♦ vt (*food*) probar; (*wine*) catar

sanction ['sæŋkʃən] n aprobación f ♦ vt sancionar; aprobar; **~s** *npl* (*POL*) sanciones *fpl*

sanctity ['sæŋktɪtɪ] n santidad f; (*inviolability*) inviolabilidad f

sanctuary ['sæŋktjʊərɪ] n santuario; (*refuge*) asilo, refugio; (*for wildlife*) reserva

sand [sænd] n arena; (*beach*) playa ♦ vt (*also: ~ down*) lijar

sandal ['sændl] n sandalia

sand: **~box** (*US*) n = **~pit**; **~castle** n castillo de arena; **~ dune** n duna; **~paper** n papel m de lija; **~pit** n (*for children*) cajón m de arena; **~stone** n

piedra arenisca

sandwich ['sændwɪtʃ] n bocadillo (*SP*), sandwich m, emparedado (*AM*) ♦ vt intercalar; **~ed between** apretujado entre; **cheese/ham ~** sandwich de queso/jamón; **~ course** (*BRIT*) n curso de medio tiempo

sandy ['sændɪ] *adj* arenoso; (*colour*) rojizo

sane [seɪn] *adj* cuerdo; (*sensible*) sensato

sang [sæŋ] *pt of* **sing**

sanitary ['sænɪtərɪ] *adj* sanitario; (*clean*) higiénico; **~ towel** (*US* **~ napkin**) n paño higiénico, compresa

sanitation [sænɪ'teɪʃən] n (*in house*) servicios *mpl* higiénicos; (*in town*) servicio de desinfección; **~ department** (*US*) n departamento de limpieza y recogida de basuras

sanity ['sænɪtɪ] n cordura; (*of judgment*) sensatez f

sank [sæŋk] *pt of* **sink**

Santa Claus [sæntə'klɔːz] n San Nicolás, Papá Noel

sap [sæp] n (*of plants*) savia ♦ vt (*strength*) minar, agotar

sapling ['sæplɪŋ] n árbol nuevo *or* joven

sapphire ['sæfaɪə*] n zafiro

sarcasm ['saːkæzm] n sarcasmo

sardine [saː'diːn] n sardina

Sardinia [saː'dɪnɪə] n Cerdeña

sash [sæʃ] n faja

sat [sæt] *pt, pp of* **sit**

Satan ['seɪtn] n Satanás m

satchel ['sætʃl] n (*child's*) cartera (*SP*), mochila (*AM*)

satellite ['sætəlaɪt] n satélite m; **~ dish** n antena de televisión por satélite; **~ television** n televisión f vía satélite

satin ['sætɪn] n raso ♦ *adj* de raso

satire ['sætaɪə*] n sátira

satisfaction [sætɪs'fækʃən] n satisfacción f

satisfactory [sætɪs'fæktərɪ] *adj* satisfactorio

satisfy ['sætɪsfaɪ] vt satisfacer; (*convince*) convencer; **~ing** *adj* satisfactorio

Saturday ['sætədɪ] n sábado

sauce [sɔːs] n salsa; (*sweet*) crema; jarabe m; **~pan** n cacerola, olla

saucer ['sɔːsə*] *n* platillo

Saudi ['saudɪ]: ~ **Arabia** *n* Arabia Saudí *or* Saudita; ~ **(Arabian)** *adj*, *n* saudí *m/f*, saudita *m/f*

sauna ['sɔːnə] *n* sauna

saunter ['sɔːntə*] *vi*: **to ~ in/out** entrar/salir sin prisa

sausage ['sɒsɪdʒ] *n* salchicha; ~ **roll** *n* empanadita de salchicha

sauté ['səuteɪ] *adj* salteado

savage ['sævɪdʒ] *adj* (*cruel, fierce*) feroz, furioso; (*primitive*) salvaje ♦ *n* salvaje *m/f* ♦ *vt* (*attack*) embestir

save [seɪv] *vt* (*rescue*) salvar, rescatar; (*money, time*) ahorrar; (*put by, keep: seat*) guardar; (*COMPUT*) salvar (y guardar); (*avoid: trouble*) evitar; (*SPORT*) parar ♦ *vi* (*also:* ~ **up**) ahorrar ♦ *n* (*SPORT*) parada ♦ *prep* salvo, excepto

saving ['seɪvɪŋ] *n* (*on price etc*) economía ♦ *adj*: **the ~ grace of** el único mérito de; ~**s** *npl* ahorros *mpl*; ~**s account** *n* cuenta de ahorros; ~**s bank** *n* caja de ahorros

saviour ['seɪvjə*] (*US* **savior**) *n* salvador(a) *m/f*

savour ['seɪvə*] (*US* **savor**) *vt* saborear; ~**y** *adj* sabroso; (*dish: not sweet*) salado

saw [sɔː] (*pt* **sawed**, *pp* **sawed** *or* **sawn**) *pt of* **see** ♦ *n* (*tool*) sierra ♦ *vt* serrar; ~**dust** *n* (a)serrín *m*; ~**mill** *n* aserradero; ~**n-off shotgun** *n* escopeta de cañones recortados

saxophone ['sæksəfəun] *n* saxófono

say [seɪ] (*pt, pp* **said**) *n*: **to have one's ~** expresar su opinión ♦ *vt* decir; **to have a** *or* **some ~ in sth** tener voz *or* tener que ver en algo; **to ~ yes/no** decir que sí/no; **could you ~ that again?** ¿podría repetir eso?; **that is to ~** es decir; **that goes without ~ing** ni que decir tiene; ~**ing** *n* dicho, refrán *m*

scab [skæb] *n* costra; (*pej*) esquirol *m*

scaffold ['skæfəuld] *n* cadalso; ~**ing** *n* andamio, andamiaje *m*

scald [skɔːld] *n* escaldadura ♦ *vt* escaldar

scale [skeɪl] *n* (*gen, MUS*) escala; (*of fish*) escama; (*of salaries, fees etc*) escalafón *m* ♦ *vt* (*mountain*) escalar; (*tree*) trepar; ~**s** *npl* (*for weighing: small*) balanza; (: *large*) báscula; **on a large ~** en gran escala; ~ **of charges** tarifa, lista de precios; ~ **down** *vt* reducir a escala

scallop ['skɒləp] *n* (*ZOOL*) venera; (*SEWING*) festón *m*

scalp [skælp] *n* cabellera ♦ *vt* escalpar

scampi ['skæmpɪ] *npl* gambas *fpl*

scan [skæn] *vt* (*examine*) escudriñar; (*glance at quickly*) dar un vistazo a; (*TV, RADAR*) explorar, registrar ♦ *n* (*MED*): **to have a ~** pasar por el escáner

scandal ['skændl] *n* escándalo; (*gossip*) chismes *mpl*

Scandinavia [skændɪ'neɪvɪə] *n* Escandinavia; ~**n** *adj*, *n* escandinavo/a *m/f*

scant [skænt] *adj* escaso; ~**y** *adj* (*meal*) insuficiente; (*clothes*) ligero

scapegoat ['skeɪpgəut] *n* cabeza de turco, chivo expiatorio

scar [skɑː] *n* cicatriz *f*; (*fig*) señal *f* ♦ *vt* dejar señales en

scarce [skeəs] *adj* escaso; **to make o.s. ~** (*inf*) esfumarse; ~**ly** *adv* apenas; **scarcity** *n* escasez *f*

scare [skeə*] *n* susto, sobresalto; (*panic*) pánico ♦ *vt* asustar, espantar; **to ~ sb stiff** dar a uno un susto de muerte; **bomb ~** amenaza de bomba; ~ **off** *or* **away** *vt* ahuyentar; ~**crow** *n* espantapájaros *m inv*; ~**d** *adj*: **to be ~d** estar asustado

scarf [skɑːf] (*pl* ~**s** *or* **scarves**) *n* (*long*) bufanda; (*square*) pañuelo

scarlet ['skɑːlɪt] *adj* escarlata; ~ **fever** *n* escarlatina

scarves [skɑːvz] *npl of* **scarf**

scary ['skeərɪ] (*inf*) *adj* espeluznante

scathing ['skeɪðɪŋ] *adj* mordaz

scatter ['skætə*] *vt* (*spread*) esparcir, desparramar; (*put to flight*) dispersar ♦ *vi* desparramarse; dispersarse; ~**brained** *adj* ligero de cascos

scavenger ['skævəndʒə*] *n* (*person*) basurero/a

scenario [sɪˈnɑːrɪəu] n (*THEATRE*) argumento; (*CINEMA*) guión m; (*fig*) escenario

scene [siːn] n (*THEATRE, fig etc*) escena; (*of crime etc*) escenario; (*view*) panorama m; (*fuss*) escándalo; **~ry** n (*THEATRE*) decorado; (*landscape*) paisaje m; **scenic** adj pintoresco

scent [sɛnt] n perfume m, olor m; (*fig: track*) rastro, pista

sceptic [ˈskɛptɪk] (*US* **skeptic**) n escéptico/a; **~al** adj escéptico

sceptre [ˈsɛptəʳ] (*US* **scepter**) n cetro

schedule [ˈʃɛdjuːl, (*US*) ˈskɛdjuːl] n (*timetable*) horario; (*of events*) programa m; (*list*) lista ♦ vt (*visit*) fijar la hora de; **to arrive on** ~ llegar a la hora debida; **to be ahead of/behind** ~ estar adelantado/en retraso; **~d flight** n vuelo regular

scheme [skiːm] n (*plan*) plan m, proyecto; (*plot*) intriga; (*arrangement*) disposición f; (*pension ~ etc*) sistema m ♦ vi (*intrigue*) intrigar; **scheming** adj intrigante ♦ n intrigas fpl

schizophrenic [skɪtsəˈfrɛnɪk] adj esquizofrénico

scholar [ˈskɔləʳ] n (*pupil*) alumno/a; (*learned person*) sabio/a, erudito/a; **~ship** n erudición f; (*grant*) beca

school [skuːl] n escuela, colegio; (*in university*) facultad f ♦ cpd escolar; ~ **age** n edad f escolar; **~book** n libro de texto; **~boy** n alumno; ~ **children** npl alumnos mpl; **~girl** n alumna; **~ing** n enseñanza; **~master/mistress** n (*primary*) maestro/a; (*secondary*) profesor(a) m/f; **~teacher** n (*primary*) maestro/a; (*secondary*) profesor(a) m/f

schooner [ˈskuːnəʳ] n (*ship*) goleta

sciatica [saɪˈætɪkə] n ciática

science [ˈsaɪəns] n ciencia; ~ **fiction** n ciencia-ficción f; **scientific** [-ˈtɪfɪk] adj científico; **scientist** n científico/a

scissors [ˈsɪzəz] npl tijeras fpl; **a pair of** ~ unas tijeras

scoff [skɔf] vt (*BRIT: inf: eat*) engullir ♦ vi: **to** ~ (**at**) (*mock*) mofarse (de)

scold [skəuld] vt regañar

scone [skɔn] n pastel de pan

scoop [skuːp] n (*for flour etc*) pala; (*PRESS*) exclusiva; ~ **out** vt excavar; ~ **up** vt recoger

scooter [ˈskuːtəʳ] n moto f; (*toy*) patinete m

scope [skəup] n (*of plan*) ámbito; (*of person*) competencia; (*opportunity*) libertad f (de acción)

scorch [skɔːtʃ] vt (*clothes*) chamuscar; (*earth, grass*) quemar, secar

score [skɔːʳ] n (*points etc*) puntuación f; (*MUS*) partitura; (*twenty*) veintena ♦ vt (*goal, point*) ganar; (*mark*) rayar; (*achieve: success*) conseguir ♦ vi marcar un tanto; (*FOOTBALL*) marcar (un) gol; (*keep score*) llevar el tanteo; **~s of** (*very many*) decenas de; **on that** ~ en lo que se refiere a eso; **to** ~ **6 out of 10** obtener una puntuación de 6 sobre 10; ~ **out** vt tachar; ~ **over** vt fus obtener una victoria sobre; **~board** n marcador m

scorn [skɔːn] n desprecio; **~ful** adj desdeñoso, despreciativo

Scorpio [ˈskɔːpɪəu] n Escorpión m

scorpion [ˈskɔːpɪən] n alacrán m

Scot [skɔt] n escocés/esa m/f

Scotch [skɔtʃ] n whisky m escocés

Scotland [ˈskɔtlənd] n Escocia

Scots [skɔts] adj escocés/esa; **~man/woman** (*irreg*) n escocés/esa m/f; **Scottish** [ˈskɔtɪʃ] adj escocés/esa

scoundrel [ˈskaundrl] n canalla m/f, sinvergüenza m/f

scout [skaut] n (*MIL, also:* **boy** ~) explorador m; **girl** ~ (*US*) niña exploradora; ~ **around** vi reconocer el terreno

scowl [skaul] vi fruncir el ceño; **to** ~ **at sb** mirar con ceño a uno

scrabble [ˈskræbl] vi (*claw*): **to** ~ (**at**) arañar; (*also:* ~ **around**: *search*) revolver todo buscando ♦ n: **S~** ® Scrabble ® m

scraggy [ˈskrægɪ] adj descarnado

scram [skræm] (*inf*) vi largarse

scramble [ˈskræmbl] n (*climb*) subida

(difícil); (*struggle*) pelea ♦ *vi*: **to ~ through/out** abrirse paso/salir con dificultad; **to ~ for** pelear por; **~d eggs** *npl* huevos *mpl* revueltos

scrap [skræp] *n* (*bit*) pedacito; (*fig*) pizca; (*fight*) riña, bronca; (*also*: **~ iron**) chatarra, hierro viejo ♦ *vt* (*discard*) desechar, descartar ♦ *vi* reñir, armar (una) bronca; **~s** *npl* (*waste*) sobras *fpl*, desperdicios *mpl*; **~book** *n* álbum *m* de recortes; **~ dealer** *n* chatarrero/a

scrape [skreɪp] *n*: **to get into a ~** meterse en un lío ♦ *vt* raspar; (*skin etc*) rasguñar; (**~ against**) rozar ♦ *vi*: **to ~ through** (*exam*) aprobar por los pelos; **~ together** *vt* (*money*) arañar, juntar

scrap: **~ heap** *n* (*fig*): **to be on the ~ heap** estar acabado; **~ merchant** (*BRIT*) *n* chatarrero/a; **~ paper** *n* pedazos *mpl* de papel

scratch [skrætʃ] *n* rasguño; (*from claw*) arañazo ♦ *cpd*: **~ team** equipo improvisado ♦ *vt* (*paint, car*) rayar; (*with claw, nail*) rasguñar, arañar; (*rub: nose etc*) rascarse ♦ *vi* rascarse; **to start from ~** partir de cero; **to be up to ~** cumplir con los requisitos

scrawl [skrɔːl] *n* garabatos *mpl* ♦ *vi* hacer garabatos

scrawny [skrɔːni] *adj* flaco

scream [skriːm] *n* chillido ♦ *vi* chillar

screech [skriːtʃ] *vi* chirriar

screen [skriːn] *n* (*CINEMA, TV*) pantalla; (*movable barrier*) biombo ♦ *vt* (*conceal*) tapar; (*from the wind etc*) proteger; (*film*) proyectar; (*candidates etc*) investigar a; **~ing** *n* (*MED*) investigación *f* médica; **~play** *n* guión *m*

screw [skruː] *n* tornillo ♦ *vt* (*also*: **~ in**) atornillar; **~ up** *vt* (*paper etc*) arrugar; **to ~ up one's eyes** arrugar el entrecejo; **~driver** *n* destornillador *m*

scribble [ˈskrɪbl] *n* garabatos *mpl* ♦ *vt, vi* garabatear

script [skrɪpt] *n* (*CINEMA etc*) guión *m*; (*writing*) escritura, letra

Scripture(s) [ˈskrɪptʃə*(z)] *n(pl)* Sagrada Escritura

scroll [skrəul] *n* rollo

scrounge [skraundʒ] (*inf*) *vt*: **to ~ sth off** *or* **from sb** obtener algo de uno de gorra ♦ *n*: **on the ~** de gorra; **~r** *n* gorrón/ona *m/f*

scrub [skrʌb] *n* (*land*) maleza ♦ *vt* fregar, restregar; (*inf: reject*) cancelar, anular

scruff [skrʌf] *n*: **by the ~ of the neck** por el pescuezo

scruffy [ˈskrʌfi] *adj* desaliñado, piojoso

scrum(mage) [ˈskrʌm(mɪdʒ)] *n* (*RUGBY*) melée *f*

scruple [ˈskruːpl] *n* (*gen pl*) escrúpulo

scrutinize [ˈskruːtɪnaɪz] *vt* escudriñar; (*votes*) escrutar; **scrutiny** [ˈskruːtɪni] *n* escrutinio, examen *m*

scuff [skʌf] *vt* (*shoes, floor*) rayar

scuffle [ˈskʌfl] *n* refriega

sculptor [ˈskʌlptə*] *n* escultor(a) *m/f*

sculpture [ˈskʌlptʃə*] *n* escultura

scum [skʌm] *n* (*on liquid*) espuma; (*pej: people*) escoria

scurry [ˈskʌri] *vi* correr; **to ~ off** escabullirse

scuttle [ˈskʌtl] *n* (*also*: **coal ~**) cubo, carbonera ♦ *vt* (*ship*) barrenar ♦ *vi* (*scamper*): **to ~ away**, **~ off** escabullirse

scythe [saɪð] *n* guadaña

SDP (*BRIT*) *n abbr* = **Social Democratic Party**

sea [siː] *n* mar *m* ♦ *cpd* de mar, marítimo; **by ~** (*travel*) en barco; **on the ~** (*boat*) en el mar; (*town*) junto al mar; **to be all at ~** (*fig*) estar despistado; **out to ~**, **at ~** en alta mar; **~board** *n* litoral *m*; **~food** *n* mariscos *mpl*; **~ front** *n* paseo marítimo; **~going** *adj* de altura; **~gull** *n* gaviota

seal [siːl] *n* (*animal*) foca; (*stamp*) sello ♦ *vt* (*close*) cerrar; **~ off** *vt* (*area*) acordonar

sea level *n* nivel *m* del mar

sea lion *n* león *m* marino

seam [siːm] *n* costura; (*of metal*) juntura; (*of coal*) veta, filón *m*

seaman [ˈsiːmən] (*irreg*) *n* marinero

seance [ˈseɪɒns] *n* sesión *f* de espiritismo

seaplane ['si:pleɪn] n hidroavión m
seaport ['si:pɔ:t] n puerto de mar
search [sɜ:tʃ] n (for person, thing) busca, búsqueda; (COMPUT) búsqueda; (inspection: of sb's home) registro ♦ vt (look in) buscar en; (examine) examinar; (person, place) registrar ♦ vi: to ~ for buscar; in ~ of en busca de; ~ **through** vt fus registrar; ~**ing** adj penetrante; ~**light** n reflector m; ~ **party** n pelotón m de salvamento; ~ **warrant** n mandamiento (judicial)
sea: ~**shore** n playa, orilla del mar; ~**sick** adj mareado; ~**side** n playa, orilla del mar; ~**side resort** n centro turístico costero
season ['si:zn] n (of year) estación f; (sporting etc) temporada; (of films etc) ciclo ♦ vt (food) sazonar; **in/out of ~** en sazón/fuera de temporada; ~**al** adj estacional; ~**ed** adj (fig) experimentado; ~**ing** n condimento, aderezo; ~ **ticket** n abono
seat [si:t] n (in bus, train) asiento; (chair) silla; (PARLIAMENT) escaño; (buttocks) culo, trasero; (of trousers) culera ♦ vt sentar; (have room for) tener cabida para; **to be ~ed** sentarse; ~ **belt** n cinturón m de seguridad
sea: ~ **water** n agua del mar; ~**weed** n alga marina; ~**worthy** adj en condiciones de navegar
sec. abbr = **second(s)**
secluded [sɪ'klu:dɪd] adj retirado
seclusion [sɪ'klu:ʒən] n reclusión f
second ['sɛkənd] adj segundo ♦ adv en segundo lugar ♦ n segundo; (AUT: also: ~ **gear**) segunda; (COMM) (BRIT: SCOL: degree) artículo con algún desperfecto; (BRIT: SCOL: degree) título de licenciado con calificación de notable ♦ vt (motion) apoyar; ~**ary** adj secundario; ~**ary school** n escuela secundaria; ~**-class** adj de segunda clase ♦ adv (RAIL) en segunda; ~**hand** adj de segunda mano, usado; ~ **hand** n (on clock) segundero; ~**ly** adv en segundo lugar; ~**ment** [sɪ'kɔndmənt] (BRIT) n

traslado temporal; ~**-rate** adj de segunda categoría; ~ **thoughts** npl: **to have ~ thoughts** cambiar de opinión; **on ~ thoughts** or **thought** (US) pensándolo bien
secrecy ['si:krəsɪ] n secreto
secret ['si:krɪt] adj, n secreto; **in ~** en secreto
secretarial [sɛkrɪ'tɛərɪəl] adj de secretario; (course, staff) de secretariado
secretary ['sɛkrətərɪ] n secretario/a; **S~ of State (for)** (BRIT: POL) Ministro (de)
secretive ['si:krətɪv] adj reservado, sigiloso
secretly ['si:krɪtlɪ] adv en secreto
sect [sɛkt] n secta; ~**arian** [-'tɛərɪən] adj sectario
section ['sɛkʃən] n sección f; (part) parte f; (of document) artículo; (of opinion) sector m; (cross-~) corte m transversal
sector ['sɛktə*] n sector m
secular ['sɛkjulə*] adj secular, seglar
secure [sɪ'kjuə*] adj seguro; (firmly fixed) firme, fijo ♦ vt (fix) asegurar, afianzar; (get) conseguir
security [sɪ'kjuərɪtɪ] n seguridad f; (for loan) fianza; (: object) prenda
sedate [sɪ'deɪt] adj tranquilo ♦ vt tratar con sedantes
sedation [sɪ'deɪʃən] n (MED) sedación f
sedative ['sɛdɪtɪv] n sedante m, sedativo
seduce [sɪ'dju:s] vt seducir; **seduction** [-'dʌkʃən] n seducción f; **seductive** [-'dʌktɪv] adj seductor(a)
see [si:] (pt **saw**, pp **seen**) vt ver; (accompany): **to ~ sb to the door** acompañar a uno a la puerta; (understand) ver, comprender ♦ vi ver ♦ n (arz)obispado; **to ~ that** (ensure) asegurar que; ~ **you soon!** ¡hasta pronto!; ~ **about** vt fus atender a, encargarse de; ~ **off** vt despedir; ~ **through** vt fus (fig) calar ♦ vt (plan) llevar a cabo; ~ **to** vt fus atender a, encargarse de
seed [si:d] n semilla; (in fruit) pepita; (fig: gen pl) germen m; (TENNIS etc) preseleccionado/a; **to go to ~** (plant) granar; (fig) descuidarse; ~**ling** n planta

de semillero; **~y** adj (shabby) desaseado, raído

seeing ['si:ɪŋ] conj: **~ (that)** visto que, en vista de que

seek [si:k] (pt, pp **sought**) vt buscar; (post) solicitar

seem [si:m] vi parecer; **there ~s to be ...** parece que hay ...; **~ingly** adv aparentemente, según parece

seen [si:n] pp of **see**

seep [si:p] vi filtrarse

seesaw ['si:sɔ:] n subibaja

seethe [si:ð] vi hervir; **to ~ with anger** estar furioso

see-through adj transparente

segment ['segmənt] n (part) sección f; (of orange) gajo

segregate ['segrɪgeɪt] vt segregar

seize [si:z] vt (grasp) agarrar, asir; (take possession of) secuestrar; (: territory) apoderarse de; (opportunity) aprovecharse de; **~ (up)on** vt fus aprovechar; **~ up** vi (TECH) agarrotarse

seizure ['si:ʒə*] n (MED) ataque m; (LAW, of power) incautación f

seldom ['seldəm] adv rara vez

select [sɪ'lekt] adj selecto, escogido ♦ vt escoger, elegir; (SPORT) seleccionar; **~ion** [-'lekʃən] n selección f, elección f; (COMM) surtido

self [self] (pl **selves**) n uno mismo; **the ~** el yo ♦ prefix auto...; **~-assured** adj seguro de sí mismo; **~-catering** (BRIT) adj (flat etc) con cocina; **~-centred** (US **~-centered**) adj egocéntrico; **~-confidence** n confianza en sí mismo; **~-conscious** adj cohibido; **~-contained** (BRIT) adj (flat) con entrada particular; **~-control** n autodominio; **~-defence** (US **~-defense**) n defensa propia; **~-discipline** n autodisciplina; **~-employed** adj que trabaja por cuenta propia; **~-evident** adj patente; **~-governing** adj autónomo; **~-indulgent** adj autocomplaciente; **~-interest** n egoísmo; **~ish** adj egoísta; **~ishness** n egoísmo; **~less** adj desinteresado; **~-**

made adj: **~made man** hombre m que se ha hecho a sí mismo; **~-pity** n lástima de sí mismo; **~-portrait** n autorretrato; **~-possessed** adj sereno, dueño de sí mismo; **~-preservation** n propia conservación f; **~-respect** n amor m propio; **~-righteous** adj santurrón/ona; **~-sacrifice** n abnegación f; **~-satisfied** adj satisfecho de sí mismo; **~-service** adj de autoservicio; **~-sufficient** adj autosuficiente; **~-taught** adj autodidacta

sell [sel] (pt, pp **sold**) vt vender ♦ vi venderse; **to ~ at** or **for £10** venderse a 10 libras; **~ off** vt liquidar; **~ out** vi: **to ~ out of tickets/milk** vender todas las entradas/toda la leche; **~-by date** n fecha de caducidad; **~er** n vendedor(a) m/f; **~ing price** n precio de venta

Sellotape ® ['seləuteɪp] (BRIT) n cinta adhesiva, celo (SP), scotch m (AM)

selves [selvz] npl of **self**

semblance ['sembləns] n apariencia

semen ['si:mən] n semen m

semester [sɪ'mestə*] (US) n semestre m

semi... [semɪ] prefix semi..., medio...; **~circle** n semicírculo; **~colon** n punto y coma; **~conductor** n semiconductor m; **~detached (house)** n (casa) semiseparada; **~-final** n semi-final m

seminar ['semɪnɑ:*] n seminario

seminary ['semɪnərɪ] n (REL) seminario

semiskilled ['semɪskɪld] adj (work, worker) semi-cualificado

semi-skimmed (milk) n leche semidesnatada

senate ['senɪt] n senado; **senator** n senador(a) m/f

send [send] (pt, pp **sent**) vt mandar, enviar; (signal) transmitir; **~ away** vt despachar; **~ away for** vt fus pedir; **~ back** vt devolver; **~ for** vt fus mandar traer; **~ off** vt (goods) despachar; (BRIT: SPORT: player) expulsar; **~ out** vt (invitation) mandar; (signal) emitir; **~ up** vt (person, price) hacer subir; (BRIT: parody) parodiar; **~er** n remitente m/f;

~-**off** *n*: **a good ~-off** una buena despedida

senior ['si:nɪə*] *adj* (*older*) mayor, más viejo; (: *on staff*) de más antigüedad; (*of higher rank*) superior; ~ **citizen** *n* persona de la tercera edad; ~**ity** [-'ɔrɪtɪ] *n* antigüedad *f*

sensation [sɛn'seɪʃən] *n* sensación *f*; ~**al** *adj* sensacional

sense [sɛns] *n* (*faculty, meaning*) sentido; (*feeling*) sensación *f*; (*good ~*) sentido común, juicio ♦ *vt* sentir, percibir; **it makes ~** tiene sentido; ~**less** *adj* estúpido, insensato; (*unconscious*) sin conocimiento; ~ **of humour** *n* sentido del humor

sensible ['sɛnsɪbl] *adj* sensato; (*reasonable*) razonable, lógico

sensitive ['sɛnsɪtɪv] *adj* sensible; (*touchy*) susceptible

sensual ['sɛnsjuəl] *adj* sensual

sensuous ['sɛnsjuəs] *adj* sensual

sent [sɛnt] *pt, pp of* **send**

sentence ['sɛntns] *n* (*LING*) oración *f*; (*LAW*) sentencia, fallo ♦ *vt*: **to ~ sb to death/to 5 years (in prison)** condenar a uno a muerte/a 5 años de cárcel

sentiment ['sɛntɪmənt] *n* sentimiento; (*opinion*) opinión *f*; ~**al** [-'mɛntl] *adj* sentimental

sentry ['sɛntrɪ] *n* centinela *m*

separate [*adj* 'sɛprɪt, *vb* 'sɛpəreɪt] *adj* separado; (*distinct*) distinto ♦ *vt* separar; (*part*) dividir ♦ *vi* separarse; ~**s** *npl* (*clothes*) coordinados *mpl*; ~**ly** *adv* por separado; **separation** [-'reɪʃən] *n* separación *f*

September [sɛp'tɛmbə*] *n* se(p)tiembre *m*

septic ['sɛptɪk] *adj* séptico; ~ **tank** *n* fosa séptica

sequel ['si:kwl] *n* consecuencia, resultado; (*of story*) continuación *f*

sequence ['si:kwəns] *n* sucesión *f*, serie *f*; (*CINEMA*) secuencia

sequin ['si:kwɪn] *n* lentejuela

serene [sɪ'ri:n] *adj* sereno, tranquilo

sergeant ['sɑ:dʒənt] *n* sargento

serial ['sɪərɪəl] *n* (*TV*) telenovela, serie *f* televisiva; (*BOOK*) serie *f*; ~**ize** *vt* emitir como serial; ~ **killer** *n* asesino/a múltiple; ~ **number** *n* número de serie

series ['sɪəri:z] *n inv* serie *f*

serious ['sɪərɪəs] *adj* serio; (*grave*) grave; ~**ly** *adv* en serio; (*ill, wounded etc*) gravemente

sermon ['sə:mən] *n* sermón *m*

serrated [sɪ'reɪtɪd] *adj* serrado, dentellado

serum ['sɪərəm] *n* suero

servant ['sə:vənt] *n* servidor(a) *m/f*; (*house ~*) criado/a

serve [sə:v] *vt* servir; (*customer*) atender; (*subj: train*) pasar por; (*apprenticeship*) hacer; (*prison term*) cumplir ♦ *vi* (*at table*) servir; (*TENNIS*) sacar; **to ~ as/for/to do** servir de/para/para hacer ♦ *n* (*TENNIS*) saque *m*; **it ~s him right** se lo tiene merecido; ~ **out** *vt* (*food*) servir; ~ **up** *vt* = ~ **out**

service ['sə:vɪs] *n* servicio; (*REL*) misa; (*AUT*) mantenimiento; (*dishes etc*) juego ♦ *vt* (*car etc*) revisar; (: *repair*) reparar; **the S~s** *npl* las fuerzas armadas; **to be of ~ to sb** ser útil a uno; ~ **included/not included** servicio incluido/no incluido; ~**able** *adj* servible, utilizable; ~ **area** *n* (*on motorway*) área de servicio; ~ **charge** (*BRIT*) *n* servicio; ~**man** *n* militar *m*; ~ **station** *n* estación *f* de servicio

serviette [sə:vi'ɛt] (*BRIT*) *n* servilleta

session ['sɛʃən] *n* sesión *f*; **to be in ~** estar en sesión

set [sɛt] (*pt, pp* **set**) *n* juego; (*RADIO*) aparato; (*TV*) televisor *m*; (*of utensils*) batería; (*of cutlery*) cubierto; (*of books*) colección *f*; (*TENNIS*) set *m*; (*group of people*) grupo; (*CINEMA*) plató *m*; (*THEATRE*) decorado; (*HAIRDRESSING*) marcado ♦ *adj* (*fixed*) fijo; (*ready*) listo ♦ *vt* (*place*) poner, colocar; (*fix*) fijar; (*adjust*) ajustar, arreglar; (*decide: rules etc*) establecer, decidir ♦ *vi* (*sun*) ponerse; (*jam, jelly*) cuajarse; (*concrete*) fraguar; (*bone*) componerse; **to be ~ on doing sth** estar empeñado en hacer algo; **to ~ to**

music poner música a; **to ~ on fire** incendiar, poner fuego a; **to ~ free** poner en libertad; **to ~ going** poner algo en marcha; **to ~ sail** zarpar, hacerse a la vela; **~ about** vt fus ponerse a; **~ aside** vt poner aparte, dejar de lado; (*money, time*) reservar; **~ back** vt (*cost*): **to ~ sb back £5** costar a uno cinco libras; (: *in time*): **to ~ back (by)** retrasar (por); **~ off** vi partir ♦ vt (*bomb*) hacer estallar; (*events*) poner en marcha; (*show up well*) hacer resaltar; **~ out** vi partir ♦ vt (*arrange*) disponer; (*state*) exponer; **to ~ out to do sth** proponerse hacer algo; **~ up** vt establecer; **~back** n revés m, contratiempo; **~ menu** n menú m

settee [se'ti:] n sofá m

setting ['setiŋ] n (*scenery*) marco; (*position*) disposición f; (*of sun*) puesta; (*of jewel*) engaste m, montadura

settle ['setl] vt (*argument*) resolver; (*accounts*) ajustar, liquidar; (MED: *calm*) calmar, sosegar ♦ vi (*dust etc*) depositarse; (*weather*) serenarse; (*also:* **~ down**) instalarse; tranquilizarse; **to ~ for sth** convenir en aceptar algo; **to ~ on sth** decidirse por algo; **~ in** vi instalarse; **~ up** vi: **to ~ up with sb** ajustar cuentas con uno; **~ment** n (*payment*) liquidación f; (*agreement*) acuerdo, convenio; (*village etc*) pueblo; **~r** n colono/a, colonizador(a) m/f

setup ['setʌp] n (*system*) sistema m; (*situation*) situación f

seven ['sevn] num siete; **~teen** num diez y siete, diecisiete; **~th** num séptimo; **~ty** num setenta

sever ['sevə*] vt cortar; (*relations*) romper

several ['sevərl] adj, pron varios/as m/fpl, algunos/as m/fpl; **~ of us** varios de nosotros

severance ['sevərəns] n (*of relations*) ruptura; **~ pay** n indemnización f por despido

severe [si'viə*] adj severo; (*serious*) grave; (*hard*) duro; (*pain*) intenso; **severity** [si'veriti] n severidad f; gravedad f;

intensidad f

sew [səu] (*pt* **sewed**, *pp* **sewn**) vt, vi coser; **~ up** vt coser, zurcir

sewage ['su:idʒ] n aguas fpl residuales

sewer ['su:ə*] n alcantarilla, cloaca

sewing ['səuiŋ] n costura; **~ machine** n máquina de coser

sewn [səun] pp of **sew**

sex [seks] n sexo; (*lovemaking*): **to have ~** hacer el amor; **~ist** adj, n sexista m/f; **~ual** ['seksjuəl] adj sexual; **~y** adj sexy

shabby ['ʃæbi] adj (*person*) desharrapado; (*clothes*) raído, gastado; (*behaviour*) ruin inv

shack [ʃæk] n choza, chabola

shackles ['ʃæklz] npl grillos mpl, grilletes mpl

shade [ʃeid] n sombra; (*for lamp*) pantalla; (*for eyes*) visera; (*of colour*) matiz m, tonalidad f; (*small quantity*): **a ~ (too big/more)** un poquitín (grande/más) ♦ vt dar sombra a; (*eyes*) proteger del sol; **in the ~** en la sombra

shadow ['ʃædəu] n sombra ♦ vt (*follow*) seguir y vigilar; **~ cabinet** n (BRIT) n (POL) *gabinete paralelo formado por el partido de oposición*; **~y** adj oscuro; (*dim*) indistinto

shady ['ʃeidi] adj sombreado; (*fig: dishonest*) sospechoso; (: *deal*) turbio

shaft [ʃɑ:ft] n (*of arrow, spear*) astil m; (AUT, TECH) eje m, árbol m; (*of mine*) pozo; (*of lift*) hueco, caja; (*of light*) rayo

shaggy ['ʃægi] adj peludo

shake [ʃeik] (*pt* **shook**, *pp* **shaken**) vt sacudir; (*building*) hacer temblar; (*bottle, cocktail*) agitar ♦ vi (*tremble*) temblar; **to ~ one's head** (*in refusal*) negar con la cabeza; (*in dismay*) mover or menear la cabeza, incrédulo; **to ~ hands with sb** estrechar la mano a uno; **~ off** vt sacudirse; (*fig*) deshacerse de; **~ up** vt agitar; (*fig*) reorganizar; **shaky** adj (*hand, voice*) trémulo; (*building*) inestable

shall [ʃæl] aux vb: **~ I help you?** ¿quieres que te ayude?; **I'll buy three, ~ I?** compro tres, ¿no te parece?

shallow ['ʃæləu] *adj* poco profundo; (*fig*) superficial

sham [ʃæm] *n* fraude *m*, engaño ♦ *vt* fingir, simular

shambles ['ʃæmblz] *n* confusión *f*

shame [ʃeɪm] *n* vergüenza ♦ *vt* avergonzar; **it is a ~ that/to do** es una lástima que/hacer; **what a ~!** ¡qué lástima!; **~ful** *adj* vergonzoso; **~less** *adj* desvergonzado

shampoo [ʃæm'puː] *n* champú *m* ♦ *vt* lavar con champú; **~ and set** *n* lavado y marcado

shamrock ['ʃæmrɔk] *n* trébol *m* (*emblema nacional irlandés*)

shandy ['ʃændɪ] *n* mezcla de cerveza con gaseosa

shan't [ʃɑːnt] = **shall not**

shantytown ['ʃæntɪtaun] *n* barrio de chabolas

shape [ʃeɪp] *n* forma ♦ *vt* formar, dar forma a; (*sb's ideas*) formar; (*sb's life*) determinar; **to take ~** tomar forma; **~ up** *vi* (*events*) desarrollarse; (*person*) formarse; **~d** *suffix*: **heart-~d** en forma de corazón; **~less** *adj* informe, sin forma definida; **~ly** *adj* (*body etc*) esbelto

share [ʃɛə*] *n* (*part*) parte *f*, porción *f*; (*contribution*) cuota; (*COMM*) acción *f* ♦ *vt* dividir; (*have in common*) compartir; **to ~ out (among** or **between)** repartir (entre); **~holder** (*BRIT*) *n* accionista *m/f*

shark [ʃɑːk] *n* tiburón *m*

sharp [ʃɑːp] *adj* (*blade, nose*) afilado; (*point*) puntiagudo; (*outline*) definido; (*pain*) intenso; (*MUS*) desafinado; (*contrast*) marcado; (*voice*) agudo; (*person: quick-witted*) astuto; (*: dishonest*) poco escrupuloso ♦ *n* (*MUS*) sostenido ♦ *adv*: **at 2 o'clock ~** a las 2 en punto; **~en** *vt* afilar; (*pencil*) sacar punta a; (*fig*) agudizar; **~ener** *n* (*also*: **pencil ~ener**) sacapuntas *m inv*; **~-eyed** *adj* de vista aguda; **~ly** *adv* (*turn, stop*) bruscamente; (*stand out, contrast*) claramente; (*criticize, retort*) severamente

shatter ['ʃætə*] *vt* hacer añicos or pedazos;

(*fig: ruin*) destruir, acabar con ♦ *vi* hacerse añicos

shave [ʃeɪv] *vt* afeitar, rasurar ♦ *vi* afeitarse, rasurarse ♦ *n*: **to have a ~** afeitarse; **~r** *n* (*also*: **electric ~r**) máquina de afeitar (eléctrica)

shaving ['ʃeɪvɪŋ] *n* (*action*) el afeitarse, rasurado; **~s** *npl* (*of wood etc*) virutas *fpl*; **~ brush** *n* brocha (de afeitar); **~ cream** *n* crema de afeitar; **~ foam** *n* espuma de afeitar

shawl [ʃɔːl] *n* chal *m*

she [ʃiː] *pron* ella; **~-cat** *n* gata

sheaf [ʃiːf] (*pl* **sheaves**) *n* (*of corn*) gavilla; (*of papers*) fajo

shear [ʃɪə*] (*pt* **sheared**, *pp* **sheared** or **shorn**) *vt* esquilar, trasquilar; **~s** *npl* (*for hedge*) tijeras *fpl* de jardín

sheath [ʃiːθ] *n* vaina; (*contraceptive*) preservativo

sheaves [ʃiːvz] *npl of* **sheaf**

shed [ʃed] (*pt, pp* **shed**) *n* cobertizo ♦ *vt* (*skin*) mudar; (*tears, blood*) derramar; (*load*) derramar; (*workers*) despedir

she'd [ʃiːd] = **she had; she would**

sheen [ʃiːn] *n* brillo, lustre *m*

sheep [ʃiːp] *n inv* oveja; **~dog** *n* perro pastor; **~skin** *n* piel *f* de carnero

sheer [ʃɪə*] *adj* (*utter*) puro, completo; (*steep*) escarpado; (*material*) diáfano ♦ *adv* verticalmente

sheet [ʃiːt] *n* (*on bed*) sábana; (*of paper*) hoja; (*of glass, metal*) lámina; (*of ice*) capa

sheik(h) [ʃeɪk] *n* jeque *m*

shelf [ʃelf] (*pl* **shelves**) *n* estante *m*

shell [ʃel] *n* (*on beach*) concha; (*of egg, nut etc*) cáscara; (*explosive*) proyectil *m*, obús *m*; (*of building*) armazón *f* ♦ *vt* (*peas*) desenvainar; (*MIL*) bombardear

she'll [ʃiːl] = **she will; she shall**

shellfish ['ʃelfɪʃ] *n inv* crustáceo; (*as food*) mariscos *mpl*

shell suit *n* chándal *m* de calle

shelter ['ʃeltə*] *n* abrigo, refugio ♦ *vt* (*aid*) amparar, proteger; (*give lodging to*) abrigar ♦ *vi* abrigarse, refugiarse; **~ed** *adj* (*life*) protegido; (*spot*) abrigado; **~ed**

housing n viviendas vigiladas para ancianos y minusválidos
shelve [ʃelv] vt (fig) aplazar; **~s** npl of **shelf**
shepherd ['ʃepəd] n pastor m ♦ vt (guide) guiar, conducir; **~'s pie** (BRIT) n pastel de carne y patatas
sherry ['ʃerɪ] n jerez m
she's [ʃiːz] = **she is; she has**
Shetland ['ʃetlənd] n (also: **the ~ Isles**) las Islas de Zetlandia
shield [ʃiːld] n escudo; (protection) blindaje m ♦ vt: **to ~ (from)** proteger (de)
shift [ʃɪft] n (change) cambio; (at work) turno ♦ vt trasladar; (remove) quitar ♦ vi moverse; **~ work** n trabajo a turnos; **~y** adj tramposo; (eyes) furtivo
shimmer ['ʃɪmə*] n reflejo trémulo
shin [ʃɪn] n espinilla
shine [ʃaɪn] (pt, pp **shone**) n brillo, lustre m ♦ vi brillar, relucir ♦ vt (shoes) lustrar, sacar brillo a; **to ~ a torch on sth** dirigir una linterna hacia algo
shingle ['ʃɪŋgl] n (on beach) guijarros mpl; **~s** n (MED) herpes mpl or fpl
shiny ['ʃaɪnɪ] adj brillante, lustroso
ship [ʃɪp] n buque m, barco ♦ vt (goods) embarcar; (send) transportar or enviar por vía marítima; **~building** n construcción f de buques; **~ment** n (goods) envío; **~ping** n (act) embarque m; (traffic) buques mpl; **~wreck** n naufragio ♦ vt: **to be ~wrecked** naufragar; **~yard** n astillero
shire ['ʃaɪə*] (BRIT) n condado
shirt [ʃəːt] n camisa; **in (one's) ~ sleeves** en mangas de camisa
shit [ʃɪt] (inf!) excl ¡mierda! (!)
shiver ['ʃɪvə*] n escalofrío ♦ vi temblar, estremecerse; (with cold) tiritar
shoal [ʃəʊl] n (of fish) banco; (fig: also: **~s**) tropel m
shock [ʃɒk] n (impact) choque m; (ELEC) descarga (eléctrica); (emotional) conmoción f; (start) sobresalto, susto; (MED) postración f nerviosa ♦ vt dar un susto a; (offend) escandalizar; ~

absorber n amortiguador m; **~ing** adj (awful) espantoso; (outrageous) escandaloso
shoddy ['ʃɒdɪ] adj de pacotilla
shoe [ʃuː] (pt, pp **shod**) n zapato; (for horse) herradura ♦ vt (horse) herrar; **~brush** n cepillo para zapatos; **~lace** n cordón m; **~ polish** n betún m; **~shop** n zapatería; **~string** n (fig): **on a ~string** con muy poco dinero
shone [ʃɒn] pt, pp of **shine**
shook [ʃuk] pt of **shake**
shoot [ʃuːt] (pt, pp **shot**) n (on branch, seedling) retoño, vástago ♦ vt disparar; (kill) matar a tiros; (wound) pegar un tiro; (execute) fusilar; (film) rodar, filmar ♦ vi (FOOTBALL) chutar; **~ down** vt (plane) derribar; **~ in/out** vi entrar corriendo/ salir disparado; **~ up** vi (prices) dispararse; **~ing** n (shots) tiros mpl; (HUNTING) caza con escopeta; **~ing star** n estrella fugaz
shop [ʃɒp] n tienda; (workshop) taller m ♦ vi (also: **go ~ping**) ir de compras; **~ assistant** (BRIT) n dependiente/a m/f; **~ floor** (BRIT) n (fig) taller m, fábrica; **~keeper** n tendero/a; **~lifting** n mechería; **~per** n comprador(a) m/f; **~ping** n (goods) compras fpl; **~ping bag** n bolsa (de compras); **~ping centre** (US **~ping center**) n centro comercial; **~-soiled** adj deteriorado; **~ steward** (BRIT) n (INDUSTRY) enlace m sindical; **~ window** n escaparate m (SP), vidriera (AM)
shore [ʃɔː*] n orilla ♦ vt: **to ~ (up)** reforzar; **on ~** en tierra
shorn [ʃɔːn] pp of **shear**
short [ʃɔːt] adj corto; (in time) breve, de corta duración; (person) bajo; (curt) brusco, seco; (insufficient) insuficiente; **(a pair of) ~s** (unos) pantalones mpl cortos; **to be ~ of sth** estar falto de algo; **in ~** en pocas palabras; **~ of doing ...** fuera de hacer ...; **it is ~ for** es la forma abreviada de; **to cut ~** (speech, visit) interrumpir, terminar inesperadamente; **everything ~**

of ... todo menos ...; **to fall ~ of** no alcanzar; **to run ~ of** quedarle a uno poco; **to stop ~** parar en seco; **to stop ~ of** detenerse antes de; **~age** *n*: **a ~age of** una falta de; **~bread** *n especie de mantecada*; **~change** *vt* no dar el cambio completo a; **~circuit** *n* cortocircuito; **~coming** *n* defecto, deficiencia; **~(crust) pastry** (*BRIT*) *n* pasta quebradiza; **~cut** *n* atajo; **~en** *vt* acortar; (*visit*) interrumpir; **~fall** *n* déficit *m*; **~hand** (*BRIT*) *n* taquigrafía; **~hand typist** (*BRIT*) *n* taquimecanógrafo/a; **~ list** (*BRIT*) *n* (*for job*) lista de candidatos escogidos; **~-lived** *adj* efímero; **~ly** *adv* en breve, dentro de poco; **~-sighted** (*BRIT*) *adj* miope; (*fig*) imprudente; **~-staffed** *adj*: **to be ~-staffed** estar falto de personal; **~ story** *n* cuento; **~-tempered** *adj* enojadizo; **~-term** *adj* (*effect*) a corto plazo; **~wave** *n* (*RADIO*) onda corta

shot [ʃɔt] *pt, pp of* **shoot** ♦ *n* (*sound*) tiro, disparo; (*try*) tentativa; (*injection*) inyección *f*; (*PHOT*) toma, fotografía; **to be a good/poor ~** (*person*) tener buena/mala puntería; **like a ~** (*without any delay*) como un rayo; **~gun** *n* escopeta

should [ʃud] *aux vb*: **I ~ go now** debo irme ahora; **he ~ be there now** debe de haber llegado (ya); **I ~ go if I were you** yo en tu lugar me iría; **I ~ like to** me gustaría

shoulder ['ʃəuldə*] *n* hombro ♦ *vt* (*fig*) cargar con; **~ bag** *n* cartera de bandolera; **~ blade** *n* omóplato

shouldn't ['ʃudnt] = **should not**

shout [ʃaut] *n* grito ♦ *vt* gritar ♦ *vi* gritar, dar voces; **~ down** *vt* acallar a gritos; **~ing** *n* griterío

shove [ʃʌv] *n* empujón *m* ♦ *vt* empujar; (*inf: put*): **to ~ sth in** meter algo a empellones; **~ off** (*inf*) *vi* largarse

shovel ['ʃʌvl] *n* pala; (*mechanical*) excavadora ♦ *vt* mover con pala

show [ʃəu] (*pt* **showed**, *pp* **shown**) *n* (*of emotion*) demostración *f*; (*semblance*)

apariencia; (*exhibition*) exposición *f*; (*THEATRE*) función *f*, espectáculo *m*; (*TV*) show *m* ♦ *vt* mostrar, enseñar; (*courage etc*) mostrar, manifestar; (*exhibit*) exponer; (*film*) proyectar ♦ *vi* mostrarse; (*appear*) aparecer; **for ~** para impresionar; **on ~** (*exhibits etc*) expuesto; **~ in** *vt* (*person*) hacer pasar; **~ off** (*pej*) *vi* presumir ♦ *vt* (*display*) lucir; **~ out** *vt*: **to ~ sb out** acompañar a uno a la puerta; **~ up** *vi* (*stand out*) destacar; (*inf: turn up*) aparecer ♦ *vt* (*unmask*) desenmascarar; **~ business** *n* mundo del espectáculo; **~down** *n* enfrentamiento (final)

shower ['ʃauə*] *n* (*rain*) chaparrón *m*, chubasco; (*of stones etc*) lluvia; (*for bathing*) ducha (SP), regadera (AM) ♦ *vi* llover ♦ *vt* (*fig*): **to ~ sb with sth** colmar a uno de algo; **to have a ~** ducharse; **~proof** *adj* impermeable

showing ['ʃəuɪŋ] *n* (*of film*) proyección *f*

show jumping *n* hípica

shown [ʃəun] *pp of* **show**

show: ~-off (*inf*) *n* (*person*) presumido/a; **~piece** *n* (*of exhibition etc*) objeto cumbre; **~room** *n* sala de muestras

shrank [ʃræŋk] *pt of* **shrink**

shrapnel ['ʃræpnl] *n* metralla

shred [ʃred] *n* (*gen pl*) triza, jirón *m* ♦ *vt* hacer trizas; (*CULIN*) desmenuzar; **~der** *n* (*vegetable ~der*) picadora; (*document ~der*) trituradora (de papel)

shrewd [ʃruːd] *adj* astuto

shriek [ʃriːk] *n* chillido ♦ *vi* chillar

shrill [ʃrɪl] *adj* agudo, estridente

shrimp [ʃrɪmp] *n* camarón *m*

shrine [ʃraɪn] *n* santuario, sepulcro

shrink [ʃrɪŋk] (*pt* **shrank**, *pp* **shrunk**) *vi* encogerse; (*be reduced*) reducirse; (*also: ~ away*) retroceder ♦ *vt* encoger ♦ *n* (*inf: pej*) loquero/a; **to ~ from (doing) sth** no atreverse a hacer algo; **~wrap** *vt* embalar con película de plástico

shrivel ['ʃrɪvl] (*also: ~ up*) *vt* (*dry*) secar ♦ *vi* secarse

shroud [ʃraud] *n* sudario ♦ *vt*: **~ed in mystery** envuelto en el misterio

Shrove Tuesday ['ʃrəʊv-] n martes m de carnaval

shrub [ʃrʌb] n arbusto; **~bery** n arbustos mpl

shrug [ʃrʌg] n encogimiento de hombros ♦ vt, vi: **to ~ (one's shoulders)** encogerse de hombros; **~ off** vt negar importancia a

shrunk [ʃrʌŋk] pp of **shrink**

shudder ['ʃʌdə*] n estremecimiento, escalofrío ♦ vi estremecerse

shuffle ['ʃʌfl] vt (cards) barajar ♦ vi: **to ~ (one's feet)** arrastrar los pies

shun [ʃʌn] vt rehuir, esquivar

shunt [ʃʌnt] vt (train) maniobrar; (object) empujar

shut [ʃʌt] (pt, pp shut) vt cerrar ♦ vi cerrarse; **~ down** vt, vi cerrar; **~ off** vt (supply etc) cortar; **~ up** vi (inf: keep quiet) callarse ♦ vt (close) cerrar; (silence) hacer callar; **~ter** n contraventana; (PHOT) obturador m

shuttle ['ʃʌtl] n lanzadera; (also: **~ service**) servicio rápido y continuo entre dos puntos: (: AVIAT) puente m aéreo; **~cock** n volante m; **~ diplomacy** n viajes mpl diplomáticos

shy [ʃaɪ] adj tímido; **~ness** n timidez f

Sicily ['sɪsɪlɪ] n Sicilia

sick [sɪk] adj (ill) enfermo; (nauseated) mareado; (humour) negro; (vomiting): **to be ~** (BRIT) vomitar; **to feel ~** tener náuseas; **to be ~ of** (fig) estar harto de; **~ bay** n enfermería; **~en** vt dar asco a; **~ening** adj (fig) asqueroso

sickle ['sɪkl] n hoz f

sick: ~ leave n baja por enfermedad; **~ly** adj enfermizo; (smell) nauseabundo; **~ness** n enfermedad f, mal m; (vomiting) náuseas fpl; **~ pay** n subsidio de enfermedad

side [saɪd] n (gen) lado m; (of body) costado; (of lake) orilla; (of hill) ladera; (team) equipo; ♦ adj (door, entrance) lateral ♦ vi: **to ~ with sb** tomar el partido de uno; **by the ~ of** al lado de; **~ by ~** juntos/as; **from ~ to ~** de un lado para otro; **from**

all ~s de todos lados; **to take ~s (with)** tomar partido (con); **~board** n aparador m; **~boards** (BRIT) npl = **~burns**; **~burns** npl patillas fpl; **~ drum** n tambor m; **~ effect** n efecto secundario; **~light** n (AUT) luz f lateral; **~line** n (SPORT) línea de banda; (fig) empleo suplementario; **~long** adj de soslayo; **~ order** n plato de acompañamiento; **~ show** n (stall) caseta; **~step** vt (fig) esquivar; **~ street** n calle f lateral; **~track** vt (fig) desviar (de su propósito); **~walk** (US) n acera; **~ways** adv de lado

siding ['saɪdɪŋ] n (RAIL) apartadero, vía muerta

siege [si:dʒ] n cerco, sitio

sieve [sɪv] n colador m ♦ vt cribar

sift [sɪft] vt cribar; (fig: information) escudriñar

sigh [saɪ] n suspiro ♦ vi suspirar

sight [saɪt] n (faculty) vista; (spectacle) espectáculo; (on gun) mira, alza ♦ vt divisar; **in ~** a la vista; **out of ~** fuera de (la) vista; **on ~** (shoot) sin previo aviso; **~seeing** n excursionismo, turismo; **to go ~seeing** hacer turismo

sign [saɪn] n (with hand) señal f, seña; (trace) huella, rastro; (notice) letrero; (written) signo ♦ vt firmar; (SPORT) fichar; **to ~ sth over to sb** firmar el traspaso de algo a uno; **~ on** vi (BRIT: as unemployed) registrarse como desempleado; (for course) inscribirse ♦ vt (MIL) alistar; (employee) contratar; **~ up** vi (MIL) alistarse; (for course) inscribirse ♦ vt (player) fichar

signal ['sɪgnl] n señal f ♦ vi señalizar ♦ vt (person) hacer señas a; (message) comunicar por señales; **~man** (irreg) n (RAIL) guardavía m

signature ['sɪgnətʃə*] n firma; **~ tune** n sintonía de apertura de un programa

signet ring ['sɪgnət-] n anillo de sello

significance [sɪg'nɪfɪkəns] n (importance) trascendencia

significant [sɪg'nɪfɪkənt] adj significativo; (important) trascendente

signify ['sɪgnɪfaɪ] *vt* significar
sign language *n* lenguaje *m* para sordomudos
signpost ['saɪnpəust] *n* indicador *m*
silence ['saɪləns] *n* silencio ♦ *vt* acallar; (*guns*) reducir al silencio; **~r** *n* (*on gun, BRIT: AUT*) silenciador *m*
silent ['saɪlnt] *adj* silencioso; (*not speaking*) callado; (*film*) mudo; **to remain ~** guardar silencio; **~ partner** *n* (*COMM*) socio/a comanditario/a
silhouette [sɪluː'et] *n* silueta
silicon chip ['sɪlɪkən-] *n* plaqueta de silicio
silk [sɪlk] *n* seda ♦ *adj* de seda; **~y** *adj* sedoso
silly ['sɪlɪ] *adj* (*person*) tonto; (*idea*) absurdo
silt [sɪlt] *n* sedimento
silver ['sɪlvə*] *n* plata; (*money*) moneda suelta ♦ *adj* de plata; (*colour*) plateado; **~ paper** (*BRIT*) *n* papel *m* de plata; **~-plated** *adj* plateado; **~smith** *n* platero/a; **~ware** *n* plata; **~y** *adj* argentino
similar ['sɪmɪlə*] *adj*: **~ (to)** parecido *or* semejante (a); **~ity** [-'lærɪtɪ] *n* semejanza; **~ly** *adv* del mismo modo
simmer ['sɪmə*] *vi* hervir a fuego lento
simple ['sɪmpl] *adj* (*easy*) sencillo; (*foolish, COMM: interest*) simple; **simplicity** [-'plɪsɪtɪ] *n* sencillez *f*; **simplify** ['sɪmplɪfaɪ] *vt* simplificar
simply ['sɪmplɪ] *adv* (*live, talk*) sencillamente; (*just, merely*) sólo
simulate ['sɪmjuːleɪt] *vt* fingir, simular; **~d** *adj* simulado; (*fur*) de imitación
simultaneous [sɪməl'teɪnɪəs] *adj* simultáneo; **~ly** *adv* simultáneamente
sin [sɪn] *n* pecado ♦ *vi* pecar
since [sɪns] *adv* desde entonces, después ♦ *prep* desde ♦ *conj* (*time*) desde que; (*because*) ya que, puesto que; **~ then, ever ~** desde entonces
sincere [sɪn'sɪə*] *adj* sincero; **~ly** *adv*: **yours ~ly** (*in letters*) le saluda atentamente; **sincerity** [-'serɪtɪ] *n* sinceridad *f*

sinew ['sɪnjuː] *n* tendón *m*
sing [sɪŋ] (*pt* **sang**, *pp* **sung**) *vt, vi* cantar
Singapore [sɪŋə'pɔː*] *n* Singapur *m*
singe [sɪndʒ] *vt* chamuscar
singer ['sɪŋə*] *n* cantante *m/f*
singing ['sɪŋɪŋ] *n* canto
single ['sɪŋgl] *adj* único, solo; (*unmarried*) soltero; (*not double*) simple, sencillo ♦ *n* (*BRIT: also: ~ **ticket**) billete *m* sencillo; (*record*) sencillo, single *m*; **~s** *npl* (*TENNIS*) individual *m*; **~ out** *vt* (*choose*) escoger; **~ bed** cama individual; **~-breasted** *adj* recto; **~ file** *n*: **in ~ file** en fila de uno; **~-handed** *adv* sin ayuda; **~-minded** *adj* resuelto, firme; **~ parent** *n* padre *m* soltero, madre *f* soltera (*o divorciado etc*); **~ parent family** familia monoparental; **~ room** *n* cuarto individual
singly ['sɪŋglɪ] *adv* uno por uno
singular ['sɪŋgjulə*] *adj* (*odd*) raro, extraño; (*outstanding*) excepcional ♦ *n* (*LING*) singular *m*
sinister ['sɪnɪstə*] *adj* siniestro
sink [sɪŋk] (*pt* **sank**, *pp* **sunk**) *n* fregadero ♦ *vt* (*ship*) hundir, echar a pique; (*foundations*) excavar ♦ *vi* (*gen*) hundirse; **to ~ sth into** hundir algo en; **~ in** *vi* (*fig*) penetrar, calar
sinner ['sɪnə*] *n* pecador(a) *m/f*
sinus ['saɪnəs] *n* (*ANAT*) seno
sip [sɪp] *n* sorbo ♦ *vt* sorber, beber a sorbitos
siphon ['saɪfən] *n* sifón *m*; **~ off** *vt* desviar
sir [sə*] *n* señor *m*; **S~ John Smith** Sir John Smith; **yes ~** sí, señor
siren ['saɪərn] *n* sirena
sirloin ['səːlɔɪn] *n* (*also*: **~ steak**) solomillo
sister ['sɪstə*] *n* hermana; (*BRIT: nurse*) enfermera jefe; **~-in-law** *n* cuñada
sit [sɪt] (*pt, pp* **sat**) *vi* sentarse; (*be sitting*) estar sentado; (*assembly*) reunirse; (*for painter*) posar ♦ *vt* (*exam*) presentarse a; **~ down** *vi* sentarse; **~ in on** *vt fus* asistir a; **~ up** *vi* incorporarse; (*not go to bed*) velar
sitcom ['sɪtkɒm] *n abbr* (= *situation comedy*) comedia de situación

site [saɪt] n sitio; (also: **building ~**) solar m ♦ vt situar

sit-in n (demonstration) sentada

sitting ['sɪtɪŋ] n (of assembly etc) sesión f; (in canteen) turno; **~ room** n sala de estar

situated ['sɪtjʊeɪtɪd] adj situado

situation [sɪtjʊ'eɪʃən] n situación f; "**~s vacant**" (BRIT) "ofrecen trabajo"

six [sɪks] num seis; **~teen** num diez y seis, dieciséis; **~th** num sexto; **~ty** num sesenta

size [saɪz] n tamaño; (extent) extensión f; (of clothing) talla; (of shoes) número; **~ up** vt formarse una idea de; **~able** adj importante, considerable

sizzle ['sɪzl] vi crepitar

skate [skeɪt] n patín m; (fish: pl inv) raya ♦ vi patinar; **~board** n monopatín m; **~boarding** n monopatín m; **~r** n patinador(a) m/f; **skating** n patinaje m; **skating rink** n pista de patinaje

skeleton ['skelɪtn] n esqueleto; (TECH) armazón f; (outline) esquema m; **~ staff** n personal m reducido

skeptic etc ['skeptɪk] (US) = **sceptic**

sketch [sketʃ] n (drawing) dibujo; (outline) esbozo, bosquejo; (THEATRE) sketch m ♦ vt dibujar; (plan etc: also: **~ out**) esbozar; **~ book** n libro de dibujos; **~y** adj incompleto

skewer ['skjuːə*] n broqueta

ski [skiː] n esquí m ♦ vi esquiar; **~ boot** n bota de esquí

skid [skɪd] n patinazo ♦ vi patinar

ski: **~er** n esquiador(a) m/f; **~ing** n esquí m; **~ jump** n salto con esquís

skilful ['skɪlful] (BRIT) adj diestro, experto

ski lift n telesilla m, telesquí m

skill [skɪl] n destreza, pericia; técnica; **~ed** adj hábil, diestro; (worker) cualificado; **~full** (US) adj = **skilful**

skim [skɪm] vt (milk) desnatar; (glide over) rozar, rasar ♦ vi: **to ~ through** (book) hojear; **~med milk** n leche f desnatada

skimp [skɪmp] vt (also: **~ on**: work) chapucear; (cloth etc) escatimar; **~y** adj

escaso; (skirt) muy corto

skin [skɪn] n piel f; (complexion) cutis m ♦ vt (fruit etc) pelar; (animal) despellejar; **~ cancer** n cáncer m de piel; **~-deep** adj superficial; **~ diving** n buceo; **~ny** adj flaco; **~tight** adj (dress etc) muy ajustado

skip [skɪp] n brinco, salto; (BRIT: container) contenedor m ♦ vi brincar; (with rope) saltar a la comba ♦ vt saltarse

ski: **~ pass** n forfait m (de esquí); **~ pole** n bastón m de esquiar

skipper ['skɪpə*] n (NAUT, SPORT) capitán m

skipping rope ['skɪpɪŋ-] (BRIT) n comba

skirmish ['skɜːmɪʃ] n escaramuza

skirt [skɜːt] n falda (SP), pollera (AM) ♦ vt (go round) ladear; **~ing board** (BRIT) n rodapié m

ski slope n pista de esquí

ski suit n traje m de esquiar

ski tow n remonte m

skittle ['skɪtl] n bolo; **~s** n (game) boliche m

skive [skaɪv] (BRIT: inf) vi gandulear

skull [skʌl] n calavera; (ANAT) cráneo

skunk [skʌŋk] n mofeta

sky [skaɪ] n cielo; **~light** n tragaluz m, claraboya; **~scraper** n rascacielos m inv

slab [slæb] n (stone) bloque m; (flat) losa; (of cake) trozo

slack [slæk] adj (loose) flojo; (slow) de poca actividad; (careless) descuidado; **~s** npl pantalones mpl; **~en** (also: **~en off**) vi aflojarse ♦ vt aflojar; (speed) disminuir

slag heap ['slæg-] n escorial m, escombrera

slag off (BRIT: inf) vt poner como un trapo

slam [slæm] vt (throw) arrojar (violentamente); (criticize) criticar duramente ♦ vt (door) cerrarse de golpe; **to ~ the door** dar un portazo

slander ['slɑːndə*] n calumnia, difamación f

slang [slæŋ] n argot m; (jargon) jerga

slant [slɑːnt] n sesgo, inclinación f; (fig)

interpretación f; **~ed** adj (fig) parcial; **~ing** adj inclinado; (eyes) rasgado

slap [slæp] n palmada; (in face) bofetada ♦ vt dar una palmada or bofetada a; (paint etc): **to ~ sth on sth** embadurnar algo con algo ♦ adv (directly) exactamente, directamente; **~dash** adj descuidado; **~stick** n comedia de golpe y porrazo; **~-up** adj: **a ~-up meal** (BRIT) un banquetazo, una comilona

slash [slæʃ] vt acuchillar; (fig: prices) fulminar

slat [slæt] n tablilla, listón m

slate [sleɪt] n pizarra ♦ vt (fig: criticize) criticar duramente

slaughter ['slɔːtə*] n (of animals) matanza; (of people) carnicería ♦ vt matar; **~house** n matadero

Slav [slɑːv] adj eslavo

slave [sleɪv] n esclavo/a ♦ vi (also: **~ away**) sudar tinta; **~ry** n esclavitud f

slay [sleɪ] (pt **slew**, pp **slain**) vt matar

sleazy ['sliːzɪ] adj de mala fama

sledge [sledʒ] n trineo; **~hammer** n mazo

sleek [sliːk] adj (shiny) lustroso; (car etc) elegante

sleep [sliːp] (pt, pp **slept**) n sueño ♦ vi dormir; **to go to ~** quedarse dormido; **~ around** vi acostarse con cualquiera; **~ in** vi (oversleep) quedarse dormido; **~er** n (person) durmiente m/f; (BRIT: RAIL: on track) traviesa; (: train) coche-cama m; **~ing bag** n saco de dormir; **~ing car** n coche-cama m; **~ing partner** (BRIT) n (COMM) socio comanditario; **~ing pill** n somnífero; **~less** adj: **a ~less night** una noche en blanco; **~walker** n sonámbulo/a; **~y** adj soñoliento; (place) soporífero

sleet [sliːt] n aguanieve f

sleeve [sliːv] n manga; (TECH) manguito; (of record) portada; **~less** adj sin mangas

sleigh [sleɪ] n trineo

sleight [slaɪt] n: **~ of hand** escamoteo

slender ['slendə*] adj delgado; (means) escaso

slept [slept] pt, pp of **sleep**

slew [sluː] pt of **slay** ♦ vi (BRIT: veer) torcerse

slice [slaɪs] n (of meat) tajada; (of bread) rebanada; (of lemon) rodaja; (utensil) pala ♦ vt cortar (en tajos), rebanar

slick [slɪk] adj (skilful) hábil, diestro; (clever) astuto ♦ n (also: **oil ~**) marea negra

slide [slaɪd] (pt, pp **slid**) n (movement) descenso, desprendimiento; (in playground) tobogán m; (PHOT) diapositiva; (BRIT: also: **hair ~**) pasador m ♦ vt correr, deslizar ♦ vi (slip) resbalarse; (glide) deslizarse; **sliding** adj (door) corredizo; **sliding scale** n escala móvil

slight [slaɪt] adj (slim) delgado; (frail) delicado; (pain etc) leve; (trivial) insignificante; (small) pequeño ♦ n desaire m ♦ vt (insult) ofender, desairar; **not in the ~est** en absoluto; **~ly** adv ligeramente, un poco

slim [slɪm] adj delgado, esbelto; (fig: chance) remoto ♦ vi adelgazar

slime [slaɪm] n limo, cieno

slimming ['slɪmɪŋ] n adelgazamiento

slimy ['slaɪmɪ] adj cenagoso

sling [slɪŋ] (pt, pp **slung**) n (MED) cabestrillo; (weapon) honda ♦ vt tirar, arrojar

slip [slɪp] n (slide) resbalón m; (mistake) descuido; (underskirt) combinación f; (of paper) papelito ♦ vt (slip) deslizar ♦ vi deslizarse; (stumble) resbalar(se); (decline) decaer; (move smoothly): **to ~ into/out o** (room etc) introducirse en/salirse de; **to give sb the ~** eludir a uno; **a ~ of the tongue** un lapsus; **to ~ sth on/off** ponerse/quitarse algo; **~ away** vi escabullirse; **~ in** vt meter ♦ vi meterse; **~ out** vi (go out) salir (un momento); **~ up** vi (make mistake) equivocarse; meter la pata; **~ped disc** n vértebra dislocada

slipper ['slɪpə*] n zapatilla, pantufla

slippery ['slɪpərɪ] adj resbaladizo

slip: ~ road (BRIT) n carretera de acceso; **~-up** n (error) desliz m; **~way** n grada, gradas fpl

slit [slɪt] (*pt, pp* **slit**) *n* raja; (*cut*) corte *m* ♦ *vt* rajar; cortar

slither ['slɪðə*] *vi* deslizarse

sliver ['slɪvə*] *n* (*of glass, wood*) astilla; (*of cheese etc*) raja

slob [slɔb] (*inf*) *n* abandonado/a

slog [slɔg] (*BRIT*) *vi* sudar tinta; **it was a ~** costó trabajo (hacerlo)

slogan ['sləugən] *n* eslogan *m*, lema *m*

slope [sləup] *n* (*up*) cuesta, pendiente *f*; (*down*) declive *m*; (*side of mountain*) falda, vertiente *m* ♦ *vi*: **to ~ down** estar en declive; **to ~ up** inclinarse; **sloping** *adj* en pendiente; en declive; (*writing*) inclinado

sloppy ['slɔpɪ] *adj* (*work*) descuidado; (*appearance*) desaliñado

slot [slɔt] *n* ranura ♦ *vt*: **to ~ into** encajar en

slot machine *n* (*BRIT*: *vending machine*) distribuidor *m* automático; (*for gambling*) tragaperras *m inv*

slouch [slautʃ] *vi* andar *etc* con los hombros caídos

Slovenia [sləu'viːnɪə] *n* Eslovenia

slovenly ['slʌvənlɪ] *adj* desaliñado, desaseado; (*careless*) descuidado

slow [sləu] *adj* lento; (*not clever*) lerdo; (*watch*): **to be ~** atrasar ♦ *adv* lentamente, despacio ♦ *vt, vi* (*also: ~ down, ~ up*) retardar; **"~"** (*road sign*) "disminuir velocidad"; **~down** (*US*) *n* huelga de manos caídas; **~ly** *adv* lentamente, despacio; **~ motion** *n*: **in ~ motion** a cámara lenta

sludge [slʌdʒ] *n* lodo, fango

slug [slʌg] *n* babosa; (*bullet*) posta; **~gish** *adj* lento; (*person*) perezoso

sluice [sluːs] *n* (*gate*) esclusa; (*channel*) canal *m*

slum [slʌm] *n* casucha

slump [slʌmp] *n* (*economic*) depresión *f* ♦ *vi* hundirse; (*prices*) caer en picado

slung [slʌŋ] *pt, pp of* **sling**

slur [sləː*] *n*: **to cast a ~ on** insultar ♦ *vt* (*speech*) pronunciar mal

slush [slʌʃ] *n* nieve *f* a medio derretir

slut [slʌt] *n* putona

sly [slaɪ] *adj* astuto; (*smile*) taimado

smack [smæk] *n* bofetada ♦ *vt* dar con la mano a; (*child, on face*) abofetear ♦ *vi*: **to ~ of** saber a, oler a

small [smɔːl] *adj* pequeño; **~ ads** (*BRIT*) *npl* anuncios *mpl* por palabras; **~ change** *n* suelto, cambio; **~holder** (*BRIT*) *n* granjero/a, parcelero/a; **~ hours** *npl*: **in the ~ hours** a las altas horas (de la noche); **~pox** *n* viruela; **~ talk** *n* cháchara

smart [smɑːt] *adj* elegante; (*clever*) listo, inteligente; (*quick*) rápido, vivo ♦ *vi* escocer, picar; **~en up** *vi* arreglarse ♦ *vt* arreglar

smash [smæʃ] *n* (*also: ~-up*) choque *m*; (*MUS*) exitazo ♦ *vt* (*break*) hacer pedazos; (*car etc*) estrellar; (*SPORT: record*) batir ♦ *vi* hacerse pedazos; (*against wall etc*) estrellarse; **~ing** (*inf*) *adj* estupendo

smattering ['smætərɪŋ] *n*: **a ~ of** algo de

smear [smɪə*] *n* mancha; (*MED*) frotis *m inv* ♦ *vt* untar; **~ campaign** *n* campaña de desprestigio

smell [smɛl] (*pt, pp* **smelt** *or* **smelled**) *n* olor *m*; (*sense*) olfato ♦ *vt, vi* oler; **~y** *adj* maloliente

smile [smaɪl] *n* sonrisa ♦ *vi* sonreír

smirk [sməːk] *n* sonrisa falsa *or* afectada

smith [smɪθ] *n* herrero; **~y** ['smɪðɪ] *n* herrería

smog [smɔg] *n* esmog *m*

smoke [sməuk] *n* humo ♦ *vi* fumar; (*chimney*) echar humo ♦ *vt* (*cigarettes*) fumar; **~d** *adj* (*bacon, glass*) ahumado; **~r** *n* fumador(a) *m/f*; (*RAIL*) coche *m* fumador; **~ screen** *n* cortina de humo; **~ shop** (*US*) *n* estanco (*SP*), tabaquería (*AM*); **smoking** *n*: **"no smoking"** "prohibido fumar"; **smoky** *adj* (*room*) lleno de humo; (*taste*) ahumado

smolder ['sməuldə*] (*US*) *vi* = **smoulder**

smooth [smuːð] *adj* liso; (*sea*) tranquilo; (*flavour, movement*) suave; (*sauce*) fino; (*person: pej*) meloso ♦ *vt* (*also: ~ out*) alisar; (*creases, difficulties*) allanar

smother ['smʌðə*] vt sofocar; (repress) contener

smoulder ['sməuldə*] (US **smolder**) vi arder sin llama

smudge [smʌdʒ] n mancha ♦ vt manchar

smug [smʌg] adj presumido; orondo

smuggle ['smʌgl] vt pasar de contrabando; **~r** n contrabandista m/f; **smuggling** n contrabando

smutty ['smʌtɪ] adj (fig) verde, obsceno

snack [snæk] n bocado; **~ bar** n cafetería

snag [snæg] n problema m

snail [sneɪl] n caracol m

snake [sneɪk] n serpiente f

snap [snæp] n (sound) chasquido; (photograph) foto f ♦ adj (decision) instantáneo ♦ vt (break) quebrar; (fingers) castañetear ♦ vi quebrarse; (fig: speak sharply) contestar bruscamente; **to ~ shut** cerrarse de golpe; **~ at** vt fus (subj: dog) intentar morder; **~ off** vi partirse; **~ up** vt agarrar; **~ fastener** n (US) botón m de presión; **~py** (inf) adj (answer) instantáneo; (slogan) conciso; **make it ~py!** (hurry up) ¡date prisa!; **~shot** n foto f (instantánea)

snare [sneə*] n trampa

snarl [snɑːl] vi gruñir

snatch [snætʃ] n (small piece) fragmento ♦ vt (~ away) arrebatar; (fig) agarrar; **to ~ some sleep** encontrar tiempo para dormir

sneak [sniːk] (pt (US) **snuck**) vi: **to ~ in/out** entrar/salir a hurtadillas ♦ n (inf) soplón/ona m/f; **to ~ up on sb** aparecérsele de improviso a uno; **~ers** npl zapatos mpl de lona; **~y** adj furtivo

sneer [snɪə*] vi reír con sarcasmo; (mock): **to ~ at** burlarse de

sneeze [sniːz] vi estornudar

sniff [snɪf] vi sollozar ♦ vt husmear, oler; (drugs) esnifar

snigger ['snɪgə*] vi reírse con disimulo

snip [snɪp] n tijeretazo; (BRIT: inf: bargain) ganga ♦ vt tijeretear

sniper ['snaɪpə*] n francotirador(a) m/f

snippet ['snɪpɪt] n retazo

snob [snɔb] n (e)snob m/f; **~bery** n (e)snobismo; **~bish** adj (e)snob

snooker ['snuːkə*] n especie de billar

snoop [snuːp] vi: **to ~ about** fisgonear

snooze [snuːz] n siesta ♦ vi echar una siesta

snore [snɔː*] n ronquido ♦ vi roncar

snorkel ['snɔːkl] n (tubo) respirador m

snort [snɔːt] n bufido ♦ vi bufar

snout [snaut] n hocico, morro

snow [snəu] n nieve f ♦ vi nevar; **~ball** n bola de nieve ♦ vi (fig) agrandarse, ampliarse; **~bound** adj bloqueado por la nieve; **~drift** n ventisquero; **~drop** n campanilla; **~fall** n nevada; **~flake** n copo de nieve; **~man** (irreg) n figura de nieve; **~plough** (US **~plow**) n quitanieves m inv; **~shoe** n raqueta (de nieve); **~storm** n nevada, nevasca

snub [snʌb] vt (person) desairar ♦ n desaire m, repulsa; **~-nosed** adj chato

snuff [snʌf] n rapé m

snug [snʌg] adj (cosy) cómodo; (fitted) ajustado

snuggle ['snʌgl] vi: **to ~ up to sb** arrimarse a uno

KEYWORD

so [səu] adv **1** (thus, likewise) así, de este modo; **if ~** de ser así; **I like swimming — ~ do I** a mí me gusta nadar — a mí también; **I've got work to do — ~ has Paul** tengo trabajo que hacer — Paul también; **it's 5 o'clock — ~ it is!** son las cinco — ¡pues es verdad!; **I hope/think ~** espero/creo que sí; **~ far** hasta ahora; (in past) hasta este momento

2 (in comparisons etc: to such a degree) tan; **~ quickly (that)** tan rápido (que); **~ big (that)** tan grande (que); **she's not ~ clever as her brother** no es tan lista como su hermano; **we were ~ worried** estábamos preocupadísimos

3: **~ much** adj, adv tanto; **~ many** tantos/as

4 (phrases): **10 or ~** unos 10, 10 o así; **~ long!** (inf: goodbye) ¡hasta luego!

♦ conj 1 (expressing purpose): ~ as to do para hacer; ~ (that) para que +sub
2 (expressing result) así que; ~ you see, I could have gone así que ya ves, (yo) podría haber ido

soak [səuk] vt (drench) empapar; (steep in water) remojar ♦ vi remojarse, estar a remojo; ~ in vi penetrar; ~ up vt absorber
soap [səup] n jabón m; ~flakes npl escamas fpl de jabón; ~ opera n telenovela; ~ powder n jabón m en polvo; ~y adj jabonoso
soar [sɔː*] vi (on wings) remontarse; (rocket, prices) dispararse; (building etc) elevarse
sob [sɔb] n sollozo ♦ vi sollozar
sober ['səubə*] adj (serious) serio; (not drunk) sobrio; (colour, style) discreto; ~ up vt quitar la borrachera
so-called adj así llamado
soccer ['sɔkə*] n fútbol m
social ['səuʃl] adj social ♦ n velada, fiesta; ~ club n club m; ~ism n socialismo; ~ist adj, n socialista m/f; ~ize vi: to ~ize (with) alternar (con); ~ly adv socialmente; ~ security n seguridad f social; ~ work n asistencia social; ~ worker n asistente/a m/f social work
society [sə'saɪətɪ] n sociedad f; (club) asociación f; (also: high ~) alta sociedad
sociology [səusɪ'ɔlədʒɪ] n sociología
sock [sɔk] n calcetín m (SP), media (AM)
socket ['sɔkɪt] n cavidad f; (BRIT: ELEC) enchufe m
sod [sɔd] n (of earth) césped m; (BRIT: inf!) cabrón/ona m/f (!)
soda ['səudə] n (CHEM) sosa; (also: ~ water) soda; (US: also: ~ pop) gaseosa
sofa ['səufə] n sofá m
soft [sɔft] adj (lenient, not hard) blando; (gentle, not bright) suave; ~ drink n bebida no alcohólica; ~en ['sɔfn] vt ablandar; suavizar; (effect) amortiguar ♦ vi ablandarse; suavizarse; ~ly adv suavemente; (gently) delicadamente, con

delicadeza; ~ness n blandura; suavidad f; ~ware n (COMPUT) software m
soggy ['sɔgɪ] adj empapado
soil [sɔil] n (earth) tierra, suelo ♦ vt ensuciar; ~ed adj sucio
solar ['səulə*] adj: ~ energy n energía solar; ~ panel n panel m solar
sold [səuld] pt, pp of sell; ~ out adj (COMM) agotado
solder ['səuldə*] vt soldar ♦ n soldadura
soldier ['səuldʒə*] n soldado; (army man) militar m
sole [səul] n (of foot) planta; (of shoe) suela; (fish: pl inv) lenguado ♦ adj único
solemn ['sɔləm] adj solemne
sole trader n (COMM) comerciante m exclusivo
solicit [sə'lɪsɪt] vt (request) solicitar ♦ vi (prostitute) importunar
solicitor [sə'lɪsɪtə*] (BRIT) n (for wills etc) ≈ notario/a; (in court) ≈ abogado/a
solid ['sɔlɪd] adj sólido; (gold etc) macizo ♦ n sólido; ~s npl (food) alimentos mpl sólidos
solidarity [sɔlɪ'dærɪtɪ] n solidaridad f
solitary ['sɔlɪtərɪ] adj solitario, solo; ~ confinement n incomunicación f
solo ['səuləu] n solo ♦ adv (fly) en solitario; ~ist n solista m/f
soluble ['sɔljuːbl] adj soluble
solution [sə'luːʃən] n solución f
solve [sɔlv] vt resolver, solucionar
solvent ['sɔlvənt] adj (COMM) solvente ♦ n (CHEM) solvente m

KEYWORD

---

some [sʌm] adj 1 (a certain amount or number of): ~ tea/water/biscuits té/agua/(unas) galletas; there's ~ milk in the fridge hay leche en el frigo; there were ~ people outside había algunas personas fuera; I've got ~ money, but not much tengo algo de dinero, pero no mucho
2 (certain: in contrasts) algunos/as; ~ people say that ... hay quien dice que ...; ~ films were excellent, but most

were mediocre hubo películas excelentes, pero la mayoría fueron mediocres

3 (*unspecified*): **~ woman was asking for you** una mujer estuvo preguntando por ti; **he was asking for ~ book (or other)** pedía un libro; **~ day** algún día; **~ day next week** un día de la semana que viene

♦ *pron* **1** (*a certain number*): **I've got ~** (*books etc*) tengo algunos/as

2 (*a certain amount*): **I've got ~** (*money, milk*) tengo algo; **could I have ~ of that cheese?** ¿me puede dar un poco de ese queso?; **I've read ~ of the book** he leído parte del libro

♦ *adv*: **~ 10 people** unas 10 personas, una decena de personas

some: **~body** ['sʌmbədɪ] *pron* = **someone**; **~how** *adv* de alguna manera; (*for some reason*) por una u otra razón; **~one** *pron* alguien; **~place** (*US*) *adv* = **somewhere**

somersault ['sʌməsɔːlt] *n* (*deliberate*) salto mortal; (*accidental*) vuelco ♦ *vi* dar un salto mortal; dar vuelcos

some: **~thing** *pron* algo; **would you like ~thing to eat/drink?** ¿te gustaría cenar/tomar algo?; **~time** *adv* (*in future*) algún día, en algún momento; (*in past*): **~time last month** durante el mes pasado; **~times** *adv* a veces; **~what** *adv* algo; **~where** *adv* (*be*) en alguna parte; (*go*) a alguna parte; **~where else** (*be*) en otra parte; (*go*) a otra parte

son [sʌn] *n* hijo

song [sɒŋ] *n* canción *f*

son-in-law *n* yerno

soon [suːn] *adv* pronto, dentro de poco; **~ afterwards** poco después; *see also* **as**; **~er** *adv* (*time*) antes, más temprano; (*preference*): **I would ~er do that** preferiría hacer eso; **~er or later** tarde o temprano

soot [sʊt] *n* hollín *m*

soothe [suːð] *vt* tranquilizar; (*pain*) aliviar

sophisticated [sə'fɪstɪkeɪtɪd] *adj* sofisticado

sophomore ['sɒfəmɔː*] (*US*) *n* estudiante *m/f* de segundo año

sopping ['sɒpɪŋ] *adj*: **~ (wet)** empapado

soppy ['sɒpɪ] (*pej*) *adj* tonto

soprano [sə'prɑːnəʊ] *n* soprano *f*

sorcerer ['sɔːsərə*] *n* hechicero

sore [sɔː*] *adj* (*painful*), que duele ♦ *n* llaga; **~ly** *adv*: **I am ~ly tempted to** estoy muy tentado a

sorrow ['sɒrəʊ] *n* pena, dolor *m*; **~s** *npl* pesares *mpl*; **~ful** *adj* triste

sorry ['sɒrɪ] *adj* (*regretful*) arrepentido; (*condition, excuse*) lastimoso; **~!** ¡perdón!, ¡perdone!; **~?** ¿cómo?; **to feel ~ for sb** tener lástima a uno; **I feel ~ for him** me da lástima

sort [sɔːt] *n* clase *f*, género, tipo ♦ *vt* (*also*: **~ out**: *papers*) clasificar; (: *problems*) arreglar, solucionar; **~ing office** *n* sala de batalla

SOS *n* SOS *m*

so-so *adv* regular, así así

soufflé ['suːfleɪ] *n* suflé *m*

sought [sɔːt] *pt*, *pp* *of* **seek**

soul [səʊl] *n* alma; **~ful** *adj* lleno de sentimiento

sound [saʊnd] *n* (*noise*) sonido, ruido; (*volume: on TV etc*) volumen *m*; (*GEO*) estrecho ♦ *adj* (*healthy*) sano; (*safe, not damaged*) en buen estado; (*reliable: person*) digno de confianza; (*sensible*) sensato, razonable; (*secure: investment*) seguro ♦ *adv*: **~ asleep** profundamente dormido ♦ *vt* (*alarm*) sonar ♦ *vi* sonar, resonar; (*fig: seem*) parecer; **to ~ like** sonar a; **~ out** *vt* sondear; **~ barrier** *n* barrera del sonido; **~bite** *n* cita jugosa; **~ effects** *npl* efectos *mpl* sonoros; **~ly** *adv* (*sleep*) profundamente; (*defeated*) completamente; **~proof** *adj* insonorizado; **~track** *n* (*of film*) banda sonora

soup [suːp] *n* (*thick*) sopa; (*thin*) caldo; **~ plate** *n* plato sopero; **~spoon** *n* cuchara sopera

sour [saʊə*] *adj* agrio; (*milk*) cortado; **it's**

~ grapes (fig) están verdes
source [sɔ:s] n fuente f
south [sauθ] n sur m ♦ adj del sur, sureño ♦ adv al sur, hacia el sur; **S~ Africa** n África del Sur; **S~ African** adj, n sudafricano/a m/f; **S~ America** n América del Sur, Sudamérica; **S~ American** adj, n sudamericano/a m/f; **~-east** n sudeste m; **~erly** ['sʌðəlɪ] adj sur; (from the ~) del sur; **~ern** ['sʌðən] adj del sur, meridional; **S~ Pole** n Polo Sur; **~ward(s)** adv hacia el sur; **~-west** n suroeste m
souvenir [su:və'nɪə*] n recuerdo
sovereign ['sɒvrɪn] adj, n soberano/a m/f; **~ty** n soberanía
soviet ['səuvɪət] adj soviético; **the S~ Union** la Unión Soviética
sow[1] [sau] (pt **sowed**, pp **sown**) vt sembrar
sow[2] [sau] n cerda (SP), puerca (SP), chancha (AM)
soy [sɔɪ] (US) n = **soya**
soya ['sɔɪə] (BRIT) n soja; **~ bean** n haba de soja; **~ sauce** n salsa de soja
spa [spɑ:] n balneario
space [speɪs] n espacio; (room) sitio ♦ cpd espacial ♦ vt (also: **~ out**) espaciar; **~craft** n nave f espacial; **~man/woman** (irreg) n astronauta m/f, cosmonauta m/f; **~ship** n = **~craft**; **spacing** n espaciado
spacious ['speɪʃəs] adj amplio
spade [speɪd] n (tool) pala, laya; **~s** npl (CARDS: British) picas fpl; (: Spanish) espadas fpl
spaghetti [spə'gɛtɪ] n espaguetis mpl, fideos mpl
Spain [speɪn] n España
span [spæn] n (of bird, plane) envergadura; (of arch) luz f; (in time) lapso ♦ vt extenderse sobre, cruzar; (fig) abarcar
Spaniard ['spænjəd] n español(a) m/f
spaniel ['spænjəl] n perro de aguas
Spanish ['spænɪʃ] adj español(a) ♦ n (LING) español m, castellano; **the ~** npl los españoles
spank [spæŋk] vt zurrar

spanner ['spænə*] (BRIT) n llave f (inglesa)
spare [spɛə*] adj de reserva; (surplus) sobrante, de más ♦ n = **~ part** ♦ vt (do without) pasarse sin; (refrain from hurting) perdonar; **to ~** (surplus) sobrante, de sobra; **~ part** n pieza de repuesto; **~ time** n tiempo libre; **~ wheel** n (AUT) rueda de recambio
sparingly ['spɛərɪŋlɪ] adv con moderación
spark [spɑ:k] n chispa; (fig) chispazo; **~(ing) plug** n bujía
sparkle ['spɑ:kl] n centelleo, destello ♦ vi (shine) relucir, brillar; **sparkling** adj (eyes, conversation) brillante; (wine) espumoso; (mineral water) con gas
sparrow ['spærəu] n gorrión m
sparse [spɑ:s] adj esparcido, escaso
spartan ['spɑ:tən] adj (fig) espartano
spasm ['spæzəm] n (MED) espasmo
spastic ['spæstɪk] n espástico/a
spat [spæt] pt, pp of **spit**
spate [speɪt] n (fig): **a ~ of** un torrente de
spawn [spɔ:n] vi desovar, frezar ♦ n huevas fpl
speak [spi:k] (pt **spoke**, pp **spoken**) vt (language) hablar; (truth) decir ♦ vi hablar; (make a speech) intervenir; **to ~ to sb/of** or **about sth** hablar con uno/de or sobre algo; **~ up!** ¡habla fuerte!; **~er** n (in public) orador(a) m/f; (also: **loud~er**) altavoz m; (for stereo etc) bafle m; (POL): **the S~er** (BRIT) el Presidente de la Cámara de los Comunes; (US) el Presidente del Congreso
spear [spɪə*] n lanza ♦ vt alancear; **~head** vt (attack etc) encabezar
spec [spɛk] (inf) n: **on ~** como especulación
special ['spɛʃl] adj especial; (edition etc) extraordinario; (delivery) urgente; **~ist** n especialista m/f; **~ity** [spɛʃɪ'ælɪtɪ] (BRIT) n especialidad f; **~ize** vi: **to ~ize (in)** especializarse (en); **~ly** adv sobre todo, en particular; **~ty** (US) n = **~ity**
species ['spi:ʃi:z] n inv especie f
specific [spə'sɪfɪk] adj específico; **~ally** adv específicamente

specify ['spɛsɪfaɪ] vt, vi especificar, precisar

specimen ['spɛsɪmən] n ejemplar m; (MED: of urine) espécimen m (: of blood) muestra

speck [spɛk] n grano, mota

speckled ['spɛkld] adj moteado

specs [spɛks] (inf) npl gafas fpl (SP), anteojos mpl

spectacle ['spɛktəkl] n espectáculo; **~s** npl (BRIT: glasses) gafas fpl (SP), anteojos mpl; **spectacular** [-'tækjulə*] adj espectacular; (success) impresionante

spectator [spɛk'teɪtə*] n espectador(a) m/f

spectrum ['spɛktrəm] (pl **spectra**) n espectro

speculate ['spɛkjuleɪt] vi: **to ~ (on)** especular (en); **speculation** [spɛkju'leɪʃən] n especulación f

speech [spiːtʃ] n (faculty) habla; (formal talk; (spoken language) lenguaje m; **~less** adj mudo, estupefacto; **~ therapist** n especialista que corrige defectos de pronunciación en los niños

speed [spiːd] n velocidad f; (haste) prisa; (promptness) rapidez f; **at full** or **top ~** a máxima velocidad; **~ up** vi acelerarse ♦ vt acelerar; **~boat** n lancha motora; **~ily** adv rápido, rápidamente; **~ing** (AUT) exceso de velocidad; **~ limit** n límite m de velocidad, velocidad f máxima; **~ometer** [spɪ'dɔmɪtə*] n velocímetro; **~way** n (sport) pista de carrera; **~y** adj (fast) veloz, rápido; (prompt) pronto

spell [spɛl] (pt, pp **spelt** (BRIT) or **spelled**) n (also: **magic ~**) encanto, hechizo; (period of time) rato, período ♦ vt deletrear; (fig) anunciar, presagiar; **to cast a ~ on sb** hechizar a uno; **he can't ~** pone faltas de ortografía; **~bound** adj embelesado, hechizado; **~ing** n ortografía

spend [spɛnd] (pt, pp **spent**) vt (money) gastar; (time) pasar; (life) dedicar; **~thrift** n derrochador(a) m/f, pródigo/a

sperm [spəːm] n esperma

sphere [sfɪə*] n esfera

sphinx [sfɪŋks] n esfinge f

spice [spaɪs] n especia ♦ vt condimentar

spicy ['spaɪsɪ] adj picante

spider ['spaɪdə*] n araña

spike [spaɪk] n (point) punta; (BOT) espiga

spill [spɪl] (pt, pp **spilt** or **spilled**) vt derramar, verter ♦ vi derramarse; **to ~ over** desbordarse

spin [spɪn] (pt, pp **spun**) n (AVIAT) barrena; (trip in car) paseo (en coche); (on ball) efecto ♦ vt (wool etc) hilar; (ball etc) hacer girar ♦ vi girar, dar vueltas

spinach ['spɪnɪtʃ] n espinaca; (as food) espinacas fpl

spinal ['spaɪnl] adj espinal; **~ cord** n columna vertebral

spin doctor n informador(a) parcial al servicio de un partido político etc

spin-dryer (BRIT) n secador m centrífugo

spine [spaɪn] n espinazo, columna vertebral; (thorn) espina; **~less** adj (fig) débil, pusilánime

spinning ['spɪnɪŋ] n hilandería; **~ top** n peonza

spin-off n derivado, producto secundario

spinster ['spɪnstə*] n solterona

spiral ['spaɪərl] n espiral f ♦ vi (fig: prices) subir desorbitadamente; **~ staircase** n escalera de caracol

spire ['spaɪə*] n aguja, chapitel m

spirit ['spɪrɪt] n (soul) alma f; (ghost) fantasma m; (attitude, sense) espíritu m; (courage) valor m, ánimo; **~s** npl (drink) licor(es) m(pl); **in good ~s** alegre, de buen ánimo; **~ed** adj enérgico, vigoroso

spiritual ['spɪrɪtjuəl] adj espiritual ♦ n espiritual m

spit [spɪt] (pt, pp **spat**) n (for roasting) asador m, espetón m; (saliva) saliva ♦ vi escupir; (sound) chisporrotear; (rain) lloviznar

spite [spaɪt] n rencor m, ojeriza ♦ vt causar pena a, mortificar; **in ~ of** a pesar de, pese a; **~ful** adj rencoroso, malévolo

spittle ['spɪtl] n saliva, baba

splash [splæʃ] n (sound) chapoteo; (of colour) mancha ♦ vt salpicar ♦ vi (also: **~**

about) chapotear
spleen [spli:n] n (ANAT) bazo
splendid ['splendɪd] adj espléndido
splint [splɪnt] n tablilla
splinter ['splɪntə*] n (of wood etc) astilla; (in finger) espigón m ♦ vi astillarse, hacer astillas
split [splɪt] (pt, pp **split**) n hendedura, raja; (fig) división f; (POL) escisión f ♦ vt partir, rajar; (party) dividir; (share) repartir ♦ vi dividirse, escindirse; ~ **up** vi (couple) separarse; (meeting) acabarse
spoil [spɔɪl] (pt, pp **spoilt** or **spoiled**) vt (damage) dañar; (mar) estropear; (child) mimar, consentir; ~**s** npl despojo, botín m; ~**sport** n aguafiestas m inv
spoke [spəʊk] pt of **speak** ♦ n rayo, radio
spoken ['spəʊkn] pp of **speak**
spokesman ['spəʊksmən] (irreg) n portavoz m; **spokeswoman** ['spəʊkswʊmən] (irreg) n portavoz f
sponge [spʌndʒ] n esponja; (also: ~ **cake**) bizcocho ♦ vt (wash) lavar con esponja ♦ vi: **to ~ off** or **on sb** vivir a costa de uno; ~ **bag** (BRIT) n esponjera
sponsor ['spɒnsə*] n patrocinador(a) m/f ♦ vt (applicant, proposal etc) proponer; ~**ship** n patrocinio
spontaneous [spɒn'teɪnɪəs] adj espontáneo
spooky ['spu:kɪ] (inf) adj espeluznante, horripilante
spool [spu:l] n carrete m
spoon [spu:n] n cuchara; ~-**feed** vt dar de comer con cuchara a; (fig) tratar como un niño a; ~**ful** n cucharada
sport [spɔ:t] n deporte m; (person): **to be a good ~** ser muy majo ♦ vt (wear) lucir, ostentar; ~**ing** adj deportivo; (generous) caballeroso; **to give sb a ~ing chance** darle a uno una (buena) oportunidad; ~ **jacket** (US) n = ~**s jacket**; ~**s car** n coche m deportivo; ~**s jacket** (BRIT) n chaqueta deportiva; ~**sman** (irreg) n deportista m; ~**smanship** n deportividad f; ~**swear** n trajes mpl de deporte or sport; ~**swoman** (irreg) n

deportista; ~**y** adj deportista
spot [spɒt] n sitio, lugar m; (dot: on pattern) punto, mancha; (pimple) grano; (RADIO) cuña publicitaria; (TV) espacio publicitario; (small amount): **a ~ of** un poquito de ♦ vt (notice) notar, observar; **on the ~** allí mismo; ~ **check** n reconocimiento rápido; ~**less** adj perfectamente limpio; ~**light** n foco, reflector m; (AUT) faro auxiliar; ~**ted** adj (pattern) de puntos; ~**ty** adj (face) con granos
spouse [spaʊz] n cónyuge m/f
spout [spaʊt] n (of jug) pico; (of pipe) caño ♦ vi salir en chorro
sprain [spreɪn] n torcedura ♦ vt: **to ~ one's ankle/wrist** torcerse el tobillo/la muñeca
sprang [spræŋ] pt of **spring**
sprawl [sprɔ:l] vi tumbarse
spray [spreɪ] n rociada; (of sea) espuma; (container) atomizador m; (for paint etc) pistola rociadora; (of flowers) ramita ♦ vt rociar; (crops) regar
spread [spred] (pt, pp **spread**) n extensión f; (for bread etc) pasta para untar; (inf: food) comilona ♦ vt extender; (butter) untar; (wings, sails) desplegar; (work, wealth) repartir; (scatter) esparcir ♦ vi (also: ~ **out**: stain) extenderse; (news) diseminarse; ~ **out** vi (move apart) separarse; ~-**eagled** adj a pata tendida; ~**sheet** n hoja electrónica or de cálculo
spree [spri:] n: **to go on a ~** ir de juerga
sprightly ['spraɪtlɪ] adj vivo, enérgico
spring [sprɪŋ] (pt **sprang**, pp **sprung**) n (season) primavera; (leap) salto, brinco; (coiled metal) resorte m; (of water) fuente f, manantial m ♦ vi saltar, brincar; ~ **up** vi (thing: appear) aparecer; (problem) surgir; ~**board** n trampolín m; ~-**clean(ing)** n limpieza general; ~**time** n primavera
sprinkle ['sprɪŋkl] vt (pour: liquid) rociar; (: salt, sugar) espolvorear; **to ~ water etc on**, ~ **with water etc** rociar or salpicar de agua etc; ~**r** n (for lawn) rociadera; (to

put out fire) aparato de rociadura automática

sprint [sprɪnt] n esprint m ♦ vi esprintar

sprout [spraut] vi brotar, retoñar; (Brussels) ~s npl coles fpl de Bruselas

spruce [spruːs] n inv (BOT) pícea ♦ adj aseado, pulcro

sprung [sprʌŋ] pp of **spring**

spun [spʌn] pt, pp of **spin**

spur [spəː*] n espuela; (fig) estímulo, aguijón m ♦ vt (also: ~ on) estimular, incitar; **on the ~ of the moment** de improviso

spurious ['spjuərɪəs] adj falso

spurn [spəːn] vt desdeñar, rechazar

spurt [spəːt] n chorro; (of energy) arrebato ♦ vi chorrear

spy [spaɪ] n espía m/f ♦ vi: **to ~ on** espiar a ♦ vt (see) divisar, lograr ver; ~ing n espionaje m

sq. abbr = **square**

squabble ['skwɔbl] vi reñir, pelear

squad [skwɔd] n (MIL) pelotón m; (POLICE) brigada; (SPORT) equipo

squadron ['skwɔdrn] n (MIL) escuadrón m; (AVIAT, NAUT) escuadra

squalid ['skwɔlɪd] adj vil; (fig: sordid) sórdido

squall [skwɔːl] n (storm) chubasco; (wind) ráfaga

squalor ['skwɔlə*] n miseria

squander ['skwɔndə*] vt (money) derrochar, despilfarrar; (chances) desperdiciar

square [skweə*] n cuadro; (in town) plaza; (inf: person) carca m/f ♦ adj cuadrado; (inf: ideas, tastes) trasnochado ♦ vt (arrange) arreglar; (MATH) cuadrar; (reconcile) compaginar; **all ~** igual(es); **to have a ~ meal** comer caliente; **2 metres ~** 2 metros en cuadro; **2 ~ metres** 2 metros cuadrados; ~**ly** adv de lleno

squash [skwɔʃ] n (BRIT: drink): **lemon/ orange ~** zumo (SP) or jugo (AM) de limón/naranja; (US: BOT) calabacín m; (SPORT) squash m, frontenis m ♦ vt aplastar

squat [skwɔt] adj achaparrado ♦ vi (also: ~ **down**) agacharse, sentarse en cuclillas; ~**ter** n persona que ocupa ilegalmente una casa

squeak [skwiːk] vi (hinge) chirriar, rechinar; (mouse) chillar

squeal [skwiːl] vi chillar, dar gritos agudos

squeamish ['skwiːmɪʃ] adj delicado, remilgado

squeeze [skwiːz] n presión f; (of hand) apretón m; (COMM) restricción f ♦ vt (hand, arm) apretar; ~ **out** vt exprimir

squelch [skweltʃ] vi chapotear

squid [skwɪd] n inv calamar m; (CULIN) calamares mpl

squiggle ['skwɪgl] n garabato

squint [skwɪnt] vi bizquear, ser bizco ♦ n (MED) estrabismo

squirm [skwəːm] vi retorcerse, revolverse

squirrel ['skwɪrəl] n ardilla

squirt [skwəːt] vi salir a chorros ♦ vt chiscar

Sr abbr = **senior**

St abbr = **saint; street**

stab [stæb] n (with knife) puñalada; (of pain) pinchazo; (inf: try): **to have a ~ at (doing) sth** intentar (hacer) algo ♦ vt apuñalar

stable ['steɪbl] adj estable ♦ n cuadra, caballeriza

stack [stæk] n montón m, pila ♦ vt amontonar, apilar

stadium ['steɪdɪəm] n estadio

staff [stɑːf] n (work force) personal m, plantilla; (BRIT: SCOL) cuerpo docente ♦ vt proveer de personal

stag [stæg] n ciervo, venado

stage [steɪdʒ] n escena; (point) etapa; (platform) plataforma; (profession): **the ~** el teatro ♦ vt (play) poner en escena, representar; (organize) montar, organizar; **in ~s** por etapas; ~**coach** n diligencia; ~**manager** n director(a) m/f de escena

stagger ['stægə*] vi tambalearse ♦ vt (amaze) asombrar; (hours, holidays) escalonar; ~**ing** adj asombroso

stagnant ['stægnənt] adj estancado

stag party n despedida de soltero

staid [steid] adj serio, formal

stain [stein] n mancha; (colouring) tintura ♦ vt manchar; (wood) teñir; **~ed glass window** n vidriera de colores; **~less steel** n acero inoxidable; **~ remover** n quitamanchas m inv

stair [steə*] n (step) peldaño, escalón m; **~s** npl escaleras fpl; **~case** n = **~way**; **~way** n escalera

stake [steik] n estaca, poste m; (COMM) interés m; (BETTING) apuesta ♦ vt (money) apostar; (life) arriesgar; (reputation) poner en juego; (claim) presentar una reclamación; **to be at ~** estar en juego

stale [steil] adj (bread) duro; (food) pasado; (smell) rancio; (beer) agrio

stalemate ['steilmeit] n tablas fpl (por ahogado); (fig) estancamiento

stalk [stɔːk] n tallo, caña ♦ vt acechar, cazar al acecho; **~ off** vi irse airado

stall [stɔːl] n (in market) puesto; (in stable) casilla (de establo) ♦ vt (AUT) calar; (fig) dar largas a ♦ vi (AUT) calarse; (fig) andarse con rodeos; **~s** npl (BRIT: in cinema, theatre) butacas fpl

stallion ['stæliən] n semental m

stamina ['stæminə] n resistencia

stammer ['stæmə*] n tartamudeo ♦ vi tartamudear

stamp [stæmp] n sello (SP), estampilla (AM); (mark, also fig) marca, huella; (on document) timbre m ♦ vi (also: **~ one's foot**) patear ♦ vt (mark) marcar; (letter) poner sellos or estampillas en; (with rubber ~) sellar; **~ album** n álbum m para sellos or estampillas; **~ collecting** n filatelia

stampede [stæm'piːd] n estampida

stance [stæns] n postura

stand [stænd] n (pt, pp **stood**) n (position) posición f, postura; (for taxis) parada; (hall ~) perchero; (music ~) atril m; (SPORT) tribuna; (at exhibition) stand m ♦ vi (be) estar, encontrarse; (be on foot) estar de pie; (rise) levantarse; (remain) quedar en pie; (in election) presentar candidatura ♦ vt (place) poner, colocar; (withstand) aguantar, soportar; (invite to) invitar; **to make a ~** (fig) mantener una postura firme; **to ~ for parliament** (BRIT) presentarse (como candidato) a las elecciones; **~ by** vi (be ready) estar listo ♦ vt fus (opinion) aferrarse a; (person) apoyar; **~ down** vi (withdraw) ceder el puesto; **~ for** vt fus (signify) significar; (tolerate) aguantar, permitir; **~ in for** vt fus suplir a; **~ out** vi destacarse; **~ up** vi levantarse, ponerse de pie; **~ up for** vt fus defender; **~ up to** vt fus hacer frente a

standard ['stændəd] n patrón m, norma; (level) nivel m; (flag) estandarte m ♦ adj (size etc) normal, corriente; (text) básico; **~s** npl (morals) valores mpl morales; **~ lamp** (BRIT) n lámpara de pie; **~ of living** n nivel m de vida

stand-by ['stændbai] n (reserve) recurso seguro; **to be on ~** estar sobre aviso; **~ ticket** n (AVIAT) (billete m) standby m

stand-in ['stændin] n suplente m/f

standing ['stændiŋ] adj (on foot) de pie, en pie; (permanent) permanente ♦ n reputación f; **of many years' ~** que lleva muchos años; **~ joke** n broma permanente; **~ order** (BRIT) n (at bank) orden f de pago permanente; **~ room** n sitio para estar de pie

stand: **~point** n punto de vista; **~still** n: **at a ~still** (industry, traffic) paralizado; (car) parado; **to come to a ~still** quedar paralizado; parar

stank [stæŋk] pt of **stink**

staple ['steipl] n (for papers) grapa ♦ adj (food etc) básico ♦ vt grapar; **~r** n grapadora

star [stɑː*] n estrella; (celebrity) estrella, astro ♦ vt (THEATRE, CINEMA) ser el/la protagonista de; **the ~s** npl (ASTROLOGY) el horóscopo

starboard ['stɑːbəd] n estribor m

starch [stɑːtʃ] n almidón m

stardom ['stɑːdəm] n estrellato

stare [steə*] n mirada fija ♦ vi: **to ~ at**

mirar fijo

starfish ['stɑːfɪʃ] n estrella de mar

stark [stɑːk] adj (bleak) severo, escueto
♦ adv: ~ **naked** en cueros

starling ['stɑːlɪŋ] n estornino

starry ['stɑːrɪ] adj estrellado; **~-eyed** adj
(innocent) inocentón/ona, ingenuo

start [stɑːt] n principio, comienzo;
(departure) salida; (sudden movement)
salto, sobresalto; (advantage) ventaja ♦ vt
empezar, comenzar; (cause) causar;
(found) fundar; (engine) poner en marcha
♦ vi comenzar, empezar; (with fright)
asustarse, sobresaltarse; (train etc) salir; **to
~ doing** or **to do sth** empezar a hacer
algo; ~ **off** vi empezar, comenzar; (leave)
salir, ponerse en camino; ~ **up** vi
comenzar; (car) ponerse en marcha ♦ vt
comenzar; poner en marcha; **~er** n (AUT)
botón m de arranque; (SPORT: official) juez
m/f de salida; (BRIT: CULIN) entrada; **~ing
point** n punto de partida

startle ['stɑːtl] vt asustar, sobrecoger;
startling adj alarmante

starvation [stɑːˈveɪʃən] n hambre f

starve [stɑːv] vi tener mucha hambre; (to
death) morir de hambre ♦ vt hacer pasar
hambre

state [steɪt] n estado ♦ vt (say, declare)
afirmar; **the S~s** los Estados Unidos; **to
be in a ~** estar agitado; **~ly** adj
majestuoso, imponente; **~ly home** n
casa señorial, casa solariega; **~ment** n
afirmación f; **~sman** (irreg) n estadista m

static ['stætɪk] n (RADIO) parásitos mpl
♦ adj estático; ~ **electricity** n estática

station ['steɪʃən] n (gen) estación f; (RADIO)
emisora; (rank) posición f social ♦ vt
colocar, situar; (MIL) apostar

stationary ['steɪʃnərɪ] adj estacionario, fijo

stationer ['steɪʃnə*] n papelero/a; **~'s
(shop)** (BRIT) n papelería; **~y** [-nərɪ] n
papel m de escribir, artículos mpl de
escritorio

station master n (RAIL) jefe m de
estación

station wagon (US) n ranchera

statistic [stəˈtɪstɪk] n estadística; **~s** n
(science) estadística

statue ['stætjuː] n estatua

status ['steɪtəs] n estado; (reputation)
estatus m; ~ **symbol** n símbolo de
prestigio

statute ['stætjuːt] n estatuto, ley f;
statutory adj estatutario

staunch [stɔːntʃ] adj leal, incondicional

stay [steɪ] n estancia ♦ vi quedar(se); (as
guest) hospedarse; **to ~ put** seguir en el
mismo sitio; **to ~ the night/5 days** pasar
la noche/estar 5 días; ~ **behind** vi
quedar atrás; ~ **in** vi quedarse en casa; ~
on vi quedarse; ~ **out** vi (of house) no
volver a casa; (on strike) permanecer en
huelga; ~ **up** vi (at night) velar, no
acostarse; **~ing power** n aguante m

stead [sted] n: **in sb's ~** en lugar de uno;
to stand sb in good ~ ser muy útil a uno

steadfast ['stedfɑːst] adj firme, resuelto

steadily ['stedɪlɪ] adv constantemente;
(firmly) firmemente; (work, walk) sin parar;
(gaze) fijamente

steady ['stedɪ] adj (firm) firme; (regular)
regular; (person, character) sensato,
juicioso; (boyfriend) formal; (look, voice)
tranquilo ♦ vt (stabilize) estabilizar;
(nerves) calmar

steak [steɪk] n (gen) filete m; (beef) bistec
m

steal [stiːl] (pt **stole**, pp **stolen**) vt robar
♦ vi robar; (move secretly) andar a
hurtadillas

stealth [stelθ] n: **by ~** a escondidas,
sigilosamente; **~y** adj cauteloso, sigiloso

steam [stiːm] n vapor m; (mist) vaho,
humo ♦ vt (CULIN) cocer al vapor ♦ vi
echar vapor; ~ **engine** n máquina de
vapor; **~er** n (buque m de) vapor m;
~roller n apisonadora; **~ship** n = **~er**;
~y adj (room) lleno de vapor; (window)
empañado; (heat, atmosphere)
bochornoso

steel [stiːl] n acero ♦ adj de acero;
~works n acería

steep [stiːp] adj escarpado, abrupto; (stair

empinado; (*price*) exorbitante, excesivo ♦ *vt* empapar, remojar

steeple ['sti:pl] *n* aguja; **~chase** *n* carrera de obstáculos

steer [stɪə*] *vt* (*car*) conducir (*SP*), manejar (*AM*); (*person*) dirigir ♦ *vi* conducir, manejar; **~ing** *n* (*AUT*) dirección *f*; **~ing wheel** *n* volante *m*

stem [stem] *n* (*of plant*) tallo; (*of glass*) pie *m* ♦ *vt* detener; (*blood*) restañar; **~ from** *vt fus* ser consecuencia de

stench [stentʃ] *n* hedor *m*

stencil ['stensl] *n* (*pattern*) plantilla ♦ *vt* hacer un cliché de

stenographer [stɛ'nɔgrəfə*] (*US*) *n* taquígrafo/a

step [step] *n* paso; (*on stair*) peldaño, escalón *m* ♦ *vi*: **to ~ forward/back** dar un paso adelante/hacia atrás; **~s** *npl* (*BRIT*) = **~ladder**; **in/out of ~ (with)** acorde/en disonancia (con); **~ down** *vi* (*fig*) retirarse; **~ on** *vt fus* pisar; **~ up** *vt* (*increase*) aumentar; **~brother** *n* hermanastro; **~daughter** *n* hijastra; **~father** *n* padrastro; **~ladder** *n* escalera doble *or* de tijera; **~mother** *n* madrastra; **~ping stone** *n* pasadera; **~sister** *n* hermanastra; **~son** *n* hijastro

stereo ['steriəu] *n* estéreo ♦ *adj* (*also*: **~phonic**) estéreo, estereofónico

sterile ['sterail] *adj* estéril; **sterilize** ['sterilaiz] *vt* esterilizar

sterling ['stə:lɪŋ] *adj* (*silver*) de ley ♦ *n* (*ECON*) (libras *fpl*) esterlinas *fpl*; **one pound ~** una libra esterlina

stern [stə:n] *adj* severo, austero ♦ *n* (*NAUT*) popa

stew [stju:] *n* cocido (*SP*), estofado (*SP*), guisado (*AM*) ♦ *vt* estofar, guisar; (*fruit*) cocer

steward ['stju:əd] *n* camarero; **~ess** *n* (*esp on plane*) azafata

stick [stɪk] (*pt*, *pp* **stuck**) *n* palo; (*of dynamite*) barreno; (*as weapon*) porra; (*walking ~*) bastón *m* ♦ *vt* (*glue*) pegar; (*inf: put*) meter; (: *tolerate*) aguantar, soportar; (*thrust*): **to ~ sth into** clavar *or*

hincar algo en ♦ *vi* pegarse; (*be unmoveable*) quedarse parado; (*in mind*) quedarse grabado; **~ out** *vi* sobresalir; **~ up** *vi* sobresalir; **~ up for** *vt fus* defender; **~er** *n* (*label*) etiqueta engomada; (*with slogan*) pegatina; **~ing plaster** *n* esparadrapo

stick-up ['stɪkʌp] (*inf*) *n* asalto, atraco

sticky ['stɪkɪ] *adj* pegajoso; (*label*) engomado; (*fig*) difícil

stiff [stɪf] *adj* rígido, tieso; (*hard*) duro; (*manner*) estirado; (*difficult*) difícil; (*person*) inflexible; (*price*) exorbitante ♦ *adv*: **scared/bored ~** muerto de miedo/aburrimiento; **~en** *vi* (*muscles etc*) agarrotarse; **~ neck** *n* tortícolis *m inv*; **~ness** *n* rigidez *f*, tiesura

stifle ['staifl] *vt* ahogar, sofocar; **stifling** *adj* (*heat*) sofocante, bochornoso

stigma ['stɪgmə] *n* (*fig*) estigma *m*

stile [stail] *n* portillo, portilla

stiletto [str'letəu] (*BRIT*) *n* (*also*: **~ heel**) tacón *m* de aguja

still [stɪl] *adj* inmóvil, quieto ♦ *adv* todavía; (*even*) aun; (*nonetheless*) sin embargo, aun así; **~born** *adj* nacido muerto; **~ life** *n* naturaleza muerta

stilt [stɪlt] *n* zanco; (*pile*) pilar *m*, soporte *m*

stilted ['stɪltɪd] *adj* afectado

stimulate ['stɪmjuleɪt] *vt* estimular

stimulus ['stɪmjuləs] (*pl* **stimuli**) *n* estímulo, incentivo

sting [stɪŋ] (*pt*, *pp* **stung**) *n* picadura; (*pain*) escozor *m*, picazón *f*; (*organ*) aguijón *m* ♦ *vt*, *vi* picar

stingy ['stɪndʒɪ] *adj* tacaño

stink [stɪŋk] (*pt* **stank**, *pp* **stunk**) *n* hedor *m*, tufo ♦ *vi* heder, apestar; **~ing** *adj* hediondo, fétido; (*fig*: *inf*) horrible

stint [stɪnt] *n* tarea, trabajo ♦ *vi*: **to ~ on** escatimar

stir [stə:*] *n* (*fig*: *agitation*) conmoción *f* ♦ *vt* (*tea etc*) remover; (*fig*: *emotions*) provocar ♦ *vi* moverse; **~ up** *vt* (*trouble*) fomentar

stirrup ['stɪrəp] *n* estribo

stitch [stɪtʃ] *n* (*SEWING*) puntada; (*KNITTING*) punto; (*MED*) punto (de sutura); (*pain*) punzada ♦ *vt* coser; (*MED*) suturar

stoat [stəut] *n* armiño

stock [stɔk] *n* (*COMM: reserves*) existencias *fpl*, stock *m*; (*: selection*) surtido; (*AGR*) ganado, ganadería; (*CULIN*) caldo; (*descent*) raza, estirpe *f*; (*FINANCE*) capital *m* ♦ *adj* (*fig: reply etc*) clásico ♦ *vt* (*have in ~*) tener existencias de; **~s and shares** acciones y valores; **in ~** en existencia *or* almacén; **out of ~** agotado; **to take ~ of** (*fig*) asesorar, examinar; **~ up with** *vt fus* abastecerse de; **~broker** ['stɔkbrəukə*] *n* agente *m/f or* corredor(a) *m/f* de bolsa; **~ cube** (*BRIT*) *n* pastilla de caldo; **~ exchange** *n* bolsa

stocking ['stɔkɪŋ] *n* media

stock: **~ market** *n* bolsa (de valores); **~pile** *n* reserva ♦ *vt* acumular, almacenar; **~taking** (*BRIT*) *n* (*COMM*) inventario

stocky ['stɔkɪ] *adj* (*strong*) robusto; (*short*) achaparrado

stodgy ['stɔdʒɪ] *adj* indigesto, pesado

stoke [stəuk] *vt* atizar

stole [stəul] *pt of* **steal** ♦ *n* estola

stolen ['stəuln] *pp of* **steal**

stomach ['stʌmək] *n* (*ANAT*) estómago; (*belly*) vientre *m* ♦ *vt* tragar, aguantar; **~ache** *n* dolor *m* de estómago

stone [stəun] *n* piedra; (*in fruit*) hueso; = *6.348 kg; 14 libras* ♦ *adj* de piedra ♦ *vt* apedrear; (*fruit*) deshuesar; **~-cold** *adj* helado; **~-deaf** *adj* sordo como una tapia; **~work** *n* (*art*) cantería; **stony** *adj* pedregoso; (*fig*) frío

stood [stud] *pt, pp of* **stand**

stool [stu:l] *n* taburete *m*

stoop [stu:p] *vi* (*also:* **~ down**) doblarse, agacharse; (*also:* **have a ~**) ser cargado de espaldas

stop [stɔp] *n* parada; (*in punctuation*) punto ♦ *vt* parar, detener; (*break off*) suspender; (*block: pay*) suspender; (*: cheque*) invalidar; (*also:* **put a ~ to**) poner término a ♦ *vi* pararse, detenerse; (*end*) acabarse; **to ~ doing sth** dejar de hacer algo; **~ dead** *vi* pararse en seco; **~ off** *vi* interrumpir el viaje; **~ up** *vt* (*hole*) tapar; **~gap** *n* (*person*) interino/a; (*thing*) recurso provisional; **~over** *n* parada; (*AVIAT*) escala

stoppage ['stɔpɪdʒ] *n* (*strike*) paro; (*blockage*) obstrucción *f*

stopper ['stɔpə*] *n* tapón *m*

stop press *n* noticias *fpl* de última hora

stopwatch ['stɔpwɔtʃ] *n* cronómetro

storage ['stɔ:rɪdʒ] *n* almacenaje *m*; **~ heater** *n* acumulador *m*

store [stɔ:*] *n* (*stock*) provisión *f*; (*depot: BRIT: large shop*) almacén *m*; (*US*) tienda; (*reserve*) reserva, repuesto ♦ *vt* almacenar; **~s** *npl* víveres *mpl*; **in ~** (*fig*): **to be in ~ for sb** esperarle a uno; **~ up** *vt* acumular; **~room** *n* despensa

storey ['stɔ:rɪ] (*US* **story**) *n* piso

stork [stɔ:k] *n* cigüeña

storm [stɔ:m] *n* tormenta; (*fig: of applause*) salva; (*: of criticism*) nube *f* ♦ *vi* (*fig*) rabiar ♦ *vt* tomar por asalto; **~y** *adj* tempestuoso

story ['stɔ:rɪ] *n* historia; (*lie*) mentira; (*US*) = **storey**; **~book** *n* libro de cuentos

stout [staut] *adj* (*strong*) sólido; (*fat*) gordo, corpulento; (*resolute*) resuelto ♦ *n* cerveza negra

stove [stəuv] *n* (*for cooking*) cocina; (*for heating*) estufa

stow [stəu] *vt* (*also:* **~ away**) meter, poner; (*NAUT*) estibar; **~away** *n* polizón/ona *m/f*

straggle ['strægl] *vi* (*houses etc*) extenderse; (*lag behind*) rezagarse

straight [streɪt] *adj* recto, derecho; (*frank*) franco, directo; (*simple*) sencillo ♦ *adv* derecho, directamente; (*drink*) sin mezcla; **to put** *or* **get sth ~** dejar algo en claro; **~ away, ~ off** en seguida; **~en** *vt* (*also:* **~en out**) enderezar, poner derecho; **~-faced** *adj* serio; **~forward** *adj* (*simple*) sencillo; (*honest*) honrado, franco

strain [streɪn] *n* tensión *f*; (*TECH*) presión *f*; (*MED*) torcedura; (*breed*) tipo, variedad *f*

♦ vt (*back etc*) torcerse; (*resources*) agotar; (*stretch*) estirar; (*food, tea*) colar; **~s** *npl* (MUS) son *m*; **~ed** *adj* (*muscle*) torcido; (*laugh*) forzado; (*relations*) tenso; **~er** *n* colador *m*

strait [streɪt] *n* (GEO) estrecho; **to be in dire ~s** pasar grandes apuros; **~-jacket** *n* camisa de fuerza; **~-laced** *adj* mojigato, gazmoño

strand [strænd] *n* (*of thread*) hebra; (*of hair*) trenza; (*of rope*) ramal *m*

stranded ['strændɪd] *adj* (*person: without money*) desamparado; (*: without transport*) colgado

strange [streɪndʒ] *adj* (*not known*) desconocido; (*odd*) extraño, raro; **~ly** *adv* de un modo raro; *see also* **enough**; **~r** *n* desconocido/a; (*from another area*) forastero/a

strangle ['stræŋgl] *vt* estrangular; **~hold** *n* (*fig*) dominio completo

strap [stræp] *n* correa; (*of slip, dress*) tirante *m*

strategic [strə'tiːdʒɪk] *adj* estratégico

strategy ['strætɪdʒɪ] *n* estrategia

straw [strɔː] *n* paja; (*drinking ~*) caña, pajita; **that's the last ~!** ¡eso es el colmo!

strawberry ['strɔːbərɪ] *n* fresa (SP), frutilla (AM)

stray [streɪ] *adj* (*animal*) extraviado; (*bullet*) perdido; (*scattered*) disperso ♦ *vi* extraviarse, perderse

streak [striːk] *n* raya; (*in hair*) raya ♦ *vt* rayar ♦ *vi*: **to ~ past** pasar como un rayo

stream [striːm] *n* riachuelo, arroyo; (*of people, vehicles*) fila, caravana; (*of smoke, insults etc*) chorro ♦ *vt* (SCOL) dividir en grupos por habilidad ♦ *vi* correr, fluir; **to ~ in/out** (*people*) entrar/salir en tropel

streamer ['striːmə*] *n* serpentina

streamlined ['striːmlaɪnd] *adj* aerodinámico

street [striːt] *n* calle *f*; **~car** (US) *n* tranvía *m*; **~ lamp** *n* farol *m*; **~ plan** *n* plano; **~wise** (*inf*) *adj* que tiene mucha calle

strength [streŋθ] *n* fuerza; (*of girder, knot*

etc) resistencia; (*fig: power*) poder *m*; **~en** *vt* fortalecer, reforzar

strenuous ['strenjuəs] *adj* (*energetic, determined*) enérgico

stress [stres] *n* presión *f*; (*mental strain*) estrés *m*; (*accent*) acento ♦ *vt* subrayar, recalcar; (*syllable*) acentuar

stretch [stretʃ] *n* (*of sand etc*) trecho ♦ *vi* estirarse; (*extend*): **to ~ to** *or* **as far as** extenderse hasta ♦ *vt* extender, estirar; (*make demands of*) exigir el máximo esfuerzo a; **~ out** *vi* tenderse ♦ *vt* (*arm etc*) extender; (*spread*) estirar

stretcher ['stretʃə*] *n* camilla

strewn [struːn] *adj*: **~ with** cubierto *or* sembrado de

stricken ['strɪkən] *adj* (*person*) herido; (*city, industry etc*) condenado; **~ with** (*disease*) afectado por

strict [strɪkt] *adj* severo; (*exact*) estricto; **~ly** *adv* severamente; estrictamente

stride [straɪd] (*pt* **strode**, *pp* **stridden**) *n* zancada, tranco ♦ *vi* dar zancadas, andar a trancos

strife [straɪf] *n* lucha

strike [straɪk] (*pt, pp* **struck**) *n* huelga; (*of oil etc*) descubrimiento; (*attack*) ataque *m* ♦ *vt* golpear, pegar; (*oil etc*) descubrir; (*bargain, deal*) cerrar ♦ *vi* declarar la huelga; (*attack*) atacar; (*clock*) dar la hora; **on ~** (*workers*) en huelga; **to ~ a match** encender un fósforo; **~ down** *vt* derribar; **~ up** *vt* (MUS) empezar a tocar; (*conversation*) entablar; (*friendship*) trabar; **~r** *n* huelguista *m/f*; (SPORT) delantero; **striking** *adj* llamativo

string [strɪŋ] (*pt, pp* **strung**) *n* (*gen*) cuerda; (*row*) hilera ♦ *vt*: **to ~ together** ensartar; **to ~ out** extenderse; **the ~s** *npl* (MUS) los instrumentos de cuerda; **to pull ~s** (*fig*) mover palancas; **~ bean** *n* judía verde, habichuela; **~(ed) instrument** *n* (MUS) instrumento de cuerda

stringent ['strɪndʒənt] *adj* riguroso, severo

strip [strɪp] *n* tira; (*of land*) franja; (*of metal*) cinta, lámina ♦ *vt* desnudar; (*paint*) quitar; (*also:* **~ down:** *machine*) desmontar ♦ *vi* desnudarse; **~ cartoon** *n* tira cómica (*SP*), historieta (*AM*)

stripe [straɪp] *n* raya; (*MIL*) galón *m*; **~d** *adj* a rayas, rayado

strip lighting *n* alumbrado fluorescente

stripper ['strɪpə*] *n* artista *m/f* de striptease

strive [straɪv] (*pt* **strove**, *pp* **striven**) *vi*: **to ~ for sth/to do sth** luchar por conseguir/hacer algo

strode [strəud] *pt of* **stride**

stroke [strəuk] *n* (*blow*) golpe *m*; (*SWIMMING*) brazada; (*MED*) apoplejía; (*of paintbrush*) toque *m* ♦ *vt* acariciar; **at a ~** de un solo golpe

stroll [strəul] *n* paseo, vuelta ♦ *vi* dar un paseo *or* una vuelta; **~er** (*US*) *n* (*for child*) sillita de ruedas

strong [strɒŋ] *adj* fuerte; **they are 50 ~** son 50; **~hold** *n* fortaleza; (*fig*) baluarte *m*; **~ly** *adv* fuertemente, con fuerza; (*believe*) firmemente; **~room** *n* cámara acorazada

strove [strəuv] *pt of* **strive**

struck [strʌk] *pt, pp of* **strike**

structure ['strʌktʃə*] *n* estructura; (*building*) construcción *f*

struggle ['strʌgl] *n* lucha ♦ *vi* luchar

strum [strʌm] *vt* (*guitar*) rasguear

strung [strʌŋ] *pt, pp of* **string**

strut [strʌt] *n* puntal *m* ♦ *vi* pavonearse

stub [stʌb] *n* (*of ticket etc*) talón *m*; (*of cigarette*) colilla; **to ~ one's toe on sth** dar con el dedo (del pie) contra algo; **~ out** *vt* apagar

stubble ['stʌbl] *n* rastrojo; (*on chin*) barba (incipiente)

stubborn ['stʌbən] *adj* terco, testarudo

stuck [stʌk] *pt, pp of* **stick** ♦ *adj* (*jammed*) atascado; **~-up** *adj* engreído, presumido

stud [stʌd] *n* (*shirt ~*) corchete *m*; (*of boot*) taco; (*earring*) pendiente *m* (de bolita); (*also:* **~ farm**) caballeriza; (*also:* **~ horse**) caballo semental ♦ *vt* (*fig*): **~ded with** salpicado de

student ['stjuːdənt] *n* estudiante *m/f* ♦ *adj* estudiantil; **~ driver** (*US*) *n* aprendiz(a)

m/f

studio ['stjuːdɪəu] *n* estudio; (*artist's*) taller *m*; **~ flat** (*US* **~ apartment**) *n* estudio

studious ['stjuːdɪəs] *adj* estudioso; (*studied*) calculado; **~ly** *adv* (*carefully*) con esmero

study ['stʌdɪ] *n* estudio ♦ *vt* estudiar; (*examine*) examinar, investigar ♦ *vi* estudiar

stuff [stʌf] *n* materia; (*substance*) material *m*, sustancia; (*things*) cosas *fpl* ♦ *vt* llenar; (*CULIN*) rellenar; (*animals*) disecar; (*inf: push*) meter; **~ing** *n* relleno; **~y** *adj* (*room*) mal ventilado; (*person*) de miras estrechas

stumble ['stʌmbl] *vi* tropezar, dar un traspié; **to ~ across**, **~ on** (*fig*) tropezar con; **stumbling block** *n* tropiezo, obstáculo

stump [stʌmp] *n* (*of tree*) tocón *m*; (*of limb*) muñón *m* ♦ *vt*: **to be ~ed for an answer** no saber qué contestar

stun [stʌn] *vt* dejar sin sentido

stung [stʌŋ] *pt, pp of* **sting**

stunk [stʌŋk] *pp of* **stink**

stunning ['stʌnɪŋ] *adj* (*fig: news*) pasmoso; (: *outfit etc*) sensacional

stunt [stʌnt] *n* (*in film*) escena peligrosa; (*publicity ~*) truco publicitario; **~man** (*irreg*) *n* doble *m*

stupid ['stjuːpɪd] *adj* estúpido, tonto; **~ity** [-'pɪdɪtɪ] *n* estupidez *f*

sturdy ['stɜːdɪ] *adj* robusto, fuerte

stutter ['stʌtə*] *n* tartamudeo ♦ *vi* tartamudear

sty [staɪ] *n* (*for pigs*) pocilga

stye [staɪ] *n* (*MED*) orzuelo

style [staɪl] *n* estilo; **stylish** *adj* elegante, a la moda

stylus ['staɪləs] *n* aguja

suave [swɑːv] *adj* cortés

sub... [sʌb] *prefix* sub...; **~conscious** *adj* subconsciente; **~contract** *vt* subcontratar; **~divide** *vt* subdividir

subdue [səb'djuː] *vt* sojuzgar; (*passions*) dominar; **~d** *adj* (*light*) tenue; (*person*) sumiso, manso subject [n 'sʌbdʒɪkt, vb səb'dʒekt] n súbdito; (SCOL) asignatura; (matter) tema m; (GRAMMAR) sujeto ♦ vt: to ~ sb to sth someter a uno a algo; to be ~ to (law) estar sujeto a; (subj: person) ser propenso a; ~ive [-'dʒektɪv] adj subjetivo; ~ matter n (content) contenido

sublet [sʌb'let] vt subarrendar

submarine [sʌbmə'riːn] n submarino

submerge [səb'məːdʒ] vt sumergir ♦ vi sumergirse

submissive [səb'mɪsɪv] adj sumiso

submit [səb'mɪt] vt someter ♦ vi: to ~ to sth someterse a algo

subnormal [sʌb'nɔːməl] adj anormal

subordinate [sə'bɔːdɪnət] adj, n subordinado/a m/f

subpoena [səb'piːnə] n (LAW) citación f

subscribe [səb'skraɪb] vi suscribir; to ~ to (opinion, fund) suscribir, aprobar; (newspaper) suscribirse a; ~r n (to periodical) subscriptor(a) m/f; (to telephone) abonado/a

subscription [səb'skrɪpʃən] n abono; (to magazine) subscripción f

subsequent ['sʌbsɪkwənt] adj subsiguiente, posterior; ~ly adv posteriormente, más tarde

subside [səb'saɪd] vi hundirse; (flood) bajar; (wind) amainar; subsidence [-'saɪdns] n hundimiento; (in road) socavón m

subsidiary [səb'sɪdɪərɪ] adj secundario ♦ n sucursal f, filial f

subsidize ['sʌbsɪdaɪz] vt subvencionar

subsidy ['sʌbsɪdɪ] n subvención f

subsistence [səb'sɪstəns] n subsistencia; ~ allowance n salario mínimo

substance ['sʌbstəns] n sustancia

substantial [səb'stænʃl] adj sustancial, sustancioso; (fig) importante

substantiate [səb'stænʃɪeɪt] vt comprobar

substitute ['sʌbstɪtjuːt] n (person) suplente m/f; (thing) sustituto ♦ vt: to ~ A for B sustituir A por B, reemplazar B por A

subtitle ['sʌbtaɪtl] n subtítulo

subtle ['sʌtl] adj sutil; ~ty n sutileza

subtotal [sʌb'təʊtl] n total m parcial

subtract [səb'trækt] vt restar, sustraer; ~ion [-'trækʃən] n resta, sustracción f

suburb ['sʌbəːb] n barrio residencial; the ~s las afueras (de la ciudad); ~an [sə'bəːbən] adj suburbano; (train etc) de cercanías; ~ia [sə'bəːbɪə] n barrios mpl residenciales

subway ['sʌbweɪ] n (BRIT) paso subterráneo or inferior; (US) metro

succeed [sək'siːd] vi (person) tener éxito; (plan) salir bien ♦ vt suceder a; to ~ in doing lograr hacer; ~ing adj (following) sucesivo

success [sək'ses] n éxito; ~ful adj exitoso; (business) próspero; to be ~ful (in doing) lograr (hacer); ~fully adv con éxito

succession [sək'seʃən] n sucesión f, serie f

successive [sək'sesɪv] adj sucesivo, consecutivo

succinct [sək'sɪŋkt] adj sucinto

such [sʌtʃ] adj tal, semejante; (of that kind): ~ a book tal libro; (so much): ~ courage tanto valor ♦ adv tan; ~ a long trip un viaje tan largo; ~ a lot of tanto(s)/a(s); ~ as (like) tal como; as ~ como tal; ~-and-~ adj tal o cual

suck [sʌk] vt chupar; (bottle) sorber; (breast) mamar; ~er n (ZOOL) ventosa; (inf) bobo, primo

suction ['sʌkʃən] n succión f

Sudan [suː'dæn] n Sudán m

sudden ['sʌdn] adj (rapid) repentino, súbito; (unexpected) imprevisto; all of a ~ de repente; ~ly adv de repente

suds [sʌdz] npl espuma de jabón

sue [suː] vt demandar

suede [sweɪd] n ante m (SP), gamuza (AM)

suet ['suɪt] n sebo

Suez ['suːɪz] n: the ~ Canal el Canal de Suez

suffer ['sʌfə*] vt sufrir, padecer; (tolerate) aguantar, soportar ♦ vi sufrir; to ~ from (illness etc) padecer; ~er n víctima; (MED) enfermo/a; ~ing n sufrimiento

sufficient [sə'fɪʃənt] *adj* suficiente, bastante; **~ly** *ad* suficientemente, bastante

suffocate ['sʌfəkeɪt] *vi* ahogarse, asfixiarse; **suffocation** [-'keɪʃən] *n* asfixia

sugar ['ʃugə*] *n* azúcar *m* ♦ *vt* echar azúcar a, azucarar; **~ beet** *n* remolacha; **~ cane** *n* caña de azúcar

suggest [sə'dʒest] *vt* sugerir; **~ion** [-'dʒestʃən] *n* sugerencia; **~ive** (*pej*) *adj* indecente

suicide ['suɪsaɪd] *n* suicidio; (*person*) suicida *m/f*; see also **commit**

suit [suːt] *n* (*man's*) traje *m*; (*woman's*) conjunto; (*LAW*) pleito; (*CARDS*) palo ♦ *vt* convenir; (*clothes*) sentar a, ir bien a; (*adapt*): **to ~ sth to** adaptar *or* ajustar algo a; **well ~ed** (*well matched: couple*) hecho el uno para el otro; **~able** *adj* conveniente; (*apt*) indicado; **~ably** *adv* convenientemente; (*impressed*) apropiadamente

suitcase ['suːtkeɪs] *n* maleta (*SP*), valija (*AM*)

suite [swiːt] *n* (*of rooms, MUS*) suite *f*; (*furniture*): **bedroom/dining room ~** (juego de) dormitorio/comedor

suitor ['suːtə*] *n* pretendiente *m*

sulfur ['sʌlfə*] (*US*) *n* = **sulphur**

sulk [sʌlk] *vi* estar de mal humor; **~y** *adj* malhumorado

sullen ['sʌlən] *adj* hosco, malhumorado

sulphur ['sʌlfə*] (*US* **sulfur**) *n* azufre *m*

sultana [sʌl'tɑːnə] *n* (*fruit*) pasa de Esmirna

sultry ['sʌltrɪ] *adj* (*weather*) bochornoso

sum [sʌm] *n* suma; (*total*) total *m*; **~ up** *vt* resumir ♦ *vi* hacer un resumen

summarize ['sʌməraɪz] *vt* resumir

summary ['sʌmərɪ] *n* resumen *m* ♦ *adj* (*justice*) sumario

summer ['sʌmə*] *n* verano ♦ *cpd* de verano; **in ~** en verano; **~ holidays** *npl* vacaciones *fpl* de verano; **~house** *n* (*in garden*) cenador *m*, glorieta; **~time** *n* (*season*) verano; **~ time** *n* (*by clock*) hora de verano

summit ['sʌmɪt] *n* cima, cumbre *f*; (*also*: **~ conference, ~ meeting**) (conferencia) cumbre *f*

summon ['sʌmən] *vt* (*person*) llamar; (*meeting*) convocar; (*LAW*) citar; **~ up** *vt* (*courage*) armarse de; **~s** *n* llamamiento, llamada ♦ *vt* (*LAW*) citar

sump [sʌmp] (*BRIT*) *n* (*AUT*) cárter *m*

sumptuous ['sʌmptjuəs] *adj* suntuoso

sun [sʌn] *n* sol *m*; **~bathe** *vi* tomar el sol; **~block** *n* filtro solar; **~burn** *n* (*painful*) quemadura; (*tan*) bronceado; **~burnt** *adj* quemado por el sol

Sunday ['sʌndɪ] *n* domingo; **~ school** *n* catequesis *f* dominical

sundial ['sʌndaɪəl] *n* reloj *m* de sol

sundown ['sʌndaun] *n* anochecer *m*

sundry ['sʌndrɪ] *adj* varios/as, diversos/as; **all and ~** todos sin excepción; **sundries** *npl* géneros *mpl* diversos

sunflower ['sʌnflauə*] *n* girasol *m*

sung [sʌŋ] *pp of* **sing**

sunglasses ['sʌŋglɑːsɪz] *npl* gafas *fpl* (*SP*) *or* anteojos *mpl* de sol

sunk [sʌŋk] *pp of* **sink**

sun: ~light *n* luz *f* del sol; **~lit** *adj* iluminado por el sol; **~ny** *adj* soleado; (*day*) de sol; (*fig*) alegre; **~rise** *n* salida del sol; **~ roof** *n* (*AUT*) techo corredizo; **~screen** *n* protector *m* solar; **~set** *n* puesta del sol; **~shade** *n* (*over table*) sombrilla; **~shine** *n* sol *m*; **~stroke** *n* insolación *f*; **~tan** *n* bronceado; **~tan oil** *n* aceite *m* bronceador

super ['suːpə*] (*inf*) *adj* genial

superannuation [suːpərænju'eɪʃən] *n* cuota de jubilación

superb [suː'pəːb] *adj* magnífico, espléndido

supercilious [suːpə'sɪlɪəs] *adj* altanero

superfluous [suː'pəːfluəs] *adj* superfluo, de sobra

superhuman [suːpə'hjuːmən] *adj* sobrehumano

superimpose ['suːpərɪm'pəuz] *vt* sobreponer

superintendent [suːpərɪn'tendənt] *n*

director(a) *m/f*; (*POLICE*) subjefe/a *m/f*

superior [su'prɪərɪə*] *adj* superior; (*smug*) desdeñoso ♦ *n* superior *m*; **~ity** [-'ɔrɪtɪ] *n* superioridad *f*

superlative [su'pə:lətɪv] *n* superlativo

superman ['su:pəmæn] (*irreg*) *n* superhombre *m*

supermarket ['su:pəmɑ:kɪt] *n* supermercado

supernatural [su:pə'nætʃərəl] *adj* sobrenatural ♦ *n*: **the ~** lo sobrenatural

superpower ['su:pəpauə*] *n* (*POL*) superpotencia

supersede [su:pə'si:d] *vt* suplantar

superstar ['su:pəstɑ:*] *n* gran estrella

superstitious [su:pə'stɪʃəs] *adj* supersticioso

supertanker ['su:pətæŋkə*] *n* superpetrolero

supervise ['su:pəvaɪz] *vt* supervisar; **supervision** [-'vɪʒən] *n* supervisión *f*; **supervisor** *n* supervisor(a) *m/f*

supper ['sʌpə*] *n* cena

supple ['sʌpl] *adj* flexible

supplement [*n* 'sʌplɪmənt, *vb* sʌplɪ'ment] *n* suplemento ♦ *vt* suplir; **~ary** [-'mentərɪ] *adj* suplementario; **~ary benefit** (*BRIT*) *n* subsidio suplementario de la seguridad social

supplier [sə'plaɪə*] *n* (*COMM*) distribuidor(a) *m/f*

supply [sə'plaɪ] *vt* (*provide*) suministrar; (*equip*): **to ~ (with)** proveer (de) ♦ *n* provisión *f*; (*gas, water etc*) suministro; **supplies** *npl* (*food*) víveres *mpl*; (*MIL*) pertrechos *mpl*; **~ teacher** *n* profesor(a) *m/f* suplente

support [sə'pɔ:t] *n* apoyo; (*TECH*) soporte *m* ♦ *vt* apoyar; (*financially*) mantener; (*uphold, TECH*) sostener; **~er** *n* (*POL etc*) partidario/a; (*SPORT*) aficionado/a

suppose [sə'pəuz] *vt* suponer; (*imagine*) imaginarse; (*duty*): **to be ~d to do sth** deber hacer algo; **~dly** [sə'pəuzɪdlɪ] *adv* según cabe suponer; **supposing** *conj* en caso de que

suppress [sə'pres] *vt* suprimir; (*yawn*) ahogar

supreme [su'pri:m] *adj* supremo

surcharge ['sə:tʃɑ:dʒ] *n* sobretasa, recargo

sure [ʃuə*] *adj* seguro; (*definite, convinced*) cierto; **to make ~ of sth/that** asegurarse de algo/asegurar que; **~!** (*of course*) ¡claro!, ¡por supuesto!; **~ enough** efectivamente; **~ly** *adv* (*certainly*) seguramente

surf [sə:f] *n* olas *fpl*

surface ['sə:fɪs] *n* superficie *f* ♦ *vt* (*road*) revestir ♦ *vi* (*also fig*) salir a la superficie; **by ~ mail** por vía terrestre

surfboard ['sə:fbɔ:d] *n* tabla (de surf)

surfeit ['sə:fɪt] *n*: **a ~ of** un exceso de

surfing ['sə:fɪŋ] *n* surf *m*

surge [sə:dʒ] *n* oleada, oleaje *m* ♦ *vi* (*wave*) romper; (*people*) avanzar en tropel

surgeon ['sə:dʒən] *n* cirujano/a

surgery ['sə:dʒərɪ] *n* cirugía; (*BRIT: room*) consultorio; **~ hours** (*BRIT*) *npl* horas *fpl* de consulta

surgical ['sə:dʒɪkl] *adj* quirúrgico; **~ spirit** (*BRIT*) *n* alcohol *m* de 90°

surname ['sə:neɪm] *n* apellido

surpass [sə:'pɑ:s] *vt* superar, exceder

surplus ['sə:pləs] *n* excedente *m*; (*COMM*) superávit *m* ♦ *adj* excedente, sobrante

surprise [sə'praɪz] *n* sorpresa ♦ *vt* sorprender; **surprising** *adj* sorprendente; **surprisingly** *adv*: **it was surprisingly easy** me *etc* sorprendió lo fácil que fue

surrender [sə'rendə*] *n* rendición *f*, entrega ♦ *vi* rendirse, entregarse

surreptitious [sʌrəp'tɪʃəs] *adj* subrepticio

surrogate ['sʌrəgɪt] *n* sucedáneo; **~ mother** *n* madre *f* portadora

surround [sə'raund] *vt* rodear, circundar; (*MIL etc*) cercar; **~ing** *adj* circundante; **~ings** *npl* alrededores *mpl*, cercanías *fpl*

surveillance [sə:'veɪləns] *n* vigilancia

survey [*n* 'sə:veɪ, *vb* sə:'veɪ] *n* inspección *f*, reconocimiento; (*inquiry*) encuesta ♦ *vt* examinar, inspeccionar; (*look at*) mirar, contemplar; **~or** *n* agrimensor(a) *m/f*

survival [sə'vaɪvl] *n* supervivencia

survive [sə'vaɪv] *vi* sobrevivir; (*custom etc*) perdurar ♦ *vt* sobrevivir a; **survivor** *n* superviviente *m/f*

susceptible [sə'septəbl] *adj*: ~ **(to)** (*disease*) susceptible (a); (*flattery*) sensible (a)

suspect [*adj, n* 'sʌspekt, *vb* səs'pekt] *adj, n* sospechoso/a *m/f* ♦ *vt* (*person*) sospechar de; (*think*) sospechar

suspend [səs'pend] *vt* suspender; **~ed sentence** *n* (*LAW*) libertad *f* condicional; **~er belt** *n* portaligas *m inv*; **~ers** *npl* (*BRIT*) ligas *fpl*; (*US*) tirantes *mpl*

suspense [səs'pens] *n* incertidumbre *f*, duda; (*in film etc*) suspense *m*; **to keep sb in ~** mantener a uno en suspense

suspension [səs'penʃən] *n* (*gen, AUT*) suspensión *f*; (*of driving licence*) privación *f*; **~ bridge** *n* puente *m* colgante

suspicion [səs'pɪʃən] *n* sospecha; (*distrust*) recelo; **suspicious** [-ʃəs] *adj* receloso; (*causing suspicion*) sospechoso

sustain [səs'teɪn] *vt* sostener, apoyar; (*suffer*) sufrir, padecer; **~able** *adj* sostenible; **~ed** *adj* (*effort*) sostenido

sustenance ['sʌstɪnəns] *n* sustento

swab [swɔb] *n* (*MED*) algodón *m*

swagger ['swægə*] *vi* pavonearse

swallow ['swɔləu] *n* (*bird*) golondrina ♦ *vt* tragar; (*fig, pride*) tragarse; ~ **up** *vt* (*savings etc*) consumir

swam [swæm] *pt of* **swim**

swamp [swɔmp] *n* pantano, ciénaga ♦ *vt* (*with water etc*) inundar; (*fig*) abrumar, agobiar; **~y** *adj* pantanoso

swan [swɔn] *n* cisne *m*

swap [swɔp] *n* canje *m*, intercambio ♦ *vt*: **to ~ (for)** cambiar (por)

swarm [swɔːm] *n* (*of bees*) enjambre *m*; (*fig*) multitud *f* ♦ *vi* (*bees*) formar un enjambre; (*people*) pulular; **to be ~ing with** ser un hervidero de

swastika ['swɔstɪkə] *n* esvástica

swat [swɔt] *vt* aplastar

sway [sweɪ] *vi* mecerse, balancearse ♦ *vt* (*influence*) mover, influir en

swear [sweə*] (*pt* **swore**, *pp* **sworn**) *vi* (*curse*) maldecir; (*promise*) jurar ♦ *vt* jurar; **~word** *n* taco, palabrota

sweat [swet] *n* sudor *m* ♦ *vi* sudar

sweater ['swetə*] *n* suéter *m*

sweatshirt ['swetʃə:t] *n* suéter *m*

sweaty ['swetɪ] *adj* sudoroso

Swede [swi:d] *n* sueco/a

swede [swi:d] (*BRIT*) *n* nabo

Sweden ['swi:dn] *n* Suecia; **Swedish** ['swi:dɪʃ] *adj* sueco ♦ *n* (*LING*) sueco

sweep [swi:p] (*pt, pp* **swept**) *n* (*act*) barrido; (*also*: **chimney~**) deshollinador(a) *m/f* ♦ *vt* barrer; (*with arm*) empujar; (*subj: current*) arrastrar ♦ *vi* barrer; (*arm etc*) moverse majestuosamente; (*wind*) soplar con violencia; ~ **away** *vt* barrer; ~ **past** *vi* pasar majestuosamente; ~ **up** *vi* barrer; **~ing** *adj* (*gesture*) dramático; (*generalized: statement*) generalizado

sweet [swi:t] *n* (*candy*) dulce *m*, caramelo; (*BRIT: pudding*) postre *m* ♦ *adj* dulce; (*fig: kind*) dulce, amable; (: *attractive*) mono; **~corn** *n* maíz *m*; **~en** *vt* (*add sugar to*) poner azúcar a; (*person*) endulzar; **~heart** *n* novio/a; **~ness** *n* dulzura; ~ **pea** *n* guisante *m* de olor

swell [swel] (*pt* **swelled**, *pp* **swollen** *or* **swelled**) *n* (*of sea*) marejada, oleaje *m* ♦ *adj* (*US: inf: excellent*) estupendo, fenomenal ♦ *vt* hinchar, inflar ♦ *vi* (*also*: ~ **up**) hincharse; (*numbers*) aumentar; (*sound, feeling*) ir aumentando; **~ing** *n* (*MED*) hinchazón *f*

sweltering ['sweltərɪŋ] *adj* sofocante, de mucho calor

swept [swept] *pt, pp of* **sweep**

swerve [swə:v] *vi* desviarse bruscamente

swift [swɪft] *n* (*bird*) vencejo ♦ *adj* rápido, veloz; **~ly** *adv* rápidamente

swig [swɪg] (*inf*) *n* (*drink*) trago

swill [swɪl] *vt* (*also*: ~ **out**, ~ **down**) lavar, limpiar con agua

swim [swɪm] (*pt* **swam**, *pp* **swum**) *n*: **to go for a ~** ir a nadar *or* a bañarse ♦ *vi* nadar; (*head, room*) dar vueltas ♦ *vt* nadar; (*the Channel etc*) cruzar a nado; **~mer** *n* nadador(a) *m/f*; **~ming** *n*

natación f; **~ming cap** n gorro de baño;
~ming costume (BRIT) n bañador m,
traje m de baño; **~ming pool** n piscina
(SP), alberca (AM); **~ming trunks** n
bañador m (de hombre); **~suit** n
= **~ming costume**
swindle ['swɪndl] n estafa ♦ vt estafar
swine [swaɪn] (inf!) canalla (!)
swing [swɪŋ] (pt, pp **swung**) n (in
playground) columpio; (movement)
balanceo, vaivén m; (change of direction)
viraje m; (rhythm) ritmo ♦ vt balancear;
(also: **~ round**) voltear, girar ♦ vi
balancearse, columpiarse; (also: **~ round**)
dar media vuelta; **to be in full ~** estar en
plena marcha; **~ bridge** n puente m
giratorio; **~ door** (US **~ing door**) n
puerta giratoria
swingeing ['swɪndʒɪŋ] (BRIT) adj (cuts)
atroz
swipe [swaɪp] vt (hit) golpear fuerte; (inf:
steal) guindar
swirl [swɜːl] vi arremolinarse
Swiss [swɪs] adj, n inv suizo/a m/f
switch [swɪtʃ] n (for light etc) interruptor
m; (change) cambio ♦ vt (change)
cambiar de; **~ off** vt apagar; (engine)
parar; **~ on** vt encender (SP), prender
(AM); (engine, machine) arrancar; **~board**
n (TEL) centralita (de teléfonos) (SP),
conmutador m (AM)
Switzerland ['swɪtsələnd] n Suiza
swivel ['swɪvl] vi (also: **~ round**) girar
swollen ['swəʊlən] pp of **swell**
swoon [swuːn] vi desmayarse
swoop [swuːp] n (by police etc) redada
♦ vi (also: **~ down**) calarse
swop [swɒp] = **swap**
sword [sɔːd] n espada; **~fish** n pez m
espada
swore [swɔː*] pt of **swear**
sworn [swɔːn] pp of **swear** ♦ adj
(statement) bajo juramento; (enemy)
implacable
swot [swɒt] (BRIT) vt, vi empollar
swum [swʌm] pp of **swim**
swung [swʌŋ] pt, pp of **swing**

sycamore ['sɪkəmɔː*] n sicomoro
syllable ['sɪləbl] n sílaba
syllabus ['sɪləbəs] n programa m de
estudios
symbol ['sɪmbl] n símbolo
symmetry ['sɪmɪtrɪ] n simetría
sympathetic [sɪmpə'θetɪk] adj
(understanding) comprensivo; (likeable)
simpático; (showing support): **~ to(wards)**
bien dispuesto hacia
sympathize ['sɪmpəθaɪz] vi: **to ~ with**
(person) compadecerse de; (feelings)
comprender; (cause) apoyar; **~r** n (POL)
simpatizante m/f
sympathy ['sɪmpəθɪ] n (pity) compasión f;
sympathies npl (tendencies) tendencias
fpl; **with our deepest ~** nuestro más
sentido pésame; **in ~** en solidaridad
symphony ['sɪmfənɪ] n sinfonía
symptom ['sɪmptəm] n síntoma m, indicio
synagogue ['sɪnəgɒg] n sinagoga
syndicate ['sɪndɪkɪt] n (gen) sindicato; (of
newspapers) agencia (de noticias)
syndrome ['sɪndrəum] n síndrome m
synopsis [sɪ'nɒpsɪs] (pl **synopses**) n
sinopsis f inv
synthesis ['sɪnθəsɪs] (pl **syntheses**) n
síntesis f inv
synthetic [sɪn'θetɪk] adj sintético
syphilis ['sɪfɪlɪs] n sífilis f
syphon ['saɪfən] = **siphon**
Syria ['sɪrɪə] n Siria; **~n** adj, n sirio/a
syringe [sɪ'rɪndʒ] n jeringa
syrup ['sɪrəp] n jarabe m; (also: **golden ~**)
almíbar m
system ['sɪstəm] n sistema m; (ANAT)
organismo; **~atic** [-'mætɪk] adj
sistemático, metódico; **~ disk** n
(COMPUT) disco del sistema; **~s analyst**
n analista m/f de sistemas

T, t

ta [tɑː] (*BRIT: inf*) *excl* ¡gracias!

tab [tæb] *n* lengüeta; (*label*) etiqueta; **to keep ~s on** (*fig*) vigilar

tabby ['tæbɪ] *n* (*also:* **~ cat**) gato atigrado

table ['teɪbl] *n* mesa; (*of statistics etc*) cuadro, tabla ♦ *vt* (*BRIT: motion etc*) presentar; **to lay** *or* **set the ~** poner la mesa; **~cloth** *n* mantel *m*; **~ of contents** *n* índice *m* de materias; **~ d'hôte** [tɑːbl'dəʊt] *adj* del menú; **~ lamp** *n* lámpara de mesa; **~mat** *n* (*for plate*) posaplatos *m inv*; (*for hot dish*) salvamantel *m*; **~spoon** *n* cuchara de servir; (*also:* **~spoonful**: *as measurement*) cucharada

tablet ['tæblɪt] *n* (*MED*) pastilla, comprimido; (*of stone*) lápida

table tennis *n* ping-pong *m*, tenis *m* de mesa

table wine *n* vino de mesa

tabloid ['tæblɔɪd] *n* periódico popular sensacionalista

---
tabloid press
---

i *El término* **tabloid press** *o* **tabloids** *se usa para referirse a la prensa popular británica, por el tamaño más pequeño de los periódicos. A diferencia de los de la llamada* **quality press**, *estas publicaciones se caracterizan por un lenguaje sencillo, una presentación llamativa y un contenido sensacionalista, centrado a veces en los escándalos financieros y sexuales de los famosos, por lo que también reciben el nombre peyorativo de* "gutter press".

tack [tæk] *n* (*nail*) tachuela; (*fig*) rumbo ♦ *vt* (*nail*) clavar con tachuelas; (*stitch*) hilvanar ♦ *vi* virar

tackle ['tækl] *n* (*fishing ~*) aparejo (de pescar); (*for lifting*) aparejo ♦ *vt* (*difficulty*) enfrentarse con; (*challenge: person*) hacer

frente a; (*grapple with*) agarrar; (*FOOTBALL*) cargar; (*RUGBY*) placar

tacky ['tækɪ] *adj* pegajoso; (*pej*) cutre

tact [tækt] *n* tacto, discreción *f*; **~ful** *adj* discreto, diplomático

tactics ['tæktɪks] *n, npl* táctica

tactless ['tæktlɪs] *adj* indiscreto

tadpole ['tædpəʊl] *n* renacuajo

tag [tæg] *n* (*label*) etiqueta; **~ along** *vi* ir (*or* venir) también

tail [teɪl] *n* cola; (*of shirt, coat*) faldón *m* ♦ *vt* (*follow*) vigilar a; **~s** *npl* (*formal suit*) levita; **~ away** *vi* (*in size, quality etc*) ir disminuyendo; **~ off** *vi* = **~ away**; **~back** (*BRIT*) *n* (*AUT*) cola; **~ end** *n* cola, parte *f* final; **~gate** *n* (*AUT*) puerta trasera

tailor ['teɪlə*] *n* sastre *m*; **~ing** *n* (*cut*) corte *m*; (*craft*) sastrería; **~-made** *adj* (*also fig*) hecho a la medida

tailwind ['teɪlwɪnd] *n* viento de cola

tainted ['teɪntɪd] *adj* (*food*) pasado; (*water, air*) contaminado; (*fig*) manchado

take [teɪk] (*pt* **took**, *pp* **taken**) *vt* tomar; (*grab*) coger (*SP*), agarrar (*AM*); (*gain: prize*) ganar; (*require: effort, courage*) exigir; (*tolerate: pain etc*) aguantar; (*hold: passengers etc*) tener cabida para; (*accompany, bring, carry*) llevar; (*exam*) presentarse a; **to ~ sth from** (*drawer etc*) sacar algo de; (*person*) quitar algo a; **I ~ it that ...** supongo que ...; **~** *after vt fus* parecerse a; **~ apart** *vt* desmontar; **~ away** *vt* (*remove*) quitar; (*carry off*) llevar; (*MATH*) restar; **~ back** *vt* (*return*) devolver; (*one's words*) retractarse de; **~ down** *vt* (*building*) derribar; (*letter etc*) apuntar; **~ in** *vt* (*deceive*) engañar; (*understand*) entender; (*include*) abarcar; (*lodger*) acoger, recibir; **~ off** *vi* (*AVIAT*) despegar ♦ *vt* (*remove*) quitar; **~ on** *vt* (*work*) aceptar; (*employee*) contratar; (*opponent*) desafiar; **~ out** *vt* sacar; **~ over** *vt* (*business*) tomar posesión de; (*country*) tomar el poder ♦ *vi*: **to ~ over from sb** reemplazar a uno; **~ to** *vt fus* (*person*) coger cariño a, encariñarse con; (*activity*) aficionarse a; **~ up** *vt* (*a dress*) acortar; (*occupy: time, space*) ocupar; (*engage in: hobby etc*) dedicarse a; (*accept*): **to ~ sb up on** aceptar; **~away** (BRIT) *adj* (*food*) para llevar ♦ *n* tienda (*or* restaurante *m*) de comida para llevar; **~off** *n* (AVIAT) despegue *m*; **~out** (US) *n* = **~away**; **~over** *n* (COMM) absorción *f*

takings ['teɪkɪŋz] *npl* (COMM) ingresos *mpl*

talc [tælk] *n* (*also*: **~um powder**) (polvos de) talco

tale [teɪl] *n* (*story*) cuento; (*account*) relación *f*; **to tell ~s** (*fig*) chivarse

talent ['tælnt] *n* talento; **~ed** *adj* de talento

talk [tɔːk] *n* charla; (*conversation*) conversación *f*; (*gossip*) habladurías *fpl*, chismes *mpl* ♦ *vi* hablar; **~s** *npl* (POL etc) conversaciones *fpl*; **to ~ about** hablar de; **to ~ sb into doing sth** convencer a uno para que haga algo; **to ~ sb out of doing sth** disuadir a uno de que haga algo; **to ~ shop** hablar del trabajo; **~ over** *vt* discutir; **~ative** *adj* hablador(a); **~ show** *n* programa *m* de entrevistas

tall [tɔːl] *adj* alto; (*object*) grande; **to be 6 feet ~** (*person*) ≈ medir 1 metro 80

tally ['tælɪ] *n* cuenta ♦ *vi*: **to ~ (with)** corresponder (con)

talon ['tælən] *n* garra

tambourine [tæmbə'riːn] *n* pandereta

tame [teɪm] *adj* domesticado; (*fig*) mediocre

tamper ['tæmpə*] *vi*: **to ~ with** tocar, andar con

tampon ['tæmpən] *n* tampón *m*

tan [tæn] *n* (*also*: **sun~**) bronceado ♦ *vi* ponerse moreno ♦ *adj* (*colour*) marrón

tang [tæŋ] *n* sabor *m* fuerte

tangent ['tændʒənt] *n* (MATH) tangente *f*; **to go off at a ~** (*fig*) salirse por la tangente

tangerine [tændʒə'riːn] *n* mandarina

tangle ['tæŋgl] *n* enredo; **to get in(to) a ~** enredarse

tank [tæŋk] *n* (*water ~*) depósito, tanque *m*; (*for fish*) acuario; (MIL) tanque *m*

tanker ['tæŋkə*] *n* (*ship*) buque *m* cisterna;

(*truck*) camión *m* cisterna

tanned [tænd] *adj* (*skin*) moreno

tantalizing ['tæntəlaɪzɪŋ] *adj* tentador(a)

tantamount ['tæntəmaunt] *adj*: **~ to** equivalente a

tantrum ['tæntrəm] *n* rabieta

tap [tæp] *n* (BRIT: *on sink etc*) grifo (SP), canilla (AM); (*gas ~*) llave *f*; (*gentle blow*) golpecito ♦ *vt* (*hit gently*) dar golpecitos en; (*resources*) utilizar, explotar; (*telephone*) intervenir; **on ~** (*fig: resources*) a mano; **~ dancing** *n* claqué *m*

tape [teɪp] *n* (*also*: **magnetic ~**) cinta magnética; (*cassette*) cassette *f*, cinta; (*sticky ~*) cinta adhesiva; (*for tying*) cinta ♦ *vt* (*record*) grabar (en cinta); (*stick with ~*) pegar con cinta adhesiva; **~ deck** *n* grabadora; **~ measure** *n* cinta métrica, metro

taper ['teɪpə*] *n* cirio ♦ *vi* afilarse

tape recorder *n* grabadora

tapestry ['tæpɪstrɪ] *n* (*object*) tapiz *m*; (*art*) tapicería

tar [tɑː] *n* alquitrán *m*, brea

target ['tɑːgɪt] *n* (*gen*) blanco

tariff ['tærɪf] *n* (*on goods*) arancel *m*; (BRIT: *in hotels etc*) tarifa

tarmac ['tɑːmæk] *n* (BRIT: *on road*) asfaltado; (AVIAT) pista (de aterrizaje)

tarnish ['tɑːnɪʃ] *vt* deslustrar

tarpaulin [tɑː'pɔːlɪn] *n* lona impermeabilizada

tarragon ['tærəgən] *n* estragón *m*

tart [tɑːt] *n* (CULIN) tarta; (BRIT: *inf: prostitute*) puta ♦ *adj* agrio, ácido; **~ up** (BRIT: *inf*) *vt* (*building*) remozar; **to ~ o.s. up** acicalarse

tartan ['tɑːtn] *n* tejido escocés *m*

tartar ['tɑːtə*] *n* (*on teeth*) sarro; **~(e) sauce** *n* salsa tártara

task [tɑːsk] *n* tarea; **to take to ~** reprender; **~ force** *n* (MIL, POLICE) grupo de operaciones

taste [teɪst] *n* (*sense*) gusto; (*flavour*) sabor *m*; (*also: after~*) sabor *m*, dejo; (*sample*): **have a ~!** ¡prueba un poquito!; (*fig*) muestra, idea ♦ *vt* (*also fig*) probar ♦ *vi*:

to ~ of or **like** (fish, garlic etc) saber a; **you can ~ the garlic (in it)** se nota el sabor a ajo; **in good/bad ~** de buen/mal gusto; **~ful** adj de buen gusto; **~less** adj (food) soso; (remark etc) de mal gusto; **tasty** adj sabroso, rico

tatters ['tætəz] npl: **in ~** hecho jirones

tattoo [tə'tu:] n tatuaje m; (spectacle) espectáculo militar ♦ vt tatuar

tatty ['tæti] (BRIT: inf) adj cochambroso

taught [tɔ:t] pt, pp of **teach**

taunt [tɔ:nt] n burla ♦ vt burlarse de

Taurus ['tɔ:rəs] n Tauro

taut [tɔ:t] adj tirante, tenso

tax [tæks] n impuesto ♦ vt gravar (con un impuesto); (fig: memory) poner a prueba (: patience) agotar; **~able** adj (income) gravable; **~ation** [-'seɪʃən] n impuestos mpl; **~ avoidance** n evasión f de impuestos; **~ disc** (BRIT) n (AUT) pegatina del impuesto de circulación; **~ evasion** n evasión f fiscal; **~-free** adj libre de impuestos

taxi ['tæksɪ] n taxi m ♦ vi (AVIAT) rodar por la pista; **~ driver** n taxista m/f; **~ rank** (BRIT) n = **~ stand**; **~ stand** n parada de taxis

tax: **~ payer** n contribuyente m/f; **~ relief** n desgravación f fiscal; **~ return** n declaración f de ingresos

TB n abbr = **tuberculosis**

tea [ti:] n té m; (BRIT: meal) ≈ merienda (SP); cena; **high ~** (BRIT) merienda-cena (SP); **~ bag** n bolsita de té; **~ break** (BRIT) n descanso para el té

teach [ti:tʃ] (pt, pp taught) vt: **to ~ sb sth, ~ sth to sb** enseñar algo a uno ♦ vi (be a teacher) ser profesor(a), enseñar; **~er** n (in secondary school) profesor(a) m/f; (in primary school) maestro/a, profesor(a) de EGB; **~ing** n enseñanza

tea cosy n cubretetera m

teacup ['ti:kʌp] n taza para el té

teak [ti:k] n (madera de) teca

team [ti:m] n equipo; (of horses) tiro; **~work** n trabajo en equipo

teapot ['ti:pɒt] n tetera

tear[1] [tɪə*] n lágrima; **in ~s** llorando

tear[2] [tɛə*] (pt tore, pp torn) n rasgón m, desgarrón m ♦ vt romper, rasgar ♦ vi rasgarse; **~ along** vi (rush) precipitarse; **~ up** vt (sheet of paper etc) romper

tearful ['tɪəfəl] adj lloroso

tear gas ['tɪə-] n gas m lacrimógeno

tearoom ['ti:ru:m] n salón m de té

tease [ti:z] vt tomar el pelo a

tea set n servicio de té

teaspoon n cucharita; (also: **~ful:** as measurement) cucharadita

teat [ti:t] n (of bottle) tetina

teatime ['ti:taɪm] n hora del té

tea towel (BRIT) n paño de cocina

technical ['teknɪkl] adj técnico; **~ college** (BRIT) n ≈ escuela de artes y oficios (SP); **~ity** [-'kælɪtɪ] n (point of law) formalismo; (detail) detalle m técnico; **~ly** adv en teoría; (regarding technique) técnicamente

technician [tek'nɪʃn] n técnico/a

technique [tek'ni:k] n técnica

technological [teknə'lɒdʒɪkl] adj tecnológico

technology [tek'nɒlədʒɪ] n tecnología

teddy (bear) ['tedɪ-] n osito de felpa

tedious ['ti:dɪəs] adj pesado, aburrido

teem [ti:m] vi: **to ~ with** rebosar de; **it is ~ing (with rain)** llueve a cántaros

teenage ['ti:neɪdʒ] adj (fashions etc) juvenil; (children) quinceañero; **~r** n quinceañero/a

teens [ti:nz] npl: **to be in one's ~** ser adolescente

tee-shirt ['ti:ʃə:t] n = **T-shirt**

teeter ['ti:tə*] vi balancearse; (fig): **to ~ on the edge of ...** estar al borde de ...

teeth [ti:θ] npl of **tooth**

teethe [ti:ð] vi echar los dientes

teething ['ti:ðɪŋ]: **~ ring** n mordedor m; **~ troubles** npl (fig) dificultades fpl iniciales

teetotal ['ti:'təutl] adj abstemio

telegram ['telɪɡræm] n telegrama m

telegraph ['telɪɡrɑ:f] n telégrafo; **~ pole** n poste m telegráfico

telepathy [tə'lepəθɪ] n telepatía
telephone ['telɪfəun] n teléfono ♦ vt
llamar por teléfono, telefonear; (message)
dar por teléfono; **to be on the ~** (talking)
hablar por teléfono; (possessing ~) tener
teléfono; ~ **booth** n cabina telefónica; ~
box (BRIT) n = ~ **booth**; ~ **call** n
llamada (telefónica); ~ **directory** n guía
(telefónica); ~ **number** n número de
teléfono; **telephonist** [tə'lefənɪst] (BRIT) n
telefonista m/f
telescope ['telɪskəup] n telescopio
television ['telɪvɪʒən] n televisión f; **on ~**
en la televisión; ~ **set** n televisor m
tell [tel] (pt, pp told) vt decir; (relate: story)
contar; (distinguish): **to ~ sth from**
distinguir algo de ♦ vi (talk): **to ~ (of)**
contar; (have effect) tener efecto; **to ~ sb**
to do sth mandar a uno hacer algo; ~
off vt: **to ~ sb off** regañar a uno; ~**er** n
(in bank) cajero/a; ~**ing** adj (remark,
detail) revelador(a); ~**tale** adj (sign)
indicador(a)
telly ['telɪ] (BRIT: inf) n abbr (= television)
tele f
temp [temp] n abbr (BRIT: = temporary)
temporero/a
temper ['tempə*] n (nature) carácter m;
(mood) humor m; (bad ~) (mal) genio; (fit
of anger) acceso de ira ♦ vt (moderate)
moderar; **to be in a ~** estar furioso; **to**
lose one's ~ enfadarse, enojarse
temperament ['temprəmənt] n (nature)
temperamento
temperate ['tempərət] adj (climate etc)
templado
temperature ['tempərətʃə*] n temperatura;
to have or **run a ~** tener fiebre
temple ['templ] n (building) templo; (ANAT)
sien f
tempo ['tempəu] n (pl tempos or tempi) n
(MUS) tempo, tiempo; (fig) ritmo
temporarily ['tempərərɪlɪ] adv
temporalmente
temporary ['tempərərɪ] adj provisional;
(passing) transitorio; (worker) temporero;
(job) temporal

tempt [tempt] vt tentar; **to ~ sb into**
doing sth tentar or inducir a uno a hacer
algo; ~**ation** [-'teɪʃən] n tentación f; ~**ing**
adj tentador(a); (food) apetitoso/a
ten [ten] num diez
tenacity [tə'næsɪtɪ] n tenacidad f
tenancy ['tenənsɪ] n arrendamiento,
alquiler m
tenant ['tenənt] n inquilino/a
tend [tend] vt cuidar ♦ vi: **to ~ to do sth**
tener tendencia a hacer algo
tendency ['tendənsɪ] n tendencia
tender ['tendə*] adj (person, care) tierno,
cariñoso; (meat) tierno; (sore) sensible ♦ n
(COMM: offer) oferta; (money): **legal ~**
moneda de curso legal ♦ vt ofrecer;
~**ness** n ternura; (of meat) blandura
tenement ['tenəmənt] n casa de pisos (SP)
tennis ['tenɪs] n tenis m; ~ **ball** n pelota
de tenis; ~ **court** n cancha de tenis; ~
player n tenista m/f; ~ **racket** n
raqueta de tenis
tenor ['tenə*] n (MUS) tenor m
tenpin bowling ['tenpɪn-] n (juego de
los) bolos
tense [tens] adj (person) nervioso;
(moment, atmosphere) tenso; (muscle)
tenso, en tensión ♦ n (LING) tiempo
tension ['tenʃən] n tensión f
tent [tent] n tienda (de campaña) (SP),
carpa (AM)
tentative ['tentətɪv] adj (person, smile)
indeciso; (conclusion, plans) provisional
tenterhooks ['tentəhuks] npl: **on ~** sobre
ascuas
tenth [tenθ] num décimo
tent peg n clavija, estaca
tent pole n mástil m
tenuous ['tenjuəs] adj tenue
tenure ['tenjuə*] n (of land etc) tenencia;
(of office) ejercicio
tepid ['tepɪd] adj tibio
term [tə:m] n (word) término; (period)
período; (SCOL) trimestre m ♦ vt llamar;
~**s** npl (conditions, COMM) condiciones fpl;
in the short/long ~ a corto/largo plazo;
to be on good ~s with sb llevarse bien

con uno; **to come to ~s with** (*problem*)
aceptar
terminal ['tɜ:mɪnl] *adj* (*disease*) mortal;
(*patient*) terminal ♦ *n* (*ELEC*) borne *m*;
(*COMPUT*) terminal *m*; (*also*: **air ~**)
terminal *f*; (*BRIT*: *also*: **coach ~**) (estación
f) terminal *f*
terminate ['tɜ:mɪneɪt] *vt* terminar
terminus ['tɜ:mɪnəs] (*pl* **termini**) *n*
término, (estación *f*) terminal *f*
terrace ['terəs] *n* terraza; (*BRIT*: *row of
houses*) hilera de casas adosadas; **the ~s**
(*BRIT*: *SPORT*) las gradas *fpl*; **~d** *adj*
(*garden*) en terrazas; (*house*) adosado
terrain [te'reɪn] *n* terreno
terrible ['terɪbl] *adj* terrible, horrible; (*inf*)
atroz; **terribly** *adv* terriblemente; (*very
badly*) malísimamente
terrier ['terɪə*] *n* terrier *m*
terrific [tə'rɪfɪk] *adj* (*very great*) tremendo;
(*wonderful*) fantástico, fenomenal
terrify ['terɪfaɪ] *vt* aterrorizar
territory ['terɪtərɪ] *n* (*also fig*) territorio
terror ['terə*] *n* terror *m*; **~ism** *n*
terrorismo; **~ist** *n* terrorista *m/f*
test [test] *n* (*gen, CHEM*) prueba; (*MED*)
examen *m*; (*SCOL*) examen *m*, test *m*;
(*also*: **driving ~**) examen *m* de conducir
♦ *vt* probar, poner a prueba; (*MED, SCOL*)
examinar
testament ['testəmənt] *n* testamento; **the
Old/New T~** el Antiguo/Nuevo
Testamento
testicle ['testɪkl] *n* testículo
testify ['testɪfaɪ] *vi* (*LAW*) prestar
declaración; **to ~ to sth** atestiguar algo
testimony ['testɪmənɪ] *n* (*LAW*) testimonio
test: ~ match *n* (*CRICKET, RUGBY*) partido
internacional; **~ tube** *n* probeta
tetanus ['tetənəs] *n* tétano
tether ['teðə*] *vt* atar (con una cuerda)
♦ *n*: **to be at the end of one's ~** no
aguantar más
text [tekst] *n* texto; **~book** *n* libro de
texto
textiles ['tekstaɪlz] *npl* textiles *mpl*; (*textile
industry*) industria textil

texture ['tekstʃə*] *n* textura
Thailand ['taɪlænd] *n* Tailandia
Thames [temz] *n*: **the ~** el (río) Támesis
than [ðæn] *conj* (*in comparisons*): **more ~
10/once** más de 10/una vez; **I have
more/less ~ you/Paul** tengo más/
menos que tú/Paul; **she is older ~ you
think** es mayor de lo que piensas
thank [θæŋk] *vt* dar las gracias a,
agradecer; **~ you (very much)** muchas
gracias; **~ God!** ¡gracias a Dios!; **~s** *npl*
gracias *fpl* ♦ *excl* (*also*: **many ~s, ~s a
lot**) ¡gracias!; **~s to** *prep* gracias a; **~ful**
adj: **~ful (for)** agradecido (por); **~less**
adj ingrato; **T~sgiving (Day)** *n* día *m*
de Acción de Gracias

Thanksgiving (Day)

i En Estados Unidos el cuarto jueves de
noviembre es **Thanksgiving Day**,
*fiesta oficial en la que se recuerda la
celebración que hicieron los primeros
colonos norteamericanos ("Pilgrims" o
"Pilgrim Fathers") tras la estupenda
cosecha de 1621, por la que se dan gracias
a Dios. En Canadá se celebra una fiesta
semejante el segundo lunes de octubre,
aunque no está relacionada con dicha
fecha histórica.*

KEYWORD

that [ðæt] (*pl* **those**) *adj* (*demonstrative*)
ese/a, *pl* esos/as; (*more remote*) aquel/
aquella, *pl* aquellos/as; **leave those
books on the table** deja esos libros sobre
la mesa; **~ one** ése/ésa; (*more remote*)
aquél/aquélla, **~ one over there** ése/ésa
de ahí; aquél/aquélla de allí
♦ *pron* **1** (*demonstrative*) ése/a, *pl* ésos/as;
(*neuter*) eso; (*more remote*) aquél/aquélla,
pl aquéllos/as; (*neuter*) aquello; **what's ~?**
¿qué es eso (or aquello)?; **who's ~?**
¿quién es ése/a (or aquél/aquélla)?; **is ~
you?** ¿eres tú?; **will you eat all ~?** ¿vas a
comer todo eso?; **~'s my house** ésa es
mi casa; **~'s what he said** eso es lo que

dijo; **~ is (to say)** es decir

2 (*relative: subject, object*) que; (*with preposition*) (el/la) que *etc*, el/la cual *etc*; **the book (~) I read** el libro que leí; **the books ~ are in the library** los libros que están en la biblioteca; **all (~) I have** todo lo que tengo; **the box (~) I put it in** la caja en la que *or* donde lo puse; **the people (~) I spoke to** la gente con la que hablé

3 (*relative: of time*) que; **the day (~) he came** el día (en) que vino

♦ *conj* que; **he thought ~ I was ill** creyó que yo estaba enfermo

♦ *adv* (*demonstrative*): **I can't work ~ much** no puedo trabajar tanto; **I didn't realise it was ~ bad** no creí que fuera tan malo; **~ high** así de alto

thatched [θætʃt] *adj* (*roof*) de paja; (*cottage*) con tejado de paja

thaw [θɔ:] *n* deshielo ♦ *vi* (*ice*) derretirse; (*food*) descongelarse ♦ *vt* (*food*) descongelar

---

KEYWORD

the [ði:, ðə] *def art* **1** (*gen*) el, f la, *pl* los, *fpl* las (*NB = el immediately before f n beginning with stressed (h)a*; a+el = al; de+el = del); **~ boy/girl** el chico/la chica; **~ books/flowers** los libros/las flores; **to ~ postman/from ~ drawer** al cartero/del cajón; **I haven't ~ time/money** no tengo tiempo/dinero

2 (+*adj to form n*) los; lo; **~ rich and ~ poor** los ricos y los pobres; **to attempt ~ impossible** intentar lo imposible

3 (*in titles*): **Elizabeth ~ First** Isabel primera; **Peter ~ Great** Pedro el Grande

4 (*in comparisons*): **~ more he works ~ more he earns** cuanto más trabaja más gana

---

theatre ['θɪətə*] (*US* **theater**) *n* teatro; (*also*: **lecture ~**) aula; (*MED*: *also*: **operating ~**) quirófano; **~-goer** *n* aficionado/a al teatro

theatrical [θɪ'ætrɪkl] *adj* teatral

theft [θeft] *n* robo

their [ðeə*] *adj* su; **~s** *pron* (el) suyo/(la) suya *etc*; *see also* **my; mine**[1]

them [ðem, ðəm] *pron* (*direct*) los/las; (*indirect*) les; (*stressed, after prep*) ellos/ellas; *see also* **me**

theme [θi:m] *n* tema *m*; **~ park** *n* parque de atracciones (*en torno a un tema central*); **~ song** *n* tema *m* (*musical*)

themselves [ðəm'selvz] *pl pron* (*subject*) ellos mismos/ellas mismas; (*complement*) se; (*after prep*) sí (mismos/as); *see also* **oneself**

then [ðen] *adv* (*at that time*) entonces; (*next*) después; (*later*) luego, después; (*and also*) además ♦ *conj* (*therefore*) en ese caso, entonces ♦ *adj*: **the ~ president** el entonces presidente; **by ~** para entonces; **from ~ on** desde entonces

theology [θɪ'ɔlədʒɪ] *n* teología

theory ['θɪərɪ] *n* teoría

therapist ['θerəpɪst] *n* terapeuta *m/f*

therapy ['θerəpɪ] *n* terapia

KEYWORD

there ['ðeə*] *adv* **1**: **~ is**, **~ are** hay; **~ is no-one here/no bread left** no hay nadie aquí/no queda pan; **~ has been an accident** ha habido un accidente

2 (*referring to place*) ahí; (*distant*) allí; **it's ~** está ahí; **put it in/on/up/down ~** ponlo ahí dentro/encima/arriba/abajo; **I want that book ~** quiero ese libro de ahí; **~ he is!** ¡ahí está!

3: **~, ~** (*esp to child*) ea, ea

---

there: ~abouts *adv* por ahí; **~after** *adv* después; **~by** *adv* así, de ese modo; **~fore** *adv* por lo tanto; **~'s** = **there is**; **there has**

thermal ['θə:ml] *adj* termal; (*paper*) térmico

thermometer [θə'mɔmɪtə*] *n* termómetro

Thermos ® ['θə:məs] *n* (*also*: **~ flask**) termo

thermostat ['θə:məustæt] *n* termostato

thesaurus [θɪˈsɔːrəs] *n* tesoro
these [ðiːz] *pl adj* estos/as ♦ *pl pron* éstos/as
thesis [ˈθiːsɪs] (*pl* **theses**) *n* tesis *f inv*
they [ðeɪ] *pl pron* ellos/ellas; (*stressed*) ellos (mismos)/ellas (mismas); ~ **say that ...** (*it is said that*) se dice que ...; ~'**d** = **they had; they would;** ~'**ll** = **they shall; they will;** ~'**re** = **they are;** ~'**ve** = **they have**
thick [θɪk] *adj* (*in consistency*) espeso; (*in size*) grueso; (*stupid*) torpe ♦ *n*: **in the ~ of the battle** en lo más reñido de la batalla; **it's 20 cm ~** tiene 20 cm de espesor; ~**en** *vi* espesarse ♦ *vt* (*sauce etc*) espesar; ~**ness** *n* espesor *m*; grueso; ~**set** *adj* fornido
thief [θiːf] (*pl* **thieves**) *n* ladrón/ona *m/f*
thigh [θaɪ] *n* muslo
thimble [ˈθɪmbl] *n* dedal *m*
thin [θɪn] *adj* (*person, animal*) flaco; (*in size*) delgado; (*in consistency*) poco espeso; (*hair, crowd*) escaso ♦ *vt*: **to ~ (down)** diluir
thing [θɪŋ] *n* cosa; (*object*) objeto, artículo; (*matter*) asunto; (*mania*): **to have a ~ about sb/sth** estar obsesionado con uno/algo; ~**s** *npl* (*belongings*) efectos *mpl* (personales); **the best ~ would be to ...** lo mejor sería ...; **how are ~s?** ¿qué tal?
think [θɪŋk] (*pt, pp* **thought**) *vi* pensar ♦ *vt* pensar, creer; **what did you ~ of them?** ¿qué te parecieron?; **to ~ about sth/sb** pensar en algo/uno; **I'll ~ about it** lo pensaré; **to ~ of doing sth** pensar en hacer algo; **I ~ so/not** creo que sí/no; **to ~ well of sb** tener buen concepto de uno; ~ **over** *vt* reflexionar sobre, meditar; ~ **up** *vt* (*plan etc*) idear; ~ **tank** *n* gabinete *m* de estrategia
thinly [ˈθɪnlɪ] *adv* (*cut*) fino; (*spread*) ligeramente
third [θɜːd] *adj* (*before n*) tercer(a); (*following n*) tercero/a ♦ *n* tercero/a; (*fraction*) tercio; (*BRIT: SCOL: degree*) título de licenciado con calificación de aprobado; ~**ly** *adv* en tercer lugar; ~ **party insurance** (*BRIT*) *n* seguro contra

terceros; ~-**rate** *adj* (de calidad) mediocre; **T~ World** *n* Tercer Mundo
thirst [θɜːst] *n* sed *f*; ~**y** *adj* (*person, animal*) sediento; (*work*) que da sed; **to be ~y** tener sed
thirteen [ˈθɜːˈtiːn] *num* trece
thirty [ˈθɜːtɪ] *num* treinta

KEYWORD

---

this [ðɪs] (*pl* **these**) *adj* (*demonstrative*) este/a; *pl* estos/as; (*neuter*) esto; ~ **man/woman** este hombre/esta mujer; **these children/flowers** estos chicos/estas flores; ~ **one (here)** éste/a, esto (de aquí)
♦ *pron* (*demonstrative*) este/a; *pl* estos/as; (*neuter*) esto; **who is ~?** ¿quién es éste/ésta?; **what is ~?** ¿qué es esto?; ~ **is where I live** aquí vivo; ~ **is what he said** esto es lo que dijo; ~ **is Mr Brown** (*in introductions*) le presento al Sr. Brown; (*photo*) éste es el Sr. Brown; (*on telephone*) habla el Sr. Brown
♦ *adv* (*demonstrative*): ~ **high/long** *etc* as de alto/largo *etc*; ~ **far** hasta aquí

---

thistle [ˈθɪsl] *n* cardo
thorn [θɔːn] *n* espina
thorough [ˈθʌrə] *adj* (*search*) minucioso; (*wash*) a fondo; (*knowledge, research*) profundo; (*person*) meticuloso; ~**bred** *adj* (*horse*) de pura sangre; ~**fare** *n* calle *f*; "**no ~fare**" "prohibido el paso"; ~**ly** *adv* (*search*) minuciosamente; (*study*) profundamente; (*wash*) a fondo; (*utterly: bad, wet etc*) completamente, totalmente
those [ðəuz] *pl adj* esos/esas; (*more remote*) aquellos/as
though [ðəu] *conj* aunque ♦ *adv* sin embargo
thought [θɔːt] *pt, pp of* **think** ♦ *n* pensamiento; (*opinion*) opinión *f*; ~**ful** *adj* pensativo; (*serious*) serio; (*considerate*) atento; ~**less** *adj* desconsiderado
thousand [ˈθauzənd] *num* mil; **two ~** dos mil; ~**s of** miles de; ~**th** *num* milésimo
thrash [θræʃ] *vt* azotar; (*defeat*) derrotar; ~ **about** *or* **around** *vi* debatirse; ~ **out** *vt*

discutir a fondo

thread [θrɛd] n hilo; (of screw) rosca ♦ vt (needle) enhebrar; **~bare** adj raído

threat [θrɛt] n amenaza; **~en** vi amenazar ♦ vt: **to ~en sb with/to do** amenazar a uno con/con hacer

three [θriː] num tres; **~-dimensional** adj tridimensional; **~-piece suit** n traje m de tres piezas; **~-piece suite** n tresillo; **~-ply** adj (wool) de tres cabos

threshold ['θrɛʃhəʊld] n umbral m

threw [θruː] pt of **throw**

thrifty ['θrɪftɪ] adj económico

thrill [θrɪl] n (excitement) emoción f; (shudder) estremecimiento ♦ vt emocionar; **to be ~ed** (with gift etc) estar encantado; **~er** n novela (or obra or película) de suspense; **~ing** adj emocionante

thrive [θraɪv] (pt, pp **thrived**) vi (grow) crecer; (do well): **to ~ on sth** sentarle muy bien a uno algo; **thriving** adj próspero

throat [θrəʊt] n garganta; **to have a sore ~** tener dolor de garganta

throb [θrɔb] vi latir; dar punzadas; vibrar

throes [θrəʊz] npl: **in the ~ of** en medio de

throne [θrəʊn] n trono

throng [θrɔŋ] n multitud f, muchedumbre f ♦ vt agolparse en

throttle ['θrɔtl] n (AUT) acelerador m ♦ vt estrangular

through [θruː] prep por, a través de; (time) durante; (by means of) por medio de, mediante; (owing to) gracias a ♦ adj (ticket, train) directo ♦ adv completamente, de parte a parte; de principio a fin; **to put sb ~ to sb** (TEL) poner or pasar a uno con uno; **to be ~** (TEL) tener comunicación; (have finished) haber terminado; **"no ~ road"** (BRIT) "calle sin salida"; **~out** prep (place) por todas partes de, por todo; (time) durante todo ♦ adv por or en todas partes

throw [θrəʊ] (pt **threw**, pp **thrown**) n tiro; (SPORT) lanzamiento ♦ vt tirar, echar; (SPORT) lanzar; (rider) derribar; (fig)

desconcertar; **to ~ a party** dar una fiesta; **~ away** vt tirar; (money) derrochar; **~ off** vt deshacerse de; **~ out** vt tirar; (person) echar; expulsar; **~ up** vi vomitar; **~away** adj para tirar, desechable; (remark) hecho de paso; **~-in** n (SPORT) saque m

thru [θruː] (US) = **through**

thrush [θrʌʃ] n zorzal m, tordo

thrust [θrʌst] (pt, pp **thrust**) vt empujar (con fuerza)

thud [θʌd] n golpe m sordo

thug [θʌɡ] n gamberro/a

thumb [θʌm] n (ANAT) pulgar m; **to ~ a lift** hacer autostop; **~ through** vt fus (book) hojear; **~tack** (US) n chincheta (SP)

thump [θʌmp] n golpe m; (sound) ruido seco or sordo ♦ vt golpear ♦ vi (heart etc) palpitar

thunder ['θʌndə*] n trueno ♦ vi tronar; (train etc): **to ~ past** pasar como un trueno; **~bolt** n rayo; **~clap** n trueno; **~storm** n tormenta; **~y** adj tormentoso

Thursday ['θɜːzdɪ] n jueves m inv

thus [ðʌs] adv así, de este modo

thyme [taɪm] n tomillo

thyroid ['θaɪrɔɪd] n (also: **~ gland**) tiroides m inv

tic [tɪk] n tic m

tick [tɪk] n (sound: of clock) tictac m; (mark) palomita; (ZOOL) garrapata; (BRIT: inf): **in a ~** en un instante ♦ vi hacer tictac ♦ vt marcar; **~ off** vt marcar; (person) reñir; **~ over** vi (engine) girar en marcha lenta; (fig) ir tirando

ticket ['tɪkɪt] n billete m (SP), tíquet m, boleto (AM); (for cinema etc) entrada (SP), boleto (AM); (in shop: on goods) etiqueta (SP); (for raffle) papeleta; (for library) tarjeta; (parking ~) multa por estacionamiento ilegal; **~ collector** n revisor(a) m/f; **~ office** n (THEATRE) taquilla (SP), boletería (AM); (RAIL) despacho de billetes (SP) or boletos (AM)

tickle ['tɪkl] vt hacer cosquillas a ♦ vi hacer cosquillas; **ticklish** adj (person)

cosquilloso; (*problem*) delicado
tidal ['taɪdl] *adj* de marea; ~ **wave** *n*
maremoto
tidbit ['tɪdbɪt] (*US*) *n* = **titbit**
tiddlywinks ['tɪdlɪwɪŋks] *n juego infantil
con fichas de plástico*
tide [taɪd] *n* marea; (*fig: of events etc*)
curso, marcha; ~ **over** *vt* (*help out*)
ayudar a salir del apuro
tidy ['taɪdɪ] *adj* (*room etc*) ordenado; (*dress,
work*) limpio; (*person*) (bien) arreglado
♦ *vt* (*also:* ~ **up**) poner en orden
tie [taɪ] *n* (*string etc*) atadura; (*BRIT: also:*
neck~) corbata; (*fig: link*) vínculo, lazo;
(*SPORT etc: draw*) empate *m* ♦ *vt* atar ♦ *vi*
(*SPORT etc*) empatar; **to ~ in a bow** atar
con un lazo; **to ~ a knot in sth** hacer un
nudo en algo; ~ **down** *vt* (*fig: person:
restrict*) atar; (: *to price, date etc*) obligar
a; ~ **up** *vt* (*parcel*) envolver; (*dog, person*)
atar; (*arrangements*) concluir; **to be ~d up**
(*busy*) estar ocupado
tier [tɪə*] *n* grada; (*of cake*) piso
tiger ['taɪgə*] *n* tigre *m*
tight [taɪt] *adj* (*rope*) tirante; (*money*)
escaso; (*clothes*) ajustado; (*bend*) cerrado;
(*shoes, schedule*) apretado; (*budget*)
ajustado; (*security*) estricto; (*inf: drunk*)
borracho ♦ *adv* (*squeeze*) muy fuerte;
(*shut*) bien; ~**en** *vt* (*rope*) estirar; (*screw,
grip*) apretar; (*security*) reforzar ♦ *vi*
estirarse; apretarse; ~**-fisted** *adj* tacaño;
~**ly** *adv* (*grasp*) muy fuerte; ~**rope** *n*
cuerda floja; ~**s** (*BRIT*) *npl* panti *mpl*
tile [taɪl] *n* (*on roof*) teja; (*on floor*) baldosa;
(*on wall*) azulejo; ~**d** *adj* de tejas;
embaldosado; (*wall*) alicatado
till [tɪl] *n* caja (registradora) ♦ *vt* (*land*)
cultivar ♦ *prep, conj* = **until**
tilt [tɪlt] *vt* inclinar ♦ *vi* inclinarse
timber ['tɪmbə*] *n* (*material*) madera
time [taɪm] *n* tiempo; (*epoch: often pl*)
época; (*by clock*) hora; (*moment*)
momento; (*occasion*) vez *f*; (*MUS*) compás
m ♦ *vt* calcular *or* medir el tiempo de;
(*race*) cronometrar; (*remark, visit etc*)
elegir el momento para; **a long ~** mucho

tiempo; **4 at a ~** de 4 en 4; 4 a la vez;
for the ~ being de momento, por ahora;
from ~ to ~ de vez en cuando; **at ~s** a
veces; **in ~** (*soon enough*) a tiempo; (*after
some time*) con el tiempo; (*MUS*) al
compás; **in a week's ~** dentro de una
semana; **in no ~** en un abrir y cerrar de
ojos; **any ~** cuando sea; **on ~** a la hora; **5
~s 5** 5 por 5; **what ~ is it?** ¿qué hora
es?; **to have a good ~** pasarlo bien,
divertirse; ~ **bomb** *n* bomba de efecto
retardado; ~**less** *adj* eterno; ~ **limit** *n*
plazo; ~**ly** *adj* oportuno; ~ **off** *n* tiempo
libre; ~**r** *n* (*in kitchen etc*) programador *m*
horario; ~ **scale** (*BRIT*) *n* escala de
tiempo; ~**-share** *n* apartamento (*or*
casa*) a tiempo compartido; ~ **switch**
(*BRIT*) *n* interruptor *m* (horario); ~**table** *n*
horario; ~ **zone** *n* huso horario
timid ['tɪmɪd] *adj* tímido
timing ['taɪmɪŋ] *n* (*SPORT*) cronometraje *m*;
the ~ of his resignation el momento que
eligió para dimitir
tin [tɪn] *n* estaño; (*also:* ~ **plate**) hojalata;
(*BRIT: can*) lata; ~**foil** *n* papel *m* de
estaño
tinge [tɪndʒ] *n* matiz *m* ♦ *vt:* ~**d with**
teñido de
tingle ['tɪŋgl] *vi* (*person*): **to ~ (with)**
estremecerse (de); (*hands etc*) hormiguear
tinker ['tɪŋkə*]: ~ **with** *vt fus* jugar con,
tocar
tinned [tɪnd] (*BRIT*) *adj* (*food*) en lata, en
conserva
tin opener [-əupnə*] (*BRIT*) *n* abrelatas *m
inv*
tinsel ['tɪnsl] *n* (guirnalda de) espumillón
m
tint [tɪnt] *n* matiz *m*; (*for hair*) tinte *m*;
~**ed** *adj* (*hair*) teñido; (*glass, spectacles*)
ahumado
tiny ['taɪnɪ] *adj* minúsculo, pequeñito
tip [tɪp] *n* (*end*) punta; (*gratuity*) propina;
(*BRIT: for rubbish*) vertedero; (*advice*)
consejo ♦ *vt* (*waiter*) dar una propina a;
(*tilt*) inclinar; (*empty: also:* ~ **out**) vaciar,
echar; (*overturn: also:* ~ **over**) volcar; ~-

off n (*hint*) advertencia; **~ped** (*BRIT*) adj (*cigarette*) con filtro

Tipp-Ex ® ['tɪpɛks] · Tipp-Ex ® m

tipsy ['tɪpsɪ] (*inf*) adj alegre, mareado

tiptoe ['tɪptəʊ] n: **on ~** de puntillas

tire ['taɪə*] n (*US*) = **tyre** ♦ vt cansar ♦ vi (*gen*) cansarse; (*become bored*) aburrirse; **~d** adj cansado; **to be ~d of sth** estar harto de algo; **~less** adj incansable; **~some** adj aburrido; **tiring** adj cansado

tissue ['tɪʃuː] n tejido; (*paper handkerchief*) pañuelo de papel, kleenex ® m; **~ paper** n papel m de seda

tit [tɪt] n (*bird*) herrerillo común; **to give ~ for tat** dar ojo por ojo

titbit ['tɪtbɪt] (*US* **tidbit**) n (*food*) golosina; (*news*) noticia sabrosa

title ['taɪtl] n título; **~ deed** n (*LAW*) título de propiedad; **~ role** n papel m principal

TM abbr = **trademark**

KEYWORD

to [tuː, tə] prep 1 (*direction*) a; **to go ~ France/London/school/the station** ir a Francia/Londres/al colegio/a la estación; **to go ~ Claude's/the doctor's** ir a casa de Claude/al médico; **the road ~ Edinburgh** la carretera de Edimburgo
2 (*as far as*) hasta, a; **from here ~ London** de aquí a or hasta Londres; **to count ~ 10** contar hasta 10; **from 40 ~ 50 people** entre 40 y 50 personas
3 (*with expressions of time*): **a quarter/twenty ~ 5** las 5 menos cuarto/veinte
4 (*for, of*): **the key ~ the front door** la llave de la puerta principal; **she is secretary ~ the director** es la secretaria del director; **a letter ~ his wife** una carta a or para su mujer
5 (*expressing indirect object*) a; **to give sth ~ sb** darle algo a alguien; **to talk ~ sb** hablar con alguien; **to be a danger ~ sb** ser un peligro para alguien; **to carry out repairs ~ sth** hacer reparaciones en algo
6 (*in relation to*): **3 goals ~ 2** 3 goles a 2; **30 miles ~ the gallon** ≈ 9,4 litros a los cien (kms)

7 (*purpose, result*): **to come ~ sb's aid** venir en auxilio or ayuda de alguien; **to sentence sb ~ death** condenar a uno a muerte; **~ my great surprise** con gran sorpresa mía

♦ with vb 1 (*simple infin*): **~ go/eat** ir/comer
2 (*following another vb*): **to want/try/start ~ do** querer/intentar/empezar a hacer; *see also relevant vb*
3 (*with vb omitted*): **I don't want ~** no quiero
4 (*purpose, result*) para; **I did it ~ help you** lo hice para ayudarte; **he came ~ see you** vino a verte
5 (*equivalent to relative clause*): **I have things ~ do** tengo cosas que hacer; **the main thing is ~ try** lo principal es intentarlo
6 (*after adj etc*): **ready ~ go** listo para irse; **too old ~ ...** demasiado viejo (como) para ...

♦ adv: **pull/push the door ~** tirar de/empujar la puerta

toad [təʊd] n sapo; **~stool** n hongo venenoso

toast [təʊst] n (*CULIN*) tostada; (*drink, speech*) brindis m ♦ vt (*CULIN*) tostar; (*drink to*) brindar por; **~er** n tostador m

tobacco [tə'bækəʊ] n tabaco; **~nist** n estanquero/a (*SP*), tabaquero/a (*AM*); **~nist's (shop)** (*BRIT*) n estanco (*SP*), tabaquería (*AM*)

toboggan [tə'bɒgən] n tobogán m

today [tə'deɪ] adv, n (*also fig*) hoy m

toddler ['tɒdlə*] n niño/a (que empieza a andar)

toe [təʊ] n dedo (del pie); (*of shoe*) punta; **to ~ the line** (*fig*) conformarse; **~nail** n uña del pie

toffee ['tɒfɪ] n toffee m; **~ apple** (*BRIT*) n manzana acaramelada

together [tə'geðə*] adv juntos; (*at same time*) al mismo tiempo, a la vez; **~ with** junto con

toil [tɔɪl] n trabajo duro, labor f ♦ vi

trabajar duramente

toilet ['tɔɪlət] n retrete m; (BRIT: room) servicios mpl (SP), wáter m (SP), sanitario (AM) ♦ cpd (soap etc) de aseo; ~ **paper** n papel m higiénico; ~**ries** npl artículos mpl de tocador; ~ **roll** n rollo de papel higiénico

token ['təʊkən] n (sign) señal f, muestra; (souvenir) recuerdo; (disc) ficha ♦ adj (strike, payment etc) simbólico; **book/record** ~ (BRIT) vale m para comprar libros/discos; **gift** ~ (BRIT) vale-regalo

Tokyo ['təʊkjəʊ] n Tokio, Tokío

told [təʊld] pt, pp of **tell**

tolerable ['tɔlərəbl] adj (bearable) soportable; (fairly good) pasable

tolerant ['tɔlərnt] adj: ~ **of** tolerante con

tolerate ['tɔləreɪt] vt tolerar

toll [təʊl] n (of casualties) número de víctimas; (tax, charge) peaje m ♦ vi (bell) doblar

tomato [tə'mɑːtəʊ] (pl ~**es**) n tomate m

tomb [tuːm] n tumba

tomboy ['tɔmbɔɪ] n marimacho

tombstone ['tuːmstəʊn] n lápida

tomcat ['tɔmkæt] n gato (macho)

tomorrow [tə'mɔrəʊ] adv, n (also: fig) mañana; **the day after** ~ pasado mañana; ~ **morning** mañana por la mañana

ton [tʌn] n tonelada (BRIT = 1016 kg; US = 907 kg); (metric ~) tonelada métrica; ~**s of** (inf) montones de

tone [təʊn] n tono ♦ vi (also: ~ **in**) armonizar; ~ **down** vt (criticism) suavizar; (colour) atenuar; ~ **up** vt (muscles) tonificar; ~~**deaf** adj con mal oído

tongs [tɔŋz] npl (for coal) tenazas fpl; (curling ~) tenacillas fpl

tongue [tʌŋ] n lengua; ~ **in cheek** irónicamente; ~~**tied** adj (fig) mudo; ~~**twister** n trabalenguas m inv

tonic ['tɔnɪk] n (MED, also fig) tónico; (also: ~ **water**) (agua) tónica

tonight [tə'naɪt] adv, n esta noche; esta tarde

tonsil ['tɔnsl] n amígdala; ~**litis** [-'laɪtɪs] n amigdalitis f

too [tuː] adv (excessively) demasiado; (also) también; ~ **much** demasiado; ~ **many** demasiados/as

took [tuk] pt of **take**

tool [tuːl] n herramienta; ~ **box** n caja de herramientas

toot [tuːt] n pitido ♦ vi tocar el pito

tooth [tuːθ] (pl **teeth**) n (ANAT, TECH) diente m; (molar) muela; ~**ache** n dolor m de muelas; ~**brush** n cepillo de dientes; ~**paste** n pasta de dientes; ~**pick** n palillo

top [tɔp] n (of mountain) cumbre f, cima; (of tree) copa; (of head) coronilla; (of ladder, page) lo alto; (of table) superficie f; (of cupboard) parte f de arriba; (lid: of box) tapa; (: of bottle, jar) tapón m; (of list etc) cabeza; (toy) peonza; (garment) blusa; camiseta ♦ adj de arriba; (in rank) principal, primero; (best) mejor ♦ vt (exceed) exceder; (be first in) encabezar; **on** ~ **of** (above) sobre, encima de; (in addition to) además de; **from** ~ **to bottom** de pies a cabeza; ~ **off** (US) vt = ~ **up**; ~ **up** vt llenar; ~ **floor** n último piso; ~ **hat** n sombrero de copa; ~~**heavy** adj (object) mal equilibrado

topic ['tɔpɪk] n tema m; ~**al** adj actual

top: ~**less** adj (bather, bikini) topless inv; ~~**level** adj (talks) al más alto nivel; ~**most** adj más alto

topple ['tɔpl] vt derribar ♦ vi caerse

top-secret adj de alto secreto

topsy-turvy ['tɔpsɪ'tɜːvɪ] adj al revés ♦ adv patas arriba

torch [tɔːtʃ] n antorcha; (BRIT: electric) linterna

tore [tɔː*] pt of **tear**[2]

torment [n 'tɔːment, vt tɔː'ment] n tormento ♦ vt atormentar; (fig: annoy) fastidiar

torn [tɔːn] pp of **tear**[2]

torrent ['tɔrnt] n torrente m

tortoise ['tɔːtəs] n tortuga; ~**shell** ['tɔːtəʃɛl] adj de carey

torture ['tɔːtʃə*] n tortura ♦ vt torturar; (fig) atormentar

Tory ['tɔːrɪ] (BRIT) adj, n (POL) conservador(a) m/f
toss [tɒs] vt tirar, echar; (one's head) sacudir; **to ~ a coin** echar a cara o cruz; **to ~ up for sth** jugar a cara o cruz algo; **to ~ and turn** (in bed) dar vueltas
tot [tɒt] n (BRIT: drink) copita; (child) nene/a m/f
total ['təʊtl] adj total, entero; (emphatic: failure etc) completo, total ♦ n total m, suma ♦ vt (add up) sumar; (amount to) ascender a; **~ly** adv totalmente
touch [tʌtʃ] n (sense) contacto ♦ vt tocar; (emotionally) conmover; **a ~ of** (fig) un poquito de; **to get in ~ with sb** ponerse en contacto con uno; **to lose ~** (friends) perder contacto; **~ on** vt fus (topic) aludir (brevemente) a; **~ up** vt (paint) retocar; **~-and-go** adj arriesgado; **~down** n aterrizaje m; (on sea) amerizaje m; (FOOTBALL) ensayo; **~ed** adj (moved) conmovido; **~ing** adj (moving) conmovedor(a); **~line** n (SPORT) línea de banda; **~y** adj (person) quisquilloso
tough [tʌf] adj (material) resistente; (meat) duro; (problem etc) difícil; (policy, stance) inflexible; (person) fuerte; **~en** vt endurecer
toupée ['tuːpeɪ] n peluca
tour ['tʊə*] n viaje m, vuelta; (also: **package ~**) viaje m todo comprendido; (of town, museum) visita; (by band etc) gira ♦ vt recorrer, visitar; **~ guide** n guía m turístico, guía f turística
tourism ['tʊərɪzm] n turismo
tourist ['tʊərɪst] n turista m/f ♦ cpd turístico; **~ office** n oficina de turismo
tousled ['taʊzld] adj (hair) despeinado
tout [taʊt] vi: **to ~ for business** solicitar clientes ♦ n (also: **ticket ~**) revendedor(a) m/f
tow [təʊ] vt remolcar; **"on or in** (US) **~"** (AUT) "a remolque"
toward(s) [tə'wɔːd(z)] prep hacia; (attitude) respecto a, con; (purpose) para
towel ['taʊəl] n toalla; **~ling** n (fabric) felpa; **~ rail** (US **~ rack**) n toallero

tower ['taʊə*] n torre f; **~ block** (BRIT) n torre f (de pisos); **~ing** adj muy alto, imponente
town [taʊn] n ciudad f; **to go to ~** ir a la ciudad; (fig) echar la casa por la ventana; **~ centre** n centro de la ciudad; **~ council** n ayuntamiento, consejo municipal; **~ hall** n ayuntamiento; **~ plan** n plano de la ciudad; **~ planning** n urbanismo
towrope ['taʊrəʊp] n cable m de remolque
tow truck (US) n camión m grúa
toy [tɔɪ] n juguete m; **~ with** vt fus jugar con; (idea) acariciar; **~shop** n juguetería
trace [treɪs] n rastro ♦ vt (draw) trazar, delinear; (locate) encontrar; (follow) seguir la pista de; **tracing paper** n papel m de calco
track [træk] n (mark) huella, pista; (path: gen) camino, senda; (: of bullet etc) trayectoria; (: of suspect, animal) pista, rastro; (RAIL) vía; (SPORT) pista; (on tape, record) canción f ♦ vt seguir la pista de; **to keep ~** of mantenerse al tanto de, seguir; **~ down** vt (prey) seguir el rastro de; (sth lost) encontrar; **~suit** n chandal m
tract [trækt] n (GEO) región f
traction ['trækʃən] n (power) tracción f; **in ~** (MED) en tracción
tractor ['træktə*] n tractor m
trade [treɪd] n comercio; (skill, job) oficio ♦ vi negociar, comerciar ♦ vt (exchange): **to ~ sth (for sth)** cambiar algo (por algo); **~ in** vt (old car etc) ofrecer como parte del pago; **~ fair** n feria comercial; **~mark** n marca de fábrica; **~ name** n marca registrada; **~r** n comerciante m/f; **~sman** (irreg) n (shopkeeper) tendero; **~ union** n sindicato; **~ unionist** n sindicalista m/f
tradition [trə'dɪʃən] n tradición f; **~al** adj tradicional
traffic ['træfɪk] n (gen, AUT) tráfico, circulación f, tránsito (AM) ♦ vi: **to ~ in** (pej: liquor, drugs) traficar en; **~ circle**

(*US*) *n* isleta; **~ jam** *n* embotellamiento; **~ lights** *npl* semáforo; **~ warden** *n* guardia *m/f* de tráfico

tragedy ['trædʒədɪ] *n* tragedia

tragic ['trædʒɪk] *adj* trágico

trail [treɪl] *n* (*tracks*) rastro, pista; (*path*) camino, sendero; (*dust, smoke*) estela ♦ *vt* (*drag*) arrastrar; (*follow*) seguir la pista de ♦ *vi* arrastrar; (*in contest etc*) ir perdiendo; **~ behind** *vi* quedar a la zaga; **~er** *n* (*AUT*) remolque *m*; (*caravan*) caravana; (*CINEMA*) trailer *m*, avance *m*; **~er truck** (*US*) *n* trailer *m*

train [treɪn] *n* tren *m*; (*of dress*) cola; (*series*) serie *f* ♦ *vt* (*educate, teach skills to*) formar; (*sportsman*) entrenar; (*dog*) adiestrar; (*point: gun etc*): **to ~ on** apuntar a ♦ *vi* (*SPORT*) entrenarse; (*learn a skill*): **to ~ as a teacher** *etc* estudiar para profesor *etc*; **one's ~ of thought** el razonamiento de uno; **~ed** *adj* (*worker*) cualificado; (*animal*) amaestrado; **~ee** [treɪ'niː] *n* aprendiz(a) *m/f*; **~er** *n* (*SPORT: coach*) entrenador(a) *m/f*; (: *shoe*): **~ers** zapatillas *fpl* (de deporte); (*of animals*) domador(a) *m/f*; **~ing** *n* formación *f*; entrenamiento; **to be in ~ing** (*SPORT*) estar entrenando; **~ing college** *n* (*gen*) colegio de formación profesional; (*for teachers*) escuela de formación del profesorado; **~ing shoes** *npl* zapatillas *fpl* (de deporte)

trait [treɪt] *n* rasgo

traitor ['treɪtə*] *n* traidor(a) *m/f*

tram [træm] (*BRIT*) *n* (*also:* **~car**) tranvía *m*

tramp [træmp] *n* (*person*) vagabundo/a; (*inf. pej: woman*) puta

trample ['træmpl] *vt*: **to ~ (underfoot)** pisotear

trampoline ['træmpəliːn] *n* trampolín *m*

tranquil ['træŋkwɪl] *adj* tranquilo; **~lizer** *n* (*MED*) tranquilizante *m*

transact [træn'zækt] *vt* (*business*) despachar; **~ion** [-'zækʃən] *n* transacción *f*, operación *f*

transfer [*n* 'trænsfə:*, *vb* træns'fə:*] *n* (*of employees*) traslado; (*of money, power*)

transferencia; (*SPORT*) traspaso; (*picture, design*) calcomanía ♦ *vt* trasladar; transferir; **to ~ the charges** (*BRIT: TEL*) llamar a cobro revertido

transform [træns'fɔ:m] *vt* transformar

transfusion [træns'fju:ʒən] *n* transfusión *f*

transient ['trænzɪənt] *adj* transitorio

transistor [træn'zɪstə*] *n* (*ELEC*) transistor *m*; **~ radio** *n* transistor *m*

transit ['trænzɪt] *n*: **in ~** en tránsito

transitive ['trænzɪtɪv] *adj* (*LING*) transitivo

transit lounge *n* sala de tránsito

translate [trænz'leɪt] *vt* traducir; **translation** [-'leɪʃən] *n* traducción *f*; **translator** *n* traductor(a) *m/f*

transmit [trænz'mɪt] *vt* transmitir; **~ter** *n* transmisor *m*

transparency [træns'pɛərnsɪ] *n* transparencia; (*BRIT: PHOT*) diapositiva

transparent [træns'pærnt] *adj* transparente

transpire [træns'paɪə*] *vi* (*turn out*) resultar; (*happen*) ocurrir, suceder; **it ~d that ...** se supo que ...

transplant ['trænsplɑ:nt] *n* (*MED*) transplante *m*

transport [*n* 'trænspɔ:t, *vt* træns'pɔ:t] *n* transporte *m*; (*car*) coche *m* (*SP*), carro (*AM*), automóvil *m* ♦ *vt* transportar; **~ation** [-'teɪʃən] *n* transporte *m*; **~ café** (*BRIT*) *n* bar-restaurant *m* de carretera

transvestite [trænz'vestaɪt] *n* travestí *m/f*

trap [træp] *n* (*snare, trick*) trampa; (*carriage*) cabriolé *m* ♦ *vt* coger (*SP*) or agarrar (*AM*) en una trampa; (*trick*) engañar; (*confine*) atrapar; **~ door** *n* escotilla

trapeze [trə'pi:z] *n* trapecio

trappings ['træpɪŋz] *npl* adornos *mpl*

trash [træʃ] *n* (*rubbish*) basura; (*pej*): **the book/film is ~** el libro/la película no vale nada; (*nonsense*) tonterías *fpl*; **~ can** (*US*) *n* cubo (*SP*) or balde *m* (*AM*) de la basura

travel ['trævl] *n* el viajar ♦ *vi* viajar ♦ *vt* (*distance*) recorrer; **~s** *npl* (*journeys*) viajes *mpl*; **~ agent** *n* agente *m/f* de viajes; **~ler** (*US* **~er**) *n* viajero/a; **~ler's**

cheque (US **~er's check**) n cheque m de viajero; **~ing** (US **~ing**) n los viajes, el viajar; **~ sickness** n mareo

trawler ['trɔːlə'] n pesquero de arrastre

tray [treɪ] n bandeja; (on desk) cajón m

treacherous ['tretʃərəs] adj traidor, traicionero; (dangerous) peligroso

treacle ['triːkl] (BRIT) n melaza

tread [tred] (pt **trod**, pp **trodden**) n (step) paso, pisada; (sound) ruido de pasos; (of stair) escalón m; (of tyre) banda de rodadura ♦ vi pisar; **~ on** vt fus pisar

treason ['triːzn] n traición f

treasure ['treʒə'] n (also fig) tesoro ♦ vt (value: object, friendship) apreciar; (: memory) guardar

treasurer ['treʒərə'] n tesorero/a

treasury ['treʒərɪ] n: **the T~** el Ministerio de Hacienda

treat [triːt] n (present) regalo ♦ vt tratar; **to ~ sb to sth** invitar a uno a algo

treatment ['triːtmənt] n tratamiento

treaty ['triːtɪ] n tratado

treble ['trebl] adj triple ♦ vt triplicar ♦ vi triplicarse; **~ clef** n (MUS) clave f de sol

tree [triː] n árbol m; **~ trunk** tronco (de árbol)

trek [trek] n (long journey) viaje m largo y difícil; (tiring walk) caminata

trellis ['trelɪs] n enrejado

tremble ['trembl] vi temblar

tremendous [trɪ'mɛndəs] adj tremendo, enorme; (excellent) estupendo

tremor ['tremə'] n temblor m; (also: **earth~**) temblor m de tierra

trench [trentʃ] n zanja

trend [trend] n (tendency) tendencia; (of events) curso; (fashion) moda; **~y** adj de moda

trespass ['trespəs] vi: **to ~ on** entrar sin permiso en; **"no ~ing"** "prohibido el paso"

trestle ['tresl] n caballete m

trial ['traɪəl] n (LAW) juicio, proceso; (test: of machine etc) prueba; **~s** npl (hardships) dificultades fpl; **by ~ and error** a fuerza de probar

triangle ['traɪæŋgl] n (MATH, MUS) triángulo

tribe [traɪb] n tribu f

tribunal [traɪ'bjuːnl] n tribunal m

tributary ['trɪbjuːtərɪ] n (river) afluente m

tribute ['trɪbjuːt] n homenaje m, tributo; **to pay ~ to** rendir homenaje a

trick [trɪk] n (skill, knack) tino, truco; (conjuring ~) truco; (joke) broma; (CARDS) baza ♦ vt engañar; **to play a ~ on sb** gastar una broma a uno; **that should do the ~** a ver si funciona así; **~ery** n engaño

trickle ['trɪkl] n (of water etc) goteo ♦ vi gotear

tricky ['trɪkɪ] adj difícil; delicado

tricycle ['traɪsɪkl] n triciclo

trifle ['traɪfl] n bagatela; (CULIN) dulce de bizcocho borracho, gelatina, fruta y natillas ♦ adv: **a ~ long** un poquito largo; **trifling** adj insignificante

trigger ['trɪgə'] n (of gun) gatillo; **~ off** vt desencadenar

trim [trɪm] adj (house, garden) en buen estado; (person, figure) esbelto ♦ n (haircut etc) recorte m; (on car) guarnición f ♦ vt (neaten) arreglar; (cut) recortar; (decorate) adornar; (NAUT: a sail) orientar; **~mings** npl (CULIN) guarnición f

trip [trɪp] n viaje m; (excursion) excursión f; (stumble) traspié m ♦ vi (stumble) tropezar; (go lightly) andar a paso ligero; **on a ~** de viaje; **~ up** vi tropezar, caerse ♦ vt hacer tropezar or caer

tripe [traɪp] n (CULIN) callos mpl

triple ['trɪpl] adj triple; **triplets** ['trɪplɪts] npl trillizos/as mpl/fpl; **triplicate** ['trɪplɪkət] n: **in triplicate** por triplicado

trite [traɪt] adj trillado

triumph ['traɪʌmf] n triunfo ♦ vi: **to ~ (over)** vencer; **~ant** [traɪ'ʌmfənt] adj (team etc) vencedor(a); (wave, return) triunfal

trivia ['trɪvɪə] npl trivialidades fpl

trivial ['trɪvɪəl] adj insignificante; (commonplace) banal

trod [trɔd] pt of **tread**

trodden ['trɔdn] *pp* of **tread**

trolley ['trɔlɪ] *n* carrito; (*also*: ~ **bus**) trolebús *m*

trombone [trɔm'bəun] *n* trombón *m*

troop [tru:p] *n* grupo, banda; **~s** *npl* (MIL) tropas *fpl*; ~ **in/out** *vi* entrar/salir en tropel; **~ing the colour** *n* (*ceremony*) presentación *f* de la bandera

trophy ['trəufɪ] *n* trofeo

tropical ['trɔpɪkl] *adj* tropical

trot [trɔt] *n* trote *m* ♦ *vi* trotar; **on the ~** (BRIT: *fig*) seguidos/as

trouble ['trʌbl] *n* problema *m*, dificultad *f*; (*worry*) preocupación *f*; (*bother*, *effort*) molestia, esfuerzo; (*unrest*) inquietud *f*; (MED): **stomach** *etc* ~ problemas *mpl* gástricos *etc* ♦ *vt* (*disturb*) molestar; (*worry*) preocupar, inquietar ♦ *vi*: **to ~ to do sth** molestarse en hacer algo; **~s** *npl* (POL *etc*) conflictos *mpl*; (*personal*) problemas *mpl*; **to be in ~** estar en un apuro; **it's no ~!** ¡no es molestia (ninguna)!; **what's the ~?** (*with broken TV etc*) ¿cuál es el problema?; (*doctor to patient*) ¿qué pasa?; **~d** *adj* (*person*) preocupado; (*country*, *epoch*, *life*) agitado; **~maker** *n* agitador(a) *m/f*; (*child*) alborotador *m*; **~shooter** *n* (*in conflict*) conciliador(a) *m/f*; **~some** *adj* molesto

trough [trɔf] *n* (*also*: **drinking ~**) abrevadero; (*also*: **feeding ~**) comedero; (*depression*) depresión *f*

troupe [tru:p] *n* grupo

trousers ['trauzəz] *npl* pantalones *mpl*; **short ~** pantalones *mpl* cortos

trousseau ['tru:səu] (*pl* **~x** *or* **~s**) *n* ajuar *m*

trout [traut] *n inv* trucha

trowel ['trauəl] *n* (*of gardener*) palita; (*of builder*) paleta

truant ['truənt] *n*: **to play ~** (BRIT) hacer novillos

truce [tru:s] *n* tregua

truck [trʌk] *n* (*lorry*) camión *m*; (RAIL) vagón *m*; ~ **driver** *n* camionero; ~ **farm** (US) *n* huerto

true [tru:] *adj* verdadero; (*accurate*) exacto;

(*genuine*) auténtico; (*faithful*) fiel; **to come ~** realizarse

truffle ['trʌfl] *n* trufa

truly ['tru:lɪ] *adv* (*really*) realmente; (*truthfully*) verdaderamente; (*faithfully*): **yours ~** (*in letter*) le saluda atentamente

trump [trʌmp] *n* triunfo

trumpet ['trʌmpɪt] *n* trompeta

truncheon ['trʌntʃən] *n* porra

trundle ['trʌndl] *vi*: **to ~ along** ir sin prisas

trunk [trʌŋk] *n* (*of tree*, *person*) tronco; (*of elephant*) trompa; (*case*) baúl *m*; (US: AUT) maletero; **~s** *npl* (*also*: **swimming ~s**) bañador *m* (de hombre)

truss [trʌs] *vt*: ~ (**up**) atar

trust [trʌst] *n* confianza; (*responsibility*) responsabilidad *f*; (LAW) fideicomiso ♦ *vt* (*rely on*) tener confianza en; (*hope*) esperar; (*entrust*): **to ~ sth to sb** confiar algo a uno; **to take sth on ~** aceptar algo a ojos cerrados; **~ed** *adj* de confianza; **~ee** [trʌs'ti:] *n* (LAW) fideicomisario; (*of school*) administrador *m*; **~ful** *adj* confiado; **~ing** *adj* confiado; **~worthy** *adj* digno de confianza

truth [tru:θ, *pl* tru:ðz] *n* verdad *f*; **~ful** *adj* veraz

try [traɪ] *n* tentativa, intento; (RUGBY) ensayo ♦ *vt* (*attempt*) intentar; (*test*: *also*: ~ **out**) probar, someter a prueba; (LAW) juzgar, procesar; (*strain*: *patience*) hacer perder ♦ *vi* probar; **to have a ~** probar suerte; **to ~ to do sth** intentar hacer algo; ~ **again!** ¡vuelve a probar!; ~ **harder!** ¡esfuérzate más!; **well, I tried** al menos lo intenté; ~ **on** *vt* (*clothes*) probarse; **~ing** *adj* (*experience*) cansado; (*person*) pesado

T-shirt ['ti:ʃə:t] *n* camiseta

T-square *n* regla en T

tub [tʌb] *n* cubo (SP), balde *m* (AM); (*bath*) tina, bañera

tube [tju:b] *n* tubo; (BRIT: *underground*) metro; (*for tyre*) cámara de aire

tuberculosis [tjubə:kju'ləusɪs] *n* tuberculosis *f inv*

tube station (BRIT) *n* estación *f* de metro

tubular ['tju:bjulə*] *adj* tubular

TUC (*BRIT*) *n abbr* (= *Trades Union Congress*) federación nacional de sindicatos

tuck [tʌk] *vt* (*put*) poner; ~ **away** *vt* (*money*) guardar; (*building*): **to be ~ed away** esconderse, ocultarse; ~ **in** meter dentro; (*child*) arropar ♦ *vi* (*eat*) comer con apetito; ~ **up** *vt* (*child*) arropar; ~ **shop** *n* (*SCOL*) tienda, ≈ bar *m* (del colegio) (*SP*)

Tuesday ['tjuːzdɪ] *n* martes *m inv*

tuft [tʌft] *n* mechón *m*; (*of grass etc*) manojo

tug [tʌɡ] *n* (*ship*) remolcador *m* ♦ *vt* tirar de; ~**-of-war** *n* lucha de tiro de cuerda; (*fig*) tira y afloja *m*

tuition [tjuːˈɪʃən] *n* (*BRIT*) enseñanza; (: *private* ~) clases *fpl* particulares; (*US: school fees*) matrícula

tulip ['tjuːlɪp] *n* tulipán *m*

tumble ['tʌmbl] *n* (*fall*) caída ♦ *vi* caer; **to ~ to sth** (*inf*) caer en la cuenta de algo; ~**down** *adj* destartalado; ~ **dryer** (*BRIT*) *n* secadora

tumbler ['tʌmblə*] *n* (*glass*) vaso

tummy ['tʌmɪ] (*inf*) *n* barriga, tripa

tumour ['tjuːmə*] (*US* **tumor**) *n* tumor *m*

tuna ['tjuːnə] *n inv* (*also:* ~ **fish**) atún *m*

tune [tjuːn] *n* melodía ♦ *vt* (*MUS*) afinar; (*RADIO, TV, AUT*) sintonizar; **to be in/out of** ~ (*instrument*) estar afinado/desafinado; (*singer*) cantar afinadamente/desafinar; **to be in/out of ~ with** (*fig*) estar de acuerdo/en desacuerdo con; ~ **in** *vi*: **to ~ in (to)** (*RADIO, TV*) sintonizar (con); ~ **up** *vi* (*musician*) afinar (su instrumento); ~**ful** *adj* melodioso; ~**r** *n*: **piano ~r** afinador(a) *m/f* de pianos

tunic ['tjuːnɪk] *n* túnica

Tunisia [tjuːˈnɪzɪə] *n* Túnez *m*

tunnel ['tʌnl] *n* túnel *m*; (*in mine*) galería ♦ *vi* construir un túnel/una galería

turban ['təːbən] *n* turbante *m*

turbulent ['təːbjulənt] *adj* turbulento

tureen [təˈriːn] *n* sopera

turf [təːf] *n* césped *m*; (*clod*) tepe *m* ♦ *vt* cubrir con césped; ~ **out** (*inf*) *vt* echar a la calle

Turk [təːk] *n* turco/a

Turkey ['təːkɪ] *n* Turquía

turkey ['təːkɪ] *n* pavo

Turkish ['təːkɪʃ] *adj*, *n* turco

turmoil ['təːmɔɪl] *n*: **in ~** revuelto

turn [təːn] *n* turno; (*in road*) curva; (*of mind, events*) rumbo; (*THEATRE*) número; (*MED*) ataque *m* ♦ *vt* girar, volver; (*collar, steak*) dar la vuelta a; (*page*) pasar; (*change*): **to ~ sth into** convertir algo en ♦ *vi* volver; (*person: look back*) volverse; (*reverse direction*) dar la vuelta; (*milk*) cortarse; (*become*): **to ~ nasty/forty** ponerse feo/cumplir los cuarenta; **a good ~** un favor; **it gave me quite a ~** me dio un susto; **"no left ~"** (*AUT*) "prohibido girar a la izquierda"; **it's your ~** te toca a ti; **in ~** por turnos; **to take ~s (at)** turnarse (en); ~ **away** *vi* apartar la vista ♦ *vt* rechazar; ~ **back** *vi* volverse atrás ♦ *vt* hacer retroceder; (*clock*) retrasar; ~ **down** *vt* (*refuse*) rechazar; (*reduce*) bajar; (*fold*) doblar; ~ **in** *vi* (*inf: go to bed*) acostarse ♦ *vt* (*fold*) doblar hacia dentro; ~ **off** *vi* (*from road*) desviarse ♦ *vt* (*light, radio etc*) apagar; (*tap*) cerrar; (*engine*) parar; ~ **on** *vt* (*light, radio etc*) encender (*SP*), prender (*AM*); (*tap*) abrir; (*engine*) poner en marcha; ~ **out** *vt* (*light, gas*) apagar; (*produce*) producir ♦ *vi* (*voters*) concurrir; **to ~ out to be ...** resultar ser ...; ~ **over** *vi* (*person*) volverse ♦ *vt* (*object*) dar la vuelta a; (*page*) volver; ~ **round** *vi* volverse; (*rotate*) girar; ~ **up** *vi* (*person*) llegar, presentarse; (*lost object*) aparecer ♦ *vt* (*gen*) subir; ~**ing** *n* (*in road*) vuelta; ~**ing point** *n* (*fig*) momento decisivo

turnip ['təːnɪp] *n* nabo

turn: ~**out** *n* concurrencia; ~**over** *n* (*COMM: amount of money*) volumen *m* de ventas; (: *of goods*) movimiento; ~**pike** (*US*) *n* autopista de peaje; ~**stile** *n* torniquete *m*; ~**table** *n* plato; ~**-up** (*BRIT*) *n* (*on trousers*) vuelta

turpentine ['təːpəntaɪn] *n* (*also:* **turps**)

trementina
turquoise ['tɜ:kwɔɪz] n (stone) turquesa
♦ adj color turquesa
turret ['tʌrɪt] n torreón m
turtle ['tɜ:tl] n galápago m; ~**neck**
(sweater) n jersey m de cuello vuelto
tusk [tʌsk] n colmillo
tutor ['tju:tə*] n profesor(a) m/f; ~**ial**
[-'tɔ:rɪəl] n (SCOL) seminario
tuxedo [tʌk'si:dəu] (US) n smóking m,
esmoquin m
TV [ti:'vi:] n abbr (= television) tele f
twang [twæŋ] n (of instrument) punteado;
(of voice) timbre m nasal
tweezers ['twi:zəz] npl pinzas fpl (de
depilar)
twelfth [twelfθ] num duodécimo
twelve [twelv] num doce; **at ~ o'clock**
(midday) a mediodía; (midnight) a
medianoche
twentieth ['twentɪθ] adj vigésimo
twenty ['twentɪ] num veinte
twice [twaɪs] adv dos veces; **~ as much**
dos veces más
twiddle ['twɪdl] vi: **to ~ (with) sth** dar
vueltas a algo; **to ~ one's thumbs** (fig)
estar mano sobre mano
twig [twɪg] n ramita
twilight ['twaɪlaɪt] n crepúsculo
twin [twɪn] adj, n gemelo/a m/f ♦ vt
hermanar; ~**bedded room** n
habitación f doble
twine [twaɪn] n bramante m ♦ vi (plant)
enroscarse
twinge [twɪndʒ] n (of pain) punzada; (of
conscience) remordimiento
twinkle ['twɪŋkl] vi centellear; (eyes) brillar
twirl [twɜ:l] vt dar vueltas a ♦ vi dar
vueltas
twist [twɪst] n (action) torsión f; (in road,
coil) vuelta; (in wire, flex) doblez f; (in
story) giro ♦ vt torcer; (weave) trenzar;
(roll around) enrollar; (fig) deformar ♦ vi
serpentear
twit [twɪt] (inf) n tonto
twitch [twɪtʃ] n (pull) tirón m; (nervous) tic
m ♦ vi crisparse

two [tu:] num dos; **to put ~ and ~**
together (fig) atar cabos; ~**-door** adj
(AUT) de dos puertas; ~**-faced** adj (pej:
person) falso; ~**fold** adv: **to increase**
~**fold** doblarse; ~**-piece (suit)** n traje m
de dos piezas; ~**-piece (swimsuit)** n
dos piezas m inv, bikini m; ~**some** n
(people) pareja; ~**-way** adj: ~**-way traffic**
circulación f de dos sentidos
tycoon [taɪ'ku:n] n: **(business)** ~ magnate
m
type [taɪp] n (category) tipo, género;
(model) tipo; (TYP) tipo, letra ♦ vt (letter
etc) escribir a máquina; ~**cast** adj
(actor) encasillado; ~**face** n letra;
~**script** n texto mecanografiado;
~**writer** n máquina de escribir; ~**written**
adj mecanografiado
typhoid ['taɪfɔɪd] n tifoidea
typical ['tɪpɪkl] adj típico
typing ['taɪpɪŋ] n mecanografía
typist ['taɪpɪst] n mecanógrafo/a
tyrant ['taɪərnt] n tirano/a
tyre ['taɪə*] (US **tire**) n neumático (SP),
llanta (AM); ~ **pressure** n presión f de
los neumáticos

U, u

U-bend ['ju:'bend] n (AUT, in pipe) recodo
udder ['ʌdə*] n ubre f
UFO ['ju:fəu] n abbr = (unidentified flying
object) OVNI m
ugh [ə:h] excl ¡uf!
ugly ['ʌglɪ] adj feo; (dangerous) peligroso
UHT abbr: ~ **milk** leche f UHT, leche f
uperizada
UK n abbr = **United Kingdom**
ulcer ['ʌlsə*] n úlcera; (mouth ~) llaga
Ulster ['ʌlstə*] n Ulster m
ulterior [ʌl'tɪərɪə*] adj: ~ **motive** segundas
intenciones fpl
ultimate ['ʌltɪmət] adj último, final;
(greatest) máximo; ~**ly** adv (in the end)
por último, al final; (fundamentally) a or
en fin de cuentas

umbilical cord [ʌm'bɪlɪkl-] n cordón m umbilical

umbrella [ʌm'brelə] n paraguas m inv; (for sun) sombrilla

umpire ['ʌmpaɪə*] n árbitro

umpteen [ʌmp'tiːn] adj enésimos/as; ~th adj: **for the ~th time** por enésima vez

UN n abbr (= United Nations) NN. UU.

unable [ʌn'eɪbl] adj: **to be ~ to do sth** no poder hacer algo

unaccompanied [ʌnə'kʌmpənɪd] adj no acompañado; (song) sin acompañamiento

unaccustomed [ʌnə'kʌstəmd] adj: **to be ~ to** no estar acostumbrado a

unanimous [juː'nænɪməs] adj unánime

unarmed [ʌn'ɑːmd] adj (defenceless) inerme; (without weapon) desarmado

unattached [ʌnə'tætʃt] adj (person) soltero y sin compromiso; (part etc) suelto

unattended [ʌnə'tendɪd] adj desatendido

unattractive [ʌnə'træktɪv] adj poco atractivo

unauthorized [ʌn'ɔːθəraɪzd] adj no autorizado

unavoidable [ʌnə'vɔɪdəbl] adj inevitable

unaware [ʌnə'weə*] adj: **to be ~ of** ignorar; ~s adv de improviso

unbalanced [ʌn'bælənst] adj (report) poco objetivo; (mentally) trastornado

unbearable [ʌn'beərəbl] adj insoportable

unbeatable [ʌn'biːtəbl] adj (team) invencible; (price) inmejorable; (quality) insuperable

unbelievable [ʌnbɪ'liːvəbl] adj increíble

unbend [ʌn'bend] (irreg) vi (relax) relajarse ♦ vt (wire) enderezar

unbiased [ʌn'baɪəst] adj imparcial

unborn [ʌn'bɔːn] adj que va a nacer

unbroken [ʌn'brəukən] adj (seal) intacto; (series) continuo; (record) no batido; (spirit) indómito

unbutton [ʌn'bʌtn] vt desabrochar

uncalled-for [ʌn'kɔːldfɔː*] adj gratuito, inmerecido

uncanny [ʌn'kænɪ] adj extraño

unceremonious ['ʌnserɪ'məunɪəs] adj (abrupt, rude) brusco, hosco

uncertain [ʌn'sɜːtn] adj incierto; (indecisive) indeciso

unchanged [ʌn'tʃeɪndʒd] adj igual, sin cambios

uncivilized [ʌn'sɪvɪlaɪzd] adj inculto; (fig: behaviour etc) bárbaro; (hour) inoportuno

uncle ['ʌŋkl] n tío

uncomfortable [ʌn'kʌmfətəbl] adj incómodo; (uneasy) inquieto

uncommon [ʌn'kɔmən] adj poco común, raro

uncompromising [ʌn'kɔmprəmaɪzɪŋ] adj intransigente

unconcerned [ʌnkən'sɜːnd] adj indiferente, despreocupado

unconditional [ʌnkən'dɪʃənl] adj incondicional

unconscious [ʌn'kɔnʃəs] adj sin sentido; (unaware): **to be ~ of** no darse cuenta de ♦ n: **the ~** el inconsciente

uncontrollable [ʌnkən'trəuləbl] adj (child etc) incontrolable; (temper) indomable; (laughter) incontenible

unconventional [ʌnkən'venʃənl] adj poco convencional

uncouth [ʌn'kuːθ] adj grosero, inculto

uncover [ʌn'kʌvə*] vt descubrir; (take lid off) destapar

undecided [ʌndɪ'saɪdɪd] adj (character) indeciso; (question) no resuelto

under ['ʌndə*] prep debajo de; (less than) menos de; (according to) según, de acuerdo con; (sb's leadership) bajo ♦ adv debajo, abajo; ~ **there** allí abajo; ~ **repair** en reparación

under... ['ʌndə*] prefix sub; ~age adj menor de edad; (drinking etc) de los menores de edad; ~carriage (BRIT) n (AVIAT) tren m de aterrizaje; ~charge vt cobrar menos de la cuenta; ~clothes npl ropa interior (SP) or íntima (AM); ~coat n (paint) primera mano; ~cover adj clandestino; ~current n (fig) corriente f oculta; ~cut vt irreg vender más barato que; ~developed adj subdesarrollado; ~dog n desvalido/a; ~done adj (CULIN) poco hecho;

~**estimate** vt subestimar; ~**exposed** adj (PHOT) subexpuesto; ~**fed** adj subalimentado; ~**foot** adv con los pies; ~**go** vt irreg sufrir; (treatment) recibir; ~**graduate** n estudiante m/f; ~**ground** n (BRIT: railway) metro; (POL) movimiento clandestino ♦ adj (car park) subterráneo ♦ adv (work) en la clandestinidad; ~**growth** n maleza, ~**hand(ed)** adj (fig) socarrón; ~**lie** vt irreg (fig) ser la razón fundamental de; ~**line** vt subrayar; ~**mine** vt socavar, minar; ~**neath** [ʌndə'niːθ] adv debajo ♦ prep debajo de, bajo; ~**paid** adj mal pagado; ~**pants** npl calzoncillos mpl; ~**pass** (BRIT) n paso subterráneo; ~**privileged** adj desposeído; ~**rate** vt menospreciar, subestimar; ~**shirt** (US) n camiseta; ~**shorts** (US) npl calzoncillos mpl; ~**side** n parte f inferior; ~**skirt** (BRIT) n enaguas fpl

understand [ʌndə'stænd] (irreg) vt, vi entender, comprender; (assume) tener entendido; ~**able** adj comprensible; ~**ing** adj comprensivo ♦ n comprensión f, entendimiento; (agreement) acuerdo

understatement ['ʌndəsteitmənt] n modestia (excesiva); **that's an ~!** ¡eso es decir poco!

understood [ʌndə'stud] pt, pp of **understand** ♦ adj (agreed) acordado; (implied): **it is ~ that** se sobreentiende que

understudy ['ʌndəstʌdɪ] n suplente m/f

undertake [ʌndə'teik] (irreg) vt emprender; **to ~ to do sth** comprometerse a hacer algo

undertaker ['ʌndəteikə*] n director(a) m/f de pompas fúnebres

undertaking ['ʌndəteikiŋ] n empresa; (promise) promesa

under: ~**tone** n: **in an ~tone** en voz baja; ~**water** adv bajo el agua ♦ adj submarino; ~**wear** n ropa interior (SP) or íntima (AM); ~**world** n (of crime) hampa, inframundo; ~**writer** n (INSURANCE) asegurador(a) m/f

undesirable [ʌndɪ'zaɪrəbl] adj (person) indeseable; (thing) poco aconsejable

undo [ʌn'duː] (irreg) vt (laces) desatar; (button etc) desabrochar; (spoil) deshacer; ~**ing** n ruina, perdición f

undoubted [ʌn'dautid] adj indudable

undress [ʌn'dres] vi desnudarse

undulating ['ʌndjuleitiŋ] adj ondulante

unduly [ʌn'djuːlɪ] adv excesivamente, demasiado

unearth [ʌn'əːθ] vt desenterrar

unearthly [ʌn'əːθlɪ] adj (hour) inverosímil

uneasy [ʌn'iːzɪ] adj intranquilo, preocupado; (feeling) desagradable; (peace) inseguro

uneducated [ʌn'edjukeitid] adj ignorante, inculto

unemployed [ʌnim'plɔid] adj parado, sin trabajo ♦ npl: **the ~** los parados

unemployment [ʌnim'plɔimənt] n paro, desempleo

unending [ʌn'endiŋ] adj interminable

unerring [ʌn'əːriŋ] adj infalible

uneven [ʌn'iːvn] adj desigual; (road etc) lleno de baches

unexpected [ʌnik'spektid] adj inesperado; ~**ly** adv inesperadamente

unfailing [ʌn'feiliŋ] adj (support) indefectible; (energy) inagotable

unfair [ʌn'feə*] adj: ~ **(to sb)** injusto (con uno)

unfaithful [ʌn'feiθful] adj infiel

unfamiliar [ʌnfə'miliə*] adj extraño, desconocido; **to be ~ with** desconocer

unfashionable [ʌn'fæʃnəbl] adj pasado or fuera de moda

unfasten [ʌn'fɑːsn] vt (knot) desatar; (dress) desabrochar; (open) abrir

unfavourable [ʌn'feivərəbl] (US **unfavorable**) adj desfavorable

unfeeling [ʌn'fiːliŋ] adj insensible

unfinished [ʌn'finiʃt] adj inacabado, sin terminar

unfit [ʌn'fit] adj bajo de forma; (incompetent): ~ **(for)** incapaz (de); ~ **for work** no apto para trabajar

unfold [ʌn'fəuld] vt desdoblar ♦ vi abrirse

unforeseen [ˈʌnfɔːˈsiːn] *adj* imprevisto
unforgettable [ʌnfəˈgetəbl] *adj*
inolvidable
unfortunate [ʌnˈfɔːtʃnət] *adj* desgraciado;
(*event, remark*) inoportuno; **~ly** *adv*
desgraciadamente
unfounded [ʌnˈfaundɪd] *adj* infundado
unfriendly [ʌnˈfrendlɪ] *adj* antipático;
(*behaviour, remark*) hostil, poco amigable
ungainly [ʌnˈgeɪnlɪ] *adj* desgarbado
ungodly [ʌnˈgɔdlɪ] *adj*: **at an ~ hour** a una
hora inverosímil
ungrateful [ʌnˈgreɪtful] *adj* ingrato
unhappiness [ʌnˈhæpɪnɪs] *n* tristeza,
desdicha
unhappy [ʌnˈhæpɪ] *adj* (*sad*) triste;
(*unfortunate*) desgraciado; (*childhood*)
infeliz; **~ about/with** (*arrangements etc*)
poco contento con, descontento de
unharmed [ʌnˈhɑːmd] *adj* ileso
unhealthy [ʌnˈhelθɪ] *adj* (*place*) malsano;
(*person*) enfermizo; (*fig: interest*) morboso
unheard-of *adj* inaudito, sin precedente
unhurt [ʌnˈhɜːt] *adj* ileso
unidentified [ʌnaɪˈdentɪfaɪd] *adj* no
identificado, sin identificar; *see also* **UFO**
uniform [ˈjuːnɪfɔːm] *n* uniforme *m* ♦ *adj*
uniforme
unify [ˈjuːnɪfaɪ] *vt* unificar, unir
uninhabited [ʌnɪnˈhæbɪtɪd] *adj* desierto
unintentional [ʌnɪnˈtenʃənəl] *adj*
involuntario
union [ˈjuːnjən] *n* unión *f*; (*also*: **trade ~**)
sindicato ♦ *cpd* sindical; **U~ Jack** *n*
bandera del Reino Unido
unique [juːˈniːk] *adj* único
unison [ˈjuːnɪsn] *n*: **in ~** (*speak, reply, sing*)
al unísono
unit [ˈjuːnɪt] *n* unidad *f*; (*section: of
furniture etc*) elemento; (*team*) grupo;
kitchen ~ módulo de cocina
unite [juːˈnaɪt] *vt* unir ♦ *vi* unirse; **~d** *adj*
unido; (*effort*) conjunto; **U~d Kingdom**
n Reino Unido; **U~d Nations
(Organization)** *n* Naciones *fpl* Unidas;
U~d States (of America) *n* Estados
mpl Unidos

unit trust (*BRIT*) *n* bono fiduciario
unity [ˈjuːnɪtɪ] *n* unidad *f*
universe [ˈjuːnɪvɜːs] *n* universo
university [juːnɪˈvɜːsɪtɪ] *n* universidad *f*
unjust [ʌnˈdʒʌst] *adj* injusto
unkempt [ʌnˈkempt] *adj* (*appearance*)
descuidado; (*hair*) despeinado
unkind [ʌnˈkaɪnd] *adj* poco amable;
(*behaviour, comment*) cruel
unknown [ʌnˈnəun] *adj* desconocido
unlawful [ʌnˈlɔːful] *adj* ilegal, ilícito
unleaded [ʌnˈledɪd] *adj* (*petrol, fuel*) sin
plombo
unless [ʌnˈles] *conj* a menos que; **~ he
comes** a menos que venga; **~ otherwise
stated** salvo indicación contraria
unlike [ʌnˈlaɪk] *adj* (*not alike*) distinto de
or a; (*not like*) poco propio de ♦ *prep* a
diferencia de
unlikely [ʌnˈlaɪklɪ] *adj* improbable;
(*unexpected*) inverosímil
unlimited [ʌnˈlɪmɪtɪd] *adj* ilimitado
unlisted [ʌnˈlɪstɪd] (*US*) *adj* (*TEL*) que no
consta en la guía
unload [ʌnˈləud] *vt* descargar
unlock [ʌnˈlɔk] *vt* abrir (con llave)
unlucky [ʌnˈlʌkɪ] *adj* desgraciado; (*object,
number*) que da mala suerte; **to be ~**
tener mala suerte
unmarried [ʌnˈmærɪd] *adj* soltero
unmistak(e)able [ʌnmɪsˈteɪkəbl] *adj*
inconfundible
unnatural [ʌnˈnætʃrəl] *adj* (*gen*)
antinatural; (*manner*) afectado; (*habit*)
perverso
unnecessary [ʌnˈnesəsərɪ] *adj*
innecesario, inútil
unnoticed [ʌnˈnəutɪst] *adj*: **to go** *or* **pass
~** pasar desapercibido
UNO [ˈjuːnəu] *n abbr* (= *United Nations
Organization*) ONU *f*
unobtainable [ʌnəbˈteɪnəbl] *adj*
inconseguible; (*TEL*) inexistente
unobtrusive [ʌnəbˈtruːsɪv] *adj* discreto
unofficial [ʌnəˈfɪʃl] *adj* no oficial; (*news*)
sin confirmar
unorthodox [ʌnˈɔːθədɔks] *adj* poco

ortodoxo; *(REL)* heterodoxo
unpack [ʌnˈpæk] *vi* deshacer las maletas
♦ *vt* deshacer
unpalatable [ʌnˈpælətəbl] *adj* incomible;
(truth) desagradable
unparalleled [ʌnˈpærəleld] *adj*
(unequalled) incomparable
unpleasant [ʌnˈpleznt] *adj* *(disagreeable)*
desagradable; *(person, manner)* antipático
unplug [ʌnˈplʌg] *vt* desenchufar,
desconectar
unpopular [ʌnˈpɔpjulə*] *adj* impopular,
poco popular
unprecedented [ʌnˈpresɪdəntɪd] *adj* sin
precedentes
unpredictable [ʌnprɪˈdɪktəbl] *adj*
imprevisible
unprofessional [ʌnprəˈfeʃənl] *adj*
(attitude, conduct) poco ético
unqualified [ʌnˈkwɔlɪfaɪd] *adj* sin título,
no cualificado; *(success)* total
unquestionably [ʌnˈkwestʃənəblɪ] *adv*
indiscutiblemente
unreal [ʌnˈrɪəl] *adj* irreal; *(extraordinary)*
increíble
unrealistic [ʌnrɪəˈlɪstɪk] *adj* poco realista
unreasonable [ʌnˈriːznəbl] *adj*
irrazonable; *(demand)* excesivo
unrelated [ʌnrɪˈleɪtɪd] *adj* sin relación;
(family) no emparentado
unreliable [ʌnrɪˈlaɪəbl] *adj* *(person)*
informal; *(machine)* poco fiable
unremitting [ʌnrɪˈmɪtɪŋ] *adj* constante
unreservedly [ʌnrɪˈzəːvɪdlɪ] *adv* sin
reserva
unrest [ʌnˈrest] *n* inquietud *f,* malestar *m;*
(POL) disturbios *mpl*
unroll [ʌnˈrəul] *vt* desenrollar
unruly [ʌnˈruːlɪ] *adj* indisciplinado
unsafe [ʌnˈseɪf] *adj* peligroso
unsaid [ʌnˈsed] *adj:* **to leave sth ~** dejar
algo sin decir
unsatisfactory [ˈʌnsætɪsˈfæktərɪ] *adj* poco
satisfactorio
unsavoury [ʌnˈseɪvərɪ] *(US* **unsavory**) *adj*
(fig) repugnante
unscrew [ʌnˈskruː] *vt* destornillar

unscrupulous [ʌnˈskruːpjuləs] *adj* sin
escrúpulos
unsettled [ʌnˈsetld] *adj* inquieto,
intranquilo; *(weather)* variable
unshaven [ʌnˈʃeɪvn] *adj* sin afeitar
unsightly [ʌnˈsaɪtlɪ] *adj* feo
unskilled [ʌnˈskɪld] *adj* *(work)* no
especializado; *(worker)* no cualificado
unspeakable [ʌnˈspiːkəbl] *adj* indecible;
(awful) incalificable
unstable [ʌnˈsteɪbl] *adj* inestable
unsteady [ʌnˈstedɪ] *adj* inestable
unstuck [ʌnˈstʌk] *adj:* **to come ~**
despegarse; *(fig)* fracasar
unsuccessful [ʌnsəkˈsesful] *adj* *(attempt)*
infructuoso; *(writer, proposal)* sin éxito; **to
be ~** *(in attempting sth)* no tener éxito,
fracasar; **~ly** *adv* en vano, sin éxito
unsuitable [ʌnˈsuːtəbl] *adj* inapropiado;
(time) inoportuno
unsure [ʌnˈʃuə*] *adj* inseguro, poco
seguro
unsuspecting [ˈʌnsəsˈpektɪŋ] *adj*
desprevenido
unsympathetic [ʌnsɪmpəˈθetɪk] *adj* poco
comprensivo; *(unlikeable)* antipático
unthinkable [ʌnˈθɪŋkəbl] *adj*
inconcebible, impensable
untidy [ʌnˈtaɪdɪ] *adj* *(room)* desordenado;
(appearance) desaliñado
untie [ʌnˈtaɪ] *vt* desatar
until [ənˈtɪl] *prep* hasta ♦ *conj* hasta que; **~
he comes** hasta que venga; **~ now** hasta
ahora; **~ then** hasta entonces
untimely [ʌnˈtaɪmlɪ] *adj* inoportuno;
(death) prematuro
untold [ʌnˈtəuld] *adj* *(story)* nunca
contado; *(suffering)* indecible; *(wealth)*
incalculable
untoward [ʌntəˈwɔːd] *adj* adverso
unused [ʌnˈjuːzd] *adj* sin usar
unusual [ʌnˈjuːʒuəl] *adj* insólito, poco
común; *(exceptional)* inusitado
unveil [ʌnˈveɪl] *vt* *(statue)* descubrir
unwanted [ʌnˈwɔntɪd] *adj* *(clothing)* viejo;
(pregnancy) no deseado
unwelcome [ʌnˈwelkəm] *adj* inoportuno;

(news) desagradable
unwell [ʌnˈwɛl] *adj*: **to be/feel ~** estar
indispuesto/sentirse mal
unwieldy [ʌnˈwiːldɪ] *adj* difícil de manejar
unwilling [ʌnˈwɪlɪŋ] *adj*: **to be ~ to do sth**
estar poco dispuesto a hacer algo; **~ly**
adv de mala gana
unwind [ʌnˈwaɪnd] *(irreg: like* wind²*) vt*
desenvolver ♦ *vi (relax)* relajarse
unwise [ʌnˈwaɪz] *adj* imprudente
unwitting [ʌnˈwɪtɪŋ] *adj* inconsciente
unworthy [ʌnˈwəːðɪ] *adj* indigno
unwrap [ʌnˈræp] *vt* desenvolver
unwritten [ʌnˈrɪtn] *adj (agreement)* tácito;
(rules, law) no escrito

KEYWORD

up [ʌp] *prep*: **to go/be ~ sth** subir/estar
subido en algo; **he went ~ the stairs/the
hill** subió las escaleras/la colina; **we
walked/climbed ~ the hill** subimos la
colina; **they live further ~ the street**
viven más arriba en la calle; **go ~ that
road and turn left** sigue por esa calle y
gira a la izquierda
♦ *adv* **1** *(upwards, higher)* más arriba; **~ in
the mountains** en lo alto (de la
montaña); **put it a bit higher ~** ponlo un
poco más arriba *or* alto; **~ there** ahí *or*
allí arriba; **~ above** en lo alto, por
encima, arriba
2: **to be ~** *(out of bed)* estar levantado;
(prices, level) haber subido
3: **~ to** *(as far as)* hasta; **~ now** hasta
ahora *or* la fecha
4: **to be ~ to** *(depending on)*: **it's ~ to
you** depende de ti; **he's not ~ to it** *(job,
task etc)* no es capaz de hacerlo; **his work
is not ~ to the required standard** su
trabajo no da la talla; *(inf: be doing)*:
what is he ~ to? ¿que estará tramando?
♦ *n*: **~s and downs** altibajos *mpl*

---

upbringing [ˈʌpbrɪŋɪŋ] *n* educación *f*
update [ʌpˈdeɪt] *vt* poner al día
upgrade [ʌpˈgreɪd] *vt (house)* modernizar;
(employee) ascender

upheaval [ʌpˈhiːvl] *n* trastornos *mpl*;
(POL) agitación *f*
uphill [ʌpˈhɪl] *adj* cuesta arriba; *(fig: task)*
penoso, difícil ♦ *adv*: **to go ~** ir cuesta
arriba
uphold [ʌpˈhəʊld] *(irreg) vt* defender
upholstery [ʌpˈhəʊlstərɪ] *n* tapicería
upkeep [ˈʌpkiːp] *n* mantenimiento
upon [əˈpɔn] *prep* sobre
upper [ˈʌpə*] *adj* superior, de arriba ♦ *n*
(of shoe: also: **~s***)* empeine *m*; **~-class**
adj de clase alta; **~ hand** *n*: **to have the
~ hand** tener la sartén por el mango;
~most *adj* el más alto; **what was ~most
in my mind** lo que me preocupaba más
upright [ˈʌpraɪt] *adj* derecho; *(vertical)*
vertical; *(fig)* honrado
uprising [ˈʌpraɪzɪŋ] *n* sublevación *f*
uproar [ˈʌprɔː*] *n* escándalo
uproot [ʌpˈruːt] *vt (also fig)* desarraigar
upset [*n* ˈʌpset, *vb, adj* ʌpˈsɛt] *n (to plan
etc)* revés *m*, contratiempo; *(MED)*
trastorno ♦ *(irreg) vt (glass etc)* volcar;
(plan) alterar; *(person)* molestar, disgustar
♦ *adj* molesto, disgustado; *(stomach)*
revuelto
upshot [ˈʌpʃɔt] *n* resultado
upside-down *adv* al revés; **to turn a
place ~** *(fig)* revolverlo todo
upstairs [ʌpˈstɛəz] *adv* arriba ♦ *adj (room)*
de arriba ♦ *n* el piso superior
upstart [ˈʌpstɑːt] *n* advenedizo/a
upstream [ʌpˈstriːm] *adv* río arriba
uptake [ˈʌpteɪk] *n*: **to be quick/slow on
the ~** ser muy listo/torpe
uptight [ʌpˈtaɪt] *adj* tenso, nervioso
up-to-date *adj* al día
upturn [ˈʌptəːn] *n (in luck)* mejora; *(COMM:
in market)* resurgimiento económico
upward [ˈʌpwəd] *adj* ascendente; **~(s)**
adv hacia arriba; *(more than)*: **~(s) of** más
de
urban [ˈəːbən] *adj* urbano
urchin [ˈəːtʃɪn] *n* pilluelo, golfillo
urge [əːdʒ] *n (desire)* deseo ♦ *vt*: **to ~ sb
to do sth** animar a uno a hacer algo
urgent [ˈəːdʒənt] *adj* urgente; *(voice)*

perentorio

urinate ['juərɪneɪt] *vi* orinar

urine ['juərɪn] *n* orina, orines *mpl*

urn [əːn] *n* urna; (*also*: **tea ~**) cacharro metálico grande para hacer té

Uruguay ['juerəgwaɪ] *n* (el) Uruguay; **~an** [-'gwaɪən] *adj, n* uruguayo/a *m/f*

US *n abbr* (= *United States*) EE. UU.

us [ʌs] *pron* nos; (*after prep*) nosotros/as; *see also* **me**

USA *n abbr* (= *United States of America*)) EE. UU.

usage ['juːzɪdʒ] *n* (*LING*) uso

use [*n* juːs, *vb* juːz] *n* uso, empleo; (*usefulness*) utilidad *f* ♦ *vt* usar, emplear; **she ~d to do it** (ella) solía *or* acostumbraba hacerlo; **in ~** en uso; **out of ~** en desuso; **to be of ~** servir; **it's no ~** (*pointless*) es inútil; (*not useful*) no sirve; **to be ~d to** estar acostumbrado a, acostumbrar; **~ up** *vt* (*food*) consumir; (*money*) gastar; **~d** *adj* (*car*) usado; **~ful** *adj* útil; **~fulness** *n* utilidad *f*; **~less** *adj* (*unusable*) inservible; (*pointless*) inútil; (*person*) inepto; **~r** *n* usuario/a; **~r-friendly** *adj* (*computer*) amistoso

usher ['ʌʃə*] *n* (*at wedding*) ujier *m*; **~ette** [-'ret] *n* (*in cinema*) acomodadora

USSR *n* (*HIST*): **the ~** la URSS

usual ['juːʒuəl] *adj* normal, corriente; **as ~** como de costumbre; **~ly** *adv* normalmente

utensil [juːˈtensl] *n* utensilio; **kitchen ~s** batería de cocina

uterus ['juːtərəs] *n* útero

utility [juːˈtɪlɪtɪ] *n* utilidad *f*; (*public ~*) (empresa de) servicio público; **~ room** *n* ofis *m*

utilize ['juːtɪlaɪz] *vt* utilizar

utmost ['ʌtməʊst] *adj* mayor ♦ *n*: **to do one's ~** hacer todo lo posible

utter ['ʌtə*] *adj* total, completo ♦ *vt* pronunciar, proferir; **~ly** *adv* completamente, totalmente

U-turn ['juːˈtəːn] *n* viraje *m* en redondo

V, v

v. *abbr* = **verse**; **versus**; (= *volt*) v; (= *vide*) véase

vacancy ['veɪkənsɪ] *n* (*BRIT*: *job*) vacante *f*; (*room*) habitación *f* libre; **"no vacancies"** "completo"

vacant ['veɪkənt] *adj* desocupado, libre; (*expression*) distraído

vacate [vəˈkeɪt] *vt* (*house, room*) desocupar; (*job*) dejar (vacante)

vacation [vəˈkeɪʃən] *n* vacaciones *fpl*

vaccinate ['væksɪneɪt] *vt* vacunar

vaccine ['væksiːn] *n* vacuna

vacuum ['vækjum] *n* vacío; **~ cleaner** *n* aspiradora; **~flask** (*BRIT*) *n* termo; **~-packed** *adj* empaquetado al vacío

vagina [vəˈdʒaɪnə] *n* vagina

vagrant ['veɪgrnt] *n* vagabundo/a

vague [veɪg] *adj* vago; (*memory*) borroso; (*ambiguous*) impreciso; (*person*: *absent-minded*) distraído; (: *evasive*): **to be ~** no decir las cosas claramente; **~ly** *adv* vagamente; distraídamente; con evasiva

vain [veɪn] *adj* (*conceited*) presumido; (*useless*) vano, inútil; **in ~** en vano

valentine ['væləntaɪn] *n* (*also*: **~ card**) tarjeta del Día de los Enamorados

valet ['væleɪ] *n* ayuda *m* de cámara

valid ['vælɪd] *adj* válido; (*ticket*) valedero; (*law*) vigente

valley ['vælɪ] *n* valle *m*

valuable ['væljuəbl] *adj* (*jewel*) de valor; (*time*) valioso; **~s** *npl* objetos *mpl* de valor

valuation [væljuˈeɪʃən] *n* tasación *f*, valuación *f*; (*judgement of quality*) valoración *f*

value ['væljuː] *n* valor *m*; (*importance*) importancia ♦ *vt* (*fix price of*) tasar, valorar; (*esteem*) apreciar; **~s** *npl* (*principles*) principios *mpl*; **~ added tax** (*BRIT*) *n* impuesto sobre el valor añadido; **~d** *adj* (*appreciated*) apreciado

valve [vælv] *n* válvula

van [væn] n (AUT) furgoneta (SP), camioneta (AM)

vandal ['vændl] n vándalo/a; **~ism** n vandalismo; **~ize** vt dañar, destruir

vanilla [və'nılə] n vainilla

vanish ['vænıʃ] vi desaparecer

vanity ['vænıtı] n vanidad f

vantage point ['vɑ:ntıdʒ-] n (for views) punto panorámico

vapour ['veıpə*] (US **vapor**) n vapor m; (on breath, window) vaho

variable ['veərıəbl] adj variable

variation [veərı'eıʃən] n variación f

varicose ['værıkəus] adj: **~ veins** varices fpl

varied ['veərıd] adj variado

variety [və'raıətı] n (diversity) diversidad f; (type) variedad f; **~ show** n espectáculo de variedades

various ['veərıəs] adj (several: people) varios/as; (reasons) diversos/as

varnish ['vɑ:nıʃ] n barniz m; (nail ~) esmalte m ♦ vt barnizar; (nails) pintar (con esmalte)

vary ['veərı] vt variar; (change) cambiar ♦ vi variar

vase [vɑ:z] n florero

Vaseline ® ['væsıli:n] n vaselina ®

vast [vɑ:st] adj enorme

VAT [væt] (BRIT) n abbr (= value added tax) IVA m

vat [væt] n tina, tinaja

Vatican ['vætıkən] n: **the ~** el Vaticano

vault [vɔ:lt] n (of roof) bóveda; (tomb) panteón m; (in bank) cámara acorazada ♦ vt (also: **~ over**) saltar (por encima de)

vaunted ['vɔ:ntıd] adj: **much ~** cacareado, alardeado

VCR n abbr = **video cassette recorder**

VD n abbr = **venereal disease**

VDU n abbr (= visual display unit) UPV f

veal [vi:l] n ternera

veer [vıə*] vi (vehicle) virar; (wind) girar

vegan ['vi:gən] n vegetariano/a estricto/a, vegetaliano/a

vegeburger ['vedʒıbə:gə*] n hamburguesa vegetal

vegetable ['vedʒtəbl] n (BOT) vegetal m; (edible plant) legumbre f, hortaliza ♦ adj vegetal; **~s** npl (cooked) verduras fpl

vegetarian [vedʒı'teərıən] adj, n vegetariano/a m/f

vehement ['vi:ımənt] adj vehemente, apasionado

vehicle ['vi:ıkl] n vehículo; (fig) medio

veil [veıl] n velo ♦ vt velar; **~ed** adj (fig) velado

vein [veın] n vena; (of ore etc) veta

velocity [vı'lɒsıtı] n velocidad f

velvet ['velvıt] n terciopelo

vending machine ['vendıŋ-] n distribuidor m automático

veneer [və'nıə*] n chapa, enchapado; (fig) barniz m

venereal disease [vı'nıərıəl-] n enfermedad f venérea

Venetian blind [vı'ni:ʃən-] n persiana

Venezuela [venı'zweılə] n Venezuela; **~n** adj, n venezolano/a m/f

vengeance ['vendʒəns] n venganza; **with a ~** (fig) con creces

venison ['venısn] n carne f de venado

venom ['venəm] n veneno; (bitterness) odio; **~ous** adj venenoso; lleno de odio

vent [vent] n (in jacket) respiradero; (in wall) rejilla (de ventilación) ♦ vt (fig: feelings) desahogar

ventilator ['ventıleıtə*] n ventilador m

venture ['ventʃə*] n empresa ♦ vt (opinion) ofrecer ♦ vi arriesgarse, lanzarse; **business ~** empresa comercial

venue ['venju:] n lugar m

veranda(h) [və'rændə] n terraza

verb [və:b] n verbo; **~al** adj verbal

verbatim [və:'beıtım] adj, adv palabra por palabra

verdict ['və:dıkt] n veredicto, fallo; (fig) opinión f, juicio

verge [və:dʒ] (BRIT) n borde m; **"soft ~s"** (AUT) "arcén m no asfaltado"; **to be on the ~ of doing sth** estar a punto de hacer algo; **~ on** vt fus rayar en

verify ['verıfaı] vt comprobar, verificar

vermin ['və:mın] npl (animals) alimañas

fpl; (*insects, fig*) parásitos *mpl*
vermouth ['vɜ:məθ] *n* vermut *m*
versatile ['vɜːsətaɪl] *adj* (*person*)
polifacético; (*machine, tool etc*) versátil
verse [vɜːs] *n* poesía; (*stanza*) estrofa; (*in bible*) versículo
version ['vɜːʃən] *n* versión *f*
versus ['vɜːsəs] *prep* contra
vertebra ['vɜːtɪbrə] (*pl* ~**e**) *n* vértebra
vertical ['vɜːtɪkl] *adj* vertical
verve [vɜːv] *n* brío
very ['verɪ] *adv* muy ♦ *adj*: **the ~ book which** el mismo libro que; **the ~ last** el último de todos; **at the ~ least** al menos; **~ much** muchísimo
vessel ['vesl] *n* (*ship*) barco; (*container*) vasija; *see* **blood**
vest [vest] *n* (*BRIT*) camiseta; (*US: waistcoat*) chaleco; ~**ed interests** *npl* (*COMM*) intereses *mpl* creados
vet [vet] *vt* (*candidate*) investigar ♦ *n abbr* (*BRIT*) = **veterinary surgeon**
veteran ['vetərn] *n* veterano
veterinary surgeon ['vetrɪnərɪ] (*US* **veterinarian**) *n* veterinario/a *m/f*
veto ['viːtəu] (*pl* ~**es**) *n* veto ♦ *vt* prohibir, poner el veto a
vex [veks] *vt* fastidiar; ~**ed** *adj* (*question*) controvertido
VHF *abbr* (= *very high frequency*) muy alta frecuencia
via ['vaɪə] *prep* por, por medio de
vibrant ['vaɪbrənt] *adj* (*lively*) animado; (*bright*) vivo; (*voice*) vibrante
vibrate [vaɪ'breɪt] *vi* vibrar
vicar ['vɪkə*] *n* párroco (de la Iglesia Anglicana); ~**age** *n* parroquia
vice [vaɪs] *n* (*evil*) vicio; (*TECH*) torno de banco
vice- [vaɪs] *prefix* vice-; ~~**chairman** *n* vicepresidente *m*
vice squad *n* brigada antivicio
vice versa ['vaɪsɪ'vɜːsə] *adv* viceversa
vicinity [vɪ'sɪnɪtɪ] *n*: **in the ~ (of)** cercano (a)
vicious ['vɪʃəs] *adj* (*attack*) violento; (*words*) cruel; (*horse, dog*) resabido; ~

circle *n* círculo vicioso
victim ['vɪktɪm] *n* víctima
victor ['vɪktə*] *n* vencedor(a) *m/f*
victory ['vɪktərɪ] *n* victoria
video ['vɪdɪəu] *cpd* video ♦ *n* (~ *film*) videofilm *m*; (*also:* ~ **cassette**) videocassette *f*; (*also:* ~ **cassette recorder**) magnetoscopio; ~ **game** *n* videojuego; ~ **tape** *n* cinta de vídeo
vie [vaɪ] *vi*: **to ~ (with sb for sth)** competi (con uno por algo)
Vienna [vɪ'enə] *n* Viena
Vietnam [vjet'næm] *n* Vietnam *m*; ~**ese** [-nə'miːz] *n inv, adj* vietnamita *m/f*
view [vjuː] *n* vista; (*outlook*) perspectiva; (*opinion*) opinión *f*, criterio ♦ *vt* (*look at*) mirar; (*fig*) considerar; **on ~** (*in museum etc*) expuesto; **in full ~ (of)** en plena vist (de); **in ~ of the weather/the fact that** en vista del tiempo/del hecho de que; **in my ~** en mi opinión; ~**er** *n* espectador(a *m/f*; (*TV*) telespectador(a) *m/f*; ~**finder** visor *m* de imagen; ~**point** *n* (*attitude*) punto de vista; (*place*) mirador *m*
vigour ['vɪgə*] (*US* **vigor**) *n* energía, vigor *m*
vile [vaɪl] *adj* vil, infame; (*smell*) asqueros (*temper*) endemoniado
villa ['vɪlə] *n* (*country house*) casa de campo; (*suburban house*) chalet *m*
village ['vɪlɪdʒ] *n* aldea; ~**r** *n* aldeano/a
villain ['vɪlən] *n* (*scoundrel*) malvado/a; (*i novel*) malo; (*BRIT: criminal*) maleante *m/*
vindicate ['vɪndɪkeɪt] *vt* vindicar, justifica
vindictive [vɪn'dɪktɪv] *adj* vengativo
vine [vaɪn] *n* vid *f*
vinegar ['vɪnɪgə*] *n* vinagre *m*
vineyard ['vɪnjɑːd] *n* viña, viñedo
vintage ['vɪntɪdʒ] *n* (*year*) vendimia, cosecha ♦ *cpd* de época; ~ **wine** *n* vind añejo
vinyl ['vaɪnl] *n* vinilo
viola [vɪ'əulə] *n* (*MUS*) viola
violate ['vaɪəleɪt] *vt* violar
violence ['vaɪələns] *n* violencia
violent ['vaɪələnt] *adj* violento; (*intense*) intenso

violet ['vaɪələt] *adj* violado, violeta ♦ *n* (*plant*) violeta

violin [vaɪə'lɪn] *n* violín *m*; **~ist** *n* violinista *m/f*

VIP *n abbr* (= *very important person*) VIP *m*

virgin ['vɜːdʒɪn] *n* virgen *f*

Virgo ['vɜːgəʊ] *n* Virgo

virtually ['vɜːtjʊəlɪ] *adv* prácticamente

virtual reality ['vɜːtjuəl-] *n* (*COMPUT*) mundo *or* realidad *f* virtual

virtue ['vɜːtjuː] *n* virtud *f*; (*advantage*) ventaja; **by ~ of** en virtud de

virtuous ['vɜːtjuəs] *adj* virtuoso

virus ['vaɪərəs] *n* (*also: COMPUT*) virus *m*

visa ['viːzə] *n* visado (*SP*), visa (*AM*)

visible ['vɪzəbl] *adj* visible

vision ['vɪʒən] *n* (*sight*) vista; (*foresight, in dream*) visión *f*

visit ['vɪzɪt] *n* visita ♦ *vt* (*person: US: also: ~ with*) visitar, hacer una visita a; (*place*) ir a, (ira) conocer; **~ing hours** *npl* (*in hospital etc*) horas *fpl* de visita; **~or** *n* (*in museum*) visitante *m/f*; (*invited to house*) visita; (*tourist*) turista *m/f*

visor ['vaɪzə*] *n* visera

visual ['vɪzjuəl] *adj* visual; **~ aid** *n* medio visual; **~ display unit** *n* unidad *f* de presentación visual; **~ize** *vt* imaginarse

vital ['vaɪtl] *adj* (*essential*) esencial, imprescindible; (*dynamic*) dinámico; (*organ*) vital; **~ly** *adv*: **~ly important** de primera importancia; **~ statistics** *npl* (*fig*) medidas *fpl* vitales

vitamin ['vɪtəmɪn] *n* vitamina

vivacious [vɪ'veɪʃəs] *adj* vivaz, alegre

vivid ['vɪvɪd] *adj* (*account*) gráfico; (*light*) intenso; (*imagination, memory*) vivo; **~ly** *adv* gráficamente; (*remember*) como si fuera hoy

V-neck ['viːnɛk] *n* cuello de pico

vocabulary [vəʊ'kæbjulərɪ] *n* vocabulario

vocal ['vəʊkl] *adj* vocal; (*articulate*) elocuente; **~ cords** *npl* cuerdas *fpl* vocales

vocation [vəʊ'keɪʃən] *n* vocación *f*; **~al** *adj* profesional

vodka ['vɒdkə] *n* vodka *m*

vogue [vəʊg] *n*: **in ~** en boga, de moda

voice [vɔɪs] *n* voz *f* ♦ *vt* expresar

void [vɔɪd] *n* vacío; (*hole*) hueco ♦ *adj* (*invalid*) nulo, inválido; (*empty*): **~ of** carente *or* desprovisto de

volatile ['vɒlətaɪl] *adj* (*situation*) inestable; (*person*) voluble; (*liquid*) volátil

volcano [vɒl'keɪnəʊ] (*pl* **~es**) *n* volcán *m*

volition [və'lɪʃən] *n*: **of one's own ~** de su propia voluntad

volley ['vɒlɪ] *n* (*of gunfire*) descarga; (*of stones etc*) lluvia; (*fig*) torrente *m*; (*TENNIS etc*) volea; **~ball** *n* vol(e)ibol *m*

volt [vəʊlt] *n* voltio; **~age** *n* voltaje *m*

volume ['vɒljuːm] *n* (*gen*) volumen *m*; (*book*) tomo

voluntary ['vɒləntərɪ] *adj* voluntario

volunteer [vɒlən'tɪə*] *n* voluntario/a ♦ *vt* (*information*) ofrecer ♦ *vi* ofrecerse (de voluntario); **to ~ to do** ofrecerse a hacer

vomit ['vɒmɪt] *n* vómito ♦ *vt, vi* vomitar

vote [vəʊt] *n* voto; (*votes cast*) votación *f*; (*right to ~*) derecho de votar; (*franchise*) sufragio ♦ *vt* (*chairman*) elegir; (*propose*): **to ~ that** proponer que ♦ *vi* votar, ir a votar; **~ of thanks** voto de gracias; **~r** *n* votante *m/f*; **voting** *n* votación *f*

vouch [vautʃ]: **to ~ for** *vt fus* garantizar, responder de

voucher ['vautʃə*] *n* (*for meal, petrol*) vale *m*

vow [vau] *n* voto ♦ *vt*: **to ~ to do/that** jurar hacer/que

vowel ['vauəl] *n* vocal *f*

voyage ['vɔɪdʒ] *n* viaje *m*

vulgar ['vʌlgə*] *adj* (*rude*) ordinario, grosero; (*in bad taste*) de mal gusto; **~ity** [-'gærɪtɪ] *n* grosería; mal gusto

vulnerable ['vʌlnərəbl] *adj* vulnerable

vulture ['vʌltʃə*] *n* buitre *m*

W, w

wad [wɔd] n bolita; (of banknotes etc) fajo

waddle ['wɔdl] vi anadear

wade [weid] vi: **to ~ through** (water) vadear; (fig: book) leer con dificultad; **wading pool** (US) n piscina para niños

wafer ['weifə*] n galleta, barquillo

waffle ['wɔfl] n (CULIN) gofre m ♦ vi dar el rollo

waft [wɔft] vt llevar por el aire ♦ vi flotar

wag [wæg] vt menear, agitar ♦ vi moverse, menearse

wage [weidʒ] n (also: ~s) sueldo, salario ♦ vt: **to ~ war** hacer la guerra; **~ earner** n asalariado/a; **~ packet** n sobre m de paga

wager ['weidʒə*] n apuesta

wag(g)on ['wægən] n (horse-drawn) carro; (BRIT: RAIL) vagón m

wail [weil] n gemido ♦ vi gemir

waist [weist] n cintura, talle m; **~coat** (BRIT) n chaleco; **~line** n talle m

wait [weit] n (interval) pausa ♦ vi esperar; **to lie in ~ for** acechar a; **I can't ~ to** (fig) estoy deseando; **to ~ for** esperar (a); **~ behind** vi quedarse; **~ on** vt fus servir a; **~er** n camarero; **~ing** n: **"no ~ing"** (BRIT: AUT) "prohibido estacionarse"; **~ing list** n lista de espera; **~ing room** n sala de espera; **~ress** n camarera

waive [weiv] vt suspender

wake [weik] (pt **woke** or **waked**, pp **woken** or **waked**) vt (also: **~ up**) despertar ♦ vi (also: **~ up**) despertarse ♦ n (for dead person) vela, velatorio; (NAUT) estela; **waken** vt, vi = wake

Wales [weilz] n País m de Gales; **the Prince of ~** el príncipe de Gales

walk [wɔːk] n (stroll) paseo; (hike) excursión f a pie, caminata; (gait) paso, andar m; (in park etc) paseo, alameda ♦ vi andar, caminar; (for pleasure, exercise) pasear ♦ vt (distance) recorrer a pie, andar; (dog) pasear; **10 minutes' ~**

from here a 10 minutos de aquí andando; **people from all ~s of life** gente de todas las esferas; **~ out** vi (audience) salir; (workers) declararse en huelga; **~ out on** (inf) vt fus abandonar; **~er** n (person) paseante m/f, caminante m/f; **~ie-talkie** ['wɔːkɪ'tɔːkɪ] n walkie-talkie m; **~ing** n el andar; **~ing shoes** npl zapatos mpl para andar; **~ing stick** n bastón m; **W~man** ® ['wɔːkmən] n Walkman ® m; **~out** n huelga; **~over** (inf) n: **it was a ~over** fue pan comido; **~way** n paseo

wall [wɔːl] n pared f; (exterior) muro; (city ~ etc) muralla; **~ed** adj amurallado; (garden) con tapia

wallet ['wɔlɪt] n cartera (SP), billetera (AM)

wallflower ['wɔːlflauə*] n alhelí m; **to be a ~** (fig) comer pavo

wallow ['wɔləu] vi revolcarse

wallpaper ['wɔːlpeipə*] n papel m pintado ♦ vt empapelar

walnut ['wɔːlnʌt] n nuez f; (tree) nogal m

walrus ['wɔːlrəs] (pl ~ or **~es**) n morsa

waltz [wɔːlts] n vals m ♦ vi bailar el vals

wand [wɔnd] n (also: **magic ~**) varita (mágica)

wander ['wɔndə*] vi (person) vagar; deambular; (thoughts) divagar ♦ vt recorrer, vagar por

wane [wein] vi menguar

wangle ['wæŋgl] (BRIT: inf) vt agenciarse

want [wɔnt] vt querer, desear; (need) necesitar ♦ n: **for ~ of** por falta de; **~s** npl (needs) necesidades fpl; **to ~ to do** querer hacer; **to ~ sb to do sth** querer que uno haga algo; **~ed** adj (criminal) buscado; **"~ed"** (in advertisements) "se busca"; **~ing** adj: **to be found ~ing** no estar a la altura de las circunstancias

war [wɔː*] n guerra; **to make ~ (on)** (also fig) declarar la guerra (a)

ward [wɔːd] n (in hospital) sala; (POL) distrito electoral; (LAW: child: also: **~ of court**) pupilo/a; **~ off** vt (blow) desviar, parar; (attack) rechazar

warden ['wɔːdn] n (BRIT: of institution)

director(a) *m/f*; (*of park, game reserve*) guardián/ana *m/f*; (BRIT: *also*: **traffic ~**) guardia *m/f*

warder ['wɔːdə*] (BRIT) *n* guardián/ana *m/ f*, carcelero/a

wardrobe ['wɔːdrəub] *n* armario, guardarropa, ropero (*esp AM*)

warehouse ['wɛəhaus] *n* almacén *m*, depósito

wares [wɛəz] *npl* mercancías *fpl*

warfare ['wɔːfɛə*] *n* guerra

warhead ['wɔːhɛd] *n* cabeza armada

warily ['wɛərɪlɪ] *adv* con cautela, cautelosamente

warm [wɔːm] *adj* caliente; (*thanks*) efusivo; (*clothes etc*) abrigado; (*welcome, day*) caluroso; **it's ~** hace calor; **I'm ~** tengo calor; **~ up** *vi* (*room*) calentarse; (*person*) entrar en calor; (*athlete*) hacer ejercicios de calentamiento ♦ *vt* calentar; **~-hearted** *adj* afectuoso; **~ly** *adv* afectuosamente; **~th** *n* calor *m*

warn [wɔːn] *vt* avisar, advertir; **~ing** *n* aviso, advertencia; **~ing light** *n* luz *f* de advertencia; **~ing triangle** *n* (AUT) triángulo señalizador

warp [wɔːp] *vi* (*wood*) combarse ♦ *vt* combar; (*mind*) pervertir

warrant ['wɔrənt] *n* autorización *f*; (LAW: *to arrest*) orden *f* de detención; (*: to search*) mandamiento de registro

warranty ['wɔrəntɪ] *n* garantía

warren ['wɔrən] *n* (*of rabbits*) madriguera; (*fig*) laberinto

warrior ['wɔrɪə*] *n* guerrero/a

Warsaw ['wɔːsɔː] *n* Varsovia

warship ['wɔːʃɪp] *n* buque *m* o barco de guerra

wart [wɔːt] *n* verruga

wartime ['wɔːtaɪm] *n*: **in ~** en tiempos de guerra, en la guerra

wary ['wɛərɪ] *adj* cauteloso

was [wɔz] *pt of* **be**

wash [wɔʃ] *vt* lavar ♦ *vi* lavarse; (*sea etc*): **to ~ against/over sth** llegar hasta/cubrir algo ♦ *n* (*clothes etc*) lavado; (*of ship*) estela; **to have a ~** lavarse; **~ away** *vt*

(*stain*) quitar lavando; (*subj: river etc*) llevarse; **~ off** *vi* quitarse (al lavar); **~ up** *vi* (BRIT) fregar los platos; (US) lavarse; **~able** *adj* lavable; **~basin** (US **~bowl**) *n* lavabo; **~ cloth** (US) *n* manopla; **~er** *n* (TECH) arandela; **~ing** *n* (*dirty*) ropa sucia; (*clean*) colada; **~ing machine** *n* lavadora; **~ing powder** (BRIT) *n* detergente *m* (en polvo)

Washington ['wɔʃɪŋtən] *n* Washington *m*

wash: ~ing-up (BRIT) *n* fregado, platos *mpl* (para fregar); **~ing-up liquid** (BRIT) *n* líquido lavavajillas; **~-out** (*inf*) *n* fracaso; **~room** (US) *n* servicios *mpl*

wasn't ['wɔznt] = **was not**

wasp [wɔsp] *n* avispa

wastage ['weɪstɪdʒ] *n* desgaste *m*; (*loss*) pérdida

waste [weɪst] *n* derroche *m*, despilfarro; (*of time*) pérdida; (*food*) sobras *fpl*; (*rubbish*) basura, desperdicios *mpl* ♦ *adj* (*material*) de desecho; (*left over*) sobrante; (*land*) baldío, descampado ♦ *vt* malgastar, derrochar; (*time*) perder; (*opportunity*) desperdiciar; **~s** *npl* (*area of land*) tierras *fpl* baldías; **~ away** *vi* consumirse; **~ disposal unit** (BRIT) *n* triturador *m* de basura; **~ful** *adj* derrochador(a); (*process*) antieconómico; **~ ground** (BRIT) *n* terreno baldío; **~paper basket** *n* papelera; **~ pipe** *n* tubo de desagüe

watch [wɔtʃ] *n* (*also*: **wrist ~**) reloj *m*; (MIL: *group of guards*) centinela *m*; (*act*) vigilancia; (NAUT: *spell of duty*) guardia ♦ *vt* (*look at*) mirar, observar; (*: match, programme*) ver; (*spy on, guard*) vigilar; (*be careful of*) cuidarse de, tener cuidado de ♦ *vi* ver, mirar; (*keep guard*) montar guardia; **~ out** *vi* cuidarse, tener cuidado; **~dog** *n* perro guardián; (*fig*) *persona u organismo encargado de asegurarse de que las empresas actúan dentro de la legalidad*; **~ful** *adj* vigilante, sobre aviso; **~maker** *n* relojero/a; **~man** (*irreg*) *n see* **night**; **~ strap** *n* pulsera (de reloj)

water ['wɔːtə*] *n* agua ♦ *vt* (*plant*) regar
♦ *vi* (*eyes*) llorar; (*mouth*) hacerse la boca
agua; ~ **down** *vt* (*milk etc*) aguar; (*fig:
story*) dulcificar, diluir; ~ **closet** *n* wáter
m; ~**colour** *n* acuarela; ~**cress** *n* berro;
~**fall** *n* cascada, salto de agua; ~**heater**
n calentador *m* de agua; ~**ing can** *n*
regadera; ~ **lily** *n* nenúfar *m*; ~**line** *n*
(*NAUT*) línea de flotación; ~**logged** *adj*
(*ground*) inundado; ~ **main** *n* cañería del
agua; ~**melon** *n* sandía; ~**proof** *adj*
impermeable; ~**shed** *n* (*GEO*) cuenca;
(*fig*) momento crítico; ~-**skiing** *n* esquí
m acuático; ~**tight** *adj* hermético; ~**way**
n vía fluvial *or* navegable; ~**works** *n*
central *f* depuradora; ~**y** *adj* (*coffee etc*)
aguado; (*eyes*) lloroso

watt [wɔt] *n* vatio

wave [weɪv] *n* (*of hand*) señal *f* con la
mano; (*on water*) ola; (*RADIO, in hair*)
onda; (*fig*) oleada ♦ *vi* agitar la mano;
(*flag etc*) ondear ♦ *vt* (*handkerchief, gun*)
agitar; ~**length** *n* longitud *f* de onda

waver ['weɪvə*] *vi* (*voice, love etc*) flaquear;
(*person*) vacilar

wavy ['weɪvɪ] *adj* ondulado

wax [wæks] *n* cera ♦ *vt* encerar ♦ *vi*
(*moon*) crecer; ~ **paper** (*US*) *n* papel *m*
apergaminado; ~**works** *n* museo de cera
♦ *npl* figuras *fpl* de cera

way [weɪ] *n* camino; (*distance*) trayecto,
recorrido; (*direction*) dirección *f*, sentido;
(*manner*) modo, manera; (*habit*)
costumbre *f*; **which ~? — this ~** ¿por
dónde?, ¿en qué dirección? — por aquí;
on the ~ (*en route*) en (el) camino; **to be
on one's ~** estar en camino; **to be in the
~** bloquear el camino; (*fig*) estorbar; **to
go out of one's ~ to do sth** desvivirse
por hacer algo; **under ~** en marcha; **to
lose one's ~** extraviarse; **in a ~** en cierto
modo *or* sentido; **no ~!** (*inf*) ¡de eso
nada!; **by the ~** ... a propósito ...; **"~ in"**
(*BRIT*) "entrada"; **"~ out"** (*BRIT*) "salida";
the ~ back el camino de vuelta; **"give
~"** (*BRIT: AUT*) "ceda el paso"

waylay [weɪ'leɪ] (*irreg*) *vt* salir al paso a

wayward ['weɪwəd] *adj* díscolo

W.C. *n* (*BRIT*) wáter *m*

we [wiː] *pl pron* nosotros/as

weak [wiːk] *adj* débil, flojo; (*tea etc*) claro;
~**en** *vi* debilitarse; (*give way*) ceder ♦ *vt*
debilitar; ~**ling** *n* debilucho/a; (*morally*)
persona de poco carácter; ~**ness** *n*
debilidad *f*; (*fault*) punto débil; **to have a
~ness for** tener debilidad para

wealth [welθ] *n* riqueza; (*of details*)
abundancia; ~**y** *adj* rico

wean [wiːn] *vt* destetar

weapon ['wepən] *n* arma

wear [weə*] (*pt* **wore**, *pp* **worn**) *n* (*use*)
uso; (*deterioration through use*) desgaste
m; (*clothing*): **sports/baby** ~ ropa de
deportes/de niños ♦ *vt* (*clothes*) llevar;
(*shoes*) calzar; (*damage: through use*)
gastar, usar ♦ *vi* (*last*) durar; (*rub through
etc*) desgastarse; **evening** ~ ropa de
etiqueta; ~ **away** *vt* gastar ♦ *vi*
desgastarse; ~ **down** *vt* gastar; (*strength*)
agotar; ~ **off** *vi* (*pain etc*) pasar,
desaparecer; ~ **out** *vt* desgastar; (*person,
strength*) agotar; ~ **and tear** *n* desgaste
m

weary ['wɪərɪ] *adj* cansado; (*dispirited*)
abatido ♦ *vi*: **to ~ of** cansarse de

weasel ['wiːzl] *n* (*ZOOL*) comadreja

weather ['weðə*] *n* tiempo ♦ *vt* (*storm,
crisis*) hacer frente a; **under the ~** (*fig: ill*)
indispuesto, pachucho; ~-**beaten** *adj*
(*skin*) curtido; (*building*) deteriorado por la
intemperie; ~**cock** *n* veleta; ~ **forecast**
n boletín *m* meteorológico; ~**man** (*irreg:
inf*) *n* hombre *m* del tiempo; ~ **vane** *n*
= ~**cock**

weave [wiːv] (*pt* **wove**, *pp* **woven**) *vt*
(*cloth*) tejer; (*fig*) entretejer; ~**r** *n*
tejedor(a) *m/f*; **weaving** *n* tejeduría

web [web] *n* (*of spider*) telaraña; (*on duck's
foot*) membrana; (*network*) red *f*

website ['websaɪt] *n* espacio Web

wed [wed] (*pt, pp* **wedded**) *vt* casar ♦ *vi*
casarse

we'd [wiːd] = **we had; we would**

wedding ['wedɪŋ] *n* boda, casamiento;

silver/golden ~ (anniversary) bodas *fpl* de plata/de oro; **~ day** *n* día *m* de la boda; **~ dress** *n* traje *m* de novia; **~ present** *n* regalo de boda; **~ ring** *n* alianza

wedge [wedʒ] *n* (of wood etc) cuña; (of cake) trozo ♦ *vt* acuñar; (push) apretar

Wednesday ['wednzdı] *n* miércoles *m inv*

wee [wiː] (Scottish) *adj* pequeñito

weed [wiːd] *n* mala hierba, maleza ♦ *vt* escardar, desherbar; **~killer** *n* herbicida *m*; **~y** *adj* (person) mequetréfico

week [wiːk] *n* semana; **a ~ today/on Friday** de hoy/del viernes en ocho días; **~day** *n* día *m* laborable; **~end** *n* fin *m* de semana; **~ly** *adv* semanalmente, cada semana ♦ *adj* semanal ♦ *n* semanario

weep [wiːp] (pt, pp **wept**) *vi*, *vt* llorar; **~ing willow** *n* sauce *m* llorón

weigh [weı] *vt*, *vi* pesar; **to ~ anchor** levar anclas; **~ down** *vt* sobrecargar; (fig: with worry) agobiar; **~ up** *vt* sopesar

weight [weıt] *n* peso; (metal ~) pesa; **to lose/put on ~** adelgazar/engordar; **~ing** *n* (allowance): **(London) ~ing** dietas (por residir en Londres); **~lifter** *n* levantador *m* de pesas; **~y** *adj* pesado; (matters) de relevancia *or* peso

weir [wıə*] *n* presa

weird [wıəd] *adj* raro, extraño

welcome ['welkəm] *adj* bienvenido ♦ *n* bienvenida ♦ *vt* dar la bienvenida a; (be glad of) alegrarse de; **thank you – you're ~** gracias – de nada

weld [weld] *n* soldadura ♦ *vt* soldar

welfare ['welfeə*] *n* bienestar *m*; (social aid) asistencia social; **~ state** *n* estado del bienestar

well [wel] *n* fuente *f*, pozo ♦ *adv* bien ♦ *adj*: **to be ~** estar bien (de salud) ♦ *excl* ¡vaya!, ¡bueno!; **as ~** también; **as ~ as** además de; **~ done!** ¡bien hecho!; **get ~ soon!** ¡que te mejores pronto!; **to do ~** (business) ir bien; (person) tener éxito; **~ up** *vi* (tears) saltar

we'll [wiːl] = **we will; we shall**

well: ~-behaved *adj* bueno; **~-being** *n*

bienestar *m*; **~-built** *adj* (person) fornido; **~-deserved** *adj* merecido; **~-dressed** *adj* bien vestido; **~-groomed** *adj* de buena presencia; **~-off** *adj* acomodado; **~-read** *adj* leído; **~-to-do** *adj* acomodado; **~-wisher** *n* admirador(a) *m/f*

wellingtons ['welıŋtənz] *npl* (also: **wellington boots**) botas *fpl* de goma

well: ~-known *adj* (person) conocido; **~-mannered** *adj* educado; **~-meaning** *adj* bienintencionado; **~-off** *adj* acomodado; **~-read** *adj* leído; **~-to-do** *adj* acomodado; **~-wisher** *n* admirador(a) *m/f*

Welsh [welʃ] *adj* galés/esa ♦ *n* (LING) galés *m*; **the ~** *npl* los galeses; **~man** (irreg) *n* galés *m*; **~ rarebit** *n* pan *m* con queso tostado; **~woman** (irreg) *n* galesa

went [went] *pt of* **go**

wept [wept] *pt, pp of* **weep**

were [wə:*] *pt of* **be**

we're [wıə*] = **we are**

weren't [wə:nt] = **were not**

west [west] *n* oeste *m* ♦ *adj* occidental, del oeste ♦ *adv* al *or* hacia el oeste; **the W~** el Oeste, el Occidente; **W~ Country** (BRIT) *n*: **the W~ Country** el suroeste de Inglaterra; **~erly** *adj* occidental; (wind) del oeste; **~ern** *adj* occidental ♦ *n* (CINEMA) película del oeste; **W~ Germany** *n* Alemania Occidental; **W~ Indian** *adj*, *n* antillano/a *m/f*; **W~ Indies** *npl* Antillas *fpl*; **~ward(s)** *adv* hacia el oeste

wet [wet] *adj* (damp) húmedo; (~ through) mojado; (rainy) lluvioso ♦ (BRIT) *n* (POL) conservador(a) *m/f* moderado/a; **to get ~** mojarse; **"~ paint"** "recién pintado"; **~suit** *n* traje *m* térmico

we've [wiːv] = **we have**

whack [wæk] *vt* dar un buen golpe a

whale [weıl] *n* (ZOOL) ballena

wharf [wɔːf] (pl **wharves**) *n* muelle *m*

KEYWORD
---

what [wɔt] *adj* 1 (in direct/indirect questions) qué; **~ size is he?** ¿qué talla usa?; **~ colour/shape is it?** ¿de qué

color/forma es?
2 (*in exclamations*): ~ **a mess!** ¡qué
desastre!; ~ **a fool I am!** ¡qué tonto soy!
♦ *pron* 1 (*interrogative*) qué; ~ **are you
doing?** ¿qué haces *or* estás haciendo?; ~
is happening? ¿qué pasa *or* está
pasando?; ~ **is it called?** ¿cómo se
llama?; ~ **about me?** ¿y yo qué?; ~ **about
doing ...?** ¿qué tal si hacemos ...?
2 (*relative*) lo que; **I saw ~ you did/was on
the table** vi lo que hiciste/había en la mesa
♦ *excl* (*disbelieving*) ¡cómo!; ~, **no coffee!**
¡que no hay café!

whatever [wɔt'ɛvə*] *adj*: ~ **book you
choose** cualquier libro que elijas ♦ *pron*:
do ~ is necessary haga lo que sea
necesario; ~ **happens** pase lo que pase;
no reason ~ ninguna razón sea la que
sea; **nothing ~** nada en absoluto
whatsoever [wɔtsəu'ɛvə*] *adj* = **whatever**
wheat [wiːt] *n* trigo
wheedle ['wiːdl] *vt*: **to ~ sb into doing
sth** engatusar a uno para que haga algo;
to ~ sth out of sb sonsacar algo a uno
wheel [wiːl] *n* rueda; (AUT: *also*: **steering
~**) volante *m*; (NAUT) timón *m* ♦ *vt* (*pram
etc*) empujar *m* ♦ *vi* (*also*: ~ **round**) dar la
vuelta, girar; ~**barrow** *n* carretilla;
~**chair** *n* silla de ruedas; ~ **clamp** *n*
(AUT) cepo
wheeze [wiːz] *vi* resollar

when [wɛn] *adv* cuando; ~ **did it happen?**
¿cuándo ocurrió?; **I know ~ it happened**
sé cuándo ocurrió
♦ *conj* 1 (*at, during, after the time that*)
cuando; **be careful ~ you cross the road**
ten cuidado al cruzar la calle; **that was ~
I needed you** fue entonces que te
necesité
2 (*on, at which*): **on the day ~ I met him**
el día en qué lo conocí
3 (*whereas*) cuando

whenever [wɛn'ɛvə*] *conj* cuando; (*every
time that*) cada vez que ♦ *adv* cuando
sea
where [wɛə*] *adv* dónde ♦ *conj* donde;
this is ~ aquí es donde; ~**abouts** *adv*
dónde ♦ *n*: **nobody knows his ~abouts**
nadie conoce su paradero; ~**as** *conj* visto
que, mientras; ~**by** *pron* por lo cual;
wherever [-'ɛvə*] *conj* dondequiera que;
(*interrogative*) dónde; ~**withal** *n* recursos
mpl
whether ['wɛðə*] *conj* si; **I don't know ~
to accept or not** no sé si aceptar o no; ~
you go or not vayas o no vayas

which [wɪtʃ] *adj* 1 (*interrogative: direct,
indirect*) qué; ~ **picture(s) do you want?**
¿qué cuadro(s) quieres?; ~ **one?** ¿cuál?
2: **in ~ case** en cuyo caso; **we got there
at 8 pm, by ~ time the cinema was full**
llegamos allí a las 8, cuando el cine
estaba lleno
♦ *pron* 1 (*interrogative*) cuál; **I don't mind
~** el/la que sea
2 (*relative: replacing noun*) que;
(: *replacing clause*) lo que; (: *after
preposition*) (el/la) que *etc*, el/la cual *etc*;
the apple ~ you ate/~ is on the table la
manzana que comiste/que está en la
mesa; **the chair on ~ you are sitting** la
silla en la que estás sentado; **he said he
knew, ~ is true/I feared** dijo que lo
sabía, lo cual *or* lo que es cierto/me temí.

whichever [wɪtʃ'ɛvə*] *adj*: **take ~ book
you prefer** coja (SP) el libro que prefiera,
~ **book you take** cualquier libro que coja
while [waɪl] *n* rato, momento ♦ *conj*
mientras; (*although*) aunque; **for a ~**
durante algún tiempo; ~ **away** *vt* pasar
whim [wɪm] *n* capricho
whimper ['wɪmpə*] *n* sollozo ♦ *vi*
lloriquear
whimsical ['wɪmzɪkl] *adj* (*person*)
caprichoso; (*look*) juguetón/ona
whine [waɪn] *n* (*of pain*) gemido; (*of*

engine) zumbido; (of siren) aullido ♦ vi
gemir; zumbar; (fig: complain) gimotear
whip [wɪp] n látigo; (POL: person)
encargado de la disciplina partidaria en
el parlamento ♦ vt azotar; (CULIN) batir;
(move quickly): **to ~ sth out/off** sacar/
quitar algo de un tirón; **~ped cream** n
nata or crema montada; **~-round** (BRIT)
n colecta
whirl [wəːl] vt hacer girar, dar vueltas a
♦ vi girar, dar vueltas; (leaves etc)
arremolinarse; **~pool** n remolino; **~wind**
n torbellino
whirr [wəː*] vi zumbar
whisk [wɪsk] n (CULIN) batidor m ♦ vt
(CULIN) batir; **to ~ sb away** or **off** llevar
volando a uno
whiskers ['wɪskəz] npl (of animal) bigotes
mpl; (of man) patillas fpl
whiskey ['wɪskɪ] (US, Ireland) n = **whisky**
whisky ['wɪskɪ] n whisky m
whisper ['wɪspə*] n susurro ♦ vi, vt
susurrar
whistle ['wɪsl] n (sound) silbido; (object)
silbato ♦ vi silbar
white [waɪt] adj blanco; (pale) pálido ♦ n
blanco; (of egg) clara; **~ coffee** (BRIT) n
café m con leche; **~-collar worker** n
oficinista m/f; **~ elephant** n (fig) maula;
~ lie n mentirilla; **~ paper** n (POL) libro
rojo; **~wash** n (paint) jalbegue m, cal f
♦ vt (also fig) blanquear
whiting ['waɪtɪŋ] n inv (fish) pescadilla
Whitsun ['wɪtsn] n pentecostés m
whizz [wɪz] vi: **to ~ past** or **by** pasar a
toda velocidad; **~ kid** (inf) n prodigio

KEYWORD

who [huː] pron 1 (interrogative) quién; **~ is
it?, ~'s there?** ¿quién es?; **~ are you
looking for?** ¿a quién buscas?; **I told her
~ I was** le dije quién era yo
2 (relative) que; **the man/woman ~
spoke to me** el hombre/la mujer que
habló conmigo; **those ~ can swim** los
que saben or sepan nadar

whodun(n)it [huː'dʌnɪt] (inf) n novela
policíaca
whoever [huː'ɛvə*] pron: **~ finds it**
cualquiera or quienquiera que lo
encuentre; **ask ~ you like** pregunta a
quien quieras; **~ he marries** no importa
con quién se case
whole [həʊl] adj (entire) todo, entero; (not
broken) intacto ♦ n todo; (all): **the ~ of
the town** toda la ciudad, la ciudad entera
♦ n (total) total m; (sum) conjunto; **on
the ~, as a ~** en general; **~food(s)** n(pl)
alimento(s) m(pl) integral(es); **~hearted**
adj sincero, cordial; **~meal** adj integral;
~sale n venta al por mayor ♦ adj al por
mayor; (fig: destruction) sistemático;
~saler n mayorista m/f; **~some** adj
sano; **~wheat** adj = **~meal**; **wholly** adv
totalmente, enteramente

KEYWORD

whom [huːm] pron 1 (interrogative): **~ did
you see?** ¿a quién viste?; **to ~ did you
give it?** ¿a quién se lo diste?; **tell me
from ~ you received it** dígame de quién
lo recibió
2 (relative) que; **to ~** a quien(es); **of ~** de
quien(es), del/de la que etc; **the man ~ I
saw/to ~ I wrote** el hombre que vi/a
quien escribí; **the lady about/with ~ I
was talking** la señora de (la) que/con
quien or (la) que hablaba

whooping cough ['huːpɪŋ-] n tos f
ferina
whore [hɔː*] (inf: pej) n puta

KEYWORD

whose [huːz] adj 1 (possessive:
interrogative): **~ book is this?, ~ is this
book?** ¿de quién es este libro?; **~ pencil
have you taken?** ¿de quién es el lápiz
que has cogido?; **~ daughter are you?**
¿de quién eres hija?
2 (possessive: relative) cuyo/a, pl cuyos/as;
the man ~ son you rescued el hombre
cuyo hijo rescataste; **those ~ passports I**

have aquellas personas cuyos pasaportes tengo; **the woman ~ car was stolen** la mujer a quien le robaron el coche ♦ *pron* de quién; **~ is this?** ¿de quién es esto?; **I know ~ it is** sé de quién es

---

why [waɪ] *adv* por qué; **~ not?** ¿por qué no?; **~ not do it now?** ¿por qué no lo haces (*or* hacemos *etc*) ahora?
♦ *conj*: **I wonder ~ he said that** me pregunto por qué dijo eso; **that's not ~ I'm here** no es por eso (por lo que) que estoy aquí; **the reason ~** la razón por la que
♦ *excl* (*expressing surprise, shock, annoyance*) ¡hombre!, ¡vaya! (*explaining*): **~, it's you!** ¡hombre, eres tú!; **~, that's impossible!** ¡pero sí eso es imposible!

---

wicked ['wɪkɪd] *adj* malvado, cruel
wicket ['wɪkɪt] *n* (CRICKET: *stumps*) palos *mpl*; (: *grass area*) terreno de juego
wide [waɪd] *adj* ancho; (*area, knowledge*) vasto, grande; (*choice*) amplio ♦ *adv*: **to open ~** abrir de par en par; **to shoot ~** errar el tiro; **~-angle lens** *n* objetivo de gran angular; **~-awake** *adj* bien despierto; **~ly** *adv* (*travelled*) mucho; (*spaced*) muy; **it is ~ly believed/known that ...** mucha gente piensa/sabe que ...; **~n** *vt* ensanchar; (*experience*) ampliar ♦ *vi* ensancharse; **~ open** *adj* abierto de par en par; **~spread** *adj* extendido, general
widow ['wɪdəu] *n* viuda; **~ed** *adj* viudo; **~er** *n* viudo
width [wɪdθ] *n* anchura; (*of cloth*) ancho
wield [wi:ld] *vt* (*sword*) blandir; (*power*) ejercer
wife [waɪf] (*pl* **wives**) *n* mujer *f*, esposa
wig [wɪg] *n* peluca
wiggle ['wɪgl] *vt* menear
wild [waɪld] *adj* (*animal*) salvaje; (*plant*) silvestre; (*person*) furioso, violento; (*idea*) descabellado; (*rough: sea*) bravo; (: *land*) agreste; (: *weather*) muy revuelto; **~s** *npl*

regiones *fpl* salvajes, tierras *fpl* vírgenes; **~erness** ['wɪldənɪs] *n* desierto; **~life** *n* fauna; **~ly** *adv* (*behave*) locamente; (*lash out*) a diestro y siniestro; (*guess*) a lo loco; (*happy*) a más no poder
wilful ['wɪlful] (*US* **willful**) *adj* (*action*) deliberado; (*obstinate*) testarudo

---

will [wɪl] *aux vb* **1** (*forming future tense*): **I ~ finish it tomorrow** lo terminaré *or* voy a terminar mañana; **I ~ have finished it by tomorrow** lo habré terminado para mañana; **~ you do it? – yes I ~/no I won't** ¿lo harás? — sí/no
2 (*in conjectures, predictions*): **he ~** *or* **he'll be there by now** ya habrá llegado; **that ~ be the postman** será *or* debe ser el cartero
3 (*in commands, requests, offers*): **~ you be quiet!** ¡quieres callarte!; **~ you help me?** ¿quieres ayudarme?; **~ you have a cup of tea?** ¿te apetece un té?; **I won't put up with it!** ¡no lo soporto!
♦ *vt* (*pt, pp* **willed**): **to ~ sb to do sth** desear que alguien haga algo; **he ~ed himself to go on** con gran fuerza de voluntad, continuó
♦ *n* voluntad *f*; (*testament*) testamento

---

willing ['wɪlɪŋ] *adj* (*with goodwill*) de buena voluntad; (*enthusiastic*) entusiasta; **he's ~ to do it** está dispuesto a hacerlo; **~ly** *adv* con mucho gusto; **~ness** *n* buena voluntad
willow ['wɪləu] *n* sauce *m*
willpower ['wɪlpauə*] *n* fuerza de voluntad
willy-nilly [wɪlɪ'nɪlɪ] *adv* quiérase o no
wilt [wɪlt] *vi* marchitarse
win [wɪn] (*pt, pp* **won**) *n* victoria, triunfo
♦ *vt* ganar; (*obtain*) conseguir, lograr ♦ *vi* ganar; **~ over** *vt* convencer a; **~ round** (*BRIT*) *vt* = **~ over**
wince [wɪns] *vi* encogerse
winch [wɪntʃ] *n* torno
wind¹ [wɪnd] *n* viento; (MED) gases *mpl*

♦ vt (take breath away from) dejar sin aliento a
wind² [waind] (pt, pp **wound**) vt enrollar; (wrap) envolver; (clock, toy) dar cuerda a ♦ vi (road, river) serpentear; **~ up** vt (clock) dar cuerda a; (debate, meeting) concluir, terminar
windfall ['windfɔːl] n golpe m de suerte
winding ['waindiŋ] adj (road) tortuoso; (staircase) de caracol
wind instrument [wind-] n (MUS) instrumento de viento
windmill ['windmil] n molino de viento
window ['windəu] n ventana; (in car, train) ventanilla; (in shop etc) escaparate m (SP), vitrina (AM); **~ box** n jardinera de ventana; **~ cleaner** n (person) limpiador m de cristales; **~ ledge** n alféizar m, repisa; **~ pane** n cristal m; **~-shopping** n: **to go ~-shopping** ir de escaparates; **~sill** n alféizar m, repisa
windpipe ['windpaip] n tráquea
wind power n energía eólica
windscreen ['windskriːn] (US **windshield**) n parabrisas m inv; **~ washer** n lavaparabrisas m inv; **~ wiper** n limpiaparabrisas m inv
windswept ['windswept] adj azotado por el viento
windy ['windi] adj de mucho viento; **it's ~** hace viento
wine [wain] n vino; **~ bar** n enoteca; **~ cellar** n bodega; **~ glass** n copa (para vino); **~ list** n lista de vinos; **~ waiter** n escanciador m
wing [wiŋ] n ala; (AUT) aleta; **~s** npl (THEATRE) bastidores mpl; **~er** n (SPORT) extremo
wink [wiŋk] n guiño, pestañeo ♦ vi guiñar, pestañear
winner ['winə*] n ganador(a) m/f
winning ['winiŋ] adj (team) ganador(a); (goal) decisivo; (smile) encantador(a); **~s** npl ganancias fpl
winter ['wintə*] n invierno ♦ vi invernar; **wintry** ['wintri] adj invernal
wipe [waip] n: **to give sth a ~** pasar un

trapo sobre algo ♦ vt limpiar, borrar; **~ off** vt limpiar con un trapo; (remove) quitar; **~ out** vt (debt) liquidar; (memory) borrar; (destroy) destruir; **~ up** vt limpiar
wire ['waiə*] n alambre m; (ELEC) cable m (eléctrico); (TEL) telegrama m ♦ vt (house) poner la instalación eléctrica en; (also: **~ up**) conectar; (person: telegram) telegrafiar
wireless ['waiəlis] (BRIT) n radio f
wiring ['waiəriŋ] n instalación f eléctrica
wiry ['waiəri] adj (person) enjuto y fuerte; (hair) crespo
wisdom ['wizdəm] n sabiduría, saber m; (good sense) cordura; **~ tooth** n muela del juicio
wise [waiz] adj sabio; (sensible) juicioso
...wise [waiz] suffix: **time~** en cuanto a or respecto al tiempo
wish [wiʃ] n deseo ♦ vt querer; **best ~es** (on birthday etc) felicidades fpl; **with best ~es** (in letter) saludos mpl, recuerdos mpl; **to ~ sb goodbye** despedirse de uno; **he ~ed me well** me deseó mucha suerte; **to ~ to do/sb to do sth** querer hacer/ que alguien haga algo; **to ~ for** desear; **~ful** adj: **it's ~ful thinking** eso sería soñar
wisp [wisp] n mechón m; (of smoke) voluta
wistful ['wistful] adj pensativo
wit [wit] n ingenio, gracia; (also: **~s**) inteligencia; (person) chistoso/a
witch [witʃ] n bruja; **~craft** n brujería; **~-hunt** n (fig) caza de brujas

KEYWORD

with [wið, wiθ] prep **1** (accompanying, in the company of) con (con+mí, ti, sí = conmigo, contigo, consigo); **I was ~ him** estaba con él; **we stayed ~ friends** nos quedamos en casa de unos amigos; **I'm (not) ~ you** (understand) (no) te entiendo; **to be ~ it** (inf: person: up-to-date) estar al tanto; (: alert) ser despabilado
2 (descriptive, indicating manner etc) con; de; **a room ~ a view** una habitación con vistas; **the man ~ the grey hat/blue eyes** el hombre del sombrero gris/de los

ojos azules; **red ~ anger** rojo de ira; **to shake ~ fear** temblar de miedo; **to fill sth ~ water** llenar algo de agua

withdraw [wɪθ'drɔː] (*irreg*) *vt* retirar, sacar ♦ *vi* retirarse; **to ~ money (from the bank)** retirar fondos (del banco); **~al** *n* retirada; (*of money*) reintegro; **~al symptoms** *npl* (*MED*) síndrome *m* de abstinencia; **~n** *adj* (*person*) reservado, introvertido

wither ['wɪðə*] *vi* marchitarse

withhold [wɪθ'həuld] (*irreg*) *vt* (*money*) retener; (*decision*) aplazar; (*permission*) negar; (*information*) ocultar

within [wɪð'ɪn] *prep* dentro de ♦ *adv* dentro; **~ reach (of)** al alcance (de); **~ sight (of)** a la vista (de); **~ the week** antes de acabar la semana; **~ a mile (of)** a menos de una milla (de)

without [wɪð'aut] *prep* sin; **to go ~ sth** pasar sin algo

withstand [wɪθ'stænd] (*irreg*) *vt* resistir a

witness ['wɪtnɪs] *n* testigo *m/f* ♦ *vt* (*event*) presenciar; (*document*) atestiguar la veracidad de; **to bear ~ to** (*fig*) ser testimonio de; **~ box** *n* tribuna de los testigos; **~ stand** (*US*) *n* = **~ box**

witty ['wɪtɪ] *adj* ingenioso

wives [waɪvz] *npl* of **wife**

wk *abbr* = **week**

wobble ['wɔbl] *vi* temblar; (*chair*) cojear

woe [wəu] *n* desgracia

woke [wəuk] *pt* of **wake**

woken ['wəukən] *pp* of **wake**

wolf [wulf] *n* lobo; **wolves** [wulvz] *npl* of **wolf**

woman ['wumən] (*pl* **women**) *n* mujer *f*; **~ doctor** *n* médica; **women's lib** (*inf: pej*) *n* liberación *f* de la mujer; **~ly** *adj* femenino

womb [wuːm] *n* matriz *f*, útero

women ['wɪmɪn] *npl* of **woman**

won [wʌn] *pt, pp* of **win**

wonder ['wʌndə*] *n* maravilla, prodigio; (*feeling*) asombro ♦ *vi*: **to ~ whether/why** preguntarse si/por qué; **to ~ at** asombrarse de; **to ~ about** pensar sobre *or* en; **it's no ~ (that)** no es de extrañarse (que +*subjun*); **~ful** *adj* maravilloso

won't [wəunt] = **will not**

wood [wud] *n* (*timber*) madera; (*forest*) bosque *m*; **~ carving** *n* (*act*) tallado en madera; (*object*) talla en madera; **~ed** *adj* arbolado; **~en** *adj* de madera; (*fig*) inexpresivo; **~pecker** *n* pájaro carpintero; **~wind** *n* (*MUS*) instrumentos *mpl* de viento de madera; **~work** *n* carpintería; **~worm** *n* carcoma

wool [wul] *n* lana; **to pull the ~ over sb's eyes** (*fig*) engatusar a uno; **~en** (*US*) *adj* = **~len**; **~len** *adj* de lana; **~lens** *npl* géneros *mpl* de lana; **~ly** *adj* lanudo, de lana; (*fig: ideas*) confuso; **~y** (*US*) *adj* = **~ly**

word [wəːd] *n* palabra; (*news*) noticia; (*promise*) palabra (de honor) ♦ *vt* redactar; **in other ~s** en otras palabras; **to break/keep one's ~** faltar a la palabra/cumplir la promesa; **to have ~s with sb** reñir con uno; **~ing** *n* redacción *f*; **~ processing** *n* proceso de textos; **~ processor** *n* procesador *m* de textos

wore [wɔː*] *pt* of **wear**

work [wəːk] *n* trabajo; (*job*) empleo, trabajo; (*ART, LITERATURE*) obra ♦ *vi* trabajar; (*mechanism*) funcionar, marchar; (*medicine*) ser eficaz, surtir efecto ♦ *vt* (*shape*) trabajar; (*stone etc*) tallar; (*mine etc*) explotar; (*machine*) manejar, hacer funcionar ♦ **~s** *n* (*BRIT: factory*) fábrica ♦ *npl* (*of clock, machine*) mecanismo; **to be out of ~** estar parado, no tener trabajo; **to ~ loose** (*part*) desprenderse; (*knot*) aflojarse; **~ on** *vt fus* trabajar en, dedicarse a; (*principle*) basarse en; **~ out** *vi* (*plans etc*) salir bien, funcionar ♦ *vt* (*problem*) resolver; (*plan*) elaborar; **it ~s out at £100** suma 100 libras; **~ up** *vt*: **to get ~ed up** excitarse; **~able** *adj* (*solution*) práctico, factible; **~aholic** [wəːkə'hɔlɪk] *n* trabajador(a) obsesivo/a *m/f*; **~er** *n* trabajador(a) *m/f*, obrero/a; **~force** *n* mano *f* de obra; **~ing class** *n* clase f obrera; **~ing-class** adj obrero; **~ing order** n: **in ~ing order** en funcionamiento; **~man** (irreg) n obrero; **~manship** n habilidad f, trabajo; **~sheet** n hoja de trabajo; **~shop** n taller m; **~ station** n puesto or estación f de trabajo; **~-to-rule** (BRIT) n huelga de celo

world [wəːld] n mundo ♦ cpd (champion) del mundo; (power, war) mundial; **to think the ~ of sb** (fig) tener un concepto muy alto de uno; **~ly** adj mundano; **~-wide** adj mundial, universal; **W~-Wide Web** n: **the W~-Wide Web** el World Wide Web

worm [wəːm] n (also: **earth~**) lombriz f

worn [wɔːn] pp of **wear** ♦ adj usado; **~-out** adj (object) gastado; (person) rendido, agotado

worried ['wʌrɪd] adj preocupado

worry ['wʌrɪ] n preocupación f ♦ vt preocupar, inquietar ♦ vi preocuparse; **~ing** adj inquietante

worse [wəːs] adj, adv peor ♦ n lo peor; **a change for the ~** un empeoramiento; **~n** vt, vi empeorar; **~ off** adj (financially): **to be ~ off** tener menos dinero; (fig): **you'll be ~ off this way** de esta forma estarás peor que nunca

worship ['wəːʃɪp] n adoración f ♦ vt adorar; **Your W~** (BRIT: to mayor) señor alcalde; (: to judge) señor juez

worst [wəːst] adj, adv peor ♦ n lo peor; **at ~** en lo peor de los casos

worth [wəːθ] n valor m ♦ adj: **to be ~** valer; **it's ~ it** vale or merece la pena; **to be ~ one's while (to do)** merecer la pena (hacer); **~less** adj sin valor; (useless) inútil; **~while** adj (activity) que merece la pena; (cause) loable

worthy ['wəːðɪ] adj respetable; (motive) honesto; **~ of** digno de

would [wud] aux vb **1** (conditional tense): **if you asked him he ~ do it** si se lo pidieras, lo haría; **if you had asked him**

he ~ have done it si se lo hubieras pedido, lo habría or hubiera hecho **2** (in offers, invitations, requests): **~ you like a biscuit?** ¿quieres una galleta?; (formal) ¿querría una galleta?; **~ you ask him to come in?** ¿quiere hacerle pasar?; **~ you open the window please?** ¿quiere or podría abrir la ventana, por favor? **3** (in indirect speech): **I said I ~ do it** dije que lo haría **4** (emphatic): **it WOULD have to snow today!** ¡tenía que nevar precisamente hoy! **5** (insistence): **she ~n't behave** no quiso comportarse bien **6** (conjecture): **it ~ have been midnight** sería medianoche; **it ~ seem so** parece ser que sí **7** (indicating habit): **he ~ go there on Mondays** iba allí los lunes

would-be (pej) adj presunto

wouldn't ['wudnt] = **would not**

wound[1] [wuːnd] n herida ♦ vt herir

wound[2] [waund] pt, pp of **wind**

wove [wəuv] pt of **weave**

woven ['wəuvən] pp of **weave**

wrap [ræp] vt (also: **~ up**) envolver; **~per** n (on chocolate) papel m; (BRIT: of book) sobrecubierta; **~ping paper** n papel m de envolver; (fancy) papel m de regalo

wreak [riːk] vt: **to ~ havoc (on)** hacer estragos (en); **to ~ vengeance (on)** vengarse (de)

wreath [riːθ, pl riːðz] n (funeral ~) corona

wreck [rɛk] n (ship: destruction) naufragio; (: remains) restos mpl del barco; (pej: person) ruina ♦ vt (car etc) destrozar; (chances) arruinar; **~age** n restos mpl; (of building) escombros mpl

wren [rɛn] n (ZOOL) reyezuelo

wrench [rɛntʃ] n (TECH) llave f inglesa; (tug) tirón m; (fig) dolor m ♦ vt arrancar; **to ~ sth from sb** arrebatar algo violentamente a uno

wrestle ['rɛsl] vi: **to ~ (with sb)** luchar (con or contra uno); **~r** n luchador(a) m/f

(de lucha libre); **wrestling** n lucha libre
wretched ['rɛtʃɪd] adj miserable
wriggle ['rɪgl] vi (also: ~ **about**) menearse, retorcerse
wring [rɪŋ] (pt, pp **wrung**) vt retorcer; (wet clothes) escurrir; (fig): **to ~ sth out of sb** sacar algo por la fuerza a uno
wrinkle ['rɪŋkl] n arruga ♦ vt arrugar ♦ vi arrugarse
wrist [rɪst] n muñeca; **~watch** n reloj m de pulsera
writ [rɪt] n mandato judicial
write [raɪt] (pt **wrote**, pp **written**) vt escribir; (cheque) extender ♦ vi escribir; ~ **down** vt escribir; (note) apuntar; ~ **off** vt (debt) borrar (como incobrable); (fig) desechar por inútil; ~ **out** vt escribir; ~ **up** vt redactar; **~-off** n siniestro total; **~r** n escritor(a) m/f
writhe [raɪð] vi retorcerse
writing ['raɪtɪŋ] n escritura; (hand-~) letra; (of author) obras fpl; **in ~** por escrito; ~ **paper** n papel m de escribir
written ['rɪtn] pp of **write**
wrong [rɔŋ] adj (wicked) malo; (unfair) injusto; (incorrect) equivocado, incorrecto; (not suitable) inoportuno, inconveniente; (reverse) del revés ♦ adv equivocadamente ♦ n injusticia ♦ vt ser injusto con; **you are ~ to do it** haces mal en hacerlo; **you are ~ about that, you've got it ~** en eso estás equivocado; **to be in the ~** no tener razón, tener la culpa; **what's ~?** ¿qué pasa?; **to go ~** (person) equivocarse; (plan) salir mal; (machine) estropearse; **~ful** adj injusto; **~ly** adv mal, incorrectamente; (by mistake) por error; ~ **number** n (TEL): **you've got the ~ number** se ha equivocado de número
wrote [rəut] pt of **write**
wrought iron [rɔ:t-] n hierro forjado
wrung [rʌŋ] pt, pp of **wring**
wt. abbr = **weight**
WWW n abbr (= World Wide Web) WWW m

X, x

Xmas ['ɛksməs] n abbr = **Christmas**
X-ray ['ɛksreɪ] n radiografía ♦ vt radiografiar, sacar radiografías de
xylophone ['zaɪləfəun] n xilófono

Y, y

yacht [jɔt] n yate m; **~ing** n (sport) balandrismo; **~sman/woman** (irreg) n balandrista m/f
Yank [jæŋk] (pej) n yanqui m/f
Yankee ['jæŋkɪ] (pej) n = **Yank**
yap [jæp] vi (dog) aullar
yard [jɑːd] n patio; (measure) yarda; **~stick** n (fig) criterio, norma
yarn [jɑːn] n hilo; (tale) cuento, historia
yawn [jɔːn] n bostezo ♦ vi bostezar; **~ing** adj (gap) muy abierto
yd(s). abbr = **yard(s)**
yeah [jɛə] (inf) adv sí
year [jɪə*] n año; **to be 8 ~s old** tener 8 años; **an eight-~-old child** un niño de ocho años (de edad); **~ly** adj anual ♦ adv anualmente, cada año
yearn [jɔːn] vi: **to ~ for sth** añorar algo, suspirar por algo
yeast [jiːst] n levadura
yell [jɛl] n grito, alarido ♦ vi gritar
yellow ['jɛləu] adj amarillo
yelp [jɛlp] n aullido ♦ vi aullar
yes [jɛs] adv sí ♦ n sí m; **to say/answer ~** decir/contestar que sí
yesterday ['jɛstədɪ] adv ayer ♦ n ayer m; ~ **morning/evening** ayer por la mañana/tarde; **all day ~** todo el día de ayer
yet [jɛt] adv ya; (negative) todavía ♦ conj sin embargo, a pesar de todo; **it is not finished** ~ todavía no está acabado; **the best** ~ el/la mejor hasta ahora; **as** ~ hasta ahora, todavía
yew [juː] n tejo
yield [jiːld] n (AGR) cosecha; (COMM)

rendimiento ♦ vt ceder; (results) producir, dar; (profit) rendir ♦ vi rendirse, ceder; (US: AUT) ceder el paso

YMCA n abbr (= Young Men's Christian Association) Asociación f de Jóvenes Cristianos

yog(h)ourt [ˈjəʊgət] n yogur m

yog(h)urt [ˈjəʊgət] n = **yog(h)ourt**

yoke [jəʊk] n yugo

yolk [jəʊk] n yema (de huevo)

---KEYWORD---

you [juː] pron **1** (subject: familiar) tú, pl vosotros/as (SP), ustedes (AM); (polite) usted, pl ustedes; ~ **are very kind** eres/es etc muy amable; ~ **Spanish enjoy your food** a vosotros (or ustedes) los españoles os (or les) gusta la comida; ~ **and I will go** iremos tú y yo

2 (object: direct: familiar) te, pl os (SP), les (AM); (polite) le, pl les, f la, pl las; **I know** ~ te/le etc conozco

3 (object: indirect: familiar) te, pl os (SP), les (AM); (polite) le, pl les; **I gave the letter to** ~ **yesterday** te/os etc di la carta ayer

4 (stressed): **I told** YOU **to do it** te dije a ti que lo hicieras, es a ti a quien dije que lo hicieras; see also **3, 5**

5 (after prep: NB: con+ti = contigo: familiar) ti, pl vosotros/as (SP), ustedes (AM); (: polite) usted, pl ustedes; **it's for** ~ es para ti/vosotros etc

6 (comparisons: familiar) tú, pl vosotros/as (SP), ustedes (AM); (: polite) usted, pl ustedes; **she's younger than** ~ es más joven que tú/vosotros etc

7 (impersonal: one): **fresh air does** ~ **good** el aire puro (t) hace bien; ~ **never know** nunca se sabe; ~ **can't do that!** ¡eso no se hace!

you'd [juːd] = **you had; you would**

you'll [juːl] = **you will; you shall**

young [jʌŋ] adj joven ♦ npl (of animal) cría; (people): **the** ~ los jóvenes, la juventud; **~er** adj (brother etc) menor;

~**ster** n joven m/f

your [jɔː*] adj tu; (pl) vuestro; (formal) su; see also **my**

you're [jʊə*] = **you are**

yours [jɔːz] pron tuyo; (pl) vuestro; (formal) suyo; see also **faithfully; mine**[1]; **sincerely**

yourself [jɔːˈsɛlf] pron tú mismo; (complement) te; (after prep) tí (mismo); (formal) usted mismo; (: complement) se; (: after prep) sí (mismo); **yourselves** pl pron vosotros mismos; (after prep) vosotros (mismos); (formal) ustedes (mismos); (: complement) se; (: after prep) sí mismos; see also **oneself**

youth [juːθ, pl juːðz] n juventud f; (young man) joven m; ~ **club** n club m juvenil; ~**ful** adj juvenil; ~ **hostel** n albergue m de juventud

you've [juːv] = **you have**

Yugoslav [ˈjuːgəʊslɑːv] adj, n yugo(e)slavo/a m/f

Yugoslavia [juːgəʊˈslɑːvɪə] n Yugoslavia

yuppie [ˈjʌpɪ] (inf) adj, n yupi m/f, yupy m/f

YWCA n abbr (= Young Women's Christian Association) Asociación f de Jóvenes Cristianas

Z, z

zany [ˈzeɪnɪ] adj estrafalario

zap [zæp] vt (COMPUT) borrar

zeal [ziːl] n celo, entusiasmo; ~**ous** [ˈzɛləs] adj celoso, entusiasta

zebra [ˈziːbrə] n cebra; ~ **crossing** (BRIT) n paso de peatones

zero [ˈzɪərəʊ] n cero

zest [zɛst] n ánimo, vivacidad f; (of orange) piel f

zigzag [ˈzɪgzæg] n zigzag m ♦ vi zigzaguear, hacer eses

zinc [zɪŋk] n cinc m, zinc m

zip [zɪp] n (also: ~ **fastener,** (US) ~**per**) cremallera (SP), cierre m (AM) ♦ vt (also: ~ **up**) cerrar la cremallera de; ~ **code** (US)

n código postal
zodiac [ˈzəudɪæk] *n* zodíaco
zone [zəun] *n* zona
zoo [zuː] *n* (jardín *m*) zoo *m*
zoology [zuˈɔlədʒɪ] *n* zoología

zoom [zuːm] *vi*: **to ~ past** pasar
zumbando; **~ lens** *n* zoom *m*
zucchini [zuːˈkiːnɪ] (*US*) *n(pl)*
calabacín(ines) *m(pl)*